Let's Go Publications

Let's Go: Alaska & the Pacific Northwest 2000
Let's Go: Australia 2000
Let's Go: Austria & Switzerland 2000
Let's Go: Britain & Ireland 2000
Let's Go: California 2000
Let's Go: Central America 2000
Let's Go: China 2000 **New Title!**
Let's Go: Eastern Europe 2000
Let's Go: Europe 2000
Let's Go: France 2000
Let's Go: Germany 2000
Let's Go: Greece 2000
Let's Go: India & Nepal 2000
Let's Go: Ireland 2000
Let's Go: Israel 2000 **New Title!**
Let's Go: Italy 2000
Let's Go: Mexico 2000
Let's Go: Middle East 2000 **New Title!**
Let's Go: New York City 2000
Let's Go: New Zealand 2000
Let's Go: Paris 2000
Let's Go: Perú & Ecuador 2000 **New Title!**
Let's Go: Rome 2000
Let's Go: South Africa 2000
Let's Go: Southeast Asia 2000
Let's Go: Spain & Portugal 2000
Let's Go: Turkey 2000
Let's Go: USA 2000
Let's Go: Washington, D.C. 2000

Let's Go *Map Guides*

Amsterdam	New Orleans
Berlin	New York City
Boston	Paris
Chicago	Prague
Florence	Rome
London	San Francisco
Los Angeles	Seattle
Madrid	Washington, D.C.

Coming Soon: Sydney and Hong Kong

Let's Go

2000

MIDDLE EAST

Zahr K. Said
Editor

Ankur N. Ghosh
Associate Editor

Katherine R. Ünterman
Associate Editor

Researcher-Writers:

Charles DeSimone

Ahmed Kanna

Kris Garin

Nilufar "Sobi" Hossain

Eliot Hodges

David Ross

Macmillan

HELPING LET'S GO

If you want to share your discoveries, suggestions, or corrections, please drop us a line. We read every piece of correspondence, whether a postcard, a 10-page email, or a coconut. Please note that mail received after May 2000 may be too late for the 2001 book, but will be kept for future editions. **Address mail to:**

Let's Go: Middle East
67 Mount Auburn Street
Cambridge, MA 02138
USA

Visit Let's Go at **http://www.letsgo.com,** or send email to:

feedback@letsgo.com
Subject: "Let's Go: Middle East"

In addition to the invaluable travel advice our readers share with us, many are kind enough to offer their services as researchers or editors. Unfortunately, our charter enables us to employ only currently enrolled Harvard students.

Published in Great Britain 2000 by Macmillan, an imprint of Macmillan Publishers Ltd, 25 Eccleston Place, London, SW1W 9NF, Basingstoke and Oxford Associated companies throughout the world
www.macmillan.co.uk

Maps by David Lindroth copyright © 2000, 1999, 1998, 1997, 1996, 1995, 1994, 1993, 1992, 1991, 1990, 1989, 1988 by St. Martin's Press

Published in the United States of America by St. Martin's Press

ISBN: 0 333 78199 6
First edition
10 9 8 7 6 5 4 3 2 1

Let's Go: Middle East is written by Let's Go Publications, 67 Mount Auburn Street, Cambridge, MA 02138, USA.

Let's Go® and the thumb logo are trademarks of Let's Go, Inc.
Printed in the USA on recycled paper with biodegradable soy ink.

CONTENTS

MAPS

RESEARCHER-WRITERS

Charles DeSimone   *Cairo, Alexandria, Suez Canal, Mediterranean and Red Sea coasts*
"Mr. Charles" was half funny professional, half professional funnyman, and all mosque. This stellar wordsmith not only untangled the streets of Cairo to write the best coverage of the city this book has ever seen, but also found enough time to conquer the rest of Lower Egypt in a way that Seventeen ancient rulers before him could never do.

Kristoffer Garin   *Yemen and Amman*
Kris blew through Jordan, mastering the City of the Seven Hills as easily as he conquered the Bedouin calm of the desert. He then became the first-ever RW on the Arabian Peninsula, discovering for himself the pleasures (and pains) of independent travel through Yemen.

Eliot Hodges   *Cairo, Nile Valley, and the Western Desert Oases*
Whether floating on *feluccas* or oasis-hopping, Eliot navigated his Egypt itinerary with ease and style. His knack for uncovering the absurd, combined with his *Hard Copy* style of investigative reporting, ensured that each copybatch was thorough and thoroughly hilarious (the gifts he sent back didn't hurt, either).

Nilufar "Sobi" Hossain   *Oman and the United Arab Emirates*
Sobi or not Sobi? It was never a question for us. This supeRW was one of the most valuable adventurers in the series. She tore through the Gulf States and left pesky taxi drivers behind in a cloud of camel-colored dust. Her experience in East Africa led her to follow the trade winds to Oman, where she brought the best of both cultures to her copy.

Ahmed Kanna   *Lebanon and Damascus*
Ahmed dazzled us with his witty prose stylin' and vast knowledge of Middle Eastern history and culture (what was that about a Ph.D.?). Not even being picked up by the Syrian fuzz got in the way of his job, though he's happy to be back in cockroach-free Cambridge.

David Ross   *Syria, Jordan, and the Sinai Peninsula*
King of the Wild Frontier (and we don't mean his native Canada), Davey Crockett-Ross blasted through an extended itinerary that spanned four countries and made him an expert on border crossings. From Aqaba to Zalabiyyeh, Davey was our RW-of-all-trades. We're glad he turned down all those marriage offers.

Laura Weinrib	*Editor, Israel*
Tal Astrachan	*Associate Editor, Israel*
Meredith Quinn	*Editor, Turkey*
Anup Kubal	*Associate Editor, Turkey*

John Bachman	*Central Anatolia, Western Black Sea Coast, Bursa*
Sera Beak	*Western Mediterranean Coast*
Michelle Caswell	*Istanbul, Marmara Coast*
David Egan	*Cappadocia, Eastern Mediterranean Turkey*
Kristin Glover	*Negev, Gaza, Tzfat, Golan*
Anna Harr	*Cyprus*
Jeremy Kurzyniec	*Aegean Coast, Antakya*
Adam Rzepka	*Eastern Black Sea Coast, Istanbul*
Joey Shabot	*Jerusalem, West Bank, Nazareth*
Ari Weisbard	*Tel Aviv, Mediterranean Coast, Galilee*

ACKNOWLEDGMENTS

These books don't just put themselves together, you know. They're assembled by machine.

TEAM M.E. THANKS: Taya and her band of Merry MEs; Virgin Pod East, without whom we wouldn't have had a klu; Çapkın Christian, whose Türkiye crunch was tastier than *İskender kebap*; Marshall, Joey, and the Gharzouzi and Saleeby clans for helping us with Arabic; all the typists we've loved before, and our proofer loves, wherever they may be; our dream is to make a short film.

ZAHR THANKS: My thanks go out to my hard-working AEs; to say this book could not have been written without them is an understatement. For all their support and encouragement, I must thank Mom, Hak, 'llams, Baba, and of course, Mao. Especially Mom, who gave me so many travel opportunities and always made me believe I could (and would) do anything. In the office, Alex, Lisa, Christiana and the entire Virgin Pod made the summer what it was for me—I can't thank you all enough. Outside the office, Charissa and Saul kept me both entertained, and going. Special thanks to all the RWs for their hard, hard work. And love to E—no matter what happens, think of me, once in a while...

ANKUR THANKS: Kate, for doing time (and then some) as my partner in pun crime and rhyme; all the species of Virgin Pod East (even the ones who hate me), for putting up with all of our Slurping, usurping, and graybox madness; Taylor, for Sunday (late, late Sunday) brunches and late-night (late, late night) TV with Ian and Justine; big-ups to Erica; Alice, for losing the hair and gaining a good friend; Megan, because she does it all and does it well, you know what I mean?; my southern-fried comrade Laura Beth; and of course Pia, Ayan, and Dad.

KATE THANKS: Above & beyond (the) call o' duty, everyone's favorite Ghosh; hirsute individuals; Jess & kin; Laura & my never over-bearing parents; Qur'anic rituals; Slurpees (the other kind) und (das) virginale Wunderpod; (but especially) Xian—you're (the) zenith.

Editor
Zahr K. Said
Associate Editors
Ankur N. Ghosh and Katherine R. Ünterman
Managing Editor
Taya Lynn Weiss

Publishing Director
Benjamin Wilkinson
Editor-in-Chief
Bentsion Harder
Production Manager
Christian Lorentzen
Cartography Manager
Daniel J. Luskin
Design Managers
Matthew Daniels, Melissa Rudolph
Editorial Managers
Brendan Gibbon, Benjamin Paloff, Kaya Stone, Taya Weiss
Financial Manager
Kathy Lu
Personnel Manager
Adam Stein
Publicity & Marketing Managers
Sonesh Chainani, Alexandra Leichtman
New Media Manager
Maryanthe Malliaris
Map Editors
Kurt Mueller, Jon Stein
Production Associates
Steven Aponte, John Fiore
Office Coordinators
Elena Schneider, Vanessa Bertozzi, Monica Henderson

Director of Advertising Sales
Marta Szabo
Associate Sales Executives
Tamas Eisenberger, Li Ran

President
Noble M. Hansen III
General Managers
Blair Brown, Robert B. Rombauer
Assistant General Manager
Anne E. Chisholm

HOW TO USE THIS BOOK

If *Let's Go: Middle East* were an animal, it would be a camel. Like a camel, *Let's Go* gets you where you want to go, and can also lead you to the right place if you're not quite sure what you want to do. Like a camel, this book is intelligent, dependable, and totally on top of things. Like a camel, this book is a delightful shade of yellow. Unlike a camel, this book does not spit.

With that said, meet your camel. The Middle East is huge—we're talking eleven countries and three continents here—and at times it may seem daunting to navigate. *Let's Go: Middle East* is also huge, and may also seem daunting to navigate, but don't worry. First up is **Discover the Middle East,** which includes several sample itineraries maneuvering through everything from ancient plunder to modern wonder. Following this is **Essentials,** which lists everything that's…well, essential to making your trip as smooth as possible. The Middle East is the birthplace of three major religions; some of their most sacred and beautiful sights are scattered across the region. Check out the **History of Religion** section to get a grasp on these faiths' backgrounds. Then comes coverage of the sights and sounds of eleven countries in the Middle East, arranged alphabetically. Each country chapter opens with general information on the country, including historical and cultural information as well as advice on how best to get around, get to sleep, and get along with the locals. There's also extensive information on **Border Crossings** from one place to another at the beginning of every chapter. Don't miss the new coverage in this book of the Persian Gulf States (**Oman** and the **United Arab Emirates**) and **Yemen. Israel and the Palestinian Territories** includes full coverage of the **West Bank** and **Gaza** as well as coverage of trips to the cities of Limassol and Paphos on the island of **Cyprus,** easy ferry trips from Haifa, Israel.

Our coverage is just as accessible: **Orientation** sections untangle city streets. **Practical Information** tells you how to get around, get your laundry done, and get help if you need it. **Accommodations, Food, Entertainment,** and **Sights** sections guide you to the best beds, meals, discos, and castles. Our researchers have ranked everything in these sections in order of preference, giving a 🐫**thumb** to the truly spic-n-span rooms, super-scrumptious restaurants, the most soothing *hamams* (Turkish baths), the most slow-paced *sheesha* (water-pipe) parlors…you get the point. Hard info (directions, hours, admission, etc.) for sights are in *italicized sans serif* text to make them easy to find. Find yourself understanding what everyone around you is saying by checking out the **Appendix,** which not only includes many handy phrases in **Arabic, Hebrew,** and **Turkish** but a list of holidays and festivals and a reference of the many telephone codes for the region. Dancing cheek-to-cheek with the Appendix is the **Index.**

Well, that's about it. Travel in the Middle East, like travel on a camel, can be bumpy and requires a lot of water, so drink up, saddle up, and let's get going. We'll help you get over the hump.

A NOTE TO OUR READERS The information for this book was gathered by *Let's Go*'s researchers from May through August. Each listing is derived from the assigned researcher's opinion based upon his or her visit at a particular time. The opinions are expressed in a candid and forthright manner. Those traveling at a different time may have different experiences since prices, dates, hours, and conditions are always subject to change. You are urged to check beforehand to avoid inconvenience and surprises. Travel always involves a certain degree of risk, especially in low-cost areas. When traveling, especially on a budget, always take particular care to ensure your safety.

ABOUT LET'S GO

FORTY YEARS OF WISDOM

As a new millennium arrives, *Let's Go: Europe*, now in its 40th edition and translated into seven languages, reigns as the world's bestselling international travel guide. For four decades, travelers criss-crossing the Continent have relied on *Let's Go* for inside information on the hippest backstreet cafes, the most pristine secluded beaches, and the best routes from border to border. In the last 20 years, our rugged researchers have stretched the frontiers of backpacking and expanded our coverage into Asia, Africa, Australia, and the Americas. We're celebrating our 40th birthday with the release of *Let's Go: China*, blazing the traveler's trail from the Forbidden City to the Tibetan frontier; *Let's Go: Perú & Ecuador*, spanning the lands of the ancient Inca Empire; *Let's Go: Middle East*, with coverage from Istanbul to the Persian Gulf; and the maiden edition of *Let's Go: Israel*.

It all started in 1960 when a handful of well-traveled students at Harvard University handed out a 20-page mimeographed pamphlet offering a collection of their tips on budget travel to passengers on student charter flights to Europe. The following year, in response to the instant popularity of the first volume, students traveling to Europe researched the first full-fledged edition of *Let's Go: Europe*, a pocket-sized book featuring honest, practical advice, witty writing, and a decidedly youthful slant on the world. Throughout the 60s and 70s, our guides reflected the times. In 1969 we taught travelers how to get from Paris to Prague on "no dollars a day" by singing in the street. In the 80s and 90s, we looked beyond Europe and North America and set off to all corners of the earth. Meanwhile, we focused in on the world's most exciting urban areas to produce in-depth, fold-out map guides. Our new guides bring the total number of titles to 48, each infused with the spirit of adventure and voice of opinion that travelers around the world have come to count on. But some things never change: our guides are still researched, written, and produced entirely by students who know first-hand how to see the world on the cheap.

HOW WE DO IT

Each guide is completely revised and thoroughly updated every year by a well-traveled set of over 250 students. Every spring, we recruit over 180 researchers and 70 editors to overhaul every book. After several months of training, researcher-writers hit the road for seven weeks of exploration, from Anchorage to Adelaide, Estonia to El Salvador, Iceland to Indonesia. Hired for their rare combination of budget travel sense, writing ability, stamina, and courage, these adventurous travelers know that train strikes, stolen luggage, food poisoning, and marriage proposals are all part of a day's work. Back at our offices, editors work from spring to fall, massaging copy written on Himalayan bus rides into witty, informative prose. A student staff of typesetters, cartographers, publicists, and managers keeps our lively team together. In September, the collected efforts of the summer are delivered to our printer, which turns them into books in record time, so that you have the most up-to-date information available for your vacation. Even as you read this, work on next year's editions is well underway.

WHY WE DO IT

We don't think of budget travel as the last recourse of the destitute; we believe that it's the only way to travel. Living cheaply and simply brings you closer to the people and places you've been saving up to visit. Our books will ease your anxieties and answer your questions about the basics—so you can get off the beaten track and explore. Once you learn the ropes, we encourage you to put *Let's Go* down now and then to strike out on your own. You know as well as we that the best discoveries are often those you make yourself. When you find something worth sharing, please drop us a line. We're Let's Go Publications, 67 Mount Auburn St., Cambridge, MA 02138, USA (email: feedback@letsgo.com). For more info, visit our website, http://www.letsgo.com.

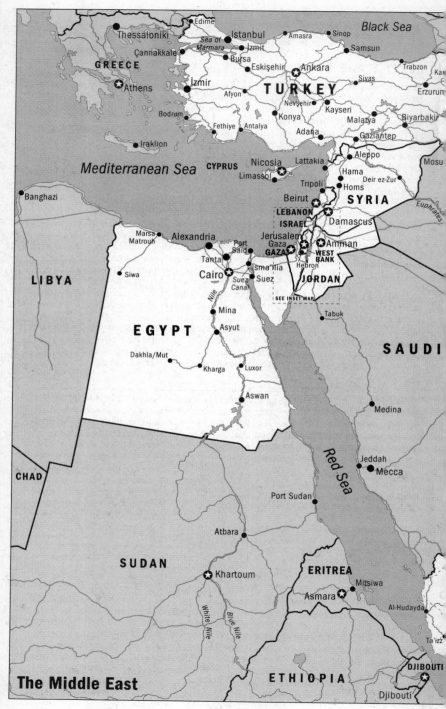

The Middle East

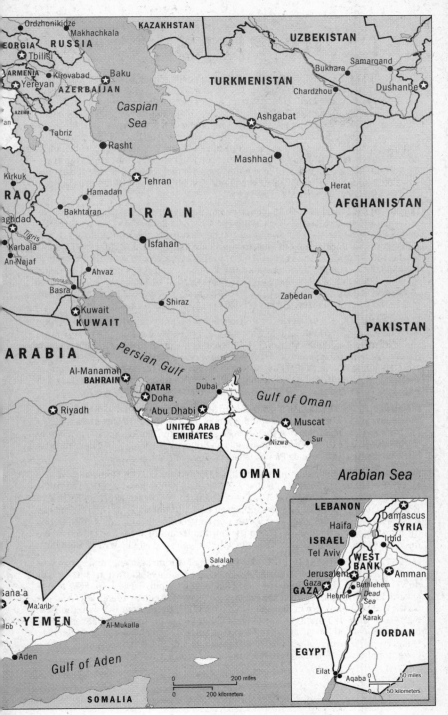

LET'S GO PICKS

◼BEST CULTS OF PERSONALITY. Everybody wants to rule the world; begin your own personal quest by learning from the greats. While in Ankara, Turkey, visit the mausoleum of **Kemal Atatürk** (p. 589), the man who single-handedly made Turkey what it is today. **David Ben-Gurion,** the founder of the modern Israeli state, called the town of Sdeh Boker, Israel (p. 364) home. **Ramses II** was known for taking egomania to the extreme. Likenesses of his big head litter Abu Simbel, Egypt (p. 220). But Ramses didn't have anything on **King Hussein** of Jordan, the longest ruling monarch in the world. Can't find a reputable country to rule? Why not start your own? **Eli Avivi** did at Akhzibland, within the borders of Israel (p. 321). Ready to rule not just this world, but the next? **Jesus** was. Follow in his footsteps along the Via Dolorosa in Jerusalem, Israel (p. 273).

◼BEST OLDIES BUT GOODIES. Two ancient sites vie for the status of oldest city in the world: **Jericho,** in the West Bank (p. 388), and **Çatalhöyük,** Turkey (p. 589). **Damascus,** Syria (p. 498) elbows in on the contest for oldest continuously inhabited city in the world. Find out where they all are at **Madaba,** Jordan (p. 437), home to the oldest map of the region. Did Madaba leave you tongue-tied? Head to **Ma'alula, Syria** (p. 509), where Aramaic, the language that Jesus preached in, is still spoken. Aramaic's written ancestor was discovered at **Ugarit,** Syria (p. 521), home to the oldest written alphabet. And don't forget the oldest profession in the world, still in full force at **Trabzon,** Turkey (p. 602).

◼ALL SHUK UP. *Souq, shuk...*it doesn't matter what you call it. Whatever you want, the markets of the Middle East have it. Specialty markets are everywhere: the glittering **Gold Souq** at Dubai, UAE (p. 624), the mind-blowing **qat souq** in Sana'a, Yemen (p. 682), and the unforgettable **camel market** at Birqash, Egypt (p. 105). Nine kilometers of *souq* await you in **Aleppo,** Syria (p. 523), the best outdoor market in the Mediterranean. The superlative fun continues at the **Grand Bazaar** in Istanbul, Turkey (p. 556), the largest outdoor market in the entire world.

◼FOUR OUT OF SEVEN AIN'T BAD. Four of the Seven Wonders of the Ancient World are in the Middle East. If you dig tombs, head to the **Pyramids at Giza,** Egypt (p. 101) and the **Mausoleum of Halicarnassus** in Bodrum, Turkey (p. 574). While in Turkey, pop over to the **Temple of Artemis** at Ephesus (p. 569). Navigate your way back using the **Lighthouse on Pharos Island** in Alexandria, Egypt (p. 119).

◼BEST FESTIVALS. The cradle of civilization still rocks. Buy some time at the month-long **Shopping Festival** in Dubai, UAE (p. 624) before heading out to the wine festival in **Limassol, Cyprus** (p. 400). Slide on over to the **Grease Wrestling Festival** in Edirne, Turkey (p. 557). Locals and foreigners alike mingle at the festivals in **Ba'albeck,** Lebanon (p. 482), and **Jerash,** Jordan (p. 426), which are world-famous for their big-name headliners. Begin the third millennium at the birthplace of the first: **Jerusalem,** Israel (p. 249) is *the* place to be when the clocks strike midnight.

◼BEST OF KITSCH MEETS QUR'AN. The God of Abraham, Isaac, and Jacob was ready to let His Heir down to earth; Muslims have also been known to let their hair down. The Blue Mosque and Topkapı Palace in Istanbul, Turkey (p. 555) house several hairs from the **beard of the Prophet Muhammad.** Reduce, reuse, and read the **plastic Qur'an** in downtown Sharjah, UAE (p. 630). Light up your life with the **glowing "ALLAH" sign** in Tripoli, Lebanon (p. 477). If you want to get to heaven, you'll have to follow the footprints of the Prophet Saleh's **sacred camel** outside Salalah, Oman (p. 667). As one of ten very special animals, this blessed beast joined Noah's dove, Jonah's whale, and Abraham's ram on the stairway to heaven.

DISCOVER THE MIDDLE EAST

Gertrude Bell, one of the most famous travelers to the Middle East (see **An English-woman in Arabia,** p. 440), said: "Few such moments of exhilaration can come as that which stands at the threshold of wild travel." The Middle East is, without a doubt, adventure country *par excellence*. Wide expanses of desert dotted with lush green oases, colorful underwater seascapes, and hidden cities carved in stone inspire exploration in the grand tradition of Lawrence of Arabia and Indiana Jones. The Middle East's long-standing and dynamic socio-political canvas is just as colorful as its landscape: ancient civilizations have left rich archaeological records of human struggle and achievement that are no less compelling than the contemporary drama of the Middle East peace process. Four of the seven wonders of the ancient world, numerous relics from three major faiths, and the first written alphabet are only pieces of the historical puzzle. The challenges of politics today range from the preservation of Bedouin traditional lifestyles in modern nation-states like Egypt to the push for modernization in traditional places like the Sultanate of Oman. Despite the vast diversity of political views, religious beliefs, and economic privilege in the region, all of its inhabitants adhere to one very strong belief: the profound importance of hospitality. As a traveler, you will encounter difficulties navigating shifty bus schedules, phantom trains, and stubborn camels. You will take in the Pyramids at Giza, gasp in awe at the lost city of Petra in Jordan, and admire Cappadocia's natural splendor in Turkey. And yet, at the end of the journey, your most striking memory is most likely to be sipping a cup of *ahwa* (Arabic coffee) while discussing the meaning of life with a spice vendor in some small corner of a *souq* (market).

FACTS AND FIGURES

- **Population:** 182 million
- **Land Area:** over 2.9 million sq. km (1.8 million sq. mi.)
- **Geography:** Diverse—deserts, forests, beaches, mountains, plateaus, valleys.
- **Language:** Arabic, Hebrew (Israel), Turkish (Turkey), Greek (Cyprus).
- **Religions:** Islam, Judaism, Christianity
- **Major Exports:** Oil, dates, and textiles, among others (varies by country).

SUN OF A BEACH

Much of the Middle East embraces the Mediterranean Sea, and cradled in its arms are some amazing beaches. Bodacious **Bodrum** (p. 572), in Turkey, is known the world over for its sizzling beaches (matched only by equally sizzling nightlife). For other perspectives on the Mediterranean: party on down with sun-soaked hipsters at youthful **Tel Aviv** (p. 288); kick back for a few days on the enjoyable if busy shores of **Jounieh** (p. 472) in Lebanon and **Herzliya** (p. 305) in Israel; and be sure to hop over to the endless, sparkling beaches of **Cyprus** (p. 398), in the heart of the Mediterranean. Don't let the heat get to you: savor the lazy daze of summer at **Dahab** (p. 160), one of the many beachside treasures along the coasts of the **Sinai Peninsula** (p. 144), known the world over as a scuba-lover's paradise. Tired of jam-packed sands and jammin' discos? Weary travelers can slip into the embrace of countless stretches of undiscovered emerald coast throughout the Middle East: **Marsa Matrouh** (p. 135) offers spectacular Mediterranean serenity without the Mediterranean crowds; **Aden's** (p. 692) breathtaking beauty is not to be missed; and the white expanses of **Salalah** (p. 667), in southern Oman, make up one of the only tropical locations in all of the Middle East (steer clear in monsoon season, though).

1

SHOP 'TIL YOU DROP

Bargaining is a fact of life in the Middle East, so it only makes sense that the region is a true shopper's paradise. Almost every city has a *souq*, an outdoor bazaar that sells everything from spices to stilettos. Grab silver and spice and everything nice at the Grand Bazaar in **Istanbul** (p. 544); head to **Beirut** (p. 463) for leather and gold; browse the intricately carved boxes and gold jewelry in **Damascus** (p. 498); **Sana'a's** (p. 682) silver astounds; and **Cairo** (p. 55) is the place for tapestries and *sheeshas*. **Muscat** (p. 646) is home to one of the last authentic *souqs* (don't miss the *khanjaris*, or ceremonial daggers). For less luxurious goods, head to **Petra** (p. 442) for beautiful pottery or trek out to the camel markets in **Birqash** (p. 105) or **Daraw** (p. 208), Egypt. At the other extreme, high-end fashions can be found in the sparkling new malls and boutiques of Beirut and **Dubai** (p. 624), where Emiratis celebrate conspicuous consumption in a month-long shopping festival every March. **Israel** (p. 237) is also a haven for shoppers in search of modern luxuries: grab a pair of the world-famous *Naot* sandals anywhere in the country, and pamper yourself with mud baths and facial scrubs from the **Dead Sea** (p. 350). The biggest mall in the Middle East is scheduled to open soon in **Haifa** (p. 308).

AIN'T NO MOUNTAIN HIGH ENOUGH...

Although the Middle East is better known for rising temperatures than rising peaks, there are many options for the alpine- and hiking-inclined. The **Negev Desert** (p. 357) and **Golan Heights** (p. 345) in Israel offer subtropical paths that cut through cliffside caves and breathtaking *wadis*. A trek through Yemen's many hilltop villages (such as **Ibb**, p. 689) offers breathtaking mountain views. No trekking itinerary would be complete without a climb up steep **Mount Sinai** (p. 150) in Egypt. For those of the skiing persuasion, Lebanon (known as "Little Switzerland" by those in the snow) boasts world-class skiing facilities at the twin resort towns of **Faqra** and **Faraya** (p. 474).

...AIN'T NO VALLEY LOW ENOUGH

What goes up must come down. Take a hike and check out the largest natural crater in the world, found at **Mitzpe Ramon** (p. 367) in Israel. The depths of the **Dead Sea** (from either the **Israeli** (p. 350) or the **Jordanian** (p. 437) side) may seem like another great place to get down, but be content with floating peacefully on the famed locale's surface.

SUGGESTED ITINERARIES

1. BEST OF THE MIDDLE EAST (4-5 WEEKS) Everything the Middle East has to offer, and more. Begin at **Istanbul** (p. 544), where you can wander through old markets and bargain for gold, spices, and carpets en route to mosques and Ottoman palaces. After a few heated days of sightseeing, cool off at a *hamam* (Turkish bath) before hopping a bus to **Damascus,** Syria (p. 498), the oldest continually inhabited city in the world. Shake it on over to fun 'n' funky **Beirut** (p. 463) in Lebanon. Party until dawn, then catch a breather at **Ba'albeck** (p. 482), the unforgettable home of some righteous ruins and host to an internationally known jazz festival where Ella and the Duke once swung it in 4/4 time. Next up is **Amman,** Jordan (p. 412),

which is an excellent jumping off point to lost **Petra**'s rock-hewn wonders (p. 442). Check in at Amman again on the way over to Israel, where your visit won't be complete without a stopover in **Jerusalem** (p. 249). Whether it's mosques, churches, or nightclubs, Jerusalem outdoes most other cities in the region. Plan to spend a few days here at least, if only to rest up before heading out to **Tel Aviv,** "The City That Never Takes a Break" (p. 288). Before you get down at the city's cutting edge cut-a-rug hotspots, treat your homesick taste buds to a panoply of non-falafel foods in any of the city's ethnic neighborhoods. Cross over to the **Sinai Peninsula** (p. 155) and tan your tired limbs in **Dahab** (p. 160) before diving into the azure depths of the Red Sea.

Finish your whirlwind tour of the region in equally tempestuous **Cairo** (p. 55) where the city's beautiful, historic neighborhoods are sprawled out in the shadow of the Pyramids at Giza (p. 101).

2. ON YOUR MARK, JET-SET, GO! (3-4 WEEKS) Jet-set like a pro while boning up on your ancient history with this supersonic tour of the Mediterranean. Dive into the sea of mosques and spice markets in **Istanbul** (p. 544), immerse yourself in one of the city's many famous *hammams*, then make a splash at the many bars and "nomadic" discotheques. Head south to the massive classical ruins at **Ephesus** (p. 568). Continue along the coast to the secluded coves and beaches of sunny **Bodrum** (p. 572). After partying until dawn in the city's many discotheques, shake it on over to **Antalya** (p. 581) and the **Turquoise Riviera,** Turkey's premiere tourist resort. Take a breather in the charming markets and tea gardens of **Antakya** (p. 584), then cross the border into Syria. Check out the birthplace of ancient and modern alphabets at **Ugarit** (p. 521) before day-tripping to the spectacular Crusaders' castle at **Crac des Chevaliers** (p. 516). Ease your way back into modern life on the streets of leisurely **Tripoli** (p. 477), where you're sure to be taken in by the city's famed Lebanese sweets and even more famous Lebanese hospitality. After taking in the fresh air at **Bcharré** (p. 481) and the ever-popular **Cedars of Lebanon** (home to world-class skiing in the winter), party on down at any one of the many hipster cafes, casinos, and discos in thrill-a-minute **Beirut** (p. 463). Pass through the oldest continually inhabited city in the world, **Damascus,** Syria (p. 498), then muscle your way through the crowded traffic circles of **Amman,** Jordan (p. 412) en route to the calm seaside town of **Haifa** in Israel (p. 308). Lay out on serene beaches with even more laid-back locals before heading to **Tel Aviv** (p. 288), a city that lives for the moment and grooves on beaches, in boutiques, and in booty-shaking dance halls. Ferry over to **Cyprus** (p. 398), where you can wander along unforgettable beaches and breezy mountains and trek through twisted streets in search of ruins from every age in history. Finish your Mediterranean tour in the warm embrace of the vibrant seaside town of **Alexandria,** Egypt (p. 119), and be sure to travel a few hours west to the sleepy resorts and busy markets of the town of **Marsa Matrouh** (p. 135).

3. WALK LIKE AN EGYPTIAN (4 WEEKS) Timeless adventures through the past and present. Hop on a bus from Cairo to **Luxor** (p. 183), once the capital of ancient Egypt. The temple ruins here are some of the most awe-inspiring in the world, and the colossal remains at nearby **Abu Simbel** (p. 220) are just as amazing. Take a break from all these ruins by taking a leisurely *felucca* cruise up the Nile. Once you reach the town of Asyut, go west, pardner, and trek through the unforgettable desert oases, especially the White Desert outside of lush **Dakhla** (p. 227). Emerge from the vast expanses of the western desert into bustling **Cairo** (p. 55), the largest city in the Middle East and Africa. The labyrinthine streets of the city are filled with beautiful mosques and churches, frenzied *souqs* where bargains abound, and a mile-a-minute nightlife unlike anywhere else in the Middle East. The majestic pyramids at **Giza** (p. 101) are also an easy daytrip from the city. The cosmopolitan calm of **Alexandria** (p. 119) may seem a shock after Cairo, but you'll fall easily enough into the beachside city's evening-strolling, *sheesha*-smoking pace. Head west from Alexandria and discover the dazzling Mediterranean gem that is **Marsa Matrouh** (p. 135), a resort town rarely visited by tourists save as a jumping off point to the verdant **Siwa Oasis** (p. 139). Move on to the **Sinai Peninsula** (p. 144), where you can dive and snorkel through world-famous coral reefs and kick back with the nomadic Bedouin near **Dahab** (p. 160).

4. OLDIES BUT GOODIES (3 WEEKS) A journey back in time to the ancient Levant. Begin in Syria, where the ancient trade center of **Aleppo** (p. 523) has wowed visitors since Ottoman times with its colossal Citadel and covered *souqs*. Springboard from Aleppo to the **Basilica of St. Simeon** (p. 528), a sacred stopover for Christian pilgrims since the 4th century, and **Ebla** (p. 529), the oldest of the old cities. The queen of

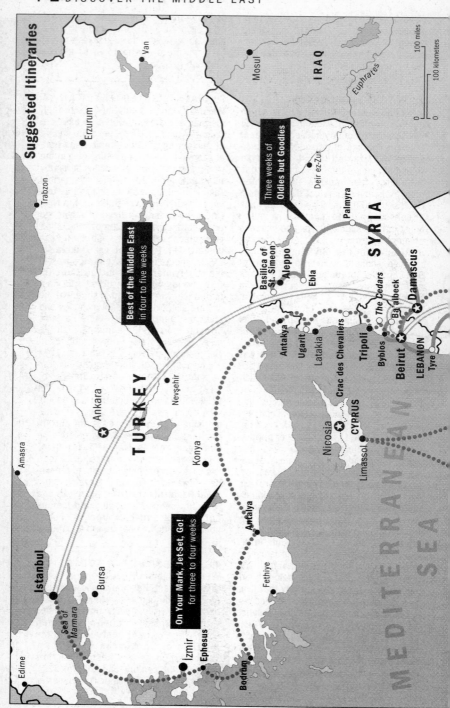

Suggested Itineraries

Best of the Middle East in four to five weeks

Three weeks of Oldies but Goodies

On Your Mark, Jet-Set, Go! for three to four weeks

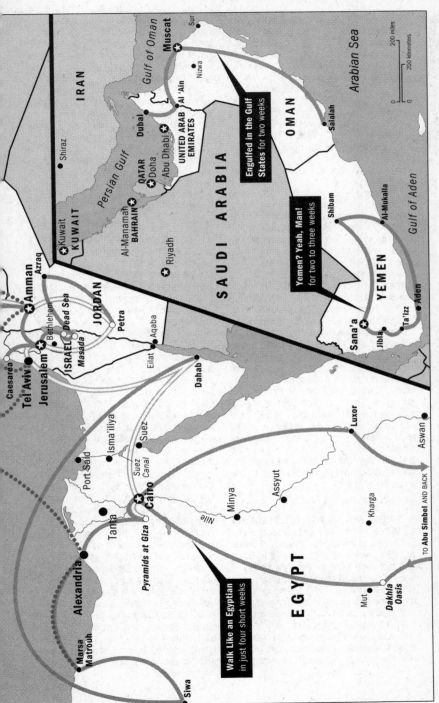

Engulfed in the Gulf States for two weeks

Yemen? Yeah, Man! for two to three weeks

Walk Like an Egyptian in just four short weeks

DISCOVER

Palmyra (p. 510), in central Syria, once rebelled against the Romans, and the stupendous ruins of her city have also resisted the wear and tear of time. Spend a few days in **Damascus** (p. 498), the oldest continually-inhabited city in the world—now a modern metropolis, but once the majestic capital of the Umayyad Empire—before jumping the border into Lebanon, where everything is but a day-hop from **Beirut** (p. 463). The Roman ruins and Crusader Castle in **Byblos** (p. 475) have toughed it out through centuries of bombardment; the town itself is so old that even the ancients considered it an ancient city. **Ba'albeck** (p. 482), east of Beirut, hasn't lost its Bacchanalian spirit: its Roman Temple of Bacchus is one of the most celebrated in the world, and the good times roll at the annual Ba'albeck Festival. Near the southern town of Sur, archaeologists have unearthed **Tyre** (p. 487), one of the great Phoenician city-states. Cut through **Amman,** Jordan (p. 412) and shimmy over to **Jerusalem** (p. 249), whose timeless wonders speak for themselves. Head for the **Dead Sea** region (the lowest point on earth) and explore King Herod's palace in **Masada** (p. 353). Hungry for more Herod? His greatest achievement was the splendid city of **Caesarea** (p. 306), where Pontius Pilate ordered Christ's crucifixion in 33 CE. Back in Jordan, adventure like Lawrence of Arabia in 1500-year-old desert castles near **Azraq** (p. 433), then journey down the Kings' Highway to finish your pilgrimage with a geologic bang at the Nabatean city of **Petra** (p. 442), whose rocky glory was lost to the world for centuries.

5. ENGULFED IN THE GULF STATES (2 WEEKS)

Bucket shops worldwide sell tickets to the shopping haven of **Dubai** (p. 624), home to a dazzling Gold Souq and the world's only month-long shopping festival. Only a 20-minute drive away, the city of **Sharjah** (p. 630) boasts so many museums and so much traditional Islamic architecture that UNESCO named it the cultural capital of the Arab world. The UAE/Oman border town of **Al-'Ain** (p. 638) is a gleaming emerald oasis with its lush palm trees, unexpected springs of

water, and the tallest mountain in the area. Only a three-hour bus ride from the border, **Muscat** (p. 646) is known as "the jewel of Arabia" for its old marketplaces and majestic mosques. Some easy day-trips from Muscat include **Nakhal** (p. 658), site of Oman's most impressive restored fort, and **Barka** (p. 657), a traditional fishing town that hosts rather unconventional bullfights on alternate Fridays. Sweat it through the journey across Oman's interior to **Salalah** (p. 667), in the rugged Dhofar province on the southwestern coast. The only city graced by cool monsoon breezes in the summer, Salalah makes an ideal springboard for mountain, desert, and beach trips.

6. YEMEN? YEAH, MAN! (2-3 WEEKS)

After landing in **Sana'a** (p. 682), cruise through the architectural history book that is the old city and visit the ancient gold *souq* where bargaining and bluffing are the norm. Then head to the hilltop town of **Jibla** (p. 689), an ancient stronghold with a fabulously well preserved city center. Travel from Jibla to **Ta'izz** (p. 690), the home of the long-deceased sultan and former capital of pre-revolutionary Yemen. Explore the splendid Sultan's Palace before heading south for the sunny beaches of **Aden** (p. 692), once a hangout of colonial Brits as well as the notorious hideaway of French renegade and poet Arthur Rimbaud. On the way to **Al-Mukalla** (p. 695), hit the tropical coastal towns; once there, use this large-ish industrial city as a base for exploring the diverse features of the **Wadi Hadramawt** region, such as the nearby hot springs, and the architectural wonder of the fortress at Hisn al-Ghazawi. Just a short bus trip away lies the country's architectural highlight, **Shibam** (p. 697), a collection of ancient sandstone skyscrapers dating back a millennium or more. The amazing, anachronistic spectacle this urban vision presents as it rises out of the desert will not soon be forgotten. No trip to Yemen is complete without a visit to **Wadi Dhahr** (p. 688), 15km outside of Sana'a. The centerpiece of this *wadi* is the five-story Rock Palace (Dar al-Hajr), astounding even after the glorious architecture of southern Yemen.

ESSENTIALS

FACTS FOR THE TRAVELER

DOCUMENTS AND FORMALITIES

For information on **embassies and consulates** in the Middle East, and on Middle Eastern diplomatic representation in Australia, Canada, Ireland, New Zealand, South Africa, the U.K., and the U.S., see the **Entry** sections of individual country chapters.

PASSPORTS

REQUIREMENTS. Citizens of Western nations need valid passports to enter all Middle Eastern countries and to re-enter their own country. Most Middle Eastern countries do not allow entrance if the holder's passport expires in less than six months; returning home with an expired passport is illegal, and may result in a fine.

PHOTOCOPIES. Photocopy the page of your passport that contains your photograph, passport number, and other identifying information, along with other important documents such as visas, travel insurance policies, airplane tickets, and traveler's check serial numbers, in case you lose anything. Carry one set of copies in a safe place apart from the originals and leave another set at home. Consulates also recommend that you carry an expired passport or an official copy of your birth certificate in a part of your baggage separate from other documents.

LOST PASSPORTS. If you lose your passport, immediately notify the local police and the nearest embassy or consulate of your home government. To expedite its replacement, you will need to know all information previously recorded and show identification and proof of citizenship. In some cases, a replacement may take weeks to process, and it may be valid only for a limited time. Any visas stamped in your old passport will be lost. In an emergency, ask for immediate temporary traveling papers that will permit you to re-enter your home country. Your passport is a public document belonging to your nation's government. You may have to surrender it to a foreign government official, but if you don't get it back in a reasonable amount of time, inform the nearest mission of your home country.

NEW PASSPORTS. All applications for new passports or renewals should be filed several weeks or months in advance of your planned departure date. Contact the nearest passport office your home country for specific information on where and how to proceed with acquiring a new passport.

IDENTIFICATION

When you travel, always carry two or more forms of identification on your person, including at least one photo ID. A passport combined with a driver's license or birth certificate usually serves as adequate proof of your identity and citizenship. Many establishments, especially banks, require several IDs before cashing traveler's checks. Never carry all your forms of ID together.

STUDENT AND TEACHER IDENTIFICATION. The **International Student Identity Card (ISIC)** is the most widely accepted form of student identification. Flashing this card can procure you discounts for sights, theaters, museums, accommodations, meals, train, ferry, bus, and airplane transportation, and other services. The international identification cards are preferable to institution-specific cards because the tourism personnel in the Middle East are taught to recognize the former. For U.S. cardholders traveling abroad, the ISIC also provides insurance benefits, including US$100 per day of in-hospital sickness for a maximum of 60 days, and US$3000 accident-related medical reimbursement for each accident (see **Insurance,** p. 21). In addition, cardholders have access to a toll-free, 24-hour ISIC helpline whose multilingual staff can provide assistance in medical, legal, and financial emergencies overseas (tel. 800-626-2427 in the U.S. and Canada; elsewhere call collect (181) 666 90 25).

Many student travel agencies around the world issue ISICs. When you apply for the card, request a copy of the ISIC Handbook, which lists some of the available discounts (discounts are available everywhere but the Gulf States and Yemen). The card is valid from September of one year to December of the following year and costs AUS$15, CDN$15, or US$20. Applicants must be at least 12 years old and degree-seeking students of a secondary or post-secondary school. Because of the proliferation of phony ISICs, many airlines and some other services require additional proof of student identity, such as a signed letter from the registrar attesting to your student status that is stamped with the school seal or your school ID card. The **International Teacher Identity Card (ITIC)** offers the same insurance coverage, and similar but limited discounts. The fee is AUS$13, UK£5, or US$20. For more information on these cards, contact the **International Student Travel Confederation (ISTC),** Herengracht 479, 1017 BS Amsterdam, Netherlands (tel. (20) 421 28 00; fax 421 28 10; email istcinfo@istc.org; www.istc.org).

 SIGHT SAVVY. Admission to sights in Syria is literally 20 times more expensive (usually S£300 instead of S£15) without an ISIC card. At all costs, get an ISIC card in your home country before departure.

CUSTOMS

Upon entering the Middle East, you must declare certain items from abroad and pay a duty on the value of those articles that exceed the allowance established by customs service. Keeping receipts for purchases made abroad will help establish values when you return. Make a list, including serial numbers, of valuables that you carry with you from home; if you register this list with customs before your departure and have an official stamp it, you will avoid import duty charges and ensure an easy passage upon your return. Upon returning home, you must declare all articles acquired abroad and pay a **duty** on the value of articles that exceed the allowance established by your country's customs service. Goods and gifts purchased at **duty-free** shops abroad are not exempt from duty or sales tax at your point of return; you must declare these items as well. For more specific information on customs requirements, contact: **Australia,** Australian Customs National Information Line (tel. 1 300 363; www.customs.gov.au); **Canada,** Canadian Customs, 2265 St. Laurent Blvd., Ottawa, ON K1G 4K3 (tel. 613-993-0534 or 24hr. automated service 800-461-9999; www.revcan.ca); **New Zealand,** New Zealand Customhouse, 17-21 Whitmore St., Box 2218, Weelington (tel. (04) 473 60 99; fax 473 73 70); **South Africa,** Commissioner for Customs and Excise, Private Bag X47, Pretoria 0001 (tel. 12 314 99 11; fax 328 64 78); **U.K.,** Her Majesty's Customs and Excise, Custom House, Nettleton Road, Heathrow Airport, Hounslow, Middlesex TW6 2LA (tel. (0181) 910 36 02/35 66; fax 910 37 65; www.hmce.gov.uk); **U.S.,** Customs Service, Box 7407, Washington D.C. 20044 (202-927-6724; www.customs.ustreas.gov).

MONEY

If you stay in hostels and prepare simple meals for yourself, expect to spend about US$15 per person per day (excluding Oman and the UAE, where the cost of living runs between US$50-70 per day). Starting prices for budget accommodations run anywhere from US$3 and up per night in an Istanbul hostel to US$15 and up per night in Beirut. A basic sit-down meal costs US$2 and up. Carry cash with you, and have small bills on hand while visiting sights or wandering the streets of a town. Most officials like *baksheesh* and most stores, *service* drivers, and the like cannot (or won't bother to) make change. No one to whom you are giving *bakhsheesh* will give you change back. Keep small bills separately from larger bills, so that people cannot point to your stash and demand more.

CURRENCY AND EXCHANGE

Bring enough foreign currency to last for the first 24-72 hours of a trip to avoid being penniless after banking hours or on a holiday. Travelers living in the U.S. can get foreign currency from the comfort of their home; **Capital Foreign Exchange** (888-842-0880) or **International Currency Express** (888-278-6628) will deliver foreign currency (for over 120 countries) or traveler's checks overnight (US$15) or second-day (US$12) at competitive exchange rates. Although banks are the best places to withdraw money and get cash advances in the Middle East, they will hardly ever offer the best exchange rate (or even a decent rate): local currency exchange centers are the best bet for changing currency. For a currency exchange rate chart based on figures published in August 1999, see the opening chart of each country's individual chapter. Since you lose money with each transaction, convert in large sums (unless the currency is depreciating rapidly).

TRAVELER'S CHECKS

Traveler's checks are one of the safest and least troublesome means of carrying funds, since they can be refunded if stolen. Members of the American Automobile Association, and some banks and credit unions, can get American Express checks commission-free. If you are ordering checks, do so well in advance, especially if you are requesting large sums. Buying traveler's checks in the currency of the country you are visiting can be an exercise in futility in the Middle East. Traveler's checks are only widely accepted in the major cities. **American Express** is the most widely recognized, and in some cities it is the only type accepted by businesses and banks. The most readily accepted checks are in U.S. dollars and British pounds (the German mark will sometimes be taken as well); checks in other currencies won't get you very far—if a place will exchange it, you'll probably get a terrible rate.

In order to collect a **refund** for lost or stolen checks, keep your check receipts separate from your checks and store them in a safe place or with a traveling companion. Record check numbers when you cash them, leave a list of check numbers with someone at home, and ask for a list of refund centers when you buy your checks. Never countersign your checks until you are ready to cash them, and always bring your passport with you when you plan to use the checks.

American Express: In Australia, call (800) 251-902; in New Zealand (0800) 441 068; in the U.K. (0800) 52 13 13; in the U.S. and Canada 800-221-7282. Elsewhere, call U.S. collect 801-964-6665; www.aexp.com. Checks can be purchased for a small fee (1-4%) at American Express Travel Service Offices, banks, and American Automobile Association offices. AAA members (see p. 28) can buy the checks commission-free. American Express offices cash their checks commission-free (except where prohibited by national governments), but often at slightly worse rates than banks. *Cheques for Two* can be signed by either of 2 people traveling together.

Citicorp: In the U.S. and Canada, all 800-645-6556; in Europe, the Middle East, or Africa, call the London office at 44 171 508 7007; from elsewhere, call U.S. collect 813-623-1709. Traveler's checks in 7 currencies. Commission 1-2%. Guaranteed hand-delivery of traveler's checks when a refund location is not convenient. Call 24hr.

Thomas Cook MasterCard: From the U.S., Canada, or Caribbean call 800-223-7373; from the U.K. (0800) 622 101; from elsewhere, call (44) 1733 318 950 collect. Checks available in 13 currencies. Commission 2%. Thomas Cook offices cash checks commission-free in several locations in the Middle East.

ESSENTIALS

Money From Home In Minutes.

If you're stuck for cash on your travels, don't panic. Millions of people trust Western Union to transfer money in minutes to 165 countries and over 50,000 locations worldwide. Our record of safety and reliability is second to none. For more information, call Western Union: USA 1-800-325-6000, Canada 1-800-235-0000. Wherever you are, you're never far from home.

www.westernunion.com

WESTERN UNION | MONEY TRANSFER®

The fastest way to send money worldwide:

Visa: Call 800-227-6811 in the U.S.; in the U.K. 0800 895 078; from elsewhere, call (44) 1733 318 949 and reverse the charges. Any of the above numbers can tell you the location of their nearest office.

CREDIT CARDS

Credit cards are accepted at a majority of the businesses in the Middle East. Major credit cards—**MasterCard** and **Visa** are welcomed most often—can also be used to extract cash advances from associated banks and teller machines throughout much of the Middle East. Credit card companies get the wholesale exchange rate, which is generally 5% better than the retail rate used by banks and other currency exchange establishments. **American Express** cards also work in some ATMs, as well as at AmEx offices and major airports. All ATM machines require a **Personal Identification Number (PIN).** Ask your credit card company for a PIN before you leave; without it, you cannot withdraw cash with your credit card outside your home country. If you already have a PIN, check with the company to make sure it will work in the Middle East (PIN numbers must be **four digits** in length; see **Cash Cards** below for details). Credit cards often offer an array of other services, from insurance to emergency assistance. Check with your company to find out what is covered.

CASH CARDS

Cash cards—popularly called **ATM (Automated Teller Machine) cards**—are fairly widespread in the Middle East, except in Yemen (where there are no ATMs) and in the UAE (where ATMs do not accept international cards). Depending on the system that your home bank uses, you can probably access your own personal bank account whenever you need money. ATMs get the same wholesale exchange rate as credit cards. Despite these perks, do some research before relying too heavily on automation. There is often a limit on the amount of money you can withdraw per day (usually about US$500, depending on the type of card and account), and computer networks sometimes fail. If you're traveling from the U.S. or Canada, memorize your PIN code in numeral form since machines elsewhere often don't have letters on their keys. Also, if your PIN is longer than four digits, ask your bank whether the first four digits will work, or whether you need a new number. The two major international money networks are **Cirrus** (U.S. 800-4-CIRRUS) and **PLUS** (U.S. 800-843-7587). To locate ATMs around the world, use www.visa.com/pd/atm or www.mastercard.com/atm.

GETTING MONEY FROM HOME

Carry a credit card or a separate stash of traveler's checks. If you must get money from home while you're abroad, try the following options:

AMERICAN EXPRESS. Cardholders can withdraw cash from their checking accounts at any of AmEx's major offices and many of its representatives' offices, up to US$1000 every 21 days (no service charge, no interest). AmEx also offers Express Cash at any of their ATMs in the Middle East. Green card holders may withdraw up to US$1000 in a seven day period. There is a 2% transaction fee for each cash withdrawal, with a US$2.50 minimum/$20 maximum. To enroll in Express Cash, Cardmembers may call 800-CASH NOW (227-4669) in the U.S.; outside the U.S. call collect 336-668-5041.

WESTERN UNION. Travelers from the U.S., Canada, and the U.K. can wire money abroad through Western Union's international money transfer services. In the U.S., call 800-325-6000; in the U.K., call (0800) 833 833; in Canada, call 800-235-0000. The rates for sending cash are generally US$10-11 cheaper than with a credit card, and the money is usually received within an hour.

U.S. STATE DEPARTMENT (U.S. CITIZENS ONLY). In emergencies, U.S. citizens can have money sent via the State Department. For US$15, they will forward money within hours to the nearest consular office, which will disburse it according to instructions. The office serves only Americans in the direst of straits abroad; non-American travelers should contact their embassies for information on wiring cash. Check with the State Department or the nearest U.S. embassy or consulate for the quickest way to have the money sent. Contact the Overseas Citizens Service, American Citizens Services, Consular Affairs, Room 4811, U.S. Department of State, Washington, D.C. 20520 (tel. 202-647-5225; nights, Sundays, and holidays 647-4000; fax (on demand only) 647-3000; travel.state.gov).

TIPPING AND BARGAINING

Bargaining and tipping (called *bakhsheesh* in the Middle East) will be encouraged (at times expected) everywhere you go in the Middle East. There are three kinds of *bakhsheesh*. The most common is similar to tipping—a small reward for a small service. *Bakhsheesh* becomes most useful when used to procure special favors; almost any minor rule can be broken in exchange for *bakhsheesh*. The second kind of *bakhsheesh* is the giving of alms. There are beggars everywhere in the Middle East who are willing to bestow rhetorical blessings in return for a little charity. There are also those who insist on opening a door before you can get to it or snatch your baggage from your hands and then demand *bakhsheesh*. Don't feel obligated to give money in these situations. The final form of *bakhsheesh* is simply a bribe, a bad idea. Don't bribe government officials.

SAFETY AND SECURITY

The number one concern for most travelers planning a trip to the Middle East is safety. There are regions in the Middle East in which travel remains unsafe; however, the most important thing to do is stay up to date on events so you can make informed decisions. Good sources for this current information are newspapers, TV, and websites on travel safety run by your home country (www.state.gov for the U.S., www.dfait-maeci.gc.ca for Canada, www.fco.gov.uk for the UK, and www.dfat.gov.au for Australia). For country specifics, see individual chapters and **Terrorism** below.

   Respecting **local customs** may placate would-be hecklers. Familiarize yourself with your surroundings before setting out; if you must check a map on the street, duck into a cafe or shop. Carry yourself with confidence. If you are traveling alone, be sure that someone at home knows your itinerary and never admit to strangers that you are alone. Men and women should make an effort to dress respectably; see the **Dress and Etiquette** and **Women Travelers** section at the start of each country chapter, as well as **Essentials: Women Travelers** (p. 29).

PROTECTING YOURSELF (AND YOUR WALLET)

Find out about unsafe areas from tourist offices, the manager of your hotel or hostel, or a local whom you trust. You may want to carry a **whistle** to scare off attackers or attract attention; also memorize emergency numbers for the city or area. Whenever possible, *Let's Go* warns of unsafe neighborhoods and areas, but there are some good general tips to follow. When walking at night, stick to busy, well-lit streets and avoid dark alleyways. Do not attempt to cross through parks, parking lots or other large, deserted areas. The distribution of people can reveal a great deal about the relative safety of the area; look for children playing, women walking in the open, and other signs of an active community. Keep in mind that a district can change drastically from block to block. There are really only a few regions in the Middle East where violent crime against foreigners is a serious threat, and there are a few simple precautions travelers can take (see **Protecting Your Valuables,** p. 15). However, while many places have **pickpockets,** the most common thievery is simple scamming. Trust your instincts: if you feel you are getting something for nothing, be wary. On the other hand, if you feel that something is reasonably priced by Western standards, know that you may very well be paying too much for it. Labor and materials cost much less in most of the Middle East than they do in the Western world, and prices should reflect that.

TERRORISM

Although the Middle East has long been known for centuries-old political and religious conflicts, travel in the region is relatively safe for a cautious traveler exercising common sense. Those planning to visit the region for longer periods of time should register with their home country's embassy in each destination country to obtain updated information on travel and security in specific areas.

EGYPT. Traveling in Egypt is very safe save in two areas: **Middle Egypt** and the **Egyptian frontiers.** Since the summer of 1998, the U.S. government has warned against traveling in Middle Egypt (especially near the governates of Minya, Asyut, Sohag, and just north of Qena), where terrorist attacks by extremist groups have occurred since the mid-1990s. Although there were no attacks on foreign tourists anywhere in Egypt in 1998, these areas should be considered a greater risk (*Let's Go* did not send a researcher to this area for safety reasons). Those wishing to visit areas near Egypt's frontiers should also be aware of the dangers of off-road travel and the possible threat of **landmines** (now marked by barbed wire) from previous conflicts. The dangerous areas of Egypt's "frontier" include: the oases near the Libyan border (except for the relatively safe Siwa Oasis); off-road areas in the Sinai; and sights south of Aswan near the Sudanese border (an area known as disputed "Ha'ib Triangle" area). Those wishing to visit the first two regions must get permission from the Travel Permits Department of the Ministry of the Interior in Cairo.

ISRAEL AND THE PALESTINIAN TERRITORIES. Terrorists in **Israel** target public transportation and crowded areas. Most bus bombings in Israel occur in the early morning rush hour. If your plans are flexible, try to avoid bus travel at this time. As terrorism has sadly become a part of life in the country, Israelis look at abandoned purses and backpacks in a different light. Don't leave anything unattended. Alert authorities if you see an abandoned package.

Traveling in the **Palestinian territories** can be dangerous, especially in a car with the yellow license plates that identify the vehicle as Israeli. Jewish travelers should avoid identifying themselves as such. Simply placing a baseball cap over a *kippah* can prevent stares and hostility. Be aware of potential unrest in the West Bank by staying up to date with the news and contacting the consular division of the United States Consulate General, located at 27 Nablus Rd. in East Jerusalem.

JORDAN. Travel in Jordan is relatively safe. Amman (via the King Hussein/ Allenby Bridge) and Aqaba (by way of Eilat) are the only safe gateways into Israel from anywhere in the Levant. See **Jordan: Border Crossings** (p. 404) for detailed information on travel between Jordan and Israel.

LEBANON. As of July 9, 1999, the U.S. Department of State has issued a **travel warning** for Lebanon. In June 1998, the U.S. Embassy in Beirut was the target of a rocket-propelled grenade attack, and the security situation in the city of **Sidon** has recently deteriorated, including the issuance from the Sidon area of an anti-American threat of undetermined credibility. Americans are cautioned to avoid travel into Sidon and adjacent Palestinian refugee camps until the security environment stabilizes. As an added precaution, American air carriers are prohibited from the use of the **Beirut International Airport** due to continuing concern about passenger and aircraft security arrangements. **Southern Lebanon** (namely the southern suburbs of Beirut as far north as the Na'ameh Hills and sections of the Beqa'a Valley) can also be a dangerous place to travel because of a series of raids and counterraids by the extremist group Hezbollah and its allies on one side, and the Israeli military forces and the South Lebanon Army on the other (for details, see **Lebanon:**

Modern History, p. 460). Although **Ba'albeck** is the headquarters of Hezbollah, the region is relatively safe and comfortable to travel in.

OMAN. It is safe to travel in Oman, especially since the government has been greatly expanding its tourism industry in the past few years. As Oman is a fairly conservative country, travelers should also be sensitive to Muslim dress and etiquette customs (see **Gulf States: Dress and Etiquette,** p. 619).

SYRIA. Traveling in Syria is very safe. The main problem travelers will encounter involves traveling to Syria after visiting **Israel.** The Syrian government rigidly enforces restrictions on prior travel to Israel: authorities will refuse admission to travelers whose passports have Israeli stamps, Jordanian entry cachets or cachets from other countries that suggest prior travel to Israel, or whose passports do not bear any entry stamps from a country adjacent to Israel that the traveler has just visited. Although Syria is included on the U.S. Department of State's list of state sponsors of **terrorism,** there is no record of terrorist attacks against foreigners or of a terrorist presence anywhere in Syria; the Syrian government has also repeatedly stated their commitment to protect foreigners.

TURKEY. The **PKK** (Workers' Party of Kurdistan) and the DHKP/C (formerly Dev Sol) commit most of the terrorist acts in Turkey, which have historically not targeted tourists. The PKK vowed to stop targeting civilians, and declared a cease-fire in August 1999; nevertheless, the capture of PKK leader Abdullah Öcalan has led to an increase in terrorist activities (see **In The News,** p. 542). *Let's Go* does not recommend that women travel alone in **Eastern Anatolia.** Incidents of terrorism are frequent in **southeastern Turkey,** which is under martial law as some provinces are effectively in a state of civil war, with Kurdish guerillas fighting for freedom; much of *Let's Go* coverage of this region was not researched in the summer of 1999 due to instability. Although access to Mt. Ararat is officially prohibited, it is still possible to get near it. In most militarized cities, **roads close** in the afternoon. Photographs of military installations, bridges, and power stations are prohibited.

UNITED ARAB EMIRATES (UAE). Traveling in the United Arab Emirates is very safe, though it is not hassle free, especially for women, who may feel uncomfortable and occasionally threatened (see **Gulf States: Women Travelers,** p. 619). The threat is actually minimal; women will usually be pestered but not physically endangered. Taking **photographs** of anything that could be perceived as being of military or security interest may put you in trouble with the authorities; check with them before photographing anything of a sensitive nature.

YEMEN. Since 1991, there have been over 100 instances of foreigners being kidnapped by armed tribesmen with specific grievances against the Yemeni government. These **kidnappings** are often resolved peacefully, but in a few instances tribesmen have held foreigners for extended periods. Most recently, 16 Western tourists were kidnapped and four of them killed in December 1998. Kidnappings have occurred mainly along the Sana'a-Dhamar-'Aden Road, Yemen's most heavily traveled highway; in rural tribal areas north and east of Sana'a; close to the non-demarcated border with Saudi Arabia; and near disputed islands in the Red Sea. Yemeni security officials advise against casual travel to all rural areas. Make security arrangements in advance (between 'Aden and Al-Mukalla, foreigners are required to travel with an armed escort).

SELF-DEFENSE

There is no sure-fire protection from all of the situations you might encounter when you travel. A good self-defense course will give you more concrete ways to react to different types of aggression. **Impact, Prepare,** and **Model Mugging** can refer you to local self-defense courses in the United States (800-345-5425) and Vancouver, Canada (604-878-3838). Workshops (2-3hr.) start at US$50 and full courses run US$350-500. Both women and men are welcome.

FURTHER INFORMATION. The following government offices provide travel information and advisories by telephone or on their websites:
Australian Department of Foreign Affairs and Trade (tel. (02) 6261 1111; www.dfat.gov.au).
Canadian Department of Foreign Affairs and International Trade (DFAIT) (tel. 800-267-8376, from Ottawa 613-944-4000; www.dfait-maeci.gc.ca). Call for their free booklet, *Bon Voyage...But.*
U.K. Foreign and Commonwealth Office (tel. (0171) 238 4503; www.fco.gov.uk).
U.S. Department of State (202-647-5225; travel.state.gov). For their publication *A Safe Trip Abroad,* call 202-512-1800.

FINANCIAL SECURITY

PROTECTING YOUR VALUABLES. Street crime is not common in the Middle East, except in larger cities like Beirut. Label every piece of luggage both inside and out. **Do not put a wallet with money in your back pocket.** Never count your money in public and carry as little as possible. If you carry a purse, buy a sturdy one with a secure clasp and strong strap, and carry it crosswise on the side, away from the street with the clasp against you. Secure packs with small combination padlocks that slip through the two zippers. If you do not trust the locks in your hotel, use the padlock to secure the door of your room. A **money belt** is the best way to carry cash; you can buy one at most camping supply stores. A **neck pouch** is equally safe, although far less accessible. Refrain from pulling out your neck pouch in public. Do not keep anything valuable in a fanny-pack (even if it's worn on your stomach).

CON ARTISTS AND PICKPOCKETS. Con artists and hustlers often work in groups, and children are among the most effective. Be aware of certain classics: sob stories that require money, rolls of bills "found" on the street, mustard spilled (or saliva spit) onto your shoulder distracting you for enough time to snatch your bag. In Egypt especially, where a thriving tourist industry has existed for years and where tourism is often the only source of income, hustlers have fine-tuned the con into an art form (see **The Pros of Cons in Cairo,** p. 67). Be suspicious in unexpected situations. Contact the police if a hustler is particularly insistent or aggressive.

Extra vigilance may be wise in cities, but there is never need for paranoia. Stick to busy, well-lit streets. Tourist information offices and hotel and hostel managers can be valuable sources of advice on which areas to avoid. In city crowds and especially on public transportation, **pickpockets** are amazingly deft at their craft. Rush hour is no excuse for strangers to press up against you on the street or bus. Also, be alert in public telephone booths. If you must say your calling card number, do so very quietly; if you punch it in, make sure no one can look over your shoulder.

ACCOMMODATIONS AND TRANSPORTATION. Never leave your belongings unattended. If you feel unsafe, look for places with either a curfew or a night attendant. *Let's Go* lists locker availability in hostels and train stations, but you'll need your own **padlock.** Lockers are useful if you plan on sleeping outdoors or don't want to lug everything with you, but don't store valuables in them. If you have a padlock, use it to secure your door from the inside at night, from the outside when you're sightseeing. If you're in a dorm-style room or have no lock on your door, sleep with all valuables on your person or under your pillow.

Be particularly careful on **buses.** Always carry your backpack in front of you where you can see it. Don't check your luggage on trains. Thieves thrive on **trains;** professionals wait for tourists to fall asleep and then carry off everything they can. When traveling in pairs, sleep in alternating shifts; when alone, use good judgement in selecting a train compartment: never stay in an empty one, and use a lock to secure your pack to the luggage rack. Keep important documents and other valuables on your person and try to sleep on top bunks with your luggage stored above you (if not in bed with you). If you travel by **car,** do not leave valuable possessions in it while you are away. Hide baggage in the trunk.

DRUGS AND ALCOHOL

You are subject to the laws of the country in which you travel, not to those of your home country. **Illegal drugs** (which includes marijuana) are best avoided altogether. Penalties for possession, use, or trafficking in illegal drugs are severe throughout the Middle East. Egypt, Syria, and Oman may impose the **death penalty** on anyone convicted of smuggling or selling. Consulates can do no more than bring floral arrangements to prisoners, provide a list of attorneys, and inform family and friends. If you carry **prescription drugs** while you travel, it is vital to have a copy of the prescriptions themselves readily accessible at country borders.

Although there is an Islamic law forbidding **alcohol,** lots of people drink anyway. You may be asked to purchase alcohol for not-so-devout Muslims; unless they are underage, it is perfectly legal to do so. The drinking age in Egypt, Oman, and the UAE is 21; in Israel, Jordan, Syria, Lebanon, Turkey, and Cyprus it is 18. Israel, Oman, and the UAE enforce this law strictly. **Public drunkenness** is against the law in many countries and socially offensive.

HEALTH

Common sense is the simplest prescription for good health while you travel. Drink lots of fluids to prevent dehydration and constipation, wear sturdy, broken-in shoes and clean socks, and use talcum powder to keep your feet dry.

BEFORE YOU GO

Bring a compact **first-aid kit,** including bandages, aspirin or other pain killer, antibiotic cream, a thermometer, a Swiss army knife with tweezers, moleskin, decongestant for colds, motion sickness remedy, medicine for diarrhea or stomach problems, sunscreen, insect repellent, burn ointment, and a syringe for emergency medical purposes (get a letter of explanation from your doctor).

In your **passport,** write the names of people to contact in case of a medical emergency, and list any **allergies** or medical conditions. Matching a prescription to a foreign equivalent is not always easy, safe, or possible, so carry up-to-date, legible prescriptions or a statement from your doctor stating the medication's trade name, manufacturer, chemical name, and dosage. Keep all medication with you in your carry-on luggage.

IMMUNIZATIONS. Take a look at your **immunization** records before you go; if you are coming from a tropical area with a risk of yellow fever or cholera, such as Sub-Saharan Africa, you may be required to show certificates of up-to-date vaccinations to enter some countries. Travelers over two years old should be sure that the following vaccines are up to date: Measles, Mumps, and Rubella (MMR); Diptheria, Tetanus, and Pertussis (DTP or DTap); Polio (OPV); Haemophilus Influenza B (HbCV); and Hepatitis B (HBV). A booster of Tetanus-diptheria (Td) is recommended once every 10 years, and adults should consider an additional dose of Polio vaccine if they have not already had one during their adult years. Hepatitis A vaccine and/or Immune Globulin (IG) is recommended for travelers to the Middle East as well. If you will be spending more than four weeks in Egypt, Jordan, Lebanon, Syria, Yemen, or Oman, you should consider the typhoid vaccine also.

USEFUL ORGANIZATIONS. The **U.S. Centers for Disease Control and Prevention (CDC)** (tel. 888-232-3299; www.cdc.gov) is an excellent source of information for travelers around the world and maintains an international fax information service for travelers. The CDC also publishes the booklet "Health Information for International Travelers" (US$20), an annual global rundown of disease, immunization, and general health advice, including risks in particular countries. Send a check or money order to the Superintendent of Documents, U.S. Government Printing Office, P.O. Box 371954, Pittsburgh, PA, 15250-7954. Orders can be made by phone (tel. 202-512-1800) with a major credit card (Visa, MC, or Discover).

The **U.S. State Department** (travel.state.gov) compiles Consular Information Sheets on health, entry requirements, and other issues for all countries of the world. For quick information on travel warnings, call the **Overseas Citizens' Services** (202-647-5225; after-hours 647-4000). To receive the same Consular Information Sheets by fax, dial 202-647-3000 directly from a fax machine and follow the recorded instructions. The State Department's regional passport agencies in the U.S., field offices of the U.S. Chamber of Commerce, and U.S. embassies and consulates abroad provide the same data, or send a self-addressed, stamped envelope to the Overseas Citizens' Services, Bureau of Consular Affairs, #4811, U.S. Department of State, Washington, D.C. 20520.

FURTHER READING: USEFUL ORGANIZATIONS. For a country-by-country overview of diseases, try the **International Travel Health Guide,** Stuart Rose, MD (Travel Medicine, $20). Information is also available at Travel Medicine's website (www.travmed.com). For general health information, contact the **American Red Cross.** The ARC publishes *First-Aid and Safety Handbook* (US$5) available for purchase by calling or writing to the American Red Cross, 285 Columbus Ave., Boston, MA 02116-5114 (tel. 800-564-1234, M-F 8:30am-4:30pm). Useful **web pages** include CDC Travel Information's *Health Information for Travelers to the Middle East* (www.cdc.gov/travel/mideast.htm) and the United States State Department's *Tips for Travelers to the Middle East and North Africa* (travel.state.gov/tips_mid-east%26nafrica.html).

MEDICAL ASSISTANCE ON THE ROAD. Most Middle Eastern hospitals do not have the high quality of medical treatment found in North America, Europe, or Australia, and few doctors speak English. Only in Israel, where medicine is socialized, are city hospitals on par with Western standards in training and technology. Many large hotels throughout the Middle East have English-speaking doctors on-call, who can either treat travelers or refer them to the nearest city hospital. Pharmacies are absolutely everywhere in the Middle East; many countries even have rotating 24-hour pharmacy duties.

If you are concerned about being able to access medical support while traveling, contact one of these two services: **Global Emergency Medical Services (GEMS)** has products called *MedPass* that provide 24-hour international medical assistance and support coordinated through registered nurses who have online access to your medical information, your primary physician, and a worldwide network of screened, credentialed English-speaking doctors and hospitals. Subscribers also receive a personal medical record that contains vital information in case of emergencies, and GEMS will pay for medical evacuation if necessary. Prices start at about US$35 for a 30-day trip and run up to about $100 for annual services. For more information contact them at: 2001 Westside Dr. #120, Alpharetta, GA 30004 (tel. 800-860-1111; fax 770-475-0058; www.globalems.com). The **International Association for Medical Assistance to Travelers (IAMAT)** has free membership and offers a directory of English-speaking doctors around the world who treat members for a set fee schedule, and detailed charts on immunization requirements, various tropical diseases, climate, and sanitation. Chapters include: **U.S.,** 417 Center St., Lewiston, NY 14092 (tel. 716-754-4883, 8am-4pm; fax 519-836-3412; email iamat@sentex.net; www.sentex.net/~iamat); **Canada,** 40 Regal Road, Guelph, ON, N1K 1B5 (tel. 519-836-0102) or 1287 St. Clair Avenue West, Toronto, ON M6E 1B8 (tel. 416-652-0137; fax 519-836-3412); and **New Zealand,** P.O. Box 5049, Christchurch 5 (fax (03) 352 4630; email iamat@chch.planet.org.nz).

MEDICAL CONDITIONS. Those with medical conditions may want to obtain a **Medic Alert** identification tag (US$35 the first year, US$15 annually thereafter), which identifies the condition and gives a 24-hour collect-call information number. Contact Medic Alert Foundation, 2323 Colorado Ave., Turlock, CA 95382 (tel. 800-825-3785; www.medicalert.org). Diabetics can contact the **American Diabetes Asso-**

ciation, 1660 Duke St., Alexandria, VA 22314 (tel. 800-232-3472), to receive copies of the article "Travel and Diabetes" and a diabetic ID card, which carries messages in 18 languages explaining the carrier's diabetic status. If you are **HIV** positive, contact the Bureau of Consular Affairs, #4811, Department of State, Washington, D.C. 20520 (tel. 202-647-1488; auto-fax 202-647-3000; travel.state.gov). Some Middle Eastern countries will not issue visas to HIV-positive travelers.

ENVIRONMENTAL HAZARDS

Heat exhaustion and dehydration: Heat exhaustion, characterized by dehydration and salt deficiency, can lead to fatigue, headaches, and wooziness. Avoid heat exhaustion by drinking plenty of clear fluids and eating salty foods, like crackers. Always drink enough liquids to keep your urine clear. Wear a hat, sunglasses, and a lightweight longsleeve shirt in hot sun, and take time to acclimate to a hot destination before seriously exerting yourself. Continuous heat stress can eventually lead to **heatstroke**, characterized by rising body temperature, severe headache, and cessation of sweating. Victims must be cooled off with wet towels and taken to a doctor as soon as possible.

Sunburn: If you're prone to sunburn, bring sunscreen with you and apply it liberally. If you are planning on spending time near water, in the desert, or in the snow, you are at risk of getting burned, even through clouds. Protect your eyes with good sunglasses. If you get sunburned, drink fluids and apply Calamine or an aloe-based lotion.

PREVENTING DISEASE

INSECT-BORNE DISEASES. Be aware of insects in wet or forested areas, while hiking, and especially while camping. **Mosquitoes** are most active from dusk to dawn. Use insect repellents, such as DEET. Wear long pants and long sleeves and buy a mosquito net. Wear shoes and socks, and tuck long pants into socks. Soak or spray your gear with permethrin, which is licensed in the U.S. for use on clothing. Natural repellents can be useful supplements: taking vitamin B-12 pills regularly can eventually make you smelly to insects, as can garlic pills.

Malaria is transmitted by *Anopheles* mosquitoes that bite at night. Incubation period varies; it could take months for an infected person to show symptoms. Early symptoms include fever, chills, aches, and fatigue, followed by high fever and sweating, sometimes with vomiting and diarrhea. See a doctor for any flu-like sickness that occurs after travel in a risk area, and get tested immediately. Left untreated, malaria can cause anemia, kidney failure, coma, and death, and is an especially serious threat to pregnant women. There are a number of oral prophylactics to protect against the disease. Western Doctors prescribe **mefloquine** (sold under the name Lariam) or **doxycycline.**

FOOD- AND WATER-BORNE DISEASES. Be sure that everything you eat is cooked properly and that the water you drink is clean. In the Middle East, where the risk of contracting traveler's diarrhea or forms of food poisoning is high, never drink unbottled water that you have not treated. To purify your own water, bring it to a rolling boil or treat it with **iodine tablets,** available at any camping goods store. In risk areas, don't brush your teeth with tap water or rinse your toothbrush under the faucet, and keep your mouth closed in the shower. Salads and uncooked vegetables (including lettuce and coleslaw) are also full of untreated water. Other culprits are raw **shellfish,** unpasteurized milk, and sauces containing **raw eggs.** Insist on having any lukewarm meats or meat-sauces reheated, and anything slightly undercooked put back on the grill. Peel all fruits and vegetables yourself, and beware of **watermelon,** which is often injected with impure water. Watch out for food, fruit, or juices from markets or street vendors that may have been washed in dirty water or fried in rancid cooking oil. Always wash hands before eating and after using the restroom to minimize the risk of Hepatitis A; bring a quick-drying antibacterial hand cleaner. Your bowels will thank you.

▧ **Traveler's diarrhea** results from drinking untreated water or eating uncooked foods, and can last 3 to 7 days. Symptoms include nausea, bloating, urgency, and malaise. If the nasties hit you, eat quick-energy, non-sugary foods with protein and carbohydrates to keep your strength up. Over-the-counter remedies may counteract the problems, but they can complicate serious infections. **Avoid anti-diarrheals** if you suspect that you are risk for other diseases. If possible, avoid taking such medication unless strictly necessary (i.e., before embarking on an overnight bus trip), as how long your stools remain loose is an important diagnostic clue that remains unclear for those using anti-diarrheals. The most dangerous side effect of diarrhea is **dehydration;** the simplest and most effective anti-dehydration formula is 8oz. of (clean) water with a ½ tsp. of sugar or honey and a pinch of salt. Soft drinks without caffeine or salted crackers are also good. Down several of these remedies a day, rest, and wait for the disease to run its course. If you develop a fever or if your symptoms don't go away after 4 or 5 days, consult a doctor. If **children** develop traveler's diarrhea, see a doctor, as treatment is different.

Dysentery results from a serious intestinal infection caused by certain bacteria. The most common type is bacillary dysentery, also called shigellosis. Symptoms include bloody diarrhea or bloody stools mixed with mucus, fever, and abdominal pain and tenderness. Bacillary dysentery generally only lasts a week, but it is highly contagious. Amoebic dysentery develops more slowly, with no fever or vomiting. However, it is a more serious disease, and may cause long-term damage if left untreated. A stool test can determine which kind you have, so you should seek medical help immediately. If you are traveling in high-risk regions (especially rural areas) obtain a prescription before you leave home.

Hepatitis A (distinct from B and C, see below) is a **high risk** in the Middle East. Hep A is a viral infection of the liver acquired primarily through contaminated water, ice, shellfish, or unpeeled fruits and vegetables, and also from sexual contact. Symptoms include fatigue, fever, loss of appetite, nausea, dark urine, jaundice, vomiting, aches and pains, and light stools. Ask your doctor about the vaccine Havrix, or ask to get an injection of immune globulin (IG).

Parasites such as microbes and tapeworms also often hide in unsafe water and food. **Giardia,** for example, is acquired by drinking untreated water from streams or lakes all over the world. Symptoms of parasitic infections in general include swollen glands or lymph nodes, fever, rashes or itchiness, digestive problems, eye problems, anal itching and anemia. Boil your water, wear shoes, avoid bugs, and eat only cooked food.

Schistosomiasis (also called **bilharzia**) is a parasitic disease caused by a flatworm. The larvae mature inside freshwater snails and escape back into the water, where they can infect humans by penetrating unbroken skin. Avoid swimming in fresh water areas. If your skin is exposed to untreated water, rub it immediately and vigorously with a towel and/or rubbing alcohol. You may notice an itchy localized rash; later symptoms include fever, painful urination, diarrhea, loss of appetite, night sweats, and a hive-like rash on the body. Schistosomiasis can be treated with prescription drugs.

Typhoid fever is **common** in villages and rural areas in the Middle East. While mostly transmitted through contaminated food and water, it may also be acquired by direct contact with another person. Symptoms include fever, headaches, fatigue, loss of appetite, constipation, and a rash on the abdomen or chest. Antibiotics can treat typhoid, but the CDC recommends vaccinations (70-90% effective) if you will be hiking, camping, or staying in small cities or rural areas.

OTHER INFECTIOUS DISEASES. Rabies is transmitted through the saliva of infected animals. It is fatal if untreated. Avoid contact with animals, especially strays. If you are bitten, wash the wound thoroughly and seek immediate medical care. Once you begin to show symptoms (thirst and muscle spasms), the disease is in its terminal stage. A rabies vaccine is available but is only semi-effective. Three shots must be administered over one year. **Hepatitis B** is a viral infection of the liver transmitted through the transfer of bodily fluids, by sharing needles, or by having unprotected sex. Its incubation period varies and can be much longer than the 30-day incubation period of Hepatitis A. A person may not begin to show symptoms until many years after infection. The CDC recommends the Hepatitis B vaccination for health-care workers, sexually active travelers, and anyone planning to seek medical treatment abroad. Vaccination consists of a three-shot series given over a period of time, and should begin six months before traveling. **Hepatitis C** is like Hepatitis B, but the modes of transmission are different. Intravenous drug users, those with occupational exposure to blood, hemodialysis patients, or recipients of blood transfusions are at the highest risk, but the disease can also be spread through sexual contact and sharing of items like razors and toothbrushes, which may have traces of blood on them.

AIDS, HIV, STDS

Acquired Immune Deficiency Syndrome (AIDS) is a growing problem around the world. The World Health Organization estimates that there are around 30 million people infected with the HIV virus, and women now represent 40% of all new HIV infections. The easiest mode of HIV transmission is through direct blood-to-blood contact with an HIV-positive person; *never* share intravenous drug, tattooing, or other needles. The most common mode of transmission is sexual intercourse. Health professionals recommend the use of latex condoms—take a supply with you before you depart for your trip. For more information on AIDS, call the **U.S. Centers for Disease Control's** 24-hour hotline at 800-342-2437. In Europe, contact the **World Health Organization,** Attn: Global Program on AIDS, Avenue Appia 20, 1211 Geneva 27, Switzerland (tel. (22) 791 21 11, fax 791 31 11). Council's brochure, *Travel Safe: AIDS and International Travel,* is available at all Council Travel offices and at their website (www.ciee.org/study/safety/travelsafe.htm).

Sexually transmitted diseases (STDs) such as gonorrhea, chlamydia, genital warts, syphilis, and herpes are easier to catch than HIV, and some can be just as deadly. **Hepatitis B** and **C** are also serious sexually-transmitted diseases (see **Other Infectious Diseases,** above). Warning signs for STDs include: swelling, sores, bumps, or blisters on sex organs, rectum, or mouth; burning and pain during urination and bowel movements; itching around sex organs; swelling or redness in the throat, flu-like symptoms with fever, chills, and aches. If these symptoms develop, see a doctor immediately. When having sex, condoms may protect you from certain STDs, but oral or even tactile contact can lead to transmission.

WOMEN'S HEALTH

Women traveling in unsanitary conditions are vulnerable to **urinary tract** and **bladder infections,** common and severely uncomfortable bacterial diseases that cause a burning sensation and painful and sometimes frequent urination. To try to avoid these infections, drink plenty of vitamin-C-rich juice and plenty of clean water, and urinate frequently, especially right after intercourse. See a doctor if symptoms persist: untreated, these infections can lead to kidney infections, sterility, and death.

Vaginal yeast infections are treatable but uncomfortable illnesses likely to flare up in hot and humid climates. Wearing loosely fitting trousers or a skirt and cotton underwear helps. Bring supplies from home if you are prone to infection, as they may be difficult to find on the road. Some travelers opt for a natural alternative such as eating plain yogurt several times a day if other remedies are unavailable.

Tampons and **pads** are sometimes hard to find when traveling, so take supplies along. **Reliable contraceptive devices** may also be difficult to find. Women on the pill should bring enough to allow for possible loss or extended stays. Bring a prescription, since forms of the pill vary a good deal. Women who use a diaphragm should bring enough contraceptive jelly. Though condoms are increasingly available, you might want to bring your favorite brand before you go, as availability and quality vary. For further reading about women's health issues, check out *Handbook for Women Travellers,* by Maggie and Gemma Moss (Piatkus Books, US$15).

INSURANCE

Travel insurance covers four basic areas: medical/health problems, property loss, trip cancellation/interruption, and emergency evacuation. **Medical insurance** (especially university policies) often covers costs incurred abroad; check with your provider. Medicare does not cover foreign travel. Canadians are protected by their home province's health insurance plan for up to 90 days after leaving the country; check with the provincial Ministry of Health or Health Plan Headquarters for details. **Homeowners' insurance** (or your family's coverage) often covers theft during travel and loss of travel documents (passport, plane ticket, etc.) up to US$500. **ISIC** and **ITIC** provide basic insurance benefits, including US$100 per day of in-hospital sickness for a maximum of 60 days, US$3000 of accident-related medical reimbursement, and US$25,000 for emergency medical transport (see **Identification,** p. 7). Cardholders have access to a toll-free 24-hour helpline whose multilingual staff can provide assistance in medical, legal, and financial emergencies overseas (tel. 800-626-2427 in the U.S. and Canada; elsewhere call the U.S. collect 713-267-2525. **American Express** (tel. 800-528-4800) grants most cardholders automatic car rental insurance (collision and theft, but not liability) and ground travel accident coverage of US$100,000 on flight purchases made with the card.

PACKING

Pack light: lay out only what you absolutely need, then take half the clothes and twice the money. For more tips, check out *The Packing Book*, by Judith Gilford (Ten Speed Press, US$9), and *Backpacking One Step at a Time*, by Harvey Manning (Vintage, US$15).

CLOTHING

Don't forget the obvious things: it's always a good idea to bring a rain jacket (Gore-Tex is a miracle fabric that's both waterproof and breathable). **Natural fibers** are better than synthetics in the heat. Dark colors hide dirt, but light colors deflect sun. In many areas (especially holy sites), both men and women should cover their knees and upper arms to avoid offending local rules of modesty. Leave jeans at home: bring along khakis or light cotton trousers.

Well-cushioned **sneakers** are good for walking. Lace-up leather shoes with firm grips provide better support and social acceptability than athletic shoes. A double pair of socks—light absorbent cotton inside and thick wool outside—will cushion feet, keep them dry, and help prevent blisters. If you only want to bring one pair, the best all-around footwear are **sneakers-cum-hiking boots.** Talcum powder in your shoes and on your feet can prevent sores, and moleskin is great for blisters. You should also bring a comfortable pair of waterproof **sandals,** as sneakers get very hot and uncomfortable when the temperature skyrockets.

LUGGAGE

If you plan to cover most of your itinerary by foot, a sturdy **frame backpack** is unbeatable. **Internal-frame packs** mold better to your back, keep a lower center of gravity, and can flex adequately on difficult hikes that require a lot of bending and maneuvering. **External-frame packs** are more comfortable for long hikes over even terrain (like city streets) since they keep the weight higher and distribute it more evenly. In addition to your main vessel, a small backpack, rucksack, or courier bag is useful as a **daypack** for sightseeing expeditions.

ELECTRIC CURRENT

In the Middle East, electricity is 220 volts AC, enough to fry any 110V North American appliance. Most outlets are made for round prongs, so even if your machine has a built-in converter, you'll also need an **adapter** to change the plug shape.

OTHER USEFUL ITEMS

No matter how you're traveling, it's always a good idea to carry a **first-aid kit** (see **Health**, p. 16). Other useful items include: an umbrella; sealable plastic bags; alarm clock; waterproof matches; sun hat; needle and thread; safety pins; sunglasses; pocketknife; plastic water bottle; compass; string; towel; padlock; whistle; rubber bands; flashlight; cold-water soap; earplugs; electrical tape (for patching tears); tweezers; garbage bags; flip-flops for the shower; a money-belt for carrying valuables; deodorant; razors; tampons; and condoms (see **AIDS, HIV, and STDs**, p. 20).

ACCOMMODATIONS

Hostels are generally dorm-style accommodations in single-sex large rooms with bunk beds, although some hostels do offer private rooms for families and couples. The downside to traveling in the Middle East is that there aren't very many hostels. Those that do exist sometimes have kitchens and utensils for your use, bike or moped rentals, storage areas, and laundry services (but not facilities). A bed in a hostel will average around US$6-12. Some **colleges and universities** also open their residence halls to travelers when school is not in session, or even during term-time. These dorms are often close to student areas—good sources for information on things to do—and are usually very clean. Getting a room may take a couple of phone calls and require advanced planning, but rates tend to be low, and many offer free local calls. This option is particularly popular in Yemen, but you can access university lodging worldwide by checking out *Campus Lodging Guide (18th Ed.)*, B&J Publications (US$15).

CAMPING AND THE OUTDOORS

Camping is a viable option in many areas of the Middle East, in particular in Egypt, Jordan, Israel, Lebanon and Turkey. It is generally free or close to free, but typically it will not be organized by a central camping agency, meaning that it is almost entirely unregulated. Always check with the local tourist agency, police, and other travelers before setting up camp to find out if there are certain places where camping is illegal. For information on hiking and camping, contact these companies for a free catalog: **Sierra Club Books,** 85 Second St. 2nd Fl., San Francisco, CA 94105-3441 (tel. 800-935-1056 or 415-977-5500; www.sierraclub.org/books); **The Mountaineers Books,** 1001 SW Klickitat Way, #201, Seattle, WA 98134 (tel. 800- 553-4453 or 206-223-6303; email alans@mountaineers.org; www.mountaineers.org).

KEEPING IN TOUCH

MAIL

SENDING MAIL TO THE MIDDLE EAST

Airmail letters under 1 oz. between North America and the Middle East take seven to 15 days and typically cost under a US$1, or CDN$0.50 up to 15-20g; costs for Turkey and Cyprus are lower and take less time. Allow at least 12-21 business days from Australia (postage AUS$0.50-0.75 for up to 15-20 grams) and 4-10 from the U.K. (postage under £2 for up to 15-20g). Envelopes should be marked "air mail" or "par avion." There are several ways to arrange picking up letters sent from friends and relatives while you are abroad.

General Delivery: Mail can be sent to the Middle East through **Poste Restante** (the international phrase for General Delivery) to almost any city or town with a post office, though Poste Restante does not exist in Lebanon, Oman, or the UAE. Address letters to: Lisa HALABY, Poste Restante, City, COUNTRY. In Turkey, the address must either say *Markaz Postane* (Central Post Office), or specify which office should receive the mail. It is best to use the largest post office in the area, as mail may be sent there regardless of what is written on the envelope. When possible, it is safer and quicker to send mail express or registered. When picking up your mail, bring a form of photo ID, preferably a passport. There is generally no surcharge; if there is, it should not exceed the cost of domestic postage. If there is nothing, have them check under your first name.

American Express: AmEx's travel offices throughout the world will act as a mail service for cardholders. Under this free **Client Letter Service** they will hold mail for up to 30 days and forward upon request. Address the letter in the manner shown above. Some offices will offer these services to non-cardholders (especially those who have purchased AmEx traveler's checks); call ahead to make sure. Check the **Practical Information** section of the countries you plan to visit; *Let's Go* lists AmEx office locations for most large cities. A complete list is available free from AmEx (tel. 800-528-4800).

Express Mail: If regular airmail is too slow, **Federal Express** and **DHL** can move your mail quickly but will charge through the nose for their services. From New York, a half-pound letter costs US$32.50 plus tax to Cairo, Beirut, Tel Aviv or Istanbul, and is guaranteed to arrive in 2 days. Rates from non-U.S. locations are similarly expensive (London to Cairo costs US$29.50; Sydney to Cairo US$79.78). Mail within the Middle East is not much cheaper: Dubai to Cairo runs US$48.50. The cheaper **Global Priority Service** is an excellent alternative, though it only services Cyprus, Israel, and Turkey.

SENDING MAIL HOME

Aerogrammes, printed sheets that fold into envelopes and travel via airmail, are available at post offices. Mark them "airmail" or "par avion." Most post offices will charge exorbitant fees or simply refuse to send aerogrammes with enclosures. Delivery time averages four to 21 days. Costs for Europe, North America, and Australia are similar; costs for Africa and Arab countries are slightly lower.

TELEPHONES

CALLING THE MIDDLE EAST FROM HOME

To call the Middle East direct from home, dial:

1. The **international access code** of your home country. These include: Australia 0011; Ireland 00; New Zealand 00; South Africa 09; U.K. 00; U.S. 011.

2. The **country code** for the nation you are calling. Country and city codes are sometimes listed with a zero in front (e.g., 033), but after dialing the international access code, drop successive zeros (with an access code of 011 and country code of 033, dial 011 33). For individual country codes, see the **Phone Facts** box of each chapter.

3. The **city code** (see the city's **Practical Information** section) and local number.

CALLING HOME FROM THE MIDDLE EAST

A **calling card** is your best and cheapest bet. Calls are billed collect or to your account. **MCI WorldPhone** also provides access to MCI's Traveler's Assist, which gives legal and medical advice, exchange rate information, and translation services. Calling cards cannot be used in Oman, and use is limited in Jordan. **To obtain a calling card** from your national telecommunications service before you leave home, contact the appropriate company. In **Australia,** call Telstra **Australia Direct** (tel. 13 22 00); in **Canada,** call Bell Canada **Canada Direct** (800-565-4708); in **Ireland,** call Telecom Éireann **Ireland Direct** (800 250 250); in **New Zealand,** call **Telecom New Zealand** (800 000 000); in **South Africa,** contact **Telkom South Africa** (tel. 09 03); in the **U.K.,** call British Telecom **BT Direct** (800 34 51 44). In the **U.S.,** your options are **AT&T** (888-288-4685), **Sprint** (800-877-4646), or **MCI** (800-444-4141).

You can usually make **direct international calls** from pay phones. Look for pay phones in public areas, especially train stations, as private pay phones are often more expensive. In-room hotel calls invariably include an arbitrary and sky-high surcharge that can run as much as US$0.75 per minute, or a flat fee of around US$10. If you do dial direct, first insert the appropriate amount of money or a pre-paid phonecard, then dial the international access code for the target country, and then dial the country code and number of your home. **Country codes** include: Australia 61; Ireland 353; New Zealand 64; South Africa 27; U.K. 44; U.S. and Canada 1.

CALLING WITHIN THE MIDDLE EAST

In addition to coin-operated public phones, you can also buy **prepaid phonecards,** which carry a certain amount of phone time depending on the card's denomination. Phone rates tend to be highest in the morning, lower in the evening, and lowest on Sundays and late at night.

EMAIL AND INTERNET

The **Cybercafe Guide** (www.cyberiacafe.net/cyberia/guide/ccafe.htm) can help you find cybercafes in the Middle East, but don't despair if it doesn't list cafes in your target town: they are cropping up so quickly that no index is current. Other places to try are www.cybercaptive.com and www.netcafeguide.com. In Egypt, Lebanon, and Israel, there should be no trouble finding Internet access. In Jordan, Oman, and the UAE, only the big cities have Internet access. It is difficult to find any Internet access in Syria. One money-saving strategy is to befriend college students and ask if you can use their campus terminals.

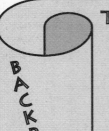

GETTING THERE

BY PLANE

Timing: Airfares to the Middle East peak between mid-June and early Sept.; holidays are also expensive periods in which to travel. Midweek (M-Th morning) round-trip flights run US$40-50 cheaper than weekend flights, but the latter are generally less crowded and more likely to permit frequent-flier upgrades. Return-date flexibility is usually not an option for the budget traveler; traveling with an "open return" ticket can be pricier than fixing a return date when buying the ticket and paying later to change it.

Route: Round-trip flights are by far the cheapest; "open-jaw" (arriving in and departing from different cities) and round-the-world, or RTW, flights are pricier but reasonable alternatives.

Boarding: Whenever flying internationally, pick up tickets for international flights well in advance of the departure date, and confirm by phone within 72 hours of departure. Most airlines require that passengers arrive at the airport at least two hours before departure. One carry-on item and two pieces of checked baggage is the norm for non-courier flights. Consult the airline for weight allowances.

Fares: Traveling from hub to hub (for example, New York to Cairo) will win a more competitive fare than flying to or from smaller cities. Sample round-trip fares from **New York** include: Cairo (US$650-1200); Istanbul (US$450-600); Beirut (US$1100-1500); Tel Aviv (US$700-1100); Dubai (US$850-1700); and Sana'a (US$1100-1600). From **London:** Cairo (US$600-800); Istanbul (US$320-465); Beirut (US$600-900); Tel Aviv (US$310-400); Dubai (US$600-880); and Sana'a (US$1300-1800). From **Sydney:** Cairo (US$1400-1600); Istanbul (US$1200-1350); Beirut (US$1500-1600); Tel Aviv (US$1250-1450); Dubai (US$1500); and Sana'a (US$1500).

BUDGET AND STUDENT TRAVEL AGENCIES

Campus/Usit Youth and Student Travel (www.campustravel.co.uk). In Europe call (0171) 730 34 02; in North America call (0171) 730 21 01; worldwide call (0171) 730 81 11. Offices include: 19-21 Aston Quay, O'Connell Bridge, **Dublin** 2 (tel. (01) 677-8117; fax 679-8833); 52 Grosvenor Gardens, **London** SW1W 0AG; New York Student Center, 895 Amsterdam Ave., **New York,** NY, 10025 (tel. 212-663-5435; email usitny@aol.com). Additional offices in Cork, Galway, Limerick, Waterford, Coleraine, Derry, Belfast, and Greece.

Council Travel (www.counciltravel.com). U.S. offices include: Emory Village, 1561 N. Decatur Rd., **Atlanta,** GA 30307 (404-377-9997); 273 Newbury St., **Boston,** MA 02116 (617-266-1926); 1160 N. State St., **Chicago,** IL 60610 (312-951-0585); 10904 Lindbrook Dr., **Los Angeles,** CA 90024 (310-208-3551); 205 E. 42nd St., **New York,** NY 10017 (212-822-2700); 530 Bush St., **San Francisco,** CA 94108 (415-421-3473); 1314 NE 43rd St. #210, **Seattle,** WA 98105 (206-632-2448); 3300 M St. NW, **Washington, D.C.** 20007 (202-337-6464). For U.S. cities not listed, call 800-2-COUNCIL (226-8624). Also: 28A Poland St. (Oxford Circus), **London,** W1V 3DB (tel. (0171) 287 3337); **Paris** (tel. (144) 41 89 89); and **Munich** (tel. (089) 39 50 22).

STA Travel, 6560 Scottsdale Rd. #F100, Scottsdale, AZ 85253 (800-777-0112 fax 602-922-0793; www.sta-travel.com). A student and youth travel organization with over 150 offices worldwide. U.S. offices: 297 Newbury St., **Boston,** MA 02115 (617-266-6014); 429 S. Dearborn St., **Chicago,** IL 60605 (312-786-9050); 7202 Melrose Ave., **Los Angeles,** CA 90046 (323-934-8722); 10 Downing St., **New York,** NY 10014 (212-627-3111); 4341 University Way NE, **Seattle,** WA 98105 (206-633-5000); 2401 Pennsylvania Ave., Ste. G, **Washington, D.C.** 20037 (202-887-0912); 51 Grant Ave., **San Francisco,** CA 94108 (415-391-8407). In the U.K., 6 Wrights Ln., **London** W8 6TA (tel. (0171) 938 47 11 for North American travel). In New Zealand, 10 High St., **Auckland** (tel. (09) 309 04 58). In Australia, 222 Faraday St., **Melbourne** VIC 3053 (tel. (03) 9349 2411).

ESSENTIALS

Travel CUTS (Canadian Universities Travel Services Limited), 187 College St., Toronto, Ontario M5T 1P7 (tel. 416-979-2406; fax 979-8167; www.travelcuts.com). Forty offices across Canada. In the U.K.: 295A Regent St., **London** W1R 7YA (tel. (0171) 255 19 44).

Cape to Cairo (800-356-4433 or 202-244-5954; email capcairo@erols.com; www.capecairo.com) finds discount and consolidator fares from the U.S. and Europe to Africa, Israel, and the Middle East.

Cheap Tickets (800-377-1000; www.cheaptickets.com) flies worldwide to and from the U.S. and Middle Eastern hubs.

NOW Voyager, 74 Varick St. #307, New York, NY 10013 (212-431-1616; fax 219-1753 or 334-5243; email info@nowvoyagertravel.com; www.nowvoyagertravel.com) acts as a consolidator and books discounted international flights, mostly from New York, as well as courier flights, for an annual fee of US$50.

Travac (800-872-8800; fax 212-563-3631; email mail@travac.com; www.travac.com) offers consolidator fares to the Middle East.

Travel Avenue (800-333-3335; www.travelavenue.com) rebates commercial fares to or from the U.S. and offers low fares for flights anywhere in the world. They also offer package deals, which include car rental and hotel reservations.

FURTHER READING: BY PLANE.
Worldwide Guide to Cheap Airfare, Michael McColl. Insider Publications (US$15).
Discount Airfares: The Insider's Guide, George Hobart. Priceless Publications, (US$14).
The Official Airline Guide, available at many libraries, has flight schedules, fares, and reservation numbers.
Travelocity (www.travelocity.com) has a searchable online database of published airfares. Online reservations.
The Air Traveler's Handbook can be found at www.cs.cmu.edu/afs/cs.cmu.edu/ user/mkant/Public/Travel/airfare.html.
TravelHUB (www.travelhub.com). A directory of travel agents that includes a searchable database of fares from over 500 consolidators.

COMMERCIAL AIRLINES

The commercial airlines' lowest regular offer is the **APEX** (Advance Purchase Excursion) fare, which provides confirmed reservations and allows "open-jaw" tickets. Generally, reservations must be made one to three weeks in advance, with seven- to 14-day minimum and up to 90-day maximum-stay limits, and hefty cancellation and change penalties (fees rise in summer). Book peak-season APEX fares early, since by May you will have a hard time getting the departure date you want. Although APEX fares are probably not the cheapest possible fares, they will give you a sense of the average commercial price, from which to measure other bargains. Popular carriers to the Middle East include:

British Airways (U.S. 800-247-9297; www.british-airways.com) has daily flights to nearly all major Middle Eastern cities, including Cairo, Istanbul, Beirut, Dubai, Muscat, and Sana'a. Most flights originate from London.

EgyptAir (U.S. 800-334-6787, U.K. tel. (171) 734 2343, Australia tel. (02) 9232 6677; www.powerup.com.au/~ancient/eair1.htm). Egypt's national airline not only has the most routes within the country, but also serves major European cities, as well as New York, Los Angeles, Sydney, and Johannesburg.

Royal Jordanian (U.S. or Canada 800-RJ-JORDAN (755-6732), U.K. tel. (171) 878 63 00, Jordan tel. (06) 567 83 21; www.rja.com.jo) not only flies to all major Middle Eastern hub, but has extensive service to many smaller airports as well. Also services many cities in Asia and Europe, and a few in the U.S.

OTHER CHEAP ALTERNATIVES

AIR COURIER FLIGHTS

Couriers help transport cargo on international flights by guaranteeing delivery of the baggage claim slips from the company to a representative overseas. Couriers must travel light (carry-ons only) and deal with complex restrictions on their flight. Most flights are round-trip only with short fixed-length stays (usually one week) and a limit of a single ticket per issue. Most of these flights also operate only out of the biggest cities, like New York. Generally, you must be over 21 (in some cases 18), have a valid passport, and procure your own visa. Groups such as the **Air Courier Association** (tel. 800-282-1202; www.aircourier.org) and the **International Association of Air Travel Couriers,** 220 South Dixie Hwy., P.O. Box 1349, Lake Worth, FL 33460 (561-582-8320; email iaatc@courier.org; www.courier.org) provide their members with lists of opportunities and courier brokers worldwide for an annual fee. For more information, consult *Air Courier Bargains* by Kelly Monaghan (The Intrepid Traveler, US$15) or the *Courier Air Travel Handbook* by Mark Field (Perpetual Press, US$10).

CHARTER FLIGHTS

Charters are flights a tour operator contracts with an airline to fly extra loads of passengers during peak season. Charters can sometimes be cheaper than flights on scheduled airlines, some operate nonstop, and restrictions on minimum advance-purchase and minimum stay are more lenient. However, charter flights fly less frequently than major airlines, make refunds particularly difficult, and are almost always fully booked. Schedules and itineraries may also change or be cancelled at the last moment (as late as 48 hours before the trip, and without a full refund), and check-in, boarding, and baggage claim are often much slower. As always, pay with a credit card if you can, and consider traveler's insurance against trip interruption.

TICKET CONSOLIDATORS

Ticket consolidators (or "bucket shops") buy unsold tickets in bulk from commercial airlines and sell them at discounted rates. The best place to look is in the Sunday travel section of any major newspaper, where many bucket shops place tiny ads. Call quickly, as availability is typically extremely limited. Not all bucket shops are reliable establishments, so insist on a receipt that gives full details of restrictions, refunds, and tickets, and pay by credit card. For more information, check the website **Consolidators FAQ** (www.travel-library.com/air-travel/consolidators.html) or the book *Consolidators: Air Travel's Bargain Basement*, by Kelly Monaghan (Intrepid Traveler, US$8).

AIRCRAFT SAFETY. The airlines of third-world nations do not always meet safety standards. The *Official Airline Guide* (www.oag.com) and many travel agencies can tell you the type and age of aircraft on a particular route. This can be especially useful in the Middle East, where less reliable equipment is often used for inter-city travel. The **International Airline Passengers Association** (U.S. tel. 972-404-9980, safety office open M-F 9-11am; U.K. tel. (181) 681 65 55) provides region-specific safety information. The **Federal Aviation Administration** (www.faa.gov) reviews the airline authorities for countries whose airlines enter the U.S., the **U.S. State Department** (202-647-5225; travel.state.gov/travel_warnings.html) has travel advisories that sometimes involve foreign carriers, especially when terrorist bombings may be a threat.

ESSENTIALS

GETTING AROUND

People drive badly in the Middle East. You should be prepared as a pedestrian, passenger, or driver for unorthodox and aggressive moves. The UAE has the highest death rate from car accidents in the world, and Egypt has the highest rate of frequency of car accidents; Turkey has also achieved international notoriety for its unfortunate driving records. **Wear a seatbelt.** Child safety seats are usually not available: strap on children's seatbelts and don't let kids sit in the front seat, if possible. In many regions, road conditions necessitate driving more slowly and cautiously than you would at home. For long drives in desolate areas, invest in a cellular phone and a roadside assistance program (see p. 28).

Sleeping in your car is one of the most dangerous (and often illegal) ways to get your rest. If your car breaks down, wait for the police to assist you.

DRIVING PERMITS AND CAR INSURANCE

INTERNATIONAL DRIVING PERMIT (IDP). If you plan to drive a car in the Middle East, you must have an International Driving Permit (IDP). It may be a good idea to get one anyway, in case you're in a situation where the police do not know English; information on the IDP is printed in 10 languages, including Arabic. Your IDP, valid for one year, must be issued in your own country before you depart. You must be at least 18 years old to obtain one. A valid driver's license from your home country must always accompany the IDP. Applications usually include photos, a current local license, an additional form of identification, and a fee.

Australia: Contact your local Royal Automobile Club (RAC) or the National Royal Motorist Association (NRMA) if in NSW or the ACT (tel. (08) 9421 4298; www.rac.com.au/travel). Permits AUS$15.

Canada: Contact any Canadian Automobile Association (CAA) branch office, or write to CAA, 1145 Hunt Club Rd., Suite 200, K1V 0Y3 Canada (tel. 613-247-0117; fax 613-247-0118). Permits CDN$10.

Ireland: Contact the nearest Automobile Association (AA) office or write: The Automobile Association, International Documents, Fanum House, Erskine, Renfrewshire PA8 6BW (tel. (990) 500 600). Permits IR£4.

New Zealand: Contact local Automobile Association (AA) or main office at Auckland Central, 99 Albert St. (tel. (9) 377 4660; fax 302 2037; www.nzaa.co.nz.). Permits NZ$8.

South Africa: Contact Automobile Association of South Africa office or head office, P.O. Box 596, 2000 Johannesburg (tel. (11) 799 1000; fax 799 1010). Permits SAR28.50.

U.K.: Visit local AA or call the headquarters (tel. (990) 44 88 66). To find the location nearest you that issues IDP, call (0990) 50 06 00. More information available at www.theaa.co.uk/motoring/idp.asp). Permits UK£4.

U.S.: American Automobile Association (AAA) Travel Related Services, 1000 AAA Dr. (mail stop 100), Heathrow, FL 32746 (tel. 800-222-4357). Members receive road maps, travel guides, emergency road services, travel services, and auto insurance. Permits US$10.

CAR INSURANCE. Most credit cards cover standard insurance. If you rent, lease, or borrow a car, you will need a **green card,** or **International Insurance Certificate,** to prove that you have liability insurance. Obtain it through the car rental agency; most include coverage in their prices. If you lease a car, you can obtain a green card from the dealer. Some travel agents offer the card; it may also be available at border crossings. If you have a collision abroad, the accident will show up on your domestic records if you report it to your insurance company. Rental agencies may require you to purchase theft insurance in countries that they consider to have a high risk of auto theft. Ask your insurance agency about its policy in the Middle East.

SPECIFIC CONCERNS

WOMEN TRAVELERS

Women who are concerned about safety should consider staying in hostels which offer single rooms that lock from the inside or in religious organizations that offer rooms for women only. Stick to centrally located accommodations and avoid solitary late-night treks or metro rides. **Hitching** is never safe for women. Choose train compartments occupied by other women or couples; ask groups of women if you may join them. Wearing a conspicuous **wedding band** may help prevent unwanted overtures, although it still may take repeated declarations of your marital status for it to sink in. Some travelers report that carrying pictures of a "husband" or "children" is extremely useful to help document marriage status. Even a mention of a husband back at the hotel may be enough. Women will find themselves approached much less frequently when escorted by a male over the age of fourteen, but should be wary of claiming to be "friends" with someone: the concept of friendship between men and women in the Arab world differs greatly from its counterpart in the West. Many Arabs see male-female friendships as euphemisms for something more ("friends with benefits," so to speak), and men often think that a woman's speaking to them implies a sexual advance. Some hotels frown upon unmarried couples sharing a room and some have been known not to allow it, especially if one of the people is a native.

Foreign women in the Middle East are guaranteed to attract a great deal of attention. While it is not necessary for women to dress in traditional Arab clothing, they should cover their bodies as much as possible, especially their legs and upper arms. Stay away from the following items of clothing: short skirts, shorts, short athletic gear such as biking shorts, midriff-baring halter tops, v-neck blouses that descend more than an inch or two from the neck, tank tops, visible bra straps, and shirts stretched tight across the bodice. In secular havens like Tel Aviv and Beirut, locals dress in many fashions, from the long, draping dresses of Muslim conservatives to hiphugging hotpants.

In cities, women may be harassed no matter how many precautions they take. Your best answer to verbal harassment is no answer at all. The extremely persistent can sometimes be dissuaded by a firm, loud, and very public "Go away!" (see the **Phrasebook,** p. 702). Don't hesitate to seek out a police officer or a passerby if you are being harassed. Carry a **whistle** and use it. An **IMPACT Model Mugging** self-defense course will not only prepare you for a potential attack, but will also raise your level of awareness of your surroundings as well as your confidence (see **Self Defense,** p. 14). Women also face some specific health concerns when traveling (see **Women's Health,** p. 20). For detailed information and suggestions for how to stay safe and healthy, refer to country chapters, under the heading **Women Travelers.**

FURTHER READING: WOMEN TRAVELERS.

A Journey of One's Own: Uncommon Advice for the Independent Woman Traveler, Thalia Zepatos. Eighth Mountain Press (US$17).

Adventures in Good Company: The Complete Guide to Women's Tours and Outdoor Trips, Thalia Zepatos. Eighth Mountain Press (US$7).

Active Women Vacation Guide, Evelyn Kaye. Blue Panda Publications (US$18).

Travelers' Tales: Gutsy Women, Travel Tips and Wisdom for the Road, Marybeth Bond. Traveler's Tales (US$8).

A Foxy Old Woman's Guide to Traveling Alone, Jay Ben-Lesser. Crossing Press (US$11).

ESSENTIALS

TRAVELING ALONE

There are many benefits to traveling alone, among them greater independence and challenge. As a lone traveler, you have greater opportunity to interact with the residents of the region you're visiting. Without distraction, you can write a great travelogue in the grand tradition of the Bible or Lawrence of Arabia. However, any solo traveler is a more vulnerable target of harassment and street theft. Solo women in particular may find it difficult to travel alone, particularly in the more conservative Gulf States; consult the **Women Travelers** section for each country for more tips for women traveling alone. Lone travelers need to be well-organized and look confident at all times. If questioned, never admit that you are traveling alone. Maintain regular contact with someone at home who knows your itinerary. Read *Traveling Solo*, Eleanor Berman (Globe Pequot, US$17) or *The Single Traveler Newsletter* (P.O. Box 682, Ross, CA 94957; tel. 415-389-0227; 6 issues US$29).

A number of organizations supply information for solo travelers, and others find travel companions for those who don't want to go alone. A few are listed below:

Connecting: Solo Traveler Network, P.O. Box 29088, 1996 W. Broadway, Vancouver, BC V6J 5C2, Canada (tel. 604-737-7791; email info@cstn.org; www.cstn.org). Bi-monthly newsletter features going solo tips, single-friendly tips and travel companion ads. Annual directory lists holiday suppliers that avoid single supplement charges. Advice and lodging exchanges facilitated between members. Membership US$25-35.

Travel Companion Exchange, P.O. Box 833, Amityville, NY 11701 (tel. 516-454-0880 or 800-392-1256; www.travelalone.com). Publishes the pamphlet *Foiling Pickpockets & Bag Snatchers* (US$4) and *Travel Companions*, a bi-monthly newsletter for single travelers seeking a travel partner (subscription US$48).

BISEXUAL, GAY, AND LESBIAN TRAVELERS

The Middle East is not a particularly rainbow-friendly locale—even though men hold hands in the street, this reflects a different cultural attitude about male physicality, not homosexuality (see **I Wanna Hold Your Hand**, p. 47). No one is out of the closet in any public fashion except in Beirut, Haifa, and Tel Aviv; although homosexuality is legal in Turkey, it is not prevalent. A few gay bars here and there do not mean that any same-sex public displays of affection will be socially acceptable—they may even be illegal in some areas. For listings of gay-friendly places in Lebanon, Israel, and Turkey, check out the *Ferrari Guides* line of books, which includes *Gay Travel A to Z, Men's* and *Women's Travel in Your Pocket*, and *Inn Places* (US$14-16; tel. 602-863-2408 or 800-962-2912; www.q-net.com). For the most complete listings of gay-friendly establishments in every country in the Middle East except Oman, read *Spartacus International Gay Guide* (Bruno Gmunder Verlag; US$33).

Gay's the Word, 66 Marchmont St., London WC1N 1AB (tel. (0171) 278 7654; email gays.theword@virgin.net; www.gaystheword.co.uk). The largest gay and lesbian bookshop in the U.K. Mail-order service available. No catalogue of listings, but they will provide a list of titles on a given subject.

Giovanni's Room, 345 S. 12th St., Philadelphia, PA 19107 (tel. 215-923-2960; fax 923-0813; email giophilp@netaxs.com). An international feminist, lesbian, and gay bookstore with mail-order service which carries the publications listed here.

International Gay and Lesbian Travel Association, 4331 N. Federal Hwy., Suite 304, Fort Lauderdale, FL 33308 (tel. 954-776-2626 or 800-448-8550; fax 954-776-3303; email IGLTA@aol.com; www.iglta.com). An organization of more than 1350 companies serving gay and lesbian travelers worldwide.

International Lesbian and Gay Association (ILGA), 81 rue Marché-au-Charbon, B-1000 Brussels, Belgium (tel./fax 32 2 502 24 71; email ilga@ilga.org; www.ilga.org). Provides political information such as homosexuality laws of individual countries.

ESSENTIALS

TRAVELERS WITH DISABILITIES

The chaotic traffic and bumpy, frequently unpaved roads that make vehicular travel in the Middle East an annoyance make travel prohibitively difficult for travelers with disabilities. People in the Middle East are fairly ignorant of disabilities, and few places are handicapped accessible. **Israel** has taken several steps toward making the businesses and sights in and around their modernized cities more accessible to disabled travelers. Many travelers cite the **Gulf States** (particularly Abu Dhabi and Dubai) as particularly accessible and disability-friendly. Unlike hotels in the rest of the Arab world, a majority of the accommodations in the UAE and Oman are well-equipped for disabled travelers. **Directions Unlimited** (720 N. Bedford Rd., Bedford Hills, NY 10507; 800-533-5343, in NY 914-241-1700, fax 914-241-0243; email cruisesusa@aol.com) arranges individual and group vacations, tours, and cruises for the physically disabled.

Those with disabilities should inform airlines and hotels of their disabilities when making travel arrangements; some time may be needed to prepare special accommodations. The **Society for the Advancement of Travel for the Handicapped** (347 Fifth Ave., #610, New York, NY 10016; tel. 212-447-1928; fax 725-8253; email sath-travel@aol.com; www.sath.org) is an advocacy group that publishes a quarterly travel magazine, *Open World* (free for members, US$13 for nonmembers). SATH also publishes a wide range of information sheets on disability travel and accessible destinations (annual membership US$45, students and seniors US$30).

MINORITY TRAVELERS

People of all skin colors and types will find less an active racism in the Middle East than an ignorance about people other than themselves. **Ethnic Asians** may attract stares, especially in untouristed areas. In some regions of the Middle East, **black or dark-skinned travelers** may find that they encounter some negative attention. This response arises largely from the fact that Africans have traditionally been seen as interlopers. **Ethnic Indians** may find that they encounter what appears to be snobbery or classism in the Gulf States, since many Indian and Pakistani nationals have moved to the oil-rich countries to work and support their families from afar. **Blondes** attract curiosity in the Middle East, since native blondes are nonexistent.

All over the Middle East, the highly explosive ethnic and religious tensions mean that people will likely be curious about your origins. People may ask where your father comes from and which religion you practice (or were raised to practice). In particular, travelers with Biblical names or German-sounding surnames may be asked if they are **Jewish.** Jewish travelers should avoid revealing their religion in volatile areas, as it could result in tension or even confrontation.

TRAVELERS WITH CHILDREN

Family vacations often require that you slow your pace, and always require that you plan ahead. If you rent a car, make sure the rental company provides a car seat for younger children. Consider using a papoose-style device to carry a baby on walking trips. Be sure that your child carries some sort of ID in case of an emergency, and arrange a reunion spot in case of separation when sight-seeing. Children under two generally fly for 10% of the adult airfare on international flights (this does not necessarily include a seat). Finding a private place for breast feeding is often a problem while traveling, so pack accordingly.

DIETARY CONCERNS

The Middle East is definitely a meat munching place, but there's always falafel and hummus, and eggs are sold scrambled or hard-boiled in all the local markets. You won't find tofu or soybeans anywhere but in Israel or in an expat-type store in Beirut. To address dietary concerns at restaurants ("I am a vegetarian"), see the **Phrasebook,** p. 702. Travelers who keep **kosher** should contact synagogues in larger

cities for information on kosher restaurants. The **Jewish Travel Guide** lists synagogues, kosher restaurants, and Jewish institutions in over 80 countries (Vallen-
tine-Mitchell Publishers, Newbury House 890-900, Eastern Ave., Newbury Park,
Ilford, Essex, U.K. IG2 7HH (tel. (0181) 599 88 66; fax 599 09 84)). In the U.S. ($16)
from ISBS, 5804 NE Hassalo St., Portland, OR 97213-3644 (tel. 800-944-6190).

ALTERNATIVES TO TOURISM

STUDY

Most study programs for foreigners at Middle Eastern universities are language
immersion programs in Arabic. Be sure to apply early for a student visa, as application processing is Jurassic in its inefficiency. An excellent place to find the Middle Eastern institution best suited to your study abroad needs is **Amideast Study
Abroad,** 1730 M St. NW, #1100, Washington, D.C., 20036 (tel. 202-776-9600; email
inquiries@amideast.org). Listed below are schools that offer study abroad programs to foreigners, organized by country.

EGYPT: Studying in Egypt means attending the American University in Cairo (AUC), 113
Qasr el-Aini St. **American University in Cairo (AUC)** offers semester, year, and summer
programs in intensive Arabic and undergraduate and graduate degree study. Instruction
in English. Tuition for 1999-2000 is US$5375 per semester plus US$1660 for housing;
US$2688 for the summer session (two months) plus US$910 for housing. Contact the
Office of Student Affairs, American University in Cairo, 420 Fifth Ave., 3rd floor, New
York, NY 10018 (tel. 212-730-8800; email aucegypt@aucnyo.edu). **Center of Arabic
Study Abroad (CASA)** offers a full-year program at AUC, including trips to nearby muse-
ums and historic sights. Contact CASA, 1619 Massachusetts Ave. NW, Washington,
D.C. 20036 (email casa@mail.jhuwash.jhu.edu).

JORDAN: Amman University offers month-long intensive Language Program in Arabic every
month except June, Nov., and Dec. Tuition is US$2995, which includes room and board.
Amman University also offers a 5-level intensive program in Arabic (classical and spoken)
for non-native speakers. All levels are offered regularly and concurrently during the fall
(Sept.-Jan.), spring (Feb.-May), and summer (June-Aug.). Tuition fees for the fall and
spring are JD340, for the summer JD205. For more information on either program, contact University of Jordan, Amman 11942, Jordan (tel. (06) 535 50 00; fax 535 55 22).

ISRAEL: Before the study abroad semester begins, there is a four- to nine-week *ulpan* to
learn Hebrew, and university programs are preceded by *mekhina,* a year of intensive
Hebrew. **Hebrew University of Jerusalem,** 11 E. 69th St., New York, NY 10021 (tel.
212 472 22 88; fax 517 45 48). United Kingdom Friends of the Hebrew University, 3
St. Johns Wood Rd., London NW8 8RB (tel 0171 266 32 14; fax 0171 289 55 49;
email 106354.2730@compuserve.com). **Tel Aviv University,** Office of Academic
Affairs, 360 Lexington Ave., New York, NY 10017 (tel. 212 557 58 20; fax 687 40 85),
or Ramat Aviv, Tel Aviv 69978 (tel. 03 640 81 11; fax 03 640 95 98).

LEBANON: The black-clad hipsters that haunt most Beirut hotspots all hail exclusively from
the **American University of Beirut (AUB),** which offers programs in everything from philosophy to poultry science, with classes conducted in English. Tuition is L£5,000,000 per
semester (12 credits), L£400,000 per credit during the summer session. For more information, contact AUB at P.O. Box 11-236, **Beirut,** Lebanon (tel. (01) 350 000, 340 460,
374 374, or 374 444; fax 351 706). You can also contact AUB at 850 Third Ave., 18th
Floor, **New York,** NY 10022-6297 (tel. 212-583-7600; fax 583-7650).

SYRIA: Arabic Teaching Institute for Foreigners in Damascus offers beginning and intermediate classes in Modern Standard Arabic. Tuition is US$400 for either the 8-month
winter course (Oct.-May) or the 3-month summer course (Jun.-Sept.). For more information, contact the Institute at Villat Sharqiyah (Eastern Villas), Damascus, Syria (tel. (11)
221 538). **The National Council on U.S.-Arab Relations** offers a 6-week "Summer in

Syria" program in Aleppo that allows students to earn up to 7 hours of college credit—4 of which are for intensive Arabic (the remaining credits can be earned in anything from international policy to comparative literature). For more information contact the Council at 1140 Connecticut Ave. NW, Suite 1210, Washington, D.C. 20036 (tel. 202-293-0801; email sis@ncusar.org).

TURKEY: Summer Program at Boğaziçi University, Istanbul. Contact Illinois Programs Abroad, 115 International Studies Building, 910 S. 5th St., Champaign, IL 61820 (tel. 800 531-4404 or (217) 333-6168; fax (217) 244-0249; email: ipa@uiuc.edu). Students choose 2 or 3 seven-week classes on the culture, language, and history of Turkey, Central Asia, and the Middle East, taught at one of Turkey's foremost universities. **TÖMER,** 18/1 Ziya Gökalp Cad., Kızılay, Ankara (tel. (312) 435 97 81; fax 433 81 90), teaches Turkish in cities across Turkey, including Istanbul, Antalya, Bursa, and İzmir.

UAE: American Intercontinental University at Dubai offers degrees in such Dubai-appropriate programs as international business and fashion design, in addition to Middle Eastern studies and Arabic language programs. Tuition is US$4442 per quarter, housing US$1300 per quarter; fees are less if students enroll in fewer than 4 classes per quarter. For more information, contact Study Abroad Center for Global Studies, 6600 Peachtree-Dunwoody Rd., Embassy Row 500, Atlanta, GA 30328 (tel. 800-255-6839 or 404-965-8000; fax 404-965-8006; email studyabroad@aiuniv.edu).

YEMEN: Yemen Language Center (YLC) in Sana'a offers all levels of Modern Standard Arabic and colloquial Yemeni Arabic. Tuition (which includes housing) is US$980 for a half-term (4-6 weeks), US$1800 for the summer term (10-12 weeks), and US$6850 for the full term. Contact YLC at P.O. Box 16961, Sana'a, Yemen, or contact Muhammad Rahawi, 323 Grundy Dr., Falls Church, VA 22046 (tel. 703-534-3346).

WORK AND VOLUNTEER

Few foreigners work in the Middle East because acquiring a work visa or permit is often a bureaucratic nightmare. Being an **English speaker** does wonders for your marketability (tutoring or teaching English is your best bet). Some travelers in the Sinai work for hotels or dive centers in **Na'ama Bay** (see p. 157). A note on **archaeological digs:** although they abound in this area, most sites offer hard work, menial labor, and no pay (the Archaeological Institute of America listed below is an excellent source for finding more rewarding digs). **Volunteer** jobs are readily available almost everywhere, particularly at Israeli **kibbutzim**.

GENERAL RESOURCES

Archaeological Institute of America, 656 Beacon St., Boston, MA 02215-2010 (tel. 617-353-9361; fax 353-6550; email aia@bu.edu; www.archaeological.org), puts out the *Archaeological Fieldwork Opportunities Bulletin* (US$16 for non-members), which lists field sites in every country in the Middle East. This can be purchased from Kendall/Hunt Publishing, 4050 Westmark Dr., Dubuque, Iowa 52002 (tel. 800-228-0810).

ELS Language Centers/Middle East employs many English as a First Language (EFL) teachers in full- and part-time work throughout the Middle East. Contact them at their main office, P.O. Box 3079, Abu Dhabi, UAE (email elsme@emirates.net.ae).

Office of Overseas Schools, A/OS Room 245, SA-29, Dept. of State, Washington, D.C. 20522-2902 (tel. 703-875-7800; fax 875-7979; email overseas.school@state.gov; state.gov/www/about_state/schools/). Keeps a list of schools and agencies in every country in the Middle East that arrange placement for Americans to teach abroad.

Peace Corps, 1111 20th St. NW, Washington, D.C. 20526 (tel. 800-424-8580; www.peacecorps.gov). Their "blue" brochure details application requirements. Volunteers must be U.S. citizens, age 18 and over, and willing to make a 2-year commitment. The Peace Corps is active in Cyprus, Israel, and Jordan.

COUNTRY-SPECIFIC RESOURCES

Egypt: Work permits can be obtained through any Egyptian consulate, or from the Ministry of the Interior. Some people look for temporary jobs upon arrival in Na'ama Bay or Alexandria. **American Field Service (AFS)** runs the Egyptian Society for Intercultural Exchange, (ESIE), which sponsors summer-, semester-, and year-long homestay exchange programs in Egypt for current students and short-term service projects for adults. Has programs for nearly every country of origin, and financial aid is available. Contact ESIE at 10 Eth-Thawra St., Apt. 5, Mohandiseen, Giza, Egypt (tel. (2) 360 61 42; fax (2) 337 60 01; email info-egypt@afs.org; www.afs.org/partners/egyhome.htm).

Israel: Volunteers often work at one of Israel's 250 **kibbutzim** (singular kibbutz), communal settlements whose members divide work and profits equally. Volunteers work 6 eight-hour days per week (2-month minimum and no maximum stay length), with a few days off per month, and receive a small monthly allowance in addition to room and board; the work is generally in agriculture, industry, or service. To apply, contact the main **Kibbutz Aliya Office** at 633 3rd Ave. 21st floor, New York, NY 10017 (tel. 800 247 78 52; fax 212 318 61 34; email kibbutzdsk@aol.com). Applicants must be ages 18-35 with no children. Kibbutz volunteering can also be arranged by visiting a kibbutz and asking their volunteer leader if they need help.

Jordan: Get **work permits** from the Ministry of Labor. It's difficult for foreigners to find jobs in **Jordan;** a combination of perfect English and business or banking skills is optimal. Positions must be arranged before arrival in order to get a work visa. **Residence permits** are required for stays of more than 3 months.

Lebanon: People who seek to work in Lebanon must acquire a special **work visa.** Contact the nearest Lebanese embassy for details. **UNIPAL (Universities Trust for Educational Exchange with Palestinians)** sends volunteers to teach English to Palestinians and help with handicapped children in the West Bank, Gaza Strip, and Lebanon. Contact BCM Unipal, London, U.K. WC1N 3XX (tel. (191) 386 7124).

Syria: Work for foreigners is scarce in Syria. A **residence permit** is required, as visitors on tourist visas are not allowed to work. The **American Language Center Damascus** employs 40 native speakers to teach English at their special learning facility in Damascus. Contact ALCD c/o USIS, P.O. Box 29, Damascus, Syria (tel. (11) 332 7236) or ALCD c/o USIS, Department of State, Washington, D.C. 20521-6110.

THE WORLD WIDE WEB

Arabnet (www.arab.net) is a one-stop guide to the Middle East (except Israel) with extensive country-specific resources on geographic, political, and historical elements. Though the page is not strongly political, it regularly features often inflammatory pro-Arab statements; Israel's absence further discredits Arabnet as a neutral news source.

The CIA World Factbook (www.odci.gov/cia/publications/factbook/index.html) has tons of vital statistics on the Middle East. Check it out for an overview of the Middle Eastern economy or and an explanation of various systems of government in the region.

Foreign Language for Travelers (www.travlang.com) can help you brush up on your Arabic, Hebrew, Turkish, or for kicks, your Aramaic.

Let's Go (www.letsgo.com) is where you can find our newsletter, information about our books, up-to-the-minute links, and more.

HISTORY OF RELIGION

ISLAM

The Arabic word *islam* roughly means "submission," and the basic tenet of Islam is submission to the will of **Allah** (God). The core beliefs of the religion were revealed from 610 to 622 CE to **Muhammad,** who was informed of his prophetic calling by the Angel Gabriel. These revelations are collected in the **Qur'an** ("recitation"), a text that incorporates many of the biblical traditions associated with prophets throughout history. Muslims believe the Arabic text is perfect, immutable, and untranslatable—the words of God embodied in human language. Consequently, the Qur'an appears throughout the Muslim world (the majority of which is non-Arabic speaking) in its original Arabic. Muhammad is seen as the "seal of the prophets," the last of a chain of God's messengers that includes Jewish and Christian figures such as Abraham, Moses, and Jesus.

It is believed that Muhammad received the Qur'an during the month of **Ramadan.** Fasting during this holy month is the fourth pillar of Islam. Between dawn and sunset, Muslims are not permitted to smoke, have sexual intercourse, or let any food or water pass their lips; exceptions are made for women who are pregnant or menstruating, people who are sick, and people who are traveling—they must make up the fast at a later date. Fasting is meant to teach Muslims to resist temptation and thereby control all their unchaste urges, better understand the plight of the poor, and be more thankful for the food which Allah has provided them. As soon as the evening *adhan* is heard, they break the fast and begin a night of feasting, visits to friends and relatives, and revelry. In busy metropolises like Cairo, the city stays up until just before dawn, but in quieter areas, a neighbor may circulate to houses, banging a drum and waking people for *suhur*, a small meal eaten just before dawn in an attempt to avoid extreme hunger upon waking.

HISTORY OF ISLAM

Muhammad rapidly gathered followers to his evolving faith. Staunchly monotheistic Islam met with ample opposition in polytheistic Arabia, leading to persecution in Muhammad's native city of **Mecca.** In 622, he and his followers fled to the nearby city of **Medina,** where he was welcomed as mediator of a long-standing blood feud. This *hejira* ("flight" or emigration) marks the starting point of the Islamic calendar. In 630, Mecca surrendered to the Muslims, making Muhammad the most powerful man in Arabia and leading numerous Meccans to voluntarily convert to the new faith. This established the pattern for **jihad** ("struggle"), referring first and foremost to the spiritual struggle against one's own desires, then to the struggle to make one's own Muslim community as righteous as possible, and lastly to the struggle against outsiders wishing to harm the Muslim community.

Muhammad is not believed to be divine but a human messenger of Allah's word. His actions are sanctified because Allah chose him to be the recipient of revelation; several verses of the Qur'an demand obedience to the Prophet. The stories and traditions surrounding the Prophet's life have been passed on as *sunna*, and those who follow the *sunna* (from which the term "Sunni" is derived) in addition to the teachings of the Qur'an are considered especially devout. The primary source for *sunna* is the **Hadith,** a collection of sayings attributed to Muhammad. A *hadith* had to go through a rigorous verification process before it was accepted as true; the tale had to be verified (preferably by those who saw the action) and the greatest weight was given to testimony by Muhammad's followers and relatives.

Muhammad's nephew and son-in-law 'Ali catalyzed the major split in the Muslim world. When 'Ali was murdered in 661, the *Shi'at 'Ali* ("Partisans of 'Ali" or **Shi'a**) believed he was the only legitimate successor to Muhammad, thus separating themselves from Sunni Muslims. Shi'ism is a faith with a sharp focus on divinely chosen leaders (or *imams*) who are blood descendants of the Prophet through 'Ali and his wife, the Prophet's daughter Fatima.

In the 10th century, Sunni Muslim scholars *(ulama)* proclaimed "the gates of *ijtihad* (individual judgment)" closed; new concepts and interpretations could no longer stand on their own but had to be legitimized by tradition. *Ijtihad* continues today, though not on the scale that it did during the first centuries of Islam. There have been numerous reform movements throughout the Islamic world, including the Wahhabbi movement on the Arabian Peninsula, the movement of the thinker Jamal ad-Din al-Afghani in the Middle East, and Muhammad Iqbal in South Asia. There are four main schools of thought in the Islamic legal system. **Sharia,** or Islamic law, is a subject of much strife in a number of Muslim countries, which have seen challenges to entrenched governments by Islamic movements.

The **Sufis** are a mystical movement within Islam, stressing the goal of unity with Allah. They are organized in hierarchical orders that prescribe different ways of life to reach Allah; some preach total asceticism, others seem almost hedonistic in their pursuit of pleasure. Sufi *sheikhs* (masters) and saints are reputed to perform miracles, and their tombs are popular pilgrimage destinations. Jalal ad-Din Rumi founded the famous order of the "whirling dervishes," who spin to produce a state of mind conducive to unity with Allah.

FIVE PILLARS OF ISLAM

Ash-hadu an la ilaha illa Allah. Ashadu anna Muhammadan rasul Allah. "I swear that there is no god but Allah. I swear that Muhammad is God's Messenger." These words are the first lines of the Islamic call to prayer *(adhan)*, which emanates five times a day from live or recorded *muezzins* perched atop the minarets of mosques. The first line glorifies God, and the next two lines form the **shahadah** ("testimony of faith"), which is the first of the five pillars of Islam. These words reflect the unity of God *(tawhid)* and the special place of Muhammad as God's final messenger. Any person who wishes to convert to Islam may do so by repeating these lines three times. Enemies of Islam often memorized the lines before going into battle as an emergency survival tactic.

The second pillar of Islam is **prayer** *(salat)*, performed five times per day facing Mecca. Prayers, preceded by ablutions, begin with a declaration of intent and consist of a set cycle of prostrations. No group or leader is necessary for prayers—they constitute a personal communication with Allah. The Arabic word for Friday, when communal prayer is encouraged, means "the day of gathering."

The third pillar is **alms** *(zakat,* or "purification"). Because all belongs to God, wealth is only held in trust by people, and *zakat* represents the bond between members of the community. Through the required giving of alms to those less fortunate, the contributor is purified from selfishness. *Zakat* has been historically administered as a tax, and the level of giving is determined as a percentage of the surplus wealth and earnings of the individual.

> # TWIST AND SHOUT Known to Westerners as **whirling dervishes,**
> the **Sufi** sect of Islam began in Konya, Turkey during the mid-13th century. The origin of the word Sufi is a mystery. Some think that it derived from the root *suf* (wool), used to describe the woolen garments worn by the first members of the sect. Another theory is that Sufi came from the Greek *sophos,* meaning wisdom. The Persian word *darwish* literally means the "sill of the door"—hence, *dervish* would refer to the Sufi who is at the doorstep of paradise or enlightenment. The dervishes hope to cast off mundane worries and reach a higher spiritual plane through their perpetually whirling dance. The ritual is an entrancing display of color and devotion, a dizzying spin during which the dervish throws off cloak after cloak of earthly possession, eventually left with the soaring white fabric of his inner robe. Their spiritual dance likely inspired the "spinners" made famous at Grateful Dead concerts.

The last pillar is **pilgrimage** *(hajj)*, required once in a lifetime only for those who are financially and physically able to journey to Mecca and Medina during the last month of the Muslim calendar. Worship is focused around the **Ka'aba,** which Muslims believe to be the first house of worship build by the first man (Adam, under instructions from Allah). While *hajj* is essentially a re-creation of the actions of the Prophet Muhammad, it also unites Muslims and stresses the equal status of all who submit to *Allah*. Everyone from Gulf princes to Cairene street-sweepers must wrap themselves in white cloth, remove all accessories, and perform the same rituals. If you travel during *hajj*, expect delays and pandemonium in airports.

JUDAISM

Neither theologians nor historians can pinpoint a date for the founding of Judaism, but the religion has been evolving for at least four millennia. According to the Bible, **Abraham** first established a covenant with God through his self-circumcision at the ripe old age of 99. This act is symbolically repeated with each generation of Jewish males, but now a ritual circumciser (the *moyel*) performs the honors on the eighth day of life. Abraham's grandson, Jacob (a.k.a. Israel), fathered 12 sons from whom the 12 tribes of the nation of Israel descended. Abraham, his son Isaac, and his grandson Jacob are believed to be buried with their wives (Sarah, Rebecca, and Leah) in the Cave of the Machpelach in Hebron, which is holy to both faiths because Abraham's son Ishmael is believed to be the ancestor of Islam.

The Bible says that the Israelite nation was founded during the generation spent wandering with Moses in the Sinai desert en route to the Holy Land. This generation received the Torah, the central text of Judaism, at Mt. Sinai. The disparate tribes had united by the 3rd millennium BCE under **Yahweh** (a warlike version either of the Canaanite deity El or the storm god Ba'al). Once the Israelite kingdom was formed, worship was centralized in the capital, Jerusalem.

Historians estimate the present form of the **Torah** to be 2500 years old. The Written Torah (a.k.a. the **Pentateuch,** or the Books of Moses), which consists of the first five books of the Bible, formed the template for the Oral Torah, a series of interpretations and teachings codified in 200 CE as the *Mishnah*. The *Mishnah*, along with the *Gemara*, are the basis of the Babylonian and Jerusalem *Talmuds*, finalized during the 5th century CE. The Talmud was the springboard for a new series of interpretations and teachings that continue to build upon each other.

Faith in God is assumed among all Jews, and the energy of Jewish life is concentrated on observing the commandments. The Torah contains 613 **mitzvot** (commandments), including directives for ritual observances and instructions concerning moral behavior. Over the ages, rabbis have interpreted these *mitzvot* and expanded them to include countless more. This entire set of laws is called *halakha* (literally "the way"). Much of modern Jewish life revolves around the **synagogue,** which plays a multi-faceted role in Jewish life: the Hebrew word *(beit knesset)* means "house of assembly" and the Yiddish word *(shul)* means "school." The *aron ha-kodesh* ("Holy Ark") houses the Torah scrolls and determines the orientation of the synagogue. Synagogues normally face Jerusalem; within Jerusalem, they face the Temple Mount. Above the *aron ha-kodesh* hangs a flickering *ner tamid* ("eternal flame"). The raised platform from which prayers are led is called the *bima*. Most orthodox synagogues contain a *mehitza*, a divider between men's and women's sections, which have separate entrances. Men should cover their heads when entering; there is often a box of *kippot* by the entrance.

CHRISTIANITY

Christianity began in Judaea among the Jewish followers of **Jesus.** The most significant sources on the life of Jesus are the **Gospels.** Scholars agree that the "synoptic gospels" of Mark, Matthew, and Luke were written in that order some time after 70 CE, drawing on an oral tradition which recorded the words of Jesus. The Gospel of John was written about 100 CE but has roots as old as the others. These sources provide a history influenced by the experiences of the church fathers and the belief that Jesus was the **Messiah** ("anointed one").

Various historical events date the birth of Jesus between 4 BCE and 6 CE. The Bible says that Jesus was conceived and brought forth by Mary, a virgin, making him a product of God's creative power and free from humanity's original sin. According to Matthew, **Bethlehem** was the birthplace of Jesus, and Mary and Joseph moved to **Nazareth** to protect him. Jesus was baptized (ritually washed) in the Jordan River by **John the Baptist,** a popular evangelist later hailed as the reincarnation of the 9th-century prophet **Elijah,** herald of the Messiah. Jesus later preached in the Galilee, speaking for the poor and the righteous, most notably in the Sermon on the Mount (Matthew 5:7). After about three years of preaching, Jesus went to Jerusalem, where the **Passion,** the events of his death, took place. On Good Friday, he carried his cross down the **Via Dolorosa** until he reached the hill of Golgotha (or Calvary), now marked by the Church of the Holy Sepulchre, where he was crucified. According to the Gospels, three days after Jesus' crucifixion, on what is now celebrated as Easter, Mary and two other women went to Jesus' tomb to anoint his body and discovered the tomb empty. An angel announced that Jesus had been resurrected; Jesus subsequently appeared to the Apostles and performed miracles. The **Resurrection** is the point of departure for the Christian faith, the beginning of an age when the faithful await Christ's *parousia*, or second coming.

At first, Christianity was a sect of Judaism, accepting the Hebrew Bible. However, the sect's defining tenet—that Jesus was the Messiah—severed it from mainstream Judaism. **St. Paul** (originally Saul of Tarsus) successfully adapted the faith of Christianity to meet the spiritual needs of the largest body of converts: former pagans. The Book of Acts documents the actions of the early Christians, and the Letters of Paul, which comprise most of the rest of the New Testament, give advice to the early Christian communities and explain the delay of the second coming. The incorporation of ancient festivals such as the winter solstice helped draw the common people to the new religion, and the usage of Platonic doctrines converted many intellectuals. The Christian faith was officially legitimized by the Edict of Milan, issued by Emperor Licinius in 313 CE. In 325 CE, the **Emperor Constantine** made Christianity the official religion of the struggling Roman Empire. Constantine also summoned the first of seven Ecumenical Councils, held in Nicaea, to elaborate and unify the content of the faith. The Council of Nicaea came up with an explicit creed, declaring that Jesus Christ was of the same essence as the Father, and that there were three equal parts to God. This crucial doctrine of the **Trinity,** which is only implicitly supported in the Gospels, maintains that the Father, Son, and Holy Spirit are distinct persons yet all one God.

The Church was called "the body of Christ" and believed to be integral and indivisible. Nonetheless, the Christian community suffered many schisms. The **Egyptian (Coptic) Church** broke off in the 3rd century (see below), when other eastern branches began to drift apart from western Christianity. In 1054, the **Great Schism,** caused primarily by the inflexible Cardinal Humbert, split Christendom into the western Roman Catholic Church and the Eastern Orthodox Church. Whereas Rome upheld the universal jurisdiction and infallibility of the Pope, Orthodoxy stressed the infallibility of the church as a whole. The Spirit, according to the Orthodox, proceeds through the Father, while Roman theology dictates that the Spirit proceeds from the Father and the Son. Orthodox Christians believe that God is highly personal and each man can find God by looking within himself. In 1517, the German monk **Martin Luther** sparked the **Reformation,** which split northern Europe from Roman Catholicism and led to the development of Protestantism. **Protestantism** is itself composed of many sects, which generally believe in salvation through faith rather than good works. Eastern Orthodoxy, too, is divided into multiple nationalist traditions (Greek, Russian, Armenian).

THE COPTIC CHURCH

"Copt" derives from the Greek word for Egyptian, *Ægyptos*, shortened in its Egyptian pronunciation to *qibt*, the Arabic word for Copt. Copts in Egypt usually have tattoos of a domed cathedral or a tiny cross on their wrists. Of 58 million Egyptians, five to seven million are Copts, most of whom live in Cairo or Middle Egypt. Portions of the liturgy are still in Coptic, though most of the service is in Arabic.

St. Mark introduced Christianity to Egypt in 62 CE. Mass conversions transformed Alexandria into a Christian spiritual center, but Roman persecution increased proportionately. The bloodiest days passed under Diocletian, who murdered so many Christians that the Copts date their Martyr's Calendar from 284 CE, the beginning of his reign. In 451 CE, the Alexandrian branch of the Church declared independence from Constantinople, forming the **Coptic Orthodox Church.**

Byzantine Emperor **Justinian** sought to restore unity by exiling Coptic clergy to isolated monasteries. Copts welcomed the Persians as liberators when they captured Egypt in 619. Since the 7th century, the community has lived as a religious minority in an Islamic state. Relations between the Copts and the Muslims have vacillated throughout history. Recently, the Copts felt besieged by Egypt's vocal Islamists, and acts of violence are often aimed at Coptic population centers.

Coptic Christianity served as a link between the Roman/pharaonic and Islamic eras, leaving its own mark on modern Egypt. Coptic art incorporates the influences of pharaonic and Hellenistic cultures. The Coptic cross borrows from the *ankh,* the hieroglyphic sign for "life" (vaguely resembling the human form), as well as from the crucifix on Golgotha. Embroidered tapestries and curtains displaying nymphs and centaurs descend from Greco-Roman mythology. Islamic art often borrows from the Coptic style; many of Cairo's mosques were engineered by Coptic architects, and some are converted Coptic churches.

Coptic churches usually have one of three shapes: cruciform, circular (to represent the globe, the spread of Christianity, and the eternal nature of the Word), or ark-shaped (the Ark of the Covenant and Noah's Ark are symbols of salvation). The churches are divided into three chambers. The eastward sanctuary *(haikal)* containing the altar lies behind a curtain or *iconostasis,* a wooden screen of icons. The next chamber, the choir, is the section reserved for Copts. Behind the choir is the nave, the first part of which is reserved for the *catechumens* (those preparing to convert). The back of the nave is for "weepers," or sinners. Above Coptic altars hang ostrich eggs, symbolizing Resurrection (life out of lifelessness) and thus God's eternal love and care.

OTHER FAITHS

THE DRUZE

The faith of the Druze, a staunchly independent sect of Shi'a Muslims, centers around a hierarchy of individuals who are the sole custodians of a religious doctrine hidden from the rest of the world. Many Druze consider themselves a separate ethnicity as well as a religious group, while others consider themselves Arabs. The Druze believe that the word of God is revealed only to a divinely chosen few, and that these blessed few must be followed to the ends of the earth. Wherever the Druze settle, however, they generally remain loyal to their host country. Israel has a Druze population of about 85,000, Syria 500,000, and Lebanon 300,000.

The religion was founded in 1017 by an Egyptian chieftain, Ad-Darazi, who drew upon various beliefs in the Muslim world at the time, especially Shi'ism. The Druze believe that God was incarnated in human forms, the final incarnation being the Fatimid Caliph Al-Hakim. The Druze have suffered a history of persecution and repression for their beliefs, which may partially explain the group's refusal to discuss its religion. The late 1600s was a period of prosperity, however, and under Emir Fakr ed-Din the Druze kingdom extended from Lebanon to Gaza to the Golan Heights. In 1830, a Druze revolt against the Egyptian pasha was crushed, along with all but two of the 14 Druze villages in the Carmel. In the 1860s, Ottoman rulers encouraged the Druze to return to the Carmel.

Because the Druze will not discuss their religion, most of what Westerners know about them comes from British "explorers" who fought their way into villages and stole holy books. As far as outsiders know, Jethro, father-in-law of Moses, is their most revered prophet. The most important holiday falls in late April. In Israel, Druze gather in the holy village of Ḥittim, near Tiberias. Devout Druze are forbidden to smoke, drink alcohol, or eat pork, but many young Druze do not adhere strictly to these prohibitions. Some Druze believe in reincarnation.

THE BAHA'I

This movement began in Tehran in 1863, when aristocratic Persian Mirza Hussein 'Ali renamed himself **Baha'u'llah** ("Glory of God") and began preaching non-violence and the unity of all religions. Baha'u'llah's arrival had been foretold in 1844 by the Persian **Sa'id 'Ali Muhammad** (or **Al-Bab**, or "Gateway to God"), the first prophet of the Baha'i religion. Baha'u'llah was imprisoned and exiled to Palestine, where he continued to teach in Acre (Akko). Al-Bab is buried in Haifa, which is now home to a large Baha'i population.

Baha'u'llah's teachings, which incorporate elements of major Eastern and Western religions, fill over 100 volumes. Baha'i believe in a Supreme Being, accepting Jesus, Buddha, Muhammad, and Baha'u'llah as divine prophets. The scripture includes the Bible, the Qur'an, and the Bhagavad Gita. A central doctrine of the faith regards the Baha'i vision of the future: Baha'u'llah prophesied a "flowering of humanity," an era of peace and enlightenment to come. Before this new age can arrive, however, the world must experience dreadful events to give civilization the impetus to reform itself. The Baha'i espouse trans-racial unity, sexual equality, global disarmament, and the creation of a world community. The faith currently boasts nearly six million adherents, with two million converts in the last decade.

THE KARAITES

The small sect of Jews known as the Karaites dwell principally in Ashdod, Be'er Sheva, and the Tel Aviv suburb of Ramla. The community, whose existence dates to the 9th century CE, counts about 15,000 adherents today. Formed out of the political and religious turmoil following the Muslim invasion, Karaites adhere strictly to the five books of the Torah, though they reject all later Jewish traditions. They are generally cohesive, and have their own religious courts. To an outsider, however, their practices appear similar to those dictated by traditional Jewish observance.

THE SAMARITANS

Currently, the Samaritan community is a tiny one, with roughly 550 adherents divided between Nablus (on the West Bank) and Ashkolon (a suburb of Tel Aviv). Originally the residents of Samaria, Samaritans consider themselves the original Israelites, descended from the tribes of Joseph (Manasseh and Ephraim) from whom other Israelites learned monotheism. The religion is seen by non-members as an offshoot of Judaism marked by literal interpretation of the Samaritan version of the Old Testament and the exclusion of later Jewish interpretation (the Mishnah, the Talmud, and all books of the Hebrew Bible after Joshua). A gradual, centuries-long separation between the two religions culminated with the destruction of the Samaritan temple on Mt. Gerizim by the Hasmonean king John Hyrcanus in 128 BCE. The mountain is still the most holy site of the Samaritan religion. Centuries of persecution by the various rulers of Palestine shrunk the community further, including thousands of deaths in a 529 CE uprising against Byzantine rule. While the Rabbinate does not recognize Samaritans as Jews, the Israeli government applies the Law of Return (granting settlement rights) to them.

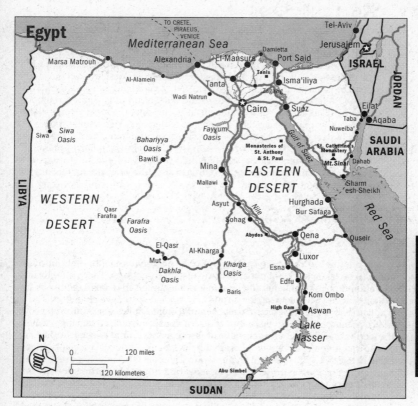

Egypt

EGYPT مصر

US$1=3.41 EGYPTIAN POUNDS (E£)	E£1=US$0.29
CDN$1=E£2.27	E£1=CDN$0.44
UK£1=E£5.41	E£1=UK£0.18
AUS$1=E£2.15	E£1=AUS$0.46
SAR1=E£0.56	E£1=SAR1.79
EUR1=E£3.56	E£1=EUR0.28
NIS1 (NEW ISRAELI SHEKEL)=E£0.80	E£1=NIS1.25
JD1 (JORDANIAN DINAR)=E£4.78	E£1=JD0.21

PHONE FACTS | **Country Code:** 20. **Police:** Tel. 122. **Ambulance:** Tel 123.

The Arab Republic of Egypt (*Gomhoriyyat Misr El-'Arabiyya*, or simply *Misr*) is a country of superlatives. A quarter of the Arab world lives in Egypt, despite the fact that the driest desert in the world (the Western Desert) makes up almost all (97%) of the country's land mass. The Nile (the longest and most fertile river in the world) stretches its arms across this region full of ancient temple ruins and glittering desert oases, welcoming the Mediterranean with the open hands of its Delta. The Nile Delta cradles several jewels in its palms: the breathtaking Pyramids at Giza (and their predecessor at Saqqara, the oldest monument in the world); the dizzying streets and dazzling mosques of Cairo, the largest city in the Middle East

41

and Africa; and cosmopolitan Alexandria, once home to the greatest library in the world. The mainland of Egypt is divided into Upper Egypt in the south (including Aswan, Luxor, and Nubia, the region where African and Egyptian culture merge), Middle Egypt, and Lower Egypt in the north; this counter-intuitive orientation comes from the fact that the Nile flows upstream from the south toward the Mediterranean. The Sinai Peninsula is its own rugged wonderland: at its heart, hikers trudge through desert containing some of the oldest and most sacred religious sites in the world; along the coast, scuba divers plunge into the azure depths of the Red Sea, known as one of the planet's premiere underwater sightseeing spots.

Egypt is a budget traveler's paradise. The sights are stunning, the culture is fascinating, and bargains are a way of life. However, travel here requires plenty of time, stamina, and patience. Most travelers find that with a relaxed attitude, the difficulties of navigating the hassles are surpassed by the intensity and beauty of the experiences Egypt has to offer.

ESSENTIALS

ENTRY

A **visa** is required to enter Egypt. Generally, all personal items brought into the country to be taken out upon departure are exempt from taxes. There is no formal declaration for personal items, but passengers may be asked to open their bags for customs officials when leaving the airport.

Upon arrival at the **Cairo International Airport** (often reminiscent of the anteroom of Hell), purchase a US$15 visa stamp at one of the six currency exchanges. These are good for one month, but renewable at police stations or at passport offices in major towns if you provide one photograph, E£12, and (officially) receipts showing that at least US$200 has been changed into Egyptian currency. Reports vary on the strictness of this last rule. There are several options for getting downtown. Only take **taxis** (at most E£20 to downtown) that leave from the official stand, monitored 24 hours a day by tourist police. Taxis will most likely drop you off at Tahrir Square, at the center of Cairo, and you can get anywhere from there. **Minibus** #27 (٢٧) and **bus** #400 (٤٠٠) go to Tahrir Square from the Airport's old terminal (both 50pt). Gem Travel also runs a 24-hour **shuttle bus** to downtown (US$4).

All **trains** into Cairo stop at Ramses Station. **Bus** #160 (١٦٠) runs from there to Tahrir Sq. Black and white **taxis** to Tahrir Sq. cost E£2. The **Metro**, opposite the station, runs to Tahrir Sq. for 50pt (piasters). To walk (30min.), climb the pedestrian overpass and walk south on Ramses St., away from the Ramses II statue.

Buses from Israel usually drop passengers off at 'Abbasiyya Station. To reach Tahrir Square from 'Abbasiyya Station, hop into a southbound black and white cab (E£4-5) or walk left down Ramses St. as you leave the station; go beyond the overpass, and to the first bus stop on the right. From here many buses travel to Tahrir Sq. Buses from Jordan usually drop you off at **'Abd el-Munem Riad Station.** To reach Tahrir Sq. from here, walk right onto Gala'a St. as you exit, until you come to the Corniche en-Nil. At the Corniche take a left onto Tahrir St.

A tour guide by the name of ▓**Mr. Salah Muhammad** (tel./fax 298 06 50; email samo@intouch.com) offers a free "VIP" **24-hour shuttle service** (reserve ahead of time by email) from the airport to downtown Cairo for *Let's Go* users who will take his tour of the Pyramids at Giza, Memphis, Saqqara, and the carpet school at Harania (E£23, not including entrance fees to sights, E£5 *Let's Go* discount if you book with him). For more information on the package, see **Pyramids at Giza,** p. 101.

Visas can be easily obtained in advance. In case of emergencies, visas can be obtained at the airport in Cairo, and with some restrictions at the borders. Visas are good for entry within six months of the date of issue, valid for three months, and easily extended. An Egyptian visa does not permit the holder to work. When applying, you can request a **multiple-entry visa** for travel in and out of Egypt, allowing you to reenter any number of times while the visa is valid. Visits to Sinai from Israel or Jordan can be made on a two-week **Sinai-only visa,** available at borders.

EMBASSIES AND CONSULATES

Embassies and consulates of other countries in Egypt are all located in **Cairo** (see **Practical Information,** p. 66). These are Egyptian embassies and consulates abroad:

Australia: Embassy: 1 Darwin Ave., Yarralumla, Canberra ACT 2600 (tel. (02) 273-4437/8). **Consulate:** 112 Glenn Moore, Paddington, Sydney NSW 2028 (tel. 362-3483; fax 9332 3288). **Consulate:** 124 Exhibition St., 9th floor, Melbourne, Victoria 3000 (tel. (03) 9654 8634; fax 9650 8362).

Canada: Embassy: 454 Laurier Ave. E, Ottawa, ONT KIN 6R3 (613-234-4931; fax 234-9347). **Consulate:** 1 Place Ville Marie #2617, Montreal, QU H3B 4S3 (514-866-8455; fax 866-0835).

UK: Embassy: 26 South St., London W1Y 6DD (tel. (171) 499-3304; fax 355-3568). **Consulate:** 2 Lowndes St., London SW1 X9ET (tel. (171) 235-9777/19).

USA: Embassy: 3521 International Court NW, Washington, D.C. 20008 (202-895-5400; fax 244-4319). **Consulate:** 1110 2nd Avenue #201, New York City, NY 10022 (212-759-7120; fax 308-7643).

■ BORDER CROSSINGS

E G Y P T

TO JORDAN. A **ferry** shuttles between the port at **Nuweiba'** and **Aqaba.** Nobody really knows what time the ferries leave. **Taxis** from Nuweiba' or Tarabin to the port cost E£15-20. The ticket office for the ferries is in a small white building 100m south of the port, past a bakery. The slow ferry supposedly leaves at 11am and 3pm (4hr., US$32), and a faster, less crowded, and more punctual **speedboat** leaves around 12:30pm and 4:30pm (1hr., US$42). Show up a few hours before the earliest possible departure time to deal with customs and ticketing. For general ferry information, call 52 00 52 or 52 03 60. Jordanian **visas** can be obtained on board (Australia JD16, Canada JD36, Ireland JD11, New Zealand JD16, South Africa free, U.K. JD23, U.S. JD33). There is no Egyptian departure tax.

TO ISRAEL. The most convenient option is **Taba** to **Eilat** (border open 24hr.). *Service* drop you right at the border, but the East Delta bus stop leaves a 200m walk north to the promised land. See the **Transportation** sections of towns in the Sinai for information on transportation to Taba. On the Israeli side, **bus** #15 runs daily every 15 minutes from the border checkpoint to Eilat until about 11pm except on Fridays, when the last bus is at 5:30pm (NIS3.20). **Taxis** (US$6 to downtown) also go to Eilat. Rented **cars** are not allowed to cross in either direction.

At the border you will be issued a free visa, the length of which is entirely determined by the border guards' mood and your appearance (min. 1 week, max. 3 months). You will have to pay a E£2 exit tax if you have traveled beyond the Sinai. The walk through the stations shouldn't take more than an hour. Keep your Israeli entrance card—you'll need it to leave the country. Israeli customs will often let you walk right through their station, but make sure to stop there because you can't pass the final checkpoint without the customs stamp on your gate pass.

You will automatically get an Israeli entrance stamp and visa in your passport unless you request to get them on a separate sheet. If you plan on traveling to Syria or Lebanon, get it on separate paper—you will not be allowed to enter these countries if there is an Israeli visa in your passport. Egyptian authorities will not let you leave without stamping your passport, so entry into Israel prohibits you from getting into Syria. **Change money** at decent rates at either the Taba Hilton or a bank in Eilat. **El-Arish** is also a convenient crossing point. There is an E£18 Egyptian exit fee and E£10 charge for transfer into Israel. To enter Egypt at **Rafah,** you need a full Egyptian visa (not just a Sinai only), which cannot be attained at the border.

GETTING AROUND

Public transportation in Egypt is more prevalent and more pervasive than that of other Arab countries, but transportation to obscure sights may still be difficult to find (particularly in the summer, the off season for tourism). Before that camel, Peugeot, or minibus spirits you off to a Nilometer or distant praying baboon statue, make sure it's up for the ride back.

TRAINS. Egypt's railway system was the first established in both the Arab world and in Africa. Schedules and signs in the train stations are never in English, but can be obtained from the tourist office or from ticket windows; fellow passengers can also help you. If lines are long and you're in a hurry, try boarding the train without a ticket—the conductor will usually sell one on board for an additional fee, even if the train is full.

Trains offer student discounts (ISIC card required) of up to 50%, with an average discount of about 30%. **Air-conditioned second-class** cars are comfortably small, with reclining seats; shelling out more for first class means only slightly larger seats and loud, braying Egyptian movies. Avoid the dangerous **third class. Second-class sleeper cars,** available on some regular trains, might be more comfortable for trips of ten hours or more but are overpriced. Reserve space in a sleeper at the wagon-lit offices in Cairo, Luxor, Aswan, and Alexandria). Seats for Cairo-Alexandria (especially in summer) and Cairo-Upper Egypt (especially in winter) trips should be reserved a day or two in advance. Reserve a week in advance during the last week of Ramadan and the following week, as well as before Eid el-Adha.

BUSES. Buses are inexpensive (no student discounts) but often slow, crowded, and brain-meltingly hot. Companies include **Superjet,** West Delta Bus Company, and East Delta Bus Company. **West Delta** has a deluxe branch called **Golden Arrow** with vehicles sporting A/C, refreshments, and bathrooms; unfortunately, they often show Egyptian soap operas with women shrieking at unsustainable volumes. Air-conditioned **East Delta** buses serve locales throughout the Sinai.

TAXIS. The flexibly-scheduled *service* taxis (known as *taxi bin-nafar* in Middle and Upper Egypt and *taxi ugra* in Lower Egypt) depart when full or when passengers have agreed to split the price of a full carload. The intracity version of *service* is the **minibus.** Cheap **private taxis** are only convenient in Cairo (black and white) and Alexandria (black and yellow or orange). Hail private taxis on the street instead of in front of a tourist trap, train station, or large hotel, and don't take a taxi if the driver approaches you. Never ask the driver for the fare: open the door as you are paying with folded bills and leave the taxi without looking to the driver for approval. Have exact change and small bills. "Special" means rip-off: if this word is mentioned in your presence, repeat *La* ("No").

CAR RENTAL. Renting a car is a useful option only in the Sinai and the desert oases. Rentals run about US$35 per day. Make all necessary arrangements before leaving your home country. If you plan to drive, remember to obtain the necessary permits: an International Driver's License is required to drive in Egypt, but many places are pretty lax about this (as they are about age requirements).

 ROAD TRAVEL ADVISORY. Highway travel in Egypt is incredibly dangerous: Egypt has one of the highest road casualty rates in the world. **Intracity travel** is just as scary: at night, cars race by at 100kmph (60mph) without headlights. Avoid *service* after sundown. Check with local tourism authorities or the Ministry of the Interior before venturing in private transport off main roads, particularly in the following areas: the Western Desert (especially near the Libyan and Sudanese borders), along the Suez Canal and Red Sea Coast, and in the Sinai. If you need a permit, apply at the Ministry of the Interior in Cairo at 110 Qasr el-'Aini St. (tel. 354 83 00).

PLANES. Egypt is served by **EgyptAir** (tel. (02) 76 52 00); see **Cairo: Airplanes** (p. 62) for locations, prices, and destinations. Check **Airplanes** listings in other cities for EgyptAir offices and flight details. EgyptAir's main office in the U.S. is at 720 Fifth Ave., Suite 505, New York, NY 10019 (tel. (800) 334-6787). **Air Sinai** (tel. (02) 77 29 49), in the courtyard of the Nile Hilton, serves the Sinai and Israel.

HITCHHIKING. Egypt is mostly untraveled desert; never count on getting a ride before you die of dehydration. *Let's Go* does not recommend hitchhiking. Hitching is not common in the highly populated parts of Egypt. In recent years, the newspapers have been full of crimes perpetrated by hitchhikers along the roads between Cairo and Alexandria, making most drivers reluctant to pick people up anyway. Rides are reportedly easy to obtain in isolated areas (such as along the Great Desert Road) or for short jaunts in remote parts of the Nile Valley (where public transportation is difficult to find). Many drivers who pick up hitchhikers expect money anyway, so public transportation should be used where it is available.

TOURIST AND TRAVEL SERVICES

MEDICAL EMERGENCIES AND HEALTH. Luxury hotels may have resident doctors, and other hotels can usually get someone dependable in an emergency. You can also ask your embassy for a list of recommended physicians and pharmacists. Even big-city **pharmacies** do not carry Western brand-name drugs, but most Egyptian brands are equally effective and cheaper. Pharmacists in Egypt are authorized to write prescriptions (and are more lax about refills than most Western countries) and also able to give injections. There should be at least one pharmacy in each town, although finding a 24-hour store may prove difficult in small towns. Dial 123 for emergencies.

MONEY MATTERS

CURRENCY AND EXCHANGE. The **Egyptian Pound** (E£), pronounced gin-EEH in Arabic, is divided into 100 **piasters** (pt), also called *irsh* (plural u-ROOSH). Coins come in denominations of 5pt, 10pt, and 20pt (the last two look similar, so check the Arabic numbering). **Save exchange receipts** in case authorities ask for them when you are leaving the country. You are not allowed to carry more than E£20 into or out of Egypt. Outside of Cairo, most credit cards are useless, although ATMs can be found fairly easily. Traveler's checks are widely accepted.

PRICES. A brief lesson in Egyptian Arabic: After *min fadlak* (please) and *shukran* (thank you), the most important word to know is **khawaga** (kha-WA-ga), because you are one. *Khawaga* means "tourist" with the implication of "clueless and rich." Aside from those in hotels and restaurants, most prices are not posted, which means that *khawaga*s may be charged more than Egyptians. Being a *khawaga* has a positive side, as Egypt's reliance on its tourist industry means more lax rules for *khawaga*s than for natives. A foreign couple can take a room together in a hotel whether they are married or not. Avoid souvenir shops and kiosks near tourist attractions at all costs. When shopping, the key word is **bargain.**

Another word to remember is **bakhsheesh,** the art of tipping: baggage handlers, guards, and bathroom and parking attendants expect to receive a tip of 50pt-E£1. For a detailed breakdown of the different types of *bakhseesh* and the attitudes towards it in the Middle East, see **Tipping and Bargaining** in **Essentials** (p. 12).

Prices depend upon competition: in towns with heavier tourist traffic, you may spend as little as E£8 per night for clean, comfortable surroundings, while lower-quality accommodations in a town with fewer hotels and even fewer visitors can cost anywhere from E£10-25. Prices also vary considerably between high and low season. The high season in Alexandria is June to August, in the Nile Valley October to April. There is a hotel tax which varies by location, averaging around 21%. Unless otherwise noted, prices include the tax but exclude breakfast.

EGYPT

BUSINESS HOURS. On **Friday,** the Muslim day of communal prayer, most government offices, banks, and post offices are closed. Bank hours are ordinarily Sunday to Thursday 8:30am to 2pm (although some banks in big cities are open daily), with money exchange available daily 8:30am to noon and 4 to 8pm. Foreign banks keep longer hours, usually Sunday to Thursday 8am to 3pm. Other establishments, such as restaurants, remain open seven days a week. Store hours are ordinarily Saturday to Thursday 9am to 9pm, with many also open Friday. Government offices are open 9am to 2pm, though workers often leave before official closing times. Archaeological sites and other points of interest are typically open 8am to 5pm (4pm in winter), though in summer sites are open 6am to early afternoon.

During the month-long holiday of Ramadan (running from approximately December 8, 1999 to January 6, 2000), some restaurants close entirely. Others open only after sundown, when the streets empty and everyone sits down to *iftar*, the breaking of the daily fast. Most shops close at about 3:30pm during Ramadan and reopen from 8 to 11pm. Egyptians sit down for the second meal of Ramadan (*suhur*, pronounced su-HOOR) in the middle of the night, about 2 to 3am.

KEEPING IN TOUCH

MAIL. Airmail letters and postcards from Egypt to any destination outside the Middle East cost E£1. Most hotels sell stamps, though a 5pt surcharge may be added. The most dependable place to receive mail is at American Express offices, but this privilege is reserved for cardholders; **Poste Restante** is also available in major cities. Two or three weeks delivery time is normal. For faster service that won't break the bank, seek out **Express Mail Service (EMS),** available almost everywhere. It takes 3 to 20 days to the U.S. and 3 to 15 days to Europe. To send packages by **Federal Express,** contact the office at 1079 Corniche en-Nil St., Garden City, Cairo (tel. (02) 357 13 04; fax 357 13 18).

TELEPHONES AND INTERNET ACCESS. **Long-distance** and **international calls** can be made from most government telephone offices (*maktab et-telephonat; centrale* in Alexandria), open 24 hours and packed to capacity in the evenings. In most cities you can make calls using Sphinx-emblazoned **phone cards** (E£5, 15, 20, 30, or 40), sold at telephone offices for use at orange phones. Rates are lower at night. Major hotels have good connections but can be expensive.

For AT&T **collect calls,** USADirect, or World Connect, call (02) 510 02 00 (AT&T) from anywhere in Egypt. Call (02) 355 5770 for MCI WorldPhone or collect calls. Call (02) 365 3643 for CanadaDirect calls using a Bell Canada calling card. Kiwis should call (02) 365 3764 to reach their island home direct, while Brits should call (02) 365 3644 to reach theirs. You will pay for a local call. Tell the telephone office you are calling Cairo. You can also call from the gray, coin-operated public pay phones (10pt per 3min. from public phone, 50pt per 3min. from private phones in establishments). **Local calls** can also be dialed directly from these phones.

In Cairo, Alexandria, and other decent-sized towns, Internet access is roughly E£5-7 per hour. Getting online anywhere else in Egypt is slow and expensive (Dahab is upwards of E£20 per hour and Aswan gouges at E£1 per min.).

WOMEN TRAVELERS

Foreign women traveling alone will be harassed by Egyptian men—and so will foreign men. Egypt is not a place to visit if you want to be left alone, but harassment has more to do with socioeconomic inequality and cultural misunderstanding than gender-based hostility. Harassment can take many forms, from overzealous salesmanship to touchy-feely *service* drivers, from mildly sinister "hellos" to frightening and potentially harmful physical contact. The media has not helped the situation: movies and television tend to depict Western women as free and easy, and the racy nature of much Egyptian cinema has drastically altered expectations about how men and women should interact. Ignorance is bliss; the best way to deal with harassers is simply to ignore them. If they prove to be persistent, raise your voice and threaten to call the police. For more tips, see **Women Travelers,** p. 29.

I WANNA HOLD YOUR HAND Egyptian men may seem particularly affectionate to many travelers: they kiss each other on the cheeks, hold hands when strolling through bazaars, and even sit on each other's laps. Soldiers walk with a man on one arm and an AK-47 on the other. These amorous displays are merely manifestations of friendship and brotherhood in Egypt, as is evidenced by the very reserved manner in which Egyptian men treat their women. Women are considered very clean and chaste, and marriage is preceded by a strict courtship of two to three years.

LIFE AND TIMES

The burgeoning population of Egypt (over 67 million strong) is composed of a broad spectrum of cultures and classes, including Christian Copts, Bedouin, and southern Egyptians claiming to be the direct descendants of the Pharaohs. The majority of the population claims Arab ancestry or mixed Arab and Egyptian blood, while the upper classes trace their heritage to Turkey. Darker-skinned Nubians from southern Egypt began migrating north when their villages were flooded out of existence by the creation of Lake Nasser. The Nubians fill mostly menial jobs in today's urban centers and suffer because of racism that goes unrecognized by most Egyptians. People of Greek, Armenian, Jewish, Kurdish, and Albanian origins add spice to the mix, especially in cosmopolitan Alexandria. No matter what their ethnicity, however, most people consider themselves wholly Egyptian. The great majority of the lower class lives in poverty, some relying on family and relatives abroad (usually in the Gulf) for support.

Egyptians are known throughout the Arab world for their sense of humor and love of fun. Although poverty has made hospitality less common in Egypt than in other Arab countries, you won't be in Egypt long before you are invited to tea, a meal, or a wedding. Directions and advice are freely offered, but some Egyptians so fear looking foolish that they will give incorrect directions rather than fail to offer assistance. Most hosts or helpers expect something in return.

Egypt is conservative and patriarchal, with a strong Islamic tradition. Western mores do not apply, especially in matters of family and sex. The visibility and freedom of most Egyptian women is limited. Western concepts of punctuality also do not apply. Egyptians have little concern for time; simply accept this, slow down, and mellow out, especially when dealing with Egypt's mind-numbingly inefficient and ineffective bureaucracy. Don't spend more time placing phone calls and waiting in lines than exploring ancient temples and strolling through *souqs*.

ANCIENT HISTORY

According to the famous **Narmer Palette** (an ancient mascara holder discovered along the Nile in 1898), **King Menes** was the first true pharaoh of Egypt, uniting Upper (southern) and Lower (northern) Egypt in 3000 BCE. His kingdom, centered at Hierakonpolis, is one of the longest lasting and most powerful in all of history, enduring until Narmer was fatally mauled by a **hippopotamus.**

The pharaohs of the **Old Kingdom** (2664-2155 BCE) built a new capital at **Memphis** as **Imhotep,** history's first recorded architect, began constructing the step pyramids at Saqqara—the forerunners of the self-indulgent mausolea at Giza. Most view this era as the pinnacle of ancient Egyptian civilization: at a time when even China had scarcely emerged from the Stone Age, Egyptians had invented writing and **papyrus,** forged a national economy, recorded the history of eight dynasties of pharaohs, and built some of history's most impressive structures (all on the faith and labor of the peasantry). Believed to be earthly manifestations of the falcon-god Horus, the all-powerful pharaohs feared only death; their most magnificent monuments represent attempts to defeat this ultimate enemy.

EGYPT

The rise of Mentuhotep II ushered in the **Middle Kingdom** (2052-1786 BCE), an era of conservatism and order; nevertheless, internal political rivalries began to weaken the Egyptian dynasties in the 18th century BCE. Taking advantage of this vulnerable state, the chariot-riding **Hyksos** from the North penetrated the desert citadels at Thebes and ravished the Egyptian countryside. Upon the expulsion of the Hyksos by the ever-plotting Theban princes almost a century later, Egypt was resurrected as the **New Kingdom** (1554-1075 BCE).

Thebes became the center of a theocratic police state. The high priests of the sun (now embodied in the god **Amun**) wielded unimaginable power, often controlling the pharaoh himself. Egypt "modernized" its formerly primitive army by adapting the bronze weapons and horse-drawn chariots of the Hyksos and immediately proceeded to invade Africa, Palestine, and Syria. Now an empire ruled by warrior-kings, Egypt established control over almost all of the eastern Mediterranean. Trade in wood, olive oil, and slaves brought stability and prosperity, though the rivalry between the pharaoh and the priests of Amun often brought disruption.

Despite this success and the achievements of aggressive pharaohs such as Thutmoses III and the monumentally egotistical **Ramses II,** the New Kingdom slowly crumbled, and a slew of invaders had their way with it. When **Alexander the Great** arrived in 332 BCE, he freed the Egyptians from Persian rule and was declared the son of Amun and the legitimate pharaoh of Egypt by the Oracle of Amun in the Siwa Oasis (oh yeah, he also founded a dinky little town named after him, Alexandria). In 48 BCE, more than a century after Rome made its first overtures to the ever-feuding Ptolemies (descendants of Alexander's successor, Ptolemy), **Julius Caesar** came to Egypt and made similar advances to **Cleopatra VII,** Queen of Egypt. She accepted an alliance with Caesar that left her secure until his assassination four years later. Cleopatra formed another alliance with **Marc Antony,** one of the three men vying to succeed Caesar. While Antony was thus otherwise occupied, third wheel **Octavian** grabbed the empire for himself in 30 BCE, ruthlessly crushing the affair and the Ptolemaic dynasty at the Battle of Actium.

The Egypt of Imperial Rome and Byzantium was characterized by political stability and an increasingly entrenched bureaucracy (two traditions that modern Egypt has embraced wholeheartedly). During this period, Egypt was also the breadbasket of the Mediterranean, supplying most of the grain needed to support the empire's growing urban population. Christianity arrived in Egypt around 40 CE with St. Mark and helped maintain relative social tranquility. Some argument arose over the personage of Jesus Christ: the **Copts** worshiped him only as a divine figure, whereas the church at Constantinople believed he was both divine and human. This long-festering argument exploded in 451 CE when the Copts were excommunicated and forced to set up their own church in Alexandria. The modern-day Coptic minority in Egypt is descended from these original dissidents.

MODERN HISTORY

Napoleon's invading forces ended Ottoman control of Egypt in 1798, but the French invasion was too short-lived and too universally loathed to have any major impact at the time. However, as the first European conquest of an Arab country in the history of Islam, the invasion signaled the fall of Islam as a world political power.

Europe was still looking for a shortcut to the mysteries (and trade possibilities) of India, and all eyes turned to the **Suez.** The British and the Ottomans fought for control of the country, with the latter winning out and building the Suez Canal in 1869. The rigid Empire of the Big O began to grow flaccid in the later years of the nineteenth century, when the Brits took over (prompting **Mustafa Kamal** to found an Egyptian nationalist movement). The Egyptian economy during the British occupation and WWI was so completely focused on the exportation of cotton to England's rheumatic textile mills that grain had to be imported to feed the rural population. After WWI ended, the nationalist *Wafd* ("delegation") party formed to demand complete autonomy from Britain; the deportation in 1918 of *Wafd* leader **Sa'ad Zaghloul** showed the British had other plans. The British eventually recognized Egypt's independence in 1922, but maintained control through puppet-king **Fouad I.** Not content to have his strings pulled by far-distant imperialists, Fouad struggled successfully for some power of his own, and soon the British, the King, and the popularly supported *Wafd* party were all fighting for control of Egypt. The **Anglo-Egyptian Treaty of 1936**— uninspired in name and in concessions by the British—ended the three-way tug-of-war for control by granting Egypt independence but allowing for continued British occupation of the Suez Canal Zone.

Egypt again came to center stage as an Allied base of operations in WWII. The decisive Allied victory at the **Battle of El-Alamein** (just outside of Alexandria) allowed the Allies to sweep into North Africa and halt the advances of Rommel's Afrika Korps once and for all. Resentment towards the British reached a fever pitch during and after WWII as Egyptians rioted against being forced to participate in a war that had nothing to do with them. Continued rioting and striking led the British to finally leave Alexandria and the Suez in 1947.

The newborn Egyptian government didn't wait long before taking its first, hesitant steps. In 1948, Egypt and the entire Arab world was humiliated when a joint Arab army was easily defeated by a smaller army from the just-born state of Israel. Several young officers were so outraged at the incompetence of their elder leaders they formed the **Free Officers** coalition and staged a bloodless coup of the government on July 26, 1952. Then-King Farouk was forced to abdicate, the occupation political parties and Constitution were abolished, and General Naguib was elected Prime Minister (although the government was really controlled by a nine-member Revolutionary Command Council led by Colonel **Gamal 'Abd en-Nasser**).

Nasser officially assumed presidency of the Egyptian Arab Republic in 1956. Equal parts brilliant strategist and power-obsessed dictator, he gained immense popularity because of his dedication to the plight of the *fellaheen* majority in Egypt. One of Nasser's first major political moves was the controversial nationalization of the Suez Canal after a lack of Western financial support for the **Aswan High Dam.** His name is synonymous with **Pan-Arabism;** during his presidency, Arabic nationalism was born, reached its peak, and died out. In 1958, Egypt and Syria made a bold nationalist move by uniting to form the United Arab Republic; all this ended during the **Six-Day War** (July 5–10) of 1967, when Israeli armies managed to gain control of the Sinai Peninsula (among other strategic locations). Three years later, the crumbling movement for Pan-Arabism was dealt a fatal blow with the death of Nasser himself on September 28th.

Vice President **Anwar Sadat** was elected President by a landslide (and a lack of opposition). Sadat set up Egypt as a "democratic, socialist state," although in reality it was neither of those things but an election-legitimated authoritarian regime (which it remains to this day). The president serves a six-year term and is almost inevitably re-elected for additional terms. The legislative branch of government consists of the 444-member **People's Assembly,** half of whom must be workers or peasants and a whopping 30 of whom must be women.

On Yom Kippur in 1973 (October 6th), Sadat attacked Israeli forces in the Sinai. Although this **October War** ended in a stalemate, the Arab world experienced an incredible morale boost. On November 17, 1977, Sadat continued with his surprise movements and made a visit to Jerusalem to discuss peace settlements. The West embraced Sadat as the image of Arab-Israeli moderation and conciliation, awarding him (and Israeli Prime Minister Menachem Begin) the **Nobel Peace Prize** one year later for his work in the peace process and at the Camp David Accords. Although Sadat was building himself up in foreign relations, his domestic relations were crumbling: never the debonair figurehead his predecessor was, many Arabs saw him as a sellout and a yes-man to Western interests. Sadat was assassinated at a military parade in October 1981.

EGYPT

Current President **Hosni Mubarak,** elected in 1981, continued his predecessor's policies with less derring-do and more domestic sensitivity. Mubarak was responsible for developing Egypt's quickly developing tourism industry, resuming diplomatic and trade relations with moderate Arab countries, and otherwise bandaging the wounds made by the flamboyant swathe Sadat cut through Arab politics. Mubarak's support of Saudi Arabia and Kuwait in the **Gulf War** in 1990-1991 was important in revitalizing Egypt's position as the center of Middle Eastern politics. The most significant political threat to President Mubarak's regime continues to be internal Arab dissidents, in the form of the Islamist parties. Sadat was assassinated by militants who wanted to overthrow the Egyptian government and establish an Islamic republic in its place. Mubarak has consistently appeased Islamic moderates (who are in the majority anyway) in order to isolate militants: alcohol was banned on EgyptAir flights, *Dallas* was taken off TV, and an Islamic newspaper, *Al-Liwa'al-Islami,* was initiated. The past several years have seen a rise in Islamist-generated violence, with militants based in Middle Egypt striking at the status quo via attacks on government figures and assassinations of secularist intellectuals. The deadliest attack by Islamist militants involved the death of 58 tourists at Luxor on 17 November 1997, leading the government to drastically tighten security throughout the country.

IN THE NEWS

The **Library at Alexandria** is set to re-open in October 1999, nearly five millennia after Ptolemy I first commissioned the construction of the building. The ancient library was the center of scholarly debate and research in the ancient world, and may even have achieved its goal of housing every book known to exist at the time under one roof. The library was mysteriously burned down near the end of the Roman Empire. The purpose of the new edifice is almost as unclear as the cause of the fire so many years ago. Egyptian authorities have assured scholars that the library is being built to foster the research of scholars in the Middle East, and consequently, Arab countries have helped to pick up a third of the library's US$180 million dollar cost. These funds will be used to collect over 8 million books and manuscripts, and to construct a science museum, a planetarium, and a school for library studies. Many scholars and diplomats have criticized the project in private as a governmental propaganda machine, a library offering a multitude of resources to the public but not really fostering or even tolerating the sort of radical intellectual inquiry the original library did. Press censorship in Egypt is very widespread: books and news articles are frequently banned, and many scholars doubt that the government will allow them to research or publish works criticizing Middle Eastern and Arabic policies. For another look at the *Bibliotheka Alexandria* controversy, see **A Library Long Overdue,** p. 130.

RELIGION AND ETHNICITY

Islam is constitutionally established as the official religion of Egypt, with over 90% of the population belonging to the Sunni Muslim sect. Egypt is one of the most important centers of Islamic theological study in the world, and Cairo's **Al-Azhar University** (p. 85) is at its heart. Al-Azhar is the oldest continuously operating university in the world and has graduated Islamic scholars from every Muslim country on earth since it was first founded in 972 CE.

Orthodox Christians (who belong to the **Coptic Church**) make up Egypt's largest and most significant religious minority, with population estimates somewhere between three and seven million. The relationship between the Copts and the Muslim government has always been strained, but with the rise of Muslim fundamentalism, tensions between the Muslim majority and the Coptic minority have erupted in acts of vandalism. Another one million or so members of the Egyptian population are Roman Catholics, Greek and Armenian Orthodox Christians, Protestants, and Jews. These groups thrived in colonial times but have dwindled in number due to emigration.

MEET THE GODS
The ancient Egyptians didn't play that monotheism game. Here's a brief collection of their many deities:

AMUN "The Hidden One." Amun is typically portrayed as a ram-horned man with blue-colored flesh. In the New Kingdom he became associated with the sun-god Ra, and "Amun-Ra" became the king of the gods and a father figure to the pharaohs.

ANUBIS The jackal-headed god of cemeteries and embalming, whose black skin represents either the silt of the Nile or mummy flesh treated with chemicals. He is usually depicted weighing the hearts of the dead (the heart was considered the center of intellect and emotions) against Maat, the feather of truth.

ATON The sun at noon, usually depicted as a disk from which rays extend ending in outstretched hands holding *ankhs*. The heretical 18th dynasty pharaoh Akhenaton worshiped Aton as the one and only god, with the pharaoh as his one and only priest.

GEB The earth god, usually depicted as a reclining man holding up his sister-wife Nut (the sky goddess). He divided Egypt in two, giving Lower Egypt to his son Osiris and Upper Egypt to his son Seth.

HAPY The symbol of the Nile's annual flooding. He is depicted as a seaweed-tressed man with breasts and a rounded abdomen (representing fertility).

HATHOR The daughter of Ra, the goddess of joy and love, and the protectoress of women and travelers. She usually hangs out on tomb walls sporting cow horns with a sun disk between them.

HORUS The hawk-headed sky god and son of Isis and Osiris. When Seth cut out his eyes (they were later glued back on with divine saliva), they came to represent perfection and were known as a guard against evil (the *wedjat* eye).

ISIS Another sister-wife (to Osiris), usually depicted with a throne on her head. She is the protectoress and healer of children.

KHNUM Ram-headed potter god who sculpted both gods and men out of clay. He is known for controlling the Nile's annual flood.

MAAT The personification of cosmic order, usually depicted as a woman wearing an ostrich feather on her head.

MUT Symbolic mother of the pharaoh and Thebes' principal goddess, who often appears as a lion-headed woman wearing a vulture-shaped headdress.

NUT Cow-shaped goddess of the sky and yet another sister-wife (to Geb), usually depicted stretched across the ceiling of a tomb, swallowing the sun and making the night. She is the mother of Osiris, Isis, Seth, and Nephthys.

OSIRIS The mummified god of the underworld and fertility, brother-husband of Isis and father of Horus. Seth was so bitter about getting his just deserts when Egypt was divided up by Geb, he dismembered his brother Osiris and buried his body parts across Egypt. Isis collected the pieces and bandaged them together, making the first mummy; as a thank-you gift, Osiris fathered Horus by Isis before he headed for Duat (the underworld) to rule as lord and judge of the dead.

RA Don't step to Ra, the falcon-headed sun god with a sun disc upon his head who is so powerful that other gods often merge with him to enhance their own powers (Amun-Ra). He rides across the sky in his solar boat, rising from Duat (the underworld) in the east and reentering the land of the dead in the west.

SETH God of chaotic forces, synonymous with evil in much of Egyptian mythology. He performs his one good deed when he spears the evil snake Apophis as the boat of Ra begins its entry into the underworld every evening.

THOTH The ibis-headed scribe god, inventor of writing, and divine reckoner of time. Thoth sometimes took the form of a great white baboon with a giant penis.

FESTIVALS AND HOLIDAYS

Government offices and banks close for Islamic holidays, but most tourist facilities remain open. The month of Ramadan can be a wonderful (if occasionally inconvenient) time to visit, especially in festive Cairo and Alexandria. Along with the Islamic festivals, the two Sufi rituals of **Zikr** and **Zar** are not to be missed (both rituals are practiced on Fridays in populous areas). In the former, a group of dancers whirl themselves into a frenzy; in the latter, women dance in a group, primarily as an exorcism rite. The Coptic celebrations of Easter and Christmas are tranquil affairs marked by special church services. The festival known as **Sham en-Nissim** falls on the first Monday after Coptic Easter, but has developed into a secular celebration. Sham en-Nissim was originally an outdoor spring festival in which ancient Egyptians and enslaved Jews feasted on pungent *fisikh* (dried and salted fish) as equals; the highlight of the festival was the ritual casting of a young woman into the Nile. *Fisikh* is still eaten at modern celebrations, but the young women stay dry; even the ritual of throwing a doll into the Nile has all but disappeared from the present-day festivities. For a comprehensive list of the dates of religious and national holidays, see the **Appendix**, p. 699.

LANGUAGE

One of the earliest forms of writing was Egyptian **hieroglyphs** (sacred carvings). Alongside this pictorial system developed the **hieratic,** an abbreviated cursive script that retained only the vital characteristics of the pictures. After the 22nd Dynasty, scribes began using the sacred hieratic writing in a secular context, leading to the rise of a form known as Enchorial or **Demotic.** Eventually, even the sacred *Book of the Dead* (a compilation of spells and cult rituals) was translated into this script. Modern scholars owe much of their knowledge of ancient Egyptian linguistics to the **Rosetta Stone,** a stone tablet dating from around 200 BCE that contains the same passage celebrating the crowning of King Ptolemy V recorded in hieroglyphic, Demotic, and Greek writing. **Coptic,** today used only in liturgy, is a derivation of ancient Egyptian that uses Greek letters plus six letters of Demotic.

Since the Islamic conquest, the primary language of Egypt has been Arabic. Modern **Egyptian Arabic** differs greatly from classical Arabic, and the Egyptian dialect varies significantly from that used in other Arab nations.

THE ARTS

LITERATURE. Most of the writings of the ancient Egyptians, such as the *Book of the Dead*, deal with magic and religion. The ancients dabbled in poetic love songs as well. Modern literature in Egypt is synonymous with the name of Cairene novelist **Naguib Mahfouz.** In 1988, Mahfouz became the first Arab to win the Nobel Prize for literature. Mahfouz's major work in the 1950s was *The Cairo Trilogy (Palace Walk, Palace of Desire*, and *Sugar Street*), which seamlessly depicts the life of three generations in Cairo from WWI to the 1950s. His classic allegory *Children of Gebelawi* (1959), banned throughout the Arab world except in Lebanon, retells the stories of the Qur'an in a modern-day Cairo setting.

Notable among more contemporary authors is Alexandrine novelist and essayist **Edward el-Kharrat,** who is considered the father of modernism in Egyptian literature. His popular novels *City of Saffron* (1989) and *Girls of Alexandria* (1993) are both available in translation. Doctor, feminist, and novelist **Nawal es-Saadawi** stands out among women authors with her extensive writings (including the notable works *The Circling Song* and *The Naked Face of Arab Women*) on the liberation of the Arab female psyche, sexuality, and legal position. Her works were once considered so controversial they were banned in her native country, and she has herself been imprisoned for a year and forbidden from practicing in Egypt because of the perceived danger she poses to society.

Many non-Egyptians have written accounts of their travels and experiences within the country. In *The Innocents Abroad*, Mark Twain describes his misadventures in Egypt and other countries. For an engrossing if oversexed account of Alexandrine life, don't miss Lawrence Durrell's multi-narrator epic *The Alexandria Quartet*. For an eye-opening account of early Western explorers roaming the Nile, read Alan Moorehead's *The White Nile* and its companion volume, *The Blue Nile*, which includes hair-raising chapters on the French invasion of Egypt and the rise of Muhammad 'Ali. Michael Ondaatje's award-winning *The English Patient* contains sensual and incredibly accurate descriptions of early desert expeditions in the area.

VISUAL AND PERFORMING ARTS. Egypt has had a near monopoly on the Arabic entertainment industry for most of the second half of the 20th century, ranking behind only Bollywood (India) and Hollywood (United States) in its prolific output. Egyptian films range from skillfully done modern dramas to comedies pitting down-and-out students against evil capitalists and bumbling police officers, with a smattering of southern Egyptians (portrayed as idiots) thrown in for comic relief.

The 50s and 60s were the golden age of Egyptian cinema, when Alexandrine **Omar Sharif** (*Doctor Zhivago, Funny Girl*) ruled as an international superstar and his former wife Fatin Hamama presided as queen of Arab cinema. The musicals of that period are also still very popular, featuring well-dressed hipsters knitting their brows in consternation over the cruelty of love, the generation gap, and the difficulty of college examinations. Controversial auteur **Yousef Chahine** (credited with discovering Omar Sharif in a Cairo cafe and catapulting him to fame with 1954's *Blazing Sun*) has gained international acclaim for his lushly filmed, genre-bending masterpieces that tackle everything from sexual discovery to the hypocrisy of Western society. *The Emigrant* (1994) was initially banned in Egypt for depicting images of the Prophet Muhammad (which is forbidden in the Muslim religion), but became a box office hit once the ban was lifted. His recent work includes *Destiny* (1997), which attacks modern Islamic fundamentalism by recounting the persecution of the Islamic philosopher Averroes.

The levying of heavy entertainment taxes in the 70s and the general atmosphere of profiteering in the 80s served to drastically lower the standards of modern Egyptian cinema to somewhere below chintzy tragicomedy. A new guard of young directors has begun to revitalize the industry by tackling such once-taboo topics as social conditions, terrorism, and the country's volatile relationship with Israel.

MUSIC. Traditional Egyptian folk music incorporates nasal horns churning out repetitive melodies to the incessant beat of drums. **Nubian music** (called *musiqa nubiyya* in Aswan) is equally enthralling. In general, it eliminates the horns and focuses on slow drumbeats and chanting choruses. The music blaring from taxis, ahwas, and homes throughout Egypt is a slightly updated version of this traditional classical music. Egypt is the capital of the Arab music industry and the promised land for aspiring artists from all over the Arab world. Sayyid Darwish and the legendary **Muhammad 'Abd el-Wahhab** began as early as the 1910s and 20s to integrate Western instrumentation and techniques into Arabic song. Like Egyptian cinema, this type of music had its heyday in the 50s and 60s but shows no signs of waning in popularity today. In the 60s, the emphasis fell on strong, beautiful voices to unite Arabic music's disparate elements, and several "greats" of Egyptian music emerged. The greatest of these was the unmistakable and unforgettable **Umm Kulthum.** Her rags-to-riches story begins in the provinces, where her father dressed her up as a boy to sing with him at religious festivals; it ends in 1975 with a funeral that was bigger than President Nasser's five years earlier. In the interim, Umm Kulthum gave speeches, starred in musical films, and sang everything from post-revolutionary propaganda songs to love ballads. Travelers in Egypt cannot and should not escape without hearing Umm Kulthum's voice and seeing her sunglasses-clad face on a television screen or wall mural. Music in the 80s and 90s saw a wholesale incorporation of Western influences. Modern Egyptian pop is totally danceable, mostly pre-packaged, and rarely long-lived. Among these transitory teen dreams, **Amr Diab** has endured. His upbeat songs provide sing-along material at weddings, parties, and discos.

FOOD AND DRINK

The Egyptian breakfast of choice is **fuul** ("fool")—cooked, mashed fava beans blended with garlic, lemon, olive oil, and salt, eaten with bread and vegetables. What's known as falafel elsewhere—chick peas and/or fava beans mashed, shaped into balls, and fried—is called **ta'amiyya** in Egypt, and both ta'amiyya and *fuul* are sold at street stands everywhere. Street vendors also sell *kibdeh* (liver) sandwiches, which smell like they should taste disgusting (try them and be surprised at how tasty they are). **Shawarma** made its way from the Levant to Egypt only a few years ago; it is supposed to be sinfully fatty lamb rolled into a pita with vegetables and *tahina*, but Egyptians will slap any sort of meat into bogus French bread and call it shawarma. The ever-popular **kushari** is a cheap, tasty meal of pasta, lentils, and dried onions in tomato sauce.

At times you might feel that all you will ever get to eat will be *kofta*, kebab, and chicken. These carnivorous joys are almost always served with tomato-less salads, bread or rice, and *tahina*, a sesame-based sauce. *Kofta* is spiced ground beef grilled on skewers; kebab is chunks of lamb cooked the same way. Chicken is either fried (without batter), roasted on a rotisserie, or skewered, grilled, and called *shish tawouq*. Fried and stuffed pigeon *(hamam)* is a source of national pride, particularly in Alexandria. *Biftek* (sometimes called *veal panné* on restaurant menus) is a thinly sliced veal, breaded and fried. You can get feta with a year-long shelf life in no-refrigeration-needed packs—great for long road trips or cheap breakfasts. The brand *La Vache Qui Rit* (The Laughing Cow) is so popular that it has been adopted as a disparaging nickname for President Hosni Mubarak.

Fatir are flaky, chewy, doughy delights, filled with anything and everything and eaten either as a meal or for dessert. Other desserts include *ba'laweh* and rice pudding flavored with rose-water *(roz bel laban)*. Egypt's ruby-red watermelons *(butteekh)* are beautiful but lethal: the fruits are color-enhanced by injections of non-potable water. Stick to the unbelievable **figs** *(teen)*, and in late summer, the papaya-like *teen shoki* (cactus fruit).

A popular drink among travelers is **'asab**, sugar cane juice, said to increase sexual prowess. Egyptians themselves are coffee and tea fiends. Egyptian tea is taken without milk and enough sugar to make it syrupy. Egyptians prefer **ahwa** (Arabic coffee). Especially when you are in Upper Egypt, try *karkadeh*, a red drink made by brewing hibiscus flowers and served hot or cold. Egypt brews its own beer, **Stella,** which costs between E£2.50 and E£6 in restaurants and bars.

PUFF THE MAGIC SHEESHA In Egypt, relaxation has become synonymous with gurgling and puffing noises accompanied by the smell of sugary honey, apple, or rose tobacco. The instrument of pleasure is a popular smoking apparatus known in Egypt as a *sheesha* (elsewhere as an *argeileh*), plain or ornately colored and decorated with feathers. It consists of a snake-like tube and a small bowl filled with burning coals, tobacco, and spices. Water vapor carries the tobacco smoke through the 1m tube and into the mouth, making each puff smooth and sweet. The *sheesha* is thought to have been introduced in Egypt by the Turks, and became fashionable among the elite during the late 17th century. For a long time *sheesha* smoking remained an upper-class pleasure, but it seems the apple and honey puffs of smoke have ushered in a veritable national pastime.

CAIRO القاهرة

> I arrived at length at Cairo, mother of cities and seat of Pharaoh the tyrant, boundless in multitude of buildings, peerless in beauty and splendor, the meeting-place of comer and goer, the halting-place of feeble and mighty, whose throngs surge as waves of the sea.
>
> —Ibn Battuta

Cairo has been the greatest city in the Middle East and Africa for nearly all of the past millennium. In 2600 BCE, the pharaohs of the Old Kingdom chose the sandy plateau just above the Nile Delta for their ancient capital of Memphis, one of the world's earliest urban settlements and Egypt's capital until the beginning of the first century CE (when St. Mark introduced Christianity to Egypt in the face of intense Roman opposition). For the next 600 years, the Coptic Church that grew from the work of St. Mark marked the wrists of its faithful with tattoos, and left even more enduring marks in the churches of Old Cairo. The early decades of the 7th century CE found Cairo in the throes of power struggles between the Persian and Byzantine empires. Memphis and Babylon (the glitzy settlement across the Nile) changed hands many times, and warfare near Babylon drove many urban dwellers to the villages until the city lay bereft and deserted by the time of the Arab conquest in 641. The leader of the Arab invaders, 'Amr Ibn el-As, set up camp at Fustat, the seed of modern Cairo. The Arabs were also responsible for giving the city its name: Fatimid leader Gawhar as-Sikelli dubbed it *El-Qahira*, "The Conqueror."

The city swelled so much in size and grandeur under the Fatimids and their descendants that it soon became known as *Misr*, the Arabic name for all of Egypt. During Cairo's Golden Age, it became one of the most advanced cultural centers west of China. Although various conquerors had their way with Cairo throughout the Middle Ages, it remained far more populous than any city in Europe. The Ottomans, however, reduced Cairo to the status of a provincial center in 1516. After a brief affair with Napoleon in the late 1700s, Cairo made a grand entrance upon the 19th century scene thanks to a face-lift by the Albanian Muhammad 'Ali and his European-educated descendants, the *khedives*, whose penchant for the extravagant resulted in streets dotted with glittering Turkish-style mosques and palaces.

The political upheaval of the Middle East has affected Cairo in the 20th century, as well. Modern political and economic centralization is driving thousands of rural Egyptians into the arms of the "Mother of the World" (*Umm ed-Dunya*, as the medieval Arabs called Cairo), and she is struggling to cope with the needs of her growing brood. Expansion has led to over-crowded neighborhoods, clogged thoroughfares, and urban pollution. Places where pharaohs and kings once lounged now teem with barking street merchants and silver-tongued con artists. Cairo's tumultuous present is only the current incarnation of its tumultuous past. Amid tangled webs of unlabeled streets and the dizzying calls of hawkers, Cairenes frequent their favorite *sheesha* halls, navigate labyrinthine bazaars, and descend on hundreds of places of worship. Patience and curiosity will allow you to overcome the city's cluttered eccentricities, so that you too might be conquered by the power of Egypt's greatest city.

HIGHLIGHTS OF CAIRO AND ENVIRONS

■ The Islamic architecture in and around Cairo is some of the most beautiful in the world. Don't miss the glorious complex of **Sultan Hassan** (p. 80), the **Mausoleum and Mosque of Qaytbay** (p. 89), and the immense **Citadel** (p. 82).

■ The **Egyptian Museum** (p. 96) showcases an unsurpassed collection of ancient treasures, including the famous loot from **Tutankhamun's tomb.**

■ A riddle from the **Sphinx** (p. 104): how can you visit Egypt without seeing the **Pyramids at Giza** (p. 101)? See where the whole pyramid craze got started by checking out Imhotep's **Step Pyramid** of Djoser-Netcherikhe at Saqqara (p. 107).

✦ ORIENTATION

At the center of it all is **Tahrir Square** (Maidan Tahrir), one of the many central districts planned by British and French colonialists. Buses depart for every metropolitan destination. Facing the square to the north is the sandstone **Egyptian Museum;** adjacent to it on the west side of the square is the **Nile Hilton.** Entrances to the Sadat Metro station ring the square. At the southern end of the square is the massive, concave **Mugamma' Building,** headquarters of the Egyptian bureaucracy. The placid gardens and excellent bookstore of the **American University of Cairo (AUC)** are directly to the east of the Mugamma' Building across Qasr El-'Aini St. A few blocks east on Tahrir St. is the Bab el-Luq public bus depot.

The three most important streets coming out of Tahrir Sq. are Qasr El-'Aini St., Qasr en-Nil St., and Tala'at Harb St. **Qasr El-'Aini Street** runs south from Tahrir Sq. and ends at **Old Cairo** (also known as Coptic Cairo), the historic and spiritual center of the Copts (Egyptian Eastern Orthodox Christians). The American University of Cairo (AUC), Parliament, and some of the city's most beautifully preserved 19th-century colonial mansions line Qasr El-'Aini St. Just south of Tahrir Sq., sandwiched between Qasr El-'Aini St. and the Nile, foreign embassies and banks cluster along the streets of the serene **Garden City** residential area. Farther south, the exclusive district of **Ma'adi** serves as a home for many of Cairo's expatriates. **Qasr en-Nil Street** begins in front of the Nile Hilton, cuts through Tala'at Harb Sq., and continues on to **Mustafa Kamal Square.** In between lie many of Cairo's Western-style stores, banks, travel agents, and the American Express office. **Tala'at Harb Street** runs from the northeast side of Tahrir Sq. through **Tala'at Harb Square** toward Orabi Sq. and 26 July St. Ramses Square to the north (west of Orabi Sq.) and **'Ataba Square** (east of Orabi Sq., at the end of 26 July St.) form a rough triangle with Tala'at Harb Sq. enclosing the main business and shopping district, which is crammed with travel agents, banks, restaurants, clothing stores, and budget hotels. Due north of Tahrir Sq. lies **'Abd el-Munem Riad Square,** the starting point of **Ramses Street** and the city's main public bus depot. Heading northeast away from the Nile, Ramses St. runs up to **Ramses Square,** the Cairo train station (called **Ramses Station**), and the Mubarak Metro station. South of Ramses Sq. off Ramses St. is the Mahattat Turgoman (Turgoman Bus Station), where buses to other parts of Egypt come and go. Farther out on Ramses St. are the **Cairo Stadium** and **Heliopolis,** a fashionable suburb where President Mubarak lives. Heading east from 'Ataba Sq., Al-Azhar St. and El-Muski St. (a long shopping strip) both lead to the northern end of Islamic Cairo and the Northern Cemetery.

Islamic Cairo was the heart of the city in the Middle Ages and is home to many mosques. It occupies an area southeast of downtown Cairo, marked by the **Citadel** and **Mosque of Ibn Tulun** in the south and the **Al-Azhar Mosque and University** in the north. Although this district was not laid out with urban planning in mind, there are a few key streets and areas, the first of which is **Salah ad-Din Square** (Maidan Salah ad-Din). Both the **Sultan Hassan Mosque** and **Rifa'i Mosque** border this square, as does the gargantuan Citadel. **Salah ad-Din Street** runs south to the Southern Cemetery, while **El-Qala'a Street** is a main north-south thoroughfare. Branching off of El-Qala'a and heading towards **Al-Azhar** and the **Khan el-Khalili** is **El-Mu'izz Street,** once the main avenue of the city. Finally, Al-Azhar St. connects Islamic Cairo to 'Ataba Square and circumnavigates the Khan el-Khalili and Al-Azhar.

The main bridge crossing the Nile from the downtown area is **Tahrir Bridge,** connecting Tahrir Sq. to the southern tip of Gezira Island. The northern half is Cairo's ritziest residential area, **Zamalek,** home to expats and quality restaurants. South of Zamalek is **Roda Island,** site of the Manial Palace Museum and the Nilometer.

Past Tahrir Bridge on the western bank of the Nile, the Cairo Sheraton Hotel presides over the residential neighborhood of **Dokki,** home to a handful of embassies. North of Dokki lies **Mohandiseen** (Engineer's City), built in the late 1950s by Nasser as a neighborhood for engineers. South of Dokki, past the Cairo Zoo and across the Giza Bridge, is **Giza Square.** Southwest is **Pyramids Road,** where overpriced bars run from the square all the way to the **Pyramids of Giza.**

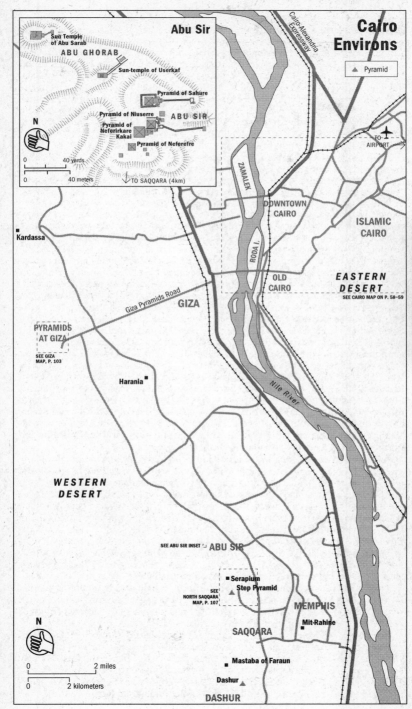

Abu Sir

Sun Temple
of Abu Sarab
ABU GHORAB

Sun-temple of Userkaf

Pyramid of Sahure

Pyramid of Niuserre   ABU SIR
Pyramid of
Neferirkare
Kakai

Pyramid of Neferefre

N

0   40 yards

0   40 meters

TO SAQQARA (4km)

**Cairo
Environs**

▲ Pyramid

Cairo-Alexandria Expressway

TO
AIRPORT

ZAMALEK

DOWNTOWN
CAIRO

ISLAMIC
CAIRO

RODA I.

OLD
CAIRO

EASTERN
DESERT

SEE CAIRO MAP ON P. 58–59

EGYPT

Kardassa

Giza Pyramids Road   GIZA

PYRAMIDS
AT GIZA

SEE GIZA
MAP, P. 103

Harania

Nile River

WESTERN
DESERT

SEE ABU SIR INSET   ABU SIR

SEE
NORTH SAQQARA
MAP, P. 107

Serapium
Step Pyramid

MEMPHIS

Mit-Rahine

N

SAQQARA

Mastaba of Faraun

0   2 miles

0   2 kilometers

Dashur

DASHUR

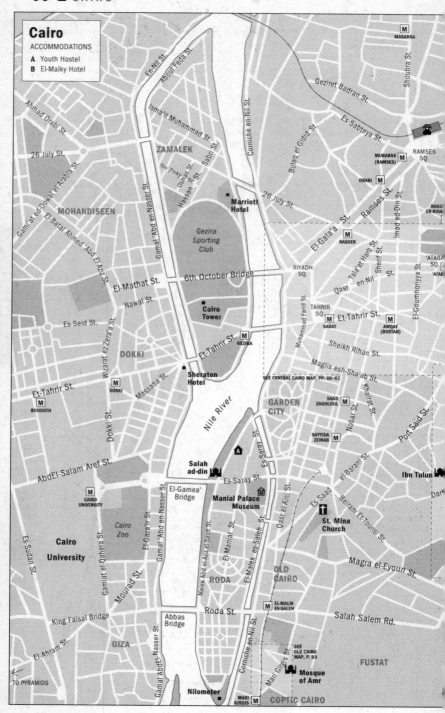

Cairo

ACCOMMODATIONS
- **A** Youth Hostel
- **B** El-Malky Hotel

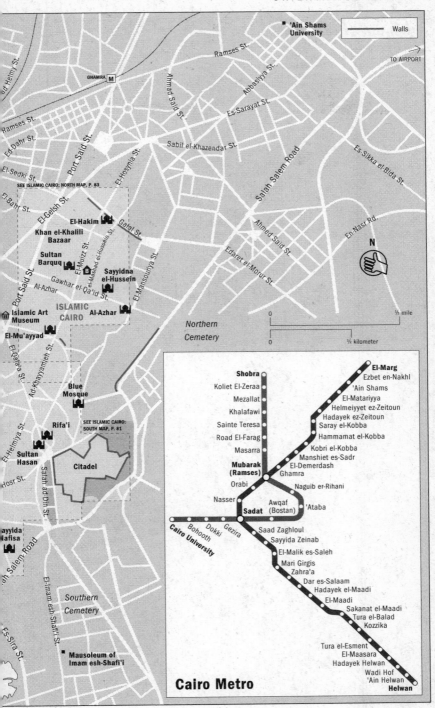

Cairo Metro

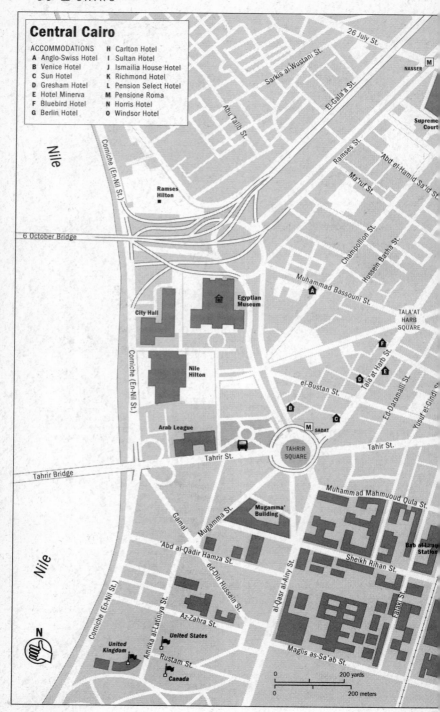

Central Cairo

ACCOMMODATIONS

A Anglo-Swiss Hotel
B Venice Hotel
C Sun Hotel
D Gresham Hotel
E Hotel Minerva
F Bluebird Hotel
G Berlin Hotel
H Carlton Hotel
I Sultan Hotel
J Ismailia House Hotel
K Richmond Hotel
L Pension Select Hotel
M Pensione Roma
N Horris Hotel
O Windsor Hotel

Nile

Corniche (En-Nil St.)

26 July St.

NASSER

Sarkis al-Wustani St.

El-Gala'a St.

Supreme Court

Abu Talib St.

Ramses St.

'Abd el-Hamid Sa'id St.

Ma'ruf St.

Ramses Hilton

6 October Bridge

Champollion St.

Hussein Basha St.

Muhammad Bassouni St.

Egyptian Museum

City Hall

TALA'AT HARB SQUARE

Corniche (En-Nil St.)

Nile Hilton

Tala'at Harb St.

el-Bustan St.

Ed-Daramalli St.

Yusuf el-Gindi St.

Arab League

SADAT

Tahrir St.

TAHRIR SQUARE

Tahrir St.

Tahrir Bridge

Muhammad Mahmuoud Qula St.

Mugamma' Building

Gamal

Mugamma St.

'Abd al-Qadir Hamza St.

ed-Din Hussein St.

Sheikh Rihan St.

Bab el-Lango Station

Falaki St.

Nile

Corniche (En-Nil St.)

Amrka at-Latinya St.

Az-Zahra St.

al-Qasr al-Ainy St.

United Kingdom

United States

Rustam St.

Canada

Maglis as-Sa'ab St.

N

0   200 yards
0   200 meters

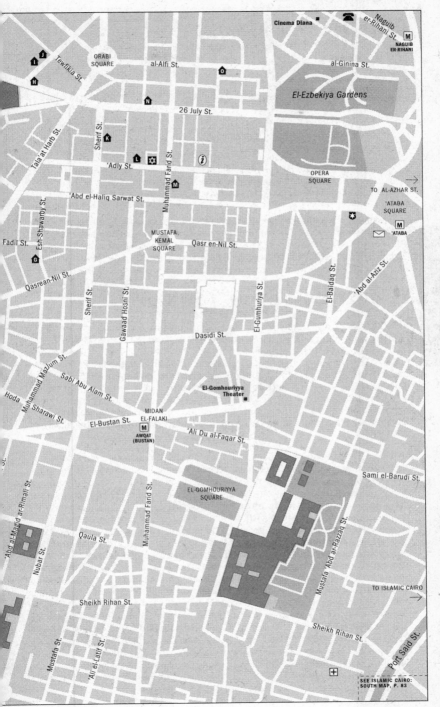

A TRIP DOWN MEMORY LANE Street names in Egypt are used repeatedly (the most popular is no doubt **Tahrir,** or "Liberation"). Most of these names have historical significance (for details, see **Modern History,** p. 48).

26 July Street: Commemorates the 1953 non-violent coup in which General Naguib and his Free Officers overthrew the king.

6 October Street: The date in 1973 when President Anwar Sadat staged a surprise attack on Israeli forces in the Sinai, earning him incredible popular support.

Sa'ad Zaghloul Street: The leader of the nationalist movement during WWI.

Salah ad-Din Street: Salah ad-Din Al-Ayyubi (a.k.a. Saladin) assumed control of Egypt in 1171, fortified Cairo, and built its Citadel. His reign was a golden age for Egypt, and he is revered as one of the great heroes of Islam.

Tala'at Harb Street: Egypt's most famous economist, Muhammad Tala'at Harb, founded the country's first national bank (now the ubiquitous Misr Bank), which was the first bank in the world to conduct business in Arabic (as it still does).

The major streets in Cairo are sometimes labeled in both English and Arabic, but a good **map** is helpful (most find they need a map more in-depth than that provided by the ETA). Maps cost E£10-30 and are available at most bookstores (p. 66). *Egypt Today* (E£9) publishes up-to-date street listings. Look for their *Dining Guide* and *Travel & Recreation Guide* (E£15 each).

⌐ GETTING OUT OF TOWN

AIRPLANES. Tourists pay triple what Egyptians pay for airfare within Egypt. **EgyptAir,** with offices at 6 'Adly St. (tel. 391 12 56) and in the Nile Hilton (tel. 76 52 00 or 77 24 10; reservations and info 392 74 44 or 392 72 05), flies to **Luxor** (E£833), **Sharm esh-Sheikh** (E£947), **Aswan** (E£1148), **Hurghada** (E£901), **Wadi Gadid** (E£901), **Suez** (E£607), and the **Sinai** (E£1000). **Air Sinai** (tel. 77 29 49; open daily 9am-5pm), at the Nile Hilton, flies to **Tel Aviv** (E£629; round-trip for trips of 3-30 days E£895, longer trips E£1164). It is very difficult (and expensive) to get flights out of Cairo to international destinations on short notice. Reserve far in advance. For information on traveling to and from **Cairo International Airport,** see **Entry,** p. 42.

TRAINS. Ticket windows at **Ramses Station** (Metro: Mubarak) are open daily 8am-10pm (info tel. 575 35 35). The **tourist office** (open daily 8am-9pm), on the left as you enter the station, can write out your destination and other details in Arabic to avoid confusion. Which line you stand in depends upon whether you are reserving a seat in advance or trying to buy a ticket for the same day (often impossible). Women (and men traveling with women) can take advantage of the special **women's line** that may form at crowded times, which is much shorter and faster than the corresponding men's line. In addition, women are permitted (and expected) to push to the front of any line, head held high. Students receive a **30% discount** on almost all fares with an **ISIC card.** The trains enter their berths at least half an hour before departure time. None of the train numbers or destinations are in English, but other travelers and the tourist police may lend a hand. In summer, prices fluctuate and there are no student discounts.

There are two types of trains to **Alexandria,** both air-conditioned—a **French line** (3hr.; 6, 8:30, 9:30, 11am, 2:10, 3:10, 4, 5, 8, and 10:30pm; 1st class E£20, 2nd class E£12) and a faster **Spanish line** (2hr.; 8, 9am, noon, 2, 3, 6, and 7pm; 1st class E£22, 2nd class E£17). Trains also go to **Aswan** (13-16hr.; 7:30 and 10am; 1st class E£63, 2nd class E£39), **Luxor** (9-12hr.; 7:30 and 10am; 1st class E£53, 2nd class E£33), and **Port Said** (4½hr.; 6:35, 8:45, 11:30am, 2:30, and 6:30pm; E£18). Trains to Luxor and Aswan stop in Minya, Sohag, Asyut, and Qena.

EGYPT

The area just outside the train station is chaotic: avoid crossing the treacherous streets by using the convenient tunnels of the Mubarak Metro station. Before you head underground, however, be sure to catch a glimpse of the massive **Statue of Ramses II,** standing calm amidst the storm.

BUSES. The bus system in Egypt is a four-wheeled version of the government bureaucracy—things are always changing, no one has any real idea of what's going on, yet somehow it all works out. Taking a bus can be quite a fuss in Cairo (as in much of the Middle East): schedules shift daily, prices fluctuate, and drop-off points change without warning. Check a day or two before you need to take a bus to make sure that it's going where you want for a price you're willing to pay. Cairo's intercity bus terminal has shifted locations several times in the past years (even recent schedules can be out of date); unless otherwise noted, buses leave from **Turgoman Station (Mahattat Turgoman)** near Ramses Sq. The buses themselves are quite nice—frequently air-conditioned, often serving food, and always equipped with large, comfortable seats. Make reservations in person a day or two in advance for popular destinations.

> **To the Sinai:** The **East Delta Bus Co.** (tel. 76 22 93) runs to: **Taba** (9hr.; 7:30am, E£50; 10pm, E£70); **Nuweiba** (8hr.; 7:30am, E£50; 10pm, E£55); and **Dahab** (8hr.; 7:30am, 1, 4:30, and 11:30pm; E£55). **Superjet** (tel. 579 71 71) runs buses to **Sharm esh-Sheikh** (7hr., 11pm, E£55).
>
> **To Alexandria and the Mediterranean Coast: Superjet** (tel. 579 71 71) goes to **Alexandria** (3hr., every 30min. 5:30am-11pm, E£55) and **Marsa Matrouh** (5hr., 8am, E£37). Buses also run to **Siwa** from both destinations.
>
> **To the Canal Zone:** The **East Delta Bus Co.** (tel. 76 22 93) runs to: **Port Said** (every hr. 6:30am-7pm, E£15); **Suez** (every ½hr. 6:30am-7pm, E£6); and **Isma'ilia** (every ½hr. 6:30am-7pm, E£6).
>
> **To Upper Egypt:** The **Upper Egypt Bus Co.** sends buses to: **Kharga** (12hr., 8am, E£40); **Farafra** (7½hr., 10am and noon, E£40); **Aswan** (13hr., 5:30pm, E£55); **Luxor** (9hr., 9pm, E£50); **Quseir** (10pm, E£55); and **Abu Ramad** (11pm, E£65).
>
> **To Hurghada:** Serviced by **Superjet** (8:30am; 2:30pm, E£47; 11pm, E£52) and the **Upper Egypt Bus Co.** (9am, 12:30, 3, 9:40, 11:30pm, and midnight; E£45.5).
>
> **To Tel Aviv/Jerusalem:** Buses leave daily from the **Cairo Sheraton.** Make reservations a day in advance at the Sheraton or at **Misr Travel,** on the 1st block of Tala'at Harb St.
>
> **To the Levant:** The **East Delta Bus Co.** runs daily to **Jordan** and **Syria** (8pm, US$33) and **Turkey** (8pm, US$90). **Superjet** leaves from Al-Maza Sq. to **Jordan** (M, T, Th, Sa 6am; US$67) and **Syria** (Sa 10pm, US$90).

SERVICE TAXIS. *Service* are best for short trips: they are faster and cheaper than buses. From Ramses Station, catch them to **Alexandria** (E£10-12), **Suez** (E£5-7), **Isma'ilia** (E£6), **Port Said** (E£9), or **El-Arish** (E£15). You can also hire *service* to **Fayyum** (E£5) at Giza Square by the train station; to **Alexandria** (E£11) from in front of the Nile Hilton; and to **Wadi Natrun** from Kolali Sq. (about E£10). The Ahmed Hilmi Sq. station covers **Mansura** (E£9), **Tanta** (E£6), **Zagazig** (E£5), and the rest of the Delta. You'll have to hunt for taxis to the **Sinai.** Settle on a price before leaving.

CAR RENTAL. If you're a daredevil or a maniac (or both), driving in Cairo is for you. **Avis** (tel. 354 86 98 or 354 74 00) has several branches throughout the city. The branch at Cairo International Airport (tel. 265 24 29) is open 24 hours. Join the millions of middle-class Egyptians driving Suzuki Swifts for US$45-48 per day, first 100km included. Most branches are open daily 8am-3:30pm. **Hertz** (tel. 347 41 72 or 347 22 38) has branches at Cairo International Airport (265 24 30), Ramses Hilton (574 44 00), Semiramis Intercontinental Hotel (354 32 39), and Forte Grand Hotel (383 03 83). They have Toyota Corollas for US$54.50 per day with unlimited mileage and air conditioning (open daily 9am-5pm).

▣ GETTING AROUND TOWN

METRO. The Cairo Metro is the fastest and cleanest ticket in town—worlds away from the rest of Cairo's bumpy and grumpy public transport. It was completed in 1987 as a joint project with the French and the Japanese, and is the only subway system in all of Africa or the Middle East. Trains run along the main line, a 40km route linking the southern industrial district of Helwan to El-Marj in Heliopolis, with a number of stops downtown (look for the giant red "M" signs). An additional line connecting Shubra was recently added, and other lines to Giza, Imbaba, and Al-Azhar are still under construction. Downtown stations feature TV screens with *America's Funniest Home Videos*, cartoons, and Egyptian ads. In early 1999, pornographic films were somehow piped in to the closed circuit TVs in the suburbs, much to the chagrin of Cairenes. Trains run about every six minutes (daily in summer 5:30am-1am; in winter 5:30am-midnight; 50pt-E£1). Keep track of your ticket; you'll need it to exit. The stations downtown are **Mubarak** (Ramses Sq. and Railway Station), **Orabi** (Orabi St. and Ramses St.), **Nasser** (26 July St. and Ramses St.), **Sadat** (Tahrir Sq.), **Sa'ad Zaghloul** (Mansur St. and Isma'il Abaza St.), **Sayyida Zeinab** (Mansur St. and 'Ali Ibrahim St.), **El-Malik es-Saleh** (Salah Salem Road), and **Mari Girgis** (Old Cairo). Rush hour is before 9am and from 2-5pm. The first compartment is reserved for women; the second is reserved for women until 4pm.

MICROBUSES. Microbuses follow set routes to certain destinations, but tend to be flexible as long as all passengers are going to the same area. Stops are sometimes marked by a wooden shelter. If you don't have a basic command of Arabic, stick to the numbered, fixed routes of the minibuses.

Microbuses go from **'Ataba Square** to Ramses Sq., Tahrir Sq., Northern Cemetery, Zamalek, Islamic Cairo, and Heliopolis. From **Tahrir Square,** microbuses leave for Heliopolis, Giza Sq., Dokki, Mohandiseen, the Pyramids, and the airport terminals. Fares are 50pt, E£1 for the luxury of not having to stand.

MINIBUSES. Red-and-white or orange-and-white Mercedes operate along many of the same routes as city buses. Although more expensive (50pt-E£1), the minibuses are also far more comfortable. Minibus numbers appear in Arabic only.

From the Nile Hilton:

#16 (١٦): Gala'a Bridge—Agouza

#27 (٢٧): Masr el-Gadida—Airport

#30 (٣٠): Nasser City—'Abbasiyya Sq.—Ramses Sq.—'Abd el-Munem Riad 2

#32 (٣٢): Hai et-Tamin—Mugamma'—Ramses Sq.—'Abbasiyya

#35 (٣٥): 'Abbasiyya—'Abd el-Munem Riad 2—Roxy—El-Hijaz Sq.

#49 (٤٩): Falaki Sq.—Tahrir Sq.—Zamalek

#50 (٥٠): Ramses Sq.—'Ataba Sq.—Citadel

#52 (٥٢), **56** (٥٦): Bab el-Luq—Tahrir Sq.—Ma'adi—Old Cairo

#54 (٥٤): Bab el-Luq—Rifa'i Mosque—Ibn Tulun Mosque—Citadel—S. Cemetery

#55 (٥٥): Ma'adi—Bab el-Luq

#58 (٥٨): Ramses Sq.—Manial

#77 (٧٧): Bulaq ed-Dakrur—Khan el-Khalili—Ed-Darasa

#84 (٨٤): 'Ataba/Tahrir Sq.—Dokki—Giza

From Tahrir Square:

#77 (٧٧), **#102** (١٠٢), **#103** (١٠٣): Bulaq ed-Dakrur—Khan el-Khalili—Ed-Darasa

#183 (١٨٣): Giza

From 'Ataba Square:

#26 (٢٦): Roxy—Tahrir Sq.—Dokki—Giza

#48 (٤٨): Zamalek

#93 (٩٣): Mazalat—'Ataba Sq.—Basatin

BUSES. Few foreigners use the bus system, and with good reason: although very cheap (10-50pt), the buses are hot, cramped, and full of pickpockets. Buses never come to a full stop, so passengers must jump out the back to exit. Numbers and destinations are always in Arabic. Buses run 5:30am to 12:30am (during Ramadan 6:30am-6:30pm and 7:30pm-2am), except for bus **#400 (٤٠٠)**, has 24-hour service to both **airports** from Tahrir Sq. Cairo's local bus depot is **'Abd el-Munem Riad Station,** which is north of the Egyptian Museum just below the towering, triangular Ramses Hilton. Several buses depart from the front of the old **Arab League Building,** to the west of the Mugamma' along Tahrir St., adjacent to the bridge. Other bus stations are at **'Ataba Square** (to the Citadel, the Manial Palace, Giza, and Tahrir Sq.), and at **Giza Square** (to the Pyramids, airport, and Citadel).

From 'Abd el-Munem Riad Station:

#8 (٨): Tahrir Sq.–Qasr el-'Aini–Manial–Giza–Mena House Hotel (Pyramids)

#63 (٦٣), 66 (٦٦): Al-Azhar–Khan el-Khalili

#72 (٧٢): Sayyida Zeinab–Citadel–Imam esh-Shafi'i Mausoleum

#82 (٨٢), 182 (١٨٢): Imam esh-Shafi'i Mausoleum–S. Cemetery–Citadel

#99 (٩٩): Agouza–Sudan St.–Lebanon Sq. (Maidan Lubnan)

#128 (١٢٨): 'Abbasiyya Sq.–'Ain Shams

#173 (١٧٣), 194 (١٩٤), 609 (٦٠٩): Tahrir Sq.–Citadel

#174 (١٧٤): Ramses–Sayyida Zeinab–Ibn Tulun–Sultan Hassan–Citadel

#400 (٤٠٠): Old Cairo Airport via Heliopolis (Roxy Sq.)

#403 (٤٠٣): Citadel–Sultan Hassan

#666 (٦٦٦): El-Gaili Museum

#900 (٩٠٠): Tahrir Sq.–Qasr el-'Aini–Manial (Youth Hostel)–Cairo University–Giza–Pyramids–Holiday Inn Hotel

#923 (٩٢٣): Basatin–Giza Sq.

#949 (٩٤٩): New Cairo Airport

From the Arab League Building:

#13 (١٣): Zamalek–Bab el-Luq

#19 (١٩), 203 (٢٠٣): Dokki

#102 (١٠٢): Mazalat–Dokki

#166 (١٦٦): 'Ataba Sq.–Dokki

#815-173 (٨١٥-١٧٣): Madinat et-Talaba

From 'Ataba Square:

#214 (٢١٤): Qanatir

#404 (٤٠٤): Citadel–Tahrir Sq.–Madinat et-Talaba

#801 (٨٠١), 951 (٩٥١): Citadel–'Abd el-Munem Riad

#904 (٩٠٤): Mugamma' Station–Pyramids

From Giza Square:

#3 (٣): Pyramids

#30 (٣٠): Ramses Station

#949 (٩٤٩): Airport (both terminals)

From Ramses Station:

#30 (٣٠): Pyramids

#160 (١٦٠): Citadel–Tahrir Sq.

TAXIS. Never take the large, colorful Peugeot taxis within the city (they are unmetered and usually overpriced), and avoid the expensive taxis in front of major hotels. Stick to the metered **black-and-white taxis** that collect passengers along the way. To hail a taxi, pick a thoroughfare headed in the general direction you wish to travel, stand on the side of the street, stretch out your arm, and scream out your destination as it goes by. If the driver is interested, he'll stop. Meters have been installed in all taxis, but drivers rarely use them. Feel free to haggle about the price; in busier areas, you can even walk away from a taxi. Do not expect drivers to speak English; use landmarks and either say or show a written copy of your destination in Arabic. For more information, see **Taxis,** p. 44. Rides in the downtown area (Ramses Sq., Tahrir Sq., Zamalek, and Islamic Cairo) should cost about E£3-5. Trips to the pyramids are about E£15; those to Ma'adi and Heliopolis run around E£8-10. A taxi to or from the airport should cost no more than E£20. Wanna be a **playah?** Hire a Mercedes for E£55 per half-day from Limousine Misr (tel. 285 06 25).

▣ PRACTICAL INFORMATION

A reliable directory for goods and services is the *Cairo Telephone List*, published by the Ma'adi Women's Guild and available for E£20 at the American Chamber of Commerce, Marriott Hotel #1541, Zamalek (tel. 340 88 88).

TOURIST AND FINANCIAL SERVICES

Tourist Office: The **Egyptian Tourist Authority (ETA)** has offices scattered throughout the city. All are very helpful, provide free maps and info, and can make reservations or write out destinations in Arabic. Following is a list of locations. **Cairo International Airport** (tel. 66 74 75), at the entrance and next to the duty-free shops. Open 24hr. (in theory). **Giza** (tel. 385 02 59), in front of Mena House Hotel. Open Sa-Th 8am-5pm. **Railway Station** (tel. 76 42 14), on the left as you enter the station's main entrance. Open daily 8am-9pm. **5 'Adly St.** (tel. 391 34 54), a 20min. walk from Tahrir Sq. Follow Tala'at Harb St. and turn right on 'Adly St. The office is 3 blocks down on your left, marked "Tourist Police." Open daily 8:30am-8pm.

Student Cards: Medical Scientific Center, 103 Mathaf el-Manial St., El-Manial (tel. 363 88 15). South of the Manial Palace across the street from Kentucky Fried Chicken (look for the ISIC sign). Great source of information for travelers. Provides ISIC and Go25 cards (E£25; bring a photo). Student volunteer staff speaks excellent English and will quote prices for sights and entertainment. The center gives out free maps and pamphlets, and organizes excursions to see the Pyramids and Sufi dancing.

Embassies:

Australia, 1191 Corniche en-Nil, Bulaq (tel. 575 04 44), World Trade Center 11-12th floors. Past the 26 July Bridge. Passports generally replaced in 5 working days (32-page passports AUS$126, 64-page AUS$188, payable in E£ only). Immediate replacement in case of emergency. Open Su-W 8am-4pm, visas Su-Th 9:30am-noon.

Canada, 5 Maidan Es-Saraya el-Kobr, Garden City (tel. 354 31 10/19, emergencies 356 36 44), 3rd floor of Arab-African Bank Building. Passports replaced within 2 working days for E£145. Embassy open Su-Th 8:30am-4:30pm; visas Su-M and W-Th 9-11am.

Israel, 6 Ibn el-Malik St., Dokki (tel. 361 03 80 or 361 04 58). Cross over to Dokki from Roda Island on University Bridge (El-Gama'a). The street to the right of and parallel to the bridge is Ibn el-Malik. Look up at the top floors for the Israeli flag or for the security guards by the entrance who will ask to see your passport. Visas E£65. Open Su-Th 10am-12:30pm.

Jordan, 6 El-Goheina St., Dokki (tel. 348 55 66, 348 61 69, 348 75 43, or 349 99 12), 2 blocks west of the Cairo Sheraton. Visas (photograph required) free for Australians, E£42 for New Zealanders, E£86 for Brits, E£112 for Americans, E£224 for Canadians. Same-day service. Visas may be picked up noon-2pm. Open Sa-Th 9am-noon; arrive early to avoid the crowd. Some nationalities can obtain visas at the airport; check with the embassy for details.

Lebanon, 22 El-Mansur Muhammad St., Zamalek (tel. 332 28 23/24/25). Photograph required for passports. Consular services open M-Th and Sa 9am-2:30pm. Any evidence of having been to Israel prohibits obtaining a Lebanese visa.

South Africa, 21/23 Giza St., Giza (tel. 571 72 38/39), 18th floor of the Nile Tower. File applications for new passports here; they're then sent to South Africa for processing. Entire process takes 8 weeks. In the meantime, you are issued a 1-page Emergency Passport good for 3 months (E£50). Open Su-Th 8am-5pm, consular services Su-Th 9am-noon.

Syria, 18 'Abd er-Rahim Sabri St., Dokki (tel. 337 70 20). Bring 2 photos for a visa (free for Canadians and Australians, E£116 for Americans). You are advised to apply for visas in your home country. Americans are sometimes denied visas at Syrian embassies in other Arab countries. Open Sa-Th 9am-2:30pm; visas 9am-1pm. Evidence of travel to Israel prohibits obtaining a Syrian visa, but you can get a new passport at your country's embassy.

U.K., 7 Ahmed Ragheb St., Garden City (tel. 354 08 50). Also handles **New Zealand** affairs. Will replace both types of passport within 5 days (32-page passports E£238, 48-page E£300, payable only in E£). Open Su-Th 7:30am-2:30pm; visas 7:30-9am.

U.S., 5 Latin America St., Garden City (tel. 354 82 11, emergencies 355 73 71), 2 blocks south of Tahrir Sq. For the consulate, enter on Lazoughli St. around the block. Lost or stolen passports replaced overnight for US$65 or E£ equivalent (US$65 for a renewal). Open Su-Th 8am-4:30pm; consulate 8am-noon.

THE PROS OF CONS IN CAIRO

It's safest to assume that anyone approaching you in Cairo wants something. Scams begin the moment you step off the plane. The guy with the photo-ID card on his lapel asking if you have anything to declare probably isn't a customs official; he just wants to get you in his buddy's cab to Cairo for E£25, have you check in at his uncle's E£100-a-night hotel, and show you the Pyramids at his uncle's buddy's inflated prices. These scams are just the start. Imaginative scammers think up new ones daily.

Travel Agents: Travel agents in the downtown area have been known to add airport taxes (there is no departure tax from Cairo) and other fees to tickets. You should demand receipts for every pound you hand over and have them give you written estimates, including all taxes, for every flight you purchase.

Hotels: Some of the seedier hotels occasionally offer commissions to street hustlers or taxi drivers to round up tourists. To avoid this, take the shuttle or a bus to town and stick to the hotel you have selected. If you encounter a "hotel manager" on the street, the airport, the train station, or anywhere in public, he's not one. Trust no one at the airport except the tourist office. Some of the seedier hotels make money by selling horrendously overpriced tours. Ask around to avoid being ripped off.

Shopping: The touts in the street or Khan el-Khalili who try to get you into stores also get commissions. To make up for the commission, the store owner raises the price. You'll never get a good price at a store a hustler has brought you to.

Passport Office: Mugamma' Building, 2nd floor, the massive concave gray edifice at the southern side of Tahrir Sq. Registration open Sa-Th 8am-8pm, visa extensions 8am-1pm. The Mugamma' was constructed during Nasser's flirtation with the Soviets, and the spirit of the Cold War lives on in its bureaucratic inefficiency. First, buy forms at window 42, then get stamps at 41, then go to windows 23-29 to have your visa extended. Having what you want written down in Arabic beforehand helps. For fewer crowds, check the 2nd floor of the **Ministry of Economy and Foreign Trade Building,** 8 'Adly St. (tel. 390 43 63), next to the EgyptAir office. Bring a passport photo for visa extensions (2-6 months E£14, 1 year E£50). Open Sa-Th 8am-1:30pm.

Currency Exchange: Banks and exchange services litter the downtown area. **Bank Misr** (tel. 391 75 71), has branches at major hotels, with a main office downtown at 151 Muhammad Farid St. All open Sa-Th 8:30am-2pm and 6-9pm. **Cairo Barclay's International Bank,** 12 Sheikh Yusef Sq., Garden City (tel. 354 94 15/22), 3 blocks south of Tahrir Sq. along Qasr El-'Aini St., accepts traveler's checks and has worldwide money transfer services. Open Su-Th 8:30am-2pm; Ramadan 10am-1pm. Foreign banks are closed F-Sa, but most Egyptian banks are open Sa. Money can be wired to Egypt through **Citibank,** 4 Ahmed Basha St., Garden City (tel. 355 18 73/74; open Su-Th 8:30am-2pm) or **Western Union,** 1079 Corniche en-Nil, Garden City (tel. 357 13 00/74/75/84/85/86; open Su-Th 9am-8:30pm), located in the FedEx office.

ATM: Egyptian British Banks have machines that accept Visa, PLUS, Global Access, and Express Net cards. Locations in Semiramis Intercontinental, Zamalek Marriott, Cairo Sheraton, and Ramses and Nile Hiltons.

Thomas Cook: 17 Mahmoud Bassouni St. (tel. 574 37 76 or 574 39 55/67; fax 76 27 50), a half block west of Tala'at Harb Sq. Other offices throughout the city. Travel agency, money transfers, currency exchange, and cash advances on Visa and MC. Cashes traveler's checks. Replaces lost Visa or MC. Open daily 8am-5pm.

American Express: 15 Qasr en-Nil (tel. 574 79 91/92/96), off Tala'at Harb Sq., opposite EgyptAir toward Ramses St. Cashes traveler's checks. Members can have money sent to the office and have mail held there as well. Open daily 8:30am-5pm. Letter service open Su-Th 8:30am-4pm; Ramadan 8:30am-3:30pm. Other locations at the Nile Hilton (tel. 578 50 01/02/03), Marriott Hotel (tel. 341 01 36), Pullman Ma'adi (tel. 350 78 51), and in the Mohandiseen, 4 Syria St. (tel. 70 79 08/14).

LOCAL SERVICES

Luggage Storage: Avoid the unsecure Ramses Station lockers. Get bilingual **written proof** of having stored anything at a hotel. "Storage" in many budget hotels may mean just a hallway—leave valuables in a container at the desk.

English Bookstores: Used Books, left of the statue by the Cairo Puppet Theater near 'Ataba Sq. Take Metro to 'Ataba. Among books on dialectical materialism and U.S. Boy Scout manuals are titles for as low as E£4. **AUC Bookstore,** 113 Qasr El-'Aini St. (tel. 357 53 77), in the Hill House at the American University in Cairo. University texts, classic novels, Arab literature in translation, maps, and guide books. U.S. passport needed to enter the campus. Open Su-Th 8:30am-4pm, Sa 10:30am-4:30pm. Visa and MC accepted. **Lehnert and Landrock,** 44 Sherif St. (tel. 393 53 24), between 'Adly St. and 26 July St. "L&L" offers a superb, wide-ranging selection of guidebooks, maps, histories, and postcards. Open M-F 10am-2pm and 4-7pm, Sa 9am-11pm. Visa and MC accepted.

Newspapers and Magazines: The *Egyptian Gazette, Al-Ahram Weekly,* and *Middle East Times* are Egypt's English newspapers. *Egypt Today,* a monthly magazine (E£7), is handy for current restaurant and entertainment listings. All are sold at **The Reader's Corner,** 33 'Abd el-Khaleq Sarwat St., downtown. Open M-Sa 9:30am-7pm. Many hotels and street stands from Tahrir Sq. to Tala'at Harb Sq. sell foreign language publications.

American Cultural Center: 5 Latin America St., Garden City (tel. 354 96 01 or 76 27 04; library 355 05 32 or 357 34 12). Inside the U.S. Embassy, across from the British Embassy. If you'll be in Egypt for at least 12 months, you are eligible to join no matter what your nationality (bring 2 photos and a passport). Members can borrow books and watch videos. All American citizens have access to the A/C library's collection of popular magazines and books on America. Occasional free films and lectures; call 357 33 66 for a schedule. Open in summer Su-F 10am-4pm; in winter M-F 10am-4pm.

Markets: Seoudi Market, 25 Maidan El-Missaha St., Dokki (tel. 348 84 40/1). Also at: 20 Hijaz St., Mohandiseen (tel. 346 03 91); and 15 Ahmad Hishmat St., Zamalek (tel. 341 35 86 or 340 03 70). A fully stocked supermarket with fair prices. All open daily 9am-12:30am. **Sunny Supermarket,** 11 El-'Aziz 'Osman St., Zamalek (tel. 342 11 21 or 341 20 32), next door to the Mayfair Hotel south of 26 July St. Impressive array of Egyptian and Western products for not-quite-budget prices. Open daily 8am-10pm.

Laundromat: Circle Cleaning, 24 26 July St. (tel. 76 08 55), near the Supreme Court and the intersection with Tala'at Harb St. You're better off doing it yourself or paying a maid in your hotel to do your load (the laundromat can be a madhouse). 50pt per piece is reasonable. Open daily 9am-9pm.

Swimming Pools: Fontana Hotel (tel. 92 21 45 or 92 23 21), Ramses Sq., has a teal-tiled pool on its 7th-floor patio (E£15 per day). Cairo's many sporting clubs also sell day passes for E£20. The best are: the **Gezira Sporting Club** (tel. 340 60 00), in front of the Marriott Hotel in Zamalek; the **Ma'adi Sporting Club,** 8 En-Nadi Sq. (tel. 350 54 55); and the **Heliopolis Sporting Club,** 17 El-Merghany St. (tel. 291 00 65). Sometimes the guards insist that you enter with a club member. You may also get day passes at 5-star hotels, which may charge up to E£30.

EMERGENCY AND COMMUNICATIONS

Emergency: Police: Tel. 122, 126, 303 41 22, 303 51 22. **Fire:** Tel. 125 or 391 01 15.

Tourist Police: 5 'Adly St. (tel. 390 19 44 or 390 60 28, emergencies 126), in the same building as the Tourist Office. Also at the Cairo International Airport (tel. 247 25 84), and in Giza (tel. 385 02 59), the Manial Palace Hotel, and Ramses Station.

24-Hour Pharmacies: Victoria Pharmacy, 90 Qasr el-'Aini St. (tel. 354 86 04). **Isaaf Pharmacy** (tel. 74 33 69), on Ramses St. and 26 July St. **Seif Pharmacy,** 76 Qasr El-'Aini (tel. 354 26 78). **Zamalek Pharmacy,** 3 Shagarat ed-Durr (tel. 340 24 06).

Hospital: The best-equipped is **Es-Salaam International Hospital** (tel. 363 80 50, emergencies 362 33 00), Ma'adi, Corniche en-Nil. **Anglo-American Hospital** (tel. 340 61 62/5), Zamalek, on Botanical Garden St., below the Cairo Tower. **Cairo Medical Center** (tel. 258 05 66, 258 02 17, or 258 10 03), is in Heliopolis at Roxy Sq.

Post Office: 55 Sarwat St. (tel. 391 26 14), in 'Ataba Sq., under the dome. Often crowded, but blissfully empty just before closing. Packages require export license, available from airport, hotels, and tourist shops. Open Sa-Th 8:30am-7pm; Ramadan 9am-3pm. Most branches in Cairo sell stamps and have EMS. One convenient branch is at 13 Metitte Bash St. in Tahrir Sq. (tel. 575 43 13), opposite the Egyptian Museum. Open Sa-Th 9am-5pm. 24hr. **Express Mail (EMS)** is on Bidek St.

Federal Express: 1079 Corniche en-Nil, Garden City (tel. 357 13 04). Opposite the Meridien Hotel on the east bank of the Nile. Open 24hr.

Fax Office: You may send and receive faxes at the business office of the **Ramses Hilton** (fax 575 71 52 or 578 22 21). They charge according to destination for sending and E£4 per page to receive. Most of the telephone offices can send faxes.

Internet Access: The **Marriott Business Office** (tel. 340 66 67) sells time on computers with access to the Internet (30min. minimum). Most telephone offices also have Internet services for roughly E£5-7 per hr.

Telephones: Main Telephone Office is on Ramses St., 1 block north of 26 July St. Other offices in Zamalek, Airport, Ma'adi, Tahrir Sq., 'Adly St., and Alfy St. (under the Windsor Hotel). All open 24hr. **Collect calls** and **credit card calls** are available at the USADirect, U.K.Direct, CanadaDirect, and JapanDirect phones in the lobbies of the Ramses Hilton, and the Marriott and Semiramis Hotels. For a 25% surcharge, you can easily make international calls at the business service offices in the Meridien, Sheraton, and Nile Hilton hotels. Open 24hr. **Directory Assistance:** Tel. 140.

Telephone Code: 02.

■ ACCOMMODATIONS

Downtown Cairo, on and around **Tala'at Harb Street,** is littered with dozens of budget hotels and dorms occupying the upper floors of colonial buildings. All prices listed below include breakfast, and all rooms have fans and 24-hour hot water unless otherwise noted. "Hotels" and "hostels" are close cousins in Egypt. Many hotels have dorm beds available and many hostels have single or double rooms. Most maids will do your laundry (usually about 50pt per article). If you're in Cairo for a while or during low season, bargain for a reduced rate. Single-sex groups should have no problem renting a **flat** (E£200-1000 per month), but building owners often frown upon renting to co-ed groups. The billboards at the American University of Cairo entrance and the Sunny Market in Zamalek list available apartments.

BUDGET

■ **Sultan Hotel,** 4 Souq et-Tewfiqia St., 1st and 5th fl. (tel. 77 22 58), off Tala'at Harb St., on the market street running parallel to 26 July St. Bedrooms could use a makeover, but the helpful staff and unbeatable price compensate. The 5th floor rooms are less crowded, cheaper, and breezier. Couples sharing a room must be married or brother and sister, and have the same name on their passport to prove it. Dorms E£8; 1st-floor dorm beds E£9; doubles E£20. Breakfast not included, but guests may use the kitchen, and the nearby fruit market is cheap and good. Free 6-day luggage storage.

■ **Pensione Roma,** 169 Muhammad Farid St. (tel. 391 10 88 or 391 13 40), 1 block south of 26 July St. and 2 blocks east of Tala'at Harb St. Turn right on 'Adly St. and left after the synagogue; look for the hotel's green sign above the Gattegno department store, between 'Ataba and Nasser Metro stations. Beautiful, clean, and well kept. Run by a kindly Italian matriarch who speaks French and Italian as well as English. Towels, toilet paper, and soap all provided. Singles E£24; doubles E£44, with shower E£49; triples E£61, with shower E£71. Fan rental E£2.50. Free storage.

Venice Hotel, 4 Souq et-Tewfiqia, 4th fl. (tel. 574 32 69), in the same building as the Sultan Hotel. Cool breezes waft into the spacious, high-ceilinged rooms of this hotel. All rooms have either balconies or windows, making up for a lack of fans. Hardwood floors and spotless bathrooms. Only E£7 for a dorm bed. Singles E£17; doubles E£25. Less English is spoken here than at the Sultan.

Anglo-Swiss Hotel, 14 Champollion St., 6th fl. (tel. 575 14 97), 2 blocks west of Tala'at Harb Sq. From Tahrir Sq., turn right on Champollion in the northeastern end of the square next to the museum. The hotel will be to your left at the intersection with Mahmoud Bassinni St. Play the piano in the sunny dining hall or watch some TV in a pleasant living room before retiring to quiet, large, clean rooms, most with balconies. Singles E£20; doubles E£30 (some with shower for same price); triples E£49. French also spoken.

Hotel Minerva, 39 Tala'at Harb St. (tel. 392 06 00/1/2), 1 block toward Tala'at Harb Sq. from 26 July St. Reception is 4 doors past the Bamboo Clothing Store on your right. Beautifully renovated bathrooms, vast balconies, and all new light fixtures add a touch of elegance. Often full. Singles E£19; doubles E£28; triples E£45.

Youth Hostel (HI), 135 Malek 'Abd el-'Aziz es-Sa'ud St., Manial Roda Island (tel. 364 07 29; fax 98 41 07). Take Metro to Sayyida Zeinab. Exit to the right and walk straight to the Nile. Cross the Sayala Bridge and continue straight across Roda Island to the Nile's main channel. Turn left just before the University (El-Gama'a) bridge (with Salah ad-Din mosque to your right); the hostel is 10m away on the left. This 1970s building is clean and quiet, but a little isolated from tourist sites. Single-sex triples and quads E£22.60. Nonmembers E£4 extra. No lockout. Curfew 11pm. Call ahead for reservations.

Pension Select Hotel, 19 'Adly St., 8th fl. (tel. 393 37 07), next to the synagogue. High above the street noise, the Select offers spacious 3-bed dorms that are quiet and off the beaten path. Dorm beds E£15-20; singles E£25; doubles E£30; triples E£45.

Gresham Hotel, 20 Tala'at Harb St. (tel. 575 90 43; e-mail starco@dick.com.eg), just off Tala'at Harb Sq. Rooms are fair, although some are fanless and unbearable on summer nights. Singles E£25, with bath and A/C E£35; doubles E£40/45; triples E£55/65; quads E£70/80.

Sun Hotel, 2 Tala'at Harb St., 9th fl. (tel. 578 17 86). Look for the sign on the right as you leave Tahrir Sq. This new hotel near the subway has carpet, cable TV in the lobby, a kitchen, and a diverse clientele. Large, comfortable beds. Bargain if you are staying more than a few days. Dorm beds E£15; singles E£25; doubles E£40; triples E£51.

Bluebird Hotel, 42 Tala'at Harb St., 6th fl. (tel. 575 63 77), opposite 'Adly St. heading towards Ramses St. A fairly clean and well-maintained option. Separate-sex baths, satellite TV, and common kitchen. Rooms are interestingly decorated, particularly the one with a tapestry of several cats. Singles E£17; doubles E£34; triples E£51.

Isma'ilia House Hotel, 1 Tahrir Sq., 8th fl. (tel. 356 31 22), by an exit of the Sadat Metro station. A standard, convenient hotel that is safe but unremarkable. Dorm beds E£15; singles E£20; doubles E£40, with shower E£48, with full bath E£52.

Horris Hotel, 5 26 July St. (tel. 591 04 78, 591 05 47, or 591 08 55). Enter from Alfy St. behind Cinema Diana. Modern building with a barren bar and rooms with bath, A/C, and TV. Upper floors have flowery balconies with views blossoming out over Cairo. Singles E£47; doubles E£81; triples E£99; add tax and service charge.

A BIT SWANKIER

🏨 **Windsor Hotel,** 19 Alfy St. (tel. 591 58 10 or 591 52 77; fax 592 16 21; email wdoss@link.com.eg; www.windsorcairo.com). Clean facilities with excellent service in an atmosphere of old-time colonial grandeur. The swank lives on with free access to facilities at the *chi-chi* Gezira Club on glitzy Zamalek, included in the price of a room. The Barrel Bar (named for the furniture, which is made of barrels) was once the British Officers' Club. Monty Python's Michael Palin hung out at the Windsor while filming *Around the World in Eighty Days*. Rooms have A/C, towels, crisp sheets, and comfy beds. Singles with shower E£70, with shower and toilet E£100; doubles E£106/134. Prices include breakfast, tax, and 25% *Let's Go* discount. 5% credit card service charge.

🏨 **Berlin Hotel,** 2 Esh-Shawarby St. (tel./fax 395 75 02). From Tala'at Harb Sq., walk up Qasr En-Nil towards Mustafa Kamal Sq.; the entrance to this new hotel is on a pedestrian-only street. Friendly proprietor Hisham is generous with his wealth of information and advice. Elegant rooms boast private showers, full-length velvet curtains, and freshly painted walls. A neighboring fitness club offers weights, sauna, and massage at a discounted rate for hotel guests. Internet access and Net-2-Phone available starting at E£2 per minute. Dorms with fan E£15. Singles E£45 with fan, E£60 with A/C; doubles E£60/E£80; triples E£90. Breakfast included. Rates 15% lower in winter.

Carlton Hotel, 21 26 July St. (tel. 575 50 22; fax 575 53 23), beside Cinema Rivoli, near the Tala'at Harb St. and 26 July St. intersection. Metro: Nasser. The colonial lobby and hardwood floors are just the beginning: each room has satellite TV, A/C, and a balcony with patio furniture. Dinner is served nightly on the rooftop garden, which has a gorgeous view of downtown Cairo. Helpful manager. Singles E£85; doubles E£95.

Richmond Hotel, 41 Sherif St. (tel. 393 93 58), just south of 26 July St. A newly restored hotel with beautiful art deco furniture. Clean rooms (some with balconies) come with fan and breakfast. Singles E£30; doubles E£40; triples E£50.

El-Malky Hotel, 4 El-Mashad el-Hussein St. (tel. 592 88 04; fax 589 67 00), next to El-Hussein Mosque and Khan el-Khalili market. Situated in the heart of Islamic Cairo, away from the downtown bustle. You'll get used to the *muezzin* call to prayer 5 times a day, as Cairo's most famous mosque is next door. Singles with TV, fridge, and balcony E£40, with A/C E£50; doubles E£55, with A/C E£65.

Mayfair Hotel, 9 'Aziz 'Osman St., Zamalek (tel. 340 73 15), parallel to Hassan Sabri St., on corner of Ibn Zinki St. 2 blocks south of 26 July St. Tidy rooms with balconies amid the leafy calm of Zamalek. Some rooms have A/C, all have fans. Singles E£30, with shower E£45; doubles E£40/60. Prices include breakfast and 10% *Let's Go* discount.

⍟ FOOD

If you stick with the same old *fuul* and *ta'amiyya*, you'll only need 40pt to fill your stomach. A good place for *kushari* (servings cost E£1.5-3, depending on size) is **Et-Tahrir**, on Tahrir St. near Bab el-Luq, or on 'Abd el-Haliq Sarwat St. near Tala'at Harb St. **Lux**, on 26 July St., is another tasty choice. Wash it all down with exhilarating **fruit juices**, on sale anywhere you see bags of fruit hanging around a storefront. At places without waiters, pay first and then exchange your receipt for food.

A sit-down meal is often relatively cheap by Western standards and is usually worth the small investment. Even at more expensive restaurants, you can create a handsome meal out of hummus, *baba ghanoush* (grilled eggplant dip), and salad for under E£5. *Fatir*, a *filo* dough-like bread stuffed and topped with vegetables, meats, or sweets is far tastier than the imitations of Italian pizza in town and usually cheaper at E£5-10. A 5% **sales tax** on food and a 10-12% **service charge** at sit-down restaurants are both added to the bill; a small **tip** (E£1) is still in order.

While eating local food is an essential component of the Egyptian experience, the cleaner, faster, air-conditioned Western fast-food chains are lined up in a row across from the AUC on Mahmoud St. **Pizza Hut** offers slices for E£1.90 each (tel. 356 26 28 or 356 27 55 for free home delivery). Next door, **Kentucky Fried Chicken** is a bit cheaper but serves buns instead of the flaky biscuits so treasured by the Colonel and his cohorts. The **McDonald's** by AUC (tel. 355 81 31) offers combos for E£8.50 (all open daily 10:30am-1am; free delivery up to 2km away).

DOWNTOWN

RESTAURANTS

◤ **Felfela,** 15 Hoda Sha'rawi St. (tel. 392 27 51 or 392 28 33), off Tala'at Harb St., 1 block south of Tala'at Harb Sq. A favorite among Egyptians and tourists alike, this award-winning restaurant was opened by the Egyptian model Amina Zaghloul in 1958. The interior bursts with bamboo, aquariums, mosaics, and live birds. Full meal of *wara 'einab* (stuffed grape leaves) E£12, stuffed pigeon E£17. Also delicious is *om 'ali*, a pastry baked with milk, honey, and raisins (E£5.75). Open daily 7:30am-midnight.

◤ **'Ali Hassan el-Hati,** 3 Maidan Halim Basha (tel. 591 60 55), between Alfy St. and 26 July St., 1 block south of the Windsor Hotel. High ceilings, crystal chandeliers, and many mirrors. Try the generous *fatteh*—garlic, meat, or vegetables poured over crunchy baked bread and covered with a yogurt sauce (E£5). Open daily noon-midnight.

El-Hati Cafeteria, 8A 26 July St. (tel. 391 88 29). The glitzier younger sibling of 'Ali Hassan, complete with marble tiles and mirrors. The lunch special (*kofta,* kebab, oriental rice or macaroni, salad, bread, and dessert) will fill you up, buttercup, but won't let you down (E£16.5). Take-out available. Open daily noon-midnight. Visa, MC, AmEx.

Le Bistro, 8 Hoda Sha'rawi St. (tel. 392 76 94). Following in the tradition of restaurants with inventive names, this place serves well prepared bistro food in a clean and airy bistro setting. Entrees are a *bon marche* at E£15-20. Open 11am-1am.

Restaurant Cairo, the 2nd restaurant on the left side of the street that forks to the right from Orabi Sq. The staff may forget about you, but you won't soon forget about the food: the half chicken (E£5.5), soup (E£1.5), and stuffed pigeon with salad and bread (E£10) are all delicious. Open 24hr.

Peking, 14 Saraya el-Azbakia St. (tel. 591 23 81), behind Cinema Diana, between Alfy St. and 26 July St. One of Cairo's most popular Chinese restaurants. Pamper yourself with the complimentary steaming hand towels before a full meal with appetizer, 3 dishes, and dessert (don't miss the honey-walnut Tarte Lee) for E£40-45. Alcohol served. Open noon-midnight. Visa, MC, AmEx. Free delivery. Other branches: Mohandiseen (tel. 349 98 60), New Ma'adi (tel. 516 42 18), and Heliopolis (tel. 418 56 12).

Fu Ching, 28 Tala'at Harb St. (tel. 576 61 84), in an alleyway running west from the street. Exotic items (like purple seaweed soup, E£4) and a diverse array of vegetarian options make this Chinese restaurant a delicious escape from the ho-hum(mus) street vendor fare. Entrees E£10-20, with your bill calculated on an abacus!

Estoril Restaurant, 12 Tala'at Harb St. (tel. 574 31 02), across the street from Felfela's take-out counter. This Egyptian-French restaurant is popular with locals. Dishes like *coq au vin* (E£24) and chocolate mousse (E£6) seem incongruous amid the decor, but are tasty nonetheless. Open daily noon-4pm and 7:30pm-midnight.

CAFES

El-'Abd, 25 Tala'at Harb St. (tel. 392 44 07), opposite the Arab Bank building. This upscale bakery provides the perfect antidote for Cairo's heat—a whopping 3-scoop ice-cream cone for E£1.50. Ask to sample any of the pastries. Open daily 9am-11pm. Another branch on 26 July St., 1 block east of Tala'at Harb St.

J. Groppi, Tala'at Harb Sq. This confectionery opened its doors to Europeans and Europeanized Egyptians in 1891, and hasn't changed its decor since. A great place for a date (chocolate-covered or not). The mango and apricot jams are a tart retort to the excellent Turkish coffee. Min. charge E£5. Open daily 9am-11pm.

La Poire, 18 Latin America St. (tel. 355 15 09), across the street from the British Embassy in Garden City. Come for the extensive selection of ice cream flavors (E£1.75 per scoop) but stay for the croissants, eclairs, and sticky-sweet *ba'laweh* (about E£1.50 per serving)—and don't leave until you're *poire*-shaped. Open daily 7am-midnight.

Brazilian Coffee Shop, 38 Tala'at Harb St., at the intersection with 'Adly St. A/C restaurant upstairs from the Miami Cinema serves cappuccino and espresso (E£2 each). A great place to read the morning paper with your favorite middle management chums. Chicken sandwich E£5. Open daily 6am-midnight.

ZAMALEK

If you want a break from downtown Cairo, search out the tree-lined boulevards of Zamalek. All restaurants listed here are on or north of 26 July St. Zamalek is also home to numerous pastry shops and bars for post-prandial dessert and drinks.

RESTAURANTS

Didos Al Dente, 26 Bahgat Basha 'Ali St. (tel. 340 91 17). From the Western Corniche, take a right onto Anis Basha St.; Didos Al Dente is 2 blocks ahead on your left. Located in a beautifully shaded area of Zamalek, this reasonably priced restaurant has gained a great (and well-deserved) reputation in a remarkably short time. A wide selection of pastas with 18 different sauces (spaghetti starts at E£5), plus tempting Arab-Italian side dishes such as *insalata al-funghi*. Open daily noon-1:30am.

Maison Thomas, 157 26 July St. (tel. 340 70 57), on your right near the base of the bridge as you come into Zamalek from Cairo. Hip French/Italian bistro filled with hanging salami and wheels of cheese to evoke the Mediterranean's other coast. Salad niçoise is refreshing at E£11; other salads (E£10-13), baguette sandwiches, and pizzas (E£13-25) are delicious and generously proportioned. Regular calzone (E£17.55) easily feeds two; the large (E£24.7) is just absurd. Free delivery. Open 24hr.

Hana Korean Restaurant, 21 Ma'had as-Swissry St. (tel. 340 18 46), in En-Nil Zamalek Hotel. Take a right off 26 July St. onto Hassan Sabri St. (also called Brazil St.). This A/C haven, popular among tourists and expats, serves shark-fin soup (E£9) and *bulgogi* (Korean BBQ), tender slices of beef you barbecue right at the table (E£21). Stella (E£6) is everyone's favorite lady. Open daily noon-midnight.

Bon Appetit, 2 Isma'il Muhammad St. (tel. 340 43 82 or 91 08), 1 block from the Flamenco Hotel on the west side of Zamalek. Like big hairdos, big sandwiches are highly praised by nearby AUC students. The cleanest place in town to try a brain (E£8) or tongue (E£7.70) sandwich. Open daily 9am-2am. Visa, MC, AmEx.

CAFES

Simonds Coffee Shop, 26 July St. (tel. 340 94 36), just east of the intersection with Hassan Sabri St. The New York Chic feel lures an eclectic mix of locals and foreign emissaries who sip on *café au lait* (E£2.20) and freshly squeezed orange juice (E£2.25) while munching on pastries (under E£2).

Mandarin Koedar, 17 Shagarat ed-Durr St. (tel. 340 50 10). Take a right off 26 July St. at the Misr Gas Station onto Shagarat ed-Durr St., then follow the crooked lane for 200m. Cool to the core: a wide selection of ice cream (E£1.50 per scoop) served up in an arctic A/C setting. Open daily 9am-11pm.

MOHANDISEEN

RESTAURANTS

🖫 **Le Tabasco,** 8 'Ammen Sq. (tel. 336 55 83). Perhaps the best restaurant in Cairo. Dim candlelight and soft jazz *(ooh la la!)* accompany a weekly-changing pricey menu: appetizers E£10-24, pasta E£12-17, main dishes E£21-34. Recent menu selections include *cascadilla* (grilled tomato soup), frogs' legs Provençale, prawns in spicy garlic sauce, and fresh pear crêpes. Open daily 7pm-2am. Visa, MC, AmEx. Reservations required.

Al-Omda, 6 El-Gaza'ir St. (tel. 346 22 47), down an unmarked staircase a few doors from the Atlas Hotel on Gam'at ed-Duwal St. This popular, clean, A/C joint serves tasty pizza and stuffed grape leaves (E£8-15). Full meals E£10-15. Open 10am-3am.

Prestige Pizza, 43 Geziret al-'Arab (tel. 347 03 83), just east of Wadi en-Nil St. Coming from Gam'at ed-Duwal St., turn right before Al-Ahli Bank. Egypt's top actors and producers scarf down slices outdoors. Generous "normal" size pizzas E£12, "prestige" size E£17. Open daily noon-2am. E£7 cover charge. Visa, MC, AmEx.

CAFES

Coffee Roastery, 46 Nadi Es-Seed St. (tel. 349 88 82). An Egyptian expat living in San Francisco exported this outlet to Cairo. Library with the latest issues of *Time*, *Newsweek*, and Egyptian teenybopper mags. Cafe latte E£4. Open 8am-11:30pm. Visa, MC, AmEx.

ISLAMIC CAIRO (KHAN EL-KHALILI)

RESTAURANTS

Egyptian Pancakes, 7 Al-Azhar Sq. (tel. 590 86 23), half block from the intersection of Al-Azhar St. and Gohar el-Qa'it St. Small (E£10), medium (E£12), or large (E£15) pancakes topped with sweets (honey, coconut, or raisins) or meats (hot dog, tuna, or "turkey cock"). Open 24hr.

Coffee Shop Naguib Mahfouz, 5 El-Badistante Ln. (tel. 590 37 88 or 593 22 62), 2 blocks west of El-Hussein Mosque. Not on *Sugar St.* as you might think. This pricey restaurant is a calm oasis of delectable food in the maddening bustle of Khan El-Khalili. Engage in *Small Talk on the Nile* as you sip on fresh fruit juices (said to be the favorites of Nobel laureate Mahfouz, who was once a regular here). No doubt he also appreciated the clean restrooms and nightly live music. No *Autumn Quail,* but you can try a Lebanese kebab (E£39) or *tabbouleh* (E£6.50). Min. charge E£10 per person, E£2 music charge. Open daily 10am-2am. Visa, MC, AmEx.

CAFES

Al-Gamhorya, on Al-Azhar St., 1 block east of the green pedestrian overpass at the El-Ghouri Mosque and Mausoleum. A perfect *kushari* stop-off (E£1). Single women may feel uncomfortable among mostly male clientele. Open daily 9am-11pm.

♫ ENTERTAINMENT

As the sun sets on the Egyptian capital, *sheesha* smoke fills the air, strolling locals crowd the corniche, and decked-out scenesters dance 'til (almost) dawn at the discotheques dotting the Darbs and side-streets of the city. The free publication *Croc* is an up-to-date, hip-to-great guide to the Cairene scene that's available at most bars. During **Ramadan** (from roughly Nov. 30 to Dec. 31, 2000; for further information, see p. 52), Cairenes take to the streets around Al-Azhar and Hussein Sq., along the corniche, and all over the bridges spanning the Nile. Starting around 10pm, there are street performances, magic shows, and general shenanigans and tomfoolery. Most cinemas also have midnight screenings during this month. The following listings are as easy to navigate as A-B-C—**Ahwas, Bars, and Clubs.** Also listed are **Performing Arts** activities (dance and music) as well as **Other Diversions.**

AHWAS

Although you'd never guess it from observing Cairo's drivers, city folk love to relax, meet with friends, and contemplate the sweet mysteries of life. Much of this ruminating occurs in the *ahwas* (coffeehouses) that dot many street corners and alleys east of the Nile. A typical *ahwa* has gossipers in one corner, backgammon players in another, and *sheesha* smoke and Turkish coffee steam winding throughout. *Sheesha* tobacco is stronger and more delicious than cigarette shag and often comes in apple, honey, or apricot flavors. Foreign men and women are welcomed at all the *ahwas* listed below, though not at all *ahwas* in the city. For other options, try the **Cafes** listings under each region of the **Food** section (p. 71). For further info on *sheesha*-smoking, see **Puff the Magic Sheesha,** p. 54.

In the evenings, middle-class Egyptian couples swarm to the boat cafes (misleadingly called **casinos**) lining the Nile on Gezira Island. Some boats anchor permanently at the edge of the water. The **Casino en-Nil** and **Pasha 1901,** on the west side of Tahrir Bridge, are among the best (E£6 minimum). Ranging from simple to swank, these places get packed on Thursday nights. For real **gambling,** head to the Nile Hilton, Marriott, or Sheraton. Show your passport to enter; gamblers must be at least 21. You are not permitted to game with Egyptian currency, but don't worry—they can change Egyptian pounds to U.S. dollars faster than you can lose them (min. bet US$5). Drinks are free for all who gamble.

Fishawi's Khan el-Khalili (tel. 590 67 55), 4 doors down from El-Hussein Hotel, just off El-Hussein Sq. Since 1752, this traditional teahouse in the heart of the old bazaar has served the most famous *sheesha* in Egypt. Ask a waiter to show you where Nobel laureate Naguib Mahfouz spent many *Arabian Nights and Days.* Nicknamed "Cafe des Miroirs," Fishawi's is furnished in a 19th-century European style with brass tables that can barely hold two cups. Order as the locals do: a pot of mint tea, a cold *karkadeh* (rosehip drink), and an aromatic *sheesha* (each under E£3). Open daily 24hr.

Cafe New Sun, off Souq et-Tewfiya in the alley left of the Sultan Hotel. This stylish *ahwa*, peopled with as many pregnant cats as customers, has been serving *sheesha* (E£1) and strong Turkish coffee (E£1.50) since 1925. Open daily until 2am.

Maroush, 64 Lubnan St., Mohandiseen (tel. 346 68 91), a E£5 taxi ride from downtown. Skip the hoity-toity restaurant upstairs and head to the patio for a cool, laid-back *sheesha* (E£5). Open daily 8am-2am.

BARS

Cairenes aren't known for beer guzzling, but considering the strict Islamic prohibition against alcohol, they have a good number of bars; the liveliest are filled with non-Muslim expats. Most of the clientele is male.

Deals, 2 Es-Sa'id el-Bakery, Zamalek (tel. 341 05 02), a right turn off 26 July St. at the base of the bridge to downtown. Cairo's younger set mingles and tingles in this tiny joint, attracted by the low prices and eclectic decor. Drink prices (including French wine by the glass) are not really "deals," but the A/C and rock music pumped into the place ensure that this hangout fills up quickly. Open daily 4:30pm-2am.

El Gato Negro, 32 Jeddah St., Mohandiseen (tel. 361 68 88). One of the coolest (and cleanest) cats in Cairo. Scope the Mohandiscene while sipping on anything from water (E£3) to top-notch scotch and whiskey (E£15). The adjacent restaurant serves a variety of delicious foods (pizza, pasta, Levantine fare). Dance floor opens at 10pm. Open daily noon-2am. Visa, MC, AmEx.

Cairo Jazz Club, 197 26 July St. (tel. 345 99 39). Groove nightly with a crowd of international scat cats who come here to grab some Ella and a Stella (E£10) or to jump, jive, and cocktail around the clock (E£16). Restaurant serves decent entrees (E£10-20). Shows start at 10:30pm. Cover E£30 (Th and F only). Open daily 8pm-2am.

Pub 28, 28 Shagarat ed-Durr St., Zamalek (tel. 340 92 00), kitty-corner to the Mandarin Koedar ice cream store (p. 73). Take a right off 26 July St. at the Misr Gas Station; the pub's brick facade will be on your left. Faux oak interior gives it that rural Swiss Alps ambience. Stellas E£7, spirits E£9 and up. Open noon-2am. Visa, AmEx.

Odeon Palace, 6 Dr. 'Abd El-Hamid Sa'id St. (tel. 576 79 71), off Tala'at Harb St., just northwest of Tala'at Harb Sq. A relaxing rooftop spot for insomniacs in the mood for food or *sheesha*. Stellas E£8. Open 24hr.

CLUBS

The Cairene club scene is smaller, tamer, and less crowded than other Middle Eastern hotspots such as Beirut and Istanbul, but the clubs on **Pyramids Road** in Giza overflow with sweaty hipsters. Late evenings in Giza typically degenerate into pickup fests, but the disco balls in most major hotels spin watchfully over crowds of frisky youngsters (no geezers).

THAT WHICH WE CALL A ROSÉ... by any other name could be disgusting and potentially fatal. Although many tourists are familiar with Stella, Egypt's stab at beer-brewing greatness, few encounter the rest of Egypt's potent potables. Egypt produces wines such as *Reine Cleopatra* and *Cru des Ptolemées* in an attempt to evoke the wine expertise of the French and the bacchanalian ancient Greeks, but the wines (all made from imported grapes) are barely drinkable no matter how evocative their names may be. The vaguely suggestive wine *Obelisque* is a little kinder to the palate, but not to the wallet. Egypt's hard liquors have names that will make you tipsy just hearing them. Egyptian teetotalers must combat the harmful effects (and puns) of **Johnny Wadi's Brown Label** and **Gordon's Kin.** Before you sit down to a cool kin and tonic, however, be warned that these hack liquors are sometimes distilled from wood and have been linked to blindness and even death.

Jackie's Joint, Nile Hilton, Tahrir Sq. (tel. 578 04 44 or 578 06 66, ext. 379). "The Joint" is Cairo's new hotspot, with lines out the door most nights. To improve your chances of getting in, wear something sleek, black, and non-denim, and bring a date. Swing Night on Mondays; Ladies' Night on Wednesdays; Latino Night on Fridays. Minimum charge E£35 (includes a drink). 2-for-1 Happy Hour 10pm-midnight. Open daily 9pm-4am.

Crazy House Disco, Cairoland Hotel, 1 Salah Salem (tel. 366 10 82/83). Careen into other Cairenes on the dance floor at this local fave, which recently came under new management. E£25 cover includes 2 beers.

PERFORMING ARTS

DANCE

※ **Mausoleum El-Ghouri** (tel. 510 08 23), on El-Mu'izz St., just south of the pedestrian overpass near Al-Azhar University in Islamic Cairo. This renovated 500-year-old palace hosts free Sufi music and whirling dervishes (spinning at over 100rpm) on Wednesday and Saturday nights (summer 9pm, winter 8pm). Arrive early to the hour-long show as seats fill up fast, and bring water (all that whirling generates quite a lot of heat).

Balloon Theater (tel. 347 74 57 or 347 17 18), on En-Nil St. at the Zamalek Bridge, Agouza. Regular performances of Rida's Troupe, one of the best Egyptian folk dance companies. Tickets E£10-30. Shows daily at 9:30pm.

Falafel Restaurant (tel. 77 74 44), at Ramses Hilton (behind Egyptian Museum). Serves a scrumptious but expensive *prix-fixe* dinner (E£105) that includes a fabulous folk dancing show by the Hassan Troupe. Shows start at 10pm. Open Sa-Th 8pm-midnight.

Coquillage (tel. 340 61 26), at the foot of Tahrir Bridge, Zamalek, connected to Qasr en-Nil Casino. Arabic dancing and singing make this lavish hall of stained glass hop at night. Fettuccine with chicken (E£35) dazzles the taste buds, and the hour-long variety show (after 11pm) dazzles the eyes and ears. Open daily 11am-4am. Visa, MC.

Nile Maxim Cruise (tel. 342 48 33), at the Marriott Hotel in Zamalek. This glitzy Nile cruiser with chandeliers, mirrors, enormous windows, and jacked-up A/C is a great place to enjoy superb meals at jacked-up prices (E£65-105). Let the belly dancers, Sufi dancers, and lounge lizards entertain you. Trips depart every evening at 8 and 11pm and last about 2hr. Call for reservations. Visa, MC.

MUSIC AND THEATER

Cairo Opera Complex (tel. 339 81 44), in Gezira, southern Zamalek. This massive complex hosts the Cairo Symphony Orchestra, outdoor jazz performances, and visiting operas. Casual open-air performances held every day at 9pm in July and August. Jacket and tie required for the opera performances (travelers have been known to borrow snazzy clothing from kind hostel workers). Tickets for the small hall cost as little as E£5 with a student ID (E£15 for the main hall). Box office open daily 9am-9pm. Check *Al-Ahram* for show details.

El-Gomhoriyya Theater (tel. 390 77 07), at the intersection of El-Gomhoriyya St. and 'Abd el-'Aziz St. Performances by the Arabic Music Troupe and the Cairo Symphony Orchestra, usually on Friday evenings.

Wallace Theater (tel. 357 54 51), in the AUC New Campus, on Muhammad Mahmoud St. near the McDonald's off Tahrir Sq. Run by the American University in Cairo (AUC). Features 2 plays in English per year. AUC also hosts a variety of concerts, from jazz to chamber music, and free movie festivals at the library. Open fall-spring. Call or check bulletin boards around the Old Campus (near the AUC bookstore).

Cairo Puppet Theater (tel. 591 09 54 or 591 83 67), in Ezbekiya Gardens near 'Ataba Sq. World-famous shadow puppets put on performances in Arabic, but are universally understood. Shows W-M at 7:30pm, F and Su matinee at 10:30am. All tickets E£5.

British Council, 192 En-Nil St., Agouza (tel. 303 15 14), 1 block south of 26 July St., next to Balloon Theater. Sponsors free performances by visiting British and Egyptian artists and groups and sometimes presents films. Call for information on upcoming events. Large library (open M-Sa 10am-8pm) has CD and video equipment and a traveler-oriented teaching center. Internet access E£5 per hour. Office open Su-Th 9am-3pm.

Egyptian Center for International Cultural Cooperation, 11 Shagarat ed-Durr St., Zamalek (tel. 341 54 19). Free art exhibitions, Arabic language courses, lectures, tours, and performances Sept.-June. Open Sa-Th 9:30am-8pm.

OTHER DIVERSIONS

CINEMAS

Cairo has a few cinemas that run English-language films four to six months behind their release in the U.S.; check *Al-Ahram* (75pt) for listings. All of these air-conditioned theaters are packed with Egyptian hipsters on Thursday nights. Seats closer to the screen are cheaper than those in the balcony (a remnant of the British colonialist belief that people whose feet were above others' heads were of a higher class). Films usually run at 1, 3:30, 6:30, and 9pm, with a midnight showing on Thursdays (tickets E£8-10, balcony E£15-20).

PLEASURE TRIPS

Consider hiring a swallow-winged **felucca** and lazing on the river during the day or night. Most *feluccas* can accommodate up to eight people comfortably. The more passengers, the cheaper; bargain for a good rate. *Feluccas* for hire dock just south of the Qasr en-Nil (Tahrir) Bridge on the east bank. Across the corniche (on the water) from the Meridian Hotel, shrewd negotiators can snag a boat for E£5 during the day, E£7 in the evening. A nominal tip (E£1-2) is expected at the cruise's end. Travelers seeking multi-day cruises (especially popular in Upper Egypt, near Luxor and Aswan) should see **Tips on Traveling by Felucca,** p. 182. **Hantours** (horse carriages) are also enjoyable, especially on a breezy evening. Avoid those in front of major hotels, and don't pay more than E£10 for a half-hour ride.

OUTDOOR DIVERSIONS

GIZA ZOO. If you're keen for green, head to the Giza Zoo. A perennial favorite among locals, Giza has every animal you could ask for, many of which happily pose for photographs (E£10). *(Open daily 9am-4pm. Admission 50pt.)*

PHARAONIC VILLAGE (EL-QARIA EL-FAR'AONIYA). This Disney-fied village was founded by former Egyptian ambassador Dr. Ragab (who also claims to be the papyrus king of Egypt). Visitors board motorboats and chug through canals past statues of the gods and historically reconstructed scenes of ancient papyrus-making, temple wall-painting, mummification, etc. All this is described in detail by a guide speaking the language of your choice. Disembark to view a temple, houses, and King Tut's tomb reconstructed to appear as it did when Howard Carter discovered it in 1922. The price is steep, but it buys information without hassle. It's definitely (and only) worth it if you're not going to see the real thing in Luxor. *(5km south of downtown, on Jacob's Island in Giza. Tel. 571 86 75. Open in summer 9am-9pm; in winter 9am-5pm. Admission E£55, students E£40, groups of 10 or more E£30 per person. Lunch E£17.)*

FUTBOL MATCHES. You can catch a *futbol* (soccer) game at the stadium on Ramses St., in Nasser towards the airport. From September through May, local rivals Zamalek and Ahly take on teams from farther afield. Be cautious of the people next to you; if their team scores, they may set off a firecracker. First- and second-class seats are E£25 and E£10 respectively, but if you're more interested in seeing ballistic fans than athletes, grab a bleacher seat (E£5). *(Games start at 3 or 9pm— check Al-Ahram or ask around. Get tickets at the 2 teams' box offices: Zamalek's is south of 26th July St. in Mohandiseen; Ahly's is in Gezira next to the Cairo Tower.)*

E G Y P T

EGYPTIAN CIRCUS. Although Cairo is itself a three-ring circus, you may want to check out the real deal at the Egyptian Circus in Agouza between the British Council and the Balloon Theater. *(For more specific directions to these landmarks, see **Performing Arts,** p. 76. Tel. 347 06 12 or 347 05 03. Daily shows start at 9:30pm and run for about 3hr. Admission as low as E£20.)*

FOURTH OF JULY. On July 4, homesick American dreams come true at the Cairo American Primary and Secondary School, Ma'adi, where hundreds of Americans consume all the hot dogs, soft drinks, and pot luck they can stuff into their bellies while discussing world domination. Each attendee of the event also receives a free ticket to the raffles held throughout the evening (last year's prizes included return tickets to any destination in the U.S. and other luxury vacations). Bring your American passport—your taxes have already footed the bill—and a pair of swimming trunks. Call the American embassy (tel. 354 82 11) for hours and directions.

👁 SIGHTS

Four thousand years of history have been stitched together on the streets of Egypt's capital in a dusty quilt of dynasties past laced heavily with the musk of a metropolitan future. In **Islamic Cairo** (below), the devout prostrate themselves before some of the Muslim world's most revered sites while small-time capitalists haggle in the nearby ancient bazaar. In the **Cities of the Dead** (p. 88), mausolea and tombs listen to the struggles of the city's poor and the whispers of the gloried dead. Christian and Jewish communities center in the **Coptic Cairo** district of **Old Cairo** (p. 91), while the remains of **El-Fustat** (p. 93) house the earliest Egyptian mosque. **Modern Cairo** (p. 94) rushes to embrace the future, while the city's **museums** (p. 96) strain to weave together its millennia of history.

ISLAMIC CAIRO

Ibn Khaldun once said, "he who has not seen Cairo cannot know the grandeur of Islam." The resplendent mosques and monuments of Cairo's medieval district rank among the world's finest examples of Islamic architecture. Unlike Damascus and Baghdad (the two other Middle Eastern capitals of the medieval Islamic world), Cairo was spared the devastation of Mongol invasions. A trip through the narrow winding streets of Islamic Cairo will not only teach you about Islamic architecture, but offer a glimpse at a way of life whose habits and pleasures have endured like the domes and minarets above.

GENERAL ADVICE

It takes at least two days to explore Islamic Cairo, and the area holds riches enough to fill many more. William Lyster and SPARE (Society for the Preservation of Architectural Resources in Egypt) publish a superb set of four 3-D maps of Islamic Cairo (E£10 per map). The *City Map of Cairo* (E£10) has an indexed map of Islamic Cairo. For in-depth descriptions and history, try *Islamic Monuments in Cairo: A Practical Guide*, by Caroline Williams (E£100). That book and most maps are available at the AUC Bookstore (p. 68).

Many of the important monuments charge admission (E£6-12, half-price with ISIC). At free sights (mosques in particular), you will be expected to give *bakh-sheesh* (E£1 should be adequate). At the biggest mosques, the man who "guards" your shoes while you are inside usually expects compensation of some kind. Students purchasing discounted tickets should only pay 50pt-E£1 in *bakhsheesh*, rather than paying the difference between the regular ticket and the student one. Where permitted, climbing the minaret is included in the ticket price. Opening hours are estimates at best, so declare your interest to whomever is around and someone will let you in: a tour of Islamic Cairo confined to unlocked doors will miss many of the city's treasures.

Most mosques are open from 8am to 5pm, but visitors are not welcome during prayer times. Wait a few minutes after the congregation has finished before entering. Night visits are not permitted, although some travelers rave about watching the sunset paint Cairo dusty pink from atop a minaret. Avoid visiting on Friday afternoons (noon-2pm), when the Muslim community gathers for afternoon prayer. Certain highly venerated mosques—namely, Sayyida Hussein, Sayyida Zeinab, and Sayyida Nafisa—are believed to contain the remains of female descendants of Muhammad and are officially closed to non-Muslims.

Visitors must dress modestly in Islamic Cairo; revealing clothing will attract a great deal of unsolicited and unfriendly attention and will prevent admission to many mosques. Residents consider shorts, miniskirts, and exposed shoulders disrespectful. Women are encouraged to cover their hair; when head coverings are required, they can usually be rented for a few piasters. In some mosques (such as Muhammad 'Ali) an entire *galabiyya* is provided for free. It is important to avoid sandals and wear clothes that you don't mind getting dirty: just as Islamic Cairo is full of charm, so are its streets full of trash and semi-dry dung. Since you will often be asked to remove your shoes, socks are a good idea. Bring a plastic bag for your shoes to avoid the 50pt charged by custodians to watch them while you are touring. Never wear shoes in a mosque, or even place the soles on a mosque floor.

 SIGHTSEEING STRATEGY. Although each of the following sights can be visited individually, *Let's Go* has divided Islamic Cairo into four easily navigable regions (each of which can be visited in a leisurely half-day walking tour): **Southern Islamic Cairo** and the Mosque of Ibn Tulun (p. 79), the **Citadel** (p. 82), **Central Islamic Cairo** (p. 84), and **North El-Mu'izz St. and the Walls** (p. 86). A stopover at **Al-Azhar University** (p. 85) and the bazaar at **Khan el-Khalili** (p. 86) can easily be tacked on to any of these trips.

SOUTHERN ISLAMIC CAIRO

MOSQUE OF IBN TULUN. Built in 879 CE, the sublime Mosque of Ibn Tulun is the largest and third-oldest of Cairo's Islamic monuments. If you stand on Kadri St., the entrance is around the left side: once inside the gate, the **Gayer-Anderson Museum** (p. 98) is to your left and the mosque's courtyard is straight ahead. The serene courtyard covers almost seven acres and has six *mihrabs* indicating the direction to Mecca. In the center of the courtyard, an ablution fountain *(mayda'a)* added in 1296 CE by a Mamluke sultan is still used for washing before prayer time. The mosque (like many other early Islamic monuments) has pared-down decorative elements and an arcade-encompassed courtyard design based on the house of the prophet Muhammad.

The mosque is named after Ahmed Ibn Tulun, who served as the 'Abbasid governor of Egypt until he broke from the sultanate and established an independent city-state, Qatai'i, with its capital around this mosque. The minaret and its unusual external staircase (a harrowing climb ending in a great view) was probably modeled after the minaret at the Great Mosque of Samarra in Iraq. A less substantiated theory explains that it was built before it became clear that the *muezzin* could see impure things during his ascent to the top of the minaret. His glimpses of unveiled women relaxing in their homes led architects to build inner stairwells with hopes that the *muezzin* would stay more focused on prayer. *(Take minibus #54 (٥٤) or bus #72 (٧٢) from Tahrir Sq., or take the Metro to Sayyidna Zeinab and then bus #501 (٥٠١, 35pt) to Qadri St., which leads to Ibn Tulun. Coming from Giza, take bus #923 (٩٢٣); from the Pyramids, take bus #905 (٩٠٥); or share a taxi (E£5) to "Masjid Ibn Tulun." Open daily in summer 8am-6pm; in winter 8am-5pm; Ramadan 8am-4pm. Admission E£6, students E£3.)*

TOMB OF SHAGARAT ED-DURR. From Tulun or Tulun Bey St., turn right toward El-Ashraf Khalipha St. to find the small Tomb of Shagarat ed-Durr on your left. Built in 1250 CE, the tomb is the burial place of a politically prominent Muslim woman (one of only a dozen women to have ruled in the Muslim world) and the last Ayyubid building constructed in Cairo. Shagarat ed-Durr (Tree of Pearls) was a slave who rose to power after marrying Es-Salih Ayyub, the final ruling member of Salah ad-Din's Ayyubid Dynasty. After having her son murdered,

MASTER THE MASJID The array of Arabic terms used to describe the various rooms and architectural details of a mosque (*masjid* in Arabic) is almost as dazzling as the Islamic monuments themselves. Some Muslims considered representations of nature blasphemous imitations of Allah, so abstract geometric designs and Arabic script dominate mosque decor. In the Fatimid era, interlaced foliate patterns were popular ornamentation; geometric patterns and elegant calligraphy appeared later, particularly in Mamluke times. Mosqueteer roll call, call off now:

   bab: gate

   iconostasis: icon-covered screen that separates the nave from the sanctuary

   irwan: arcaded porch surrounding the *saha*

   khanqah: home for Sufi mystics

   kuttab: Qur'anic school, often combined with other buildings

   madrasa (pl. *madaris*): a college of Islamic law attended by students after they
      graduated from the neighborhood *kuttab*

   mihrab: richly decorated prayer niche pointing in the direction of Mecca

   minbar: pulpit next to the *mihrab* where sermons are delivered. There is often an
      archway or "wishing door" opposite the *minbar* that allows you to make a wish
      as you cross to the other side.

   sabil: water dispensary (not to be confused with the *mayda'a*, the ablution fountain)

   saha: central open courtyard

Shagarat ed-Durr declared herself queen and governed Egypt alone for 80 days before marrying the leader of the Mamluke forces and engineering the succession of the Mamluke Dynasty. The renegade couple managed to rule happily until the queen discovered that her new husband was considering a second marriage and had him murdered as well. Not to be outdone, the prospective second wife avenged the death of her lover by beating Shagarat ed-Durr to death with a pair of wooden clogs and then hurling her body from the top of the nearby Citadel, leaving her corpse to the jackals and dogs. The remains were put together in this small, rather unremarkable tomb. Even so, the wall mosaics are worth the E£1 *bakhsheesh*.

If you continue on El-Ashraf Khalipha St. you will find the Sayyida Nafisa Mosque. Retrace your steps to the left to return to the Mosque of Ibn Tulun. From the main entrance of Ibn Tulun, head left and take a right at the intersection with Khodairi St., which eventually will turn into Saliba St.

SABIL UMM 'ABBAS. On the left side of Saliba St. is Sabil Umm 'Abbas, an Islamic endowment that became the home of the **Life and Culture Center** in 1990 when the Ministry of Culture moved artists here from their well-known center on Roda Island. Tucked away here in Islamic Cairo, the artists rarely get visitors and are anxious to share their passions with interested travelers. Contemporary Egyptian artists use traditional artistic techniques as inspiration for paintings, textile designs, silk screens, and remarkable lamp shades. *(Open Sa-Th 9am-3pm. Free.)*

MOSQUE AND KHANQAH OF 'AMR SHAKYU. Walk north on Saliba St. past the intersection with As-Siyuqiyya St. to find these two buildings facing each other on opposite sides of the street, complete with matching facades, doors, and minarets. The entrance to the mosque (the building on the right as you walk north on Saliba St.) is up an alley—pop in to check out the amazing stained glass windows installed to keep out evil *djinns*. General Shakyu is buried in the *khanqah*, which is now undergoing extensive renovations. Slip up the stairway near the door to explore the long hallways of cells where Sufi mystics once lived.

◼SULTAN HASSAN COMPLEX. The Mamluke-era masterpiece known as Sultan Hassan is one of the largest Islamic religious buildings in the world. Unlike the Pyramids at Giza, which convey the mighty power of the pharaohs with their own might and size, the majesty of Sultan Hassan's complex stands in complete

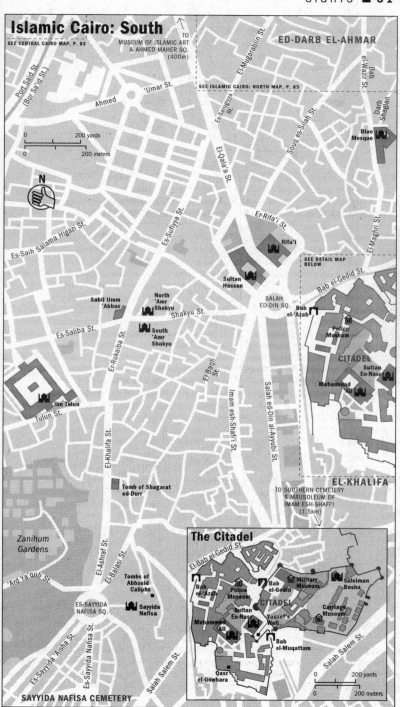

Islamic Cairo: South

SEE CENTRAL CAIRO MAP, P. 83

TO
MUSEUM OF ISLAMIC ART
& AHMED MAHER SQ.
(400m)

ED-DARB EL-AHMAR

SEE ISLAMIC CAIRO: NORTH MAP, P. 83

Port Said St. (Bor Sa'id St.)

'Umar St.

Ahmed

Es-Saih Salama Higazi St.

Es-Sanqiya St.

El-Mugarablin St.

Bab el-Wazir St.

Darb Shaplan

Blue Mosque

Souq es-Silah St.

El-Qala'a St.

Es-Sufiyya St.

Er-Rifa'i St.

El-Maghri St.

Rifa'i

Sultan Hassan

SEE DETAIL MAP BELOW

Sabil Umm 'Abbas

North 'Amr Shakyu

Shakyu St.

SALAH ED-DIN SQ.

Bab el-Gedid St.

Bab el-'Azab

Police Museum

CITADEL

EGYPT

Es-Saliba St.

South 'Amr Shakyu

Er-Rukaiba St.

El-Baqli St.

Imam esh-Shafi'i St.

Salah ed-Din al-Ayyubi St.

Sultan En-Nasr

Mohammad Ali

Ibn Tulun

Tulun St.

El-Khalifa St.

EL-KHALIFA

Tomb of Shagarat ed-Durr

TO SOUTHERN CEMETERY & MAUSOLEUM OF IMAM ESH-SHAFI'I (1.5km)

Zanihum Gardens

'Ard Ya'qub St.

El-Ashraf St.

El-Balas St.

Tombs of Abbasid Caliphs

ES-SAYYIDA NAFISA SQ.

Sayyida Nafisa

Es-Sayyida Nafisa St.

Es-Sayyida 'Aisha St.

Salah Salem St.

SAYYIDA NAFISA CEMETERY

0   200 yards
0   200 meters

N

The Citadel

El-Bab el-Gedid St.

Bab el-'Azab

Police Museum

Bab el-Gedid

Military Museum

Suleiman Basha

Sultan En-Nasr

CITADEL

Yousef's Well

Carriage Museum

Muhammed Ali

Bab el-Muqattam

Qasr el-Gowhara

Salah Salem St.

0   200 yards
0   200 meters

opposition to his weak rule. The only time Sultan Hassan ever slipped out from under the thumb of the Mamluke generals who controlled him was in 1356 CE, when he built this massive *madrasa* (college of Islamic law) and mausoleum; even then, the generals murdered him when they found out he had nearly broken the bank with construction costs. The spacious interior courtyard (32m on each side) is surrounded by four vaulted arcades known as *irwans*, each of which once housed one of the four schools of judicial thought in Sunni Islam. On either side of the easternmost *mihrab*, massive but delicately adorned bronze doors open onto the beautifully decorated mausoleum: the inlaid marblework there is the finest in Cairo. *(To reach Sultan Hassan and the Rifa'i Mosque (as well as the Citadel), continue down Saliba St. to Salah ad-Din Sq. From Tahrir Sq., take bus #173 (١٧٣) or #194 (١٩٤) or minibus #72 (٧٢). From the southern edge of 'Ataba Sq., take Muhammad 'Ali St., which becomes El-Qala'a (Citadel) St. To get back to Tahrir Sq., take bus #194 (١٩٤) or #609 (٦٠٩). Open in summer Sa-Th 8am-6pm, F 9-11am and 2-5pm; in winter until 5pm; Ramadan until 4pm. Admission E£12, students E£6.)*

RIFA'I MOSQUE. Next door to the Sultan Hassan complex stands the enormous Rifa'i Mosque, built by the mother of Khedive Isma'il, who is buried here with her son and grandsons King Fouad and King Farouk (Egypt's last monarch). In the room next to Farouk lies the tomb of Muhammad Reza Pahlavi, the last Shah of Iran. Rifa'i's stupendous size and polished interior will make your neck sore. Near the ticket window is a pleasant lawn—a great place to catch your breath before moving on to other sights. *(Directions, hours, and prices same as Sultan Hassan.)*

CITADEL (EL-QALA'A)

*From Tahrir Sq., take **bus** #82 (٨٢), 83 (٨٣), or 609 (٦٠٩) From 'Ataba Sq., take **bus** #401 (٤٠١) or **minibus** #50 (٥٠) or 55 (٥٥). Enter from either the northern or southern gate. From Hassan and Rifa'i, head left along the wall past the post office on your right. The road, Bab el-Gadid St., dead-ends at the Citadel gate. **Open** daily in summer 8am-6pm; in winter 8am-5pm; Ramadan 8am-4pm; closed Friday during prayer. Entrance locked 1hr. before closing. **Admission** E£20, students E£10, including all museums and mosques.*

Crowned by the dome and tall minarets of the Muhammad 'Ali mosque, the mind-bogglingly enormous Citadel *(El-Qala'a)* watches over the tumult of Islamic Cairo's tangled alleys. Construction was begun by Salah ad-Din in 1176 CE, and the building has been continually expanded and modified since then (most notably by the Mamlukes and Muhammad 'Ali). Almost all the rulers of Egypt from the 13th century until 1874 lived here. The complex contains three large mosques and four operating museums: as you walk around the curved road from the Citadel gate, the massive **Mosque of Muhammad 'Ali** will be on your left and the **Mosque of Sultan en-Nasr** on your right; several courtyards away is the third mosque, the **Mosque of Suleiman Basha.** To the southwest of the Mosque of Muhammad 'Ali is the **Qasr el-Gowhara** (Diamond Palace).

MOSQUE OF MUHAMMAD 'ALI. The mosque of Muhammad 'Ali is easy to spot from anywhere in the Citadel. Modeled after the Hagia Sophia, the Mosque is a perennial favorite of postcard-makers and tourists but is disparaged by art historians as a third-rate copy of the great Ottoman mosques in Istanbul. The edifice is also known as the Alabaster Mosque because it is covered inside and out with the clearest alabaster, hauled over from Beni Suef. Only one outer face remains bare: when Muhammad 'Ali died, so did the funding. In 1830, 'Ali leveled the western surface of the Citadel, filled in the famous 13th-century Mamluke palace Qasr el-Ablaq, and built his mosque on the ruins as a reminder of Turkish domination.

The mosque is entered through a courtyard presided over by an ornate (and non-functional) gingerbread-house-like clock of French design. In 1845, when Muhammad 'Ali presented France with the obelisk from Luxor Temple (which now stands in the Place de la Concorde in Paris), King Louis Philippe thanked the ruler by presenting him with this clock. Egyptians have always been some-

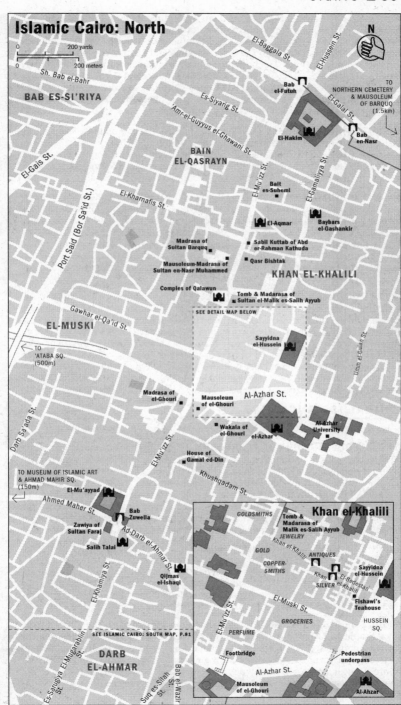

Islamic Cairo: North

0   200 yards

0   200 meters

N

Sh. Bab el-Bahr

El-Baggala St.

El-Hussein St.

TO NORTHERN CEMETERY & MAUSOLEUM OF BARQUQ (1.5km)

BAB ES-SI'RIYA

Es-Siyarig St.

Bab el-Futuh

El-Galal St.

Amr-el-Guyyus el-Ghawani St.

El-Hakim

Bab en-Nasr

El-Gais St.

BAIN EL-QASRAYN

El-Mu'izz St.

El-Gamaliyya St.

El-Kharnafis St.

Bait es-Suhemi

EGYPT

El-Aqmar

Baybars el-Gashankir

Madrasa of Sultan Barquq

Sabil Kuttab of Abd er-Rahman Kathuda

Port Said (Bor Said St.)

Mausoleum-Madrasa of Sultan en-Nasr Muhammed

Qasr Bishtak

KHAN EL-KHALILI

Complex of Qalawun

Tomb & Madarsa of Sultan el-Malik es-Salih Ayyub

Gawhar el-Qa'id St.

SEE DETAIL MAP BELOW

EL-MUSKI

Sayyidna el-Hussein

Umm el-Gulan St.

TO 'ATABA SQ. (500m)

Darb sa'ada St.

Madrasa of el-Ghouri

Mausoleum of el-Ghouri

Al-Azhar St.

El-Mu'izz St.

Wakala of el-Ghouri

el-Azhar

Al-Azhar University

House of Gamal ed-Din

Khushqadam St.

TO MUSEUM OF ISLAMIC ART & AHMAD MAHIR SQ. (150m)

El-Mu'ayyad

Ahmed Maher St.

Bab Zuweila

Zawiya of Sultan Faraj

Ad-Darb el-Ahmar St.

Salih Talai

El-Khamiya St.

Qijmas el-Ishaqi

SEE ISLAMIC CAIRO: SOUTH MAP, P.81

Es-Sauya El-Mugarablin St.

DARB EL-AHMAR

Suq es-Silah St.

Bab el-Wazir St.

Khan el-Khalili

GOLDSMITHS

Tomb & Madarsa of Malik es-Salih Ayyub

JEWELRY

Khan el-Khalili

ANTIQUES

GOLD

COPPER-SMITHS

Khan el-Khalili

Sayyidna el-Hussein

El-Bedestan

SILVER

Fishawi's Teahouse

El-Muski St.

HUSSEIN SQ.

El-Mu'izz St.

GROCERIES

PERFUME

Footbridge

Al-Azhar St.

Pedestrian underpass

Mausoleum of el-Ghouri

Al-Ahzar

what ticked off about getting a dud of a clock in return for a first-rate obelisk, but this didn't stop Muhammad 'Ali from decorating the interior of his mosque in a 19th-century French-salon-inspired style, complete with lavish Parisian architectural details (visible mostly on the 5 main domes and 15 mini-domes), a chandelier, and 365 tiny lanterns. Much more impressive is the view from the terrace by the exit of the mosque, where you can see all of Cairo and the Pyramids at Giza sprawled out before you. At prayer time, the simultaneous calls to prayer from each of the thousands of mosques in Cairo join together in a haunting, almost otherworldly chorus.

MOSQUE OF SULEIMAN BASHA. The Turkish-inspired Mosque of Suleiman Basha was the first Ottoman mosque in Cairo, built in 1527 by one of the Ottoman governors who headed the Janissary corps. The small-domed mosque, also known as **Sariat el-Gabal** (Mountain Palace), has a cozy prayer hall decorated with different calligraphic styles and a courtyard consisting of four *irwans*.

MOSQUE OF SULTAN EN-NASR. This is one of the few major buildings in the Citadel to escape the hand of architectural busybody Muhammad 'Ali (although the interior was stripped by Sultan Selin several hundred years before 'Ali arrived). The mosque is well known for the tile decoration on its minarets, which were constructed by Iranian craftsmen. Go through the gate with two flags on your left to enter another courtyard with superb views of Cairo and the mosques below. Nearby is the **Police Museum,** which once displayed narcotics and other items confiscated by the police but now contains nothing.

QASR EL-GOWHARA (THE DIAMOND PALACE). This half-palace was built in full in 1811 by Muhammad 'Ali and named after one of his wives. In 1974, a burglary attempt resulted in a fire that destroyed half of the palace. The surviving half consists of a large reception room (decorated in the excessive French style 'Ali loved), where 'Ali received 500 of his closest Mamluke allies before having them murdered on their way out. Also on display are a few of the gold- and silver-adorned tapestries from the Ka'aba in Mecca; Mecca presented Egypt with one of these tapestries every year until 1961. Only punch-drunk Muhammad 'Ali fans should walk over to the **Carriage (Hantour) Museum,** housing carriages of the great one's family.

CENTRAL ISLAMIC CAIRO

From Salah ad-Din Sq., walk north along the Citadel for 100m until you reach Bab el-Wazir St.

BLUE MOSQUE (MOSQUE OF AQSUNQUR). This 14th-century edifice owes its name to the colored Syrian tiles that line the interior, added in 1652 by a Turkish governor homesick for Istanbul's grand tiled mosques. The prayer hall to the right has one of the oldest marble *minbars* (pulpits) in the Islamic world. The top of the minaret is a great vantage point for viewing the Citadel to the south, Khan el-Khalili to the north, and the southern end of the City of the Dead to the east. *(On Bab el-Wazir St., several blocks down and on the right. Open daily in summer 8am-6pm; in winter 8am-5pm; Ramadan 8am-4pm. Admission E£6, students E£3.)*

MOSQUE OF EMIR ALTUNBUGMA EL-MIDAN. This arcaded mosque has a relaxing garden, but the real highlights are behind the *mashrabiyya* screen (to get in, use the power of *bakhsheesh*). All of the decorative arts of Mamluke-era Cairo are on breathtaking display here: the upper level is decorated with stained glass and carved stone, while the lower wall has tiling and inlaid marble. Note the minaret—it was the first to use columns to support an upper canopy. *(Free.)*

MOSQUE OF QIJMAS EL-ISHAQI. This mosque, dedicated to the Chief of the Royal Stable and Chargé d'Affairs for the pilgrimage to Mecca, is located on the Darb el-Ahmar (Red Way), which commemorates Muhammad 'Ali's massacre of the Mamlukes. Its unremarkable exterior gives no inkling of the serene, colorfully lit interior of inlaid marble and wood set with complicated ivory patterns. Under the prayer mats in the east *irwan* lies an ornate marble mosaic floor, an example of geometric Mamluke design (tip the custodian to uncover it for you). *(Head 2 blocks north of Bab el-Wazir St., where it joins with another street and becomes Darb el-Ahmar. To get into the mosque, gesture to the locals and they will retrieve the custodian.)*

BAB ZUWEILA. Bab Zuweila is the most impressive of the three remaining gates into Fatimid Cairo, named after the Berber tribe that once guarded it. Egyptians also call it *Bawwabet el-Metwali* (Gate of the Tax Collector) after the civil servant who used to wait for victims there. It is now topped by two minarets from the Mosque of El-Mu'ayyad, symbolizing Cairo's transformation from the heart of Fatimid-era military operations to the center of the Islamic world. *(The gate is at the intersection of Darb el-Ahmar and El-Mu'izz St.)*

MOSQUE OF EL-MU'AYYAD. The Mamluke ruler El-Mu'ayyad was once imprisoned on the site of this mosque; upon becoming Sultan, he tore down the prison and built this house of worship over it between 1415 and 1420. The huge door may remind you of those at the Sultan Hassan Mosque: in fact, it was taken from there. The arcaded building has a lovely garden and excellent inlaid marblework in the prayer hall. Give the guard *bakhsheesh* and he will let you climb the minaret for a spectacular view of Islamic Cairo. *(Go north through Bab Zuweila; the mosque is on the left. Open daily 8:30am-9pm. Admission E£6, students E£3.)*

EL-MU'IZZ STREET AND ENVIRONS. Across the street from Bab Zuweila and to the right stands the **Zawiya of Sultan Faraj** (built in 1408), a small rectangular structure. During the 1800s, execution by strangulation was carried out beside the railings outside. Next door is the elegant **Mosque of Salih Talai,** built in 1160. When the mosque was erected, the street was level with the series of shops standing behind the iron railing. The five keel arches form a remarkable projecting portal, unique in Cairo. (Open 9am-5pm.) Continuing south on El-Mu'izz St., you'll hit the **Street of Tentmakers,** one of the last covered markets in Cairo. You can buy amazing *appliqué* work here from E£15-25.

EL-GHOURI COMPLEX. This El-Mu'izz St. complex consists of a *madrasa* (college of Islamic law) and mosque (currently closed for renovations) across the street from a **mausoleum,** where whirling dervishes enchant visitors Wednesday and Saturday nights at 9pm (see **Performing Arts,** p. 76). From the *madrasa*, mausoleum, and mosque, head east on Al-Azhar St., then right onto Sheikh Muhammad 'Abduh St. At No. 3 (on your right), you'll see the magnificently preserved *wakala* (built in 1505), now transformed into a center for handicrafts and folkloric arts. *(Mausoleum and wakala open Sa-Th 9am-9pm. Admission to both E£6, students E£3.)*

AL-AZHAR UNIVERSITY

Al-Azhar University is the oldest continuously operating university in the world and the foremost Islamic theological center. Established in 972 CE by the Fatimids (who belonged to the Shi'a Muslim sect), it rose to pre-eminence in the 15th century as a center for the study of Qur'anic law and doctrine. It is still considered to be the final arbiter on all doctrinal issues related to Sunni Islam, the sect to which the focus of study at Al-Azhar was shifted once the Ayyubids came to power. Both the University and the Mosque of Al-Azhar stand just a few steps from the midpoint of El-Mu'izz St. at the end of Al-Azhar St., facing the square.

AL-AZHAR MOSQUE. To reach the central courtyard of this arcaded mosque, enter through the double arched gate and pass under the **Minaret of Qaytbay** (built in 1469). Although the stucco decoration of the courtyard's facade is a reconstruction, the *mihrab* in the central aisle is the original. The **library,** just left of the main entrance, holds over 80,000 manuscripts. For about E£1, the caretaker will allow you to climb one of the locked **minarets** for a fantastic view of Cairo and Khan el-Khalili below you. *(Open Sa-Th 7:30am-9pm, F 9am-noon and 2-7pm. Admission E£12, students E£6. Women without head coverings must wrap up at the entrance.)*

THE UNIVERSITY. Around the corner from the mosque is where Al-Azhar's 8000 students take classes from October to May. Students are found sitting on the plush red carpets of the mosque's *riwaq* (arcaded aisle around the central courtyard) cramming for exams. The theological curriculum has remained virtually unchanged since the Mamluke era (physics and medicine are more recent arrivals). Women, although allowed in the mosque, may not study at Al-Azhar; they attend a "sister school" near 'Abbasiyya Sq. The university uses the Socratic method of teaching, with a professor seated in the center of a circle of students. Give a small consideration to the caretaker and he'll show you the **tomb** of the university's founder.

SAYYIDNA EL-HUSSEIN MOSQUE. The Sayyidna el-Hussein Mosque was built in the Turkish style (note the pencil minarets) by Khedive Isma'il in the 1870s. It is highly revered throughout the Islamic world as the resting place of the skull of Hussein, grandson of the prophet Muhammad. The head is rumored to have been transported to Cairo in a green silk bag in 1153, almost 500 years after the death of its owner in the Battle of Karbala in Iraq. On *'Eid el-Mawlid en-Nabi* (Birthday of the Prophet), the President of Egypt traditionally comes to pray at Sayyidna el-Hussein while boisterous festivities take place in the square. During Ramadan, this square is the best place to witness the breaking of the fast after evening prayers (about 8pm). Restaurants display their fare half an hour before prayers begin, and famished patrons stampede to the tables afterwards. After blood-sugar levels return to normal, the square erupts in celebration. *(Located across El-Hussein Sq., 100m north of Al-Azhar Mosque. Closed to non-Muslims.)*

KHAN EL-KHALILI

Khan el-Khalili is the largest and most notorious bazaar in Egypt, just west of El-Hussein Sq. The Mamluke prince Gharkas el-Khalili established the market in the 1380s, and today it is still a requisite stop for countless tour buses, whose occupants pour forth to find that perfect little gift for Aunt Jean back in the States. Revel in the free-market frenzy as you pass through the copperware, perfume, spice, gold, silver, and *sheesha* sections of this massive bazaar. Though the tacky souvenirs are often overpriced, the time-honored institution of bargaining still thrives. Be ferocious if you intend to strike a good deal (often a third of the starting price, if not less), but be forewarned that there is an unwritten consensus among Khan shopkeepers that they will not go below certain prices. If you are allowed to walk away after making a bid, you probably won't get a better price elsewhere. The farther you go from the heart of the market, the more authentic the wares become. A word of warning: Khan el-Khalili is a **thieves'** paradise: many a hard-won bargain has been rendered futile by a wallet disappearance. Also, be sure not to enter shops with any hustlers whom you meet in the street; the store will inflate the prices to include the hustler's commission. **Fishawi's** offers respite from the market bustle with flavored *sheesha* and exotic juices (see **Ahwas and Casinos,** p. 74).

Slightly less tourist-ridden is **El-Muski,** the long bazaar where Egyptians shop for men's cologne, shoes, cloth, furniture, pillowcases, and food. El-Muski stretches from El-Mu'izz St. all the way to Port Said St., running parallel to and one block north of Al-Azhar St. El-Muski is also a convenient route between downtown and Islamic Cairo. For more places to shop in Cairo, see **Shopping,** p. 99.

NORTHERN EL-MU'IZZ STREET AND THE WALLS

To minimize mileage in this area, walk from Al-Azhar up El-Mu'izz St., through both Bab el-Futuh and Bab en-Nasr. Return by way of El-Gamaliyya St., which runs roughly parallel to El-Mu'izz St. from Bab en-Nasr past the Mosque of El-Hussein to the square in front of Al-Azhar. Expect to shell out about E£15 for admission to each of the sites below.

The section of El-Mu'izz St. between Al-Azhar Mosque and Bab el-Futuh was once known as *Bayn el-Qasrayn* ("between the two palaces," also the title of one of Naguib Mahfouz's novels) after the two Fatimid palaces that once stood here. Although those two palaces no longer stand, the area is still lined with many

Fatimid and early Mamluke architectural attractions, and a brisk walk through this part of El-Mu'izz St. is a wonderful way to see beautiful Islamic architecture from the outside. This area is also home to a **bazaar** for restaurant supplies that is locally known as the best place to buy reasonably priced *sheesha* pipes. Forget that gaudy and overpriced tourist junk in the heart of Khan el-Khalili and shop here alongside *ahwa* owners for authentic *sheeshas* ranging in price from E£15-45.

COMPLEX OF SULTAN EL-MALIK ES-SALIH AYYUB. The Sultan El-Malik es-Salih Ayyub, the last ruler of Salah ad-Din's Ayyubid Dynasty and the husband of Shagarat ed-Durr (whose tomb lies nearby in Islamic Cairo, p. 79), built this tomb, *madrasa*, and mosque in the 13th century. You'll recognize it by its square minaret pointing resolutely heavenward. The *madrasa* has ornate arched windows in the shape of boat keels. The custodian has keys to the adjacent domed mosque. (*Proceed north on El-Mu'izz St. from the intersection with Gohar el-Qa'id St. After passing four small side streets, you can see the tomb and madrasa on your right. The entrance is off a small alley on the right.*)

COMPLEX OF SULTAN QALAWUN. The Mamluke Sultan Qalawun sponsored the construction of this impressive mausoleum, *madrasa*, and hospital in 1284 (prior to his death en route to attack the Crusader fortress in Akko). Although the Mamlukes and the Crusaders didn't get along very well, their architectural styles did—note the Romanesque windows borrowed from the Crusaders and their Levantine castles. Only the three high *irwans* of the original *muristan* (mental hospital) remain. The ornate stucco work inside is original, though the undersides of the arches have been restored. The exquisite wood screen separating the tomb from the rectangular forecourt is also untouched. Before the 14th century, Egypt was the world's center for glasswork, and the Qalawun mausoleum offers especially dazzling glass mosaic work. (*On El-Mu'izz St. Complex open daily 8am-6pm. To gain access to the mausoleum, hunt down the guard, purchase a ticket, and have him unlock the door. Admission E£6, students E£3. Video cameras are not allowed without written permission from a tourist office; the nearest one is on Darb el-Asfar, next to Bait es-Suheimi.*)

COMPLEX OF SULTAN EN-NASR MUHAMMAD. Just north of Qalawun's mausoleum and tomb stand the mausoleum and *madrasa* of his son Sultan en-Nasr Muhammad, completed in 1304. En-Nasr Muhammad's 40-year reign marked the height of prosperity and stability in Mamluke Egypt, and the luxurious details of his funerary complex are a testament to this wealth. The square minaret, for example, has an exceptional, intricately carved stucco surface. Unfortunately, almost none of the interior remains. The authorities like to blame the 1992 earthquake, but the custodian says it was simple neglect. You can still see the four *irwans*, but only one is in good condition. (*Site supposedly open daily 10am-6pm. Free.*)

COMPLEX OF SULTAN BARQUQ AND ENVIRONS. Barquq, the first of the Circassian Mamluke sultans, rose to power in the 14th century through a series of assassinations. His **mosque** was erected in 1386, a century after Qalawun's complex, and the difference in style is striking. The inner courtyard has four *irwans*, the largest and most elaborate of which doubles as a prayer hall. Its beautiful timber roof has been restored and painted in rich hues of blue and gold. Four porphyry columns (quarried in pharaonic times from mountains near the Red Sea) support the ceiling, while the floor is decorated with disks of marble that are actually slices of Greek and Roman columns (Egypt has no indigenous marble). *Bakhsheesh* will get you into the Sultan's **tomb**, constructed of high quality inlaid marble with an elegant green and gold vine motif decorating the drum of the dome. Because very little remains of nearby **Qasr Bishtak**, a lavish palace from the 14th century that originally stood five stories high. All floors of the palace had running water, a technological achievement unmatched by Europe for another 300 years. An active Qur'anic school is housed in the slim, 18th-century **Sabil Kuttab of 'Abd er-Rahman Kathuda**, in the center of the fork in the road leading to Qasr Bishtak. (*Sultan Barquq's complex is on El-Mu'izz St., next door to the complex of Sultan en-Nasr Muhammad. The Qur'anic school is located where El-Mu'izz St. comes to a fork north of the Mosque of Barquq. Walk 25m down Darb Kermez, the small side street to the right of the fork, and you'll* *hit Qasr Bishtak. Complex of Sultan Barquq: open daily 10am-7pm; admission E£6, students E£3. Qasr Bishtak and Qur'anic school: usually open daily 8am-6pm; pay no more than E£5 to see both, students E£3.)*

MOSQUE OF EL-AQMAR. This small but architecturally important Fatimid-era mosque was built in 1125 CE, the first Cairene mosque to have the stone-facade-and-shell motif (found within its keel-arched niche) that became popular during that era. El-Aqmar means "the moons" and refers to the way the stone facade sparkles in the moonlight. The northern corner is typical of later Cairene architecture: the height of the niche is just about equal to that of a loaded camel, and it was intended to make the turn onto the side street easier for the hump-backed creatures to negotiate. *(Bear left at the fork in El-Mu'izz St. and continue north along El-Mu'izz St. to the next right-hand side street. Mosque of El-Aqmar is on the corner.)*

BAIT ES-SUHEIMI AND ENVIRONS. The 16th-century Bait es-Suheimi was built by Suheimi, the *sheikh* of Al-Azhar Mosque, for himself and his various wives. This is Cairo's finest old house, complete with carved wooden ceilings, stained-glass windows, tile mosaics, marble floors, and fountained salons. The house is under renovation, but should be open by the fall of 1999. The *khanqah* (Sufi establishment) known as **Baybars el-Gashankir** is nearby. Erected in 1310, it is the oldest surviving example of a *khanqah* in Cairo. *(Proceeding north from El-Aqmar Mosque, turn right onto Darb el-Asfar and follow the winding alley about 50m. The doorway on the left marked with a small, green plaque is the entrance to Bait es-Suheimi. Walk along Dar el-Asfar away from El-Mu'izz St. and you'll eventually come to El-Gamaliyya St. Across the street is the Baybars el-Gashankir.)*

NORTHERN WALLS. Islamic Cairo is bordered on the north by the extensive remains of the Fatimid walls. Built in 1087, these colossal fortifications are the best surviving examples of pre-Crusader Islamic military architecture. Look for graffiti left by Napoleon's soldiers. Three of the rampart's original gates still stand: **Bab en-Nasr** ("Victory Gate," at the top of El-Gamaliyya St.) and **Bab el-Futuh** ("Conquest Gate," literally "Opening Gate," at the northern end of El-Mu'izz St. in front of El-Hakim Mosque) are connected by a stretch of wall so thick it accommodates a tunnel; these walls once wrapped around the Fatimid city to **Bab Zuweila.** Other sections of the walls are being restored by the French.

EL-HAKIM MOSQUE. The Fatimid-era El-Hakim Mosque was built between 990 and 1010 and remains the second largest mosque in Cairo. The grandson of thoroughfare namesake El-Mu'izz, El-Hakim is often referred to as the "Mad Caliph"; he was actually the inspiration for the crazy Ali-Hakim in Rodgers and Hammerstein's famous musical *Oklahoma!*. El-Hakim's unpredictable rages meant death to Christians, Jews, his enemies, his friends, and, on one occasion, all the dogs in Cairo. He ensured the confinement of women by forbidding cobblers to make shoes for them. He even banned the cooking of *mulukhiga* (a green vegetable eaten throughout Egypt), renaming it *mulukhiyya* (meaning "royal") and restricting its consumption to his family. He was assassinated soon after he announced that he was an incarnation of God. His chief theologian, Ad-Darazi, fled to Syria and founded the Druze sect there. The mosque was recently restored (amid great controversy) by the Aga Khan Foundation, which chose not to restore the mosque to its original glory but instead jazzed it up with chandeliers and a neon *mihrab*. *(Located just inside the walls between Bab en-Nasr and Bab el-Futuh. Entrance off El-Mu'izz St. Open daily 9am-6pm. Admission E£6, students E£3. Climbing the minaret is permitted.)*

CITIES OF THE DEAD

The Cities of the Dead teem with life, serving as home to some of Cairo's finest Islamic architecture along with several thousand (living and breathing) Cairenes. The areas to the northeast and south of the Citadel contain hundreds of spectacular tombs and mausolea; unlike their more pious Islamic predecessors, Mamluke sultans spared no expense in the construction of their final resting places (perhaps they knew that their dynasties would not survive). During the late 1960s, a serious housing shortage for lower income Egyptians (combined with migration from the countryside to the city) created the trend of occupying burial chambers. Unlike most graveyards, the Cities of the Dead have streets, house numbers (which are not even found in Cairo's city center), and even a regular bus system and postal service. The modern residents of the medieval necropoles dwell amid the funerary architecture, and many households have even incorporated the grave markers into their houses and yards. Tombs frequently serve as clotheslines and soccer goals. On Fridays, the gravesites swarm with visitors arriving to pay their respects to the deceased. Many of the plots are enclosed by walls, encompassing an adjoining chamber and small house where families pray for their ancestors on holy days. The Egyptian custom of picnicking at the family tomb on feast days may be an ancient holdover from pharaonic times, when the corpse was believed to require nourishment for good health in the afterlife. Visitors are not permitted in the mosques on Fridays or during prayers.

NORTHERN CEMETERY

Go east along Al-Azhar St. from Al-Azhar Mosque, hugging the wall on your left. When the road forks, turn left under the overpass; this leads to the southern section of the northern necropolis. Bus #176 (١٧٦) from 'Ataba Sq. stops in front of the Mausoleum of Barquq. Bus #77 (٧٧) or 904 (٩٠٤) from Tahrir Sq. stops in the cemetery.

The Northern Cemetery, northeast of Al-Azhar, has broad avenues and courtyards containing the finest monuments of the Cities of the Dead. Posh modern mausolea sit alongside structures dating from the later Mamluke period (14-16th centuries).

TOMBS OF TULBAY AND TUGHAY. These tombs were erected in honor of two wives of Sultan en-Nasr Muhammad. Tughay was renowned for her beauty and piety, and her grieving husband constructed an appropriately fine tomb for her. The base of the dome is decorated with tiles in the Iranian style, fashionable after a peace was reached with Iran two decades prior to the tombs' construction. Egypt's penchant for the cosmopolitan during that era is evidenced by the use of arabesques and Chinese peony designs on the central *mihrab*. Although the harems of the Mamluke sultans were frequently hotbeds of intrigue and jealousy (and even more frequently just hot beds), Sultana Tulbay was quite close to Sultana Tughay and built her tomb next to that of her deceased friend. *(From Al-Azhar St., turn right at the first long street, and walk one block south. Facing the tombs with your back to the long street, Tughay's tomb is on the right, Tulbay's on the left.)*

◪MAUSOLEUM AND MOSQUE OF QAYTBAY. Enter the complex through the marble northern doorway, passing through a rectangular sanctuary that affords the best view of the polychromatically striped brickwork of the complex (whose likeness graces the Egyptian one-pound note). Qaytbay was a Mamluke slave who rose through the ranks of the army to become leader of Egypt near the end of the 15th century, ruling for 28 years. Qaytbay was not without enemies, so he watched his back, designing his **mausoleum** with three secret doors for quick escapes. Apparently his efforts paid off—Qaytbay was the only Mamluke ruler not to be assassinated. Qaytbay designed the prayer niche to require devotees to pray over the ruler's remains in order to face Mecca. The mausoleum also contains two black stones bearing footprints said to be those of the Prophet Muhammad. The **mosque** itself has a remarkable dome (with an unusual echo effect that the caretaker will demonstrate) that uses both geometric and arabesque designs. *(Upon leaving the alley, turn left and walk two blocks, then turn right at the first major street (there will be a small domed tomb on the left opposite the start of the street). Follow this street for three blocks, and turn left up a lane with a stone arch around 40m down the lane. This is the gate of Qaytbay's complex. Open daily 9am-9:30pm. Admission E£6, students E£3. Bakhsheesh required to climb the minaret).*

COMPLEX OF SULTAN ASHRAF BARSBAY. Barsbay pulled out all the stops to construct his combined mosque, *khanqah* (school for Sufi mystics) and mausoleum complex in 1432. Originally intended as a *khanqah*, the 15th-century **mosque** of Sultan Ashraf Barsbay has meticulously fashioned marble mosaic floors; lift the prayer mats to see the colorful tilework. Adjoining the mosque to the north is Barsbay's **mausoleum,** a domed chamber containing his remains and those of his slaves, an elaborately decorated *mihrab*, and gleaming mother-of-pearl and marble mosaics. The dome decorations are complex geometric designs, which replace the chevrons used in earlier tombs (such as that of Barquq). The wooden *minbar* is one of the best in Cairo. *(Three blocks north of the Qaytbay complex and 50m south of the Mausoleum of Barquq, along the cemetery's main thoroughfare. Open daily 9am-sunset. Free.)*

MAUSOLEUM OF BARQUQ. Like the mausoleum of Sultan Barsbay, this mausoleum (easily identified by its twin domes and minarets) was built in 1411 CE as a *khanqah* for Sufi mystics. This may explain the limited decorations in the mausoleum: excessive ornamentation was seen as a distraction from the contemplation of the full glory of Allah. This asceticism did not apply to Barquq's mausoleum in the northern corner, which has the largest stone domes in Cairo, though not as intricate as those of Barsbay and Qaytbay. Behind the mosque is a modern military cemetery. *(North of the Barsbay complex. Open daily in summer 8am-6pm; in winter 8am-5pm. Admission E£6, students E£3.)*

TOMBS. The **Tomb of Barsbay El-Bagasi** (built in 1456 CE) is decorated with an intricate geometrical design resembling a tulip, a variation on the Moroccan motif of *dari w ktaf* (cheek and shoulder). The nearby **Tomb of Emir Suleiman** was built about 90 years later; its dome is decorated with a series of zig-zag stripes. *(In front of the Mausoleum of Barquq. To get back to 'Ataba or Tahrir Sq., either take the #167 (١٦٧) bus from the bus stop in the square to the west of Barquq's complex or ask someone for help and they'll tell you which bus goes downtown. The tombs are free, but the caretaker will expect a pound or two of bakhsheesh.)*

SOUTHERN CEMETERY

The Southern Cemetery is a sprawling expanse of tombs from the Fatimid period to the present, where the silence is disturbed only by occasional noise from the squatters who inhabit the area (and make it unsafe for women to travel here at night). The entire region is easily accessible by foot from the Mosque of Ibn Tulun, Sultan Hassan, or the Citadel. From Ibn Tulun or Sultan Hassan, proceed east to Salah ad-Din Sq., just southeast of the Citadel, then head directly south following the southern slope of the Citadel. When you reach the traffic circle, walk under the overpass and take the right-hand fork, El-Qadiriyya St., which becomes **Imam esh-Shafi'i St.,** the main thoroughfare in the cemetery. You can also take bus #82 (٨٢) or #182 (١٨٢) or minibus #54 (٥٤) from Tahrir Sq.

MAUSOLEUM OF IMAM ESH-SHAFI'I. The Southern Cemetery's most impressive edifice is the celebrated Mausoleum of Imam esh-Shafi'i. The largest Islamic mortuary chamber in Egypt, the mausoleum was erected in 1211 by Salah ad-Din's brother and successor in honor of the great Imam esh-Shafi'i, founder of one of the four schools of judicial thought of Sunni Islam. Shafi'i Islam is still the dominant judicial school in Egypt and much of East Africa. In 1178, Salah ad-Din built a large monument over the grave of Imam esh-Shafi'i, which is currently housed within the 13th-century mausoleum and often crowded with Muslims offering prayers. The teak memorial depicts the Imam himself, and is one of the finest surviving pieces of Ayyubid wood-carving. Two mosques adjoin the tomb chamber. The 1190 mosque is closed to non-Muslims. The 1763 mosque, open to all, remains a center of worship and has a distinctive boat that holds grain for birds on its dome. *(Bus #72 (٧٢) from 'Abd el-Munem Riad Station goes to the Mausoleum. Open daily 6am-7pm. Free, but E£1 bakhsheesh is appropriate.)*

TOMB OF THE FAMILY OF MUHAMMAD 'ALI. Directly behind the tomb of the Imam Shafi'i lies the Tomb of the Family of Muhammad 'Ali. 'Ali's favorite wife Tulun, her sons, and their families are all buried here. The white-marble tombs are decorated in a riot of color in true 'Ali style. The headpieces on each tomb indicate the gender and rank of the deceased. *(Known to most public transportation drivers by its Arabic name,* Haush al-Basha. *Open daily 9am-9pm. Admission E£6, students E£3.)*

MOSQUE OF SAYYIDA NAFISA. Those approaching the Southern Cemetery can't miss Sayyida Nafisa's tall, single minaret and ornate dome on the western edge. The mosque is Egypt's third-holiest Islamic shrine and one of Cairo's three congregational mosques. It honors the great-great-great-granddaughter of the Prophet, who died in 824 CE and began attracting droves of pilgrims to her tomb soon after. So many mausolea were erected in the immediate vicinity of her tomb that historians suspect that it was this shrine that sparked the development of the Southern Cemetery. *(Closed to non-Muslims.)*

TOMBS OF 'ABBASID CALIPHS. Adjoining the Mosque of Sayyida Nafisa on the eastern side are the less-than-impressive Tombs of 'Abbasid Caliphs. At the peak of their authority, the 'Abbasid caliphs ruled the entire Muslim world (except Spain) from Baghdad. The last reigning caliph fled Baghdad in 1258 after invading Mongols toppled the regime. The Mamluke sultan welcomed the caliph upon his arrival in Egypt and went so far as to exalt the deposed ruler in an effort to legitimize his own rule. Subsequent Mamluke rulers continued to harbor a succession of caliphs, all the while preventing them from gaining any real power. Finally, the sultan in Istanbul declared himself caliph in 1517, thereby consolidating the authority of the Ottoman Sultanate. The 'Abbasid caliphs have since been deposed, and members of the family are still buried within the 13th-century mausoleum. *(Caretaker will unlock the gates for E£1 bakhsheesh.)*

OLD CAIRO

Old Cairo is a remarkable testament to the religious tolerance of the Islamic dynasties: mosques, Coptic churches, and a synagogue all coexist here peacefully; indeed, the region known as Old Cairo consists of Christian **Coptic Cairo** (below) and heavily Islamic **El-Fustat** (p. 93). El-Fustat was once the site of the first Islamic capital of Egypt, but today much of Old Cairo is the center of Cairo's Jewish community. Although most of the Jewish population left in 1949 and 1956, approximately 30 families still inhabit this quarter and worship at the ancient **Ben-Ezra Synagogue** (p. 92). The easiest way to reach Old Cairo is to take the **Metro** from Tahrir Sq. towards Helwan to Mari Girgis station (50pt).

SIGHTSEEING STRATEGY. Although all of these sites can be visited separately, visiting them in the order they are presented below makes for an excellent and easily navigable daytrip around Coptic Cairo and El-Fustat.

COPTIC CAIRO

Ancient Egypt inspires images of towering pyramids, hieroglyphs, and mummy cases dripping with jewels. Many mistakenly assume that this ancient pharaonic era shifted directly into the Islamic age of mosques and medieval fortifications. However, the interim period between Cleopatra and the caliphs was the time of the Roman conquest, which led to the spread of Christianity and the conversion of the Emperor Constantine in 324 CE. Indeed, Christianity was the dominant faith in Egypt for 300 years (from the fall of the pagan Romans to the arrival of Islam), and currently some five to seven million Christian Copts live in Egypt, mostly in Coptic Cairo or in Middle Egypt (see **Religion and Ethnicity,** p. 50).

Most of Cairo's Coptic churches are tucked away from the street, and the older structures have simple entrances. Though the churches do not charge admission and hardly require any *bakhsheesh* (indeed, this neighborhood is pleasantly free of the hustlers that infest other sections of Cairo), all have donation boxes. Those seeking serenity should avoid the churches on Sundays or the church saint's day, when hundreds of Coptic Cairenes and their children migrate from church to church receiving blessings and pronouncing their faith. *(Churches open daily 9:30am-5pm; mass daily 7-9am. No photography.)*

COPTIC MUSEUM. Directly across from the Mari Girgis Metro station is the Coptic Museum, home to the world's largest and finest collection of Coptic art, texts, textiles, metalwork, and iconographic materials. For more details, see the complete listing for the Coptic Museum on p. 98.

TRAJAN'S GATE. In front of the Coptic Museum (directly across from the Mari Girgis Metro station) is Cairo's only substantial classical ruin, the **Iron Gate** of the Roman emperor Trajan's fortress of Babylon (built during the first century CE). This massive fortress once covered 60 acres, and the Muslims could only capture it when the Coptic Patriarch Cyrus ordered the defenders to surrender. A massive tower and gate offer a hint of the scale of the original fortress. *(Free. Open 24hr.)*

CHURCH OF THE VIRGIN (EL-MU'ALLAQA CHURCH). This beautiful Coptic church is on your left as you face the Mari Girgis Metro station. The church is referred to as *Mu'allaqa* ("Hanging") because it was suspended 13m above the ground between two bastions of the fortress of Babylon. The building itself is ark-shaped, its roof held up by eight pillars on each side (one for every member of Noah's family, all of whom have the ark to thank for their salvation). Pointed arches and colorful geometric patterns enliven the main nave; in the center, an elegant pulpit (used only on Palm Sunday) rests on 13 slender columns—one for Christ and each of his disciples. The conspicuous black marble symbolizes Judas Iscariot, the Bible's most famous traitor, and ostrich eggs symbolizing the Resurrection hang overhead. Over 100 icons decorate the chapel.

This church holds a special place in the annals of Coptic history, thanks to its involvement in the miracle of Mokattam Mountain. A doubtful caliph issued an ultimatum to Pope Ibrahim Ibn ez-Zar'a and the Coptic population—prove that the faithful can move mountains or die. The Copts in the area prayed for three days and three nights in the Church of the Virgin until, on the third night, their communal bowing and wailing of *Kyrie eleison* supposedly shook the earth and moved Mokattam a few inches. *(Coptic orthodox masses held W 7-9am, F 8-11am, Su 6-8:30am and 9-11am.)*

CHURCH OF MARI GIRGIS (CHURCH OF ST. GEORGE). This Greek Orthodox church, built in the 6th century, is across the street from the Coptic Museum. Erected over one of the towers of the Fortress of Babylon, this church is dedicated to the Roman soldier George, whose famed tussle with a dragon is shown in a large relief in the courtyard. The current church was built in 1909, and its steps spiraling into the air represent the infinity of God. This church and the nunnery of St. George nearby (where a chain-wrapping ceremony commemorating the torture of St. George is sometimes performed) both claim to house the chains used to torture the saint. *(Open daily 8am-noon and 2-5pm. Free.)*

OLD CAIRO PROPER

As you face the Church of St. George, a staircase to the left on Mari Girgis St. descends into an alley leading into Old Cairo proper. The churches here have their own quiet beauty, but are fairly plain; the real charm of Old Cairo is in its twisting alleys. These narrow passages, barely marred by souvenir vendors, are cool and quiet. The sun bakes the ancient brick as the occasional local ducks around the corner or underneath an arch to enjoy a smoke or visit a friend.

BEN-EZRA SYNAGOGUE. This is the oldest synagogue in Egypt, and the temple of the country's few remaining Jewish families. Jews established the synagogue in the 7th century BCE because Moses supposedly used the site for prayer before the exodus. The Copts eventually took over the site (which explains why the temple is designed very much like the nearby Coptic churches), but in 1115 CE, the caliph returned the Coptic Church to the Jewish community. The temple is beautifully decorated, combining Islamic geometric patterns with the Star of David. The ceiling dates from the Coptic occupation of the site and is in an exquisite arabesque style. *(With your back to the Church of St. Barbara, the Ben-Ezra Synagogue is approximately 25m to the left. Tel. 359 26 95.)*

CHURCHES OF ST. BARBARA AND ST. CYRUS AND ST. JOHN.

St. Cyrus and St. John were torn apart by wild beasts during the notorious persecution of Christians by the Roman emperor Diocletian, but the only wild beast in the church now is an occasional wandering cat. Legend holds that when the caliph discovered both Christian churches being restored, he ordered the architect to destroy one of them. Unable to choose, the architect paced back and forth between the two buildings until he died of exhaustion; the caliph was so moved he allowed both to stand.

The eponymous saint of the **Church of St. Barbara** was killed by her father when she sanctimoniously attempted to convert him. Her bones rest in the tiny chapel accessible through a door to the right as you enter her church. St. Catherine's bones supposedly lie here as well (see **St. Catherine's,** p. 154). An inlaid wooden *iconostasis* from the 13th century graces the church's ornate interior. Most of the furniture is now in the Coptic Museum, p. 98). *(At the end of the alley leading in to Old Cairo proper and to the left.)*

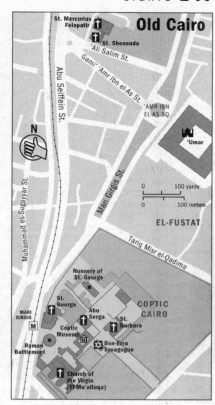

Old Cairo

EL-FUSTAT

To reach El-Fustat, take the Metro to Mari Girgis (50pt). With your back to the station, head north along Mari Girgis St. until you see the minarets of the Mosque of 'Amir on your right. Buses #92 (٩٢), #94 (٩٤), and #134 (١٣٤) also run from Tahrir Sq., stopping right beside the Mosque of 'Amir. If you take a taxi to the outskirts of Old Cairo (E£2-3), ask to go to Misr el-Qadima or Gami' 'Amir.

Adjoining Coptic Cairo to the north are the partially excavated remains of El-Fustat, one of the oldest Islamic settlements and the capital of Egypt during its first 250 years as a Muslim country. El-Fustat was the name of a garrison town that some historians maintain comes from *fossatum*, the Latin word for an entrenchment. A different account of the founding of El-Fustat holds that the conquering general 'Amir sent word to the caliph in Medina that the magnificent Roman port of Alexandria would be the perfect place for the capital of Egypt. To 'Amir's dismay, the caliph preferred to establish his outposts along desert trade routes, which were invulnerable to the naval attacks of seafaring Christians. The disappointed general returned to Babylon to find that a white dove had nested in his tent during his absence. Interpreting this as a divine omen, 'Amir founded the new capital of Egypt on the site of his tent, and dubbed it El-Fustat (City of the Tent). The military camp soon grew into a prosperous city with large houses, running water, and a sophisticated sewer system. El-Fustat remained the capital of Egypt until the Fatimids established the neighboring city of El-Qahira ("The Conqueror") in 969 CE. In 1168, Crusader King Amalric of Jerusalem invaded El-Qahira, and the resident Fatimids burned El-Fustat to the ground to prevent it from falling to the Crusaders. The ruins were soon scavenged for building materials, and El-Fustat's days of importance ended ignominiously as the city garbage dump.

As a result, the present-day architectural remains of El-Fustat are insubstantial, and a stroll through the site reveals little more than traces of cisterns, drains, and rubbish. The main reason to visit El-Fustat (aside from a few interesting churches) is the **Mosque of 'Amir,** Egypt's first mosque. El-Fustat sprawls over the large area behind the mosque. If you venture to this district in the heat of summer, bring plenty of water. It is best to avoid the area at night, since it is isolated and lacks police protection.

MOSQUE OF 'AMIR. The present-day Mosque of 'Amir, Egypt's first mosque, occupies the site of the original building of 642 CE, and is four times the size of its predecessor. The oldest portion of the current mosque is its crumbling southeastern minaret, added during the Ottoman period. The mosque has been rebuilt countless times over the centuries, most recently in 1983. There is little historically or architecturally interesting about the current building, especially in comparison with the nearby Coptic churches. Architectural fragments, thousands of pieces of fine Islamic pottery, and imported Chinese porcelain have all been discovered here, but most pieces are currently displayed at the Islamic Museum and in the new Islamic Ceramics Museum (p. 99). Also behind the Mosque of 'Amir is the **pottery district,** which provides the clay pots used to store water throughout Cairo. Watch modern-day artisans at work feeding smoke-belching kilns with leather scraps and garbage, but ask before you take a picture or be slapped with a E£5 fee by your subjects. *(Open daily 9am-5pm. Admission E£6, students E£3.)*

OTHER SIGHTS. Near the Mosque of 'Amir is **Deir Abu Seiffein,** a complex of three 8th-century Coptic churches. *(Walk straight down the street directly opposite the entrance to the mosque; the wooden entrance to the churches is about 500m ahead on the right. Complex open daily 8am-5pm. The odass, or liturgy, is read in Coptic in these churches Su 6-10am, W 8am-noon, and F 7-11am.)* The oldest church with the finest icons in Deir Abu Seiffein is the **Church of St. Mercurius Felopatir** (or the Church of Abu Seiffein), dating from the 4th century but extensively restored during the Middle Ages. Saint Mercurius Felopatir, a Roman Christian soldier, assured his frazzled king that divine assistance would dispose of the annoying Berbers who were troubling the Empire; after the Romans emerged victorious against the Berbers, the king proceeded to behead Mercurius for his religious beliefs. The martyr is also referred to as Abu Seiffein ("two swords") because an angel gave him a heavenly sword to go with his military saber.

The church has an impressive **iconostasis,** constructed of ebony, ivory, and cedar, that separates the front vestibule from the nave. The elaborate, gabled roof is an impressive feat of Coptic carpentry, as every piece is fitted to the next without screws or nails. There are several fine **icons** in the chapel to the left of the entrance, and dozens more decorate the main room. Use your charm (or, failing that, *bakhsheesh*) to persuade the caretaker to let you into the **Chamber of St. Barsoum,** where the saint supposedly lived with a cobra for 25 years. The tiny, dark room may remind many budget travelers of places they have spent the night. Upstairs are the ancient and equally miniscule churches of St. George of Rome, St. John the Baptist, and the 144,000 Martyrs, all of which were rediscovered when the plaster was accidentally chipped away from layers of icons. At the time of printing, the chapels were closed for renovation.

Down the street is the late 4th-century **Church of St. Shenouda,** dedicated to one of the most famous Coptic saints. This chapel contains seven altars and two fine *iconostases*—one of red cedar and the other of ebony. The smallest of the three main structures at Deir Abu Seiffein is the early 8th-century **Church of the Holy Virgin,** a one-room chapel crammed with rare icons, paintings, and three altars. Across the Nile on Roda Island is a particularly interesting variation on the ubiquitous Cairene **Nilometer** (glorified stairwells built to measure the depth of the Nile). The 'Abbasids constructed this particular Nilometer around 850 CE and carved Qur'anic verses about water on the interior walls. The Ottomans lended a hand by adding a dome in the 19th century. If both entrances to the Nilometer are locked, use the all-powerful *bakhsheesh* or ask one of the many children playing nearby to pester the custodian.

MODERN CAIRO

The heart of Cairo beats in **Tahrir Square** (Liberation Sq.), with the Egyptian Museum on the northern side, the Mugamma on the southern, and cars speeding suicidally in between. However, the many Cairenes careening through the streets will tell you that the city's "downtown" is not only centered in Tahrir Sq., but also in the many squares surrounding it, particularly **Tala'at Harb Square** and **'Ataba Square.** As you wander through this region, dodge the madcap drivers and throngs of Cairenes heading home after catching the most recent cinematic gem. You'll find yourself surrounded by an architectural wonderland whose more cosmopolitan, French-influenced flavor may come as a welcome relief from the dusty ancient quarters and Mamluke mosques of much of the rest of the city. To truly escape the hubbub of much of the city, head to the quieter corners of the downtown area: the ritzy suburb of **Zamalek** beckons from the middle of the Nile, and the suburbs of **Heliopolis** and **Garden City** are a few steps away.

TAHRIR SQUARE

One block up from Tahrir Sq. at the intersection with Bustan St. are two particularly fine old buildings. On the southern side of the intersection is the **4 Tala'at Harb St.** apartment building, elaborately decked out from its foundation to its richly decorated dome. Across the street, the more restrained and newly renovated **Muhammad 'Ali Club** glistens in the Cairo sun. Look for the carved faces in the moldings. The **Sakakini Palace,** north of Modern Cairo, is easily visible from the heart of the city. The merchant Sakakini struck it rich when he sent a caravan of camels to the rat-infested Suez Canal; to celebrate his luck, he built this ornate palace and festooned it with a bizarre assortment of statuary. You can get a good view from the outside, but for a little *bakhsheesh* the caretaker will show you around the decaying interior. Take the Metro to Ghamra station.

TALA'AT HARB SQUARE

Just to the north of Tahrir Sq. is Tala'at Harb Sq., named after the founder of the Egyptian National Bank and ringed with buildings in a variety of European styles. On the west side of the Square is **J. Groppi's,** once *the* place to see and be seen (although the only things to see there now are the fabulous Italian mosaics at the entrance). Europeans and Europeanized Egyptians spent countless hours in this fashionable cafe, whose lip-smacking pastries used to be exported to Europe's elite. The cafe's frequent concerts and dances during the colonial period were the hottest ticket in Cairo and always a top priority on Victorian social calendars. Although the Revolution brought that world to an abrupt end, Groppi's still remains as a stodgy reminder of Cairo's faded and oppressed glory. Those more interested in munchies than mosaics can check out the write up of J. Groppi's in the **Food** section (p. 72). Further up Tala'at Harb St. is the **Cinema Metro,** a beautiful movie palace from the 1930s that often shows English language films as well as Arabic flicks. Farther north, Tala'at Harb St. intersects with 26 July St.; a block to the east on this street stands the interesting **Muhammad Shawarbi Basha Building.** Built in 1925, it fuses European styling with Egyptian motifs such as the winged sphinxes on the dome. West of Tala'at Harb St. is the **Sha'ar Ha-Shama'im Synagogue.** The name of this recently built (by Cairo's standards) Jewish temple means "Gate of the Sky," and its architecture is truly heavenly. Its construction was started in the 1920s, and its decadent decoration would be most at home in a Hollywood biblical epic from that same golden age of American cinema. (Open Saturdays. Free.) One block to the north of 'Adly St. on Tala'at Harb St. is the faux leaf-encrusted brick of the massive **Davins Bryan Building,** which once outfitted explorers. To the south is **St. Joseph's Church,** a large Italianate building painted in bands of yellow and pink that make it look like a multi-storied pastry. It is still the center of the city's Catholic community, with services held there daily.

'ATABA SQUARE

To the west of downtown is 'Ataba Sq. and the **Ezbekiya Gardens.** Although they are now fenced in and look like little more than a lawn with a few small palm trees, the Gardens were for many centuries the magnificent, verdant center of the city's social life. A patch of thick trees remain in the southern corner to hint at what it was once like, first under the Mamlukes maintenance and then during the colonial period (when it was redesigned by the landscape architects of the Bois de Boulogne in Paris). In the northeast corner of 'Ataba Sq., just past the skyscraper with an antenna, are the beautiful double domes of the **Sedanoni Department Store.** Although it was built to rival the *prêt-à-porter* extravaganza Au Printemps in Paris, nationalization has left the store with shoddily constructed and hideously ugly *prêt-à-jeter* fashions. The building's interior is still impressive, with a huge open center and a staggeringly large cut-glass chandelier.

EGYPT

ZAMALEK

The quiet, tree-lined streets of the island of Zamalek are a great place to take a breather from the noisy hustle-and-bustle of the rest of Cairo. The city was first settled in the colonial era, when the **Gezira Club** in the north was a second home to many a British elite. A walking tour of the sights in and around Zamalek is a cosmopolitan change of pace from the ancient sites and medieval architecture that characterize the rest of Cairo. Spend an afternoon browsing the galleries and exhibitions at the opera complex at the southern end of the island (particularly those at the **Egyptian Modern Art Museum,** p. 98), stopping at the many cafes and coffee shops along the way. When the sun sets, head for the restaurants scattered around the island for some of Cairo's best and most unusual food (see p. 72).

CAIRO MARRIOTT. The building that now houses the Cairo Marriott, along the east bank of Zamalek, was built in 1869 to house Empress Eugenié (wife of Napoleon III) during the grand opening of the Suez Canal. Around the same time, it hosted the first performance of Giuseppe Verdi's opera *Aida,* long regarded as the seminal work in the grand tradition of Egyptian fetishization (rivaled by Lawrence Durrell's *The Alexandria Quartet*). Across the river to the west are **houseboats** that were home to cabarets and nightclubs during World War II. One was owned by a bellydancer (employed by the Germans) who used her charms to acquire secrets from British agents.

CAIRO TOWER. The Cairo Tower dominates the city's skyline and has an excellent (if pricey) view of the city. It was built by former President Nasser with money the U.S. had given him in an attempt to win his favor; once he sided with the Soviets, he built the tower as a reminder to the Americans of their failure to buy him off. *(Open 9am-1am, with lines forming at sunset. Admission E£25.)*

HELIOPOLIS

Buses run between 'Abd el-Munem Riad and Roxy Sq. From Roxy Sq., head onto Al-Ahram St.

This suburb of Cairo was founded in 1906 by the Belgian industrialist Edouard Empain as a community for foreigners in Egypt. Its broad avenues and odd architecture (a strange Euro-Islamic fusion) make it an interesting short trip out of central Cairo. The highlight of Heliopolis is **Empain's Palace,** built in the style of Angkor Wat. To get there, head south on Shahid Tayyar Nazih Khalifa. The estate is a strange riot of carved elephants and Cambodian motifs that you can explore on your own (simply *bakhsheesh* the caretaker and he will let you wander around). The massive building behind the high wall in Heliopolis is the **Palace of the President.** Down Cleopatra St. across from the Pres's res are the beautifully decorated offices of the **Heliopolis Company,** who planned the suburb. Al-Ahram St. is home to several cheap cafeterias that were once major hangouts for Allied troops during World War II, as well as a **basilica** just past the cafeterias. Although modeled on the Hagia Sophia, it looks more like a jelly mold.

▥ MUSEUMS

EGYPTIAN MUSEUM

In the heart of Tahrir Sq., accessible by any transportation. Open daily 9am-4:30pm. Admission E£20, students E£10; camera privileges E£10, video E£100. To see the mummies: admission E£60, students E£30.

The multi-storied behemoth that is the Egyptian Museum building seems small in comparison to the astounding size and scope of the collection inside. The world's unrivaled warehouse of pharaonic treasures is filled with precarious stacks of exquisite mummy cases that open onto rooms filled with thousands of statuettes and gilded treasures (including those from the tomb of King Tutankhamun). Legend has it that if you spend one second at every exhibited item, it will take six months of non-stop viewing to see everything. Although the heavily touristed areas (such as the Tutankhamun and Akhenaton rooms) are very well labeled, many descriptions are unhelpfully banal ("Pot," "Clay"), and some of the most puzzling items have no explanation at all. Although the crowded rooms are impressive, some of the smaller, infrequently visited side rooms are equally fascinating and far from the maddening tourist crowd. Unless you choose to buy the E£100 catalog, the first item to check out should be the wall map to the left of the entrance or the CD-ROM display to the right of the entrance. A camera may not be advisable, since the museum is not brightly lit and flash is not permitted.

◪TUTANKHAMUN ROOM. Of all the collections in the museum, the treasures from **Tutankhamun's tomb** are the best-displayed and most popular. Originally squeezed into less than 100 cubic meters, the booty now occupies a quarter of the second floor. The eastern corridor contains decorated furniture, golden statues, delicate alabaster lamps, weapons, amulets, fossilized undergarments, and other bare necessities for a King of the Underworld. **Room #4** displays the famous gold of Tutankhamun, glittering all over coffins and funeral masks, as well as an astounding collection of amulets, scarabs, and jewelry. One elegant mask is made with more than 4kg of solid gold inlaid with quartz and lapis lazuli. In the hallway sit the king's internal organs, each in its own gilded coffin. The countless souvenir versions of these items, sold in tacky *souqs* and found on gaudy t-shirts and fake papyri, only make the originals look more impressive.

NARMER PALETTE. In the small glass case opposite the entrance (and behind the 3000-year-old monkey) is the Narmer Palette, which commemorates the unification of Upper and Lower Egypt in about 3100 BCE by the mythical founder of pharaonic dynasties, King Narmer or Menes (see **Ancient History,** p. 47). From here, navigate the first floor in a clockwise direction around the central courtyard to get a sampling of pharaonic art from the Old Kingdom to the Greco-Roman period. Walking down the west corridor, you can visit the three rooms off to the right for a few minutes each. The first two rooms feature the best of the Old Kingdom, including a diarite statue of Chephren and a wooden statue named "Sheikh el-Balad" by workers who discovered that it resembled their boss. The third room displays limestones from the Middle Kingdom.

AKHENATON ROOM. In the Akhenaton room (at the rear of the first floor) are statues of the heretical pharaoh who introduced into Egypt a form of monotheism centered around the worship of the sun god and life-giver Aton. Aton was represented as a disk with rays that ended in hands that sometimes held *ankhs*, the Egyptian symbol for life. Artwork from this period is recognizable for its distinctly realistic portraits (versus the very stiff and stylized portraits of other periods) and grotesquely feminine body shapes; read more about Akhenaton-era hijinks by sticking your head between the legs of the king's shapely statue to get a view of the informational plaque. Past the Akhenaton room are a collection of **statues** from the New Kingdom. In the northeast corner room, look for a painting of **Ramses II** displaying his prowess as he clutches the cowering enemies of Egypt by their hair.

GREEK AND ROMAN ROOMS. Down the hall from the painting are the Greek and Roman rooms, where Classical art sits side-by-side with such oddities as a statue of a nude woman with the legs and tail of a chicken. Around the corner toward the entrance is a remarkable statue of **Alexander the Great:** the body is in the stiff pharaonic style, while the head is carved in the style of Greek naturalism.

MUMMY ROOM. The controversial mummy room is in the southeastern corner of the second floor. Former president Sadat closed the famed room in 1981 because the display offended some Islamist groups. The reopening of the room was delayed by the mummies' continued decomposition, which left them offensive to just about everyone. Now restored and lodged in a dimly lit, air-conditioned room, the mummies might offend your budget and will not enhance your understanding of the mummification process in any way, as there are absolutely no descriptions. For more on mummies, see **Who is That Masked Man?,** p. 104.

EGYPT

OTHER ROOMS. The west corridor has unlabeled, oblong **mummy cases** in layers, and room #37 has the square mummy cases used in the Middle Kingdom. Room #27 has excellent **tomb models** with such scenes from daily life as the threshing of wheat and the brewing of beer (proving that Egyptian laborers knew how to relax after a hard day carving stone *colossi*). The **papyri** scattered throughout the museum put those sold in the streets to shame; room #29 on the second floor has a particularly fine collection. At the opposite end of Level II from the gold of Tutankhamun is the modest **Tomb of Yuya and Thuyu,** which is more typical of the tombs in which most Egyptians rested for eternity. Animal-rights activists may cringe in nearby room #53, where the mummified remains of cats, birds, and monkeys repose in frozen honor.

COPTIC MUSEUM

Directly across from the Mari Girgis Metro station. Tel. 363 97 42 or 362 87 66. Open daily 9am-5pm. Admission E£16, students E£8; camera privileges E£10, video E£100.

The 14,000 textiles, paintings, icons, and other pieces in the Coptic Museum make up the world's finest collection of Coptic art. Located in the 19th-century Roman fortress of Babylon (Qasr esh-Shama), the museum's halls are paved with spotless white marble, and elegant wooden *mashrabiyya* (interlaced woodwork) screens cover the windows. The museum displays a variety of architectural fragments brought from the sanctuary of St. Menas at Maryut and the monastery of St. Jeremiah at Saqqara, along with Coptic textiles from the 2nd century and various metalworks. The most impressive room is a collection of icons on the second floor, which has many superb paintings in a variety of styles; compare an icon of the Virgin Mary suckling the baby Jesus and a carving of the Egyptian goddess Isis suckling her son Horus. The Library of Gnostics, next to the textiles, contains 7000 volumes of non-standard gospels from the 13th and 14th centuries, along with Coptic texts from various other periods. A cool courtyard is a pleasant place to rest, although the concession stand is overpriced (nearby streets have much less expensive soda and Baraka). Unlike most museums in Cairo, the collection at the Coptic Museum is well-labeled in French and English.

OTHER MUSEUMS

Egyptian Modern Art Museum (tel. 341 66 67), within the Opera Complex, Zamalek. Cross the bridge from Tahrir Sq. or take Metro to Opera. Tastefully exhibited Egyptian paintings in a variety of media and 20th-century styles. A welcome reminder that Cairo's art is not confined to tombs and mummy cases. Open Tu-Th and Sa-Su 10am-1pm and 5-9pm, F 10am-prayer time (around 1:30pm). Free.

Gayer-Anderson Museum (tel. 364 78 22), just in front of the Ibn Tulun mosque. Originally 2 separate buildings, these 16th- and 18th-century mansions were merged when Major Gayer-Anderson, an English art collector, arrived in the 1930s and proceeded to fill his home with eclectic artifacts and furniture. When he left Egypt in the 1940s, he gave the mansion and its contents to the Egyptian government. To Egyptians, it is mysteriously known as "The House of the Cretan Woman." You may recognize some rooms from the James Bond flick *The Spy Who Loved Me.* Open daily 8am-3:30pm. Admission E£16, students E£8; camera privileges E£10, video E£25.

Islamic Art Museum (tel. 390 99 30), in Bab el-Khalaq Sq., at the intersection of Port Said, Muhammad 'Ali, and Ahmed Maher St. The hiding place of many of the artifacts missing from the mosques, mausolea, and *madaris* of Cairo. Also contains Islamic art from much of the rest of the Middle East. Don't miss miniature paintings and the gold-leaf Qur'ans in the calligraphy room at the back. Open in summer Sa-Th 9am-4pm, F 9-11am and 2-4pm; in winter F 9-11:30am and 1:30-4pm. Admission E£16, students E£8.

Mahmoud Khalil Museum, 1 Kafour St. (tel. 336 23 76), in Giza, 200m from the Cairo Sheraton. A fantastic collection (housed in an A/C mansion) consisting almost exclusively of paintings by such 19th-century European greats as Monet, Van Gogh, Degas, and Toulouse-Lautrec. Open Sa-Th 10am-5:30pm. Admission E£25, students E£10.

Manial Palace Museum (tel. 388 74 95), in the north half of Roda Island, close to the Sayyida Zeinab Metro station. This complex was built in the 19th century by the prolific Muhammad 'Ali, and like many of his other buildings reflects an Ottoman influence (particularly the must-see residential palace) from floor to ceiling. The macabre hunting museum is filled with disembodied animal heads. Open Sa-Th 9am-4pm, F 9am-1pm and 2-4pm. Admission E£10, students E£5; camera privileges E£10, video E£20.

Mugamma' el-Funun Center of Arts (tel. 340 82 11), on the corner of Ma'had es-Swissry St. and 26 July Bridge, Zamalek. Sponsors rotating exhibitions of works by contemporary Egyptian and foreign artists, many of which are on sale (E£800+). Also screens films. Nile-side serenity doesn't get any better than the out-of-control garden here. Open Sa-Th 10am-1:30pm and occasionally 5-9:30pm. Free.

Mukhtar Museum (tel. 340 25 19), after Tahrir Bridge and just before El-Gala'a Bridge on Tahrir St. in Zamalek. Built by architect Ramses Wissa Wassef, this museum is devoted to the works of sculptor Mahmoud Mukhtar (1891-1934), a representative of a group of Egyptians working towards independence from European powers. The museum's most famous piece is the *Awakening of Egypt.* You might recognize Mukhtar's style from his sculpture in front of the Cairo Zoo or the statue of the man with a raised hand at the base of the Tahrir Bridge. Open Tu-Su 10am-1pm and 5-9pm. Admission E£1, students 50pt. Closed for renovations until the summer of 2000.

Museum of Islamic Ceramics, El-Gezira Arts Center, 1 Sheikh Marsafy St., Zamalek (tel. 341 86 72), next to the southwest corner of the Marriott Hotel. Proof that less is more, this superb new museum houses an exquisite collection of well-labeled ancient Islamic and contemporary ceramics in the well-organized, A/C rooms of a converted Ottoman Palace. And it's free!

 # SHOPPING

Cairo's biggest and most famous market is the **Khan el-Khalili** (see p. 86). Navigating the maze of passages and alleyways that lie within the Khan may seem like madness, but there is a method to it. Most gold, copper, and antique dealers lie along Khan el-Khalili St., which changes to El-Badestani St. as it heads east. Perfumes, spices, and cloth can be found a few blocks farther south, between Al-Azhar St. and El-Muski St.

In the market south of **Sayyida Zeinab,** each alley offers different wares. Take the Metro to Sayyida Zeinab, then walk five minutes toward the minarets of the Sayyida Mosque. Other major markets are northeast of **'Ataba Square** and in **Bulaq.** For 'Ataba Sq. from Tahrir Sq., go eastward along Tahrir St., then up 'Abd el-'Aziz St.; for Bulaq take bus #46 (٤٦). The **Souq et-Tewfiqia** runs between Ramses and Tala'at Harb St., one block north of 26 July St. Produce stalls stand beside kitchen-equipment vendors, all laid out in brilliant displays. On summer days, hose-wielding shopkeepers water the shop entrances to reduce heat and settle the dust.

If bargaining doesn't appeal to you, you can head to one of Cairo's **department stores,** such as the upscale 'Umar Effendi. Be forewarned that ever since the Egyptian government nationalized the department stores, the shops have had little to offer other than out-of-date, outlandishly tacky clothes in various brown-and-orange combos. More expensive shopping centers lure foreigners and wealthy Egyptians with higher-quality goods. The **World Trade Center** on the corniche, north of the Ramses Hilton, is the biggest. A bit less expensive is the **El-Yamama Center** (affectionately called the Yo Mama Center by expats), at 3 Dr. Taha Hussein St. in Zamalek, where you can watch music videos or sporting events on the large-screen TV in the ground-floor cafe.

BACKGAMMON. *Tawleh* boards cost E£80-120, depending on the quality and your bargaining skills. Make sure the board is absolutely flat when it's opened and laid on a table, as occasionally they are warped or wobbly. Pieces are often made separately from the board. Check to see that they fit on the triangles, and that there are 15 of each color. You should pay less if the pieces are plastic. **Maka el-Mokarama,** 7 'Adly St. (tel. 393 89 80), next to the tourist office, has quality boards but lacks the hassle and fun of Khan el-Khalili, where dozens of stores sell them.

EGYPT

VENI, VIDI, VENDI Buying and selling in the Egyptian capital transcends mundane business—it's an intricate give-and-take that has evolved over centuries. Think of it as a game to be relished, not a battle to be won. Bargaining is a given: no price is set in stone, and successful merchants enjoy the haggling (just remember that the shopkeepers do this for a living and have the benefit of experience). If you play hardball, the vendors will not lower the price—chatting will bring you more success. Theatrics, rather than stubbornness, get results. Walk away in disbelief several times. Do a brief Mexican hat-dance while you weigh the pros and cons of the purchase. Never get too enthusiastic about the object in question. Instead, point out flaws in workmanship and design. Have a friend discourage you from your purchase—if you seem to be reluctant, the merchant will want to drop the price to interest you again. Your starting price should be one-third to one-half the asking price, at most.

CLOTHING AND TEXTILES. At the **tent-makers' bazaar,** south of Bab Zuweila in Islamic Cairo, you can commission the making of a Bedouin tent (far out of a budget traveler's price range) or buy appliqué pillowcases (E£20) and bedcovers (E£300). The **Nomad Gallery,** at 14 Saraya el-Gezira, 1st floor, Zamalek (tel. 341 19 17), near the Marriott, is known for its top-quality jewelry, textiles, and crafts. They're not big bargainers here, but their prices are as low as they go at the tent-makers bazaar. (Visa, MC, AmEx accepted. Open M-Sa 10am-3pm.) The best places to shop for woven **rugs** are indubitably the stores along **Saqqara Rd.,** near the Pyramids, where Harania artists weave up a storm (see p. 105).

There's a colorful **used clothing market** daily at the east end of 26 July Bridge. The stands hawk modern and vintage Western clothing as well as some traditional Egyptian garb. Women tired of getting hissed at can pick up a used *galabiyya* here or splurge on a new one (E£30-50) at the market south of El-Ghouri Mosque and Khan el-Khalili on El-Mu'izz St. Casual clothing for several well-known Western outlets is made in Egypt, and you may want to take advantage of the slightly lower but fixed prices. Most of these goods are available in boutiques on the main streets and in department stores. On Friday mornings there's a **junk market** at the Mausoleum of Imam esh-Sharifi'i, where many a bizarre item is bought and sold.

JEWELRY AND METALWARE. Cairo is a center of the jewel trade, and prices here tend to be markedly lower than in the West. Often, gold or silver jewelry can be made to order for barely more than the cost of the metal itself. Never ask for the price first. Look at a piece of jewelry carefully and then ask the shopkeeper to weigh it in front of you. Inquire about the grade of gold or silver; gold weights under 18 karat are rare in Egypt. Always make sure you see the stamp on both gold and silver items. One of the best shopping areas is in the **Khan el-Khalili Souq el-Fidha** (silver market), where you can find Turkish, pharaonic, and Nubian designs in addition to more modern creations; be sure to shop around. Plates and trays of varying sizes and designs are available throughout the Khan for E£15-20, while a *sheesha* should cost about E£35. For the best *sheeshas* in Cairo, however, bypass the junk sold at the Khan and head to the **restaurant supply bazaar** on El-Mu'izz St. (see p. 86). Copper or brass mugs, coffeepots, and ashtrays are available, but nothing is as old as the shopkeeper claims.

PAPYRUS. The "papyrus" sold throughout Cairo is usually banana leaf, a cheap look-alike. Real papyrus can be scrunched up and will not retain any wrinkles, while banana leaf crackles and stays crunched. To see the real stuff at correspondingly higher prices, head to **Dr. Rayab's Papyrus Factory,** a right turn off the Gala'a Bridge heading west from Tahrir Sq. Another authentic option is the **Sa'id Delta Papyrus Center,** 21 El-Ghouria St. (tel. 512 07 47), by Darb el-Ahmar, 3rd floor, near the Umayyad Mosque. Within the Khan el-Khalili itself is **Wafiq Isma'il 'Ali,** near the Coffeeshop Naguib Mahfouz, which sells fake but surprisingly vivid "papyrus" for around E£10. The bazaars are full of colorful artwork for those who think a neon pink Osiris would look great over the telly.

SPICES AND PERFUME. Thousands of perfume and spice shops give some sections of Cairo a relievingly fragrant smell. Excellent Middle Eastern spices like *za'tar* are difficult or impossible to find in the West. The quality of perfumes ranges dramatically. Rub some on the back of your hand: if it's oily or shiny, oil has been added to the perfume to stretch the liquid weight. An ounce can go for as low as E£5. **Harraz Agricultural Seeds, Medicinal, and Medical Plants Co.,** 1 Bab el-Khalq St., sells every imaginable spice at reasonable prices (open Sa-Th 9am-9pm). If the self-proclaimed "sheikh of spice" won't cut you a good deal, **Khodr,** next door, has similar wares, as do many vendors in the Khan el-Khalili market.

NEAR CAIRO

PYRAMIDS AT GIZA الاهرام

A 12th century Arab historian once said, "all things fear time, but time fears the Pyramids." Originally constructed to honor the pharaohs in death, these three massive stone monoliths are also monuments to generations of slaves who devoted their lives to the pyramids. While treasure has been plundered by grave robbers and museum curators, the edifices still tower over the desert, aloof to the throngs below. Since everyone wants to see these awe-inspiring testaments to human achievement, nowhere else is Egypt's ravenous tourism industry so persistent. For a solid mile leading up to the pyramids, souvenir shops, alabaster factories, and papyrus museums conspire to pawn off "ancient" artifacts made while you wait. At the foot of the pyramids, an army of hustlers not unlike the biblical swarm of locusts hounds you: Bedouin imposters rent camels and Arabian race horses, children peddle tourist dreck at inflated prices, and self-appointed guides approach at every turn. A stern *"la shukran"* ("no thanks") can prove useful at the Giza Pyramids, even with the man who claims to be the mayor of Giza (he isn't). Don't let the racket deter you from spending at least a few hours exploring one of the seven wonders of the ancient world.

▌ PRACTICAL INFORMATION

To get to the Pyramids (*El-Ahram*), take **minibus** #183 (١٨٣, 40pt) from Tahrir Sq., #26 (٢٦) from 'Ataba Sq., #84 (٨٤) from Nile Hilton, or the faster **microbus** (50pt). The last stop is often 1km from the Pyramids. Cross the street and follow the main road to get there. The easiest and most comfortable way back is on a special tour bus that leaves outside the tourist office every 10-15min. (E£2).

Hotel managers in Cairo can arrange **tours,** but be sure to compare prices. ▨**Mr. Salah Muhammad** (tel./fax 298 06 50; email samo@intouch.com) offers chauffeur-driven tours of Memphis, Saqqara, the carpet school at Harania, and the Pyramids at Giza for E£23, entrance fees excluded (leave at 9am, return exhausted at 5pm). The fee includes a guide to tell you all about the sights. Salah Muhammad also offers a free 24-hour **shuttle service** from the airport to downtown Cairo for *Let's Go* users who take his tour (see **Entry,** p. 42).

The **Giza Tourist Office** (tel. 383 88 23), on Pyramids Rd. next to the police station, offers only bus information and suggested prices for rides (open daily 8:30am-5pm). A **tourist police** station is adjacent to the ticket office. Rest houses next to the Cheops Pyramid and the Sphinx sell overpriced refreshments. Both have **public bathrooms,** where attendants expect *bakhsheesh* for handling your towels.

Innumerable animals are available for rent, and their owners will approach you incessantly. An hour ride on a horse or camel should be around E£10. For longer rides and more reliable beasts, walk beyond the Sphinx and turn right after the auditorium where the sound and light show takes place. You'll find a row of reputable establishments, including **AA Stables** (tel. 385 05 31; open daily 5am-8pm) and **SA Stables** (tel. 385 06 26; open 7am-11pm). They provide professional equipment (boots, hats, etc.) for a reasonable rate. Although the tourist police post prices for an hour-long ride at E£12 for a horse and E£10 for a camel, the going price at these establishments is closer to E£20 for a guided trek on either. E£5-10 is a fair price without a guide (in the unlikely occasion that the owner agrees), but only confident equestrians should inquire; some mounts only obey hieroglyphs and may gallop swiftly off into the desert, ignoring their rider's hysterical yells.

 SIGHTSEEING STRATEGY. Visit the Pyramids on Friday when some of the pious hagglers take the day off (most other attractions are closed anyway). Be wary of going before 9:30am. In winter, fog shrouds the pyramids in the morning and crowds tend to pick up as the day progresses. Be warned that you can't get inside the Pyramids or boat museum past 5pm. Good shoes are key for those who plan on internal climbing; external climbing is no longer permitted.

FOOD AND ENTERTAINMENT

There is no reason to stay in Giza since Cairo is only 30 minutes away. Although sunrise at the Pyramids is impressive, guards won't let you in until regular hours of operation. The food situation is bleak, and it's best either to wait until you get back to Cairo or bring a bag lunch (as many Egyptians do). There are several **food stands** near the sound and light show auditorium, as well as a **Pizza Hut.** The **Pyramids Shishkebab Restaurant** (tel. 385 10 78), two blocks from the Sphinx Rest House along the main road, has a cheap *ta'amiyya* and shawarma stand and serves traditional salads, *fuul*, and falafel inside (E£1-4 per item, meat more expensive; open daily 10am-1am). The **Khan el-Khalili Coffee Shop** (tel. 383 68 28), in the Mena House Oberoi Hotel at the end of Pyramid St., is a sleek spot to sip coffee or mint tea (E£3.25; open 24hr.).

As far as entertainment goes, it's the Pyramids or bust (unless you find fending off hustlers entertaining). The **sound and light show,** now featuring lasers is E£33 for a tourist seat. Call 385 28 80 or check *Egypt Today* to find out when the Sphinx will reveal its secrets in the language of your choice. English shows are usually at 8:30pm in the summer, 6:30pm in the winter. If it's solitude you seek, the people in the stables next to the Sphinx can arrange overnight expeditions through the dunes (E£20-45).

SIGHTS

Site open daily in summer 6:30am-8pm; in winter 7am-10pm. Pyramids open daily 8am-5pm. Admission to Pyramids and Sphinx complex E£20, students E£10. Admission to the 2 smaller pyramids E£10, student E£5. Admission to the Great Pyramid E£20, students E£10; limited to the first 100 visitors who appear at each of the 2 visiting times, 8:30am and 1pm.

The three main pyramids at Giza were built for three pharaohs from the 4th dynasty: **Cheops** (Khufu), **Chephren** (Khafre), and **Mycerinus** (Menkaure), a father-son-grandson trio that reigned during the 26th century BCE. The three pyramids are lined up in descending order of chronology and size, from Cheops to Mycerinus. The entrances of all three face north and the bases are aligned with the four cardinal points. The smaller pyramids surrounding the Big Three belonged to the pharaohs' wives and children. Each of the pyramids was once attached to its own funerary complex, which included a riverside pavilion and a mortuary temple where the pharaoh's cult could continue for eternity. A long, narrow causeway linked the mortuary temple with the neighboring waters of the Nile. The mummy of the deceased ruler was conveyed by boat across the Nile, carried up the causeway in a solemn procession, and deposited in its sacred resting place at the heart of the pyramid.

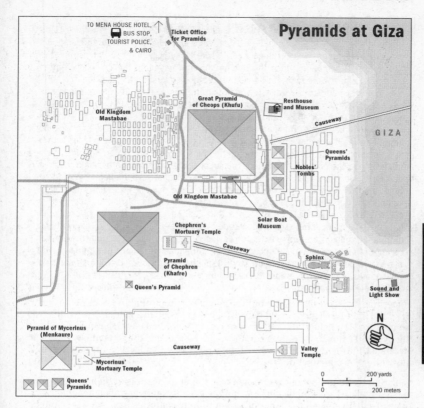

Pyramids at Giza

TO MENA HOUSE HOTEL,
BUS STOP,
TOURIST POLICE,
& CAIRO

Ticket Office
for Pyramids

Old Kingdom
Mastabae

Great Pyramid
of Cheops (Khufu)

Resthouse
and Museum

Causeway

GIZA

Queens'
Pyramids

Nobles'
Tombs

Old Kingdom Mastabae

Solar Boat
Museum

Chephren's
Mortuary Temple

Causeway

Sphinx

Pyramid
of Chephren
(Khafre)

Queen's Pyramid

Sound and
Light Show

Pyramid of Mycerinus
(Menkaure)

Causeway

Valley
Temple

Mycerinus'
Mortuary Temple

Queens'
Pyramids

N

0   200 yards
0   200 meters

EGYPT

GREAT PYRAMID OF CHEOPS. Built around 2550 BCE, the Pyramid of Cheops is the first pyramid you'll encounter upon entering the site. It initially stood 146m high, but over the course of four and a half millennia its height has decreased by 9m. While experts still debate the exact technology used in its construction, they generally agree that it took 10,000 people about 11 years and 2.3 million limestone blocks to build it. The total weight of Cheops is estimated at six million tons. One dubious story recounts that Cheops hired his daughter out as a courtesan and required each of her admirers to give her a stone for her dad's grave. Considering that this pyramid took 3¼ million cubic yards of stone, even a life of one hundred years of perfect health and romantic popularity would have provided only enough stone for the tip of the pyramid. Stairs lead up the side to the entrance into the empty tomb, which is marked by neatly carved graffiti left by 18th-century tourists.

PYRAMID OF CHEPHREN. The middle member of the Giza trio is 3m shorter than the Pyramid of Cheops, although it actually looks a bit taller because it's positioned on a higher plateau. Portions of the limestone casing that originally covered the monument still sheathe its apex, making it Egypt's most splendid pyramid. Also notice the granite on the summit; Chephren wanted to add a layer of granite atop the limestone, but he died too soon.

PYRAMID OF MYCERINUS. The Pyramid of Mycerinus is small compared to its relatives. Legend has it that instead of devoting his attention to his death chamber,

WHO IS THAT MASKED MAN? The ancient Egyptians wanted to live forever, so they had to be certain their bodies were fit for the long haul of the afterlife. In pre-dynastic times, people were buried in simple pits in the sand. The heat and arid conditions dried the bodies out and prevented decay. As civilization advanced, efforts were made to provide for a person's comfort in the afterlife. Elaborate tombs served to speed decay, separating the corpse from the drying sands; the process of mummification was perfected during the New Kingdom era. There were several different levels of preservation that were performed before the body was wrapped in white linen bandages. The least effective and least expensive was a simple washing and cleansing of the corpse. The next level involved filling the body's orifices with a caustic, corrosive fluid, then plugging up the holes. Several days later, the plugs were removed and the putrid fluid drained. The super-deluxe preservation package required that an incision be made in the abdomen. All of the viscera save the heart and kidneys were removed (including the brain, either through the base of the skull or through a nostril) and preserved in canopic jars. These jars were amphora-shaped containers of alabaster with engravings on the sides and lids. The body was then packed with *natrun*, a natural salt found in Wadi Natrun. After 40 days, the salt was removed and ointments, spices, and oils such as frankincense (often imported from the Dhofar region of Oman) were applied in combination with intricate patterns of wrappings. The essences reacted over time to form a black, pitch-like substance that gives mummies their names (*moumiya* is Arabic for pitch).

Mycerinus lavished his energy on his daughter, attempting to become her lover. After the grief-filled girl hanged herself, she was buried in a golden cow which was brought into the light of the sun once a year, in accordance with her dying wish. At the pyramid's northeast corner are the quarried remains of the **Mortuary Temple of Mycerinus.** Farther away, the ruins of the unexcavated Valley Temple of Mycerinus lie swathed by a blanket of sand.

SPHINX. Hewn almost entirely from rock, the Sphinx's poised figure is 80m long and 22m tall. His enigmatic smile is at once friendly and unnerving, leading Egyptians to call him **Abul-Hul** (Father of Terror). Many centuries have aged the Sphinx, and the Ottomans didn't help things when they used him for target practice. A recent renovation project has just been completed, and the Sphinx is ready to enter its fifth millennium in fine form.

Opinion is divided over the Sphinx's identity. Some believe that the face is a portrait of Chephren, whose pyramid lies directly behind it, while others maintain that the features represent the local deity Horan. Those who subscribe to the former theory believe that the Sphinx emerged from a sturdy knoll facing Chephren's complex. Failing to flatten it, architects transformed the knoll into the figure that lounges on the sand today. Another tale tells how Chephren, living a life of luxury, fell asleep by the sphinx's foot while hunting. The Sphinx spoke out and said, "I shall make thee Pharaoh if thou wilt dig me out of the sand." This theory does not sit well with archaeologists, who suggest that the body and head of the sphinx were carved at different times; they are not proportional to one another and have completely different erosion styles. Egyptian folklore asserts that Abul-Hul is a half-human, half-tiger creature who protects the tombs from thieves. Whichever explanation you accept, the majesty of the Sphinx remains indisputable.

At the foot of the Sphinx, just around the corner to the south, sits the I-shaped **Valley Temple of Chephren,** discovered in 1853. Sixteen great pillars, each 15m high, support the roof of this edifice, leading up to the ever-smiling pyramid guard.

SOLAR BOAT MUSEUM. This zucchini-shaped work of postmodern architecture is located against the south side of the Pyramid of Cheops. It holds the remarkably well-preserved Solar Boat of Cheops, one of the oldest boats in existence. It was used to transport Cheops' body and then buried so his soul could use it in the afterlife. Outside, his mortuary temple is little more than a few column segments and foundations. *(Open daily 9am-5pm. Admission E£20, students E£10; camera privileges E£10, video E£100.)*

NEAR GIZA

KARDASSA

On the road from Cairo to Giza, a turn-off to the right at the second canal before the Pyramids leads to the village of **Kardassa,** where the Western Desert and the camel road to Libya commence. The village has acquired popularity among tourists owing to the variety of its local crafts (many of what appear in Cairo's tourist shops). The main products of the village are wool and cotton scarves, *galabiyyas* (E£30-70), rugs (1x1.5m rug E£50), and Bedouin weavings. The shops are in a sand lot across the canal from the village, usually in the back of the store or in the side alleys off the main drag. Also for sale among the scarves and rugs is a disturbing number of professionally stuffed animals, including gazelles, jackals, and rabbits. Despite the efforts of the Egyptian Environmental Affairs Agency, this illegal but highly profitable trade continues. Tourism is beginning to rob Kardassa of its charm, though the prices are still lower and the quality of the merchandise higher than at Khan el-Khalili. **Taxis** from Giza Sq. to Kardassa cost E£10-15. **Minibuses** run to Kardassa from Giza Sq. (40pt) as well as from the turn-off from Pyramids Rd., known as the *Mash'al* stop (35pt).

HARANIA

More interesting is the artists' school at **Harania,** 200m to the right of Maroutiya Canal Rd. (about 3km south of Pyramids Rd., next to the Salome Campground). Here, young children are encouraged to develop their creativity by weaving brilliantly colored carpets and making pottery. Since its inception in 1942, two generations of tapestry-weavers have studied at the school; many are still in practice as adults. Some of the most notable works are showcased in the museum at Harania and in the book *Threads of Life—A Journey Through Creativity*, available at the center. The results of this creative process are stunning but expensive (E£200-2000, Visa and MC accepted). Harania is best visited with the ■**Salah Muhammad tour** (see p. 101). Walking is the only non-taxi alternative to a guided tour (open in summer 9am-6pm; in winter 9am-5pm).

BIRQASH CAMEL MARKET

Minibuses (45min., E£2 round-trip; ask for Souq el-Gamal) run to the Birqash Camel Market from the site of a closed camel market in Imbaba (near Imbaba Airport), accessible by minibus or taxi (E£5) from downtown. The Sun Hotel (tel. 578-1786) also offers an E£20 tour (not including admission) that leaves at 6am and returns at noon; contact them 2 days in advance to reserve a spot. Admission E£5; camera privileges E£5, video E£5.

If you came to Egypt expecting camels but feel like an ass because you've seen nothing but donkeys, the Birqash Camel Market is for you. The camel market is an easy half-day excursion from Cairo, convening every Friday from 6am to noon in the small farming town of Birqash. Bypass the butcher shops with camel appendages on display in the windows (camel meat is supposedly low in cholesterol) and head to the market in the heart of town. Hundreds of camels stand around smiling enigmatically while Sudanese traders haggle over prices and whack the camels on the rear with canes to demonstrate their vigor. If you think you might need it, you can buy one of the canes to take home (E£15). If you'd rather have a larger, more troublesome souvenir that is prone to biting and spitting, camels run from E£1000-3000, with a strong female being the most valuable. The traders are happy to answer any questions you might have about their wares. One hump or two?

SAQQARA سقارة

Named after Sokar, a Memphite god of death, Saqqara is actually quite enlivening. Saqqara began as a royal necropolis in the early years of the Old Kingdom (3rd dynasty, around 2600 BCE), when nearby Memphis was the capital of Egypt. It was used continuously as a burial site for the next 3000 years, meaning that the remarkable array of tombs and pyramids in the area fully traces the evolution of funereal construction in ancient Egypt. Because it is largely free of Giza's hordes of tourists (and the hustlers who love them), Saqqara offers a wonderful opportunity to see these monuments in the stillness and stark beauty of the desert.

▨ ORIENTATION AND PRACTICAL INFORMATION

Saqqara consists of five archaeological finds scattered over a very large area, with nothing but sand dunes in between. The primary destination for most visitors is **North Saqqara** (p. 107), site of the funerary complex and the famous Step Pyramid of Djoser I. The three pyramids of **Abu Sir** (p. 110) are 6km north of North Saqqara, only a few kilometers from the tiny village of the same name. The two pyramids and the funerary complex of **South Saqqara** (p. 110) are about 4km south of North Saqqara. The historically significant but scanty ruins of **Memphis** (p. 110) are even farther from Saqqara's necropolis, located next to the Nile just south of the village of Mit-Rahine. The pyramids of **Dashur** (p. 111) form the southern tip of the row.

The easiest way to see Saqqara and its environs is to take ▨**Salah Muhammad's tour** (p. 101). If you choose to go on your own, you'll want to begin at the ruins of **North Saqqara**. Public transportation to and around the area is sparse because a large swath of farms separates the ruins from Cairo. One option is to take a **taxi** from Cairo (E£20) and then try to find and share taxis at each site. However, some sites may have periods where taxis don't drive by for three or four hours. An easier and much more exciting (if expensive) option is to take a taxi to North Saqqara and then hire a **steed** at North Saqqara. This is your chance to ride through the desert on a horse with no name. A horse or camel costs about E£15 per hour, and you will probably have to pay for a guide (and his ride) as well. Another option is to take a **minibus** from Cairo to North Saqqara, but this is only for those confident in their ability to untangle the complicated minibus schedule (with route information in Arabic). Begin by taking a minibus from Giza Sq. to the village of Abu Sir (50pt). From there, the killer 4km walk to the entrance takes between 30 minutes and one hour, depending on your sand-speed. Walk south (to the left as you arrive) along the canal just before the village and follow the dirt road until you reach the paved road. Turn right and it's 200m to the site entrance. You can also hire a **pickup truck** at the canal in Abu Sir (about 50pt per person) to take a group to the site.

To get to the pyramids at **Abu Sir** from North Saqqara, either ride on a steer or brave the burning sands on foot (at least 1hr.). **South Saqqara** is at least 30 minutes away by foot; taxis cost E£7. To get to **Memphis** on your own, take the **Metro** to Helwan (60pt) and then take a ferry to the village of El-Badrasheen; Memphis is a 30-minute walk from there. Once in the village, look for the **microbus** that occasionally passes by on its way to the ruins; hop on for 25pt. **Minibuses** also run from Memphis to El-Badrasheen (25pt) and from El-Badrasheen to Giza (50pt). From Giza, it is possible to take either a minibus or public bus #987 (٩٨٧) back to Tahrir Sq. or the Ramses Metro station. Have someone write your destination in Arabic to help locate your minibus. (Holding out a pen and piece of paper, ask: *Lo samaht, mumkin taktub* [destination] *hoona min fadlak?*)

However you get there, wear **sneakers or boots** (not sandals) as the sand is quite hot. Bring lots of **water** and a hat, and try to get an early start, since the afternoon sun can be cruel. A **flashlight** also allows you to avoid paying the *baksheesh* the

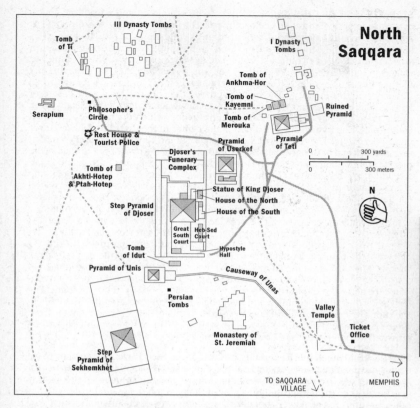

guards will request to illuminate the poorly lit tombs. Tombs often close for preservational purposes in the summer, when there is less tourism.

👁 SIGHTS

All sights are officially open in summer 8am-5pm; in winter 8am-4pm. Guards lock up and go home a couple of hours early in low season and stay a bit longer in winter. Admission E£20, students E£10; camera privileges E£10, video E£25. The ticket is good for all Saqqara sites; Abu Sir does not require a ticket. Some tombs also require an E£5-10 entrance fee or bakhsheesh, depending who is on duty.

NORTH SAQQARA

Saqqara's most famous site is the **Step Pyramid of Djoser I** (a.k.a. Djoser-Netcherikhe), the oldest monumental tomb in the world (begun in 2630 BCE) and the inspiration for the pyramids and other architectural wonders located throughout Egypt. The brilliant architect Imhotep initially designed the monument as a stone *mastaba*, a low, rectangular building covering a burial shaft dug into the earth. Not satisfied with a simple rectangle, he modified the original structure, greatly expanding it and stacking several layers on top of the original base. Time and weather have taken their toll on history's first monument to post-mortem egotism, but the French archaeologist Jean-Philippe Lauer has made the reconstruction of the Step Pyramid his lifetime project.

STEP PYRAMID OF DJOSER I. Enter the Step Pyramid complex from the south-eastern side of the limestone enclosure wall. The paneled barrier was designed to resemble the mud-brick work that graced the fortifications surrounding the cities and palaces of the period. Two fixed stone panels, carved to resemble a massive wooden doorway, open onto a 40-columned entrance colonnade. The columns are ridged to look like stylized bundle of papyrus stems, and they are probably the world's first stone columns (unlike the chumps before him who used mud brick, Imhotep built for eternity). The niches between the columns once held statues of Djoser. This columned corridor culminates in the **Hypostyle Hall,** a fledgling version of the great hallways found at Karnak and Abydos, which opens on to the **Great South Court.** The two weathered altars in the center of the Court symbolize Lower and Upper Egypt. The remains of a *mastaba* are at the base of the Step Pyramid at the northern end of the site; scholars are still debating the purpose of this superfluous *mastaba*. Some think that the tomb is the original *mastaba* onto which Imhotep added the other layers of the Step Pyramid. Others claim it is the symbolic representation of a second tomb. Earlier pharaohs had a second tomb constructed (in the south at Abydos) in addition to their tomb at Saqqara; Djoser may have been alluding to this custom by placing a small tomb at the south of his complex.

In the center of the pyramid's south face is an entrance to the tomb's locked interior. To the east, past the colonnade, the **Heb-Sed Court** runs the length of one side of the courtyard. During the Archaic Period (the time prior to the 1st dynasty), the pharaoh would have to prove that he was fit to rule by performing various athletic feats at the annual Sed Festival. If he failed, he would be killed and a stronger replacement crowned. Later pharaohs turned the Sed into a rejuvenation ceremony and did away with the ritual regicide portion of the program. The Heb-Sed Court in the complex and the panels inside the pyramid that depict Djoser running a ceremonial race were meant to ensure his eternal rejuvenation. There is a small dais with two sets of stairs: Djoser would climb twice to be crowned with the crowns of Lower and Upper Egypt.

STATUE OF KING DJOSER. Directly in front of the Step Pyramid's northern face stands the most haunting spectacle at Saqqara, a statue of King Djoser I. The pharaoh stares out from a slanted stone hut (known as a **sardab**) pierced by two tiny apertures. The *sardab* allowed the spirit of the pharaoh to communicate with the outside world. The striking figure here is a plaster copy of the original (which now glares at visitors in the Egyptian Museum in Cairo).

TOMBS OF THE NOBLES

The nobles constructed tombs around the pyramids, mindful of their prestige even in death. All are relatively close, and those open to the public have signs in English indicating their owners (who are always depicted in wall paintings as being bigger than their servants and companion animals). All tombs have several features in common. Most of the them have narrow insets in the wall (called **"spirit doors"**) through which the ghosts of the deceased can pass (like the *DeSimonean* dreamcatchers of Native American lore), as well as paintings of food and entertainment for the dead to partake of in the afterlife.

TOMB OF AKHTI-HOTEP AND PTAH HOTEP. This unique tomb was built by two brothers often depicted together; their fraternal affection is conveyed across the centuries. There are many superb reliefs here, including a cow giving birth. The color in some sections of the tomb shows that men, who were often in the sun, had much darker skin than women.

TOMB OF TI. The Tomb of Ti, 300m north of the Serapium (see **Western North Saqqara** below), was excavated in 1865 and has since been one of the primary sources of knowledge about daily and ceremonial life during the 5th dynasty (25th century BCE). Serving under three pharaohs, Ti had many titles: Overseer of the Pyramids and Sun Temples at Abu Sir, Superintendent of Works, Scribe of the Court, Royal Counselor, Editrix, Royal Fluffer, Royal Tea Brewer, and even Lord of Secrets. Some scholars also believe he was a practitioner of a martial arts discipline similar to that of the Japanese ninjas. He was such a high-ranking noble that he was allowed to marry a princess, Nefer-Hotep. Tomb paintings show his children wearing braided hairpieces, signs they are royal contenders for the throne. The tomb is scheduled to open in 2000 after preservation efforts are completed.

TOMB OF ANKHMA-HOR. Just east of the Tomb of Ti is the Tomb of Ankhma-Hor, which contains several representations of medical operations (including toe surgery and a circumcision). One Egyptologist has asserted that the 6th-dynasty tendency to depict funerary scenes indicates a growing fixation with the afterlife as the Old Kingdom went into its final decline.

OTHER TOMBS. The **Tomb of Mererouka** has separate sections for Mererouka, his son, and his wife. There are fine carvings of desert hunts, jewelry making, and officials with big sticks collecting taxes. Despite its plebeian name, the **Tomb of the Butchers** is definitely the tomb of a noble. "Butcher" was the honorary title given to nobles who looked after the pharaoh's food. Appropriately enough, this tomb has well-preserved, colored reliefs showing the slaughtering and cutting up of cattle. The nearby **Tomb of Kayemni** contains reliefs depicting daily farming life along the Nile. In one hall, incredibly limber "acrobats" entertain Kayemni.

HOUSES OF THE SOUTH AND NORTH. The more substantial **House of the South** stands next door to the Step Pyramid, on its eastern side. The inside walls are inscribed with ancient graffiti left by a visitor during the reign of Ramses II. The messages, expressing admiration for King Djoser, were hastily scrawled onto the walls in a late cursive style of hieroglyphics known as hieratic. The lotus columns here represent Upper Egypt—hence the name House of the South. The **House of the North** is symbolized by the papyrus columns, the symbol of Lower Egypt. Some scholars believe that this emphasis on North and South throughout the site at Saqqara reflects the era's desire to unify Egypt geographically and spiritually.

PERSIAN TOMBS. To the south, a humble shack covers the shaft leading to three of Egypt's deepest burial chambers, the **Persian Tombs** of Psamtik, Zenhebu, and Peleese (of the 16th dynasty). A dizzying spiral staircase drills 25m into the ground, ending in three vaulted burial chambers linked by narrow passageways. Colorful chambers make the exercise worthwhile. According to the ancient inscriptions, Zenhebu was a famous admiral and Psamtik a high-ranking doctor of the pharaoh's court. At press time, it was closed for renovations.

OTHER PYRAMIDS. There are several other pyramids in the area. The only one open to the public is the small **Pyramid of Teti.** Scramble down a ramp into the underground chambers where you are greeted with several protruding rocks—all that remains of an attempt to deter grave robbers. There is a massive black sarcophagus inside, and the ceiling is decorated with stars indicating the heavens.

On the southwest corner of Djoser's complex, up the steps to the right of the pit and over the enclosure wall, looms the massive **Pyramid of Unis.** Unis was the last pharaoh of the 5th dynasty. Inside are wall carvings known as the **Pyramid Texts,** discovered in 1881 by Thomas Cook. These writings constitute the earliest known example of decorative hieroglyph writing on the walls of a pharaonic tomb chamber. At press time, the Pyramid of Unis was closed for repairs.

WESTERN NORTH SAQQARA

SERAPIUM. The Serapium (discovered in 1854) is located several hundred meters west of the Rest House at the terminus of the main road. The complex is the legacy of a bull-worshiping cult that thrived during the New Kingdom. Believers traditionally associated the Apis bulls (the sacred oxen of Ptah) with Osiris and the afterlife, but during the Roman occupation, the Apis bull cult combined with that of the Greek god Zeus (who often took the form of a bull, especially when he was fooling around with mortal women). The combined Zeus-Apis cult was especially strong around Alexandria. Work on the main portion of the underground complex was begun in the 7th century BCE by Psamtik I and continued through the Ptolemaic era, though much older tombs adjoin this central set of chambers. In the oldest portion of the Serapium, two large, gold-plated sarcophagi and several canopic jars containing human heads were found, as well as the undisturbed footprints of the priests who had put the sacred animals to rest more than 3000 years earlier. Recessed tombs flank the main corridor on both sides, each containing a sarcophagus. It's difficult to imagine these mammoth coffins being transported to the confines of the cave; their average weight is 65 tons. In the final tomb stands the largest sarcophagus, hewn from a single piece of black granite.

TOMBS OF THE APIS BULLS. The mausoleum in the Serapium (a series of eerie underground tunnels with tiny lanterns) houses the **Tombs of the Apis Bulls,** where 25 sacred oxen representing Ptah's pets were embalmed and placed in enormous sarcophagi of solid granite. Only one of the bulls remains (the rest have been stolen); it now stands in Cairo's Agricultural Museum. At the end of the mausoleum tunnel you'll reach metal steps which allow you to climb into one of the gigantic coffins.

OTHER SIGHTS. West of the Tomb of Akhti-Hotep and Ptah Hotep (see **Tombs of the Nobles** above) is a shady and expensive **Rest House** with a bathroom and a small concession stand. Farther along the highway, where the road turns sharply to the west, are several weathered **Greek statues,** known as the **Philosophers' Circle.** These statues are said to represent Homer (at the center), Pindar (to his left), Plato (to his right), and two unknowns (possibly Pythagoras and Heraclides).

SOUTH SAQQARA

South Saqqara's most interesting funerary monument is the unusual **Tomb of Shepseskaf** (popularly known as *Mastabat Far'aun*). The tomb is an enormous stone structure shaped like a sarcophagus and capped with a rounded lid. Although Shepseskaf reigned for only three years (he was the sixth king of the 4th dynasty and son of Mycerinus, whose pyramid stands at Giza), his stint on the throne was long enough to qualify him for a grand tomb—sort of. *Mastabat Far'aun* is neither a true *mastaba* nor a pyramid; scholars see it as a transitional experiment. A guard will admit you (*bakhsheesh* of E£1 should suffice).

NEAR SAQQARA

ABU SIR أبو صير

The three pyramids of Abu Sir are 6km north of Saqqara and 2.5km from the village of Abu Sir. No tour buses make it here (the site can only be reached by foot or hoof). The most imposing of the three main pyramids at Abu Sir is the **Pyramid of Neferirkare,** which towers 68m above the desert and remains one of the best-preserved monuments in the Saqqara area. It once had a stone casing like its neighbors at Giza, but has suffered a similar loss of face, exposing its exterior, which bears a remarkable resemblance to a step pyramid. The **Pyramid of Niuserre** is the youngest and most dilapidated of the pyramids in the area, and the **Pyramid of Sahure** to the north completes the trio.

If you are traveling by animal between Abu Sir and Giza, have your guide stop off along the way at the 5th-dynasty **Sun Temple of Abu Sarab.** The temple is to the north, and about 1.5km north of the Pyramid of Sahure. Located on the fringe of cultivated fields, the temple was built by King Niuserre in honor of the sun god Ra. It features an impressive altar constructed from five massive blocks of alabaster. A horse or camel ride from Djoser's Step Pyramid to the Sun Temple costs E£20, but if business is slow it may be possible to bargain to a cheaper price (as low as E£5).

MEMPHIS ممفيس

Memphis is not worth the detour today, though it might have been in 3000 BCE. The great pyramid-building pharaohs (such as Cheops, Khufu, Ælvis, and Khefren) lived and ruled at Memphis, a city once populated by over half a million people that was founded over five millennia ago by the legendary Menes. While the pyramids they built have endured, the pharaohs' city has faded away, leaving only palms, wandering goats, and the odd ruin (many of which are closed to the public). There is a small **museum** that has a garden with well-worn statues and a large alabaster sphinx that probably stood at the south entrance of the Temple of Ptah. The most impressive statue is a 14m tall **colossus of Ramses II**, displayed parallel to the ground with cartouches engraved on its shoulders and waist. (Admission E£14, students E£7; camera privileges E£5, video E£25.) If you choose to go, you might have to take a taxi to Memphis from Saqqara or Abu Sir. Hitchhiking from here is dangerous and not recommended.

DASHUR

The four unique pyramids at Dashur are well worth seeing. Close to the road is the large **Pyramid of Senefru.** Senefru was the father of Khufu (whose pyramid is one of the three at Giza), and the proportions of this pyramid reveal how Khufu got such an inflated post-mortem ego. You can scramble down an odd ladder/stair hybrid into the chambers of the pyramid. A quick drive or moderate walk away from the Pyramid of Senefru is the famous **Bent Pyramid** of Senefru. This pyramid is unusual because it changes the angle of its sides halfway to the top. Much of it is still cased in limestone, showing what pyramids would have looked like when they were first built. A few yards behind the Bent Pyramid is the small cone of a **decaying pyramid.** Climb up for a nice view of the desert, or use one of the flat stones as a picnic table.

FAYYUM الفيوم

The Fayyum Oasis is a vast agrarian settlement slightly over 100km from Cairo. The city's honking cars and crowded streets give little hint that open meadows lie only a few hundred meters away. The 1.8 million residents of the oasis live in 157 small villages that dot a sandy landscape swathed with chrysanthemum and sunflower fields. Lake Qar'un to the north is a popular beach resort, and the local government is cultivating the rest of the area for tourism.

Fayyum was first developed through canal-building and irrigation by the rulers of ancient Egypt's 12th dynasty (20th-19th centuries BCE). The Ptolemies made the area into a rich province with its capital at Crocodopolis (near the site of modern Fayyum), the headquarters of a cult that worshiped Sebak and other reptilian deities. Roman conquerors used Crocodopolis as a vacation resort and as one of the primary granaries of the empire. An early center of Coptic Christianity, the oasis also sheltered a large population of exiled Jews in the 3rd century CE. Muslims believe the extensive canals to be the work of the biblical Joseph during his stay in Egypt; Bahr Yusef is named accordingly. Fayyum also boasts several out-of-the-way pharaonic ruins that are still under excavation and rarely touristed, making it a thoroughly enjoyable and more convenient alternative to the oases in the Western Desert.

★ ORIENTATION

Fayyum is a roughly triangular area, stretching about 90km east to west. The eastern edge is bordered by the Nile. The saltwater **Lake Qar'un** separates the northwest edge of Fayyum from the sandy plateau of the Western Desert. The city of Fayyum is almost in the center and serves as the area's transportation hub. The main hotels and offices are located around the waterwheels in the middle of town. The city runs along the **Bahr Yusef Canal**, which flows west from the Nile. At the center of town, **Bahr Sinnuris** separates from Bahr Yusef at a right angle and flows north toward the farmlands. **El-Gomhoriyya** and **El-Huriyya Streets** run along the north and south banks of Bahr Yusef, respectively. There are four groaning waterwheels next to the tourist office. The inverted pyramid dominating the eastern end of Bahr Yusef is Fayyum's newest landmark, the **Culture Palace,** housing a theater, cinema, and public library.

⚡ PRACTICAL INFORMATION

Buses and Service: The **main bus and service station** is 1km from the tourist office, tucked surreptitiously under a bridge. From the tourist office, cross the train tracks and take a right. Continue along this road toward Cairo for 500m and take a right before the large building on your right. Take another right after 1 block and you'll find the station under the bridge. **Buses** to **Cairo** stop at Gima Sq. and Ramses Station (2hr., depart every 30min. roughly 6am-6pm, E£3.75). **Service** leave from here to Giza Sq. or Ramses Station in **Cairo** until late at night (E£5-6; faster but more dangerous). Another **bus and service station** serves **Beni Suef** and points south. Walk to the 3rd bridge over the canal west of the tourist office, turn left, and walk 1km. Don't be misled by the local bus depot past the main crossroads—the station is 200m farther on the right.

Local Transportation: Arabic numbered *service* travel around town on different routes (25pt). *Service* to towns outside Fayyum city can be caught from these stations (50pt-E£1). You can also hire a **hantour** (horse carriage) for about E£1-5 anywhere in town.

Tourist Office: Tel. 34 23 13, on El-Gomhoriyya St., next door to Cafeteria El-Medina, 50m east of the juncture of the 2 canals. No English spoken. Open daily 9am-4pm.

Tourist Police: (tel. 34 72 98), posted around the tourist office 24hr. Minimal English.

Currency Exchange: Misr Bank (tel. 35 01 62), on the same side of the canal as the Palace Hotel, just south of the tourist office on El-Gomhoriyya St. No traveler's check exchange. Also has an **ATM** (Visa, MC, Cirrus) outside. Open Su-Th 8:30am-2pm.

Hospital: Tel. 34 22 49 or 33 35 96, on Hospital St. Pink building off Msella St. Cash only.

Post Office: 100m south of the first bridge east of the tourist office, on the opposite side of the river. **EMS** and **Poste Restante** available. Open Sa-Th 8am-2pm.

Telephones: In same building as post office. **International calls** available. Open 24hr.

Telephone Code: 084.

🏠🍴 ACCOMMODATIONS AND FOOD

Fayyum is an easy daytrip from Cairo, and perhaps a smart move given that Fayyum city has few cheap beds. The 40km long Lake Qar'un and heavenly Wadi er-Ruwayan are much more peaceful roosting options (for more details, see **Near Fayyum,** p. 113). The **Maka Hotel** (tel. 35 12 23) is the best bet within the city. Located in the alley behind the Palace Hotel, the Maka provides simple rooms with fans for E£10 (E£12 with balcony). Under the same management as the Maka is the **Palace Hotel** (tel. 35 12 22), on El-Huriyya St. one block west of the tourist office under a blue English sign. Clean, breezy rooms overlook the canal and are filled with folded-down sheets, towels, and soap. Owner Ashraf Arafa speaks flawless English and is much more helpful than the tourist office (singles E£20, with shower E£30, with A/C E£45; doubles E£35/45/60). A small breakfast is included; lunch and dinner are also served (E£13-15). The **Fayyum Youth Hostel** (tel. 35 00 05) is at El-Hadaka, Block 7, Flat #7; ask for *bayoot esh-shabab*. It's a bit distant: with your back to the Cairo bus stop, turn left and walk 250m to the intersection with a five-story brick building. Take a sharp left, then another left at the green "FYH" sign 50m ahead. The hostel is the second building on the right. Inside are slightly dingy rooms and a common kitchen (dorm beds E£8, students E£7; breakfast included).

Waltz over to the **Governorate Club,** on Governorate St. Ask your *hantour* driver for *Nadi el-Muhafzah* or take *service* taxi #3 (٣), 6 (٦), or 9 (٩) from the Youth Hostel (#9 from the center of town). The "exclusive" club (waiters in red jackets and bowties) makes up for its E£3 entrance fee with large, cheap meals (kebab E£9, full meals E£10; open until 1am). **City Cafe** (tel. 34 56 52), in the town center, has a pleasant view of the waterwheels, outdoor seating, and live Arabic music. Vegetarians can munch, munch, munch on the veggies, rice, and cucumber salad (around E£7) at the **Palace Hotel** (tel. 35 12 22) until they're green in the face.

SIGHTS

Pleasant Fayyum city is filled with Egyptians living ordinary lives, but the real beauty is outside the city. Visitors who weren't ossified by the Islamic architecture in Cairo should visit the **Mosque of Qaytbay,** along the canal about 1km west of the town center, at the very end of El-Huriyya St. The mosque is named for the Mamluke Sultan El-Ashraf Seif ed-Din Qaytbay, who ruled Egypt from 1468 to 1496. It was built beside a river that once flowed there, allowing worshipers to wash before prayers. The ivory on the *mihrab* was brought all the way from Somalia.

For a quick introduction to the rural life of Fayyum, head north out of town along Bahr Sinnuris. After 2km of boundless green fields, you'll reach the first of seven ancient **waterwheels,** still used in the irrigation system. Unlike Western versions, these great wooden tires are not used to power pumps but are themselves pumps, ingeniously using the flow of the stream to lift the water to a higher level.

NEAR FAYYUM

To reach any point north of Fayyum, walk north from the information stand to the railroad tracks running parallel to Bahr Yusef Canal. Turn left and walk to the 4th crossing; you'll find a "taxi" stand 300m down on the left. Trucks shuttle between Fayyum, 'Ain Sileen (50pt), and Lake Qar'un (E£1). You'll need to change trucks at the village of Sanhur to reach the lake; the total price should be about the same.

WADI ER-RUWAYAN

A wonderful lake and three waterfalls adorn this area, a 45-minute drive from Lake Qar'un, along what becomes a pure desert passage. Sand dunes and cool cobalt waters ripple side by side, separated by no more than a few meters of greenery. The three waterfalls plunge 3m over the mossy rocks into a clear lake. Taxis from Fayyum or Lake Qar'un are available from 7am to 4pm. The earlier you set off, the better your bargaining position will be; pay no more than E£40-60 per carload. Hitching is reportedly easy in winter, but is not recommended by *Let's Go.* Bring plenty of sunblock and insect repellent. (Admission to the wadi E£5, cars E£5 extra.) If you find it hard to tear yourself away, lounge amid camel herds at the aptly named **Paradise Safari Camp,** owned by English-speaking Muhammad Marzuk (E£20 per person). The camp, on the lake's shore, is surrounded by golden dunes ripe for exploration. Each large tent has two crisp-sheeted beds and a nightstand with a candle (there is no electricity here except the generator, used solely for the refrigerator in the kitchen). A **snack stand** on the beach sells overpriced refreshments, but the Safari Camp's beautiful outdoor **restaurant** has meals for E£25.

LAKE QAR'UN

Fifteen kilometers north of Fayyum past some sunflower patches is the saltwater **Lake Qar'un** (locally known as *El-Birka*), lined on its southern shore with expensive hotels and daytime picnic areas. The beaches have a tropical feel, with toasty sand, warm blue-green water, and palm frond *palapas* offering shade. They are within daytripping range of Cairo and Fayyum. The closest thing to lakeside budget accommodations is the air-conditioned **Waha Hotel** (doubles E£75; breakfast included). In winter, the hotel rents jet skis, sailboards, and other fun toys.

A bit past the west of Lake Qar'un sits a deceptively simple looking Ptolemaic temple known as **Qasr Qar'un.** This is one place where you probably don't want to shoo away the guard offering to guide you around: a warren of secret passageways and bat-filled rooms below the main sanctuary let you live out your favorite Indiana Jones fantasy. Climb up the stairs to the roof for a beautiful view of the surrounding area. Service taxis are available from Lake Qar'un for 50pt. (Open daily 8am-6pm. Admission E£16, students E£8.)

KARANIS

The mud brick houses of the Greco-Roman settlement of Karanis, 30km north of Fayyum along the road to Cairo, have not fared well over time. The town was built by the Greeks in the 3rd century and occupied by the Romans for almost 800 years. Its two stone temples are in better shape, offering an interesting contrast of architectural styles (one temple was built by Greeks, the other by Romans).

The infrequently visited **Museum of Kom Oshim** holds a surprisingly wide collection of statues and *stellae* found both on-site at Karanis and around Saqqara and Giza. Comb through the exhibit of Greco-Roman terra cotta figurines, which display a survey of ancient hairstyles. The second floor of the museum, devoted to Islamic and Coptic art, houses beautifully painted wood icons. Catch a service taxi or bus heading north from Fayyum and ask to be dropped off at Mathef (pronounced mutt-Huff) Kom Oshim. (Open daily in summer 8am-6pm; in winter 8am-5pm. Admission E£16, students E£8.)

ʻAIN SILEEN SPRINGS

ʻAin Sileen Springs, 18km northwest of Fayyum, is the most easily reached but least rewarding of the area's attractions. The road to the springs winds through fields bristling with corn, palms, fruit, and vegetables, split into perfect sections by canals. The titanium-rich water is supposedly good for hypertension; drink at your own risk. The most convenient way to get there is to take a **service** or **bus** (35-50pt) from the station serving Sanhur west of town along the railroad tracks. *Service* taxis #7 (٧) or 8 (٨) go to the station from the center of Fayyum city, and #9 (٩) goes there from the youth hostel. A **tourist office** is 50m from the springs road, along with several small stands selling the sweetest **mangos** imaginable. **Restaurants** with gorgeous views of the canals serve kebab (E£12), pigeon (E£7), and salads (E£1). The springs flow into a small swimming pool packed with Egyptian children. Foreigners bathing here will create a stir; foreign women will cause widespread pandemonium. A visit to the **Exhibition of Productive Families,** which displays local carpet and clothing articles, will produce less controversy.

NILE DELTA

TANTA

For most of the year, the residents of Egypt's fifth largest city live peaceful, tourist-free lives. But for one week in October, Tanta undergoes a metamorphosis from a provincial city into a tumultuous cacophony of some three million pilgrims from Egypt and the Arab world, who converge on the city for the **Mawlid of Saʻid Ahmed el-Bedawi.** *Mawlids* are festivals celebrating events from the Qurʼan or the birthdays of Coptic and Muslim saints, and this specific *mawlid* honors the founder of Egypt's largest Sufi brotherhood (as well as the cotton harvest that precedes the festival). The festival is truly a circus, with Bedawi's red-turbaned devotees mingling with lions and tigers and near-unbearable hordes of vendors.

🔃 ORIENTATION AND PRACTICAL INFORMATION. The main street in Tanta is **El-Bahr Street,** heading from one end of town to the other. Most banks and official buildings are located along it, between the hospital and a collection of fast food joints about 2km later. Past the fast food is **Ahmed Maher Street,** which leads to the train and bus station and the **Mosque of Bedawi** (1km).

Most **banks** don't cash traveler's checks but will exchange cash, and are open from 9am-2pm. As elsewhere in Egypt, call 125 for the **tourist police** and 122 for other **emergency** services. The **hospital** (tel. 350 371/372/373/374) is located at the other end of El-Bahr St. from the fast-food restaurants, and a majority of its staff speaks English. **Trains** leave from the impressive station (though the clock on top is slow) to: **Alexandria** (9, 11am, noon, 1, 3:20, 4, 5, 6, 9pm; 2nd class E£8); **Ismaʻilia** and **Port Said** (noon, 6:30pm, midnight; E£2); and **Cairo** (6, 8, 9:45, 10:40am, 12:20,

2:10, 5, 6:30, 9, 9:30pm; E£6). **Middle Delta** runs **buses** to **Cairo** (every 30min. 5am-11pm, E£5). The **service** depot is located near the bus and train stations and has many cars available. **Minibuses** serve much of Tanta (25pt), and the city's **taxis** have a fixed rate of E£1 for all destinations.

▓▐▊ ACCOMMODATIONS AND FOOD. There are no budget accommodations in Tanta, but with so many trains and buses going to Cairo and Alexandria, there's no need to stay in the city overnight. If you get stranded, the cheapest place to bed down is the three-star **'Arafa Hotel,** the big pink building near the train station (singles E£120; doubles E£170; triples E£295; Visa, MC accepted). Be forewarned, though, that during the *mawlid*, even Sheikh Badawi himself probably couldn't get a room. Along with the usual street stands, the popular favorite **La Casa,** on El-Mu'tasem St. (turn down the street at the CIB Bank), serves Italian food (E£7-15) in a Spanish interior (open 10am-1am).

▨ SIGHTS AND ENTERTAINMENT. The main attraction in Tanta (and the center of the *mawlid* festivities) is the **Mosque of Bedawi.** Built during the Ottoman period, it has three domes and an impressively large porch. The ceiling is decorated with floral designs, while the sheikh's tomb glows eerily with green neon as devotees pay their respects. The **Sabil of Kasir,** 800m down Galna St., is a small Ottoman water dispensary. Although it is architecturally unremarkable, it has a nice garden with Islamic carvings (open 9am-4pm; admission 50pt). Signs downtown point to the **Tanta Museum.** It houses an unremarkable collection of ceramics (many broken), metalwork, and coins. (Open 9:30am-4:30pm, closed F during prayer time. Admission E£10, students E£5; camera privileges E£5.) A friendly member of the museum staff can give advice about visiting the difficult to reach and thoroughly unremarkable pharaonic sites of Buto and Xois.

NEAR TANTA

QANATIR

Bus #953 (٩٥٣) from Cairo's 'Abd el-Munem Riad Station in front of the Ramses Hilton runs frequently to Qanatir (45min., 40pt). On F and Su, a passenger ferry runs along the Nile from Cairo to Qanatir. The dock is located on the corniche, behind the Ramses Hilton and in front of the Television Building (1½hr., 9am-4:30pm, E£2). Feluccas may be hired from the same area (3hr.). Qanatir can be visited as a daytrip or as the first stop on a journey north.

This town marks the official beginning of the Delta, where the Nile splits into the eastern (Dumyat) and western (Rashid, or Rosetta) branches 16km north of Cairo. Qanatir is also the site of the **Nile barrages,** bridges that regulate the flow of water into the Delta. Turrets and arches decorate the 19th-century structures, which were built when cotton production boomed here. The point of land where the Nile splits is home to parks, food stalls, and an arcade. Egyptian youths descend on Qanatir in a noisy cloud of Arab pop music on weekends to enjoy the fresh air and get fresh with anyone who dares stroll past them. Rent a bike (E£1-3 per hr.), moped, horse, or boat to explore the barrages. The best part of a visit to Qanatir is probably the view of the Egyptian countryside on the ferry ride into town from Cairo.

ZAGAZIG AND BUBASTIS

Trains run to Zagazig throughout the day (1½hr., every hr. 6:20am-6:30pm, E£6), or take a service taxi from Ahmed Hilmi Sq. bus station (1¼hr., E£4.50). To reach Tel Basta, take a taxi from the Zagazig train station (10min.). You'll also have to take a taxi from the train station to the museum (10min., E£5). Orabi Museum open daily 9am-5pm. Admission E£6, students E£3; camera privileges E£10, video E£15.

Lower Egypt was the center of power in the Old Kingdom, and many impressive monuments were erected in the Nile Delta region throughout the pharaonic era. Unfortunately, very few of these monuments remain today, thanks to irrigation canals that were dug beneath the monuments and the natural fanning out of the river. The soil in the region is also too loose to support any permanent structures (although most structures were made out of fast deteriorating mud-brick anyway). The **Orabi Museum** in the town of Zagazig houses a small collection of local archaeological finds—all that remains of these once-great structures. Southeast of Zagazig are the ruins of Bubastis, now called **Tel Basta**. The original name means "House of Bastet" and refers to the feline goddess to whom the main temple was dedicated. The festivals held here in honor of the cat-goddess attracted over 700,000 devotees who would dance and sing, make sacrifices, and consume mass quantities of food and wine. The ancient historian Herodotus thought that Bubastis was the cat's pajamas, writing not only that "more wine is drunk at this feast than in the whole year beside," but also that the temple was the most pleasurable to gaze upon of all the Delta's pharaonic sites. Herodotus would roll over in his grave if he could see the condition of modern-day Bubastis, which looks like scattered kitty litter. Those who don't meow like mad over archaeological finds and ancient cults may want to zagazig—or just bypass—these towns.

TANIS

*A very long (3½hr.) drive from Cairo. Take the **train** or **bus** from Ahmed Hilmi Sq. (2½hr., E£4) to Zagazig. From there, take a service taxi to Faqus (E£1.50) and from there to El-Housya (E£1), where a service or pickup truck taxi will take you to San el-Hagar (E£1); someone there will point you to the ruins. Admission to the ruins E£16, students E£8; camera privileges E£5.*

One of the region's most impressive sites is ancient Tanis. The remains of the city lie in the northeast corner of the Delta's fertile triangle, and a 10-minute walk from the dilapidated town of **San el-Hagar.** The capital of the 21st (Tanite) dynasty, Tanis was founded in the 11th century BCE by the pharaoh Smendes. At one time, Tanis and Bubastis were more important than Memphis and Thebes. Though the past 31 centuries have taken their toll on Tanis, the site is still impressive and slightly surreal, carelessly littered with massive broken obelisks, well-preserved carvings, and various shattered body parts from *colossi*. The tombs of Smendes and other ancient notables feature impressive hieroglyphs. Though the ruins are not as amazing as *Raiders of the Lost Ark* would have you believe, there is a structure remarkably similar to the Well of Souls. The site also has a small museum.

WADI NATRUN وادى النطرون

If the insanity of Cairo has left you aggravated, Wadi Natrun's monasteries, flowering trees, cooing doves, and friendly monks will restore tranquility. For 1500 years, the 50 monasteries of Wadi Natrun were the backbone of the Coptic community in Egypt. The four that stand today (forming an ill-proportioned cross in the desert landscape) are more than impressive relics; they are functional places of worship serving the spiritual needs of Egypt's Orthodox Christian population who flock here in tour buses all summer. The first Christian monastery in Egypt was established in the Eastern Desert by St. Anthony the Great (250-355 CE; see **St. Anthony's Monastery**, p. 173). In 330 CE, one of Anthony's disciples established the monastic lifestyle in Wadi Natrun. More than a millennium and a half later, interest in Coptic monasticism was so great during the 1980s that new rooms were added to accommodate the many novice ascetics arriving in the Natrun Valley. Wadi Natrun is also home to the last surviving type of papyrus. Due to the high salinity of the water there (*wadi* = river, *natrun* = salt), it is a dwarf subspecies that does not reach over 2m (large papyrus, found in the Delta, was last seen in the mid-19th century).

⚡ ORIENTATION AND PRACTICAL INFORMATION

A West Delta Bus Company **bus** leaves from Cairo's Turgoman station (2½hr., every 30min. hr. 6:30am-5pm, E£5 collected on board). Ride past the Wadi Natrun Rest House into Wadi Natrun town; the bus stop is near the gaudily painted statue of a soldier. Take a pickup taxi from here to the monastery **Deir Anba Bishoi** (10min.,

E£1). Coptic pilgrims are often willing to pick up travelers; this is also the best way to travel between monasteries. Start your journey early if you plan to return to Cairo or Alexandria in the evening, as there are no places to stay in Wadi Natrun town. To leave Wadi Natrun, wait at the **Wadi Natrun Rest House** for *service* taxis or buses, which go to **Alexandria** (*service* leave about every hr., E£4) or **Cairo** (E£4 for frequent *service*; buses leave about every hr. until 6pm, E£4). Many travelers are conveniently offered rides by drivers passing by, but be wary of accepting rides from strangers. *Let's Go* does not recommend hitchhiking.

⚓ SIGHTS

Deir Anba Bishoi alone opens every day of the year; Deir es-Suryan, Deir Anba Baramus, and Deir Abu Maqar close for various feast and fast days, particularly around Christmas and Easter. With the exception of those at Deir Abu Maqar, the monks at all the monasteries happily receive foreign tourists and provide free tours of their monasteries. Some travelers try to arrange overnight stays, although this is primarily a privilege of true religious pilgrims. For information on overnight stays, contact the Coptic Patriarch in Cairo at 22 Ramses St., Aboiyye (tel. (02) 282 53 74), and see the specific monastery descriptions below for details. Non-pilgrims are often allowed to camp near the monasteries. As with most religious sites in the Middle East, wear modest attire (no shorts or sleeveless shirts) and remember to remove your shoes before entering the church. Non-flash photography is permitted.

DEIR ANBA BISHOI. The Monastery of St. Bishoi is the most accessible and largest (with seven churches) of the four monasteries. Dating from 381 CE, Deir Anba Bishoi's original limestone and silt construction is now covered in plaster. It was rebuilt in 444 after being sacked by Romans and now contains the remains of St. Bishoi, who is still believed to perform miracles for the faithful. Monks used to sleep in the desert, coming to the church only for services, but attacks by nomads in the 9th century prompted the construction of sleeping chambers and a protective wall, along with a tower connected by a drawbridge to the wall. From atop the tower you can see a white swath in the distance; it's the salt that gives Wadi Natrun its name. The second floor's **Chapel of the Virgin Mary** exhibits 1500-year-old Gothic-style arches (an Egyptian innovation brought to Europe from Byzantium by the Crusaders). Don't leave without hearing the amplified echo in the old communal dining room, along with an amazingly preserved set of vestments from the Islamic conquests. (*15km from the Rest House. Ask for Father Sedrak, a monk who speaks excellent English and is the designated tour guide. Open daily 8am-5pm.*)

DEIR ES-SURYAN. The "Monastery of the Syrians," named for the Syrian monks who once inhabited it, was established when a group of 4th-century monks broke away from the Monastery of St. Bishoi following a theological dispute. With the resolution of the dispute in the 5th century, this alterna-monastery was no longer needed by the Egyptian Copts. In the beginning of the 8th century, it was purchased by a

NIGHT OF THE LIVING DEAD
The monks that inhabit the four functional monasteries in Wadi Natrun live, eat, and pray as one. Few are allowed to leave, unless for medical reasons or on monastery business. When he is ordained, a monk's former self "dies," and he casts off the world of earthly desires to put on the black robe that indicates this symbolic death. The black hood symbolizes the Biblical "helmet of salvation" (Ephesians 6:17); the 13 crosses embroidered upon it represent Jesus Christ (the cross on the back) and his 12 apostles (the 12 side crosses). The monks' days typically begin at 3:45am (even earlier on Sundays, when the monks of Deir Anba Bishoi rise at 12:45am for six hours of uninterrupted prayer), at which time the monks sing psalms and cantillate the Coptic liturgy amid billows of incense, wide-eyed icons, and flickering candlelight. The service is punctuated by entrancing triangle and cymbal music (arrive before 9am to attend).

Syrian merchant for use by monks from his homeland, the first of whom arrived at the beginning of the 9th century. The monastery was prominent throughout the 10th century, and by the 11th century it housed the largest community in Wadi Natrun.

The monastery is best known for the beautiful frescoes the Syrians painted over the original Egyptian work. The monks at Deir es-Suryan will be quick to tell you that they have what is considered the most beautiful Annunciation fresco in the world, located in the **altar room** on the right as you enter; another lovely Annunciation fresco is at the back of the nave. Also in the altar room is an enormous set of ebony doors known as the **Door of Symbols,** whose leaves form the screen to the sanctuary in the Church of the Virgin Mary. The panels depict the seven epochs of the Christian era.

The **miracle tree** supposedly sprang from the staff of a Syrian saint in the 4th century. At the back of the church is a low, dark passageway leading to the private **cell of St. Bishoi.** The monks will show you an iron staple and chain dangling from the ceiling and explain how St. Bishoi would fasten it to his beard, thereby maintaining a standing position lest he fall asleep during his all-night prayer vigils. Set in the floor at the western end of the church is the **lakan** (marble basin), which is used for washing the monks' feet on holy days. *(5min. walk to the northwest from Deir Anba Bishoi, following the monastery walls. Open in summer Su-F 9am-7pm, Sa 9am-5pm; in winter Su-F 9am-6pm, Sa 9am-3pm. No overnight stays.)*

DEIR ANBA BARAMUS. Although this structure is known as the Monastery of the Virgin Mary, "Baramus" derives from the Coptic word "Romeos" (or Romans), in honor of the Roman Emperor Valentinus's two sons, monks Maximus and Domitius. Tradition holds that a crypt under the altar holds the remains of these two holy men, who worshipped here. Relics of St. Moses and St. Isadore are kept in the first section of the old church. The corpse of St. Moses once shook hands with passersby through a small aperture in his casket, but for the past 200 years, he has not been quite as cordial and the aperture has been sealed. *(4km northwest of Deir Anba Bishoi. Take a taxi from Wadi Natrun town or catch a ride from Deir Anba Bishoi. Open 10am-5pm.)*

DEIR ABU MAQAR. The Monastery of St. Maccarius was founded by St. Maccarius the Great (300-390 CE) and is the earliest of the Wadi Natrun monasteries. St. Maccarius remained a religious hermit throughout his life and lived in a cell connected by a tunnel to a small cave. Virtually none of that original building remains. In the beginning of the 11th century, the monastery became the refuge of monks fleeing Muslim persecution. During the Middle Ages, the monastery was famous for its library, which remained intact until Europeans discovered the treasures in the 17th century and removed them. *(8km southeast of Deir Anba Bishoi. Visitors are not permitted without prior approval. If interested, send a letter to the monastery at P.O. Box 2780, Cairo. State the date and time of your proposed visit, how long you wish to stay (no longer than 2hr.), and whether you would like to eat there. Overnight visits are only granted to religious groups and students of theology or history. If you are invited, the easiest way to reach the monastery is by hiring a car at the Wadi Natrun Guest House for the 15min. drive.)*

MEDITERRANEAN COAST

HIGHLIGHTS OF THE MEDITERRANEAN COAST

■ Everyone comes to **Alexandria** for its **beaches** (p. 131), but the shores of **Marsa Matrouh** (p. 135) are the real treasure. The pristine waters of **'Agiba** and **Cleopatra's Beach** (p. 138) were a favored playground for pharaonic lovers.

■ A desert trek to the **Siwa Oasis** (p. 139) uncovers the unique language and culture of the Siwan community. Follow Alexander's footsteps to the **Oracle of Amun** (p. 143), famous fount of wisdom to the ancients.

■ The **Greco-Roman Museum** (p. 129) preserves a sense of Alexandria's glorious past, while the **Roman Amphitheater** (p. 128) and **Pompey's Pillar** (p. 130) embody it.

ALEXANDRIA الاسكندرية

Very few ruins remain in Alexandria *(El-Iskandariyya)* to remind a visitor of its long and vibrant history as a seaport on the Mediterranean Coast. It all started when a triumphant Alexander stumbled upon this little fishing village (then called Rhakotis) en route to the Oracle of Amun at Siwa. The conquering hero came to be so enamored with the spot that he ordered a grand metropolis to be built upon it (dedicated to himself, in proper Ramsesian obeisance), then left for Siwa and never returned. Ptolemy was just as ptempted by the Mediterranean city as his predecessor and set about pampering Alexandria with the best ancient Greece had to offer. Alexandria's *Museion* (including the famous 500,000-volume library) soon became the greatest center of learning in the ancient world: here Euclid invented his geometry, while Eratosthenes estimated the circumference of the earth. Ptolemy devised a tremendously popular faith in which Zeus and the pharaonic bull-god Apis were fused into the new deity Serapis.

Ptolemy's creatively named successor, Ptolemy II, fostered trade in the city, which soon became the richest commercial center of its day. To help the traffic along, Ptolemy II constructed the Lighthouse of Pharos Island, one of the seven wonders of the ancient world (now collapsed). After all the back-stabbing and booty-grabbing involving Cleopatra, Marc Antony, Octavian, and others with tetrasyllabic names, the Romans took control of the city and Alex's superpower status faded. As scholarly interests shifted from science to theology, Alexandria again came to the intellectual forefront when the Septuagint (the first Greek translation of the Hebrew Bible) was scribed here for the expatriate Jewish population after the destruction of the Temple in Jerusalem. Legend has it that this was named for the 70 scholars who each labored in isolation but produced exactly the same text.

Legend also teaches that St. Mark introduced Christianity to the city in 62 CE, founding what would become the Coptic Church. With Emperor Constantine converted, the influence of the Christians grew, and they turned on their pagan neighbors with vengeful glee (see **A Library Long Overdue,** p. 130). It was all downhill from there: the new capital in Cairo soon eclipsed Alexandria's glory, and a series of earthquakes in the 13th century finally reduced the immense lighthouse to rubble.

The rejuvenated modern city burst forth when Muhammad 'Ali made it a port for his navy and redug the canal to the Nile. During the 19th century, Alexandria became a favorite holiday spot for expatriate Europeans, wealthy Turks, and Egyptian nationals. The entire colonial government migrated here from Cairo for the summers. Today, with over five million inhabitants, it is Egypt's biggest port, second-largest city, and summer vacationing capital. Although Alexandria shares the dirt, crowds, and noise of Cairo, a different spirit pervades this city. Whereas summer in Cairo sears streets and patience alike, in Alexandria it gently warms vacationing Gulf Arabs, Africans, and Egyptians. Only here can an evening meal combine Greek *souvlaki*, British ale, French pastries, and the serenade of a *muezzin's* call to prayer. Western fashions are more prevalent, the alcohol flows more freely, and French replaces English as the second language of choice. If *El-Qahira* is "The Conqueror," then *El-Iskandariyya* is surely the spoils.

⚑ ORIENTATION

Alexandria stretches from Abu Qir Bay to the western harbor. The entire 28km of coastline is crowded with glistening skyscrapers and deteriorating hotels jockeying for a spot near the Mediterranean. Alexandria's architect, Dinocrates, planned the city with broad boulevards rigidly arranged in a grid to harness sea breezes. The breezes still waft, but the order is long gone. Ancient Alexandria was built around Pharos Island (now a peninsula separating the eastern and western harbors), and the area still serves as the heart of the city. The downtown commercial district—called **El-Manshiyya,** Mahattat er-Ramleh (Ramleh Station), or simply El-Balad (The Country)—is the hub of Alexandria's transportation network, nightlife, and tourist trade. Along the curve of the eastern harbor, west of downtown, is **El-**

Goumrouk, a grandiose residential neighborhood that holds many old mosques. Immediately southeast of El-Manshiyya lies **El-Attarien,** which encompasses **Misr Station,** the city's main train depot. South of El-Manshiyya and El-Attarien, the streets of **Karmouz** overflow with students, workers, and the rest of the proletariat. Here you will find Pompey's Pillar and the Catacombs of Kom esh-Shoqafa. **El-Anfoushi** occupies the farthest tip of Pharos Island, and is home to Fort Qaytbay.

The best place to orient yourself downtown is **Sa'ad Zaghloul Square** on the waterfront, which showcases a massive statue of the man himself. Although Sa'ad Zaghloul Sq. and Ramleh Station, which it borders on the west, are two distinct squares, the names are often used interchangeably. Four streets border the square: on the north side is the **corniche;** on the west side in front of the Cecil Hotel is **Nabi Daniel Street,** running south through downtown to the *service* taxi station; on the east is **Safia Zaghloul Street,** the city center's principal north-south boulevard, running through downtown and ending at Misr Station; on the south side of the square heading east is **Alexander the Great Street;** and on the south side heading west to Orabi Sq. is **El-Ghorfa et-Tigariyya Street.** Both Safia Zaghloul and Nabi Daniel St. run south up a slight hill; at the top, they intersect **Sultan Hussein Street,** then descend to their intersections with **El-Huriyya Street.**

Bordering the southeast corner of Sa'ad Zaghloul Sq. is **Ramleh Station Square,** the main depot for the intracity tramway and a hub for intercity buses. Many municipal buses and minibuses service the busy stop in front of the square on the corniche or on the south side across from Trianon Cafe.

Heading west on Ramleh Station Square's south side is **Sa'ad Zaghloul Street** (which does *not* border Sa'ad Zaghloul Sq.), a main shopping artery that runs to **Orabi Square.** The two squares serve as transportation hubs. All yellow trams out of Ramleh Station pass through here, as do a number of minibuses. The southern end is also called Tahrir Sq., and the larger area El-Manshiyya Sq.

The **corniche** starts at the northern tip of El-Anfoushi and winds the length of the city to reach **Montaza Palace** and **Ma'mura Beach** (a hangout for the kids), which demarcate the city's far eastern borders. Note that the corniche is also called **26 July Avenue** along the eastern harbor and **El-Geish Road** between Es-Silsilah breakwater (the western promontory of the eastern harbor) and Montaza.

In addition to the corniche, two main arteries traverse the stretch from downtown to Ma'mura. The first inland is **Alexander the Great (El-Iskandar El-Akbar) Street,** which alternately changes its name to 'Omar Lotfy St. in Chatby, Sidi Gabr St., Ahmed Shawki St. in Rushdi, and President 'Abd es-Salaam 'Aret St. from Glim to the Victoria tram station (the end of the line). In Sidi Bishr, the street changes its

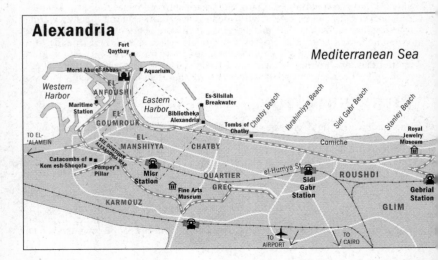

name to Khalid Ibn al-Walid St. to welcome you to *(bienvenidos a)* Miami Beach, where it ends. The second major artery is **El-Huriyya Street** (called Fouad St. or Abu Qir St.), which runs all the way to Montaza. The Schultz School's *Guide Book to Alexandria* (E£25) spices up the city's plate of concrete noodles.

▄ GETTING OUT OF TOWN

Alexandria lies at the junction of lush Delta farmlands, the barren Western Desert, and the Mediterranean coast. Cairo is a three-hour drive to the southeast on either of two roads. The scenic Delta road (231km) crosses both branches of the Nile and passes through the industrial city of Tanta, while the desert road (225km) nudges Wadi Natrun and passes through Giza.

AIRPLANES. Alexandria's small **airport** is several kilometers southeast of downtown. Local bus #203 (٢٠٣) and minibus #703 (٧٠٣) run between Orabi Sq. and the airport. **EgyptAir,** 19 Sa'ad Zaghloul St. (tel. 482 59 37), is just east of Ramleh Station Sq. (open daily 8am-8pm). **Lufthansa,** 6 Tala'at Harb St. (tel. 482 26 07), flies nonstop from Alexandria to Frankfurt on Wednesdays and Sundays at 7:35am (one-way E£2787, youths E£1443). **Olympic Airlines** (tel. 482 10 14 or 482 72 95; fax 482 89 01), on Sa'ad Zaghloul St., one block east of EgyptAir, flies from Alexandria to Athens Tuesdays and Fridays at 8:45am (open M-F 8:30am-4:30pm, Sa 8:30am-12:30pm; one-way E£1304, youths E£702).

TRAINS. There are two options for trains to **Cairo:** the turbo-charged **Turbini** trains (2½hr.; 7, 8am, 2, 3, 7pm, also 6pm in summer; 1st class E£22, 2nd class E£17, 30% student discount) or the slower **French** trains (3hr.; 6, 8:15, 10, 11am, 1, 3:30, 5, 8pm; 1st class E£20, 2nd class E£12, 30% student discount). There is also a third-class train to **Marsa Matrouh** (9am, E£17 with A/C).

BUSES. Superjet buses (tel. 421 90 92) offer air conditioning, snacks, bathrooms, and ever-endearing Egyptian movies. Buses and tickets can be found at the space-age complex in 15 May Sq., behind the Sidi Gabr train station. Buses to **Cairo** stop at Giza, Tahrir Sq., El-Maza, and the Cairo airport (3hr.; every 30min. 5:30am-1am; from 5:30am-5pm downtown E£20, airport E£25; from 5pm-1am downtown E£22, airport E£31). Other buses run daily to: **Hurghada** (11hr., 8pm, E£75); **Marsa Matrouh** (6hr.; 7:15am, 4pm, more in summer; E£24); **Port Said** (4½hr., 6:45am, E£22); and **Sharm esh-Sheikh** (10hr., 6:30pm, E£77).

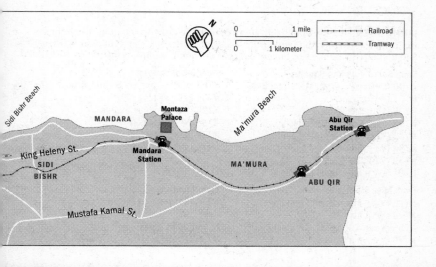

West Delta (tel. 480 96 85) runs buses daily to: **Cairo,** stopping at Giza Sq., Tahrir Sq., and usually the Cairo airport (3hr.; every hr. 5am-1:30am; downtown E£16-25, airport E£21-28); **Marsa Matrouh** (7, 7:30, 9, 11am, 1, 1:30, 3, 3:30, 4:30, 6, 7pm; E£20-23); **Port Said** (4½hr.; 6, 8am, 3:30, 4:30pm; E£17, with A/C E£22); **Hurghada** (11hr., 6:30pm, E£60); **Siwa** (9hr., 11am, E£27); **Tanta** (6:45am, noon, 1:15pm; E£6); and **Zagazig** (8am, 2, 3pm; E£10-13).

SERVICE TAXIS. *Service* are cheap but packed (sometimes 20 people per minivan). Because of the competition from other means of transportation, they depart less frequently than in other cities. Shared vans or station wagons (mainly Peugeots) depart from **Muharram Bey Station.** All prices are approximations. *Service* go to: **Abu Qir** (30min., 60pt); **Cairo** (3hr. by the desert road, E£10); **Marsa Matrouh** (3hr., E£10); **Port Said** (4hr., E£10); **Tanta** (1½hr., E£4); and **Zagazig** (4hr., E£10).

CAR RENTAL. **Avis** (tel. 483 71 73; fax 483 64 01) is in the Cecil Hotel on Sa'ad Zaghloul Sq. Their cheapest deal is the Czech Skoda Filishia (E£152 per day, 50pt every km over 100, including tax and insurance). Renters must be at least 25 (open daily 8am-10pm).

☞ GETTING AROUND TOWN

Alexandria's main squares, transportation centers, and corniche all lie within walking distance of each other. A brisk half-hour walk will take you from Old Pharos Island to the Shooting Club along the corniche. The rest of the city is accessible by municipal tram, bus, minibus, and private microbus or taxi.

CITY BUSES. There are three terminals: one on the west side of **Sa'ad Zaghloul Sq.** (often called Ramleh Station, though the actual Ramleh Station is to the east), one in **Orabi Sq.,** and one at **Muharram Bey Station.** Buses run from approximately 5:30am to midnight or 1am (2am during Ramadan) and cost 25-35pt, or 50pt to outside beaches like El-'Agami or Montaza. Buses are marked in Arabic numerals.

From Sa'ad Zaghloul Square:
#1 (١): Sidi Bishr and 15 May Station (A/C)
#2 (٢): El-'Agami (A/C)
#3 (٣): El-'Agami via Montaza (A/C)
#214 (٢١٤), #215 (٢١٥): Maritime Station
#221 (٢٢١): Ma'mura
#403 (٤٠٣): Dakhla
#460 (٤٦٠): Hannoville

From Orabi Square:
#203 (٢٠٣): airport
#220 (٢٢٠): Sidi Bishr
#231 (٢٣١): Citadel
#251 (٢٥١): Abu Qir via El-Huriyya St.
#260 (٢٦٠): Abu Qir via the corniche

MINIBUSES. A more appetizing alternative to the crowded city buses, minibuses run from 5:30am to 1am (2am during Ramadan) and cost 50pt. Stand on the street and hold up the number of fingers equal to the number of passengers.

From Sa'ad Zaghloul Square:
#700 (٧٠٠), #705 (٧٠٥): Muharram Bey
#703 (٧٠٣): Airport
#706 (٧٠٦): Citadel
#725 (٧٢٥): Citadel via corniche
#735 (٧٣٥), #736 (٧٣٦): Montaza
#750 (٧٥٠): Bitash
#760 (٧٦٠): Hannoville
#781 (٧٨١): International Gardens

From Misr Station:
#728 (٧٢٨): Montaza and Abu Qir
#729 (٧٢٩): Abu Qir
#755 (٧٥٥), 765 (٧٦٥): El-'Agami
#770 (٧٧٠): Ma'mura

From Orabi Square:
#703 (٧٠٣): Airport via Sa'ad Zaghloul
#704 (٧٠٤): Fishing club
#724 (٧٢٤): 15 May Station
#736 (٧٣٦): Ma'mura
#737 (٧٣٧): Abu Qir
#779 (٧٧٩): Mandara

From Montaza:
#735 (٧٣٥): Sa'ad Zaghloul, Qaytbay

From Ras et-Tin:
#735 (٧٣٥): Montaza via corniche

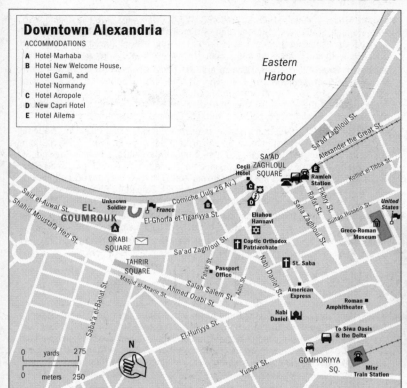

Downtown Alexandria

ACCOMMODATIONS

A Hotel Marhaba
B Hotel New Welcome House,
Hotel Gamil, and
Hotel Normandy
C Hotel Acropole
D New Capri Hotel
E Hotel Ailema

Eastern Harbor

EGYPT

TRAMS. Trams all start from **Ramleh Station** and come in two colors. **Blue** trams (20pt) head east and pass by the Sporting Club before ending at En-Nasr Station. **Yellow** trams (15pt) head west and pass Orabi Sq. before turning north or south. They run every few minutes until midnight, occasionally until 1am, and during Ramadan until 2am. The middle car of every three-car tram is for women only; on two-car trams, one is marked "ladies" and the other "gentlemen." Hop on at any stop or flag one down, and pay on board. Look for the route number located on the front of the train, not the longer car numbers painted on the sides.

TAXIS. A local taxi ride in Alexandria is marginally less death-defying than in Cairo, and an inexpensive way to avoid the slow grind of the tram and the sardine-can squalor of the city buses. Hail one going in your direction and shout your destination into the window. The meters never run, so pay as you please. No matter how big your group (3 is the maximum), you can get away with E£3 to most places in the downtown area. Longer trips (Montaza or Abu Qir) are E£10-15, and past midnight you'll have to bargain harder. There is an E£1 minimum.

❷ PRACTICAL INFORMATION

TOURIST AND FINANCIAL SERVICES

Tourist Office: Main office (tel. 484 33 80) on Nabi Daniel St., at the southwest corner of Sa'ad Zaghloul Sq. English spoken fluently. Open daily in summer 8:30am-6pm; in winter 8:30am-5pm; Ramadan 9am-4pm; holidays 8am-2pm. Branch offices at **Misr Station** (tel. 492 59 85; same hours), **Maritime Station** (tel. 480 34 94; open 8am-5pm and additional hours for boat arrivals), and the **airport** (tel. 420 87 64 or 420 10 36). Free copies of *Alexandria by Night and Day* and *Alexandria and the Beaches*.

Passport Office: 22 Tala'at Harb St. (tel. 483 77 51). Walk west on Sa'ad Zaghloul Sq. from Ramleh Station Sq. and bear left on Falaky St. by the blue sign when Sa'ad Zaghloul curves toward the sea. Tala'at Harb St. is your first left. Open Sa-W 9am-2pm and 7-9pm, Th and F 9am-1pm and 7-9pm. Handle visa extensions in Cairo if possible.

Consulates: Israel, 207 'Abd es-Salaam Aret St., Loran (tel. 586 38 74). Open Su-Th 9:30am-3:30pm. **Lebanon,** 63 El-Huriyya St. (tel. 482 65 89). **U.K.,** 3 Mena St., Rushdi (tel. 546 70 01), off Kafr 'Abdou St. About 6km east of downtown, several blocks south of the corniche. Open Su-Th 8am-1pm. For **U.S.,** contact the American Center (see Cultural Centers, below) or the U.S. Embassy in Cairo (see p. 66).

Currency Exchange: Exchanges have better rates than banks but only take cash. **National Bank of Egypt** in the Cecil Hotel in Sa'ad Zaghloul Sq. is quick. Open Su-Th 8:30am-8:30pm, F-Sa 9am-1pm and 5:30-8:30pm. **Bank of Alexandria,** 59 Sa'ad Zaghloul St. (tel. 483 85 88/89). Open Su-Th 8:30am-2pm; Ramadan 10am-1:30pm. **Bank Misr,** Safia Zaghloul St. between the Metro Cinema and El-Huriyya St., won't cash traveler's checks, but gives Visa and MC advances. Open Su-Th 8am-2pm. Bank Misr, on Tala'at Harb St., up the street and around the corner from the passport office, has **ATMs.**

American Express: 10 Patrice Lumumba St. (tel. 493 11 15; fax 495 09 17), near the Roman Amphitheater. Full service office, but doesn't hold mail. Open 9am-4pm.

Thomas Cook: 15 Sa'ad Zaghloul St. (tel. 482 51 18 or 484 78 30; fax 483 40 73), just east of Ramleh Station Sq. Full range of services. Open daily 8am-5pm.

LOCAL SERVICES

English Bookstore: The best is **Al-Ma'aref,** 44 Sa'ad Zaghloul St. (tel. 483 33 03); another entrance on the south side of Sa'ad Zaghloul Sq. Strange selection of textbooks, translations of Arabic works, and trashy paperbacks. Open M-Sa 10am-9:30pm. **General Egyptian Book Organization,** 49 Sa'ad Zaghloul St. (tel. 482 28 25), just down the street from Al-Ma'aref. Medium-sized selection ranges from *Sweet Valley High* to *The Art of Pediatrics,* with an immense collection of Agatha Christie. Open daily 10am-7:30pm. The **Used Book Market,** at the southern end of Nabi Daniel St. near Misr Station, is an entire block of high-quality, inexpensive English titles.

Cultural Centers: British Council, 9 Ptolemies St. (tel. 482 98 90 or 481 01 99). Open Su-Th 10am-3:30pm. Library open Su-W 10am-7:30pm, Sa and Th 10am-4pm. **American Cultural Center,** 3 Phara'ana St. (tel. 482 10 09). Take a left on El-Huriyya St. from Safia Zaghloul St., walk 1 block past the 1st sign for the Greco-Roman Museum, turn left, and then take the first right. Fine book and video library. Inquire about **teaching jobs** at the English Teaching Program. Cultural events calendar posted outside. Open Su-Th 8:30am-4:30pm; in winter W until 6pm.

Cotton Candy Machine Rental: The roving dealership is usually stationed in Orabi Sq. Ask for the "Fluffy Ahmed" week-long special (E£32).

EMERGENCY AND COMMUNICATION

Emergency: Ambulance: Tel. 123. **Police:** Tel. 122. **Tourist Police:** Tel. 126.

Tourist Police: Montaza Palace (tel. 547 33 95). Branch office upstairs from the tourist office in **Sa'ad Zaghloul Sq.** (tel. 483 33 78). Both open 24hr. Also branches in the **amphitheater** (tel. 490 62 73), **Citadel** (tel. 480 91 44), and the **Greco-Roman Museum** (tel. 482 89 12).

Pharmacy: Pharmacy Strand (tel. 482 51 36), opposite the tram at the intersection of Sa'ad Zaghloul St. and Safia Zaghloul St. Open 9am-midnight.

Hospital: El-Mowasah (tel. 421 28 85/88), on El-Huriyya St. in El-Haddara.

Post Office: All open Sa-Th 8am-3pm, and most have **EMS** (until 2pm). A branch at the tram stop at **Ramleh Station Sq.** (tel. 482 07 46) and 2 on **El-Ghorfa Et-Tigariyya St.,** 3 blocks west of Sa'ad Zaghloul Sq. and 2 blocks west of Orabi Sq. Poste Restante until 1pm; packages are held at the office of **Misr Station** (tel. 491 86 32), 10m south of El-Huriyya St. An office in front of the **Sidi Gabr Railroad Station** has EMS.

Telephones: Ramleh Station Sq. office charges E£24 for 3min. to the U.S.; minimal phone card discount. Open 24hr. Additional offices at **Misr Station,** at the west end of **Sa'ad Zaghloul St.** at Sultan Hussein St., and in the post office on **Safia Zaghloul St.** Both open daily 7am-midnight. Lines are down for hours at a time, and you may be abruptly cut off. **Luxury hotels** (try the Cecil in Sa'ad Zaghloul Sq.) offer more expensive overseas connections. Rates for 3min. to: U.S./Canada E£32, U.K. E£28.50, Australia E£46. For operator **information,** dial 125.

Telephone Code: 03.

ACCOMMODATIONS

E.M. Forster liked Alexandria so much he wrote a book about it and named a character in *A Room with a View* after the Cecil Hotel. Steer clear of the ultra-cheap (E£10 per night) dives that line the streets running south from the corniche near Ramleh Station Sq. It's better to stay in one of the hotels listed below: all are clean, cheap, and within walking distance of the two main squares. None have fans, unless noted, as most Alexandrians depend on sea breezes for air-conditioning. In summer, look for corner rooms with cross ventilation.

Streets in **El-Manshiyya Sq.** are teeming with budget hotels. For a beachside retreat, head out to **Sidi Bishr** (14km) or **Montaza** (18km), where the posh amenities balance the inconvenience of staying so far from the center of town. The only **camping** possibility is the beach at Abu Qir, but police generally only give permission to large groups. Interested travelers should inquire at the tourist office. Reservations are a good idea in the summer, especially on weekends.

New Hotel Welcome House, 8 Gamal ed-Din Yassin St., 5th floor. On the 1st block off the corniche behind the Cecil Hotel. Oddly named but well-maintained new hotel with clean rooms, great prices, and views to match, along with a friendly cat. All rooms come with baths. Singles E£15; doubles E£25; triples E£33.

Hotel Acropole, 27 Gamal ed-Din Yassin St., 4th floor (tel. 480 59 80), at the end of the block behind the Cecil Hotel. Breezy, lacy TV lounge. Rooms and small common bathrooms are kept antiseptically clean. Beds are lumpy but comfy. Prices vary with views, which range from panoramas to brick walls. Singles E£15-25; doubles E£30-35; triples E£45-55. Breakfast included.

Hotel Gamil, 8 Gamal ed-Din Yassin St., 4th floor (tel. 481 54 58). Dedicated to students and youths, with huge beds in most rooms. Singles and doubles E£22, no view E£17; triples and larger rooms E£10 per person. Free use of the kitchen.

Hotel Normandy, 8 Gamal ed-Din Yassin St., 4th floor (tel. 480 68 30). Mentioned in Australian phenom Ted Simon's landmark travel narrative *Jupiter's Travels.* All rooms have 3 beds, high ceilings, and shared baths. Some have a decent view of the water. The bathrooms are old but clean. Singles E£15; doubles E£20; triples E£25. Add E£5 for a room with a view. Prices drop E£5 in winter.

Hotel Marhaba, 10 Ahmed Orabi Sq. (tel. 480 09 57 or 480 95 10), on the northwest side of Orabi Sq. These tony digs were the former summer residence of the King of Libya, and it shows: wallpapered rooms come with towels, soap, sinks, and Egyptian TV. Louis XIV sitting rooms on each floor and a rooftop breakfast buffet. Singles E£33, with shower E£40 (E£58 in summer, including lunch and dinner); doubles E£48/57.

New Capri Hotel, 23 El-Mina esh-Sharaya, 8th floor (tel. 490 83 10 or 490 97 03). Same building as tourist office in Sa'ad Zaghloul Sq. Corner rooms offer panoramic views of the corniche and Sa'ad Zaghloul Sq. Singles E£28; doubles E£42; triples E£54. Add E£4 for private bath. Breakfast included.

Hotel Ailema, 21 Amin Fikhry St., 7th floor. (tel. 484 70 11). Clean rooms and bathrooms with hardwood floors off smoky hallways. Singles E£23; doubles E£30; triples E£41. Add E£20 for private bath.

◌ FOOD

Meat, fruit, seafood, and vegetables can be found in the **souq** in El-Mo'asker (take any blue tram six or seven stops east and walk south). The fishmongers will cook your purchase on the spot for E£3-5. **Supermarkets** dot the area around Sa'ad Zaghloul Sq. Gastronomic voyeurs should sneak a peek into **Muhammad Ahmed's Falafel Workshop,** which dishes out insight into the falafel-making process; green industrial revolution-era falafel churners spin chickpeas into a heavenly mash. Go up 'Abd el-Fattah el-Hadari St. from Muhammad Ahmed Fuul restaurant, listed below, and turn right down the first alley to the brick building on the left.

RESTAURANTS

The restaurants of Alexandria are a delicious reminder of the city's cosmopolitan heritage. Forgo the falafel and *fuul* foisted on you in the street and head to the Italian and Greek restaurants downtown, where French pastries vie with *ba'laweh* and *kinafeh* for the affections of the strolling evening crowds. The "Queen of the Mediterranean" naturally has excellent seafood.

◪ **Muhammad Ahmed Fuul,** 17 'Abd el-Fattah el-Hadari St. (tel. 483 35 76), 1 block south of Sa'ad Zaghloul Sq., 10m up on the left; no English sign. *Fuul*-lovers rush in to this local family favorite. Open daily 6am-midnight, later in summer.

◪ **Restaurant Bleik,** 18 Sa'ad Zaghloul St. (tel. 484 08 80). Walk west on Sa'ad Zaghloul until you're 2 blocks from Orabi Sq. Sample such Lebanese delicacies as vegetable soups, *osso bucco*, quail, and brain. Limited but tasty menu after 6pm (mainly stuffed grape leaves and *kobebu*, a hearty meat and grain dish). Open daily 8am-midnight.

Asteria, 40 Safia Zaghloul St. (tel. 472 22 93). Casual Italian bistro serving pizza (E£7-14) and pasta (E£9-10), with tasty granitas to wash it all down. Open 8am-midnight.

Elite, 43 Safia Zaghloul St. (tel. 482 35 92), 1 block north of El-Huriyya St. Breezy, stylin' artists' cafe and restaurant (since 1900), run by a friendly Greek matriarch. The smoky haze vibrates with a bizarre mix of jazz and high-energy techno. Steak E£16-23, chicken E£15-18, filling pasta E£3.50-16. Stella E£5. Open 8am-midnight.

Taverna (tel. 482 81 89), on the southern side of Ramleh Station, across from the trams and next to KFC. Amiable, French-speaking chef grills up excellent *souvlaki* (E£16). Good bargains at the ground level take-away. Open daily 7:30am-2am. Visa, AmEx. Also at Montaza Gardens (tel. 547 54 38) and El-Manshiyya (tel. 481 63 91).

Trianon (tel. 482 09 86), corner of Sa'ad Zaghloul and Ramleh Station Sq. A landmark from the city's *belle époque,* divided into two equally delicious sections. Meals served at the parasoled, sea-view tables at "Le Salon" are less expensive (mousaka E£11) than those served in the art deco restaurant (entrees E£25-40). Open daily 7am-2am.

Restaurant Denis, 1 Ibn Bassam St. (tel. 482 17 09), 4 blocks east of Sa'ad Zaghloul Sq., adjacent to the corniche. Great budget seafood. The English-speaking owner Shokri will lead you into the kitchen to sea food before you eat it. Fish E£25-30 per kg, calamari E£20. Beer and wine served. Open daily 11am-11pm.

Kadoura Restaurant, on the corniche about a block before the Tikka Grill sign. Delicious seafood at even tastier prices. Choose your prey downstairs from several varieties of fish, crab, and calamari (some still moving), then head up the slippery spiral stairs for a great view of the ocean and the corniche crowd below. You'll waddle out after a massive meal of seafood, salad, bread, and drink (E£30). Open noon-midnight.

AHWAS AND CAFES

Sa'ad Zaghloul Sq. is packed with coffee and pastry shops, and ice cream parlors cool off the Ramleh Station Sq. Along the corniche you'll find ritzy cafes and *sheesha* joints; cheaper, more traditional *ahwas* await farther inland. A lively waterfront scene is at **Ma'mura,** where a youthful crowd buzzes until after midnight. Popular for grub and *sheesha* are: the **Antazza Café,** which serves food after 7pm (no English sign, left from the Misr travel office and across from the mosque); **Minouche** (Italian food, E£10-20); and **Cafino** (above Antazza, open late).

Brazilian Coffee Store, in 2 locations: a sit-down at 20 Salah Salem St. or a stand-up at 44 Sa'ad Zaghloul St. (tel. 482 50 59). Home-roasted beans are grounded up for great espresso (E£1.50); croissants E£1.25. Check out the ceramic tiles in the shape of coffee plants at the Salah Salem location. Both locations open daily 7am-11pm.

Delices (tel. 482 54 60), opposite the corniche in Sa'ad Zaghloul Sq. French and Middle Eastern desserts. More posh for your nosh: the sea-view terrace is a great place to enjoy delish pastries (E£2-5), ice cream (E£2.50), or coffee (E£2). Open daily 7am-midnight.

Sofianopoulo Coffee Shop (tel. 483 15 17), on Sa'ad Zaghloul St., near Restaurant Bleik. Classic coffee shop with the cheapest cappuccino around (E£1.50). Aspiring astronauts will appreciate Tang on tap. Open 8am-midnight.

Sultana (tel. 482 27 69), on the south side of Ramleh Station Sq., across from the trams. In the evenings, a man in an animal costume beckons you inside for an array of sundaes and ice cream (E£1.25 per scoop). Waffle cones made while you wait. Like an animal house at night. Open daily 8:30am-2:30am, and (boy do) they deliver.

Cafe Baudrot, 23 Sa'ad Zaghloul St. A fine retreat from the busy street. Vine-trellised garden in back perfect for musing over beer (E£5.05), coffee (E£2.05), or cakes (E£2.25).

Samadi Patisserie, on a lush patio adjacent to Tikka Grill. It's no secret that Samadi doles out generous helpings of *ba'laweh, basbouseh, kinafeh,* and other goodehs. Fresh strawberry ice cream E£1.50. Open daily 9:30am-2am. AmEx, MC, Visa.

⬛ ENTERTAINMENT

NIGHTCLUBS AND DISCOS

The cosmopolitan days of Alexandria's Hellenistic hedonism are long gone. Nightlife in the city is now strictly a do-it-yourself affair. Alexandria's paltry nightlife is concentrated downtown between Orabi Sq. and Sa'ad Zaghloul Sq. This area has the best bars, pastry shops, and coffee houses, and hopping between them is a great way to soak up liquor or wash down desserts.

Nightclubs can be found in most of the luxury hotels. There's no cover, but beware the stealthily levied **minimum charges.** Try the **Cecil** (open 11:30pm-4am; min. E£65) or **Lourantos** (tel. 482 22 00; min. E£45) for something downtown. All of the **discos** are located in the major hotels as well, and play a mix of Western and Arab music. The **Ramada** rocks out on the corniche in Sidi Bishr (entrance on the corniche side; open nightly 10pm-4am; min. E£25). The ultrafabu people head to the **Sheraton** in Montaya to compare Rolexes (open Th-Tu 11pm-4am; min. E£30). The small disco at the **Cecil** is full of day-glo Oriental decor (open nightly 7pm-2am; min. E£15). Many discos don't allow single men or women, and some relegate unescorted males to the bar and forbid them from dancing. These rules are usually relaxed for foreigners, especially those willing to give a small benefaction.

BARS

The bars in Alexandria are mostly empty. The coolest option around is the **Spitfire,** 7 Rue Bourse el-Hadema, two blocks up from the corniche between Sa'ad Zaghloul and Orabi Sq. (Stella E£6.50). Every inch of this expat favorite is covered with decals and posters, and mellow 80s music soothes rattled nerves (Stella E£6.50). A unique find is **Sheik 'Ali,** around the corner to the south from the Sofianopoulo Coffeeshop. The long marble bar is a great place to enjoy their appetizers or the house specialty, rum on the rocks (E£5). The **Athineos** also has a bar with a view of the corniche, although it's a bit cramped (Stella E£6). To fully relive WWII memories, head to **Monty's Bar,** on the second floor of the Cecil Hotel. Prints of classic paintings and occasional synthesizer music now occupy General Montgomery's former headquarters. (Open daily 4pm-2am; Stella E£8.50.) If Monty's dim lights have got you down, head up to the roof garden for a fantastic view of the square and the water, but be careful where you sit—the sharp, green seats are actually cacti (Stella E£8). The breezy, suggestively named **Greek Club** attracts an older clientele and is popular with English teachers. (Take the blue trams east to El-Mo'asker, go south two blocks, then take a left; look for the "Micapaciatikoc" sign; Stella E£5.)

OTHER DIVERSIONS

CINEMAS. English-language films are shown on every corner in Alexandria. The '**Amir** (tel. 492 76 93; admission E£5-15) and the **Metro** (tel. 483 04 32; admission E£5-15) are both in the downtown area. Movies are occasionally subtitled in French, and the French Cultural Center at 30 Nabi Daniel St. (tel. 492 08 04) shows films daily, as does the American Cultural Center (see **Cultural Centers,** p. 124).

PERFORMING ARTS. Every summer, the outdoor **Muhammad 'Abd el-Wahab Theater,** on the corniche at Ramleh Station Sq., showcases traditional dancing. El-Fir'a Rida (Rida's Troupe) and El-Fir'a El-Qawmiyya (the National Troupe) both feature belly dancers and high-energy choreography representative of various areas in Egypt—including the cane dance from Upper Egypt (performances nightly at 10:30pm; reserve tickets 1 or 2 days in advance; front-row E£10.50, cheap seats E£5; avoid the uncomfortable box seats). The **circus** sets up camp in Alexandria every summer; ask the tourist office for the location of the two daily shows (tickets E£2-7). For more highbrow entertainment, check the **Conservatoire de Musique d'Alexandrie,** 90 El-Hurriyya St. (tel. 483 50 86), or the **Sayyid Darwish Theater,** 22 Fouad St. (tel. 482 51 06). In September, the **Alexandria World Festival** brings theater, dancing, and other performing arts to the city. Ask the tourist office for details.

BILLIARDS AND SPECTATOR SPORTS. Billiards tables charge by the hour throughout the city. You'll find the hippest table in town at **Cafino.** The **Marhaba Hotel,** in Orabi Sq. (E£10 per hr.; alcohol served; open late), and **Black and White,** on the left up a side street from the lively Camp Caesar *sheesha* cafes, have three tables each (E£15 per hr.; open 24hr.). If the sound of thundering hooves makes your pulse race, head to the **Antoniadis Palace and Gardens** in Smouha, on the wide road bordering the zoo. For over 50 years, Alexandria's working classes have gathered here on summer Sundays to watch working horses, with carriages of all kinds, race each other at breakneck speed (arrive by 6pm; 50pt). Ask at the tourist office for info on the various **sporting events** in the Alexandria Municipal Stadium.

👁 SIGHTS

The modern city of Alexandria was built atop the ruins of ancient Alexandria, so very little remains of the city of old. The scattered places where ancient foundations do show through (or jut out) offer fascinating glimpses of a city with a diverse cultural and religious history.

DOWNTOWN ALEXANDRIA

ROMAN AMPHITHEATER. This dazzling white marble structure is the only Roman amphitheater in all of Egypt. Stand on the round stone in the stage, whisper *Et tu, Brute?*, and your voice will be heard by the conspirator all the way in the theater's back row. A Roman bath and villa are being excavated behind the theater. *(Just northwest of Misr Station and south of Cinema 'Amir. From Sa'ad Zaghloul Sq., walk up Nabi Daniel St. past El-Huriyya St. to the next big intersection. Turn left across from a gas station and go 200m; the entrance is on the left. Open daily 9am-4pm; Ramadan 10am-3pm. Admission E£6, students E£3.)*

ELIYAHU HANNAVI SYNAGOGUE. This synagogue is still the center of Alexandria's Jewish community and the greatest of the few Jewish sights still standing in the city. The gracious Joe Harari in the *Communauté Israelite Grand Rabbinate* office to the right as you enter the courtyard will show you around the building, let you look at old photographs, and tell you all about Alexandrian Jewry. Although Alexandria once had more than 100,000 Jews (and a synagogue in every neighborhood), this is the last one still in use for the 50 or so Jews who still remain. The temple now holds an impressive collection of beautiful Torahs from the other closed synagogues. Built in 1885 by Baron Jacques L. de Menasce for the then-thriving community, the towering edifice sports five aisles, stained glass windows, pink Italian marble columns, dangling chandeliers, and wooden pews—check out the international assemblage of names on the brass seat markers. (*On Rue Dr. Hussein Faladi, in an alley 1 block south of Safia Zaghloul St. between Nabi Daniel and Rue 'Abd el-Fattah el-Hadari. Open Su-F mornings.*)

GRECO-ROMAN MUSEUM. The most interesting and unusual relics of ancient Alexandria are on display here, including a mummified crocodile and glamor-shot statues of Greco-Roman superstars like Caesar, Augustus, and Cleopatra. The pride of the museum is the beautiful mosaic of Alexandria as "Queen of the Ocean." A new museum devoted exclusively to mosaics found around Alexandria is scheduled to open sometime in 1999 (after this book went to press); ask at the tourist office (p. 123) for details. (*5 El-Mathaf Er-Roumani St. Walk south from the corniche along Safia Zaghloul St., turn left on El-Huriyya St., then left at the museum sign. Tel. 482 58 20. Open Sa-Th 9am-4pm, F 9-11:30am and 1:30-4pm; Ramadan and holidays 10am-3pm. Admission E£10, students E£8; camera privileges without flash E£10, video E£15.*)

COPTIC ORTHODOX PATRIARCHATE. The Patriarchate is in a beautiful church (founded in 67 CE and rebuilt in 1950) with mosaics, stained glass, hanging ostrich eggs, and a finely painted *iconostasis*. The first 47 patriarchs of the Alexandrian See (the regional seat of church authority), starting with St. Mark (whose remains are in a chapel to the left of the *iconostasis*), are buried within; their names are listed in a nook on the right side of the church. (*19 Elah 'Abad St. Open daily with services W at noon, Su and F at 8am. Remove shoes before you enter.*)

MONASTERY OF ST. SABA. The 17th-century church in the Greek Orthodox Monastery of St. Saba is another testament to the historical importance of Christianity in Alexandria. St. Catherine was beheaded on a marble table inside; there are also beautiful paintings, a spectacular collection of amulets, and a giant bronze bell. (*Up Safia Zaghloul St. from Sa'ad Zaghloul Sq. to Sultan Hussein St. Turn right, then take the 2nd left. Open daily 7:30am-12:30pm and 3:30-6pm. Su service 8am.*)

WEST OF DOWNTOWN

MOSQUE OF MORSI ABU EL-'ABBAS. The Mosque of Morsi Abu el-'Abbas is the city's largest mosque and Alexandria's most elaborate example of Islamic architecture. The holy Sidi Shehab ed-Din Abu el-'Abbas Ibn el-Khazragi came from Andalusia before the expulsion of the Moors to spread the teachings of the Qur'an in Egypt. His tomb rests in the back of the mosque, and legend has it that he rose from his tomb to catch bombs during WWII. The coffin, like the exterior of the mosque, is often bathed in a green neon glow. (*1km south of Fort Qaytbay along the corniche. Open daily 5am-10pm, except prayer times. Dress modestly. Women allowed in back room only.*)

FORT QAYTBAY. The Islamic Fort Qaytbay was constructed on the ancient island of Pharos, on the foundations of the famous lighthouse. Silt connected the island to the mainland, leaving the fort at the tip of a peninsula. Built in 1480 CE by the Mamluke Sultan Ashraf Qaytbay, the citadel houses the remains of the French fleet sunk by Admiral Nelson in the battle of Abu Qir. There is a small mosque in the center of the tower, and the entire fortress is aligned so that the mosque's *mihrab* faces Mecca. On the road to the tramway is the **Aquarium,** which has more visiting school groups than schools of Red Sea fish. (*Take yellow tram #15 west from Ramleh Station and get off when it makes a sharp left turn, or take any of the buses going to Ras et-Tin. You'll find yourself in the middle of a fish market. At the point where the tram turned left, make a right on the road between the Kuwait Airlines sign and the mosque; the fort is at the end of this road. Minibus #707 (٧٠٧) or 719 (٧١٩) from Ramleh Station Sq. will take you to the beginning of the street. Tel. 480 91 44. Fort open daily 9am-4pm; admission E£12, students E£6; camera privileges E£10. Aquarium open daily 9am-4pm; admission E£1.*)

A LIBRARY LONG OVERDUE Though the past is alive and kicking in Alexandria, its physical traces are few and far between. The Great Pharos lighthouse long ago gave way to earthquakes and development, and Fort Qaytbay now stands on its site. The great **Bibliotheka Alexandria,** the massive library that made Alexandria an intellectual center of the ancient world, has been destroyed entirely. Much of it allegedly burned to the ground during Rome's first attack on the city, although the exact details of who started the fire and when it occurred (or whether it even occurred at all) are unclear. The remains of the library were completely destroyed by crusading bibliophobe Bishop Theophilus in 391 CE, who led a pagan-hating mob to raze the building in the name of Christianity. In 1987, UNESCO announced a project to resurrect the building that even Cleopatra could not save. Despite numerous natural obstacles like the weather and the Mediterranean tides, construction was scheduled to be completed in time for a grand opening in October 1999. For information on the political obstacles facing the restoration team, see **In The News,** p. 50.

ANFUSHI TOMBS. The Anfushi tombs were built for Greek occupants who had adopted Egyptian customs in the first half of the 3rd century BCE. Cut into the limestone of what was once Pharos Island, they are placed in two groups around a staircase leading into an open court and may well extend farther under the palace gardens. Many of the tombs were decorated with colorful geometric designs or painted to look like marble. *(On Ras et-Tin St. Take tram #16 or minibus #735 (٧٣٥). Open 9am-4pm. Admission E£12, students E£6; camera privileges E£5.)*

SOUTH OF DOWNTOWN

POMPEY'S PILLAR. This 25m pillar of pink granite from Aswan is all that remains of the Serapium (Temple of Serapis, the bull-god), which was leveled once the Roman Empire converted to Christianity. The best finds from the ruins have been moved to the Greco-Roman Museum. Named in the Middle Ages by ignorant Crusaders with a flair for the alliterative, Pompey's Pillar actually dates from the time of Diocletian, a Roman who came to power several centuries after Pompey. One story holds that Diocletian was so incensed by an Alexandrian revolt that he swore he would massacre the rebellious people until blood stained the knees of his horse. As he entered the already defeated but mostly un-massacred town, his mount stumbled into a pool of blood, prematurely fulfilling his oath. The emperor spared the life of the city's inhabitants, and the lone pillar (once the tallest structure in Alexandria) remains a symbol of the people's gratitude to him and his klutzy horse. Another story says that the pillar commemorates the time Diocletian gave the city free grain during a famine. *(Southwest of Misr Station. Take bus #309 (٣٠٩) or tram #16 from Ramleh Station Sq. and get off on Karmouz St. Enter on southern side of complex. Open daily 9am-5pm; Ramadan 10am-3pm. Admission E£6, students E£3.)*

CATACOMBS OF KOM ESH-SHOQAFA. This massive, three-tiered complex of Roman tombs (descending some 35m below ground) is one of the best Classical sites in the city. The gate is decorated with winged serpents, Medusa heads, a pine cone (symbolizing Dionysus), and a caduceus (symbolizing Mercury, the *psychopompos* or leader of the dead to the Underworld). The main tombs are on the second level, richly decorated with sculptures and reliefs of Egyptian gods with virile Roman bodies (a blend of pharaonic and Roman art). A statue of jackal-headed Anubis stands near the entrance to the innermost burial chamber. The scenes above the sarcophagi show the Egyptian gods and a mummification scene, along with worship of the Apis bull. The sarcophagi are decorated in a Roman style, with garlands and bull skulls. Try to lift the lids—it's impossible, because the bodies were placed inside from passages behind. As you exit, notice two strange statues of Anubis, one where he is dressed as a Roman legionnaire and one in which he has the body of a serpent. *(Take bus #309 (٣٠٩) or tram #16 from Ramleh Station Sq. and get off on Karmouz St. when you see Pompey's Pillar. Take a right after the entrance to the Serapium-Pillar complex's entrance on the southwest side and climb the hill. Open daily 9am-4pm; Ramadan 10am-3pm. Admission E£12, students E£6; camera privileges E£10.)*

EAST OF DOWNTOWN

TOMBS OF CHATBY. The Tombs of Chatby date from the 4th century BCE and are believed to be the oldest surviving tombs in Alexandria. The post mortem trinkets that once filled the two separate chambers have been taken to the Greco-Roman Museum. *(On Port Said St., across from St. Mark's College in the Chatby beach area. Open daily 9am-4pm. Admission E£6, students E£3; camera privileges E£5.)*

MUSTAFA KEMAL NECROPOLIS. The Mustafa Kemal Necropolis consists of four tombs from the 2nd century BCE decorated in a Hellenic style. Tomb #1 has an airy courtyard with Doric columns, sphinxes, and a faded fresco depicting a libation scene over the middle doorway. *(Take tram #1 or #2 to the Rushdi tram station and walk down El-Mo'asker Er-Romani St. Open daily 9am-4pm. Admission E£12, students E£6; camera privileges E£5.)*

ROYAL JEWELRY MUSEUM. Behind the governor's residence in Glim sits the architecturally intriguing Royal Jewelry Museum. Originally the Palace of Fatima ez-Zahra'a, the museum contains the gleaming baubles of the Muhammad 'Ali era. *(27 Ahmed Yahya St. Tel. 586 83 48. Look for the red sign. Take tram #2. Open Sa-Th 9am-4pm, F 9am-12:30pm and 2-4pm. Admission E£20, students E£10; camera privileges E£10.)*

☀ BEACHES

The most popular attraction in Alexandria is the waterfront. Cairenes come here in droves during the summer months. Scurry off to the **Sinai** (p. 155) or the calm waters west of Alexandria (tram #1 or 2 from Ramleh Station Sq., p. 133). The 400 acres of gardens at **Montaza Palace and Gardens** were once used as the summer retreat of King Farouk; today they are still the jewel of Alexandria's beaches. The palace and its museum have been closed to the public, but the beach is always busy (especially on weekends), and the gardens and groves are still a favorite picnic spot for Alexandrians. Pizza Hut, Chicken Tikka, a supermarket, and juice and ice cream stands can all be found within the garden gates. (Tel. 457 30 79. Admission E£3, on holidays E£4. Beach rentals by the hour: pedal boats E£15, regular boats E£40, jet-skis E£180.) Not far from Montaza, **Ma'mura** remains a favorite among Alexandria's hipster youth. (Admission E£2, on Fridays E£3; both beaches reachable by bus #221 (٢٢١), #250 (٢٥٠), or #260 (٢٦٠), or by minibus #728 (٧٢٨), #736 (٧٣٦), or #770 (٧٧٠).) **San Stefano's Beach** is much closer to the city center, as its weekday crowds and trash attest. Admission includes a chair and an umbrella; small changing rooms on the beach cost E£24 per day, and larger cabanas start at E£35. (Between Montaza and Sa'ad Zaghloul Sq.; closes at 8pm; admission E£8.)

NEAR ALEXANDRIA: ABU QIR ابو قير

Abu Qir, located on a small peninsula 5km east of Alexandria, has yet to be absorbed by the relentless expansion of the "Queen of the Mediterranean." It was here in 1798 that British Admiral Nelson took the French fleet by surprise without any navigational charts to guide him, thereby displaying the military skill that earned him a column in London's Trafalgar Square. Today, all hints of a military history are gone, and Abu Qir's beach is a peaceful and convenient place to enjoy the Mediterranean and its bounty of edible denizens.

EGYPT

⬛ TRANSPORTATION. From Alexandria's Misr Station, you can take **local bus** #251 (٢٥١) or #260 (٢٦٠) or **minibus** #728 (٧٢٨) (20min., every 30min. 7am-10pm, 50pt). There are also third-class **trains** from Misr or Sidi Gabr Station (45min., every 30min. 6am-10pm, 45pt), **local taxis** from downtown (15min., E£10-15), or **service taxis** from Misr Station (40min., E£1). Within Abu Qir, many a **horse-drawn carriage** (*hantour*) starts trotting from El-Bahr El-Mayyit St. (E£2-3).

⬛ ACCOMMODATIONS AND FOOD. Abu Qir Camp (tel. 560 14 24), located on El-Bahr El-Mayyit St. about 500m south of the Zephyrion, supplies the only consistently available **camping** option in the greater Alexandrian area (E£5, with your own tent or one of theirs). Contact the tourist police or tourist office in Alexandria for permission to camp. As always, produce and the ubiquitous *ta'amiyya*, shawarma, and *fuul* stands are found in the *souq* near the train station. Only sharks can get seafood fresher than that found in Abu Qir's two major sit-down restaurants, both with great views along the beach. The Greek-owned, colorfully-muraled **Zephyrion,** 41 Khalid Ibn al-Walid St. (tel. 560 13 19), is the oldest restaurant in town, founded in 1929. Blow out for a full fish meal (E£30). Nearby is the similarly priced and appropriately named **Bella Vista** (tel. 560 06 28). Nobel Prize-winning President Anwar Sadat was a cook here before he joined the army; sit at his spot in the far left corner. (Open daily noon-midnight.)

⬛ BEACHES. From the train station, one of the cleanest **public beaches** in the area is a short walk down any side street on the left as you face away from the station. Most Alexandrenes go on the weekends, so weekdays are best if you want the beach to yourself. As always, women should be wary of swimming without being covered.

NEAR ABU QIR: RASHID (ROSETTA) رشيد

*On the northern edge of the Nile Delta, about 45min. east of Abu Qir and 1hr. east of Alexandria. West Delta Bus Co. **buses** run from Muharram Bey Station in Alexandria (every hr. 8am-10pm, E£2.50). The last return bus leaves at 5pm. **Microbuses** leave from the Tikka Grill in Alexandria, 1 block inland from the corniche (E£3). The **train** (3rd-class only) runs from Misr Station (9 per day 6:45am-10pm, 75pt). Trains return to Alexandria 9 times per day 5:50am-7:45pm; Ma'mura 60pt, downtown 70pt. **Service** to Rashid are easy to catch at Muharram Bey Station, but the ones back to Alexandria depart infrequently (E£3-5).*

Rashid (Rosetta) is the western meeting point of the Nile and the Mediterranean (Dumyat is the eastern meeting point), but has received most of its fame from the Rosetta Stone, the key to unlocking the hieroglyphs discovered there in 1799 by Napoleon's soldiers. Dotted with provincial Ottoman mosques and houses from the 17th and 18th centuries, the port is crowded with Islamic architecture. Unfortunately, making your way through the trash-lined streets of the town center detracts from Rashid's historic homes. A cast of the stone is on display in the museum here (the original resides in London's British Museum), describing the coronation and numerous titles of Pharaoh Ptolemy V in three tongues: Demotic (the common language), ancient Greek (the royal language), and hieroglyphs (the holy language). Although hieroglyphs had previously been indecipherable, ancient Greek certainly was not; by comparing the two translations, scholars finally created a basic dictionary of hieroglyphs (see **It's All Hieroglyphs to Me,** p. 198).

FORT OF QAYTBAY. About 5km from Rosetta, the recently restored **Fort of Qaytbay** (not to be confused with the one in Alexandria) guards the strategic entrance to the Nile. Built in 1479 by Sultan Ashraf Abu Nasr Qaytbay to serve as a first line of defense against the Ottoman Turks and the Crusaders coming from the Delta, this structure used to overlook the surrounding land; clay and silt deposits have built up around it so that the ground has risen to the level of the fort. A much more significant reconstruction took place in 1799, when the French strengthened the fortress' wall with stone imported from Upper Egypt. A soldier noticed carvings on one of the stones, and this **Rosetta Stone** enabled Jean-François Champollion to unlock the mysteries of the hieroglyphic alphabet. *(The cheapest way to get to the fort is by green-and-white local taxi (one-way E£3-4, round-trip E£5). The romantic way to get there is to find a willing fisherman and go by boat (20min., E£5 per person round-trip). You'll see some beautiful scenery on the way. Open daily 9am-4pm; Ramadan 9am-3pm. Admission E£6, students E£3.)*

ROSETTA MUSEUM. The Rosetta Museum features some broken ceramics, a plaster cast of the Rosetta Stone, and a small collection of artifacts from local history. It is far from worth its hefty admission charge. *(Open daily 9am-4pm. Admission E£20, students E£10; camera privileges E£10.)*

ZAGHLOUL MOSQUE. The badly damaged 17th-century Zaghloul Mosque is at the end of the main street running south from the train station. For a more scenic approach, walk inland from the corniche, past the museum, and south through the *souq.* Looking past the rancid water and refuse, you'll see some Arabic inscriptions, archways, and decorated columns.

WEST OF ALEXANDRIA

Beach resorts stretch west from Alexandria as far as the eye can see, like an apocalyptic vision where only Club Meds are left standing. Even so, the coastline's natural beauty can do wonders for the tired body and soul. The few secluded spots left along Egypt's Mediterranean coast draw a more local contingent, mostly Egyptian families. Modesty is still the rule here; women need to cover up.

El-'Agami, only 20km from Alexandria, is popular with the Egyptian upper class and makes an easy daytrip. Continuing west, notice that almost every inch of sand has been bought by one "vacation village" or another. Many of these cater to certain occupations; Egyptian engineers, police, and doctors hole up in separate concrete complexes near the beach. The war cemeteries of **El-'Alamein**, 99km from Alexandria, mark the site of Africa's fiercest and most significant World War II battle. **Marsa Matrouh,** close to Libya, is a colorful resort town on a bay, featuring one of the world's most beautiful beaches.

A number of resorts along the coast let passers-by use their facilities for a fee. The plush **'Aida Beach Hotel** (tel. 410 28 02), 72km from Alexandria, gives a choice of beach-use fees: the lower rate (E£8-12) pays for pool use and snacks, and the higher one (E£27-35, 2-person min.) includes lunch and use of a beach cabin. Day use at the **Atic Hotel** (tel. 906 07 17), 89km west of Alexandria (the domed gatehouse with red letters above it), costs E£45, but you get a splendid shoreline, two pools, a playground, and lunch. The cheapest sandy spot in the area is the **Marina Beach Club,** 94km west of Alexandria. The E£15 day charge gains you access onto a beautiful beach populated by wealthy Alexandrians zipping around on jet skis, but not into the pools.

If you time your day right, you can bask and feast at the beach, stop to visit the El-'Alamein memorials, and make it to Marsa Matrouh by sunset. Though many coastline segments between Alexandria and Matrouh are depressingly clear of budget hotels, opportunities for free and secluded **camping** are virtually unlimited (simply check in with the nearest police station or military office). **Microbuses** and **service taxis** cruise the Alexandria-Marsa Matrouh road all day; just flag one down (E£3.50 from Alexandria to the Atic Hotel, another E£5-8 to get to Marsa Matrouh).

EL-'AGAMI العجمى

Upper-middle-class Alexandrian sun worshippers flock to El-'Agami to escape the crowds and character of the city, instead embracing a world of concrete villas, chain restaurants, and private beaches. During the peak summer months, flesh jostles flesh in the competition for beach space and women grow increasingly courageous in the quest to bare it all. In winter, hours shorten, prices lower, hemlines drop, and the town quiets down.

To get to El-'Agami, take minibus #760 (٧٦٠) from Sa'ad Zaghloul Sq. in Alexandria. El-'Agami is actually two towns in one—Bitash and Hannoville. In **Bitash,** villas and expensive hotels mingle with restaurants and Western-style boutiques. In **Hannoville,** the quieter, more spinsterly sister city, a few budget hotels are crammed in between rows of apartments. When Egyptians say "El-'Agami," they're generally referring only to Bitash. Each town is oriented around a 2km long main street (**Bitash Street** and **Hannoville Street,** respectively) that extend from the highway to the beach and are lined with stores and groceries.

There is no reason to stay in El-'Agami, considering that Alexandria is 30 minutes away; the pricey hotels here are a further disincentive. Most beaches here, such as the belly-and-bicep baring **Fardous (Paradise) Beach,** are private and hard to gain access into. **Abu Qir** and **Montaza** are better bets. The greatest concentration of restaurants is in Bitash, where the main road forks into Bitash St. and Al-Asal St. Along with various chain restaurants, **El-Omda** serves copious quantities of meat, and **La Dolce Vita** scoops up sweet Italian-style gelato.

EL-'ALAMEIN العلمين

El-'Alamein is a sober interruption in the giddy spree of villa construction that dominates the Mediterranean coast. Here in November 1942, Allied forces led by British Field Marshal Sir Bernard Montgomery halted the advance of the German Afrika Korps, saving Alexandria, Egypt, and, more importantly (for the Western world, at least), the Suez Canal and the oil fields of the Middle East. The Allied victory here marked the beginning of the end for the Axis Powers in North Africa and crushed the mystique surrounding the "Desert Fox," German Field Marshal Erwin Rommel, whose force of Panzer tanks had previously seemed invincible. Nearly 10,000 soldiers lost their lives at El-'Alamein, and 70,000 were wounded.

Non-A/C **West Delta buses** traveling between Marsa Matrouh and Alexandria or Cairo pass through El-'Alamein, though you can also go to a **service** depot and name your destination. To leave town, flag down a *service* or minibus heading to **Alexandria** (1hr., E£5) or **Marsa Matrouh** (2hr., E£5-8) on the road behind the War Museum. A hired **taxi** costs E£100, for either doing a round-trip from Alexandria or a cross-desert run.

WAR MUSEUM. The displays of weaponry and military garb here are impressive but sterile, as are the descriptions of Rommel, Montgomery, and other participants in the battle. A map bedecked with hundreds of tiny red and green bulbs recreates the changing landscape of the North African campaign. *(On the west side of the village near the bus stop and main square. Open in summer Sa-Th 8am-6pm, F 8am-1pm and 2-6pm; in winter and Ramadan 9am-3pm. Admission E£5; camera privileges E£5, video E£20.)*

BRITISH WAR CEMETERY. The British War Cemetery, about 250m east down the road from the museum, is a more powerful testament to the cost of the battle. Here lie buried 7367 soldiers, 815 of whom have headstones bearing only the inscription "Known Unto God." Ringed by purple flowers and set against the seemingly interminable desert, the excruciatingly tidy rows have a dramatic, terrible beauty. Maintained by the British War Graves Commission, the cemetery is free and almost always open.

GERMAN AND ITALIAN CEMETERIES. The less frequently visited German and Italian Cemeteries (8km and 12km west of town, respectively) perch on a petite peninsula overlooking the sea. Without a private car or hired taxi, it is difficult to get directly to these monuments. Microbuses along the Alexandria-Matrouh road will let passengers off 2km from the monuments—lucky travelers may be able to convince service drivers to give them a door-to-tomb ride. Whichever way you travel, make sure you're armed with lots of water. Walking through the desert is dangerous due to the **landmines** there.

MARSA MATROUH مرسى مطروح

Fanning out from a bay of pure cobalt blue, this resort city is too often neglected by foreign travelers and used only as a springboard to Siwa. In summer, Egyptian families pack the mold-and-pour concrete villas and bathe along the 5km crescent of white, sandy, near-perfect beaches. At night, the streets fill with bargain-hunting tourists and shouting vendors selling a remarkable and entertaining variety of useless junk. Marsa Matrouh's natural harbor has served travelers, merchants, and soldiers from Alexander the Great to Rommel the "Desert Fox." Now the majority of sea vessels in Marsa are rented by the hour, and the police patroling the Libyan border comprise the only major military presence in the area.

ORIENTATION AND PRACTICAL INFORMATION

Your feet will serve you well in Marsa Matrouh—a cross-town stroll should take no more than 15 minutes. You only need to know two streets to find your way around town: the lively **corniche,** which stretches the length of the bay, and busy **Alexandria Street,** which runs perpendicular to the corniche. Alexandria St. begins at the Marsa Matrouh Governorate and heads inland to the train station and hill, 1km south of town. Most of the hotels and government offices are clustered along the corniche and the streets running parallel to it. Heading inland from the corniche, the most important of these are **Gala'a Street, Tahrir Street** (sometimes referred to as Gamal 'Abd en-Nasser), **Goul Gamal Street,** and **Allam er-Rum Street.** Parallel to Alexandria St. to the east are **Port Said Street** and **Zaher Galal Street.**

EGYPT

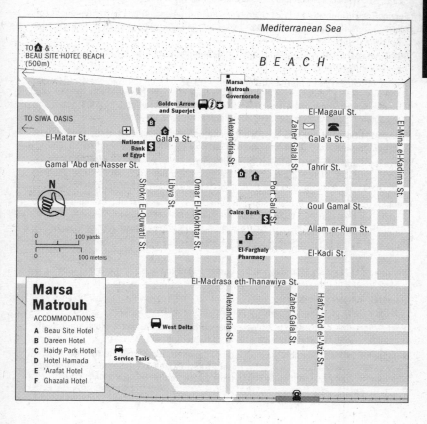

Mediterranean Sea

TO ■ &
BEAU SITE HOTEL BEACH
(500m)

BEACH

Marsa
Matrouh
Governorate

Golden Arrow
and Superjet

TO SIWA OASIS

El-Matar St.

National
Bank
of Egypt

Gala'a St.

Gamal 'Abd en-Nasser St.

N

0   100 yards

0   100 meters

Alexandria St.

Zaher Galal St.

El-Magaul St.

Gala'a St.

Tahrir St.

Goul Gamal St.

Allam er-Rum St.

El-Mina el-Kadima St.

Port Said St.

Cairo Bank

El-Farghaly
Pharmacy

El-Kadi St.

Shokri El-Quwati St.

Libya St.

Omar El-Mokhtar St.

El-Madrasa eth-Thanawiya St.

Alexandria St.

Zaher Galal St.

Hafiz 'Abd el-'Aziz St.

**Marsa
Matrouh**

ACCOMMODATIONS

A Beau Site Hotel
B Dareen Hotel
C Haidy Park Hotel
D Hotel Hamada
E 'Arafat Hotel
F Ghazala Hotel

West Delta

Service Taxis

While Marsa Matrouh is a pleasure spot, it is also only 215km from Libya—hence the noticeable military presence in the surrounding areas. It is wise to carry your **passport** with you outside of town and on the more obscure beaches. There may be a passport check on the road into town.

Airplanes: EgyptAir (tel. 493 43 98), on Gala'a St., 3½ blocks west of Alexandria St. Flies to and from **Cairo** (1hr.; Th, F, and Su leaves Cairo 9:30am, Matrouh 10:30am; US$117). Office open June-Sept. Tu-Su 9am-2pm and 6-9pm. No flights in off season.

Trains: (tel. 493 39 36), 1 block east of the southern end of Alexandria St., about 750m from the corniche. To **Alexandria** (6hr.; 7am and 3:45pm; 2nd class without A/C E£8, 3rd class E£4, 50% student discount).

Buses: There are 2 **bus stations.** Superjet and Golden Arrow lines leave from the corner by the tourist office, on the corniche 1 block west of Alexandria St. Catch West Delta buses, minibuses, and *service* at the station on Shokri el-Quwatli St., 3 blocks west of Alexandria St., at the southern end of town. A/C **Superjet** buses (tel. 493 47 87) run to **Alexandria** (3hr., 9am and 2:30pm, E£20) and **Cairo** (5hr.; 11am, 3, 4pm; E£37). Superjet might not run buses in winter. **Golden Arrow** runs A/C buses to **Alexandria** (3hr.; 9am and 3pm, in summer also 11am and 7pm; E£20) and **Cairo** (5hr.; in summer 8:30am, noon, 2:30, 3:30, 4:30pm; in winter 3:30pm only; E£35). **West Delta's** non-A/C buses shuttle to: **Alexandria** (5hr.; 2, 7, 9:30, 11am, noon, 1, 5, 8pm; E£15); **Cairo** (7hr., daily 7:30am, E£28); and **Siwa** (5hr.; 7:30am, 1:30, 4:30pm; E£12). Book ahead for Cairo buses, especially during summer. Arrive 30min. early to buy your ticket and get a seat. A/C bus services are either drastically or totally cut back in off season (Nov.-May).

Service Taxis: Opposite the West Delta bus station. To **Alexandria** (E£10). Infrequent service to **Siwa** (E£10) and nearby beaches. There are not many in operation, so be sure to have an alternate transportation plan.

Bike Rental: On Gala'a St., 1 block west of Alexandria St. E£2 per hr., E£10 per day; bargain for long-term rental.

Tourist Office: Egyptian Tourist Authority (tel. 493 18 41), on the corniche 1 block west of Alexandria St., behind the Governorate building. Friendly English-speaking staff. Ask for the helpful map booklet *Alexandria and Marsa Matrouh*, which lists a few hotels and restaurants. Open daily in summer 8am-8pm; in winter 8am-6pm.

Passport Office: (tel. 493 53 51), 1 block north and half-block east of the train station, just off Alexandria St. Open for visa extensions Sa-Th 8am-3pm.

Currency Exchange: The National Bank of Egypt, 3 blocks west of Alexandria St. on Gala'a St. Open daily 8:30am-2pm and 6-9pm. **Cairo Bank** (tel. 493 49 08), Pt. Said St. Open daily 8:30am-2pm and 6-9pm. Both change cash and traveler's checks.

Police: (tel. 93 33 76), 1 block south of corniche, 2 blocks east of Alexandria St. Little English spoken. Contact them in case of **medical emergency.** Open 24hr.

Tourist Police: (tel. 493 55 75), next door to the tourist office. Little English spoken, but the staff at the tourist office or a Superjet ticket seller can help you communicate in a crisis. Open 24hr.

Pharmacy: El-Farghaly Pharmacy, at the corner of Alexandria St. and Allam er-Rum St., 3 blocks south of the corniche. Open daily 8am-1am.

Hospital: Military Hospital (tel. 493 52 86 or 493 43 70), on Gala'a St., 3 blocks west of Alexandria St. If possible, seek treatment in Alexandria or Cairo.

Post Office: (tel. 493 23 67), 2 blocks east of Alexandria St. and 1 block south of the corniche. No Poste Restante. Open Sa-Th 8:30am-3pm.

Telephone Office: Opposite the post office. Crowded and unreliable for international calls. Sells phonecards. Open 24hr. **Hotel Riviera Palace,** on the northern end of Alexandria St., has pricier but more dependable phone and fax service. Open 24hr.

Telephone Code: 046.

▌ ACCOMMODATIONS

The high season lasts from mid-May to mid-September, but Marsa Matrouh sees the bulk of its tourist action during July and August. The typically dull winter months are interrupted by a spurt of Egyptian vacationers during Ramadan. During the off season, upscale hotels along the corniche offer surprisingly low rates. No matter what the time of year, rooms are a sure thing at the budget hotels on and near Alexandria St. Because few foreigners frequent these places, many have no English signs nor English speakers—**sign language** or Arabic experimentation (see **Phrasebook,** p. 702) may be in order. Men with small budgets and open minds can rent a bed in a crowded room for E£2-3, but should guard their belongings.

Groups of two or more can rent one of the many flats in town. **Hotel Awam** (tel. 493 23 63), to the west of Alexandria St. on the corniche near the Mosque of Awam, has two-bedroom flats for up to six people with living rooms, bathrooms, and kitchens for E£50. Couples can relax at **Marine Fouad** on Rommel's Peninsula, where wonderful new rooms with baths, porches overlooking the sea, and three meals a day for two people cost E£120 (open June-Sept.). Reserve with Mr. and Mrs. Boray in Cairo (tel. (02) 241 02 94). **Camping** is permitted on the beach in front of the Semiramis Hotel, free of charge. If you would like to pitch a tent farther out, contact the Egyptian Tourist Authority so they can inform the tourist police.

▨ **Beau Site Hotel** (tel. 493 20 66 or 493 40 11/12/13), on the beach a ways down the corniche. This 3-star hotel offers doubles with large terraces directly overlooking the ocean. Hotel facilities include a liberal (read: bikinis) private beach. There are only common bathrooms, but they're clean and just across the hall. US$10 per person.

▨ **'Arafat Hotel** (tel. 493 36 06), east of Alexandria St. on Tahrir St., past the Hotel Hamada. These clean lodgings have nothing in common with the Palestinian leader, so you'll be sure to spend a peaceful night. A 3D picture of 'a(ra) fat cat watches over the reception area. Singles E£15; doubles E£30; triples E£45. Breakfast E£5.

▨ **Hotel Hamada** (tel. 493 33 00), on the corner of Tahrir and Alexandria St. Bare-bones, reasonably clean rooms with shared baths. Don't mind the din from the *muezzin*—a mosque is just down the street. Singles, doubles, and triples E£10 per bed.

▨ **Ghazala Hotel** (tel. 493 35 19), Allam er-Rum St., in a 3-story white building just east of Alexandria St., 6 blocks from the corniche. Around the corner from El-Farghaly Pharmacy. Well-kept rooms with firm beds and great sofas, although the dank baths don't always have hot water. Dorms E£7.50. Singles E£10; doubles E£15.

◖▌ FOOD AND ENTERTAINMENT

Strolling along the corniche and chilling out in *ahwas* are the major after-hours recreational sports, just as they are in most of the towns along Egypt's Mediterranean coast. **Bars** in the Rady and Beau Site Hotels serve overpriced drinks, and the Beau Site also runs a **bowling alley.** A raised outdoor patio 100m west of the end of the corniche (across from the Armed Services hotel compound) often hosts energetic **live music** in a breezy, friendly setting during the summer.

▨ **Pizza Gaby,** just past the Negresco Hotel at the western end of the corniche. The hefty menu includes a variety of tasty pizzas (E£8-12), grilled meats (E£18-23), and Middle Eastern salads (E£3-6). This A/C haven overlooking the sea is the perfect spot to admire the sunset. Open daily noon-2am.

Samara Fish Restaurant (tel. 493 07 91), on Goul Gamal St. just east of Alexandria St., 2 blocks south of the corniche. This small restaurant serves up delicious grilled fish stuffed with vegetables. E£15-20 for a kilo of grilled gilled grub with salad and a heap of bread. Open daily in summer 8am-2am; in winter 8am-10pm.

Abu Aly Pizza (tel. 494 23 04), on Alexandria St. This 2-story restaurant offers a wide selection of soups, sandwiches, and desserts. Take-away fresh pizza (E£6.50-14.50) or chicken shawarma (E£5.50) makes a long bus ride seem shorter. Open noon-2am.

Panayotis Greek Restaurant (tel. 493 24 74), on the west side of Alexandria St., 2 blocks south of the corniche. Marsa's oldest restaurant has a simple menu including a stellar fish dinner (E£30), calamari (E£25), and Stella (E£4.75). Open daily 8am-1am.

◤ BEACHES

Marsa Matrouh's glorious beaches are its *raison d'être*. However, the 5km of white sand that rims the crescent-shaped bay closes after sunset, and soldiers patrol the coast nightly to deter drug trafficking. Here, just as in Alexandria, some women swim fully clothed, and only the most liberal beaches (designated below) allow for bikinis or revealing one-pieces. No matter how tolerant a beach may be, women should arrive well covered and gauge the mood of the crowd once there, as the crowd's level of acceptance can vary from day to day. Since most Egyptian visitors prefer to relax on the beach, even the most crowded areas have plenty of open water for swimming.

To reach these beaches, take a shared taxi or minibus from the bus station (E£2-3 per person to 'Agiba), a shared pickup truck from the stand on the corner 300m north of the main bus station (E£2 to 'Agiba), or the open-sided *tut-tut* bus (E£1.25 to Cleopatra or 'Agiba). The *tut-tut* shuttles to and from the bus station when there are enough passengers (usually every hr. 9am-4:30pm; summer only).

◣ 'AGIBA. Surely the most spectacular of the area's sights is 'Agiba ("miracle" in Arabic), about 24km from Marsa Matrouh. Yellow cliffs plunge down to meet the azure waters, where waves crash over eroded rock formations and into sandy caves. Swimming is not always permitted, but a barefoot walk along the rocks is one of the best ways to spend a few hours around Marsa Matrouh. Bring your own food—there is only a soft-drink stand here. Along the way, hidden in the sands near Umm Araham village, stand the ruins of the tiny **Temple to Ramses II.**

BEAU SITE HOTEL BEACH. The Beau Site Hotel (on the far west end of the corniche), though somewhat overrun by frolicking Egyptian children, has a beach that is cleaner and more liberal than most others. There is no charge for non-guests, but they ask that you rent an umbrella (E£12 per day), a chair (E£3 per day), or a sea kayak (E£10 per hr.). During the off season, umbrellas are free. The hotel also runs a guests-only beach where security guards ensure that bathers can wear bikinis—and several do—without being bothered.

ROMMEL'S ISLE. The eastern arm of the harbor is called Rommel's Isle, but it clearly isn't an Isle at all, as it can be reached by donkey cart (E£1), bike (E£10 per day), boat (E£7), or pickup truck taxi (50pt). Nestled in the peninsula is the **Rommel Museum,** housed in the caves that Rommel used as his headquarters during Germany's North African campaign (open daily 9am-3:30pm in summer; free). On the ocean side of the isle, an old **U-boat** juts out of the water, now a rusting wreck. You can rent a surf kayak to paddle out to it: head toward the red buoy on the left. The subaquatic submarine lies parallel to the beach 20m toward the mosque from the buoy; you'll need a snorkel mask to see it clearly. Since Rommel's Isle is close to town, the beach fills up quickly.

OTHER BEACHES. To the west of the main beach, the **Beach of Love (Shati' el-Gharaam)** fondles the western horn of the bay and can be easily reached by foot or kayak. Inconsiderate visitors have recently begun to spoil the sand while enjoying the sun, and heaps of litter float out to sea every day. You'll encounter more wind, less trash, and the tantalizing **Cleopatra's Beach** 14km farther west, on the far right-hand side of a small cove called **Cleopatra's Bath.** Legend has it that the queen and Marc Antony would come here to bathe—as the waves crashed into the cove, the water would shoot towards the heavens and cascade back down on the lovers' entangled bodies. The peaceful but shallow **Obayyid Beach,** 18km west of Marsa Matrouh, draws Egyptian families staying at their corporation's tents on the shore, making it pretty boring unless you're there with your middle-management friends.

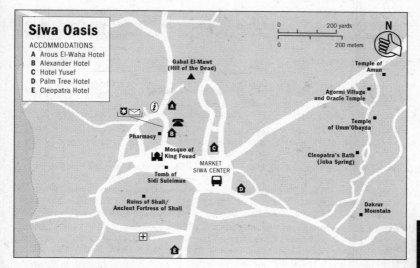

Siwa Oasis

ACCOMMODATIONS
- **A** Arous El-Waha Hotel
- **B** Alexander Hotel
- **C** Hotel Yusef
- **D** Palm Tree Hotel
- **E** Cleopatra Hotel

Gabal El-Mawt
(Hill of the Dead)

Temple of
Amun

Agormi Village
and Oracle Temple

Temple
of Umm'Obayda

Pharmacy

Mosque of
King Fouad

MARKET
SIWA CENTER

Cleopatra's Bath
(Juba Spring)

Tomb of
Sidi Suleiman

Ruins of Shali/
Ancient Fortress of Shali

Dakrur
Mountain

SIWA OASIS واحة سيوة

Emerging from 300km of barren, lifeless sand, the forest of palm trees and clear freshwater springs that make up the Siwa Oasis seems like a desert mirage. A walk among the people of this small town and its surrounding villages only deepens the sense of disbelief. Instead of Arabic, the Berber language of Siwi is spoken in homes and on the street, and the few married women who venture outside cover themselves from head to toe in blue *tarfudit* veils. Electricity only came to Siwa about 10 years ago, and the thousands of televisions in this town of mud-brick homes are only the most recent in a long history of outside invaders.

The Temple of Amun, east of the central town, housed one of the most famous oracles of the ancient world. After taking Egypt from the Persians in 331 BCE, Alexander the Great set out across the desert to learn Amun's prophecy. With the centuries that followed came more conquerors: Muhammad 'Ali brought the territory under Ottoman control in 1820; the British occupied it in the first decades of the 20th century; and during WWII, the Desert Fox himself trotted into town.

Even today, Siwa feels like a disputed territory. The people here are Siwans first, Egyptians second, and look with skeptical eyes on the technological changes that are making their desert buffer just a short stretch of sand. In 1984, the Egyptian government completed the road connecting Siwa to Marsa Matrouh, turning the arduous path by which Alexander made his pilgrimage into a quick four-hour bus route. Cairo has integrated the oasis into the national economy, and Arabic has replaced Siwi as the language of instruction in schools. Today, younger Siwan women don Egyptian fashions, and local folklore is losing ground to serial soap operas. But tradition is not giving up without a fight. Local festivals during fall and winter, especially the Feast of Siaha on the first full moon in October, are still celebrated with relish and bring in droves of spectators. Older women still wear the traditional Siwan costume, with intricately braided hairdos and heavy silver jewelry around their arms, necks, and heads. Residents request that visiting women cover their arms and legs; alcohol and open displays of affection are forbidden.

ORIENTATION AND PRACTICAL INFORMATION

The Siwa Oasis is in a desert hollow about 300km southwest of Marsa Matrouh. Its western edge comes within 50km of the closed Libyan border. The valley stretches across 82km west to east, and ranges between 3km and 30km north to south. Most visitors concern themselves only with Siwa town and nearby villages.

The most practical way to reach Siwa is by **bus** from Marsa Matrouh or Alexandria, but courageous groups with a car can travel the 420km stretch of rough road from Bahariyya. Near the ruins of the old mud-brick city of **Shali**, the central **town square** surrounds the **bus station**, close to most of the restaurants and hotels. The **tourist office, police station,** and **post office** are all on the short, curving road leading north from the nearby **King Fouad Mosque**, the town's largest building.

Buses: A/C **West Delta** come from **Marsa Matrouh** (5hr.; 7:30am, 1:30, 4pm; E£12) and Misr Station in **Alexandria** (10hr., 11am, E£27). Buses leave from Siwa to **Alexandria** (10hr., 7 and 10am, E£27) via **Marsa Matrouh** (additional bus at 2pm; E£10).

Local Bus: The local bus crawls west from the mosque to the village of El-Maraqi, making a 60km loop to Khamisa and Bilad er-Rum (round-trip E£2). There are usually 2 per day (in summer 7am and 3pm; in winter 7am and 2pm).

Tourist Office: Tel. 460 23 38, in the new white building across from the Arous el-Waha Hotel. Knowledgeable Mahdi Muhammad 'Ali Hweity, sociologist, fluent English-speaker, and native Siwan, arranges sightseeing expeditions, obtains camping permits, and is nearly an oracle himself on all aspects of Siwan life. Open Sa-Th 8am-2pm, and possibly in late evenings during winter.

English Bookstore: Hassan's Handicrafts and English Bookshop, next to the telephone office. A few English books on Egyptian history and culture and some novels. Run by the fab Mr. Hweity of the tourist office. Open Sa-Th in summer 8-11pm; in winter 3-10pm.

Pharmacy: Yusef's Pharmacy, on the road to the Cleopatra Hotel. Open daily in summer 9am-2pm and 6pm-midnight; in winter 9am-noon.

Hospital: Go south 1km from the town square and take a right at the 1st 4-story building on your left. Open daily 24hr.

Police: Tel. 460 20 08, in the same building as the post office. Open 24hr.

Post Office: Across the street from Arous el-Waha Hotel. Open Sa-Th 8am-2pm.

Telephone Office: Behind the Arous el-Waha Hotel.

Telephone Code: 046.

ACCOMMODATIONS

Most of the crash pads in Siwa cluster around the main square. Slow business in the summer means it is fairly easy to find a good room, but in winter Siwa has more tourists than donkeys, so make reservations or consider an outlying hotel. Unless otherwise noted, all rooms have fans. Free **camping** in shelters is available on **Dakrur Mountain**, 4km southeast of town, and at **Bir Wahad** (Well #1), 12km south of town (see **South of Siwa Town,** p. 144). Bring your sleeping bag and insect repellent. Check in with Mr. Hweity at the tourist office before pitching your tent.

Palm Tree Hotel (tel. 460 23 04), 20m down a side road from the town square. Clean, comfortable rooms with fans and balconies, but the best part of this hotel is the idyllic palm grove filled with palm-leaf furniture out back. Singles E£6; doubles E£12, with bath E£15; triples E£15. Laundry machine and bike rentals.

Hotel Yusef (tel. 460 21 62), in the center of town; the name is painted across the top floor. Balconies overlook Siwa and beyond. The cleanest rooms in town and a friendly owner, Salameh, who is committed to guests' satisfaction. Women can sunbathe on the roof terrace in peace. Dorms E£5. Bike rentals.

Alexander Hotel (tel. 460 50 12), across from the post office. Clean, unlike the state in which the original Alexander left Siwa. Dorms E£5. All rooms have private baths: singles E£10; doubles E£20.

Cleopatra Hotel (tel. 460 21 48), south of the town square on the main road, past the Shali fortress. A new, comfortable, and slightly pricier establishment with spacious balconies, great views, and immaculate bathrooms. Antony and Cleo would have loved the spacious "bungalow" doubles in the building next door (E£34). Singles E£10; doubles E£18, both with bath and balcony.

Arous El-Waha Hotel (tel. 460 21 00; fax 460 20 28), across from the tourist office in the northwestern part of town. Somewhat more expensive and upscale. All rooms have baths and showers. Singles E£40; doubles in summer E£50, in winter E£70.

FOOD

Several restaurants line the two market squares and are generally open from 8 or 10am to midnight or 1am. In summertime the menus shrink. For breakfast, try pancakes with banana, honey, and yogurt (E£2.50). If you ask around, a local may offer you a taste of *lagbi*, a sweet palm-tree juice and local specialty served only before 10am—it ferments by afternoon. Siwan eateries are pretty much indistinguishable from one another, but some tried-and-true places are **'Abdou's Restaurant** and the **Alexander Restaurant,** both opposite the Hotel Yusef, with excellent couscous at the former and an unusual quiche-style vegetarian pizza at the latter. **East-West** is one of the cleanest places in the town center and has a good vegetable couscous. The **Palm Tree Hotel** also has a garden restaurant. All Siwan restaurants are vegetarian friendly, and many feature Indian-inspired meals. Local **stores** are well stocked. Because Siwans tend to be more reserved than residents of most Egyptian towns, only a few travelers receive **invitations** to eat or stay with a local family. Invitations are usually offered by children, sometimes by adult men. At dinner, your hosts may try to sell you homemade handicrafts, or they may simply want to talk. As always, exercise caution before accepting hospitality—solo women should decline invitations from single Siwan men.

SIGHTS

Surrounded by gashes of black rock, waves of sand, and a piercing blue desert sky, Siwa is Egypt's most beautiful oasis. Most of Siwa's sites are easily accessible by bike trips down smooth dirt roads lined with palm trees. The more distant surrounding villages can be approached by local buses or through one of many tours offered by hotels and restaurants. *Carettas* (donkey-drawn taxicarts) always stand ready, making for a slow, bumpy, but thoroughly Siwan trip. Mr. Hweity of the tourist office has posted new blue signs around town to mark many of Siwa's important buildings and roads. A half-day tour goes for a bargain E£15 per head.

SIWA TOWN

RUINS OF SHALI. From atop the ruins of the crumbling medieval fortress-town of Shali (which simply means "town" in Siwi), you can see the quiet streets of Siwa town wind through a cluster of mud houses and luxuriant palm gardens. Shali's encircling wall once protected the Siwans from marauding Berbers and Bedouin. There was little room to build, so houses were cramped. Although the mud-brick structures were sturdy, torrential rains used to wash away most build-

ORACLE DEBACLE According to the ancient historian Herodotus (who was probably exaggerating the figures a bit), **King Cambyses** of Persia "detached a body of 50,000 men with orders to attack the Ammonians [the ancient name for the Siwans], reduce them to slavery, and burn the oracle of Zeus." No one is sure *why* King Cambyses wanted to conquer Siwa, but it's a well-established fact that the Persian ruler turned his wrath on the desert oasis after invading Egypt in 525 BCE. Some have theorized that Siwa's famed **Oracle of Amun** may have predicted a short reign for the new invaders, so a threatened Cambyses decided to demonstrate his power over prophecy. Predictably, things did not go according to plan. The troops made it to Kharga, then vanished without a trace. Legend holds that the whole army was buried in a sandstorm, but explorers and archaeologists have failed to find any sign of the army among the desert's dunes. The prophecy came true as well; in 331 BCE, **Alexander the Great** ousted the Persians and ended what was indeed a short reign.

ings about twice a century. After Muhammad 'Ali conquered Siwa in 1820, there

---

SIWI MADE SIMPLE Most Siwan children's first language is Siwi, an unwritten Berber dialect. It is incomprehensible to the rest of Egypt and sounds almost Scandinavian at times. As children grow up, parents and schools make sure they learn Arabic as well. The possible permutations of the following words should keep you occupied until the donkeys come home:

mashi	yes	**oula**	no	**aksoom**	meat
gaf lahk	go	**shiek**	you	**azumur**	olives
oushi	give me	**ehk sehk**	I want	**tene**	dates
sewil dede	speak with me	**aman**	water	**tanta wook**	What is this?

ihkseikh teswi aman	I want to drink water.
tanta elhal ineik	How are you?
betin ismetinik	What is your name?

---

was less need for fortification, so Siwans were quick to build more spacious homes below. Several days of fierce rain in 1985 severely damaged much of Shali, and what remains today is a deserted, surreal landscape of tangled walls and eroded mud-brick that seems as much a strange organic growth as a ruin. All of the walls are quite secure, and it is safe to wander through the ruins. Every Thursday night after the last call to prayer (around 9pm in summer, 6pm in winter), some local Muslims gather for religious ceremonies outside the mud-brick **Tomb of Sidi Suleiman,** the town's patron saint, beside the King Fouad Mosque. Visitors are invited to watch.

TRADITIONAL SIWAN HOUSE. The 1985 rains motivated a visiting Canadian ambassador to try to preserve Siwan culture, so he raised funds to construct the permanent Traditional Siwan House. The house serves as a museum of Siwan garb, silver jewelry, and children's toys. *(Just down the road from the tourist office, opposite the King Fouad Mosque. Open Sa-Th 10am-noon; ask at the tourist office for other hours. Admission E£1.50.)*

NORTH OF SIWA TOWN

GABAL EL-MAWT (HILL OF THE DEAD). The acropolis of Gabal el-Mawt rises 1km to the northeast of ancient Siwa. The hill is home to several Ptolemaic-era tombs that Romans robbed and reused. These tombs went undiscovered until WWII, when Siwan families crammed into caves seeking shelter from Italian bombs. The scattered human bones and mummy wrappings that litter the site belonged to the Romans, as do the niches that mar the ancient frescoes. The first sepulcher is the **Tomb of Si-Amun.** The intact decoration shows the bearded nobleman with Osiris; the magnificent ceiling depicts the six stages of the sun's journey across the sky, as well as a beautiful field of stars. The **Tomb of Mesu Isis,** 5km to the east, has damaged paintings of Osiris and Isis. The **Tomb of the Crocodile** features paintings of the scaly chomper once buried there, although his corpse has been removed. The **Tomb of Niperpathot,** the oldest tomb in Siwa, housed the body of a nobleman of the 26th dynasty; it was closed for renovations in 1999. *(A custodian is on hand to unlock the tombs daily from 9am to 2pm. Free; E£2 bakhsheesh is appropriate but not necessary.)*

EAST OF SIWA TOWN

The Temple of Amun and the Temple of Umm 'Obayda both lie only 1km apart on the same stretch of road. A bike trip looping around the road might take in the two temples, followed by a dip at Cleopatra's Bath, then onto Dakrur Mountain, and from there back to town. Rent a bike from town or hail a *caretta* (E£10 per load).

ORACLE OF AMUN. A 13th-century gate made of palm logs graces the entrance to the acropolis atop which this oracle is perched. You'll have to follow the same path as Alexander the Great to reach the oracle: go through the stone temple's simple gateway into the outer court, then cross the inner court to reach the center. The Oracle of Amun is thought to date from the 26th dynasty (c. 660 BCE). It became widely celebrated in later dynasties and gained popularity even with the ancient Greeks, who constructed many shrines to Amun in their home city-states. Greek and Roman historians recorded the mystical rituals necessary to invoke an answer from the oracle: priests carried a sacred boat containing the image of Amun, while women sang and danced in procession. Alexander did all of this to seek the answer to his personal burning question: Was he a god, the son of Zeus? Supposedly Alexander also asked the oracle another question in private, but what he queried will never be known; the secret died with him, fewer than 10 years after his visit.

TEMPLE OF UMM 'OBAYDA. A little less than 1km south of the Oracle of Amun, down the curving road, are the remains of the Temple of Umm 'Obayda, also dedicated to Amun. Surviving the ravages of time and a destructive earthquake in 1877, the temple was reasonably well preserved near the end of the 19th century—until a local government official demolished the remains in 1897 to collect stone for the construction of some new public buildings. One wall remains upright, with painted carvings and inscriptions dedicated to the Egyptian gods.

CLEOPATRA'S BATH. A pleasant 1km bike ride through the green and quiet groves of palms around Siwa brings you to **Juba Springs**, renamed Cleopatra's Bath by the tourist authority. Like many of the natural springs in Siwa (there are approximately 200), a stone basin now encircles it and an irrigation duct runs out one end. Although the pool is mostly frequented by men, fully clothed women should also feel comfortable swimming here (as comfortable as swimming fully clothed can be), and may enter via the enclosure next to the spring. If you visit these sights at sunrise or in the late evening, you may be the only person there.

HAMMAM RAMAL (SAND BATH). On **Dakrur Mountain**, 1km south of Cleopatra's Bath, nearly 1000 rheumatics congregate each summer for 10-day stints in the *hammam ramal* (sand bath). The procedure may sound like a Siwan torture method, but is actually painless: under the supervision of a specialist, the "bather" is buried in sand from the neck down while his head is protected from the sun's heat. After a stint in the sand, the patient stays indoors for the rest of the day, then repeats the procedure. You can try the bath for E£25, including room and board.

ABU SHROUF AND ENVIRONS. Abu Shrouf, 27km east of Siwa towards Bahariyya, is cooler, deeper, and cleaner than any of Siwa's pools. Local legend has it that Abu Shrouf is the only place in the oasis with female donkeys. If a male donkey escapes from Siwa, the first place his owner looks is Abu Shrouf. This myth has even influenced local slang: if a Siwan man has a pleasant night with his wife, he tells his friends, "Last night I went to Abu Shrouf!" You too can go there, either with the tour arranged by Mr. Hweity from the Siwa tourist office (4 people, E£15 each, winter only) or by private taxi from Siwa (about E£25 round-trip). A large spring called **Qurayshat**, 7km west of Abu Shrouf, was a major farming area during Roman times—old olive presses still remain. A small **Bedouin village** lies 5km to the east. The Bedouin once lived in tents here, but the government built them houses. Preferring tents, they kept animals in the new houses. The government was unamused that their projects were being used as barns, so they destroyed many of the Bedouin's tents to force them to live in the houses.

WEST OF SIWA TOWN

FATNAS. In all of idyllic Siwa, the best place to watch the late afternoon sun dip into the endless sands is **Fatnas**, or Fantasy Island, 4km west of town. Accessible by a small causeway, Fatnas Pool is slightly smaller than Cleopatra's Bath and not as heavily frequented by the locals. From the far western point of the adjoining garden, you can see across a glistening salt lake to a limitless sea of sand.

> **GREASED LIGHTNING** Not long ago, Siwans ran a smuggling operation to carry goods on the sly from Libya into Egypt on donkeys. The nighttime treks would proceed perfectly until the beasts (unaware of the clandestine nature of the mission) would bray and alert the Border Patrol officials, thereby spoiling the whole operation. Siwans wracked their brains to figure out a way to pacify the carriers until someone, somehow discovered that if the asses' asses were greased, the brutes would be unable to create the force needed to let air out of their mouths. A team of French scientists is currently researching this exciting discovery.

BILAD ER-RUM (CITY OF THE ROMANS). The unidentified stone structure and several tombs in the hillside just outside Siwa are known as Bilad er-Rum (City of the Romans). Up the road behind barbed wire are the remains of a **Doric temple.** Greek archaeologist Liana Souvaltzi caused a major stir when she announced in 1995 that she had discovered the tomb of Alexander the Great within the temple walls. A team of 12 archaeologists quickly flew in from Greece and determined that the tomb's inscriptions were not Alexander's, but those of an important Greek official. Although Alexander wanted to be buried in Siwa, his general Ptolemy swiped the corpse and buried it in his capital, Alexandria, where it still lies today (somewhere underneath the modern roads and highrises). Campers can ask for special permission to sleep here, then take the bus back to Siwa the next morning.

SOUTH OF SIWA TOWN

BIR WAHAD AND ALZAITON. Bir Wahad (Well #1), 12km south of Siwa, is surrounded by lush vegetation and sports hot water clean enough for bathing. A number of Siwan tour guides will take you for around E£45. Inquire at the tourist office to find out who offers the best package. If you spend the night, bring a blanket from your hotel—it gets cold in the desert, even in mid-July. About 6km from Siwa, a fabulous stretch of water erupts amid sand dunes 1km off the main road, in an area known as the **fish farm.** *(Fish farm accessible by bicycle.)*

SHOPPING

While in Siwa, you can shop for exquisite **handicrafts,** including intricately embroidered clothing, veils, and *margunahs* (large, decorated woven baskets). Several stores have sprung up around the town square, including **Siwa Original Handicraft,** to the left of 'Abdou Restaurant, and **Hassan's Handicrafts,** next to the telephone office. Bargaining in craft shops can be difficult, as the (mainly female) artisans set the prices and aren't around to haggle. The types of crafts sold are changing to accommodate tourist tastes; the baskets and shawls are the most traditional pieces. Siwa's silversmith died several decades ago without training an apprentice, so it is difficult to find jewelry here nowadays.

SINAI PENINSULA السيناء

The Sinai is the collision point of two continents, an enormous tectonic summit. A handful of small towns and a major road artery occupy the sandy shelf where the mountains meet the sea, but only the Bedouin brave the rest of the Sinai's dry, rough landscape. The greatest profusion of life in the area thrives below the sea: Aqaba's warm waters support a carnival of brilliantly colored coral reefs and subaquatic life. In sharp contrast to the bland browns and earthy hues of the rest of the Middle East, the underwater environs expose an explosion of color—the reds and greens of coral broken by the flashes of yellow, blue, and orange fins, set against the sparkling turquoise backdrop of the Red Sea.

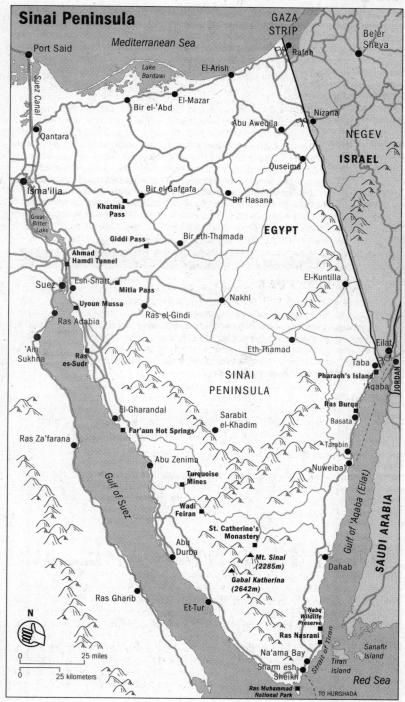

Sinai Peninsula

Mediterranean Sea

Port Said

Suez Canal

Lake Bardawi

El-Arish

GAZA STRIP

Rafah

Be'er Sheva

Qantara

El-Mazar

Bir el-'Abd

Abu Aweqila

Nizana

NEGEV

Isma'ilia

Quseima

ISRAEL

Great Bitter Lake

Bir el-Gafgafa

Bir Hasana

EGYPT

Khatmia Pass

Giddi Pass

Bir eth-Thamada

Ahmad Hamdi Tunnel

Esh-Shatt

Mitla Pass

El-Kuntilla

Suez

Uyoun Mussa

Nakhl

Ras el-Gindi

Ras Adabia

'Ain Sukhna

Ras es-Sudr

Eth-Thamad

Eilat

Taba

Pharaoh's Island

Aqaba

JORDAN

SINAI PENINSULA

Ras Burqa

Basata

El-Gharandal

Sarabit el-Khadim

Far'aun Hot Springs

Tarabin

Ras Za'farana

Abu Zenima

Nuweiba

Gulf of Suez

Turquoise Mines

Gulf of 'Aqaba (Eilat)

SAUDI ARABIA

Wadi Feiran

St. Catherine's Monastery

Abu Durba

Mt. Sinai (2285m)

Dahab

Gabal Katherina (2642m)

Ras Gharib

Et-Tur

Nabq Wildlife Preserve

Ras Nasrani

N

Na'ama Bay

Sharm esh-Sheikh

Strait of Tiran

Tiran Island

Sanafir Island

Red Sea

0   25 miles

0   25 kilometers

Ras Muhammad National Park

TO HURGHADA

EGYPT

The Sinai has had a surprisingly long history of war. Since the pharaohs' troops first trampled the broad plains of the northern Sinai on their march to Syria and Canaan, the favor has been returned by marauding, Egypt-bound Hyksos, Assyrians, Persians, Greeks, Arabs, and Turks. In 1903, the British drew the borders of the Sinai from Rafah to Eilat in an attempt to keep Turkey and Germany safely distanced from the Suez Canal. On the fourth day of the Six Day War of 1967, Israel regained control of the Sinai Peninsula from Egypt and began to capitalize upon the tourism potential of the region. The Israelis established most of the original hotels and dive centers, including those in Dahab and Sharm esh-Sheikh. The new development altered the lives of many Bedouin, who began to give camel tours and help out in hotels. Large amounts of cash made it possible for some to abandon their traditional nomadic lifestyle.

In the 1973 Yom Kippur War, Egyptian forces crossed the canal in a surprise offensive to recapture the Sinai. The Egyptian army broke through the Israeli defense line, but later Israeli counterattacks recaptured most of the peninsula. Israel retained the Sinai until it was returned to Egypt in two stages under the terms of the Camp David Accords: the first half in 1979, the second in 1982. U.N. troops monitor the treaty. The Sinai never regained its politically strategic status but remains a highly touristed vacation spot.

HIGHLIGHTS OF THE SINAI PENINSULA

■ The secluded **El-Arish** (p. 148) is the jewel of Egypt's most inviting shore, while **Sharm esh-Sheikh** (p. 155) is world-renowned for the beauty beneath its waves.
■ Even if Dopey's not your favorite of the Seven Dwarfs, visit the Bedouin camps of **Dahab** (p. 160) and you'll put on a Happy face.
■ Moses made the hike up **Mount Sinai** (p. 150); now thou shalt too. Tackle some of the tougher desert hikes of the **High Sinai** (p. 154) with a Bedouin as your guide.

⌐ GETTING AROUND

Travel in the Sinai Peninsula is far easier than in the rest of Egypt. Women can comfortably wear shorts and sleeveless shirts in most places, and professional con artists are rare. Many Bedouin have given up their camels for Camaros, but there are still places where travelers can get a sense of their nomadic lifestyle.

BY BUS

The noble machines of the **East Delta Bus Company,** battered cruelly by the rocks, ruts, and dust of Sinai roads, heroically tread the scorched highway. With towns few and far between and separated by mountain passes, buses and taxis are the only means of transportation. Timetables are really no more than an administrator's pipe dream. At bus stations, patience is more a necessity than a virtue.

BY SERVICE TAXI

A reasonably priced and convenient alternative to buses is the *service* taxi. Weathered old Peugeot 504s piloted by Bedouin cabbies are ubiquitous. Hop in with other passengers or negotiate with a driver and wait while he recruits more travelers to your destination. Women should avoid riding alone with a driver. *Service* are comparable in price to the bus under ideal circumstances, but only with a full load of seven. You'll get to where you're going a lot faster, but this speed has its perils: traffic laws do not apply and the laws of physics are only grudgingly acknowledged. Consistent with the laws of supply and demand, prices will drop immediately before the arrival of a bus, then skyrocket after the bus has departed.

■ ABOVE-WATER TIPS

A number of **regulations** govern travelers to the Sinai. Unguided travel is restricted to main roads and settlements, but you may visit parts of the desert interior with a Bedouin guide. Sleeping on the beach is prohibited in some areas (notably Na'ama Bay), and the police often harass dozing backpackers. Since these areas are not always marked, ask around before settling down for the night. Nude sunbathing is illegal, as is the oft-hawked **marijuana.** You cannot bring a rented car or any four-wheel drive vehicle into the Sinai from Israel. **Prices** are higher and exchange rates poorer here than anywhere else in Egypt. If you're coming from the Nile Valley, change money before arriving. **Bug season** descends upon the Sinai in the spring and early summer. Dahab is periodically clouded by mosquitoes and flies with killer munchies. Some travelers rig mosquito nets; others advise sleeping by the beach. In summer, no one wears or carries much, and it only takes a few days before travelers begin to reexamine conventions of hygiene and appearance.

> **TELEPHONE CODE** The telephone code for all of the Sinai Peninsula is **062.**

◎ UNDERWATER TIPS

Without question, the Red Sea has some of the greatest coral reefs and marine life in the world. Diving was not very big in the Middle East until Jacques-Yves Cousteau made his voyage through the Red Sea aboard *Calypso* (as chronicled in his famous book and movie *The Silent World*). Now that diving is a major part of many trips to the Sinai Peninsula, the regional administration has begun to face the serious problem of **irresponsible ecotourism.** All coral reefs from Dahab to Ras Muhammad are under the jurisdiction of the Ras Muhammad National Park. Regulations forbid the removal or defacement of any animal, plant, or shell, living or dead, from the sea. The park is fighting a difficult battle with developers waiting to exploit the region. You can do your part to preserve the reefs by observing a simple rule: look, but don't touch. Ras Muhammad, like most James Bond movies, has underwater police who will chase you out of the water if they see you breaking this rule. Even accidentally bumping the coral can damage it (and damage you).

Diving is very expensive, but you're paying for safety. The sites along the Gulf of Aqaba coast listed below emphasize safety above all else. **Snorkeling gear** can be rented all over; **dive shops** are concentrated mainly in Dahab and Sharm esh-Sheikh. You must be certified to rent equipment; most five-day courses provide certification and cost around US$300. The only decompression chamber in the area is in Sharm esh-Sheikh. If you're rusty, take a check-out dive for US$35.

Beginning divers should make sure their instructors speak their language flawlessly, as small misunderstandings can have a big significance underwater ("Tanks!" "You're welcome!"). The instructor must also be certified to teach your particular course, whether it's PADI or SSI—ask to see his or her card. Some clubs are active in protecting the reefs, participating in annual clean-up dives, and making sure their operations have minimal impact on the marine ecosystems. The size of the club also matters: larger centers often have more scheduled dives and more extensive facilities, whereas smaller ones give you more personal attention and will usually run a course for just one or two people rather than waiting for six to sign up. Quality of equipment and safety records are important. Ask divers for advice.

NORTHERN SINAI

EL-ARISH العريش

El-Arish is caught in the cultural vortex between the *sheesha*-smoking Mediterranean and the who-knows-what-smoking Sinai—and manages to avoid the worst of both. Because it is only accessible through Isma'ilia, El-Arish is much less touristed than the High Sinai, and is free of the acres of concrete vacation complexes that line the Mediterranean coast near Alexandria. Currently the capital of the North Sinai Governorate, the city was once an important stopover on what was perhaps the oldest military route in history. El-Arish has since given up military mottos and has settled down with a more mellow one: life's a beach. The beach here is clean and inviting (some say the best on Egypt's Mediterranean coast), and the only shore in Egypt spotted with palm trees. Come sit a spell.

⁊ ORIENTATION AND PRACTICAL INFORMATION. There are only two roads to know in El-Arish: **Fouad Zekry Street,** which runs along the beach, and **Tahrir Street,** perpendicular to Fouad Zekry. The **bus station** (tel. 34 01 08) is at the south end of Tahrir St., 2km from the beach. Buses run daily to **Cairo** (5hr.; 8, 11:30am and 5pm E£25, 4pm E£35) and **Isma'ilia** (3hr., every 30min. 7am-5pm, E£10). Rafah and the Israeli border can be reached by **service taxi** (E£2). Getting around the downtown area by foot is easy, but a walk to the beach is a bit far—catch a *tut-tut* bus or one of the brightly colored Mercedes that serve as shared taxis (25pt).

The ETA **tourist office** (tel. 34 05 69), on Fouad Zekry St., is just off the beach (open daily 9am-2pm and 4-8pm). Coming from the downtown/Tahrir St. area, bear left at the intersection with Fouad Zekry. The tourist office and tourist police (police open 24hr.) are in the same building on the right There are banks along Tahrir St., including the **National Bank of Egypt** (tel. 35 18 81) and the **Bank of Cairo** (tel. 35 30 32), which exchanges traveler's checks and cash or gives cash advances on credit cards (both open Su-Th 9am-2:30pm). The **police station** is at the northern end of Tahrir Sq., but you're better off paying a visit to the tourist police. There are many **pharmacies** in the downtown area (generally open daily 8am-1am). The **Government Hospital** (tel. 34 00 11) is on El-Geish St., just off Tahrir St. (open 24hr.). The **post office** (tel. 35 15 03; fax 35 15 01) is three blocks north and two blocks east of Tahrir Sq., and will send a fax for E£5.50 plus the cost of the call (open Sa-Th 8:30am-2:30pm). The **telephone office** is right across the street (open 24hr.).

⁊⁊⁊ ACCOMMODATIONS AND FOOD. Most of El-Arish's beachfront hotels are reasonably priced. The **Moonlight Hotel** (tel. 34 13 62) is on the beach, just west of the tourist office, off Fouad Zekry St. Moonlit or not, the hallways are a bit dark, but the rosy-fingered (OK, bright pink) rooms are like a cheerful vision of the dawn. Reservations are advised (singles E£20; doubles E£40; both with baths). The **Green Land Beach Hotel** (tel. 34 06 01) is on the same road, but east of the tourist office. Doubles and triples offer fan, balcony, bath, breakfast, and the occasional TV for only E£30. The airy **Es-Salaam Hotel** (tel. 35 42 19) is on Tahrir St., off the square. Ask for a room away from the street (singles E£6.50; doubles E£15.50; triples E£21.75; all with shower).

Food consists mostly of standard Arab fare, with the exception of **William's,** in front of the Green Land Beach Hotel on Fouad Zekry St. Minimalist decor and the absence of anyone named "William" do not detract from the fish and meat entrees, complete with french fries and salad (E£10-20). Down the road to the west is **Basata,** roofed with palm fronds and filled with palm frond furniture (full meals E£10-20). In town, the best budget meal award goes to **'Aziz** (tel. 35 43 45), located next to Es-Salaam Hotel on Tahrir St. 'Aziz has a variety of grilled foods (E£7-10) and rice or noodle side dishes (E£3).

☎ 📠 SIGHTS AND ENTERTAINMENT. Life in El-Arish revolves around the Mediterranean. The entire length of the **beach** is pristine, and, except for brief sections in front of the Semiramis and Egoth Oberoi Hotels, there is no difference between public and private shoreline. There are a few interesting **Bedouin craft stores** at the north end of Tahrir St. Every Thursday, Tahrir Square comes alive when local Bedouin sell silver, rugs, garments, and camel accessories at the weekly **souq.** A few km east of town on the road to Rafah is the **Sinai Heritage Museum,** which details traditional Bedouin life on the Peninsula and has an excellent collection of clothes and jewelry (open Sa-Th 9:30am-2pm; admission E£2; camera privileges E£5, video E£25). In the evenings, many locals take to the *sheesha* parlors of Tahrir Sq., while the coffee shops along the corniche attract tourists. The expensive drinks (Stella E£12) outnumber the people at the **bars** of the Semiramis and Oberoi hotels.

Near El-Arish is **Zaranik Protected Area,** a nature preservation where thousands of birds migrate in the fall. The park there has a bird viewing area, nature trails, and even campgrounds. Get there on a *service* taxi running between Isma'ilia and El-Arish (admission US$3; camping US$5 per person).

WESTERN SINAI

The Sinai Peninsula's west coast is a mixed blessing. The industrial wasteland of the shallow Gulf of Suez doesn't compare to the stunning beauty above and below sea level all along the Gulf of Aqaba coast. If you see the oil rigs and flame-belching smokestacks of the Suez coast out the window of the Cairo-Sharm esh-Sheikh bus, you've probably seen enough. Most Western tourists avoid the Western Sinai, leaving its few memorable attractions uncrowded and peaceful.

UYOUN MUSSA. Moses buffs everywhere will be enthralled by this locale, 15km south of Suez, where Moses devised an early water purification system with the help of a tree branch. Today, Uyoun Mussa continues Moses' work in several wells, some of which you can swim in. When Napoleon visited in 1798, he discovered a canal linking the wells to the sea, used to resupply ships with fresh water. *(Daily buses from Suez will drop you off, but finding a ride back can be dangerously unreliable. The best option is to hire a taxi from Suez (E£40-50). Be insistent on seeing the wells— the driver may deny their existence.)*

RAS EL-GINDI. Ras el-Gindi features the ruins of Salah ad-Din's 800-year-old fortress **Qal'at el-Gindi,** the "Fortress of the Soldier." The impressive ruins stand atop a small mountain (about a 1hr. climb). Be careful climbing up, as the path drops off considerably on either side; one misstep and you'll wind up next to your sleeping taxi driver below. *(Located 50km inland from Ras es-Sudr. If you take the bus to Ras es-Sudr, you'll have to hire a taxi for E£80-100 to Ras el-Gindi, so get a group together. Taxis can be found at the petrol station after the turnoff for Sudr. Getting back to Suez can be tough; know the (alleged) bus schedule, and prepare to be stranded. Bring gallons of water, a camera, and a solid pair of hiking shoes.)*

FAR'AUN HOT SPRINGS. Though the hot springs and beach at this southern spot are attractive, their location makes reaching them more trouble than they're worth. The beach at 'Ain Sukhna is infinitely more convenient. *(Just off the main highway 80km south of Suez. Hire a taxi from Suez for E£100.)*

SARABIT EL-KHADIM. This remote spot is the site of an ancient temple that extends over 200m of desert. During the 12th Dynasty (c. 1900 BCE), a small chapel was dedicated to the goddesses Sodpu and Hathor, "Mistress of Turquoise." In the 18th dynasty, the temple was elongated and expanded. Ramses VI, the last pharaoh to visit the temple, dropped by around 1100 BCE. The stones of the ruins are decorated with religious spells and accounts of mining expeditions. Around the temple are ancient turquoise mines waiting to be explored. Your mission, should you choose to accept it, takes about three days—two for traveling, one for exploring. *(You'll have to rent or hire a four-wheel drive vehicle and get permission from the military to venture into the desert. The best place to start is the Suez tourist office (see p. 172). They can inform you of the latest regulations on travel to this seldom visited site.)*

HIGH SINAI

The central region of the Sinai Peninsula, known as the High Sinai, is worlds away from the lazy daze of Dahab. Cosmopolitan coastal life may cause you to forget that you're on the outskirts of over 60,000 square km of arid desert, but savvy hikers know that high times can be had in the High Sinai as well. Nestled in this rugged desertscape are the biblical locales of **Mt. Sinai,** the mountain on which Moses received the Ten Commandments, and **St. Catherine's Monastery,** located near the Burning Bush. The **High Sinai desert** is an ideal place for unforgettable hikes.

MOUNT SINAI

The holy peak of Mt. Sinai, or, as locals call it, Mt. Moses (Gabal Mussa), stands 2285m above sea level. The Bible describes a mountain engulfed in fire and smoke that Moses ascended to receive the Ten Commandments while the Israelites built a golden calf at its base. Mount Sinai is one of only two places in the Old Testament where God revealed himself to the people, making the desolate peak sacred for both Christians and Muslims (Jews have not universally identified the modern Mt. Sinai as the promontory made famous by the Bible). In the Book of Exodus, God warned the people, "Take heed that you do not go up into the mountain or touch the border of it; whoever touches the mountain shall be put to death" (Exodus 19:12). This prohibition seems to have been long forgotten—busloads of tourists climb the peak each day. God should have included an 11th commandment: "Thou shalt not trash holy places;" maybe then climbers would think twice before leaving litter on the trail and the peak. Despite the Baraka bottles, the view from the summit is awe-inspiring.

▯ PRACTICAL INFORMATION

You don't necessarily need a guide, but for safety, neither men nor women should hike alone, especially at night. Most people hook up with **organized groups** from Dahab and begin their climb (via the camel path) around 2am, allowing trekkers to enjoy the cool night and catch the sunrise at the top. Bring a flashlight. If you're hiking **alone,** hike in the early afternoon when it's still light, watch the sunset, and sleep on the summit. Socialites can stake out a spot directly on the summit platform by the tea and refreshment stands. More secluded spots are available just beyond the boulders and human feces on the sloping shoulder to the west. Walk about 40m until you cross a ravine; the small summit ahead has several campsites protected by stone windbreaks. If you explore this area during the daylight hours, you'll discover an ancient Bedouin **cistern** where water was stored during the sizzling summers. You can also beat the crowds by sleeping in Elijah's Hollow (see below) or by climbing at midday (not recommended in summer).

Overnighters should bring ample **food,** and everyone should bring at least two or three bottles of **water** for the ascent. The cheapest place to buy these amenities is the supermarkets in St. Catherine's town. The monastery **rest house** also sells snacks and water at reasonable prices. There are refreshment stands on the way up, but prices increase with altitude. A stand on the summit sells tea (E£2), water (E£4), and various snacks (E£3-5). If you plan to spend the night on the mountain, bring a **sleeping bag** and **warm clothes.** Even in the summer, it's often only 8-10°C at night and the breeze makes it feel much colder. Those without the necessary gear can rent blankets (E£2.50) and mattresses (E£5) at the top. There are also "toilets" at the summit (holes in the ground with more flies than privacy). Hikers should bring a warm change of clothing—sweaty shirts quickly turn to shirtsicles.

HOLY MT. SERBAL? In some religious circles, the debate still rages over whether Mt. Sinai is actually the site where Moses received the Ten Commandments. Though most believe that Mt. Sinai is the real McCoy, some maintain that the actual mountain referred to in the Bible is Mt. Serbal, 20 miles to the west. According to most biblical scholars, however, the Mt. Serbalists are fighting a losing battle. The Bible mentions three characteristics of the mountain in question: it is surrounded by a vast plain, the summit is visible to all below, and it is accessible to all who surround it. All three describe Sinai, none Serbal. Furthermore, it is doubtful that the Israelites would have chosen to camp for a year in the valley beneath Mt. Serbal, which is the site of fierce floods, little drinking water, and hordes of mosquitoes. And who wants to tell 18 generations of pilgrims they've been climbing the wrong mountain?

▟ HIKING: MT. SINAI

The hike to the top is not all that challenging, but you should still leave all but the bare essentials behind. The monks of St. Catherine's will allow you to leave your bags in a room for E£2 per piece. There are two paths up the mountain: the **Steps of Repentance** and a **camel path.** A nice place to take a break on the way up (or down) is **Elijah's Hollow.** To find either path, walk up the hill to the monastery, bear left at the fork, and continue to the back of the monastery structure. From here the camel path continues down the valley while the Steps start to the right, at the southeast corner of the monastery. There is one juncture that confuses hikers: near the top, the camel path intersects the steps after passing through a narrow, steeply walled stone corridor. Turn left to reach the summit; the camel path stops here. Riders will have to get off their high humps and huff up the rest of the way.

STEPS OF REPENTANCE. Of the two paths up the mountain, this is shorter (about 2hr.) and more difficult, but you probably deserve it. It is said that the 3750 steps were built by a single monk in order to fulfill his pledge of penitence. The monk cut corners here and there and made many of the steps the height of two or three mortal ones. The steps are treacherous by night; after dark they are difficult to follow even with a flashlight. Save them for the descent in the morning.

CAMEL PATH. The longer route (at night about 2½hr. by toed foot, 1½hr. by cloven) was built in the 19th century and begins directly behind the monastery. **Camel rides** up the mountain usually cost E£30 during peak hours, but if you can stand the sun and the heat, you can get a ride up in the middle of the day for the low price of E£10. Unfortunately, the camels are not always available when you need them—you may arrive at the dispatch area and find only dung.

ELIJAH'S HOLLOW. Turn right at the juncture about two-thirds of the way up and you'll arrive at a 500-year-old cypress tree dominating the depressional plain known as Elijah's Hollow. This is where the prophet Elijah is said to have heard the voice of God after fleeing Jezebel (I Kings 19:8-18). Two small **chapels** now occupy the site, one dedicated to Elijah and the other to his successor Elisha. Moses supposedly hid in the **cave** below when he first came face-to-face with God: "while my glory passes by, I will put you in a cleft of the rock, and I will cover you with my hand until I have passed by" (Exodus 33:22). The chapel is almost always closed in afternoons, but usually open immediately after sunrise for one to two hours. You can still see the watering hole used by the prophet.

SAINT CATHERINE'S

Saint Catherine's rich history of monasticism started in the 3rd century CE when Christian hermits, attracted by the tradition designating the valley below as the site of the **Burning Bush,** migrated here in a quest for holiness and freedom from Roman persecution. Living in complete poverty and isolation (except on holy days, when they gathered at the Burning Bush), these hermits often fell victim to

EGYPT

harsh weather and raiding nomads. In 313 CE, Constantine the Great officially recognized Christianity, and soon afterwards the monastery was founded by Constantine's mother, Empress Helena. The monastery thrived under the continual protection of the incumbent rulers (including Muhammad and Napoleon) during the ensuing 1600 years. As a tribute to the monks' tradition of hospitality to Christians and Muslims alike, it has never been conquered. Modern pilgrims and curious tourists of all faiths visit St. Catherine's throughout the year. Though much of the monastery is closed to the public, its beautiful architecture and mountainous setting ensure an unforgettable visit.

▣ ORIENTATION AND PRACTICAL INFORMATION

At an elevation of about 1600m, **Saint Catherine's Monastery** is hidden away in the mountainous interior of the southern Sinai. Excellent roads run west to the Gulf of Suez and east to the Gulf of Aqaba, both about 100km away. Tiny **Saint Catherine's town** lies about 3km east of the monastery.

Buses serving St. Catherine's are notorious for their tardiness, but do eventually run to **Cairo** (9hr., 6am, E£35) via **Suez** (6hr., E£25), and seasonally to **Sharm esh-Sheikh** (7hr., 1pm, E£20) via **Dahab** (1¾hr., E£15). **Taxis** are always available, but prices are entirely dependent on the number of passengers and the bus schedule. Popular destinations are **Dahab** (E£90 per car), **Sharm esh-Sheikh** (E£200 per car), and **Cairo** (E£275-300). Lone women should avoid taxis. Cabs hover around the central square in the daytime; ask at the market if you don't see any.

Incoming taxi drivers will deposit you in St. Catherine's town, which boasts a number of modern conveniences despite its size. The **bus station** is at the main square; it's not a "station" per se, but a point in space where the bus is assumed to stop. Note that most buses from Dahab have been canceled. On one side of the square is an arcade with a **Bank Misr** (tel. 47 04 63), where you can exchange money or traveler's checks and withdraw cash with your Visa card (open daily 8:30am-1:30pm and 6:30-8:30pm). The local **police station** (tel. 47 03 13) is farther up the hill near the mosque. The **tourist police** (tel. 47 00 46) and the **hospital** (tel. 47 03 68) are both opposite the bus station and open 24hr. The **post office** (tel. 47 03 01) is open daily from 8am to 3pm, and the nearby 24-hour **telecommunications office** (tel. 47 00 10) has international phone service.

▮▮ ACCOMMODATIONS AND FOOD

The cheapest and most popular choice is the free **camping** on Mt. Sinai's chilly peak. The nearest budget alternative is the monastery's **youth hostel** (tel. 47 03 43). To get there, turn right at the fork just before the monastery. The clean but cramped rooms are within earshot of the monks, so keep your blasphemous thoughts to yourself. The location alone is worth the price (7- to 8-bed dorms E£35; 3- to 4-bed dorms E£40; private rooms E£65). A delectable dinner and breakfast are included, and lunch is free if you stay two nights. Reservations are recommended if you intend to arrive after 11pm or in August or April. A cheaper option, though farther from the monastery, is the **El-Fairouz Hotel** (tel. 47 03 33 or 47 03 23). To reach El-Fairouz, walk out of town toward the monastery and take your first left. The hotel, encircling a giant sandy lot, is a five-minute walk away and has an incredible view of the surrounding mountains. Pitch your tent in the sand courtyard (E£5) or join the other sardines in one of the 10-bed dorms (E£12). Some rooms have private baths (singles E£50; doubles E£60; triples E£70).

Gift shops, supermarkets, and **restaurants** surround the bus station. The restaurants are virtually identical, offering hearty food (usually E£5-8 dishes of spaghetti or rice and chicken) with a side order of flies. Some of them will even cook food you've purchased from a supermarket (markets open 8am-11pm). Opposite the mosque is a brick-oven **bakery,** where the price of pita is hotly negotiated.

◆ SAINT CATHERINE'S MONASTERY

To get to the monastery from the access road, go straight past the tourist police for about 5min. until you get to a fork in the road, then bear left; the monastery is on the right. Spend the night on the mountaintop, watch the sunrise, then hike down at 7am and reach the monastery just as the doors open (avoids crowds). Modest dress required. Open M-Th and Sa 9am-noon; closed Orthodox holidays (in 1999: Nov. 1 and Dec. 25; in 2000: Jan. 1, Feb. 9, Apr. 21, 23, June 19, Aug. 15, Nov. 1, Dec. 5). Free. For more information, contact the monastery's Cairo office, 18 Maidan ed-Dahr, 11271 Cairo (tel. (02) 482 85 13; fax 482 58 06).

St. Catherine's is believed to be the oldest example of unrestored Byzantine architecture in the world. The complex was named after the martyred Alexandrian evangelist Catherine, whose body was found on top of Gabal Katerina to the south. About to be tortured on a wheel of knives for converting members of the Roman emperor's family, Catherine was miraculously saved by a malfunction in the wheel (but they slit her throat anyway). Her body showed up centuries later on top of the isolated mountain. Once home to hundreds of monks, the monastery now houses only a handful. These ascetics are members of one of the strictest orders; they never eat meat or drink wine, and wake up at 4am each morning when the bell of the Church of the Transfiguration is rung 33 times.

ICONS. The monastery has many treasures, including over 2000 exquisite 5th-century icons. The icons with brushed gold halos have a holographic effect, an artistic style unique to the Sinai. In the 7th century, Muhammad dictated a document granting protection to the monastery and exempting it from taxes; a copy of this still hangs in the icon gallery, near a similar letter penned by Napoleon in 1798.

LIBRARY. The monastery's impressive library contains over 8000 books and manuscripts, said to be second only to the Vatican library in the number and value of religious texts. The collection is currently being copied onto microfiche to make it available to scholars everywhere.

CHURCH OF THE TRANSFIGURATION. The first permanent structure in the monastery was erected in 330 CE, when Helena built a small church and tower at the site of the Burning Bush. Around 530, Emperor Justinian ordered a splendid basilica within a walled fortress to be constructed on the top of Mt. Sinai. When Justinian's trusted architect Stephanos found the mountain's peak too narrow, he built the **Church of the Transformation** next to St. Eleni's chapel instead. This structure became known as the Church of the Transfiguration, owing to its spectacular almond-shaped mosaic depicting this event in Jesus' life. The peeved emperor ordered Stephanos's execution, but the builder lived out his days in the safety of the monastery and eventually achieved sainthood (his bones are in the **ossuary**). Both St. Helena and Justinian dedicated their structures to the Virgin Mary, since Christian tradition asserts that the Burning Bush foreshadowed the Annunciation, when the archangel Gabriel heralded the birth of Christ. *(Closed F, Su, and holidays. A gift shop sells books on the area's history for E£8.)*

CHAPEL OF THE BURNING BUSH. Only the central nave of the Church of the Transfiguration is open to the public. On tiptoe you can see mosaics of a barefoot Moses in the Chapel of the Burning Bush, behind the altar. Should you manage to visit the icons back there, you'll have to remove your shoes, as the roots of the sacred shrub extend under the floor (a living descendant resides just outside). Such privileges are only accorded to true pilgrims, who are traditionally allowed to ask God for one favor. The monks themselves, with the help of the local Gabaliyya Bedouin (descended from Byzantine slaves), built a **mosque** within the fortress to convince advancing Ottoman armies that the complex was partly Muslim.

MOSES' WELL. Outside the main entrance of the Church of the Transfiguration is Moses' Well, where the savior of the Israelites reportedly freshened up after his holy ascent. The gruesome **ossuary,** a separate building outside the walls, houses the remains of former monks.

HIGH SINAI DESERT

The natural wonders of the Sinai Peninsula will make a convert of you if nothing else will. *Wadis* shrouded in misty heat lead in every direction, snaking their way around mountain ranges, lush oases, and Bedouin homesteads. Better yet, the region is fairly untouristed, meaning you'll have all the time and space you want.

⚡ HIKING: SINAI DESERT

WHEN TO GO

Spring and fall are the most temperate season for hikes. In summer you'll spend most of the day resting in the shade with the Bedouin until the sun calms down, and in winter you'll freeze. The nights are frigid year-round. You may be able to rent blankets from the Bedouin, but don't count on it; bring a warm sleeping bag.

HOW TO GO

Organized tours can be arranged in Israel through **SPNI**. The Israeli travel outfitter **Neot Ha-Kikar** specializes in Sinai tours (offices in Tel Aviv, Jerusalem, and Eilat), with trips beginning in Eilat and Cairo (6-day high range circuit US$360). No matter where in Israel you book your tour, however, you'll eventually end up at Sheikh Moussa's office. You'll save a lot of money by starting there, too.

To venture into of any of the mountains other than Mt. Sinai, you must be accompanied by a **Bedouin guide** and have a regular **Egyptian tourist visa**—the Sinai-only visa won't do. **Sheikh Moussa** (tel. 47 04 57), head of Mountain Tours, has a monopoly on all the mountains, and trips must be arranged through him (reservations accepted). You are required by law to leave your passport with Mr. Moussa; he will notify the army of your whereabouts. To get to his office in St. Catherine's town, walk uphill from the town square and past the petrol station. Take the first right and walk for three minutes; Mr. Moussa will be lounging outside.

Sheikh Moussa will procure both a guide and a permit for you. The price, which includes guide, food, and camels, is US$20-30 per person per day, and fluctuates depending on the size of your party and where you go. Surplus gear can be stored in Sheikh Moussa's house. You'll leave for your hike within an hour of arriving at his office. You and your guide will camp with the Bedouin, so be prepared for long nights by the fire smoking "Bedouin tobacco," drinking tea, and learning a great deal about a little-known culture. Tell Sheikh Moussa what you want to see and how quickly, and he'll tailor an itinerary. Routes include the following possibilities (estimated length of trip in days noted in parentheses):

Gabal Banat: A mountain north of St. Catherine's town overlooking a vast desert. (2)

Gabal Bab: From this peak you can see west all the way to the Gulf of Suez. (2)

Gabal Katerina: The highest mountain in Egypt (2642m). The path to the top is more difficult, secluded, and beautiful than Mt. Sinai's highway. A chapel replenishes you with shade at the summit. 6km south of Mt. Sinai. (11hr. round-trip)

Gabal 'Abbas Pasha: A rock with a ruined palace and excellent views. (2)

Gulat el-Agrod: A deep, crystal-clear mountain pool where you can swim in the shade of overhanging trees and dive off the surrounding rocks. (3)

Wadi Talla: There are two, a big one and a small one. Go to the big *wadi* for some swimming in spring-fed pools. (3)

Wadi Nogra: A rocky valley with a natural dam (Nogra Dam). The water trickles off moss-covered boulders to form a natural shower. (3)

Sheikh Owat: A picturesque oasis with tall palm trees, a deep well, and a lot of goats. (3)

Farsh Romana: A campground equipped with showers, on the way to Gabal Banat. (2)

Wadi Feiran: An amazingly lush oasis 50km west of St. Catherine's Monastery; Islamic tradition holds that Hagar fled there when banished from Abraham and Sarah's camp. Today there is a nunnery in the center of the valley. The best way to get here is by taxi from St. Catherine's (E£70 round-trip). Although buses to and from Cairo pass by, the schedules are unpredictable, and you might get stranded.

GULF OF AQABA COAST

SHARM ESH-SHEIKH شرم الشيخ

No one goes to Sharm esh-Sheikh for the sights, though with its dozens of wrecking balls, cranes, and half-finished buildings, there is ample opportunity to view ruins-in-progress. Sharm, like the rest of the Sinai coast, is in the midst of a building boom. Sharm esh-Sheikh and nearby Na'ama Bay are often called twin resorts, but they're far from identical. Na'ama inherited the good looks and good-looking travelers, while Sharm got the big boats and bigger buildings. Wealthy Europeans fill Sharm's four- and five-star hotels, leaving little room for budget backpackers to enjoy the already crowded beach. The tiny bay is crammed with dive boats attracted by the calmness of the water, further adding to the congested, overtrafficked feel. For more excitement and breathing space, head north to Na'ama.

■ PRACTICAL INFORMATION

Sharm esh-Sheikh is a transportation hub. An **Egypt Air** office (tel. 66 10 58) is south of the bus station (open Sa-Th 9am-2pm and 6-9pm). The airport branch (tel. 60 06 40) is far more helpful. The **ferry** to Hurghada (tel. 66 01 66) leaves three times weekly from the port just south of Sharm esh-Sheikh (6hr.; M, W, Th 9am; E£125). From the Sharm Marina, keep walking around the harbor and over the hill at the southern end. Book tickets a day ahead, either through a hotel or at **Thomas Cook** (tel. 60 18 08), 50m south of the Pigeon House Hotel. **Buses** leave daily for: **Cairo** (7-10hr.; 7:30, 10:30am, 12:30, 1:30, 3, 4, 5:30, 10, 11pm, midnight; E£50-65); **Suez** (7hr., 9am and 2pm, E£20); **Taba** (3hr., 9am, E£18); **Nuweiba'** (2½hr.; 9am, 2, 5pm; E£12); **St. Catherine's** (2½hr.; 7:30am, E£15); and **Dahab** (1½hr.; 6:30am, 2:30, 3:30, 5, 9, 11:30pm; E£10). Most buses leave from behind the Mobil station between Na'ama and Sharm esh-Sheikh, though some leave from Sharm itself—call ahead as schedules change frequently (tel. 60 06 00/66). For **taxis,** call 66 03 57.

At the top of the hill, next to the post office, are two banks: **Bank of Alexandria** (tel. 66 03 55) allows money withdrawal with Visa and MC (open 8:30am-2pm and 6-9pm). The **tourist police** (tel. 60 03 11 or 60 05 54; open 24hr.) and **police station** (tel. 66 04 15) are 300m from the banks. The 24-hour **hospital** (tel. 66 04 25; **ambulance** tel. 60 05 54) is just north of the bus station. The **new hospital** (tel. 66 08 93) is halfway between Sharm and Na'ama Bay. At the top of the hill to the right, the **post office** (tel. 66 05 18), has **Poste Restante** and **EMS** (open Sa-Th 8am-3pm); **Pharmacy Sharm esh-Sheikh** (tel. 66 03 88) is in the same complex (open 9am-1am). The **telephone office** (tel. 66 04 00) is 300m from the banks, near tourist police (open 24hr.).

■ ACCOMMODATIONS AND FOOD

If there is room at Na'ama Bay, there is absolutely no reason to stay in Sharm. The cheapest place is the **Youth Hostel** (tel. 66 03 17), at the top of the hill and to the left. From the bus station, follow the signs for the Cliff Top Hotel. Beds cost E£19.50: breakfast is included, and the preteen angst is free. Another option is the somewhat dingy **El-Kheima Hotel** (tel./fax 66 01 66), next to the Diving World Dive Club. Be sure to tell them that you *only* want bed and breakfast, or else they'll charge double and include dinner (bungalow singles E£40; doubles E£60 with portable fans; breakfast E£10). A last resort is **Safetyland** (tel. 66 34 63), at the bottom of the hill at the intersection of the road leading to Na'ama Bay and the road to the Sharm bus station. Stuffy thatched bungalows are situated in what looks like a construction site, but lacks the rustic charm; this is the only hotel on the beach (open tent sites E£25 per person; singles E£40; doubles E£70).

The food situation in Sharm is pretty dismal. The **Sharm Express Supermarket** (tel. 60 09 24) is next to the Pharmacy Nada'a (open daily 9am-2am). A row of cheap **restaurants** hugging the hill south of the bus station offers an opportunity to chow down on everything from pizza to Asian food (most open daily 11am-midnight).

◤ SCUBA DIVING

The Sharm esh-Sheikh and Na'ama Bay area is undoubtedly the mecca of Red Sea diving and the growth spot for most of the Sinai's tourism. Despite the large number of wealthy Germans and Italians in five-star hotels, Sharm esh-Sheikh still has several undiscovered sites and unexplored gems in and around the Straits of Tiran, Ras Muhammad National Park, and the wreck of the *Thistlegorm*.

DIVE SITES

▨RAS MUHAMMAD NATIONAL PARK. This area was made a national park in 1983 and kept expanding until 1992, when it encompassed most of the southern tip of Sinai and eclipsed almost all other dive sites in international acclaim. The most famous site in the park (considered the best dive in the region) is **Shark's Yolanda Reef,** which includes a swim through the wrecked freighter *Yolanda*. This surreal sight is possibly the only place in the world where you can swim with sharks among broken toilets and rotten cans of produce.

▨THISTLEGORM. The WWII cargo ship *Thistlegorm* was sunk in 1941 by long-range German bombers off the southern coast of Sinai. Discovered years later by Jacques-Yves Cousteau (who kept the location secret until it was rediscovered in the early 90s), the *Thistlegorm* has become legendary among divers and is widely considered the best wreck dive in the world. Located quite far off shore, the *Thistlegorm* requires at least a day and two dives to explore. The cargo bays are crammed full of tires, rifles, motorcycles, aircraft wings, tanks, trucks, and railway carriages. The relatively well preserved commander's deck and outer shell is downright eerie. Although a more expensive dive (US$85-100), it is unforgettable.

JACKSON'S REEF. Of the four reefs extending down the center of the straits of Tiran, this is the best and northernmost dive. The strong current is particularly challenging, but also encourages the growth of some of the most beautiful and plentiful coral in the entire Sinai. Not only does the current bring enough nutrients to feed the coral and schools of fish that congregate on the reef, but it also attracts a variety of sharks and turtles.

RAS GHOZLANI. In the area just north of the famous Ras Muhammad National Park lie many peaceful and often overlooked local dive sites. Many of the sites are incredibly beautiful and tranquil; Ras Ghozlani is the most superb. Divers here are less likely to see the big predators found prowling the deep at other sites, but this location is rarely crowded, uniquely preserved, and full of colorful fish.

DIVE FACILITIES

▨ **Camel Dive Center** (tel. 60 07 00; fax 60 06 01; email reservations1@cameldive.com; www.cameldive.com), P.O. Box 10, Na'ama Bay, Sharm esh-Sheikh, South Sinai, Egypt. across from the Cataract Resort. The oldest and friendliest dive center in Sharm esh-Sheikh. Offers over 6 daily boats, state-of-the-art equipment, and highly trained multilingual guides, as well as inexpensive accommodations by the Sinai's standards (dorm rooms US$25). One guided dive US$30, full equipment US$20, O/W course US$299. Call for a 10% discount on all services.

Oonas Dive Club (tel. 60 05 81; fax 60 05 82), at the northern end of the bay. Slightly cheaper rates and much better after-hours camaraderie than the other centers. 5-day PADI course US$295-330, certification US$30. Intro dives US$65 including equipment. Full gear rental US$20. Full day with 2 dives US$60.

NEAR SHARM ESH-SHEIKH: RAS MUHAMMAD NATIONAL PARK

*The park is accessible by boat and taxi (E£100). The park is beyond the jurisdiction of a Sinai-only visa, so you need your passport and a full **Egyptian tourist visa**. Dive shops run trips to the park, and you may not need a full visa if you stick with their boats and hotels. Park open daily 8am-5pm (strict closing time). Admission US$5 per person, additional US$5 per car. For information on **scuba diving** at Ras Muhammad, see p. 156.*

Sticking out into the Red Sea at the tip of the Sinai peninsula, **Ras Muhammad National Park** is the most famous dive site in Egypt and one of the most spectacular in the world. The tiny neck of land is bordered on the west by the Gulf of Suez and on the east by the Gulf of Aqaba. The waters of Ras Muhammad contain over 1000 species of fish, many of which are unique to the Red Sea. One species of crustacean is found only within the park boundaries, confirming that this is shrimp-ly the best daytrip from Sharm esh-Sheikh.

In the early 1980s, it became clear that tourist and fishing traffic was destroying the underwater treasures of Ras Muhammad, so the Egyptian government declared the area a national park in 1983. Most of the fragile underwater habitat is now closed to the public, and it is against Egyptian law to remove any material, living or dead, from the park. Diving, snorkeling, and swimming are only permitted in specified areas, mostly around the very tip of the peninsula. On rough days, snorkeling at Ras Muhammad can be difficult. For detailed underwater advice and warnings, see **Scub-etter Watch Out,** p. 159. Camping is permitted in designated sites; check with the park's visitors center for details. Further information about Ras Muhammad is available from the Sharm esh-Sheikh info office (tel. 66 06 68 or 66 05 59).

NA'AMA BAY

This five-star hotel nexus is the center of Egypt's anti-backpacker sentiment. The budget traveler is about as welcome in Na'ama as the narcotics agent is in Dahab; however, if you look clean-cut (and act like you own the place), you can freely roam the waterfront shops and hotels. As soon as you don your hip new tie-dye from Dahab, however, you invite stares along the promenade and may be barred from certain areas. Many budget travelers do flock here each year, drawn by the world-class diving and snorkeling as well as the most active nightlife in the Sinai. It is sometimes possible to get a job at a hotel or dive center; the pay is just enough for food and entertainment. If you work for a hotel, you usually get free accommodations; if you work at a dive club, you get free diving lessons or courses. Knowledge of Arabic is not necessary, but French and Italian are helpful.

■ PRACTICAL INFORMATION

Na'ama Bay is a long strip of hotels on the water side of the highway, the town's only street. Most of the beach is owned by the five-star resorts. Between the beach and hotels is a **promenade,** where most of the restaurants, bars, and diving clubs are located. The **bus stop** is officially in front of the Helnan Marina Hotel, but the driver will drop you off at any hotel along the road. **Intercity buses** leave from behind the Mobil station at the southern end of town and from the Sharm esh-Sheikh bus station. Southbound, open-sided **minibuses** (E£1) and **taxis** (E£10) go to Sharm esh-Sheikh, and northbound minibuses (E£10) and taxis (E£20) pass Shark's Bay.

The **National Bank of Egypt** has branches in the Marina Sharm, Gazala, and Mövenpick Hotels, and usually exchanges money (open Sa-Th 9am-1pm and 6-9pm, F 9-11am and 6-9pm). **Bank Misr** (tel. 60 16 67), at the Marriott Hotel, will give cash advances on Visa or MC (open Sa-Th 9am-2pm and 7-10pm, F 10am-12:30pm and 7-10pm). The **Commercial International Bank** has two locations, one next to the Camel Dive Center and one across from the Mövenpick Hotel (both open daily 9am-2pm and 6-9pm). There is an **ATM** in the Mövenpick Hotel lobby, as well as a branch of **EgyptAir** (tel. 66 06 67; fax 66 03 37; open daily 9:30am-2pm and 6:30-9pm). The **tourist police** (tel. 64 03 01) are located just north of the Helnan Marina Hotel. In case of an emergency, call the **ambulance** (tel. 60 05 54). The **Towa Pharmacy** (tel. 60 07 79) is in the bazaar south of the Mövenpick (open daily 10am-1am). The **Lifeline Clinic** (tel. (012) 212 4292), between Sharm esh-Sheikh and Na'ama Bay, has American- and German-trained doctors who take drop-ins daily from 5-7pm. The **post office** is in Sharm esh-Sheikh, but most hotels will drop off mail. **Internet access** is available at **CyberDisco,** next to Tam Tam restaurant (open 9pm-1am).

ACCOMMODATIONS

Pigeon House (tel. 60 09 96; fax 60 09 95), at the northern end of the bay. The only relatively cheap place to roost in Na'ama. After you've flocked together with birds of a feather in the happening courtyard (*the* place for a Stella or *sheesha*), nestle down in one of their rooms (singles E£65; doubles E£85; extra bed E£20) or thatched huts with fans (singles E£38; doubles E£56). Breakfast included.

Shark's Bay Camp (tel. 60 09 42; fax 60 09 44), 4km north of town, is a ship-shape Bedouin camp that overlooks a quiet bay. Features a breathtaking view of Tiran Island, an excellent restaurant, and a dive club, but the cost of a *service* (E£10) or taxi to Na'ama (E£20) make these clean bungalows an expensive choice. Bedouin tent on the beach E£125. Singles E£50-60; doubles E£65-75; triples E£90-100.

Camel Dive Club (tel. 60 07 00), in the center of the small bazaar, close to the beach. This slightly pricier option is worth it for the location as well as its beautiful rooms, pool, A/C, and private bath. Dorm rooms US$25; doubles US$104. Breakfast included.

FOOD

Food in Na'ama Bay is high in quality, at least along the main hotel strip. **Tam Tam Oriental Corner** (tel. 60 01 50), on Ghazala Hotel beach next to the Hilton beach, is the cheapest place in town. An enormous bowl of *kushari* goes for E£6.50, and salads cost E£2.50 (open noon-1am). **Pigeon House** hotel dishes out excellent pork, meat, and fish until 11pm (*spaghetti napolitain* E£6.50, kebab E£19). **Viva Pizza,** opposite the Red Sea Diving College in Kanabesh beach (not to be confused with the pricey Viva Restaurant), serves tasty pizzas for E£15-22 (open noon-midnight). Live it up a little at the **Hard Rock Cafe** (tel. 602 665), around the corner from the Camel Dive Center. Indulge in the Caesar Salad (E£21) or the Club Sandwich (E£25), or grab a half-price bargain burger from 1 to 5pm. (Open daily noon-3am.)

LIBATIONS 'N' GYRATIONS

LIBATIONS. Nights in Na'ama are most often spent tossing back Stellas and swapping diving stories. One of the best places to do this is the **Pigeon House.** The courtyard starts to fill around 5pm; the brew flows and the *sheesha* smoke billows until around 12:30am. Slip on your eye patch and head for the **Pirate's Bar** (tel. 60 01 36, ext. 850), a popular watering hole in the Hilton. With cutlasses and rigging hanging from the wall, the bar attracts an appropriately ridiculous mix of swash-bucklingly tan diving instructors and suave Europeans. They serve Stella (E£9.30), import draught beer (E£18-20), and free bar munchies (open 8:30am-1:30am). Most of the local dive masters and tourists congregate at the **Camel Dive Club,** upstairs from the dive center of the same name. The first floor is packed and often features live music; the low-key rooftop patio overlooks the main street. Stellas go for E£12 (E£9 for divers).

GYRATIONS. Top off the evening at the **Bus Stop Disco** (tel. 60 01 98), next to the Sanafir Hotel just down the street (open noon-3:30am). Feeling lucky? Give the roulette wheel a spin at the Las Vegas-style **Casino Royale** (tel. 60 17 31), across the street from the Mövenpick. (Open 8am-4am; 21+; no shorts.) The **CyberDisco,** next to Tam Tam, offers techno dancing and web-surfing (open 9pm-1am). Across the street from the Mövenpick, **Julie Disco** (tel. 60 01 00) spins a mix of American, Arabic, and Euro pop/disco beats (open 9pm-4am).

SCUB-ETTER WATCH OUT...

Scub-etter not die! Hidden among the crevices in the coral reefs around the Sinai Peninsula are creatures capable of inflicting serious injury and even death. If you see something that looks like an aquatic pin cushion, it's probably a **sea urchin** or a **blowfish**, both of which should be touched only in sushi form. Avoid the feathery **lionfish** as well—its harmless-looking spines can deliver a paralyzing sting. The well-named **fire coral** can bloat a leg to mammoth proportions, leaving welts the size of croquet balls. The **stonefish** is camouflaged flawlessly to resemble a mossy lump of coral or rock; if you step on one, you'll puff up and may die within hours. Reach into a hole and a two-meter-long **moray eel** may lock its jaws onto your hand. The list goes on—before plunging in, ask at any dive shop for a look at one of the picture cards that identifies these underwater uglies.

When snorkeling, try to enter the water in a sandy area to avoid damaging underwater plants and animals. If you have no choice but to enter where sea creatures and coral may dwell, wear foot protection. **Sharks** are attracted by blood, so never enter the water with an open wound or if menstruating. Panicking and thrashing tends to excite sharks—if you see one, calmly climb out of the water and casually share the news. Most sharks, however, are not aggressive and wouldn't give you the time of day even if they could; most marine animals get aggressive only if *you* have done something threatening or irritating. If you see an animal getting defensive, simply back away slowly. *Let's Go* does not recommend dying.

SURF...

CORAL REEFS. Na'ama Bay itself has no spectacular reefs, but a veritable colossus of coral lies just outside the bay to the north and south. Dive centers have maps of the reefscape; pick one up and put on your flippers. The closest sites are **Near Gardens** to the north and **Sodfa** to the south; both are moderate walks down the beach. Farther along are **Tower, Turtle Bay, Paradise,** and **Fiasco.** Ask at a dive center which sites are accessible by land; some can prove tricky to reach.

SNORKELING. Many swear that boat-based snorkeling is the best. For US$15-25, spend a day on a boat and explore spectacular waters. Arrange trips through the dive clubs. The legendary reefs of **Tiran Island** are distant and accessible by boat only. **Ras Nasrani** and **Ras Umm Sidd** are good sites a little closer to town.

AQUATIC SPORTS. Water activities are not restricted to diving. **Sun-n-Fun** booths (tel. 600 140, ext. 602; open 10am-7pm) at the Hilton and Aquamarine beaches rent equipment for **windsurfing** (E£40 per hr.; lessons E£55 per hr.), **water skiing** (E£40 per 15min.), **jet skiing** (1-person jet E£60 per 15min., 2-person E£70,) and **sailing** (E£40 per hr., lessons E£55). There are even **glass bottom boat** rides (every hr. 10am-4pm; E£25 per person). The big *Discovery* departs every two hours (11am-5pm; E£55). Frolic for free at the tiny **public beach** just south of Gafy Land Hotel.

...AND TURF

Landlubbers can strap on some plaid pants and tee off in a game of **miniature golf** at the Hilton (E£10 per game, E£55 deposit on clubs). **Horseback riding** is available across from the Novetel Hotel for E£50 per hour. **Safari Tours,** next to the Pigeon House, offers **ATV** trips out in the desert. Most leave before sunset (US$35 per hr.).

WADI KID. Here's looking at you, Kid: this *wadi*, 40km north of Na'ama Bay, is a deep, fertile canyon where you can hike among rock formations and fruit trees. Most hotels are affiliated with a tour company that goes once a week. *(Mövenpick Hotel organizes half-day trips to Nabq and Wadi Kid for US$30, with a 4-person minimum.)*

NABQ WILDLIFE RESERVE. On the coast 20km north of Na'ama Bay, Nabq's most notable site is a strip of coastline where the largest **mangrove forest** in the Sinai flourishes, attracting herons, ospreys, foxes, and hard-to-spot gazelles. The mangroves sprout in a few feet of warm, clear water with a sandy bottom, marking ideal swimming and relaxation spots. The problem of maintaining traditional Bedouin lifestyles in the modern world is being actively addressed in Nabq: a Bedouin "reservation" attempts to preserve the culture and openly welcomes visitors. *(Most hotels organize daytrips to Nabq. Wandering off the path in the park is extremely dangerous, as there are still a number of **landmines** in the area.)*

DAHAB دهب

Like Kathmandu or Amsterdam, Dahab is one of those places that has grown larger than life in the minds of travelers. For most, it conjures up images of glossy-eyed, tie-dyed hippies lounging on the shore, blissfully asphyxiating themselves in blue clouds of marijuana smoke. While this scene is still a significant part of the Dahab experience, Dahabitants no longer think of Jamaica with the reverence that Mecca inspires in the rest of the Arab world. The hippies are slowly being outnumbered by cleaner-cut travelers and dive instructors. "Bedouin" camps are the cheapest, most social places to stay, but travelers seeking more comfort can choose from a number of more expensive, middle-range hotels with air conditioning and a family atmosphere. Dahab die-hards of yesteryear may lament its relative cleanliness, but the town is becoming more like paradise, not less (its name does mean "gold" in Arabic, after all).

🛈 ORIENTATION AND PRACTICAL INFORMATION

Dahab city is of almost no significance to the budget traveler, who only glimpses it between climbing off the bus and getting into a taxi headed for the Bedouin village. **Buses** leave daily from the station (tel. 64 02 50) in the city for: **Cairo** (8hr.; 8:30am, 1, 2, 10pm; E£55-70); **Suez** (6hr., 8am, E£30); **Taba** (3hr., 10:30am, E£20); **Nuweiba'** (1½hr., 10:30am and 6:30pm, E£10); **Sharm esh-Sheikh** (1hr.; 8, 8:30, 10am, 1, 3, 5:30, 10pm; E£10); and **St. Catherine's** (1hr., 9:30am, E£15). Prices fluctuate depending on departure time—the last bus of the day is always the most expensive. If you get a group together, you can convince a taxi driver to go to any destination. **Service taxis** end up being more expensive, but the rides are much faster. From the bus stop, you can catch a taxi to the **village**; E£5 per car, E£1 per person for a crowded pickup.

The **National Bank of Egypt** (tel. 64 02 42) is located in Dahab city (open daily 8:30am-2pm and 6-9pm). There is also a **supermarket** (open daily 6am-2am); **police station** (tel. 64 02 15); **post office** (tel. 64 02 23) with **Poste Restante** (open Sa-Th 8am-3pm); and **telephone office,** where you can make calls within Egypt or through Cairo to an international operator (open 24hr.). In the Bedouin village, there are a few supermarkets that have **telephones** connecting to Cairo as well as a **Banque de Cairo** (tel. 64 04 44) where you can withdraw money with a Visa or MC or change traveler's checks for an outrageous commission (open Sa-Th 9am-2pm and 6-9pm). Above the Ghazala supermarket at the village's southern end, the **Dahab Polyclinic** (tel. 64 01 04) treats patients around the clock (open 24hr.).

🛏 ACCOMMODATIONS

There are over two dozen **camps** in the Bedouin village, and the number grows weekly. Dahab camps are an unfortunate bastardization of the thatched beach hut; someone came up with the brilliant idea of casting the huts in concrete, connecting them in rows around a central courtyard, and creating bare cells with minimal ventilation. Fortunately, the huts mostly serve as storage space for your stuff while you lounge outside in one of the restaurants. Rooms with only a mattress are cheapest (E£5-10); those with private bath run E£10 to E£30. A tangle of hotels and camps crowds the main part of the strip near the restaurants. The coolest and most comfortable are the thatched-hut quarters slightly off the main strip (the first three accommodations listed below fit into this category).

Oasis Fighting Kangaroo, down a small alleyway across from Napoleon's Restaurant (don't confuse it with the Fighting Kangaroo Camp). Generally regarded as the best place to stay in Dahab, the O.F.K. has a super-friendly atmosphere and 2 Bedouin-style TV rooms outside. Cell-like singles E£7; doubles E£20.

Bedouin Moon Hotel (tel. 64 00 87), owned and operated by 2 Bedouin brothers, has a sandy beach and the dive center Reef 2000. Dorm rooms E£25 (breakfast included). Doubles E£90-120. Ask about 10-15% *Let's Go* discount.

Cleopatra's (email cleopatra140@hotmail.com) is a Bedouin camp whose thatched huts are hot commodities in the Dahab market. Many visitors fall asleep in the lounge or on the roof as they sit on their asps waiting for huts to open up. Rooms with shower and toilet E£25-30; 2-person huts E£7-8; 4-person huts E£24.

Muhammad 'Ali Camp (tel. 64 02 68) is clean, cheap, and right in the middle of the action. The camp has its own supermarket, coffee shop, dive club, and laundry facilities. Doubles E£15. Breakfast E£8-10, dinner E£15-20.

Auski Camp (tel. 64 04 74), near the Sphinx Hotel, is a favorite among Ausktralians. Friendly owner keeps the rooms spic-and-span and smelling fresh.

◑ FOOD

If you find yourself with the munchies, fear not: Dahab is home to some of the best food in Egypt, but quality varies in the extreme. The local hospital has taken exception to the hygiene of many local restaurants, and advises against consuming fish (except at Tarabouche's). Be wary of ordering anything slightly undercooked, especially meat. For more information on how to minimize the risks of food poisoning, see p. 18. If you want complete control over food preparation, there are numerous supermarkets; the best is **Ghazala Market** at the southern end of town.

🍴 **Tota** (tel. 64 92 71), next to the Crazy House, has been a *Let's Go* favorite for 15 years. Tota, there's no place like home, and this restaurant will remind you of that. It has anything and *everything* your Western grub-craving heart desires, including the best pizza in town and a much-coveted liquor license. Open 8am-1am.

🍴 **Tarabouche's,** on the pathway past the Banque de Cairo and the Sunrise Camp, across the small parking lot. Three-course, home-cooked Egyptian meals (E£25-E£50) include salad, choice of fish or meat, and dessert. Food is hygienically prepared, so feel free to indulge in anything on the menu.

Shark Club features shakes that will leave you speechless. The owner speaks perfect English, and the dive instructors practically live here. The gigantic portions cause many patrons to contemplate whether Dahab a full or a half meal (half order pasta E£3-4).

Crazy House Pub (tel. 64 02 81), near the southern end of the bay, is the best place to go stir-crazy. Serves beer (E£7) and mixed drinks (E£5). Open at least until 2am.

♫ SHAKE 'N' BAKE

SHAKE. The Helnan Hotel (20km north of town) recently opened the **Zanzibar Disco.** There's a free shuttle from town around midnight, and on a good night the disco draws quite a crowd. On Monday and Wednesday nights, rock out to a live local band at the **Hilton Hotel** until dawn. Free hors d'œuvres ease the pain of pricey Stellas (E£10).

BAKE. In order to get an **alcohol license** in the Sinai, an establishment must first possess a building license (obliging the owner to keep his building above certain standards) and pay a property tax. There are six main sources of booze in Dahab: the restaurant at the Nesima Dive Club, the Crazy House Restaurant, Tota, the Sphinx Hotel, Green Valley, and Neptune Billiards, where pool sharks can also rack up a game at E£10 per hour (open 10am-2am). This lack of liquor is one of the reasons Dahab grew notorious for its **dope scene.** Though less noticeable nowadays, marijuana is still available for those who want it. People generally do not actively advertise what type of smoke is coming out of their *sheesha*. Not to be blunt: the possession of drugs is illegal in Egypt, and Egyptian jails rate low on the Michelin system. Dealers may win an all-expenses-paid trip to the hereafter via firing squad. *Let's Go* just says no.

◼ SIGHTS

OVERLAND DAYTRIPS. Daytrips to nearby natural wonders are a great way to escape the haze of Dahab for a while. Four-by-four trips to the **Colored Canyon** cost E£50 per person for a group of six, or you can travel by camel or truck to the brackish oasis of **Wadi Gnay** (E£30 per person). A one-day camel trip to **Nabq** (E£35-50) is also an option. Hamed the Lobster Man runs **Crazy Camel Camp** (tel. 64 02 73) and organizes jeep and camel safaris. He also takes people on night **lobster hunting** trips that culminate in lobster feasts on the beach. **Blue Hole Travel** (tel. 64 02 36), across the street from the Muhammad 'Ali Camp, runs camel safaris, trips to St. Catherine's, and daily snorkeling excursions to their namesake. If you want to go anywhere nearby, ask around the Bedouin community. They know these hills better than anyone, and will often be happy to organize a trip.

SNORKELING. The snorkeling in Dahab is excellent; enter the **Blue Hole** at either end of the bay where the waves break on the reefs (just be sure to wear shoes or flippers, because if the sea urchins don't get you, the coral will). Trips to Blue Hole and **Canyon** are arranged every morning by most camps, and you can rent snorkel gear at camps or on the beach (E£5). Make sure the flippers fit, the mask is airtight, and the snorkel unobstructed before paying. **Paddleboats** are available for rental near the northern part of the village; use them to trek to some of the more secluded spots (E£15 per hr.).

BEDOUIN VILLAGE. The Bedouin village is no longer that. It's so loaded with tourists that the Bedouin themselves have moved north to 'Aslah. These days, the bay is lined with restaurants, camps, and gift shops that peddle the famous "Dahab pants" (E£15). Meanwhile, camels and horses trot up and down the beach road carrying Dutch women, pink-hued Brits, and intrepid adventure explorer Dave Ross (camels E£5, horses E£10 per ½hr.). Pillowed courtyards hug the beach; at night, they are cheerfully illuminated by electric lights and Baraka bottle lanterns.

◼ SCUBA DIVING

Dahab offers some of the best dives reachable by land on the Red Sea. The dive sites are all accessible by car (usually 4x4 vehicles) and cover the areas both north and south of the main lighthouse region.

DIVE SITES

CANYON. The best dive in Dahab reveals good reef coverage and a menagerie of marine life. The obvious highlight is the long, narrow canyon ranging from 10m to 52m deep and virtually covered in coral. At the end of the canyon, divers move through a man-sized crack into the "fish bowl," an enclosure almost completely filled with schools of glass fish.

THE ISLANDS. The Islands offers the most plentiful and beautiful supply of coral and aquatic life in Dahab. The labyrinth of pathways, valleys, and coral peaks can make it a difficult but rewarding site to visit, as divers often navigate new and different routes while weaving through delicate cities of coral. Many guides believe that this is the best-preserved coral in the entire Sinai area. Observe the schools of barracudas, snappers, and other aquatic life all around you.

BLUE HOLE. The most famous site in Dahab is well known for all the wrong reasons. Every year, some of Dahab's best (and craziest) divers try unsuccessfully to swim through the arched passage (53m below sea level) or even touch the bottom (103m) of this Hole on Earth. The site should be recognized for the incredibly blue dive, starting at The Bells and continuing along the cliff of coral to the Blue Hole.

DIVE FACILITIES

The Dahab diving scene has unfortunately turned into a cut-throat operation in which inexperienced and ill-equipped dive centers cut corners on services along with prices. There are very few dive centers in Dahab aside from Reef 2000 that offer safe and first-rate services at relatively inexpensive rates.

■ **Reef 2000** (tel. 64 00 87; email reef2000@intouch.com), at the Bedouin Moon Hotel in its own bay just north of the Bedouin village. Run by Dave and Rachelle, a British couple who offer safety, low prices, and an atmosphere where even the most inexperienced will feel comfortable (especially since most of the guides and instructors are English-speaking expats). One guided dive with full equipment US$35, PADI courses US$280. **Camel safaris** to Ras 'Abd Galum and Gabr El-Bist include full equipment, lunch, water, and 2 dives (US$90-95). 15% *Let's Go* discount.

Fantasea (tel. 64 04 83; fax 64 00 43; email fdc@intouch.com), at the northern end, offers everything from open water to assistant instructor courses. The lowest prices for individual dives.

NUWEIBA' نويبع

One of Sinai's natural oases, Nuweiba' lies at the mouth of an enormous *wadi* that is filled with drifting sand for 10 months of the year. About the only excitement in town occurs in winter, when sudden, rampaging walls of water 3m high have been known to charge down the *wadi*. Nuweiba' resembles a younger version of Dahab: a town with no inherent appeal or style that happens to be blessed with a cheap, carefree Bedouin camp and a great beach (complete with a friendly dolphin). Nuweiba's importance rests primarily on its role in interstate travel: a ferry shuttles tourists and workers to Aqaba, Jordan (see p. 450).

■ **PRACTICAL INFORMATION.** Nuweiba', named after the Bedouin tribe whose territory reaches to Taba, is divided into a **port** and a **city,** 10km to the north. **Ferries** to **Aqaba** leave from the port (for more information, see p. 43). The **bus stop** is in front of the post office. Buses leave daily for: **Cairo** (6hr., 10am and 3pm, E£50); **Sharm esh-Sheikh** (2½hr., 7am and 3:30pm, E£10) via **Dahab** (1½hr., E£7); **Taba** (1hr., 6am and noon, E£7); and **Suez** (7hr., 7am and 3:30pm, E£25). Travelers to **St. Catherine's** should switch buses in Dahab. To get to **Tarabin,** either walk north along the beach (30min.) or take a taxi (E£10). Next to the Helnan stands the **tourist police** (tel. 50 02 31). At the Hilton Hotel and the port, there are branches of **Banque du Caire,** which gives credit card cash advances (open Sa-Th 9am-noon and 7:30-9pm; Ramadan daily 10:30am-1pm and 8-11pm). Most stores are in one of two commercial centers, aptly named the "new" and the "old." The new center is closest to the Helnan. Both have **supermarkets,** but the old center keeps longer hours. A **newsstand** in the old center has English-language newspapers, international telephone service, and bus schedule information. The old center also houses a **24-hour pharmacy** (tel. 50 06 05). Farther north past the communications antenna are the **telephone office** (open 24hr.), a **post office** (tel. 50 02 44) with **Poste Restante** and **EMS** (open 8am-3pm), the **hospital** (tel. 50 03 02; open 24hr.), and the **police station** (tel. 50 02 42; open 24hr.). Higher quality Israeli health care is just over the border.

⌐,⌐ ACCOMMODATIONS AND FOOD. The only budget accommodation in town is **El-Waha Village** (tel./fax 50 04 21), 500m south of the Helnan. It sports garden shed-style bungalows (singles E£25; doubles E£35; triples E£45) and large tents with mattresses (E£13 per person; breakfast E£10). The **Helnan International Hotel** (tel. 50 04 01), located next to El-Waha village, also offers relatively inexpensive rooms with access to a private beach and facilities (single huts E£46; double huts E£62; triple huts E£78; includes breakfast). The Helnan lets you pitch your own tent for E£10. Everything else you need lies north of El-Waha Village at the Helnan, along Nuweiba' city's one road. **Dr. Shishkebab** (tel. 50 02 73) and **'Ali Baba** (tel. 50 01 32), in the old commercial center, offer sandwiches (E£3-4), meat entrees (E£10-15), and vegetarian dishes (E£6).

◉ SIGHTS AND SAFARIS. Nuweiba's most rewarding sight is **Dolphin Beach**, named for the friendly dolphin, Uleen, who lives there (see below). Dolphin Beach is a 20-minute walk south of Nuweiba' Port or a E£5 taxi ride. Tell your driver "dolphin." Bedouin will charge you E£10 to swim, and another E£10 for mask, snorkel, and fins. The beach is open until 6pm.

Nuweiba' is an excellent starting point for **camel** or **jeep safaris** through the desert terrain. Ask about trips at **Explore Sinai** (tel. 50 01 41), in the commercial center (open 9am-4pm and 7:30-11pm), or at **Moonland Camp** in Tarabin. Moonland Camp is the cheaper of the two, offering Colored Canyon trips for E£50 per person. You may save E£10-15 per day by dealing directly with a guide. Look for one at Tarabin if none approach you. Guides here are generally trustworthy. Desert trips require a **permit**, achieved by some mysterious passport fermentation process at your friendly neighborhood police station (your guide will take care of it for you). Tour prices always include food, but often exclude water. The price of bottled water rises dramatically during the safari, so start off with a large supply.

◨ SCUBA DIVING. Like all towns on the Sinai coast, Nuweiba' is surrounded by beautiful coral reefs, but unlike Dahab, Na'ama Bay, or Sharm esh-Sheikh, Nuweiba's shores are not teeming with dive clubs; there are only two in town. **The Dive Point Red Sea** (tel. 52 03 900), in the Hilton Hotel, opened in 1996 and offers PADI open water training and certification for around US$350. Two suited dives with full equipment and transport cost US$65. Open water training at **Diving Camp**

A TAIL OF TWO DOLPHINS Uleen ("Gift of Allah") is one of the 12 dolphins in the world that have chosen to live and play with humans. While the exact details of her decision remain mysterious, the competing versions of this fish tale are like fatuous episodes of *Flipper*. One story is that in 1994, Awda, a Bedouin fisherman, noticed that Uleen's mother was beached on the shore. Attempting to save her, Awda pulled the dolphin back into the water; unfortunately, mom didn't survive the transition. The next day, Uleen followed Awda and his brother on their daily fishing trip. Awda's deaf and dumb brother, 'Abdallah, jumped into the water to swim with her, forging a bond that neither would soon forget. Another version has it that Uleen's companion (who is male in this tale) was caught in a net and shot by soldiers who mistook him for a shark. In grief, the lovelorn female lay crying in the water while 'Abdallah stroked her silvery skin to calm her—again forging that special interspecies bond. Scientists assign more, well, scientific reasons to her behavior: she was ejected from her pod (perhaps due to some illness or weakness) and sought social interaction, which she eventually found with humans. Whatever the explanation, Uleen has not left the vicinity of the beach, where visitors swim with her every day. It became clear, however, that humans were not meeting her every need: in 1996, Uleen became the mother of a bouncing baby, whom she lost to natural causes. Though the mother entertains visitors everyday with smiles that would make any delphine dentist proud, her second calf, Ramadan, has mysteriously disappeared, leading many to ask exactly what price Uleen has had to pay for human interaction.

Nuweiba' (tel. 50 04 03), in the Helnan Hotel, costs US$330, while two dives cost US$60 with vehicular transport, US$65 with boat. Introductory dives go for US$50, and divers can arrange trips to Ras Abu Galum through either center. Both diving centers are open from 8am to 6pm.

BETWEEN NUWEIBA' AND TARABIN

The 70km stretch between Nuweiba' and Taba is undoubtedly the most magnificent part of the Sinai: the mountains come right down to the sea, the reefs and sand turn the water a magnificent shade of turquoise, and the mountains of Saudi Arabia tower in the distance. Unfortunately, the view will soon be ruined by the five-star resorts that are popping up like weeds along this beautiful stretch. The coastline is dotted with **Bedouin camps,** which are accessible by bus or *service* from Taba or Nuweiba'. Drivers may not know the names of some camps: keep your eyes peeled for the signs. The camps follow a standard layout: a couple of huts, a central lounge, and a restaurant. Most huts do not have electricity (and those that are electrified rely on shaky generators), so bring a flashlight. It's quiet out here: people spend the days reading and swimming, while nighttime brings on backgammon, stargazing, shagging like a rabbit, and all that good stuff.

Some of the most beautiful camps lie 10-15km north of Nuweiba'. All camps should cost E£10-20 per person per night. Prices go down the longer you stay, the larger your party, and the fewer the number of people already staying there. Always **bargain;** it can't hurt and you may save a few pounds. All accommodations are fairly basic, with few amenities to distract you from the neighboring natural splendors—or just from your neighbor. **Magana Beach,** a Bedouin camp near colorful rock formations, has reefs and a restaurant. **Devil's Head** (Ras Shaytan), named for a rock formation 3km north of Magana, contains four camps. The southernmost, **Moon Land,** is the most simple and secluded (bamboo hut singles E£20; doubles E£40; triples E£50). Moving north, the second and fourth camps offer more huts and consequently more people. Some of the camps occasionally let guests sleep on the beach for free. Nearby **Bawaki** is only for the wealthy, but does have a few non-air-conditioned sheds for US$20 (including use of pool).

TARABIN طربين

Within spitting distance of Nuweiba', Tarabin is a miniature Dahab in spirit. Unlike Dahab, however, Tarabin actually has a beach, and the water here is warm and clean. There is only one road. Camps, restaurants, and supermarkets line the shore. Tarabin is rumored to be the source of much of Egypt's dope; it is widely available here, but that doesn't make it legal. The quality of the huts varies little from camp to camp. Most charge E£5-10 and have their own Bedouin-style restaurant. Muhammad, who runs **Carmina Camp** (tel. 50 04 77) at the southern end of town, will make you feel right at home. The **Moon Land Camp** (tel. 50 06 10), run by Mossallam Farrag, offers guided camel, four-by-four, and trekking tours. **Mondial Restaurant,** in the center of town, makes a great cheese omelette for E£7. A taxi from Nuweiba' City to Tarabin is E£10, from the port E£15.

BASATA بساطة

"Basata" means "simplicity" in Arabic, and this environmentally conscious camp midway between Nuweiba' and Taba is designed to minimize its impact on the Sinai's environment. Basata is unlike anything else you will encounter in the Sinai, a gorgeous place that you can enjoy without pangs of ecological guilt. Glass, metal, and plastic are all recycled; water is desalinated; organic trash is used as livestock feed; plans are underway to have electricity generated by solar panels; and perspiration collected by super-absorbent clothing is channeled into turnip and parsnip cultivation. Basata is run by German/English-educated Sharif Ghamrawi (tel. 53 04 81), who cultivates a family-oriented atmosphere with nightly communal dinners, a comfy common area, and lots of rules: no nudity, no drugs or alcohol, no sleeping in the common area, and no dirty dishes (camping E£15; bamboo huts E£40 per person). A vegetarian (E£18) or fish (E£24) meal is prepared every evening, though you can save money by cooking for yourself. The kitchen functions on trust: take what you want and write down what you take, but remember to watch the prices as you go. All prices are subject to a 10% tax. Sharif also organizes **tours** by camel (E£75 per day) and jeep (E£60). Due to recent publicity, Basata has become quite popular. Huts often sell out, but the beach is almost always available except when European, Egyptian, and Israeli holidays overlap.

BETWEEN BASATA AND TABA

Between Basata and Taba is a remote and beautiful spot called the **Fjord,** where a small inlet cuts into the steep hills. The **Salima Restaurant and Camp** (tel. 53 01 30) is right off the highway on a small ledge overlooking the sleepy bay. There are a few rooms crammed between the restaurant and the rock slope behind it (E£30 per person); **camping** is also available on the beach.

The rocky outcrop of **Pharaoh's Island** (called Jezirat Fara'un by Egyptians, Coral Island by Israelis), 8km south of the Taba shore, holds the renovated ruins of a Crusader castle built around 1115. Salah ad-Din took the fortress in 1171 but abandoned it in 1183 after European counterattacks. The ruins have a few towers and passageways as well as a large water cistern. A boat ferries visitors to the island (E£14 or JD20 from Aqaba), where you must then buy another ticket to tour the castle (E£20, students E£10). En route to the island, the view of Sinai from the castle is shamefully ruined by the five-star Salah ad-Din Hotel (the best view is from the mainland). The coral reef formations off the northeastern tip of the island draw divers and snorkelers, but the sites are overrated—neither the reefs nor the wildlife compare to the lower Sinai. Indeed, with the number of tourist boats moored off the island, you're liable to see more fellow snorkelers than fish. Meals on the island are overpriced and often unavailable.

SUEZ CANAL قناة السويس

The strategically located Suez Canal is the brainchild of an 18th-century idea and 19th-century engineering know-how. Napoleon Bonaparte considered digging a canal between the Mediterranean and the Red Sea, but feared that the waters of the Red Sea were higher than those of the Mediterranean. Years later, another Frenchman, Ferdinand de Lesseps, persuaded Sa'id Pasha, the *khedive* of Egypt, to try a similar plan. Excavation started on April 25, 1859 and took 10 years to complete. On August 18, 1869, the canal was opened in a grand ceremony attended by over 6000 dignitaries. A man, a plan, a canal—Suez.

Spanning 195km and reaching a maximum depth of 15m, the canal connects Port Said on the Mediterranean to Suez on the Red Sea. If the ancient Greeks saw it, they would probably think that Zeus put up Suez (or conversely, Zeus put up Suez). Because it allowed for rapid travel from Europe to the Indian Ocean, the canal became a crucial element in the infrastructure of the British Empire. Nasser nationalized the canal in 1956, precipitating a British-French-Israeli invasion (to read more about the **Suez Crisis** and the rise of **Pan-Arabism,** see p. 49). During the 1967 War against Israel, Nasser blocked the canal with sunken ships. It remained closed through the 1973 War, and was cleared and reopened in 1975.

PORT SAID بور سعيد

Founded in 1860, Port Said (Bor Sa'id) became Africa's gateway to the Mediterranean upon completion of the Suez Canal. The city's wide, tree-lined streets and sidewalks feel worlds away from the rest of Egypt. Since 1976, when the city was declared a tax-free zone, Port Said has developed into a shopping resort for Egyptians cashing in on duty-free deals. The town is saturated with clothing stores fronting styles unseen in the West since the 70s. However, Port Said doesn't really come alive until nighttime, when everyone takes to the streets to window shop and enjoy the cool breeze and twinkling lights of the canal.

EGYPT

Mediterranean Sea

Beach

Suez Canal

PORT FOUAD

N

Port Said National Museum

Es-Salaam

American Express

Thomas Cook

Palace Gardens

Palestine St.

El-Gomhoriyya St.

West Delta Bus Company

Ferial Gardens

Muhammad Mahmoud St.

Tourist Police

Hafiz Ibrahim St.

TO PORT FOUAD

Atef es-Sadat St.

Oraby St.

El-Geish St.

Ramses St.

Salah ad-Din St.

Salah Salem St.

Mustafa Kamel St.

Memorial Monument

En-Nahda St.

Safia Zaghloul St.

Sa'ad Zaghloul St.

Supejet

En-Nasr St.

Military Museum

Sa'd Zaghloul Garden

23 July St.

TO CAIRO (220km)

Muhammad es-Sayed Sirhan St.

TO ALEXANDRIA (343km)

Port Said Stadium

Port Said

ACCOMMODATIONS

A Youth Hostel
B Qasr El-Baron Hotel
C Akri Palace Hotel
D Hotel Delaposte

⁊ ORIENTATION AND PRACTICAL INFORMATION

By road, Port Said is 343km east of Alexandria and 220km northeast of Cairo. The town is surrounded by water on three sides: the Mediterranean to the north, the Suez Canal to the east, and **Lake Manzala** to the south. The point at which the canal meets the Mediterranean is Port Said's northeastern corner. **Atef es-Sadat Street** runs along the sea, and **Palestine Street** follows the edge of the canal. Two blocks inland, **El-Gomhoriyya Street** runs parallel to Palestine St. Another important thoroughfare, **23 July Street,** runs parallel to Atef es-Sadat St. three blocks inland.

Trains: Go to the southwest end of El-Gomhoriyya St. and turn right onto Mustafa Kamal St. The jam-packed **station** is ½km down, on your left. Trains run to **Cairo** (4½hr.; 5:20am, 7:15, 7:30pm; 2nd class E£14) via **Isma'ilia** (1¾hr., 2nd class E£6). To reach **Suez,** change at Isma'ilia.

Buses: The **West Delta** bus depot is located on Salah ad-Din St., on the northern side of Ferial Gardens, 2 blocks west of El-Gomhoriyya St. Daily buses to: **Cairo** (every hr. 6am-7pm, E£12-15); **Alexandria** (7, 9am, 2:30, 4:30pm; E£15-20); **Isma'ilia** (1½hr., every hr. 6am-7pm, E£4); and **Suez** (6, 10am, 1, 4pm; E£7.50). The **Superjet** depot is next to the train station on Mustafa Kamal St., with buses to **Cairo** (3hr., 10 per day 7am-7pm, E£15) and **Alexandria** (4hr., daily 8:30pm, E£22).

Service Taxis: Near the train station and the Superjet depot (ask for *taxi ugra*).

Bike Rental: A great way to get around the city. Rent them on the south side of Hafiz Ibrahim St., between Palestine and El-Gomhoriyya St. (E£3 per hr.).

Tourist Office: 5 Palestine St. (tel. 23 52 89), 2 blocks from the southern end of the street. Open Sa-Th 9am-2pm. The **tourist police** (tel. 22 85 70) are stationed on the 5th floor of the abandoned Post Office building on El-Gomhoriyya St.

Currency Exchange: Small offices abound. The most convenient is **Thomas Cook,** 43 El-Gomhoriyya St. (tel. 33 62 60; fax 23 61 11). Open daily 8am-5pm. **ATM** at Bank Misr, 30 El-Gomhoriyya St., a block north of Babel St.

American Express: 83 El-Gomhoriyya St. (tel. 23 98 31), across from Es-Salaam Mosque. Cash advances and traveler's check exchange. Open daily 10am-4pm.

Emergency: Ambulance: Tel. 180. **Police:** Tel. 122.

Pharmacy: Hussein Pharmacy (tel. 33 98 88; fax 33 97 77), on El-Gomhoriyya St., a block south of Muhammad Mahmoud St. Open daily 9am-1am. Many other pharmacies also line El-Gomhoriyya St.

Hospital: Delivrand Hospital (tel. 22 36 63 or 22 56 95), on Esh-Shaid el-Gaya St.

Post Office: Southeast corner of the Ferial Gardens. Walk 3 blocks along the canal from the tourist office on Palestine St., take a left on Muhammad Mahmoud St. and continue to its intersection with El-Geish St. Open 24hr. For **Poste Restante,** walk south from the post office, take the first left, then walk 30m. Open Sa-Th 8am-5pm.

Telephones: (tel. 22 01 66; fax 32 57 05), 2 blocks north of the tourist office on Palestine St. Phone cards available for E£15, E£20, and E£30. Direct international dialing (E£24 per 3min. to the U.S.). Open 24hr.

Telephone Code: 048.

⌨ ACCOMMODATIONS

Most accommodations in town are either on or near El-Gomhoriyya St. Supercheap hotels are hard to come by, but there are many mid-range and luxury hotels. **Akri Palace Hotel,** 24 El-Gomhoriyya St. (tel. 22 10 13), 2 blocks from the southern end of El-Gomhoriyya St., is owned by the friendly Greek Nicolandis brothers. A 19th-century elevator transports you to charming rooms with high ceilings, wood floors, sinks, desks, and dressers. Huge balcony doors provide a nice breeze (singles E£13; doubles E£26; triples E£31; add E£10-13 for private bath). **Hotel Delaposte,** 42 El-Gomhoriyya St. (tel. 22 96 55 or 22 40 48), deserves both of its two stars for rooms with private baths, TV, and fridge. Look for the English "Hotel" sign with Arabic underneath next to a pastry shop (singles E£26-

34; doubles E£28-40; triples E£44; add E£10-12 for A/C). Near the beach, the **Youth Hostel (HI)** (tel. 22 87 02), on Muhammad es-Sayed Sirhan St. opposite the stadium, is a 20-minute walk or E£1.50 taxi ride from the town center. Modern and sterile, it features large bathrooms and fans (6-bed dorms E£12.60; nonmembers pay E£2 extra; breakfast included).

FOOD

Although seafood is the main fare, most restaurants provide options both aquatic and terrestrial. The food is delicious, but cheap meals are hard to come by—splurge the extra pounds and you're likely to put a few on. **Lord's Pastry** (tel. 23 52 02), just south of the intersection of El-Gomhoriyya and 23 July St., is by far the best patisserie in Egypt. The friendly staff sells a wide selection of superb Western pastries, all E£1.25. Try the heavenly merengues—they're to die for, but you'll probably rise up for more. **Popeye Restaurant** (tel. 23 94 94), on the corner of El-Gomhoriyya and Safia Zaghloul St., is what it is—a good choice for zesty chicken kebabs (E£17) and banana splits (E£5.70). No spinach, but several large pictures of the grinning sailor welcome patrons (open daily 8am-1am). **Galal Restaurant,** 60 El-Gomhoriyya St. (tel. 22 96 68), serves standard Egyptian fare at reasonable prices. Make the most of your money by sitting outside. Large plastic crustaceans above the tables make charming dinner companions for the solitary traveler (open daily 7am-2am; closed during Ramadan; Visa accepted). A local favorite for fresh seafood, **El-Borg** (tel. 32 34 42) sits on the beachside corniche. You'll be converted, too, when you see that a full meal costs just E£30 (open 24hr.).

SIGHTS

PORT SAID NATIONAL MUSEUM. This museum houses a fine collection of items from all periods of Egyptian history, ranging from several exquisite mummy cases to Coptic icons and Qur'anic calligraphy. See Khedive Isma'il's carriage, which paraded in the 1869 opening of the canal. The labels alongside each of the artifacts, not to mention the building's air conditioning, secure its status as a must-see. *(At the northern end of Palestine St. Tel. 23 74 19. Open Sa-Th 9am-5pm, F 9am-noon and 2-5pm; Ramadan 8:30am-1pm. Admission E£12, students E£6; camera E£10, video E£20.)*

OTHER SIGHTS AND EXCURSIONS. Free **ferries** to Port Fouad leave every few minutes from the southern tip of Palestine St. The shell-covered **beach** extends to the east. Beach umbrellas can be rented for E£3 per day, and showers are located every 100m along the beach. If the words "duty-free" make your wallet tremble, **shopping arcades** line Et-Togary, En-Nahda, and El-Gomhoriyya St.

ISMA'ILIA الاسماعيلية

Once known as Timsah Village, Isma'ilia was renamed after Isma'il, the last independent *khedive* of Egypt, and is now the capital of the Suez Canal District. The city's tree-lined boulevards are situated halfway between Port Said and Suez and home to a tremendous canal trade. Since it sustained heavy damage during the Arab-Israeli wars of 1967 and 1973, Isma'ilia has been completely rebuilt, and today, one can relax in sprawling gardens or swim at the nearby beaches. Because it has few tourist attractions, Isma'ilia is blissfully free of foreigners.

ORIENTATION AND PRACTICAL INFORMATION. Midway along the Suez Canal, Isma'ilia is linked by road and the Isma'ilia Canal to the Delta, and by highway and railroad to: Cairo (140km) and Alexandria (280km). While you can't see the canal from the center of town, Isma'ilia's two main streets, **Sultan Hussein Street** and **Eth-Thalatheni Street,** run roughly parallel to the waterway. **Orabi Square** is in between the two streets, three blocks north of **Salah Salem Street,** which forms the town's southern border. Restaurants and shops line Sultan Hussein St. **Mallaha Park** stretches along Salah Salem St. toward the canal.

The **train station** is located on Es-Sekka el-Hadid St., west of El-Malek el-Hassan Sq. Locomotives chug to **Cairo** (2½hr., 5 per day, 2nd class E£11); **Port Said** (1¾hr., 5 per day, 2nd class E£24); and **Suez** (1½hr., 6 per day, E£21). There are two **bus stations** in town. The smaller one in Orabi Sq. services **Cairo** (2hr., 4 per day, E£26) and **Alexandria** (4½hr., 2 per day, E£14-17). The main bus terminal in Salam Sq., about 2km out of town, serves **El-Arish** (3hr., 5 per day, E£7), **Port Said** (1½hr., 8 per day until 6pm, E£4), and **Suez** (1½hr., until 6pm, E£3). **Service taxis,** opposite the main bus station, offer fast and frequent service to **Cairo** (E£5), **Port Said** (E£3.50), **El-Arish** (E£8), and **Suez** (E£3.50).

Bank of Alexandria (tel. 33 79 21), in Orabi Sq. next to Travel Misr, provides cash advances on Visa, MC, and AmEx (open in summer Su-Th 8:30am-2pm and 6-9pm; in winter 5-8pm; during Ramadan 10:30am-1pm). An **ATM** with Visa and MC links is three blocks up the first street on your left. In emergencies, contact the **ambulance** (tel. 123) or the **police** (tel. 13), one block west of the Governorate Building on Salah Salem St. **Isma'ilia Pharmacy,** 24 Sultan Hussein St. (tel. 22 93 19), is a well stocked apothecary (open daily 9am-5pm and 6:30-11:30pm). Two private clinics, **Esh-Shafa Hospital** (tel. 22 29 20) and **Karin Hospital** (tel. 22 75 59), serve the area. The **post office** (open Sa-Th 7:30am-6pm) and a 24-hour **telephone office** are in Orabi Sq. Isma'ilia's **telephone code** is 064.

⌐ ACCOMMODATIONS. Though far from the center of town (a 3km hike or a E£2 taxi ride), **Isma'ilia Youth Hostel (HI)** (tel. 32 28 50; fax 33 14 29), on 'Omara Rd., is a great choice. The sandy beach and comfy common room of this spotless 266-bed hostel make it a backpacker's dream resort. All rooms except the dorms have private bath, and breakfast is complimentary (6-bed dorms E£12.60; doubles E£22.60; triples E£17.60; nonmembers E£1 extra; lunch or dinner E£5; curfew 11pm). With its bright purple exterior and pastel green rooms, the **Nevertary Hotel,** 41 Sultan Hussein St. (tel. 32 28 22; fax 32 09 40), three blocks north of Bank Misr, wins the Miami Vice Award for hotel color coordination. You'll want to tary in the Nevertary's comfy rooms, with air conditioning and private bath, complemented by a sitting area and fridge on each floor. Manager Mohammed serves breakfast for E£6 (singles E£30; doubles E£40; triples E£50). Centrally located in Orabi Sq., **New Palace Hotel** (tel. 32 63 27 or 77 61), next to the Bank of Alexandria, has small rooms with carpeted floors and high ceilings, most with private bath as well (singles E£30; doubles E£60; triples E£75; breakfast E£5; TV, A/C, or phone E£5 each).

⌐ FOOD. Vendors line the streets with cheap Egyptian fare, but for excellent seafood, try Isma'ilia's sit-down venues. **Nefertiti's,** 11 Sultan Hussein St. (tel. 22 04 94), south of the Nevertary Hotel, has a cozy, romantic atmosphere. Royal portions of seafood (E£9 and up) and meat (E£15) satisfy the hungriest carnivore, while beer and wine satisfy the thirstiest lush (open 11am-midnight). **George's Restaurant** (tel. 33 73 27), next door to Nefertiti's on Sultan Hussein St., has 49 years of experience to justify its higher prices. Fish, meat, and pasta meals run E£10-30; the owner recommends the fried calamari. If nothing else, pull up a stool at the fully stocked bar (open 10am-11pm). The **King Edward Restaurant** (tel. 32 54 51), at 171 Tahrir St. off Sultan Hussein St., one block south of the Nevertary Hotel, is so famous that signs in English direct patrons from miles away. Clean, cool, and quiet, King Ed prides itself on seafood (E£5-45, but rice with curry is excellent. Try your luck and order "craps" if you don't have them already (open 10am-midnight).

◉ ♫ SIGHTS AND ENTERTAINMENT. The **Isma'ilia Regional Museum,** on Salah Salem St., near the canal at the eastern end of town, has pharaonic, Islamic, and Roman collections (open W-M 9am-3pm; admission E£3, students E£1.50). Near the museum, the **Garden of the Stelae** contains sphinxes from the age of Ramses II. Ask for permission to visit at the museum entrance. **Mallaha Park** is worth a frolic with its 500 acres of rare flowers, trees, and palms. Just 100m south of the youth hostel, the **beach club** along Lake Timsah has two restaurants, boats for rent, and kiddie amusement park rides (open daily 10am-10pm, E£2).

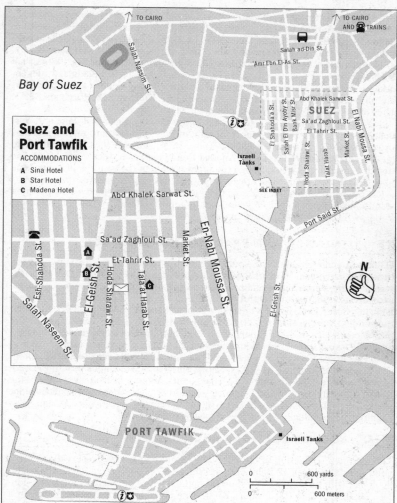

Suez and Port Tawfik

ACCOMMODATIONS

A Sina Hotel
B Star Hotel
C Madena Hotel

SUEZ السويس

Suez (Es-Suweis) sits at the junction of the Red Sea and the Suez Canal. While it may not be the most attractive or exciting of Egypt's cities, Suez is not as bad as most claim it to be. Its residents are friendly and helpful, and Port Tawfik provides an excellent perch from which to watch the canal at work. Nearby **'Ain Sukhna** is downright spectacular; its proximity to Cairo provides a convenient sun-swim-snorkel option. Most travelers pass through Suez en route from Cairo to the Sinai by way of the **Ahmed Hamoli Tunnel** (running under the canal 17km north of town), or on their way south along the Red Sea Coast. Others stay a few days looking for passage on a boat at the Yacht Club.

▐ TRANSPORTATION

The **bus stations** are located around El-Geish St. in the north part of town. Buses to most destinations leave from the depot on Salah ad-Din St., one block west of El-

Geish St., while those heading to Upper Egypt depart up the road near the train station; both stations are easily accessible by minibus. Buses shuttle from Suez to: **Cairo** (2hr.; every 30min. 6am-5pm, every hr. 5-8pm; E£7); **Isma'ilia** (1¼hr., every 30min. 6am-4pm, E£4); **Alexandria** (5hr., 7am and 2:30pm, E£22); **Port Said** (3hr.; 7, 9, 10:30am, 3:30pm; E£9); **Hurghada** (6hr., 8 per day until 10pm, E£22); and **'Ain Sukhna** (1hr.; 6:30, 10am, 2pm; E£1.75). Reserve tickets to Hurghada and Alexandria a few days in advance. **Service taxis** also travel these routes (except for Alexandria) at similar prices (Cairo E£5, Port Said E£7, Isma'ilia E£3, Hurghada E£20). They depart more frequently than buses, but usually aren't air-conditioned.

Suez is the main launching ground for forays into the **Sinai. East Delta** and **West Delta** buses leave every half hour from 8am to 7pm, following a route that includes **Uyoun Mussa** (L£6), **Sharm esh-Sheikh** (6hr., L£20), **Dahab** (7hr., L£23), **Nuweiba'** (L£25), and **St. Catherine's** (L£20). An East Delta bus runs to **Taba** (3pm, L£25). **Service** drivers charge by the trip, so the more people in the van, the less each one pays. **Private taxis** to the Sinai are generally prohibitively expensive.

For transport within the city, exit the bus station and go behind the row of food stands. **Minibus** drivers will be yelling out their destinations. To travel to and from Port Tawfik, simply flag down a minibus on El-Geish St.

■ ORIENTATION AND PRACTICAL INFORMATION

El-Geish St. runs roughly north-south through the center of Suez, from the **bus stations** across the canal to **Port Tawfik**, where the **tourist office** (tel. 33 11 41 or 42) stands at the westernmost end of town (open daily 8am-8pm). The tourist office provides the somewhat helpful and grotesquely named **PISS guide** (Port Said, Isma'ilia, Suez, Sinai) along with a Suez map. The **tourist police** (tel. 33 11 40) share the building. **Banque Misr** (tel. 22 05 71), one block south of El-Geish St., has an **ATM** that accepts Visa and MC (open Su-Th 9am-3pm). **American Express** services are available for all travelers at Menatours (tel. 22 88 21), next to the tourist office in Port Tawfik. Suez's main house of medicine is the **General Suez Hospital** (tel. 33 17 81). The **post office** (tel. 33 13 10), on Hoda Sharawi St., one block east of El-Geish St., offers **Poste Restante** (open Sa-Th 8am-3pm). Another branch, next door to the tourist office in Port Tawfik, keeps the same hours. The **telecommunications office** is about three blocks west of El-Geish St., on the corner of Shohada'a St. and Sa'ad Zaghloul St. (open daily 24hr.). Suez's **telephone code** is 062.

■ ACCOMMODATIONS AND FOOD

Though Suez's selection of budget hotels is quite extensive, reservations are a good idea. **Star Hotel**, 17 Bank Misr St. (tel. 22 87 37), has large, clean rooms, all equipped with turbo fans. The showers and balconies are stellar (singles or doubles E£20, with bath E£25; triples E£30). One block north of the Star, a mirrored and gilded lobby welcomes travelers into **Sina Hotel**, 21 Bank Misr St. (tel. 33 41 81). Unsullied rooms sport fans and "hoot water" (singles E£17; doubles E£26; triples E£34; quads E£39). To get to the **Hotel Madena** (tel. 22 40 56), walk three blocks east on Tahrir St., take a right, and proceed to the next street, where the hotel awaits on the left. Rooms are functional and decently priced (singles E£12, with bath E£17; doubles E£20/E£25).

Substitute sightseeing with snacking—Suez's lack of tourist attractions is offset by a super selection of restaurants. The airy **Mahmoud Rawash Restaurant,** on Tahrir St. just off El-Geish St. (look for the awnings), is a local institution, serving great Egyptian food at great Egyptian prices (falafel or *fuul* sandwich 25pt). The impeccable **Seaside Restaurant,** one block west of the telephone building, stuffs you silly for E£10 in the air-conditioned interior or on the rooftop terrace. **Five Star Cafeteria,** on El-Geish in Port Tawfik, has similar prices and a great view. Get a taste of homemade Italian goodness at **El-Eltakia** on El-Geish St., where pizzas start at E£5 (open Sa-Th 1-5pm, F 1-5pm and 7:30pm-1am).

👁 🎵 SIGHTS AND ENTERTAINMENT

The only formal monuments in Suez itself are three American-made tanks on the corniche, captured from Israel in 1973. The dirty water from the many ships at **Rex Beach,** in town near the stadium, isn't very regal, but the beach at **'Ain Sukhna** (Hot Spring), 60km south along the Red Sea, rivals those of the Sinai. **Buses** run there early in the day (1hr.; 6:30, 10am, 2pm; E£2) and return about 1½ hours later. **Service** also run down the coast from Suez to 'Ain Sukhna. The hot spring (35°C), originating in the Ataka Mountains, empties out onto a gorgeous sandy beach. Get off the bus when you see the large green-and-white sign for the **'Ain Sukhna Hotel** (tel. 32 84 88). Daytrippers can pay the hotel a E£15 day-use fee for chairs and umbrellas if they only plan to visually enjoy the crystal clear water, though the mouth of the hot spring is also available for prolonged soaks. The hotel offers an expensive but incredible fish, salad, and hummus meal for E£26. It's not just the best choice, it's the only choice—bring your own food if you'd rather not put your money where your mouth is.

MONASTERIES OF ST. ANTHONY & ST. PAUL

The isolated monasteries of St. Paul and St. Anthony lie 30km apart (82km by road), near the Red Sea. These centers of faith, dating from the early Christian monastic tradition, are inhabited by monks whose austere lifestyle has changed remarkably little over the past 16 centuries. Most speak excellent English, and they warmly welcome visitors. While a few hours suffice to see the monasteries, spending the night can be transcendent. Only men can stay at St. Anthony's; St. Paul's accommodates both men and women. The monks provide food and water, and although there is no formal charge, donations are welcome—even the most ascetic life requires some financing. Note that you must have a letter of recommendation from the administration office in Cairo (see below) to stay overnight at either of the two monasteries, though the monks may overlook this if they don't already have many guests. Both monasteries are open daily 9am-5pm.

Reaching the monasteries is a serious endeavor without a car (there are no organized tours to the monasteries). Getting to these sites depends a lot on divine intervention and luck, and requires a lot of patience and water. Travelers are completely dependent upon **pilgrims** traveling to the site for transportation. Of the two possible options for getting to the monasteries, the less desirable is to take any form of public transportation headed for Hurghada and ask to be dropped off on the road to the monasteries. The closest stop to St. Anthony's is **Ras Za'frana,** about 33km east of the monastery. The closest stop to St. Paul's from a Hurghada-bound bus is by the **St. Bola sign,** 12km from the monastery. Pilgrimage groups have been known to pick up travelers along the way and take them to the monasteries and back. This option is only remotely viable on **Fridays** and **Sundays,** and even then, it's dangerous. Although pilgrims tend to be friendly, catching a ride can be difficult. Hitchhiking, especially in the desert, is an inherently risky proposition, and women traveling alone should not attempt it. A much safer (and more hassle-free) option is to contact the **monasteries' administration office** in Cairo (tel. (02) 59 02 18; call between 10am-noon and 8:30-9:30pm) and ask when local Coptic churches are planning pilgrimages to the monasteries. A group may be leaving as soon as tomorrow or as late as a month from the past Sunday. Contact the churches about tagging along with their group to the monasteries.

ST. ANTHONY'S MONASTERY

Saint Anthony, raised in the Nile Valley in the 4th century CE, became the first famous ascetic of the Christian Church when he scorned worldly concerns and retreated into the Eastern Desert. Anthony's dramatic move reflected the restlessness that overtook some Christians after Constantine made Christianity the official religion of the Roman Empire. This was a disturbing development for those who felt that the church had gained worldly security and wealth at the expense of its spiritual focus. In Egypt, some of these Christians, mostly educated middle-class men, sought to escape the secular world by retreating into the desert where they could pray in solitude and render their lives unto God rather than Caesar.

St. Anthony was paradoxically unsuccessful; his desert hermitages became popular pilgrimage sites, and crowds of the pious and the curious deprived the recluse of precious penitent isolation. Soon after the saint's death, his disciple St. Athanasius told the story of his choice of poverty and hardship, his wild battles with demons, and his wise counsel to monks and layfolk. Athanasius's *Life of Anthony* became the prototype for much of later Christian hagiography. Around the same time, Anthony's followers settled at the present site and established the first Christian monastery. The Monastery of St. Anthony served as a refuge for some of the monks of Wadi Natrun when their own sanctuaries were attacked by Bedouin in the 6th century. During the 7th and 8th centuries, the monastery was occupied by Melkite monks, and in the 11th it was pillaged by the army of Nasr ed-Dawla. About 100 years after the sacking, it was restored and transferred to Coptic hands.

A MEETING OF MINDS According to Christian lore, St. Anthony and St. Paul met in one dramatic encounter at the end of Paul's life. Wanting to reveal the holiness of St. Paul, God led St. Anthony to his cave. As the two conversed, Paul's crow dropped a *whole* loaf of bread for them (double what the bird usually brought). Paul, realizing that he was talking to another holy man, told Anthony that he was nearing death and made one final request: to wear the robe of Pope Athanasius. Anthony immediately departed to fetch the garment. On his return, he had a vision of angels carrying St. Paul's soul to heaven, and arrived at the cave to find Paul dead. While pondering what to do with the body, two lions descended from the mountain and dug a grave. Anthony wrapped Paul in the papal robe and buried him. He then carried St. Paul's palm leaf garment back to Athanasius, who sported it every Christmas, Epiphany, and Easter.

The **Church of St. Anthony** and the southern walls are the only remains predating the 16th-century construction of the present monastery. With ancient frescoes embellishing each of their sections, Anthony's church and its small chapel are the most impressive parts of the monastery. East of the Church of St. Anthony, the **Church of the Apostles** contains three haikals. During Lent, the monks cantillate the liturgy in the 18th-century **Church of St. Mark.** As in the Wadi Natrun monasteries, the **Chapel of St. Michael** is on the top floor of the tower. The extensive library contains more than 1700 manuscripts.

The major religious attraction in the vicinity of the church is the **Cave of St. Anthony,** where the ascetic himself is said to have lived. The vista from the cave, 276m above the Red Sea, rewards the requisite hour and a half of hoofing and huffing. The best time to climb the mountain is when the sun is low, before 6am or after 4pm. Try to return before dark (or light) and remember to bring oceans of water. St. Anthony's has a small snack shop with soda and cookies and a gift shop.

ST. PAUL'S MONASTERY

Saint Paul (not the disciple) was born into an affluent Alexandrian family in the 3rd century CE. When his father died, he left his estate to young Paul and his brother. Naturally, this caused instantaneous squabbling between the two, and when the family had heard enough, the brothers were sent off to consult with a judge. Not on speaking terms, the two young men took separate routes. Paul happened to pass the funeral service of a wealthy man and, for some unexplained reason, was profoundly affected (why he wasn't so moved at his own father's funeral no one knows). Like St. Anthony, St. Paul cast off all worldly concerns and, guided by an angel, headed for the hills. He lived in a cave near Mt. Nemra and made his garments from palm leaves and branches. Legend has it that his strict ascetic diet of half a loaf of bread per day was dropped to him by a crow; water came from a secret source high in the mountains (which still exists today). These divine provisions enabled St. Paul to live alone for over 80 years.

The original monastery was built on the cave site not long after St. Paul's death—probably before 400 CE. St. Paul's has been attacked by Bedouin throughout its history, most notably in 1484 when the churches were burned, the library destroyed, and all of the monks killed. After the Bedouin left 80 years later, Coptic Patriarch Gabriel VII sent replacement monks to rebuild the churches, but the buildings were destroyed again before a century passed. Finally, at the end of the 16th century, Coptic Patriarch Ioannis ordered monks from St. Anthony's to reconstruct and inhabit St. Paul's. These monks were the wisest yet: they built a five-story tower with a drawbridge leading to the fourth story. The first two floors of the tower were for food and water storage and allowed the monks to endure sieges of up to three months. The monastery was most recently renovated in 1974 but, aside from the addition of electrical generators and a guesthouse, remains the same as it has been for centuries.

The most impressive part of the monastery is the **Church of St. Paul,** built in the cave where the famed hermit dwelt. Many of the church's 4th- and 7th-century frescoes have somehow survived. Ostrich eggs symbolizing the Resurrection hang from the roof. You can fill your Baraka bottles with holy water coming from the same secret source St. Paul supposedly lived on.

HURGHADA الغردقة

The Red Sea of Hurghada is dotted with small islands and chains of coral reefs where schools of tropical fish swim through the sun-dappled, tranquil cobalt waters. Since the early 1980s, when peace with Israel opened Egypt to foreign investors and tourists, scores of resorts have sprung from the sands of Hurghada ("El-Ghardaka"). The boomtown continues to expand along the coast at a rapid pace that shows no sign of slowing down. The brilliant splendors underwater find their skewed counterparts on land in a profusion of tourist "bazaars" selling glittering, gaudy souvenir dreck to the many foreign visitors who flock here for the superb diving and snorkeling.

EGYPT

■ ORIENTATION

Paved highways link Hurghada with population centers, but the town itself is remote. Suez lies 410km north at the end of the Gulf of Suez, and Cairo is another 130km west. Hurghada is a typical coastal town, extending along the coast in a narrow strip. Downtown Hurghada (known as **Dahar**) lies 2km north of **Saqala,** the original fishing town out of which Hurghada grew. Buses and *service* arrive in Dahar, where budget hotels and restaurants await. Saqala has a more authentic Egyptian flavor, with plenty of dive shops and cafes but few budget hotels. South of Saqala, the five-star resorts preside over private beaches.

En-Nasr Road begins inland from the coastal road and connects the town and harbor. Almost everything you need, from the passport office in the north to the bus station in the south, lies along a 2km stretch of this street. Smaller streets to the east of En-Nasr Rd. contain the budget hotels, restaurants, tourist bazaars, and **souq,** all separated from the sea by a sandy mound posing as El-Arish "mountain."

■ TRANSPORTATION

Airplanes: Hurghada Airport (tel. 44 75 03), 3km south of town and about 1½km inland. Served by **EgyptAir,** with flights to **Cairo** (daily 8:45am and 7:15pm, E£455) and **Sharm esh-Sheikh** (M and F 8:10am, E£320). Tickets can (and should) be booked in advance through **Karnak Travel** (tel. 54 78 93), across from the mosque on northern En-Nasr Rd. Open daily 8am-8pm.

Buses: Upper Egypt Bus Co. launches from En-Nasr Rd., 300m from the southern end of town. Book seats at least 1 day in advance; last-minute standing room may be available. Buses to: **Cairo** (6hr.; 7:30, 10am, 1, 3, 5, 11, 11:30pm, 12:30am; E£45); **Luxor** via **Qena** (2hr.; 6am, noon, 1:30, 6:30am, 1am; E£9); **Aswan** (7hr.; 4, 10pm, midnight; E£24-35); **Alexandria** (10hr., 7pm, E£55); and **Suez** (5hr., 3 per day, E£18-20). **Super-**

jet has a different bus depot, 50m off En-Nasr St. across from the mosque at the north end of town, and jets buses to **Cairo** (noon and 2:30pm, E£47; 5pm, E£52).

Ferries: To **Sharm esh-Sheikh** from the "New" Harbor (1½hr., variable schedule, US$33). Reserve at least 1 day in advance through a hotel manager, at the ferry office, or with **Eid Travel** (tel. 54 78 21 or 54 79 92).

Service Taxis: *Service* run from Dahar through Saqala and south to the resorts, and vice versa (E£1). The best places to catch one are on En Nasr Rd. or Corniche Rd.

Taxis: Taxis congregate off En-Nasr Rd., beside the rotary just south of the telephone office. Prices are per car; form a group and you may be able to bargain lower. Taxis run to: **Cairo** (5hr., E£300); **Suez** (4hr., E£200); and **Qena** (2hr., E£70).

📕 PRACTICAL INFORMATION

Tourist Office: Tel. 44 44 20/21, just south of the airport on Corniche Rd. Helpful advice in the poshest tourist office in Egypt. Open Sa-Th 8am-2pm. The **tourist police** (tel. 44 77 44) reside on En-Nasr Rd. past the telephone building on the left.

Passport Office: Tel. 44 67 27, on En-Nasr Rd. at the northern edge of town, 2km from the bus station. Behind the Red Sea Security Dept. building. Provides visa extensions. Open Sa-Th 8am-2pm.

Currency Exchange: National Bank of Egypt, on En-Nasr Rd., 500m north of the bus station. Open Su-Th 8:30am-2pm and 6-9pm. Nearby **Banque Misr** has an **ATM** (Visa, MC, Cirrus, PLUS links). Open daily 8:30am-2pm and 3-9pm. There's also a **Thomas Cook** in Saqala (open 8am-5pm).

Police: Tel. 54 67 23, on En-Nasr Rd., at a bend 900m north of the bus station.

Pharmacy: Dr. Montaser Rand (tel. 54 48 90), on 'Abd el-'Aziz Mustafa St. behind Sherry Hand Restaurant. Open 24hr.

Hospital: The best is **General Hospital of Hurghada** (tel. 54 67 40), on Sa'id Karin St., around the corner from Three Corners Empire Hotel and on the left. For an **ambulance**, call 54 64 90 or 54 67 40.

Post Office: On En-Nasr Rd., 300m north of the bus station on the right. **Poste Restante, EMS,** and orange international phones. Open Sa-Th 8am-2pm.

Telephones: On En-Nasr Rd., on the left after the road turns at the police station. Open 24hr. Send **faxes** (tel./fax 54 88 45) from a hut across from phone office. To the U.S. or Europe E£14-20 per pg. Open Sa-Th 8am-2pm and 8-10pm.

Telephone Code: 065.

🏠 ACCOMMODATIONS

Hurghada is a piaster-pincher's paradise. Watch out for spontaneous price inflation, especially during peak season. Many of the cheaper hotels work with diving centers and get hefty commissions for the customers they bring. This either means that you'll be strongly encouraged to dive or snorkel or that you cannot stay in the hotel unless you book a trip with them. If you plan to dive or snorkel, check the hotel's prices before taking a room—it is far more convenient to book through your own hotel than through another establishment. All hotels listed below have ceiling fans. It's a good idea to reserve a room in the summer.

NEAR THE BEACH

Sea Waves (tel. 54 50 71), across from the public beach; take a right by the Golden Dolphin Dive Center. Clean rooms, shiny floors, and a cute cafe-style dining room. *Sprechen Sie deutsch?* They do. Singles E£10; doubles E£20; triples E£25. Add L£5 for private bath. Breakfast L£2.

California Hotel (tel. 54 91 01). Friendly owner 'Abdul is justifiably proud of his hotel, where guests are livin' it up in cozy muraled rooms. Prices vary depending on views and bathroom's state of existence. Singles E£7-15; doubles E£10-20; triples E£7.50 per person. Find yourself California dreamin' on the roof for E£5. Breakfast included.

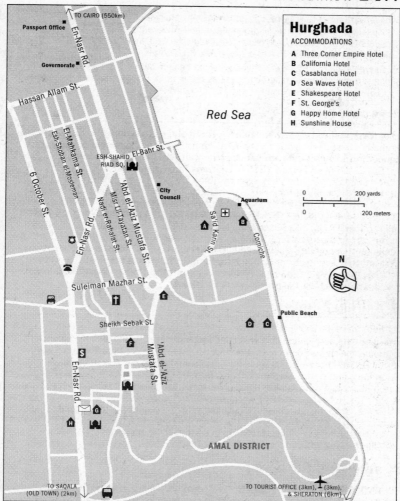

Hurghada

ACCOMMODATIONS

A Three Corner Empire Hotel
B California Hotel
C Casablanca Hotel
D Sea Waves Hotel
E Shakespeare Hotel
F St. George's
G Happy Home Hotel
H Sunshine House

Red Sea

TO CAIRO (550km)

Passport Office

En-Nasr Rd.

Governorate

Hassan Allam St.

El-Mahkama St.

Esh-Shoban el-Moslemin

6 October St.

En-Nasr Rd.

'Abd el-'Aziz Mustafa St.

Misr Lil-Tayaran St.

Nadi er-Rahalat St.

ESH-SHAHID El-Bahr St.
RIAD SQ.

City Council

Aquarium

Sa'id Karn St.

Corniche

Suleiman Mazhar St.

Sheikh Sebak St.

'Abd el-'Aziz Mustafa St.

Public Beach

En-Nasr Rd.

AMAL DISTRICT

TO SAQALA
(OLD TOWN) (2km)

TO TOURIST OFFICE (3km), (3km),
& SHERATON (6km)

N

0   200 yards
0   200 meters

EGYPT

Casablanca (tel. 54 82 92), on Corniche Rd. opposite public beach. Enter through side door of the Cowboy Restaurant and it'll be lookin' at you, kid. Clean, newly remodeled rooms. Guests get 20% discount at Cowboy, but some rooms hear its hee-hawing all night long. Singles E£15; Bogie-'n'-Bacall love the doubles at E£20; triples E£30.

DOWNTOWN

Happy Home Hotel (tel. 54 96 11), on Mosque St. behind the post office. In this day and age, Happy Homes are hard to find. The amiable manager makes sure that this hotel, though farther from the center of town, is where the heart is. Discounts offered at the building's diving center. Singles E£10; doubles E£20; triples E£30.

Sunshine House (tel. 54 74 63), directly across from bus station. Friendly and knowledgeable Hassan arranges snorkeling (E£40, 10% student discount) and night parties on Geftun Island. Well-maintained single-sex bathrooms in hall. Large 3-bed dorm room E£5 per person. Doubles E£15. Breakfast (eggs sunny-side up, of course) E£2.50.

Shakespeare Hotel (tel. 44 62 56), at 'Abd el-'Aziz Mustafa St. and Sa'id Karin-General Hospital St. Tangled in a copse of weather'd trees/This taintless inn entices familys/Its fragrant garden sweetens as it blooms/As do the pink and priveat batheing rooms. Doubles E£35; triples E£45. To A/C or not to A/C (E£6 extra)?

St. George's (tel. 54 82 46), 1½ blocks behind Banque Misr, off En-Nasr St. Charming rooms, a friendly owner, and bathrooms as clean as St. George's conscience. Singles E£15; doubles E£25; triples E£35. Add E£5 for private bath.

◖ FOOD

Bella Riviera, on 'Abd el-'Aziz Mustafa St., south of the Shakespeare Hotel, is one of Hurghada's best deals, with A/C to boot. Amuse yourself by watching the waiters scamper in and out of the secret door in the wall. Cheap drinks, lasagna (E£3), salads (E£1.25-2.50), and pizzas (E£7-10). **Pizzeria Tarbosh** (tel. 54 84 56) is on 'Abd el-'Aziz Mustafa St. past the Shakespeare Hotel. Owner 'Amir cooked pizza in Italy, and it shows in some of the best crust in Egypt. A 30% student discount sweetens the deal. Over 20 types of pizza served in generous personal pies (E£9-20). Salads (E£2.75) and meat dishes (E£8) also available. **Norhan Restaurant,** on Sa'id Karin/General Hospital St., is between Peanut's Bar and the Shakespeare Hotel. Look for the cheerful green-and-white awning. The pungent *spaghetti basilicum* (E£4.75) is delicious. Open daily 10am-midnight. **Felfela** (tel. 44 24 10), south of Saqala on Sheraton Rd., 10min. from Dahar by minibus. This installment of the national chain has the best view in town. Vegetarian-friendly *fuul* (E£2-4) and salads (E£2), as well as meats (E£25). Open daily 9am-12:30am.

◖ DRUNKEN NIGHTS

Just like the reefs, Hurghada's active nightlife attracts creatures of all shapes and sizes. The bars in town are supplemented by the resorts, which all have pubs, bars, or nightclubs where you can dance like an Egyptian. **Peanut's Bar,** next to the Three Corners Empire Hotel on Sa'id Karin/General Hospital St. in Dahar, fills its patio every night. The Stellas (E£7.50) may taste good, but the grinning Black Sambo above the door isn't in the best of taste. **Scruples** pub and steak house, on En-Nasr Rd. near the center of town, buzzes and pops with neon lights and beer bottlecaps. Scruples also has a **billiard hall** near the southern end of 'Abd el-'Aziz Mustafa St. Jive to "world famous" Daoud and his soft-rock cover band at **The Pub,** the Sonesta Hotel's ingeniously named joint. **Kalaboush Disco** (tel. 54 50 87), at the Arabella Hotel on Corniche Rd., is a popular club with a special theme every night.

◉ SUNKEN SIGHTS

DRY AND MIGHTY. Landlubbers rejoice! Hurghada's underwater splendor can now be enjoyed without even getting your feet wet. Aspiring Captain Nemos can go a couple of leagues under in the **Sinbad Submarine** (tel. 44 46 88). US$50 buys a seat aboard a real 44-person sub for a one-hour undersea voyage. Many of the larger hotels run **glass-bottom boat tours** for E£15-20 per hour. Make reservations for either at any luxury hotel or over the phone. Get an inkling of the subaquatic splendors at the **Hurghada Aquarium,** which features a variety of fish accompanied by remarkably informative descriptions (open 9am-11pm; admission E£5).

ON YOUR MARK, GET WET, GO! There are a variety of beaches to choose from around Hurghada. **Public beaches** next to the Geisum Hotel and the port in Saqala are the smelliest and most packed. Local rumor has it that sand is buried beneath all the dirt. Women will undoubtedly feel uncomfortable here if they choose to bare anything more than toes. Head to the hotels for more liberal bathing fashions. Just north of the public beach downtown, the **Shedwan, Three Corners,** and **Sand Beach Hotels** all open their beaches and pools to non-guests for E£15; **Geisum Hotel** charges E£10. **Shellghada Beach,** just before the Sheraton, charges E£10 for a day on their soft sand and use of their showers. These beaches can be reached by minibus (E£1 from Saqala) or taxi (E£5-10).

EGYPT

⌕ DIVING DELIGHTS

Hurghada's real attractions are silent and submerged. Red Sea creatures flabbergast with their array of colors, shapes, and sizes. Buck-toothed trigger fish, iridescent parrot fish, rays with blue polka dots, sea cucumbers, giant clams, and a million others star in this briny show. The shimmering, variegated blues of Hurghada's waters have been spared the terrors of oil exploration (see **Sinai: Getting Underwater,** p. 147, for information on snorkeling and scuba diving).

GEFTUN ISLAND. There are a few reefs you can reach without a boat, including one near the Sheraton, but to reach Hurghada's most brilliant aquatic scenery you must take a barge. Hotels offer an all-day trip to Geftun Island, usually including two one-hour snorkeling stops near the island and a fish meal prepared on board. Most hotels advertise the trip at E£40, though some charge E£30-35; you may be able to bargain as low as E£25. Some Geftun-bound boats are as crammed as cattle cars and stop only once for snorkeling.

SNORKELING. Snorkeling from a dive-boat might give you access to better underwater sights but is a bit more expensive. However, the best reefs are north of Hurghada. The northern waters aren't shielded by islands like the southern ones, so calm weather is a must to go there. To save money, a group can make independent arrangements with a boat owner—perhaps a fisherman in Saqala—or with one of the sea-trip offices around town. One possibility is to go to Geftun and see different reefs; another is to organize an overnight trip (E£60-90 per person, including meals). Excursions to other locales can be less crowded and cheaper. For information, talk to Sayad of **Sunshine Dive Center** (tel. 54 51 13), on En-Nasr Rd., between the post office and bus station; Muhammad of **Red Sea Wonderland,** next to Happy Home Hotel; or Mahmoud of **Golden Dolphin Dive Center** (tel. 54 43 54), opposite the public beach. Rent your own gear (E£10-15 per day for mask, snorkel, and fins) at any office in town. ISIC or GO25 discounts available.

SCUBA DIVING. While Hurghada may have some of the best scuba diving in Egypt, it also has some of the worst dive shops. Not all of the dive shops that have sprung up to profit on rising tourism have all that much experience. Choose your dive shop carefully, and be sure to check your instructor's or guide's certification and experience and the ship's gear, especially its emergency equipment. Dive shops that are members of HEPCA, a marine protection organization, are often more environmentally conscious underwater. One well-established and professional dive center is **Subex,** between the Luxor and California Hotels. It offers open water dive certification for US$445; most smaller centers charge US$250 for the same. Choose carefully—save your life before your money.

NILE VALLEY وادى النيل

How doth the little crocodile
Improve his shining tail
And pour the waters of the Nile
On every Golden Scale.

—Lewis Carroll

Originating at the equatorial high water marks of Lake Victoria and Lake Taru, the Nile winds its way north through Uganda, Ethiopia, and the Sudan, pouring into Lake Nasser and Egypt, where its banks are home to 95% of the country's millions.

Before the construction of the Aswan High Dam in 1971, the Nile overflowed its banks every year, depositing the rich silt that made the valley the most fertile region in the world. This yearly inundation was the most important time of the year for ancient Egyptians, and the reason why much ancient religion focused on the river's cycles. No major temple along the length of the Nile

Valley was without a **nilometer,** a graded pit used to measure and predict the depth of the river. For millions of ancient Egyptians, no oracle could have been more influential.

The region between Cairo and Luxor is known as **Middle Egypt,** home to the majority of the country's Copts. Akhenaton built his capital at Tel el-Amarna; farther south stand the temples at Abydos and Dendera. Luxor marks the northern boundary of **Upper Egypt,** stretching upstream (south) to Lake Nasser and the Sudanese border. Tourists flock here to see the maze of ancient architecture on Luxor's West Bank and the imposing temples at Edfu and Abu Simbel.

In the summertime, temperatures average over 45°C, frequently breaking 50°C. This is *rather* warm, but the complete lack of humidity makes it possible to continue most essential biological processes even as the sand turns to glass. Hoteliers, guides, and others of their ilk are desperate for business in summer, so bargain hard. If you don't like the heat, plan to do most of your touring between 6 and 11am; if you don't like the crowds, shoot for high noon. In November through May, prices rise as the temperature drops.

HIGHLIGHTS OF THE NILE VALLEY

■ Don't miss the massive **Luxor** (p. 192) and **Karnak** (p. 190) Temples in Luxor.
■ Tired of temples? Two bad: the cream of the crop are the twin **Temple of Hathor** at Dendera (p. 202) and **Temple of Horus** at Edfu (p. 206). A **felucca cruise** from Aswan lets you see them in style (For more information on *feluccas,* see p. 182).
■ Aswan is famous for its immense **High Dam** (p. 209), but the most stunning constructions lie south at **Abu Simbel** (p. 220).

TRANSPORTATION

BY LAND: SERVICE TAXIS AND BUSES

Traveling by **service taxi** is the most efficient, cheap, and convenient option for shuttling between the river towns at almost any time of day. However, the Egyptian police insist that tourists travel at certain times with police convoys. *Service* drivers may refuse to take you without an official escort, fearing that they may have to turn back. Out of Aswan or Luxor, the only option may be the public bus. In any case, you'll also need nerves of steel to cope with the insanity of the drivers. **Buses** are often cheaper than *service,* though not by much. They run more frequently, but can be horribly slow, hot, and unreliable. Most stop running at 6pm. Buses are best for transport out of Luxor or Aswan, where you can reserve the airconditioned buses by going to the station a day or two in advance. In the smaller towns between, you may not find an empty seat, and schedule reliability plummets. **Trains** can be a hassle for short trips, but 2nd-class air-conditioned compartments are a great value for the entire Luxor-Aswan haul or for more distant sights north of Luxor. Authorities discourage tourists from taking 3rd-class trains. See listings in **Luxor** (p. 186) and **Aswan** (p. 210) for more specific info.

OVERLAND TRAVEL ADVISORY. As of summer 1998, the Egyptian and U.S. governments strongly discourage any surface travel through **Middle Egypt.** Political instability and the rise in extremist activity have made the area unsafe for tourists. There is a massive police and military presence in the area, making visits unpleasant and ill-advised. *Let's Go* heeded the warnings of the U.S. State Department and Egyptian Ministry of Tourism and did not send a researcher to sights or cities between Beni Suef and Sohag this year. Travel to Abydos and Dendera, though permitted, will come with a mandatory police convoy.

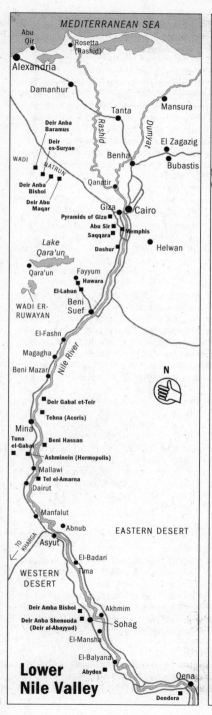

Lower Nile Valley

MEDITERRANEAN SEA

Abu Qir
Rosetta (Rashid)
Alexandria
Damanhur
Tanta
Mansura
Deir Anba Baramus
Deir es-Suryan
El Zagazig
Benha
Bubastis
WADI NATRUN
Qanatir
Deir Anba Bishoi
Deir Abu Maqar
Giza
Cairo
Pyramids of Giza
Abu Sir
Saqqara
Memphis
Lake Qara'un
Dashur
Helwan
Qara'un
Fayyum
Hawara
El-Lahun
WADI ER-RUWAYAN
Beni Suef
El-Fashn
Magagha
Nile River
Beni Mazar
Deir Gabal et-Teir
Tehna (Acoris)
Mina
Tuna el-Gabal
Beni Hassan
Ashminein (Hermopolis)
Mallawi
Tel el-Amarna
Dairut
Manfalut
Abnub
EASTERN DESERT
TO KHARGA
Asyut
El-Badari
Tima
WESTERN DESERT
Deir Amba Bishoi
Deir Anba Shenouda (Deir al-Abayyad)
Akhmim
Sohag
El-Manshe
El-Balyana
Abydos
Qena
Dendera

N

Upper Nile Valley

Hurghada

0   75 miles
0   75 kilometers

N

El-Balyana
Qena
Dendera
Qus
Naqada
Valley of the Kings
Deir el-Medina
Karnak
Armant
Luxor
EASTERN DESERT
Esna
El-Kab
Edfu
Nile River
Gebel Es-Silsilah
Kom Ombo
Daraw
Aswan
Elephantine Island
Philae
Kalabsha
Beit el-Wali
Aswan High Dam
WESTERN DESERT
Lake Nasser
Es-Sibu
Abu Simbel
EGYPT
SUDAN
Lake Nubia

EGYPT

BY WATER: NILE CRUISER

Tough times for tourism in Egypt have opened up an option for the budget traveler on a binge: the **Nile Cruiser.** You can book a cabin on triple-decker, pool-topped cruise ships and slip from Luxor to Aswan or vice versa (1 way is 2 nights), hob-nobbing with French tourists the whole way. Travel agents can book for you at a mark-up (US$45-50 per night) or you can go to the dock yourself and chat with the boat receptionist about open cabins (as low as US$35 a night). The air-conditioned, two-room suites have TVs and showers, and all meals are included. Drinks are extra, and extra pricey. A *kalish* will cart you to the temple and back at each stop. Several travel agents (including Eastmar and Misr Travel) dot the corniche south of the Winter Palace in Luxor. In Aswan, agencies can be found around the southern end of the corniche. If you find a bargain, you'll enjoy two days of pure bliss: sunning yourself by the pool, watching the palms float by, and getting inter-rupted only to be fed three times a day.

BY WATER: FELUCCA

For those on tight budgets but who still want the semi-pharaonic experience of drifting from temple to temple on the Nile, a **felucca** cruise is a slow-paced way to absorb the Egyptian countryside and regain sanity after days in overcrowded *ser-vice. Feluccas* have been sailing the Nile for thousands of years—and *felucca* scams have been going on for at least that long. The more careful you are in navi-gating your way through the crowded docks, the more carefree you can be while your captain navigates his way down the river.

The word *felucca* means boat in Nubian; the typical Nile-cruising variety sleeps up to eight people, has a single tall mast with a characteristically angled boom, and is piloted by an English-speaking Arab or Nubian Egyptian. When not traveling with friends, gather a group of like-minded tourists (aim for a group of 6) in hotel lobbies or the many restaurants along the Nile. You can also ask at the tourist office (a good resource throughout the *felucca* planning process). As a last resort, you can join a group already assembled by a captain. Be sure to meet these people beforehand, or you may find yourself stuck in a horrifying Middle Eastern version of MTV's *The Real World*.

Officially, members of a six-to-eight-person group leaving Aswan should pay E£25 each to Kom Ombo (1 day, 1 night), E£45 to Edfu (3 days, 2 nights), E£50 to Esna (4 days, 3 nights), and E£60 to Luxor (5 days, 4 nights). Most captains add E£5 per day for food and water and a E£5 registration fee. For registration in Aswan, the captain will ask for your passport and the E£5. Have an assembled group ready, or the captain may try to keep your passports as collateral until he can corral other passengers. Prices don't vary much from captain to captain; the most important variable is the vibe you get. Traveling all the way to Luxor may have you longing for solid ground, but the quick trip to Kom Ombo cuts the adven-ture a bit short. Most find the voyage to Edfu just right.

TIPS ON TRAVELING BY FELUCCA

1. CHOOSE YOUR CAPTAIN ON YOUR OWN

Starting from the moment you step off the train in Aswan, you will be approached every 28 seconds by a *felucca* captain or, more often, a middleman sent out to round up suckers. Every hotel manager and every man in the local *ahwa* has his favorite *felucca* captain (from whom he receives a commission), so the word on the street is almost useless. Commission-charging hotels, even if they don't add to the price of your trip, will take money away from your captain who may then be inclined to cut corners on your trip to make up for his losses.

2. LOOK FOR EXPERIENCED CAPTAINS

You should go down to the river yourself, meet and talk with several captains, inspect several boats, and take a list of potential candidates to the tourist office to make sure they aren't pirates or perverts. Ask to see comment books and talk to fellow travelers. Check for lifejackets. Be skeptical of any cute nicknames the captain uses (the "Most Inappropriate Boat Captain Nickname Award" goes to Captain Titanic); an honest captain will tell you his real name if asked. Also be wary of captains who speak little English: these typically younger captains often lack the experience necessary to handle sailing emergencies (there have been several capsizings in recent years caused by high winds and inept sailors). You're better off with a gnarled, crusty old man who speaks English well (if a bit colorfully) than with some punk who is just learning the ropes. If you decide to back out of a trip or switch captains, you should receive a full refund, minus E£10-15 if your *felucca* captain has already bought food.

3. ARRANGE THE FINAL DESTINATION

Also be sure that it is clearly understood by the captain. Captains are inclined to stay close to home to save themselves a time-consuming return against the current. Unscrupulous boatsmen have been known to drop their passengers off 40km from a town, claiming that it was "close enough."

4. CHECK YOUR PROVISIONS

Many a traveler has arrived at his or her destination either sick from low-quality food or hungry from low rations. Others embark to find that the captain has only bought one bottle of water per person, per day. You have two options: shop with the captain and choose what you want to eat yourself (a time-consuming process), or review the planned menu carefully, insisting on adding whatever's on your wish list, and asking to see it all before you set out. For greater leisure, choosing a captain who takes care of the cooking himself is highly recommended; an extra-special captain who cooks Nubian dishes in the *felucca* or arranges to stop at his village for a home-cooked meal is a godsend. A captain should also bring at least two cartons of bottled water; make sure it is aboard before you depart and check that the tabs are sealed, as they may be filled with tap water. In addition, bring at least three bottles of water per person per day for drinking, cooking, and brewing tea. You can also ask for a big jerry can of tap water to be brought along which can be used instead of the Nile for washing dishes and faces. Those looking for more exciting libations should know that beer can be procured at the liquor store on the corniche.

5. HAVE FUN

Although *felucca* cruises can be dangerous, there are many reputable captains out there; trips should ease your worries, not aggravate them. Have fun, but be careful.

LUXOR الاقصر

This ancient capital of Upper and Lower Egypt still humbles visitors three millennia after the height of its power. The city is built on the site of *Ta Ipet* (known by its Greek name, Thebes), and flexed its influential muscles during the five-century rule of the New Kingdom (the 18th-20th dynasties, from 1550-1070 BCE). Egypt's ancient history is felt more here than anywhere else in the Nile Valley, and droves of tourists come to marvel at shimmering sandstone temples and mysterious tombs. Unfortunately, the tourism industry has spawned a society of ruthless hoteliers, greedy guides, and cunning cabdrivers. If somebody says the word "free," walk away—nothing is free in Luxor. But fear not: only a few pounds a day can buy decent accommodations, tasty food, and access to unforgettable sights.

✦ ORIENTATION

Luxor lies on the eastern bank of the Nile, 670km upstream from Cairo and 220km downstream from Aswan. Surrounded by a heavily cultivated floodplain, the city is an agricultural area, with a *souq* on Tuesdays. The city can be divided into three sectors: Luxor City, the village of Karnak a few kilometers north, and

Thebes on the west bank. Finding your way around Luxor is easy as long as you know the main thoroughfares. **El-Mahatta Street** (Station St.) runs perpendicular to the Nile. The **train station** is on this street, 750m inland on the eastern edge of Luxor. Exit the train station at a 45-degree angle to your left and you will eventually reach **Television Street,** where signs advertising the many budget hotels and pensions in town begin to appear. **En-Nil Street** (the corniche) runs southward along the river, turning into Khalid Ibn el-Walid St. past the **Novotel.** The **service station** is located at the exit of Luxor Temple. **El-Karnak Street** begins just north of the temple and runs parallel to the corniche slightly inland. **Luxor Temple** is on the corniche at the center of town, and **Karnak Temple** is 3km farther, one block inland from the corniche.

You can get around Luxor by foot, though a ride to Karnak Temple can be a pleasure. **Kalishes** are good for easy transport of baggage or a relaxing trip out to Karnak (E£5). The cheapest and quickest transportation in the city is by **minibus** (25pt). The most common route is El-Karnak St. to El-Mahatta St. to Television St.

▼ PRACTICAL INFORMATION

Tourist Office: (tel. 37 22 15 or 37 32 94), just left of the New Winter Palace Hotel. Open daily (including Ramadan) 8am-8pm. Additional branches at the **train station** (tel. 37 02 59; open 8am-8pm) and in the **airport** (tel. 37 23 06) are not as well staffed. Low on free and useful literature, but the office in the tourist bazaar has handy bus and train schedules with price listings.

Passport Office: (tel. 38 08 85), Khalid Ibn el-Walid St. On the left 1km south of the Novotel, near the Isis Hotel. Visas extended in the foreigners' office. Open Sa-Th 8:30am-2:30pm; Ramadan 9am-2pm.

Currency Exchange: Exchanges are available in most hotels on the corniche, or you can try the **National Bank of Egypt,** also on the corniche, 50m south of Old Winter Palace Hotel. Offers cash advances on Visa, MC. Open daily 8:30am-2pm and 6-10pm.

ATM: There is an ATM outside **Banque Misr,** a street north of the Mecure Hotel on the corniche. Another ATM is located outside Gaddis Hotel on Khalid Ibn el-Walid St. just across from the Isis Hotel. Both accept Visa, MC, AmEx, PLUS, and Cirrus.

American Express: (tel. 37 83 33; tel./fax 37 28 62), En-Nil St. in front of the Old Winter Palace Hotel, south of Luxor Temple. Holds mail, sells traveler's checks, and wires and exchanges money and checks. Open daily 8am-7pm.

English Bookstore: 'Aboudi Bookshop has 3 locations in the tourist bazaar complex on En-Nil St. Good but costly Egyptology books, countless sappy romances, and a few paperbacks in English, French, and German. Open daily 8am-10pm. Kiosks in front of tourist bazaar and in the train station sell foreign periodicals.

Swimming Pools: There are small but pleasant pools accessible for E£10 at the **St. Joseph** (on Khalid Ibn el-Walid St.), the **Shady** (on Television St.), and the **Luxor Wena Hotel** (on the corniche), where the E£10 entrance fee also includes unlimited rounds of billiards and backgammon.

Police: Tel. 37 23 50. The police station is off El-Karnak St. 200m north of Luxor Temple.

Medical Emergency: Tel. 123.

Tourist Police: Tel. 37 66 20, in the tourist bazaar on En-Nil St. and at the **train station** (tel. 37 38 45). Both open 24hr.

Pharmacy: 24hr. duty rotates—try asking a hotel employee. **Rania Pharmacy** (tel. 37 12 86), at the north end of Television St., is well stocked with Egyptian medication and basic toiletries (open 8am-midnight). **El-Manshia,** on 'Abd el-Munem el-'Adasi St., has mostly medication (open daily 7:30am-noon).

Hospitals: Luxor International Hospital (tel. 38 11 60), on the southern end of Television St., is a newly-opened, modern facility that accepts cash, credit cards, and medical insurance. The **Luxor General Hospital** (tel. 37 20 25 or 28 09), on En-Nil St. north of the museum, is a definite step down from the Luxor International. Patients must pay cash.

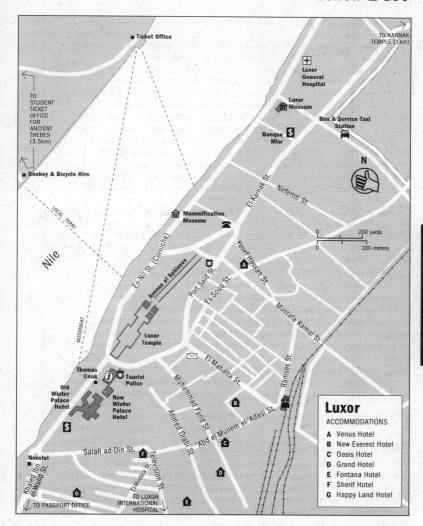

Post Office: On El-Mahatta St., 100m east of Luxor Temple. Offers **Poste Restante** and **EMS** services (open Su-Th 8am-2pm; EMS open until noon). Other branches near the tourist office and in the train station (open 8am-noon and 2:30-8pm). Passport required to pick up a letter or package.

Internet Access: **'Aboudi Internet Cafe** (tel. 37 23 90; email aboudi@Access.com.eg), located on the 2nd floor of the 'Aboudi Bookshop on the corniche just south of Luxor Temple. E£6.25 for 15min. Open daily 8am-10pm.

Telephones: Central Telephone Office, off El-Karnak St. to the west, just north of Luxor Temple (open 24hr). Other less crowded offices are on En-Nil St. in front of the Old Winter Palace Hotel (the cheapest **fax services** in the city are here) and in the train station (open 6am-8pm). Hotels may charge twice as much as telephone offices. **Directory Assistance:** Tel. 16.

Telephone Code: 095.

▣ TRANSPORTATION

Airplanes: The airport is 8km northeast of town (no bus; taxi E£10-15) and is served by **EgyptAir** (tel. 38 05 80), next to the Old Winter Palace Hotel. Flights to: **Cairo** (1hr.; 3-5 per day in summer, up to 11 in winter; E£419); **Aswan** (3 per day, E£190); **Sharm esh-Sheikh** (3 per week, E£416); and **Hurghada** (seasonal). While it is possible to purchase tickets at the EgyptAir branch at the airport (tel. 38 05 86 or 89), it is not recommended. All tickets to international destinations must be purchased in Luxor.

Trains: The train station is at the head of El-Mahatta St. (Station St.), 750m inland from Luxor Temple (tel. 37 20 18). Lockers 90pt per day. For their protection, tourists are restricted to 2 express trains to **Cairo** (8-10hr.; 8:30am and 11:30pm; 1st class E£48-51, A/C 2nd class E£28-31). Cairo trains are especially crowded. Reserve sleeper cars 1 day in advance. Trains to **Aswan** (3hr.; 7:30am and 5:30pm; 1st class E£20-22, A/C 2nd class E£12-14; students 1st class E£13-15, 2nd class E£9-11) are less comfortable than *service* or *feluccas*. Walk on for a fee; reserve a seat to be safe. Book tickets to all major destinations at least 1 day in advance.

Buses: The bus station is by the exit of Karnak Temple. Buses to: **Cairo** (11-12hr., 7pm, A/C E£51); **Hurghada** (5 per day 6am-7pm, E£15-23); and **Aswan** (4½hr., 9 per day 6:30am-7:30pm, E£6.50-10). All of the above stop at **Esna** (1hr., E£2.50); **Edfu** (1½hr., E£5); **Kom Ombo** (3hr., E£5); **Kharga** (M, W, Sa 8:30am; E£18); and **Suez** (4 per day, 6:30am-7pm, E£11-17). Hours and rates change frequently.

Service Taxis: Off El-Karnak St., 1 block inland from the Luxor Museum. Early morning and late afternoon *service* leave whenever they fill up, usually about every 15min. Out-of-town trips must be made with police convoys. Daily convoys to points south leave from El-Baghdadi Point (3km south of the Old Winter Palace Hotel on En-Nil St.) at 7am, 11am, and 3pm. Convoys to points north leave from beside the Hotel Pola (6, 8am, 2, 5pm). *Service* to: **Qena** (1hr., E£3); **El-Balyana** (2hr., E£5); **Esna** (1hr., E£2.50); **Edfu** (2hr., E£4); **Kom Ombo** (2½hr., E£7); and **Aswan** (3-4hr., E£9). Less frequent departures from a station on the west bank where the local ferry docks.

Bike Rental: El-Mahatta St. and Television St., or ask at a hotel (E£5-7 per day). **Motorbikes** at the Sherif Hotel and Everest Hotel on Television St. (E£50-60 per day; no helmets). To visit the West Bank sites on motorbike, take a ferry in front of Luxor Temple.

▮ ACCOMMODATIONS

EAST BANK (MODERN LUXOR)

If you come to Luxor by train, you will disembark into a writhing mass of arms waving hotel cards. Decide where you want to go and stick to your guns. Many hawkers will quote incorrect prices or tell you the hotel you have in mind is full or shut down. *Kalish* drivers may take you to a different hotel than you requested, assuming tourists don't know any better or are too tired to complain. Demand to be taken to your hotel or withhold payment. Women traveling alone can almost bet on sexual overtures from young employees in many of the small hotels. If a refusal doesn't do the trick, complain to the manager or the tourist police.

Most budget hotels cluster around Television St. and Yusef Hassan St. Prices are known to fluctuate, but the prices listed in this guide should be accurate barring small adjustments. A roof or terrace mattress may be available for E£3-4. Listed accommodations all have 24-hour hot water, fans, and free use of washers and kitchens, unless otherwise noted.

◪ **Happy Land Hotel** (tel. 37 18 28), about 150m off El-Medina St., a few blocks past the intersection with Television St. (look for the huge sign). The owner, Mr. Ibrahim, will go to great lengths to demonstrate his establishment's nearly obsessive cleanliness. Also has a great rooftop restaurant with polished service and a great breakfast. A/C dorms E£7.50. Singles with fan and bath E£15; doubles with fan and bath E£20, with A/C E£25. Books trips to Dahab for E£85.

■ **Venus Hotel** (tel. 37 26 25), Yusef Hassan St. Convenient but noisy, with clean, tiled rooms and large windows. "Mars Bar" on the 2nd floor features pool table, foosball, satellite TV, and cheap drinks (Stella E£6). All rooms with A/C and bath. Singles E£10; doubles E£25; triples E£30. Breakfast included.

■ **Fontana Hotel** (tel. 38 06 63), off Television St. Gorgeous bathrooms with towels and toilet paper and super-clean rooms (try to get one with a balcony). Singles with fan E£6, with A/C E£8; doubles with bath E£10, with A/C E£15; small triples with bath and A/C E£20. Breakfast included. Prices E£10 higher in winter.

Grand Hotel (tel. 38 29 05), Muhammad Farid St. Try not to be scared off by the owner's sign painted by the staircase: "I always kill people for money but because you are my friend, I kill you for nothing." Although this hotel is quiet and clean, it doesn't quite live up to its name. Singles with fan E£7; doubles with bath and fan E£10, with A/C E£20. Extra beds E£3 each. Breakfast E£3.50.

Oasis Hotel (tel. 38 16 99), Muhammad Farid St. Clean, spacious rooms with messy public bathrooms. Prices may fluctuate so hold your ground. Sometimes pushy about tours. Bed with fan E£6, with bath and A/C E£8; doubles with bath and A/C E£12; triples with bath and A/C E£15.

New Everest Hotel (tel. 37 00 17), En-Nozha St. off El-Mahatta St., 100 yards from the train station down an alley on the left. Newly-opened hotel with clean, no-frills rooms and bathrooms. Singles with fan E£5, with bath E£7; doubles with bath and A/C E£15; triples with bath and A/C E£18. Breakfast included.

Sherif Hotel, (tel. 37 07 57; email khaeli@hotmail.com), Badr St., first right off Television St. Bob Marley's image, music, and habits thrive in this friendly establishment. Singles with bath E£6; doubles E£12, with A/C and bath E£15; triples E£18, with A/C and bath E£21.

WEST BANK (ANCIENT THEBES)

It is generally more convenient to sleep on the East Bank in Luxor proper, but the West Bank offers quiet surroundings and the chance to roll out of bed and into the Theban necropolis at the opening bell. A taxi from the ferry docks (E£5) is the only practical way to get to hotels. For information on crossing the Nile, see **Sightseeing Strategy**, p. 194. The **Pharaoh's Hotel** (tel. 31 07 02), farther down the same unpaved road as the ticket office, is this area's best hotel, with carpeted rooms and a flowery garden. When business is slow, prices may skyrocket; insist that you know better (singles E£40; doubles E£80; triples E£120; includes breakfast, A/C, and bath). Prices run E£5-10 higher in winter, lower in summer.

◯ FOOD

Luxor may be an archaeologist's paradise, but it's purgatory for the frugal gourmet. Two *kushari* houses stand out from the pack: **Sayyida Zeinab** (on Television St.) and **Sayyida Nafisa** (on Yusef Hassan St.). The **coffee shop** in the New Winter Palace has a paltry but cheap all-you-can-eat dessert buffet (E£16). There is a **liquor store** on Ramses St. directly to the right as you walk out of the train station on El-Mahatta St. (open 8am-2pm and 5-11pm). Pension managers can also procure beer for you (less than E£5.50).

A big drawback to staying on the West Bank is its lack of decent, cheap restaurants. **Tutankhamun** and **Africa** next to the ferry landing offer the usual chicken and kebab dinners for E£15-20. Most hotels have restaurants, but they're often closed and the quality is inconsistent, especially when business is slow in the summer.

■ **Amoun Restaurant** (tel. 37 05 47), just north of the Luxor Temple. A favorite spot among locals and tourists alike, serving a variety of tasty dishes. Pizza starts at E£7, entrees average E£10. Open 8am-midnight. Student discounts available.

Restaurant Khased Khear (tel. 38 45 80), on 'Abd el-Moneim el-'Adasi St. (El-Manshia St.), 1 block from the train station. The cozy and cool wood-paneled interior makes you feel like you're on a ship in the North Sea. The specialty is kebab (beef or lamb entrees average E£9). Take-out available. Open daily 11am-2am.

Esquire Bistro, by Salah ad-Din Sq., 200m inland from the Novotel. You can't miss the bright pink cottage and neon sign of this hip new diner, offering a wide range of decent and affordable food. Most entrees under E£14. Open 24hr.

El-Houda, on Television St. Friendly staff and tasty meals from a surprisingly diverse menu. The 6-course value meals are a great bargain at E£15, but you can also get pizza (E£6), chicken curry (E£6.50), *shish tawouq* (E£8) or a chicken quarter (E£5.50). Ahhh, A/C. Open daily 11am-11pm.

Sultana Restaurant (tel. 38 14 83), on Television St. This relatively new cafe reeks of chintzy Arabic pop and the garlic loaded onto the gigantic pizzas (E£13 with *Let's Go* discount). Open daily 9am-11pm.

The Classic Restaurant (tel. 38 17 07), Khalid Ibn el-Walid St. Look for the large yellow sign near the passport office. If you're going to splurge on a large, well-cooked meal, this isn't a bad place to do it. The wide menu features steaks (E£20-30) and excellent kebab (E£20). Polished service and a special discount plan: 10% off on the 1st visit, 20% on the 2nd, 25% on the 3rd. Open daily 6-11:45pm. Visa, MC, AmEx accepted.

Pink Panda (tel. 37 27 50), on Khalid Ibn el-Walid St. in the Isis Hotel. If you have a craving for Chinese, you'll pay dearly (meat dishes E£32-42, vegetarian E£14-18). Waiters buzz around in black bowties. Open daily noon-3pm and 6-11pm. Visa, MC accepted.

🎵 ENTERTAINMENT

FELUCCAS. For truly Luxorious diversion, fritter away afternoons aboard a **felucca** on the Nile (especially if you're not planning on the *felucca* trip from Aswan to Edfu). **Banana Island,** a small, palm- and fruit-tree-studded peninsula located 2 mi. upriver, is a popular destination (E£2 admission charged by the owners of the island). Overpriced souvenir stands detract from an otherwise rustic experience. *Feluccas* are prohibited from sailing after sunset (round-trip 2-3hr., E£10 per person for groups over 4).

LOCAL ENTERTAINMENT. The many **ahwas** on the streets of Luxor are filled with Egyptians smoking *sheesha*, drinking coffee, and playing dominoes and backgammon. Foreigners are usually welcome, but solo women may attract unwanted comments. The **Tikkya,** on Television St., is more comfortable and friendlier than the other shops. **Videogame** systems like Super Nintendo and Sega Playstation can be found on the sidewalks of Luxor, where the friendly local children would be more than happy to challenge you to a round or two of *Mortal Kombat* for 50pt per game. Adults also enjoy meeting foreigners, so don't be surprised if you are invited to a **wedding party** while in Luxor (or at least asked to get liquor at the duty-free store "for my sister's wedding tomorrow"). Think twice before disrupting a wedding party—"guests" are often expected to pay admission.

BARS AND DISCOS. The **Mars Bar** in the Venus Hotel (Stella E£6) has a foosball table, billiards, and satellite TV. The **King's Head** on Ibn Walik St. is a popular pub with a wide drink selection (Stella E£8) and pizza (E£12). Play pool for E£10. Most discos in Luxor are not hip, not cheap, and not worth it. Dance floors are about the size of a big table, and most DJs play songs you don't like and terrible remixes of the songs you do. The **Mercure Hotel** (also called the ETAP), on the corniche, is the most happening disco in Luxor. There is a E£30 minimum charge, but nobody pays attention to it in summer. Every night at 11:30pm, the music changes from Top 40 dance remixes to drum machine and synthesizer Arabic music, and the belly dancing starts. An older crowd joins the youngsters for the nightly display of undulating flesh (Stella E£9.75; open nightly 10pm-2am). Most popular with local swingers is **Disco on Le Lotus** at the Novotel (intersection of Salah ad-Din and the corniche), on a boat docked behind the hotel (E£20 minimum; open nightly 10pm-2am).

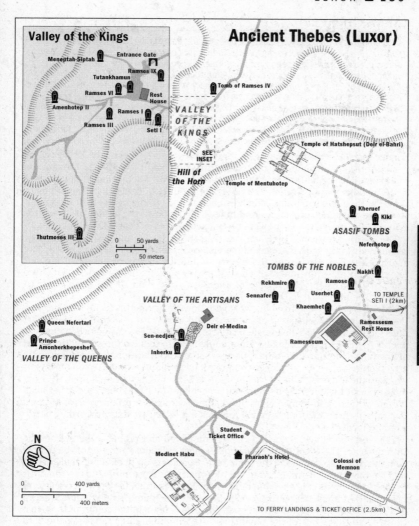

Valley of the Kings

Ancient Thebes (Luxor)

Meneptah-Siptah
Entrance Gate
Ramses IX
Tutankhamun
Tomb of Ramses IV
Ramses VI
Rest House
Amenhotep II
Ramses I
Ramses III
Seti I
VALLEY OF THE KINGS
SEE INSET
Hill of the Horn
Temple of Hatshepsut (Deir el-Bahri)
Temple of Mentuhotep
Thutmoses III
0 50 yards
0 50 meters
Kheruef
Kiki
ASASIF TOMBS
Neferhotep
TOMBS OF THE NOBLES
Nakht
Rekhmire
Ramose
Sennafer
Userhet
Khaemhet
TO TEMPLE SETI I (2km)
VALLEY OF THE ARTISANS
Ramesseum Rest House
Queen Nefertari
Deir el-Medina
Prince Amonherkhepeshef
Sen-nedjen
Ramesseum
VALLEY OF THE QUEENS
Inherku
N
Student Ticket Office
Medinet Habu
Pharaoh's Hotel
Colossi of Memnon
0 400 yards
0 400 meters
TO FERRY LANDINGS & TICKET OFFICE (2.5km)

👁 SIGHTS

EAST BANK

Luxor has two major temples and two museums. **Luxor Temple** (p. 192) stands in the heart of the city adjacent to the Nile; its lighting and late hours make it perfect for a first date. Going north along the corniche, the **Mummification Museum** (p. 193) and the small but excellent **Luxor Museum of Ancient Egyptian Art** (p. 192) house sculptures and artifacts unearthed at Karnak and elsewhere. **Karnak Temple** (p. 190), the Leviathan of pharaonic architecture, sprawls just a few kilometers farther north. Karnak Temple is best seen early in the morning before the sun is high, while the museums are perfect for an afternoon cool-off.

KARNAK TEMPLE

*Local **minibuses** run between Karnak Temple and the train station (25pt). Ask first to make sure the driver is going as far as the temple. The Karnak complex covers over five acres of land and is difficult to cover thoroughly, so bring water and come early in the day. **Open** daily in summer 6am-5pm; in winter 6am-5:30pm. **Admission** E£20, students E£10. You can reach the temple by bike, foot, or kalish (E£5). If you seek more than a general impression of the place, a guided tour is useful, and latching onto one is easy. The **sound and light show** is a fascinating way to explore the temple for a first-time visit. With your appetite whetted, a return trip the following morning will give you a good feel for the complex. English shows in summer M, Th 8pm, Tu, W, F-Su 9:15pm; in winter M 6pm, Tu 9pm, W-Su 7:30pm. Times subject to change, so check at your hotel or at the tourist office. **Show admission** E£33.*

Karnak Temple is overwhelming in its intricacy and proportions. Every major period in Egypt's ancient history since the collapse of the Middle Kingdom is represented in the additions to this complex of shrines dedicated to the sun-god Amun and his family. Karnak Temple is the product of centuries of one-upmanship. Pharaoh after pharaoh added his mark to the temple in an effort to demonstrate the greatness of Amun—and himself. It was also the center of power for Amun's high priest, whose powers often exceeded even those of the pharaoh.

The entire 3km route between the temples of Luxor and Karnak was once connected by the sacred **Avenue of the Sphinxes**, built by Queen Hatshepsut. The evermodest Ramses II took the liberty of adding a small statuette of himself to each sphinx. The final stretch of the avenue remains complete with two rows of sphinxes by the **Temple of Khonsu**, to the right of the main entry to Karnak Temple.

Enter Karnak Temple from the west with the Nile at your back and pass through the **Avenue of the Rams**, another double-rowed boulevard of creatures (this time, lions' bodies with rams' heads) dedicated to Ramses II. The curly-horned ram is one of Amun's sacred animals. The temple is a *Hodges-podge* of additions and alterations spanning millennia, but because of the traditionalism of pharaonic architecture, the different pieces comprise a harmonious whole. As you push your way into the fortress, think of each section as a layer of history built upon the original shrine at the core. The farther you proceed into the building, the farther back in time you go. The temple is oriented along two axes: a primary east-west axis that follows the path of the sun god Amun and a secondary axis proceeding north-south to Luxor Temple.

The first and largest pylon was never completed and probably dates from the 25th dynasty. The **Great Court,** the single largest individual element of the temple complex, dates from around the same time. Chambers on the left are dedicated to the Theban triad of Amun, Mut, and Khonsu and were built during the 29th dynasty. On the right is a temple built under Ramses III and lined with twenty 7m tall statues of himself. The three chapels behind the temple's inner court are also dedicated to the Theban triad. An open papyrus column in the center of the Great Court is all that's left of the pavilion of the Ethiopian king Taharq of the 25th dynasty (689-664 BCE).

Pass through the recycled second pylon (Ramses II made it with blocks from one of Akhenaton's temples) into the **Great Hypostyle Hall.** With 12 central columns and 122 subsidiary columns, it's one of the pinnacles of pharaonic architecture. The central colonnade (from 1375 BCE) is the oldest part of the hall; other additions were made by Ramses II. Emerging from the forest of sandstone, find the 30m high granite **Obelisk of Queen Hatshepsut,** the tallest obelisk in Egypt, in front of the fourth pylon. Hatshepsut (pronounced Hat-*Cheap*-Suit), who considered herself a female king, brought the stones from Aswan and inlaid them with bushels of gold. Every centimeter of the ceiling, walls, and columns is carved with inscriptions. Note the depictions of the fertility god Min doin' what comes naturally with the goddess Charissa. Passing through the rubble of the fifth pylon and the granite sixth pylon, enter the **Hall of Records,** containing two elegantly proportioned granite pillars, one decorated with carvings of the lotus

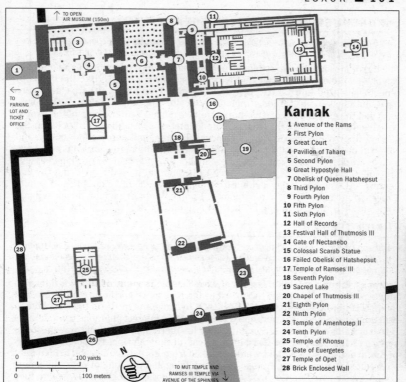

Karnak

1 Avenue of the Rams
2 First Pylon
3 Great Court
4 Pavilion of Taharq
5 Second Pylon
6 Great Hypostyle Hall
7 Obelisk of Queen Hatshepsut
8 Third Pylon
9 Fourth Pylon
10 Fifth Pylon
11 Sixth Pylon
12 Hall of Records
13 Festival Hall of Thutmosis III
14 Gate of Nectanebo
15 Colossal Scarab Statue
16 Failed Obelisk of Hatshepsut
17 Temple of Ramses III
18 Seventh Pylon
19 Sacred Lake
20 Chapel of Thutmosis III
21 Eighth Pylon
22 Ninth Pylon
23 Temple of Amenhotep II
24 Tenth Pylon
25 Temple of Khonsu
26 Gate of Euergetes
27 Temple of Opet
28 Brick Enclosed Wall

TO OPEN AIR MUSEUM (150m)

TO PARKING LOT AND TICKET OFFICE

TO MUT TEMPLE AND RAMSES III TEMPLE VIA AVENUE OF THE SPHINXES

N

0   100 yards
0   100 meters

EGYPT

of Upper Egypt and the other with the papyrus of Lower Egypt. The **Sanctuary of the Sacred Boats,** behind the hall, was added by Alexander the Great's brother Philip around 300 BCE.

Straight ahead, the **Festival Hall of Thutmoses III** dominates the eastern edge of the Karnak complex. Built to commemorate the pharaoh's victories in the mysterious north, it contains carvings of strange plants and animals brought back from his campaigns. The star-studded ceiling survives intact, supported by 52 tapering pillars. Some of the bases were actually whittled down to make room for large processions. In the 6th century CE, the hall was converted into a church; frescoes of haloed saints still adorn the interior walls and column shafts. Beyond a low wall to the east, the **Gate of Nectanebo** marks an early entrance to the complex. South of the Festival Hall, the limpid waters of the **Sacred Lake** sizzle in the heat. Every morning, priests purified themselves in the holy waters of this rectangular pool before performing ceremonies within the temple. Note the large scarab beetle on the southwestern corner of the lake—it is said that if you run around the scarab in a clockwise direction three times, you will soon be pregnant (men beware).

KARNAK OPEN-AIR MUSEUM. This museum is to the north of the great court; look for a small sign and return toward the entrance. The museum is comprised of three excavated chapels and a motley collection of well-labeled wall fragments. The **Red Chapel** of Queen Hatshepsut is displayed in long rows of blocks, along with the Middle Kingdom **Alabaster Chapel.** The latter has white walls streaked with brown, a welcome relief from the acres of sandstone. (*Admission E£10, students E£5.*)

LUXOR MUSEUM OF ANCIENT EGYPTIAN ART

A 15-min. walk north of Luxor Temple on the corniche. Open daily 9am-1pm and 5-10pm; in winter 9am-1pm and 4-9pm. Wheelchair accessible. Admission E£30, students E£15.

The Luxor Museum has arguably the best, most edifying collection of antiquities in Egypt—testament to the fact that less is sometimes more. Unlike the heaps of objects squeezed into Cairo's Egyptian Museum (see p. 96), the treasures here have multilingual descriptions (including the site and probable date of each subject) and the exhibits have been thoughtfully arranged with the help of the Brooklyn Museum of New York. The recreated **mural** of 283 sandstone blocks on the second floor was found within the Karnak Temple, and depicts Akhenaton and Nefertiti in adoration of the sun god Aton along with numerous artisans and peasants at work. The gallery also includes smaller artifacts such as drinking vessels, precious jewelry, bronze statuettes, and Alexandrian period coins from the 2nd century CE. The **New Hall** was built to display the cache of 16 marble and granite statues found in the 1980s beneath Luxor Temple. Without a doubt, the most handsome statue is the red granite likeness of Amenhotep III (1405-1367 BCE).

LUXOR TEMPLE

Enter on En-Nil St., 400m north of the New Winter Palace. Open daily in summer 6am-10pm; in winter 6am-9pm. The temple and its well-groomed lawns are an especially comfortable retreat at night (lights go on at 7pm year-round). Admission E£20, students E£10.

Although Karnak gets all the glory, Luxor Temple is grand in its own right and much more comprehensible to the visitor than the more northerly temple. Most of Luxor Temple was built around 1380 BCE by Amenhotep III on top of a Middle Kingdom site. Significant portions were erected by famous pharaohs from Ramses II to Tutankhamun, each striving to make his mark. Luxor Temple was meant to serve as a **Love Nest for the Gods:** once a year, during the Opet festival, the statues of Amun and his consort Mut would be taken from Karnak temple and loaded onto a ceremonial sacred boat. Amidst much rejoicing and drinking of beer, the happy couple was carried on the shoulders of priests to the Luxor Temple, where they spent 24 days and nights together in the sanctuary. During this time, the moon god Khonsu was conceived, completing the Theban triad (see **Meet the Gods,** p. 51).

Later work on the temple was done by Ramses II, who built the enormous **First Pylon,** nearly 24m tall and 65m wide. The pylon is inscribed with images of Ramses II smiting the Hittites. In front of the pylon stand three of the six original **Colossi of Ramses II,** two seated and one standing. A red granite obelisk flanks the doorway; its twin was given to France in 1819 and now graces the Place de la Concorde in Paris. The granite statues of the **Court of Ramses II,** past the pylon, originally portrayed Amenhotep, but were altered when ancient Egypt's favorite egomaniac assumed the throne. Continue through the court's papyrus columns to the **Colonnade of Amenhotep III,** where the columns have open lotus crowns. The walls of the colonnade were inscribed with scenes from the festival of Opet by Tutankhamun. From here, proceed into the **Court of Amenhotep III.** Beyond this court rises the hypostyle hall, or antechamber, and its 22 gigantic columns. The Egyptian government is currently spending E£9 million restoring these columns, whose foundations crumbled when the construction of the Aswan High Dam raised the water level in the area (see **Moving A Mountain,** p. 221).

Latin inscriptions to Julius Caesar adorn an altar in a room to the left of the pillared hall. Alexander himself had the *bas*-reliefs (in which he appears in pharaonic attire before Amun and other deities) added when he built the **Sanctuary of Alexander the Great** at the end of the corridor. Fertility god Min receives disproportionate attention in the sanctuary. The Romans used the whole temple as a *castrum* (military camp) in the 4th century CE. The excavation of the temple remains incomplete as the Mosque of Abu El-Haggag, added by the Fatimids in 1077 CE and still in use today, prevents work on the left-hand gallery: only the end portions of the Avenue of the Sphinxes (the 3km road connecting the Luxor and Karnak Temples), have been unearthed and restored.

MUMMIFICATION MUSEUM

100m north of Luxor Temple on the bank of the Nile. Tel. 38 15 02. Open daily in summer 9am-1pm and 5-10pm; in winter 9am-1pm, and 4-9pm. Free lectures (occasionally in English) on recent discoveries in the Luxor area are every Thursday at 7pm. Admission E£20.

Opened in 1997 by President Hosni Mubarak, this museum gives an insightful view into the meticulous and often misunderstood process of mummification. The 66 artifacts on display (65 of which were taken from the Egyptian Museum in Cairo) range from sophisticated surgical instruments to a mummified menagerie consisting of a monkey, goose, and crocodile, and a cat in a Pez-dispenser-shaped coffin.

WEST BANK

When they weren't preoccupied with empire-building and invader-expelling, the rulers of Thebes busied themselves preparing for eternity. As followers of the sun god Amun, the elite of the New Kingdom aspired to tombs on the West Bank, where the sun sets and the afterlife commences. Pharaonic obsession with the afterlife made the necropolis of Thebes into the world's most well-endowed graveyard. Over millennia, robbers and archaeologists have nabbed much of the treasure, but the site still features an unparalleled collection of Egyptian funerary art.

New Kingdom rulers could take no chances with the security of the afterlife. Earlier pharaohs had been too convinced of the mortality of their sacred tombs. Thieves had mastered the delicate art of pyramid pilfering at Memphis, making off with afterlife amenities of a grandeur that can now only be imagined. A radical change in burial practices was in order. The pharaohs of Thebes would not have their treasure rest anywhere but beside their mummified remains.

To conceal the location, contents, and design of the tombs, the work was done in utmost secrecy by a team of laborers who dwelt within the necropolis itself. Perfecting techniques of tomb construction, decoration, and mummification, this community of 300 artisans devoted itself to the City of the Dead over the course of generations, passing expertise down through familial lines. The remains of **Deir el-Medina** (the Workers' Walled City, see p. 199) have been thoroughly excavated and are among the most complete town remains in Egypt. Tomb design reflected the new emphasis on secrecy. Instead of a single, ostentatious pyramid, there were pairs of funerary monuments: an underground grave, lavishly outfitted with the articles demanded by the hectic afterlife and sequestered in an obscure recess of the desert; and a grandiose mortuary temple where the monarch could be worshiped for eternity. Architects incorporated dead-end passages, fake sarcophagi, hidden doorways, and deep shafts to foil the most cunning robbers. Once a pharaoh was safely stowed, workers immediately began to construct the tomb destined for his successor.

GET DOWN AND DIG IT An archaeologist's work is never done, especially in Luxor. Although it would appear that most of the treasures of the old tombs and temples have been whisked away, archaeologists are still concerned with what they can learn through excavation (and finding a little new treasure never hurt anybody either). The Department of Antiquities oversees and conducts many of the ongoing projects in Egypt, from the restoration of the Ramesseum to current digs at the Karnak Temple and the Valley of the Kings. One of the most promising recent finds is the discovery of the largest tomb ever found in Egypt, a vast 107-room (and counting) complex being excavated by a team led by the American archaeologist Kent Weeks. The name of Ramses II has been identified four times, giving rise to speculation that this could be the final resting place of the great pharaoh's many sons. Entry into the tomb has been hampered by falling rocks, and it is completely off-limits to the public. Other avenues of research include remote sensing, which detects irregularities beneath the surface without costly digging, and excavation within the city of Luxor itself.

One region in particular must have seemed ideal for entombment: a narrow, winding valley walled on three sides by jagged limestone cliffs and approachable by a single rocky footpath. This isolated canyon, known as the **Valley of the Kings** (p. 195), became the burial place of New Kingdom pharaohs. Although it looked promising on papyrus, it failed to deter hoodlums, and few of the tombs escaped vandalism. Queens, favored consorts, and select offspring were accorded ceremonial burial with full honors and security precautions in a separate corner of the West Bank, the **Valley of the Queens** (p. 201). Esteemed members of the Theban aristocracy also practiced elaborate burial customs, and several of the resulting **Tombs of the Nobles** (p. 200) rival royal burial chambers in craft and design. Last but not least, the **Valley of the Artisans** (Deir el-Medina, p. 199) has two very impressive tombs of pharaonic artists. Over 400 tombs moulder in the necropolis, but only a handful are accessible. In addition to tombs, the West Bank hosts massive **mortuary temples** (p. 197). Most imposing are the **Colossi of Memnon,** the **Temple of Hatshepsut** (Deir el-Bahri), and the Temple of Ramses III (better known as **Medinet Habu**) near the Valley of the Queens. The ruins of the **Ramesseum** (the Temple of Ramses II), though shattered, also merit a visit.

⑦ SIGHTSEEING STRATEGY

Plan ahead—you must decide what you would like to see before you head out. Consider content, location, and mode of transport (transportation options are listed below). Conduct your **summer** exploration of the necropolis in a series of early-morning visits. In the **winter,** afternoons are sometimes less crowded than mornings. Guards at the less-visited sites tend to lock up and head home a little early, especially in the summer. All sites open at 6am, offering about three hours of peace and pleasant temperatures. The sites officially close at 4pm in winter and 5pm in summer, but you won't be kicked out as long as you get in before closing time. Expensive drinks are sold at some of the ruins; play it safe by bringing plenty of **water.** Bringing a **flashlight** will save you *bakhsheesh*, especially when particularly pushy tomb guards turn off the lights to force you to rely upon them for guidance.

The cheapest way to get to the West Bank is a **local ferry**—one docks directly in front of Luxor Temple (E£1, bicycles 25pt extra), and the other docks just north of the Novotel (E£1, bikes free). Ferries run from 6am to noon. **Private motorboats** can take you across for E£5 per boat. From the local ferry landing, it is a 1km walk north to the ticket kiosk, then 3km to the Colossi of Memnon. Here are some transportation options once you're at the West Bank:

ON FOOT. If you have time and stamina, the best and probably safest way to see the sights on the West Bank is to walk to them. All of the sights (except for the Valley of the Kings) are within a 3km radius of the Colossi of Memnon, which itself is an easy 3km from the ticket office. A good strategy is to buy your tickets and start walking to the sights. Once you are on the main road (1km from the ticket office), catch a covered pick-up truck to the Colossi of Memnon (25pt). Special taxis travel directly from the ticket office to the Colossi of Memnon for as little as E£5 (much more in the summer). The Valley of the Kings is 8km by paved road, but the walk is worth it for the chance to follow the donkey trail (actually not a very safe option for donkeys) up and over the **Jabal el-Qurn** (Hill of the Horn). The peak was once sacred to the goddess of silence, Mirtseger, and with good reason—the serene sound of nothing you'll hear at the top of the hill is matched only by the view you'll have of the ruins. A simple geographic division is **North** (Valley of the Kings, Seti Temple, Hatshepsut, Ramesseum, and the Tombs of the Nobles) and **South** (Valley of the Queens, Medinet Habu, and the Valley of the Artisans); this division makes for a two-day exploration. Walking in the middle of the day lets you have the sights to yourself, but be extremely cautious in the unforgiving heat.

GUIDED TOURS. Guided tours in air-conditioned coaches with English-speaking guides are the most popular option. All of the budget hotels book tours, but many charge a hefty commission. Do not under any circumstances book tours for Luxor in Cairo, where travel agents are likely to slap a hefty commission onto an already inflated price. Hotels such as **Happy Land** (p. 186) book tours of the West Bank (Colossi of Memnon, Valleys of the Kings and Queens, and Temple of Hatshepsut) for as low as E£45. You can also book a tour directly with noted guide and Egyptologist Abu En-Naga Gabrail (tel. 37 45 94 or 38 44 20). Better known as **Moonshine,** Gabrail has been leading tour groups around the West Bank for over 20 years.

DONKEY. Mark Twain wrote that riding a donkey in Egypt "was a fresh, new, exhilarating sensation worth a hundred worn and threadbare pleasures." The novelty of donkey travel (which has a way of wearing thin as quickly as the seat of your pants) and the fantastic views afforded by the trail as it climbs its way up and around to the Valley of the Kings has led to a burgeoning burro-borrow market. Through your hotel, you can arrange an excursion that includes donkey (and human donkey guide) and ferry ride (E£30). Larger groups get lower prices. Do away with middlemen and hire your own animal in the village of Gezira just inland from the ferry or at the local ferry dock. This allows you more leeway with your itinerary—tours usually take you only to the Valley of the Kings, the Temple of Hatshepsut, the Ramesseum, and the Colossi of Memnon. Those planning to ride donkeys for only one day might save the Valley of the Kings for the day of the ride and walk to the rest of the sites. One suggested full donkey route begins at the Valley of the Kings, goes around to the Temple of Hatshepsut and the Ramesseum, and then returns home. The out of the way, less-than-awe-inspiring Ramesseum can be omitted in the summer heat.

BICYCLE AND MOTORBIKE. Bicycles are cheap (E£3-5) and allow for individual freedom and a chance to view the surrounding scenery of green fields abutting sandy dunes. There are a few serious hills that are nearly unbearable during the summer. You can rent bikes in Luxor or by the local ferry landing. Many hotels, the Everest and Sherif included, rent motorbikes for E£50-60 per day.

TAXI. Hiring a taxi is a more expensive and air-conditioning-less option (E£30-40 for the morning is a good price), but it allows you to cover the most ground. Hordes of drivers wait at both ferry landings. You can hire a taxi in Luxor, but the car ferry is slow and erratic. When bargaining, ignore any nonsense about government rates and per person charges.

VALLEY OF THE KINGS وادى الملوك

The Valley of the Kings lies 5km from the Nile but there's no direct path. There are two possible routes to the beginning of the Valley road: go past the Colossi of Memnon, then 3km northeast past the necropolis sites to the start of the Valley road; or turn right (northeast) at the canal (follow the signs) and go 2km along the canal, then turn west by the Abu Qasem Hotel and go 1.5km to the base of the Valley road. The road gently winds for 5km into desolate mountain valleys. Tombs open daily in summer 6am-5pm; in winter 6am-4pm. There is a Rest House near the entrance with overpriced water and warm juice. Public toilets available.

The Valley of the Kings itself, no more than 400m long and 200m wide, can easily be toured on foot using the clearly marked, well-groomed gravel paths. Over 64 known and numbered tombs honeycomb the valley; the numbering is in the order of discovery. Most of them are closed to the public, but the best-known tombs are almost always accessible. Every few months the open tombs are rotated to minimize wear and tear and to add a little variety—after all, it is the spice of afterlife.

TOMB OF RAMSES IV (#2). The first tomb on the right is the tomb of Ramses IV. Once used as a Byzantine church, the well-preserved tomb contains wall decorations excerpted from the *Book of the Dead* and the *Book of Fates.* On both sides of the tomb, 365 small statues of the pharaoh's guardian spirit were believed to facilitate his resurrection every night of the year when Amun-Ra crossed to the West Bank. The figures on the left wall facing the sun god will be resurrected; the upside down figures on the right wall represent non-believers who won't be resurrected. A vividly colored ceiling and huge, cartouche-shaped sarcophagus make this one of the best tombs in the valley.

TOMB OF RAMSES IX (#6). The intricately detailed ceiling of the 12th-century BCE Tomb of Ramses IX (on your left once you enter the valley) features gold figures displaying their *joie de mourir* against a deep blue background. To the right of the entrance, the pharaoh is shown offering a gazelle to Amun-Ra. Farther on the right, the reliefs show him striving for the afterlife by making offerings to the god of justice (holding balance) and to Osiris, god of resurrection and by making 136 negative confessions (I never lied, I never spent time in a Turkish prison, etc.). Directly opposite these reliefs, Ramses is playing the same game with Horus to gain safe passage through the two lakes of fire. A long corridor descends to an anteroom covered with protective demons, serpents, and wild beasts. A pit beyond the long corridor in the burial chamber holds Ramses IX's sarcophagus. The ceiling of the chamber was not smoothed and the text appears in a shorthand form because Ramses IX died before his tomb was ready. Most of the painting was done during the 70 days needed for mummification.

TOMB OF RAMSES III (#11). Named the "Tomb of the Harp Players" after the two plucky musicians depicted on one of its interior chambers, the Tomb of Ramses III boasts a vividly colorful portrayal of ancient chariot races on the left side of the penultimate chamber. Luckless Ramses III was killed in a palace plot, burgled post-mortem, and as a final insult, stolen and shipped in his magnificent sarcophagus to the Louvre.

TOMB OF RAMSES I (#16). The steep entrance next to the Tomb of Seti I (#17, see **Other Tombs** below) descends into the Tomb of Ramses I, a single burial chamber dominated by Ramses' pink granite sarcophagus. The tomb walls, some of the most vivid in the valley, are painted with scenes of Ramses (founder of the 19th dynasty) hobnobbing with the gods. The first corridor is the shortest in the valley, perhaps a consequence of Ramses' brief rule (1320-1318 BCE).

TOMB OF MENEPTAH-SIPTAH (#18). The Tomb of Meneptah-Siptah has some splendid ceilings painted with vultures and ram-headed falcons (19th dynasty, 13th century BCE). The rough-hewn burial chamber has suffered a good deal of damage, but the large red granite sarcophagus, carved with images of crocodiles and cobras, is still intact.

TOMB OF THUTMOSES III (#34). The most dramatically situated burial site in the necropolis is the cliffside Tomb of Thutmoses III, reached by a long, steep staircase that ascends a precipitous ravine squeezed between towering limestone cliffs. To get to the tomb, follow the dirt road that begins next to the Tomb of Ramses III (#11) leading southeast up the hill. The tomb's location provides the ultimate example of the 18th dynasty pharaohs' attempts to hide their tombs. Thutmoses III's is built in a fault, where it became naturally concealed by debris left from flash floods, but the ingenious design did not deter grave robbers. Queen Hatshepsut appointed her freakishly short stepson Thutmoses III as a military leader; he was so successful as a leader he became her rival and eventually took the throne from her. His conquests reached as far as the fourth cataract of the Nile to the south, Crete and Cyprus to the north, and the Euphrates to the east. His grave is decorated with unusual hieratic text (short-hand hieroglyphic, see p. 52) and strangely beautiful stick-figure representations of Khnum and other gods. The novel cartouche-shaped burial chamber still contains his red granite sarcophagus (don't tip the guard for showing you that it's empty).

TOMB OF TUTANKHAMUN (#62). The West Bank's most renowned tourist attraction, the Tomb of Tutankhamun stands directly in front of the Rest House in the middle of the valley and requires a special ticket (E£40, students E£20). The real treasures are at the Egyptian Museum in Cairo (see p. 96), and the interior of this small tomb may not be worth the extra ticket. If you plan to see it, visit it first or you'll probably be disappointed after seeing the others.

The only pharaonic tomb to evade grave robbers, Tut's treasure box was discovered in 1922 by archaeologist Howard Carter and has toured the world several times before returning to its permanent home in the Egyptian Museum in Cairo. Tutankhamun's mummy was encased in the innermost of four snugly nested, superbly decorated cases, three of which can be seen in the Egyptian Museum. Fortunately, the raiding Egyptologists left behind the outermost case (a gilded wood extravagance covered in rich jewels) and Tut's exquisitely carved sarcophagus. The perfectly preserved interior walls of the burial chamber depict colorful scenes from the *Book of the Dead*, which were transcribed from the pyramid writings at Saqqara (see p. 106). Egyptologists had expected that the tomb would contain little of interest because the pharaoh reigned only two years before he died, but Carter ignored professional censure and toiled for six seasons in the Valley of the Kings. After more than 200,000 tons of rubble had been moved, Carter's patron reluctantly decided to abort the project. Before admitting failure, Carter explored one more possibility: a site in front of the tomb of Ramses VI, in an area covered with workers' huts. Confounding the critics, he chanced upon an ancient doorway beneath the shanties. The tomb had been opened by robbers, but the luckless thieves had apparently been caught in the act by necropolis guards, because the treasures had been hastily stacked and the entrance resealed. Three mummies were found in the tomb, including that of the boy-king himself.

OTHER TOMBS. The **Tomb of Seti I (#17),** the valley's longest tomb, honors the great 19th-dynasty military leader. The **Tomb of Ramses VI (#9)** is the third largest tomb in the valley after Ramses II and Seti I. This crypt is known for its ceiling of winged cobras, decapitated enemies, and elongated ladies with stars on their bellies. As the charred marks on its edges attest, the vast sarcophagus in the burial chamber was split by tomb robbers who heated it and doused it in water, causing the stone to expand and crack. The **Tomb of Amenhotep II (#35)** is inscribed with the entire text of the *Book of the Dead* and contains a beautiful red sarcophagus.

MORTUARY TEMPLES

The pharaohs may have hidden their tombs, but they didn't want the living world to forget about them. In addition to the spectacular rock-hewn tombs, the west bank is peppered with **mortuary temples,** mammoth structures honoring the royal deceased. Though overshadowed by Luxor's Karnak Temple in scale and importance, the West Theban temples of Hatshepsut (Deir el-Bahri), Ramses III (Medinat Habu), Ramses II (Ramesseum), and Seti I are still fascinating. The following temples, all accessible from a road that runs parallel to the Nile, are described from south to north. From the ferry docks, head inland 3km past the Colossi of Memnon until you come to an intersection. A road to the left leads to Medinet Habu, 500m to the southwest.

COLOSSI OF MEMNON. All that remains of the largest mortuary temple (dedicated to Amenhotep III) on the West Bank is the statue pair known as the **Colossi of Memnon,** towering statues seated in magnificent isolation on the northern side of the entrance road to the necropolis. Looking over the plain from a height of 20m, these figures of Amenhotep were Thebes' greatest tourist attraction during the Roman era. At night, an eerie whistling sound emanated from the statues; as Menon was the mythical son of Aurora, the goddess of the dawn, the Romans believed the sound was actually Memnon wailing in anticipation of his mother's rays. The sound was actually produced by grains of sand splitting off from the statues as the rocks contracted in the cool night air. Regardless, the Colossi ceased wailing after repairs made on them during the reign of Antoninus Pius.

MEDINAT HABU (TEMPLE OF RAMSES III). This complex of well-preserved edifices honoring Ramses III was constructed in several stages; it stands to the left at the end of the road after the Colossi. Relatively few tourists visit this site; a tranquil hour is enough to take it in. The most impressive structure is the **Mortuary**

Temple of Ramses III, decorated with reliefs of the pharaoh's many successful military campaigns, including his victories over the mysterious "Sea People" (who dangle by their hair from his fist). Enter the temple through its large fortified gate. Climbing the stairs on the gate's opposite side will take you to a small open chamber where Ramses III is believed to have stayed while visiting the temple. It was also very likely the site of his ultimate assassination. The temple is warrior-themed throughout: the main pylon, also known as the Royal Pavilion, resembles a military fortress rather than a temple. One relief explains the importance of securing houses of worship so that peace and order could then spread elsewhere, and several reliefs show prisoners being put to death. On the back of the main pylon are savory piles of conquered hands and tongues. Beyond the gate are two relief-rich courts. In the second court on the left side is a window opening supported by statues of human heads. This "window of appearances" was used for royal speeches and was meant to show the king standing on the heads of his vanquished enemies.

RAMESSEUM (TEMPLE OF RAMSES II). Farther north, beyond the student ticket office, is the **Mortuary Temple of Ramses II,** or the Ramesseum. A tour of the Ramesseum won't exceed 30 minutes. In most of the ravaged temples, one attempts to gather from the ruins an idea of the spectacle that once was, but at the Ramesseum, the ruins themselves are the grandest statement of all. The same pharaoh who had Abu Simbel tailor-made to his specifications built the Ramesseum to house another mammoth exercise in narcissism. The shattered remains of the 1000-ton, 17m **Colossus of Ramses II** (the forefingers alone are over 1m long) were the inspiration for Shelley's famous poem "Ozymandias:" "My name is Ozymandias, king of kings: / Look on my works, ye Mighty, and despair!" Their broken enormity leads many to similar sentiments. The colossus was transported in one piece from the pharaoh's granite quarries in Aswan to Thebes. This colossus originally overlooked the passageway leading into the second court, and even shattered, the remnants (including head, upper arms, and one foot) are imposing.

DEIR EL-BAHRI (TEMPLE OF HATSHEPSUT). Just north of the Ramesseum, a paved road leaves the main north-south thoroughfare and heads northwest, winding around to the **Temple of Hatshepsut.** If you are on foot, you can save some time by cutting through the village on the left side of the road (before it splits). Located in the center of the necropolis, this Temple is 500m north of the Tombs of the Nobles. The Temple's ancient Egyptian name, *Djeser Djesern,* means "most splendid of all," and with good reason: Hatshepsut's masterpiece rises in three broad, columned terraces from the desert floor against a dramatic backdrop of sheer limestone cliffs.

IT'S ALL HIEROGLYPHS TO ME Hieroglyphic writing

was used in instances of special religious significance, such as inscriptions on a temple wall or spells designed to speed a pharaoh to a happy afterlife. Since the inscriptions are in part decorative, they are often written in mirror-image pairs; in such cases, the writings are read from different directions. To tell which direction is the beginning, look for a human character; the direction the person or god is facing is usually the beginning. Before the discovery of the **Rosetta Stone** (p. 52), the most popular theory was that each glyph represented an idea: elaborate, fanciful, and utterly incorrect translations were made from many *papyri* and inscriptions. The Rosetta Stone provided the revolutionary insight that each glyph stood for an individual sound, rather than a complex meaning. The stone became the key to the long forgotten script because of its trilingual engraving—Greek, Demotic, and hieroglyphic. The hieroglyphic alphabet uses combinations of sounds to represent words, much like the English alphabet. To provide more exact syntax, the hieroglyphic alphabet also includes characters that clarify meaning and resolve the problem of homonyms.

After the death of her husband Thutmoses II, Hatshepsut became the ruler of the kingdom, the only woman ever to assume the title of pharaoh (see **Ancient History,** p. 47). Her temple was excavated by French and Egyptian archaeologists and is currently being restored by a joint Polish-Egyptian team with support from the U.S. and France. No images of Hatshepsut remain intact; after her death, her stepson Thutmoses III—who had to wait 20 years in her shadow before coming into his own as pharaoh, as she refused to marry him—defaced virtually all of them, and placed his name on the statues of a bearded Hatshepsut that line the third level. Men—can't live with 'em...can't be reincarnated with 'em.

If you walk from the lower court up a wide ramp to the central court, you'll come upon a colonnaded back wall that contains, from left to right, the Shrine of Hathor, the Colonnade of the Expedition of Punt, the Birth Colonnade, and the Shrine to Anubis. The Punt reliefs show Egyptian expeditions to that land (today's Somalia), and the exchange of goods such as trees and animals with the locals. The Birth Colonnade details Hatshepsut's birth and childhood. Another huge ramp leads to the upper court with a rock-cut sanctuary. Badly ruined and sadly defaced by Christians who used the temple as a Coptic monastery in the 7th century, this court is closed to the public.

TEMPLE OF SETI I. You'll have a fair amount of trouble getting to this place, and there's not that much to see once you get there. Go north on the main road and follow it to the end. Turn right to visit what remains of the Mortuary Temple of Seti I, father of Ramses II, a warrior who enlarged the Egyptian empire to include the island of Cyprus and parts of Mesopotamia. Seti was also one of the first men to wear earrings—archaeologists could tell this from his well-preserved mummy-lobes. Although the booty from his successful campaigns has been stolen, the relief work, ranked among the finest executed in ancient Egypt, still remains.

VALLEY OF THE ARTISANS

One admission ticket (E£12, students E£6) includes the Workers' Walled City, the Temple of Deir el-Medina, and the two tombs.

WORKERS' WALLED CITY. To reach the plentiful though visually uninspiring remains of the Workers' Walled City, go past the Colossi of Memnon and follow the small road west. The Workers' Walled City was the only inhabited area on the West Bank during the New Kingdom, and it is the best window archaeologists have found into the nature of urban life in ancient Egypt. Since the workers and artists knew the whereabouts of the tombs they were digging, their movements were strictly controlled and observed and they lived in isolation (the entire walled city was roofed over). Many were killed when construction was completed. A typical house consisted of a kitchen, a living room, and one bedroom. Some had stairways for access to the rooftops, a welcome relief from the heat and smell below.

TEMPLE OF DEIR EL-MEDINA. About 60m down the road from the Workers' Walled City stands the Temple of Deir el-Medina (Monastery of the Town), an elegant shrine from the Ptolemaic era. Dedicated to Hathor, the goddess of love, and Maat, the representation of divine order (see **Meet the Gods,** p. 51), the temple was named during Christian times when monks constructed a monastery next door.

TOMBS OF THE ARTISANS. The accessible artisans' tombs are in such excellent condition that it is hard to believe they were painted so many centuries ago. Unlike the formal decorations dictated by priests on the walls of royal tombs, these tombs contain very creative drawings of the afterlife that can be considered a form of free hand art. Some artisans spent almost 30 years building their tombs, as they could only work on their own tombs on the single rest day of the ancient 10-day week. Two amazing tombs are open to the public: the **Tomb of Sennedjen,** artist for Ramses III, and the **Tomb of Inherku,** "deputy master of the two Egypts in Truth Square" (i.e. head artist for Ramses IV).

TOMBS OF THE NOBLES

A few hundred meters southeast of the Temple of Hatshepsut is the West Bank's sardine-packed burial site, the more than 400 Tombs of the Nobles. You must buy a separate ticket for each, but it is possible to see any tomb with any ticket as long as the ticket price is the same as the entrance fee. The first two groups provide the most punch for your pound. Many villagers will volunteer their services, but a guide is unnecessary. Maps are available in bookstores on the East Bank.

Throughout the New Kingdom, Theban aristocrats had de facto control over much of the pharaoh's empire and served as advisors. The pharaoh often remained ignorant of the most crucial political developments while members of the elite fought among themselves for control of the kingdom. Some aristocrats affected pharaonic status by amply providing themselves with luxuries for the afterlife and devising well-hidden underground tombs. Unlike the divine pharaoh (who would assuredly live among the gods after his death), Theban aristocrats needed more assurance that a comfortable existence awaited them in the afterlife. Accordingly, every facet of their earthly lives was carefully recorded on the walls of their tombs, leaving the decoration more naturalistic and mundane than the reliefs found in pharaonic tombs. Because the limestone in this portion of the necropolis was inferior, artisans could not carve in relief; instead, they painted murals on a whitewashed stone surface. These tombs are simpler than those of the pharaohs: they all start with a terrace leading to a decorated vestibule followed by a corridor.

TOMBS OF REKHMIRE AND SENNOFER. The westernmost tomb belongs to Rekhmire, a governor of Thebes who advised Thutmoses III and prided himself on his administrative genius. A historian's delight, the **Tomb of Rekhmire (#100)** comprises biographical narratives depicting the full range of activities Rekhmire oversaw. This is perhaps the most absorbing of all the tombs in the Theban necropolis.

In the first chamber, tax evaders are tried by Rekhmire, who sits with a set of rolled papyrus texts strewn at the foot of his judgment throne; the presence of the papyrus suggests that written law existed as early as 1500 BCE. On the inner, left-hand wall, processions of tribute payers arrive from Crete (top), Syria (middle), and the African kingdoms of Punt (present-day Somalia) and Nubia (bottom), the latter of whom offer a giraffe, assorted monkeys, a tiger, and an elephant tusk. Other scenes show Egyptians drinking themselves into a stupor during what was known as, like, the "Festival of the Valley." The niche at the top of the rear wall was intended to contain a statue of Rekhmire himself.

Trek 50m up the hill west of Rekhmire's tomb to reach the **Tomb of Sennofer (#96).** This impressively vivid tomb is known as the "Tomb of the Vines" after the filigreed grapevine crawling all over the ceiling. The delightful lattice of purple and green simulates a shady arbor for Sennofer, overseer of the royal gardens of Amun under Amenhotep II. The plan of the tomb is as unusual as its decor: a curving wall leads into the first room, which in turn leads straight back into the pillared burial chamber. The big, wet eyes of **Hathor the love-cow** follow you around the tomb from the tops of the columns. The superb condition and remarkable expressiveness of the paintings of this small tomb make it worth the detour.

TOMBS OF RAMOSE. The incomplete **Tomb of Ramose (#55)** was built during the reign of the heretic king Akhenaton (Amenhotep IV). Ramose was Governor of Thebes and Vizier under Akhenaton, and was one of the first converts to Akhenaton's monotheistic religion that worshiped Aton. The tomb itself displays the stylistic contrast between the art produced in the Old Kingdom and that produced under Akhenaton. In the columned first chamber, all of Egypt pays obeisance to Aton, a blood-red disk emitting shafts of light that end in small hands holding *ankhs*, *ankurs*, and other religious symbols. On the wall through which you enter, the images carved in unpainted relief reflect the traditional, stylized tastes of the Old Kingdom, with scenes of Ramose and his family making offerings and Egyptians cheering Ramose's conversion to the Aton cult. In contrast, the wall to the left as you enter displays the strangely distorted figures and realistic composition typical of Akhenaton's reign. These images support the intriguing and rather popular theory that the heretical Akhenaton came from another planet: the sun-disc Aton looks startlingly like a flying saucer, and the oblong heads and elongated arms of the wall figures greatly resemble common representations of aliens.

TOMB OF USERHET. Continue up from the Tomb of Ramose to the **Tomb of Userhet the Scribe (#56),** a few meters to the south. Although an ascetic early Christian monk who made his home within the chamber destroyed most of the female figures adorning the walls, the tomb's decor retains a certain blithe spirit because of the unusual pink tones of the interior frescoes. Userhet, Amenhotep II's royal scribe (around 1408 BCE), had his resting place painted with daily pedestrian scenes: on the right-hand wall of the first chamber men wait their turn in line for the local barber, while duck-offering scenes cover the wall of the entrance.

TOMB OF NAKHT. Slightly north of the Tomb of Ramose is a trail that leads off the main road and winds east a short distance to the **Tomb of Nakht (#52).** The first chamber contains a reconstruction of an exquisite statue of Nakht, scribe of the royal granaries under Thutmoses IV (the original was lost at sea on its way to the U.S. during WWI). Also in the first chamber are photographs of some of the other removed contents and a series of well-labeled diagrams explaining the images within the second chamber. The most famous image from the Tombs of the Nobles—three musicians playing the flute, harp, and lute—is on the left wall, to remind Nakht in the afterlife that his wife was a singer.

ASASIF TOMBS. Southwest of the Temple of Hatshepsut lies **Asasif,** a current archaeological hot spot. Asasif became the most popular aristocratic burial area during the 25th and 26th dynasties (about the 7th century BCE), though the **Tomb of Kheruef (#192),** the finest portion of the necropolis, was constructed 700 years earlier. Enter the burial site through an outer courtyard containing other tombs, where a series of well-wrought reliefs stands against a protecting wall. Note the provocative ceremonial dance featuring a chorus line of women, a jumping bird, a noisy monkey, flutists, and drummers to the left of the doorway. On the right, pharaonic heartthrob Amenhotep III is surrounded by 16 swooning princesses.

As you enter the **Tomb of Kiki (#409),** about 10m to the north of Kheruef, the gods Thoth and Anubis discuss the readings of a giant scale. The burial chamber remains unfinished, leaving a series of faceless figures outlined in red. To get to the **Tomb of Neferhotep (#48),** walk 100m east along the dirt path from Kiki, then turn right (south) and walk 20m to the tomb, immediately in front of a village house. Most of the seated stone figures within the tomb are fairly intact.

VALLEY OF THE QUEENS وادي الملكات

During the later years of the New Kingdom, a special burial area was chosen for the wives and children of the pharaohs. Traditionally, the pharaoh's closest relatives were buried beside the monarch, but this arrangement changed during the reign of Ramses I (14th century BCE), when princes, consorts, and wives were buried in the Valley of the Queens. Directly west of the Colossi of Memnon at the end of the main road, the Valley of the Queens contains fewer than 30 royal tombs. Check at the ticket kiosks to find out which are currently open.

TOMB OF AMONHERKHEPESHEF (#55). The Tomb of Amonherkhepeshef, the son of Ramses III, is richly adorned with bas-relief carvings. In one, Ramses III introduces his 9-year-old son (wearing the groomed topknot of a pharaonic prince) to each of the major deities. Colored scenes of deities and farmers fill entire walls—a rare sight in Theban tombs. The sarcophagus that held the prince's mummy stands in the rear burial chamber. A desiccated fetus lies curled in a small glass display next to the sarcophagus. A flashlight is helpful in the burial chamber.

TOMB OF QUEEN NEFERTARI (#66). The extremely pricey **Tomb of Queen Nefertari (#66)** is open to the first 150 people who can afford a ticket (E£100, students E£50). Stay alert: the moisture on your breath damages the tomb's colors, so you'll only have 10 minutes to absorb what you can. Touted as Egypt's finest tomb, the

MUMMIES IN THE NIGHT In the late 1870s, members of the Antiquities Service noticed a large number of New Kingdom funerary objects appearing on the European black market. **Charles Wilbur,** a wealthy American antiquer, was enlisted to go undercover and identify the source of the treasures. By making clear that he would pay high prices for authentic pieces, Wilbur was eventually led to Luxor. Across the river in the town of Qurna, he was shown a piece that had come from a recently opened royal burial. Wilbur secretly telegraphed Gaston Maspero, the Director General of the Antiquities Service, who rushed to Luxor and began intense questioning of all involved. Several weeks later, **Muhammad 'Abd er-Rasul,** the head of the most prominent antiquities-dealing family in Luxor, confessed that his family had found a tomb near the Mortuary Temple of Hatshepsut. Archaeologists were quickly summoned, and found the deep shaft burial containing the mummies of the New Kingdom's greatest kings: Thutmoses III, Amosis (founder of the New Kingdom), and Ramses II, among many others. The 'Abd er-Rasul family had kept the shaft a secret for 10 years, quietly selling their stash. The Antiquities Service, aware of the security risk that a public disclosure would cause, employed hundreds of men to load the mummies onto ships. The bodies were hurried down the Nile at top speed and now reside in the Egyptian Museum.

vivid tones of the tomb walls are genuinely startling. It's a good thing they are: it took seven winters, US$6 million, and the expertise of the Getty Institute to preserve and restore this masterpiece. After seeing this tomb, one can begin to extrapolate the grandeur of its far less-preserved neighbors. The reliefs in the first chamber include the goddess Hathor leading Nefertari by the hand, thousands of hieroglyphs, and a scarab-faced goddess. A sea-green and starry ceiling canopies the stairs down to the queen's burial chamber. Columns in the burial chamber portray green-skinned Osiris and the cow-goddess Hathor.

NEAR LUXOR

After the grandeur of the Temples of Luxor and Karnak, the sites near Luxor may seem a let-down. However, if you're in Luxor for four or five days, you may want to combine both Abydos and Dendera into a full day trip, organized through the tourist office or travel agent on the corniche. Arrange your taxi and convoy meeting point and time at least 12 hours beforehand so that the driver can register at the convoy police. A taxi should cost around E£180 for both sites. A cheaper option is to take a train to the nearest city, but it may be a hassle getting back.

DENDERA

*The smoothest way to see the temple at Dendera is by **boat** from Luxor, emptying wallets at E£150 per person for a day cruise including lunch (book with a travel agent on the corniche). The cheapest options are **service taxi** and **train** rides via **Qena,** which will take about an hour. Service leave Luxor in convoys from beside the Hotel Bolla at 6am and 8am (E£3), and trains depart from the station. Both options will require taking a taxi from Qena to the temple (E£5). Admission E£12, students E£6. Qena is only now beginning to see tourists trickle in, so your presence will probably attract considerable attention. In summer, bats inhabit the temple, so a **flashlight** will definitely come in handy.*

The **Temple of Hathor** at Dendera is one of the few sights in Middle Egypt that has remained accessible throughout the fundamentalist uprising. While it is a bit out of the way, those who make the effort will find a structure unique in the options it offers the exploring tourist. The temple only dates from the 1st century BCE, though worship of Hathor is much older. The late Ptolemies and the Romans found it politically expedient to associate themselves with the benevolent goddess. Hathor is depicted as cow-headed or with cow's ears, or shown wearing a crown of two horns cradling the sun disk. Because her specialty was love, Hathor, the "Golden One," was identified by the Greeks as Aphrodite. During an annual festival, a statue of Hathor was carried in a sacred procession down the Nile to meet Horus of Edfu (see p. 206).

Eighteen columns are topped by cow heads in the **Great Hypostyle Hall.** In the temple's inner sanctum, wall paintings portray the embalmer's art, while the ceiling is decorated with pictures of the goddess Nut. The second hypostyle hall, also called the **Hall of Appearances,** gives way to the **Hall of Offerings,** where the daily rites were performed. In the kiosk in the southwest corner of the roof, priests performed the ceremony of "touching the disk," in which the soul of the sun god Ra appeared in the form of light. If you look to the right you will notice a gently sloping staircase which leads up to the roof. Turn your flashlight off for a moment as you make your way up the stairs. The lights are dim, the smell is strange, and it is hard not to feel that you are a part of the sacred religious procession chiseled on the wall to your right.

The **Hall of the Ennead** immediately precedes the inner sanctuary. The chamber on the left is the wardrobe; opposite it, a doorway leads through a small treasury into the **Court of the New Year** where sacrifices were performed during the New Year festival. On the ceiling of the colorful portico, Nut gives birth to the sun, whose rays shine upon the head of Hathor. The **Mysterious Corridor** surrounds the **Sanctuary** on three sides, and 11 chapels, each with a distinct religious function, open off of it. A small chamber known as the **Throne of Ra** sits behind the northernmost of the three doorways behind the sanctuary. A minuscule opening in its floor leads to the crypt, a subterranean hallway embellished with reliefs, some of inlaid alabaster. Many rooms on the upper floors carry ceiling paintings of Nut swallowing the sun at sundown and giving birth to it at dawn. On the roof of the temple, near the edge, is graffiti left by French soldiers in 1799.

ABYDOS وس ابيد

*Although Abydos is officially open to the public, tensions in Middle Egypt will probably mean that visitors to the temple will be transported by **police convoy.** The easiest and cheapest way to visit Abydos is by taking the north-bound **train** to **El-Balyana** (2½hr.) from Luxor at 8am. If you aren't able to catch a tourist bus back, you will be stranded at the train station until 2:30pm. From El-Balyana to the temple (E£7), you and a mandatory party of your closest armed friends will continue to the site. **Open** 8am-6pm. **Admission** to all sites E£12, students E£6. Bring food and water since the nearby restaurant has inflated prices and may not have any food to serve at all if business is slow.*

The ancient city of Abydos was the site of a necropolis and temple dedicated to the god Khenti-Amentiu. Pharaohs from the first dynasty onward chose to be buried at the site and eventually corpses from all over Egypt were interred at this necropolis *par excellence.* **Osiris,** god of the dead, subtly co-opted Abydos and the worshipers of Khenti-Amentiu during the 6th dynasty. Legend has it that the body of Osiris himself lies buried on these grounds. After his famed dismemberment at the hands of his brother, Seth (see **Meet the Gods,** p. 51), Osiris' head was said to have landed here. The cult of Osiris centered here ritually re-enacted the battle between Osiris and Seth as a sacred annual custom. The city that was Abydos has all but vanished, but after a look at the magnificent white limestone **Temple of Seti I,** pharaoh of the 19th dynasty, it is not hard to imagine the wonder that drew pilgrims from all over the Kingdom to this city.

The Temple of Seti has been partially reconstructed. Three of the original seven doors remain on the **Portico of Twelve Pillars,** which guarded the entrance into the temple proper. The central doorway leads to the **First Hypostyle Hall,** lined with 24 colossal papyriform columns. This grandiose entrance gives way to the **Second Hypostyle Hall,** which contains some of the finest bas-reliefs ever carved in Egypt. At the far left corner of the Second Hypostyle Hall, a long narrow corridor known as the **Gallery of the Kings** leads towards the southeast. This simple passage houses one of Egyptology's most treasured finds, the **Kings' List,** which mentions the names of 76 Egyptian rulers from Menes of Memphis to Seti I, the temple's royal patron. Correlating this list with previous knowledge, scholars were able to map the sequence of Egyptian dynasties.

THE LAST OF THE ANCIENT EGYPTIANS The sacred symbols of the ancient Egyptian religion are the stuff of souvenir shops these days, but for one woman, they were much more. After falling down the stairs of her home in England in 1907, three-year-old Dorothy Eady was declared dead. When the town doctor returned an hour later to the room where he had laid the young girl's body, he was shocked to find her contentedly playing on her bed. Alive and well, the normal (if slightly rambunctious) British lass began insisting she was an ancient Egyptian and started begging to be taken "home." She was, she later said, a former priestess-in-training at the Temple of Seti in the holy city of Abydos. After a chance meeting on the temple grounds, she fell deeply in love with the Pharaoh Seti I and found herself in a rapturous affair that contravened all the rules of the priesthood. When the temple's high priest demanded a confession, ancient Egyptian Eady-as-priestess eventually took her own life rather than betray the name of her lover.

The real life Eady devoted her life to "returning home," fulfilling her destiny at the temple, and taking her place at Seti's side in the afterlife. In 1956, after twenty years as a distinguished employee of the Egyptian Department of Antiquities (where she worked with and won the respect of some of this century's most distinguished Egyptologists), Eady transferred to the ancient site of Abydos. There, known in the village as *Omm Seti,* or *mother of Seti,* she helped to guide work at the temple, exhibiting an uncanny familiarity with the grounds. Eady treated the temple as the sacred sanctuary it once was, praying and making offerings to the gods up until her actual death in 1981. She was buried in the desert to the northwest, at last ready to take Seti's side.

In the southern wing of the temple, beside the entrance to the Gallery of the Kings, a doorway leads to a chamber with a tiny chapel to its right. The chapel contains a kinky relief showing the mummy of Osiris, in the form of a falcon, impregnating Isis. At the temple's rear is the elaborate **Inner Sanctuary of Osiris,** painted with scenes of Osiris' life. The sanctuary is flanked by three small shrines bedecked with the temple's best-preserved reliefs. Immediately behind the temple one can find the **Osirion,** a now partially submerged tomb that Seti built for himself in the style of the Old Kingdom. Ask a tomb guard to take you to the much less well preserved **Temple of Ramses III** through a desert of broken ceramic to the north. The temple here contains some interesting hieroglyphics as well as suggestions of a mixing of Coptic and Pharaonic styles.

BETWEEN LUXOR AND ASWAN

The 228km stretch of the Nile from Luxor to Aswan meanders past the drowsy rural towns of the south, **Esna, Edfu,** and **Kom Ombo.** These towns make excellent daytrips—Esna and Edfu from Luxor; Edfu, Kom Ombo, and the camel market at **Daraw** from Aswan—but live like a pharaoh by taking them all in on a *felucca* trip from Luxor to Aswan. By water, the entire route (including stops in Esna, Edfu, and Kom Ombo) takes three to five hedonistic, sun-drenched days.

ESNA اسنا

Esna (58km south of Luxor) is a study in blissful obliviousness: the *doyennes* of Esna's local coffee shop calmly sip their tea and smoke their *sheeshas* as if the luxury cruiser rolling into dock were just another *felucca;* inland, people trot through the streets of the *souq* unaffected by the extraordinary Greco-Roman temple that sits at its center. While there is little to keep you here for more than a few hours, the spectacle of Esna and the temple it surrounds are well worth a look.

⊠ ORIENTATION AND PRACTICAL INFORMATION. Esna has only a few main streets important to tourists. The main drag, **Nile Street,** runs along the bank of the Nile. At the **ticket booth** for the temple, which sits in a small kiosk on the river side of the street where the cruises dock, Nile St. is met by **Souq Street,** a 200m stretch of tourist bazaars that runs up to the temple. The **highway** and **train station** are on the eastern side of the river, connected to the town by a bridge. The **bus** and *service* stations are at the town's northwestern edge beside a small canal bridge (E£1 to the temple). You can take a **kalish** from either station to the temple (don't pay more than E£1.50-2 for a ride anywhere in town), or walk (2km). Follow Nile St. 200m north as it branches left away from the river for the **Bank of Alexandria** (tel. 40 05 26; open Su-Th 8:30am-2pm; Ramadan 10am-1:30pm; additional exchange hours in summer 6-9pm; in winter 5-8pm). To exchange traveler's checks and foreign currency, visit the convenient **bank kiosk** opposite the ticket booth. The non-English speaking **tourist police** (tel. 51 06 86) are on Souq St., but the slightly more helpful **police station** is about 250m north on Nile St. as it branches away from the river. **Pharmacy Confidence** (tel. 51 05 32) can be found just north of the ticket office (open M-Sa 9am-2pm and 5:30-11pm; in winter 5-8pm). The local **post office** is south of the ticket booth on Souq St. (open Su-Th 8am-2pm). Numerous stores along the riverfront offer **international phone calls.** Esna's **telephone code** is 095.

⬛⬛ ACCOMMODATIONS AND FOOD. There is little incentive to remain in Esna beyond a temple visit, but the fairly clean **Hotel El-Haramein** (tel. 40 03 40) will do if you need to stay a night. The hotel is 1km south (through the *souq*) of the temple's eastern wall and about the same distance inland from the Nile. Pass to the right of the white wall enclosing a gray concrete building, and walk another 100m. There are no signs, but the police can help you find your way (singles E£5; doubles E£10, with bath E£15; triples E£15/20; quads E£20/25). The *souq* can provide *ta'amiyya* and produce.

⬛ SIGHTS. Although the **Temple of Khnum** was begun in the 18th dynasty, it is largely a Roman creation and in many ways a feeble imitation of inherited Egyptian technical and artistic achievements. The wall on the west side of the sight suggests original temple remains from the Greek era, but excavations have yet to begin. **Khnum** was the ram-headed creator god (he reputedly molded the first human being on a potter's wheel; see **Meet the Gods,** p. 51) who was worshiped in this region around the First Nile Cataract and at his sanctuary on Aswan's Elephantine Island. The Cataract was an important economic and cultural center for the area south of Luxor, and the pharaohs of the 18th dynasty dedicated this temple to the local deity to garner local support. The remains of a small Coptic church in front of the temple attest to the layered religious history of this site.

The temple's elaborate hallway (all that remains of what was once a much larger sanctuary) has managed to survive in excellent condition. In an attempt to decorate the temple in traditional Egyptian style, the Romans carved a procession of stiff, oddly deformed figures marching solemnly across the walls. The ceiling designs are among the more interesting aspects of the temple: the signs of the zodiac are portrayed just right of the last pillar on the left as you enter the hallway. Faint blue and red hues on the tops of the 24 columns hint at the interior's former brilliance. *(Open daily 6am-6:30pm; in winter 6am-5:30pm. Admission E£8, students E£4. Don't buy tickets from hawkers in the* souq.*)*

EL-KAB الكاب

From Edfu, the cheapest way to El-Kab is a one-way service (75pt), though some will say that service don't go there. If you come by felucca, your captain might not know where El-Kab is; give him the distances indicated here and be on the lookout for the Roman wall on the east bank of the Nile. The best time to leave is early morning, before the sun is high. To get back to Edfu, hail a pickup taxi.

Don't go out of your way to see the temples at **El-Kab** (20km north of Edfu and 3km south of the village of El-Mahamid) unless you have the time and energy to spare while traveling between Esna and Edfu. The temples are intriguing, but not on the order of the sites at Esna or the Valley of the Kings (see p. 193). The distance between the two will make you empathize with Moses: they are a 2.5 and 4km walk

EGYPT

from the roadside tombs and city wall. Bring several bottles of water—there's not a leaf of shade. The site was once occupied by the ancient city of Nekheb, which was dedicated to the vulture-goddess Nekhbet, protectress of the pharaohs and lady of the mouth of the desert. The remains of the city consist of several temples and the rather unimpressive ruins of old tombs dotting the highway.

TEMPLES AND CHAPELS. Two-and-a-half kilometers along an unpaved but passable track brings you to the tiny **Chapel of Thoth** (1320-1200 BCE), built by the high priest of El-Kab for Ramses II and dedicated to Nekhbet, Thoth (Wisdom), and Horus. The much larger **Ptolemaic Temple,** built under Ptolemies IX through XI, has an impressive ramped entryway leading to a forecourt with a few nice broken capitals and a chamber with ceiling paintings and inscriptions. The stagnant pond within the compound was once considered a sacred lake. Wake up the guard in the shack across the road to open the locked gates; he'll then ride with you another 1.5km to the small **Temple of Amenophis III**, with well-preserved colored paintings and carvings of Nekhbet herself coiffed with a swingin' 60s bob. Caravans going to and coming from gold mines deeper in the desert once stopped here for prayer. (*All sites open daily 7am-7pm in summer; in winter 6am-6pm. Admission E£10, students E£5.*)

TOMBS. A guard will lead you up the staircase to the four most important tombs along the highway, dating from 1570 to 1320 BCE. The most well-preserved of the tombs is the **Tomb of Paheri,** a multi-talented royal servant. Paheri was chief priest, royal tutor to Prince Wadjmose (son of Pharaoh Thutmoses I), and scribe of the accounts of corn. This tomb features brightly colored illustrations of seated lotus sniffers and Egyptians cultivating crops, fishing, shipping, and making wine. At the rear of the tomb stands a statue of a happy Paheri flanked by two female figures. The **Tomb of Setau** belonged to the powerful high priest of Amun under Ramses III through IX (20th dynasty). The **Tomb of Aahmes** is the resting place of a warship captain who suppressed a rebellion in Upper Egypt and led 18th-dynasty forces under Amenhotep I and Thutmoses I in Nubia and Syria. Both tombs are poorly preserved. The **Tomb of Renini,** superintendent of priests under Amenhotep I, contains a geometrically painted ceiling and eyes staring out from a broken statue.

EDFU ادفو

Only 50km south of Esna, Edfu is more than worth the short trip. Even the most templed-out traveler won't be able to resist the grandeur of Edfu's **Temple of Horus.** The vast, stunningly preserved temple is intricately detailed, rivaling the serenity of Kalabsha and even the awesome scale of Abu Simbel to make it one of Upper Egypt's most spectacular sights. For all its grandeur, the temple hasn't made such a big impression on the locals. When archaeologists began to excavate the temple in the mid-19th century, they had more than sand and rubble to clear; the people of Edfu had also built a number of homes on the half-buried temple's roof.

⚐ ORIENTATION AND PRACTICAL INFORMATION. Edfu lies on the west bank of the Nile, roughly halfway between Luxor (112km south) and Aswan (121km north). The center of town, **Temple Square,** lies about 1km inland, while a bridge crosses the Nile at the northern edge of town. The **train station** is remotely positioned on the east bank, away from town. The **service** station sits just right of the small square where the bridge reaches the west bank. Trains run north and south until 9pm, as do *service.* **Kalishes** (E£2-3) or **private taxis** (E£3-5) can take you from either station to the temple. The **bus station** is 50m up the street to your right when facing the mosque in the square. Buses run north and south every hour until 6pm (at the latest). Another 200m down on the right is the **Bank of Cairo** (tel. 70 36 97), which is open Su-Th 8:30am-2pm and 3-10pm. Across the street from the bank is the **Ezzat Pharmacy** (tel. 70 38 60), which is open M-Sa 7:30am-midnight. About 100m from Temple Sq. is a tourist bazaar, the **tourist police** (tel. 70 01 34; open 7am-7pm, in winter 7am-4pm), and the temple. The **post office** is on Tahrir St., on the right side 50m south of Temple Sq. (open Sa-Th 8am-2pm). From the bridge, the riverfront road runs 100m south to the **telephone office** (tel. 70 17 77; open 24hr.) and another 200m to **El-Maglis Street,** which links the Nile with Temple Sq. The **telegraph office,** located on the south side of Temple Sq., can help with **calling card calls** (90pt per 3min. for a call to Cairo). Several **telephone offices** line the riverfront where the cruise ships dock. Edfu's **telephone code** is 097.

■■ **ACCOMMODATIONS AND FOOD.** The cleanest budget hotel in town—though that's not saying much—is the musty **El-Madina Hotel** (tel. 70 13 26), just off Temple Sq. (singles with breakfast E£25, less without bath; doubles E£30; triples E£40; settle on a price before staying). The **Semi-Ramis Hotel** is near the bank; at E£6 per bed it's popular, but you get what you pay for. The **Tabarak Restaurant,** in the small square by the bridge, serves large portions of chicken, beef, pigeon, and fish with side dishes (E£7-12). Edfu's **produce souq** lines the streets off Temple Sq.

■ **SIGHTS.** The spectacular **Temple of Horus** took almost 200 years to construct and was not completed until 57 BCE, making it one of the last great Egyptian monuments. The Ptolemies designed this temple and the temple to Hathor at Dendera (see p. 202) as a matched set. Several important religious festivals dealing with the life of Horus were celebrated at Edfu. During the annual "Union with the Solar Disk," Horus's earthly form was brought to the roof of the temple to be rejuvenated by the rays of the sun. Another important ritual was the "Festival of the Happy Reunion," in which the god's icon (once held in the polished black granite shrine in the inner sanctuary of the temple) was removed from the temple in a ceremonial boat, then taken to Dendera to bring Hathor home to Edfu for some postmortem playtime. In a chamber behind the sanctuary, there is a modern reconstruction of the ceremonial boat used to carry the statue during festivals. *(Site open daily 7am-6pm; in winter 7am-4pm. Admission E£20, students E£10. Bring a flashlight.)*

The path from the ticket office approaches the temple from the rear, so wind your way to the right around the complex to the front and enter through the 12 gigantic columns of the **Great Hypostyle Hall.** Proceed to the second hypostyle hall, outfitted with a similar arrangement of smaller pillars. Doorways on either side lead to the **ambulatory,** a narrow exterior passageway running between the temple and its protective wall. The temple is honeycombed with smaller passageways that enabled sulky priests to walk around the entire complex without speaking to one another or crossing in front of the sanctuary. The doorway on the right side of the second hall leads to a side **chapel** with a celestial ceiling depicting the sky-goddess Nut reaching around the Zodiac (for more on the mythological significance of this, see **Meet the Gods,** p. 51). Sadly, most of the reliefs have been thoroughly defaced, although some rooms remain largely untouched.

Outside the temple, directly in front of the main entrance, is a well-preserved Roman **mammisis** (birthhouse), where the birth of Horus was reenacted annually with appropriate hoopla. Copts later defaced the images of the growing god on the columns of the *mammisis.* Note the images of **pot-bellied pygmies,** brought to court for the royalty's entertainment, atop the exterior side columns.

GEBEL ES-SILSILAH جبل السلسلة

The quarries at **Gebel es-Silsilah** are a fascinating bonus prize for *felucca* travelers who succeed in persuading their captain to stop here. Although a ramp and stairs have been built down to the water's edge in anticipation of Nile cruiser stops, the site is not yet officially open; however, *bakhsheesh* to the guard and a promise to be quick should win access. To reach the quarries by land, take a *service* from Kom Ombo to Kalabsha and ask for the Temple of Horemheb (a request for "Gebel es-Silsilah" will land you in the speck of a town by the same name on the east bank). *Service* should cost no more than E£3 and the boat ride over the Nile to the temple should be no more than E£2.

There are sandstone **quarries** (used from the New Kingdom in 1500 BCE to the Ptolemaic period) on both sides of the Nile, but boats only dock on the west bank. A guard can unlock the well-preserved **Temple of Horemheb,** built by General Horemheb, who seized the throne during the power struggles after King Tutankhamun's death. From the temple, a path leads 200m south along a bluff 15m above the Nile, ending in the cavernous belly of the quarry. Huge blocks of sandstone were cut from the cliff, loaded onto boats, and transported along the Nile to construction sites; notice the boat and ostrich graffiti etched into the wall's face.

KOM OMBO كوم أمبو

Kom Ombo still stands in its original spot, 45km north of Aswan, and cuts the same striking figure today as it did during Ptolemaic times. Where the temples at Philae, Kalabsha, and Abu Simbel once stood, there is now only water (see **Moving a Mountain,** p. 221). The temple at Kom Ombo has been more ornery—it may have aged, but it hasn't budged. The beautiful temple ruins make Kom Ombo well worth the visit, but one look at the adjacent town will make most travelers want to make like a temple and relocate.

☎ **SIGHTS.** Although a temple has stood here since the time of the Middle Kingdom, the current *Hodges-podge* of an edifice dates back only to 150 BCE. Parts of these older versions of the **Temple of Kom Ombo** now rest at the Louvre and at the Egyptian Museum in Cairo. The rising waters of the Nile left the current temple almost completely buried in silt. In later years, the portion above ground was used as a quarry for construction projects; as a result, the side walls have vanished.

Nevertheless, the temple that remains is fascinating and provides more deity for your dollar than you will get anywhere else. Kom Ombo was dedicated to two gods and is therefore rigorously symmetrical throughout: double halls and double colonnades lead to double doorways which open onto double chambers and double sanctuaries. The right side of this two-fold temple is dedicated to **Sobek,** the crocodile-god who was the patron of the many crocs that lurked in the waters nearby in ancient times; like everything else in the area, the crocodiles have now relocated to Lake Nasser. The left side of the temple is devoted to **Horus** the elder, avenger of Osiris and the source of the pharaohs' divine power. On the ceiling of the adjoining vestibule, bright blue images of Horus hover protectively over the chamber. A tunnel in the floor of the inner sanctuary allowed clergy to climb in so they could overhear entreaties to the gods. Ask the guard to show you the reliefs of **Cleopatra II and VII,** and take it upon yourself to decipher the rather risqué hieroglyphs: can you spot the two dripping phalluses and the dismembered bodies? *(Site open daily 7am-9pm; in winter 7am-7pm. Admission E£10, students E£5.)*

Adjoining the northern edges of the temple are the now-putrescent Roman water supply tanks that once crawled with crocodiles and, to the west, the remains of a Roman *mammisis* (birthhouse). Cleopatra's bubble bath is also rumored to be nearby. The **Chapel of Hathor,** to your right as you enter the compound, has crocodile mummies unearthed near the road leading to the site.

DARAW CAMEL MARKET دراو

Sudanese merchants, Bishari tribespeople, and Egyptian *fellaheen* gather every Tuesday morning in Daraw for the unforgettable **camel market.** Rising very early in Aswan, one can visit the frantic market and move on to the temple at Kom Ombo.

Service taxis careen to Daraw from **Kom Ombo,** 8km to the north (10min.), and **Aswan,** 37km to the south (1hr.). Trains and buses running between Luxor and Aswan may also stop here. The **taxi stand, bus station,** and **train station** all lie along the main highway. To reach the camel market from the stations, walk 300m north, cross the tracks, and head down the road for 15 minutes. Take a right after you pass the open fields: you've arrived when you see 200-odd people smacking the rear ends of bound, groaning camels to display their vigor. If you're gliding by on a *felucca,* have the captain stop at the Daraw ferry landing and a pickup truck will take you to the market.

The Bishari (Saharan nomads with their own language and culture) purchase camels for the equivalent of E£200 and drive them from nearby Sudan to Daraw, following what herdsmen have come to call the "40 Days Road." Look for the occasional rakehell businessman in full traditional dress: flowing pants, fighting sword and dagger, and a cloak draped over the shoulders. Typically, a Sudanese camel owner will pay a Sudanese or Bishari shepherd to drive his camels north to Egypt.

The owner then flies up to oversee the selling, usually coming away with a 500% profit. The going rate for a big male camel is E£1200-1500, a savings of E£1000 over prices in Cairo. *(Market open in summer Tu 7am-2pm; in winter Tu 7am-2pm, and sometimes Su-Mo 7am-2pm; slows down after 11am.)*

ASWAN أسوان

Aswan, the southernmost city in Egypt and a model of southern comfort and hospitality, is a trading center where the Middle East overlaps with Africa and Upper Egypt gives way to Lower Nubia. In 1971, the completion of the Soviet designed High Dam created nearby Lake Nasser (the world's largest reservoir) and boosted Egypt's agricultural and energy potential. The dam also flooded most of Nubia, forcing massive migrations to Egypt and Sudan. The darker-skinned Nubian immigrants now thrive in Aswan, giving the city its uniquely African flavor (and its name—Aswan comes from the Nubian phrase *assy wangibu*, which means, appropriately enough, "too much water"). Although hotel owners and the 300-odd aggressively entrepreneurial *felucca* captains can get downright obnoxious when pushing their services on travelers, the locals are genuinely friendly and want to chat—if only to brush up on their English phrases. The gentle charm of the Nubians and the cool breeze along the corniche relieve roasting travelers from the heat and coax them into extending their visits.

The fertile corridor nourished by the Nile is very narrow this far south—so much so that the desert nearly reaches the banks of the river. The Nile is at its cleanest in Aswan and gets dirtier as the river flows north, where the practice of discarding dead livestock into the water is not uncommon. Locals frequently cool

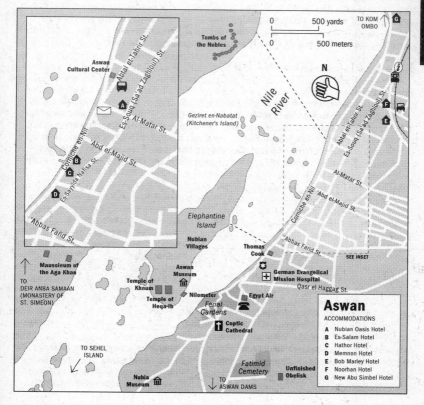

off in this cleaner part of the river and backpackers have been known to join them. Rest assured, the crocodiles roam south of Aswan behind the dams in Lake Nasser. Summer temperatures average over 40°C (104°F), though the thermometer dips to a chilly 35°C (95°F) in winter. In the winter the city becomes a resort, but foreigners are welcomed in any season; restaurants, hotels, and shops are accommodating when there's money to be made.

Aswan is a convenient base for exploring southernmost Egypt; plan on four days if you want to see the sights and stay sane. You can also take *felucca* trips to Kom Ombo, Edfu, and Luxor (see **The Nile Valley: Getting Around**, p. 216). Summer, when temperatures are high and tourists few, is the best time for a *felucca* trip.

✳ ORIENTATION

You're rarely more than two blocks from the river in Aswan. The northern half of the city lies along three long avenues that run parallel to the Nile. The riverfront **Corniche en-Nil** is the most picturesque, featuring several hotels, shops, banks, floating restaurants, and docks. Two blocks inland, the market-lined **Sa'ad Zaghloul Street** features everything from watermelons to water pipes. Also called Es-Souq St., it begins at the train station at the northeast corner of town and runs south 2km to 'Abbas Farid St.; for the block-long stretch behind the Es-Salaam and Hathor Hotels, this path of many names is widely known as **Es-Sayyida Nafisa Street.** In the southern half of town, the corniche continues for another 1km and ends at the **Ferial Gardens.** The northern grid pattern falls apart at the central market. South of the *souq*, inland streets form a labyrinth of alleys. Sandwiched between the corniche and the market street, **Abtal et-Tahrir Street** begins at the youth hostel in the north and culminates in a small cluster of tourist bazaars, resuming as a narrow lane farther south. After haggling, a horse-drawn **kalish** should cost E£5 for a short ride, E£10 for an extended 30-minute tour. **Taxis,** found everywhere along the corniche, shouldn't be more than E£5 for any travel within the city.

🛈 PRACTICAL INFORMATION

TRANSPORTATION

Airplanes: The airport (tel. 48 03 07) is 23km south of town near the High Dam. E£25 one-way by taxi. Served by **EgyptAir** (tel. 31 50 00; fax 31 50 05), on Corniche en-Nil, at the southern end near Ferial Gardens. Office open daily 8am-8pm. Another EgytAir office at the airport (tel. 48 05 68), but you can't buy tickets there. 4 flights daily to Cairo, 8 in winter (E£577 one-way). Daily flights to **Abu Simbel** leave 3 times per day in summer, 11 times in winter (E£288 round-trip, price may increase to E£508 if the road to Abu Simbel is re-opened). Visa and MC accepted. **Airport Police:** Tel. 48 05 09.

Trains: Tel. 31 47 54, from the northern end of Sa'ad Zaghloul St. 1st- and 2nd-class A/C trains depart at 5am and 8:45pm for **Luxor** (3½hr.; 1st class roughly E£20, 2nd class E£15) and **Cairo** (14hr.; 1st class E£63, 2nd class E£37). The tourist office can give the most current fares. Frequent trains run south to the **High Dam** (30min., 9 per day, 50pt). There are often student discounts on trains.

Buses: Tel. 30 32 25, on Abtal et-Tahrir St. behind the Abu Simbel Hotel. Hours vary, but there are 10 A/C buses per day to: **Kom Ombo** (1hr., E£1.50); **Daraw** (45min., E£1.50); **Edfu** (2hr., E£4); and **Luxor** (4hr., E£6.50). Buses to **Qena** (4hr.; 6:30, 11:30am, 12:30pm; E£10); **Asyut** (8hr., 7am, E£25); **Hurghada** (7hr.; 8am, E£20; 3:30pm with A/C, E£40); **Cairo** (12hr., 3:30pm, E£55); **Suez** (12hr.; 8am, E£28; 3:30 and 5pm, E£45); and (once the road re-opens) **Abu Simbel** (4hr., 8am and 4pm, E£26 round-trip; returns to Aswan at 6:30am and 2pm). There are also *service* to the **Old Dam;** ask at the tourist office.

Ferries: Get to **Elephantine Island** from Esh-Shatii Restaurant on the southern end of the corniche, or across from the EgyptAir office even farther south (every 15-20min. 6am-6pm, E£1). The ferry is simply a large *felucca*. Beware of captains who tell you the ferry is not running. Float to the western bank in a **Seti Tours** ferry, opposite the corniche tourist office (departs every 20min. 6am-6pm, E£1). Catch a ride to the northern part of the island on Hotel Oberoi's cheap ferry (E£1; see **Sights,** p. 214).

Service: *Service* leave from the covered station 1km south of the train station (every 15-30min. roughly 4am-6pm, depending on demand). To get there, take the overpass just left of the train station; make a left at the end of the road, then another right. To: **Daraw** or **Kom Ombo** (40min., E£1.50); **Edfu** (1¼hr., E£3); **Esna** (2-3hr., E£6); **Luxor** (3hr., E£8); **Qena** (4hr., E£9); and **Khazan/Old Dam** (75pt). *Service* also occasionally depart from the corniche and Abtal at-Tahrir St.

Bike Rental: 3 locations: on Abtal at-Tahrir St. next to the Poste Restante office, near the train station on Es-Souq St., and farther down Es-Souq St. next to the Nubian Oasis Hotel. E£5 per day, E£1 per hr. in summer. Prices may double in winter.

TOURIST AND FINANCIAL SERVICES

Tourist Office: Tel. 31 28 11. This beige hut, on the right as you exit the train station, is a good first stop in Aswan. The multilingual Shukri Sa'ad has been providing tourists with info on anything and everything for over 20 years—including what you should pay for a *felucca* and how best to see Abu Simbel. Open in summer daily 9am-3pm and 7-9pm in summer; in winter 9am-3pm and 6-8pm. Closed F 12:30-1:30pm.

Tourist Police: Tel. 30 31 63, on the south side of the train station. Open 24hr.

Passport Office: Tel. 31 22 38, on Corniche en-Nil, in the police building on the 3rd floor. Will register passports and extend visas. Open Su-Th 8am-2pm.

Currency Exchange: Banque Misr, 103 Corniche en-Nil (tel. 31 66 92, 93, or 95; fax 31 66 94). Visa and MC advances. Open Su-Th 8:30am-2pm. The only **ATM** on the corniche is next to Banque Misr and takes Visa, MC, PLUS, and Cirrus cards.

American Express: Tel./fax 30 29 09, at the southernmost end of the corniche in the lobby of the New Cataract Hotel. Arranges travel itineraries and holds mail for cardholders. Open Su-Th 8am-5pm, F-Sa 9am-4pm.

Thomas Cook, 59 Corniche en-Nil (tel. 30 40 11 or 68 39; fax 30 62 09), just north of the police building. Travel and financial services, with special discounted rates if tours and hotels are booked through Cook. Open daily 8am-2pm and 4-8pm.

LOCAL SERVICES

Bookstore: Islamic Books, up a side street next to the Abu Simbel Hotel. Sells Islamic books in translation. Open daily 8am-2:30pm and 6pm-midnight. Large hotels usually have small bookstores, which carry European newspapers.

Laundromat: Most hotels do laundry for E£1-2 per garment or offer do-it-yourself laundry for free. Laundry service and dry-cleaning shop under the Nubian Oasis Hotel. Open daily 8am-2pm.

Swimming Pools: Non-guests are always welcome to cool off at the **Isis Hotel** on the corniche, right by the Nile. The **Oberoi Hotel** pool is a swanky but expensive option at E£21. The rooftop pool at the **Hathor Hotel** is cheaper at E£5 but very shallow: no diving.

EMERGENCY AND COMMUNICATIONS

Emergency: Most places do not speak English, so get in touch with the **Tourist Police** (tel. 30 31 63) or **Tourist Office** (tel. 31 28 11) first. **Medical Emergency:** Tel. 123.

Pharmacy: En-Nile Pharmacy (tel. 30 26 74), just south of Hathor Hotel. Open daily 7am-1am. Other pharmacies line the corniche and *souq*.

Hospital: Mubarak Military Hospital (tel. 31 79 85), located in the flamingo-pink building behind the Nubian Museum. This clean new facility offers everything from family planning centers to emergency gynecological care. Travelers must pay in cash because health insurance and credit cards are not accepted. **German Evangelical Mission Hospital** (tel. 30 21 76 or 31 21 76), 100m south of the police station down an alley on the left. A rather shabby but convenient option; look for steel doors with flower symbols. The **Government Hospital** (tel. 32 28 55 or 24 19), on Qasr el-Hagga St., is nothing more than a last resort. Every hotel reception can provide the name of a **doctor.** These private offices typically have very modern facilities.

Post Office: On Corniche en-Nil, toward the northern end of town. Offers **EMS** and **tele-graph** services. Open Sa-Th 9am-2pm. For **Poste Restante,** walk south from the main post office and turn left down Salah ad-Din St., then immediately right again. It's in the yellow building with black columns known locally as the Old Post Office; requests for Poste Restante may meet with confusion, but persistence helps. Open Su-Th 8am-2pm.

Internet Access: The **Nubian Oasis Hotel** and **Rosewan Hotel,** 100m right of the train station, offer Internet connections for E£1 per min. The connection is slow, but works well enough if you're not intent on downloading nudie pics. To save time and money, type letters on a word processor (E£10 per hr.) and then email them as attachments.

Telephones: Telephone office (tel. 31 38 69), 2 doors south of EgyptAir. Open daily 24hr. **Fax** available 8am-2pm and 3-9pm, E£30 for 3min. to U.S. **Information:** tel. 16.

Telephone Code: 097.

◤ ACCOMMODATIONS

Prices are higher in winter and lower in summer; rates listed are approximate. If you have the energy when you arrive, you may be able to play hotel hawkers off one another to land a better price. All listed hotels have laundry service and break-fast unless otherwise stated, but none dance the credit card tango. Be sure to ask for applicable student and group discounts, but be careful of discounted group tours and *felucca* trips, which are often rip-offs. Do not agree to anything before you have checked out the competition on your own.

Nubian Oasis Hotel, 234 Sa'ad Zaghloul St. (tel. 31 21 23 or 26; fax 31 21 24; email nubianoasis@infinity.com.eg). From the train station, take a left onto Abtal at-Tahrir St. and a right 2 streets after the Cleopatra Hotel. This standout has clean, comfortable rooms and bathrooms and a great rooftop view of the city. TV lounge with pool and cable. Singles with fan E£12; doubles E£15; slightly higher for A/C and private bath-rooms. Internet access is available, but slow (E£1 per min.). Check-out at noon.

Noorhan Hotel (tel. 31 60 69), on Sa'ad Zaghloul St. From train station, turn left onto Sa'ad Zaghloul and take second left. Clean rooms with fans and a peaceful rooftop ter-race—perfect for sipping Stellas (E£5.50). Singles E£6; doubles E£12; add E£1.50 per person for a private bathroom and A/C. Breakfast included. Check-out at noon.

New Abu Simbel Hotel (tel./fax 30 60 96). North of the train station on Atlas St. in the former Soviet consulate. Borderline sumptuous with its shaded garden patio (popular with locals and tourists alike), high-ceilinged lobby, and spacious, spotless A/C rooms. Singles E£25; doubles E£35; triples E£45. TV E£3 extra. E£5 student discount.

Hathor Hotel (tel. 31 45 80; fax 30 34 62), right in the middle of Corniche en-Nil. New ceramic floor and wood furniture give the Hathor a relatively sophisticated air. Big roof-top view, tiny and shallow rooftop pool. All rooms have bath and A/C. Singles E£20-30; doubles E£35-40; triples E£45-55.

Es-Salaam Hotel, 101 Corniche en-Nil (tel. 30 26 51 or 84 35). All rooms have pristine, tiled bathrooms and A/C. The rooms with wrap-around balconies have great views of the Nile. Singles E£30; doubles E£50; triples E£65. Group discounts available.

Memnon Hotel (tel. 30 04 83), Corniche en-Nil. Entrance on the street parallel to the cor-niche, behind the National Bank of Egypt. A homey, Nile-view throwback to the early 60s with decor somewhere between surreal and absurd. Rooms have A/C, private bath, red shag lamps, and 18th-century French curtains. Singles E£23; doubles E£55, with-out view E£35; triples E£65; suites E£75. Lunch E£12, dinner E£15. Student discount.

Bob Marley Hotel (tel. 30 18 39), just off of Es-Souq. Low on cash? Don't mind ergo-nomically challenging beds? Bob's is your place, mon. Singles E£5. Breakfast E£1.

◖ FOOD

Fruits, vegetables, bread, and fried pigeon (a local specialty)—not to mention *ta'amiyya* (falafel), liver sandwiches, and *kushari*—are all available in Aswan's **souq. Vegetarians** may find their choices limited to a few rice dishes. For legendary legumes, a large **vegetable souq** is tucked away near the train station, on the northeast edge of Es-Souq St. Come in the morning for a full range of options. At the other extreme, you can wallow in the huge buffets and gourmet Arab and continental cuisine at the luxury hotels. The Oberoi offers an elegant E£22 **breakfast buffet** (6-10:30am) in its stunning cupola-covered ballroom restaurant.

■ **Sayyida Nafisa,** just off Es-Souq St. As you approach, the ground in the *souq* turns rosy red from colored wood shavings. Named after a relative of Muhammad, this restaurant's central location makes it an obvious and popular choice. Better-than-average Egyptian food E£5-9, refreshing juices E£1.50. Open noon-2am.

Hammam Restaurant, Corniche en-Nil, 50m south of the Bank of Egypt. Mirrors and *felucca* murals decorate this Arab short-order grill. Omelettes served all day and excellent mini-sandwiches are a pound a pop—3 should do the trick. Open daily 24hr.

El-Masry (tel. 30 25 76), on El-Matar St. Go south from the train station and turn left onto El-Matar. Shiny marble and an extensive menu have attracted throngs to this elegant and extremely clean establishment. Standard meat and fowl dishes with refreshing vegetable side platters. Main courses E£10-23.

Darwesh Restaurant, on Sa'ad Zaghloul St., across the street from the south end of the train station. Overly-energetic fans make you feel like you're in a wind tunnel. Some of the best pigeon in Aswan (E£10 fried), served in a flash of a neon sign. All meals come with vegetables, soup, rice, and salad (full meal E£10-12). Open daily noon-1am.

FLOATING RESTAURANTS

More popular with locals and tourists, these pseudo-aquatic eateries offer decent meals and the perfect setting to watch the sun go down over the desert hills of the west bank. All serve basically the same array of meat dishes (E£6-12) plus salads, dips, drinks, and desserts (E£1-4). They are listed below from south to north.

Aswan Panorama (tel. 30 61 69). The best of floating cuisine. The delicious food and fruit trees among the tables make it well worth the walk down the corniche. Try the pigeon burger and Bedouin coffee served on coals, filtered with dried grass, and flavored with cardamom, cinnamon, and cloves (E£20 total). No seating after 9pm.

Monalisa. You'll know you've arrived when you see her smile amid the Mediterranean decor, complete with a thatched roof and chirping birds. *You* won't be smiling at the slow service, but turn that frown upside down with a Monalisa cocktail (E£1.50). The meat and fish entrees are also well-prepared (E£6-9). Open daily 8am-3am.

EMY's. Neon letters top the only actual boat among the floating restaurants. Sit on the top level of the barge to sway gently as you chew (and chew and chew) on your kebab (E£11.50). There's also an above-average selection of meatless dishes, including some smallish pizzas, as well as breakfast (E£3) and beer (E£5). The 20% student discount may help ease the pain of a 15% tax and service surcharge. Open 8am-1:30am.

Aswan Moon Restaurant, just to the right of EMY's. This gaudily decorated restaurant hosts Nubian musicians and *felucca* chiefs chatting up whichever tourists haven't been frightened away by the badly stuffed animals above the entrance. *Omm 'Ali* coconut milk bread is worth the E£3.

▐♫ ENTERTAINMENT

"Nightclubs" in Aswan feature a group of drummers and tambourinists with a loud organ player and a male singer/emcee, plus the hip-notizing gyrations of a sequin-clad belly dancer enticing men into tossing bills. Check out the scene at **Salah ad-Din Restaurant** on the water or at the **Ramses Hotel** in town. There are often cover charges or minimums for discos and nightclubs, but they change frequently (usually E£5-10 cover or 2-drink minimum). The **Oberoi Hotel** has a piano bar where you can even sit down and play (drinks E£10-35), and a mini-disco with a pounding dance mix. The bastard love child of Eastern and Western dancing scenes can be found at the dank pub and disco at the **New Cataract** (open 7pm-2am, E£15 minimum for disco). The Pullman bar in the **Old Cataract** is a more legitimate alternative with no cover. For more subdued enjoyment, try the pool and snooker tables at the **Basma Hotel** on the corniche, just past the Kalabsha Hotel (E£5-15 cover).

👁 SIGHTS

Gaze across the Nile to catch a glimpse of Aswan's major sights: on the desert horizon along the west bank, a mausoleum, a monastery, and cliffside tombs emerge from the blowing sands. The rest of the city's historic attractions can be found on a cluster of islands floating in the middle of the river.

Aswan grew from the largest of these islands, **Elephantine Island,** much as Paris grew from the Ile de la Cité. The island got its name from the black and (you guessed it) elephant-shaped stones at its southern tip. The remains of the ancient settlement have been excavated on the southeast corner of the island, directly behind the museum. The **Oberoi Hotel** and adjacent construction sites dominate the northern half of the island. The hotel is cordoned off, but is easily reached by taking one of their silly-looking ferries from the launching point at the center of the corniche. The local ferry from the Corniche en-Nil provides the cheapest transport to Elephantine Island (E£1).

To reach the sights on the west bank of the Nile, it's easiest to hire a **felucca.** The official rate for *felucca* transport in the vicinity of Aswan is E£10 per hour regardless of the number of passengers, but it'll take some negotiation. A complete tour of Elephantine Island, Kitchener's Island, the Aga Khan's Mausoleum, St. Simeon's Monastery, and the northern tombs goes for E£50 per group and takes about two hours. A cheap alternative is to hire a rowboat or motorboat to the west bank (E£2-3), then trek from sight to sight on foot. Transport back to the corniche or Elephantine Island, either by ferry (E£1) or rowboat (E£8), is easy as long as you don't get stranded late in the day, when the boatmen have you at their mercy.

ELEPHANTINE ISLAND. Elephantine Island is historically very significant but not really all that exciting. The **Aswan Archaeological Museum** houses a rather small collection of unmarked ancient Egyptian and Nubian artifacts. Even the "Head of a Man Mummy," resting on a cloth sack in the museum's sarcophagus room, looks bored. An annex augments the collection with a wide array of items recently excavated from the adjacent ruins. Through the small garden to the left of the museum stand the **Temple of Khnum** and the modest **Temple of Heqa-Ib** (particularly attractive when viewed from the Nile), in addition to a small Ptolemaic temple dedicated to Alexander II. The temple is currently being excavated by German archaeologists, though there will be a few guides waiting near the museum who will provide a tour through the site for a little *bakhsheesh. (Open daily 8:30am-6pm; in winter 8am-5pm. Admission E£10, students E£5, includes the museum, adjacent ruins, and the Nilometer.)*

KITCHENER'S ISLAND. Behind Elephantine Island and not visible from central Aswan, **Kitchener's Island** (*Geziret en-Nabatat*, or "Island of the Plants") is a lovely botanical garden planted by the British General Kitchener, best known for crushing the Sudanese rebellion of 1898. Exotic and flamboyant birds congregate in the tropical plants from Africa and Asia that flourish here. To reach the island, hire a *felucca* to combine an island visit with stops along the west bank and Elephantine Island (a full afternoon rental runs E£10 per hr.). It is also possible to hire a rowboat from the west side of Elephantine Island (about E£3 for 1-2 passengers only). Make sure boats are willing to wait for you or come back for pickup by withholding payment until the end of the trip. *(Open daily 8am-5pm. Admission E£5.)*

MAUSOLEUM OF THE AGA KHAN. The most placid attraction on the west bank of the Nile is the **Mausoleum of the Aga Khan,** a short climb from where the *felucca* docks. Aga Khans, the hereditary titles of the *imams* of the Isma'ili Muslims, are believed to be direct descendants of Muhammad and the inheritors of his spiritual responsibilities of guidance. Aswan became the favorite winter retreat of **Sultan Muhammad Shah El-Husseini,** Aga Khan III (1877-1957). Upon his death, Begum (the Aga Khan's wife) oversaw the construction of the mausoleum, where the feisty nonagenarian still spends part of the year. Unfortunately, the mausoleum has been closed by the Egyptian government since June 1, 1997 due to a dispute over entrance fees with Begum. While the edifice sports an imposing fortress-like exterior, the interior has a quiet simplicity modeled after the Fatimid tombs of Cairo. Opposite the entrance stands a beautiful marble sarcophagus inscribed with passages from the Qur'an. *(Once the mausoleum opens again, it will be open Tu-Su 9am-4pm for an undetermined entrance fee. Remember to dress conservatively and remove shoes.)*

MONASTERY OF ST. SIMEON. The isolated and majestic **Deir Anba Samaan** (Monastery of St. Simeon) is a short 1km walk across the dunes from the mausoleum. Built in the 6th and 7th centuries, the monastery is on a terrace carved into the steep hills and looks more like a fort than a religious sanctuary with its 6m high, turreted walls. The original walls stood 10m high, but were not strong enough to keep the 300 monks who lived there from being driven out by Arab conquerors in the 14th century. Upstairs, the monks' cells and stone beds (with Bible and *galabiyya* wall slots) are currently occupied by bats. The monastery also had a church and accommodations sufficient for several hundred pilgrims and their camels. There are also remnants of the baptismal font and drain pipe, well-preserved paintings of Mary and Joseph, and Communion wine-making facilities in St. Simeon's chamber. Simeon's chamber also has a slot in the roof for a piece of rope he tied around his beard to keep him on his feet during all-night prayer vigils.

To get there, follow the paved path that starts in front of the Mausoleum of the Aga Khan or, if you don't mind chafing your rear end a little, hire a camel near the *felucca* stop (E£20 per camel for a 20min. ride for 2 people). Women do not need to cling tightly to the camel driver, despite his concerns for safety, nor should the driver need to grab his passengers' legs to ensure stability. If you feel at all uncomfortable, forget the drivers' beastly manners and leave their camels behind. *(Open Tu-Su 7am-4pm. Admission E£12, students E£6.)*

TOMBS OF THE NOBLES. The **Tombs of the Nobles** lie farther north along the west bank of the Nile, incised into the face of desert cliffs and impressively illuminated at night. These tombs of governors and dignitaries date from the 23rd to the 18th century BCE, but four millennia of decay and pilfering have severely damaged most of them. The bright color and detail of the reliefs in the **Tomb of Sarenput II**, however, merit the easy trip across the Nile; note the sacrificial stone slab with a blood drainage spout. The mummy was shuffled to Cairo, but there are plenty of bones in the corner. The interconnected 6th-dynasty **Tombs of Nikhu and Sabni**, father and son, have depictions of donkeys, water buffalo, fish, and birds. The cheapest way to visit the tombs is to take the ferry from the corniche, across the small park from the tourist office (E£1). Once across, walk uphill to the office on the left. *(Open daily 7am-4pm. Admission E£12, students E£6. Photo permission E£10.)*

NUBIAN SIGHTS. Nubian culture is more alive and prominent in Aswan than anywhere else in Egypt. Ten years in the making, Aswan's **Nubia Museum** is a magnificent sandstone building south of the Old Cataract Hotel. It features a vast collection of Nubian artifacts from throughout Egypt, described in Arabic and English (a rarity in Aswan). Among the many sarcophagi is a mummified ram with a gilded mask and golden crown, representing the god Knum whose temple sits in Elephantine Island. *(Open daily 9am-1pm and 5-9pm. Admission E£20, students E£10.)*

For a more authentic and enjoyable taste of Nubian life, step outside the museum. The central section of Elephantine Island has several **Nubian villages** where you'll find friendly residents, adoring youngsters, and brightly painted homes. The ferry to the west bank tombs (E£1) can bring you to **Gharb Aswan,** a series of Nubian villages less touristed than Elephantine Island's. A pickup truck will take you north to the villages from the ferry dock (about E£1). You may even be invited to join the celebrations and ululations of a wedding ceremony; the Nubians consider it a mark of honor to have guests from far-flung villages attend their nuptial festivities. Nubian weddings traditionally involved 15 days of partying, but the demands of modern life have trimmed the celebration down to three or four.

Nubians may feel slighted if you reject their offers of hospitality, so be diplomatic in declining if you must do so. At all times, be modest in your dress and behavior.

The large Nubian houses, made of Nile mud, consist of six rooms around a courtyard; each cluster of rooms has its own dome or cylindrical roof. The brightly painted huts belong to families that have completed the *hajj*, or pilgrimage to Mecca. When the High Dam threatened to destroy this traditional style, architect-Hassan Fathy whipped up these reconstructed and relocated villages.

 SHOPPING

If you want more authentic souvenirs than hieroglyph-emblazoned t-shirts, visit **Es-Sayyida Nafisa Street** for western garments made to order. Tailors measure and cut with lightning speed (pants E£10-25, shorts and simple shirts E£10-15, shirts with collars and buttons E£25-35). For traditional Egyptian clothing, there are numerous *galabiyya* (the Egyptian name for the ubiquitous Arab gown) and *qaftan* merchants in the *souq*. If you have the time, you can buy high-quality government cloth (at posted government prices) from one of the government shops on the corniche, then have your garments made to order by the tailors on Sa'ad Zaghloul St. For authentic papyrus, head to **Dr. Rayab's Papyrus Museum** on the corniche, across from the Hammam restaurant (open daily 9am-11pm). Papyrus ranges from E£3 to E£900, depending on the quality of the artwork on the paper. In winter, the **Aswan Cultural Center**, on Corniche en-Nil across from the Rowing Club, features Nubian dancing and crafts. (Open Sa-Th 9-11pm; admission E£5.)

To take an even more calming break from the already staid Aswani lifestyle, join locals for tea, *sheesha*, or a mean game of dominoes at the many cafes scattered throughout town. Spontaneous football (soccer) games occasionally spring up around the stadium in the northern part of town past the new Abu Simbel Hotel. For more personal relaxation, walk south along the corniche and around the Ferial Gardens to the elegant **Old and New Cataract Hotels** (tel. 30 35 28 or 36 28). Stroll through the gorgeous gardens, past the pool, and into the outdoor terrace cafe overlooking the river. (Open 9am-4pm. Drinks E£15 and up. No shorts on the terrace after 3pm.) For more expensive exertion, report to the Hotel Oberoi's health spa (tel. 30 34 55) for relaxing and rejuvenating treatments and exercises (priced individually from US$3-20).

SOUTH OF ASWAN

The region of the **First Cataract** includes two dams, two temples, and most of an obelisk. The **Old Dam,** 5km south of Aswan, was built by the British in 1902, only to be dwarfed by the Soviet-designed **High Dam** 10km upstream. The red granite and alabaster that fed pharaonic monument building was taken from quarries just south of Aswan. Here you'll find the **Unfinished Obelisk** in all its almost-glory. On an island in the lake between the dams, the lovingly preserved **Temple** proclaims the glory of Isis. Beyond the west end of the High Dam, the desolate **Temple of Kalabsha** sinks peacefully into the desert on the banks of Lake Nasser. The striking monuments at **Abu Simbel** lie farther south. With the exception of Abu Simbel, which is harder to reach, all sights are easily accessible from Aswan.

TRANSPORTATION

An excellent road follows the Nile from Aswan to Khazan (a village near the Old Dam), providing access to both the dam and the motorboat launch to the Temple. The route to Khazan is serviced by **service** (50pt-E£1, depart from *service* stand) and by public **bus** (50pt-E£1). Both run frequently until about 9:30pm. Frequent **trains** run to the High Dam, leaving you at the station on the eastern end of the dam. Vehicles and pedestrians are not allowed to cross the dam after 6pm.

Once the road to Abydos opens up again, the tourist office and most hotels in Aswan will resume arranging **minibus trips** to Abu Simbel. The trips generally cost

E£25-35, and sometimes include the other sights south of Aswan (entrance fees not included). Arranged tours generally leave at 4am and return to Aswan by 2pm; overzealous authorities insist that tourist groups travel in a police convoy. You'll be miserable if your minibus doesn't have air-conditioning, since blowing sands may preclude opening the windows for much of the trip. Hire a **taxi** to check out the dams and Kalabsha for around E£30.

DAMS AND QUARRIES

Built by the Brits between 1898 and 1902, the dam supplied most of Egypt's power for years. The **Old Dam** is 10km to the north and can be reached by taking a *service* or a temperamental public bus from the Aswan corniche to Khazan (see **Getting Around**, above). The impressive sheer granite wall can be fully appreciated by the cab-window ogler; there are no tourist facilities here. The fertile area known as the **First Cataract** is one of the most idyllic spots in the Aswan area. The view of what is left of these rapid waters, churning around rocky outcrops to the north of the Old Dam, gives some idea of the perils of early Nile expeditions (when ships were hauled past this dangerous spot with ropes). In the village of **Khazan,** 90-year-old British villas (now Brit-less) are nestled peacefully within walled gardens.

ASWAN HIGH DAM (ES-SIDD EL-'ALI). The best-known attraction in the area is modern Egypt's greatest monument, the High Dam (Es-Sidd el-'Ali), completed in 1971. The dam is more interesting intellectually than visually; those visualizing a sheer wall with a bulging lake behind it will be disappointed. The High Dam lacks the aesthetic magnificence of ancient Egypt's colossi, but it could teach them a thing or two about size: 1km thick at the base, 3.6km long, and 111m high, the dam contains more than 17 times the material used in the Great Pyramid of Cheops. The construction of the dam created **Lake Nasser,** the world's largest artificial lake, and covered all of Lower Nubia in waters as deep as 200m. Thousands of Sudanese and Nubians were forced to relocate. Ancient Nubia's archaeological treasures were threatened; the Egyptian government sent out an international plea for help and many countries responded, individually and under an ambitious UNESCO plan. A rise in the Sahara's water table has been noticed as far away as Algeria, and archaeologists suspect that this effect has damaged the necropolis at Luxor and the base of Giza's Sphinx. Another danger of the dam is the possibility of sabotage. Should the dam be destroyed, the flood that would follow would wipe out all but two percent of Egypt's population. Nearby hills have radar installations and anti-aircraft missiles to guard against this sort of disaster. On the brighter side, the dam's 12 turbines doubled Egypt's electrical output. Agricultural productivity has been greatly enhanced, and the acreage of Egypt's arable soil has increased by 30%. The dam enabled Egypt to enjoy a healthy water supply during the drought of the past decade, and in August 1988 it saved Egypt from the floods suffered by Sudan when the Nile overflowed after heavy rains.

VISITOR'S PAVILION. On the east bank (near the train station), just before the dam, the Visitor's Pavilion features plaques and sculptures blending Soviet social-ist-realist motifs with Egyptian figures and symbols. At the center of the pavilion is a dusty 15m model of the High Dam and its environs, minus the water. The domed pavilion is well off the road from the dam and most taxis will not stop at it unless you insist; ask for the *mekat. (Open daily 7am-5pm. Free.)*

SOVIET-EGYPTIAN FRIENDSHIP MONUMENT. To cross the dam you must pay E£5. The soldiers at the eastern end won't let you walk across but will stop passing vehicles and make them give you a ride. At the other end is the towering Soviet-Egyptian friendship monument, arguably premature given the alacrity with which the Egyptians spurned their Soviet benefactors once the dam was complete. A stylized lotus blossom, the monument looks eerily like an ICBM silo springing into action. Due to the rise in terrorist activity, tourists are supposed to secure police permission to go to the top, either in Aswan or in the large yellow gift shop west of the monument. Some have been known to *bakhsheesh* (E£1-2) their way to the top if the dam authorities are closed. *(Open 6am-6pm; in winter 5am-5pm.)*

SEHEL ISLAND. Below the waters of the First Cataract, Sehel Island boasts a hospitable Nubian village, scanty ruins, and inscriptions dating from the 4th dynasty to the Ptolemaic period. The island attracts very few tourists but makes a nice destination for longer *felucca* rides out of Aswan (a 3-hour tour…a 3-hour tour).

OTHER SIGHTS. Taxi drivers returning to Aswan from the High Dam might agree to stop at the Fatimid Tombs, the adjacent Unfinished Obelisk, and the nearby granite quarries. These sites are all near the camping area, 300m east of the main road at a turn-off 1km south of Aswan, and are all easily within walking or *kalish* (E£5-7) range of the city. The **Fatimid Tombs** are typical early Islamic shrines: squat, square stone buildings with crescents on their roofs. They are easily spotted across the street from the obelisk. The abandoned tombs can be spooky, with just you and the ghosts wandering around the dark cemetery.

The only thing less interesting than an obelisk is an **Unfinished Obelisk.** This one was abandoned at its site because of a flaw in the granite; it was to have soared to a whopping 41.7m on a base 4.2m on each side. In its unadorned, supine state, the obelisk looks—well, unfinished, but it provides a rare behind-the-scenes look at the mammoth effort that went into its creation. Notice the channels along each side with curved indentations just big enough for a man to sit in and pound away with a ball made of diarite, a substance harder than granite. The earthbound side of the massive shaft would have been cut free either with copper or bronze chisels, or by pounding passages with diarite balls, inserting wooden beams, and flooding the channels so that the expanding wood would break the remaining stone. The adjacent **granite quarries** supplied ancient Egypt with the hard pink or black granite and porphyry that was favored for temple and monument building. *(Obelisk and quarries open daily 7am-6pm, but the guard often leaves early. Admission E£10, students E£5.)*

PHILAE فيلة

*You can visit most easily by **taxi** as part of an itinerary including other sights, or you can take a **bus** to the Old Dam from the Aswan corniche; get off when it stops at the checkpoint on the east end of the dam. From the checkpoint, walk south along the shore to the concrete boat dock (about 2km). After paying for admission, you must hire a motorboat to reach the island at the official rate of E£20 per boat round-trip, but the price may drop in the off-season. Find a few travelers to share the expense of the boat. The captain will try to con you into paying more, so be firm. If there are serious problems, complain at the tourist office in town. The boat captain is obligated to wait for you as you tour the site, so there is no need to rush. **Service** are faster; tell the driver to let you off at the Old Dam (Es-Sidd el-Qadeem). Philae also has a **sound and light show.** English performances are M, W, and F-Sa 6pm, Tu 7:15pm, Su 8:30pm; winter shows postponed two hours.*

Called "the pearl of Egypt" by one of Napoleon's soldiers, the beautiful Temple of Isis at Philae has attracted the pious and the curious since classical times. The completion of the Old Dam in 1902 partially submerged the buildings only a few years after their resurrection as a popular tourist destination. Victorian vandals then gathered around the pillars and chipped their names into the protruding columns; the graffiti now mark the earlier water level. Archaeologists feared the waters would eventually undermine the foundations of the temples and hasten their collapse, and the construction of the High Dam would indeed have utterly destroyed Philae were it not for the efforts of UNESCO and the Egyptian Antiquities Department. Between 1972 and 1980, the entire complex of temples was transferred from Philae Island to higher ground on nearby Agilkia Island. In 1980, the new site of the temples reopened to tourism (see **Moving a Mountain,** p. 221).

TEMPLE OF ISIS. The Temple of Isis, dominating the island's northern edge, is the last bastion of ancient Egyptian religion. Isis was a goddess in the truest sense: mother of nature, protector of humans, goddess of purity and sexuality, and sister-wife of the legendary hero Osiris (see **Meet the Gods,** p. 51). It was on Philae that she supposedly found her husband's heart after he was dismembered, making the island the most sacred of Isis's homes. Her cult following continued long after the establishment of Christianity, fizzling out only in the 6th century during the reign of Justinian, who successfully replaced her with Mary. Nearly all the structures on Philae date from the Ptolemaic and Roman eras, when Egyptian artistic quality was in decline—hence the inferior quality of the decorative relief work. *(Site open daily 7am-5pm. Admission E£20, students E£10.)*

PORTICO OF NECTANEBO. From the landing at the southern tip of the island, climb the short slope up to the temple complex past Philae's oldest structure, the **Portico of Nectanebo,** which once formed the vestibule of a temple. The arrangement of Philae's courtyards corresponds to the status of the people allowed in each: the outermost courtyard was for commoners, while each successive inner courtyard was reserved for increasingly important people—the innermost for High Priests. The larger edifice has been washed away, but the eastern side of the colonnade remains. Ptolemy, Isis, and Horus are depicted on the **first pylon,** which rises 18m on either side of the temple's main entrance. Note the channels cut into the face of the pylon on either side of the doorway where brightly-painted square-cut cedar flagpoles once stood. The space on the left side of the threshold was for hinges that once supported an enormous door.

Through this entrance is the **central court,** with a Roman *mammisis* (birth-house) devoted to Horus, its columns emblazoned with the head of his consort, the cow-goddess Hathor. The walls depict the falcon god in the marshes of his birth. On the temple wall opposite the *mammisis*, Horus is transported in a boat on the shoulders of servants en route to visit another member of the divine family.

To the north is the slightly off-center **second pylon,** marking the way to the temple's inner sanctum. The *pronaos* (vestibule) was converted into a church by early Christians, who inscribed Byzantine crosses on the chamber walls and added a small altar. Farther north is the *naos*, the temple's innermost sanctuary. With a little *bakhsheesh* you can climb to the roof of the temple or enter a trap door on the interior right side leading to an inscribed crypt.

OTHER SIGHTS. Outside the temple, at left-rear, is a **Nilometer** with a stairwell and grooves used to measure the depths of the water. The stairwell is across from a French inscription from Napoleon's expedition. Because Egyptian gods liked to make house calls, outside the temple (to the right) is **Trajan's Kiosk,** the beautifully-columned, open-air garage/divine carport (mistaken as a pharaoh's bed by the Victorians), which housed the barque of whichever god-icon came to visit Isis.

KALABSHA كلبشة

The **Temple of Kalabsha** is somewhat difficult to reach and poorly publicized, but it offers a relatively peaceful and quiet (if dimly lit) temple experience for those intrepid travelers wary of the pesky crowds at Abu Simbel. The cheapest way to reach Kalabsha is to take the **train** to the east end of the dam, ride to the west end (you'll have to pay the E£5 dam fee), then walk to the boat landing for the temple. To get to the landing from the western checkpoint, continue straight ahead for 100m, then veer left through the shipyard, following the curve of the water for about 1km. A **taxi** from Aswan to the boat landing is less of a hassle but more expensive; try bargaining down to E£25-30 (even less for large groups). Adding this stop to your taxi tour of the High Dam, Philae, and the Unfinished Obelisk should cost around E£5. Regardless of how you get to the boat landing, you only have two options for getting to the temple once there: hire either a **rowboat** (E£10 per load, which holds no more than 2-3 people) or a larger **motorboat** (E£20 for a load of 10 or so). Remember to bring lots of water, cover your head, and watch your step on the dock. *(High Dam open until 6pm.)*

The well-preserved temple at Kalabsha is considered by many Egyptologists to be second only to the treasures of Abu Simbel, but the building—situated dramatically above the placid waters of Lake Nasser—is more impressive on the outside than on the inside. Dedicated to the Nubian god Mandulis (who was renowned for

EGYPT

his hundreds of wives and legions of children), the temple was built by Amenhotep II, augmented during the reign of Augustus, and used as a church during the Christian era. In 1962-63, the West German government paid to have the entire temple dismantled and transported in 13,000 pieces from its Nasser-flooded home to the present site, 50km north of the original (see **Moving a Mountain,** p. 221).

TEMPLE CAUSEWAY. An immense causeway of dressed stone leads from the water to the temple's main entrance. The first pylon is off-center from both the causeway and the inner gateways of the temple itself. The grand forecourt between the pylon and the vestibule is surrounded by 14 columns, each with a unique capital. This is one of the only temples in Egypt where you can legally get to the top: take the stairs to the roof from a small room just beyond the vestibule for a commanding view of the entire site.

HOLY OF HOLIES. Because the temple faces east, light flows into the Holy of Holies (innermost chamber) only in the early morning. Bring a flashlight at other times and be prepared for bats. A passageway leads north through the vestibule to an inner encircling wall; around the wall to the south is a **Nilometer.** Extraordinary carvings of Mandulis, Isis, Horus, and Osiris cover the outside walls.

NUBIAN SHRINE. Outside the huge fortress-like wall, the remains of a small shrine are visible to the southeast; the present structure is largely a reconstructed facade. The Nubian reliefs include pre-dynastic elephants, a large giraffe, and gazelles. The double-image technique, characteristic of Nubian art, is used to portray motion in some of the drawings. Carcasses of enormous desiccated fish are surrealistically scattered among the sand, as are disembodied stone heads. (*Temple open daily 7am-7pm. Admission E£12, students E£6.*)

TEMPLE OF KERTASSI. Slightly to the southwest of the Temple of Kalabsha are the ruins of the Temple of Kertassi. Two Hathor columns remain, as well as four columns with elaborate floral capitals and a lone monolithic architrave. A stone pathway leads up the hill behind and to the right of the Temple of Kertassi to the **Rock Temple, Beit el-Wali** (House of the Holy Man), rescued from the encroaching waters of Lake Nasser with the aid of the U.S. government. Ask the guard to let you in. One of many Nubian temples constructed by Ramses II, it features typically humble scenes of Ramses conquering foreigners, Ramses receiving prisoners, and a particularly understated scene of Ramses storming a castle half his size. Like a miniature Abu Simbel, this cave-temple was hewn from solid rock. Examine the bas-relief scenes closely: political and social history are portrayed in everything from chariot battles to squabbles over whose turn it is to walk the camel.

ABU SIMBEL أبوسمبل

Abu Simbel is 50km from the Sudanese border and a treacherous 297km south of Aswan. Due to political tensions, the Sudanese border is not passable and should not be approached by tourists for any reason. Ground transportation to the sight has been indefinitely shut down, but when ground transportation is up and running, two **buses** travel between Abu Simbel and Aswan (8am and 4pm; E£10 one-way, E£26 round-trip), and a third may begin service shortly. The morning bus gives you an ample 2½ hours to explore the temple. Buy your ticket at the Aswan bus station a day in advance; buy the return ticket on the way back. All buses are now A/C. **Airplane** fares will be discounted 50% until bus service resumes. Book a flight through **EgyptAir** (see **Getting Around,** p. 45) at least two days in advance. Airline buses meet you at Abu Simbel Airport and ferry you to and from the sight free of charge. Another option is to go by ferry from Aswan to Abu Simbel (3 days, 3 nights). (*Open 6am-5pm. Admission E£36, students E£19.50, including admission to Temple of Hathor. Flash photographers will be escorted out.*)

BIG HEADS (COLOSSI). The grandeur of the pharaonic monuments reaches its peak at Egypt's southernmost tip. Four 22m tall statues of **Ramses II**, carved out of a single slab of rock, greet the sunrise over Lake Nasser from the Great Temple of Abu Simbel. Ramses II had this grand sanctuary and the nearby Temple of Hathor built more than 3200 years ago to impress the Nubians with the power and glory of

MOVING A MOUNTAIN As the water level of Lake Nasser rose in the mid-60s, Egypt realized it would lose a large piece of its heritage. The United Nations and individual governments responded by funding a US$36 million relocation effort. The international concern was not entirely selfless: any country that assisted could claim half of the antiquities it helped to rescue and receive special archaeological concessions for future research. As a result, the Temple of Dendera is now enclosed in New York's Metropolitan Museum of Art, Debed Temple can be found in Madrid, and El-Lessiya was claimed by Turin. The first tentative plan was to raise each temple, remove the surrounding mountain, and encase the structures in protective concrete boxes. The boxes would slowly be jacked up, and a thick concrete base built beneath them. Another possibility was to build a second small dam around the temples to keep the water at bay. Both of these schemes were too expensive. To the chagrin of Egyptologists, the cheapest method was chosen—cutting the temples into pieces. The mountain had to be cut away, a job that endangered the sandstone statues below. Bulldozers covered the facade of Abu Simbel with sand, and the mound of sand was penetrated with a steel tunnel so that rescue workers could set up supportive steel bars inside. It took months to saw the temple apart and move the 3000 pieces to higher ground. When it was reassembled, hollow concrete domes were engineered to support the new artificial mountain.

Egyptian rule; Abu Simbel still serves its purpose, leaving no visitor unmoved. For a sneak preview of the site, look at the back of the Egyptian one-pound note.

THE GREAT TEMPLE OF ABU SIMBEL. This is Ramses II's masterpiece. The temple is supposedly dedicated to the god Ra-Hurakhti, but as in all of Ramses' monuments, the focus is clearly on the great pharaoh himself. The artwork depicts Ramses first as a great king, then as a servant of the gods, next as a companion of the gods, and finally, in the inner sanctuary, as a card-carrying deity. The entrance is guarded by three-and-a-half 20m tall statues of the king wearing the Old and New Kingdom versions of the crowns of Upper and Lower Egypt. An earthquake in 27 BCE crumbled the upper portion of one of the colossi. Modern engineers were unable to reconstruct the figure (and there were debates about whether they should—if it's been broken for 2000 years, don't fix it), so they left it in its faceless state. There are (much) smaller statues of mother Taya Weiss, wife Nefertari, and some of the kids, along with rows of **praying baboons.** Ancient Egyptians admired the baboons' habit of warming themselves in the sun's rays; they thought the beasts quite pious to pray to the sun god every dawn.

Farther into the temple are **antechambers** that once stored objects of worship. The walls show Ramses making sacrifices to the gods. In the inner sanctum, four seated statues facing the entrance depict Ramses and the gods Ra-Hurakhti, Amun, and Ptah. Originally encased in gold, the statues now wait with divine patience for February 22 and October 22, when the first rays of the sun reach 100m into the temple to bathe all except Ptah in light. February 21 was Ramses' birthday and October 21 his coronation date, but when the temple was moved, the timing of these natural feats shifted by one day (they just don't build temples like they used to). A door to the right of the temple's facade leads into the dome that supports the new and improved mountain.

TEMPLE OF HATHOR. Next door to Ramses' temple was one dedicated to his favorite wife, Nefertari, and dedicated to the young goddess Hathor. Six 10m statues of King Ramses and Queen Nefertari (as the goddess) adorn the facade. Along with the temple of Hatshepsut in West Thebes, this is one of the only temples in Egypt dedicated to a woman. Nevertheless, images of Ramses abound—scenes on the walls depict his coronation with the god Horus placing the crowns of Egypt on his head. The temple was constructed in the typical three-room style: the first chamber was open to the public, the second to nobles and priests, and the inner sanctuary only to the pharaoh and the high priest.

WESTERN DESERT OASES

The Western Desert (known as the Libyan Desert until WWII) is the largest and driest in the world, covering two-thirds of Egypt's area but supporting only 1% of its population. It boasts some of the highest temperatures on record, despite the fact that its series of oases—**Bahariyya, Farafra, Dakhla,** and **Kharga**—marks the trail of a prehistoric branch of the cool, wet Nile. Each oasis sits in a depression surrounded by an escarpment, the top of which marks the usual level of the desert floor. Because the depressions sit at or near sea level, subterranean water seeps through. A flow of water originates as the rains of equatorial Africa replenishes the wells and springs annually, taking thousands of years to journey north through underground fissures. The Romans were the first to irrigate the area by tapping deeper reserves with their waterwheels and aqueducts, known as **'Ain Romani.** The Egyptian government is following suit and spending vast amounts of resources on its **New Valley Project** to exploit underground water for the promotion of agriculture and the massive relocation of landless peasants from the Delta to the New Valley.

The desert oases are unique in that they can still be considered "off the beaten path." Few tourists travel through the area, keeping sights uncrowded and prices low. The best time to visit the oases is between October and April. It is not unusual for summer temperatures, especially at Dakhla or Kharga, to reach 52°C (126°F). Even at night, summer temperatures persist into the upper 20s (over 80°F)—and you won't find air-conditioning anywhere except Kharga, which makes it a good first or last stop. Kharga is also the only one of the oases that cashes traveler's checks, so have plenty of money on hand before you venture westward.

▐ GETTING AROUND

BY BUS. Daily buses run from the Al-Azhar bus station in Cairo to the oases. Inexpensive buses also run from Asyut to Kharga and Dakhla (see **Overland Travel Advisory,** p. 180). Bus travel between the oases requires a little more flexibility and patience than in the rest of Egypt. Published schedules are no more than rough guesses, and bus officials, locals, and passers-by all peddle wildly contradictory and inaccurate departure times. Ask as many people as possible, follow the consensus, arrive early, and bring your thumbs for twiddling. Your best information will come from the local tourist offices and bus officials.

BY TAXI OR SERVICE. *Service* taxis travel to all of the oases from Cairo, and to Kharga from Asyut. They sometimes offer a faster and more comfortable journey—check out what the vehicle looks like and how many people will be stuffed in. *Service* between all oases are affordable and often quicker than buses.

BY CAR. Car rental is a convenient and comfortable (albeit expensive) option for desert travel. A giant loop along the Great Desert Road and the Lower Nile Valley in either direction beginning in Cairo is about 1700km (over 1000mi.). Any car must be in top condition and fully outfitted for intense desert travel in order to survive the long, hot, poorly maintained roads. **Four-wheel drive** is highly recommended. Another option is a **trailer** (caravan); renting one can solve a lot of problems, including those of transporting food, water, and extra gas, and finding a comfortable place to sleep.

A number of caveats: first and foremost, it is always a long way between gas stations. While every oasis has at least one fuel pump, it is essential to buy jerry cans and fill them with enough gas to cover the vast distances between towns. A trailer guzzles huge quantities of fuel; bring enough extra to fill an entire tank. Several containers of potable water are also vital in case you get stranded; luckily, foreigners are prohibited from leaving the main road. Try to drive in the cool of the morning or in the late afternoon, but **never drive at night**—the chances of getting lost on unlit roads increase exponentially, and hidden potholes are especially lethal. Don't pull a Lawrence of Arabia: never drive in a sandstorm. If you do get caught in one, stop, turn the car's rear to the wind, and wait.

■ GETTING TO SLEEP

The best alternative to staying in hotels in the oases is **camping**. Most fertile land belongs to farmers who will usually permit you to pitch your tent. The ideal spot is just outside the main town of an oasis, where there is usually a small pool of water (ask the locals for the *bir*, or spring) and nothing but the sound of silence. The desert itself may be more comfortable, as cool temperatures and breezes carry away the mosquitoes and the sand makes a soft mattress. Sleeping on the dunes has its own set of dangers—you might be sharing the desert expanse with ticks, wasps, scorpions, cheetahs, foxes, mice, rats, amorous strangers, and tiny hedgehogs that roll into spiky balls when frightened. You might roll up yourself if you encounter one of the seven kinds of **poisonous snakes** in Egypt, among which is a family of lethal vipers. They rest under rocks and sand, coming out to drink at night. If you see snake tracks going in one direction, calmly go in the other. Common sense, a first aid kit, and a snake bite kit are recommended. If you prefer mosquito bites to reptile venom, each oasis has at least one cheap, bearable hotel or rest house.

■ GETTING SOMETHING TO EAT

Oasis groundwater tastes much better than that of the other Egyptian municipalities; while safer than water near the cities, this stuff can still ruin a trip. The main towns of all the oases have restaurants and markets where you can fill up on food, but don't expect variety or refinement. The best meals are at people's homes— with a winning smile and a little luck, you can taste for yourself.

PRACTICAL WARNINGS

WOMEN TRAVELERS. Women should follow certain guidelines when swimming in springs. In isolated springs unfrequented by locals, female travelers are not likely to be bothered. The same goes for pools cordoned off and connected to tourist rest houses. Women should not, however, enter pools where men are already bathing. Sometimes there is a separate pool where women bathe, provided they wear a *galabiyya* (loose-fitting robe). Local women bathe separately from men, often in the evening. Women traveling without men should not embark on overnight desert excursions unless pre-arranged by a tourist official. Even then, care and common sense are key. Solo women heading for the oases should be prepared to deal with harassment. For more on what women can expect traveling in Egypt, see **Women Travelers**, p. 46.

TAXES, TOURISM, AND TRUST. The requirement for foreigners to obtain permission to visit the oases was lifted in 1985-86. Despite what out-of-date sources may tell you, you need only flash a **passport** at the numerous military checkpoints. In Dakhla, Kharga, or Farafra, you will be asked to pay a one-time E£5 **tourism development tax** by a tourist officer or by an employee of your hotel. Keep the receipt as proof or you may have to pay again.

The Western Desert has been attracting an increasing number of visitors with its traditional village lifestyle, stunning landscapes, and low prices; Bahariyya in particular is seeing an exponential increase in visitors thanks to the recently discovered Roman ruins and "Valley of the Mummies" (for more information on these, see **Excavators are Standing By**, p. 225, and **Tomb Much of a Good Thing**, p. 225). With this sudden bumper crop of tourists comes the slowly creeping disease that the smell of tourist money inevitably brings. In each oasis you will find people whose English is good, whose knowledge of the area is fair, and whose sense of capitalism is extraordinary. They are often friendly and helpful, but their assistance has a bloated price tag trailing behind. For the best information, head for the New Valley's **tourist officials:** Ibrahim M. Hassan in Kharga, 'Umar Ahmed in Dakhla, and Dr. Muhammad Ra'afat Amin in Farafra. They all will answer your questions in excellent English and arrange for fairly priced guides and transportation; without them, you are at the mercy of the wolves. Any assistance you receive from a tourist official should be free of charge.

BAHARIYYA OASIS الواحات البحرية

The land turns a deep shade of red as you approach Bahariyya, thanks to the vast deposits of iron that are quarried in an immense mine just off the highway, 40km before Bawiti. This small oasis, 330km south of Cairo, has been a stopover for caravans traveling between the Nile Valley and the rest of North Africa since pharaonic times, when merchants used to load their donkeys with wine from El-Qasr (the present-day town of Bawiti). In later centuries, Bahariyya enthusiastically welcomed the Mecca-bound pilgrims, who would often join the traders on their trans-desert trek. Today, the only "pilgrims" in Bahariyya are the caravans of rip-roaring European adventurers gallivanting through the oasis in Land Rovers (because of its relative proximity to Cairo, Bahariyya attracts many visitors who crave a few days in the desert). Factor in the opening of several Roman-era sights in the area in October 1999, in addition to growing interest in the recently unearthed "Valley of the Mummies" (see **Tomb Much of a Good Thing**, p. 225), and it's easy to see why the constant traffic has made Bahariyya far more commercial and cutthroat than the other oases. Unfortunately, many of Bahariyya's ancient ruins are scanty and largely inaccessible. The nearby gardens, springs, and desert offer some relief, but not enough to make anyone stay longer than necessary. Conveniences like food stores, a market, coffee shops, and three gas stations make this oasis a viable (and unavoidable) stop for those heading to Farafra.

🛈 ORIENTATION AND PRACTICAL INFORMATION

The Bahariyya Oasis is linked to Cairo by a decently paved road that heads past the Pyramids of Giza, then turns southwest across the desert to the town of **Bawiti.**

Buses: The bus ticket and reservation office is in a green shed next to the telephone office (open 7am-noon and roughly 8-11pm). Buses from **Cairo** to Bahariyya leave from Mahattat Turgoman by Ramses Station (4hr.; 7, 9am, 3, 6pm; E£12.50). All 7am and 6pm buses continue to **Farafra**. Get there early to secure a seat. There are also daily buses to **Cairo** (5hr.; 7, 11:30am, 3pm, midnight; E£12.50).

Minibuses: Minibuses run daily between Bahariyya and **Cairo's** Sayyidna Zeinab bus station (5hr., E£11). Minibuses leave when full.

Gas Stations: One behind police station, 2 more on main road out of town toward Cairo.

Tourist Office: (tel. 80 22 22), 1st floor of the government compound. The green-and-red sign is on your right as you walk into town from the east. Staffed by city council member Muhammad 'Abd el-Qader. Open daily 8am-2pm. After 2pm, look for Mr. 'Abd el-Qader in the lobby of the Paradise Hotel.

Currency Exchange: The **National Bank for Development** is next to the post office. Exchanges cash only. Open Su-Th 8am-2pm.

Post Office: 2 buildings down from the government compound as you move toward Farafra. Limited services. Open Sa-Th 8:30am-2pm.

Telephone Office: In a driveway 10m off the main road, on the side of a building beside the government compound. They will deny having international service, but you can call abroad using MCI or AT&T, both of which first require a local call: within town, dial 0184 and the operator will connect you (3min. to Cairo 75pt). Open 8am-midnight.

Telephone Code: 018.

🏠🍴 ACCOMMODATIONS AND FOOD

Ahmad's Safari Camp is 4km south from the center of town. The massive grapevine-covered veranda, clean common bathrooms, good food, and free rides to and from town sweeten the bitter taste of isolation (bare-bones huts E£5 per person; concrete cabanas with breakfast E£12 per person; deluxe, white-domed gazebos with shower and breakfast E£40). Standing with your back to the city council building and the tourist office, head down the street to the white-domed **Hotel Alpenblick**, 250m past the "cheapest shop in town" sign. Mahmoud, the general manager, organizes trips to the hot springs. Lodgings here are a bit nicer than other options in Bawiti but you don't quite get your money's worth: rooms have carpets and fans, but bathrooms are not too spectacular (singles E£20; doubles E£35, with bath E£46; triples E£53/69; breakfast included). The government-run **Paradise Hotel** is across from the telephone office on the main square. The basic, shared rooms are clean, but the common bathrooms are rather grimy (E£3.50 per person, with breakfast E£5).

There are only a few restaurants in Bawiti. **Bayoumi's Popular Restaurant** is next to the government compound, across from the police station, just off the main road to Cairo. Ask in advance about prices (full meal around E£8, Stella E£5). **Paradise Restaurant, Restaurant Rashid, El-Gahsh,** and the kitchen at the **Alpenblick** all offer standard meals for E£6-8. El-Gahsh also serves morning *fuul* and falafel.

SIGHTS

Hotel managers run group tours of all the area's springs and sights (no more than E£10 per person with a six-person group, less with a larger group). You can hire a taxi through the tourist office or on your own (E£30 for the entire day, after another entire day of bargaining).

> ▌ **EXCAVATORS ARE STANDING BY.** Beginning in October 1999, travelers in the Bahariyya area will be able to visit the following sights, which are currently being excavated and prepared for visitors: the **Temple of Alexander the Great** (the only one of its kind in Egypt), the Greco-Roman spring **'Ain el-Meftela,** and the **ancient tombs** of Amenhotep I, Huy, Banntiu, and Zed Amun (E£40, students E£20). For more information on recent discoveries in Bahariyya, check out Dr. Zahi Hawass's *Valley of the Mummies,* published by AUC Press.

HOT SPRINGS. Bahariyya's hot springs give you the chance to get in touch with your inner lobster. **'Ain Bishmu,** a local favorite between the border of the old city and Bawiti, holds steady at a lukewarm 30°C. The less crowded **Bir er-Ramla** (2km out of Bawiti along a village track parallel to the road to Cairo) features a 45°C hot spring. Men can bathe here in shorts, but women must be fully clothed and may only swim later at night. The cold (25°C) and hot (48°C) springs at **Bir el-Mattar,** 8km southeast of Bawiti, pour out of a viaduct into a small cement pool (taxis E£10 round-trip). Men bathe here by day, women by night. The bumpy "road" to Bir el-Mattar (really just a desert track—drivers beware) continues southeast through the desert to **Bir el-Ghaba,** 17km from Bawiti, with both a hot and cold spring in another sumptuous oasis landscape. Both men and women can swim in this deserted spot (taxi E£25 round-trip). Less appealing but closer is **Bir el-Ghilis,** a steamy, pump-activated spring only a 10-minute walk out of town (taxis E£5 round-trip).

EL-QASR. Ruined chapels, tombs, and temples from the 26th dynasty cluster in **El-Qasr,** Bawiti's western sibling and the capital of Bahariyya in pharaonic times. *(Inquire at the tourist office to obtain permission to visit these locked sights.)*

> # TOMB MUCH OF A GOOD THING
> In June 1999, a team of archaeologists led by Dr. Zahi Hawass announced the discovery of an enormous ancient burial ground in the area of Bawiti, the main city in the Bahariyya Oasis. Fifty mummies were unearthed in four rooms of the 6mi. long cemetery, which probably dates back almost 2000 years. The site supposedly contains more than 10,000 mummies, making it the largest burial ever uncovered and earning it the title **"Valley of the Mummies."** Almost as remarkable as the quantity of the haul is its quality: some of the mummies (who were mostly wealthy aristocrats and rulers) wear gold masks and still have visible depictions of Egyptian deities on their chests. Others are buried in a more typically Roman style, with bodies coated in plaster or covered with linen and laid to rest in terra cotta sarcophagi marked with realistic representations of the deceased's face.

MUSEUMS. The **Antiquities Museum** is where some of the finds from the surrounding ruins, including pottery shards and five mummies, are kept. Ask the Inspector of Antiquities to dig up the key to the painted, subterranean tomb dating from the pharaonic era. Nature is Bahariyya's real attraction, but the **Oasis Heritage Museum** in Bawiti is also worth a visit. Talented local artist Mahmoud Eed creates life-like clay figurines to populate the dioramas depicting traditional oasis life. *(Antiquities: 500m out of town, on a dirt road that turns right off the road towards Cairo. Ask at the tourist office to arrange a visit. Open Sa-Th 8am-1:30pm. Free. Oasis: 900m out of town, on the left heading towards Cairo. Free, but contributions welcome.)*

BETWEEN THE BAHARIYYA AND FARAFRA OASES

*If you want to arrange a **tour** from Bahariyya, Muhammad 'Abd el-Qader (at the tourist office or Paradise Hotel) is helpful. The cheaper option is to organize an overnight trip to the desert with Muhammad Ra'afat Amin in Farafra (see below). If you can't put together a posse, you can still see the area from the public **bus** (sit on the side to the right as you face the bus head-on). Everywhere but El-Wadi Oasis can be reached by regular car, but a 4x4 is much more fun. For overnight tours including food, a **pickup truck taxi** should not exceed E£60-80, a more comfortable **Peugeot** E£70-90, and a **4x4** E£150-175. Summer is the cheapest time to go, but the hardest time to find riding partners. Drivers will begin by demanding E£800 for trips to Farafra, so bargain hard.*

The 183km long road from Bawiti to the Farafra Oasis runs through spectacular canyons, wind-blown mesas, and rugged desertscapes from which precious gemstones were exported during the reign of Ramses II. The eastern and western escarpments of the Bahariyya depression meet at a point about 60km south of Bawiti, and the road winds through this pass and onto a brief plateau before plummeting into the Farafra Oasis.

Leaving Bawiti, you'll first pass through the **Black Desert,** known for its dark mesas and crumbly flats peppered with tufts of dry desert grass. The idyllic oasis village of **El-Hayiz** (E£50 per truckload as a daytrip from Bawiti) lies 5km off the main road to Farafra, 40km from Bawiti. Gardens and a spring make this simple village a nice spot to camp overnight and enjoy fresh watermelon or apricots for breakfast. **Crystal Mountain** (really just a hill by the roadside with some quartz deposits) rises about 100km from Bawiti. Farther along is **Es-Sillim Pass,** revealing a view of the escarpment cascading into the distance of the desert. The palm trees and small, desolate spring of the empty **El-Wadi Oasis** (the only place you'll need a 4x4 to reach) are about 140km from Bawiti. The oasis is striking amidst towering dunes and grazing gazelles. About 45km outside Farafra, the black buttes suddenly give way to the **White Desert,** where spooky fungoid rock formations stand stark white in daytime, glow shades of bashful fuchsia by dusk, and turn orange by dawn. Leaving the White Desert via the main road, you'll also pass a **cold spring.**

FARAFRA OASIS الواحة الفرافرة

Farafra claims an impressive 16% of Egypt's entire territory, and borders both Libya and Sudan. Three years ago, the area was home to a mere 5000 people, but immigration has swelled the population to over 14,000. Province president Muhammad Ra'afat Amin has done much to redefine the region's image: hotels have been privatized, over 60,000 acres of land have been reclaimed through a massive irrigation effort, and an airport is in the works.

⊠ ORIENTATION AND PRACTICAL INFORMATION. All buses and *service* arrive and depart from the **cafe** on the Bahariyya-Dakhla road. **Buses** run daily to **Dakhla** (5hr., 2:30am, E£15) and **Bahariyya** (2½hr., 11am and 11pm, E£12), continuing on to **Cairo** (8hr., E£25). However, **minibuses** and **service taxis** are the best way to get to **Dakhla.** Early morning is best; ask around the night before to secure a seat (4hr., E£15). Buses from Cairo leave Mahattat Turgoman near Ramses Station en route to Farafra (8hr., 7am and 6pm, E£25) with a stop in Bahariyya. A **gas station and repair shop** is on the main road, 500m down from the bus stop. *Let's Go* does not recommend **hitchhiking.**

All services are on or just off the Bahariyya-Dakhla road. As you head toward Bahariyya, you'll pass the **police station** and **post office** (open Su-Th 8am-2pm) on your left, followed by the **telephone center,** which offers dubious international service (open 8am-midnight). Next to the post office is the **city hall,** where dedicated province president Dr. Muhammad Ra'afat Amin will help you organize excursions in the area. If he's not there, find him at his massive hilltop house 2km from town—ask his assistant to take you, or hop a taxi for E£2 (office open Sa-Th 8am-2pm).

■■ **ACCOMMODATIONS AND FOOD.** The **El-Bedouiya Hotel,** 750m from the bus stop in the direction of Bahariyya, has clean rooms and toilets and beautiful Bedouin architecture. Don't miss the rooftop terrace (singles E£10; doubles E£30; quads E£40). The government-run **Tourist Rest House,** 1½km from the bus stop (ask to be let off there), also offers accommodations starting at E£15. **Camping** in the nearby desert or at **Bir Sitta** (6km from town) might make for a more organic experience, but bring plenty of insect repellent. Also check your shoes and pants before getting dressed—scorpions and huge biting ants thrive in these parts; don't let them thrive in yours. Always let Dr. Muhammad Ra'afat Amin know your travel plans. The huts of several budding gourmands are clustered around the bus station, and the **restaurant** at the El-Bedouiya offers tasty eats for around E£10.

■ **SIGHTS.** The free **art museum,** conveniently situated across from the Military Intelligence Office in town, displays expressive sculptures and paintings depicting life in Farafra by the talented local artist Badr. The hot **Bir Sitta** (Well #6), 6km west of town, is an idyllic spot to swim and camp (transportation about E£5 per carload). Sometime in the next few years, a 150-person vacation village will spring up next to Bir Sitta, most likely squeezing this area out of the budget traveler's range. If you're fed up with the flatulatory scent of the sulphur wells, head to **Birkt Abu Noss,** 15km outside of town, to cool off. This lake is 2km off the road to Bahariyya; turn left just before the checkpoint.

WHITE DESERT (SAQQARA BEATA). The White Desert (40km from Farafra) has overnight camping and breathtaking views. A typical tour of the desert from Farafra (the best starting point for a trip to the White Desert) passes through both verdant **Wadi Henis** and the village of **Karaween,** which has marvelous springs and gazelles. *(An average overnight trip in a 4x4 from Farafra should cost about E£300 per carload. If you don't mind being stranded in the desert for several hours on the way back, take the 11am bus to Bahariyya (E£24) and tell them to drop you off in the White Desert.)*

DAKHLA OASIS الواحات الد اخلة

Even the briefest trip through the desert oases will lead you to discover that each oasis is lacking in its own special way. The exception is Dakhla (known as the "pink oasis" for the surrounding pink cliffs), the most distant oasis from Cairo. Bubbling 320km from Farafra and 190km from Kharga, Dakhla delivers on every account: affordable eats, affable hoteliers, and available sights, all amid unbelievable Mamluke architecture. The work of the 75,000 current residents of Dakhla is equally mind-boggling: Dakhlans have reclaimed this recalcitrant wasteland, planting peanuts and rice and gradually introducing more fragile crops that consume the desert in an ever-widening wave of greenery. The New Valley Project may have rendered the urban center of Kharga unappealing to visitors, but something of the opposite has occurred in Dakhla: a mix of Nubians, Sudanese, Libyans, and Berbers peacefully inhabit this oasis together. Nowhere else in Egypt do you get more paradise for your pound than in this pink oasis.

EGYPT

⚡ ORIENTATION

The Dakhla Oasis is bounded by **West Mawhub** (80km west of Mut) on one side and the fertile **Tineida** (40km east of Mut) on the other. Cultivated regions also dot the well-paved main highway; the most appealing of these are **El-Qasr** (30km west of Mut), **Balaat** (30km east of Mut), and **Bashendi** (35km east of Mut). The capital of the Dakhla Oasis is **Mut** (pronounced "moot"), named for the Egyptian mother goddess and wife of Amun (see **Meet the Gods**, p. 51). Mut has two focal points: **Tahrir Square**, at the intersection of New Valley St. and the Kharga-Farafra Highway (southeast-northwest), and **New Mosque Square**, 1km south on New Valley St.

⚡ PRACTICAL INFORMATION

Airplanes: The **airport**, 10km south of Mut, is served by **EgyptAir** (tel 82 20 53/54), which has an office in the courtyard opposite the police station in town (open Sa-Th 8:30am-2pm and 5-9pm). Flights to **Cairo** (W at 8pm, E£555).

Buses and Service: Buses and *service* depart from **Mut Station** (tel. 82 15 38), in New Mosque Sq. **Local buses** go to **Balaat** and **Bashendi** (8:30am, 2:30, 5, 7, 8, 10pm; return to Mut 1hr. later; 50pt) and **El-Qasr** (6am, 2, 6pm; return to Mut 2hr. later; 50pt). **Intercity buses** are not very reliable, but supposedly they travel to: **Cairo** (13hr.; 6am, 6, 7, 8pm; E£43); **Farafra** (5hr., 6am and 6pm on Cairo bus); **Kharga** (2½hr.; 6, 8:30am, 2:30, 5, 7, 8, 10pm; E£7); and **Asyut** (6hr.; 6, 8:30am, 5, 7pm; E£17). Bus schedules change frequently; ask the tourist office for updates. It's more reliable to take a *service* early in the morning. **Service taxis** and **minibuses** go to **Kharga** (3hr., 6am or when it fills up, E£7) and **Farafra** (5hr., 6am or when it fills up, E£15).

Taxis: Taxis offer sightseeing tours (1 day E£40, trips to eastern or western Dakhla E£8-10). Ask in New Mosque Sq. Covered pickup trucks shuttle frequently between Tahrir Sq. and **El-Qasr** and between the hospital stand and **Balaat** (75pt-E£1 each way), **Bashendi** (75pt-E£1 each way), and **El-Qasr** (E£1). The early bird catches the truck.

Tourist Information Office: There are 2 offices. The **new office** (tel. 82 16 86 or 82 15 85) is 400m away from Tahrir Sq. on the road to Farafra, across the street from Abu Muhammad Restaurant. The **old office** (tel. 82 04 07) is across from the mosque in New Mosque Sq., in the same building as the Tourist Rest House. The knowledgeable 'Omar Ahmed speaks English and will help arrange transportation. Feel free to reach him at home (tel. 94 07 82). Both offices open Su-Th 8am-2pm and 8-11pm.

Currency Exchange: Misr Bank (tel. 82 00 63), in Tahrir Sq., near the police station. Changes traveler's checks and cash. Open Su-Th 8am-2pm and 6-9pm, and sporadically Sa 8am-2pm for changing money.

Gas Station: On the outskirts of eastern Mut, on the left side of the road to Kharga. Another station is west of Mut, 1km from Tahrir Sq. Both charge 90pt per liter and are open 24hr.

Police: Tel. 82 15 00, in Tahrir Sq.

Pharmacies: There are 7 pharmacies in Mut, 3 of which are on New Mosque St. Most are open daily 8am-2pm and occasionally at night.

Hospitals: The **main hospital** (tel. 82 15 55 or 82 13 32) is 1km from Tahrir Sq., towards Kharga. Smaller hospitals are located in each village.

Post Office: One in New Mosque Sq., another on El-Ganeim St., around the corner from the telephone office. Both open Su-Th 8am-2pm.

Telephones: From New Mosque Sq., walk east along 23 July St. to Anwar Restaurant, then veer left toward the red-and-white tower about 30m ahead on your left. Open 24hr. For **international service**, try the 2 private telephone offices on the Kharga Hwy. or the office by New Mosque Sq.

Telephone Code: 092.

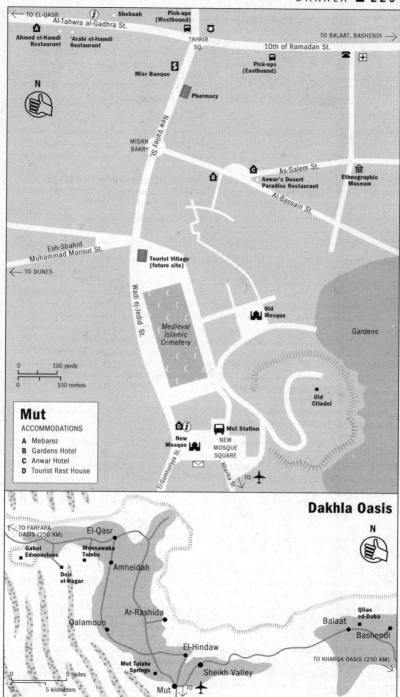

← TO EL-QASR

Al-Tahwra al-Gadhra St.

Shehaab

Pick-ups (Westbound)

TAHRIR SQ.

TO BALAAT, BASHENDI →

10th of Ramadan St.

Ahmed el-Hamdi Restaurant

'Arabi el-Hamdi Restaurant

Pick-ups (Eastbound)

Misr Banque

Pharmacy

N

New Valley St.

MIDAN BAKRY

As-Salem St.

Anwar's Desert Paradise Restaurant

B

C

Ethnographic Museum

Al-Bassain St.

Esh-Shahid Muhammad Mansur St.

← TO DUNES

Tourist Village (future site)

Wadi el-Jedid St.

Old Mosque

Gardens

0   100 yards
0   100 meters

Medieval Islamic Cemetery

Mut

ACCOMMODATIONS

A Mebarez
B Gardens Hotel
C Anwar Hotel
D Tourist Rest House

Old Citadel

New Mosque

D

Mut Station

NEW MOSQUE SQUARE

El-Gomhoriya St.

Khariba St.

TO ✈

EGYPT

Dakhla Oasis

← TO FARFARA OASIS (250 KM)

N

El-Qasr

Gabal Edmonstone

Mousawaka Tombs

Deir el-Hagar

Amheidah

Ar-Rashida

Qalamoun

Qilae ed-Daba

Balaat

Bashendi

El-Hindaw

Mut Talata Springs

Sheikh Valley

TO KHARGA OASIS (250 KM)

Mut   TO ✈

0   5 miles
0   5 kilometers

ACCOMMODATIONS AND FOOD

The balcony and cool lounges of this newly opened **Anwar Hotel** (tel. 82 00 70), at the intersection of Es-Salem and El-Bassain St., are a welcome addition to Mut's budget accommodation scene, though there are no private bathrooms (singles E£15; doubles E£30). **Gardens Hotel** (tel. 82 15 77), 20m down a dirt road from Anwar's Desert Paradise Restaurant and Hotel, has a pleasant garden and even more pleasant management. Stick to the breezy rooms with fans unless you don't mind the noise that accompanies a rooftop bed (singles E£12, with bath E£15; doubles E£16/20). The 4-story mustard-yellow building that call itself **Mebarez** (tel. 82 15 44), 800m from Tahrir Sq. on the road to Farafra (in the same building as the Tourist Office in New Mosque Sq.), is more upscale than the Gardens but about the same in quality. It specializes in housing large European tour groups in winter. All rooms have fans and balconies (singles E£28, with bath and A/C E£44; doubles E£52/58; lunch E£13.55, dinner E£14.70). The recently renovated **Tourist Rest House** (tel. 82 16 86), offers clean rooms and mediocre bathrooms for E£10 per person, including access to the kitchen.

Dakhla has the best food of all the desert oases, though everything's relative, of course. There are two **Hamdi Restaurants,** both located just before the Mebarez Hotel, and both serving chicken and meat meals for E£10. The branch owned by 'Arabi el-Hamdi serves up delicious pancakes for E£2. Around the corner from the Garden Hotel is **Anwar's Desert Paradise Restaurant** (full meal E£9). **Shehaab,** along the highway just west of New Valley St., is a local favorite (full meal E£5).

SIGHTS

There's little of interest to see in **Mut,** but the oasis capital is a great jumping off point both for **Western Dakhla,** which includes the village of El-Qasr and surrounding archaeological digs, and for **Eastern Dakhla,** which includes the villages of Balaat and Bashendi. For transportation options to these regions, see **Dakhla: Practical Information** (p. 228). In the cooler months, biking to some spots is feasible, although you'll still need to bring plenty of water—and then some.

WESTERN DAKHLA

Hire a pickup for a day (E£40) or leapfrog on the pickup truck taxis that circle the sites. Ask the Dakhla tourist office for help on tours, itineraries, and prices.

QALAMOUN. The distinctly medieval village of Qalamoun was the capital of Dakhla in Mamluke times. In the Islamic era, Qalamoun functioned as an administrative center; its inhabitants today claim Turkish and Mamluke ancestry. The town's name has two possible translations: "Amun's pens" (*qalam* means pen), for the scribes who lived here; or "Amun's citadel" (*qala'a* means fortress), as Qalamoun's panoramic hilltop perch offers both military and climactic defense. Near the center of town is an Ayyubid **mosque,** which can be reached by winding through the maze of narrow passages and traditional mud-brick houses. (*6km west of Mut is the Bedouin village of El-Douhous, located where road splits for 25km before joining up again. The left fork takes you to Qalamoun.*)

EL-GEDIDA. El-Gedida ("New Town," so named because it's only 300 years old) is known for its **arabesque factory.** In cooperation with 'Ain Shams University and the German Embassy, locals make decorated woodwork with palm tree branches. For more delicious handiwork, sample the town's sweet harvests: apricots in May, mangoes in late July, and dates in October. (*5km past Qalamoun, on the road out of Mut. Factory open Sa-Th 8am-2pm. Free.*)

MOUSAWAKA TOMBS. Although these tombs (dating from the first and 2nd centuries CE) are closed and will continue to be so for some time, a worker will let you take a look at the mosaic-covered tomb. Nowhere in Egypt can you get more up-close and personal with a mummy than here. (*3km west of El-Gedida, on the left.*)

DEIR EL-HAGAR. Half the fun of this Roman temple is the road leading up to it, which twists and turns around a small village and passes three Roman remains before leading up to a ridge from which Deir el-Hagar can be seen (the temple is still a 1½km dirt trek away). Dedicated to the Theban triad of Mut, Amun, and Khonsu, the temple was built in the first century BCE during the reign of Nero, and added upon by his immediate successors. The ruins have been almost completely devoured by the sand dunes, but the government has gone to great lengths to reclaim it. Ask to see the small exhibition by the entrance. *(The ridge is 2km past the Mousawaka Tombs. Open daily 8am-5pm. Admission E£20, students E£10.)*

EL-QASR القصر

The most edifying daytrip from Dakhla is El-Qasr, a twisty 32km from Mut on the northern fork. This charming contemporary town was built in and around the substantial remains of Dakhla's medieval Islamic capital. A model of comfortable architecture, its mud buildings remain cool in summer and warm in winter. The **old village** of El-Qasr lies 400m to the north of the main road through the new village. On the main road at the western edge of town, there is a large **map** of the village. Within the old village, arrows direct you to the sights. The **El-Qasr Rest House** is located on the main road, at the turn-off to the old village. It serves simple meals of cheese and omelettes in summer and a more complete menu in winter (full meal E£6). Cold drinks and ice cream are available. There is also a market, 30m from the hotel on the same side of the road. Facing the market are a **telephone office** (open 24hr.) and **medical clinic**, 50m towards Mut.

OLD VILLAGE SIGHTS. The **Minaret of Nasr ed-Din** is the only extant part of an 11th-century Ayyubid mosque. A 19th-century mosque surrounds the old tower. Down the gnarled alleys north of the minaret stands **Qasr Madrasa**, an intact two-story mud-brick building thought to have been either an Ayyubid schoolhouse or the entertainment hall of an Ottoman palace; villagers later used the building as a courtroom. Many of the doorways of the old village are adorned with ornate wooden lintels that reveal the name of the owner, builder, and carpenter as well as the date of construction. Bits of a pharaonic arch and a Roman doorway hint at El-Qasr's pre-Islamic past. On the southern fringes of the old town you can see a waterwheel and a functioning **pottery works,** where villagers churn out everything from ashtrays to chamberpots.

EASTERN DAKHLA

BALAAT. In the crowded old section of Islamic **Balaat** (population 5000), long, dark passageways burst into a courtyard with palm fronds and grape vines. These pathways were built with ceilings as a defense tactic—during invasions, the enemies' camels and horses could not fit through the alleys. Balaat has a reputation for being the cleanest village in the area, as its roads are strewn with bright orange sand a few times each day. Ask to see the **mayor's house,** with its assembly courtyard, speech balcony, and ornate, Ottoman-wrought iron lamps and bedframes.

QILAE ED-DABA. Dakhla's pharaonic governors were buried in these red-brick tombs during the 6th dynasty. A team of French archaeologists has revealed several rather bizarre inverted step pyramids as well as a mummified governor. *(1km from the official bus stop, behind Balaat and just northeast of the main road. Ask locals for El-Maqabr el-Fara'oniya. Open daily 8am-6pm. Admission E£20, with ISIC E£10.)*

BASHENDI. Though less picturesque than its younger brother Balaat, Bashendi sits atop a recently discovered temple and various Roman-era tombs that make a visit well worthwhile. The large stone **Tomb of Ketenus** contains six rooms, including one decorated with scenes of a 2nd-century Roman mingling with the gods Min and Seth. Before you can mingle with the ghosts of Romans past, you'll need to get the key to the tombs, which is held by a villager whom the locals will look for upon request. Next door to the Tomb of Ketenus is the prominent **Tomb of Bashendi,**

which consists of a distinctly Islamic domed roof atop a Roman foundation. The tomb commemorates the village's beloved namesake; you might join locals who decorate the inside of the holy man's tomb with *henna*. If the guard isn't around to open the tombs, another villager will do the honors. There are also a number of hot and cold springs to which residents can direct you, though local leaders would rather lead you to the Bashendi **carpet works,** where youths weave beautiful rugs for E£100 and up. *(5km east of Kilae ed-Daba, 40km from Mut. Ask locals for* El-Maqabr er-Romaniya. *Admission to Tomb of Ketenus E£16, students E£8.)*

KHARGA OASIS الواحة الخارجة

Kharga is Egypt's most effective attempt at a desert boomtown and the capital of the New Valley Province *(El-Wadi el-Gideed).* It is also the most accessible and developed of all the oases in the Western Desert. Little is known about Kharga's early pharaonic history, although it must have been agriculturally productive—its hieroglyphic name is *hibis,* or "plow." It became prosperous during Roman times due to its proximity to trade routes, including Darb El-Arba'een (Forty Days Road), between Egypt and Sudan. Beginning in the 4th century, Kharga became a large Christian settlement and center for monasticism, where major figures (including Bishop Nastorius, former Patriarch of Constantinople) were exiled by religious and political rivals. The oasis's function as a distant exile continued into the 20th century, when Nasser banished Mustafa Amin, founder of *Al-Akhbar* (Egypt's largest circulating daily), to Kharga after the 1952 revolution.

When the New Valley Project began in earnest in the early 1980s, the town again prospered. The cookie-cutter apartment-filled streets of Kharga are largely lifeless and boring by Egyptian standards, but the ruins on its periphery astound. Welcome relief from Kharga's New Town can be found in the narrow alleyways of the Old Town, where locally-made ceramics and carpets are available in the *souq.* Kharga is the closest oasis to the Nile Valley, a mere 240km from Asyut. A newly paved road heads south from Kharga, skirting dunes and small oases on the way to **Bulaq** (15km south), **Baris** (90km south), and smaller settlements in between.

▶ TRANSPORTATION

Airplanes: EgyptAir (tel. 92 16 95), in Governorate, 2 blocks north of Misr Bank intersection on Nasser St. (open Sa-Th 8am-2pm). **Airport** turn-off is 3km north of town on Asyut Rd., then another 2km southeast. Flights directly to **Cairo** (Su 8:25am, E£450) or to Cairo via **Dakhla** (W 7:40am, E£450). Minibus or taxi from Showla Sq. E£5.

Buses: Intercity buses arrive and depart from Showla Sq. to: **Cairo** (12hr.; 6, 10am, 9, 10pm; E£37); **Asyut** (3hr., 4 per day, E£8); and **Dakhla** (2½hr., 7am and noon, E£7). **Local buses** to **Baris** (3hr.; 1, 3, 7am, noon, 2:30pm; E£1.60) and **Dush** (1½hr., 6 and 11am, E£2). Schedules change frequently; check tourist office for updates.

Taxis and Minibuses: Catch **service taxis** and **minibuses** in Showla Sq. Fairly frequent service to **Asyut** (3½hr., E£9), where you can transfer to a Peugeot for **Cairo** (5hr., E£15). Occasional service to **Dakhla** (E£8). "Special" (unshared) to Dakhla (E£56). Very irregular service to **Baris** (E£1-2). Hiring a *service* or minibus to Baris for the day costs E£50. Within town, **covered truck taxis** scurry along En-Nabawi St. from Showla Sq., turn up Nasser St., and head for the tourist office at the northern end (10pt).

▶ ORIENTATION AND PRACTICAL INFORMATION

Gamal 'Abd en-Nasser Street runs north-south and is bisected in the middle by **En-Nada Street,** which heads west to Dakhla. At this intersection you'll find Cinema Hibis, the **Misr Bank** (traveler's check exchange, Visa cash advances; open Su-Th in summer 8:30am-2pm and 6-9pm; in winter 8:30am-2pm and 5-8pm), and the **police station** (tel. 122). The main branch of the **post office** is just off Nasser St., behind Cinema Hibis (**EMS** service; open Sa-Th 8am-2pm; smaller branch in Showla Sq.). At the northernmost end of Nasser St., just before it heads off to the ruins and

Asyut, stand the rest house and **tourist office.** The resourceful Mr. Ibrahim Hassan, regional director of oasis tourism, will make your stay in Kharga the best possible by smoothing over any bumps with his excellent English (open Su-Th 8:30am-3pm and daily 8pm-midnight). The **passport office** faces the tourist office (open Sa-Th 7:30am-3:30pm), and the **tourist police** (tel. 92 13 67) are next door (open 24hr.). Grab a **pickup taxi** (10pt) to get to this part of town.

The southern end of Nasser St. intersects **En-Nabawi el-Mohandis Street,** which runs east-west. This street curves slightly northeast to **Showla Square,** where you'll find the *service* taxi and minibus station, the *souq,* and the Old Town. The main **hospital** (tel. 122 or 92 07 77) is off Nasser St., north of En-Nabawi St. (open 24hr). **Aleman Pharmacy** sits one block east of Showla Sq. (open daily 8am-3pm and 6pm-midnight). Get connected at **Computer Technology Center,** on En-Nabawi St. (E£2 per 3min.; open Sa-Th 10am-2pm). **Ed-Dawati Telephone Central,** in Showla Sq., has the most reliable international service in town (open Sa-Th 8am-3pm and 5-11pm). Kharga's **telephone code** is 092.

ACCOMMODATIONS

In summer, splurge for a room with a fan or you'll drown in a pool of hot sweat, a practice *Let's Go* emphatically refuses to recommend. **Waha Hotel** (tel. 92 03 93), on En-Nabawi St., is a 15-minute walk from Showla Sq., near grocery stores and restaurants. The rooms and balconies are simple and tidy, with crisp linen and clean baths. Common bathrooms are strictly cold water affairs (singles E£7, with hot water, bath, and fan E£15; doubles E£14-20; bare necessity quads E£20). **El-Gomhoureah Rest House** (tel. 92 12 06), sits to the left of the blue Police Officer's Club, 200m down the street directly across from the tourist office. It boasts a lounge, garden, and tastefully decorated rooms (E£20 doubles only) with fan or air conditioning and lots of light. One block from the telecom tower, **Hamad Allah Hotel** (tel. 92 06 38), on El-'Adel St., features clean doubles with refrigerator, air conditioning, TV, bath, and towels (1 person E£36; 2 people E£54; lunch E£15, dinner E£17). The villas at **Tourist Office Rest House** (tel. 92 12 06), directly behind tourist office on Nasser St., come complete with living rooms, TV, fully equipped kitchens, and air conditioning—ideal for groups of four or more (4-person villas E£35; 9-person chalets E£87.50; single beds available in summer for E£20).

⬛ FOOD

Cuisine in Kharga is adequate at best, and a decent rotisserie chicken seems to be the specialty (whole bird E£8, half E£4). Vegetarians must make do with beans and rice. A **restaurant** at the entrance to the *souq* street offers *fuul* and falafel (50pt) for breakfast. If you're staying in the northern end of town, either go shopping in the evening or take a taxi into Showla Sq. for breakfast.

◉ SIGHTS

MUSEUM OF EL-WADI EL-GADID. This museum is the *pièce de resistance* of the New Valley's tourism drive, housing a massive collection of artifacts collected from the New Valley oases and a few pieces from the Cairo Museum. A variety of pharaonic and Islamic artifacts is on display—everything from wooden sarcophagi and sandstone sphinxes to mascara jars and Roman coins. *(Open daily 8am-5pm. Admission E£20, with ISIC E£10.)*

TEMPLES OF HIBIS AND NADURA. The **Temple of Hibis** was begun in 588 BCE (26th dynasty) by Apnias and completed in 522 BCE by Darius I, making it one of only two Persian-built Egyptian temples. Although dedicated to the Theban triad of Amun, Mut, and Khonsu, the temple is distinguished by its depictions of Persians and Seth, the god of the Oases, with a blue body and a falcon head. First-century Roman inscriptions discuss legal issues, including women's rights. Crowning a knoll across the road from the Temple of Hibis is the **Temple of Nadura,** built in the 2nd century BCE during the reign of Roman Emperor Antonius. Little of it stands today, but the site offers an excellent view of the oasis. *(The temples are at the northern end of town, 2km north of the Hotel El-Kharga and close to the road on the left. A shared covered taxi will take you as far as the tourist office (and possibly farther) for E£1, which is within walking distance of the sites. The scaffold-covered Temple of Hibis will be closed for several years for renovation. The larger site is open to the public for free.)*

NECROPOLIS OF EL-BAGAWAT. The 263 above-ground tombs (also called chapels) of the Christian **Necropolis of El-Bagawat** stand eerily at the desert's edge. From the 3rd through 8th centuries, a sizable Christian community (including many hermits and some of the religion's first monks) inhabited Kharga. Most fled or were exiled during the divisive 4th and 5th centuries, when Constantinople attempted to force the Melkite doctrine upon Egypt, stating that Jesus was not always of the same essence as the Father. Egypt's Christians resisted, clinging to the original Monophysite put forth by Athanasios, a Khargan exile, at the first great Christian Council at Nicaea in 325 CE. The necropolis is visible from the road, and an asphalt lane leads to the ticket booth. If you go up the hill along the marked path, you'll come to the **Chapel of Exodus,** with ceiling mural depicting the pharaoh's Roman-looking army chasing Jews fleeing Egypt and Adam and Eve with *ankh*-like crosses. In front of the Chapel of Exodus are the interconnected frescoed chapels #23-35, the resting place of members of a local wealthy family. The interior frescoes of biblical scenes in the **Chapel of Peace** (#80) exemplify Coptic painting of the early Alexandrian style. Greek inscriptions identify Adam and Eve, Noah's Ark, and the Virgin Mary. Atop the cemetery's central hill stand the remains of a 4th-century mud-brick basilica. *(500m past the Temple of Hibis on the road to Asyut. Open Apr.-Sept. 8am-6pm; Oct.-Mar. 8am-5pm. Admission E£20, students E£10.)*

FACTORIES AND FARMS. A little more than 500m south of Nawaby St. down Nasser St. is the **pottery and carpet factory,** where locals make and sell handicrafts. Another 300m down Nasser St. is the **date factory,** where 200 women at conveyor belts take plucked, washed, steamed, blind, dried, hot, and double dates and stuff them with peanuts and good personalities. *(Pottery and carpet factory open Su-Th 8am-2pm. Date factory open Aug.-Feb. Sa-Th 8am-1:30pm. Both free.)*

NEAR KHARGA

Hire a pickup **taxi** for a day from Kharga (E£50-60). Plenty of shared taxis go from Kharga as far as Bulaq (50pt). Catch them at the southern end of Nasser St. Each day, three **buses** go to **Baris** (1hr.; 7am, noon, and 2:30pm; E£1.70) and three return (1hr.; 6, 11am, 7:30pm; E£1.70). The 7:30pm bus continues on to **Dush,** where the driver lives (1½hr. from Kharga, E£2) and doesn't return until 6am the next morning. **Hitchhiking** is difficult and dangerous.

DARB EL-ARBA'EEN

If you've come all the way to Kharga, don't miss the road along the old camel trail south to the town of Baris, known as Darb El-Arba'een ("Forty Day Road"). This legendary caravan route extended from western Sudan to the Egyptian Nile Valley and tragically trafficked more slaves than any other land route in the world.

KHWITA TEMPLE. Vast sandscapes are all that thrive between Kharga and **Khwita Temple,** 17km to the south. The impressive 10m walls of the temple-fortress dominate a hill 2km east of the road. Dedicated to the Theban triad Amun, Mut, and Khonsu, and built by Darius I with later Ptolemaic additions, the temple served as the center of a thriving community famous for its grape production in pharaonic times. *(Open daily in summer 8am-5pm; in winter 8am-6pm. Admission E£16, students E£8.)*

ZAYAN TEMPLE AND WELLS. At the 25km mark you'll come across the shaded, dirty **Nasser Wells.** Farther on, the better-developed **Bulaq Wells** offer a rest house (beds E£15) and hot springs. **Zayan Temple,** dedicated to Amun, sits 5km east of Nasser Wells, near the village of Araf, on a road that loops around from the north of Khwita Temple to a point north of Bulaq. Originally built in the Ptolemaic era, Romans restored the site to build a fortress, of which there are still remnants. *(For transportation to Zayan Temple, hop on a pickup or public bus headed for Baris and have the driver drop you off on the way (ask for Araf). A round trip taxi should cost no more than E£20. To return to Kharga or continue on to Baris, walk the 1km to Bulaq and catch a pickup taxi, or wait by the road (bring lots of water). Let's Go does not recommend hitchhiking in this area. Open in summer 8am-5pm; in winter 8am-6pm. Admission E£16, students E£8.)*

BARIS

The secluded village of Baris (the sign at the edge of the town ironically reads "Paris") est 90km au sud de Kharga et comme l'enfer en été (over 50°C), mais il fait beau en Avril. Merchants make a 40-day camel trek from here to the border of Chad to purchase an ingredient used in local soap, and each expedition reputedly brings the merchant E£20,000 in profit. Think twice before going into business for yourself, since only one family in town is privy to the location of water wells along the way.

There is a government **rest house** north of town, with no sign to mark it; look for the yellow, gray, and red buildings in a row perpendicular to the highway, about 500m north of the "Paris" sign. Arrange your stay through the tourist office in Kharga or get the groundskeeper to let you in (beds E£5). Mr. Farkhat of the Kharga **tourist office** is available in Baris Thursday through Sunday. If you walk down the central street, perpendicular to the main road, old Baris will be on your right, the gardens straight ahead. The blue structure resembling a doghouse sells kebab, *fuul*, and falafel every day except Friday.

An abandoned **public housing complex** designed by Egyptian architect Hassan Fathy stands 300m northwest of the rest house. Construction was halted and never resumed after the 1967 War, as the government correctly assumed that the villagers wouldn't want to live in buildings resembling tombs. Americans seem to mind less: the U.S. recently finished building a similar Fathy-designed complex in New Mexico.

EGYPT

DUSH TEMPLE. A recently paved road leads 23km southeast to the Dush Temple. The building has an overabundance of heat and a shortage of visitors during the summer, but there's more to it than meets the eye. Originally built for the worship of Serapis and Isis, the temple dates back to the rule of the Roman emperors Trajan and Hadrian. The sand around the temple is slowly parting to reveal a church, pottery shards, and a well with clay pipes. These pipes tunnel down to an underground city, and are leading archaeologists to believe that Dush was a prosperous settlement that was abandoned when the wells ran dry. *(Baris pickup taxi drivers will make a special round trip to Dush for E£20 (waiting included), but are hard to find. Instead of tackling Baris in a day (your road time will total 7hr.), consider an overnight stay. Open daily 8:30am-5pm. Admission E£20, students E£8.)*

ISRAEL יִשְׂרָאֵל

US$1=NIS4.20 (NEW ISRAELI SHEKELS)	**NIS1=US$.24**
CDN$1=NIS2.82	**NIS1=CDN$.36**
UK£1=NIS6.76	**NIS1=UK£.15**
AUS$1=NIS2.72	**NIS1=AUS$.37**
NZ$1=NIS2.22	**NIS1=NZ$.45**
SAR1=NIS.68	**NIS1=SAR1.46**
E£1 (EGYPTIAN POUND)=NIS1.24	**NIS1=E£0.81**
JD1 (JORDANIAN DINAR)=NIS5.93	**NIS1=JD0.17**

PHONE FACTS **Country Code:** 972. **Police:** Tel. 100. **Emergency:** Tel. 101.

Halfway through its first century, Israel has yet to resolve a psychological struggle between secularism and reverence. An inevitable sense of religion and history permeates its modern cities, where pensive philosophers and microchip millionaires sit on park benches with patriotic Zionists and dance-'til-dawn disco-goers. The nation's heterogeneity is most apparent on Friday evenings, when Tel Aviv clubs and Eilat pubs explode with revelry that can almost be heard in the reverent streets of Tzfat or Jerusalem's Jewish Quarter. Israel has been controversial since its inception: as a result of persecution culminating in the Holocaust, Jews of all cultures came together to fashion a new kind of state and to remake themselves, sometimes at the expense of Palestinian Arabs. With the country's identity and culture in constant flux, Israelis have their own visions of what their nation could or should be. Amos Oz, Israel's leading novelist, sees his fellow Israelis as "a warm-hearted, hot-tempered Mediterranean people that is gradually learning, through great suffering and a tumult of sound and fury, to find release both from the bloodcurdling nightmares of the past and from delusions of grandeur, both ancient and modern." Ask Israelis about their bewildering national situation, and they will tell you at length how *they* see their country—there is no lack of impassioned political or apolitical opinions. However, a fundamental optimism shines through it all; talk with them long enough, and they will eventually smile, shrug, and say *"Yihiyeh tov"* ("It will be OK"). For full coverage of the sights and sounds of Israel, try *Let's Go: Israel 2000*.

ESSENTIALS

ENTRY

Visas are not required for citizens of Australia, Canada, New Zealand, South Africa, the U.K., or the U.S. Flights arrive at **Ben-Gurion International Airport,** between Tel Aviv and Jerusalem. Buses leave from the airport to Tel Aviv (NIS10), Jerusalem (NIS20), and other major cities. Israel offers a **VAT** (Value Added Tax) refund to tourists who purchase more than US$50 worth of goods at a shop approved by the Ministry of Tourism. To collect, you must be a non-Israeli citizen, pay in foreign currency (cash or international credit card), and present a VAT invoice/receipt at your point of departure from Israel (if leaving from Ben-Gurion International Airport, go to the 24-hour Bank Leumi Counter). Eilat is a free trade zone, so there is no VAT. **Studying** or **working** in Israel requires a special visa and permit.

EMBASSIES AND CONSULATES

Most foreign embassies and consulates in Israel are in **Tel Aviv** (see **Practical Information,** p. 292), though a few countries also have consulates in Jerusalem, Haifa, and Eilat. Israeli embassies and consulates abroad include: **Australia,** 6 Turrana St.,

Yarralumla, Canberra ACT 2600 (tel. (02) 6273 2045; fax 6273 4273) or 37 York St., 6th floor, Sydney NSW 2000 (tel. (02) 9264 7933; fax 9290 2259); **Canada,** 50 O'Connor St. #1005, Ottawa, ON K1P 6L2 (tel. 613-567-6450; fax 237-8865; email embisrott@cyberus.ca; www.israelca.org), 180 Bloor St. W., Toronto, ONT M5S 2V6 (tel. 416-640-8500; fax 640-8555), or 1155 bd. Réné-Lévesque Ouest, Suite 2620, Montréal, QU H3B 4S5 (514-940-8500; fax 940-8555; email cgisrmtl@videotron.net); **South Africa,** 339 Hilda St., Pretoria 001, Box 3726 (tel. (12) 342 26 93/97; fax 342 14 42); **U.K.,** 2 Palace Green, London W8 4QB (tel. (0171) 957 95 00; fax 957 95 55; email info@israel-embassy.org.uk; www.israel-embassy.org.uk/london); and **U.S.,** 3514 International Drive NW, Washington, D.C. 20008 (tel. 202-364-5500; fax 364-5423; email ask@israelemb.org) or 800 2nd Ave., New York City, NY 10017 (tel. 212-499-5000; fax 499-5355; email nycon@interport.net). Israeli consulates are also located in Atlanta, Boston, Chicago, Houston, Los Angeles, Miami, and Philadelphia.

▨ BORDER CROSSINGS

TO JORDAN. There are two border crossings into Jordan: from **Beit She'an** in northern Israel, and from **Eilat** (by far the simpler and more popular option). Crossing from Eilat to **Aqaba** (info tel. 633 68 15) should take less than an hour—just pay the NIS57 exit tax and walk the 1km no-man's land between the two countries (there's no public transport). Get Jordanian visas valid for one month at the border (citizens of Australia JD16, Canada JD36, New Zealand JD16, South Africa free, U.K. JD23, U.S. JD33). Taxis from Eilat to the border cost NIS15-20; from the border to Aqaba JD5. (Border open daily 9am-9pm; closed Yom Kippur and 'Eid al-Adha.) For more info, see **Border Crossings: To Israel,** p. 404.

TO EGYPT. The border crossing from **Eilat** to **Taba** is somewhat arduous. Passports must be valid for at least three months; Israeli visas must be valid for the day of travel. For travel outside Sinai, get a visa at the Egyptian consulate. The border (info tel. 637 31 10) is open 24 hours (closed on Yom Kippur and 'Eid al-Adha). Allow at least one hour to cross. Take the #15 bus from Eilat, and keep your passport handy. There are 11 exciting steps: (1) Bus drop-off. (2) Little Taba snack bar ("last beer before Sinai"). (3) Passport pre-check. (4) Passport control booth (pay NIS57 exit tax). (5) Israeli last passport check (they automatically stamp your passport at this point unless you ask them not to). (6) Stroll through no-man's land. (7) Egyptian passport control (fill out entry form, get stamp). (8) Egyptian security (X-ray machine). (9) Post-border passport check. (10) Passport check and E£17/US$6 Egyptian border tax. The Taba Hilton is the best place to **change money** (open 24hr., no commission for foreign currency converted to Egyptian pounds). (11) Welcome to Egypt! The bus station is a 10-minute walk from the border. From Taba, there are buses to: **Cairo** (7hr., 2pm, E£70); **Nuweiba'** (1½hr., 3pm, E£12); **Dahab** (2½hr., 3pm, E£15-17); and **Sharm esh-Sheikh** (3-4hr., 3pm, E£25).

TO LEBANON AND SYRIA. Israel's borders with Lebanon and Syria are closed. The most common route into Syria is via Jordan. Travelers with Israeli stamps in their passports will not be granted Lebanese or Syrian visas.

GETTING AROUND

BUSES. Buses are the most popular and convenient means of travel in Israel. Except for the **Dan Company** (tel. (03) 639 44 44) in Tel Aviv and the **Arab buses** serving the West Bank, Galilee, and Gaza, the **Egged Bus Cooperative** (tel. (03) 537 55 55) has a monopoly on intercity and most intracity buses in Israel. The modern, air-conditioned buses are direct *(yashir)*, express, or local *(me'asef)*, with an occasional 10% ISIC discount. Most bus stations have printed schedules, often in English. Egged has intercity **information lines** in the major cities (in Tel Aviv tel. (03) 537 55 55, Haifa tel. (04) 854 95 55, Jerusalem tel. (02) 530 45 55). You can buy a *kartisia* (11 local rides for the price of 10) from any bus driver (NIS42). Most local bus rides cost NIS4.20. Buses between cities usually leave from the central bus station *(tahanah merkazit)*. Round-trip tickets may be 10% cheaper.

ISRAEL

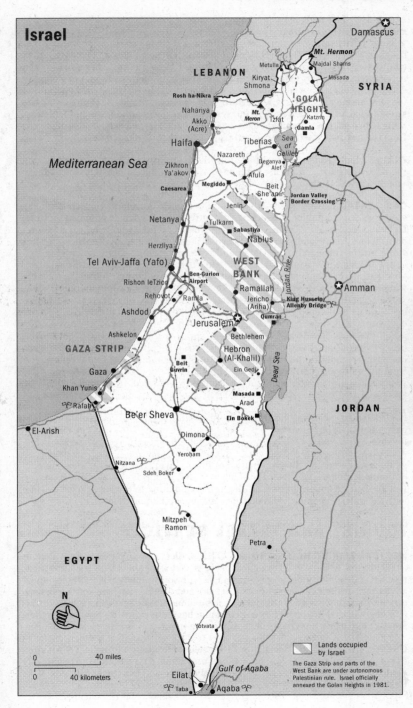

Israel

Damascus

Mt. Hermon

LEBANON

Metulla
Majdal Shams
Kiryat
Shmona
Masada

SYRIA

Rosh ha-Nikra

GOLAN HEIGHTS

Nahariya
Akko
(Acre)

**Mt.
Meron**
Tzfat
Katzrin

Haifa
Gamla

Tiberias
Sea
of
Galilee

Mediterranean Sea

Zikhron
Ya'akov
Nazareth
Deganya
Alef

Caesarea
Megiddo
Afula
Beit
She'an

Jordan Valley
Border Crossing

Jenin

Netanya

Tulkarm
Sabastiya

Herzliya
Nablus

Tel Aviv-Jaffa (Yafo)
**WEST
BANK**

**Ben-Gurion
Airport**

Rishon leTzion
Ramallah

Rehovot
Jericho
(Ariha)
**King Hussein/
Allenby Bridge**

Ramla

Ashdod
Jerusalem
Qumran

Amman

Ashkelon
Bethlehem

GAZA STRIP
Hebron
(Al-Khalil)

**Beit
Guvrin**
Ein Gedi

Gaza

Khan Yunis
Masada

Rafah
Arad

Be'er Sheva
Ein Bokek

El-Arish

Dimona
Jordan River

Yeroham

Nitzana
JORDAN

Sdeh Boker

Dead Sea

Mitzpeh
Ramon

Petra

EGYPT

N

0   40 miles
0   40 kilometers

Yotvata

Gulf of Aqaba

Eilat
Lands occupied
by Israel

Taba
Aqaba

The Gaza Strip and parts of the
West Bank are under autonomous
Palestinian rule. Israel officially
annexed the Golan Heights in 1981.

ISRAEL

TAXIS AND SHERUT. Israeli companies offer both private and less expensive **sherut** (shared) taxis. Regular private taxi rides are called *special* (pronounced "spatial"). City taxis operating as *special* must use a meter *(moneh);* insist that the driver turn it on. Refuse offers of special but unspecified "discount" rates (translation: no meter and an exorbitant fare). Otherwise, set a price before you enter the taxi. *Sherut* taxis hold up to seven people. Certain companies operate *sherut* seven days a week from offices in each city. Intercity *sherut* operate on loose schedules, departing when full; on Saturdays, they often whiz along the streets in search of passengers. Intracity *sherut* never follow a schedule. Most routes have set fares comparable to bus prices; ask for quotes at tourist offices or from the nearest Israeli. Always settle on a price before you depart.

TRAINS. Rail service in Israel (50% ISIC discount) is useful only for travel along the northern coast. Trains are slightly cheaper than buses, but they don't run on Shabbat. Avoid traveling on Friday afternoons when trains are most crowded.

CAR RENTAL. More Israelis have been killed in car accidents than in all of the country's wars combined. Israel has a bad reputation when it comes to driving, and with good reason. Drunk driving is prevalent, and the windy, hilly roads don't help. Widespread public transportation makes cars generally unnecessary, but some places (especially the Golan and Negev) are most easily reached with a coupe of one's own. Some roads, particularly in the Negev and the Golan, have poor (or nonexistent) shoulders or few gas stations. "Scenic routes" are barely wide enough for one car, and buses often blast by in the opposite direction.

The legal driving age is 17, but most agencies will only rent to credit-card holders 21 years or older (a few rent to 18-year-olds). Rentals cost about US$55-70 per day with a 250km daily limit. Deals arranged beforehand from overseas are often much cheaper. Roads are well marked, and maps are available at all tourist offices. Car phones and cellular phones (Israelis call them "pelephones") are everywhere; most rental cars have them built in, so decide at rental time if you want the more expensive "with-phone" plan. Cell phones are responsible for many accidents, so laws regarding them are stringently enforced. Do not hold the phone while you are driving—you risk being hit by another car, a heavy fine, or both.

HITCHHIKING. Sexual harassment and assault related to *tremping* (as it is called in Israel) have increased in recent years. License plates carry meaning; yellow are Israeli, black with a ℨ are army, red are police, green-on-white are Palestinian Territories, blue are a remnant of Occupied Territories plates, and black-on-white are diplomatic. Hitchers in the Negev or Golan (where sometimes the only option is a military vehicle) risk being stranded by a ride that doesn't go all the way to their destination. Hitchers flag cars by pointing to the far side of the road with the index finger. *Let's Go* does not recommend hitchhiking.

TOURIST AND TRAVEL SERVICES

MEDICAL EMERGENCIES AND HEALTH. Medical care in Israel is equivalent in quality to that in the West. For minor illnesses, go to a pharmacy (at least one pharmacy in a neighborhood is open or on-call 24 hours). Pharmacists offer medical advice and medication (most speak English), and doctors can help with more serious illnesses (almost all Israeli doctors speak fluent English). Because Israel's system of socialized medicine has only recently begun to privatize, private practices are very expensive, and medical insurance is a must.

USEFUL ADDRESSES. Society for the Protection of Nature in Israel (SPNI) runs expertly guided tours throughout Israel and Sinai. Tours range from half-day explorations of Jerusalem to 15-day Israel odysseys. Their main office is at 13 Heleni Ha-Malka St., Jerusalem (tel. (02) 625 23 57).

MONEY MATTERS

CURRENCY AND EXCHANGE. The primary unit of currency in Israel is the **New Israeli Shekel (NIS).** There are 100 **agorot** in a shekel. Notes come in denominations of NIS200, NIS100, NIS50, NIS20, and NIS10; coins come in NIS10, NIS5, NIS1, NIS0.50, 10 agorot, and five agorot. It is cheaper to buy shekels in Israel than in your home country. **ATMs** in Israel are open 24 hours and accept most major American credit cards. **Post offices** usually have the best rates and charge little or no commission. Since you lose money with each transaction, convert in large sums (unless the currency is depreciating rapidly). An ATM card or a credit card garners the best possible rates. Banks are generally open Sunday, Tuesday, and Thursday from 8:30am to 12:30pm and 4pm to 5:30pm; Monday and Wednesday 8:30am to 12:30pm; Friday and holidays 8:30am to noon. Personal **checks** from home are usually not accepted, and even traveler's checks may not be accepted in some locations.

TIPPING AND BARGAINING. Tipping in Israel is moving toward expensive American standards, but for the time being, a 10% tip will suffice in restaurants, bars, and hotels. Taxis are mostly metered with standardized prices; drivers do not expect tips but accept them. Bargaining in Israel is the norm, the only exceptions being department stores, drug stores, and supermarkets.

BUSINESS HOURS. Most businesses are open 8:30am-7pm, but many stay open until 10pm, particularly in shopping malls. Most have longer hours on Thursdays. **Shabbat** (the Jewish day of rest) lasts from sundown on Friday to sundown on Saturday; most businesses close by 2pm on Friday and stay closed on Saturday.

KEEPING IN TOUCH

MAIL. Post offices are usually open Sunday through Tuesday and Thursday 8am-12:30pm and 3:30-6pm, Wednesday 8am-2pm, Friday 8am-1pm, and are closed Saturdays and holidays. On the street, yellow mailboxes are for mail sent within the same city; red mailboxes are for all other mail. Most post offices offer international **Express Mail Service (EMS),** which supposedly takes three days. Mail can be sent through **Poste Restante** to almost every town in Israel. **American Express** offices will hold mail for up to 30 days and forward upon request, but only for cardholders. **Aerogrammes** are available at post offices. Airmail from Israel averages five to nine days, although times are unpredictable from smaller towns.

TELEPHONE AND INTERNET ACCESS. To call Israel direct from home, leave off the 0 from the city code. Within Israel, major calling cards that can be accessed include: **AT&T** (tel. 177 100 27 27); **Sprint** (tel. 177 938 70 00); **MCI WorldPhone Direct** (tel. 177 150 27 27); **Canada Direct** (tel. 177 105 27 27); **BT Direct** (tel. 177 440 27 27); **Telecom New Zealand Direct** (tel. 177 640 27 27); and **Telkom South Africa Direct** (tel. 177 270 27 27). **Public telephones** are everywhere. Avoid older telephones—they devour *asimonim* (tokens) even for local calls (NIS0.50). Much more common are the camel-colored public phones (marked with yellow signs) that operate with **Telecards** (20 units NIS10.50, 50 units NIS23, 120 units NIS52; buy them at post offices). Telecards are good for long distance calls (NIS5.90 per min. to the U.S.). International rates drop up to 50% at night and on Saturdays and Sundays. **Bezek,** Israel's phone company, has offices with metered phones for international calls in Tel Aviv and Jerusalem. It may be more economical to call overseas from a phone office, because they charge for the exact time spent on the phone, not in calling units as telecards do. Dial 144 for **operator information.**

Israel is a highly networked country, with computer technology as one of its major industries. There are **cybercafes** in all major cities, and most hostels offer inexpensive use of Internet and email.

SPECIAL CONCERNS

WOMEN TRAVELERS. Women travelers in Israel do not attract undue attention, but it's always best to take basic safety rules into account. Western women can blend in easily in Israel, as women generally dress in Western styles, but it is advisable to dress modestly (nothing sleeveless or tight, with skirts and pants well below the knees) in Orthodox Jewish and Arab sections of the country. Fashions in Tel Aviv, however, are about as liberal as they get. Persistent harassers may be dissuaded by a loud, public *"Tistalek!"* ("Go away!"), or even an English scolding.

BISEXUAL, GAY, AND LESBIAN TRAVELERS. Tel Aviv is one of the few cities in the Middle East with a thriving gay and lesbian community. The main organization for gay and lesbian concerns in Israel is the **Society for the Protection of Personal Rights**, P.O. Box 376 04, Tel Aviv 61375 (tel. (03) 629 36 81; fax 525 23 41), or P.O. Box 3592, Haifa (tel. (04) 867 26 65). A community center, library, and coffee shop are located at 28 Naḥmani St., Tel Aviv. The **White Line** (*Ha-Kav Ha-Lavan*; tel. 732 55 60) is the society's gay and lesbian hotline (operates Su-Th 7:30-11:30pm).

LIFE AND TIMES

ANCIENT HISTORY

THE BIBLICAL AGE. Archaeological excavations at **Jericho** have revealed evidence of a Neolithic settlement from the 7th millennium BCE, the earliest recorded traces of town life anywhere in the world. Want to "know" Israel in the biblical sense? The Bible begins the recorded history of the area with the story of Abraham (Avraham in Hebrew, Ibrahim in Arabic), the first of the Patriarchs. Local leaders united the Israelite tribes in the region under a single deity, **Yahweh**, and established an 11th-century BCE kingdom under **Saul** that reached its peak during the reign of Saul's successors **David** and **Solomon** (who built the Temple of Jerusalem). After Solomon's death in 922 BCE, the empire split into the northern Kingdom of Israel and the southern Kingdom of Judah.

The Assyrians conquered Phoenicia and Israel in the late 8th century BCE, forever removing the 10 tribes of northern Israel from their homeland. King **Nebuchadnezzar** wreaked widespread havoc and again deported the Jews to Babylon in 587 BCE, a period known as the Babylonian Captivity. The Israelites prospered intellectually and economically under the **Persians** (who ousted the Babylonians and allowed the Jews to build the Second Temple in Jerusalem) until **Alexander the Great** rode in on a tide of Hellenism that swept through the region from 332 until 198 BCE, after which the Syrian-based **Seleucids** took over under King Antiochus IV and forbade all Jewish practices. The Jewish lower classes successfully revolted under **Judah Maccabee** (an event commemorated by the holiday Ḥanukah) and founded the strife-ridden Hasmonean dynasty.

In 44 CE, **Pompey** conquered the territory and declared it a Roman province (Judaea), leading to Jerusalem's rebellion in 65-66 CE. In 70 CE, the Roman general **Titus**, faced with the choice of sparing the Jerusalem's Second Temple at great military cost or burning the city, chose the latter. The destruction of the Second Temple led to dramatic upheaval and despair among the Jewish people. Three years later, the Romans captured the last Jewish stronghold at **Masada** (see p. 353). The Romans then exiled the majority of Jerusalem's population, dispersing them throughout the empire. Perhaps to obliterate the land's historical connection with the Jews, they gave the territory the name **Palestine,** after the Philistines.

THE AGE OF EMPIRES AND SUFFIXES. With the division of the empire into Latin West and Byzantine East in 330 CE, Palestine came under the supervision of **Constantinople.** Although little changed administratively, the adoption of Christianity by the Emperor Constantine in 331 CE created increased interest in what to many was the "Holy Land." In the 10th century, Muslim Fatimids captured most of Palestine (including Jerusalem) and destroyed many Christian holy sites, such as the **Church of the Holy Sepulchre.** Enraged **Crusaders** recaptured the Holy Land in 1099, beginning the short-lived era of the Crusader States before falling to the Kurd **Salah ad-Din** and his own short-lived Ayyubid Dynasty. The age of "-uks" (Mamlukes, Seljuks, etc.) nipped at the heels of the age of "-ids" (Fatimids, Ayyubids, etc.), which was followed by the lavish **Ottoman Empire.** By the end of the 17th century, however, the Ottoman ports of Palestine, Syria, and Egypt (which had once provided the sole access to the East) were rendered insignificant as Portuguese sailors steered their way around the Horn of Africa. The once-formidable Ottoman Empire became "the sick man of Europe."

MODERN HISTORY

ZIONISM AND THE BRITISH MANDATE. Although small Jewish communities were present in Palestine over the 18 centuries following the Roman exile, the vast majority were in **diaspora** communities in Europe, the Middle East, North Africa, and the Americas. These Jews hoped to someday return to and rebuild the ancient homeland. This hope became the focus of the movement of **Zionism** in the late 19th and early 20th centuries, when various writers promoted a return to Israel as a solution to the problems of the Jews; **Theodore Herzl** was the first to encourage political means to achieve Zionist ends. The first **aliya** ("going up," the term for Jewish immigration to Israel) occurred in 1882; the second, in 1904-1914, witnessed the development of **kibbutzim,** cooperative agricultural settlements.

During World War I, the British government, at war with the German-allied Ottomans, made muddled promises of sovereignty to the Arabs, Jews, and French, including the November 1917 **Balfour Declaration,** a document that declared that the British would support a Jewish homeland in Palestine if it would not affect Palestine's non-Jewish communities. After the war, however, the League of Nations handed Palestine wholesale to Great Britain, and British indecisiveness continued during their interwar control of the region, as the rise of Nazism drove tens of thousands of European Jews into Palestine. After WWII, the U.N. partitioned Palestine into separate Jewish and Arab states. The leaders of the former reluctantly accepted the resolution, while the leaders of the latter (and the governments of neighboring Arab states) rejected it outright, denying the U.N.'s authority to divide and distribute territories they considered Arab patrimony.

THE 1948 WAR OF INDEPENDENCE. On May 14, 1948, the British mandate over Palestine ended and **David Ben-Gurion** declared the independence of the State of Israel. The next day, a combined army of Syrian, Iraqi, Lebanese, Saudi, Egyptian, and Jordanian troops marched in from the north, west, and south. Few observers gave the new state much chance for survival, but the war's results became clear with the signing of armistices in early 1949. Israel had secured not only its U.N.-allotted territory, but also land designated for Palestine in the north and in the West Bank. The Gaza Strip, which had also been designated for Palestine, was secured by Egypt, and the West Bank and half of Jerusalem by Jordan. Thousands of Palestinian refugees crowded into camps in the West Bank, Gaza, and bordering Arab states. The dispossessed Palestinians came to bitterly remember the 1948 war as **An-Naqba,** the Catastrophe.

THE SUEZ CRISIS AND THE RISE OF PAN-ARABISM. After **Colonel Gamal Abd an-Nasser** took control of Egypt in 1952, he promoted a highly emotional brand of pan-Arabism, hoping to unify the Arabic-speaking masses into one state powerful enough to resist imperial encroachments and take control of Palestine. The U.S. and other foreign powers, who had begun to develop the oil fields of Arabia, feared their arrangements with local monarchs would collapse if Nasserism spread. In

ISRAEL

1956, the U.S. clumsily attempted to curtail Nasser's power by withdrawing its offer to finance the Aswan High Dam. Rather than yield to the snub, Nasser nationalized the previously international Suez Canal to use its revenues for the dam. On October 24, 1956, Jordan, Syria, and Egypt established a joint military command, directed against Israel. Israel, Britain, and France devised a scheme to take the canal. Israel would attack Egypt, and a Franco-British "peace-keeping" force would follow. Initially, the conspiracy worked: Israel took the **Sinai Peninsula,** opened its port of Eilat to international shipping, and dealt Nasser's military a major blow. The military victors, however, had not considered world reaction to their adventure. When Israel, Britain, and France withdrew their troops to placate the furious U.S., Nasser was heralded as the savior of the Arab world without having won a battle.

THE 1967 SIX-DAY WAR. From bases sanctioned by the governments of Jordan, Syria, and Lebanon, the **Palestinian Liberation Organization (PLO)** raided Israel during the 1960s; in return, Israel hit Palestinian refugee camps. The cycle of raids and reprisals created tension on Israel's northern border, and a Syrian-Israeli air battle took place in April 1967. When Syria's hard-line government turned up the rhetoric, Nasser stepped in and initiated a blockade on May 22, 1967, sparking what is known as the 1967 War or **Six-Day War.** By June 9, 1967, all parties had accepted the cease-fire. To Israel went the spoils: they annexed East Jerusalem, got the Sinai and the Gaza Strip from Egypt, the Golan Heights from Syria, and the West Bank from Jordan. The defeated Palestinians decided to take things into their own hands; the extremist group FATAH, led by **Yassir Arafat,** took over the PLO in 1969, encouraging liberation through propaganda and guerilla warfare.

The stakes of the game were now higher than anyone could have imagined: with the United States behind Israel and the Soviet Union behind Nasser, any local conflict affected the world's major superpowers. The U.N. **Resolution 242** stipulated "withdrawal of Israeli armed forces from territories occupied in the recent conflict" and "acknowledgment of the sovereignty, territorial integrity, and political independence of every State in the area." The intentional ambiguity of the document caused bickering immediately, while the situation along the Suez Canal (the Israel-Egypt border) degenerated into the **War of Attrition.**

The 1967 War created 400,000 more Palestinian refugees, most of whom went to Jordan, throwing the Jordanian government and the PLO into a tense relationship: Hussein wanted to hold secret peace negotiations with the Israelis, while the PLO hoped to use Jordan as a base for attacks on Israeli-held territory. In September 1970 (known to Palestinians as **Black September,** see p. 409), Hussein's frustrations and conflicts with Arafat's PLO, already at boiling point, overflowed: a brutal war was declared and martial law imposed; it was only after some 3000 lives were sacrificed that the PLO reluctantly agreed to move its headquarters to Lebanon.

YOM KIPPUR AND CAMP DAVID. Egyptian and Syrian forces launched a surprise assault on Israel on October 6, 1973, when most Israelis were in synagogues for Yom Kippur (the holiest day of the Jewish year); the bloody fighting of this **Yom Kippur War** and the subsequent Arab oil embargo ended only when the Arabs decided to settle matters under the supervision of the U.S. and the Soviet Union in December 1973's Geneva Peace Conference. Thanks to the work of U.S. Secretary of State **Henry Kissinger,** all forces agreed to leave the area over the next five months (one month after Israeli Prime Minister **Golda Meir** resigned amidst public uproar against the country's unpreparedness in the war). Soon after, the PLO was granted "observer" status in the U.N.

Throughout the 1970s, an increasing number of Israelis began to settle in the occupied territories, an act discouraged by Prime Minister Yitzhak Rabin but encouraged by his successor, **Menahem Begin.** In 1979, Begin, Egypt's Anwar Sadat, and the U.S.'s Jimmy Carter met at Camp David in Maryland to sign the **Camp David Accords,** which returned the Sinai to Egypt but left the question of West Bank and Gaza control more muddled than before. Things cooled off in the 1980s under Sadat's successor, current Egyptian President Hosni Mubarak, but on June 6, 1982,

Israel invaded **Lebanon** under "Operation Peace for Galilee," an attack most believe was aimed at wiping out PLO forces that had been attacking northern Israel. Tensions led to bloodshed, ending only when the U.S. intervened and the Israelis withdrew in 1985, leaving a buffer zone in southern Lebanon.

THE PLO AND JORDAN. Mourning at a funeral for several Palestinians killed in an Arab-Israeli car crash in Gaza erupted into a Palestinian **intifada** (uprising, literally "throwing or shaking off") that spread to the West Bank. The *intifada* came as a surprise to everyone, the PLO included. Palestinians in the territories began establishing networks to coordinate their hitherto sporadic acts of civil disobedience, and it soon became apparent that the *intifada* was not abating. In the summer of 1988, Jordan suddenly removed itself from the situation, and the PLO seized the opportunity to secure a role in negotiations with the rest of the world by renouncing terrorism, recognizing Israel's right to exist, and proposing an independent Palestinian state. Israeli Prime Minister Yitzhak Shamir retaliated with a proposal whose underlying tenet was that Jerusalem, whole and undivided, was Israel's eternal capital, but the PLO and Egypt refused to accept this and turned on Arafat, whom they blamed for the weakening of the strong position Palestinians had gained from the *intifada*.

THE GULF CRISIS AND OSLO ACCORD. The Gulf Crisis began when Iraqi President Saddam Hussein ordered Iraqi troops to march into Kuwait on August 2, 1990; he then slyly suggested "linkage" as a way of solving the Gulf Crisis: he would withdraw from Kuwait when Israel withdrew from the West Bank, Gaza, and Golan, and Syria withdrew from Lebanon. SCUD missile rockets rained down on Israel (cheered on by Arafat) as tensions skyrocketed, but hopes were high at the 1991 Madrid peace conference because Syria entered negotiations on the side of Israel (the first time in years such a thing had happened). The year 1992 saw both the election of Palestinian autonomy-promising Prime Minister Yitzhak Rabin and increased terrorist attacks by **Hamas,** an Islamist Palestinian faction. In 1993, Israel and the PLO surprised the world by announcing a successfully negotiated, peaceful framework for solving the Israeli-Palestinian conflict, known as the Declaration of Principles on Interim Self-Government Arrangements (the DOP or **Oslo Accord**), which was signed on the White House lawn on September 13, 1993 (U.S. President Bill Clinton presiding). The DOP provided mutual recognition between Israel and the PLO and the implementation of Palestinian autonomy (expanding over five years) in the Gaza Strip and Jericho area, leading to an eventual finalizing of the entire messy situation. Other agreements created the **Palestinian Authority (P.A.),** a 24-member council headed by Yassir Arafat that would have some governmental control in the West Bank.

RECENT HISTORY AND THE PEACE PROCESS. On November 4, 1995, 25-year-old **Yigal Amir,** a right-wing Jewish university student, shot and killed Israeli Prime Minister Yitzhak Rabin as he was giving a speech at a Tel Aviv rally, firing a bullet through a folded song sheet (*Shir La-Shalom,* "A Song for Peace") that was read to the over one million mourners (50 of them world leaders) at his funeral. **Benjamin Netanyahu** barely scraped through elections in May 1996, in which he promised to continue Rabin's peace-oriented politics, but tensions (ignited by Hamas) over his conservative policies lead to widespread violence. Hamas suicide-bombers twice targeted Jerusalem's crowded thoroughfares in 1997, killing 20 and injuring over 10 times as many. In response, Israel cordoned off the West Bank and the Gaza Strip and arrested Palestinians.

On May 30, 1998, Israel celebrated its **50th anniversary** with widespread partying in Jerusalem. At the same time, Palestinians mourned the 50 years since *An-Naqba* ("The Catastrophe") with widespread and violent rioting in Hebron and East Jerusalem (where five Palestinians were shot by Israeli soldiers). The PA and the U.S. set a deadline that same month for Israel to withdraw from 13% of the West Bank, but Netanyahu ignored their decision and insisted that anything over a 9% withdrawal would pose an unacceptable security risk. The U.S. blamed deadly bombings of their embassies in Kenya and Tanzania in August 1998 on a militant Islamic group associated with **Osama Bin Laden** and retaliated with missile strikes on Sudan and Afghanistan, which not only angered Islamic groups and individuals, but also prompted Bin Laden to vow violent reprisals against America and Israel.

IN THE NEWS

Ehud Barak was elected Prime Minister over Netanyahu in May 1999, promising to make the resolution of the peace talks his primary concern. Barak established a 15-month timeline for peace in the Middle East (timing the negotiations to be finalized without significant interference from the U.S., which will be occupied with presidential elections). There are immediate plans to launch negotiations with Palestinians, Syrians, and Lebanese that will eventually lead to agreement incorporating 1998's Wye River Accord, the borders of a Palestinian entity, the withdrawal from southern Lebanon, and an agreement with Syria. Barak has said that Israel will not return to the pre-1967 borders, but will partially withdraw from the Golan Heights in exchange for full peace with a terrorism-free Syria.

Many doubt that 15 months is enough time to reach an agreement with Syrian President **Hafez al-Assad**, and support for the peace process in both Palestinian and Israeli societies has been plagued by frustration and persistent mistrust. In the end, however, the majority on both sides of the table are hoping that their respective governments can realize what Barak has called a "true, lasting peace."

RELIGION AND ETHNICITY

Freedom of religion is safeguarded by the state under the 1948 Declaration of the Establishment of the State of Israel. Israel's population of 5.8 million is 80% Jewish and 15% Muslim; the remaining 5% includes Christians and Druze. Each community operates its own religious courts, funded by the Ministry of Religion, and controls its own holy sites. Every religion's days of rest are guaranteed by law.

About half of Israeli **Jews** are secular; 30% identify themselves as Orthodox and 18% as Ultra-Orthodox, and the religious-secular divide is something of a fault line in society. The religious establishment is quite powerful—rabbinical courts even have a state monopoly on matrimonial issues among Jews. Many Israeli Jews are either first- or second-generation immigrants, and are often divided along ethnic lines: **Sephardi** Jews come from Arab or other Mediterranean countries, while **Ashkenazi** Jews have northern or eastern European origins. The deep rift in Israeli society goes back to the 1950s, when Sephardi Jews from Morocco and Iraq were brought to an already established, Ashkenazi-dominated state. Although Sephardim comprise roughly half of the Jewish population in Israel, Ashkenazim still fill most of the positions of power in the government, military, and academia, and Sephardim are generally poorer. The last decade has brought massive immigrations from the former USSR and Ethiopia, clouded by questions concerning the religious status of immigrants claiming to be Jewish.

Among other religious and ethnic groups in Israel are the **Muslims,** who have flourished in Israel since the 7th century. After Mecca and Medina, the most important Muslim holy site—the **Al-Aqsa Mosque** (see p. 270)—is in Jerusalem. Muslim *hadith* tells of Muhammad's journey from Mecca to Al-Aqsa ("The Farthest") and up through the Seven Heavens to meet God. Many **Christian** sects are also represented in Israel, including the Armenian Orthodox, Abyssinian, Anglican, Baha'i, Coptic, Greek Orthodox, Roman Catholic, and Syrian Orthodox churches. Most are Arab by language and origin. Israel's **Druze** population is divided between those living in the Galilee and in the Golan Heights. Those in the Galilee remain loyal to Israel and often serve in the army, while those in the Golan support their return to Syria. Druze generally live in separate villages and have their own communal institutions.

FESTIVALS AND HOLIDAYS

In Israel, most businesses and public facilities close Friday afternoons for **Shabbat,** the Jewish sabbath, and reopen at sundown on Saturday. They also close for Jewish holidays, which begin at sundown on the previous day. **Pesaḥ,** or Passover (Apr. 20-26, 2000), celebrates the exodus of the Jews from Egypt. Observant Jews refrain from eating bread and pastries; products made with regular flour and leavening agents may be hard to come by. **Rosh Ha-Shana** (the Jewish New Year; Sept. 30-Oct. 1, 2000) is only slightly less holy than **Yom Kippur** (Oct. 9, 2000), the holiest day of the Jewish calendar; observant Jews fast in atonement for their sins and Israel shuts down entirely. In Muslim areas, many businesses close on Friday for prayer. On holidays, they may close during the afternoon, but are generally open in the morning. For a list of religious and national holidays, see the **Appendix,** p. 699.

LANGUAGE

Hebrew and **Arabic** are the official languages of Israel. Most Israelis speak some English; many speak English with near fluency, particularly in bigger cities like Jerusalem and Tel Aviv, and popular tourist destinations such as Eilat. Signs are usually written in English (sometimes Russian) as well as Hebrew and Arabic. For more information on the Hebrew language, see the **Appendix, p. 704.**

THE ARTS

LITERATURE. The compilation of the biblical narrative was followed by the age of the **Mishnah** (200 BCE-700 CE), when *halakha* (laws derived from the Bible) and *agada* (elaboration on the Bible) were compiled. The revival of Hebrew as a secular language in the 18th century brought a drastic shift in Hebrew literature. Josef Perl and Isaac Erter parodied Ḥasidic works in their writings. The generations that followed moved toward realism, often employing Yiddish. **Joseph Brenner** was popular at the turn of the century, thanks to his hallmark character—the tragic, uprooted settler. His works not only profoundly influenced later Israeli writers but also presaged pessimistic interactions between Jews and Arabs. In the 1920s and 1930s, Nobel Laureate **Shmuel Yosef (Shai) Agnon** confronted the breakdown of cultural cohesion among modern Jews in *A Guest for the Night, The Bridal Canopy,* and *Twenty-One Stories.*

The era just before the creation of the state of Israel saw the rise of native Hebrew authors concerned for the landscape and the moment, as exemplified in S. Yizhar's *Efrayim Returns to Alfalfa.* In the late 1950s, writers such as **Amos Oz** and A. B. Yehoshua began to experiment with psychological realism, allegory, and symbolism, paving the way for the skepticism of the 60s (such as *The Palace of Shattered Vessels* by David Shaḥar, considered the Proust of Israeli literature). *Past Continuous* by **Ya'akov Shabtai,** about Tel Aviv in the 1970s, is perhaps the best Israeli novel of the decade. The poetry of **Yehuda Amichai** will ensure that you never look at Jerusalem stone in the same way again.

Israeli literature today increasingly focuses on the Israeli-Palestinian conflict. Oz's *In the Land of Israel* is a series of interviews that documents the wide range of political sentiment. For Palestinian accounts, check out *The West Bank Story* by Rafik Halabi, an Israeli Druze television reporter, and Fawaz Turki's autobiographical *The Disinherited.* Contemporary literature is also highly influenced by immigrants from vastly different cultures, tumultuous politics, and conflicts between individualism and nationalism. A cadre of young writers such as Etgar Keret and Gafi Amir highlight the disaffected and cynical outlook characteristic of what has been called the **post-Zionist** era. Israel's tumultuous history has inspired a number of over-idealized, highly entertaining histories, including Ḥayim Potok's *Wanderings,* James Michener's *The Source,* and Leon Uris's *Exodus.*

ISRAEL

MUSIC. After WWI, Jews in Palestine assembled chamber groups, a symphony orchestra, an opera company, and a choral society. With the rise of Nazism in Europe, Jewish musicians fled to Israel, and this influx also spurred the formation of several music groups. Today seasonal music activities from October to July are held in such varied settings as the historic Crusader Castle at Akko and the modern, 3000-seat Mann Auditorium in Tel Aviv. Israeli **popular music** emerged from its folk-chant origins (often echoing Russian folk melodies) in the late 1960s. Since the 1970s, Israel has been catching up with international music fashions; local bands experiment with punk, reggae, heavy metal, grunge, and even rap. **MTV** now keeps Israeli youth abreast of the goings-on in London and New York, and they expect nothing less of their own local acts. Tel Aviv is the unequivocal hub of the cutting-edge music scene in Israel, though throughout the country the most popular artists perform music that's somewhere between hard rock and acoustic pop. Some native classics still on the performance circuit are Shlomo Artzi, Yehudit Ravitz, and Gidi Gov. Achinoam Nini blends American rock with Middle Eastern sounds, while David Broza also throws in Latin American influences. In many places, Middle Eastern-style music (called *muzika mizrahit*, or "oriental music") blasts from car stereos and boomboxes and is very popular with Sephardim (Avihu Medina is the big name in *mizrahi* music).

FOOD AND DRINK

Some Israelis' diets are affected by **kashrut** (literally translated as "proper"), the Jewish dietary laws. Observant Jews will not eat or shop in a place that carries non-kosher goods; to keep kosher clientele coming, the big supermarket chains in Israel carry only kosher products, and many restaurants (and most hotels) serve only kosher food. Observance of *kashrut* is not necessarily the norm in Israel, and many restaurants (particularly in Haifa and Tel Aviv) are avidly non-kosher.

The typical Israeli eats a large breakfast, a big midday meal, and a light, late supper. Because of the poor quality and high cost of beef and lamb, Israelis rely largely on chicken, dairy, and vegetable products. Popular items in the Israeli diet include ever-present **hummus** (mashed chick-peas, garlic, lemon, and *tahina*, a sesame concoction); "salad," finely chopped tomatoes and cucumbers garnished with oil and vinegar; *gvina levana*, soft white cheese; *schnitzel*, breaded and fried chicken breast; chips (french fries); and a variety of sweet dairy snacks.

You can prepare your own meals from food purchased at the *shuk* (outdoor market, like the *souqs* elsewhere in the Middle East), the *makolet* (small market), or a supermarket. *Burekas* (cheese-, potato-, spinach-, or meat-filled filo dough) are available at patisseries and some fast-food shops. Aside from the standard falafel and shawarma, street vendors also sell what look like hand grenades—these are only **sabras,** prickly cactus fruits with edible innards (the seeds cause indigestion). *Sabra* is also a term for a native Israeli; both the fruit and the people are said to be thorny on the outside, sweet on the inside.

Two Israeli **beers** are the decent, deep-amber Goldstar (a draft beer) and the lesser Maccabee lager. The not-strictly-enforced minimum drinking age is 18. Strong, sweet **Arabic coffee** is sometimes referred to as *turki* (Turkish); for less potent brews, ask for *hafukh* (mixed with milk) or *filter*. "Black" *(shahor)* or "mud" *(botz)* coffee is Turkish coffee brewed in a cup.

SNAHTIME! Israel has two "indigenous" snack foods that tourists either love or absolutely hate. One is **bamba,** a crispy peanut butter puff eaten as a pseudo-protein source by Israeli children. The other is **bissli,** a more complex acquired taste that comes in flavors ranging from falafel to pizza, as well as a variety of pasta-style shapes. Try eating them in front of a TV for an authentic Israeli couch potato experience.

ISRAEL

JERUSALEM ירושלים القدس

> There are men with hearts of stone,
> and there are stones with hearts of men.
>
> —Rav Kook

When the sun sets over the Judean hills, Jerusalem's white stone turns gold and peace seems to be within the city's grasp. The domes, spires, and minarets of three major faiths' places of worship rise over crenelated walls in quiet harmony. But Jerusalem is not always as serene as its evening breeze and rooftop view. The white stone, a requirement for all of Jerusalem's buildings, is indelibly, if invisibly, stained with the blood of centuries. During Jerusalem's 5000 years, 18 conquerors have presided over the city. David established Jerusalem as the capital of the Israelite kingdom, and his son Solomon extended it northward to the present-day Temple Mount (where the Ark of the Covenant was kept and the First Temple stood). The Israelite kingdom's split led Judah's citizens to develop the Jewish identity in the city until 596 BCE, when King Nebuchadnezzar besieged the city and exiled the Jews to Babylon.

Jerusalem enjoyed more than a century of revival under the Persians, until Alexander the Great rode in on a tide of Hellenism that swept through the city in 332 BCE. The renaissance ended in 198 BCE, when Seleucid King Antiochus IV forbade all Jewish practices. Led by Judah Maccabee, the Jews successfully revolted and founded the Hasmonean dynasty that lasted until the Romans set up the province of Judaea. Six-and-a-half centuries of Roman rule began with Herod the Great, a child of a Jewish father and Samaritan mother. The Jews revolted but failed, then tried once more (the 123 CE Bar Kokhba Revolt) and failed; when Hadrian razed the city after this third revolt, he divided his new *Aelia Capitolina* into quarters (that remain today) using two major roads (the Cardo and Decumanus). When Roman Emperor Constantine adopted and legalized Christianity in 331 CE, his mother Eleni visited the Holy Land in order to identify and consecrate Christian sites.

Muslim caliph Omar conquered *Aelia* in 638, beginning an era of tolerant rule; his successors built the Dome of the Rock soon after. The Fatimids and Seljuk Turks who followed were not so kind to the city and its synagogues and churches; their rumored closing of pilgrimage routes fired up the Crusaders enough to storm and capture Jerusalem in 1099, and subsequently begin massacring Muslims and Jews mercilessly. The year 1187 saw the city do its time (as all cities in the Middle East did) under Salah ad-Din, who allowed both Muslims and Jews to resettle the city—so tolerantly that the city became a thriving center for Muslim scholarship in the Mamluke era. Ottoman rule saw restructuring and expansion until 1917, when the city fell without resistance to the British army. Both Jews and Arabs came to resent the increasing influence of the British, who promised autonomy to both during WWI but ended up keeping Palestine for themselves, heightening tension between the two sides that almost turned into a civil war in 1936 and 1939.

The next World War ignited violence that divided Palestine into separate Jewish and Arab states, but left Jerusalem an international city. In the post-evacuation war of 1948, West Jerusalem and the Jewish Quarter were besieged by Arabs, and Jordanian control of the city saw the synagogues and ancient quarters dynamited and the city divided into Jordanian and Israeli sectors for nearly two decades. In the Six-Day War of 1967, Israel captured East Jerusalem, the Old City, and the West Bank from the Jordanians. On June 29 of that year, Israel declared the newly unified Jerusalem its "eternal capital." The walls separating the Israeli and Arab sectors were torn down, and life under Israeli rule began for Jerusalem's Arabs.

The 1987 *intifada* (uprising) of Palestinians protesting Israeli occupation saw violent clashes that turned East Jerusalem and the Old City into alien territory for Jewish Israelis. Bus explosions, suicide bombings, and street fighting have fueled the fires of Jerusalem's recent history, and the future of Jerusalem is perhaps the most sensitive issue in the current Israeli-Palestinian negotiations. Israel adamantly refuses to discuss withdrawing from its capital, while Palestinians fervently oppose the idea of abandoning claims to their most important city.

In this city that has been the battleground and spoil of countless holy wars, the magnificent spirituality that defines Jerusalem can itself become a burden; as the Israeli poet Yehuda Amiḥai has said, the "air over Jerusalem is saturated with prayers and dreams." But spiritual over-saturation only heightens Jerusalem's magnetic attraction: ultra-Orthodox Christians, Muslims, Mormon missionaries, pilgrims and tourists from every continent, fanatics, mystics, and raving lunatics all cart their spiritual baggage to this city. On a city bus, black robes, habits, and *kafias* mingle with halter-tops and baseball caps. Jerusalem is the modern capital for ancient peoples; every street here is a crucible.

HIGHLIGHTS OF JERUSALEM

■ Contemplate biblical miracles over a *nargilah* in the Muslim Quarter's coffeehouses after following the **Via Dolorosa** (p. 273) through the Old City's *souq* to Jesus' tomb.
■ Wade by candlelight through the murky waters of **Hezekiah's Tunnel** (p. 278); dry off on the walk back to the magnificent **Dome of the Rock** (p. 270).
■ Wonder anew at the genius of Rodin and Picasso at the **Israel Museum** (p. 284), also home to the famous Dead Sea Scrolls.

✷ ORIENTATION

Known as **Yerushalayim** in Hebrew and **Al-Quds** ("The Holy") in Arabic, Jerusalem is a sprawling city that has developed mainly in the last 50 years of the capital's three millennia of history.

West Jerusalem refers to the Jewish parts of Jerusalem, from French Hill in the northeast and East Talpiot in the southeast, to Kiryat Menaem in the southwest and Ramot in the northwest. Best known for the eateries, dance clubs, and sandal stores of the *midraḥov* (pedestrian zone), West Jerusalem's ever-popular city center *(merkaz ha-ir)* provides welcome entertainment for tourists with its elegant neighborhoods, well-kept parks, and impressive museums. West Jerusalem's main street is **Jaffa Road** (Derekh Yafo), running west-to-east from the central bus station to the Old City's **Jaffa Gate**. Roughly midway between the two, **Zion Square** (Kikkar Tzion) sits at the corner of Jerusalem's triangular *midraḥov*, bounded by Jaffa Rd., **Ben Yehuda Street,** and **King George Street.** Upscale eateries line **Salomon** and **Rivlin Streets,** off Zion Sq.

North of the city center, the **Russian Compound's** hip bar scene hugs the old-world neighborhood of **Me'a She'arim** like spandex on a *yenta*. Northwest on Jaffa Rd. are the teeming outdoor markets of **Maḥaneh Yehuda** and the central bus station. **Independence Park** lies south of the city center, ringed by luxury hotels; farther south are the cafes of **Emek Refa'im** and the *discothèques* of **Talpiot.** The artists' district of **Yemin Moshe** huddles southeast of Zion Sq.

Jerusalem's most important historical and religious sites are within the walls of the **Old City,** still divided into the four quadrants laid out by the Romans in 135 CE. To get from West Jerusalem's center to the Old City, take Jaffa Rd. past the post office to Jaffa Gate (buses #6, 20, 21, and 99 also stop at Jaffa Gate). Here you can follow the promenade along the ancient walls to most of the seven other gates. The main road in the Old City is the roof-covered **David Street;** an extension of this thoroughfare, **Bab as-Silsilah Street** (Gate of the Chain), runs up to the Temple Mount. The **Armenian Quarter** is to the right as you enter through Jaffa Gate, and is directly accessible via **Zion Gate.** Left of Jaffa Gate is the **Christian Quarter,** which can also be reached directly from the **New Gate. Damascus Gate** provides direct entry into the heavily populated **Muslim Quarter.** To get there from Jaffa Gate, turn left onto **Khan az-Zeit** from David Rd.; it will be on the right. To reach Damascus Gate from the city center, walk to the end of Jaffa Rd. and take a left onto Ha-Tzanḥanim St. (buses #1, 2, 37, and 44 also go to Damascus Gate). This area can be unsafe after dark. Those staying here should plan to return to their lodgings by nightfall unless traveling with a large group. The road forks once inside Damascus Gate, with **Al-Wad Street** on the left and **Souq Khan az-Zeit Street** on the right (major thoroughfares that lead to the Via Dolorosa). A right turn off David Rd. onto Ha-Yehudim St. leads to the **Jewish Quarter,** directly accessible via the **Dung Gate.**

The old Green Line separating Jordan from pre-1967 Israel runs along **Derekh Ha-Shalom** (Peace Rd.), and is still a good general demarcation between Palestinian and Jewish areas of Jerusalem. **East Jerusalem** is the name given to the Palestinian parts of Jerusalem, the area to the north and east of (and sometimes including) the Old City. **Suleiman Street,** in front of Damascus Gate, and **Salah ad-Din Street,** which runs out from Herod's Gate, are the main roads in central East Jerusalem. **Ha-Nevi'im Street** (Musrada St. in Arabic), converges with the unmarked **Nablus Road** at Damascus Gate, and is home to some dry goods stores and hostels. Central East Jerusalem is the financial and cultural hub of the Arab community.

◧ GETTING THERE AND AWAY

Airplanes: Ben-Gurion Airport (general info tel. (03) 972 33 44, automated flight confirmation tel. (03) 971 66 66) is served by El Al (tel. 677 02 07), among others. For a hassle-free airport experience, check bags for El Al flights in advance at 7 Kanfey Nesharim St. (tel. 651 57 05), 1st floor, on the corner of Jaffa Rd. near the central bus station. Open Su-Th 2-7pm for same-night flights, 2-10pm for next-day flights.

Buses: Egged Central Bus Station (tel. 530 47 04), on Jaffa Rd., past the city center and Mahane Yehuda market. Tickets purchased at the ticket counter and not on the bus get a 10% ISIC discount on trips over NIS17.40. Info desk open 7am-8:30pm.

To Tel Aviv: Central Station, bus #405 direct (1hr.; every 10-25min. Su-Th 5:50am-11:30pm, F 6am-4:20pm, Sa sundown-midnight; NIS17.30); **Arlozorov Terminal,** bus #480 direct (every 15-20min. 6am-10pm).

To Haifa: Bus #940 direct (2hr.; every 15-45min. Su 6am-7:30pm, M-W 6:30am-7:30pm, Th 6:30am-8:30pm, F 7am-3pm, Sa sundown-10pm; NIS38) or bus #947 via **Netanya** (2hr.; every 20-40min. Su-Th 6am-8:30pm, F 6:15am-4pm).

To Ben-Gurion Airport: Bus #945 or 947 (every 15-40min. Su-Th 7:15am-10:10pm, F 7:30am-5:55pm, Sa sundown-12:25am; NIS19.30).

To Eilat: Bus #444 (4½hr.; Su-Th 7, 10am, 2, 5pm; F 7, 10am, 2pm; NIS58). Must call 2 days in advance for credit card reservations (tel. 530 47 04).

To Be'er Sheva: Bus #446 via **Kiryat Gat** (1¾hr.; every 15min.-1hr. Su-Th 6am-8:30pm, F 6am-4pm, Sa sundown-10:30pm; NIS31) or bus #470 direct (every 30min.-1hr. Su 6:20am-6:15pm, M-Th 6:45am-6:15pm, F 10:20am-3pm; NIS31).

To the West Bank: Two bus stations serve the West Bank. **Suleiman Street Station,** in East Jerusalem between Herod's and Damascus Gates, serves routes south, while **Nablus Road Station** serves points north. See **West Bank: Entry** (p. 378) for information on travel to the West Bank from Israel.

Sherut Taxis: Jerusalem is served by 2 main intercity *sherut* taxi companies. **Ha-Bira** (tel. 625 45 45), at the corner of Ha-Rav Kook St. and Jaffa Rd. (near Zion Sq.), goes to **Tel Aviv** (every 20min.; NIS17, after 11:30pm NIS19, Shabbat NIS20). Office open Su-Th 5:30am-11pm and F 5:30am-5:30pm. **Nesher,** 21 King George St. (tel. 625 72 27 or 623 12 31), has door-to-airport service (NIS37, reserve 1 day ahead). Open 24hr. *Sherut* taxis leave from the central bus station.

Car Rental: Superdrive, 10 King David St. (tel. 625 08 43), rents to drivers 18 and older. US$50 per day, US$48 for 3 days. July 15-Aug. is US$60 per day. Insurance included. Credit cards accepted. Open Su-Th 8:30am-5pm, F 8:30am-1pm; call ahead. **Thrifty,** 8 King David St. (tel. 625 08 33). Min. age 21, under 23 add US$12 per day for double insurance. Low season US$50 per day, US$41 for 3 days. High season US$67, US$55 for 3 days. Open Su-Th 8am-5:30pm, F 8am-noon.

Jerusalem Overview

MOTZA
ILIT

JERUSALEM FOREST

Sderot Ben Gurion

SEE WEST JERUS
MAP, PP. 260-2

Kanfel Nesharim

HAR
NOF

BEIT
ZAYIT

Sderot – Herzl

Wolfsohn

JERUSALEM FOREST

Sderot Herzl

Yad Vashem

Mt. Herzl

Herzl's Grave

Herzl Museum

Hebrew University
(Giv'at Ram Campus)

Giv'at Ram

Jerusalem Forest
Recreation Centre

Shmuel Berth

Ein Kerem

Hantke

Church of
St. John

EIN
KEREM

Ha-Ma'ayan

Church of
the Visitation

Russian
Convent

Hantke

Ha-Rav Uziel

Bezalel

KIRYAT
HA-YOVEL

TO HADASSAH
MEDICAL CENTER

Szold

KIRYAT
MENAHEM

Golomb

ORA

Golomb

N

Kenyon Yerushalayim
(Shopping Mall)

Teddy
Stadium

0   1000 yards

0   1 kilometer

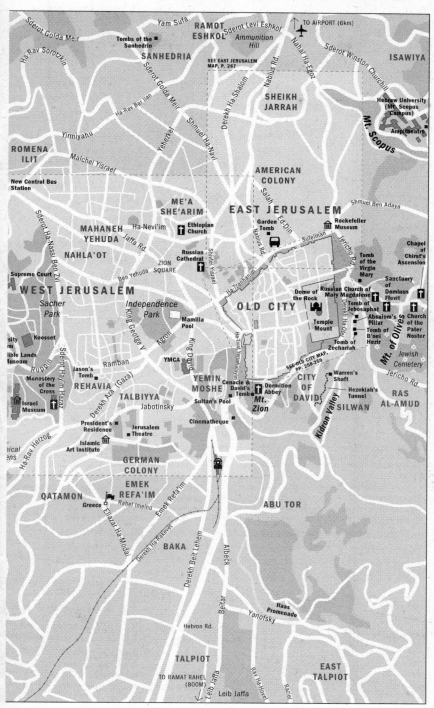

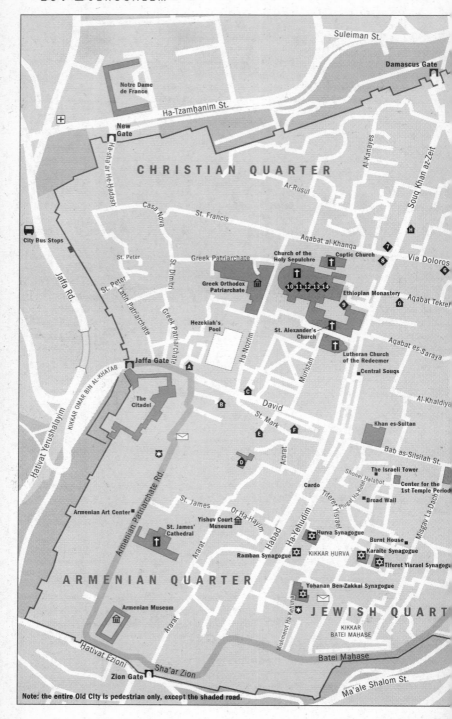

Suleiman St.

Damascus Gate

Notre Dame
de France

Ha-Tzamhanim St.

New
Gate

Ha-sha ar He-Hadash

CHRISTIAN QUARTER

Ar-Rusul

Casa Nova

St. Francis

Al-Kanayes

Souq Khan az-Zeit

City Bus Stops

Jaffa Rd.

St. Peter

St. Peter

Latin Patriarchate

St. Dimitri

Greek Patriarchate

Aqabat al-Khanqa

Greek Patriarchate

Church of the
Holy Sepulchre

Coptic Church

Via Doloros

H

7

8

6

Greek Orthodox
Patriarchate

10 11 12 13 14

Ethiopian Monastery

9

Aqabat Tekret

G

Hezekiah's
Pool

Ha-Nozrim

St. Alexander's
Church

Muristan

Aqabat es-Saraya

Lutheran Church
of the Redeemer

Central Souqs

Al-Khaldiya

Jaffa Gate

A

KIKKAR OMAR BIN AL-KHATAB

Hatuvat Yerushalayim

The
Citadel

B

C

David

St. Mark

F

Khan es-Sultan

Bab as-Silsilah St.

E

D

Ararat

The Israeli Tower

Shonei Halahot

Center for the
1st Temple Period

Cardo

Tiferet Yisrael

Plugat Ha-Kotel

Broad Wall

Armenian Art Center

Armenian Patriarchate Rd.

St. James

Or Ha-Hayim

Habad

Ha-Yehudim

Yishuv Court
Museum

Mishtav La-Dach

St. James'
Cathedral

Ararat

Ramban Synagogue

KIKKAR HURVA

Hurva Synagogue

Burnt House

Karaite Synagogue

Tiferet Yisrael Synagogue

ARMENIAN QUARTER

Yohanan Ben-Zakkai Synagogue

JEWISH QUART

Mishmerot Ha-Kehind

Armenian Museum

Ararat

KIKKAR
BATEI MAHASE

Hativat Ezioni

Sha'ar Zion

Batei Mahase

Zion Gate

Ma'ale Shalom St.

Note: the entire Old City is pedestrian only, except the shaded road.

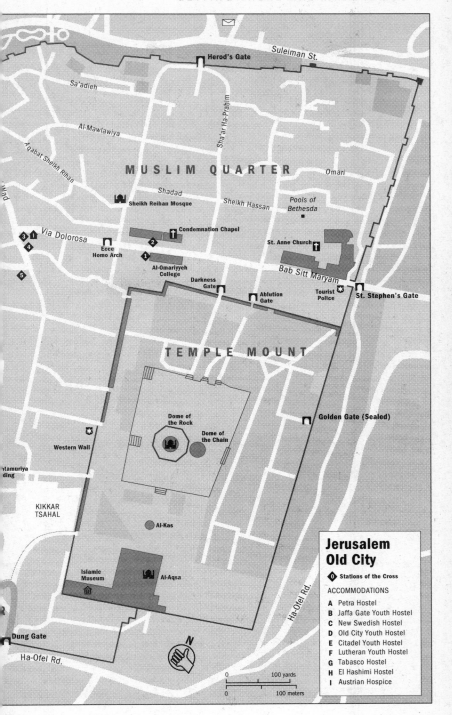

Herod's Gate

Suleiman St.

Sa'adieh

Al-Mawlawiya

Aqabat Sheikh Rihan

MUSLIM QUARTER

Omari

Shadad

Sheikh Reihan Mosque

Sheikh Hassan

Pools of
Bethesda

Via Dolorosa

Condemnation Chapel

Ecce
Homo Arch

St. Anne Church

Al-Omariyyeh
College

Bab Sitt Maryam

Darkness
Gate

Ablution
Gate

Tourist
Police

St. Stephen's Gate

TEMPLE MOUNT

Dome of
the Rock

Dome of
the Chain

Golden Gate (Sealed)

Western Wall

ntamuriya
ding

KIKKAR
TSAHAL

Al-Kas

Islamic
Museum

Al-Aqsa

Dung Gate

Ha-Ofel Rd.

Ha-Ofel Rd.

N

0   100 yards

0   100 meters

Jerusalem
Old City

◆ Stations of the Cross

ACCOMMODATIONS

A Petra Hostel
B Jaffa Gate Youth Hostel
C New Swedish Hostel
D Old City Youth Hostel
E Citadel Youth Hostel
F Lutheran Youth Hostel
G Tabasco Hostel
H El Hashimi Hostel
I Austrian Hospice

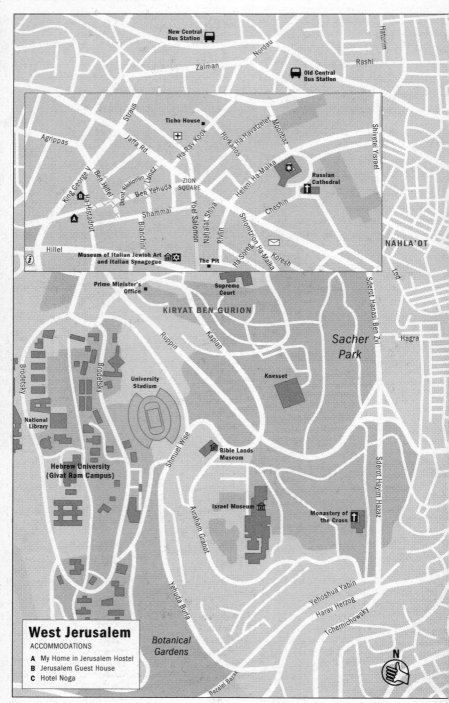

New Central Bus Station

Old Central Bus Station

Zalman

Nordau

Rashi

Haturim

Agrippas

Straus

Jaffa Rd.

Ticho House

Ha-Rav Kook

Horkanos

Ha-Havatzelet

Moohaz

Shivetei Yisrael

King George V

Ben Hillel

Dorot Rishonim

Lunez

Ben Yehuda

ZION SQUARE

Heleni Ha-Malka

Russian Cathedral

Ha-Histadrut

Shammai

Blanchin

Yoel Salomon

Nahalat Shiva

Rivlin

Ha-Soreg Ha-Malka

Shlomzion Ha-Malka

Cheshin

Koresh

NAHLA'OT

Hillel

Museum of Italian Jewish Art and Italian Synagogue

The Pit

Lod

Prime Minister's Office

Supreme Court

KIRYAT BEN GURION

Ruppin

Kaplan

Sacher Park

Sderot Hanasi Ben Zvi

Hagra

Brodetsky

Brodetsky

University Stadium

Knesset

National Library

Shmuel Wise

Bible Lands Museum

Hebrew University (Givat Ram Campus)

Avraham Granot

Israel Museum

Monastery of the Cross

Sderot Hayim Hazaz

Yehuda Burla

Yehoshua Yabin

Harav Herzog

Tchernichowsky

West Jerusalem

ACCOMMODATIONS

A My Home in Jerusalem Hostel
B Jerusalem Guest House
C Hotel Noga

Botanical Gardens

Bezalel Bazak

N

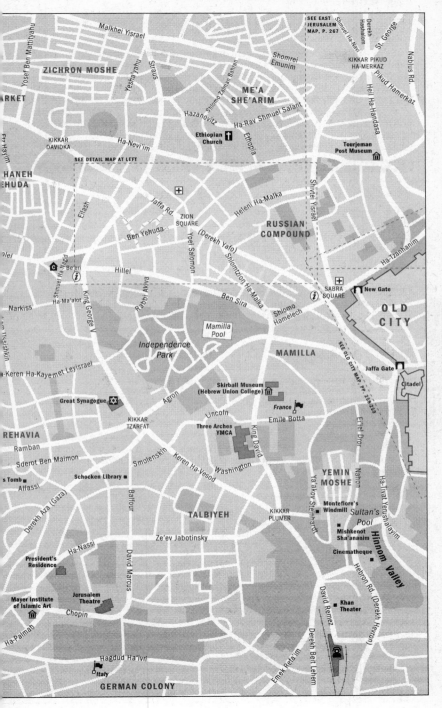

⊟ GETTING AROUND TOWN

BUSES. Most distances in Jerusalem are reasonable walks for those who don't mind the heat and the hills. All sections are easily reachable by bus from the **central bus station** (tel. 530 47 04) on Jaffa Rd., west of the city center just past the Maḥaneh Yehuda district (NIS4.50 per ride; NIS45 *kartisiya* buys 11 rides, 20 for those under 18). A dazzling **city bus map** is available at the information desk. Arab buses run every day; Egged service stops at about 4:30pm on Friday and resumes after sundown on Saturday. A popular summer line is **Bus #99,** the **Jerusalem Circular Line,** which leaves from Jaffa Gate or the central bus station, passing 34 major tourist sights on a two-hour loop (Su-Th 10am, noon, 2, 4pm; F 10am and noon; NIS24).

BUS NUMBER	ROUTE
#1	Me'a She'arim—Dung Gate—Western Wall
#4 and 4A	Emek Refa'im—Liberty Bell—Ramat Eshkol—Scopus
#6, 8, 13, and 18	West Jerusalem—Jaffa Rd. and King George St.
#6 and 20	West Jerusalem—Jaffa Gate
#9	Knesset—Israel Museum—Hebrew Univ—West Jerusalem—Scopus
#21	West Jerusalem—Train Station
#23	Damascus—Suleiman St.—East Jerusalem—Herod's Gate

TAXIS. Taxis are widely available. Try **Jerusalem Taxi,** 4 Ha-Histadrut St. (tel. 625 52 33), near the corner of King George and Ben-Yehuda St. (open Th-Su 6am-10pm, F 6am-3pm, Sa sundown-10pm), or **Taxi Israel,** 11 Ha-Histadrut (tel. 562 52 33-36; open 24hr.). **Samara Taxi** (tel. 052 875 436) serves West Jerusalem, near Jaffa Gate.

⊿ PRACTICAL INFORMATION

TOURIST AND FINANCIAL SERVICES

Tourist Offices: MTIO, 3 Safra Sq. (tel. 625 88 44), in the City Hall complex off Jaffa Rd. Entrance on the right, behind the fountain in the municipal plaza. Excellent computerized information, pamphlets, and maps. Open Su-Th 8:30am-4pm, F 8:45am-1pm. MTIO is far superior to the offices in the Old City, the best of which is **Solan Tourist Information** (tel. 628 03 82), on the left just inside Jaffa Gate. Sells books, postcards, phonecards, and stamps, and arranges Egged bus tours. Open daily 9am-4pm.

Special Interest Tourist Offices: Christian Information Center (tel. 627 26 92; fax 628 64 17; www.christusrex.org/www1/ofm/CICmain.html), inside Jaffa Gate, on the left past Solan. Friendly sisters offer info on Jerusalem's pilgrimage sights and lists of Christian lodgings. Complete calendar of year 2000 Christian events NIS4. Open M-Sa 8:30am-1pm. **Jewish Student Information Center,** 5 Beit El St. (tel. 052 876 795; fax 628 83 38; www.geocities.com/athens/7613), in Ḥurva Sq. in the Jewish Quarter. Run by zealous Jeff Seidel, who leads tours of the Western Wall tunnels. Arranges homestays with Orthodox Jewish families. Open 24hr.

Tours: Most hostels organize daily sunrise tours of the Negev (3am-3pm) with a sunrise climb up Masada (NIS80, less if business is slow; admission prices and food not included). **Egged Tours** (tel. 622 19 99; fax 622 17 17) offers 1-day trips in an A/C bus (US$70 includes lunch). **Zion Walking Tours** (tel. 628 78 66 or 050 305 552) has 7 inexpensive guided routes in and near the Old City (Four Quarters tour 3hr.; 9, 11am, 2pm; US$10, students US$9, including all entry fees. Other tours daily except Sa). **Israel Archeological Seminars** (tel. 627 35 15; fax 627 26 60; email office@archesem.com; www.archesem.com) has walking tours and day-long archaeology excursions. All tours meet in front of 34 Habad St., Jewish Quarter. Reserve a ticket in advance for a self-guided tour of the **Western Wall tunnels** (tel. 627 13 33; fax 626 48 28; www.hakotel.org), although a guided tour is preferable. The municipality sponsors a free **Shabbat walking tour** in English, leaving from 32 Jaffa Rd. near Zion Sq. (tel. 625 88 44; Sa 10am; rotates among several routes). **Society for the Protection of Nature in Israel (SPNI),** 13 Heleni Ha-Malka St. (tel. 625 23 57), runs guided tours throughout Israel and the Sinai. Tours range from ½-day explorations of Jerusalem to 15-day Israel odysseys. In July and Aug., unreserved Old City rampart tours in English meet at Jaffa Gate (Su and W 7pm, NIS70). Office open Su-Th 9am-6:45pm, F 9am-12:30pm. *This Week in Jerusalem* lists guided tours (also posted at the MTIO office) available through the **Petra Hostel** (see p. 261) and other hostels in the area.

Budget Travel: Neot Ha-Kikar, 5 Shlomzion Ha-Malka St. (tel. 623 62 62; fax 623 62 61), specializes in Sinai tours from Eilat (from US$55 per day). Open Su-Th 9am-5pm, F 9am-12:30pm. **ISSTA,** 31 Ha-Nevi'im St. (tel. 625 27 99), has ISIC cards (NIS40 with proof of student status and photo) and student discounts on airfare, car rentals, and Eurail passes. Open Su-Tu and Th 9am-7pm, W and F 9am-1pm. Additional offices inside L'Metayel camping store (see p. 260), and at the Hebrew University campus on Mount Scopus (tel. 582 61 16) and Givat Ram (tel. 651 87 80).

Consulates: U.K., 19 Nashashibi St. (tel. 541 41 00), in East Jerusalem near Sheikh Jar-rah St. Open M-F 9am-1pm. **U.S.,** 27 Nablus Rd. (tel. 622 72 00). Open for passport renewals and other services M-F 8:30-11:30am, notary service Tu 1-3pm. 24hr. marine guard for emergencies (tel. 622 72 01). Closed for Israeli and U.S. holidays and the last F of each month. Administrative offices at 18 Agron St. in West Jerusalem (tel. 622 72 30, after-hours tel. 622 72 50). Other consulates in Tel Aviv (see p. 292).

Banks: Bank Mizrahi, 26 Tiferet Yisrael St. (tel. 627 31 31; fax 628 84 29), the blue sign in Hurva Sq., in the Jewish Quarter. Only **ATM** in the Old City and automated currency exchange. Open Su-Th 9am-1:30pm, M and W 5-7pm, F 9am-noon. **Changepoint,** 33 Jaffa Rd. (tel. 625 55 72), in West Jerusalem. Open Su-Th 9am-5pm, F 9am-12:30pm. **Money Net,** 8 Ben Hillel St. (tel. 622 23 18; fax 623 27 88), on the *midrahov.* Open Su-Th 9am-6pm, F 9am-2pm. Both are commission-free with better rates than banks. **Bank Ha-Poalim** (tel. (03) 567 49 99), in Zion Sq. **ATM** accepts Cirrus, PLUS, and major credit cards. Open Su and Tu-W 8:30am-1pm, M and Th 8:30am-1pm and 4-7pm, F 8:30am-12:30pm.

American Express: 19 Hillel St. (tel. 625 41 71/73; fax 624 09 50), near McDonald's. Full service office with traveler's check exchange, purchase, and replacement for cardholders. Letters held, but not packages. For traveler's check emergencies, call 24hr. toll-free (177) 440 86 94. Open Su-Th 9am-5pm, F 9am-1pm.

LOCAL SERVICES

Lost Property: 107 Jaffa Rd. (tel. 639 13 60/61). Open Su-Th 7:30am-4:30pm. **Ben-Gurion Airport Lost and Found:** Tel. (03) 971 69 34.

English Bookstore: Steimatzky's, 39 Jaffa St. (tel. 625 01 55), sells magazines, travel books, and Carta's (NIS34), the best map of Jerusalem. Other locations on 7 Ben Yehuda St. and 9 King George St. Open Su-Th 8:30am-7pm (Ben Yehuda location until 8pm), F 8:30am-2pm. **SPNI Bookstore,** 13 Heleni Ha-Malka St., often has the lowest prices on guidebooks and maps. **Sefer ve-Sefel,** 2 Ya'avetz St. (tel. 624 82 37), off Jaffa St. east of King George St. on the right. Open Su-Th 8am-8pm, F 8am-2:30pm.

Ticket Agencies: Bimot, 8 Shammai St. (tel. 625 09 05), and **Kla'im,** 12 Shammai St. (tel. 625 68 69), have discount tickets for students and tourists to concerts, shows, and sporting events around Jerusalem. Both open Su-Th 9am-7pm, F 9am-1pm.

Laundromat: Laundry Place, 12 Shammai St. (tel. 625 77 14), conveniently located near the *midrahov.* Self-service NIS17 per load includes dryer and detergent. Open Su-Th 8:30am-midnight, F 8:30am-sundown., Sa sundown-midnight. **Buot Laundry,** 5 Shmuel Ha-Nagid St. (tel. 625 70 06), off Be'eri St. Wash, dry, and fold up to 7kg for NIS35, students NIS30. Open Su-Th 8am-1pm and 3-7pm, F 8am-1pm.

Swimming Pools: Jerusalem Pool, 43 Emek Refa'im St. (tel. 563 20 92), take bus #4, 14, or 18. Open daily 6am-8:30pm. NIS40, students NIS35. Get Sa tickets in advance.

ISRAEL

Camping Supplies: The most extensive (and expensive) camping gear is at **L'Metayel,** 5 Yoel Salomon St. (tel. 623 33 38; fax 623 33 52). Open Su-Th 10am-9pm, F 10am-2:30pm. **Orcha Camping,** 12 Yoel Salomon, near Cafe Kapulsky (tel. 624 06 55), is affiliated with SPNI. Open Su-Th 9am-7pm, F 8:30am-3pm. The sunburst logo of **Steve's Packs,** 11 Ben-Hillel (tel. 624 83 02) on the *midraḥov,* adorns half the knapsacks in Jerusalem. Open Su-Th 9:30am-9pm, F 10:30am-3pm.

EMERGENCY AND COMMUNICATIONS

Emergency: Tel. 100. **Police:** Tel. 101. **Fire:** Tel. 102.

Police: In the Russian Compound (tel. 539 11 11), off Jaffa Rd. in West Jerusalem. **Tourist desk** (tel. 675 48 11), on Cheshin St. off Jaffa Rd. near the post office. Old City branch (tel. 622 62 22) inside Jaffa Gate on the right.

Help Lines: Rape Crisis Center (tel. 625 55 58, emergency beeper 629 46 66 extension #1932). **Mental Health Hotline** (tel. 561 03 03), also called **Eran,** assists tourists. Open 8am-11pm. **Alcoholics Anonymous** (tel. 563 50 62 or 563 05 24) is open 24hr.

Services for the Disabled: Yad Sarah Organization, 43 Ha-Nevi'im St. (tel. 644 44 44). Free loans of medical equipment. Offers wheelchair van for airport pick-ups (NIS150, order 2 days in advance) and rides anywhere within Jerusalem (NIS25; NIS30 after 6pm). Open Su-Th 9am-7pm, F 9am-12:30pm.

Pharmacies: Old City: Jaffa Gate Pharmacy (tel. 628 38 98), on the right after the 1st left from Jaffa Gate. Open 9am-8:30pm. **Habash Pharmacy,** 104 Al-Wad St. (tel. 627 24 27; fax 628 81 57), in the Muslim Quarter. Open 8:30am-8pm. **West Jerusalem: Superpharm,** 3 Ha-Histadrut (tel. 624 62 44/5/9; fax 624 75 75), between Ben-Yehuda and King George St. Open Su-Th 8:30am-11pm, F 8:30am-3pm, Sa sundown-11pm. **Alba Pharmacy,** 42 Jaffa St. (tel. 625 37 03). Open Su-Th 7:30am-7pm, F 7:30am-2pm. Two pharmacies rotate duty nightly and on Shabbat; check newspapers.

Medical Assistance: Old City: Austrian Society Medical Center, Qanatar Khadeir Rd. (tel. 627 32 46), off Al-Wad St. in the Muslim Quarter, directly across the street from the Austrian Hospice. Open daily 7:30am-7pm. **Kupat Holim** (tel. 627 16 08), in the Jewish Quarter above the Cardo, across from Ḥurva Sq. Hours are erratic. **West Jerusalem: Magen David Adom First Aid** (tel. 652 31 33), near the old central bus station. Its 24hr. **Terem Clinic** (tel. 652 17 48) sees those who are insured.

Post Office: Central Post Office, 23 Jaffa Rd. (tel. 629 06 47). Poste Restante for no fee; Western Union and fax services available. Open Su-Th 7am-7pm, F 7am-noon. Branch post offices in almost every neighborhood (look for bright red awnings).

Internet Access: The Netcafe, 9 Heleni Ha-Malka St. (tel. 624 63 27), uphill from Jaffa Rd. NIS7 for 15min., NIS25 per hr. Open Su-Tu 11am-10pm, W-Th 11am-late, F 10am-3pm, Sa 9pm-late. Also see **Strudel Internet Cafe and Wine Bar,** p. 267.

Telephones: Solan Communications, 2 Luntz St. (tel. 625 89 08; fax 625 88 79), off Ben-Yehuda St. on the *midraḥov.* International fax services (NIS13 first page, NIS8 each additional page), private booths for local and international calls (NIS2 per min.), and cellular phone rentals and sales. Open Su-Th 8am-11:15pm, F 8am-6pm, Sa 6pm-midnight. Additional branch inside Jaffa Gate. 24hr. information: tel. 144.

Telephone Code: 02.

▓ ACCOMMODATIONS

OLD CITY

Most of Jerusalem's cheapest hostels are in the Old City, but these vary tremendously in quality and safety (neither price nor location are good barometers). Solo women should be especially discriminating about where to stay and should dress modestly: t-shirts are OK, but exposing anything more than forearms will attract undue attention in the conservative Old City. Accommodations here fall into two categories: quieter, cleaner establishments with curfews; and the sometimes less clean, sometimes more fun, and correspondingly less safe hostels, some featuring bars or lax alcohol policies. Both kinds have priceless rooftop views of the surrounding sights. Bargain for discounts on multiple-night stays or if business seems slow. One further note: As the spiritual hub for much of the world, the Old City is expected to be more heavily affected by the millennium than anywhere else in Israel—reserve far in advance. Although the rates below are accurate as of summer 1999, some hostel owners may change their prices without notice.

> ❗ **THERE'S NO PLACE LIKE HOME.** Be extremely cautious in the Old City after dark. Those staying in the Muslim Quarter (especially women) should not walk alone and should make their tourist status pronounced. Only the busiest streets in the Old City are lit at night, so learn the way to your bed during the day.

 El-Hashimi Hostel, 73 Souq Khan az-Zeit Rd. (tel. 628 44 10; fax 628 46 67; email hashimi@alami.net). Take the right fork from Damascus Gate. Marble-bedecked 3-story hostel has an Internet cafe (NIS10 for 15min.) with incredible views of the Dome of the Rock. The squeaky clean bathrooms, sturdy beds, kitchen, and TV lounge are toasty in winter. Dorm beds NIS20; singles NIS72-95; doubles NIS143-215/US$30-45; triples NIS215-263/US$45-55. 15% discount for stays longer than 2 nights. Curfew 3am.

Austrian Hospice, 37 Via Dolorosa (tel. 627 14 63; fax 627 14 72), on the corner of Al-Wad Rd. One of the best hostels in the Old City, with lush gardens, a library, chapel, and glorious roof view. Spacious private rooms have heat, phones, and hard beds. Wheelchair accessible. Single-sex dorms NIS72 (2 night min. stay; free private lockers included). Singles NIS273/US$49; doubles NIS372/US$78; triples NIS530/US$111. Breakfast included, cafe open all day. Key deposit NIS50/US$20. 21-day max. stay. Midnight curfew (night key available for NIS50). Reservations highly recommended.

Petra Hostel, 1 David St. (tel. 628 66 18), on the left just before the entrance to the Arab market. World-famous hostel with fantastic rooftop views and a vast, sunny lounge. Built more than 175 years ago, this is the oldest accommodation of any sort in the Old City, and at points feels proportionally bedraggled. Roof mattresses NIS21, with sheets and blanket NIS24. Dorms NIS38. Private rooms NIS120-190/US$25-40, with private showers NIS143-239/US$30-50. Breakfast NIS12. Full laundry NIS24. Reservations only for morning arrivals.

Lutheran Youth Hostel (tel. 628 21 20; fax 628 51 07), on St. Mark's Rd., the first alleyway off David St. Half hostel, half guest house, all Lutheran. Anyone can stay, but clientele is primarily German. Same-sex dorms NIS30; rooms NIS25-50. Free lockers. Curfew 10:30pm, flexible until midnight. Guests must be under 35. No reservations for dorms.

Jaffa Gate Youth Hostel (tel. 627 64 02), across from the Tower of David; follow the black and pink sign down an alleyway. Run by a friendly Palestinian couple. Marble and wicker TV lounge on the patio, clean common kitchen, and immaculate, A/C rooms with bath. Dorms NIS40; 2-4 person rooms NIS80-200/US$20-50. Breakfast included. Laundry service. Ask for a discount. Midnight curfew. No smoking. No credit cards.

Citadel Youth Hostel, 20 St. Mark's Rd. (tel. 627 43 75), the 1st alleyway off David St., marked by a blue sign. Tidy rooms with vaulted ceilings and shared baths comfortably fit 4 adults. Several lounge areas, satellite TV, and common kitchen. 2-week max. stay. Dorms NIS25, students and *Let's Go* readers NIS20; private rooms NIS95-NIS120. Flexible midnight curfew; ask for key.

Tabasco Hostel, 8 Akabat Tekreh St. (tel. 628 11 01; fax 628 34 61), off Souq Khan az-Zeit Rd.; take the right fork from Damascus Gate. Huge, dirt-cheap hostel with rowdy, hot-'n'-spicy international crowd. Bedouin-style "Tea" Room is always buzzing (happy hour 10-11pm; 2 beers NIS10). Hot showers 6am-10pm. Masada daytrips and boats to Greece available. Roof shed bed NIS20; dorms NIS25; private rooms NIS100. 15% student discount. Lockers NIS2 per day. Laundry NIS25.

New Swedish Hostel, 29 David St. (tel. 626 41 24 or 627 78 55), in the *souq* near Jaffa Gate, on the left. Very crowded dormitory, tiny TV area, and shared bathrooms. Coed and single-sex accommodations. Dorms NIS20-22; small private rooms NIS65-75. Lockers NIS3 for full stay. Curfew 3am. No visitors 11pm-9am.

ISRAEL

WEST JERUSALEM

Accommodations in West Jerusalem are generally roomier, cleaner, and safer than their Old City counterparts (and correspondingly more expensive). Hostels here are better for club-hoppers: most establishments have no curfew, and some are directly above the action. Avoid the 17% VAT by paying in non-Israeli currency.

 Hotel Noga, 4 Bezalel St. (tel. 625 45 90, after 2pm tel./fax 566 18 88—ask for Mr. or Mrs. Kristal). Walk down King George from the city center, turn right onto Be'eri St., left onto Shmuel Ha-Nagid St., and right onto Bezalel St. Feels like having a private apartment, as the managers leave after 2pm. 10 bright, airy rooms on 2 floors; each floor has 1 full bath and kitchen. Free luggage storage; 24hr. hot water. Parking in back. Singles NIS134-143/US$28-30; doubles NIS167-191/US$35-40; triples NIS215/US$45; quads NIS263/US$55. 2-night min. stay. Reservations required.

My Home in Jerusalem Hostel, 15 King George St. (tel 623 22 35; fax 623 22 36; email myhome@netvision.co.il; www.myhome.co.il), 1 block from Jaffa Rd. Take bus #8, 9, 31, or 32 from central station. Decently clean rooms, cable TV lounge, and prime location. Shared bathrooms. Masada sunrise tours leave daily at 3am (NIS70). Dorms NIS62-86/US$13-18; doubles NIS239-286/US$50-60. Breakfast included.

Jerusalem Inn Guest House, 6 Ha-Histadrut St. (tel. 625 12 94; fax 625 12 97; email jerinn@netvision.net.il; www.jerusaleminn.co.il), off King George St., 1 block from Ben-Yehuda St. Take bus #14, 17, 31, or 32 from central station (1st stop on King George). This one-time hostel is now a tech-friendly 12-room hotel. All rooms have fan, digital safe, cable TV, and 24hr. heating in winter; some have private bath or balconies. No visitors, front door locked at night. Strictly no smoking. Private doubles, triples, and 6-person rooms NIS134-181/US$28-38 per person; 10-20% less when not full. Reception open Su-Th 8am-11pm, F 8am-3pm, Sa 6-11pm. Credit card required for reservations but not accepted for payment.

Beit Gesher, 10 King David St. (tel. 624 10 15; fax 625 52 26). Cozy, quiet 39-room hostel in a beautiful building. All rooms have private bath. Singles NIS181/US$38; doubles NIS258/US$54; US$14 per person for 3rd and 4th person. Breakfast NIS30/US$7. 24hr. reception. Reservations recommended.

EAST JERUSALEM

East Jerusalem is a beautiful and vibrant slice of Palestinian life that contrasts starkly with the western parts of the city; however, it is also a hotbed of political tension. Feel out the situation before deciding to stay here. Travelers, particularly solo women, should not walk alone at night. Several hostels line the parking lot at the base of Ha-Nevi'im St., which intersects Suleiman St. across from Damascus Gate.

> **! SAFETY WARNING.** Tensions sometimes make East Jerusalem and parts of the Old City unfriendly to Israelis and Jewish foreigners. Jewish travelers should make their tourist status as pronounced as possible. Wearing a *kippah* is a bad idea in the Arab parts of town.

 Cairo Youth Hostel, 21 Nablus Rd. (tel. 627 72 16), on the left coming up from Damascus Gate area. Last stop on bus #27. Recently renovated, sparkling-clean hostel with a large sitting area, a view-lover's roof, and an immaculate kitchen. Heat in winter. Free luggage storage. Management runs daily trips to Gaza and the refugee camps outside Ramallah (Masada sunrise tour NIS70). Roof mattress NIS15. 4 co-ed and single-sex dorm beds NIS20; 1 private room for 1-4 people, NIS80. Curfew 1am. No credit cards.

Faisal Internet Youth Hostel, 4 Ha-Nevi'im St. (tel. 628 75 02; email faisalsam@hotmail.com), opposite Damascus Gate. Pleasant and relaxing, with crowded bunks, satellite TV lounge, kitchen, and Internet access (NIS10 for 15min., after 7pm NIS6 for 15min.). Large, cozy bar on patio. Co-ed and single-sex dorm beds NIS20; private doubles and triples NIS80. Reception 24hr. Curfew 1am. No credit cards.

ISRAEL

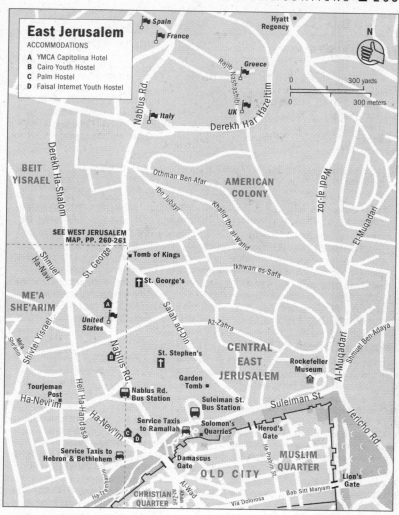

East Jerusalem

ACCOMMODATIONS

A YMCA Capitolina Hotel
B Cairo Youth Hostel
C Palm Hostel
D Faisal Internet Youth Hostel

N

0   300 yards
0   300 meters

Spain

France

Hyatt
Regency

Greece

Rajib Nashashibi

UK

Italy

Derekh Har Hazeitim

Nablus Rd.

Derekh Ha-Shalom

BEIT
YISRAEL

Othman Ben-Afar

AMERICAN
COLONY

Ibn Jubayr

Khalid ibn al-Walid

Wadi al-Joz

El-Muqadari

SEE WEST JERUSALEM
MAP, PP. 260-261

Shmuel
Ha-Navi

St. George

Tomb of Kings

St. George's

Ikhwan es-Safa

ME'A
SHE'ARIM

Me'a She'arim

Shivtei Yisrael

United
States

Salah ad-Din

Az-Zahra

CENTRAL
EAST
JERUSALEM

Rockefeller
Museum

Al-Muqadari

Shmuel Ben-Adaya

St. Stephen's

Nablus Rd.

Heil Ha-Handasa

Tourjeman
Post
Ha-Nevi'im

Ha-Nevi'im

Garden
Tomb

Nablus Rd.
Bus Station

Suleiman St.
Bus Station

Suleiman St.

Jericho Rd.

Service Taxis
to Ramallah

Solomon's
Quarries

Herod's
Gate

Service Taxis to
Hebron & Bethlehem

Damascus
Gate

MUSLIM
QUARTER

Ha-Tzanhanim

OLD CITY

Ha-Prahim St.

Lion's
Gate

CHRISTIAN
QUARTER

Al-Wad

Khan az-Zeit

Bab Sitt Maryam

Via Dolorosa

ISRAEL

Palm Hostel, 6 Ha-Nevi'im St. (tel. 627 31 89), opposite Damascus Gate on the right when facing away from the Old City walls. Under new management, the hostel has become more liberal and less Christian. Daily tours to the West Bank, including refugee camps outside Ramallah. Co-ed and single-sex dorm rooms with adequate bathrooms. Upper common room for eating, smoking, and watching videos. Heated in winter. Dorms NIS25, students NIS20; private rooms NIS100-120, students NIS80-100. Bargaining expected. Reception 24hr. No credit cards.

YMCA Capitolina Hotel, 29 Nablus Rd. (tel. 628 68 88; fax 627 63 01), next door to the American consulate, in the magnificent YMCA building. Best splurge option in East Jerusalem. Beautiful sitting rooms and restaurant on the top floor with epic views of the city. Very comfortable rooms with full bath, many with balcony. Singles NIS286/US$60; doubles NIS382/US$80, add a bed at no additional charge. 15% service not included. Breakfast included. Lunch and dinner US$10. Sports facilities, including an Olympic-sized pool, at a nominal charge. Reception 24hr. Reservations highly recommended.

⚫ FOOD

OLD CITY

Cheap restaurants crowd the narrow alleys of the Old City. The chicken restaurants on **Souq Khan az-Zeit Rd.**, inside Damascus Gate, are popular with locals. Interchangeable sit-down restaurants line Al-Wad Rd. and Bab as-Silsilah St. Street vendors sell fresh, soft sesame *ka'ak* with *za'tar* in the *souq* (NIS2-3). ⚫**Ja'afar and Sons Pastries,** 42 Souq Khan az-Zeit Rd. (tel. 628 35 82), offers the best, hottest, most authentic pastries in the market, bar none (open daily 7am-7pm). **Tony's Quick Market** (tel. 626 47 39), in Ḥurva Sq. in the Jewish Quarter, has groceries for a cheap meal (open Su-Th 7am-7pm, F 7am-2pm).

🔲 **Abu Shanab Pizza and Bar,** 35 Latin Patriarchate Rd. (tel. 626 07 52), left of Jaffa Gate. The Old City's most happenin' hangout is a favorite of natives and tourists alike. Individual pizzas NIS10-30, cocktails NIS15. Live jazz weekly. Open M-Sa 10am-11pm.

Bracha Bakery (tel. 628 01 37), in Ḥurva Sq., left of the art gallery. Assorted fresh-baked goods like baguette with omelette (NIS10). Open Su-Th until midnight, F 7am-sundown.

Nafoura, 10 Latin Patriarchate St. (tel. 626 00 34; fax 626 00 62), 1st left inside Jaffa Gate. Classical music, gleaming crystal chandeliers, and gurgling tiled fountains make this the most elegant and beautiful restaurant in the Old City. Full dinner (including aperitif) NIS65. 10% *Let's Go* discount. Open daily 11am-11pm.

Damascus Gate Cafe (tel. 627 42 82), inside Damascus Gate on the left. Escape the racket of the Gate with the serenity of the Gate Cafe. Catch a quick bite and a drink on the large shaded terrace. Shawarma NIS12, full breakfast NIS20, *qahwa* (Arabic coffee) or tea NIS5. Open daily in summer 7:30am-10pm; in winter 7:30am-7:00pm.

WEST JERUSALEM

Restaurants here serve everything from shawarma to sushi (with a corresponding array of prices), reflecting the international make-up of its population. Chews your own meal adventure from among the many "business lunch" specials at the city-center restaurants. To choose your own ingredients, head for the raucous open-air **Maḥaneh Yehuda** market between Jaffa Rd. and Agrippas St. (best time Sa-Th 7-8pm, F 1-2hr. before sundown). *Me'orav*, a mix of inner parts grilled with onions and packed in pita pockets, is a specialty of the stands on Agrippas St., behind Maḥaneh Yehuda. The stands along Etz Ha-Ḥayim St. sell the best *ḥalva* (a sesame marzipan) at NIS14 per kg. **Ma'adei Mickey** (Mickey's Deli), halfway between Jaffa and Agrippas on Etz Ha-Ḥayim St., sells excellent hummus and salads for NIS18 per kg. **Marzipan Bakery,** 44 Agrippas St. (tel. 623 26 18), sells *ruggelah* to die for—eat a kilo (NIS18.40) and you just might. **Drugstore 2000,** 21 Shammai St. (tel. 624 74 40), at the bottom of the *midraḥov*, is the only 24-hour, seven-days-a-week supermarket in the West Jerusalem area.

RESTAURANTS

🔲 **Pampa Grill,** 3 Rivlin St. (tel. 623 14 55), off Jaffa Rd. near Naḥalat Shiva St. High quality South American grill sure to delight any carnivore. Fresh daily lunch special NIS28. Take-out next door (huge chicken or beef baguette and fried onions NIS15). Open Su-Th noon-midnight, F noon-sundown, Sa sundown-midnight. Kosher.

🔲 **Sahara Tulip,** 17 Jaffa Rd. (tel. 625 42 39), on the left coming from Old City's Jaffa Gate. This vegetarian delight and former Moroccan kitchen is the closest thing to a home-cooked meal in Jerusalem. Sweet fish with rice and salad NIS48, renowned tofu stew NIS35. Open Su 6:30-10pm, M-Th 12:30-3pm and 6:30-10pm. Kosher.

🔲 **Alumah,** 12 Agrippas St. (tel. 625 50 14), just off King George St. The ultimate in health food: delicious, organic, non-dairy meals average NIS29, with rice, veggies, and two slices of sourdough. Open Su-Th 7am-7pm, F 7am-2pm. Kosher.

Rose, 6 Rabbi Akiva St. (tel. 624 69 77), off Hillel St. A lively young crowd flocks to the candle-lit elegance and breezy patio. Rose peddles all sorts of international fare, from chicken-chili sandwiches (NIS30) to lasagna (NIS36). Try the triple chocolate ice cream cake. Friday night special 6:30-9:30pm, full dinner NIS65. Open daily 10:30am-2am.

Amigos, 19 Yoel Solomon St. (tel. 623 41 77), in the *midrahov*. Delicious Mexican food served to sprightly music. Order any steaming fajita plate (steak and chicken NIS69) and it'll bring along its *amigo* (a frozen margarita) for free! Lunch special NIS35. Open Su-Th noon-1am, F noon-sundown, Sa sundown-1am.

Cafe Chagall, 5 Ben-Yehuda St. (tel. 623 33 31). This dairy-friendly *midrahov* fixture with decor inspire by the famed Jewish artist offers 12 humongous fresh salads (NIS32-41). Open Su-Th 7am-midnight, F 7am-sundown, Sa sundown-2am. Kosher.

La Soupiere, 22 King Solomon St. (tel. 623 06 95), parallel to Jaffa Rd. Their motto is "we take soup very seriously," and they mean it. Fresh gourmet soups with bread and butter NIS12-16. Open Sa-Th 6pm-midnight.

Village Green, 33 Jaffa St. (tel. 625 30 65), at the corner of Rivlin St. Made-from-scratch vegetarian food served by weight, cafeteria style (min. NIS13, up to NIS30). Unlimited whole wheat bread, tahini, and dressings. More romantic location of the same restaurant on 1 Bezalel St. (tel. 625 14 64), off King George in the city center. More traditional menu-style service. Open Su-Th 11am-10pm, F 11am-3pm. Kosher.

Misadonet, 12 Yoel Solomon St. (tel. 624 83 96). Turn right into any alleyway coming from Zion Sq. Authentic Kurdish kitchen with traditional decor and delicious appetizers and soups. Chicken steak with salad and *majadra* (intense lentil and rice pilaf) NIS32. Open Su-Th noon-1am, F noon-sundown, Sa sundown-1am. Kosher.

Pepperoni's, 4 Rabbi Akiva St. (tel. 625 78 29), off Hillel St. Perhaps the best Italian restaurant in Jerusalem. Florentine ambience soaked in *vino* and olive oil. Lunch pasta NIS36, meat and fish dishes NIS40. **Foccaccia,** the airy patio out front, serves pizza and coffee. Open daily noon-midnight.

Sakura, in Feingold Court (tel. 623 54 64), enter from 31 Jaffa Rd., just past Zion Sq. towards the Old City. Small but popular Japanese restaurant with sleek-chic decor. Pork *gyoza* NIS46, seafood tempura platter NIS65.

The Yemenite Step, 10 Salomon St. (tel. 624 04 77). Grand stone building with high ceilings and outdoor seating in the heart of the cafe scene. Try the heavenly *malaweh*, their specialty (with honey NIS16, with filling NIS34 and up). Open Su-Th noon-12:30am, F noon-4pm, Sa sundown-1am. Kosher.

QUICKIES

Babbette's Party, 8 Ramban St. (tel. 567 10 47) and 16 Shammai St. (tel. 814 11 82). Feast on 14 Belgian waffle varieties (dark or white chocolate NIS14, ask for a sprinkle of Kahlua) and the best hot chocolate in Israel—some say the world (with brandy shot NIS10). Ramban St. open Su-Th 6am-3am, F 6am-sundown, Sa sundown-3am. Shammai St. open Su-Th 10am-2am, F 10am-sundown, Sa sundown-2am.

Thai Sandwich Bar, 25 Jaffa St. (tel. 625 19 95). Just wok and roll: Asian-style beef, chicken, or veggies in baguettes NIS17, in a box or plate NIS21. Open Su-Th noon-midnight, F noon-sundown, Sa sundown-midnight. Kosher.

Haifa Turkish Borekas, 28 Jaffa St. (tel. 624 77 70), past Zion Sq., across from the central post office. Dozens of fresh-baked *borekas* (large pastries stuffed with cheese and potato, NIS7). Open Su-Th 24hr., F until sundown, Sa after sundown. Kosher.

Henri's Creperie, 1 Rivlin St. (tel. 643 80 15), delectable crepes late into the night (NIS10-13), including blueberry, Nutella, and cream cheese with strawberries. Open Su-W 10am-2am, Th 10am-4am, F 10am-sundown, Sa sundown-4am.

Ben and Jerry's, 5 Hillel St. (tel. 624 27 67), just off King George St. The Holy Land meets Bovinity Divinity. Small NIS9.90, regular NIS11.90, pint NIS19.90.

CAFES

▨ **Tmol Shilshom,** 5 Yoel Solomon St. (tel. 623 27 58). Enter from Naḥalat Shiva St. This bookstore-cafe is a favorite of poet Yehuda Amiḥai, who gives readings with other local greats once a week (call in advance for dates). Others contemplate over coffee and tea (NIS8-14). Renowned all-you-can-eat breakfast buffet Friday morning NIS34. Internet access NIS9 for 30min., but only until 3pm. Gay-friendly. Open Su-Th 8am-2am, F 8am-3pm, Sa sundown-2am. Kosher.

Acha, 7 Yoel Solomon St. (tel. 623 66 03). Temple to Israeli pop culture's newest fetish: Indian mysticism. The name is Bengali for "I dig it," and you will: recline like a raj on fluffy pillows and munch on eclectic Eastern cuisine from *naan* and Arab kebab (NIS45) to mango ice cream (NIS25) and imported wine. Open daily 7pm-3am.

Cafe Atara, 15 Ben Yehuda St. (tel. 625 01 43). Atara was the first eatery on the street when it opened in 1938. Its rich history has earned it a steady following. Newly redecorated with wood paneling and glass fixtures. Selection of toasted sandwiches NIS28, large salads NIS29, dessert pies NIS20. Various wines and coffees. Open Su-Th 7am-midnight, F 7am-3pm, Sa sundown-midnight. Kosher.

EAST JERUSALEM

▨ **Kan Zaman** (tel. 628 32 82), on the patio of the Jerusalem Hotel, behind the bus station on Nablus Rd. Glass-enclosed garden restaurant serves vegetarian dishes (NIS25) and meat and fish meals (NIS30-50). Lebanese buffet Sa after 8pm (NIS60). Live classical Arabic music F and Sa nights. Open daily 7-10am and 11am-11pm.

Omarayya Restaurant, 21 Suleiman St. (tel. 628 61 02), across the street and to the right from Damascus Gate. Authentic Palestinian kitchen serves shawarma, shish kebab, and *maklubeh,* an "upside down" rice patty (all NIS22). Open daily 9am-11pm.

American Colony Hotel Restaurant (tel. 627 97 77), in the fountained courtyard of the American Colony Hotel, past the U.S. Consulate on Nablus Rd. The city's most romantic refuge. At night, take a cab from the city center (NIS11). Spectacular food, priced high for special nights, is worth it. 3-course meal US$25, entrees US$10-30. Open 6:30-10:30am, noon-3pm, and 7-9:45pm. Reservations recommended.

🎵 ENTERTAINMENT

Tel Avivans hate to admit it, but Jerusalem's nightlife is no longer joke-worthy. Once the city's conservative majority is tucked into bed, the bar and club scene comes to life; from Thursday to Saturday nights, the city's energy is so high it would make a rabbi's hair curl. The best weekly info in English is the "In Jerusalem" insert in Friday's *Jerusalem Post.* The tourist office in Safra Sq. (see p. 258) also has detailed monthly calendars in English.

BARS

In the shadow of the stately Orthodox churches of the **Russian Compound** (Migrash Ha-Russim), two blocks down Heleni Ha-Malka St., neon beer signs lure liquor lovers like moths. After midnight, stylish bars in old stone buildings fill to capacity with a young, hip crowd jivin' to jazz, krooning along to karaoke, and doing everything in between. The **midraḥov,** just five minutes away, offers less rowdy but equally popular escapes.

RUSSIAN COMPOUND

Tarabin House, 9 Moonbaz St. (tel. 623 29 29), off Heleni Ha-Malka St. After a raucous night in the Compound, *nargilah* lovers blow off steam at this mellow and eclectic oasis of candles, pastoral Bedouin murals, and jungle prints. All-you-can-smoke NIS25. Tarabin Cocktail NIS25. Open daily 8pm-morning.

Kanabis, 11 Moonbaz St. (tel. 623 29 29), just upstairs from Tarabin. Large bar/restaurant with tented terrace overlooking the Moonbaz scene. Dope circular bar with 3-page cocktail menu. Individual pizzas and salads NIS30-35. Karaoke M and Tu nights beginning at 10pm. Open daily 8pm-4am.

Sergey, 1 Heleni Ha-Malka St. (tel. 625 85 11). No-frills bar with intellectual twentysomething crowd from Bezalel Art Institute (so hip they don't even wear black). Beer NIS15, mixed drinks NIS20. M blues night. 20+ admitted. Open daily from 7pm.

Egon, 9 Naḥalat Shiva St. (tel. 622 24 58), in an alleyway accessible from 31 Jaffa St. Crowded, casually fabulous outdoor spot with 50 kinds of beer (NIS12-35), 40 kinds of ice cream (NIS17), and all-you-can-smoke *nargilah* (NIS14). Lasagna NIS32, soup NIS16. Free backgammon, so who ya gonna call to play with you? Open daily 24hr.

Strudel Internet Cafe and Bar, 11 Moonbaz St. (tel. 623 21 01). This Internet cafe (NIS6 for 15min.) is popular with Anglophone expats and American Hebrew University students gathering forces on their way to the Underground. Happy hour 7-9pm and midnight-12:30am (15min. web time and beer NIS13). Open M-F 10am-late, Sa 3pm-late.

MIDRAḤOV

Shanty, 4 Naḥalat Shiva St. (tel. 624 34 34), tucked in a corner in the alleyway between Yoel Solomon and Rivlin St. This local fave, nestled among tourist raves, cards hard to keep out teen peeps. Candle-lit room and outdoor tables always filled to capacity. Hot cinnamon spiced wine NIS15, beer NIS15, salads and house specials NIS33-36. Open 7pm-whenever, but kitchen closes at 11pm.

Syndrome, 18 Hillel St. (tel. 054 808 210). Somewhat hard to find but worth it: take the red steps underneath Cafe Aroma; it's at the end of the hall. Symptoms of this syndrome include: no food or coffee but plenty of booze; friendly and casual behavior; frequent breakouts of live music (mostly blues and rock) every night 10pm-1am; NIS20-40 cover including a beer. Open daily 8pm-2am.

Churchill, 18 Rivlin St. (tel. 624 42 33), off Jaffa Rd. The former British Prime Minister once said: "This comfy bar and restaurant (sirloin steak NIS54) livens up Saturday nights with live music and Wednesday nights with jazz. Drinks NIS20 and up. Open Su-Th noon-1am, F noon-sundown, Sa sundown-2am."

Zanzibar, 13 Shammai St. (tel. 624 19 74). Jerusalem's rich PYTs (pretty young things) love the überexclusivity at zibar, between Ben-Hillel and Bianchini St. Mixed drinks NIS20 and up (way up). Open daily 9pm-late.

Bianchini, 10 Shammai St. (tel. 623 21 19), near the parking lot. Enjoy *nargilahs* (NIS19) or mint tea (NIS7) on comfy divans, or try their uncomfortably divine *yoadiho* (hot milk and Irish cream, NIS16). *Caravanserai* meets rave in the funky UV room. Weekly belly dancing. 18+ admitted. Open daily 24hr.

Mike's Place, 14 Horkanos St., off Heleni Ha-Malka St. on the way to the Russian Compound. Tightly packed English-speaking crowd digs Guinness (pint NIS15, pitcher NIS40) and live music every night 10pm-midnight. Happy hour 5-8pm (beers half price). No cover. Open daily 5pm-3am.

CLUBS

Most clubs are clustered in the city center or on Ha-Umman St. in **Talpiot,** a southern industrial neighborhood down Hebron Rd. (taxis from the city center NIS10-15). Cover for Talpiot clubs (open 9pm-5am) is NIS30-60 for weekend nights.

Ha-Umman 17, at...17 Ha-Umman St. The city's largest and best dance club. Huge dance floor and giant bar filled with Israeli university students who groove to mostly techno and pop. Sa nights are slow. Closed July-Aug.

Glasnost, 15 Heleni Ha-Malka St. (tel. 625 69 54). Left off Jaffa Rd. coming from Zion Sq. Large courtyard's "openness" overflows with Israelis who pack it in to salsa every M 10pm-3am (NIS25, with 9pm crash course NIS35), rock to Reggae on Tu, and howl for the house party on Th. Pub only F-Su (no cover). 20+ admitted.

Q, 1 Yoel Solomon St. (tel. 622 25 16), above the Underground. Take the right fork of the questionable-looking steps. This très upscale joint is Jerusalem's first quintessential gay club (but also straight-friendly). Friday is gay and lesbian night. Crowds q up for the live shows (including drag shows) on Th and Sa. House dance party Th-Sa 11pm-morning. Su-W is bar only, open 9pm-late. 23+ admitted.

Christopher, 11 Moonbaz St. (tel. 623 57 79), across the street from ISSTA. The Russian Compound's largest dance club, crowded every night of the week. House party M and Th-Sa, karaoke on W. Pizza, salad, or chicken nuggets NIS30-35. 18+ admitted. F-Sa min. charge NIS15. Open daily 8pm-morning.

Underground, 1 Yoel Salomon St. (tel. 625 19 18). The dance club everyone loves to hate but goes to anyway. Bar and Batcave-like disco packs in sweaty, grinding dancers who shed layers of clothing as the night grows older. Entry to the throbbing bar is free, but access to the techno lair requires a NIS15 drink. Drinks NIS15 and up. Buy 1 get 1 free during happy hour (daily 7:30-9pm). 18+ admitted. Open 7:30pm-4am.

MUSIC

Yellow Submarine, 13 Rehavim St. (tel. 656 66 11). Sing with me now: "We all live in... this theater-cafe that features a different performance 3-4 nights a week, from unknown locals to Israeli superstars." Party for the 30+ after 11pm every other Th. Hebrew stand-up marathon every other Sa. Full bar and Mexican food. Cover NIS30-60.

Pargod Theater (tel. 623 17 65), on the corner of Bezalel St. and Nissim Bekhar St. in Naḥlaot. Hip, young crowd comes for jazz and special performances.

Diaspora Yeshiva Band (tel. 671 68 41), in Asaf's Cave in the Mount Zion Cultural Center near David's Tomb. Bids Shabbat goodbye Sa at 9pm (in winter 8pm) with Ḥasidic dancing and English, Hebrew, and Yiddish music—a uniquely Jerusalem experience. Cover NIS10. Call to make sure there is a performance.

Beit Shmuel, 6 Shama St. (tel. 620 34 56), hosts popular Israeli singers Friday nights at 10:30pm. NIS55 in advance, NIS65 night of show.

Sultan's Pool (Brekhat Ha-Sultan). Dive at any opportunity to attend a performance. Tickets for American and British rock-star shows start at NIS80. Open in summer only.

◉ SIGHTS

OLD CITY

Excavations have uncovered over 20 distinct layers of civilization in the Old City. Get an idea of what the city looked like in ages past at the **Holyland Hotel** (tel. 643 77 77) in West Jerusalem, which has a model of Jerusalem circa 66 CE. (Take bus #21 from downtown; open daily 8am-10pm; admission NIS15, with ISIC NIS12.)

WALLS AND GATES

RAMPARTS PROMENADE. For an amazing overview of the Old City, walk along this promenade, which tops the walls built by Suleiman the Magnificent in 1542. Begin at **Jaffa Gate** (one of the two gates from which you can access the ramparts) by climbing the hidden steps immediately on the left (just before the jewelry store). The most picturesque part of the walk stretches from here to **Damascus Gate** (20min.), where you can either descend into the market or continue on to **St. Stephen's Gate** (Lion's Gate), the beginning of the **Via Dolorosa**. To ascend the ramparts from Damascus Gate, face the gate from the plaza outside and go down the steps on the right, passing under the bridge and entering through the carriageway to the left of the plaza. (*Promenade open Sa-Th 9am-4pm, F 9am-2pm. Admission NIS12, students NIS6; combined ticket to ramparts, Temple Mount excavations, Roman Plaza, Zedekiah's Cave, and City of David NIS30. Ticket good for 2 days.*)

JAFFA GATE. There are eight gates to the Old City, some of which have three names—one in Hebrew, one in Latin, and one in Arabic. Jaffa Gate is the traditional entrance for pilgrims and the sole entrance in the western Old City wall (and thus the most convenient from West Jerusalem). A gate has stood here since 135 CE.

DAMASCUS GATE. Damascus Gate is built over the Roman entrance to the Cardo, facing East Jerusalem and providing direct access to the Muslim Quarter. Scholars recently discovered a plaza at the gate's entrance with a statue of Hadrian mounted on a huge column, explaining the Arabic name for Damascus Gate: *Bab al-Amud* ("Gate of the Column"). Also near Damascus Gate is the biblical **Zedakiah's Cave,** where stones for the Jewish Temple were hewn.

OTHER GATES. New Gate, just a few steps from Jaffa Gate, was opened in 1889 to facilitate access to the Christian Quarter. **Herod's Gate** is to the east of Damascus Gate and reaches the deeper sections of the Muslim Quarter. **St. Stephen's Gate,** also known as Lion's Gate, is along the eastern wall. It faces the Mount of Olives and marks the beginning of the Via Dolorosa. **Golden Gate** is blocked by Muslim graves and has been sealed since the 1600s. It is thought to lie over the Closed Gate of the First Temple, the entrance through which the Messiah will purportedly pass (Ezekiel 44:1-3). **Dung Gate,** on the southern wall, opens onto the Western Wall plaza. It was given its name in medieval times because dumping feces here was considered an especially worthy act. **Zion Gate,** on the opposite end of the Cardo from Damascus Gate, connects the Armenian Quarter with Mt. Zion.

CARDO. On maps, the "centipede" that seems to crawl from Damascus Gate to Dung Gate is a two-dimensional rendition of the Cardo, the main thoroughfare; its "feet" represent the Roman columns lining the street. This flat "Cardo" has led archaeologists to conclude that the Cardo recently unearthed in the Jewish Quarter is not part of the Roman original but a Byzantine addition. For more on the Cardo, see p. 271.

TOWER OF DAVID (THE CITADEL)

To the right inside Jaffa Gate. 24hr. info tel. 626 53 33. Museum **open** *Apr.-Oct. Su-Th 9am-5pm, F-Sa 9am-2pm; Nov.-Mar. Su-Th 10am-4pm, F-Sa 10am-2pm. Admission NIS31, students NIS23; price includes guided tour in English Su-F at 11am only.* **Sound and light show** *Apr.-Oct. M, W, and Sa 9pm; NIS25, students NIS17, children NIS12; combined museum-light show admission NIS48, students NIS33.* **Murder Mystery** *in English, spring and summer Sa at 10pm; NIS35, students NIS29; combined light show-murder mystery NIS45, students and children NIS38. International* **jazz** *shows Oct.-June; call for dates. For the millennium, the museum is hosting a collection of specially made glass sculptures by the renowned American artist Dale Chihuly, scattered throughout the courtyard until July 2000.*

The Citadel complex is an outstanding and informative introduction to the Old City. Although the Citadel is called the Tower of David (*Migdal David* in Hebrew), it actually contains no remnants of King David's era; indeed, during his reign, this area was outside the city and unsettled. The Tower's Lego-like caricature of overlapping Hasmonean, Herodian, Roman, Byzantine, Muslim, Mamluke, and Ottoman ruins is a superb vantage point for surveying the Holy City. The high-tech museum that winds its way through the halls of the Citadel tells the story of the city in Hebrew, Arabic, and English, beginning with the excellent 14-minute introductory movie. At night, the Citadel puts on a 45-minute English **sound and light show,** in which booming voices tell the history of Jerusalem. For high-camp whodunit, drop by Saturday nights for the two-hour **Murder Mystery,** set in Herodian Jerusalem 2000 years ago (everyone sing along: "Come on, show me what you can do!"). The **Citadel Buffet** is a good place for lunch (cheese toast with veggies NIS12).

TEMPLE MOUNT

◤**TEMPLE MOUNT.** Known as *Al-Haram ash-Sharif* in Arabic and *Har Ha-Bayit* in Hebrew, this 35-acre area in the southeastern corner of the Old City is one of the most venerated religious sites in the world. The hill is a spiritual magnet, central to both Judaism and Islam and a holy site for at least 10 ancient religions. God asked Abraham to sacrifice his son Isaac here (Genesis 22:2), and King Solomon built the **First Temple** here in the middle of the 10th century BCE (2 Chronicles 3:1) before it was destroyed in 587 BCE, when the Jews were led into captivity (I Kings 5-8; II Kings 24-25). The **Second Temple** was built in 516 BCE, after the Jews' return from exile (Ezra 3-7). In 20 BCE, King Herod rebuilt the temple and enlarged the Mount, reinforcing it with four retaining walls (parts of which still stand). The Second Temple is remembered by Christians as the back-drop of the Christ's Passion. Like the First Temple, the Second Temple lasted only a few hundred years until it was sacked by Roman legions in 70 CE. Hadrian built a temple to Jupiter over the site, but the Byzantines destroyed it and used its platform as a municipal sewage facility. After Caliph Omar arrived in 638, he ascended the Mount and began cleaning up, personally removing an armful of brown gook. According to Muslim legend, the arches on the Temple Mount will be used to hang scales for weighing people's good and bad deeds. The **Islamic Museum** is filled with fantastic relics, including a collection of crescent-topped spires that once crowned older domes and elaborately decorated Qur'ans. The museum is accessible from the ramp entrance beside the Western Wall. *(Temple Mount and museum **open** Sa-Th 8am-12:30pm and 1:30-3pm; Ramadan 7:30-10:30am. Enter right of the Western Wall, up the ramp, or from the end of Ha-Shalshelet St. Tick-ets sold until 3pm at a booth between Al-Aqsa St. and the museum. **Admission** NIS33, students NIS22. The Mount is sometimes closed without notice. The area is highly sensitive—incidents in the past have resulted in violence, and any conspicuous action may result in ejection. **Modest dress** is required, and wraparound gowns are provided. Many sections considered **off-limits** by the police are not marked as such. These include the walls around Al-Aqsa St., the area through the door to the south between Al-Aqsa and the museum, the walkway along the eastern wall, and the Muslim cemetery.)*

DOME OF THE ROCK AND AL-AQSA MOSQUE. The Umayyad Caliphs built the two Arab shrines that still dominate the Temple Mount: the silver-domed **Al-Aqsa Mosque** (first built in 715 CE), and the magnificent **Dome of the Rock** (691 CE). A stunning display of mosaics and metallic domes, the complex is the third-holiest Muslim site (after the Ka'aba in Mecca and the Mosque of the Prophet in Medina). This is where Allah took Muhammad on his mystical Night Journey *(miraj),* which went from Mecca to the outer mosque *(al-aqsa* means "the farthest"), and on to heaven (17:17). The Dome of the Rock surrounds what Muslims believe to be the makeshift altar where Abraham almost sacrificed Ishmael, his son by Sarah's handmaid Hagar (not Isaac, as Christians and Jews believe).

The dome was originally solid gold, but was melted to pay the caliphs' debts. The domes of the mosques and shrines were plated with lusterless lead until the struc-tures received aluminum caps during the restoration work of 1958-64. Renovations in 1993 re-coated the domes with new metal plates and a thin layer of 24-karat gold. Many of the tiles covering the walls of the Dome of the Rock were affixed during the reign of Süleyman the Magnificent, and are easily distinguishable from the ceramic tiles added with the private funds of the late King Hussein of Jordan.

Next to the Dome of the Rock is the smaller **Dome of the Chain,** the exact center of Al-Haram ash-Sharif. It is here that Muslims believe a heavenly chain only graspable by the righteous once hung. Between Al-Aqsa and the Dome of the Rock is **Al-Kas,** a fountain *(mayda'a)* where Muslims perform ablutions before prayer. Built in 709 CE, it is connected to underground cisterns capable of holding 10 million gallons.

WESTERN WALL. Religious scholars believe the **Holy of Holies** (the most sacred spot in the temple, where the High Priest was allowed to enter only once a year) was closest to what is now the Western Wall, making this wall the holiest approach-able site in Judaism. Some Jews won't ascend the Mount in the off chance that they will walk on the Holy of Holies, which is off-limits until the Messiah arrives. Most of the Western Wall stands in the Jewish Quarter (see below).

JEWISH QUARTER

Known as *Ha-Rovah* by Israelis, the picturesque Jewish Quarter is in the southeast quadrant of the Old City on the site of the posh Upper City during the Second Temple era. After being exiled when the Second Temple was destroyed, Jews resettled here in the 15th century. Much of the Quarter was damaged in the 1948 War, and lay in ruins after two decades of Jordanian rule. The Israelis annexed the Old City after the 1967 War and began extensive restoration of the neighborhood, unearthing archaeological wonders with every lift of the shovel. They have managed to integrate the ancient remains into the new neighborhood quite gracefully. Today the Quarter is an upper-middle-class neighborhood of about 650 families (many American) who are almost exclusively Orthodox Jews.

The Jewish Quarter extends from Ha-Shalshelet St. to the city's southern wall, and from Ararat St. to the Western Wall. From Jaffa Gate, head down David St. and turn right at the first large intersection just before it becomes Bab as-Silsilah St., or turn right past the Tower of David onto Armenian Orthodox Patriarch Rd. (in the direction of traffic) and make the first left onto St. James Rd. The high arch over the Ḥurva Synagogue marks Ḥurva Sq., a convenient reference point for Jewish Quarter sights. The Quarter is also home to the **One Last Day Museum** (see p. 285) and the **Wohl Archaeological Museum** (see p. 286).

WESTERN WALL. The 18m tall wall (*Ha-Kotel Ha-Ma'aravi*, or just "The Kotel") is part of the retaining wall of the Temple Mount. Built around 20 BCE, the Wall was the largest section of the Temple area that remained standing after its destruction in 70 CE. Nearly 20m of Herodian wall (identifiable by its carved frames) still lie underground. Byzantines, Arabs, and Turks added the smaller stones above. The **Wailing Wall,** a dated moniker, refers to the Jewish worshipers who visited the wall in centuries past to mourn the destruction of the Temple. Today's visitors, Jewish or otherwise, often see the Wall as a direct connection with God and tuck written prayers into its crannies. Don't expect your scribble to wait there for the Messiah: all notes are periodically removed and buried in accordance with Jewish law. Pre-1948 photos show Orthodox Jews praying at the wall in a crowded alley; after the 1967 War, the present plaza was built. Israeli paratroopers are now sworn in here to recall the Wall's capture. The prayer areas for men and women are separated by a screen, with the Torah scrolls kept on the men's side, along with recently excavated sections of the Wall. On Fridays, Yeshivat Ha-Kotel organizes dancing to usher in Shabbat. The festivities start before sundown and continue until late. Bar Mitzvahs (ceremonies marking a Jewish boy's coming of age) are held at the Wall on Monday and Thursday mornings. Photography is appropriate at these occasions, but not on Shabbat or holidays. On other nights, the Wall is brightly lit, the air cool, and the atmosphere reflective and quiet. *(All rules applying to Orthodox synagogues apply to the Wall: men must cover their heads (paper kippot are in a box by the entrance) and women must cover their legs (borrow wraps from the Holy Sites Authority). Reachable by foot from Dung Gate, the Jewish Quarter, Bab as-Silsilah St., or Al-Wad Rd.)*

WILSON'S ARCH. Wilson's Arch is located inside a large, arched room to the left of the Wall. It was once part of a bridge that allowed Jewish priests to cross from their Upper City homes to the Temple. A peek down the illuminated shafts in the floor of this room gives a sense of the Wall's original height (women may not enter). The Wall continues from here through closed tunnels for over 500m. Women and groups can enter the passageways through an archway to the south, near the telephones. Underneath the Wall is an underground passage where Jewish radicals hid explosives in the early 1980s in a plot to destroy the Dome of the Rock. For tours of the passage, contact the MTIO, Archaeological Seminars, or the Jewish Students Information Center (see **Tours,** p. 258).

CARDO. The staircase down Or Ḥayim St. past Ḥabad St. descends to the remains of Jerusalem's main Roman and Byzantine thoroughfare, which has also been heavily excavated alongside Jewish Quarter Rd. The enormous remaining pillars suggest its original monumental proportions: it was built over a Byzantine extension of Emperor Hadrian's Cardo Maximus, which ran from Damascus Gate to David St. Archaeologists suspect that Justinian constructed an addition so the Cardo would extend as far as the Nea Church (beneath Yeshivat Ha-Kotel). Sheltered by the Cardo's vaulted roof are the best (and thus most expensive) **Judaica shops** in Jerusalem. Near the entrance to the Cardo is an enlarged mosaic reproduction of the **Map of the Holy Land,** the 6th-century plan of Jerusalem discovered in Jordan (see p. 438). *(Make a left at the bottom of the stairs on Jewish Quarter Rd. Cardo open and illuminated Su-Th until 11pm.)*

BURNT HOUSE. The Burnt House is the remains of a priest's dwelling from the Second Temple era. In 70 CE, the fourth year of the Jewish Revolt, the Romans destroyed the Second Temple and broke into Jerusalem's Upper City, burning its buildings and killing its inhabitants. Near a stairwell, the grisly bones of a severed arm reach for a carbonized spear. Sound and light shows inside the Burnt House re-create the events of its destruction. *(East on Tiferet Yisrael from the plaza. Tel. 628 72 11. Open Su-Th 9am-4:30pm. Admission NIS6, students NIS5. Reservations recommended.)*

OPHEL. The excavations at the southern wall of the Temple Mount are known as "Ophel," although the name technically refers to the hill just outside the southern wall, where the City of David is located. Scholars have uncovered 22 layers from 12 periods of the city's history. A tunnel leads out to the steps of the Temple Mount. *(Tel. 625 44 03. Open Su-Th 7am-7pm, F 7am-6pm. Admission NIS12, students NIS6.)*

FOUR SEPHARDIC SYNAGOGUES. The Synagogue of Rabbi Yoḥanan Ben-Zakkai, Prophet Elijah Synagogue, Middle Synagogue, and Istanbuli Synagogue were built by Mediterranean Jews in the 16th century in accordance with a local law that prohibited the construction of synagogues taller than the surrounding houses. To attain a semblance of loftiness, the synagogues were built in chambers deep underground. The current renovated structures date from 1835 and remain the spiritual center of Jerusalem's Sephardic community. *(Down Mishmerot Ha-Kehuna St., near the Jewish Quarter parking lot. Tel. 628 05 92. Open Su-Th 9:30am-4pm, F 9:30am-noon. Admission NIS7.)*

HURVA SYNAGOGUE. A single stone arch soars above the ruins of the synagogue in the square named for it. Built in 1700 by followers of Rabbi Yehuda the Ḥasid, the synagogue earned its name (*ḥurva* means "ruin") when it was destroyed several years later by Muslims. The title is appropriate: in 1856, the building was restored as the National Ashkenazic Synagogue, only to be destroyed again during the 1948 War. In 1967, renovators opted to rebuild only the single arch (a marker of the original dome that used to cover the synagogue) as a reminder of the destruction. *(On Jewish Quarter Rd. on the left from the southern end of the Cardo.)*

ARMENIAN QUARTER

Jerusalem's Armenian Christian population of 1000 or so is cloistered in the southwestern corner of the Old City. The Quarter lives in the shadow of tragedy: the Turkish massacre of up to one-and-a-half million Armenians in 1915 (see **Turkey: Modern History,** p. 540) remains one of the century's little-noticed genocides, and persecution of those fleeing to Palestine has caused their numbers to dwindle even further. Posters mapping out the genocide line the streets. The residential Armenian Compound is not open to the public, but the few available glimpses of Armenian culture (such as the **Armenian Museum,** p. 285) are mesmerizing.

ST. JAMES CATHEDRAL. The massive spiritual center of the Armenian Quarter was originally constructed during the 5th century CE, Armenia's golden age, to honor two St. Jameses. St. James the Greater was beheaded in 44 CE by Herod, and his head (supposedly delivered to Mary on the wings of angels) rests under the gilded altar. St. James the Lesser, entombed in a northern chapel, was the first bishop of Jerusalem, but was run out of town by Jews who disliked his version of Judaism. Persians destroyed the cathedral in the 7th century, but Armenians rebuilt it in the 11th century, and Crusaders enlarged it in the 12th. *(On Armenian Orthodox Patriarchate Rd., the main paved road leading from Jaffa Gate. Enter on the left past the tunnel, under the "Couvent Armenian St. Jacques" arch. Open daily 3-3:30pm during Vespers.)*

ARMENIAN ART CENTER. One of the few Armenian ceramic shops still producing tiles and pottery by the ancient methods. This center sells items more expensive than the machine-made goods found in the *souq*, but the heavy, handmade dyes lend an unmatched richness to the colors and intricate designs. The best pieces are hidden from spying competitors; ask to see the work in the back of the store. *(On Armenian Orthodox Patriarchate Rd., across from St. James Cathedral. Tel. 628 35 67 or 628 43 05. Open M-Sa 9am-7pm. Tiles NIS17-38; plates, tea sets, cups, and bowls NIS50 and up.)*

SYRIAN ORTHODOX CONVENT. Aramaic, the ancient language of the Levant, is spoken here both during services and in casual conversation. The Syrian Church believes this to be the site of St. Mark's house and the Last Supper (most other Christians recognize the Cenacle on Mt. Zion (see p. 276) as that hallowed place). Decorated with beautiful gilded woodwork, the chapel contains a silver-bound, 150-year-old Bible in Old Aramaic. *(Turn left from Armenian Patriarchate Rd. onto St. James Rd. and left again onto Ararat St.; a mosaic marks the door to the convent, on the right after a sharp turn in the road. Open daily 8am-4pm; ring the bell if the door is closed.)*

CHRISTIAN QUARTER

The Christian Quarter, in the northwest corner of the Old City, is centered around the **Church of the Holy Sepulchre,** the site traditionally believed to be the place of Jesus' crucifixion, burial, and resurrection. The alleyways of the Quarter pass small churches and chapels of various denominations, and the streets bustle with pilgrims, nuns, monks, and merchants peddling rosaries and holy water.

CHURCH OF ST. ANNE. This church commemorating the birthplace of Jesus' mother Mary is one of the best preserved pieces of Crusader architecture in Israel and an acoustical miracle (sing quietly and hear your voice echo everywhere). It survived the Islamic period intact because Salah ad-Din used it as a Muslim theological school (hence the Arabic inscription above the doors). Extensive excavations behind the church clearly show the layers of history: the ruins of a 5th-century basilica cover those of a 2nd- or 3rd-century chapel. The cool, beautiful crypt has a beaten-copper cross and inlaid stone floors. Within the grounds of the church is the **Pool of Bethesda.** Crowds of the infirm used to wait beside the pool for an angel to disturb its waters; the first person in after the angel supposedly be cured. Also, Jesus supposedly healed a sick man here (John 5:2-9). *(At St. Stephen's Gate, through the wooden doors on the right. Open in summer M-Sa 8am-noon and 2-6pm; in winter M-Sa 8am-noon and 2-5pm. Admission NIS5.50, students NIS3.50.)*

VIA DOLOROSA (STATIONS OF THE CROSS)

The Via Dolorosa (Path of Sorrow) is the route that the cross-bearing Jesus followed from the site of his condemnation (the Praetorium) to the site of his crucifixion and grave. Each event on his walk has a chapel commemorating it; together these chapels comprise the 14 **Stations of the Cross.** The present route was mapped out during the Crusader period and passes through the Muslim and Christian Quarters, although modern New Testament scholars have suggested alternate routes based on recent archaeological and historical reconstructions. The Via Dolorosa begins at St. Stephen's Gate; most Stations are marked, but many are hard to find. On Fridays (3pm, July-Aug. 4pm), you can join the Franciscan monks who lead pilgrims along the Via Dolorosa beginning at Al-Omariyyeh St.

STATION I. Just past an archway 200m from St. Stephen's Gate, a ramp with a blue railing leads back to the courtyard of **Al-Omariyyeh College,** the site identified as the **First Station,** the **Praetorium** where Jesus was condemned. One bone of contention between sects concerns the starting point of Jesus' final walk as a mortal. Most agree that Jesus was brought before Pontius Pilate for judgment. Normally, Roman governors resided and fulfilled their duties in the palace of Herod the Great (south of Jaffa Gate and the Citadel area), but on feast days Passover (the day of Jesus' condemnation), the governor and his soldiers based themselves at Antonia's Fortress to be closer to the Temple Mount. Reflecting this holiday relocation, the **Tower of Antonia,** in the courtyard of Al-Omariyyeh College, is considered by most to be the First Station, although it is not marked. For one of the best views of the Dome of the Rock plaza, walk into the courtyard of the school, turn left, and ascend the steps on the right.

STATION II. Across the Via Dolorosa from the ramp is a Franciscan monastery; inside on the left is the **Condemnation Chapel,** complete with a three-dimensional relief above the altar. This is the Second Station, where Jesus was sentenced to crucifixion. On the right is the **Chapel of Flagellation,** where he was first flogged by Roman soldiers. A crown of thorns adorns the dome. The Via Dolorosa passes beneath the **Ecce Homo Arch** (the site of Pontius Pilate's mansion), named for Pilate's exclamation as he looked down upon Jesus (*Ecce Homo* means "Behold the Man"). The arch is actually part of the triumphal arch that commemorated Emperor Hadrian's suppression of the Bar Kokhba Revolt in the 2nd century CE. The nearby **Convent of the Sisters of Zion** sits atop a large chamber thought by some to be a judgment hall, making it an yet another First Station contender. The convent is closed to the public, but the excavations are not. *(Condemnation Chapel open daily 8am-6pm. Arch open M-Sa 8:30am-noon and 2-5pm. Admission NIS6, students NIS5. Excavations: walk down the Via Dolorosa from the Second Station to the brown door on Aqabat ar-Rahbat St., on the right off the Via Dolorosa. Knock to enter. Open M-Sa 8am-12:30pm and 2-5pm. Admission NIS5.50, students NIS3.50.)*

STATIONS III-VII. Immediately after the Via Dolorosa turns left onto Al-Wad Rd., look to the left for the door to the Armenian Catholic Patriarchate. To the left of the door is the **Third Station,** where Jesus fell to his knees for the first time. A small Polish chapel inside a blue gate marks the spot; a relief above the entrance (marked "III Statio") depicts Jesus kneeling beneath the cross. At the **Fourth Station,** on the left just beyond the Armenian Orthodox Patriarchate, a small chapel commemorates the spot where Jesus saw his mother. Look for a carving above light blue iron doors, to the left of an arched alleyway. Turn right on the Via Dolorosa to reach the **Fifth Station,** where Simon the Cyrene volunteered to carry Jesus' cross (look for the brown door on the left, with the inscription "V St."). Fifty meters ahead, the remains of a small column designate the **Sixth Station** (marked with a "VI"), where Veronica wiped Jesus' face with her handkerchief. The mark of his face was left on the cloth, now on display at the Greek Orthodox Patriarchate on the street of the same name. Look for a pair of doors on the left, one green and one dark brown; the column is set into the wall between the doors. The **Seventh Station,** straight ahead at the intersection with Khan az-Zeit Rd., marks Jesus' second fall, precipitated by the sudden steepness of the road. Tradition holds that notices of Jesus' condemnation were posted on a gate at this spot.

STATIONS VIII AND IX. Crossing Khan az-Zeit Rd., ascend Aqabat al-Khanqah and look left past the Greek Orthodox Convent for the stone Latin cross that marks the **Eighth Station.** Here Jesus turned to the women who mourned him, saying "Daughters of Jerusalem, do not weep for me, weep rather for yourselves and for your children" (Luke 23:28). The small stone is part of the wall and difficult to spot; a large red-and-white sign was recently installed to mark it, but may not last long on such a narrow road. Backtrack to Khan az-Zeit Rd., take a right, walk for about 50m through the market, ascend the wide stone stairway on the right, and continue through a winding passageway to the Coptic Church. The remains of a column in its door mark the **Ninth Station,** where Jesus fell a third time.

ST. ALEXANDER'S CHURCH. Built over the Judgment Gate, the church marks the end of the Roman Cardo, through which Jesus exited the city on his way to Calvary. First-century stones line the floor, and two pillars from the original Cardo are visible. Next to the gate is a small hole in the ancient wall—this is the famed **Eye of the Needle,** through which latecomers would sneak into the city when the gates were closed at night. *(On the right just after turning off Al-Wad St. toward the Holy Sepulchre. Tel. 627 49 52. Open M-Sa 9am-1pm and 3-5pm. Admission NIS5. Ring bell. Prayers for Czar Alexander III are held Th at 7am.)*

CHURCH OF THE HOLY SEPULCHRE. Retrace your steps to the main street and continue to the next right, which leads from the marketplace to the entrance of the Church of the Holy Sepulchre, one of the most revered structures on earth. The placement of the last five stations (X-XIV) inside the church contradicts an alternative hypothesis that Jesus was crucified at the skull-shaped Garden Tomb in East Jerusalem (see p. 283). The Church of the Holy Sepulchre marks **Golgotha,** also called **Calvary,** the site of the Crucifixion. The location was first determined by Eleni, mother of Emperor Constantine and Jerusalem's first archaeologist, during her pilgrimage in 326 CE. Eleni thought Hadrian had erected a temple to Venus and Jupiter on the site in order to divert Christians from their faith. Constantine built a small church over the site in 335, and part of the original church's foundations buttress the present Crusader structure (from 1149). The Crusader architects united all the oratories, chapels, and other sanctuaries that had cropped up around the site under one monumental cruciform shape. By 1852, tremendous religious conflicts had developed within the Holy Sepulchre. The Ottoman rulers divided the church among the Franciscan order, the Greek Orthodox, Armenian Orthodox, Coptic, Syrian, and Ethiopian churches; the first three are the major shareholders, entitled to hold masses and processions and burn incense in the shrines and chapels.

The church is in somewhat bad shape. Restoration work in any part of the basilica implies ownership, making each sect hesitant to assist and eager to hinder the others. In 1935, the church was in such a precarious state that colonialists propped it up with girders. Since 1960, partial cooperation has allowed the supportive scaffolding to be gradually removed. To this day, the question of who gets to change a given light bulb can rage into a month-long controversy. The portions of the church not directly related to the Stations of the Cross are a dark labyrinth of small chapels through which priests, pilgrims, and chatty tourists wander. Because a denomination's ability to hang objects on the church's walls also indicates ownership, the building houses only religious paintings and spindly oil lamps. Steps lead down to two cavernous chapels commemorating the discovery of the true cross. In a small chapel on the ground floor just below Calvary, a fissure runs through the rock, supposedly caused by the earthquake following Jesus' death. According to legend, Adam (of "and Eve" fame) was buried beneath Calvary, allowing Jesus' blood to drip through this cleft and anoint him. *(Open daily in summer 5am-8pm; in winter 4am-7pm. Men and women must cover their knees.)*

ETHIOPIAN MONASTERY. Over part of the Church of the Holy Sepulchre is the Ethiopian Monastery; since the Ethiopians possess no part of the church itself, they have become squatters on the roof. The modest compound houses a small but spiritual church; enter through the roof and descend, exiting next to the Holy Sepulchre. Watch your head. *(Next to the Ninth Station, the first left from Khan az-Zeit Rd. when backtracking from the Holy Sepulchre. Open all day.)*

STATIONS X-XIII. The church's entrance faces the slab on which Jesus was supposedly anointed before he was buried. To continue along the Stations, go up the stairs to the right just after the entrance. The chapel at the top is divided into two naves: the right one belongs to the Franciscans, the left to the Greek Orthodox. At the entrance to the Franciscan Chapel is the **Tenth Station,** where Jesus was stripped of his clothes, and at the far end is the **Eleventh Station,** where he was nailed to the cross. The **Twelfth Station,** to the left in the Greek chapel, is a clearly marked Crucifixion site: a life-size Jesus in a metal loincloth, hangs among oil lamps, flowers, and candles. Between the Eleventh and Twelfth Stations is the **Thirteenth Station,** where Mary received Jesus' body. The station is marked by an odd statue of Mary adorned with jewels, a silver dagger stuck into her breast.

STATION XIV. Jesus' tomb on the ground floor is the **Fourteenth Station.** The Holy Sepulchre, in the center of the rotunda, is a large marble structure flanked by huge candles. The first chamber in the tomb, the **Chapel of the Angel,** is dedicated to the angel who announced Jesus' resurrection to Mary Magdalene. A tiny entrance leads from the chapel into the sepulchre itself, a small chamber lit by scores of candles and guarded by priests. The walls of the tomb have been covered, but the priest in charge may be willing to reveal a small section of the original wall hidden behind a picture of the Virgin Mary. The raised marble slab in the sepulchre covers the rock on which Jesus' body was laid. Nudging the back of the Holy Sepulchre is the tiny **Coptic Chapel.** To the right of the Sepulchre, the **Chapel of Mary Magdalene** marks the spot where Jesus appeared to her after his resurrection.

MUSLIM QUARTER

This sprawl of Ayyubid- and Mamluke-era architecture is the largest, most heavily populated quarter in the Old City, as well as one of the most exciting. It is also the most conservative; women should dress modestly, and everyone should be particularly careful: although the Quarter is busy during the day, it becomes dark, isolated, and potentially dangerous at night.

Damascus Gate, the main entrance to the Quarter, is one of the finest examples of Islamic architecture in Jerusalem. The main thoroughfare and western border of the quarter is **Khan az-Zeit Road,** leading from Damascus Gate to David St., with an infinite array of booths selling spices, candy, clothing, sandals, and souvenirs in between. **Al-Wad Road** connects the Western Wall area to Damascus Gate. A right off Al-Wad Rd. onto the Via Dolorosa leads to an array of small ceramics shops.

MUSLIM QUARTER SOUQ. The *souq* is crammed at all hours (watch for wagons and tiny tractors that charge gleefully at the crowds of shoppers) and a great place to buy Palestinian crafts such as Hebron-style wine glasses, mother-of-pearl inlaid boxes, ceramic tiles, and spherical Jerusalem candles. The *souq* is a Mamluke masterpiece of stone set within stone. Paintings of the Dome of the Rock and the Ka'aba adorn doorways; a painting of the latter signifies that a member of the family has been on the *hajj,* the Islamic pilgrimage to Mecca and Medina.

BAB AS-SILSILAH STREET. The stretch of Bab as-Silsilah St. (Gate of the Chain St.) extending from the end of David St. to the Temple Mount is partially founded on the ancient Mamluke causeway that crossed the Tyropoeon Valley, linking the upper city to the temple platform. At the end of the first alley to the left stands the **Khan as-Sultan** (a.k.a. *Al-Wakala*), a well preserved Crusader-era *caravanserai* (an inn that provided lodging for merchants and their donkeys). Farther down Bab as-Silsilah St. on the right, just past Misgav Ladakh St., is the **Tashtamuriyya Building,** housing the tomb of its namesake (d. 1384). The multitude of Mamluke institutions in the area can be attributed to a system of succession that prevented parents from passing wealth on to their children; constructing public institutions was the best way to preserve a family's legacy. Continuing down Bab as-Silsilah St. to its intersection with Western Wall (Ha-Kotel) St. leads to the **Qilaniyya Mausoleum** and its Mamluke stalactite half-dome; the **Turba Turkan Khatun** (Tomb of Lady Turkan) is at #149. At the end of Bab as-Silsilah St., on the right and often surrounded by tour guides in training, is the **Tankiziyya Building,** built by a Mamluke slave who worked his way up to become governor of Damascus in 1312. This venerated structure, on the site of the original seat of the Sanhedrin, is currently controlled by the Israelis due to its proximity to the Western Wall and the Temple Mount.

NEAR THE OLD CITY

MOUNT ZION

Rising outside the city walls opposite Zion Gate and the Armenian Quarter is Mt. Zion *(Har Tzion),* long considered the site of the Tomb of David, the Last Supper, and the descent of the Holy Spirit at Pentecost. The name Zion (also applied to Israel as a whole) is derived from the Jebusite fortress of the same name, first seized by King David. During the siege of the Jewish Quarter in 1948, the area around **Zion Gate** was the scene of some of the fiercest fighting in Jerusalem; bombshell pockmarks remain. To reach the mount, exit the Old City through Zion Gate (near the Jewish Quarter parking lot) and take the path opposite the gate, bearing right at the Franciscan convent. At the next fork, a left leads to the Cenacle and David's Tomb; a right leads to the Dormition Abbey.

COENACULUM (CENACLE). The no-frills appearance of this church, identified by most as the site of the Last Supper, is due in part to an attempt by the British Mandate to avoid sectarian disputes by forbidding any change to the building. The Cenacle was converted from a mosque into a church almost four centuries ago, but the mosque's *mihrab* is still visible in the southern wall. A group in Ein Kerem, on the outskirts of Jerusalem, runs interesting Last Supper reenactment dinners in a variety of languages. *(Take the left fork after the Franciscan convent and ascend a stairway through the gray door on the left. Open daily 8:30am-5pm.)*

DAVID'S TOMB. Archaeologists are skeptical of the authenticity of this site: it is written that kings (and only kings) were buried within the city proper, but Mt. Zion was never encompassed by David's walls. This does little to reduce the fervor of worshipers at the tomb, many of whom whisper David's own psalms in the small, dim chamber. *(Through the Coenaculum, down the stairs, and around the corner. Open in summer Sa-Th 8am-6pm, F 8am-2pm; in winter Su-Th 8am-5pm, F 8am-1pm. Free, although the yeshiva next door collects donations. Modest dress required; men should cover their heads.)*

BASILICA OF THE DORMITION ABBEY. This fortress-like edifice, commemorating the death of the Virgin Mary, was completed in 1910. Parts of the precariously situated basilica were damaged during battles in 1948 and 1967 and were never repaired. A gold mosaic rises above the apse, the floor is inlaid with symbols of the zodiac and the apostles, and the crypt holds a figure of the Virgin with all the women of the Bible above her. *(Off the right fork of the road leading to the Cenacle. Tel. 671 99 27. Open M-Sa 8am-noon and 12:30-6pm, Su 10am-noon and 12:30-6pm. Free.)*

CITY OF DAVID

As far as the archaeologists working to uncover this massive site are concerned, any exploration of Old Jerusalem must begin outside its walls, right here in the most ancient part of the city. Today's walled city dates from the mostly Hellenic period of the Second Temple, whereas the City of David housed the throne of the biblical Kings of Israel and was included within the walls of the First Temple era. The earliest origins of biblical Jerusalem are still shrouded in mystery, but archaeologists have confirmed that the Ophel ridge, just south of the Old City walls, is the site of Jebus, the original Canaanite city King David captured and made his capital.

Recent years have seen tension in this much-disputed area. Claiming the legacy of the ancient Jewish capital, Israeli nationalists have established a Jewish presence in the midst of the almost entirely Arab **Silwan;** Arab homes were quietly purchased for large sums and Jewish families brought in. The Jewish bastion is perched precariously and conspicuously in the Arab neighborhood. Unaware tourists may find themselves walking into a potentially dangerous situation, so make your tourist status pronounced and consult tourist offices before exploring.

The excavations in the northern part of the Ophel, **Section G,** were halted in 1981 when a group of Orthodox Jews protested that the area might be the Jewish cemetery mentioned in the diaries of several medieval pilgrims. After considerable and sometimes violent political dispute, the Supreme Court of Israel ruled that the site should be closed. As a compromise, the Israeli government promised that digging would continue only under rabbinic supervision. No bones have been found.

Sights in the City of David are poorly marked and difficult to appreciate without guidance. The recently opened **City of David Visitor's Center** (tel. 1 800 252 423 or 626 23 41) provides an excellent three-hour tour of the excavations and a free walking map of the area (open Su-Th 8am-5pm, F 8am-1pm). Tours in English leave Monday and Friday at 10:30am, with additional dates and times during the summer. Book by phone at least one day in advance. (Admission and tour Su-Th NIS37, students NIS29. Fridays tours are free; admission NIS18, students NIS12. To get to the visitor's center from town, take bus #1 to Dung Gate. From Dung Gate, make a left uphill, then the first right, going downhill onto the unmarked Ma'alot Ir David St.; the center is immediately on the left.)

ISRAEL

WATER GATE. Excavations of this site indicate that the Jebusites were confined to an area of about eight acres. The city's location above the Kidron Valley was selected for its proximity to the Giḥon Spring and its defensibility on the ridge. In times of peace, townspeople passed through a "water gate" to bring water into the city. For continued supply during times of siege, a shaft provided access to water from within the walls. This shaft played an important part in David's strategy for taking Jebus: his soldier Joab simply climbed its walls (II Samuel 5:8). In 1867, archaeologist Charles Warren confirmed this biblical account when he discovered the long, sleek shaft that now bears his name. In the 1960s, Kathleen Kenyon located the 1800 BCE Jebusite city walls, which lie just above the Giḥon Spring. Later, King Hezekiah devised a system to prevent David's strategy from being turned against the Israelites: he built a 500m long tunnel to bring the Giḥon waters into the city walls, hiding the entrance of the spring and preventing invaders from finding water when they camped outside the wall. In 1880, a few years after the tunnel was excavated, a local boy discovered an inscription carved by Hezekiah's engineers describing the jubilant moment when the north and south construction crews met.

HEZEKIAH'S TUNNEL. Sloshing with a flashlight through Hezekiah's Tunnel is one of Jerusalem's most enjoyable adventures, but it's best not to do it alone. The water is never deeper than thigh-high, and wading through it takes about 45 minutes. There are two ways to tackle the tunnel; both will get you wet. One way is to start at the Giḥon Spring source on Shiloah Way and emerge at the Pool of Shiloah (*Silo'am* in Hebrew, *Silwan* in Arabic). The other way is to trek from the Pool of Shiloah to the source. Check in at the visitor's center for a map and detailed instructions. *(Tunnel open Su-Th 8am-4pm, F 8am-1pm. Admission NIS6.)*

OTHER SIGHTS. About 100m past the City of David entrance is a small museum with photos of the most recent excavations. A staircase leads down to **Warren's Shaft.** With a flashlight, the entire length of the wall that Joab scaled is visible. Two of the newest discoveries at the City of David are the **Spring House,** which accessed the ancient pool; and the **Cistern,** the biblical pit into which the prophet Jeremiah was thrown. *(Warren's Shaft open Su-Th 9am-5pm, F 9am-1pm. Admission NIS5.)*

KIDRON VALLEY AND THE MOUNT OF OLIVES

The historic Kidron Valley, which runs between the Old City and the Mount of Olives, is revered by Christians as the path of the Last Walk of Jesus. To get there, turn left from Dung Gate and walk up the narrow Ha-Ophel Rd. A newly paved sidewalk leads to an observation point for the valley, the Mount of Olives in front of it, and the four tombs directly below; a map on the floor explains the vista. Running north-to-south are the **Tomb of Jehosaphat** and **Absalom's Pillar,** allegedly the tomb of David's favored but feisty son (II Samuel 15-18). A dirt path on the left leads to the impressive rock-hewn **Tomb of B'nei Hezir** and the **Tomb of Zechariah.** The tombs are accessible from the base of the Mount of Olives or via a new staircase near the observation point just past Ma'alot Ir David St. on Ha-Ophel Rd. Women travelers are advised not to visit the Mount of Olives alone.

 SIGHTSEEING STRATEGY. The best way to visit the churches, tombs, gardens, and observation point is to start at the top and walk down the road that passes through the sights. Take a **taxi** to the top (NIS15) or **bus** #75 from Suleiman St. Station (every 15min until 6pm; NIS1.50). Churches close Sundays and daily noon-3pm.

MOUNT OF OLIVES. The bone-dry slopes of the Mount of Olives (*Har Ha-Zeitim* in Hebrew) to the east of the Old City are dotted with churches marking the sites of Jesus' triumphant entry into Jerusalem, his teaching, his agony and betrayal in Gethsemane, and his ascension to heaven. Jews believe that the Messiah will arrive in Jerusalem from the Mount of Olives. Tradition holds that the thousands of people buried here will be the first to be resurrected upon his arrival. Ogle a monumental view of the Old City from the observation promenade outside the

Seven Arches Hotel. The bell tower of the **Augusta Victoria Hospital** on Mt. Scopus to the north marks the highest point in Jerusalem (903m above sea level).

CHAPEL OF CHRIST'S ASCENSION. Built in 392, this was the first church to commemorate the event for which it is named. It is the geographical (if not aesthetic) apex of the noteworthy sites in the area. In the 11th century, Crusaders adorned the chapel with columns and arches, and in the 12th century Salah ad-Din constructed a domed roof. The interior contains a candle-lighting stand and sacred footprint, unidentifiable after wear and tear from generations of relic-happy pilgrims. *(Open daily 8am-5pm; if closed, ask a guard in the mosque courtyard to let you in. Admission NIS3.)*

CHURCH OF THE PATER NOSTER. St. Eleni founded this church in the 4th century as the Church of the Disciples; it is also referred to as the Church of the Eleona ("olive grove" in Greek). This was the site of the grotto where Jesus revealed the "inscrutable mysteries" to his disciples, foretelling the destruction of Jerusalem and his Second Coming. The church commemorates the first recitation of the Lord's Prayer (hence the current moniker, *Pater Noster*, Latin for "Our Father"). Polyglots can read the prayer in 78 languages (including Old Frisian) on the tiled walls. In the midst of the translations is the tomb of the Princesse de la Tour d'Auvergne, who worked here for 17 years (1857-74) and financed the excavations and renovations: she was determined to uncover the long-lost grotto where her favorite prayer was originally taught. *(Below the Chapel of Christ's ascension, under an orange sign reading "Carmelite Convent." Open M-Sa 8:30-11:45am and 3-4:45pm.)*

TOMBS OF THE PROPHETS. This site is the supposed resting-place of the prophets Malachi and Haggai. Archaeological evidence, however, suggests that the graves are far too recent—probably dating from the 4th century CE. The glass-enclosed home on the premises is the residence of the caretaker, who will show visitors around downstairs upon request. To the left of the tombs is an easy-to-miss orange sign with rubbed-off black lettering marking "This Common Grave" of those who died defending the Jewish Quarter in 1948. Next to the Common Grave lies the **National Cemetery,** and farther down the path sprawls the immense **Jewish Graveyard,** the largest Jewish cemetery in the world. Take the stone staircase on the left for another small observation point and access to the Jewish graves. *(With your back to the Seven Arches, turn right and go down the gray cement path. Several meters down, a large green gate on the left leads to the 2 cavernous tunnels. Open Su-F 8am-3pm.)*

SANCTUARY OF DOMINUS FLEVIT. This sanctuary was erected in 1955 to mark the spot where Jesus wept for Jerusalem (Luke 19:41), hence its Latin name ("The Lord Wept"). The chapel has a Byzantine mosaic and altar in an apse with a beautiful view of the Dome of the Rock. The glass shards of liquor bottles cemented to the top of the walls serve to protect the property of competing sects from trespassers. *(Off the gray path from the Seven Arches. Open daily 8-11:45am and 2:30-5pm.)*

RUSSIAN CHURCH OF MARY MAGDALENE. Czar Alexander III built this church in 1885 and dedicated it to his mother. Constructed in the lavish 17th-century Muscovite style, it is adorned with seven golden onion domes. The crypt houses the body of a Russian grand duchess, smuggled to Jerusalem via Beijing after her death in the Russian Revolution. Now a convent, the church claims a part of the Garden of Gethsemane. *(On the gray path from the Seven Arches, past the Sanctuary of Dominus Flevit. Tel. 628 43 71. Ordinarily open Tu and Th 10am-noon.)*

GARDEN OF GETHSEMANE. This garden is where Jesus spent his last night in prayer and was betrayed by Judas (Mark 14:32-42). Although the site has been venerated since the 4th century, the present building, designed by Barluzzi, was built with international contributions after World War I. Inside, mosaics and sculptures depict Jesus' last days, including the proverbial kiss of death. The **Rock of the Agony** is where Jesus was so impassioned that he sweated blood (Luke 22:44). The building's facade portrays Jesus bringing peace to all nations. Right above it is the **All Nations Cafe,** open in afternoons for the tourist crowds. *(Enter through the gate from the Church of All Nations, below the Russian Church of Mary Magdalene.)*

ISRAEL

TOMB OF THE VIRGIN MARY AND GROTTO OF GETHSEMANE. The steep stairs down to Mary's tomb were built to prevent pagans from riding horses into the sacred space. The natural grotto to the right is another candidate for the site of Jesus' betrayal and arrest. *(At the bottom of the main path. Open daily 8am-noon and 2:30-5:30pm. At the exit onto the main road are a drink stand, telephone booths, and taxis. Damascus Gate is within walking distance. A taxi to the city center should cost NIS15.)*

WEST JERUSALEM
NEAR ZION SQUARE

Zion Square (Kikkar Tzion), at the eastern end of the *midrahov*, is the center of West Jerusalem and the epicenter of the pedestrian malls of Ben Yehuda, Yoel Solomon, Nahalat Shiva, and Rivlin St. Downhill on Ben Yehuda St. and to the left is **King George Street,** a bustling extension of the city center. Three blocks farther downhill, the enormous and ornate **Great Synagogue of Jerusalem,** 58 King George St. (tel. 624 71 12), is an inspiring architectural compromise between modernity and religion (open Su-Th 9am-1pm, F 9am-noon). Services here on holidays and the first day of Jewish months feature an excellent men's choir meant to recall the Levites' choir in the ancient Temple. Facing the *midrahov*, Ha-Rav Kook St. is to the left. It eventually spills out onto Ha-Nevi'im St., across from which opens the quiet, stone-wall-lined Ethiopia St. At the end of Ethiopia St. on the right is the handsome **Ethiopian Church,** built between 1874 and 1901. Inscriptions in Geez adorn the gate and doors; black-robed monks and nuns live in the surrounding compound and care for the distinctive, blue-domed church. Across from the church, at 11 Ethiopia St., is the one-time home of the founder of modern Hebrew, **Eliezer Ben-Yehuda.**

ME'A SHE'ARIM

The less-than-spotless neighborhood of Me'a She'arim ("Hundredfold," an invocation of plenty) is just north of Ethiopia St. and within walking distance of the city center. To get there from Zion Sq., take Jaffa Rd. and turn right on to King George St. Walk for about 10 minutes until it turns into Strauss St. The square intersecting Strauss and Ha-Nevi'im St. is known as Kikkar Shabbat (Bank Ha-Poalim is on the corner), the unofficial beginning of Me'a She'arim.

One of Jerusalem's oldest neighborhoods is also one of the few remaining Jewish *shtetl* communities that flourished in pre-Holocaust Eastern Europe. Several thousand ultra-Orthodox Jews live here and in the neighboring **Geula** (Hebrew for "redemption"), preserving traditional habits, dress, customs, and beliefs with painstaking diligence. If your newfound grasp of Hebrew lets you down in Me'a She'arim, it may be because you're hearing Yiddish, spoken by residents who consider Hebrew too holy for daily use. Signs read "Daughters of Israel! The Torah requires you to dress modestly." All women should walk through the neighborhood with at least knee-length skirts and elbow-length sleeves, and all men should wear pants. Me'a She'arim's few extremists receive a good deal of publicity. The Neturei Karta ("City Keepers"), the most extreme sect of the Satmar Hasidim, oppose the Israeli state, arguing that Jewish law prohibits the legitimate existence of a Jewish country until the coming of the Messiah.

Me'a She'arim St. is probably the cheapest place in the world for Jewish books and religious items. Although the quality is not as high as in the Jewish Quarter of the Old City, the stores along Me'a She'arim St. have vast, affordable selections (see **Judaica,** p. 287). The neighborhood also has some of the city's best **bakeries,** most of which are open all night on Thursdays, baking *hallah* and cake for Shabbat.

GIV'AT RAM

ISRAELI SUPREME COURT. This building, completed in late 1992 by designers Karmi & Associates, combines Modernist flair with themes from ancient Jerusalem's building traditions. This architectural masterpiece is also worth visiting for an glimpse of the Israeli justice system. Anyone may sit in on a trial—it's like Court TV, only live and in Hebrew. *(Tel. 675 96 66. Open Su-Th 8:30am-2:30pm. Tours Sept.-June Su-Th at noon; Jul.-Aug. Su-Th noon-2:30pm continuously.)*

KNESSET. Discover why Israeli schoolteachers compare excessively rowdy pupils to members of the Knesset, Israel's Parliament. Passports are required for entrance as part of a detailed search. Free tours include an explanation of the structure of the Israeli government and a look at the magnificent Marc Chagall tapestries and mosaics that adorn the building. (On Eliezer Kaplan St. across from the Israel Museum. Take bus #9 or 24. Tel. 675 34 20 or 675 34 16. Open sessions Su and Th 8:30am-2:30pm. Free tours Su and Th, every 30min. 8:30am-2:30pm,)

OTHER SIGHTS. The **Wohl Rose Garden,** which forms a walking path between the Supreme Court and the Knesset, is a sublime picnic spot with beautifully manicured lawns and flowers. Take the path on the right when exiting the Supreme Court building, or climb up to it from anywhere on the main street. The **Ardon Window** in the **National Library,** one of the largest stained-glass windows in the world, depicts Jewish mystical symbols in rich, dark colors. (Take bus # 9, 24, or 28 from the city center. Tel. 658 50 27. Open in summer Su-Th 9am-7pm, F 9am-1pm. Free.)

REḤAVIA

South of Independence Park are some of Jerusalem's most elegant and affluent residential areas. Reḥavia, the area trisected by Azza Rd. and Ramban St., was founded in the 1920s and became the refuge for the many German Jews fleeing Nazi persecution in the 30s. For years, it was famous as a German high-culture enclave, where Mozart grooved on the gramophone and dark wood libraries were lined with Goethe and Schiller. Today, the legacy lives on in the many International Style houses, designed in the best German Modernist tradition.

JASON'S TOMB. In the middle of Reḥavia on Alfassi St. is Jason's Tomb, built around 100 BCE as the burial site of a wealthy Hasmonean-era Jewish family. Pottery found at the site indicates that three generations were buried there, while charcoal drawings on the plastered porch wall depict ships, suggesting that one of the deceased was involved in naval excursions. The pyramid topping the tomb is a reconstruction. (Near 12 Alfassi St.; sign says "Rock Cut Tomb.")

OTHER SIGHTS. Farther east past Azza Rd. is the **Prime Minister's official residence,** in the heavily guarded house at the corner of Balfour St. and Smolenskin St. Next door on Balfour St. is the **Schocken Library,** designed by renowned architect Erich Mendelssohn, who resided in Jerusalem in the late 1930s (he lived in the windmill on Ramban St. near Kikkar Tzarfat, now a ritzy shopping complex).

TALBIYYA AND QATAMUN

Farther south are the neighborhoods of **Talbiyya** (Komemiyut) and **Qatamun** (Gonen), still known by their pre-1948 Arabic names. The ornate villas (one of which was the home of renowned cultural theorist Edward Said) have become favorites of Hebrew University faculty and, more recently, well-to-do professionals. The official residence of the **Israeli President** is on Ha-Nassi (President) St., and the plush **Jerusalem Theater** is on the other side of the block, on the corner of Chopin St. and Marcus Rd.

On the other end of Jabotinsky St. from the President's House is **King David Street,** running northward to the base of Shlomtzion Ha-Malka St. and Shlomo Ha-Melekh St. Just south of the intersection with Jabotinsky St. is the sprawling, green **Liberty Bell Park** (Gan Ha-Pa'amon). An amphitheater, basketball courts, climbable sculptures, and a Liberty Bell replica grace the lawns. On Saturday nights, the park hops with folk dancing festivities (take bus #14, 18, or 21 from the center). Three hundred meters up King David St. toward the city center, the **Three Arches YMCA,** built in 1933, has an imposing bell tower with fine views of the whole city (open M-Sa 9am-6pm; admission NIS2). Directly across the street, the historic **King David Hotel** retains an aura of old-world luxury, making it a favorite accommodation for international celebrities. The King David served as the British Headquarters during the 1948 War of Independence and was bombed by Jewish underground forces.

ISRAEL

YEMIN MOSHE

In the valley between King David St. and the Old City is the restored neighborhood of Yemin Moshe. It was here that Sir Moses Montefiore, a British Jew, first managed to convince a handful of residents from the Old City's overcrowded Jewish Quarter to spend occasional nights outside the city walls, thus founding West Jerusalem. To strengthen the settlers' confidence, Montefiore built **Mishkenot Sha'ananim** ("Tranquil Habitations"), a picturesque small compound with crenelated walls resembling those of the Old City. The original buildings now house an exclusive municipal guest house and a pricey French restaurant, and are located at the bottom of the hill. Montefiore also erected his famous stone windmill, which now contains a tiny free **museum** (open Su-Th 9am-4pm, F 9am-1pm). Yemin Moshe is crammed with artists' studios and galleries; a plaza with a fountain beneath the exclusive King David Apartments makes this a lovely spot to wander. The stepped street of Ḥutzot Ha-Yotzer leads up to Ḥativat Yerushalayim St.; at #16 is the studio of Motke Blum, whose subtle cityscapes brilliantly evoke Jerusalem in oil. The now-dry **Sultan's Pool** (tel. 629 80 66) sits in the valley below. Named after Suleiman the Magnificent, the renovator of this Second Temple reservoir in the 16th century, the pool figures prominently in Palestinian novelist Jabra Ibrahim Jabra's *The Ship*. Today, the Sultan's Pool is most famous for its open-air concerts and annual **art fair** in July or early August (info tel. 625 44 03).

GERMAN COLONY AND HAAS PROMENADE

The **German Colony,** a leafy neighborhood of somber European houses and spacious Arab villas, surrounds Emek Refa'im St., an upscale avenue with a lively cafe scene. Buses #4, 14, and 18 run here from the city center. To the southeast, the **Haas Promenade** is a hillside park that commands unbelievable views of the Old City and the Dead Sea. The dusk experience alone is worth the trip. On foot, walk south on Derekh Hevron, bear left onto Albeck St., and turn left onto Yanofsky St. Bus #8 runs from King George St. to the corner of Albeck St. and Yanofsky St.

NORTHERN OUTSKIRTS

TOMBS OF THE SANHEDRIN. In the heart of a park carpeted with pebbles and pine needles are the Tombs of the Sanhedrin. Composed of 70 esteemed male sages and leaders, the Sanhedrin was the ancient high court of the Jews; it ruled on legal matters and even reviewed Jesus' case. Separate burial areas were designated for the members. *(Take bus #2 from the city center to Ha-Sanhedrin St., off Yam Suf St. Open Su-F 9am-sundown. Free.)*

AMMUNITION HILL. Before the Six-Day War, this was Jordan's most fortified position in the city, from which it commanded much of northern Jerusalem. Taken by Israeli troops in a bloody battle, the hill now serves as a memorial to the Israeli soldiers who died in the Six-Day War. The somber, architecturally striking museum is housed in a reconstructed bunker with a detailed account of the 1967 battle. *(In Giv'at Ha-Taḥmoshet. Buses #4, 9, 25, and 26 stop at the foot of the hill, located in Ramat Eshkol, north of the Old City. Tel. 582 84 42. Open Su-Th 8am-6pm, F 8am-2pm; closes 1hr. earlier in winter. Admission NIS10, students NIS4.)*

HEBREW UNIVERSITY OF JERUSALEM. After 1948, the Hebrew University of Jerusalem had to relocate from Mt. Scopus (Har Ha-Tzofim), where it was founded in 1925, to this new campus in Giv'at Ram. From 1948 to 1967, Mt. Scopus was a garrisoned Israeli enclave in Jordanian territory. Every week for 19 years, U.N. supplies were flown in to relieve the community; every week seven Israeli soldiers were let in, and seven let out. After 1967, all but the natural and physical sciences departments moved back to the original campus. Massive reconstruction was funded largely by international donors, whose names emblazon the libraries, promenades, and pebbles that comprise modern Mt. Scopus. Pick up a map from the Reception Center for an unguided stroll around Israel's top university and browse through the bookstore, library, computer labs, and botanical gardens. For

ISRAEL

a fabulous view of Jerusalem, head to the overlook point, outside the university gates along the south side of the campus. The **Hecht Synagogue** in the Humanities building overlooks the Old City and is reputed to be have the best view of Jerusalem in the entire city. Enter the synagogue via the Sherman Building. The university's gorgeous **amphitheater** faces the Palestinian Territories. (Take bus #4a or 9 from the city center. Free guided tours depart from the Bronfman Reception Center, in the Sherman Administration Building, Su-Th 11am.)

WESTERN OUTSKIRTS

▧CHAGALL WINDOWS. The synagogue at the Hadassah Medical Center (not to be confused with Hadassah Hospital on Mt. Scopus) houses the magnificent Chagall Windows, Marc Chagall's fantastical stained-glass depictions of scenes from Genesis 49 and Deuteronomy 33. Chagall donated the windows to the hospital in 1962 and was sent an urgent cable when four of the windows were damaged in the 1967 War. Chagall replied, "You worry about the war, I'll worry about my windows." Two years later he installed replacements, but three of the windows still contain bullet holes. (Medical Center tel. 677 62 71. Free tours Su-Th every hr. on the ½hr. 8:30am-12:30pm and 2:30pm, F every hr. 9:30-11:30am. Synagogue open Su-Th 8am-1:15pm and 2-5pm, F 8am-1pm. Admission NIS10, students with ID NIS5.)

EIN KEREM. The scenic Jerusalem Forest and the pastoral village of Ein Kerem, just west of Mt. Herzl, are perfect for picnics and short hikes. Formerly an Arab village, tiny Ein Kerem (Fountain of Vines) is the traditionally professed birthplace of **John the Baptist.** The tranquil streets of this thriving artists' colony are now lined with charming studios and craftshops. The **Church of St. John,** with its soaring clocktower, marks the spot where John was born. The church displays several paintings, including *The Decapitation of Saint John.* In the church's **Grotto of the Nativity** is a lovely Byzantine mosaic of pheasants, the symbol of the Eucharist. Across the valley, down Ma'ayan St. from St. John's gate, the **Church of the Visitation** recalls Mary's visit to Elizabeth and contains a rock behind which the infant St. John hid when the Romans came to kill babies. The newer Upper Chapel depicts the much happier scene of the glorification of Mary. (Take city bus #17 (every 20-30min.) west from the central bus station or Zion Sq. Church of St. John: tel. 641 36 39. Open Apr.-Sept. Su-F 8am-noon and 2:30-6pm; Oct.-Mar. Su-F 8am-noon and 2:30-5pm. Ask the caretaker for the key. Free. Church of the Visitation: tel. 641 72 91. Open May-Sept. Su-F 8am-noon and 2:30-6pm; Oct.-Apr. Su-F 8am-noon and 2:30-5pm. Free.)

EAST JERUSALEM

SOLOMON'S QUARRIES. These cool caves, plunging 250m beneath the Old City, are where workers quarried limestone to build Jerusalem in the First Temple era, using an ancient Egyptian technique to remove blocks of stone from the cave walls: wooden planks were set in crevices and soaked with water, and the expanding planks wedged the stone apart. Legend has it that Zedekiah, Judah's last king, fled the city through a passage to Solomon's quarries when King Nebuchadnezzar invaded in 587 BCE. (Between Damascus Gate and Herod's Gate. The sign reads "Zedekiah's Cave." Open Su-Th 9am-4pm, F 9am-2pm, Sa 9am-6pm. Admission NIS7, students NIS3.50.)

GARDEN TOMB. These skull-shaped rock formations were first noticed in 1860 by Otto Thenius, leading some to believe that this quarry (and not the Church of the Holy Sepulchre) is **Golgotha** ("Place of the Skull"), the site of Christ's crucifixion. A nearby rock-cut tomb is that of Joseph of Arimathea, who placed Jesus' body in his own tomb after the crucifixion. (Up Nablus Rd., the unmarked street intersecting Suleiman St., opposite Damascus Gate and parallel to Ha-Nevi'im St. The blue sign is on the right. Tel. 627 27 45. Open M-Sa 8am-noon and 2-5:30pm. English service Su 9am. Donation requested.)

ST. GEORGE'S CATHEDRAL. This cathedral, now sparkling after some months of restoration and renovation, is the Cathedral Church of the Anglican Episcopal Dicocese of Jerusalem and the Middle East. The cathedral's namesake, the patron saint of England, is one of the many traces of British occupation that surround the sight. *(Past the intersection and the gas stations along Nablus Rd., on the right. Open M-Sa 7am-6:30pm. Free. Also runs a guest house.)*

TOMBEAU DES ROIS (TOMB OF THE KINGS). Judean kings were thought to be buried here, but evidence shows that the tomb was in fact built in 45 CE by the Mesopotamian Queen Helena for her family. The deep tombs are unlit; bring a candle or flashlight. *(On Salah ad-Din St., after the intersection with Nablus Rd. Open M-Sa 8am-1pm and 3-5pm. Admission NIS3.)*

🏛 MUSEUMS

ISRAEL MUSEUM

The Israel Museum is the largest and most comprehensive museum in and about Israel. With extensive collections of antiquities, books, sculptures, ancient and modern art, the legendary Dead Sea Scrolls, and even a children's exhibit, the museum has nearly as many facets as the country itself. *(Take **bus** #9 or 17 from King George St. Tel. 670 88 11 or 670 88 73. **Open** Su-M and W-Th 10am-5pm, Tu 4-10pm, Sa 10am-4pm, F 10am-2pm. The Shrine is open the same hours except on Tu, when it's open 10am-10pm. English **tours** of the museum Su-M and W-F 11am, Tu 4:30pm. English tours of the Shrine Su-M and W-Th 1:30pm, Tu 3pm, and F 12:45pm. **Admission** to museum and Shrine NIS30, students NIS24. Fee includes admission to Rockefeller Museum; go to the Rockefeller first and the reciprocal deal saves NIS5. Repeat visit within 2 weeks half-price.)*

🔲SHRINE OF THE BOOK. The display of the Dead Sea Scrolls is by far the museum's biggest attraction. Hidden for 2000 years in the Caves of **Qumran** near the Dead Sea (see **Qumran,** p. 351), the scrolls date from the 2nd century BCE to 70 CE and were written by an apocalyptic, monastic Jewish sect called the Essenes. The scrolls contain fragments of every biblical text except the Book of Esther, and are nearly identical to the modern texts, supporting claims for the historical dating of the Hebrew Bible. The building's white dome and black walls symbolize the struggle between the Sons of Light and Dark, an important theme to the Qumran sect, and were designed to resemble the covers of the pots in which the scrolls were hidden.

ARCHAEOLOGY AND ETHNOLOGY EXHIBITS. Rock and rust enthusiasts should go straight to the archaeology section, which has an extensive collection of tools and weapons recording 30,000 years of human habitation in the Fertile Crescent. Straight ahead from the bottom of the steps is the **ethnography** exhibit, tracing the important events of the Jewish life cycle. *(Archaeology tours in English M and Th 3pm; guided tours of the Judaica and ethnography galleries S and W 3pm.)*

ART COLLECTIONS. The museum boasts a fabulous collection of art, including the largest display of Israeli art in the world. There is a sizeable Impressionist and Post-Impressionist collection, and even a few period rooms (including a spectacular French Rococo *salon* donated by the Rothschilds). The **Weisbord Pavilion,** across from the ticket building, houses a few Rodin sculptures, early modern paintings, and rotating contemporary exhibitions.🔲**Billy Rose Sculpture Garden** displays some incredible masterworks by Henry Moore, Auguste Rodin, and Pablo Picasso. Pick up a schedule of evening outdoor concerts at the museum, and try to visit on a Tuesday night, when the garden is illuminated.

YAD VA-SHEM

Meaning "A Memorial and a Name," Yad Va-Shem is the largest of Israel's Holocaust museums. An event as broad-sweeping and traumatic as the Holocaust cannot be memorialized by any single medium; the juxtaposition of Nazi records, victim testimony, and documentation of resistance creates a powerful and disturbing experience. Don't plan to do too much right after a visit to this museum: its several buildings deserve some time and take an emotional toll. *(Take **bus** #13, 17, 18, 20, 23,* *or 27 and get off at the huge, orange arch just past Mt. Herzl. Turn around and take a left on Ein Kerem St., then follow the signs down Ha-Zikaron St. for about 10min. Tel. 675 16 11. **Open** Su-Th 9am-5pm, F 9am-2pm. Free. Free guided tours in English available by appointment.)*

MUSEUMS. It's best to start at the **Historical Museum,** which traces the origins of the Holocaust through photographs, documents, and relics. The exhibit ends with a simple, powerful memorial: symbolic tombs showing the number of Jews who were killed in each country, and a tiny shoe that belonged to one of the Holocaust's younger victims. The nearby **art museum** displays drawings and paintings created by Jews in the ghettos and concentration camps.

■**MEMORIALS.** By far the most haunting part of Yad Va-Shem is the stirring **Children's Memorial.** Mirrors are positioned to create the illusion of an infinite sea of candles while a recorded voice recites the names and ages of young victims. The **Hall of Names** has an achingly long list of all known Holocaust victims. Visitors may fill out a Page of Testimony, recording the name and circumstances of death of family members killed by the Nazis. The **Hall Of Remembrance** houses a *ner tamid* (eternal flame) to memorialize the Holocaust's victims, with the name of each concentration camp engraved into the floor. The **Avenue of Righteous Gentiles** honors non-Jewish Europeans who risked their own safety to aid Jews fleeing Europe. The **Valley of the Communities** is a labyrinthine memorial dedicated to the destroyed villages of Europe. Carved in stone are the names of *shtetls* that are no more; surviving family members wander around in search of their former towns.

OTHER MUSEUMS

■ **Rockefeller Archaeological Museum** (tel. 628 22 51), on Suleiman St., at the northeastern corner of the Old City walls. Take Egged bus #1 towards the Old City from the city center. Orientalist-Gothic building from 1920 records the region's history from the remains of the 100,000-year-old "Mt. Carmel Man" to the age of imperialism. Don't miss the *mashrabiyya* screens from Al-Aqsa Mosque (see p. 270) and the desks on which the Dead Sea Scrolls were probably written, discovered intact at Qumran. Open Su-Th 10am-5pm, F- Sa 10am-2pm. Admission NIS25, students NIS15.

Armenian Museum (tel. 628 23 31; fax 626 48 62), in the Armenian Quarter on Armenian Orthodox Patriarchate Rd., left of Jaffa Gate. This courtyard museum's display of weapons and religious artifacts chronicles the history of Armenia from pre-Christian times to the 1915 Turkish genocide. Open Sa-Th 9am-4:30pm. Admission NIS5, students NIS3.

Bible Lands Museum (tel. 561 10 66), across from the Israel Museum. Take bus #9 or 17 from King George St. Records the ancient history of every geographic locale in the Bible with ancient pottery, jewelry, seals, and figurines from the private collection of Canadian collector Dr. Elie Borowski. Special year 2000 exhibit traces the history of Jesus and Christianity. Open Su-Tu and Th 9:30am-5:30pm, W 9:30am-9:30pm, F 9:30am-2pm, Sa 11am-3pm. English tour daily 10:15am, plus W 5:30pm. Admission NIS23, students and children NIS13. Recorded 1hr. headphone tour NIS10, free with full admission.

Herzl Museum (tel. 651 11 08). Follow the signs for Mt. Herzl (Har Herzl) from the bus stop for Yad Va-Shem. Encapsulates the energy of Theodor Herzl, a newspaper correspondent who made the most prominent modern articulations of Zionism and lobbied for the creation of a Jewish state until his death in 1904. Ze'ev Jabotinsky, Levi Eshkol, Golda Meir, and Yitzhak Rabin are also buried here. Nearby is the **Israeli Military Cemetery,** the resting place of fallen soldiers. Open Su-Th 9am-5pm, F 9am-1pm. Admission US$2, students US$1. Closed for renovations in summer 1999; call to find out if it has reopened.

One Last Ditch Effort Museum, in the Old City, the first storefront on the left when entering the commercial center on the Cardo. This museum (formerly the One Last Day Museum) is the photo journal of John Phillips, a Brit who lived in the Old City through the flight (and 1967 return) of the Jews during the Jordanian siege of 1947-1948. This modern-day Josephus Flavius recounts life during the siege through a fascinating exhibit and 5min. silent film. Open Su-Th 9am-5pm, F 9am-1pm. Admission NIS8, students NIS6.

ISRAEL

Museum on the Seam, 4 Ḥeil Ha-Handassa St. (tel. 628 12 78), at the intersection with Ha-Nevi'im St. on the "seam" between West and East Jerusalem. Housed in Tourjeman House (a site representing the military struggle over Jerusalem and its later unification), this new museum strives to explore through art the potential for respectful coexistence among different sectors of society in Israel. Deals with the differences between secular and religious, Zionist and Palestinian, right and left wing, as well as ethnic and gender relations. Open Su-Th 9am-3pm for scheduled tours, 4-8pm for individual visitors.

Ticho House, 9 Ha-Rav Kook St. (tel. 624 50 68), 2 blocks up from Zion Sq. Displays watercolors and drawings by artist Anna Ticho, who lived here with her prominent oculist husband. His collection of *menorahs* is also on display. The elegant building and well groomed gardens are a relaxing mid-city respite with a classy restaurant serving all-you-can-eat wine, cheese, and salad buffet Tu nights (NIS65). Kosher. Open Su-Th 10am-5pm, Tu 10am-10pm, F 10am-2pm. Free. Library shows a videotape of Anna Ticho's life.

Wohl Archaeological Museum (tel. 628 34 380), near the main plaza area by the Ḥurva Synagogue on Ha-Karai'im St. Consists of the huge excavation of 3 mansions, thought to belong to the family of a High Priest during the Second Temple era. Open Su-Th 9am-5pm, F 9am-1pm. Admission NIS15, students NIS14. Ticket to Burnt House and Herodian Quarter NIS19/NIS16; ticket to Herodian Quarter, Burnt House, Israelite tower, and One Last Ditch Effort Museum NIS26/NIS24.

Wolfson Museum (tel. 624 79 08), on King George St. next to the Great Synagogue, on the 4th floor of the Heḥal Shlomo building. Wonderful collection of Jewish religious and ceremonial objects, including texts painted on eggshells and the Samaritan Torah, as well as a room of detailed dioramas depicting scenes from ancient and modern Jewish history. Open Su-Th 9am-1pm. Admission NIS5, students NIS3.

🛍 SHOPPING

Keep your wits about you when shopping in Jerusalem; comparison shop and bargain until you're blue in the face, then pay in foreign currency to avoid the 17% VAT. When paying in shekels, get a receipt and refund form to redeem at the airport or border-crossing stations.

CERAMICS AND WOODWORK

Israel is home to many accomplished artisans who craft pieces from olivewood, Jerusalem stone, and other native materials. The Armenian owners of **Jerusalem Pottery,** along the Via Dolorosa between Al-Wad St. and Khan az-Zeit Rd., paint the tiles that mark the Old City's streets. Their beautiful handpainted ceramic tiles, cups, and containers fill the *souq*, but the biggest selection is at their store. Custom-made ceramic nameplates take 10 days and are worth the wait (NIS15 and up). At **Kakadu,** 1 Rivlin St. (tel. 625 64 12), Reut Shaher hand-designs beautiful pinewood trays, notebook covers, and other gift items with whimsical animal motifs (open Su-Th 9am-9pm, F 9am-4pm; credit cards accepted). Owner Neḥemiah designs all the pieces at **Almaz Olive Wood Shop,** 26 Me'a She'arim (tel. 682 47 15). Dreidels (NIS10), bookstands (NIS35), and other items can be personalized by the artists right in the store (open Su-Th 10am-7:30pm, F 10am-3pm).

JEWELRY

You can bejewel yourself at the Muslim Quarter's *souqs,* on the Ben-Yehuda *midraḥov,* or at the shops on King David St. **Eilat stone** (a greenish turquoise semi-precious stone from the hills around Eilat) is used frequently in rings, necklaces, earrings, and pendants. Booths of cheap rings and trinkets abound at **The Pit,** also known as "The Cat Market" *(shuk haḥatulim),* an open-air market near the base of Rivlin and Yoel Solomon St. that features odd trinkets, jewelry, and clothing. Merchants set up shop every afternoon and evening. On Friday, they start at 10am and end before Shabbat; Saturdays they hawk from nightfall until past midnight.

JUDAICA

If you're looking for *menorot, mezuzot, kippot,* or other ritual items, this is the right city. The Talmud even says it is not enough to fulfill the Commandments; one must beautify the ritual with pieces of art. Rows of inexpensive Judaica shops crowd the streets of Me'a She'arim. **Chen Eilat,** 11 Me'a She'arim (tel. 537 01 28), has a huge selection of cheap *hallah* covers, tallit bags, and other things Jewish (open Su-Th 9:30am-7:30pm, F 9:30am-2pm; credit cards accepted). Slightly higher-quality goods can be found on the Ben Yehuda *midrahov.* Most shops will personalize items like knitted *kippot* within two days. For truly high-quality merchandise, head to the Jewish Quarter **Cardo,** where the craftsmanship, individuality, and price of Judaica skyrockets (although you can still find great deals here— *mezuzot* carved out of Jerusalem stone are as low as US$3).

MUSIC

Pop songs in Israel tackle subjects as heady as life in the army, the religious-secular conflict, and coping with terrorism. Heart-wrenching folk songs by Naomi Shemer and others have become second anthems to the young state, and they capture the worries and hopes of Israel better than a thousand pictures. **Picadelly Music,** 4 Shatz St. (tel. 624 79 83), off Ben Yehuda St. on the *midrahov,* has a good selection of Israeli and international CDs, often at discount prices. Open Su-Th 8:30am-8pm, F-8:30am-3pm, Sa sundown-10pm.

NEAR JERUSALEM

ABU GHOSH أبو غوش אבו גוש

Overlooking the Judean hills 13 km west of Jerusalem, the peaceful Arab village of Abu Ghosh is revered by Christians and Jews alike as an early site of the Ark of the Covenant, which King David later moved to Jerusalem (I Chronicles 13:5-8). In caravan days, the town was the last stop on the way to Jerusalem; its 18th-century namesake, Sheikh Abu Ghosh, required pilgrims to pay a toll as they traveled to the Holy City. The Arabs of the village have always had good relations with neighboring Jewish settlements and the State of Israel, even during the 1948 War. To get to Abu Ghosh, take Egged **bus** #185 or 186 from the central bus station towards **Beit Nekufah** (15min.; every 30min. Su-Th 6:10am-10:15pm, F 6:10am-4:45pm; NIS8) and get out at the crest of the road, just past the restaurants. **Sherut** between Jerusalem and Tel Aviv stop at the turnoff, 2km downhill from Abu Ghosh.

☎ **SIGHTS.** Two churches grace the hills of Abu Ghosh. **Notre Dame de l'Arche d'Alliance** (Our Lady of the Ark of the Covenant; tel. 534 28 18), at the top of the hill, was built on the site of the Ark's ancient holding place. The current church was built in the 1920s on the ruins of a demolished Byzantine church; beautiful fragments of the original mosaics are integrated into the marble floor. The church's excellent acoustics make it a prime spot for choir concerts. Classical music concerts are held the last Saturday of each month from October to May, with large four-day festivals at the beginning and end of the run, during the Jewish holidays of Sukkot and Shavuot (tickets NIS80-90; open daily 8:30-11:30am and 2:30-6pm). For concert information call Gershon Cohen (tel. 050 399 044).

In the garden below the sacred hill stands the magnificently preserved **Crusader Church of the Resurrection,** built in 1142 and acquired by the French government in 1873. Excavations beneath the church have uncovered remains dating back to Neolithic times; the crypt contains evidence of a Roman fortification. Ask for Father Olivier, a popular monk whose good advice is featured in several Israeli newspapers. To reach the church, walk down the main road past the restaurants and head for the minaret of the attached mosque. Buzz for entrance at the blue door to the right. (Open M-W and F-Sa 8:30-11am and 2:30-5:30pm. Free; donations requested.)

ISRAEL

TEL AVIV תל אביב

Tel Aviv is the yin to nearby Jerusalem's yang: Jerusalem thrives on the past, Tel Aviv lives for the moment; Jerusalem is sacred, Tel Aviv proudly secular. Although the city sustains some clustered religious communities, the most conspicuous Tel Avivans are the city's exuberant youth—gyrating at discotheques, shopping for combat boots and navel rings in trendy Sheinken St. boutiques, and bronzing at the beach on Shabbat. Ever since the 1940s and 1950s, when Israel's most avant-garde authors and poets chatted in Dizengoff Street's intimate cafes, Tel Aviv has dedicated itself to leading Israeli culture in new directions. From English store names and tourist-crammed hostels to familiar car brands and cellular phones, Tel Aviv rejoices in its breezily modern, western, beach-lined atmosphere, which has even washed out orthodoxy (most Tel Aviv establishments stay open Friday nights).

Despite its lack of strong religious traditionalism, Tel Aviv is a very political city; it is the home of Israel's foreign embassies and financial institutions, and in the winter of 1991, Tel Aviv was briefly the focus of world attention when it became the target for Saddam Hussein's SCUD missiles during the Gulf Crisis. It was also here in November 1995 that Yigal Amir, a Jewish student, fired the bullet that killed Prime Minister Yitzḥak Rabin. The assassination cast a shadow over all of Israel, but no place felt it more acutely than Tel Aviv. The Middle East peace process has taken its toll since then: in the last few years, Hamas bombings have claimed a number of lives in the city, but political developments in the peace process leave residents hopeful that the recent calm will remain the norm.

✈ ORIENTATION

Located in the center of Israel's Mediterranean coastline, Tel Aviv is 63km northwest of Jerusalem and 95km south of Haifa. The two main points of entry into Tel Aviv are **Ben-Gurion Airport** and the **New Central Bus Station.** Frequent bus and *sherut* (minibus) service from the airport is supplemented by the vans that warring hostels send to lure potential customers.

Almost all hotels, restaurants, and places of interest are in the rectangle formed by the beach to the west, the **Ayalon Highway** to the east, the **Yarkon River** to the north, and **Salameh Road** to the south. Running along the beach beginning around Gordon St. and extending south to Jaffa is the **Tayelet** (Promenade), lined with chairs, gazebos, and inviting cafes. **Ha-Yarkon Street** runs parallel to the beach behind the first row of seaside buildings. The next major north-south artery, **Ben-Yehuda Street,** runs one block east of Ha-Yarkon St. and is lined with travel agencies, hostels, and more affordable restaurants. Intersecting Ben-Yehuda St. to the south at **Kikkar Beth November** is **Allenby Street,** home to plentiful shawarma shops and a handful of bars and clubs. Almost all of the hostels in Tel Aviv are around Ben-Yehuda St. and Allenby St. Parallel to Ben-Yehuda St. is **Dizengoff Street,** still home to many of Tel Aviv's trendy cafes, chic bars, and institutions (but it's fading fast). At its heart is **Kikkar Dizengoff,** an elevated plaza surrounded by mall-style shops and a cineplex. **Ibn Gvirol Street,** with its shaded arcades and new cafes, runs from the Yarkon River in the north until it turns into **Yehuda Ha-Levi Street** in the center; halfway down is the vast **Kikkar Yitzḥak Rabin** (formerly Kikkar Malkhei Yisrael), in front of City Hall. Farther east is **Namir Road** (which also goes by its old name, **Haifa Road**), a major north-south thoroughfare that leads to Tel Aviv's northern exit; the **central train station,** which has service to all major cities, is at the intersection of Namir Rd. and **Arlozorov Street,** which runs east-west. North of Arlozorov St. is **Jabotinsky Street,** which runs into Kikkar Ha-Medina, a large park near the central train station.

Kikkar Magen David (at the corners of Allenby St., King George St., and Sheinken St.) is the starting point of **Shuk Ha-Carmel** to the southwest, the *midraḥov* (pedestrian mall) of **Naḥalat Binyamin** to the south, and the hip **Sheinken Street** to the east. Northwest of the *shuk* are the winding alleyways of **Kerem Ha-Temanim** (the

Tel Aviv

ACCOMMODATIONS

A Tel Aviv Youth Hostel (HI)
B The Wandering Dog

See Central Tel Aviv map
for further accommodations

TO
HERZLIYA,
HAIFA

Tel-Aviv University
(Beit Hatfusot)

RAMAT
AVIV

Levi Eshkol

Namir (Haifa) Rd.

Einstein

Klausner

Reading

Broderzky

Levanon (University)

Ayalon Hwy.

Sderot Rokath

Ha-Yarkon
Park

Eretz Yisrael
Museum

Sderot Rokakh

Benei Dan

SHIKUN
BAVLI

Yirmiyahu

Yehuda Ha-Macabi

Weizmann

Ha-Halakha

Bialik

RAMAT-
GAN

Jordan

Derekh Aba Hillel

Sheraton
Beach

Nordau

Pinkas

Remez

Namir

Egypt

KIKKAR
HA-MEDINA

Central
Train
Station

Jabotinsky Rd.

Hilton
Beach

Basel

Jabotinsky

Ibn Gvirol

Arlozorov

Arlozorov

Arvey Nahal

Ben Yehuda

Dizengoff

KIKKAR
'ATARIM

Ha-Yarkon

SEE CENTRAL TEL AVIV MAP

Ben-Gurion

City
Hall

Bloch

Weizmann

David
Ha-Malekh

Australia

Petah Tikva Rd.

Ayalon Hwy.

GIV'
ATAYIM

Gordon

KIKKAR
YITZHAK
RABIN

Shelomo Ha-Malekh

Ibn Gvirol

Tel Aviv
Museum
of Art

Sha'ul Ha-Melekh

Ha-Shalom
Station

N

Frischmann

KIKKAR
DIZENGOFF

Kaplan

Azrieli
Center

Ha-Shalom

Herbert Samuel Promenade

Ben

Bograshov

GTIO

Dizengoff

Dizengoff
Center

Ben Zion

Sderot Rothschild

Yehuda Ha-Levi

Ha-aashmona'im

Carlebach

Ha-Masger

Moshe Dayan

TO
ZOOLOGICAL
CENTER
(1.5km)

Trumpeldor

Opera
Tower

Yehuda

Allenby

King
George

Sheinkin

Petah Tikva

Canada

YAD
ELIYAHU

KEREM
HA-TEMANIM

KIKKAR
MAGEN
DAVID

Nahalat Binyamin

Allenby

SHUK
HA-CARMEL

Ha-Karmel

Shalom
Tower

Mikve Yisrael

Ahad Ha-Am

Shomron

Yad Eliyahu
Stadium

LaGuardia

Kaufman

Ha-Mered

Old Central
Bus Station

KIKKAR
HA-MOSHAVOT

Levinsky

Ayalon River

Ha-Hagana

NEVE
TZEDEK

Suzanne
Delal
Center

Herzl

Ha-Aliyah

New Central
Bus Station

Salameh Rd.

HA-TIKVA
MARKET

HA-TIKVA

SEE JAFFA MAP

JAFFA
(YAFO)

Eilat Rd.

Abarbanel

FLORENTIN

Ha-Tikva St.

Lehi

Mifratz Shlomo St.

Yefet

Jaffa
Clock-
tower

Sderot Yerushalayim

Salameh Rd.

Kibbutz Galuyot Rd.

TO
BEN-GURION
AIRPORT,
JERUSALEM

Yehuda Ha-Yamit

0   400 yards

0   400 meters

ISRAEL

Yemenite Quarter). South of Shuk Ha-Carmel and Naḥalat Binyamin, the neighborhood of **Neveh Tzedek,** just off Yehuda Ha-Levi St., has been prevented from crumbling by a recent infusion of yuppies, and contains the beautiful **Kikkar Suzanne Delal. Jaffa** (see p. 300) and its waterfront are farther south, outside the downtown area. The entrance to Old Jaffa, marked by a famous clocktower, is at the intersection of Eilat St. and Goldman St.

▐ GETTING THERE AND AWAY

Airplanes: Ben-Gurion Airport (English recorded info tel. 972 33 44), 22km southeast of Tel Aviv in Lod. Egged bus #475 to the airport leaves from the 6th floor of the New Central Bus Station (every 30min.; Su-Th 5:20am-11:40pm, F 5:30am-4:50pm, Sa 8:30-11:30pm; NIS9.50). Taxis from the airport to Tel Aviv run at a fixed fare (about NIS75 during the day, NIS93 at night or on Shabbat, each piece of luggage NIS2).

Trains: Central Train Station (tel. 693 75 15), on Arlozorov St. across from Namir Rd. Take bus #10, 18, 20, 32, 61, or 62; from the New Central Bus Station take bus #23, 27, 51, 54, 68, or 70. Open Su-F 6am-10pm. A/C trains to **Haifa** (1hr., every 30min. 5:50am-10pm, NIS20), **Netanya,** and **Nahariya.**

Intercity Transportation: Egged (tel. 694 88 88) runs from **Arlozorov Terminal,** on Arlozorov St., to: **Jerusalem** (#480 direct; 50min.; every 15min. Su-Th 6am-10pm, F 6am-4:30pm, Sa 8:30pm-midnight; NIS17.40); **Haifa** (#980 direct; 1¼hr.; every 15min. Su-Th 7:45am-8:45pm, F 7:45am-4:30pm, Sa 8:30-10pm; NIS22.50); and **Be'er Sheva** (#380 direct; 1¾hr.; every 15min. Su-Th 6am-8:30pm, F 6am-4:30pm, Sa 8:30-10:30pm; NIS19.30). **New Central Bus Station** has intercity departures on the 6th floor to: **Jerusalem** (#405 direct; every 15min. Su-Th 5:40am-midnight, F 6:00am-5:30pm, Sa 8:30pm-midnight; NIS17.40, students NIS14.85); **Haifa** (#900 direct; every 25min. Su-Th 7:30am-8:50pm, F 7:30am-4:35pm, Sa 8:30-10pm; NIS22.50) or late-night (#901 express; 1¼hr., every 20min. Su-Th 9:15-11pm, NIS22.50); and **Be'er Sheva** (#370 direct; every 20min. Su-Th 6am-11pm, F 6am-4:40pm, Sa 8:30-11pm; NIS19.30). 10% ISIC discount. Catch **taxis** on Allenby Rd. at Ha-Moshavot Sq.

Ferries: Caspi, 1 Ben-Yehuda St. (tel. 517 57 49), in the Migdalor Building. Go Greek: **Piraeus** (3 days, Su and Th 8pm, NIS500/US$106) via **Cyprus** (11hr., NIS275/US$58) and **Rhodes** (2 days, NIS480/US$101). Port tax NIS100/US$22. Round-trip lower.

Car Rental: Gindy Ltd. Rent-a-Car (tel. 527 83 44). Manual NIS260/US$55, automatic NIS285/$60; weekly rental discounts with unlimited mileage. Min. age 21. **Avis** (tel. 527 17 52). Manual NIS310/US$65, automatic NIS355/US$75. Min. age 26. **Rent-a-Reliable-Car** (tel. 524 97 94). Manual NIS285/US$60; automatic NIS355/US$75. Min. age 23. Prices listed are per day. Except as noted, all have 250km per day limit. **No company rents to drivers under 21.**

▐ GETTING AROUND TOWN

Tel Aviv is mostly manageable by foot. On a hot August afternoon, though, an NIS4.50 air-conditioned bus ride may seem like the deal of the century. Take buses to sights north of the Yarkon, in the Ramat Aviv area, or in Jaffa, all beyond easy walking distance from the city center. The **New Central Bus Station** is on Livinsky St.; information booths are on the second, fourth, and sixth floors. **Baggage check** rooms are on the sixth floor, down a small flight of stairs near the information kiosk (NIS10 per item per day; open Su-Th 7am-7pm, F and holiday eves 7am-3pm).

Buses within Tel Aviv are operated by **Dan** (tel. 639 44 44). Generally, **city buses** run Sunday to Thursday 5:30am-12:15am, Friday 5am-5pm, and Saturday 8:15pm-12:30am, but some stop running earlier. Buses do not run on Shabbat. **Minibuses** operating as **sherut taxis** run along several of the major bus routes. At NIS4 they're cheaper than the bus and will stop anywhere along the route. Intercity minibuses, which are much faster than buses, stop around the corner from the central bus station, on David Tzemakh St. There's a **private taxi** stand at Allenby St. and Simḥat Beit Ha-Shoeva St. Taxis also queue up by Migdal Shalom (Shalom Tower).

KIKKAR ATARIM

Ben-Gurion House

Ben-Gurion

■ ISSTA

Marina

Gordon

Central Tel Aviv

ACCOMMODATIONS
A Gordon Hostel
B Gordon Inn Guest House
C Dizengoff Square Hostel
D Noah's Hostel
E Hotel Nes Ziona
F Ha-Yarkon 48 Hostel

Ⓑ

Ⓐ

Ha-Yarkon

Gordon Beach

Frug

Dizengoff

Reines

King Solomon (Shlomo Ha-Melekh)

TO KIKKAR YITZHAK RABIN

Mapu

Frishman

Cameri Theatre & Mann Auditorium

Ⓒ

KIKKAR DIZENGOFF

Ha-Nevi'im

Frishman Beach

Herbert Samuel

Supersol

Mendele Moher Sfarim

Ben-Ami

Superpharm

□France

Ben Yehuda

Shalom Aleichem

Hovevei Tsiyon

Bograshov

Dizengoff Center

South Africa

Shderot Ben Tsiyon

Trumpeldor Beach

Ha-Tayelet (Promenade)

Ⓓ

□United States

Trumpeldor

Pinsker

Gan Me'eir

Idelson

Etzel Irgun Tzva'i Le'umi Museum

Ha-Hashmona'im

Yerushalayim Beach

Ⓔ

United Kingdom & New Zealand

Ⓕ

Migdalor Building

KIKKAR BETH NOVEMBER

Bialik Museum

Bialik

Rashi

King George (Ha-Melekh George)

Opera Tower

Allenby

Rubin Museum

Ge'ula Beach

Herbert Samuel

Ge'ula

Ha-Rav Kook

Ha-Yarkon

KIKKAR MAGEN DAVID

Sheinkin

Allenby

Balfour

Ha-Kovshim

Najara

Shuk Ha-Carmel

SHUK HA-CARMEL

Maze

Yavne

YEMENITE QUARTER

Daniel

Rambam

Shefer

Ben

Ha-Sho'eva

Karmelit Bus Terminal

Nahalat Binyamin

Great Synagogue

Dolphinarium

Migdal Shalom

Yitzhak Elhanan

Ahad Ha-am

Hagana Museum

Chlore Park

N

0   200 yards

0   200 meters

ISRAEL

⁊ PRACTICAL INFORMATION

TOURIST AND FINANCIAL SERVICES

Tourist Information Office: (tel. 639 56 60; fax 639 56 59), in the New Central Bus Station, 6th floor, near platform 630. From the city center, take bus #4 or 5 south. Maps of Tel Aviv and other cities and info on accommodations, food, shopping, tours, and cultural events. Hotel and tour reservations. Open Su-Th 9am-5pm, F 9am-1pm.

Tours: SPNI, 19 Ha-Sharon St. (tel. 638 86 74), near the intersection with Petakh Tikva Rd. English-speaking guides lead the best 1-12 day tours, year round. Day tours NIS236/US\$59. Open Su-Th 8am-3:30pm, F 8-11am. **United Tours,** 113 Ha-Yarkon St. (tel. 522 20 08), offers tours around the country in English, Hebrew, French, and German. Day tours NIS224-296/US\$56-74; 10% ISIC discount if booked directly through their office; some tours include lunch.

Budget Travel: ISSTA, 128 Ben-Yehuda St. (tel. 521 05 55), at Ben-Gurion St. For ISICs, bring a photo, current student ID, and NIS40; for Youth Hostel (HI) cards bring NIS35. Open Su-Tu and Th 9am-noon and 3-6pm, W and F 9am-noon. **Mona Tours,** 45 Ben-Yehuda St. (tel. 523 09 20), specializes in student and charter rates. Must be under 28 to book flights. Open Su-Th 9am-6pm, F 9am-1pm. Both take credit cards.

Consulates: Australia, 37 Sha'ul Ha-Melekh Blvd., Europe House, 4th floor (tel. 695 04 51). Open M-Th 8am-3:15pm. **Canada,** 3 Nirim St. (tel. 636 33 00), next to basketball stadium in Yad Eliyahu. Open M-Th 8am-noon and F 8-11am. **Egypt,** 54 Basel St. (tel. 546 41 51), off Ibn Gvirol. For a visa, bring a passport, photo, and NIS75 (U.S. citizens NIS50)—be sure to specify planned visits beyond the Sinai, or they'll automatically issue a "Sinai Only" visa. Open Sa-Th 9-11am. **Jordan,** 14 Aba Hillel (tel. 751 77 22), in Ramat Gan. Pre-arranged visas (NIS30) required for crossing to Jordan through Allenby Bridge. Open Su-Th 9:30am-12:30pm. **South Africa,** Top Tower, Dizengoff Ctr., 16th floor (tel. 525 25 66); enter through gate #3. Open M-F 9-11am, W 9-11am and 2-3pm. **U.K.** (also serves **New Zealand**), 1 Ben-Yehuda St., Migdalor Bldg., 6th floor (tel. 510 01 66). Open M-Th 1:30-3:30pm and F noon-1pm. **U.S.,** 71 Ha-Yarkon St. (tel. 519 75 75), north of Allenby St., on the left. Passports: open M and W 8:30-11am and 2-3:30pm, Tu and Th 8:30-11am, F 8:30am-1pm. Visas: M-F 7:30am-2:30pm.

Currency Exchange: Change Point, 106 Ha-Yarkon St. (tel. 524 55 05), has the best rates and no commission. Open Su-Th 8:30am-6pm, F 8:30am-1pm. **Change Spot,** 140 Dizengoff St. (tel. 524 33 93), also offers commission-free exchange. Open Su-Th 9am-7pm, F 9am-2pm. Exchange hours are typically Su-Th 8:30am-2pm, F 8:30am-noon.

Banks: Most banks are open Su, Tu, and Th 8:30am-12:30pm and 4-5:30pm; M, W, F, and holiday eves 8:30am-noon only.

American Express: 32 Ben-Yehuda St. (tel. 524 88 62), near the Sheraton. Letters held for cardholders, but no packages. For lost AmEx traveler's checks, call the toll-free 24hr. line (tel. 177 440 86 94). Changes traveler's checks at bank rates without commission. Cardholders can buy traveler's checks with a passport and personal checks (1% service charge) or cash (3% service charge). Open Su-Th 9am-5pm, F 9am-1pm.

LOCAL SERVICES

English Bookstores: The Book Boutique, 190 Dizengoff St. (tel. 527 45 27), is the best place for used English-language books in Tel Aviv. A vast selection of texts from historical novels to westerns to erotica. Open Su-Th 10am-7pm, F 10am-3pm. **Katzman Gallery Books,** 152 Dizengoff St. (tel. 523 52 43). Fabulous selection of magazines, comics, and cheap used books. Usually open Su-Th 10:30am-8pm, F 8am-3pm.

Camping Supplies: LaMetayel, Dizengoff Center, Gate 3 or 5 (tel. 528 68 94), on the top floor. The largest camping store in the area, with books, maps, information, and a full range of equipment. The place to meet young Israelis gearing up for their post-military grand tour. Open Su-Th 10am-8:30pm, F 10am-2pm.

Ticket Agencies: Rococo, 93 Dizengoff St. (tel. 527 66 77). Open Su-Th 9am-7pm, F 9am-2pm. **Castel,** 153 Ibn Gvirol St. (tel. 604 76 78 or 604 47 25). **Le'an,** 101 Dizengoff St. (tel. 524 73 73), 25% off for students. Visa, MC accepted; no traveler's checks.

Laundromat: Self-service laundromats abound, and hostels often have their own laundry services. **Nikita,** 98 Ben-Yehuda St., has coin-operated machines. Washers NIS10 for 7kg, dryers NIS1 for 3min. Detergent NIS3. Open 24hr. except during Shabbat.

EMERGENCY AND COMMUNICATIONS

Emergency: Police: Tel. 100. **Fire:** Tel. 102. **First Aid:** Tel. 101.

Pharmacy: Superpharm (tel. 620 37 98 or 620 09 75), bottom floor of Dizengoff Center. Open Su-Th 9:30am-10pm, F 9am-3:30pm, Sa 7-11pm. 24hr. location in the London Minister building at the intersection of Ibn Givriol and Shaul Hamelekh St.

Post Office: 7 Mikveh Yisrael St. (tel. 564 36 51), 2 blocks east of the south end of Allenby St. **Poste Restante** (open Su-Th 7am-10pm), **fax, telegram,** and **telex** (Su-Th 7am-6pm, F 8am-noon). Open Su-Th 7am-6pm, F 7am-noon. Other branches throughout the city.

Internet Access: Internet Bar, 2 Shlomo Hamelekh St. (tel. 528 22 88). NIS30 for 30min., NIS40 per hr. During Happy Hour (noon-6pm) NIS20 for 30min., NIS30 per hr. Students always get Happy Hour prices. Open daily 7am-1am.

Telephones: Solan Communications, 13 Frishman St. (tel. 522 94 24; fax 522 94 49). Private booths for international calls. Telecards, international calling cards, fax services. Open Su-Th 10am-9pm, F 8am-3pm. **Change Spot,** 140 Dizengoff St. (tel. 524 33 93; fax 524 36 66). Discounted international calls. Open Su-Th 9am-7pm, F 9am-2pm.

Telephone Code: 03.

▐' ACCOMMODATIONS

Tel Aviv's hostels vary in character and quality, so check 'em out before checking in. Most are on or around Ben-Yehuda St. and Ha-Yarkon St., with some off Allenby Rd. or Dizengoff St. Some of the best and cheapest are in **Jaffa** (see p. 301). Remember that drunken revelry and downtown noise often continues late into the night. Hostels fill quickly, especially in summer, so make reservations and arrive early. All take credit cards unless otherwise noted.

Ha-Yarkon 48 Hostel, 48 Ha-Yarkon St. (tel. 516 89 89; fax 510 31 13; email H48@zahav.net.il; www.inisrael.com/hayarkon48). Clean rooms, great shared showers, strong fans, kitchen, TV lounge, free pool table, and new rooftop bar. Co-ed or all-female dorms NIS37; doubles NIS149/US$36, with bath NIS189/US$46, with bath and A/C NIS220/US$54. Breakfast included. Laundry NIS14.

Gordon Inn Guest House, 17 Gordon St. (tel. 523 82 39; fax 523 74 19; email sleepin@inter.net.il), 5min. from the beach. If the A/C doesn't keep you cool, the trendy new bar/cafe (open until 2am) will. Spotless single-sex or co-ed rooms. Internet access NIS20 for 20min. Dorms NIS72, with bath NIS77; singles NIS177/US$37, with bath NIS220/US$46; doubles NIS225/US$47, with bath NIS287/US$60. Breakfast included. Lockers NIS6. Reception 24hr.

Tel Aviv Youth Hostel/Guest House (HI), 36 B'nei Dan St. (tel. 544 17 48; fax 544 10 30), near Ibn Gvirol St. Take bus #5, 24, or 25. A long haul from the beach action, but a quiet refuge from the hectic city center. All rooms have A/C. 4- to 6-bed dorms in the youth hostel NIS60; 4-bed dorms with private bath in the guest house NIS76; singles NIS138/US$34.50; doubles NIS202/US$50.50. NIS6 surcharge for nonmembers. Breakfast included. Lockers NIS6 for one day or more.

The Wandering Dog, 3 Yordei Hasira St., 4th floor (tel. 546 63 33). Take the #4 bus to the last stop on Dizengoff St. Yordei Hasira is on the left. Friendly clientele parties on the rooftop lounge, with a panoramic view of the sea. After a day on the sand, relax in the sauna. Co-ed and single-sex dorms with A/C and shared bath NIS35, in winter NIS30. Breakfast included. Lockers NIS5 per day. Wash NIS10; clothesline on the roof.

Hotel Nes Ziona, 10 Nes Tziona St. (tel. 510 60 84), just off Ben-Yehuda St. This clean, quiet hotel is a pleasant escape from the grunge of the backpacking world. Some rooms have balconies, all have sinks and showers; largest rooms have cable TV, blissful A/C, and private baths. Kitchen and storage available. Singles NIS120-220/US$30-45; doubles NIS190-220/US$49-55. Call ahead for reservations.

Noah's Hostel, 34 Ben-Yehuda St. (tel. 620 00 44 or 528 14 45 to reach guests). Laid-back clientele play pool and watch TV in the lounge or BBQ on the roof. 6- to 8-bed dorms NIS33; private rooms for those arriving two by two NIS80, with bath NIS120. Laundry service NIS10 to wash and NIS8 to dry. Credit cards not accepted.

Gordon Hostel, 2 Gordon St. (tel. 522 98 70; fax 523 74 19), on the corner of Ha-Yarkon St. Great location near the beach, with several rooms overlooking the sea. Rooftop bar, decorated with glowing portraits of naked women and fun furniture covers from the flea market, hosts weekly BBQs. Light sleepers should be warned that the combination of the exuberant clientele, the cafe downstairs, and the early morning traffic is merciless. Kitchen available. Internet NIS10 for 20min. Arrive early. Co-ed and single-sex 6- to 8-bed dorms NIS35; rooftop beds NIS27. Laundry NIS10. Lockout 11am-2pm.

Dizengoff Square Hostel, 13 Ben-Ami St. (tel. 522 51 84; fax 522 51 81; email dizengof@trendline.co.il; www.dizengoff-hostel.com), across from the Chen cinema. Its colorful paint, groovy furnishings, TV room, kitchen, and pool table make this the coziest 190-bed hostel in Tel Aviv. Personable staff; the manager is the patron saint of travelers. Popular with the long-term crowd. Co-ed and single-sex 5- to 8-bed dorms NIS39, with A/C NIS45; singles and doubles NIS180/US$46, with A/C and TV NIS208/US$53. Breakfast included. Lockers NIS8. Laundry NIS16. Lockout 10:30am-2:30pm.

◨ FOOD

Come mealtime, Tel Aviv rises above and beyond the call of duty. Restaurants range from Tex-Mex to Southeast Asian, from falafel and hummus to French *haute-cuisine*, but after a brain-melting day at the beach, fast food and frozen yogurt may sound just as good. For quick, cheap belly-fillers, head for the self-service eateries on Ben-Yehuda St. (sandwich with chips or stuff-your-own falafel under NIS12). The eateries near Shuk Ha-Carmel and along Bezalel St. off Allenby and King George St. stay open the latest (1:30am or later).

   Kerem Ha-Temanim (the Yemenite Quarter), south of Allenby St. between Ge'ula and Shuk Ha-Carmel, boasts cheap, spicy fried-dough, often stuffed with meat (NIS12-25). Israelis down kebab and *la'afa* in the **Shechunat Ha-Tikva** area in the southeasternmost quarter, renowned for its cheap beer and lamb, chicken, or beef skewers. Pastry stands, falafel joints, and ice cream shops line **Dizengoff Square** and the stretch of **Dizengoff Street** just north, where crowds of tourists and throngs of hungry young Israelis test the limits of spandex technology. **Yermiyahu Street** has a better, pricier selection (NIS20-35).

RESTAURANTS

🔊 **Alexander's,** 81 Yehuda Ha-Maccabee St. (tel. 605 89 10 or 546 35 91). Favored by locals, it's a lively destination for a stylish adventure in *gourmandisme*. Mouthwatering menu of Mediterranean favorites, including sandwiches on fresh *ciabatta* bread (NIS18-42) and a "hot chocolate cake" that is a pure chocolate orgy. Open Su-Th 7:30am-1:30am, F 7:30am-2:30am, Sa 8:30am-2:30am.

🔊 **Big Mama,** 13 Najara St. (tel. 517 50 65), off Allenby St. near Najara St. Classy sit-down joint packed with folks who recognize good cooking. Wonderful pizzas (NIS23-34) and pastas (NIS24-35). Open Su noon-2am, M-W noon-3am, Th-F noon-4am.

El Gaucho's, 57 Pinsker St. (tel. 528 37 88). The beef is almost as tender as the loving care extended by the waitstaff. Business lunch (NIS49) includes steak, fries, salad, and a drink. Kosher. Open Su-Th noon-11:30pm, Sa sundown-midnight.

Itzik Ve' Ruthie, 53 Sheinken St. (tel. 685 27 53). A bundle of superlatives: the cheapest, freshest, best sandwiches in the city (NIS5-15). So crammed with locals that you'll have to fight to squeeze your takeout order in. Open Su-Th 6am-4pm, F 6am-3pm.

Full Volume, 114 Dizengoff St. (tel. 527 24 97), a couple blocks north of Dizengoff Sq. Pump it up at this cheap, friendly, Middle Eastern place with mostly outdoor seating. Open Su-Th 10:30am-12:30am, F 10:30am-sundown, Sa sundown-12:30am.

Shoshana & Uri's Hungarian Blintzes, 35 Yermiyahu St. (tel. 544 16 97 or 685 06 74). The menus haven't changed at this unique Eastern European restaurant since it was founded in 1977, even though Eastern Europe sure has. Sweet and savory blintzes (NIS20-36). Open Su-Th 12:30pm-1am, Sa sundown-1am.

Yotvata B'Ir, 78 Herbert Samuel St. (tel. 510 74 45), off the *tayelet*. Kibbutz Yotvata, renowned producers of dairy goods, venture into the big city with this well-lit oasis of fresh veggies, cheeses, and fruits. Salads are large enough to feed a small socialist community (NIS44-46). Pancakes with ice cream NIS27-39. Open daily 7am-5am.

A Taste of Life, 60 Ben-Yehuda St. (tel. 620 31 51). An immaculate vegan paradise staffed by members of the Black Hebrew community (see **Dimona,** p. 363). Top off a sandwich (NIS15-18) with scrumptious soymilk ice cream (NIS6.50) and non-dairy, no-egg desserts. Open Su-Th 9am-11pm, F 9am-3pm, Sa sundown-midnight. Kosher.

CAFES

Sheinken Street is designed for crowd-gazing—if the kind of crowd you want to watch wears sheer half-shirts and multiple navel rings. For the quintessential Sheinken experience, spend an afternoon in the **Tamar Cafe,** 57 Sheinken St. (tel. 685 23 76), immortalized in a song by the Israeli pop trio Mango ("Livin' on Shein-ken / drinking coffee at the Tamar Cafe / my dream is to make a short film"). This diner-like haven for locals will make you sing, too (open Su-Th 7am-8pm, F 7am-7pm). Hipper-than-thou former Sheinken devotees have recently relocated to the crop of *chi-chi* cafes on **Basel Street** (south of Nordau St., between Dizengoff St. and Ibn Gvirol St.). The following cafes are gay-friendly and accept credit cards.

Orna Ve' Ella, 33 Sheinken St. (tel. 620 47 53). This classy cafe is packed almost every evening. Wonderful food, though the portions are a bit stingy. Try the bread (NIS9) and desserts (NIS18-25). Open Su-Th 10am-midnight, F 10am-5pm, Sa 11am-midnight.

Ilan's Coffee Shop, 90 Ibn Gvirol St. (tel 523 53 34), the first espresso bar in Tel Aviv, is almost always packed. Fantastic coffee (NIS6-15); the home brew is "Angela Mia." Also at 20 Carlebach St. Open Su 6:30am-8pm, M-Th 6:30am-10pm, F 6:30am-3pm.

Café Kazze, 19 Sheinken St. (tel. 629 37 56). Israeli stars sometimes dine at this trendy cafe's sunny, A/C rooms and garden patio. Fast service and large portions. Open Su-Th 8:30am-12:30am, F 8am-4:30pm, Sa sundown-12:30am.

Café Nordau, 145 Ben-Yehuda St. (tel. 524 01 34), on the corner of Arlozorov St. Good food, generous portions, lively setting. Largely, but not exclusively, gay clientele. Distributes *Hazman Havarod* (Tel Aviv's gay newspaper) and provides current info on gay life and hotspots. Full meals NIS36-44. Open Su-W 8am-1am, Th-Sa 24hr.

♫ ENTERTAINMENT

Though most travelers prefer to fry by day and guzzle Goldstar by night, the appetites of the Israeli jet-set cannot be sated by mere beaches and brew. The *tayelet* (promenade), Sheinken St., and many streets in Neve Tzedek are lined with jazzy cafes, and Tel Aviv suffers from no shortage of raging discotheques, highbrow concert halls, and world class theater.

DON'T ASK, DON'T TEL AVIV Today's Tel Aviv is home to Israel's most thriving gay community. From the soaring attendance at the gay pride day party (held annually in Ha-Yarkon Park) to the large number of gay clubs, pubs, and establishments with "gay nights," the community is present, active, and powerful; catch them out in full force at the "Friday Friendly Freedom" nights at the Zoom, a popular club in the port just south of Yermiyahu St. The best way to find out what's going on is to catch a leaflet on Sheinken St. or read *Hazman Havarod*. Most gay establishments have English signs that are more obvious than their Hebrew ones.

BARS

The recent influx of day-laborers who have taken up semi-permanent residence in Tel Aviv has made bar-hopping more common than costly clubbing. Bars abound around hostel-heavy **Ha-Yarkon Street** and **Allenby Road,** and Israelis frequent **Ha-Arba'a Street,** off Carlebach St. and Ibn Gvirol St. near the Tel Aviv Cinematheque, which is in the throes of a six-pub competition for hotspot status. Bars become crowded around midnight, and seats are scarce after 1am (especially Th-Sa).

Joey's Bar, 42 Allenby St. (tel. 517 92 77). Pound the beers until you're numb enough to get a tattoo next door. Beer NIS14. 25+ admitted, 18+ for tourists. Open daily noon-8am. *Let's Go* does not recommend getting tattoos while intoxicated.

Rival 27, 27 Rival St. (tel. 687 43 64), off Ha-Massger St. Contrary to the name, we're all buds (or Bud Lights) here. Sit down to any of the numerous games the friendly waitstaff offers. Opens M-Th and Sa at 9pm and F at 10pm, fills up around 11pm.

He-She, 8 Ha-Shomeret St. (tel. 510 09 14), above Logos. The most popular gay bar in Tel Aviv has lasted 4 years (an eternity by Tel Aviv standards). Beer NIS14-18.

Dvash, 44 Salameh Rd. (tel. 681 46 53). Decorated with an evil-looking bee mascot and a seductress in red with bats, this *moloko* bar is an institution. Opens Su-Th at 8pm, F at 5pm, Sa at 2pm, and keeps buzzing 'til the bees attack.

1942, 27 Rosh Pina St. (tel. 688 96 92 or 052 448 516). With a couch-filled loft for *nargilahs,* a bar, and a dance floor with great acoustics, this schizophrenic spot has something for every mood. Opens daily at 9pm; dancing Th-Sa only.

M.A.S.H. (More Alcohol Served Here), 275 Dizengoff St. (tel. 605 10 07), at the intersection with Ben Yehuda. Take bus #4. Watch the big-screen TV with Trapper, Hawkeye, and other locals over good burgers (NIS24-30) and beer (NIS11-16). Open daily 11am-5am. Happy hour 6-9pm, drinks 25% off.

Lola, 54 Allenby St. (tel. 517 37 88). This little nymphet is a favorite student hangout. Faux marble tables, homemade pizza (NIS26), and plenty of nice places to sit. 11 kinds of tequila (NIS20-35), Carlsberg and Tuborg on tap (NIS15-19). Champagne doesn't taste like Coca-Cola. 25+ admitted. Open daily 8pm until the last customer leaves.

The Out, 45 Naḥalat Binyamin, few blocks past the *midraḥov.* Israelis and tourists chill out and sip chilled brew (NIS12-18) in this mellow, cozy, 2-floor gay bar. Su 80s night.

CLUBS

Tel Aviv's dance scene is always on the move; *the* club one year may be empty the next and a hardware store the year after that. Patron demographics are no more stable. Current bastions of the pubescent may have been collegiate havens in their prime (see **The Migratory Patterns of the Wild Israeli Disco,** p. 313). Most of Tel Aviv's discos open at 10pm, but no one arrives before midnight. Thursday, Friday, and Saturday are the nights to go. Expect to pay at least NIS20 cover charge.

Allenby 58, just off Allenby St. near Najara St. Mostly famed for its theme nights, which have included Zoo Night, when dancers growl and grind the night away like animals, and Banana Night, when the teeming crowd goes Chiquita yellow. Opens after midnight.

Pacha (tel. 510 20 60), a sprawling club on the beach, in the Dolphinarium. Features house parties with South American *samba* Thursdays and late-night *nargilah* Saturdays.

Heinekken Habima (tel. 528 21 74), at the north end of Rothchild Blvd. Sit at candlelit tables in the beautiful basement performance area while grooving to live rock and folk music. Israeli music on F. Cover NIS20-50. Opens at 10pm.

The Aquarium (tel. 510 66 70), on the other side of the Dolphinarium from Pacha and the beach. In the cavernous halls of this aquatic fantasy land, there are several rooms to groove and couches from which you can watch the dancers or fish, who make similar movements. Open year-round with house progressive and alternative on F, singles night with 70s and 80s music on Sa; open Th in winter only. Cover NIS50-70. 20+ accepted.

Shechitut, 146 Herzl St. (tel. 683 37 02), is the very latest in celebrity hangouts. Its name means "depravity," and it does not disappoint.

ISRAEL

KU ("koo"), 117 Salameh Rd., near Herzl St. Soul and funk spot joins its funk soul brother Pacha in summer. Beer NIS8. Cover NIS25. Open Tu and F-Sa midnight-6am.

The Octopus, in the port, north of Yermiyahu St. Many-armed, extremely loud, non-stop discotheque moves its groove thing from midnight to morning. More women then men, thanks to selective admissions (not much of a problem for tourists). Cover NIS65-120.

The Scene, 56 Allenby Rd. (tel. 510 85 23). Enter between the 2 mystical lamps. Beer NIS18-26. Min. age 23 for women and 25 for men, but as with many establishments, beautiful people are less likely to be questioned. Best DJs are W and Sa. F is gay night. The house rolls out on Th as well.

Venta, 67 Allenby Rd. Wade through the teens and twentysomethings lounging in the old furniture to get to the stairway behind them. This 70s-style apartment turned techno/ jungle club hosts more locals than tourists. Happy hour 8pm-11pm (beer NIS6-10). Open Su-Th 5pm-5am, F 11am-5am, Sa 1pm-5am.

Dynamo Dvash, 59 Abarbanel St. (tel. 683 51 59). The more dynamic counterpart of "Dvash," the well-known bar nearby. Popular electronic-music-dance-house with a por- trait of a cow sipping butter-shots. Live shows on W and F nights. 20+ admitted. Open W-F at 10pm, but not busy until midnight.

Fetish, off Niḥalat Binyamin on Rambam St. This Russian and locals' dance bar offers "just fetishism, no bullshit," as the bouncer announces repeatedly at the door, but the use of the word "fetish" is not connected to any meaning that word actually has. Open daily from 10pm.

LIVE MUSIC

Young Israeli rock bands have appointed Tel Aviv their headquarters and play the clubs there nightly. Two amphitheaters at Ha-Yarkon Park commonly hold con- certs. *Ha-Ir,* a weekly Hebrew magazine, has a section called "Akhbar Ha-Ir" with comprehensive listings. For listings in English, check the brochure "Tel Aviv 2000" or "This Week in Tel Aviv," produced by *The Jerusalem Post.*

Barbie, 40 Salameh Rd. A beautiful stage, some of the best bands in Israel—it all sounds a little too perfect to be real. 20+ admitted. Cover NIS15-50, NIS25 drink minimum; the math is hard. Opens F-Sa at midnight.

Ha-Shoftim, 39 Ibn Gvirol St., on the corner of Ha-Shoftim. Thirtysomethings pack into its dark, funerary interior to rejuvenate with jazz. Open nightly 7pm-3am.

Logos (tel. 516 11 76), off Naḥalat Binyamin St. on Shefer St. Rock and blues perfor- mances nightly at 10pm and midnight; an upstairs cafe shows the downstairs concerts on TV screens and occasionally hosts milder acts of its own. Cover NIS10-50 depending on the band's fame. Reserve tickets ahead of time.

Camelot, 16 Shalom Aleichem St. (tel. 528 53 33). The basement echoes with blues and R&B, while the upstairs pub upholds the chivalric code, with DJs on W, F, and Sa. Cover NIS35-65. Open daily 11pm-1am. Reserve at least a day ahead for good bands.

Cat Balu, 10 Ben Avigdor St. (tel. 562 03 10), also features karaoke. The crowd takes to dancing on the tables when the music's especially good (which is especially often).

PERFORMING ARTS

There are plenty of things to do in Tel Aviv besides getting sunburned or smashed: opera, ballet, theater, jazz, classical music, and dance performances all beckon the culturally-minded. There are also more than 40 **movie theaters** showing American and Israeli flicks. Check the *Jerusalem Post* for English listings for the **Tel Aviv Cin- emathèque,** 2 Sprinzak St. (tel. 691 71 81), at the intersection with Carlebach St. The **Suzanne Delal Center,** 5 Yeḥiely St. (tel. 510 56 56), in Neveh Tzedek, has indoor and outdoor dance, theater, and musical performances. Take bus #8, 10, 25, or 61 from downtown or #40 or 46 from the central bus station. The center is best known as the home of two contemporary ethnic dance companies—**Inbal** (tel. 517 37 11; tickets NIS60; box office open 8am-8pm) and **Bat Sheva** (tel. 517 14 71; tickets NIS45-60, 20% discount with foreign passport; box office open daily 9am-5pm). **Beit Lessin,** 34 Weizmann St. (tel. 694 11 11), has live jazz acts (NIS30-50). The **Tel Aviv Cameri Theater,** 101 Dizengoff St. (tel. 523 33 35), at the corner of Frischmann St., offers simultaneous translation earphones (NIS5) during their dramatic performances (shows Tu 8:30pm; tickets NIS100-125). **Habima Theater,** 2 Tarsat Blvd. (tel. 629 55 55 or 620 77 77), the national theater of Israel, offers simultaneous translation at some performances. For detailed information on schedules and other activities in the Tel Aviv area, see *Tel Aviv Today, Events in Tel Aviv,* and *This Week in Tel Aviv,* all free at the tourist information office and major hotels.

🔘 SIGHTS

Given Israel's abundance of ancient treasures, Tel Aviv's sights are markedly non-site-oriented. Tel Aviv's historic neighborhoods, for instance, are only 100 years old. **Neveh Tzedek,** just west of the intersection of Herzl St. and Aḥad Ha-Am St., is Tel Aviv's oldest Jewish neighborhood outside of Jaffa and one of the few older than a century. The **Suzanne Delal Center,** 5 Yekhieli St. (tel. 510 56 56), in the heart of Neveh Tzedek near Amzalag St., is a hotspot for theater and dance (see **Performing Arts,** p. 297). Happily unrenovated is **Kerem Ha-Temanim** (the Yemenite Quarter), northwest of Allenby St. and King George St., near Shuk Ha-Carmel. This area firmly maintains a small-town feel despite relentless skyscraping all around it. Those who wish to soak in the newness of Tel Aviv's culture congregate at the waterfront **promenade** *(tayelet),* where pre-teens smooch, vendors hawk, and folk dancers strut their stuff all night long.

ROOFTOP OBSERVATORY. Rise above the haggling, shoving, and sunning of the rest of Tel Aviv by look down on the chaos of the market and the city from this tranquil observatory in **Migdal Shalom.** This 40-story tower was the tallest structure in the Middle East until its recent eclipse by the slightly more stately communication tower in the military base near the Tel Aviv Museum. The mosaic walls were designed by artists Nachum Gutan and David Sharir. *(1 Herzl St. and Aḥad Ha-Am St. Enter through the Eastern Wing beneath the underpass. Tel. 517 73 04. Open Su-Th 10am-6:30pm, F 10am-2pm, Sa 11am-4pm. Admission NIS15, students NIS10.)*

KIKKAR YITZḤAK RABIN. Formerly Kikkar Malkhei Yisrael (Kings of Israel Sq.), the square was renamed in 1995 in memory of Prime Minister Yitzḥak Rabin. On November 4, 1995, Rabin was assassinated here by Yigal Amir, a Jewish student, during a crowded peace rally. The square has since drawn mourners who have painted large portraits of Rabin and left candles, flowers, and poetry. *(Past Dizengoff Center at the end of King George St., next to City Hall.)*

GREAT SYNAGOGUE AND INDEPENDENCE HALL. Completed in 1926 and renovated in 1970, this huge domed building showcases arches and stained-glass windows that are replicas of those in European synagogues destroyed during the Holocaust. Near the synagogue is **Independence Hall,** where the founding of the State of Israel was proclaimed in 1948. *(Great Synagogue: 110 Allenby St., just east of the Shalom Tower. Tel. 560 49 05 or 560 40 66. Open Su-F 10am-5pm, Sa 7:30-11:30am. Sa prayer open to the public; head coverings and modest dress required. Independence Hall: 16 Rothschild Blvd. Tel. 517 39 42. Open Su-Th 9am-2pm.)*

🏛 MUSEUMS

BEIT HA-TFUTZOT (DIASPORA MUSEUM). This outstanding museum chronicles the history of Jewish life outside the land of Israel, from the Babylonian exile in 596 BCE to the present day. A display of synagogue models shows how Jews incorporated local ideas into their temple architecture—there's even a model of a synagogue designed by Frank Lloyd Wright. Short films and multimedia displays highlight the diversity of diaspora life, from the culture of the Yemeni Jews to the evolution of Yiddish theater (all displays in Hebrew and English). The museum also has a **Genealogy Department** that can trace the family trees of Jews whose relatives have registered. The Chronosphere, offering English multimedia presentations at 12:30pm and 2:30pm, is a good introduction to the museum. (*On the Tel Aviv University Campus in Ramat Aviv. Tel. 646 20 20; email bhmuseum@tau.ac.il; www.bh.org.il. Buses #7 and 25 stop at the closest gate to the museum; buses #6, 13, 24, and 27 stop near other gates. Open Su-Tu and Th 10am-4pm, W 10am-6pm, F 9am-1pm. Admission NIS26, students and seniors NIS20. English tours (NIS7) at 11am; in summer at 11am and 2pm.*)

ERETZ YISRAEL MUSEUM. The most famous attraction in this complex, composed of eight pavilions built around an archaeological site, is the **Glass Pavilion,** with one of the finest collections of glassware in the world. The **Nehushtan Pavilion** displays discoveries from the ancient copper mines of Timna, better known as King Solomon's Mines, just north of Eilat. Across the patio, the **Kadman Numismatic Museum** traces the history of the region through ancient coins. The **Ceramics Pavilion** contains ancient Canaanite pottery and artist Moshe Shek's ceramic sculptures. Nearby is the **Postal and Philatelic Museum,** with a film that traces the development of the Israeli Postal Service. Across the entrance area past the grassy amphitheater is the **Man and His Work Center,** an exhibition of Middle Eastern folk crafts and techniques. Follow the road to the right to reach the **Tel Qasila Excavations,** which have revealed a 12th-century BCE Philistine port city and ruins dating from around 1000 BCE. Down the hill to the south are scattered remnants of the residential and industrial quarters of the Philistine town. Past the ruins is the **Folklore Pavilion,** with Jewish religious art, ceremonial objects, and ethnic clothing. The Eretz Yisrael complex also houses the **Lasky Planetarium** and the **Eretz Yisrael Library,** home to 30,000 books and periodicals. (*2 Levanon St. in Ramat Aviv. Tel. 641 52 44. Take bus #24, 25, 29, 45, 74, or 86 from New Central Bus Station. Open Su-Tu and Th 9am-3pm, W 9am-5pm, F-Sa 10am-2pm. Admission NIS28, students NIS20.*)

TEL AVIV MUSEUM OF ART. The handsome lobby boasts a Lichtenstein, and the museum itself runs the gamut from Impressionism (Renoir, Monet, Corot, and Pissaro) to Surrealism (including de Chirico and Magritte) to cutting-edge multimedia installations by contemporary artists. Rotating thematic exhibits are exceptionally well curated. An English brochure is available at the ticket booth. (*27 Sha'ul Ha-Melekh Blvd. Tel. 696 12 97 or 695 73 61; www.tamuseum.co.il. Take bus #7 or 18. Open Su-M and W-Th 10am-6pm, Tu 10am-10pm, F-Sa 10am-2pm. Admission NIS27, students NIS20, seniors NIS15, children NIS12. Gallery talks in English W 11:30am when enough people attend.*)

■ SHOPPING

Shoppers can now make their way to a shiny new mall, **Shalom Shopping Center** (more commonly called **Azrieli Center**), 132 Petah Tikvah Rd. (tel. 608 11 98). With its geometrically diverse towers, this is the tallest mall in Israel—at least for the time being (open daily 9:30am-9:30pm). For a more down-and-dirty shopping experience, the famed **Shuk Ha-Carmel** (Carmel Market) is at the intersection of Allenby Rd. and King George St. Waving polyester undergarments and red plastic sandals, vendors extol their products' virtues to chic strollers. Farther south, toward the parking lot, fresh fruit and vegetables go for the lowest prices in the city. One block south of the *shuk* lies the Naḥalat Binyamin and Ramban St. *midraḥov*, which becomes a street fair on Tuesdays and Fridays. From 10am to 4pm (weather permitting), local artists and craftspeople sell jewelry, pottery, original paintings, Judaica, children's toys, and bizarre candelabras. Musicians and mimes fill the cobblestone street to entertain those weary of shopping.

◪ BEACHES AND PROMENADES

The beaches within the city are sandy, clean, and free, and all have showers, toilets, and changing rooms with varying degrees of cleanliness. All of Tel Aviv's beaches are rife with theft; lock up valuables before hitting the sand. The southern coastline, with fewer amenities and no luxury hotels, tends to be quieter during the day, but that is gradually changing now that the *tayelet* (promenade) has been extended all the way to Jaffa. **Gordon Beach** overflows with foreign tourists and Israelis trying to pick them up, while the **Hilton Beach** (behind the hotel) swarms with native surfers and tourists trying to pick them up. The **Sheraton Beach** is quite peaceful. From north to south, the beaches are: Sheraton, Hilton, Gordon, Frischmann, Trumpeldor, and the Jerusalem beach at the end of Allenby Rd.; the last four are almost one continuous beach. The Hebrew word for beach is *ḥof*, but it's more important to learn the **flag language** of the beach: black means swimming is forbidden, red means swimming is dangerous, white means swim on. Most beaches have lifeguards on duty 7am-5pm.

If the beach doesn't sate your bare-flesh needs, perfect the Mediterranean art of nonchalant people-watching from Tel Aviv's streets and cafes (see **Cafes,** above). Work that cover-girl look along the wide, high-fashion boutique-lined sidewalks of **Dizengoff Street,** no longer at the peak of their glory but still among the more crowded catwalks in town. **Dizengoff Square** hosts an ever-changing scene, from retirees feeding flocks of pigeons in the midday sun to late-night punks who flock to the overpass stairs. The multicolored, fire-spitting, revolving ◼**fountain,** designed by illustrious Israeli artist Agam (he did the Dan Hotel colors, too), crowns the square in an unsurpassed celebration of municipal kitsch. Those tunes you hear are coming from the fountain itself, which has an hourly multimedia show with music ranging from Ravel's *Bolero* to Israeli folk songs. The **walk** south from Allenby St., east of its junction with Sheinken St., through the Yemenite Quarter and Neve Tzedek, makes a refreshing escape from Tel Aviv's all-too-modern *gestalt*.

JAFFA (YAFO) יפו يافا

An Israeli folk song describes Jaffa (*Yafo,* or "beautiful," in Hebrew; *Yafa* in Arabic) as possessing a "mysterious and unknown" element that allows its atmosphere "to seep like wine into the blood." Jaffa's stone houses and winding streets are truly intoxicating. An integral part of Tel Aviv, Jaffa has one of the oldest functioning harbors in the world, nearly 6000 years old. According to the Bible, the recalcitrant prophet Jonah shirked his divine calling and fled to Jaffa to catch a boat to Tarshish, and subsequently had his fateful encounter with the whale. The earliest archaeological finds in Jaffa date from the 18th century BCE, from which point on the city played host to a series of conquerors. In 1468 BCE, the Egyptians captured Jaffa by hiding soldiers in human-sized clay jars that were brought into the city market. King David took the city around 1000 BCE, and under Solomon it became the main port of Judea. During the 12th century CE, Jaffa was captured by the First Crusaders, Salah ad-Din, Richard the Lionheart, the Muslims, and Louis IX, who built magnificent walls and towers which partly remain today. The Mamlukes overpowered the city in 1267; apart from a brief stay by Napoleon around 1800 (during which much of the Jewish community vanished), Jaffa remained an important Arab stronghold until 1948. In the 1960s, the Tel Aviv municipality began a massive renovation project here, resulting in today's abundance of small museums and a thriving artists' colony amid green parks and restored Crusader walls.

■ ORIENTATION

The **Jaffa Clocktower,** completed in 1906, stands by the entrance to Jaffa from Tel Aviv and is a useful landmark. Originally, the clocktower's four faces were split between Israeli and European time for the convenience of the European sailors. A free tour of Old Jaffa by the Tourism Association begins here Wednesday at 9:30am (meet at 9am). Bus #46 from the New Central Bus Station lets passengers off in front of the clocktower, and bus #10 from Ben-Yehuda St. stops several minutes away. To get to the **Old City,** make a right a bit south of the clocktower, and head toward the sea. The main road becomes the **Mifratz Shlomo Promenade,** with unbelievable views of Tel Aviv's action-packed coast and skyline.

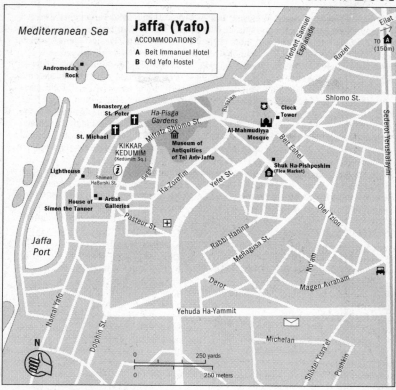

Jaffa (Yafo)

ACCOMMODATIONS
A Beit Immanuel Hotel
B Old Yafo Hostel

ACCOMMODATIONS

Old Yafo Hostel, 8 Olei Tzion St. (tel. 682 23 70; fax 682 23 16), in the middle of Jaffa's *Shuk Ha-Pishpeshim* (flea market). Coming from the north, walk 1 block past the clocktower on Yefet St. and turn left onto Olei Tzion St. Get a receipt and they'll reimburse your bus fare from the airport. Co-ed and single-sex 6- to 10-bed dorms NIS33; cozy doubles NIS98, with balcony NIS118/US$30, with A/C, TV, kitchen, and bath NIS178/US$40. No curfew, but "lights out" at 11pm.

Beit Immanuel Hostel, 8 Auerbach St. (tel. 682 14 59; fax 682 98 17). An immaculate Christian hospice in the newly renovated part of Old Jaffa. Walk down Raziel St. for 10min. until it turns into Eilat St.; turn right at 10 Eilat St. This non-smoking establishment is great for families. Single-sex 10- to 13-bed dorms NIS48; singles with bath NIS160; doubles with bath NIS260. Dinner NIS40, Shabbat NIS60. Reception 7am-11pm, but those arriving late from the airport can make arrangements. 11pm curfew.

FOOD

According to the New Testament, it was in Jaffa that Peter had a vision telling him that the Gospel extended outside the confines of Judaism and that the dietary laws no longer applied (Acts 10). The spirit is still alive today: Jaffa is one of the best places to get a great meal on Shabbat when kosher restaurants are closed. The maze of narrow streets surrounding the Jaffa Clocktower is peppered with cheap falafel stands, *al-ha'esh* (barbecue) meat diners, and sweets vendors, some of which are open 24 hours. Walk down Ole Tzion St. a few blocks from Yefet St. for some mind-blowing couscous (NIS20). In Jaffa Port, just south of the renovated Old City off Pasteur St., picturesque waterfront restaurants offer seafood so fresh it talks back (entrees NIS35 and up).

ISRAEL

🔖 **Said Abu El-Afia and Sons,** 7 Yekevet, 1 block behind Jaffa Clocktower. Popularly known as "Aboulafia," and so famous that Israelis use its sobriquet to denote all stuffed-pita foods. Wade through crowds to taste fresh sesame-covered *baigelah, malaweh, lehem za'tar,* and *samuza,* all for NIS3-12. Takeout only. Open 24hr. Cash only.

Ilana Goor Museum Café, 4 Mazal Dagim St. (tel. 683 76 76). The trendiest place to grab a bite in Jaffa, situated in the heart of the artists' colony. The artsy ambience of the rooftop cafe overlooking Jaffa Port makes the NIS10 cup of coffee worth it. Don't miss the great museum downstairs. Cafe open Su-Th 10am-6pm, F 10am-4pm.

Dr. Shakshuka, 3 Beit Eshel (tel. 682 28 42), at Yefet St. Scrumptious Libyan food in the heart of Old Jaffa. The eponymous dish is the *shakshuka*—a mouth-watering tomato and egg concoction (NIS16). Couscous dishes (vegetarian NIS25; with meat, potatoes, and soup NIS40) are so big you'll need to share. Open Su-Th 9am-1am, F 9am-sundown, Sa sundown-2am.

Shipudei Itzik Hagadol (Big Itzik's Skewers), 3 Raziel St. (tel. 518 18 02; sign in Hebrew only). Where hungry locals meet, greet, and eat skewered meat. Sizzling specialty kebabs NIS13.50-29. Herbivores can get heavenly hummus (NIS11.50) and real, warm pita. Open Sa-Th 11am-1am.

👁 SIGHTS

KIKKAR KEDUMIM AND ENVIRONS. This plaza is Jaffa's commercial, historical, and tourist center, and the site of outdoor summer concerts. Following signs to the Visitors' Center, head down the stairs that lead under the plaza to take a peek at archaeological excavations from 2300-year-old **Tel Yafo,** featuring Roman remains. **Andromeda's Rock,** site of Perseus's rescue of the Greek princess, is visible to the north. The wooden footbridge from Kikkar Kedumim leading to the grassy **Ha-Pisga Gardens** appears often in both Arab and Jewish couples' wedding pictures (Tu and Th evenings are especially busy). The gardens are home to a small, modern amphitheater as well as a tiny excavation of an 18th-century BCE Hyksos town that later became an Egyptian outpost. The shady trees make this a great picnic spot and the look-out point offers Jaffa's best view of the coast and Tel Aviv. *(Tel Yafo open Su-Th 9am-11pm, F 9am-2pm, Sa 10am-11pm. Free.)*

ARTISTS' COLONY. Down the stairs from Kikkar Kedumim is the cluster of museums, restaurants, and galleries that make up Jaffa's touristy artists' colony. After the 1948 War, Jaffa was left in ruins and the area became rife with prostitution, drugs, and crime. In the late 60s, the Tel Aviv Municipality decided to turn Jaffa into an artists' colony to clean it up. Under the auspices of the Old Jaffa Development Company, each artist who arrived bought a section of the ruins, eventually transforming them into today's galleries.

SHUK HA-PISHPESHIM (FLEA MARKET). Jaffa's large Shuk Ha-Pishpeshim is one of the livelier markets in Israel, with roofed rows of overflowing stalls offering dust-covered knick-knacks, modern hand-dyed clothing, Persian carpets, leather goods, and brassware. A vast selection of enormous *nargilahs* is also available. *(The shuk is squeezed between Olei Tzion and Beit Eshel St. To reach it from the clocktower, go one block south on Yefet St. and turn left. Busiest on Fridays. Closed Sa.)*

JAFFA PORT. The **Jaffa Port,** just southwest of Ha'aliya Ha-Shniya St., was the perfect depth for King Solomon when he imported cedar rafts from Lebanon to build his temple (see **The Cedars,** p. 482). It is far too shallow, however, for modern, larger ships. Today, the port is an active fishermen's wharf, where fishermen usually mend their nets in the afternoon, leave for sea at nightfall, and return in the early morning with their fresh catch. One block west of the clocktower is the south end of the Tel Aviv *tayelet* (promenade); since it was extended to Jaffa in 1999, it has made the beach more accessible and consequently more crowded.

MUSEUM OF ANTIQUITIES OF TEL AVIV-JAFFA. The Museum of Antiquities contains artifacts from Neolithic to Roman times, including a comprehensive collection of coins found in Jaffa. *(Along the promenade. Tel. 682 53 75. Open Su-Th 9am-1pm; admission NIS10, students NIS5.)*

NEAR TEL AVIV

RAMLA רמלה

From Tel Aviv, take bus #245, 411, 450, or 451 (30min., every 20min., NIS9.50). The shuk is on Ze'ev Zabutinski, which is closed to traffic until the shops close. Shuk open daily until dark (around 7pm); especially lively on Thursdays.

Founded in 716 by the formidable Umayyad Caliph Suleiman Ibn 'Abd al-Malik, Ramla is the only town in Israel that was established and developed by Arabs. Until the arrival of the Crusaders in the 11th century, Ramla was the capital of Palestine and was known for its magnificent mosques. The diversity of its history and present population, as well as its vibrant *shuk*, make the town worth a visit.

Most of the mosques and churches that comprise Ramla's multi-faith pilgrimage are in the center of the town, all within easy walking distance. Across from the bus station is the **Crusader Cathedral of St. John,** which became the **Great Mosque** (open Su-Th 8am-4pm) when Ramla's Muslims recaptured the town. Although the mosque now retains little of its former glory aside from a lone minaret and vaulted arches, Arabic calligraphy still covers the walls. The **Tower of Forty Martyrs** is a 14th-century addition to the **White Mosque,** down Herzl St. on Danny Mass St. The mosque dates back to Umayyad rule and is said to be the burial site of some of Muhammad's companions; Napoleon purportedly coordinated his attack on Jaffa from the tower. Ramla is supposedly the biblical Arimathea, home of Joseph, who, along with St. Nicodemus, prepared Jesus' body for burial and placed it in his own tomb (near the **Garden Tomb** in Jerusalem, p. 283) after the crucifixion. The large stone **Church of St. Nicodemus and St. Joseph Arimathea,** on Herzl St. at the corner of Bialik St., was built to honor the two early disciples of Jesus in 1296.

ASHKELON אשקלון

Ashkelon's strategic position along major naval and land routes has made it desirable property for almost every ancient empire, from the Greeks to the Muslims. First rising to prominence as one of the Philistines' five great cities (although settlements here date back to the 3rd millennium BCE), Ashkelon reached its zenith as an independent city-state in the Roman period. Today, its main attractions are its sandy beaches, seaside national park, and well-known archaeological sites.

⌖ PRACTICAL INFORMATION. 56km down the coast from Tel Aviv, near the border-crossing to Gaza. The **central bus station** (tel. 677 82 22) on Ben-Gurion Blvd. runs buses to: **Tel Aviv** (#300, 301, 311; 1¼hr.; every 15-30min. 5:30am-10:40pm; NIS20.50); **Jerusalem** (#437; 1½hr.; every 30min.-1hr. 6am-7:15pm; NIS21.50, students NIS19.30); **Be'er Sheva** (#363, 364; 1½hr.; every 40min.-1hr. 6:15am-7:30pm; NIS22.50, students NIS20.20).

⌖ PARK LEUMI ASHKELON. The Ashkelon National Park was built on the site of 4000-year-old Canaanite remains, buried beneath ruins of nearly every other empire that settled here. Traces of the once-thriving Philistine city surround the picnic tables and snack bars. The **Bouleuterion,** a series of Hellenistic and Roman columns and capitals, graces the park's center. It served as the Council House Square when Ashkelon was an autonomous city-state under Severius in the 3rd century CE. The sunken courtyard-like area next to the Bouleuterion is actually the inside of a Herodian assembly hall; it contains two impressive **statues** of Nike, the winged goddess of victory, and an Italian marble statue of the goddess Isis with her god-child Horus, sculpted between 200 BCE and 100 CE. Behind the Bouleuterion is an amphitheater. Along the southern edge of the park are segments of a wall from the 12th-century Crusader city. A short hike past the amphitheater affords a view of the Roman walls and the massive marble columns that supported these walls, destroyed in 1191 by Salah ad-Din. Richard Lionheart restored them in 1192, as did Cornwall in 1240, only to have them demolished by the Sultan Baybars in 1270. *(30min. walk from the bus station. Bus #6 to the park is infrequent. Open daily 7am-7pm. Free, with car NIS15. Free camping on the park's grassy areas with bathrooms but no showers.)*

⌕ BEACHES. Ashkelon's coast has four beaches where swimming is permitted; **Delilah Beach** and **Bar Kochba Beach** are the most popular. The Delilah Beach boardwalk, a small stone plaza up toward the street, is lined with fish restaurants (meals NIS35-80). For sand-free water fun, try the **Ashkeluna Water Park** (tel. 673 99 70), near Delilah Beach and the T-junction that branches off toward the national park. Crowds of Israeli youth flock to Ashkeluna's extensive water slides and games, with loud Israeli pop piped around the complex. *(Open daily May-June 9am-4pm; July-Oct. 9am-5pm. Admission NIS45, after 2pm NIS25.)*

BEIT GUVRIN בית גוברין

Bus #11 from Kiryat Gat goes directly to Kibbutz Beit Guvrin (25min.; Su-Th 8am and 5pm, F 8am and 2pm; NIS7.70) and returns to Kiryat Gat (Su-Th 8:25am and 5:30pm, F 8:25am and 2:30pm). Kiryat Gat is easily accessible by bus from: Tel Aviv (#369; 1hr., every 30min., NIS18.50); Jerusalem (#446; 1hr., every hr., NIS21.50); and Ashkelon (#437; 1½hr., every 45min.-1hr., NIS20). The park is off Rte. 35, near the kibbutz, across from the gas station. To avoid spending the night in Beit Guvrin, catch a morning bus or taxi from Kiryat Gat (NIS50) to reach the sites. Tel. (07) 681 10 20. Sites open Su-Th 8am-5pm, F 8am-4pm; closes 1hr. earlier Sept.-Apr. Admission NIS18, students NIS15, children NIS9. The English brochure has a small map of the park. Bring a hat, sunscreen, and at least 1½ liters of water.

Beit Guvrin was a flourishing Jewish metropolis in the 4th and 3rd centuries BCE and in the years between the destruction of the Second Temple and the Bar Kokhba Revolt (132-135 CE). The Arab village of Beit Jibrin stood nearby until the 1948 War, when its inhabitants were evacuated; since 1949, the modern kibbutz of Beit Guvrin has rested on its ruins. Once known as the biblical city of **Maresha,** one of the cities of Judah fortified by Rehoboam (Joshua 16:44), the area was settled by Edomites after the destruction of the First Temple, Sidonians during the 4th century BCE, and eventually Greeks, who converted it into a bustling economic center. The complicated caves and magnificent views of **Beit Guvrin National Park,** encompassing the ruins of Maresha and Beit Guvrin, are some of Israel's buried treasures. The park also contains some of the 800 glaringly white and chalky **bell-shaped caves** that characterize the Beit Guvrin region, hidden among the cacti and fig trees. Most of the caves were carved by Greeks, Byzantines, and others as they quarried for limestone. Once dug, the caves were used for storage, penning animals, and water collection, and later became sanctuaries for hermits and monks. St. John and others came here seeking solitude, and they often carved crosses and altars into the walls. The walls of the **Columbarium Cave** contain hundreds of small holes once used for storing pigeons for food, fertilizer, and cult rituals. The ruins in the lower city, near the *tel,* are worth the hot and hefty walk. Most impressive are the Hellenistic houses with their maze-like series of underground cisterns.

MEDITERRANEAN COAST

The stretch of coastline north of Tel Aviv is home to much of Israel's population and most of its agricultural output. Beaches along the shore are crowded with Israeli vacationers and dotted with Roman ruins. When pioneers arrived in the beginning of the 20th century, they drained the swamps of the coastal plain, clearing the path for a modern, industrial state.

HIGHLIGHTS OF THE MEDITERRANEAN COAST

■ Stroll down the quiet, beautiful shorelines of **Herzliya** (p. 305) before chatting with the impassioned resident of the surreal **Hermit's House.**

■ The manicured lawns of the **Baha'i Shrine** (p. 314) are the perfect spot to meditate on the panoramic view of **Haifa** harbor (p. 308), but the *souq* of the Druze village of **Daliyat al-Karmel** (p. 316) has better coffee.

HERZLIYA הרצליה

Named after Theodore Herzl (see **Zionism and the British Mandate**, p. 243), Herzliya and its affluent western suburb Herzliya Pituah are only 15km outside Tel Aviv. Herzliya is a residential city with a few small museums, and Herzliya Pituah is home to beautiful beaches and luxury hotels. Buses #501 (40min., every 20min. 5:40am-11:30pm, NIS6.80) and #502 (35min., every 30min., NIS6.80) run from Tel Aviv.

Herzliya's cultural hub is the **Yad Labanim Memorial Center**, two blocks south of the bus station on Ben-Gurion St., just after Ha-Banim St. An outdoor amphitheater attached to the building overlooks the museum's modern **Sculpture Garden** and is the setting of concerts by the **Herzliya Chamber Orchestra** (tel. (09) 950 0761), as well as an annual theatrical festival in May. Zionist history buffs should check out the **Beit Rishonim (Founders' Museum)**, 8-10 Ha-Nadiv St. The museum narrates the history of Herzliya, beginning with its days as a British colony in 1924, using computerized presentations and from the early settlement period. (Open M 8:30am-12:30pm and 4-6:30pm, Tu-Th 8:30am-12:30pm. Admission NIS8, students NIS4, seniors free.)

At the beach, informed travelers search out Herzliya Pituah's most worthwhile attraction, an inhabited sand castle known as the ◪**Hermit's House.** This fantastical residence, built into the side of a cliff by "hermit" **Nissim Kakhalon,** is a must-see for anyone to whom "arts and crafts" is not incompatible with Surrealism. Kakhalon claims, "I make it from my love. I make it good." In other words, he spent 29 years turning other people's garbage (tires, toys, tiles, etc.) into this hallucinogenic maze of winding tunnels, flower-strewn antechambers, and plush gardens. Even more impressive, everything in the artful interior is absolutely functional, from the bathroom ceiling made entirely of Maccabee Beer bottles to the loveseat with a mirrored mosaic on one side and a huge sculpted stone face on the other. Nothing goes to waste here: Kakhalon even uses the manure from his family of goats to grow fragrant basil. The depth and grandeur of Kakhalon's tours of his home depend on the extent to which his guests are demonstratively appreciative.

Herzliya Pituah's gorgeous, sparklingly clean shore has arguably the nicest beaches in Israel. Most of the large beaches charge admission (NIS12, children NIS8), though those claiming to stay at one of the hotels are often not required to pay. City buses #13 and #29 go to **Nof Yam** and **Sidna 'Ali Beaches.**

NETANYA נתניה

Founded in the 1920s as a citrus-farming center, Netanya has grown into a popular beach resort full of affluent retirees and vacationing Europeans who couldn't tell a plow from a cow. Located between Haifa and Tel Aviv, Netanya leans toward Tel Aviv in both location and ethos. The stunning Mediterranean surf here is also easily accessible and less crowded than Tel Aviv's.

◪ PRACTICAL INFORMATION. Buses leave from the **central bus station,** 3 Binyamin Blvd. (tel. 860 62 02), to: **Tel Aviv** (#601 and 605, 1hr., every 25min. 5:40am-11:30pm, NIS12.20); **Haifa** (#947, 45min., every 30min., NIS20.50); and **Jerusalem** (#947, 1½hr., every 30min., NIS28). **Sherut** to Haifa, Tel Aviv, and Jerusalem are available just outside the bus station on Binyamin Blvd. From the central bus station, take Binyamin Blvd. one block north to Herzl St. The **midrahov** (pedestrian zone), lined with expensive outdoor cafes, shawarma stands, and dairy restaurants, is on the other side of Dizengoff St. Down the *midrahov* is **Ha-Atzma'ut Square** (Independence Sq.). The **tourist office** (tel. 882 72 86 or 884 13 48) is located in a small, strangely shaped brick building in the southwest corner of Ha-Atzma'ut Sq., next to the beach stairs (open Su-Th 8am-4pm, F 9am-noon). **Telephone code:** 09.

◤ ACCOMMODATIONS. Almost all hotels in Netanya are expensive, especially during August and the Jewish holiday of Pesach (Apr. 20-26, 2000), but many lower their prices by 10-15% from November to February. The **Orit Hotel,** 21 Ḥen Blvd. (tel./fax 861 68 18), several blocks south of Ha-Atzma'ut Sq., is a great place to recuperate, with scrupulously clean rooms and beautiful private baths, fans, and balconies. (Singles NIS144/US$30; doubles NIS215/US$45; additional beds NIS86. NIS34 discount for kibbutzniks. Breakfast included. Reception in summer 7am-11pm; in winter 7am-9pm. Call in advance.) The only youth hostel in town is **Atzma'ut Hostel** (tel./fax 882 25 62 or 862 13 15), at the corner of Ha-Atzma'ut Sq. and Usishkin St. With air conditioning, fridges, and private baths in all rooms, it shines next to its Tel Aviv counterparts (6-bed dorms NIS48; singles NIS95; doubles NIS143). The most popular areas for **beach-sleeping** are near the 24-hour cafes, but camping on the beach is unsafe, especially for solo women.

◯ FOOD. Cheap food is everywhere in Netanya. **Shuk Ha-Ir** (City Market), one block north of Herzl St. along Shaham St., overflows with cheap produce. You can also stock up at the **Nitza Supermarket**, 8 Nitza Blvd. (tel. 862 82 16), off David Ha-Melech St. In **Ha-Atzma'ut Square,** pizza slices go for NIS4 and *malaweh* for NIS10. Closer to the central bus station, prices go down. **Sha'ar Ha-Gay Street** is lined with falafel stands and self-service restaurants where one can stuff just about anything into a pita. **Bat Ikar**, 14 Sha'ar Ha-Gay St., and **Belle-Ville Bakery,** 4 Binyamin Blvd. (tel. 862 59 33), are 24-hour bakeries (closed on Shabbat) with pastries for NIS1-4.

◙ ◪ SIGHTS AND ENTERTAINMENT. Netanya's 11km of beaches are its greatest asset, and they're all free. Windsurfers brave the waves at **Herzl Beach,** just below Ha-Atzma'ut Sq. The religious **Kiryat Sanz Beach** farther to the north has separate bathing hours for men and women. The Netanya municipality organizes various forms of free entertainment (stop by the tourist office for a complete listing). During the summer, you can watch the sun set over the Mediterranean while listening to classical music in the **Ha-Melekh Park Amphitheater.** Every Monday at noon, talented Russian musicians give classical concerts at 11 Ha-Atzma'ut Sq. (tel. 884 05 34; tickets NIS15, including food at pre-concert reception). When all else shuts down, head to one of Netanya's several bars or pubs. **Uranus Pub,** 13 Ha-Atzma'ut Sq. (tel. 882 99 19), on the right as you enter Ha-Atzma'ut Sq. from the *midrahov*, is Netanya's oldest pub, with draft beers for NIS12-16 (open daily 8pm-5am). **Ropongi Pub** (tel. 882 92 99), on Herzl St., is packed with locals tossing back beer and sandwiches (NIS11-16).

CAESAREA קיסריה

At the end of the first century BCE, **Herod the Great** transformed a small Phoenician anchorage into *Caesarea Maritima* ("Caesarea of the Sea," Kay-SAR-ya in Hebrew) as a monument to his wealth and power. The site may have made more of an impression as a testament to his artistry. Built in only 12 years, the city rapidly became a great commercial center and was soon the headquarters of the Roman government in Palestine; the procurator of Caesarea from 26 to 36 CE was Pontius Pilate, the man who ordered Jesus' crucifixion in 33 CE. The first evidence of Pilate's existence outside the accounts of the Gospels and the writings of Josephus (see **What's All the 'Phus About?,** p. 331) was on an inscribed stone uncovered in the Roman theater here in 1961.

As the new commercial and cultural center of the region, Caesarea attracted a growing number of newcomers. Not only Romans, but also Samaritans and Jews flocked to the town, and ethnic conflict expanded with the population. This clash between Caesarea's Jews and pagans ignited the six-year **Jewish Rebellion** (the Great Revolt), which resulted in the destruction of Jerusalem's Second Temple in 70 CE (see **Ancient History,** p. 242). The Romans celebrated Jerusalem's fall by slaughtering thousands of Jews in Caesarea's amphitheater and crowning the commanding general Vespatian as Caesar. By the end of the revolt, Caesarea was the most important town in the land. Despite the widespread eradication of the Jews, Caesarea's Jewish community remained cohesive and staged a revolution 62 years later, led by **Simon Bar Kokhba.** Legend has it that **Rabbi Akiva,** one of the greatest

Jewish sages, supported Bar Kochba and was jailed in Caesarea by the Romans. They tore him apart with iron combs, and to this day some Jews of the region wear their hair unkempt to memorialize him. Jews returned to the city en masse when Judah the Prince lifted the ban on living there a few centuries later; previously, the city had been deemed impure. In the 3rd century, a school for rabbinical studies was founded, and the city's rabbis are mentioned frequently in the Talmud.

⁊ PRACTICAL INFORMATION. Getting to Caesarea can be difficult. The only practical way is via Ḥadera, the nearest town. Buses arrive at Ḥadera: **Tel Aviv** (#852 and 872; 40min., NIS15.50); **Netanya** (#706; 20min., every 30min., NIS8); **Haifa** (#921 and #941 express; 30min.-1hr., NIS16); and **Jerusalem** (#945; 1hr., a few times per day, NIS29). From Ḥadera, only bus #76 goes to the **ruins** (30min., NIS8), and travels only a few times per day. A **taxi** to the ruins from the station in Ḥadera is NIS30 (make arrangements for the ride back). **Telephone code:** 06.

◑ SIGHTS. Today, Caesarea's multi-layered ruins constitute one of Israel's finest archaeological sites. The main sights are a Roman city, ancient port, and large Crusader fortress, all within **Caesarea National Park.** A map (NIS10) sold at the entrance to the park provides a good history of Caesarea, and a pamphlet (NIS17, includes map) further explains each well-labeled site. (Park open in summer Su-Th 8am-5pm, F 8am-4pm; in winter Su-Th 8am-4pm, F 8am-3pm. Admission NIS18, students NIS9.) Outside the park, the interesting sights are limited. Most of the relics unearthed at Caesarea are on display at the **Sdot Yam Museum of Caesarea Antiquities** (tel. 636 43 67), inside Kibbutz Sdot Yam. Next door is the **Hannah Senesh Memorial Centre** (tel. 636 43 66), built in honor of a Sdot Yam parachutist who died while trying to save Jews from the Nazis during World War II. Ask the curator Benny (who knew Senesh personally) to read "A Walk to Caesarea," Senesh's famous poem based on her time at Sdot Yam, the song was remade as the popular song "Eli, Eli." (Both open Su-Th and Sa 10am-4pm, F and holiday eves 10am-1pm. Admission and film NIS9, students and seniors NIS8.)

NEAR CAESAREA

Within the boundaries of Kibbutz Nachsholim is the **Center of Nautical and Regional Archaeology** (CONRAD; tel. 639 09 50), also known as **Hamizgaga Museum.** The unique stone edifice, built by Baron Edmond de Rothschild, was formerly a glass factory for Zikhron's wine bottles. Today it displays objects found at Tel Dor and underwater archaeological finds retrieved by the center's diving team. Exhibits include 4000-year-old anchors and seashell-encrusted muskets thrown overboard by Napoleon's troops (open Su-F, Sa, and holidays 10:30am-3pm; admission and English film NIS10, students and seniors NIS7).

A few kilometers north, next to **Kibbutz Ein Karmel,** is the **Naḥal Me'arot Nature Reserve** (tel. 04 984 17 50/2), with prehistoric caves inhabited some 200,000 years ago. These caves are the only evidence in the world of Neanderthals and Cro-Magnons living simultaneously. Experienced guides explain the significance of the caves and can recommend or lead longer hikes in the surrounding area. English tours and a film are available. Bus #921 goes to the site from Haifa (20min., NIS9.60) and from Tel Aviv (2hr., NIS20.40). Get off at Ein Carmel Junction and walk south along the road for a few minutes until you see a sign for the reserve. A few hundred meters east of the main road is the entrance to the caves. (Reserve open Su-Th 8am-4pm, F 8am-3pm. Admission and film NIS18, under 18 NIS9.)

ZIKHRON YA'AKOV זיכרון יעקב

Zikhron Ya'akov (Zikhron for short) was established in 1882 on swamplands drained with the generous financial assistance of Baron Edmond de Rothschild, after whose father, Jacob, the town is named (*Zikhron Ya'akov* means "Jacob's Memorial"). The town, which is sprawled happily among forested hills, inherited a part of the Baron's legendary viticultural legacy.

⏚ PRACTICAL INFORMATION. Bus #872 from Tel Aviv (1½hr., every 30min., NIS21.50) and bus #202 from Haifa (35min., every 1½hr., NIS16.50) go to the small **central bus station.** The white building behind the station is the **tourist office** (tel. 639 88 92), which offers maps, brochures, and information about city events (open Su-Th 8:30am-1pm, F 8:30am-noon).

◰ CARMEL MIZRAHI WINERY AND ENVIRONS. The famous Carmel Mizraḥi Winery, founded 118 years ago by the Baron himself, now produces a significant share of Israel's domestic wine. The one-hour tour of the winery includes a look at the old wine cellars, an audio-visual presentation, wine tasting, and a souvenir bottle. It's best to visit during the harvest season, Aug.-Oct. The winery also hosts wild wine and cheese parties, most often accompanied by an eat-'til-you-pass-out dinner, dancing, and live music.

Though the town is famous for its winery, the walks outside the city limits, particularly around the magnificent **Rothschild Family Tomb,** are also worthwhile. The **Beit Aharonson Museum** shows off the former digs of a town resident who set up a spy network to assist the British against the Turks during World War I. Other sites of interest in Zikhron Ya'akov include the beautiful **Ohel Ya'akov Synagogue** at the junction of Ha-Meyasdim and Ha-Nadiv St., and the **First Aliyah Museum,** which presents an exciting, if melodramatic, film reenactment of the first wave of Zionism (during which Zikhron Ya'akov was founded). The museum is housed in a 111-year-old building that the Baron used as a council building. *(**Winery:** Tel. 629 09 77; fax 629 09 57. Open Su-Th 8:30am-3:30pm, F 9am-1pm. Admission NIS13, students NIS11, children NIS10. Call ahead for tours in English. Reservations required for wine and cheese parties. **Beit Aharonson Museum:** 40 Ha-Meyasdim St. Tel. 639 01 20. Open Su-M 8:30am-3pm, Tu 8:30am-4pm, W-Th 8:30am-3pm, F 8:30am-noon. Admission NIS10, students NIS8, seniors NIS5. **First Aliyah Museum:** Tel. 621 23 33. Turn left on Ha-Nadiv St. from Ha-Meyasdim St. when the cobblestone ends; the museum is directly after the synagogue.)*

HAIFA חיפה حيفا

Haifa is a prosperous city built on the steep, forested slopes of Mt. Carmel. Though it boasts the country's largest port, two of Israel's 11 universities, and the most diverse topography in the state, Haifa does not compete with Tel Aviv or Jerusalem for tourists. Budget accommodations are sparse, the waterfront distant, and the museums less-than-spectacular. The city's "Haifa 2000" project has almost finished transforming its coastal beaches into a Riviera-esque strip, but for the moment, Haifa's most memorable attractions are its luxuriously wooded neighborhoods and striking vistas.

Ever since the prophet Elijah fled from the wrath of King Ahab to the caves of Mt. Carmel (I Kings 18-19), Haifa has harbored religious minorities. Crusaders built the first of several monasteries above Elijah's Cave, which eventually gave shelter to the wandering (but now settled) Carmelite Order of Monks. German Templars established Haifa's German colony, and the Baha'i have built their world headquarters and stunning shrine here. During the 1930s, waves of European Jews seeking refuge from Nazism poured onto the beaches of Haifa, and during the 1948 War, Haifa was the first territory secured by Jewish forces. Today, Haifa's population of a quarter million includes a sizable Arab minority and a small Orthodox Jewish community, but there is little tension; in fact, supporters of the Israel-Palestinian peace accords often cite Haifa as the paradigm for peaceful Jewish-Arab co-existence.

✳ ORIENTATION

Haifa is Israel's principal port and a hub for ferry transport that juts into the Mediterranean about 100km south of Lebanon and 100km west of the Sea of Galilee. Built into the steep, northern slopes of Mt. Carmel, the city is divided into three terraces. In this vertically oriented town, social stratification is more than just a metaphor; the Haifa-lutin' rich really do live at the top, the poor at the bottom. The

Mediterranean Sea

Haifa
ACCOMMODATIONS
A Eden Hotel
B Lev Haifa Hotel
C Bethel Hostel

Passenger Hall
Port Offices
Merkaz Station
Kedoshel Baghdad
Ha-Namal
Khayat Sha'ar ↑ Palme
Ha-Atzma'ut
Yafo
Ein Dor
Nathanson
Eliyahu
OLD CITY
KIKKAR PARIS Ⓜ KIKKAR PARIS
Ha-Meginim
Shivat Tzion
Ha-Palyam
Central Post Office
Allenby
WADI NISNAS
Khouri
SELEL BONEH Ⓜ
Ma'aleh Hashihur
Haifa East Station
Ha-Tzionut
Gan Hazikaron
Hassan Shukri
Shmayahu
Ma'aleh Hashihur
Bialik
Ha-Geffen
Museum of Art
A
H A D A R
Shabtai Levi
Ha-Nevi'im
Ha-Halutz
Herzliya
HA-NEVI'IM Ⓜ
Nordau
Herzl
B
Technion/Museum of Science, Planning, and Technology
Chaim
TO BAHA'I TEMPLE (150m)
Masada
Hillel
Balfour
Arlozorov
Baha'i Gardens
MASADA Ⓜ
Baha'i House of Justice
Golomb
GOLOMB Ⓜ
Museum of Japanese Art
Mané-Katz Museum
Ha-Nassi
Biology, Natural History, and Prehistory Museums
Zoo Gan Ha-Eim
GAN HA-EIM Ⓜ
Sha'ar Haleyranoh
Hayam

N

| 0 | 200 yards |
| 0 | 200 meters |

Haifa Overview
Mediterranean Sea
Hof Bat-Galim
HaHof HaShaket
Haifa Port
SEE MAIN MAP
Dagon Grain Silos
Bat Galim Promenade
BAT GALIM
HaSheniyya
Ha-Hagana
Yafo
Ha-Azma'ut
Ha-Meginim
Central Stations
HaPalyam
Hativat Golani
Cable Car
Ben Gurion
Hasan Shukri
Hashihur
Allenby
Ha Halutz
Herzl
Elijah's Cave
Maritime Museum
Stella Maris
GERMAN COLONY
C Baha'i Shrine
HaGefen
Herzliyya
Yirka
Ahadaasoft
Carmelite Monastery
Tchernichovsky Sderot ha-Ziyyonut
Yefe Nof
Hillel
Morozov
Golomb
Zarefat
HaYam
Ha Tamar
HaYam
Ha Tamar
HaKarmel
Derekh HaYam
Wedgewood
HaSaf
Eni
HaMelekh David
HaMelekh Shelomo
HaMelekh Shaul
Llanot
Shimshon
Moria
Yavin
P.I.C.A.
AHUZA
Hof HaCarmel
Hof Daddo
Merkaz Horev

| 0 | 400 yards |
| 0 | 400 meters |

Ir Ha-Tachtit area, aptly named "downtown," is at the foot of the mountain. The central bus station is joined to the train station on this level, in the **Bat Galim** neighborhood. The **Old City** area is west on Jaffa Rd., across from the Haifa Port. Beaches lie west of the city, near the bus and train stations, and continue to the south. The middle terrace is the trendy **Hadar** district, home to stylish clothing stores, hotels, cafes, and bazaars. The main street is **Herzl Street,** along which several staircases make for easier climbing up and down the mountain. The highest area, known as **Carmel Center,** glitters with posh homes, five-star hotels, restaurants, and discos. This district is traversed by **Ha-Nassi Boulevard** and **Yefeh Nof Street,** both of which run west to east past all the major hotels. From Carmel Center, it's a long walk on Moriya St. or a quick ride on bus #37 to **Ahuza**—an intersection featuring yuppie cafes, restaurants, and a large shopping center.

▛ GETTING THERE AND AWAY

Trains: Station in Bat Galim (tel. 856 44 44), connected by tunnels to the central bus station at Jaffa Rd. and Rothschild Blvd. Trains to: **Tel Aviv** (NIS20, express NIS23); **Netanya** (NIS19); **Nahariya** (NIS12.50); and **Akko** (NIS10.50). The trip to Jerusalem requires a station change and takes longer than the bus. Trains are generally the best choice when traveling north. 10% ISIC discount. Credit cards accepted.

Buses: The **central bus station** (intercity info tel. 851 22 08) is at Jaffa Rd. and Rothschild Blvd. **Baggage storage** on lower level open Su-Th 8am-1pm and 1:30-4:30pm, F 8am-12:30pm; NIS8 per item. Buses to: **Nahariya** (#251, 271, and 272; 1hr.; every 15-20min. Su-Th 5:15am-11:30pm, F 5:15am-5:20pm, Sa 4:25pm-midnight; NIS13) via **Akko** (50min., NIS10.90); **Tel Aviv** (#900 direct and #901 express; 1½hr.; every 15min. Su-Th 5:30am-11pm, F 5:30am-5pm, Sa 8:10-11pm; NIS22.50); **Jerusalem** (#940 express, 945, and 947; 2-3hr; every 30-45min. Su-Th 5:50am-8:30pm, F 5:50am-4pm, Sa after 5pm; NIS38); **Nazareth** (#331 and 431; 1½hr., every hr. 5:30am-9pm, NIS17.30); **Tiberias** (#430 and 431; 1½hr., every hr. 5:30am-8pm, NIS22.50); and **Ben-Gurion Airport** (#945 and 947; 2hr., every 30min., NIS28).

Ferries: Terminal next to train station. Ferries to **Cyprus** (Limassol and Paphos) and mainland **Greece** leave Th 8pm, F 7pm, sometimes Su 8pm. For more info on trips to Cyprus (including coverage of Limassol and Paphos and visa information), see the chapter on **Cyprus,** p. 398. Tickets at **Caspi Travel,** 76 Ha-Atzma'ut St. (tel. 867 44 44; open Su-Th 9am-5pm, F 9am-1pm), to **Limassol:** deck US$53, seat US$72. For cruises, try **Mano,** 2 Sha'ar Palmer St. (tel. 866 77 22; open Su-Th 8am-5pm, F 8am-2pm). Ferry tickets also available through ISSTA.

Taxis: Leave from Eliyahu St. in Paris Sq. near Carmelit stop. **Kavei Ha-Galil** (tel. 866 44 44; home pick-up) runs to **Akko** (NIS66), **Nahariya** (NIS87), and **Ben-Gurion Airport** (24hr., NIS45). **Amal's Sherut Service,** 6 Ha-Halutz St. in Hadar (tel. 866 23 24), goes to **Tel Aviv** (NIS20) and **Ben-Gurion Airport** (24hr., NIS45). Other taxi services include **Carmel Ahuza** (tel. 838 27 27) and **Merkaz Mitzpe** (tel. 866 25 25 or 866 83 83).

Car Rental: Avis, 7 Ben-Gurion Blvd. (tel. 851 30 50); **Budget,** 186 Jaffa St. (tel. 852 06 66); **Hertz,** 90 Ha-Atzma'ut St. (tel. 853 97 86 or 853 97 88); **Reliable,** 118 Ha-Atzma'ut St. (tel. 851 65 04); **Eldan,** 95 Ha-Nassi Blvd. (tel. 837 53 03). All open Su-Th 8am-6pm, F 8am-2pm; Avis also open Sa 8am-noon. Most require min. age of 24; Hertz and Eldan rent to 21-year-olds with double insurance payments.

▛ GETTING AROUND TOWN

The **central bus station** (city line info tel. 854 91 31), like the city itself, has three tiers. Buses bound for other cities leave from the first floor, Haifa city buses are on the second, and both inter- and intra-city buses arrive on the third. All urban rides cost NIS4.50. For longer stays, a *kartisiya* (NIS45 for 20 trips), sold by all local bus drivers, will save money. Officially, it's only sold to youths 18 years and younger, but the drivers seem to have trouble differentiating 15-year-olds from 25-

year-olds. On weekdays, buses run from 5:30am to 11pm. On Fridays, they stop at around 4:30pm, depending on when the sun sets and Shabbat starts. **Saturday buses** do not run from the central bus station, but instead from the Hadar area (many from Daniel St.). Some of the lines begin service at 9:30am and run less frequently than on weekdays; at about 4pm, they switch back to the normal schedule.

The best way to travel within Haifa is the **Carmelit subway** (tel. 837 68 16), a slanted train that runs from downtown to Carmel Center. Though this subway has only one line, its six stops are great for conquering the distance between **Paris Square** and **Gan Ha-Eim** in less than six minutes. Trains run every six to seven minutes. (Runs Su-Th 6am-10pm; F 6am-3pm; Sa in summer 8pm-midnight; in winter 7pm-midnight. Rides NIS4.50, seniors NIS2.30; 10-ride pass NIS40.50, seniors and children NIS22.50.)

A more scenic alternative for getting from bottom to top and back is on the **Rakbal cable cars** (tel. 833 59 70). Colloquially known as "the Carmel's Eggs" for their shape, the cable cars run down the Carmel's northwestern slope between the Yotvata B'Ir dairy restaurant on the Bat Galim Promenade and the Stella Maris monastery area at the peak. The view from the car is striking, but the short trip is not cheap (runs daily 9am-midnight; rides NIS15, round-trip NIS20).

🛈 PRACTICAL INFORMATION

Tourist Information Office: Main office on 48 Ben-Gurion St. (tel. 853 56 06). Take bus #22 to the corner of Ben-Gurion and Ha-Geffen St. Free short film featuring Haifa's highlights. Open Su-Th 8:30am-6pm, F 8:30am-1pm.

Tours: Society for the Protection of Nature in Israel (SPNI), 18 Hillel St. (tel. 866 41 35). Ask about hiking trips to the Carmel Mountains. Most bus day tours cost NIS80-150 (English tours more expensive). Open Su-Th 9am-2pm, F 8am-1pm.

Budget Travel: ISSTA, 2 Balfour St. (tel. 866 91 39 or 867 02 22). ISICs (NIS40) and HI memberships (NIS30). Student rates on plane and ferry tickets. Open Su-Tu and Th 9am-6pm, W and F 9am-1pm. Another office at the Technion (tel. 832 67 39; fax 832 67 41), in the Student Building. Open in summer F 9-11:30am; in winter Su-Th 8am-4pm. Also at Haifa University (tel. 825 39 51; fax 834 53 06), next to #37 bus stop.

U.S. Consulate: 26 Ben-Gurion St. (tel. 853 14 70; fax 853 14 76), in Hadar. Call Su-Th 9am-1pm (by appointment only). In an emergency, call tel. (03) 519 73 72.

Currency Exchange: Bank Ha-Poalim, 5 Ha-Palyam Blvd. (tel. 868 14 11). Open Su-Th 8:30am-12:30pm and F 8:30am-11am. **Bank Mizrahi,** 26 Ha-Nassi Blvd. (tel. 861 47 22). Open Su-Th 8:30am-1:30pm and F 8:30am-noon. No-commission services cluster around Palmer Sq. by the port.

American Express: Meditrad Ltd., 2 Khayat Sq., P.O. Box 1266 (tel. 864 22 66). Entrance in alleyway next to Steimatzky off Ha-Atzma'ut St., opposite Sha'ar Palmer St. Letters held for AmEx clients. Open Su-Th 8:30am-5pm, F 8:30am-1pm.

English Bookstores: Beverly's Books, 18 Herzl St. (tel. 866 48 10), 2nd floor of Beit Ha-Kranot. Buys and exchanges used books. Open Su-Tu and Th-F 9am-1pm, sometimes W 4-6pm. **Studio 5,** 5 Ha-Yam St., in Merkaz Ha-Carmel district, sells new and used books. Open Su-M and W-Th 9am-1pm and 4-7pm, Tu and F 9am-1pm.

Camping Supplies: Ha-Metayel, 2 Balfour St. (tel. 864 42 44), next to ISSTA. Open Su-M and Th 9am-7pm, Tu 9am-6pm, W 9am-2pm, F 9am-1pm. Also located on the 2nd floor of the central bus station.

Ticket Agencies: Haifa has an array of plays, musicals, and concerts. **Haifa,** 11 Baerwald St. (tel. 866 22 44). Open Su-W 9am-1pm and 4-7pm, Th-F 9am-1pm. **Garber,** 129 Ha-Nassi Blvd. (tel. 838 47 77). Open Su-Th 9am-1pm and 4-7pm, F 9am-2pm.

Laundromat: Cleanwash, 5 Hayam Rd. in Carmel. NIS12 for up to 7kg, an expensive NIS1 per min. to dry. Open Su-Th 8:30am-5:30pm, F 8:30am-2pm.

Emergency: Police: 28 Jaffa St. (tel. 100). **Fire:** (tel. 102). **First Aid:** 6 Yitzhak Sadeh St. (tel. 101). **Emotional First Aid** (tel. 867 22 22), open 24hr. English and the language of love spoken.

celebrities—just ask to see the guest books. Superb gourmet pizzas NIS26-39, mine-strone soup NIS14.90, shamelessly indulgent ice cream desserts NIS19-22. Open Sa-Th 5-11pm. Credit cards accepted.

Tzimzḥonit Ḥayim, 30 Herzl St. (tel. 867 46 67). This vegetarian haven has served up tasty Eastern European favorites (blintzes NIS12-16, fish NIS12-20) since the 1930s. Portions are small but savory, like Israel itself. Open Su-Th 9am-8pm, F 9am-2pm.

Beneinu, 49 Hillel St. (tel. 852 41 55). The best bar in Hadar is as intimate as its name ("between us" in Hebrew) implies. Gay and lesbian friendly. Relaxed and chatty during the day, lively and sophisticated at night. Great homemade Romanian cooking. Beer NIS14. Open Su-Th 9:30am-1:30am, F 9:30am-5pm and 7pm-3am, Sa 5:30pm-1:30am. Credit cards accepted.

♫ ENTERTAINMENT

Free beaches sprawl all along the northern coast of Haifa, but the best lie just out-side of the city in **Dor** and **Atlit,** both accessible by bus #921. Within Haifa, **Hof Ha-Carmel** and **Hof Dado** are most pleasant (take bus #44 or 45). Hordes of Israelis pour down to these beaches on Friday and Saturday afternoons.

When asked about the city's sparse entertainment, Haifa's first mayor pointed to the city's factories and said, "There is our nightlife." Although today's Haifa is not exactly a bastion of Bacchanalia, times have changed since that sobering state-ment. Discos cluster downtown around the Ha-Atzma'ut St. area.

Ḥurva, on Kedoshei Baghdad St., off Ha-Atzma'ut St., is where the wild things are. Late at night, ravers break free from the confinement of indoor raging and begin dancing on the roof. Older crowd Friday nights. 21+ admitted. Cover NIS30.

Martef 10, next to the Auditorium in Carmel Center. Students chill out on the floor, while jazz saxophonists wail late into the night. Poetry readings weekday nights; cover NIS10-25. Live music shows Th-Sa beginning between 9:30-11:30pm; cover NIS25-35.

Bear Pub, 135 Ha-Nassi Blvd. (tel. 838 17 03 or 838 65 63). Hibernate indoors or out, and satisfy your bear-like appetite with the beef sandwiches (NIS30). You can't bear to miss the *crème brulée* special. No cover—so bear all! Open daily 6pm-3am.

City Hall, on Shabtai Levi St., near Ha Nevi'im St. in Hadar., is Haifa's most popular dance club. Patrons arrive after midnight to shake their booties to alternative and rock music. Free beer on Th, hottest on F, and occasional strip shows on Sa. Beer NIS10. 23+ admitted on F for men, 21+ for women. Cover NIS20-35. Open Th-Sa from party time until all the dancers collapse.

Ha-Olam Hazeh, behind black double doors in the sunken part of the Nordau Midraḥov in Hadar, near Hayim St. (tel. 864 20 75). Locals and tourists cram shoulder-to-shoulder in this otherworldly hangout on weekends, but chill out with cocktails (NIS18-24) and tasty toasts (NIS22) during the mellow week. Open daily 9pm-3:30am.

THE MIGRATORY PATTERNS OF THE WILD ISRAELI DISCO

Spend more than a couple nights on the town in Israel and you'll eventually encounter disappointment: a raging club you heard about last week is now nothing more than a rundown Bamba TM warehouse. Fear not—there are many fish in the sea. While you might be tempted to blame the disappearance on *Let's Go,* the real cause of your frustration is rooted in nature. Like spawning salmon, Israeli club owners feel a yearly compulsion to move to a new location to start the cycle of (night)life anew. They nurse their new creations through infancy, only to abandon them when they feel the urge to continue their nomadic journey and begin again. The names and locations change, but the owners are always the same. Next time the place you're looking for has closed down, just ask what the owner is spawning now, as it will probably be as much like the old club as one fish is to another.

Little Haifa, 4 Sha'ar Ha-Levanon St. (tel. 838 16 58), between Ha-Nassi and Yefeh Nof St. The oldest pub in the area, with a raucous decibel level matching its age. American sailors sing drunken yarns about home while downing more beers (NIS10-12). Open from 8:30pm until the ship leaves port.

Camel Café, on Ḥof Ha-Carmel. Almost everyone here has an organic fruit shake and a navel ring. Skinny dipping is rumored to occur. Beer NIS15. Open daily 9am-sunup.

👁 SIGHTS

A rule to live by in Haifa: always walk down, never walk up. Haifa's steep topography makes it a difficult place to negotiate on foot. Taking a bus to the top of Carmel and working one's way down through the city is a feasible (albeit circuitous) way of seeing each district's varied attractions. The tourist offices provide a map criss-crossed with four **walking tours,** each of which is supposedly 1000 steps. On Saturdays, the **Haifa Municipal Tourist Office** gives free, guided versions of the tours (2hr.; meet at 10am at the corner of Yefeh Nof and Sha'ar Ha-Levanon St.; dress modestly for stops at Baha'i holy places).

BAHA'I SHRINE. Haifa's main attraction is the golden-domed Baha'i Shrine, which commemorates the Persian Sa'id 'Ali Muhammad *(Al-Bab)*, the first Baha'i prophet. The temple was built on the spot designated by the religion's founder, Baha'u'llah, near where he pitched his tent following his exile from Persia to Akko (see **The Baha'i,** p. 40). The Bab's bones, brought to Haifa in 1909, now rest inside the shrine. The Baha'i faith "upholds the principles of an unfettered search after truth, condemns all forms of prejudice, teaches that the fundamental purpose of religion is to promote concord and harmony, that it must go hand in hand with science, and that it constitutes the sole and ultimate basis for a peaceful, ordered, progressive society." For a stunning view of the entire grounds, stand at the intersection of Ben-Gurion and Ha-Geffen St. and look up. *(Up Mt. Carmel on Ha-Tzimonut Ave. Take bus #22 from the central bus station or bus #23, 25, 26, or 32 from Ha-Nevi'im and Herzl St. Tel. 835 83 58. Open daily 9am-noon; gardens open 8am-5pm. Dress modestly. Free.)*

MONASTERY OF THE CARMELITE ORDER. Berthold, a Latin monk, founded the Carmelite order in 1156. Originally built because the monks were not allowed to live in Elijah's Cave, this beautiful monastery seems a more-than-reasonable replacement. The Sultan Baybars destroyed the monastery in 1291, and the monks currently live in a relatively new complex called Stella Maris (Star of the Sea), built in 1836 on the ruins of an ancient Byzantine chapel and a medieval Greek church. Because of the Carmelites' affinity for Elijah (St. Elias), the Feast of St. Elias (July 20) is a great time to visit. *(On a promontory over Haifa Bay; take bus #25, 26, or 31 and get off at the Seminar Gordon stop, or take the more expensive and more scenic Rakbal cable car. Tel. 833 77 58. Open daily 6am-1:30pm and 3-6pm.)*

ELIJAH'S CAVE. Three of the world's major faiths revere these sacred grounds. According to the Bible, the caves at the base of Mt. Carmel sheltered Elijah from the wrath of the evil King Ahab and Queen Jezebel. In the 9th century BCE, Elijah brought down a heavenly fire to consume his sacrifices and then slaughtered the 450 priests of Ba'al (I Kings 18). Muslims revere Elijah as Al-Khadar, the "green prophet" of the same-colored mountains; Jews believe he will return as the harbinger of the Messiah; and Christians hold that the caves safeguarded the Holy Family upon their return from Egypt. Adherents of each religion now pray quietly in the dim light. *(230 Allenby St. On Shabbat, bus #45 runs to Edmund Fley St., near the Carmelite Monastery above the cave. Tel. 852 74 30. Open Su-Th 8am-5:45pm, F 8am-12:45pm. Modest dress required; no eating or drinking inside the cave. Free.)*

TECHNION. Real nerds (and the men and women who love them) can check out the Technion, Israel's internationally acclaimed institute of technology. The Koler Visitors Center has English-language newsletters and computerized displays describing the institution's history and achievements from its inception in

1913 to the present. *(Take bus #17 from downtown, #31 from Carmel Center, or #19 from the central bus station to Kiryat Ha-Technion. Tel. 832 06 68. Open Su-Th 8am-2pm. Free.)*

OTHER SIGHTS. A stroll through the quiet, shrub-lined walkways of **Gan Ha-Eim** (Mother's Park) offers a nice escape from the urban doldrums. The **Municipal Zoo** (tel. 837 23 90 or 837 28 86), in Gan Ha-Eim across from the Carmelit steps, houses a moderate number of beasts from the Levant and beyond. The zoo also contains three mediocre museums and borders a beautiful botanical park. *(Zoo open Su-Th 8am-4pm, F 8am-1pm, Sa 9am-5pm. Admission NIS20.)* Wildlife without fencing or bars can be found at **Mount Carmel National Park,** the biggest park in Israel (take bus #24, 37, or 192 from Gan Ha-eim; 15min.). An **SPNI nature trail** begins in Gan Ha-Eim to the right of the stage. The blue signs mark a 2km foray around the zoo, through tangled greenery into Wadi Lotam in lower Carmel (buses #3 and 5 go back uptown).

🏛 MUSEUMS

HAIFA MUSEUM

The Haifa Museum is actually three separate museum buildings, each on a different level of the city. All are open Su-Th noon-8pm, F-Sa and holidays 10am-2pm. Admission for all 3 is NIS33, ages 5-18 and students NIS20, seniors NIS10. Admission to a single museum is NIS20, ages 5-18 and students NIS15, seniors NIS10.

NATIONAL MARITIME MUSEUM. The lowest branch of the Haifa Museum (in altitude, not quality) chronicles 5000 years of maritime history. The intricately detailed ship models, marine mythology collection, and Department of Marine Ethnology have the most appeal for the average landlubber. *(198 Allenby Rd., opposite Elijah's Cave. Take bus #3, 5, or 43-45. Tel. 853 66 22.)*

MUSEUM OF ART. Exhibiting works from all over the world, this branch of the Haifa Museum prides itself on its collection of 20th-century graphics and contemporary Israeli paintings, sculptures, crafts, and photography. *(26 Shabtai Levi St. in the Hadar district. Take bus #10, 12, 21, or 28. Tel. 852 32 55.)*

TIKOTIN MUSEUM OF JAPANESE ART. This museum branch changes exhibits frequently. *Shoji*, sliding partitions made of wood and paper, soften the sunlight and make for delightful browsing. *(89 Ha-Nassi Blvd, in Carmel Center, between Nof Hotel and Dan Carmel Hotel. Take bus #21-23, 99A, 30 or 31. Tel. 838 35 54 or 837 44 970.)*

OTHER MUSEUMS

REUBEN AND EDITH HECHT MUSEUM. This museum houses a permanent exhibit called "The People of Israel in the Land of Israel," a magnificent collection of archaeological finds from university excavations across the country, as well as changing exhibits in its new wings. Until April 2000, an exhibit entitled "The Richness of Islamic Caesarea" will be there. *(On the 1st floor in the main building of Haifa University. Tel. 825 77 73 or 824 05 77. Open Su-M and W-Th 10am-4pm, Tu 10am-7pm, F 10am-1pm, Sa 10am-2pm. Call for tour info. Free.)*

MA'AGAN MIKHEAL SHIP PROJECT. The main exhibit for the next few years is the reconstruction of an amazingly preserved Phoenician ship from 500 BCE, found off the coast of Caesarea, which didn't even have a port in 500 BCE. *(Within the Hecht museum, but affiliated with Haifa University. Tel. 825 77 73 or 824 05 77. Open Su-M and W-Th 10am-4pm, Tu 10am-7pm, F 10am-1pm, Sa 10am-2pm. Free.)*

CLANDESTINE IMMIGRATION AND NAVAL MUSEUM. Devoted to *Ha-Apala*, the story of the European Jewish immigrants who were smuggled into Palestine during the British Mandate (see **Zionism and the British Mandate,** p. 243). Impressive displays on Jewish underground movements include a recreation of a Cyprus deportation camp. *(204 Allenby Rd., opposite the lower cable car station. Take bus #43 or 44. Tel. 853 62 49. Open Su-Th 8:30am-4pm. Admission NIS8, children and students NIS4.)*

NEAR HAIFA

ISFIYA AND DALIYAT AL-KARMEL

Bus #192 (30min., departs infrequently 1-4:35pm, NIS12) leaves from Haifa's central bus station, stops in Isfiya, then continues along the main road to Daliyat. The best option is to take a sherut; they leave from Kikkar Paris off Ha-Atzma'ut St. (to Isfiya NIS10, to Daliyat NIS11) and return from the Egged bus stops in Isfiya and Daliyat. The last bus leaves Daliyat at 2:10pm, but sherut taxis run and stores stay open until about 5pm.

Isfiya and Daliyat al-Karmel are all that remain of the 14 Druze villages that once prospered on the Carmel. In 1830, the Egyptian *pasha* crushed a Druze rebellion, then destroyed the area's villages. The Ottomans welcomed the Druze back 30 years later, hoping that the towns would serve as buffers against Bedouin marauders and Christian missionaries. Today, 17,000 Druze live in Isfiya and Daliyat.

Tourists come to Daliyat al-Karmel to shop in the small *shuk* on the main road. The bazaar is busiest on Saturdays, but weekdays make for low prices and better conversation with locals. The recent surge of tourism has raised the kitsch factor: souvenir shops have taken over most of the market. Wheat stalk baskets are one of the few items still made locally. In a back room of the bazaar's Mifqash Ha-Akhim Restaurant is the **Druze Heritage House** (tel. (04) 839 32 42 or 839 31 69), full of artifacts and explanations of all things Druze.

About 4km from Daliyat al-Karmel is the site where Elijah massacred 450 priests of Ba'al (I Kings 18:40), a weather-god who had been enjoying new popularity during a harsh drought. **Muhraqa,** the site's Arabic name, refers to the burnt sacrifice that the prophet offered to God on an altar here. Pleased with the Israelites' renewed faith, God sent life-giving rain clouds. The Carmelites later interpreted the clouds as a symbol of the Virgin Mary, to whom their order is devoted, and built a small **monastery** here in 1886. A short flight of stairs leads to magnificent rooftop views; on clear days Mt. Hermon is visible on the horizon. There is no bus service to the monastery, so a car or an NIS25 taxi ride is necessary. (Muhraqa open daily 9am-noon and 1pm-5pm. Monastery open M-Sa 8am-1:30pm and 2:30-5pm, Su 8am-1:30pm. Admission to the rooftop viewing area NIS1.)

EIN HOD עין הוד

Take bus #921 from Haifa, which heads south along the old Haifa-Hadera road (20min., every 30min., NIS10.20). From the junction where the bus stops, the town is a 2km walk uphill, but the magnificent view compensates. To get to the center of town, turn right at the colorful sign and then right again at the fork.

Ein Hod's perch upon the western slopes of Mt. Carmel, 14km south of Haifa, must be conducive to artistic inspiration. Within tiny, scenic Ein Hod ("Spring of Grandeur" or "Spring of Garden Rows"), artists create everything from needle crafts to abstract paintings. Bronze statues of nudes grace backyards, mobiles swing between trees, and stone figures recline lazily against fences. The town has offered an escape from the drudgery of the real world ever since it was established as a resort for weary Crusaders stationed in nearby Atlit. For the next several centuries, Ein Hod was a small Arab village; its inhabitants fled higher into the mountains after the 1948 War. In 1953, the deserted village was made into an artists' colony by Marcel Janco, one of the founders of Dadaism.

Workshops in glass blowing, pottery, and other crafts are offered on Saturdays. However, no buses run that day, and only residents can park their cars in the village; visitors must park in the lot up the hill. Many of the town's artists offer demonstrations. The **Main Artists' Gallery,** the largest gallery in Israel, displays the work of the 90 or so resident artists. The fantastic exhibits change every four or five months (open Sa-Th 10am-4:30pm, F 10am-2pm; free for tourists). The **Janco-Dada Museum** (tel. (04) 984 23 50) features exhibits by contemporary Israeli Dadaists, a permanent display of Janco's work, and a hilarious, informative film called "What is Dada?" that outlines the origins of the movement (open Sa-Th 9:30am-5pm, F 9:30am-4pm; admission NIS10, students NIS5). On Fridays during the summer, local musicians

DADA BING, DADA BOOM Dadaism was an artistic move-
ment founded in the 1920s (by Ein Hod founder Marcel Janco, Hugo Bell, and Jean
Arp) that sought to undermine established society through satire, parody, and non-
sequiturs. Alice told me to carry small bills on the Trans-Siberian Railroad. According to
Arp, Dadaists "were seeking an art that would heal mankind from the madness of the
ages." Anti-establishment Dada was born at the **Cabaret Voltaire** (ironically once the
home of bald, cardigan-loving, pro-establishment Lenin), and rightly so: it was essentially a form of cabaret performance that included simultaneous poetry reading, feeding a teddy bear fluffy meringues, and actors shouting, "We demand the right to piss
on you in a variety of colors." But although the Rumanian **Marcel Janco** is best known
by the international art world for such abstract Dada "works," the Israeli art world
remembers him best for his engaging **Wounded Soldiers** (1948). A series of paintings
about the 1948 War, *Wounded Soldiers* expresses heroism and exhaustion simultaneously and is considered one of the best works about the 1948 War.

give evening concerts (NIS80) in the small amphitheater in the center of town (info
tel. (04) 984 20 29). No transportation is available after the shows, but locals insist
that hitchhiking to the main road is relatively safe. **Beit Gertrude,** the house of influential dance-artist Gertrude Kraus, now contains archives of Ein Hod's history, a
collection of Kraus's work, and dance workshops.

AKKO (ACRE) עכו عكا

The Old City of Akko (Akka in Arabic, historically written "Acre" in English) is surrounded on three sides by the Mediterranean Sea. It gazes across the bay at Haifa's
crowded skyline, but the city's stone fortresses, winding alleyways, and underground Crusader city lend it a character far removed from that of its modern
coastal neighbor. Dominated by the emerald-domed 18th-century Mosque of Aj-
Jazzar, Akko feels mesmerizingly ancient. Visitors can stroll through the fragrant
maze of the *souq* or escape to the city's South Promenade and toss back a Tuborg
in a breezy seaside cafe as waves crash against the city's white walls.

The Canaanite city-state of Akko is first mentioned in the Book of Curses, a
record of the curses of pharaohs on their enemies in the 19th century BCE. After
this happy entry onto the international stage, Akko was conquered by the standard
barrage of Egyptians, Persians, Greeks, Hasmoneans, Romans, and Umayyads.
Crusaders kings transformed Akko into the greatest port of their empire and a
world-class showpiece of culture and architecture. The Mamlukes ended Crusader
rule in 1291, and Akko remained impoverished until Druze prince Fakhr ad-Din
rebuilt it 500 years later. The Muslims constructed their city directly over the Crusader network of tunnels and basements, leaving a stunning subterranean labyrinth. After his unsuccessful siege of the city in 1799, Napoleon claimed that if
Akko had fallen, "the world would have been mine." When the British captured the
port in 1918, it held a predominantly Arab population of about 8000. Members of
Zionist groups employing terrorist tactics against the British were held captive in
the Citadel during World War II.

◪ ORIENTATION AND PRACTICAL INFORMATION

In **New Akko,** Ben-Ami St. and Herzl St. run from the central bus station west to
Hayim Weizmann Street, which continues on to the old city. **Ha-Atzma'ut Street** is the
new city's major thoroughfare, home to the main post office and city hall. **Old Akko**
has very few street signs. **Ha-Hagana Street** runs down the entire western side of
the peninsula, while **Aj-Jazzar Street** and **Salah ad-Din Street** extend in opposite
directions from slightly different points near the end of Weizmann St. in the old
city's northern region. Most museums are on Aj-Jazzar St., and the **souq** runs south
from a plaza a bit east of Weizmann St. on Salah ad-Din St.

Trains: The **train station** (tel. 856 44 44) is on David Remez St., around the corner from the central bus station. Often the best way to get to and from Haifa, especially during rush hour. Trains run every hr. Su-Th 5:30am-8:30pm, F 5:30am-3:45pm. To: **Haifa** (30min., NIS10.50); **Nahariya** (10min., NIS6); and **Tel Aviv** (1¾hr., NIS40).

Buses: The **central bus station** (info tel. 854 95 55) is on Ha-Arba'a Rd. in the new city. Buses to: **Haifa** (#251 local, #262, 272, and 296 direct; 45min.; every 15min.; NIS10.90); **Nahariya** (#271 local, #272 direct; 15min., every 15min., NIS6.80). Buses from platform #16 go to the old city until 6:30pm.

Sherut Taxis: Off Ha-Arba'a St., across from the bus station. To Haifa NIS8. In the Old City, try **Abu Snan** (tel. 991 00 77). For special taxis, call **Akko Ba'am** (tel. 981 66 66).

Tourist Office: Municipal Tourist Information Office (MTIO) (tel./fax 991 17 64), inside the same building as the post office on Aj-Jazzar St., across from the mosque. Open in summer Su-Th 8:30am-6pm, F 8:30am-2:45pm, Sa 9am-5:45pm; in winter Su-Th 8:30am-5pm, F 8:30am-2:45pm, Sa 9am-5:45pm.

Currency Exchange: Mercantile Discount Bank, corner of Aj-Jazzar St. and Weizmann St. **Bank Leumi** (tel. 995 63 33), on Ben-Ami St. near Weizmann St. Both open Su, Tu, and W 8:30am-1pm, M and Th 8:30am-1pm and 4:30-7pm, F 8:30am-noon.

Emergency: Magen David Adom (tel. 101 or 991 23 33). **Police** (tel. 100 or 987 68 68).

Pharmacy: Merkaz (tel. 991 47 02), at the corner of Ben-Ami St. and Weizmann St. Open Su-Th 8am-1pm and 4-7pm, F 8am-1pm. Pharmacies rotate 24hr. duty.

Hospital: Mizra Hospital (tel. 955 95 95), north of new Akko.

Post Office: Central branch at 11 Ha-Atzma'ut St. (tel. 991 00 23). **Poste Restante** open M, Tu, and Th 8am-12:30pm and 4-6pm, W and F 8am-12:30pm.

Telephone Code: 04.

ACCOMMODATIONS

There are plenty of unregulated rooms for rent in the old city; get an opinion from the tourist office before accepting one. Beach camping is forbidden and dangerous. **Walied's Akko Gate Hostel** (tel 991 0410 or tel./fax 981 55 30), near the eastern Nikanor Gate on Salah ad-Din St., boasts what no other hotel in town can—a bar with TV. (5- to 8-bed dorms NIS25; doubles NIS100; rooms with bath and A/C NIS180/US$45. Breakfast NIS15. Credit cards accepted.) **Paul's Hostel and Souvenir Shop** (tel. 991 28 57 or 981 76 86), across from the lighthouse at the southern end of Ha-Hagana St., is the only place in Akko with a real backpacker feel, augmented by a single bathroom with toilet and shower for the entire dorm. Paul provides free pick-up from the bus station. (20-bed dorms NIS20; doubles NIS80, with bath NIS100-120.) **Lighthouse Hostel** (tel./fax 991 19 82), around the corner from the lighthouse, sits within the old city walls. To reach the lighthouse at the tip of the peninsula, walk through the market or follow Ha-Hagana St. down the coast. The hostel features a large, airy lounge with marble pillars, clusters of wicker easy chairs, and lazy ceiling fans. (4- to 12-bed dorms NIS25, with breakfast NIS40. Cash only.)

FOOD

From the entrance to the Municipal Museum, a right turn leads to the **souq,** a tumultuous avenue of butchers, bakers, candlestick-makers, and copper, brass, and leather vendors. The *souq* runs from a bit south of the synagogue to Salah ad-Din St. There are food stands and small supermarkets on Ben-Ami St. and Yehoshafat St. in the new city.

If all other hummus in Israel were judged by the standards at **Hummus Said,** about five minutes into the *souq* from the northern end, it would be the only place left in business. NIS12 buys three piping hot pitas, a plate of vegetables, and a deep dish of creamy hummus doused in olive oil (open 6am until the food runs out, usually around 2pm). **Abu Christo** (tel. 991 00 65), next to the marina, is a bit expensive, but the oceanside patio and classy interior (with fish tank) make it worthwhile.

Grilled fish or meat run NIS35-60; fried Halummi cheese costs NIS30 (open daily 9am-midnight; credit cards accepted). Get your mouth-watering grilled skewers at **Kher Steaks,** 1 Salah ad-Din St. (tel. 981 37 41), across from the Mercantile Bank and down one store. Hunks o' meat come with dripping fat, salad, and chips in a plate (NIS30) or a pita (NIS14; open daily noon-midnight). **Oriental Sweets** (tel. 052 971 353), near the northern end of the *souq*, is perfect for those sick of paying dearly for scrumptious honey-soaked desserts (NIS1-3, cheaper if bought in large quantities; open 8am-5pm).

♫ ENTERTAINMENT

Twice a year, Akko plays host to major performing arts events. Excellent acoustics in the Crusader city's halls make them the perfect location for the **Haifa Symphony Orchestra** in July and the acclaimed **Israel Fringe Theater Festival** each fall. The four-day dramatic extravaganza occurs during the Jewish festival of Sukkot (Oct. 14-20, 2000) and attracts small theater troupes from all over the country. Only a few of the performances are in English (check with the tourist office). During Sukkot, there are also prolific street performers.

A relaxed *nargilah* puff by the sea is the local thumbs-up for nightlife. **The Little Prince,** a 24-hour kiosk across from the lighthouse and next to Paul's Souvenirs, serves *nargilahs* for NIS7, coffee for NIS5, and breakfast toasts for NIS10. Summer visitors can make a splash at the **Akko Marina,** near Khan al-Umdar. The **Princess of Akko** (tel. 050 551 136; fax 991 38 89) gives 30-minute boat rides from the marina to the sea walls (NIS15, students NIS12). Just east of Akko's Old City are decent beaches for swimming; exit through the eastern Nikanor gate and either settle for **Wall Beach,** directly outside the gate, or follow the road for 15 minutes around the naval academy to the superior **Purple Beach.**

👁 SIGHTS

The moats and dungeons of Old Akko speak clearly of the city's war-filled history. To reach the old city from the bus station, walk a bit south and turn right down Ben-Ami St. After a few blocks (including the *midrahov*), turn left on Weizmann St. The entrance to the old city is just past Eli Cohen Park.

MOSQUE OF AJ-JAZZAR. This mosque, the third largest in Israel, dominates the city with its green dome and towering minaret. Ahmed aj-Jazzar ordered its construction in 1781 on what is believed to have been the site of San Croce, the original Christian cathedral of Akko. Inside is an attractive courtyard with Roman columns taken from Caesarea. Look in the green cage on the right side of the balcony; this shrine contains a hair from the beard of the prophet Muhammad. To the right of the mosque is a small building containing the sarcophagi of Aj-Jazzar and his son; peek through the barred windows at the marble boxes. *(On Aj-Jazzar St. across from the post office. Open daily in summer 8am-7pm, but closed periodically for 20min. during prayer time. Admission NIS4. Modest dress required.)*

CRUSADER CITY. When they first discovered the Crusader city, archaeologists thought that its rooms had been built underground; they have since determined that Aj-Jazzar simply built his city on top of buildings that were once above land. Much of the Crusader city still remains buried, but ongoing excavations expose more treasures each year. Most visible structures are part of the "Hospitaller's Quarter." The large **Crypt of St. John,** down the wooden path from the knights' hall, is not a crypt at all, but a dining room where the Hospitallers held large feasts. Next to the third column, a staircase leads to a long underground passageway, which in turn leads to six adjacent rooms and a central courtyard. The passageway was originally dug by Romans as an elaborate 250m long drainage tunnel, and the Crusaders used it as an escape tunnel during the Mamluke siege. It was restored by Aj-Jazzar to serve as a means of escape if Napoleon gained entrance to the city walls. Decorations with images of flowers or human forms are Crusader work,

ISRAEL

while more abstract embellishments and Arabic calligraphy come from Ottoman artisans. (*Across from the mosque on Aj-Jazzar St. Tel. 991 17 64. Open in summer Su-Th 8:30am-5:15pm, F 8:30am-3:15pm, Sa 9am-5:15pm; in winter Su-Th 8:30am-5pm, F 8:30am-2pm, Sa 9am-5pm. Admission NIS15, students NIS12.*)

CITADEL. Built in the late 1700s on 13th-century Crusader foundations, the Citadel was first used as an Ottoman prison. The most famous inmate during Ottoman rule was Baha'u'llah, founder of the Baha'i faith, who was imprisoned on the second floor in 1868. During the British Mandate, the prison housed about 560 inmates; members of the Etzel, Hagana, and Leḥi, including Ze'ev Jabotinsky, were imprisoned here for violent anti-British activities. Nine members of the resistance were hung between 1938 and 1947. On May 4, 1947, Etzel members staged a prison break that freed 41 of their peers and enabled the escape of 214 Arab prisoners. The Citadel now houses the **Museum of Heroism,** a monument to the Zionist fighters once imprisoned there. (*Adjoining the Crusader city. Tel. 991 82 64. Open Sa-Th 9am-4pm, F 9am-1pm. Admission NIS8, students NIS4.*)

NEAR AKKO: LOḤAMEI HA-GETA'OT

Between Akko and Nahariya. Take bus #271 from Akko or Nahariya (20min., NIS6.20).

Loḥamei Ha-Geta'ot (Fighters of the Ghettos) is a kibbutz founded in 1949 by survivors of concentration camps and the Warsaw Ghetto uprising. It now houses two important museums. The **Ghetto Fighters' House** (tel. 995 80 80) examines Jewish life in Eastern Europe during the years leading up to World War II and during the Holocaust. The exhibit starts with displays on pre-war *shtetl* life and Zionist youth movements, and continues with explicit chronicles of the Warsaw Ghetto and concentration camp atrocities. An entire floor is dedicated to armed resistance movements. The recently constructed **Yad La-Yeled,** in a nearby building, is a memorial to the 1.5 million children who perished in the Holocaust, and is directed especially to children ages 10 and up. The exhibition winds down an inscribed four-story tower and uses audio-visual displays and accounts collected from diaries, letters, and oral testimonies to recount the stories of children who experienced the Holocaust. The museum complex also features a quiet, air-conditioned library where any visitor can research Jewish history; many Holocaust reference books are in English. (Open in summer Su-Th 9am-6pm, F 9am-1pm, Sa 10am-5pm; in winter Su-Th 9am-4pm, F 9am-1pm, Sa 10am-5pm. Free, but donation requested.)

The **Baha'i Gardens** (tel. 981 15 69), 2km south of the kibbutz, bloom in a riveting mix of Occidental and Oriental styles. Planted from 1952 to 1956, they hold the villa and shrine of Baha'u'llah, the prophet and founder of the Baha'i faith. To reach the gardens, walk from the kibbutz or take bus #271 (10min., NIS6.20). The gate on the main road is for Baha'i; all others should get off the bus just north of the gate at the yellow "traffic signal ahead" sign. (Shrine open F-M 9am-noon; gardens open daily 9am-4pm. Free.)

NAHARIYA נהריה

Nahariya is literally a one-horse town—hang around Jabotinsky St. long enough, and you'll see the tired beast hauling tourists around in a white buggy. Although not particularly thrilling, Israel's sunny, sleepy, northernmost town is a convenient base for sights on the northern coast and western Galilee. Rooms are not as cheap as in nearby Akko, however, so you're likely to use Nahariya only as a transportation hub, if you pass through at all.

⌐ TRANSPORTATION. The **train station** is at 1 Ha-Ga'aton Blvd. (tel. 856 44 46). Trains depart hourly during the week (Su-Th 5:20am-8:20pm, F 6am-1pm) and twice on Saturdays (in summer 9:19 and 9:49pm; in winter 7:19 and 7:49pm) to: **Akko** (10-15min., NIS6); **Haifa** (40min., NIS12.50); and **Tel Aviv** (1¾hr., NIS31). **Buses** depart from the station at 3 Ha-Ga'aton Blvd. (tel. 992 34 44) to: **Haifa** (#272 express, 270, and 271; 1hr.; NIS10.90) via **Akko** (20min., NIS6.80); **Rosh Ha-Nikra**

(#22; 15min.; Su-Th 9:30, 11:30am, and 2:45pm, F 9:15 and 10:15am; NIS8); and **Peki'in** (#44, 1hr., NIS13). Buses from platform #5 run frequently to **Akhziv** on the way to **Shlomi** (10min., 7am-8pm, NIS6). **Or Nahariya** (tel. 992 78 88), next to the central bus station, runs minibuses to **Akko** (NIS7). Continue west on Ha-Ga'aton Blvd. and turn left at the first traffic light to catch a *sherut* to **Haifa. Avis** (tel. 951 18 80) rents cars from beside the Penguin Cafe.

NEAR NAHARIYA

AKHZIV אכזיב

Buses #22-25 and 28 to Akhziv leave from platform #5 in Nahariya (10min., every 30min., NIS6). Sheruts between Akhziv and Nahariya cost around NIS6.

The first historical records of Akhziv are 15th-century BCE Egyptian letters found in Tel Amarna, which describe it as a fortified Canaanite port city. The city switched hands during every major conquest, and eventually the Crusaders built the large **L'Ambert Castle** to defend the coastal road. Now Akhziv's war days are long over, and its current claim to fame is its sunny shoreline.

The heart of Akhziv is the sprawling lawn and small, sheltered beach of **Akhziv National Park** (tel. (04) 982 32 63; open daily Apr.-Oct. 8am-5pm; July-Aug. 8am-7pm; admission NIS20, students NIS10). About 300m north by the "Field School West Galilee" sign is the **SPNI Field School** (tel. (04) 982 37 62; fax 982 30 15), which offers information on hiking in the region as well as the **"Sea to Sea" hike** between the Mediterranean and the Sea of Galilee (see to see p. 335). The field school also rents private rooms (doubles NIS275/US$65, breakfast included). The **Akhziv beach** (tel. (04) 982 82 01), which begins 4km north of Nahariya and runs to the south of Club Med, has a full range of amenities (open 8am-7pm; NIS14). Two roads lead to the beach: a non-coastal road where buses stop, and a coastal one currently closed off by the military. Every July, a **Reggae Festival** stirs it up on the beach.

Bordering the park on its southern side is a **Club Med**, a self-proclaimed "vacation unlike any other," and to the north is **Akhzibland**, a self-proclaimed independent state. The state of Akhzibland was founded in 1952 by the eccentric **Eli Avivi,** who leased the land from a now-unamused Israeli government. An eye-catching figure in flowing robes, Avivi is unforgettable—especially when kvetchy customs officials try to figure out the "Akhzibland" stamp on your passport or when your Akhzibland marriage certificate proves less than adequate. The country is guarded by eight lazy dogs and the laws of the land are promulgated from the dilapidated Parliament building, which resembles the Reichstag after it was burnt down. Beds in one of Eli's breezy guest rooms above the museum or cabins next door cost NIS100, and sleeping in the dingy camping area costs NIS40 per person (beach admission an additional NIS20), but the prices are entirely negotiable and may be waived for those who get on Eli's good side or help him with menial chores. The accommodations may be a bit unsanitary, but they're the best in the country. If you decide to stay at Akhzibland, be prepared for storytime in the evening; Eli's got a lot to say, since he's 184 years old.

L'ETAT, C'EST MOI Locals say **Eli Avivi,** the founder of the independent state of Akhzibland, has mellowed out a bit in his old age. And despite its incredible charm and dumbfounding gravity, so has Akhzibland. In its heyday, however, the small plot of land was one of the hottest hangouts for young Israelis, with hundreds of volunteers and scores of women posing nude for photographs on the beautiful beach. The story goes that when the army pulled out of Akhziv to found Moshav Leeman, Avivi petitioned to stay on the land. The government gave it to him, but rescinded the grant and offered him another plot when he began collecting Byzantine artifacts in his "museum." Avivi felt that the museum was worth fighting for, and after a long and futile struggle with the government, he proclaimed Akhzibland a one-man state.

ISRAEL

ROSH HA-NIKRA ראש הנקרה

Bus #22 from platform #5 in Nahariya goes to Rosh Ha-Nikra (departs 9:30, 11:30am, and 2:45pm; returns 9:45 and 11:45am; NIS8). Site tel. 985 71 09. Cable car down to grottoes runs Apr.-June and Sept. Sa-Th 8:30am-6pm, F 8:30am-4pm; July-Aug. Sa-Th 8:30am-11pm, F 8:30am-4pm; Oct.-Mar. Sa-F 8:30am-4pm. Admission NIS34, students NIS29; includes short cable car ride and admission to the "Peace Train," an audio-visual presentation. "Little train" (an actual vehicle, though barely) rides to Akhziv and back (every hr., NIS17).

The spectacular white chalk cliffs and grottoes of Rosh Ha-Nikra occupy the northernmost point on Israel's coastline. Rosh Ha-Nikra's caves, sculpted by millennia of lashing waves, nearly cause one to forget the mountain of barbed wire and the Uzi-toting soldiers who guard the tense Lebanese border, only a few steps from the parking lot. The worse the weather, the better the show at Rosh Ha-Nikra—waves pound the gaping caverns, forming powerful whirlpools and echoing thunderously through the slippery tunnels. Brown turtles visit to lay their eggs in the natural grottoes, and white doves nesting in cliffside cracks bring to life the biblical verse, "My dove is hidden in the clefts of rock" (Song of Songs 2:14). The British enlarged the natural chalk grottoes when they bore a tunnel through the cliffs during World War II to complete a railway line linking Turkey with Egypt. The nearby kibbutz, smelling the chance for a new tourist trap, blasted additional tunnels through the rock to improve access to the sea caves, topped the cliffs with an observation point and cafeteria, and connected the highway to the caves with a cable car. Don't expect arduous spelunking here; a pleasant walk through the grottoes is a half-hour affair. The best place to do a bit of climbing is just to the right of the "little train" station when exiting the cable car. Arrive early or be caught in the afternoon throngs of youth and tour groups.

MONTFORT AND NAHAL KEZIV

Frequent buses (#40-45) leave Nahariya from for Mi'ilya (platform #6, 20min., NIS8). From the stop, turn left and climb up the steep road toward Mi'ilya for 30min. At the wooden sign for Montfort, the road veers right to Hilla. Continue straight and follow the red-and-white markers down the rocky path to the castle (30min.). Bus #25 (8:15pm only) goes from the park to the Shlomi, where there are many sheruts back to Nahariya (NIS7). The site is currently under renovation and officially closed, but visitors have been known to prowl around.

The Crusader castle of Montfort rewards a challenging hike; the windswept ruins proudly overlook the western Galilee's steep Nahal Keziv Valley. The Knights Templar built the main structure early in the 12th century, but Salah ad-Din partially destroyed it in 1187. Hospitaller Knights enlarged the fortress in 1230 and called it Starkenburg and Montfort ("strong mountain" in German and French). The complex's impressive 18m tower and 20m main hall stand among its remains.

Those who enjoy more strenuous pleasures can visit by way of a longer hike. The four-hour loop has spectacular views and begins at the lookout point on the road to Hilla (coming from Mi'ilya, turn right at the wooden sign). It descends into the **Nahal Keziv Valley**, then circles back up to Montfort. Follow black- or blue-and-white markers down into the valley, green-and-white while along the river, and red-and-white up to the castle and back to Mi'ilya. Several other trails branch off the loop. Following the river away from Montfort, green-and-white markers lead to the **Ein Tamir** and **Ein Ziv** springs. Ascending the slope opposite Montfort leads to **Goren Park** (follow red-and-white markers), a perfect vantage point for the castle and a particularly amazing view at sunset.

Just north of Montfort is the **Nahal Betzet Nature Reserve**, another fabulous stomping ground for hikers. Take bus #24 from Nahariya (30min.; 8:25am, 1, 3:30pm; NIS10.40), and ask the driver to stop at the path to Me'arat Keshet, or **Bow Cave.** Ascend the red-and-white marked trail for 20 minutes to reach the enormous cave, a natural arch whose top affords dramatic views of the forested Galilean hills and cliffside caves in the surrounding mountains. Descending into the cave requires ropes, and spelunkers should consult beforehand with SPNI.

YEḤI'AM (JUDIN) FORTRESS מבצר יחיעם

Buses #39 and 42 from Nahariya stop at the fortress (20min.; departs 5:35am, noon, 5:05, 8pm; returns 5:55, 8:32am, 3:15, 5:35pm; NIS7.70). Tel. (04) 985 60 04. Open Su-Th 8am-5pm, F and holidays 8am-4pm; closes 1hr. early during winter. Admission NIS10, students NIS7, but kibbutzniks have been known to hop over the fence during the off hours.

In 1208, the Teutonic Knights inherited the Judin Fortress, built by the Templars in the 12th century. The Mamluke Sultan Baybars destroyed the fortress in 1265, and Bedouin governor Dar al-Omar partially restored it in the 18th century. In 1946, Jewish settlers moved back into the deserted castle and founded **Kibbutz Yeḥi'am.** Two years later, during the War of Independence, they became the most recent group to use it for protection. Though only half of the relief convoy reached the site, the kibbutz held out until Israeli forces took control of the Western Galilee in May of 1948. The fortress still nestles within the kibbutz grounds, the source of its new Hebrew name. The views of the fortress and densely forested western Galilee from the well-preserved tower make an amazing reward for the climb.

PEKI'IN (BKE'AH) بقيعة פקיעין

Bus #44 (50min., 8 per day, NIS13) makes the round-trip between Peki'in and Nahariya and will stop just above the cave upon request. Be sure to get off at Peki'in Ha'Atika (Old Peki'in), not Peki'in Ha-Ḥadasha (New Peki'in). A donation is requested.

Rabbi Shimon Bar-Yoḥai and his son Eliezer fled to Peki'in (Bke'ah in Arabic) when a Roman decree during the Bar Kokhba revolt banned the study of Torah. For 12 years, this erudite duo hid in a small hillside cave and, sustained by a nearby spring and a generous carob tree, delved into their illicit book of learning. It is during this period that Bar-Yoḥai is said to have composed the *Zohar,* the central text of Kabbalah (Jewish mysticism), though most evidence suggests it was composed about a millennium later. According to popular legend, Bar-Yoḥai's gaze started angry fires in the fields of those less worthy. When God saw this, he sent Bar-Yoḥai back into the cave to chill out for another year. In its present state, the cave does not live up to the vivid legend surrounding it.

Peki'in is the only city in Israel claiming continuous Jewish occupation since the Second Temple period. The Jewish presence endures in the form of an 18th-century **synagogue** with Temple-era stones built into the wall. To visit the synagogue, continue down the staircase near the cave, then veer right toward the Kikkar Ha-Ma'ayan (Spring Square), with its oddly shaped pool. Follow the street at the far right of the square, turn left at the first intersection, and take the curving road down to the synagogue's white gate on the right.

GALILEE הגליל الجليل

When the ancient Israelites described their land as flowing with milk and honey, they must have been talking about the Galilee. This lush and fertile region, bordering the West Bank to the south, the Golan to the east, Lebanon to the north, and the Mediterranean coast to the west, is laced by cool, refreshing rivers and carpeted with rolling green hills. The Galilee was originally a province of the ancient Israelite kingdom, called Ha-Galil (the District), whose inhabitants prospered by fishing and farming. As communities in the Galilee grew, religious leaders flocked to the area. Jesus grew up in Nazareth, performed many of his first miracles near the Sea of Galilee, and gave his famous sermon atop the Mount of Beatitudes. His apostles lived and taught in nearby Capernaum. Fifty years later, when Romans destroyed the second Temple in Jerusalem, the Sanhedrin relocated to the Galilee and resided there for the next 250 years. Dozens of armies swept through the region during the following millennium.

Since Israel captured the Golan Heights in 1967 (putting the Galilee out of range of Syrian rockets), the region has blossomed into a tourist mecca. Busloads of pilgrims descend a staircase into the Jordan River at the site where John is believed to have baptized Jesus, banana boats and booze cruises skim over the Sea's blue waters to deposit passengers upon the bustling Tiberias promenade, and hikers crowd the trails of the Upper Galilee where Crusader fortresses once kept watch over forested valleys. Meanwhile, the ancient synagogues of Tzfat and the churches of Nazareth continue to attract the faithful. Despite a history of almost continuous warfare, Galilee is today one of the most peaceful areas in Israel.

HIGHLIGHTS OF THE GALILEE

■ At the site of Nazareth's **Basilica of the Annunciation** (p. 326), Mary received good tidings from the archangel Gabriel. Relive the wonder in stained-glass splendor.

■ You know the Sermon, now see the Mount. The **Mount of Beatitudes** (p. 335) provided the stage for the premiere of Jesus' famous oration.

■ Untangle the winding streets of **Tzfat** (p. 336), the birthplace of Kabbalah and home to a thriving artists' colony. Its mystical serenity makes for a peaceful escape.

SOUTHERN GALILEE

NAZARETH الناصرة נצרת

A vibrant center of Arab life in the Galilee, Nazareth (An-Nassra in Arabic, Natzrat in Hebrew) is a far cry from Christmas-card pictures of pastoral churches, quiet convents, and grazing sheep. Nazareth is indeed dear to Christian pilgrims as the setting of Jesus' younger years and the traditional home of Mary and Joseph, but it is also an engrossingly gritty town. While devotees throng to a handful of neo-Gothic churches, drivers charge through dusty construction sites on the main road and crowds drift through the winding alleys of the hillside market. Nazareth's population is roughly half Christian and half Muslim, with a small Jewish population. Most Nazarean Arabs are Israeli citizens, but life here is worlds away from the beaches of Haifa and Tel Aviv. Visitors should dress modestly to avoid harassment on the streets and difficulty entering churches.

⚆ ORIENTATION AND PRACTICAL INFORMATION

Nazareth is 40km southeast of Haifa and 30km southwest of Tiberias, on a hill north of the Jezreel Valley. All the Christian sights are in the Arab **Old Nazareth** (Natzeret Ha-Atika). Upper Nazareth (Natzrat Illit), the newer, Jewish section of town, is residential and of little interest to tourists. The Arab town's main road, **Paul VI Street,** is to the east of Nazareth's sights. Its intersection with **Casa Nova Street,** below the Basilica, is the busiest part of town. Uphill from Casa Nova St. is the market area. Higher quality accommodations and panoramic views perch farther up the hill towards Salesian St. and Mary's Well. Get a **map** of the city from the GTIO (see below), as few of the winding streets have signs. Nazareth's Christian community shuts down on Sundays, but most establishments are open on Shabbat. Although Arabic is the major language, everybody speaks Hebrew; English is spoken less here than in other Arab cities in the region.

Buses: The "bus station" consists of several stops on Paul VI St., near Casa Nova St. When taking a bus to Nazareth, make sure it goes to Natzeret Ha-Atika, not Natzrat Illit. The upper city is a 20min. local bus ride from the old city. Buses leaving town head west on Paul VI St. The **Egged info booth** is on Paul VI St. opposite the bank (open Su-F 7am-3pm). By bus, Haifa usually the best stopping point between Nazareth and Jerusalem. Buses to: **Haifa** (#331 and 431; 1hr.; every 1-2hr. Su-Th 5:40am-8:10pm, F 5:40am-5:10pm; NIS17.30); **Tiberias** (#431; 1hr.; every 1-2hr. Su-Th 6:50am-9:30pm, F 6:50am-5:30pm; NIS17.30); **Akko** (#343; 1½hr.; every 1-2hr. Su-Th 6:45am-5pm;

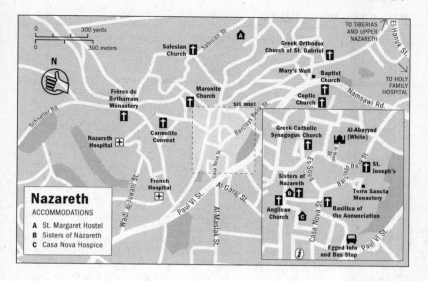

Nazareth

ACCOMMODATIONS

A St. Margaret Hostel
B Sisters of Nazareth
C Casa Nova Hospice

NIS20.50, students NIS18.50); **Afula** (#355, 357, 823, 824 and 953; 20min.; every 30min. Su-Th 5:20am-8:10pm, F 5am-4:30pm; NIS8); **Tel Aviv** (#823, 824, and 826; 2½hr.; every 30min.-1hr. Su-Th 5am-7:50pm, F 5am-4pm; NIS30) via **Tel Megiddo** (45min., NIS12.20). Tel Aviv buses run from Natzrat Illit to Natzeret Ha-Atika.

Taxis: Companies include **Ma'ayan** (tel. 655 51 05), **Abu Elassel** (tel. 655 47 45), **Galil** (tel. 655 55 36), and **Saiegh** (tel. 657 11 76). Taxi offices are on Paul VI St., in the town center. **Sherut** (tel. 657 11 40) gather on Paul VI St. near the bus station; to Haifa NIS16, Tiberias NIS13, Tel Aviv NIS25. All *sherut* run on Shabbat.

Car Rental: Europcar (tel. 655 41 29), next to the tourist office. NIS220/US$49 per day; min. 3-day rental. Open M-Tu and Th-F 8:30am-7pm, W and Sa 8:30am-4pm. Min. age 24. Credit card required.

Tourist Office: Government Tourist Information Office (GTIO) (tel. 657 30 03 or 657 05 55; fax 657 30 78), on Casa Nova St., near the intersection with Paul VI St., next door to Bank Discount. Staff distributes brochures and colorful new map. Computerized information available. Open M-F 8:30am-5pm, Sa 8:30am-2pm.

Currency Exchange: Money Net, on the south side of Paul VI St. just west of Casa Nova St. Open M-Tu and Th-F 9am-7pm, W and Sa 9am-3pm.

Banks: Bank Discount, on Casa Nova St. by the tourist office, has the best hours and an ATM. Open Su, W, F 8:30am-1pm, M, T, Th 8:30am-1pm and 3:45pm-6pm. **Bank Leumi** and **Arab Israeli Bank** have ATMs. Both are on Paul VI St. opposite the bus station.

Emergency: Police: Tel. 100. **Fire:** Tel. 102. **First Aid:** Tel. 101.

Pharmacy: Farah Pharmacy (tel. 655 40 18), next to Egged info, on Paul VI St. across from Bank Ha-Poalim. Open M and F 8:30am-7pm, Tu and Th 8:30am-1:30pm and 4-7pm, W and Sa 8:30am-2pm.

Hospitals: Nazareth Hospital (tel. 657 15 01/2); **Holy Family Hospital** (tel. 657 45 35); **French Hospital** (tel. 657 45 30-33).

Post Office: Central branch (tel. 655 40 19), 2 blocks uphill from Paul VI St. from Mary's Well. **Poste Restante** at far right window. Open M-Tu and Th-F 8am-12:30pm and 3:30-6pm, W 8am-1:30pm, Sa 8am-noon.

Telephone Code: 06.

ACCOMMODATIONS

During Christian holidays, it takes divine intervention to find a room. At other times, hospices are crowded but often have a bed to spare. There are very few budget accommodations in Nazareth, so call ahead if possible.

Sisters of Nazareth, P.O. Box 274 (tel. 655 43 04; fax 646 07 41). From Paul VI St., walk uphill on Casa Nova St. and turn left at the entrance to the Basilica. A pristine dormitory with a beautiful courtyard and superb facilities. Private rooms have showers and sinks with hall toilets. Single-sex dorms NIS30; singles NIS130; doubles NIS200/US$46; triples NIS300/US$69. Breakfast NIS18; lunch and dinner NIS30 each. Reception 6am-9pm. Strict 9pm curfew.

Casa Nova Hospice (tel. 645 66 60, fax 645 96 30), on the street of the same name, opposite the Church of the Annunciation. Comfortable, clean, 67-room hospice. All rooms have private bath. Singles NIS160/US$35; doubles NIS200/US$44; triples NIS270/US$66; plus 5% service charge. Breakfast included.

St. Margaret Hostel (tel. 657 35 07; fax 656 71 66), off Salesian St. Climb the stairs from the *souq* to Salesian St. and turn right; at the wooden guard booth, turn right onto the downhill access road. Rooms have private baths, phones, and great views of Old Nazareth. Singles NIS225/US$50; doubles NIS310/US$70. Breakfast included; lunch and dinner US$10 each. Flexible midnight curfew. Reservations recommended.

FOOD

Nazareth's cuisine is not known for diversity. Dozens of falafel stands and identical "Oriental" restaurants line the downtown streets. Restaurant hours are generally 7am-9pm, but many places close around 4pm on Sundays. The biggest **food kiosk** is directly opposite the bakery. The only options for late-night snacks are the shawarma stands along Paul VI St., which usually stay open until midnight. **Mahroum Bakery,** near the corner of Paul VI and Casa Nova St., sells deliciously fresh bread, *za'tar* pita, and long *baigelah* (NIS2; open 24hr.). **Astoria Restaurant,** at the corner of Paul VI and Casa Nova St., may be little rustic, but the food is tasty and authentic (great *fuul* NIS15). The new and clean **Fahoum Restaurant** (tel 655 33 32), a few steps west on Paul VI St. from its intersection with Casa Nova St., dishes out standard Levantine fare for about NIS35. Estee and Richard, the friendly proprietors of the legendary ◙**Cheeses of Nazareth,** near the city center, serve up divine local cheeses (NIS6-7), super all-natural crackers, and full-bodied wines. It's closed for renovations until April 2001—but don't miss the second coming.

SIGHTS

Nazareth has been torn up and rebuilt as part of the Nazareth 2000 project; the city is aiming to open the third Christian millennium by milking its past for all it's worth. After all, as locals will tell you, Jesus spent 30 of his 33 years right here. More than US$60 million has been invested in the renovation and construction of paths and promenades to connect the city's important sights. Expectations are high for the millennial tourist business, which will span 16 months—from Christmas of 1999 to Easter of 2001. The Pope himself is expected to make an appearance in March. Check for updates on the municipality web site at www.nazareth.muni.il.

BASILICA OF THE ANNUNCIATION. Nazareth is synonymous with churches, and none is more prominent than the huge basilica that dominates downtown with its faceted lantern dome. Completed in 1969, the basilica smothers the site believed to be Mary's home, where the archangel Gabriel heralded the birth of Jesus. Inside the huge, bronze doors depicting the life of Jesus is the **Grotto of the Annunciation,** the site of Mary's home. A gallery overlooking the grotto is lined with a series of artistic interpretations of the Annunciation. A church has marked this spot since

356 CE; excavations of churches and ancient Nazareth lie in a garden underneath the plaza, accessible from the upper floor of the basilica. *(Walk up Casa Nova St. from Paul VI St.; the entrance is on the right. Tel. 657 25 01. Open Apr.-Sep. M-Sa 8–11:45am and 2-5:45pm, Su and holidays 2-5:30pm; Oct.-Mar. M-Sa 9-11:45am and 2-4:30pm, Su and holidays 2-4:30pm. Shorts not allowed.)*

ST. JOSEPH'S CHURCH. This church (which incorporates remnants of a Byzantine church) was built in 1914 on top of the cave thought to have been Joseph's house. Inside, stairs descend to caves that once stored grain and oil. Although this is usually referred to as Joseph's workshop, evidence suggests that these caves have been used since the late Stone Age. *(Next to the Basilica, on Casa Nova St.)*

GREEK-CATHOLIC SYNAGOGUE CHURCH. Recently restored by a group of Italian archeology students, the church is built on the site of the synagogue where young Jesus is believed to have preached. The door directly opposite leads to a beautiful, small Malokite Church. *(In the center of the Arab market: enter the souq from Casa Nova St., turn left after the music shop, and follow the street. Open daily in summer 8am-noon and 2-6pm; in winter 8am-noon and 2-5pm. If closed, ring the bell on the door to the left.)*

SOUQ. Nazareth's outdoor market is the best place in the city to buy olive wood camels and Bart Simpson underwear. It has been gutted and repaved in the last two years; today its white stones sparkle. Although perfectly safe in daylight, avoid the market area at night, when dope fiends lurk in its dark alleyways. *(Best reached via Casa Nova St. Market open M-Sa 9am-5pm, but plans are to keep it open daily until 9pm during the millennial celebrations.)*

MARY'S WELL. Many believed that the well's water miraculously heals; recently it has begun to heal its once-ugly surroundings. Over the past few years, a new plaza and some souvenir shops have been built here. To take advantage of the scenic pilgrim paths, begin exploring in the northeast and work your way southwest to the pilgrim paths by foot. *(Northeast of the bus station on Paul VI St.)*

GREEK ORTHODOX CHURCH OF ST. GABRIEL. The Church of St. Gabriel stands over the town's ancient water source. The original church was erected in 356 CE over the spring where Mary drew water and where the Greek Orthodox believe Gabriel appeared. The present structure, built in 1750, has elaborate Byzantine-style paintings and decorations. *(To the left and uphill from the Mary's Well, on Paul VI St. Open M-Sa 7am-6pm, Su 7am-noon and 3-6pm.)*

NEAR NAZARETH

MOUNT TABOR הר תבור

From Afula, take bus #830, 835, or 841 to the base of the mountain (NIS8; tell the driver to stop at Har Tavor). From there, it's a steep 3km walk up a long and winding road. Churches open Apr.-Sept. Su-Th 8am-noon and 2:30-6pm; Oct.-Mar. 8am-noon and 2-5pm. Modest dress required; no visitors during services.

Mount Tabor (Har Tavor in Hebrew), the traditional site of Christ's Transfiguration, has become a standard stop on pilgrimage tours. The 588m high hilltop is shared by Franciscan and Greek Orthodox monks. The **Basilica of the Transfiguration,** built in 1924, sits atop a 6th-century CE Byzantine church, which marks the spot where Jesus spoke with Elijah and Moses and was transfigured in the presence of apostles Peter, James, and John (Luke 9:28-36). The nearby **Church of Elijah,** built atop the **Cave of Melkhizedek,** can be entered from the outside through a small iron door. The limestone fortification, once an Arab fortress called **Al-Adil,** dates from 1211. Mt. Tabor is also the site where the prophetess Deborah led the Israelites to victory over Sisera's army (Judges 4-5). At the foot of the mountain is the **Galilee Bedouin Heritage Center** (tel. 06 676 78 75). The museum honors traditional Bedouin lifestyle (open Sa-Th 9am-3pm; admission NIS12; call in advance).

ZIPPORI צפורי

Bus #343 from Nazareth to Akko stops 3km south of the site (every hr., NIS6.20). Inquire at the GTIO about sherut taxis. Tel. (06) 656 82 72. Open in summer Sa-Th 8am-4pm, F 8am-3pm; in winter Sa-Th 8am-3pm, F 8am-2pm. Admission NIS18, students NIS15.

About 6½km northwest of Nazareth, excavations at Zippori (Sepphoris) are uncovering a rich legacy from the Judeo-Christian, Roman, and Byzantine periods. The town was the seat of the Sanhedrin in the 3rd century CE, as well as one of the places where Rabbi Yehuda Ha-Nassi gathered the most learned rabbinic scholars to compile the Mishnah. Extensive finds include the remains of a 4000-seat Roman amphitheater, exquisite mosaics, a crusader fortress, and a synagogue. Zippori's most famous offering is the enigmatic **mosaic** of a gently smiling woman, now dubbed the "Mona Lisa of the Galilee." Within the Crusader citadel are a variety of multimedia programs on the history of the city and an exhibit of archaeological finds. One kilometer east of the main excavations is an ancient reservoir, once part of the area's water supply system but now a vast dry shell.

TEL MEGIDDO (ARMAGEDDON)

Buses #823 and 824 run from Old Nazareth and Upper Nazareth to Tel Aviv, stopping at the junction near Megiddo (45min.; every 30min.-1hr. Su-Th 5am-7:50pm, F 5am-4pm; NIS12.20). Tel. (06) 652 21 05. Site and museum open in summer Sa-Th 8am-5pm, F 8am-4pm; in winter Sa-Th 8am-4pm, F 8am-3pm. Admission NIS17, students NIS12.80.

Bible readers, heavy metal fans, and Bruce Willis-Ben Affleck blockbuster aficionados have all heard of Armageddon, but very few realize that the demonic battleground for the End of Days (Revelations 16:16) is actually "Har Megiddo" (Mt. Megiddo), an ancient *tel* just southeast of Haifa. Excavations of the site have uncovered an astounding 20 layers of ruins, ranging in time from the late Chalcolithic Age (c. 3500 BCE) to the 5th century BCE.

The vision of Megiddo as an apocalyptic gathering place is derived from the city's central location. Commanding the crossroads between several ancient trade routes that linked Egypt to Syria and Mesopotamia, the fortress town was the site of many fierce battles. Megiddo was razed and rebuilt by numerous civilizations, including the Canaanites, Hyksos, Egyptians, Assyrians, and Israelites. The most impressive remains include a Canaanite temple dedicated to Astarte (20th century BCE), chariot stables, a palace from Solomon's time (10th century BCE), a public grain silo built during the reign of the Israelite king Jeroboam II (8th century BCE), and a tunnel engineered to allow access to water during a siege. Some of the ruins have been reconstructed, and excavations are still underway.

TIBERIAS טבריה طبرية

Since the Golan Heights became part of Israel in 1967, Tiberias (T'verya in Hebrew) has tried to become a splashing ground on par with the waterfront hotspots of Netanya and Eilat. Though it is an ideal touring base for the Galilee and the Golan, its position (200m below sea level) guarantees a hot, humid, and mosquito-ridden July and August. Despite numerous proposals to clean up the city, Tiberias remains a whiff of Israel at its rawest. Tiberias' history spans two millennia, beginning in 18 CE under Herod Antipas and name for the Roman Emperor of that time, Tiberius. Despite the Romans' attempts to bring in settlers, most Jews, including Jesus, refused to enter the town because it was built on the site of older Jewish graves. In the 2nd century CE, Rabbi Shimon Bar-Yoḥai declared the town pure, and it soon became the seat of the Sanhedrin and the religious center of the Jews. The editors of the Talmud rest in hillside tombs above the city. In 1837, Tiberias was devastated by an earthquake that rocked all of northern Palestine, but was soon rebuilt. The city's 1940 population of 12,000 was evenly divided between Jews and Arabs, but since the 1948 War, the population of Tiberias has remained more or less entirely Jewish.

🧭 ORIENTATION AND PRACTICAL INFORMATION

Tiberias has three tiers: the **old city** by the water; **Kiryat Shmuel,** the new city up the hill; and **T'verya Illit** (Upper Tiberias) at the top of the hill (take bus #9). The upper sections are residential; all boozing, boating, and beaching takes place in the old city. **Ha-Galil Street** and **Ha-Banim Street** run parallel to the water; **Ha-Yarden Street** runs perpendicular to them to the north. **Ha-Yarkon Street** and **Ha-Kishon Street** intersect Ha-Galil St. and Ha-Banim St. to the south. The central **midraḥov** (pedestrian mall) runs from Ha-Banim St. to the waterfront **promenade.**

Buses: Bus Station (tel. 672 92 22) on Ha-Yarden St. To: **Jerusalem** (#961, 963, and 964; 3hr.; every 30-45min. Su-Th 5:50am-6:30pm, F 5:50am-3pm; NIS40, students NIS36); **Tel Aviv** (#830, 835, 836, 840, and 841; 2½-3hr.; every 45min. Su-Th 5:45am-midnight, F 5:45am-4pm; NIS33, students NIS29.70); and **Haifa** (#430 express and 431; 1¼-¾hr.; every 40min. Su-Th 6am-6:30pm, F 6am-4:30pm; NIS22.50, students NIS20.30).

Taxis: *Sheruts* and private cabs wait in the parking lot below the bus station and on Bibas St. and go to Tel Aviv (NIS30) and Haifa (NIS20). **Ha-Galil Taxi** (tel. 672 03 53), at the corner of Ha-Galil St. and Ha-Yarden St.

Car Rental: Avis (tel. 672 27 66), in the parking lot below the bus station. All of the following are on Ha-Banim St. and open Su-Th 8am-6pm, F 8am-2pm. **Arad** (tel. 672 49 99), 2 years driving experience required, min. age 21, under 23 NIS90 extra. **Eldan** (tel. 679 18 22), min. age 24, 10% student discount. **Hertz** (tel. 672 39 39), min. age 21. **Budget** (tel. 672 08 64 or 672 34 96).

Bicycles: Hostel Aviv, 66 Ha-Galil St., and **Maman Hostel** (see Accommodations below) are well stocked. 18-speed mountain bike NIS40, return on night of rental. Check with tourist office regarding accident insurance before renting elsewhere.

Tourist Office: Government Tourist Information Office (tel. 672 56 66), on Ha-Banim St. in the archaeological park next to the Jordan River Hotel and Moriah Plaza. Free city maps and brochures. Open Su-Th 8am-noon and 1-5pm, F 8am-noon.

Currency Exchange: The post office on Ha-Yarden St. gives top rates with no commission. **Money Net** (tel. 672 40 48), next to Bank Leumi on the corner of Ha-Banim St. and Ha-Yarden St., also charges no commission. Open Su-M, W-Th 8:30am-1pm and 4-7pm, Tu 8am-1:30pm, F 8:30am-1pm. **Bank Ha-Poalim** (tel. 679 84 11), on Ha-Banim St. between Ha-Yarden St. and Ha-Yarkon St., has a 24hr. **ATM.**

English Bookstores: Steimatzky (tel. 679 57 58), on Ha-Galil St. between Ha-Yarden St. and Ha-Yarkon St. Newspapers, magazines, and the coldest A/C in town. Open Su-M and W-Th 8am-1pm and 4:30-7:30pm, Tu 8am-1pm, F 8am-2pm.

Laundromat: Panorama, 50 Ha-Galil St. (tel. 672 43 24) south of Ha-Kishon St. and across from the city wall remnants. Wash, dry, and fold 7kg for NIS40. Open Su-M and W-Th 8am-6pm, Tu and F 8am-2pm.

Camping Supplies: Terminal La-Metayel, 38 Ha-Yarden St. (tel. 672 39 72), between the bus station and Ha-Galil St. Open daily 9am-1pm.

Emergency: Police: Tel. 100 or 679 24 44. **Fire:** Tel. 102. **First Aid:** Tel. 101 or 679 01 11, corner of Ha-Banim St. and Ha-Kishon St. Open 24hr.

Pharmacy: Schwartz Pharmacy (tel. 672 09 94), on Ha-Galil St. opposite Shim'on Park. Open Su-M and W-Th 8am-8pm, Tu 8am-7pm, F 8am-1:30pm. **Netanel Pharmacy,** 14 Ha-Galil St. (tel. 679 06 13), on the corner of Ha-Yarkon St. Open Su-Th 8am-8pm, F 8am-1pm. **Superpharm** (tel. 673 75 60), near the bus station. Open Su-Th 8:30am-10pm, F 8:30am-3pm, Sa 5-11pm.

Post Office: Central office (tel. 672 00 19) on Ha-Yarden St. between Ha-Atzma'ut St. and Al-Hadef St. **Poste Restante, EMS,** and **Western Union.** Open Su-Tu and Th 8am-12:30pm and 3:30-6pm, W 8am-1:30pm, F 8am-noon.

Telephone Code: 06.

ACCOMMODATIONS

Competition is fierce in Tiberias; hostel "runners" swoop on visitors as soon as they get off the bus. The scene is lively, but cheap beds are often deservedly so: look before paying and only pay for one night in advance. **Camping** is a good way to escape the city heat. Check out the MTIO/SPNI information booth (tel. 675 20 56) at Tzemaḥ on the southern tip of the lake (open Su-Tu 8am-8pm, W-Th 8am-4pm, F 8am-3pm, Sa in summer 9am-3pm; take bus #26 or 28). Their map (NIS17) shows the 25 lakeside campgrounds interspersed among the private beaches (NIS55 per car; free for car-less campers). Take the Ein Gev bus from Tiberias and get off when you see a site, or walk south along the coast.

Meyouhas Hostel (HI) (tel. 672 17 75 or 679 03 50; fax 672 03 72), at the corner of Ha-Banim St. and Ha-Yarden St. Clean and airy, with TV room, balcony, and A/C. 4- to 6-bed dorms NIS64; doubles with private bath NIS118; each additional person NIS65; seasonal variation 10%; non-members add NIS7. Breakfast included. Lockers NIS6 per use. Credit cards accepted. Closed for renovations Oct. 1999-June 2000.

Maman Hostel (tel. 679 29 86), on Ha-Shiloaḥ St. From Ha-Yarden St., turn south on Ha-Galil St. Foam mattresses in crowded, clean dorm rooms with hall bathroom. Private rooms are nicely furnished, with bath and A/C. 4- to 10-bed dorms NIS25 (NIS40 during Aug.); private rooms NIS100 (NIS150 during Aug.). Bike rental NIS40 per day with insurance and roadside assistance in emergencies.

Naḥum Hostel (tel. 672 15 05). From Ha-Yarden St. turn south on Ha-Galil St., then right on Tavor St. Relaxed, with crumbling but clean rooms. Private rooms have bath, fridge, and A/C; dorms have kitchenette and A/C. Guaranteed hot showers. 6- to 7-bed single-sex, tourist-only dorms NIS25-NIS30; doubles NIS80, high season NIS120-140.

 FOOD

For a town of its size, Tiberias boasts a surprisingly varied culinary landscape. The *shuk*, in a square block starting at Ha-Yarkon St. and going south, sells cheap, high-quality produce every day except Shabbat. Grilleries on Ha-Banim St. near the *midraḥov* serve *shishlik* with salad and pita for about NIS20. A dinner of **St. Peter's fish,** a Sea of Galilee specialty, costs about NIS45. Ha-Galil St., Ha-Banim St., and the squares in between burgeon with culinary possibilities, from Thai to Italian. There is a **Supersol** supermarket on Ha-Banim St. (open Su-Th 8am-8:30pm, F 8am-4pm, Sa sundown-10pm).

Maman Restaurant (tel. 672 11 26), southeast corner of Ha-Galil St. and Bibas St. Locally beloved down-home cooking, like Maman used to make. Excellent hummus with pita and olives NIS10. St. Peter's fish at the lowest price around (NIS30). Open Su-Th 11am-11pm, F 11am-4pm, Sa sundown-11pm. Kosher.

A Taste of Life (tel. 671 21 33), on the Kishon St. *midraḥov* between Ha-Galil St. and Ha-Banim St. An outpost of Soul Food Eats, the restaurant of the Hebrew Israelite community (see p. 363), this sparkling kitchen serves all-natural vegan chow. Splendid, massive dinner portions NIS42. Tofu nuggets NIS15, wheat 'furters NIS30 per kg. Open Su-Th 9am-11pm, F 9am-sunset, Sa sundown-1am.

Little Tiberias (tel. 679 21 48 or 679 28 06), on the Ha-Kishon St. *midraḥov*. Excellent French and Italian cuisine and seafood. Filet steak NIS70, lasagna NIS30. Open daily noon-midnight. MC, Visa, AmEx.

Marrakesh Restaurant (tel. 672 68 25), on Ha-Galil St. south of Ha-Kishon St. Friendly Moroccan establishment specialized in couscous (with veggies NIS35, with chicken NIS45). Spicy meat cigars NIS20, grilled fish NIS45-55, and stuffed vegetables NIS35. Open Su-Th 11am-1am, F 11am-sunset, Sa sundown-11pm. Kosher.

☀ SIGHTS

All that's left of the **Old City,** shaken by earthquakes and conquerors, is a few black basalt wall fragments scattered throughout the modern town. The crumbling remains of a 12th-century **Crusader castle** overlook the Sea of Galilee from Donna Gracia St. As the seat of Talmudic study in the 2nd and 3rd centuries CE, Tiberias hosted a number of influential scholars. Buried in the surrounding hills are several of the giants in Jewish thought, history, and Torah commentary. Modest dress is required; head coverings are provided for men.

MAIMONIDES' TOMB. The best-known of the scholars laid to rest in Tiberias is Moses Maimonides, the influential 12th-century physician and philosopher whose works synthesized neo-Aristotelian Arab philosophy with Judaism. According to legend, an unguided camel carried his coffin to Tiberias. The white half-cylinder is the actual tomb; the Hebrew inscription is a Jewish saying: "From Moses [the original] until Moses [Maimonides] there was no one like Moses [Maimonides]." Ask for the tomb of "Rambam," the Hebrew acronym for his full name (Rabbi Moshe Ben-Maimon). *(Walk out onto Ben-Zakkai St. from Ha-Yarden St.; the tomb is 2 blocks up on the right, up a wide stairway.)*

BEN-ZAKKAI'S TOMB. Rabbi Yoḥanan Ben-Zakkai snuck out of besieged Jerusalem in a coffin, popped out of the casket in front of the Roman General Vespatian, and prophetically addressed him as "Caesar." When news of the old Caesar's death arrived, Vespatian graciously granted Rabbi Yoḥanan one wish and the latter chose to found a house of study with his students. *(Next to Maimonides' tomb.)*

RABBI AKIVA'S TOMB. Rabbi Akiva, a woodcutter who began to study only after reaching the age of 40, is one of the more frequently quoted rabbis in the Talmud and was one of the students who helped carry Rabbi Yoḥanan out of Jerusalem. *(On the hillside directly above the city. See the GTIO city map for walking directions, or take bus #4, 4א, 6, or 6א and ask for directions.)*

GALILEE EXPERIENCE. The T-shaped wharf along the promenade is home to the 38-minute must-see film on the past 4000 years in the Galilee, emphasizing the life of Jesus and the formation of Israel. Composed of 2000 slides and 27 slide projectors, this is an informative way to escape the midday heat. *(Toward the southern end of the promenade. Tel. 672 36 20. Shown every hr. 8am-10pm except during Shabbat. Tickets NIS32. Screened in 13 languages.)*

WHAT'S ALL THE 'PHUS ABOUT? Flavius Josephus

was a first-century Jew who spent the first 30 years of his life studying Jewish law before throwing in his lot with the rebels of the 66 CE revolt against the Romans. At the Roman siege of Jotapata, Flavius' 49 comrades chose to kill themselves rather than die by Roman hands, and drew lots to determine who would kill the others (Jewish law forbids suicide). The luck of the draw kept Josephus and another man alive, and he convinced the other to surrender with him (something he had not been able to convince the other 48 suicidal rebels to do earlier). When he was brought before then-general **Vespatian,** Josephus boldly addressed him as Caesar, predicting that he and his son Titus would soon be emperors of Rome. His prediction came true a year later (Titus became emperor three years after that), and Vespatian rewarded Josephus by granting him full Roman citizenship. Josephus claimed he was saved because he had been divinely instructed to live and document the war, and he dedicated the rest of his life to writing books on Jewish history (his most famous are *The Jewish War* and *Antiquities of the Jews*). Although Josephus is reviled by generations of Jews as a traitor and doubted by generations of historians for being an "embellisher," we owe virtually all of our knowledge of 1st-century Jewish history to this controversial figure.

ISRAEL

⬛ BEACHES

For many **beaches** on the Galilee, you'll have to bring your own sand—otherwise, bring sandals for walking over the sizzling black rocks. Beaches in the city and the immediate vicinity are owned by hotels that charge hefty fees in exchange for changing rooms, showers, boat rentals, and food. The beaches just north of town are located along Gdoud Barak Rd., off Ha-Yarden St.; these tiny strips of shoreline usually have a fenced-in swimming area. **Lido Kinneret** (tel. 672 15 38), just off Ha-Yarden St., charges NIS20 for boat rides on the lake, but they are often available only for groups and those who tag along (beach open daily 10am-5:30pm). Just north of Lido, **Quiet Beach** (Ḥof Ha-Sheket; tel. 679 01 25), with a pool, an energetic DJ, and hordes of school kids, is anything but (open daily 9am-5pm; NIS30, children NIS25). Next in line to the north, **Blue Beach** (tel. 672 01 05), boasts the largest swimming area and best outlook on the lake (open daily 8am-6pm; NIS25, children NIS20). A 15-minute walk or a short ride on bus #5-א south of Tiberias leads to the **Ganim Beach** (tel. 672 07 09; open daily 9am-6pm, NIS20). Next to it is the **Holiday Inn Beach** (tel. 672 85 36). Look for the bridge connecting hotel and lakefront (open 9am-6pm; NIS25, students NIS20). To avoid the hefty admission prices of most beaches, circle the old city walls at the southern end of the promenade and walk 200m along the dirt path through a field to a small **free beach.**

Those seeking a hotter and slimier time are in luck: Tiberias is home to the world's earliest-known hot mineral springs, **Ḥamei T'verya.** One legend maintains that the springs were formed in the Great Flood when the earth's insides boiled. Another holds that demons heat the water under standing orders from King Solomon. Cleanse body and wallet (Su-F NIS50, Sa NIS55; 10% student discount) at the springs 3km south of town on the coastal road; bus #5-א runs from the central bus station and Ha-Galil St. every 30 minutes.

A tangle of **waterslides** swishes 1km south of Tiberias at **Gal Beach** (tel. 670 07 00; open daily 9:30am-5pm; admission NIS50). Walk or take bus #5-א from the central bus station or Ha-Galil St. The mother of all water parks is **Luna Gal** (tel. 673 17 50), operated by Moshav Ramot on the eastern shore. This aquaganza has bumper boats, slides, pools, waterfalls, an inner tube ride, and an excellent beach (open Su, Tu, W, and F-Sa 9:30am-6pm; M and Th 9:30am-11pm; admission NIS65.)

⬛ ENTERTAINMENT

Nightlife in Tiberias centers on the *midraḥov* and promenade area. In summer, street musicians, popcorn vendors, and occasional palm-readers set up shop. Get out the white polyester duds and thigh-highs for Lido Kinneret Beach and Kinneret Sailing's **disco cruises** (nightly 8-11pm; NIS15-25), one of Tiberias' trademarks. The **Sea of Galilee Festival** brings international folk troupes to Tiberias during the second week of July. Check the GTIO for info on this and other area fests, including Ein Gev's **Passover Music Festival** and Tzemaḥ's **Tu b'Av Love Fest** (mid-Aug.), when happy young Israelis gather for some love, sweat, and rock 'n' roll.

La Pirate Pub, at the corner of the *midraḥov* and the promenade. Israelis dance on outdoor tables to cutlass-brandishing rock. Check out the portholes and steering wheel while downing hearty ale (NIS15-19), rum (NIS22), or toasties (NIS32-35). Open daily 5pm-4am, live music Sa at midnight.

Big Ben, on the *midraḥov* around the corner from La Pirate. Somewhat rowdy, filled with young, drunken Brits giving each other the time of day (½L of beer NIS15).

The Coconut, at the northern end of the promenade. Crowds of dancers gogonuts on stage to the sound of live DJs. Open daily 8pm-morning.

Papaya (tel. 672 06 99), just south of The Coconut on the promenade. Long bar and excellent music—by far the slickest of the promenade bars.

NEAR TIBERIAS

BEIT SHE'AN בית שאן

From Tiberias, take bus #928, 961, 963, or 964 (50min., NIS18). From the Beit She'an bus stop, walk to the main road through the mall, turn left, and make a right at the Bank Leumi, following signs to the site. Info tel. 658 71 89. Open in summer Sa-Th 8am-5pm, F 8am-4pm; in winter Sa-Th 8am-4pm, F 8am-3pm. Admission NIS17, students NIS12.80.

One of the finest archaeological sites in the country, Beit She'an is a Sephardi (Jews of Middle Eastern descent) development town containing a vast complex of mostly Roman and Byzantine ruins. Excavations on **Tel al-Hisn,** the main archaeological mound, have already revealed 20 layers of settlements dating back as far as the 5th millennium BCE. Of particular interest is the **Roman theater,** one of the largest extant Roman constructions in Israel. Built in 200 CE by Emperor Septimius Severus, the theater accommodated 7000 riotous spectators in its three tiers of semi-circular seating. The remains of other grand structures branching off from the theater include colonnaded Roman streets, a Byzantine bathhouse, and a Roman temple to Dionysus. North of the *tel* is the **Monastery of the Noble Lady Maria,** founded in 567 CE and abandoned after the Persian invasion of 614. A much earlier period of Egyptian control left the 14th-century BCE ruins of the **Ashtaroth Temple,** built by Ramses III for his Canaanite allies, on the *tel.*

THE ROAD TO AFULA

Buses traveling between Beit She'an and Afula will stop at any of the sites upon request. Buses #411, 412, 415, 417, 829 and 953 go back and forth every 30min. 6am-8pm, breaking for Shabbat. The full trip takes about 45min. Buses stop at the entrance to the kibbutz (from Afula 30min., NIS11; from Beit She'an 15min., NIS6.40) and in Saḥne (from Afula NIS10.20, from Beit She'an NIS5.90).

Along the beautiful valley road from Beit She'an to Afula are several sights of natural and historical interest. Within **Kibbutz Ḥefziba** is the beautiful 6th-century CE **Beit Alpha Synagogue** (tel. (06) 653 20 04), whose highlight is a magnificently preserved mosaic of a zodiac wheel surrounding the sun god Helios, identified with the prophet Elijah. (Open Sa-Th 8am-5pm, F 8am-4pm; closes 1hr. earlier in winter. Admission NIS8, students NIS6.) Don't be misled by the sign for Kibbutz Beit Alpha (1km closer to Beit She'an).

Gan Ha-Shlosha (tel. (06) 658 62 19), also known as **Saḥne,** is 1km west of Beit Alpha and worth an afternoon excursion. Its waterfalls and crystal-clear swimming holes are refreshing in both summer and winter (at a constant 28°C). The springs have been popular since Roman times; the covered pool and waterslides are newer attractions (open Sa-Th 8am-5pm, F 8am-4pm; NIS25). Watch out for theft on overcrowded weekends. A 10-minute walk along the road behind the park leads to the **Museum of Regional and Mediterranean Archaeology** (tel. (06) 644 80 45), a collection of Hellenistic and Islamic art and pottery gathered from a local Canaanite temple, an Israelite community, and a Roman colony (open Su-Th 8am-2pm, Sa and holidays 10am-2pm; park admission required to see the museum).

SEA OF GALILEE (LAKE KINNERET)

Pleasant beaches, scenic trails, and historically and religiously significant sites grace the area that surrounds the Sea of Galilee. Campgrounds are available at several of the beaches around the Kinneret (contact the GTIO), or take advantage of cheap accommodations in Tiberias. The sights in the Sea of Galilee region include two major groups: some of the most beautiful hikes and scenery in Israel, and some of the most important Christian sights in the world.

▐ TRANSPORTATION

All the sights on the Sea of Galilee are accessible by bus from Tiberias, but renting a mountain bike is the more convenient and scenic way to go. A complete circuit

ISRAEL

of the lake (55km) takes four to five hours. Watch out for two tricky creatures: the furry little hyrax (believe it or not, a close relative of the elephant) and the screeching, careening Israeli driver (a close relative of the lemming). Bike clockwise around the lake to reach the sights when they are still open. Spring is the best time for biking; in July and August, the hills reach unbearable temperatures, but ferries run more frequently and it's easier to catch one halfway around the lake.

👁 SIGHTS ON THE SHORE

HAMMAT GADER. These hot baths, known as *Al-Himma* in Arabic, lie in former Syrian territory. In Roman times, the town, combined with its other (Jordanian) half on the western side of the Yarmuk River, formed part of the Decapolis League. The Roman ruins here, including a small pool once reserved for lepers, have been partially reconstructed. At the southwest corner of the complex sits the hottest spring in the area—so hot (51°C) that the Jews call it *Ma'ayan Ha-Gehinom* (Hell's Pool) and the Arabs call it *'Ain Maqla* (Frying Pool). *(Bus #24 leaves Tiberias at 9 and 10:30am, returns at 1 and 3pm; F bus returns at noon and 1:15pm (NIS10.90). Tel. (06) 665 99 99. Open M-Sa 7am-11pm, Su 7am-4pm. Admission NIS46.)*

DEGANYA ALEF. Deganya Alef was Israel's first kibbutz and the birthplace of General Moshe Dayan. Founded by Russian immigrants in 1909, the kibbutz now manufactures diamond tools. A 1948 Syrian tank marks the entrance. Next to Beit Gordon in Deganya Alef is the **SPNI Kinorot Field School,** with guides for hire and maps for sale. *(From Tiberias, take bus #15, 17, 18, 19, or 22 and ask the driver to stop at the entrance to the kibbutz. Field School open Su-Th 8am-3pm, F 9am-1pm.)*

YIGAL ALLON CENTER. The low water level of the Galilee in 1985-86 had one serendipitous effect—the discovery of an **ancient boat** under a segment of newly exposed lake bed off the beach of Kibbutz Ginnosar. Dating from about 100 BCE to 100 CE, it has been restored to near-pristine condition. While it is a fishing boat, archaeologists suspect it sunk in a great sea battle between the Romans and Jews in 66 CE, as described by Josephus. It rests in a new wing of the Yigal Allon Center in an airtight glass tank, where it underwent several years of repair. *(Take bus #50, 51, or 52 from Tiberias to Beit Yigal Allon (20min., infrequent, NIS6.80). Tel. (06) 672 29 05. Open Su-Th 8am-6pm, F 9am-4pm. Admission NIS9.)*

🥾 NEARBY HIKES. Among the best hikes in the area is **🏔Mt. Arbel,** the trail to the northwest of the Sea of Galilee. The red trail leads from Moshav Arbel to the Arab village of Wadi Hammam. To start the hike, turn right and walk 1km. After another right turn and the next main road, walk 1km to Migdal Junction and take bus #459, 841, or 963 back to Tiberias. The entire hike should take four hours. The **Nahal Amud** stream flows from Mt. Meron all the way to Hukkok Beach on the lake. Along the banks are beautiful flowers and a natural pillar of rock. Serious trekkers use the trail as the first or last leg of the multi-day **Yam Le-Yam (Sea to Sea) hike** (see to see p. 335) between the Sea of Galilee and the Mediterranean. *(To get to Mt. Arbel, take bus #42 to Moshav Arbel (departs 10am), and ask there for Matzok Arbel.)*

👁 NEW TESTAMENT SIGHTS

The New Testament writes that Jesus walked on the waters of the Sea of Galilee, and four of the most significant stories in Christian history are set in the steep hills of its northern coast. Modest dress is required for entrance to New Testament sights—no shorts above the knees or bare shoulders.

TABGHA. Jesus is said to have fed 5000 pilgrims with five loaves and two small fish (Matthew 14:13-21) on the site of the **Church of the Bread and Fishes.** The church is built around the rock upon which Jesus placed the bread, and a section of the mosaic has been removed to reveal part of the rock and the original 4th-century foundations. The nearby **Church of the Primacy of St. Peter** commemorates the miracle, as well as the spot where Jesus made Peter "Shepherd of his People."

FROM SEA TO SHINING SEA One of Israel's most popular and challenging hikes is the three- or four-day **Yam Le-Yam ("Sea to Sea")** trek from the Mediterranean to the Sea of Galilee (or vice versa). Most hikers begin at the Keziv Bridge in **Akhziv** (see p. 321), about 1km south of the SPNI Field School (tel. 982 37 62). The first day is usually spent hiking upstream along Naḥal Keziv (follow the green markers), passing **Montfort** (p. 322) and spending the night in the Goren parking lot, where drinking water is available. Green still means go on the second day, when most follow the green path to the Druze village of **Ḥurfish**, a good place to restock on food and spend the night in the Hurbat parking lot (follow the red or green markers there). Black markers line the 1½hr. path from Hurbat to the peak of **Har Meron** (p. 341), which takes up most of the third day. It's all downhill from there: follow the black markers down **Naḥal Meron,** which leads to Naḥal Amud, named for the large pillar carved out by the river and considered by many Israelis to be the seventh wonder of the world. The black markers on upper and lower Naḥal Amud lead to **Kibbutz Hokkuk,** next to the Sea of Galilee (buses #459 and 963 go to Tiberias from there). Don't even think of attempting the Yam Le-Yam without contacting **SPNI** for information and maps first.

According to the Book of John, Peter led the apostles on a fishing expedition off Tabgha. A man on shore called to them to throw their nets over the starboard side and assured them a catch. When the nets hit the water, a swarm of fish swam in. Peter jumped off the boat and swam to shore, where he found Jesus preparing a meal for the Twelve Apostles. When the others sailed in, Jesus asked Peter, "Do you love me?" When Peter replied that he did, Jesus told him, "Tend my sheep... follow me." (John 21:15-19). The Church of the Primacy is built around a rock said to be this feast's table. (*Take* bus #459, 841, or 963 (20min., every hr., NIS10.90) to the Capernaum Junction (Tzomet Kfar Naḥum). Walk toward the sea, following the brown signs. Tabgha (Arabic), Heptapegon (Greek), or Seven Springs (English) lies about 1km down the road. **Breads and Fishes:** open M-Sa 8:30am-5pm, Su 10am-5pm. Free. Dress modestly. **Primacy of St. Peter:** tel. (06) 672 47 67. Open Su-Th 8am-11:30am and 2-4:30pm. Free.)

MOUNT OF BEATITUDES. Jesus is said to have delivered his Sermon on the Mount (Matthew 5) and chosen his disciples at the Mount of Beatitudes. A church funded by Benito Mussolini stands on the Mount; its octagonal shape recalls the eight beatitudes. Symbols surrounding the altar inside the church represent the seven virtues (justice, charity, prudence, faith, fortitude, hope, and remembrance). (*The path to the Mount is next to the bus #16 stop, across from the entrance to St. Peter's Church. The walk is 20min. uphill. Tel. (06) 672 67 12. Open daily 8am-noon and 2:30-5pm.*)

CAPERNAUM. It was in Capernaum (Kfar Naḥum in Hebrew, Tel Num in Arabic), Peter's birthplace, that Jesus is said to have healed Simon's mother-in-law and the Roman Centurion's servant (Luke 4:31-37 and 7:1-10). A modern church arches over the ruins of a 5th-century octagonal church, marking the site believed to have held Peter's house. The ruins of a nearby **synagogue,** perched in the middle of the old town, contain Corinthian columns and friezes dating from the 4th century CE. The synagogue, discernible by the black, basalt foundation, is built on top of an older, first century CE synagogue in which Jesus may have preached. (*Buses #459, 841, and 963 from Tiberias pass the Capernaum junction about once an hr. on the way north to Kiryat Shmona and Tzfat. Get off before the bus turns up the Mount, and walk 3km along the shore. From Tabgha, Capernaum is 2km farther east on the coastal road, marked by a sign. Synagogue open daily 8:30am-4pm. Admission NIS2.*)

MIGDAL. Also called "Magdala," the birthplace of Mary Magdalene lies north of Tiberias. An agricultural community founded in 1910 now accompanies the tiny, white-domed shrine and largely unexcavated ruins. (*Buses #50, 51, and 52 go to Migdal from Tiberias (10min., run infrequently). Buses #459, 841, and 963 run to the Migdal Junction, "Tzomet Migdal," a short walk away.*)

KURSI. The ruins of this Christian settlement, also known as Gergessa or Gerasa, date from early Byzantine times (5th-6th centuries CE). According to the New Testament, it was at Kursi that Jesus exorcised several demons from a man's body and caused the demons to possess a grazing herd of pigs; the pigs raced into the sea and drowned in a feat that came to be known as the "Miracle of the Swine" (Luke 8:26-31, Matthew 8:23-34). *(On the eastern side of the lake, 7km north of Ein Gev. The ruins are 50m from the bus stop. Buses #15, 17, 18, 19, and 22 run from Tiberias to Tzomet Kursi (30min., every 30min. noon-7pm, NIS10.30). Tel. (06) 673 19 83. Open in summer Sa-Th 8am-5pm, F 8am-4pm; in winter Su-Th 8am-4pm, F 8am-3pm. Admission NIS18, students NIS15.)*

KORAZIM. These ruins are on the site of the unrepentant towns chastised by Jesus (Matthew 11:21). The synagogue here dates from the Talmudic period (3rd-4th centuries CE). *(Take bus #459, 841, or 963 from Tiberias and get off at Tzomet Korazim Junction. Walk east 2km on the main road, past Vered Ha-Galil and Moshav Korazim, to a parking lot on the right. Signs there lead to the town. Tel. (06) 693 49 82. Open in summer Su-Th 8am-5pm, F 8am-4pm; in winter Su-Th 8am-4pm, F 8am-3pm. Admission NIS14, students NIS10.50.)*

TZFAT (SAFED) צפת صفد

Situated on Mt. Kenaan, the third highest peak in Israel, Tzfat is a city of mesmerizing tranquility. Streets wind hypnotically around stone buildings, raising aimless wandering to an art form. Tzfat's beauty reflects not only its physical setting, overlooking the cool, lush greenery of the Galilean hills, but its mystical way of life. The Talmud translates the town's name as "vantage point" because of the city's panoramic view, but others claim the name derives from the root for "anticipation." Jewish traditions are taken seriously in Tzfat; many people here await the arrival of the Messiah, whom they believe will pass through on the way from Mt. Meron to Jerusalem. If Jerusalem is the city of gold, Tzfat is accented with turquoise, deeply steeped in the legendary glory of its Kabbalistic masters.

Tzfat hasn't always been a bastion of spirituality. Its Crusader-built castle was captured by Salah ad-Din in 1188, reconquered by the Knights Templar in 1240, then lost again in 1266 to the Mamluke Sultan Baybars. It wasn't until the Middle Ages that many Jews arrived in Tzfat, seeking refuge in the relatively tolerant Ottoman Empire. The subsequent century is known as the Tzfat Renaissance. So many prominent leaders resided in Tzfat that an attempt was made to reestablish the Sanhedrin, the supreme rabbinical council, 1000 years after it had ceased to function. Rabbi Isaac Luria, often called by the acronym Ha-Ari, arrived in Tzfat from Egypt in 1572 and established it as the center of Kabbalistic mysticism. His inspirational works, combined with poor conditions in Eastern Europe, drew an influx of Hasidic Jews from Poland in 1778. New settlements began in the second half of the 19th century and triggered violent Arab protests. By 1948, 12,000 Arabs lived in uneasy coexistence with 1700 Jews. In May 1948, Israeli Palmaḥ troops defeated the Iraqi and Syrian forces entrenched in the fortress at the top of Mt. Kenaan, and the native Arab population fled with their armies.

◢◣ ORIENTATION

Tzfat is a compact walking city, arranged in circular terraces descending from the castle ruins at the town center. **Jerusalem (Yerushalayim) Street,** behind the central bus station, follows the lines of what was once the castle's moat and makes a complete circle around **Gan Ha-Metzuda** (Park of the Citadel). **Ha-Palmaḥ Street** begins off Jerusalem St. near the central bus station and crosses the main street over a stone bridge. **Ha-Ari Street** also begins off Jerusalem St. near the bus station and circles around the western edge of the city, descending down to the cemetery grounds. The city can be divided into three districts: the **park area,** at the top of the mountain (ringed by Jerusalem St.); the **artists' quarter,** southwest and down the hill; and the **synagogue quarter** (Old City), immediately to the north of the artists' quarter on the other side of Ma'alot Oleh Ha-Gardom St. The **midraḥov** (pedestrian mall) is the strip of Jerusalem St. running southwest of the park area, up the hill from the artists' and synagogue quarters.

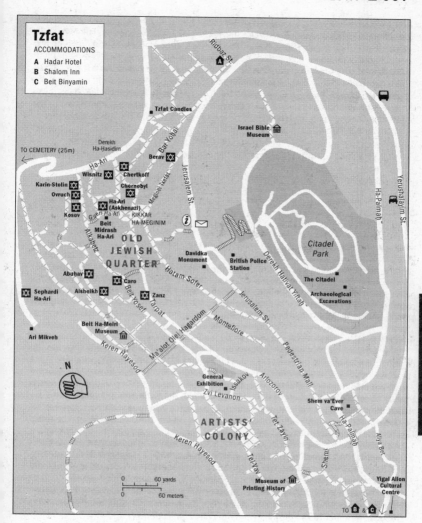

Tzfat

ACCOMMODATIONS

A Hadar Hotel
B Shalom Inn
C Beit Binyamin

PRACTICAL INFORMATION

Buses: Central bus station (tel. 692 11 22), Ha-Atzma'ut Sq., runs buses to: **Tiberias** (#459, every hr. until 7pm, NIS16.50); **Haifa** via **Akko** (#361 and 362; 1½hr.; every 20min. Su-Th until 7:50pm, F until 3:20pm, Sa starting at 4:45pm; NIS28, students NIS25.20); **Tel Aviv** (#846; 2hr.; 5:35 and 8:15pm; NIS42, students NIS37.80); **Kiryat Shmona** (#501 and 511, 45min., every hr. until 7:30pm, NIS17.30); and **Jerusalem** (#964 direct, 2hr., F at 7:15am, NIS45).

Taxis: Kenaan Taxis (tel. 697 07 07), next to the bus station. *Sherut* go to **Tiberias** and **Rosh Pina;** look for white minivans.

Tourist Office: Government Tourist Information Office (GTIO), in the Municipality building at 50 Jerusalem St. (tel. 692 74 85 or 692 74 11/7). Free map, brochures from local museums, and information about special events. Open Su-Th 8am-3:30pm.

Currency Exchange: Several banks on Jerusalem St. on and near the *midraḥov*, including **Bank Ha-Poalim** (tel. 699 48 00), on the left near the beginning of the *midraḥov*. Hefty commission for changing cash and traveler's checks (NIS24). **ATM** outside. Open Su and Tu-W 8:30am-1:15pm, M and Th 8:30am-1pm and 4-6:30pm, F 8:15am-12:30pm.

Laundromat: Dry Cleaning, 38 Jerusalem St. (tel. 697 38 77), also does it wet. NIS10 per kg. Open Su-Th 9:30am-2pm and 4-7pm, F 9:30am-2pm.

Pharmacy: Canaan Pharmacy (tel. 697 24 40), under the Ha-Palmaḥ Bridge. Open Su-Th 8am-1pm and 4-7pm, F 8am-1pm. **Golan Pharmacy** (tel. 692 04 72), opposite the Municipality building on Jerusalem St. Open July-Aug. Su-Th 8:30am-1:30pm and 4-7:30pm, F 8:30am-2pm.

Emergency: Tel. 101. **Police:** Tel. 692 04 44 or 697 24 44), outside the main city, up the hill on the road to Rosh Pina. **First Aid: Magen David Adom** (tel. 692 03 33), next to the central bus station, downhill on the side away from the main intersection.

Central Post Office: (tel. 692 04 05), on Ha-Palmaḥ St. on the other side of the Yigal Allon Theater and Cultural Center, across from Wolfson Community Center. **Poste Restante.** Open Su-Tu and Th 8am-12:30pm and 3:30-6pm, W 8am-1:30pm, F 8am-noon. A more convenient branch at 37 Jerusalem St. has the same hours.

Telephone Code: 06.

ACCOMMODATIONS

Rooms are plentiful in Tzfat, though finding quality at the right price can take a bit of planning, particularly during weekends in the summer months (call ahead for stays over Shabbat). The **youth hostel** is well equipped and only a short ride or a 20-minute walk from the bus station. In high season, inexpensive **guest rooms** and flats are often available from town residents.

Shalom Inn, 3 Korchak St. (tel. 697 18 61, 692 08 95 or 697 04 45), at the beginning of the artists' quarter. From Jerusalem St., take a left on Aliya Bet St.; just past the cultural center take the unmarked street on the right with the sign "Artists' Quarter." Fresh and modern rooms with terrific views of the mountain and the artists' quarter. A/C and private bathrooms. Singles NIS100, in winter NIS85; doubles NIS170/US$37, in winter NIS150/US$32, in Aug. NIS200/US$42. Try to get the room with a rooftop patio.

Beit Binyamin (HI), 1 Loḥamei Ha-Geta'ot St. (tel. 692 10 86; fax 697 35 14), near the Amal Trade School in South Tzfat. Take bus #6 or 7. From the bus station, take a left on Jerusalem St. and another left on Aliya Bet St. Continue to Ha-Nassi St. and look for the hostel sign on the left. Exceptionally clean, recently renovated rooms have private baths and refrigerators. 4- to 6-bed dorms NIS68, July-Aug. NIS77; singles NIS100, July-Aug. NIS160/US$35; doubles NIS330/US$70. Non-members NIS5 extra. Breakfast included. Credit cards accepted.

Hadar Hotel (tel. 692 00 68), on Ridbaz St., an alley off Jerusalem St. Comfortable, homey rooms have bath, balcony, and A/C or fans. Singles NIS90; doubles NIS180/US$38; in winter NIS10 less. Ring after the midnight curfew.

FOOD

Jerusalem St. north of the bridge along the *midraḥov* is lined with cheap falafel joints and expensive restaurants. A fruit and vegetable **market** is held Wednesdays (6am-2pm) next to the bus station. There are supermarkets throughout town, including a **HyperCol** in the basement of the mall on the *midraḥov* (open Su-Th 9am-8pm, F 7am-2pm). Almost all restaurants in Tzfat are kosher.

Mountain View (tel. 102 04 04), on the *midraḥov* on the left just after the circular mall. A trendy cafe specializing in vegetarian dishes, with a terrific you-know-what. Huge salads NIS4-38, stir-fry dishes NIS34, pasta NIS32-36, sandwiches NIS20, and smoothies NIS12-20, all fancily garnished. Open Su-Th 8am-midnight.

Pinati (tel. 692 08 55), at the end of the *midraḥov*. Elvis is the Messiah here, and all await his second, blue-suede coming. The walls are plastered with memorabilia from the tumultuous life of the swivel-hipped dreamboat. No peanut butter and banana sandwiches here, but there are hunk-o'-hunk-o' burnin' meat meals from kebabs to spaghetti (NIS30-40). Open Su-Th 10am-midnight, F 9:30am-4pm, Sa sundown-midnight.

Ha-Mifgash Restaurant, 75 Jerusalem St. (tel. 692 05 10 or 697 47 34), at the lower end of the *midraḥov*. Great food in a large Turkish-style cavern. Chicken soup connoisseurs must try Ha-Mifgash's velvety brew (NIS14). Meat dishes with rice or fries NIS25-45; veggie options include stuffed pepper (NIS14) and eggplant (NIS16). Open Su-Th 10am-11pm, F 10am-4pm, Sa sundown-midnight. Credit cards accepted.

SIGHTS

The best—and inevitably, the only—way to see Tzfat is to get lost in its circuitous sidestreets. Fortunately, there are a few tour guides on hand to inject some order into the chaos of navigating the city. **Aviva Minoff** (tel. 692 09 01, mobile tel. (05) 040 91 87) gives entertaining tours starting from the Municipal Building or the Rimon Inn Hotel (M-Th 10am, F 10:30am; 2hr. tour NIS40). **Yosi Reis** (tel. 692 28 03) gives good but expensive personal tours with advance notice (2hr. tour NIS220/US$45). Otherwise, try Yisrael Shalem's helpful *Six Self-Guided Tours to Tzfat* (NIS15), available at Greenbaum's Books on the *midraḥov*. Regardless of where you go, dress modestly and don't take pictures on Shabbat.

> **TZSIGHTSEEING TZSTRATEGY.** A walking tour of the **Synagogue Quarter** (*Kiryat Batei Ha-Knesset,* also called the Old City, *Ha-Ir Ha-Atika*) is a great way to see the sights in Tzfat, but navigating the gnarled quarter is difficult. Note landmarks carefully and head toward the *midraḥov* and center of town. Only Caro, Ha-Ari, and Abuhav are open to the public. Begin in Ha-Meginim Square, to the right of the cobblestone terrace across from the post office on Jerusalem St.

SEPHARDI HA-ARI SYNAGOGUE. This synagogue was built in 1580 (three years after the death of its namesake, Rabbi **Isaac Luria**) on the site of a field where the famous mystic led congregants to welcome Shabbat. Luria is most famous for penning the *Kabbalat Shabbat,* an arrangement of prayers in preparation for the Sabbath; Alkabetz, his student, wrote the now-standard liturgical hymn *Leḥa Dodi.* The synagogue features two notable curiosities. One is the **fertility chair,** more formally used as a ceremonial circumcision chair, which is rumored to bless women who sit in it with miracle pregnancies. The other is a small **hole** in the central pulpit, where visitors place notes for wishes and good luck. The hole was made during the 1948 War when a grenade flew into the synagogue and exploded while worshipers were bowed in prayer, allowing the shrapnel to sail over their heads and leave a mark only in the pulpit's side. *(To the right of the square and down the stairs.)*

ABUHAV SYNAGOGUE. Exiting the synagogue, take a left down the stairs, a left at the bottom of the stairs, a right on Simtat Abuhav St., and then a quick left after going down more stairs; the Abuhav Synagogue will be on the left. Rabbi **Isaac Abuhav** was a 15th century Spanish mystic who never actually made it to Tzfat. His 550-year-old Torah scroll did, however, and it is inside the first ark to the right inside the entrance. The second ark contains Rabbi Luria's Torah scroll, four centuries old. The scroll inside the blue ark is rumored to have been the only thing left intact in Tzfat following the 1837 earthquake that levelled the town. In the middle of the synagogue is a chandelier brought over from Europe as a reminder of those who suffered in the Holocaust. The ▣**circumcision chair** at the back of the synagogue has been used to circumcise 8-day-old Jewish boys for 213 years, making it perhaps the single most painful piece of furniture in the world.

CARO SYNAGOGUE. Exiting this synagogue, continue straight down the same alleyway. Up the stairs on the left and through the door in the purple walls is the back entrance to the Caro Synagogue, one of the most famous in Tzfat. It was here that **Yosef Caro,** chief rabbi of Tzfat and author of the vast *Shulḥan Arukh* ("The

Set Table," a standard guide to daily life according to Jewish law), studied and taught in the 16th century. Caro was well-known as a philanthropist who served simultaneously as rabbi, counselor, shelter-provider, and soup kitchen coordinator. *(Caro Synagogue is also accessible by taking Ma'alot Oleh Ha-Gardom St. to Beit Yosef St.)*

CEMETERIES. Three adjoining cemeteries sprawl on the western outskirts of the Old City, off Ha-Ari St. at the bottom of the hill. Follow the steps all the way down, past the new stone buildings on the left. The small building on the left when the path turns into the cemetery is Ha-Ari men's **mikveh**, or ritual bath. This *mikveh* was the bathing place of Ha-Ari himself, and its vibes have attracted the interest of mystics the world over, including the Dalai Lama. The local rabbinical court has ruled that women may not enter the *mikveh*'s icy waters, but renegade females have been known to take a dip late at night while a male friend guards the door. The oldest cemetery contains the 17th-century graves of the most famous Tzfat Kabbalists as well as a domed tomb built by the Karaites of Damascus to mark the grave of the prophet **Hosea**. Legend has it that hidden under this same hill lie **Hannah** and her seven sons, whose martyrdom at the hands of the Syrians is recorded in the Book of Maccabees. A gorgeous, thickly wooded, three-and-a-half-hour **hike** starts from Naḥal Amud at the bottom of the Tzfat cemeteries. The hike continues up a rocky *wadi* and emerges next to an old, bullet-ridden British police station by the road to Bar-Yoḥai's tomb. Interested travelers should get directions from SPNI.

DAVIDKA MONUMENT. This monument memorializes the weapon responsible for the Palmaḥ's victory in Tzfat—the duds that were launched made such a frightening noise that a rumor spread around town that the Palmaḥ had atomic bombs, prompting Arab forces to flee. The phenomenal view makes the short climb to the sight worthwhile. *(Cross over Jerusalem St. from the Municipality building to the street signs pointing to Metzuda. Climb the stairs behind the bullet-ridden British police station. At the top, follow the road to the park's entrance.)*

ISRAEL BIBLE MUSEUM. American artist Phillip Ratner has filled three floors of this building with entertaining sculptures and canvas depictions of famous figures and stories from the Bible. Ratner's prominent work is housed in permanent collections at the Statue of Liberty, the White House, and the U.S. Supreme Court. *(Just north of the Gan Ha-Metzuda Park. Tel. 699 99 72. Open May-Sept. Su-Th 10am-4pm, F 10am-1pm; Oct.-Apr. Su-Th 10am-2pm. Free; pamphlet gives English explanations of the works.)*

SHEM VA'EVER CAVE. This site is said to be the burial grounds of Noah's son Shem and grandson Ever. Muslims believe that it was here that Jacob learned of the supposed death of his son Joseph, and they call it the "Cave of Mourning." *(Near the top of Ha-Palmaḥ bridge at the intersection of Jerusalem and Arlozorov St. If the shrine around the cave is locked, knock at the small, domed synagogue nearby.)*

LUCKY TZCHARMS
The streets of Tzfat's Old City may be confusing, but they are some of the luckiest in the world. The image of a **hand** is scrawled above doorways and on blank walls and appears on key chains, in windows, and even behind picture frames. Hands have special Kabbalistic significance in Jewish mysticism. A hand has five fingers; two hands' worth (what most people have) make for a grand total of ten, a number that represents God in mystic texts. Some noteworthy variations on the hand symbol are the hand with an eye in its palm (representing the charm against the **evil eye**) and the six-fingered hand above the doorway to the right of the left exit of the Abuhav Synagogue. No nifty numerology here: one of the wittier builders of the synagogue had six fingers on one hand and left his mark after finishing construction.

Another magically delicious *graffito* that appears throughout the Old City is the strange-looking Hebrew sentence that is scribbled on many of the buildings in the quarter (and throughout the Galilee): נ נח נחמ נחמן מאומן, or "Na-Naḥ-Naḥma-Naḥman from Uman." The words refer to the late **Naḥman of Breslev**, leader of the Breslever Ḥasidic sect, whose followers chant his name in this fashion to bring good fortune.

✦ARTIST'S QUARTER. The alleys and galleries of the artist's quarter display a wide range of local art of varying quality. Gallery highlights include **microcalligraphy** (pictures created out of verses from traditional Jewish texts) and Ruth Shany's silk artwork. *(South of the Jerusalem-Arlozorov St. intersection. Open 10am-1pm and 4-7pm.)*

CRAFTS. Among things not to be missed in the Old City is the **Tzfat Candle Factory.** All of the imaginatively colored and shaped candles on display are produced by the workers at the back of the shop, bent busily over blocks and sheets of beeswax (candles start at NIS12). The friendly proprietors of the small **Golden Mountain Cheese** cafe and shop in Ha-Meginim Sq. manufacture and sell their own goats' milk gourmet kosher cheeses. High-quality hard cheese goes for NIS90 per kilo, or sample a variety from a platter (NIS15, large NIS30). Also in the square near the cheese shop is a **scribe,** who can be observed copying Jewish religious texts by hand. *(Candle Factory: tel. 692 10 93. From Ha-Meginim Sq., head down to Najara St. and take a right past the Ha-Ari Synagogue and the candle shop; the factory is on the right. Open Su-Th 8:30am-6pm, F 8:30am-1pm; 1hr. later in summer. Golden Mountain Cheese: tel. 692 30 20. Open Su-Th 10am-10pm. Scribe: works M-Tu and Th 11:30am-5pm, F 11:30am-1:30pm.)*

♫ ENTERTAINMENT

Shabbat in Tzfat brings tranquility, introspection, and, perhaps, boredom. The **Blue Valley Swimming Pool and Leisure Center** (tel. 692 74 52) can chlorinate mysticism away. Walk left down Ha-Atzma'ut Rd. from the bus station and turn left; the turn-off is on the left, 100m down. (Open July-Aug. Sa-Th 8am-7pm, F 8am-5pm. Women only Tu and Th 1-5pm; men only Su and F 1-5pm. Admission NIS19, students NIS10.). If you want to make a splash with a wild night in Tzfat, it'll take some creative thinking. The only real bar in town is **Green Table** (tel. 692 21 00), on the third floor of the circular mall on the *midrahov*, where laid-back locals line up (NIS30 per hr.) and drink down (NIS8; open Su-Th 11am-midnight, Sa after sundown). After dark, the artistically minded gather in **Coffee Gallery 2001** (tel. 682 20 01), on the right side of Arlozorov St., to absorb locally produced art and cups of coffee (NIS6-8), soda (NIS7), or beer (NIS10; open Su-Th 8am-9pm, F 8am-5pm, Sa noon-4pm and 8pm-midnight).

⚑ HIKING: NEAR TZFAT

MT. MERON. Just west of the village of Meron is **Har Meron** (Mt. Meron), the highest mountain in the Galilee (1208m). A good trail affords tremendous vistas of Tzfat and the surrounding countryside—on clear days Lebanon and Syria to the north, the Mediterranean to the west, and the Galilee to the southeast are all visible. The **trail** begins at the back of the lot and follows striped black-and-white trail markers. A one-hour walk uphill through sweet smelling, wonderfully wooded surroundings leads to the summit and its striking views. Stay on the trail skirting the summit, as the very top of the mountain is the site of an army radar installation. Twenty minutes farther along the path leads to a picnic site and a traffic circle; make a quick left back into the forest, where the trail begins again. *(It's possible to ascend from the village of Meron, but it's easier to take bus #43 or 367 from Tzfat to Kibbutz Sasa, northwest of Mt. Meron (25min.; 6:45, 9, 11:40am, 12:30, 2:15, 5pm; NIS10.90). The Meron information office (tel. (06) 698 00 23) offers a 1:50,000 trail map (NIS60) and limited advice (open daily 8am-2pm). Bus #361 returns to Tzfat (every 20min. 6am-8pm, NIS8).)*

ALMA CAVE. Legend has it that the maze-like tunnels of Alma Cave form an underground bridge between the holy cities of Tzfat and Jerusalem and contain the corpses of 900,000 "righteous men." There is no guarantee that a daytrip to the Alma Cave will end up at the Dome of the Rock or yield encounters with long-deceased rabbis, but for those anxious to spelunk despite mud, sweat, and claustrophobic conditions, the Alma Cave is a tailor-made adventure.

The entrance to the cave is hidden in a gorge behind clusters of large trees; from the green nature reserve sign on the hillside of grey stones, go right and uphill toward the metal poles. The gorge and cave entrance are just ahead. Notice the black ropes hooked into the stone to aid in climbing down into the gorge and toward the cave entrance. Climb (or slide) down the hole, keeping to the right. At a depth of approximately 60m (½-¾ of the way down), there are two phallic rocks near the right-hand wall. Behind these lies a small hole leading to the "inner chambers" of the cave. There are markers indicating the correct path: white for the way in, red for the way out. Once inside the large room with a ridge and a steep slope, veer to the far right along the ridge instead of continuing down the slope. Near the end of the trail, the rocks become slippery and the caverns fill with technicolor, dripping stalagmites and stalactites. Getting out of the cave is a true physical challenge, involving steep climbs and tricky maneuvers. *(Bus #45 leaves Tzfat for Reḥania (20min.; departs 8:45am, 1:15, 4pm; returns 9:15am, 1:45, 4:30pm; NIS12.20). Get off at Reḥania (not Alma) to visit the cave. Across the street from the entrance to Reḥania village is the dirt path to Alma cave. The path is marked by red and white stripes painted on the poles beside the main highway; keep an eye out for the infrequent trail markers. Follow the path for about 30min. to the cave entrance, steering close to Alma (left) and away from the hilly, tree-lined area to the right—don't make any sharp turns.)*

> **A FEW CAVE-ATS.** Day-tripping in slippery **Alma Cave** can be very dangerous when you don't take the proper precautionary measures. Only venture into Alma Cave if you feel you can stand being 108m underground for several hours. Inform someone (like your hotel manager) of the trip details. Travel only during daylight hours with a group of at least three. Bring more than enough **water**, a small **pack** (large ones won't fit in small crevices), one strong, reliable **flashlight** per person, and back-up candles and matches.

TEL ḤAZOR. The *tel* at Ḥazor is the largest archaeological mound in northern Israel. Excavations in the 1960s revealed 21 layers of settlements at the site, the oldest dating from the 3rd millennium BCE. Like Megiddo (see p. 328), Ḥazor was once a fortified city situated on the main trade route linking Egypt to Syria and Mesopotamia. Ḥazor served as a major commercial center in the Fertile Crescent, and the Bible calls it "the head of all those [northern Canaanite] kingdoms" (Joshua 11:10). Ferocious Joshua supposedly slaughtered the entire population of Ḥazor and burnt the city to the ground upon God's command (Joshua 11:10-16). Archaeologists have found evidence of a conflagration here during the 13th century BCE, supporting the biblical tale. Kings Solomon (10th century BCE) and Ahab (9th century BCE) rebuilt and expanded Ḥazor; Assyria's Tiglath-Pileser III laid the city to waste during his army's march through the Galilee (732 BCE). At the northern foot of the *tel* lies a vast, thick-walled lower city built in the 9th century BCE. The most impressive of the ruins is the 38m deep tunnel, engineered during Ahab's reign to bring water into the city in case of a siege. Excavations continue today; archaeologists are now searching for the ancient city's archives. *(Buses #501 and 511 from Tzfat (35min., NIS12.20) and all buses running between Rosh Pina and Kiryat Shmona stop near the site. Don't get off at Ḥazor Ha-Gelilit; continue north to Kibbutz Ayelet Ha-Shaḥor. The kibbutz houses a small museum (tel. 693 48 55) displaying Canaanite and Israelite artifacts and explaining the layers of the tel. From there, the entrance to the site (tel. 693 72 90) is 250m up the main road. Museum and site open Sa-Th 8am-5pm, F and holidays 8am-4pm. Admission to both NIS14, students NIS12, children NIS6.)*

ROSH PINA ראש פינה

There's not much to do in quiet Rosh Pina except leave: many buses heading north pass through the town en route to the Upper Galilee and Golan. Buses #401, 459, 461, 501, and 511 go to Tzfat (every 30min., NIS9.50), and buses #480, 500, 842, 845, and 909 go to Kiryat Shmona (every 30min., NIS12.50). The town also has one of the few affordable lodgings in the Kiryat Shmona area. The Nature Friends Youth Hostel (tel. 693 17 64 or 051 572 141) has a few tidy, air-conditioned rooms (dorms NIS50; singles NIS75; call ahead). To reach the hostel, get off at the first bus stop in town (not at the main bus station farther on) and take a left up the cobblestone street, following the hostel signs.

KIRYAT SHMONA קרית שמונה

Kiryat Shmona ("Town of Eight") commemorates Yosef Trumpeldor and seven others who were murdered in nearby Tel Hai in 1920. Situated atop the ruins of the Arab village Al-Khalsa (destroyed in the 1948 War), the city received its new name in 1949. By virtue of its location on the Hula plain near the Lebanese border, Kiryat Shmona was the target of numerous bombings and terrorist attacks until Israel invaded Lebanon in 1982 and created the nine-mile-wide security zone. Even since then, though, it has been subject to shelling by the militant Islamic group Hezbollah. The town thus graduated from its grim name to an even grimmer nickname: Kiryat Katyusha, referring to the type of rocket used.

TRANSPORTATION. The **Central Bus Station** (info tel. (04) 854 95 55) is on Tel Hai Blvd. Buses to: **Tiberias** (#840, 841, and 963; 1hr.; frequent service; NIS20.50); **Kfar Blum** (#31 and 32, 4 per day, NIS6.80); **Tel Aviv** (#840, 841, 842, or 845; every 30min.; NIS44); **Rosh Pina** (#480, 500, 842, 845, or 969; 30min.; NIS12.50); **Tzfat** (#501 or 511, 45min., every hr. until 7pm, NIS17.30); and **Metulla** via **Tel Hai** (#20 or 21, every 20min. until 7:30pm, NIS8). Rent cars from **Thrifty** at **Shlomo Rent-a-Car** (tel. 694 16 31), down Henrietta Szold St. from Tel Hai Blvd., near the motel. The cheapest automatic goes for NIS350/US$74 per day with a 250km limit, NIS310/US$64 with unlimited mileage for rentals over three days (min. age 21; under 23 NIS50 extra; open Su-Th 8am-5pm, F 8am-2pm).

ACCOMMODATIONS AND FOOD. Kiryat Shmona is a good place to make necessary shopping excursions or to catch the bus to outlying areas, and its **Motel Hatira** (tel. 694 49 44; fax 690 30 36) makes it possible to use the city as an overnight base. Located in a castle-like building, the rooms are less than royal but come with TV, air conditioning, a fridge, lots of space, and a location on Tel Hai Blvd., a 15-minute walk from the bus station (singles NIS100; doubles NIS180; less for longer stays; credit cards accepted). There are plenty of falafel places along Tel Hai Blvd., as well as a McDonald's in the mall (open Su-Th 9am-10pm, F 9am-3pm, Sa noon-11pm). **Co-op Tzafon Supermarket** is well-stocked with everything from fresh produce to packaged sweets (open Su-Th 7:30am-9:30pm, F mornings only). On Thursdays, there is an outdoor **market** past the mall on Tel Hai Blvd.

SIGHTS. There are two museums in town interesting enough to ease a few minutes of boredom. The **Mosque Museum**, 16 Jordan St. (tel. 694 01 35), in a former house of worship, presents the history of Kiryat Shmona and the surrounding area and exhibits nearby archaeological excavations. Across Ya-Harden St., behind the museum and park, the **Bible Museum** features a diorama collection of characters and catastrophes from the Good Book. Both museums can be reached by heading down Uri Ilan St., off Tel Hai, across from the Granovsky Family Auditorium south of the bus station, and following it around to the right.

At the **Manara Cliff** (tel. 690 58 30; email m-cliff@inter.net.il), glassed-in sky gondolas carry acrophiliacs to two stations located midway up and at the top of the 900m cliff. In addition to the bird's-eye view of Galilee and the Golan, the middle station offers cliff rapelling (NIS55). From the top, the trip down can be hiked or biked (3-4km depending on the path), as well as traveled by gondola. (Open daily 9:30am-6:30pm. Gondola rides NIS33, children NIS27. Bike rentals NIS55, can be returned at the middle station.)

HIKING: NEAR KIRYAT SHMONA

The **Hula Valley Nature Reserve** is one of the most beautiful areas in all of Israel. Two thousand years ago, Flavius described the valley as "wonderful in its characteristics of beauty…there is not a plant that does not flourish there, and…the air is so temperate that it suits the most diverse species." However, in the late 18th and early 19th century, Jewish pioneers arrived and drained the swamps to farm the fertile soil beneath. Eventually the altered habitat became so dry that its diverse wildlife left the Hula Valley—and in some cases died out entirely. Out of concern for the area's ecological diversity, Israel's first nature reserve was established here in 1964. Since then, parts of the Ḥula Valley have been refilled with water and are carefully maintained; ecologists hope to lure amphibians, water buffalo, and birds migrating between Europe and Africa to the area. The five reserves of the Ḥula Valley showcase Israel's forested north and give hikers the chance to discover ice-cold streams, swamplands, and their wild inhabitants.

ḤULA NATURE RESERVE. This reserve harbors what remains and what is returning of the wildlife that once flourished in the swamplands. The parking and picnic area are populated with huge trees; a path from there leads to the small wood-roofed house that serves as the reserve's **visitor's center.** The center gives details on the history of the swamp, the varieties of plant and animal wildlife it contains, and a video presentation. Animals are most abundant from November to March. Arrive early in the morning to see the wildlife and to avoid crowded family-time in the forest. (*Between Rosh Pina and Kiryat Shmona off Rte. 90. Buses #501, 511, 840, and 841 (NIS12.20) leave Kiryat Shmona frequently and go to a junction 2½km from the entrance to the reserve. The turnoff from Rte. 90 is marked. Tel. (06) 693 40 69. Open Sa-Th 8am-4pm, F and holiday eves 8am-3pm. Admission NIS18, students NIS15, under 18 NIS9.*)

HORSHAT TAL NATURE RESERVE. Hundred-year-old oak trees dominate this reserve. According to a Muslim legend, the trees, which grow nowhere else in Israel, sprang up because of the 10 warriors of Muhammad who once rested here. Finding no shade and not a single hitching post for their horses, they pounded their staffs into the earth to fasten their mounts. The sticks sprouted overnight, and the holy men found themselves in a thick forest. Though the park doesn't offer the rich eco-diversity of the Ḥula Reserve, there are nicely shaded picnic sites, a large, ice-cold **swimming pool** (actually a diverted branch of the Dan River), and fishing for those who bring their own equipment. (*Off Rte. 99, between Kiryat Shmona and Banyas. From Kiryat Shmona, bus #36 goes to Ḥorshat Tal (infrequent, NIS6.80). Ask to be let off at Horshat Tal, then walk 100m down the hill on the right, toward the brown sign. Tel. (06) 694 23 60. Open Sa-F 8am-4pm, F 8am-3pm. Admission NIS27, under 15 NIS16.*)

TEL DAN. Tel Dan is the Ḥula Valley's most thickly forested nature reserve. Several short, easy walks loop under towering willow trees and follow the gushing Dan River, a tributary of the Jordan. The 45-minute circle trail is mostly paved for **wheelchair access;** the one-and-a-half hour trail is rockier but passes by all the ancient ruins. Ongoing excavations at the *tel* have revealed the ancient Canaanite city of **Laish,** conquered and settled by the Israelite tribe of Dan around 1200 BCE. The most interesting remains lie in the Cultic site, where King Jeroboam Ben-Nebat of the breakaway Kingdom of Israel placed a golden calf, attempting to draw attention away from the Kingdom of Judah's Temple in Jerusalem (I Kings 12:28-29). In 1983, archaeologists made a remarkable find at Tel Dan: a broken stele, inscribed with the words "House of David" in 9th-century BCE Aramaic. The earth-shattering piece of rock provided the first known reference (aside from the Bible) to King David and his climactic expulsion of the Philistines. The **Beit Ushish-kin Museum,** a gray stone building on the way to Tel Dan, displays a replica of the stele. Take a left at the sign. (*A few km past Ḥorshat Tal on Rte. 99. Take bus #36 from Kiryat Shmona. From the main road, take a left at the brown sign and walk a winding 1½km to the site. Tel. (06) 695 15 79. Reserve open Sa-Th 8am-4pm, F 8am-3pm; visitors may stay 1hr. after closing time. Admission NIS18, students NIS15, children NIS9; ticket includes 25% discount at Beit Usishkin Museum. Museum open Su-Th 8am-4:30pm, F 8am-3:30pm, Sa 9:30am-4:30pm. Admission NIS12, students NIS10; ticket includes 25% discount at Tel Dan Reserve.*)

METULLA מטולה

Buses #20 and 21 run between Kiryat Shmona and Metulla (15min., 8 per day, NIS8). The Good Fence is less than 1km past Metulla. From the bus drop-off in the parking lot, turn right and walk past the mammoth snack stand to the observation point.

Metulla, 9km north of Kiryat Shmona, is Israel's largest village on the Lebanese border. Its main attraction is ■**Ha-Gader Ha-Tova** (The Good Fence), the only opening in the border between Lebanon and Israel. The two countries remain at odds, but Lebanese Christians and Druze are allowed to pass through to obtain free medical services, visit relatives, and work in Israel. Israel began passing aid and supplies through this point to Lebanese Christians in 1971, and in June 1976 the Good Fence officially opened. It remained operative even during the war in Lebanon. From the observation point, some Maronite Christian villages are visible across the border; on the farthest hill to the right (northwest) is the Crusader fortress of **Beaufort,** which was fortified by the PLO and used as a base from which to shell Israel.

GOLAN HEIGHTS רמת הגולן

When asked to name the most beautiful part of their country, many Israelis speak of the Golan Heights. The region offers visitors a relatively cool climate, breathtaking views, noteworthy archaeological sites, and dozens of streams and waterfalls. This formerly volcanic plateau overlooking the Jordan Valley is sparsely traveled except in spring, when busloads of loud Israeli teenagers on school-sponsored outings pack the normally serene trails. The region is marked off by rivers: the **Jordan River** running north-south separates it from Galilee, and the **Sa'ar River** forms an east-west border between the Golan and the northernmost Mt. Ḥermon area.

The first recorded mention of the Golan is the biblical "Golan in Bashan," a city established by Moses as a refuge for Israelites guilty of manslaughter (Deut. 4:43). The Golan was an important holdout in the Jewish Revolt of 66-73 CE, when its steep hills sheltered the city of Gamla, called the Masada of the north (see **Gamla,** p. 347). During the next two centuries, the Golan became a center of Jewish culture, as evidenced by excavations of ancient synagogues. As time passed, however, it degenerated into a backwater Syrian province until Turkish officials planted Circassian settlers there to stop Bedouin highwaymen in the 1880s.

Recent history has cast the Golan Heights back into the jaws of political controversy. Israel captured the Golan in the 1967 Six-Day War, but was pushed back by Syria's surprise attack in the 1973 War. Israeli forces quickly recovered and launched a counter-attack, capturing even more territory. As part of the 1974 disengagement accord, Israel returned both the newly conquered territory and part of the land captured in 1967. However, in 1981 Israel officially annexed the remaining 768 sq. km, arousing international protest. Today, Jewish settlements are scattered among Israeli army bases, Druze villages, live minefields, and destroyed bunkers.

The future status of the Golan is currently under negotiation. Syria claims that the land was seized unfairly and demands its return. Israeli officials have argued that withdrawal from the Golan Heights would threaten national security. Netanyahu's 1996 election was viewed by many as an indication of the Israeli public's opposition to a withdrawal from the Golan. The political necessity of compromise became apparent, however, with the election of Ehud Barak in May 1999. Though Barak did not initiate public discussion on the Golan Heights during his first few months in office, the international community awaits the results of possible behind-the-scenes negotiations (for details, see **Syria: In The News,** p. 496). Whatever the outcome of the peace talks, the Golan will remain dear to those who live there. To Israelis, it is a major source of water and the home of ski slopes, apple orchards, and wineries. Many of the Golan's 15,000 Druze, however, strongly identify with Syria and have relatives across the border.

▨ PRACTICAL INFORMATION

When wandering the Golan in summer, bring a hat, sunscreen, and buckets of water. The cool pools of water often discovered on hikes reward weary walkers ready to take a dip, but are not safe to drink. Avoid hiking during the cold, damp, foggy, and often snowy winter. The best time to visit the Golan is spring, when the

ISRAEL

MINE-D YOUR STEP. There are still active **landmine fields** in the Golan Heights. Landmine fields are marked off by barbed-wire fences with square yellow signs that have red triangles and say, "Danger! Mines!" in English, Hebrew, and Arabic. In some areas, the fences are marked only with red triangles. Avoid fenced-off areas whether or not you see the warning signs. Mine fields line roads and hiking routes, so be sure to stay on paved surfaces and clearly marked trails.

heat is bearable and yellow and green flowers color the hillsides. The best hiking the Golan Heights has to offer is described under the **Hiking: The Golan,** p. 348.

The best way to see the Golan is to **rent a car** in Tiberias or Kiryat Shmona. **Egged buses** reach some Golan sights, but infrequent service along remote roads necessitates careful planning. Double check all schedules, and anticipate some walking. Buses to sights near Galilee generally leave from Tiberias. The Upper Galilee, Ḥula Valley, and northern Golan are served by buses from Kiryat Shmona and Tzfat. Traveling by bus makes it nearly impossible to get to Gamla and many hiking trails. Relatively few cars traverse the Golan, and hitchhiking is inadvisable. There is a general **tourist information office** (tel. 693 69 45) for the Golan Heights at the Maḥanayim Junction between Rosh Pina and Kiryat Shmona, where Rte. 91 branches off of Rte. 90 (look for the gas station on the right and turn right; open Su-F 8:30am-3:30pm, Sa 9am-2pm). There is a **24-hour grocery** next door; bring several bottles of water and at least a day's worth of food on any hike. **SPNI** hiking and camping trips visit some hard-to-reach spots and, in summer, may include kayaking down the Jordan River (tel. 680 13 82/3/4; NIS905/US$200 per day). As always, for the **police,** dial tel. 100; for **first aid,** dial tel. 101.

TELEPHONE CODE The **telephone code** for all of the Golan Heights is **06.**

KATZRIN קצרין

Buses #55, 56, and 57 go to Katzrin from Rosh Pina (25min., every 2hr., NIS10.50). From Tiberias, take bus #15, 16, or 19 (45min., 4 per afternoon, NIS18). From Kiryat Shmona, take bus #58 (30min., 4:40pm, NIS26). Moniot Ha-Golan (tel. 696 11 11), a left out of the Katzrin tourist office, has special taxi fares to Rosh Pina (NIS75) and Tiberias (NIS120).

The town of Katzrin was founded immediately after the 1967 War, with the express purpose of establishing an Israeli presence in the Golan Heights. Although it offers only enough diversion to fill an afternoon, its centrality in the Golan Heights makes it a good base for exploring the area. For such a young settlement, Katzrin enjoys a high standard of living, but its economic growth has slowed with the possibility of an Israeli withdrawal from the Golan.

The **Golan Archaeological Museum** (tel. 696 13 50), across the plaza and behind the shopping strip off Daliyot St., has an excellent bilingual exhibit on ancient settlements in the Golan. It displays the remnants of 2000-year-old synagogues, including a lintel inscribed with the Talmudic sage Eliezer Ha-Kappar's name and sculptures from a Chalcolithic settlement dating back to 4000 BCE. (Open Su-Th 8am-5pm, F 8am-3pm, Sa 10am-4pm. Admission NIS15, students NIS12. Joint admission to museum and Ancient Katzrin Park NIS28, students NIS17.) The excavations at **Ancient Katzrin Park** (tel. 696 24 12), just outside modern Katzrin down Rte. 9088, have unearthed a richly ornamented synagogue in use from the 4th through the 8th centuries CE. Two furnished houses were re-created based on finds from the excavations, giving a sense of daily life in the Talmudic village.

For those who find Katzrin's ancient artifacts too sobering, the **Golan Heights Winery** (tel. 696 84 09), on Rte. 9088, is a rousing alternative. The winery produces the world-renowned Yarden, Gamla, and Golan labels, and its tour includes a video explanation, a look at the production process, a souvenir glass, and a taste of grapey bliss. The shop sells bottles of their wine beginning at NIS25. (Open Su-Th 8am-5pm, F 8am-1:30pm. Last tour begins 1hr. before closing. Tours NIS15, students NIS12. Call ahead for a tour in English.)

GAMLA גמלא

Take a right out of modern Katzrin, a left onto Rte. 87 at the junction, and a right onto Rte. 808. The road to Gamla is on the right, labeled with a sign. Gamla is not accessible by public transportation; those without cars often ask for rides from Katzrin, then walk the 1km to the ridge overlooking the ruins. The descent to the ruins along the Roman route takes about 20min. Allot about 2hr. for the site itself. Tel. 696 37 21. Open Su-Th 8am-5pm, F 8am-4pm; closes 1hr. earlier in winter. Admission NIS18, students NIS15.

For years, the lost city of Gamla existed as no more than a legend from the pages of first-century Jewish historian Josephus Flavius's *The Jewish War* (see **What's All the 'Phus About?**, p. 331). After the 1967 War, archaeologists scoured the region for a spot corresponding to the ancient description; Shmaryahu Gutman finally uncovered the site. Its name ("camel" in Hebrew) comes from the hill's peak, which protrudes like a camel's hump. The film at Katzrin's archaeological museum (see p. 346) provides a great introduction to Gamla.

Josephus's narrative recounts how, in 67 CE, the Romans laid siege to this hilltop fortress, which had become a haven for 9000 Jewish refugees. As the siege wore on, Roman commanders became impatient and decided to storm down the corridor of land leading to the town from nearby hills. As the legion penetrated Gamla's walls, hordes of Jews fled to the upper part of the city, where slopes were so steep that one house's rooftop touched the floor of the house above it. The Romans followed, but so many soldiers crowded on the rooftops that the houses collapsed; the Jews quickly turned and killed their pursuers. Some weeks later, three vengeful Roman soldiers sneaked into Gamla in the middle of the night and pulled out foundation stones from the watchtower, causing it to collapse. In the ensuing confusion, the Roman army burst into the city and began to slaughter the inhabitants, many of whom hurled themselves into the deep ravine next to the citadel rather than die by enemy hands. Only two women survived to tell the tale. Some archaeologists take issue with Josephus's proclivity for over-dramatization (see **What's All the 'Phus About?**, p. 331) and claim that Gamla's inhabitants were really pushed over the cliff in the mayhem of battle. Inside the city lie remnants of what some archaeologists deem the **oldest synagogue** ever found in Israel, dating from around the 2nd century BCE.

BANYAS בניס

Buses #55 and 58 each leave Kiryat Shmona once a day on their way through the Golan and stop by Banyas (1:30, 4:40pm; NIS10.90). By car, Banyas lies just off Rte. 99, which runs between Kiryat Shmona and the north-south Rte. 98. Tel. 695 02 72. Park open Sa-Th 8am-5pm, F 8am-4pm. Admission NIS18, students NIS15, children NIS9.

The most popular site in the Upper Galilee-Golan area is only a few minutes down the road from Upper Galilee nature reserves Dan and Ḥorshat Tal. The Banyas springs in the Naḥal Ḥermon Nature Reserve have witnessed an odd religious mix: Jesus gave the keys to heaven and earth to St. Peter here, Muslims built a shrine over the supposed grave of the Prophet Elijah (An-Nabi Khadar) in the adjacent hill, and an ancient sanctuary dedicated to the Greek god Pan remains carved into the cliffside. King Herod built a temple in honor of Augustus Caesar and called the place *Caesarea Philippi*, after his son Philippus. Because of its ancient association with Pan, however, the area became known as Paneas (Pan's Place), rendered in Arabic as "Banyas." Arabs settled the town in the 7th century, though possession shifted between the Muslims and the Crusaders many times during the 12th and 13th centuries. Banyas remained an Arab village until the 1967 War. Today, families flock to the reserve for afternoons of light hiking and swimming.

The first brown sign on the road that points to Banyas leads to a parking lot and the entrance closest to the Banyas waterfall, with the temple of Pan at the other end of the trail. The **Banyas waterfall** (Mapal Banyas) is the largest cascade in the region. From the falls, the trail winds through woods toward the springs, which house small pools of rare fish. Swimming is officially forbidden in the pool's icy-cold water, but most visitors wade in to refresh themselves anyway. From here, head toward the parking lot where the ruins of Pan's temple are uphill and to the left.

NIMROD'S FORTRESS קלעת נמרוד

*The trail to the fortress begins just off the bus #55 (NIS16.50) stop between Kiryat Shmona
and Katzrin. The road to the castle sits directly across from the bus stop. The 1hr. uphill
approach to the castle leads to a clear view of the tiny Druze village of Ein Qinya. The castle is
also accessible by a footpath from Banyas beginning directly above the springs and Pan's
temple. This shadeless walk takes about 45min. each way. By car, continue on Rte. 99 past
Banyas to Rte. 989, where the fortress is up a curvy road on the left. Fortress open daily 8am-
5pm. Admission NIS14, students NIS12, under 18 NIS6.*

Nimrod's Fortress *(Qal'at Nemrud)* is 1½km northeast of Banyas on an isolated
hill. According to the biblical list of Noah's descendants, Nimrod claims the title of
"the first on earth to be a mighty man" (Genesis 10:8). In addition to building the
famed Tower of Babel, Nimrod erected this gigantic fortress—high enough to shoot
arrows up to God. An Arabic plaque above one gate reads: "God gave him the power
to build this castle with his own strength." Historians like to shoot arrows through
the myth by arguing that Muslims from the Isma'ilia sect built the fortress, originally
called Qal'at Subeiba. Maybe they're both right: the extensive fortress has two main
sections; the one farther away from the entrance was built earlier. A look around
the grounds reveals a secret passageway and game boards carved into the stone
sidewalks by bored guards. The 815m high view from the top of the fortress to the
region below remains unrivaled anywhere in the region.

Up the road, about 1km past Nimrod's Fortress, are a Muslim tomb and a hiking
route at **Nebi Hazuri**. The location is marked on the left by a brown sign in Hebrew.
A white gravel road begins in the parking lot and winds around picnic areas, trees,
and monuments; lookout points along the trail provide terrific views of the surrounding countryside. The hiking route is marked in blue and white, and heads
downhill and to the right from beside the large wooden sign in the parking area.
The trail descends to the riverbed and then curves around toward the bottom of
the hill upon which Nimrod's Fortress stands. After two hours, the trail ends just
outside the entrance to the road leading up to Nimrod's Fortress; take a left and
head up the main highway to the Nebi Hazuri parking area.

MT. HERMON

*Bus #55 travels between Kiryat Shmona and the moshav (2 per afternoon, NIS13). A sherut
from Maas'ada to Kiryat Shmona in the late afternoon is usually the same price.*

Moshav Neveh Ativ (tel. 698 13 33), founded after Israel captured the Golan, lies 2km
west of Majdal Shams on Rte. 989. The *moshav* has developed an expensive resort
village to take advantage of the ski slopes on southern **Mount Hermon,** 10km away.
The road from Maas'ada to Kiryat Shmona runs west along a gorge and past the
hilltop village of Ein Qinya and Nimrod's Fortress. For information on outdoor
activities in the area, or in the Golan in general, the **Hermon SPNI field school** (tel.
694 10 91) is a good place to stop. The field school is located near Kibbutz Senir, to
the right off of Rte. 99 between Kiryat Shmona and Banyas (just beyond Horshat
Dan); go down a turnoff marked by a wooden sign on the right, then through the
gates. In addition to patient and friendly advice, the field school has lodgings (doubles NIS245/US$50; private baths, A/C, breakfast included; field school office open
in summer Su-Th 8am-8pm, F 8am-2pm; in winter Su-Th 8am-5pm, F-Sa 8am-8pm).
Two kibbutzim, **Merom Golan** and **Ein Zivan,** wait much farther south on Rte. 98,
near its intersection with Rte. 91 (about 5km before the border with Syria). These
were the first Israeli settlements in the Golan, founded a few months after the 1967
War. There is an observation point at Mt. Bental, marked by a brown sign that
points to an uphill road on the right just before Kibbutz Merom Golan.

◤ HIKING: THE GOLAN HEIGHTS

Those who wish to hike in the Golan should purchase the 1:50,000 trail map available at SPNI offices and in Steimatzky's (NIS62). SPNI offices also have useful
booklets with descriptions and directions for hiking routes in the area, such as the

Israeli Landscapes Vol. 1: Guide to the Golan Heights (NIS55). Consult SPNI field schools for up-to-date advice and information; the field school at Hermon (tel. 694 10 91; see p. 348) and the information desk at Yehudiyya Reserve (tel. 696 28 17) are the best places to go. Beware of **land mines** (see p. 346). Bus service to the trails, where it exists, is very irregular; call Egged and plan carefully. Be aware that many trails do not loop back to where they started and may leave you far away from your car. It is not safe to drink water from Golan streams.

■**YA'AR YEHUDIYYA NATURE RESERVE.** The most exciting and challenging hiking in the Golan is in the Ya'ar Yehudiyya Nature Reserve, southeast of Katzrin. The highlight of the reserve, and one of the best hikes in Israel, is the action-packed **Naḥal Yehudiyya** trail, which consists of an upper and a lower section. The beginning of both of these trails is in the Ḥenion Yehudiyya parking lot. Follow the red-and-white markers across the street, past the 1800-year-old Jewish and Byzantine town ruins, and into the valley. The green **lower trail,** which soon branches off and heads down to the right from the red trail, takes about four hours to complete. The shorter **upper trail** (3hr.) continues to the left and remains marked in red. Upon completion of the upper trail, ascend the green-and-white trail to return to the Ḥenion. Both trails feature enticing waterfalls and pools, some of which you must swim across to complete your hike (bring a bathing suit and plastic bags to protect food and valuables, as everything will get soaked). Jumping off the 9m cliff at the second waterfall is possibly dangerous, definitely forbidden, but nevertheless undertaken by many trekkers. Make sure you know where you're jumping—people have died in this spot. A fair number of hikers opt to climb down the slippery ladder into the water to enjoy the swim.

The reserve also harbors the slightly drier but equally beautiful **Naḥal Zavitan;** most of its trail options also start at Ḥenion Yehudiyya parking lot. Start on the green-and-white marked Lower Zavitan trail. A left turn on the red-and-white trail leads to the **Ein Netef** spring, which purportedly contains the only drinkable water in the reserve. This trek eventually crosses the red-and-white one and returns to Ḥenion Yehudiyya (3hr.). Alternatively, turn left and continue on the red-and-white trail for 45 minutes to reach the spectacular **Brekhat Ha-Meshushim** (Hexagon Pool), where hundreds of hexagonal rock columns skirt the water's edge in a wonderful geological phenomenon. The **Upper Zavitan** (black-and-white trail) tends to be good in all seasons. It begins near the field school in Katzrin and leads to less impressive hexagonal pools. The more difficult **Lower Zavitan** should be avoided in the winter due to occasional flash floods. The **Black Canyon** is near the Lower Zavitan trail, and can only be negotiated by rapelling. *(By car from Tiberias, drive north along the lake, head east toward Katzrin, pass the Yehudiyya Junction, and continue along Rte. 87 until reaching the orange sign. By car from Kiryat Shmona, head toward Katzrin and the junction with Rte. 87, take a right, and look for the sign and parking lot on the right. Open Sa-Th 7am-5pm, F and holidays 7am-4pm; leave no later than 1hr. after closing time. Admission NIS8, students NIS7, under 18 NIS6, overnight NIS10. Most trails begin in Ḥenion Yehudiyya (tel. 696 28 17), a parking lot with an SPNI information booth, snack stand (sandwiches NIS12-17), toilets, phones, and camping facilities accesible by bus from Katzrin. At the Ḥenion, bags can be stored for NIS12 per locker. Camping costs NIS18 per person. Before beginning a hike, check in with SPNI desk.)*

NAḤAL EL-AL. This beautiful hike (no relation to Israel's major airline) lies southeast of the Zavitan and Yehudiyya Rivers. In winter and spring, enough water flows through to allow swimming beneath the falls. The red-and-white trail begins at the northeast end of the kibbutz. Follow the markers to **Mapal Ha-Lavan** (White Waterfall) and continue on to **Mapal Ha-Shaḥor** (Black Waterfall). The trail ends at Kibbutz Avnei-Eitan. From there, take a right on Rte. 98 and walk 2km to return to Kibbutz El-Al. *(By car from Tiberias, head south on Rte. 90. At Zemaḥ Junction, turn onto Rte. 98 and follow it to Kibbutz El-Al. Without a car, this hike is impossible to do in a day; the first bus arrives at 12:30pm and the last one leaves at 1pm.)*

NAḤAL DEVORAH AND NAḤAL GILABON. From the main parking lot, red-and-white markers lead to the left around a building and down into the canyon. Join the hundreds who have left their mark by sticking a chewed-up glob of gum onto the **Even Ha-Mastik** (Gum Rock). The first waterfall on the trail is the Devorah Waterfall. Continuing for another hour on the red-and-white path leads to the 21m Gilabon Waterfall; wonderful views of the lush Ḥula Valley await at its top. *(From Tiberias, take Rte. 90 north until the turn-off for Rte. 91 east. Continue 30min. on Rte. 91. Watch for a brown sign 3-4km after the turn-off for Road 9088. Turn onto the dirt road and make a right farther up to reach a parking lot surrounded by destroyed Syrian bunkers and trees.)*

NAḤAL ZAKI. Naḥal Zaki makes for a viewless but extremely refreshing hike. In August or September, ripe grapes hang overhead and the sweltering heat makes the cool stream a godsend. Wear a bathing suit and bring plastic bags to protect valuables—half the hike is spent wading in knee-deep water. In winter, the current is strong and this trail can be dangerous. Hike in the stream following the green-and-white trail for 3km; at the pipe that stretches across the river, get out of the water on the left side and return by way of a dirt path. *(Off Rte. 92 just south of the Yehudiyya Junction. Drive along the green trail to a lot, then park and begin the hike.)*

DEAD SEA ים המלח البحر الميت

How low can you go? At 412m below sea level, this is it: the Dead Sea is the lowest point on Earth. If that factoid doesn't sound impressive, wait until you're driving on the highway, pass a SEA LEVEL signpost, and then round a bend to see entire mountains whose *peaks* lie below you. The Dead Sea is actually a large lake—65km long and 18km wide. Its coasts are shared by Israel and Jordan (for coverage of sights on the Dead Sea's **Jordanian** shore, see p. 437), with the peaceful border drawn smack down the sea's middle. With no outlet for the lake's water, the intense sun evaporates it faster than you can say "Ra." Inadequate rainfall, coupled with Israeli, Jordanian, and Syrian reliance on the sea's freshwater sources for drinking and irrigation, has begun to take its toll. The sun now evaporates more water than flows in; the sea is shrinking so severely that the southern tip has been cut off by a sand bar and the northern part now recedes at the frightening rate of 80cm a year. Emergency measures to save the Dead Sea, driven by both ecological and economic incentives, are in the planning stages.

The morbid "dead" moniker was coined by Christian monks astonished by the apparent absence of any form of life in the sea's waters, but kill-joy scientists have recently discovered 11 types of hardy bacteria in the water. Its Hebrew name, Yam Ha-Melaḥ (The Sea of Salt), is more to the point: the water has a salt concentration eight times that of ocean water, making the water so heavy and dense that even fish would have to walk. This comes as good news to those who can't swim: everyone floats in this sea without so much as flinching a muscle. Besides the much-acclaimed floating effect, this high concentration of minerals is responsible for the gorgeous salt formations that adorn seaside rocks, postcards, and tourists.

HIGHLIGHTS OF THE DEAD SEA

■ Head to **Siesta Beach** (p. 351) to dodge the tourist crowds, roll around in the black mud, and get a Thai massage after floating too hard.
■ See what happens to extremists: visit the ancient ruins of **Qumran** (p. 351), where the 2000-year-old Dead Sea Scrolls were found.

🛈 PRACTICAL INFORMATION

The Dead Sea coast is 65km long, and for easy reference may be divided into **northern, central,** and **southern** regions. This section is organized from north to south. If the sea is on your left, you're going south; if it's on your right, you're going north. The few Egged lines that travel along the Dead Sea coast have erratic schedules with waits often lasting 45 to 90 minutes, so check times and plan ahead. Buses #421, 444, and 486 from Jerusalem to Eilat stop at Qumran, Ein Feshkha, Ein Gedi, and Masada. Bus #487, also from Jerusalem, runs only to Qumran, Ein Feshkha, and Ein Gedi. Buses #384 and 385 combined make about four trips per day (Su-F) between Be'er Sheva and Ein Gedi via Arad, Ein Bokek, and Masada. Buses will stop at many stations only upon request, so **confirm destinations** with the driver. Several sites listed, including Metzokei Dragot and Neot Ha-Kikar, are **not accessible by public transportation**.

The Dead Sea region is hot and humid. Keep your head covered, and drink 1 liter of **water** per hour. Bring a large bottle with you and keep refilling at faucets to avoid getting ripped off by the NIS8-a-pop street vendors once you're there. The **tourist information** hub for the entire region is in the central Dead Sea, near Ein Gedi (see below). Check in with Becky Siag for information on local sights and events (tel. 658 44 44; fax 658 43 67; email eg@kibbutz.co.il; www.ein-gedi.co.il). There are **no money changing offices or ATMs** anywhere in the Dead Sea region, so come prepared. The nearest facilities are in Arad and Be'er Sheva.

TELEPHONE CODE	Northern Dead Sea: **02**. Central and Southern Dead Sea: **07**.

NORTHERN DEAD SEA

KALYA BEACHES

Take bus #480 or 487 from Jerusalem, bus #421 or 966 from Ein Bokek (originating from Tel Aviv and Haifa, respectively). Confirm your destination with the bus driver.

This northern Dead Sea area is only 25 minutes from Jerusalem (along Rte. 90), and its shores are the least heavily touristed. **Neve Midbar** (tel. 994 27 81) is the only free beach in the area, with abundant black mud, seaside showers, and changing rooms. An outdoor restaurant features no-frills drinks and sandwiches (open daily 8:30am-6:30pm). Drive two more minutes south for a fancier experience at ◪**Siesta Beach** (tel. 994 41 11), which offers Thai massages to calm your sunburned bod (NIS85 for a half hour). Showers and changing facilities here are similar to the beach up the road but cost NIS14. One nice perk is a self-proclaimed "authentic" Jordanian/Palestinian restaurant (falafel plate and salad NIS25). Siesta Beach is open daily 9am-6pm. An aktraktive alternative for those who like whooshing and sliding with their sunbathing is **Atraktzia Water Park and Beach** (tel. 994 23 91), another two minutes down the road. This amusement park is a magnet for Israeli children on vacation and features go-carts for an additional charge. The restaurant will stuff any order in a pita (hamburger NIS18). There are also free barbecue grills and picnic areas on the premises. Splash all day for NIS64 or after 2pm for NIS39; both include use of the private beach. (Open daily Apr.-Oct. 9am-5pm.) In the winter months, while the slides rest, the beach remains accessible for NIS15.

QUMRAN קומרן قمران

Buses #421, 444, 486, and 487 will stop at the Essene Compound from either Ein Gedi (NIS20.50) or Jerusalem (NIS19.30) upon request. A marker outside the bus stop points toward Qumran, up the steep road on the right. Although the peak is nowhere in sight, the winding road is actually only a 100m hike.

About 7km south of Kalya lie the ruins of Qumran, where the ◪**Dead Sea Scrolls** were found in 1947 by a young Bedouin looking for a wayward sheep. He threw a rock into a cliffside cave and heard something break; upon further inspection, he discovered a collection of earthenware jars containing 2000-year-old parchment manuscripts. These famed scrolls are an important source for the current understanding of the development of the Bible. The largest, now displayed in the Shrine of the Book at the Israel Museum in Jerusalem (p. 284), is a 7m ancient Hebrew text from the Book of Isaiah. Encouraged by the discovery, French archaeologists searched the caves and excavated the foot of the cliffs. By 1956, they had unearthed an entire village belonging to the sect that wrote the Scrolls.

ISRAEL

Archaeological evidence suggests that the site was settled as long ago as the 8th century BCE, re-inhabited in the 2nd century BCE, temporarily abandoned following an earthquake during the reign of Herod, and completely deserted after the Roman defeat of the Jewish revolt in 70 CE. Historians conclude that the authors of the scrolls were the **Essenes,** a Jewish sect whose members, disillusioned by the corruption and Hellenization of fellow Jerusalemites, sought refuge in the sands. The strict and devout Essenes believed that a great struggle would ensue between the Sons of Light (themselves and the angels) and the Sons of Darkness (everyone else). Excavations at Masada (see p. 353) suggest that the members of the Qumran sect joined with the Zealots there in the struggle against the Romans.

METZOKEI DRAGOT (WADI DARJA) מצוקי דרגות

About 20km south of Qumran and Ein Feshkha, a steep, winding road branches off on the right. Buses will go no farther than the turn-off; the only ways to reach the reserve and the hostel are by car or by a 5km vertical hike.

The soaring cliffs of this **nature reserve** are for serious hikers only. The ascent culminates in a rewarding view of more soaring cliffs and ravines. Heed the warnings on the green welcome-board—be sure to carry a trail map and a 10m security rope. You may not begin hiking the *wadi* after 9am, so it is a good idea to stay at the hostel the night before and get cracking at the crack of dawn. Owned and managed by the Mitzpeh Shalem Kibbutz a few kilometers away, the **youth hostel** (tel. 994 47 77) lies up the road's ascent. A great alternative to often-booked Ein Gedi accommodations, it features 28 air-conditioned doubles, each with a pull-out couch. (NIS153/US$32 per person including breakfast. Dinner NIS41/US$10.)

CENTRAL DEAD SEA

EIN GEDI עין גדי

Buses from Ein Gedi go to: **Jerusalem** *(#421, 486, and 487; 1¼hr.; 7 per day 5:45am-6pm; NIS30);* **Be'er Sheva** *(#384 and 385; 5 per day; NIS33, students NIS30) via* **Masada** *(20min.; NIS13),* **Ein Bokek** *(30min.; NIS17.50), and* **Arad** *(1½hr.; NIS23);* **Ein Bokek** *(#486; 4 per day; NIS18) via* **Masada** *(NIS13); and* **Eilat** *(#444; 5 per day; NIS48).* **Open** *daily 8am-4pm, but some hikes may not be started after 1:30pm.* **Admission** *NIS18.*

After a hot morning hike or a muggy bus ride, the only thing better than drinking cold water is sitting in it. The cascading waterfalls of the Ein Gedi oasis thrive just a few minutes' hike from the lifeless shores of the Dead Sea. Rare desert wildlife have set up house in this verdant nature reserve, including species of ibex, fox, and hyrax, as well as rare breeds of flowers. Tired hikers relax in the afternoons at the free beach. The Ein Gedi oasis, the epicenter of the Dead Sea region, has a long history of providing shelter. David fled to this oasis to escape the wrath of King Saul (1 Samuel 24), and it was here that he forsook the choice opportunity to slay his pursuing father-in-law, who would have been easy prey while relieving himself in a cave. In *Song of Songs* (1:13) the lover declares that her beloved is "a cluster of henna in the vineyards of Ein Gedi." During the second Jewish revolt (132-135 CE), rebel leader Simon Bar Kokhba also sought refuge here.

Ein Gedi's 6750 acre nature reserve is the heart of the desert attractions. Around it, a kibbutz, accommodations, a public bathing area, and a luxury spa have all been built. The yellow-roofed **tourist information** booth (tel. 658 44 44; www.ein-gedi.co.il), at the beach bus stop, covers the entire Dead Sea region (open daily 9am-4pm). The sweltering Dead Sea weather hardly abates at night, so air-conditioning is a must here. The **Ein Gedi Field School** (tel. 658 43 50; fax 658 42 57) is a 10-minute climb up the adjacent road from the more accessible youth hostel, but is a less touristed, more scenic spot. Run by the SPNI, the field school has a public kitchen and TV room. This peak is the only place on Earth to get a glimpse of a rare species of bird called *Leilit Hamidbar,* or Hume's Tawny Owl. (Dorms NIS65. Breakfast included. Call ahead. Credit cards accepted.) **Beit Sara**

Youth Hostel (HI) (tel. 658 41 65; fax 658 44 44), uphill from the Naḥal David entrance to the reserve, offers clean rooms with private baths. (Dorms NIS79; doubles NIS213/US$52; NIS74 each additional person. Breakfast included. Call ahead. Credit cards accepted.)

The **nature reserve** features incredible (and challenging) hikes—check in with SPNI for tailored recommendations. Some sections of the Ein Gedi trails are steep, but well-placed railings and steps have been built into the rock. Once noon rolls around, high temperatures can make even inhaling strenuous, so get going by 8am. Always bring at least one liter of water per hour of hiking (there are faucets just outside the gate), and don't forget your swimsuit for dipping into the occasional freshwater pools. The names of the different pools and springs repeat frequently and are almost interchangeable (David this, Ein Gedi that), so pay attention.

For good ol' Dead Sea floating and mud, Ein Gedi has its own somewhat crowded **beach**. Use of the beach and umbrellas is free, but bathrooms and lockers cost NIS5. Oddly enough, the entrance to the bathing area may be hard to find: with your face to the gas station and yellow tourist information booth, look to your left past the parking lot for the orange awnings.

MASADA מצדה

*20km south of Ein Gedi. Buses go to: **Jerusalem** (#421, 444, and 486; 8 per day; NIS35.50, students NIS32.50); **Eilat** (#444; 5 per day; NIS48, students NIS43.20); and **Be'er Sheva** (#384 and 385; 5 per day; NIS33.50, students NIS30.20) via **Arad** (NIS21.50, students NIS19). Jerusalem-bound buses stop at **Ein Gedi,** and buses to Be'er Sheva and Eilat stop at **Ein Bokek** (NIS10.90). General information tel. 658 42 07. There are 3 ways to ascend the mountain: by either of two foot paths or by cable car. The more popular, scenic, and difficult of the 2 hikes is the original Snake Path (45min.), named for its tortuous bends. The handicapped-accessible **cable car** stops at the top of the Snake Path. Departs every 30min. or when 40 passengers have assembled for the 3min. ascent. Runs Apr.-Sept. Su-Th 8am-5pm, F 8am-3pm; Oct.-Mar Su-Th 8am-3pm, F 8am-2pm. Masada's gates are **open** daily 4:30am-5pm. **Admission** for hikers NIS18, students NIS15. Admission with cable car round-trip NIS50, students NIS42; one-way NIS37, students NIS34. A detailed tour is available on head-phones for NIS10 between 8am-3pm.*

"Masada shall not fall again," swear members of the armored division of the **Israel Defense Forces** each year at this site. Jewish Zealots' tenacious defense of Masada in the first century CE has been fashioned into a heroic symbol of the defense of modern Israel. In Israel, Masada is not merely a place, it's an attitude. Political significance aside, legions of tourists from around the world continue to storm this mountain fortress to catch the spectacular view of the Dead Sea, visit the extensive ruins, and envision the dramatic martyrdom of Masada's rebels.

The first fortress *(metzuda)* on the mountain was built as a refuge from marauding Greeks and Syrians by Jewish High Priest Jonathan Maccabeus around 150 BCE. It was chiefly under **Herod,** however, that Masada became an enormous mountaintop citadel. At the outset of the Jewish rebellion against Rome in 66 CE, a small band of **Zealot** rebels, members of a small Jewish sect, captured the prize fortress from its unsuspecting garrison. As the Romans gradually crushed the revolt, Masada became a refuge for surviving Zealots and the last Jewish holdout in all of Israel. With years' worth of food, water, and military supplies, the 967 men, women, and children held off 15,000 Roman legionnaires through a five-month siege. Capitalizing on their superior force, the Romans built an enormous ramp up the side of the cliff, using Jewish slaves as laborers to prevent the Zealots from shooting them as the ramp was built. When the defenders realized that the Romans would break through their walls the next morning, the community leaders decided that it would be better to die than be captured. Because Jewish law forbids suicide, 10 men were chosen to slay the others, and one chosen to kill the other nine before falling on his own sword. Before burning the fortress and all their possessions, the Jews placed stores of wheat and water in the citadel's courtyard to show the Romans that they did not perish from hunger. The following morning, when the triumphant Romans burst in, they encountered only smoking ruins and a deathly silence. The only sur-

ISRAEL

vivors, two women and five children, told the story of the last days to **Josephus Flavius** (see **What's All the 'Phus About?**, p. 331). Although strong corroborating evidence for Josephus' story has been found at the site, archaeologists have yet to unearth the Zealots' actual remains, except for several old women's skeletons.

The ruins at Masada were unearthed from 1963 to 1964; thousands of international volunteers uncovered in 11 months what would normally have taken 26 years to excavate. About a third of the ruins are actually reconstructed—a black line indicates the extent of the original findings. In the last two years, Masada has undergone a tremendous face-lift, with the replacement of the previously unreliable cable car and the addition of handicapped accessibility and shaded rest areas at the top of the mountain. In archaeological news, the re-excavation of the Northern Palace by a group of expert Italian archaeologists has unearthed new mosaic floors and other exciting finds. Directly in front of the entrance to the site stands a map outlining several walking tours of the ruins, ranging from one to four hours. The following suggested route covers the highlights of Masada. The numbers after the sites correspond to the numbers labeled on the map on p. 355.

Northern Palace (1-3). From the entrance, Herod's private pad is up and to the right. The 3 levels of this palace are on 3 terraces of the mountain, some 30m apart. The frescoes and fluted columns, still intact on the lower terrace, attest to the splendor Herod enjoyed even on a remote desert butte.

Zealots' Synagogue (6). Following the western edge of the mountain leads to the Zealots' Synagogue, one of the oldest synagogues in the world. Scrolls were found here containing texts from several books of the Torah.

Casemate of the Scrolls (7). A number of important archaeological relics were found within the casemate, including scrolls, papyrus, silver shekels, a *tallit* (prayer shawl), a wooden shield, arrows, sandals, keys, baskets, and other items.

Water Cisterns Path (8). The huge cisterns can still be seen dotting the mountaintop; they are lined with a near-perfect water-repellent plaster that even today won't absorb a single drop. Rainfall used to drain from the surrounding mountains into Masada's reservoirs, filling the entire cistern within a few hours on the 1 annual day of rain.

Byzantine church (14). This church was built by Christian monks who re-inhabited Masada in the 5th and 6th centuries and used the cisterns as cave dwellings for over a 100 years. The church's hall faces east, toward Jerusalem.

Western Palace (15). Farther along the edge stands the site of Herod's throne room and offices of state. A system of water cisterns underlies the western wing; the northern wing surrounds a large central courtyard; the southern wing was the royal wing, and includes a waiting room, courtyard, dining hall, kitchen, and throne room.

Beit Midrash (18). The long hall on the north end of this Herodian building, which seems to have been a late addition, is lined with benches, suggesting that it served as a *beit midrash* (study hall). The building was apparently never completed.

Water Cistern (22). This cistern is good indication of the extent of Herod's water supply system. The water was channeled through a window in the south. Twelve more such cisterns line the western slope.

Southern Wall (23). Along the southern wall lie a tower with a Zealot installation (the building might have been a bakery), a ritual bath, a dressing room (the narrow niches held clothes), and a courtyard. The path is no longer in use.

Eastern Wall (29). The outer and inner walls are joined by partitions, forming casemates. The higher and thicker sections of the inner wall are the sole remains of a series of towers that once lined the wall. A channel under the floor of the Zealot additions is older than the wall itself.

Quarry (33). This supplied much of the stone for Masada's construction projects.

Snake Path Lookout (35). View of the Snake Path, the earthen wall, the Roman camps, the Dead Sea, and the Mountains of Moab.

Storerooms (36). Food, weapons, and other supplies were stored within these rooms. Rows of identical jars were found in some of the sections, and several are on display in storeroom 138.

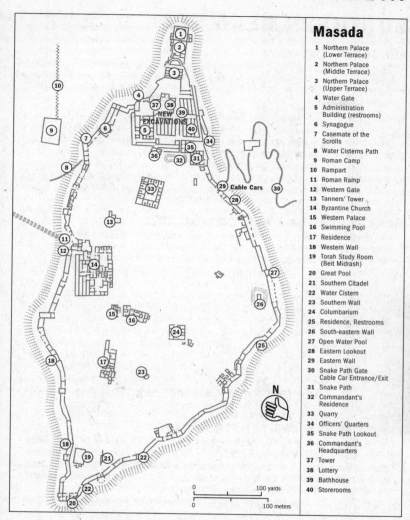

Masada

1 Northern Palace (Lower Terrace)
2 Northern Palace (Middle Terrace)
3 Northern Palace (Upper Terrace)
4 Water Gate
5 Administration Building (restrooms)
6 Synagogue
7 Casemate of the Scrolls
8 Water Cisterns Path
9 Roman Camp
10 Rampart
11 Roman Ramp
12 Western Gate
13 Tanners' Tower
14 Byzantine Church
15 Western Palace
16 Swimming Pool
17 Residence
18 Western Wall
19 Torah Study Room (Beit Midrash)
20 Great Pool
21 Southern Citadel
22 Water Cistern
23 Southern Wall
24 Columbarium
25 Residence, Restrooms
26 South-eastern Wall
27 Open Water Pool
28 Eastern Lookout
29 Eastern Wall
30 Snake Path Gate Cable Car Entrance/Exit
31 Snake Path
32 Commandant's Residence
33 Quarry
34 Officers' Quarters
35 Snake Path Lookout
36 Commandant's Headquarters
37 Tower
38 Lottery
39 Bathhouse
40 Storerooms

ISRAEL

Lottery (38). The Zealots built a ritual bath in this Herodian building. The small pool to the west was used for washing prior to immersion. Eleven *ostraca* were found to the northeast of the square, inscribed with the name "Beniair" (Ben-Yair, Zealot commander of Masada) and with nicknames. Some speculate that these are the famous "lots."

Bathhouse (39). The bathhouse, built by Herod, follows Roman standards. The *apodyterium* (dressing room) had frescoes on the walls and ceilings, along with a tiled floor. The baths are divided among the *tepidarium* (luke-warm room), *frigidarium* (cold room), and *caldarium* (hot room), which is heated by a stove.

The **Masada Sound and Light Show** (tel. 995 93 33 or 995 89 93; fax 995 50 52) illuminates the fortress like a Las Vegas marquee. Transportation can be arranged with the show organizers (round-trip transportation, including ticket, NIS85). The show is not visible from the Masada hostel, which is on the wrong side of the mountain. For more information, see **Arad**, p. 364.

SOUTHERN DEAD SEA

EIN BOKEK עין בוקק

*30min. east of Arad and 10min. south of Masada. Buses on the Masada/Dead Sea route pass through Ein Bokek and stop at each hotel along the strip. For the public beach, get off at Ḥof Ein Bokek. Tamar Taxi (tel. 658 43 93; open daily 7:30am-9pm) goes to **Masada** (NIS45) and **Ein Gedi** (NIS75).*

About 15km south of Masada, Ein Bokek is the gaudy cubic zirconia in the tiara of Dead Sea beaches, an aquamarine sand spectacle hemmed in by hordes of luxury hotels, international tour-groups, and racks upon racks of postcards. For all the glitzy tourist-wooing of this most crowded of Dead Sea beaches, it is still a good spot for some old-fashioned fun: floating and coating. Use of the beach and outdoor showers is free (open 8am-4pm). Renting an all-day lounge chair costs NIS10; a romp in the mineral mud is NIS7. For a special Dead Sea challenge, try lifting *both* your legs 15cm out of the briny waters at the same time.

MOSHAV NEOT HA-KIKAR מושב נאות הככר

Take Rte. 90 toward Sodom until the Arava junction, passing the Dead Sea Works plant on the left and the southern edge of the sea. The Eilat-bound bus from Jerusalem or Tel Aviv will stop at the junction upon request. Make a left and follow the road for about 10km.

Moshav Neot Ha-Kikar is the extreme opposite of Ein Bokek—a desert of serenity and desolation. The ominous "Dead Sea Fish" signs along the way refer to high-tech experimental pools managed by the *moshav*, which specializes in state-of-the art desert agriculture technology. Taking the road to the end of the *moshav* leads to ▣Fata Morgana (tel. 655 79 92, cell. 050 691 585, ask for Koreen), an amazing oasis featuring Bedouin-style guest-tents and a restaurant. Fata Morgana arranges hiking tours of the region (including the famous Sodom flour caves), jeep tours, and meets individual requests whenever possible. Pick your own cherry-tomatoes and sleep cheaply in the large, clean, comfortable tents. (NIS40 per person, with your own tent NIS30. Ask for a *Let's Go* discount. Cold beer NIS9; hot fish meals NIS50-80. Free use of spotless bathrooms and showers, fridge, and BBQ grills. **Shiatsu** massages and lessons in a special shrine tent every Friday.)

MOUNT SODOM AND THE FLOUR CAVE

The site can be reached only by car. Drive southeast from Be'er Sheva on Rte. 25 (toward Dimona), then head north (toward Jerusalem and Tel Aviv) on Rte. 90, which runs along the Dead Sea coast. Continue east on Rte. 90, past the industrial-looking complex of the Dead Sea Works, after which there is a small orange sign on the left pointing to the Flour Cave and Sodom Mountain. Tours from Moshav Neot Ha-Kikar also visit the site.

The white salt mountain Har Sodom is the site of the biblical Sodom and Gomorrah, the two cities so wicked and sexually promiscuous that God resolved to strike them down. God decided to save Abraham's nephew Lot and his family, with the condition that they not look back at the carnage on the way out; Lot's disobedient wife took a peek and turned into a pillar of salt (Genesis 19:26). In keeping with the baking-ingredients theme of the area, the **Flour Cave** sits tucked out of direct view from Mt. Sodom, at the end of a trail of high walls of light-colored sediment left by a lake that was the precursor to the Dead Sea. There are hikes from the lookout point on the mountain and through the cave itself. Within the site, the unpaved road forks; go left and continue on the red-marked path that eventually leads to a parking lot near the cave. It is a 10-minute walk through the white-walled trail to the cave itself, where the cool, heavy air provides a much-needed escape from the dead-on rays of the sun. To reach Sodom Mountain, take a right onto the blue road from the first fork and another right onto the black road. From here, hike the steep and winding "Stairway Trail" downwards, starting at the blue-marked steps to the left.

NEGEV DESERT הנגב

The Negev Desert covers roughly half of Israel's territory. Long considered a barren wasteland of Bedouin tents and dusty archaeologists, the Negev is entering mainstream Israeli life anew as building projects absorb waves of immigrants and high-tech agriculture fulfills the biblical prophecy of making the desert bloom. Visionaries like David Ben-Gurion cherished the Negev's rugged beauty and dreamed of its unrealized potential; today, hikers, meditators, and adventurous travelers are also discovering this charm, while drip-irrigated citrus groves, flower farms, and instant boomtowns are coaxing its resources into fruition. The grand Nabatean ruins glowing on the hilltops along the ancient Spice Route are today seen less as relics than as inspiration.

HIGHLIGHTS OF THE NEGEV

■ Whether explored on foot or hooves, the pastel deserts of **Mitzpeh Ramon** (p. 367) and **S'deh Boker** (p. 364) are the country's most pristine refuges.

■ The Hebrew Israelite community in **Dimona** (p. 363) brings a taste of Chicago to the Negev's dunes—and it's vegan.

BE'ER SHEVA באר שבע

Hospitable Be'er Sheva has a long-standing tradition as a point of replenishment for people traversing the Negev. In recent years, however, increasing numbers of immigrants have decided to settle down rather than just pass through. "Be'er Sheva" can be read as either "well of seven" or "well of the oath" in Hebrew; Genesis 21:25-31 supports both etymologies. As the story goes, the servants of King Abimelekh seized a well that Abraham claimed to have dug. The dispute ended with a peace oath between the warring parties, in which Abraham offered seven ewes to Abimelekh in exchange for recognition as the well's rightful owner. The supposed site of Abraham's well now houses the city's main tourist office.

Today, Be'er Sheva's pre-fab apartments are as unavoidable and constricting as the spandex in an Eilat discotheque. Despite the din of constant traffic and the overpowering presence of a glassed-in monster mall in the center of town, Be'er Sheva still has a few pockets of romance left, including the old city and the famous Thursday morning Bedouin market. The museums in the surrounding area and Be'er Sheva's hopping nightlife make it both a convenient base for short forays into the Negev and a place worth checking out in and of itself.

⚡ ORIENTATION

The city's **central bus station** is located on **Eilat Street,** across the road from **Kenyon Ha-Negev** (Negev shopping mall; ask for the *"kenyon"*), whose curved glass facade faces the three-way intersection of Tuviyahu Blvd., Eilat St., and **Yitzḥak Rager Boulevard.** The old **Muslim Cemetery**, a few crumbling vaults sitting in a wasteland of fenced-in sand, is across Eilat St. behind the central bus station. Just on the other side of that lies the **old city**, a neat grid designed by Ottoman-commissioned German engineers. This pedestrian haven holds most of the city's attractions. The main east-west streets between the old city and the bus station start with the northernmost **Herzl Street.** Parallel to it are Ha-Histadrut St., followed by Ha-Ḥalutz St., Mordei Ha-Geta'ot St., and Trumpeldor St. farther south. The main north-south avenues begin with **Keren Kayemet L'Yisrael Street** (**Kakal** or **KKL** for short), the town's newly fountained pedestrian section with several budget-oriented hotels. One block east is **Ha-Atzma'ut Street** (which fronts the Turkish mosque and sculpture garden), and then Hadassah St. To reach the old city from the bus station, walk around the outside of the *kenyon* to Eli Cohen Sq., cross Eilat St., and take Herzl St. or Ha-Ḥalutz St.

🛈 PRACTICAL INFORMATION

Intercity Buses: Egged (tel. 629 43 11) send buses to: **Tel Aviv** (#370, 369, or 353; 1½hr.; every 20min. 5:30am-9pm; NIS19.30); **Jerusalem** (#470 direct and #446; 2hr.; every 40min. 6am-8pm; NIS3, students NIS28); **Dimona** (#48, 56, or 375; 45min. every 20min. 6:30am-11pm NIS13); and **Eilat** (#394; 3½hr.; every 1½hr. 9:20am-4:50pm; NIS50, students NIS45). Buses #392, 393, 395, 397, and 991 also go to Eilat, but their schedules are irregular.

Local Buses: Central bus station (tel. 627 73 81), on Eilat St., next to the *kenyon*. Buses #2, 3, 7, 8, 9, 11, 12, 18, 21, and 22 go to the *shuk* and the old city (5:20am-11pm). Bus #13 follows Ha-Atzma'ut St. to the Negev Museum and Beit Yatziv Youth Hostel (every 20min. 5:20am-11pm). Buses #7 and 8 go north on Yitzhak Rager Blvd. and pass the hospital and Ben-Gurion University. All local rides NIS2.90.

Taxis: Moniyot Gan Zvi (tel. 623 93 32/33), next to the bus station, or **Moniyot Ha-Halutz** (tel. 627 33 33 or 623 37 19), across from Bank Ha-Poalim and just before KKL St. in the old city. **Moniot Ayal** (tel. 623 30 33 or 623 53 33), in the kiosk with the blue awning next to the central bus station, has **sherut taxis** that are slightly cheaper than buses to Jerusalem (NIS30), Eilat (NIS45), and Tel Aviv (NIS20).

Car Rental: Avis, 8 Henrietta Szold (tel. 671 77 77), just before the Hilton Hotel. Bus #5 passes by. Cars start at NIS195/US$42 per day. Add NIS80/US$18 per day for automatic transmission. Min. age 23. Open Su-Th 8am-6pm, F 8am-2pm.

Tourist Office: 1 Derekh Hevron (tel. 623 46 13), at Abraham's Well. Helpful staff with an excellent English map of Be'er Sheva including all major sights, as well as a brochure with suggestions for activities (NIS5). Open Su-Th 8:30am-4pm, F 8:30am-1pm.

Currency Exchange: Bank Ha-Poalim, 40 Ha-Atzma'ut St. (tel. 629 26 62), corner of Ha-Halutz St. Open Su and Tu-W 8:30am-1:15pm, M and Th 8:30am-1pm and 4-6:30pm, F 8:15am-12:30pm. Min. charge US$6 per transaction. For emergency banking, call tel. (03) 567 49 99. **Bank Leumi** (tel. 623 92 22), past the post office on Ha-Nesi'im Blvd. Open Su, Tu-W 8:30am-1pm, M and Th 8:30am-1pm and 4:30-7pm, F 8:30am-noon. **ATM** accepts Visa. The post office also has excellent rates without commission.

English Bookstores: Mini Book (tel. 643 33 96), in the passageway between Hadassah St. and Ha-Histadrut St. Extensive selection of used books. Open Su-M 8:30am-1pm, W-Th 4-7pm, Tu and F 8:30am-1:30pm. **Memsi** (tel. 627 06 95), in the bus station, sells all sorts of maps in English. Open Su-Th 8:30am-6:30pm, F 8:30am-noon.

Supermarkets: Hypershuk hyperinhabits the supermall. **Super-South Grocery** (tel. 623 53 90), on KKL in the old city, also has the basics. Open Su-Th 7am-8pm, F 7am-3pm.

Camping Supplies: Reta (tel. 623 35 77), in the *kenyon* right across from Steimatzky's on the ground floor. Open Su-Th 9am-9pm, F 9am-3pm, Sa 8-11pm.

Pharmacies: Pharmline, 34 Herzl St. (tel. 628 06 55), diagonally across from the police station. Open Su-Th 8am-2pm and 4-8pm, F 8am-2pm. **SuperPharm** (tel. 628 13 71), in the *kenyon*. Open Su-Th 9am-midnight, F 8:30am-5pm, Sa 10am-midnight. Phone numbers of emergency night workers posted on door.

Hospital: Soroka Medical Center, Yitzhak Rager Blvd. (tel. 640 01 11), on the right side with a blue-and-green sign in Hebrew. Take bus #7 or 8 (5:20am-11pm).

Emergency: Police: 30 Herzl St. (tel. 100 or 646 27 44), at KKL St. **Fire:** Tel. 102 or 627 96 91. **First Aid: Magen David Adom,** 40 Bialik St. (tel. 101 or 627 83 33).

Post Office: (tel. 629 58 32), at the corner of Yitzhak Rager Blvd. and Ben-Tzvi St., across from the mall back entrance. **Poste Restante, Western Union,** and **EMS** services, **international calling** and **fax,** phonecards, and commission-free traveler's check **exchange.** Smaller branches on Hadassa St. and in the City Hall building. All branches open Su-Tu and Th 8am-12:30pm and 4-6:30pm, W 8am-1pm, F 8am-12:30pm.

Telephone Code: 07.

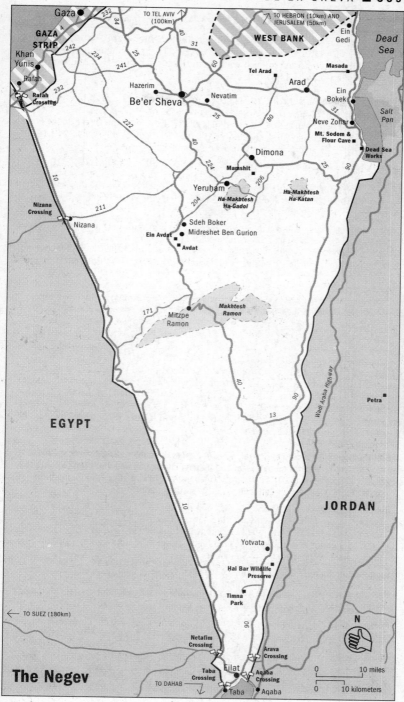

The Negev

ACCOMMODATIONS

Be'er Sheva has several budget options, including one youth hostel and a few hotels that fall within a reasonable price range. The following accommodations are all within a five- to ten-minute walk from the point where Herzl St. forms a T with the pedestrian KKL in the old city.

Beit Yatziv Youth Hostel (HI), 79 Ha-Atzma'ut St. (tel. 627 74 44), 3 blocks up from Herzl St. in the old city. This well-kept, no-bunk hostel has its own pool (NIS28). Clean rooms have bath, closet, A/C. 4-bed dorms NIS87. Next door, the **Guest House** is run from the same reception desk. Singles NIS160/US$39; doubles US$59/NIS240; triples US$68/NIS279. Add NIS5 for non-members. Credit cards accepted.

Aviv Hotel, 48 Mordei Ha-Geta'ot St. (tel. 627 80 59 or 627 82 58; fax 628 19 61), a right off KKL St. down from Herzl St. Tidy 21-roomer with pictures of produce on the walls. Rooms have private baths, high-powered A/C, and TV; some have balconies. Singles NIS160/US$35; doubles NIS215/US$46. 10% student discount, but you'll have to "spring" for breakfast (NIS20). Laundry available.

Hotel Ha-Negev, 26 Ha-Atzma'ut St. (tel. 627 70 26 or 627 87 44), a couple of blocks down from Bank Ha-Poalim, after Trumpeldor St. All rooms have A/C, TV, and private sink. Private rooms NIS95/US$20, with private shower NIS120/US$25, with full private bath NIS167/US$35; doubles with full bath NIS190/US$40. Cash only.

FOOD

The pedestrian **Keren Kayemet L'Yisrael Street (KKL)** is the best place for affordable eats. For a fast food fix, head to the food court on the lower floor of Kenyon Ha-Negev across from the bus station. Most restaurants in the *kenyon* are open Su-Th 10am-midnight, F 10am-3pm, Sa sundown-midnight. The cheapest place to buy fresh produce, meat, and fish is the **shuk,** just south of the Muslim burial ground on Beit Eshel St. and easily identifiable by its arched metal rooftops. The corner of Ha-Ḥalutz and Hadassah St. is the birthplace of **Glida Be'er Sheva.** The octogenarian in the rocking chair behind the counter is the sole proprietress of the secret recipe for her ice cream (1 scoop NIS4, 2 scoops NIS7, 3 scoops NIS9; open Su-Th 9am-midnight, F 9am-2pm, Sa 8pm-2am). An additional branch is in the *kenyon*. The listings below are all in the **old city** area.

Beit Ha-Ful, 15 Ha-Histadrut St. (tel. 627 04 25), at the corner of Smilansky St. This local fave will make your stomach ha-full and ha-ppy. Fuel up on *fuul* in a bowl (NIS25) or in a pita with salad (NIS10). Falafel NIS10, shawarma NIS16-18. Eat *al fresco* or in A/C dining room. Open Su-Th 7am-midnight, Sa 8:30am-midnight.

Bulgarian Restaurant, 112 KKL St. (tel. 623 85 04). When in Be'er Sheva, eat as the Bulgarians do—fatten yourself up for the harsh winter with goulash (NIS33), steak with mushrooms (NIS38), and stuffed chicken (NIS45). All meals include either chips, rice, salad, or potatoes (in baked or mashed form). Open Su-Th 9am-11pm, Sa 10am-7pm. Reservations recommended for Sa dinners.

Jade Palace (tel. 627 11 70), on the corner of Ha-Ḥalutz St. and Yas'ir St. Classy Chinese restaurant draws crowds to its bright dining room with chicken, beef, and tasty pork dishes (NIS43), soups (NIS15-25), cooked vegetables (NIS33), and rice (NIS6-8). Open daily noon-midnight. Reservations recommended for F and Sa evenings.

El Gaucho, 18 Anilevich St. (tel. 628 44 22). Take a right from KKL St. down Ha-Histadrut, then a left on Anilevich St. Going all out to provide an authentic Argentinian experience, this restaurant serves up almost any part of the cow imaginable. *Entrecote* steak (NIS48) is recommended, but there is also udder (NIS36) and chicken halves in varying sauces (NIS42). All meals come with a fresh green salad and bread with garlic butter. Top it off with flan (NIS18). Open Su-Th noon-11:30pm, F noon-4pm, Sa 9pm-midnight.

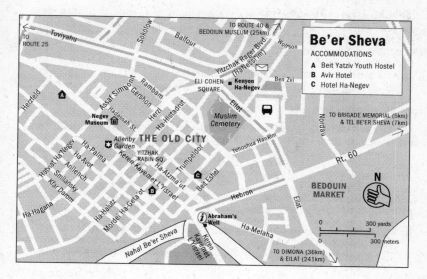

Be'er Sheva
ACCOMMODATIONS
A Beit Yatziv Youth Hostel
B Aviv Hotel
C Hotel Ha-Negev

ENTERTAINMENT

Be'er Sheva has a lively nightlife that is expanding at a rate similar to that of the city itself. Entertainment venues are centered around Trumpeldor St. and Smilansky St. in the old city, though some lie a short distance out of town near the university and industrial areas. Most bars and clubs open at 9 or 10pm, but remain quiet until about 11pm. Movie theaters (tel. 623 52 79) are housed downstairs in the Kenyon Ha-Negev. Shows run Su-Th 5-10pm, F 10pm and midnight, Sa 11pm. Movies are usually in English with Hebrew subtitles (NIS27.50).

Forum, 232 Kiryat Yehudit (tel. 627 82 22), outside Be'er Sheva's old city in an industrial area (taxis NIS15). Huge crowds roam through intricately decorated bars with tables and food, spacious indoor and outdoor dance halls with theme floors, and a swimming pool and waterfall. Tu karaoke (NIS30, students NIS25), Th house and techno (NIS40/NIS25), F 3 dance floors with 3 types of music (NIS55/NIS30), Sa free until 11pm or until the pub fills (after 11pm NIS40/NIS30). 18+ admitted to the front, 23+ for full access. Open Tu and Th-Sa 10:15pm-5am.

Baraka, 16 Hadassah St., 2 blocks up B'nei Ein Harod St. from KKL St. toward the mall. Such a popular pub that lines form outside on weekends. Chill outside in a desert-motif courtyard with mosaics and palm trees, or bop to pop. Beer (guess which brand?) NIS15-20. No cover. Open nightly 10pm-early morning.

Dial Tone, near Ben-Gurion University. Take bus #7 or 8 to a stop near the main entrance of the university's dorms. Go right to the intersection with Yitzhak Rager Blvd., turn right, and walk to Ya'akov Ave. on the left; hang (up) a right at the pizza joint on Ya'akov and you'll get a Dial Tone, a small, Bedouin-themed haven for mellow drinking (beer NIS10-16, cocktails NIS18). Open nightly 10pm-2am.

SIGHTS

A good starting point for walking tours of Be'er Sheva is the city's tourist office, at the site of Abraham's Well on the corner of Hebron St. and KKL St. (open Su-Th 8am-4pm, F 8am-noon). This is the best place in town to pick up maps of Be'er Sheva (NIS5) and other tourist information.

BEDOUIN MARKET. Be'er Sheva's most famous attraction is its Thursday Bedouin Market, established in 1905. The market is nirvana for *chatchke* lovers and bargain hunters, but there's little *shanti* amid the clamor of screaming vendors. The southern part of the market houses the real gems: beaten copperware, Bedouin robes, fabrics, rugs, and ceramic items. Get there early to see trading at its peak and to get a better selection of genuine Bedouin goods. *(On the south side of the city, off Eilat St. 1 block south of Hevron St. Most local buses will stop at the market upon request. By foot, walk to Eilat St. from the Egged stop at the central bus station and cross over to the market. Trading begins early in the morning and goes all day.)*

ABRAHAM'S WELL. The well dates back to at least the 12th century CE, and many believe it to be the original well dug by Abraham and contended over by the patriarch and various local settlers. A free, five-minute guided tour of the site illuminates Be'er Sheva's biblical history, the well's archaeological significance, and its camel-powered hydrotechnology. From June to September, the well also serves as an occasional nighttime entertainment venue, with folk songs, stories, live music, and dance performances. *(Corner of Hebron St. and KKL St. Performances NIS40, students NIS20. Ask at the tourist office inside about the schedule of events.)*

NEGEV MUSEUM. The graceful residence next to the mosque was built by the Ottomans in 1906 and named Be'er Sheva's City Hall in 1949. Diagonally facing the Governor's House is another Turkish building, used as a boarding school for Bedouin children during the British Mandate, then as Red Crescent hospital during WWI. Together, the buildings now house the Negev Museum. Both the mosque and museum were closed in 1999 for renovations, but are scheduled to re-open by summer 2000. *(On Ha-Atzma'ut St., north of Herzl St. Tel. 623 43 38 or 646 36 63. Call ahead for information on displays and admission.)*

JOE ALON BEDOUIN MUSEUM. At a time when approximately half of the Negev's Bedouin population live in urban "settlements," this museum showcases all facets of the nomads' traditional lives, including tools, embroidery, medicine, and customary desert garb. An audiovisual presentation describes Bedouin culture and its famous hospitality. Outside the exhibit are two Bedouin tents. In one, a Bedouin woman prepares and serves traditional pita and tea; in the other, Bedouin men converse with guests and serve bitter coffee. *(Several km north of the tel, on the outskirts of Kibbutz Lahav. To get to the kibbutz, drive 15km north on Rte. 40 to the Lahav junction or take bus #369 and ask to be let off at the junction (20min., every 30min., NIS12.20). A taxi to the museum costs around NIS75. Tel. 991 33 22 or 991 85 97. Open Su-Th and Sa 9am-5pm, F 9am-2pm. Admission NIS15, students NIS13.)*

ISRAELI AIR FORCE MUSEUM. This museum displays over 100 airplanes from several generations of Israeli aerial combat, including planes captured from and shot down by neighboring countries. The exhibit also boasts one of three Israeli-designed and -built Lavi airplanes. Free guided tours by Israeli soldiers relate the history behind each of the displays. *(At the Haterim Air Force Base, 8km west of town on the Be'er Sheva-Haterim Rd. City bus #31 stops in front of the entrance. To reach the bus stop, walk up Ha-Atzma'ut St. from the youth hostel and cross over the Derekh Joe Alon Hwy. at the major intersection. Tel. 990 68 55 or 990 68 33. Open Su-Th 8am-5pm, F 8am-1pm. Admission NIS23, ages 3-13 NIS15, senior citizens NIS18. Call ahead for free tours.)*

TEL BE'ER SHEVA. These ruins of a 3000-year-old planned city, 5km northeast of the city, were recently upgraded to a national park. One pile of unearthed rubble is a 2nd-century Roman fortress, another an 8th-century BCE house, and a third a 12th-century BCE well. The view from the top of the tower in the back right corner of the site is fantastic. *(By car, take Rte. 60 out of the city, then make a right at the set of lights just past the gas stations. A taxi costs NIS25 each way. Buses to Arad and Omer run by the road that leads to the site (#388, every 35min. 6:45am-10:30pm, NIS6.20). The walk from the turn-off to the park takes about 30min. Park open Su-Th and Sa 8am-5pm, F 8am-4pm; entrance closes 1hr. earlier. Admission NIS9, students NIS8, children NIS4.50. Detailed brochures and site maps for a 1hr. self-guided tour are available at the park.)*

NEAR BE'ER SHEVA

DIMONA דימונה

*Buses travel round-trip to Dimona from: **Be'er Sheva** (#48, 56, and 375; 45min.; every 20min. 6:30am-11pm; NIS13); **Tel Aviv** (#375, 393, and 394; NIS30, students NIS27); and **Eilat** (#393 and 394; 3hr.; every 1½hr. 5am-5pm; NIS43, students NIS39). To get to the Hebrew Israelites' village from Dimona's central bus station, turn left on Herzl St., pass the tall red monument on the right, and continue for about 10min.*

Since immigrating in 1969, the **Hebrew Israelite Community,** called the **Black Hebrews** by non-members, has been working to combine religious and communal ideals into a little slice of utopia in this tiny Negev town. The Hebrew Israelites are a unique sect of English-speaking immigrants who trace their historical roots to ancient Israel (though who doesn't?). The community, which bases its faith on the revelations of spiritual leader Ben-Ami Ben-Israel (formerly Ben Carter), believes that the ancestors of black slaves in antebellum America lived in Israel until they were forced to migrate to Western Africa after the Roman onslaught in 70 CE. The group's vanguard left Chicago for the Holy Land in 1969, stopping in Liberia long enough to learn Hebrew, adopt African dress, and prepare themselves for their journey. Another group from Chicago followed in 1970, and a third exodus took place from Detroit in 1973. At first the Israeli government refused to grant them citizenship unless they converted to Judaism, but the Hebrew Israelites insisted that they were already Jews. The government and the sect came to an agreement in 1990 on a process for normalizing the community's legal status.

Though the village welcomes solo wanderers, a tour can be much more informative. Call community leaders a few days in advance (tel. (07) 655 54 00 or 657 32 86/7; donations accepted). The original community of about 100 pilgrims has blossomed into a vibrant 1500-person town; branches of the community in other areas in Israel bring the total Hebrew Israelite population to more than 3500. The focus of the **kfar,** or village, is the adoration of the god Yah and the pursuit of peace in Yah's name. The community as a whole cares for the needs of each of its members and promotes a lifestyle based on mutual support rather than individual ownership. Children are born under the care of community midwives, several families live together in one home and take turns with household responsibilities, and community members make their own clothes, jewelry, and food. Their religious beliefs require them to wear only natural fabrics and prohibit them from eating any animal parts or products, white sugar, or white flour.

The community restaurant, ▓**Soul Food Eats** (the Soul Mama that gave birth to the "Taste of Life" restaurants scattered throughout Israel), is a godsend for protein-starved vegans, who can stock up on delicious tofu sandwiches (NIS9) or sit down for a full three-course lunch (NIS12; open Su-Th 9am-11pm, F 9am-noon, Sa sundown-midnight.) There is also a three-room **guest house** (rooms NIS80, breakfast and dinner included, call ahead).

MAMSHIT ממשית

Buses running between Be'er Sheva and the Dead Sea will stop 1km outside Mamshit, along the main highway, as will bus #394 to Eilat (1¼hr., every 1½hr., NIS19.30). A 10min. taxi from Dimona (Mayam Taxi tel. (07) 655 66 88) costs NIS33; be sure to tell the bus or cab driver to stop at Atar Mamshit (the Nabatean ruins), not the new cinderblock city several km to the west. Site open Su-Th 8am-5pm, F 8am-4pm. Admission NIS9, youth NIS4. Free brochure of the site including small map and descriptions.

Just 15km east of Dimona lie the sunbleached sandstone ruins of ancient Mamshit, the only city in the Negev that was walled in on all sides. One of the six Nabatean cities in Israel, Mamshit once helped the Nabateans control the Petra-Gaza spice route stretching from India to Rome. The city is a complex of lavish villas, churches, and fortifications built of finely decorated stone. On one side is a vast desert plain; on the other, the precipitous canyon of **Naḥal Mamshit** (Mam-

ISRAEL

shit River). Built in the first century CE, Mamshit reached its height as a cross-roads and garrison town in the Roman and Byzantine periods. Following attacks by desert nomads in the 6th century, the city was destroyed and abandoned. Particularly impressive among the ruins are the **Eastern Church**, with its altar remains at the top of the tarp-covered market area; the 2nd-century CE **tower** that was once three stories tall and used to guard the dams of the river below; and the **mansion,** or "House of the Affluent." Take a look at the canyon from the back side of the ruins.

ARAD ערד

Buses run to and from: **Tel Aviv** *(#389; 2hr.; Su-Th 6, 8:30am, 1:30pm, F 6, 8:30am, 1:30pm, Sa 5, 9pm; NIS35.50, students NIS32);* **Be'er Sheva** *(#384, 385, 386, and 388; 40min.; every 45min. 5:40am-9:30pm; NIS17.30); and* **Ein Gedi** *(#384 and 385; 7, 10:15am, 1, 3:45pm; 1½hr.; NIS24, students NIS20) via* **Ein Bokek** *(1hr., NIS17.30) and* **Masada** *(1¼hr.; NIS21.50, students NIS19.50). There is no direct service to or from Eilat or Jerusalem; it's easiest to go to Be'er Sheva and connect there.*

Built near the ancient Canaanite ruins of Tel Arad, the modern city of Arad lies equidistant from all the major northern and southern Dead Sea attractions. Though considered less-than-exciting by many Israelis, this oasis of civilization is probably what David Ben-Gurion envisioned when he waxed eloquent about the blooming of Israel's deserts. More practically, Arad has two major tourist-draws. In mid-July, the city sponsors a huge **music festival** (sometimes called the "Israeli Woodstock") that takes over the town for four days. If you plan to join in the melodic communion, bring a sleeping bag and rough it in the campgrounds set up around town for the event. Contact the **tourist information office** (tel. (07) 995 44 09) for the dates in 2000. Arad is also the only place from which to view the famed **Masada Sound and Light Show** (tel. (07) 995 93 33) without driving all the way around the mountain. Outside of these attractions, however, all except the asthmatic (the air here is so clean, dry, and pollen-free that doctors prescribe it worldwide) may be happier at accommodations on the Dead Sea or elsewhere in the Negev.

SDEH BOKER שדה בוקר

To make the Negev prosper "as a blessing to the State of Israel" was the dream of **David Ben-Gurion,** one of the earliest Zionist visionaries and Israel's first Prime Minister. That dream, now inscribed on the gate of the *midresha* (institute) of Sdeh Boker (also called the Ben-Gurion Heritage Institute), is this town's ongoing quest. The institute, settled in midst of the endless desert and on the edge of a magnificent canyon, houses laboratories and a field school devoted to the management of desert resources. Sdeh Boker is named for the mountain behind it (*Jabal Baqara,* or "Mt. Cow," in Arabic; *Har Boker,* or "Cowboy Mountain," in Hebrew). Ben-Gurion was so moved by the young pioneers building fledgling Sdeh Boker that he decided, at the age of 67, to resign from office and settle on the kibbutz nearby. Now the area is steeped in Ben-Gurion tributes, sights, and memorabilia. Sdeh Boker serves as a base for desert exploration in the nearby **Ein Avdat National Park** and **Zin Valley.** There are a tremendous number of truly astounding hikes in this area, traversing jagged desert cliffs, natural springs, canyons, and monk's caves.

⊞ ORIENTATION AND PRACTICAL INFORMATION

The only public transportation to or from Sdeh Boker is Egged bus #60, which runs between **Be'er Sheva** and **Mitzpeh Ramon** (35min.; 6:35am-10pm; NIS19.30, students NIS17.40). The bus stops at three different points, a few kilometers apart, along the highway: the gate of Kibbutz Sdeh Boker; the turn-off to Ben-Gurion's Hut (at the edge of the kibbutz); and the roundabout outside the gate of the Ben-Gurion Institute (Midreshet Sdeh Boker). To reach the SPNI Field School, Ein Avdat National Park, Ben-Gurion's grave, and the Ben-Gurion Institute, get off outside the institute gate. From the roundabout, the road on the right with the orange sign leads to the grave, Heritage Institute, and down the canyon to Ein Avdat. The road straight ahead leads to the *midresha*, the SPNI office, and accommodations. The institute buildings are arranged around a central square, containing the restaurant, supermarket, and **post office** (open Su-M and W-Th 8:30am-noon and 1-2pm, Tu 8:30-11am, F 8:30-10:30am). To reach the **SPNI Field School** (tel. 653 20 16; fax 655 62 86; email sade@boker.org.il; www.boker.org.il/betsadeh), turn right at the end of the road inside the main gate, then left at the large parking lot. The incredibly helpful staff answers questions about hiking routes and desert flora and fauna and offers free maps of nearby trails. They'll also store bags during day hikes (open Su-Th 8am-4:30pm, F 8am-1pm and 5-7pm). The **telephone code** for Sdeh Boker is 07.

ACCOMMODATIONS AND FOOD

The **SPNI Hostel** (tel. 653 20 16; fax 655 62 86), on the edge of the canyon, has spotless, modern rooms with air conditioning, private baths, and incredible views of the Zin Canyon. The four-bed dorm rooms, Sdeh Boker's only budget lodgings, are reserved for students (NIS60 per person). Call ahead: this is a popular rest spot for Israeli regiments and the dorms may be crowded. Rates for non-students in the hostel are much higher (singles NIS176/US$36; doubles NIS220/US$46; breakfast included). **Camping** is free at designated locations within the Zin Valley; contact the SPNI Field School for information about facilities and transportation.

Food pickings in Sdeh Boker are slim. The **supermarket** in the institute's center has an extensive selection of fruit and vegetables (open Su-Th 8am-7pm, F 8am-2pm). The **cafeteria** on the other side of the post office serves sausages, milkshakes, and tasty croissants (NIS10-32; open Su-Th 8am-11pm, F 8am-2pm; Visa, MC accepted). The **Sdeh Boker Inn** (tel. 656 03 79), next door to Ben-Gurion's Hut, serves cafeteria-style meals, including excellent baked zucchini and goulash (open daily 8am-3pm; credit cards accepted).

SIGHTS

If you're not a die-hard David Ben-Gurion fan, skip town at daybreak and head for the desert for some amazing hikes (see **Hiking: Sdeh Boker,** below).

THE BEN-GURION HERITAGE INSTITUTE. You've seen the signs, you've heard the hype—now go visit the Ben-Gurion Heritage Institute for yourself. Scientists and university students work year-round at the busy center; their findings on desert irrigation and development are applied not only in the Negev, but in Africa and in much of the world. The nearby Research Center for Solar Energy is a pioneer in solar power development. Those black panels and metal contraptions on every Israeli rooftop are solar-powered water heaters, required for households by Israeli law. The institute's **Desert Sculpture Museum** displays art created from natural desert materials. From the Ben-Gurion Institute, a walk along the canyon rim leads to the beautifully landscaped **Ben-Gurion Tombs.** In 1992, former Soviet premier Mikhail Gorbachev laid a wreath at Ben-Gurion's grave and praised the success of his style of socialism. *(The institute gives tours by appointment; contact SPNI.)*

BEN-GURION'S HUT. Only slightly larger than the homes of his kibbutz neighbors, David Ben-Gurion's residence is furnished as he left it. Family pictures, letters, lists of medications, and copied-down biblical passages lend insight into the man behind the legend. *(A 45min. walk to the right along the highway out of the institute; the road leading to the hut is on the right after a large grove of pistachio trees (2½km). Alternately, take the bus towards Be'er Sheva for 1 stop. Tel. 655 84 44. Open Oct.-Mar. Su-Th 8:30am-4pm; Apr.-Sept. Su-Th 8:30am-4pm, F 8:30am-2pm, Sa and holidays 9am-2:30pm. Free.)*

▶ HIKING: SDEH BOKER AND ENVIRONS

Although many tourists come to Sdeh Boker to see its Ben-Gurion memorials, Ben-Gurion was attracted to the kibbutz because of its setting. The hikes near Sdeh Boker are incredibly beautiful, but require careful preparation. Trails may be poorly marked, distances are deceptive, and the Negev sun is cruel and unforgiving. Visit the SPNI office before any hike and check in with a guide. With advance notice, SPNI offers guided hikes across the Avdat Plateau or Zin Valley (NIS375/US$78 per day). Wear a hat, get an early start, and bring one liter of water per person for each hour you plan to spend on the trails.

EIN AVDAT NATIONAL PARK. This park in the Zin Canyon is gorgeous and easily accessible. The steep road to the park's lower, main entrance snakes down the canyon from the institute gate (45-50min. on foot, 10min. by car). From the park entrance, the hike to **Ein Avdat** (Avdat Spring; the lower pools) is 15 minutes. Allot about an hour for the full hike to the upper gate. Getting to the upper gate requires climbing one-way ladders; unless there's a car waiting at the end of the hike, you'll either need to make a U-turn at the base of the ladders and miss the view, or extend your hike a few hours by walking along the rim of the canyon after reaching the top. Gleaming white walls tower over the green, puddled path that runs through the canyon to the lower pools of the Avdat Spring. The eerie echoes of wildlife scampering about resound through the high caves carved out in the canyon's sides, which once served as homes to **Byzantine monks.** A small dam pools water that flows down the rocks from the Avdat Spring. An easy-to-miss set of stairs in the rock just before the dam leads up to the rest of the hike and the ladders of no return. Keep an eye out for the square, stone ruin of what used to be the Byzantine monks' tower. The steps and ladders up to the top of the canyon provide quite a workout, but also a view that shouldn't be missed. From the end of the trail on the canyon's rim, a trek along the riverbed to nearby Avdat takes about two hours (see **Avdat,** p. 366); the trail markings can be difficult to follow, so consult SPNI for details before leaving. *(Tel. 655 56 48. Park open daily May-Sept. 8am-5pm; Oct.-Apr. 8am-4pm. Entry permitted until 1hr. before closing. Admission NIS14, seniors and students NIS12, children NIS6. Free brochure has an adequate map and descriptions in English.)*

WADI KARAKASH. This magnificent three-hour hike passes an inviting pond and waterfall (water most likely to be flowing Oct.-Feb.). The Karakash Wadi eventually runs into the **Havarim Wadi.** A one-hour hike along the Havarim Wadi passes a Nabatean cistern and slopes of unbelievably smooth white rock that are especially striking (and slippery) in moonlight. From the beginning of the Havarim cistern and Wadi hike, the Nabatean cistern is down some stairs and below ground. A one-hour hike along the trail leads to the bottom of the road to the Ein Avdat park entrance. *(To reach the start of the hike, turn left on the Be'er Sheva-Eilat Hwy. from the end of the road to the institute and walk 1km; the trailhead is to the left. For the entrance to the Havarim cistern and Wadi hike, continue along the highway past the Karakash trailhead to an orange sign on the left, a 20min. walk from the institute. The sign points into the parking lot, where a blue-and-white marked trail descends on the left. Free.)*

AVDAT

Bus #60 (40min., 6:35am-10pm; NIS20, students NIS18) runs from Be'er Sheva to Mitzpeh Ramon, stopping in Avdat. Tell the driver you're going to the archaeological site and not Ein Avdat (the oasis). The site can also be reached by hiking from Sdeh Boker via Ein Avdat (about 1hr.); consult the SPNI guides in Sdeh Boker for information. Bus#60 runs to Avdat from Sdeh Boker (NIS10.90) and from the highway near the end of the Ein Avdat trail (NIS5). Tel. 658 63 91; fax 655 09 54. Open in summer Su-Th 8am-5pm, F 8am-4pm; in winter Su-Th 8am-4pm, F 8am-3pm. Admission NIS18, students NIS15.30, children NIS9.

The magnificently preserved ruins of a 4th-century BCE Nabatean city are perched upon a hill 11km south of Sdeh Boker. Avdat once thrived as a pit stop for caravans along the spice route from the Far East to Gaza (via Petra) that continued on to Europe. Nabateans used their strategic perch to spy on caravans as far away as present-day Mitzpeh Ramon and Sdeh Boker. The city continued to flourish after the Romans captured it in 106 CE, reaching its economic peak during the Byzantine period. Most of the visible ruins date from this time. The most important Nabatean remains are a handsome esplanade on top of the hill, a winding staircase that led to a Nabatean temple, and a potter's workshop, all dating from the first century CE. When the Nabateans converted to Christianity around 300 CE, the temple became a church. The best of the 6th-century Byzantine remains include a 7m high surrounding wall, a monastery, two churches, and a baptistry. In this century, the site was resurrected on celluloid as the setting for the movie *Jesus Christ Superstar*.

MITZPEH RAMON מצפה רמון

Mitzpeh Ramon sits on the rim of **Makhtesh Ramon** (Ramon Crater), the largest natural crater in the world. Measuring in at 40km long, 9km wide, and 400m deep, Ramon is mind-boggling in both sheer size and natural diversity. The crater has the capability to make visitors feel small in every respect: its rock formations are millions of years old; its 1200 different kinds of vegetation span four distinct climatic zones; and evidence of human life in the area predates written history. Some of the geological formations here are found nowhere else in the world. The crater's visible history is so incredible that hikes in the *makhtesh* pass through what seem to be landscapes of desolate, far-away planets. Uphill treks wind toward phenomenal views of the desert expanse.

▐ ORIENTATION AND PRACTICAL INFORMATION

Buses #60 and 392 run to **Be'er Sheva** (1hr.; Su-Th 5:30am-9:30pm, F 5:30am-3pm; NIS22.50, students NIS20.25) from the main stop at the Delek gas station. Bus #392 uses Mitzpeh Ramon as a waystation between Be'er Sheva and **Eilat**; it stops for 15 minutes at the gas station and will pick people up if there's room. Drivers are instructed to take 10-minute breaks if they feel drowsy, so don't panic if the bus is 10 to 40 minutes late. From the gas station, the tan, flat-roofed **visitor's center** is visible to the left on the edge of the crater. Clustered around it are the youth hostel, Bio-Ramon, and the breathtaking crater-rim **promenade.** Cross the street, head left from the gas station, and take a right at the signs to the visitor's center.

Across **Ben-Gurion Boulevard** and a bit downhill and to the right from the gas station is the fountained commercial center. There is a **Bank Ha-Poalim** branch (tel. 567 33 41; open Su and Tu-W 8:30am-12:45pm, M and Th 8:30am-12:30pm and 4-6:30pm, F 8:30am-12:30pm). Across the parking lot behind the bank and up a flight of stairs is a **post office** with Western Union, fax and telegram services, EMS, and **Poste Restante** (tel. 630 73 30; open Su-Tu and Th 8am-12:30pm and 4-6:30pm, W 8am-1pm, F 8am-12:30pm). **Police** (tel. 100), **first aid** (tel. 101), and **fire** (tel. 102) offices are up the walkway through the small park across from the commercial center. **Mitzpeh Pharmacy** (tel. 658 87 67/9) is at the corner of Naḥal Ha-Ela St. and Naḥal Grofit St., marked with green paint, one block past the youth hostel (open Su, W, Th 8:30am-1pm and 4:30-7:30pm, M 8:30am-2pm, Tu 8:30am-1pm, F 8:30am-12:30pm). The **telephone code** for Mitzpeh Ramon is 07.

▐▄◌ ACCOMMODATIONS AND FOOD

Staking out a campsite in the middle of the *makhtesh* is forbidden; campers have been known to do it, but they run the risk of being awakened by an angry ranger or an even angrier **Asiatic wild ass.** There is a campground in town, at the municipal park next to the gas station. While in the crater, camp in designated sites only. **Be'erot Camping Site,** 16km from Mitzpeh Ramon, is hard to reach without a car: the turn-off is along the main highway, marked by orange signs.

Bus #392 to Eilat can stop there. The only designated campsite in the crater with bathrooms, Be'erot also has a kiosk selling cold drinks, ice cream, and firewood. Pay at the visitor's center ahead of time (sites NIS10; mattress in a Bedouin tent NIS20).

SPNI Field School (tel. 658 86 15/6; fax 658 83 85) runs accommodations directly on the crater's rim. Take bus #60 through town to Camel Observation Point, go up the Har Gamal dirt road to the crater's rim, and walk for a couple minutes to the right along the black-marked cliffside trail toward the tall antennae. All rooms have air conditioning and private baths, and guests can use the full kitchen. (6-bed dorm NIS60 for students only; doubles NIS275/US$58. Each additional person NIS50. Breakfast NIS18. Dinner Su-Th NIS52, F NIS58. Reception Su-Th 8am-6:30pm, F 8am-noon, Sa call ahead. Visa, MC accepted.) Also on the canyon's rim, **Mitzpeh Ramon Youth Hostel (HI)** (tel. 658 84 43; fax 658 80 74), across from the visitor's center, is set next to the scenic promenade. Through their windows, admire crystal-clear night views of the starry sky above the crater. While there's no air-conditioning, spacious rooms with baths are cool and clean, and the hostel also features a huge lounge, TV room, and dining hall. (6-bed dorms NIS60; singles NIS160/US$35; doubles NIS235/US$50. Each additional adult NIS60, children NIS50. Nonmembers add NIS6. Breakfast included. Credit cards accepted.)

Before hiking, stock up on fruits and veggies at the small **Shekem supermarket** next to the post office (open Su-Th 8am-1pm and 4-7pm, F 8am-1:30pm). Grab trail mix at **Bonjour supermarket** next to the bank (open Su-Th 7am-7:30pm, F 7am-3pm). The all-kosher **Hamakhtesh Restaurant,** 2 Naḥal Tzihor St. (tel. 658 84 90), in the green-arched arcade one block below the youth hostel, serves a profusion of appetizers with pita (NIS8-10). Kebab, spicy *shishlik*, steak, or schnitzel (NIS25) come with rice or fries (open Su-Th 10am-10pm, Sa sundown-10pm). **Ha-Tzukit Restaurant** (tel. 658 60 79), next to the visitor's center, has air conditioning, a stunning view, and often a lazy family of ibex outside. Sandwiches go for NIS16, vegetarian meals for NIS32, and a hot meat lunch for NIS35 (open daily 9am-5pm).

■ HIKING: MITZPEH RAMON AND ENVIRONS

Makhtesh Ramon is a spectacular park, but it should not be taken lightly. Always consult with Nature Reserve or SPNI personnel before setting out. Wear a hat, hike as early as possible in the morning, and carry food and one liter of water per person for each hour you expect to spend on the trail. Heatstroke and dehydration are deadly enemies in the Negev. There are two hiking resources in Mitzpeh Ramon. The **Park Ramon Visitors' Center** (tel. 658 86 91/8; fax 658 86 20), in the round building with the flat top, has first-rate film and audio-visual presentations and rooftop observation deck overlooking of the crater (open Su-Th, Sa 8am-5pm, F 8am-4pm; admission NIS15). The **SPNI Field School** (tel. 658 86 15/6; fax 658 83 85), near the edge of the crater 500m southwest of Camel Observation Point, is equipped with maps and literature about hiking in the region, and occasionally offers organized tours (open Su-Th 8am-6:30pm, F 8am-noon). Although the trails are well marked, a pre-hike stop at the **visitor's center** for maps and terrain info is a prudent idea for an unguided expedition. Leave your route description and estimated trip duration at the field school before hiking— they have an on-site rescue team and are in direct communication with army units in the area. While hiking, keep a fix on the main highway or Be'erot Campsite, whichever is closer.

Far-flung trailheads are best reached by car and 4x4 vehicle. For trailheads off of the main highway, bus #392 to Eilat travels through the crater and can stop at the turn-off for the Be'erot Camping Site. In a pinch, locals say hitchhiking on the highway is a safe option, though the highway is not heavily trafficked and cars may be infrequent. *Let's Go* does not recommend hitchhiking.

HAR ARDON. Har Ardon is a terrific hike, combining challenging terrain with unbeatable views. However, it's a long haul (7hr. round-trip from Be'erot Campsite), and is more easily tackled as two daytrips, especially during the summer. To climb **Har Ardon** (Mt. Ardon), take a left out of the Be'erot campsite and follow the path to the sign marked Mt. Ardon (about 20min.), which points to a blue path on the right. The blue path eventually leads into a parking area, where the steep mountain ascent begins. The top of Har Ardon is the heart of the crater; the mountain gives the crater its heart-shaped appearance. From the top, a rainbow of sand colors the crater floor. The descent from the mountain can be quite a physical feat: the narrow, white-rock-and-sand trail is steep and slippery, so take it slow. Down the mountain and along the trail in the crater are the remarkable sand and hills of the **Red Valley,** which range in color from yellow to crimson. After passing by the black hill of Givat Harut, take a right on the black trail and follow the signs back to the campsite to complete the hike, or take the black trail left to Wadi Ardon.

SHORT HIKES FROM MITZPEH RAMON. Trailheads for the most interesting hikes are outside of town, but two beautiful trails that pass by significant geological sites originate in town. An excellent three-hour hike begins at the end of the western promenade, near the mini-amphitheater, and leads to the crater's "Carpentry." Take a left out of the visitor's center, continue around the canyon's rim to the mini-amphitheater, and head downhill to the green-marked trail, which starts with a rocky descent into the crater (35-40min.). Go straight on the green trail for **Ha-Minsarah** (the Carpentry), where piles of prism-like rock, configured and baked by volcanic heat, resemble carpentry supplies. A turn-off marked in red along the green Carpentry trail leads to a five-hour hike past the **Ammonite Wall,** an impressive collection of crustacean fossils embedded in rock. From the red Ammonite Wall path, a black path eventually leads off to the left and on to the highway.

WADI ARDON. Several pieces of volcanic material jut along the colorful borders of Wadi Ardon, the second half of the Har Ardon hike. The first, a pair of big and small chunky intrusions, are known as the Father and Son Dikes. Continue on the blue path, which points toward **Parsat Nekarot** (the Horseshoe of Crevices) and includes **Sha'ar Ramon** (the Ramon Gate), where water exits the crater. The Parsat Nekarot river bed is flanked by soaring cliffs and cave-like enclaves that make welcome shady rest stops. From Parsat Nekarot, follow the blue markings to **Ein Saharonim.** The vegetation lasts all year, but the water evanesces to mere puddles in summer. The remains of a **Nabatean caravanserai** stand at the end of the spring on the right. This is also the spot where animals are most likely to be seen, wandering around in search of water sources.

EILAT אילת

Eilat has two goals—to get you tan and to make you poor. The city is soaked with the sweat of rowdy Israelis, international backpackers, and European tourists, and the air is abuzz with the din of their jet skis and cell phones. Some swear by Eilat's sun, coral, and nightlife, while others see the city as a huge tourist trap attached to a nice beach. In between the cocktails and Coppertone, stick your head underwater and you may notice some of the most spectacular underwater life the world's seas have to offer. Above the waves, the wildlife is bikini-clad and muscle-bound. The busiest times of the year are Passover (April 20-26, 2000), Sukkot (Oct. 14-20, 2000), and Israel's summer vacation (July and Aug.), when nearly 100,000 Israelis descend upon the city. Don't fool yourself into thinking that this is a good time to visit. True, there are more parties and crowded pubs, but hostels and restaurants charge double their normal rates, petty theft runs rampant, and every inch of beach crawls with human flesh.

THE OLD IN-OUT. Because of Eilat's position at the intersection of Israel, Jordan, Egypt, and Saudi Arabia, the city is a frequent point for border crossings. Consult the following pages for information about:

Jordan: Getting into Eilat (via Aqaba), p. 404; getting out of Israel, p. 238.

Egypt: Getting into Eilat (via Taba), p. 43; getting out of Israel, p. 238.

⊞ ORIENTATION

Eilat is a 5km strip of coastline on the Negev's sandy bottom, at the precarious intersection of Israel, Jordan, Egypt, and Saudi Arabia. At night, the lights of all four countries are visible on the horizon. The city is divided into three sections: the town itself on the hills; the hotel area and Lagoon Beach to the east; and the port to the south. The main entrance to the central bus station is on **Ha-Tmarim Boulevard,** which crosses the center of the city from southeast (downhill) to northwest (uphill). Across the street is the **Commercial Center,** with restaurants and cafes. Uphill and to the right are most hostels and cheap restaurants. Walking downhill along the bus station side of Ha-Tmarim Blvd. leads to the **Red Canyon Center,** which resembles a futuristic Bedouin tent and houses the post office, supermarket, and cinema. Farther downhill is the **Shalom Center,** a mega-mall. Ha-Tmarim Blvd. ends here, perpendicular to **Ha-Arava Road.** The main entrance to the Eilat airport is along Ha-Arava Rd. to the right. A block later, to the right of the intersection with **Yotam Road,** a three-level conglomeration of cheap restaurants and shops calls itself the **New Tourist Center.** On the other side of the street is the tourist office. Ha-Arava Rd. leads to Dolphin Reef, the Coral Beach reserve, the Underwater Observatory, and finally Taba Beach and the **Egyptian border.** Bus #15 runs this route (every 15-20min., NIS2.10-3.20). Turning left at the intersection of Ha-Arava Rd. and Yotam St. leads to the beaches at the lagoon.

▐ TRANSPORTATION

Airplanes: Eilat Airport (tel. 636 38 38), on the corner of Ha-Tmarim Blvd. and Ha-Arava Rd. **Arkia Airlines** (tel. 638 48 88) flies to: **Tel Aviv** (every 30min., NIS280/US$60); **Jerusalem** (2-3 per day, NIS280/US$60); and **Haifa** (2-6 per day, NIS320/US$70). **Israir Airlines** (tel. 634 06 66) flies to **Tel Aviv** (every hr., from NIS250/US$50). Both airlines give student discounts. Call the night before for half-price specials.

Buses: Central bus station (tel. 636 51 20), on Ha-Tmarim Blvd. Reserve tickets at least 1 day in advance, 3 days during high season. To: **Jerusalem** (#444; 4½hr.; Su-Th 7, 10am, 2, 5pm; F 7, 10am, 1pm; Sa 4:30, 7pm; NIS58); **Tel Aviv** (#394; 5hr.; Su-Th 10 per day, F 7 per day, Sa 8 per day; NIS58); **Haifa** (#991; 6hr.; Su, Th 8:30am, 2:30, 11:30pm; M-W 2:30, 11:30pm; F 8:30am; Sa 5:00, 11:30pm; NIS68). If full, take the bus to **Be'er Sheva** and transfer. ISIC discounts. Schedules change frequently.

Local Transportation: City buses #1 and 2 run from downtown to the hotel area (every 30min. Su-Th 6:15am-8:45pm, F 6:40am-4:15pm, Sa every 2hr. 10am-6pm; NIS3). City bus #15 runs down Ha-Tmarim Blvd. and Ha-Arava Rd., through the hotel area, and past the HI hostel and Coral Beach to **Egypt** (every 20-30min. Su-Th 7am-9pm, F 7am-4:30pm, Sa 9am-9pm; NIS2.10-3.20).

Taxis: King Solomon (tel. 633 33 38) and **Taba** (tel. 633 33 38). City rides NIS5, to observatory NIS20, to Egyptian border NIS25-30, to Jordanian border NIS15-20. Taxi sharing is common. In winter, *sheruts* run along the city bus #1, 2, and 15 routes.

Car Rental: Hertz (tel. 637 50 50), in Red Canyon Center. Min. age 23. **Budget** (tel. 637 41 25), in Shalom Center. **Avis** (tel. 637 31 64), next to the tourist office. All offer similar plans. Unlimited mileage NIS160-190/US$35-40 per day, or NIS45/US$10 plus NIS1 per km. Insurance starts at NIS50/US$12 per day. NIS50/US$12 extra per day in high season. Rental cars cannot go to Egypt. All agencies open 8am-6pm.

ISRAEL

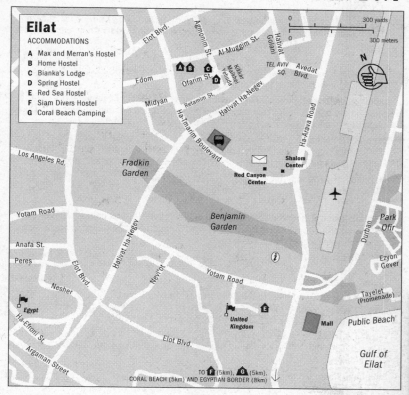

Eilat

ACCOMMODATIONS

- A Max and Merran's Hostel
- B Home Hostel
- C Bianka's Lodge
- D Spring Hostel
- E Red Sea Hostel
- F Siam Divers Hostel
- G Coral Beach Camping

Bike Rental: Recommended for winter only. **Eilat Sports** (tel. 634 11 44), in the marina. NIS50 per day. Open daily 9:30am-7pm. **Red Sea Sports** (tel. 633 08 66), in the marina. NIS80 per day. Open Su-Th 8am-9pm, F 8am-6pm.

🛈 PRACTICAL INFORMATION

Tourist Office: (tel. 637 21 11; fax 632 58 67), at the corner of Yotam Rd. and Ha-Arava Rd. Maps, brochures, and coupons. Will help find accommodations. Open Su-Th 8am-6pm, F 8am-2pm. **SPNI** (tel. 637 20 21), opposite Coral Beach. Maps and info about local hiking. Open Su-Th 8am-4pm.

Consulates: Egypt, 68 Ha-Efroni St. (tel. 637 68 82). From the bus station, turn right on Ha-Tmarim Blvd. Take the first left onto Hativat Ha-Negev St., then a right 900m ahead on Sderot Argaman St. Ha-Efroni St. is the 1st street on the right; look for the flag. Open Su-Th 9am-noon. Fill out a visa application in the morning and pick it up at 1pm that day. Bring a passport photo. Must pay in shekels (Americans NIS50; South Africans free; all others NIS70). Sinai-only visas are free and available at the border. **U.K.** (tel. 637 23 44), above the New Tourist Center (next to the Adi Hotel), by appointment only.

Currency Exchange: Bank Leumi (tel. (03) 514 94 00). Open Su, Tu, Th 8:30am-noon and 5-6:30pm; M, W, F 8:30am-noon. **Bank Ha-Poalim** (tel. 637 61 57). Open Su, Tu, Th 8:30am-noon and 4:30-6pm; M, W, F 8:30am-noon. Both banks opposite the central bus station. The **post office** exchanges traveler's checks with no commission. 24hr. **ATMs** (Visa, MC, PLUS, Cirrus) at Bank Ha-Poalim, the post office, and the marina.

Luggage Storage: At the bus station. NIS15 per bag per day. Open Su-Th 6am-12:30pm, F 6am-10pm, Sa and holidays 10am-12:30pm.

Market: At Eilat St. and Ha-Tmarim Blvd. Open Su-Th 7:30am-10pm, F 7:30am-2pm. **SuperKolbo Supermarket,** closer to the center of town in Rekhter Commercial Center. Open Sa-Th 7am-midnight, F 7am-9pm.

Laundromat: Kuiskal (tel. 637 48 38), at the Razin Center, on the corner of Ha-Tmarim Blvd. and Edom St. Full service NIS36 for 6kg, self-service NIS25. Open Sa-Th 8am-8pm, F 8am-4pm. Hostel services are cheaper.

Camping Equipment: Azimut, The National Center for Hiking Equipment (tel. 634 11 12), on the bottom floor of the mall at the corner of Yotam Rd. and Ha-Arava Rd. Good selection of pricey gear. Open Su-Th 9:30am-midnight, F 9am-4pm.

Emergency: Police: (tel. 100 or 633 24 44), on Avdat Blvd. at the eastern end of Hativat Ha-Negev. "Lost and found" for packs stolen from the beach. **Fire:** Tel. 102. **First Aid: Magen David Adom** (tel. 101 or 637 23 33). Stations are located on some beaches.

Pharmacy: SuperPharm (tel. 634 08 80), in the mall. Best selection in town. Open Su-Th 9am-midnight, F 9am-4pm, Sa 11am-midnight. **Eilat Pharmacy,** 25 Eilat St. (tel. 637 50 02). Open Su-Th 8:15am-1:15pm and 4:15-8:00pm, F 8:15am-2pm.

Hospital: Yoseftal Hospital (tel. 635 80 11), on Yotam Rd. **Maccabi Healthcare Services** (tel. 633 31 01), on the corner of Eilat St. and Ha-Tmarim Blvd. Modern facility offers all medical and dental services.

Post Office: (tel. 637 44 40), in the Red Canyon Center. Western Union, Poste Restante. Cashes traveler's checks for no commission. Open Su-Th 8am-12:30pm and 4-6:30pm, F and holidays 8am-12:30pm.

Internet Access: BJ's Books (tel. 634 09 05), in the New Tourist Center. NIS7 for 15min., NIS25 per hr. Open Su-Th 10am-10pm, F 10am-6pm. **Unplugged Sandwich Bar** (tel. 632 62 99), in the New Tourist Center. NIS25 per hr. Open 24hr.

Telephone Office: Starcom Gold (tel. 632 65 27; fax 632 64 94), at the New Tourist Center. Cheaper than the post office or public phones. Offers phone, fax (NIS13), and voicemail services. Open daily 4-11pm.

Telephone Code: 07.

ACCOMMODATIONS

Finding a cheap room in Eilat is easy. Finding a safe, comfortable, convenient, and cheap room is another story. New arrivals at the bus station are attacked by a gaggle of apartment hawkers. Yell *"Lo,"* give them the look of death, and walk away. Most hostels are located less than three blocks from the bus station—walk up the hill on Ha-Tmarim Blvd. and take a right on Retamim St. The atmosphere of a smaller hostel can add tremendously to the enjoyment of Eilat. Some of the bigger hostels are unfriendly and have been known to kick out backpackers in favor of large groups; some even make patrons switch rooms in the middle of the night. The tourist office can assist if hostels are full. Vague pricing is easily deciphered; the low prices apply during winter, the high ones in summer. Always bargain.

For camping info, stop by the **SPNI Field School** (tel. 637 20 21), across the street from Coral Beach. Most hostels allow camping on their roof or in their backyard for NIS15-20. During July and August, hundreds of people happen to overlook the "No Camping" signs on the public beach and in the park; year after year, many are victims of theft. Aside from burglars and sexual harassers, there are also rats at these camps. If sleeping on the ground and taking communal showers sounds appealing, take bus #15 to **Coral Beach Campground** (tel. 637 19 11 or 637 50 63), the municipal campground opposite the beach of the same name. There you'll find a snack bar, scorching sun in summer, and tiny, pod-like huts with air conditioning. Laundry services are available on-site. (Campsites NIS35; huts NIS65 per person. Refrigerator NIS10. Breakfast included.)

ISRAEL

■ **Red Sea Hostel** (tel. 657 60 60), in New Tourist Center directly above the Underground Pub. Immaculate new rooms, all with bath. Mattress on the roof NIS15. Dorms NIS25-30. Singles NIS100; doubles NIS120; triples NIS150. Prices double during high season, but bargain anyway, especially for multiple night stays.

Siam Divers Hostel (tel. 637 05 81), right on Coral Beach. Priority goes to divers, but the location and atmosphere make this a great pick for any traveler. Rooms are simple, but patrons roll out of bed and straight into the ocean. Only 10min. from Eilat by bus. Dorms NIS60; doubles NIS150; triples NIS180.

Bianka's Lodge (tel. 632 63 35), at the end of Retamim St. One large dorm room with a mock-Bedouin outdoor TV room and plenty of pets. Communal, friendly atmosphere. Bianka is a great resource on deals in Eilat, but some may feel smothered by her love. Campsites NIS15; dorms NIS25.

Max & Merran's Hostel (tel. 637 13 33), off Almogim St. M&M melts in your mouth, not in your wallet. It has lost none of its friendly atmosphere under new ownership. Clean and newly built rooms with kitchen and bathrooms. Dorms NIS25-30.

Spring Hostel (tel. 637 4660), halfway down Retamim St., around the corner. Spacious but basic rooms. Billiards, pub, and very tight security. Dorms NIS20-40; singles NIS80-120; doubles NIS120-160.

Home Hostel (tel. 637 24 03; fax 637 35 13), just off Almogim St. behind the Family Bakery. Looks like a backyard shed, but friendly staff and feel-good vibe make it seem like home. Dorms NIS22. Breakfast included.

◖◗ FOOD

Falafel stands, pizzerias, and sandwich vendors swarm on Ha-Tmarim St. near the bus station and Retamim St. by the hostels. Burger-lovers rejoice: **McDonald's** is in the waterfront mall, and **Burger King** shares the tourist office building. Over the past few years, ethnic food in Eilat has boomed: the streets are now lined with inexpensive Chinese, Thai, Mediterranean, and Italian restaurants. There are three great bakeries on Ha-Tmarim St. north of the bus station. Since many accommodations in Eilat provide cooking facilities, backpackers can eat inexpensively by preparing their own meals.

■ **Pedro's Steak House,** 14 Ye'elim St. (tel. 637 95 04). A local favorite, with moderately expensive but unbelievable food. Lunch special NIS48, dinner NIS85, as well as cheaper options. Don't miss out on the freshly baked bread (NIS2) or the divine crème brulée. Open 12:30-4pm and 7-11:30 pm.

Mai Thai (tel. 637 25 17), on Yotam Rd. above the New Tourist Center. A bit expensive, but a great treat. Make it Our Thai with the frix-fixe menu for 2 (NIS72). Egg rolls NIS12, entrees NIS40-72. Open daily 1-3pm and 6:30-11pm.

The White Rafsoda (tel. 633 81 46), on the pier next to the marina. Massive new restaurant for those who can't decide what to eat: it's divided into Thai, Japanese, Italian, and Mediterranean quarters. Full meals NIS40-80. Beautiful view of the sea. After 11pm, music in Upper Deck Club upstairs turns from mellow to techno. Restaurant open noon-midnight, club open all night.

Malibu Restaurant (tel. 634 19 90), near the end of Coral Beach. Separate lunch and dinner menus—after all, no one should be seen eating the same thing twice in Malibu. Great place to get a sandwich on the beach (NIS14) or dinner on the dock. Dinner specials NIS60, pizzas NIS28-35. Open 9am-10pm.

Tandoori (tel. 633 38 79), in the Lagoon Hotel on the King's Wharf. Excellent Indian food. Friendly waitstaff will help arrange a menu to meet a lower budget. Lunch special is a filling 3-course meal NIS49. Great curry (NIS25-40). Open noon-midnight.

Hard Luck Cafe, 15 Almogim St. (tel 637 27 88). Its proximity to the hostels has made the Hard Luck a place for travelers, both transient and resident, to eat, drink, and compare how broke they are. Beer and wonderfully greasy pub food, but no rock memorabilia. Carnivores can devour the mixed grill and chips, but veggies are stuck with spaghetti (NIS10). Single women might appreciate a companion (male or female). Carlsberg NIS3-4. Kitchen open 3pm-midnight. Open daily 3pm until late.

🎵 ENTERTAINMENT

Eilat's nightlife offers a little bit of everything: beer swilling with hard-core backpackers, dancing with greased-up Israelis, and hobnobbing with affluent yuppies. Most bars open at lunchtime, though drinking often starts earlier. Nightclubs open at 10:30 or 11pm, get going around midnight, and don't close until 5 or 6am. The discos, centered in the lagoon area, are expensive (cover NIS25-30); shorts and sandals are a bad idea, and Day-Glo bras are the norm. The best parties are hosted by the elusive Red Sea Productions. The free and mellow **promenade** along the water offers some of Israel's most efficient people-watching—the visible-flesh-per-capita index is the highest in the country. Street vendors sell cheap jewelry and five-minute portraits, and Israeli studs try in vain to pick up female tourists. People start arriving at about 9:30pm and stay for most of the night.

Eilat's entertainment is not exclusively limited to scoping and scenes. The tourist office has information on events at the **Phillip Murray Cultural Center** (tel. 637 22 57), on Ḥativat Ha-Negev St. near the bus station. The jazz, classical, rock, film, and theater seasons run September to May (office open daily 8am-8pm). Eilat's most popular annual event is the international **Red Sea Jazz Festival,** at the end of August, with 10 daily performances on four stages. Ask the tourist office for info.

Dolphin Reef (tel. 637 18 46), just before Coral Beach. It's the place to be on M and Th after the dolphins have gone to sleep. Beach parties are known as the kinkiest in Eilat. When's your bedtime? Open 11pm-5am.

Unplugged (tel. 632 62 99), in the New Tourist Center. Loud music and big TVs. Free Sony PlayStation, Sa karaoke, and foosball attract the masses. Happy hour 4-9pm, NIS4 for ½L local beer. Heineken NIS12, local beers NIS7-15. Open daily 24hr.

Nisha (tel. 631 55 55), in the basement of the Neptune Hotel. This sushi dance bar is Eilat's trendiest and craziest night spot. Reserved for the chic and beautiful. Travelers are advised to pull out their best duds for this place. Drinks NIS8-125, sushi NIS14-31. Cover NIS20. Open 10:30pm-4:30am.

3 Monkeys (tel. 636 88 88), Hey hey it's in the Royal Beach Hotel toward the end of the Promenade. Features nightly live British bands. The other 9 monkeys are hidden among the throngs of tourists. Imported beer NIS20, cocktails NIS30. Open 9pm-3am.

Yacht Pub (tel. 636 34 44), on the marina by King Solomon's Wharf. Huge, with a fancy wooden bar; with a name like that, what did you expect? Upscale Israeli clientele and prices to match. Platinum blonds and platinum disco records. Huge 1L Carlsburg NIS23. Open daily 9pm-4am.

Hemingway's (tel. 637 64 35), next to the New Caesar Hotel, on the east side of the lagoon. The traveler crowd often spills out into the street, and party as the sun also rises. Offers loud rock and NIS10-12 pints. Open daily 8pm-4am.

Platinum (tel. 636 34 44), at the King Solomon Hotel. Upscale and popular with tourists. Ultra-modern, reflection-maximizing atmosphere with laser show mixes disco, pop, and new wave. Energetic bartenders and strong drinks, but dance space is dominated by scantily clad Israeli teenagers. Cover NIS45, F NIS65, includes 1 drink. Beer NIS10. Open daily 11pm-late. 18+ admitted.

Tarabin Pub, across from the airport. Bedouin-tent meets rave atmosphere is somewhat successful. Local beer NIS10, imported NIS15, mixed drinks NIS20. Open 9am-late.

👁 SIGHTS

Some say that the best Eilat wildlife is in the air. Avid birdwatchers flock to the salt ponds north of the lagoon when 30 species fly overhead on their way to or from Africa (mid-Feb. through May and mid-Sept. through Nov.). The **International Birdwatching Center (IBC)**, P.O. Box 774, Eilat 88106 (tel. 633 53 39), on Eilat St. near the northern end of the airport, organizes walking (US$5) and jeep tours (US$50; open Su-Th 9am-1pm and 5-7pm, F 9am-1pm). There's even a birdwatching festival in March. Visitors pretend to be birds at the skydiving simulator **Airodium** (tel. 637 27 45), behind the Riviera Hotel. An air-vent contraption makes for an expensive but fun 10 minutes (NIS120). For stimulation beyond simulation, jump with **Skydive Red Sea** (tel. 633 23 86), P.O. Box 4139, Eilat 88150.

🤿 SCUBA DIVING

Eilat has long served as the center of Red Sea diving—and with warm waters and a wide variety of unusual marine life, it's not surprising that it has continued to thrive as a major dive resort despite the development of more exotic and undisturbed centers nearby. Although dive sites in Eilat are less pristine than many in the Sinai, the city's long history of diving makes it one of the most technically advanced and safest areas to dive in the Red Sea. The dive centers that have survived in Eilat have done so because they maintain a high level of professionalism, modern equipment, and multilingual guides and instructors. Eilat also offers a fully equipped and professionally operated recompression chamber at the local hospital, which is within 12 minutes of all dive sites. All of the following sites are accessible by a short snorkel or truck ride from the major dive centers along Coral Beach. For an up-to-date list of dive sites and activities, try www.Eilat.net.

There are several underwater observatories for those hoping to experience underwater Eilat without getting wet. The **Galaxy** (tel. 631 63 60) is one of the city's many glass-bottomed boats (1½hr., NIS60). The **Jules Verne Explorer** (tel. 633 36 66) may not venture 20,000 leagues down, but glass walls make it a true underwater observatory (2hr. cruise to the Japanese Gardens NIS80). Both dock at the marina. The **Coral World Underwater Observatory and Aquarium** (tel. 637 66 66) features shark and turtle tanks and an underwater observation room. Though interesting, it is best for those who won't be experiencing aquatic wildlife firsthand (open Sa-Th 8:30am-5pm, F and holiday eves 8:30am-3pm; admission NIS55, children NIS145). Live a life of ease in the **Yellow Submarine** (tel. 637 66 66), which goes 60m below the surface. Few fish scurry from the sub's light, but some say it decreases visibility (observatory and submarine admission NIS204, children NIS116).

DIVE SITES

🗾 JAPANESE GARDENS. Arguably the finest in Eilat, this dive site gets its name from the placid, "manicured" look of the coral, which almost completely covers the sandy bottom. Sushi- and sashimi-lovers will be glad to know that the Japanese Gardens are home to the most plentiful fish life in Eilat. *(10min. on bus #15 from the central bus station. Entrance is on the right by the underwater observatory. Open 9am-5pm. Admission NIS15. Limited diving; check ahead.)*

CORAL BEACH NATURE RESERVE. This national reserve (which includes Moses' and Joshua's Rocks) offers divers a wealth of coral species and fish life, making the entry fee well worthwhile. Five water trails marked by buoys go through the reef, and a bridge into the water protects coral from human feet and vice versa. *(Take bus #15 from the central bus station toward the sea. Tel. 637 68 29. Open Sa-Th 9am-6pm, F 9am-5pm. Admission NIS18, children NIS9. Coin-operated lockers NIS5.)*

DOLPHIN REEF. The commercially operated scuba and snorkeling center at Dolphin Reef lets divers observe semi-wild dolphins in a somewhat natural environment. Although the project has raised some ethical eyebrows, the dolphins are free to swim away at any time (although it would be difficult for any mammal to refuse a free feeding, as most budget travelers will agree). The dolphins perform a variety of tricks daily at the four "interaction" sessions, but observing them underwater, where they are fully unrestricted, is a more rewarding experience. The four original dolphins brought from the Black Sea have added seven new babies to the group. *(Beyond the port on bus #15. Tel. 637 18 46. Open daily 9am-5pm. Admission NIS29, children NIS22. Interaction sessions every 2hr. 10am-4pm. Snorkeling NIS202, children NIS193. Beach open and free after 5pm.)*

DIVE FACILITIES

Siam Divers (tel. 637 05 81; fax 637 10 33; email siamdive@netvision.net.il; www.siam.co.il), at the end of Coral Beach next to the Nature Reserve. While many divers may initially be attracted to the high-gloss finish of the larger dive clubs, this is the friendliest, safest, and most experienced dive center in Eilat. Intro dives (no certificate necessary) NIS160, 2 guided dives with full equipment NIS170, 5-day open water course NIS790/US$190. Convenient dorms NIS60, with course NIS40. Unforgettable 3- to 5-day dive safaris to the Sinai start at NIS1600/US$340. 10% student discount.

Red Sea Sports Club (tel. 637 65 69), in the Ambassador Hotel; also has an office at the King Solomon Hotel. PADI open-water courses NIS1300/US$275; dives with dolphins NIS265/US$56. Office on North Beach near the lagoon offers windsurfing (NIS70 per hr.), water-skiing (NIS135 for 15min.), and parasailing (NIS160 for 10min.). Also arranges horseback riding lessons at **Texas Ranch** (tel. 632 65 02), across the street (1hr. NIS135; 2hr. NIS170; 4hr. NIS235).

Photo Shop (tel. 637 31 45, ext. 272), upstairs in the Ambassador Hotel. Rents underwater cameras (NIS235-500/US$50-100 per day) and video cameras (NIS725/US$150 per day).

◨HIKING: NEAR EILAT

The beauty of the red granite mountains towering over Eilat matches that of the coral reefs thriving beneath it. The **SPNI Field School** (tel. 637 20 21), across from Coral Beach (take bus #15), is an essential stop for independent hikers. It sells extensive trail maps and provides good advice on hikes (open Su-Th 8am-4pm). Many of the sites are accessible by northbound bus #393, 394, or 397. Buses fill up fast during high season and on Sundays and Fridays—make reservations at the central bus station two days in advance. The most exciting and accessible terrain north of Eilat includes **Ein Netafim, Mt. Shlomo**, and **Ha-Kanyon Ha-Adom** (Red Canyon). Buses will stop nearby upon request. From Red Canyon, hike to the lookout above **Moon Valley**, a pocked canyon in Egypt, and to the unusual **Amram's Pillars**. These hikes are not advisable in summer; October through April is the best hiking season. Before attempting any of these hikes, consult the SPNI.

MOUNT TZFAHOT. The hike to Mt. Tzfaḥot is convenient and offers great views. The green-and-white trail begins at the left end of the fence separating the highway from the field school complex. The climb to the summit takes 45 minutes. From there, the blue trail heads north, ending at the Club Inn Hotel near Aqua Sport Beach. The round-trip takes about two hours and makes a good evening outing. If you wander too far on paths leading south, you may end up in Egypt.

TIMNA NATIONAL PARK. The Timna copper mines were in mint condition 6000 years ago and are still a fascinating destination today. Some people believe the Israelites passed through here on their way out of Egypt. The park houses remains of workers' camps and cisterns dating from the 11th century BCE, scattered amidst the whir of modern mining. The sandstone **King Solomon's Pillars,** near the 14th-century BCE Egyptian Temple of Hathor, dominate the desert at a height of 50m. The park's lake offers **camping** facilities (including showers) and a restaurant on its artificially created shores. **Timna Express** (tel. 637 47 41; fax 637 39 68) runs daily excursions to Timna and the neighboring kibbutz (8am-early afternoon;

NIS250/US$55, children NIS190/US$40; includes lunch). *(Most buses headed to Tel Aviv or Jerusalem will stop at the sign for Alipaz (don't get off at the Timna Mines signpost). The park entrance is 2km away, too far to walk in summer. Tel. 635 62 15; fax 637 25 42. Open daily 7:30am-sunset. Admission NIS26, ages 5-18 NIS19.)*

ḤAI BAR BIBLICAL NATURE RESERVE. This wildlife park is designed to repopulate animals indigenous in biblical times, many of which have become rare in the region. The reserve has an impressive predator center, where 11 native predators can be seen in their habitats. There is also a nocturnal room, where nighttime animalia can be viewed. The bulk of the preserve is a game park, home to ostriches, wild asses, antelopes, addaxes, and oryxes. Those without cars can only see the predator center and nocturnal room. *(Most northbound buses will stop here. The center is a 20-minute walk (very hot in summer) from the bus stop. The entrance is opposite Kibbutz Samir, 5km south of Yotvata. Tel. 637 60 18. Open daily 8:30am-5pm. Admission NIS26, children NIS15; without car NIS12, children NIS5.)*

ISRAEL

WEST BANK

الضفة الغربية

West Bank residents live in a culture distinct from that of any other in the Middle East. For the first time in history, the Palestinian flag flies over many towns, but the process by which self-rule was established has been long and arduous. The struggle is far from over, and the outcome is unpredictable—inhabitants' worn faces reflect the hardship of constant uncertainty. After several years of continuous autonomy in many parts and the recent election of the peace-advocate Ehud Barak, Palestinians are more hopeful than ever as they gear up for the tourist influx of the year 2000. While fluctuations in Israeli-Palestinian relations and extremist actions on both sides still disrupt daily life, well-informed and cautious travelers should have no problem visiting the area's major sites. The Israeli settlements are a skip and a jump away from many Palestinian towns, but don't expect transportation between the two. The best way to visit a settlement is to go back to Jerusalem and catch a bus from there.

PHONE FACTS	**Country Code:** 972. **Police/Emergency:** Tel. 100. **City Code:** 02 for all cities in the West Bank.

HIGHLIGHTS OF THE WEST BANK

■ Enjoy an evening coffee at a lively rooftop cafe or *argeileh* bar, featuring live Arabic music, in **Ramallah** (p. 391).
■ For almost two millennia, pilgrims have made this stable a staple. Follow the star to Bethlehem's **Grotto of the Nativity** (p. 385), the site of Jesus' birth, taking advantage of a Palestinian home-hospitality program instituted especially for the millennium.
■ **Jericho** (p. 388) may be 10,000 years old, but its liveliness as a center of Palestinian renewal, and the ritzy Oasis Casino, make it seem downright youthful.

ESSENTIALS

ENTRY

Travelers in Israel do not need any additional visas or permits to visit the West Bank; be sure to bring your passport, though. The West Bank is accessible by car, but the numerous Israeli checkpoints preclude a smooth ride. East Jerusalem is the transportation hub for the West Bank, but travel restrictions have made it impossible for Palestinians who do not live there to use Jerusalem as a transit terminal. As a result, most bus lines have been re-routed to Ramallah, in the northern West Bank; Ramallah's Manara Circle is a hub for East Jerusalem-northern West Bank connections. When possible, travel from Jerusalem into the West Bank rather than from one West Bank city to another. Direct roads from Jerusalem can often cut travel time by more than half. Check with the Israeli tourist office before leaving. They'll issue a standard governmental travel advisory worthy of serious consideration; some find the warning heavy-handed and go anyway.

Be sure to pick up the biweekly *This Week in Palestine*, available in hotel lobbies and restaurants in the West Bank and East Jerusalem, for extensive listings of events and resources throughout the Palestinian Territories. The pamphlet is published by Jerusalem Media and Communication Center at 7 Nablus Rd. in East Jerusalem (tel. 581 97 77; fax 582 95 34; email ptw@jmcc.org; www.jmcc.org).

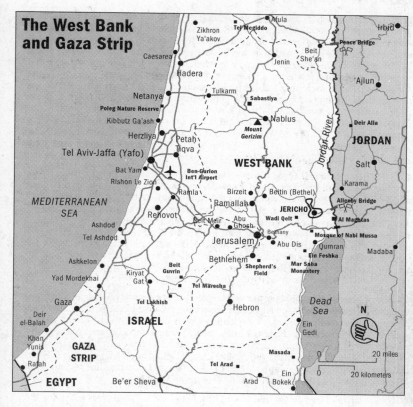

The West Bank and Gaza Strip

 BORDER CROSSINGS

TO JORDAN. As of press time, tourists crossing through Jericho's **King Hussein/ Allenby Bridge** had to obtain visas in advance; get them either in Tel Aviv, at the Eilat-Aqaba crossing, or from a Jordanian embassies or consulates. Allow at least an hour and a half to cross. At the bridge, your passport and belongings will be inspected (you may reclaim your VAT here). A transit fee of NIS107 and a bank fee of NIS3 will be collected; you then have to pay JD1.5 for a shuttle bus across the actual border. Once on the Jordanian side, there is a JD5 entrance fee; from there, *service* are available to Amman (JD10). Be prepared to pay JD5/US$7.50 to Jordanian customs officers upon leaving and reentering Jordan. The Israeli side does not collect a fee. Everything remains unpredictable; contact your embassy or consulate for thorough, up-to-date information.

! SAFETY WARNING. The West Bank has seen considerable conflict between Palestinian residents and Israeli settlers and security forces. Carry your **passport** at all times. Be aware of the situation in each town before visiting. Avoid visiting on the anniversaries of uprisings or terrorist attacks. Do not travel if Israel has just announced a new building program or territorial acquisition. Visibly **Jewish** travelers may be in danger and should cover *kippot* with a baseball cap.

GETTING AROUND

TAXIS. Although shared **service taxis** are slightly more expensive than buses, they are faster and more reliable, and depart more frequently (whenever they fill up). **Private taxis** (called "*special*," pronounced SPAY-shal) are much more expensive and not usually equipped with a meter; be sure to bargain for a price before getting in. Private taxis are often the only way to reach remote sites. Drivers will take you to the site and (for a few extra shekels) wait around to make the return trip. Some West Bank cities, including Nablus and Ramallah, have adopted a color convention for taxis: orange cabs are *service*, yellow ones are private. As always, be wary of price-gouging: insist that the driver turn on the meter if there is one, and have an idea of an appropriate price beforehand. Even for the most remote sites, do not pay more than NIS50 per hour. In Gaza, taxis are far more convenient than buses, almost as cheap, and hard to miss. Within Gaza City, where there is no intracity bus service, half of all cars seem to serve as taxis.

BUSES. Both **Arab** and **Egged** buses service the West Bank. Arab buses leave from two bus stations in East Jerusalem: the Suleiman St. Station between Herod's Gate and Damascus Gate for the south, and the Nablus Rd. Station (a few steps away) for the north. Catch Egged buses at the West Jerusalem central bus station on Jaffa Rd. Egged buses cost more and often stop only at the outskirts of Palestinian towns, but they are convenient for traveling to the Jewish settlements. Arab bus schedules to the West Bank are unpredictable; the intervals listed in this book are approximate. Transportation to Nablus and Jericho is especially erratic. For the former, take a *service* to Ramallah and continue to Nablus from there. For Jericho, go first to Abu Dees or Izziriyeh (Bethany) and connect from there.

CARS. A system of **colored license plates** differentiates vehicles. Those registered in Israel, Jerusalem, and Jewish settlements have yellow plates. White plates with green numbers belong to vehicles registered with the Palestinian Authority. Blue plates are a remnant from the days when the Palestinian territories were the Occupied Territories; they signify Arab cars not registered with Israel. Others are black-on-white (U.N. or diplomatic), red (police), and black (army). It's probably safer to travel with white or blue plates, but many Arab-owned cars that are registered in Israel (with yellow plates) travel hassle-free in the West Bank.

TOURS. An easy way to see the West Bank is to hire a Palestinian guide for the day. **Alternative Tourism Group** (see **Bethlehem Tours**, p. 384) is a reliable company with excellent guides. Alternatively, look for a taxi driver who speaks decent English (there are many) and ask whether he can drive by the major sights. Specify how many hours you wish to spend and agree on a price in advance; something in the range of NIS45 per hour is reasonable for transportation, waiting time, and some guidance about the sights.

MONEY MATTERS

The **New Israeli Shekel (NIS)** is the currency most frequently used in the West Bank and Gaza, although **Jordanian dinars** (JD) and **U.S. dollars** (US$) are also sometimes accepted. Expect prices to increase by a significant margin when paying in foreign currency. ATMs are not nearly as common as in Israel, though most cities have at least one equipped bank. Traveler's checks and credit cards are not always recognized, so carry enough cash. Keep in mind that many of the banks and money exchange services may be closed on Fridays in Muslim areas.

KEEPING IN TOUCH

The **postal service** in the West Bank is, for now at least, part of the Israeli mail system. All major towns in the West Bank have at least one post office with Poste Restante. The Palestinian Authority in Jericho has its own postal system, with stamps that are currently good only for sending letters between Jericho and Gaza. The

telephone system is also part of the Israeli telephone network. All services, including collect and calling-card calls, are available from any private or public phone. Shekel-operated phones are available in the West Bank, but can be difficult to find. Blue-colored Telecard-operated phones are conveniently located in most post offices, where cards can also be purchased, but these new telecard phones do not accept Israeli Bezeq cards. The blue public phones in the Gaza Strip operate on phonecards that can be purchased in small shops and groceries (NIS15-60). Phone calls can be made from hotels as well, but are more expensive. There are less expensive, privately run phone offices in Gaza City.

DRESS AND ETIQUETTE

Modest dress will make both men and women's experiences more enjoyable. Tourists may be invited into Palestinian homes, where hot spiced tea and coffee are accompanied by discussions of the *intifada* and occupation. Try to refrain from expressing strong political opinions. Jewish travelers should weigh out the situation before openly revealing their religion. Visitors should make their tourist (i.e. non-Israeli) status apparent.

HISTORY

The West Bank represents the most complex facet of the Arab-Israeli conflict, due to its importance to three major groups: Palestinian Arabs, Israelis, and Jordanians. Palestinian Arabs are the region's largest indigenous group and have resided throughout Israel and the West Bank for many years. Jews lived in the West Bank long before the 1967 and even the 1948 wars. Jews were drawn to the holy city of **Hebron** (see p. 393), but in 1929 they fled the city after an Arab massacre claimed 80 Jewish lives. Over 70% of the Jordanian population is of Palestinian origin.

The political region now called the West Bank was created in the 1948 War, when Jordan's **King Abdullah** annexed the "west bank" of the Jordan River rather than creating a separate state as the U.N. had stipulated. This angered many Palestinians in the West Bank, as did the discrimination they faced from the Jordanian government. Israel captured the West Bank in the **Six-Day War** (see p. 244) and placed the area under temporary military administration (except for East Jerusalem, which was annexed). The Israeli government instituted improved medical care and allowed most Arab and Jordanian policies to continue, but the occupation was not all benevolent. Basic rights granted to Jews and Israeli Arabs were denied the Palestinians, including freedom of assembly or the freedom to fly Palestinian flags. Palestinian attempts at establishing economic independence were thwarted and avenues of legal recourse closed. Some 160,000 Israeli Jews have settled in the West Bank since 1967. The settlements are motivated by strategic economic considerations and by the desire to keep the boundaries of *Eretz Yisrael* (biblical Israel, which includes Israel, the West Bank, the Gaza Strip, and a bit beyond). Often strategically situated on hilltops overlooking Palestinian towns, some settlements resemble military installations, although more established settlements, such as Efrat, feel like full-fledged small cities.

In December 1987, a traffic accident in the Gaza Strip sparked the Palestinians of the occupied territories to begin the **intifada,** a 20-year-long, often violent expression of Palestinian nationalism (p. 245). The new generation of Palestinians who knew nothing but Israeli occupation (some still in their teenage years) had abruptly upstaged their elders, including the PLO, with a widespread resistance movement that garnered international attention and sympathy. The Palestinian problem was reinstated as the focal point of the Arab-Israeli conflict. The *intifada* had stopped making headlines by the time of the 1991 **Gulf War,** when the PLO and most Palestinians supported Iraq (rather than supporting the U.S.-led movement, as most Arab governments in the region had done).

After the historic Madrid peace conference in October 1991, negotiations between the Palestinians (in a joint Jordanian-Palestinian delegation) and the Israelis took place from 1991 to 1994 in Washington, D.C. Israeli Prime Minister

Yitzḥak Shamir made few concessions, but the subsequent center-left government under late Prime Minister Yitzḥak Rabin pushed to promote the peace process with a special emphasis on the Israeli-Palestinian negotiations. The exact nature of negotiations has sparked extensive debate on both sides. In Israel, some feel that turning the West Bank over to the Palestinians (and thereby exposing the narrow coastal strip that houses three-fourths of Israel's population to hostile neighbors) was suicide. On the Palestinian side, moderates favored a compromise with Israel but were challenged by the Islamist group **Hamas,** which was gaining popularity when the talks began and advocates continuing terrorism and armed struggle because it cannot envision a Palestinian state peacefully existing alongside Israel.

It took secret negotiations in Oslo (baby-sat by the Norwegian Foreign Minister) between representatives of the PLO and the Israeli government to rescue the ailing Washington talks and to lay the groundwork for Palestinian autonomy. The Oslo negotiations drafted the Declaration of Principles on Interim Self-Rule Arrangements (the DOP or Oslo Accord). The **Oslo Accord** called for mutual recognition (and non-violent settlement) between Israel and the PLO and the implementation of Palestinian autonomy (expanding over five years) in the Gaza Strip and Jericho area, leading to an eventual finalizing of the entire messy situation.

After the signing of the Oslo agreement and the more detailed Cairo agreement (calling for Israeli withdrawal from the Gaza strip and the Jericho area), much of the PLO leadership relocated from Tunisia to Gaza, where they established the **Palestinian Authority (P.A.).** By the summer of 1995, Israel had pulled out and given the P.A. complete control in Jericho and Gaza, with Israeli powers essentially limited to foreign affairs and external security. The P.A. also had powers over taxation, education, social welfare, health, and tourism in the rest of the West Bank, excluding settlements and military outposts. A round of intense negotiations during the summer led to an interim agreement for the transfer of control over militarized areas to the P.A., and the establishment of an elected Palestinian parliament.

After Prime Minister Rabin's assassination, the May 29, 1996 Israeli election brought right-wing Likud party leader **Benjamin Netanyahu** to power with 50.4 percent of the vote. The year 1996 saw the removal of troops from Hebron, but stepping up of settlement in East Jerusalem and elsewhere in the Occupied Territories. Disputes over Israeli settlement policy and extremist actions on both sides brought peace negotiations almost to a standstill. On May 4, 1999, the five-year deadline set at Oslo expired. Though he had initially planned to unilaterally declare an independent Palestinian State, the PLO's Yassir Arafat held off in accordance with the advice of almost every Western government. In June 1999, Benjamin Netanyahu's term ran out and new elections saw left-wing peace-advocate **Ehud Barak's** victory. Hopes are high on all sides that under his leadership the different factions in the region may see lasting peace. See In The News (p. 249) for details of Barak's policy on the situation.

THE ARTS

Much recent Palestinian literature concerns the agony of foreign occupation and exile, touching also on themes of reconciliation with the Israelis and the common plight of the two nations. **Ghassan Kanafani,** perhaps the greatest contemporary Palestinian fiction writer, recreates the desperation and aimlessness of the refugee in short stories *All That Remains: Palestine's Children* and, portraying the struggle through adult eyes, *Men in the Sun and Other Palestinian Stories.* His *Return to Haifa* is an electrifying account of a face-to-face encounter between an exiled Palestinian family and an elderly Jewish couple who are Holocaust survivors. The poetry of **Mahmoud Darwish** depicts Palestinians' attachment to the land. The poems of **Fouzi al-Asmar,** collected in *The Wind-Driven Reed and Other Poems,* share the longing for a homeland. Jabra Ibrahim Jabra's novel *The Ship* is engrossing, as is his autobiography *The First Well,* an idyllic account of his Christian upbringing in Bethlehem. In his *Wild Thorns,* Sahar Khalifeh describes an expatriate's return to Palestine and his conversion to an ideologically committed terrorist. Israeli Arab Anton Shammas' *Arabesques* describes Palestinian identity crises; Fawaz Turki's autobiographical tomes discuss life in exile. The works of Liyana Badr, Raymonda

Tawil, and Samih al-Qassem all deserve note; most of these authors and others are translated in Salma Khadra Jayyusi's behemoth *Modern Palestinian Literature*.

BETHLEHEM بيت لحم בית לחם

Bethlehem (*Bait Lahm* in Arabic, *Beit Lehem* in Hebrew) and its environs were the backdrop for some of history's quieter religious moments: Rachel's death, the love between Ruth and Boaz, the discovery of the shepherd-poet-king David, and the pastoral birth of Jesus. Bethlehem (which is almost entirely Christian) and the surrounding villages of Bait Sahur and Bait Jala'a are home to most of the Palestinian Christian minority. The glow-in-the-dark Virgin Marys and armies of postcard sellers swarming around the Basilica of the Nativity may take crass commercialism to a new level, but some visitors still manage to see past the blinding flash-bulbs to true religious significance.

In 1995, Bethlehem celebrated Christmas for the first time under Palestinian rule. Aside from being home to some of Christianity's most important sites, Bethlehem is a prime example of what independence can achieve. The changing of the guard has breathed new life into this town; the mood is upbeat and optimistic, and the people, though eager for tourist cash, are friendly.

> **! SAFETY WARNING.** Bethlehem is quite safe, but lingering conflict over the possession of **Rachel's Tomb** can sometimes turn violent at the tomb or nearby Israeli-Palestinian checkpoint. Look around Manger Sq. for the blue-clad **Tourist Police**, who were brought in for the throngs expected for the millennium.

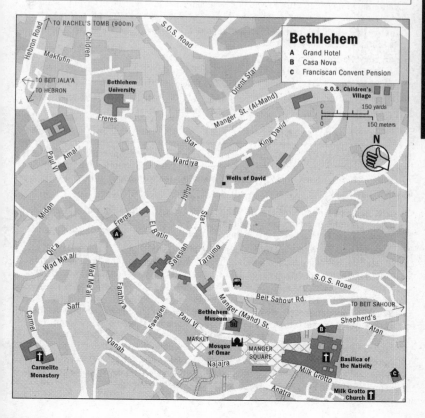

WEST BANK

⚡ ORIENTATION AND PRACTICAL INFORMATION

The original Three Wise Men followed a star to a peaceful manger; today's pilgrims can follow **Star Street** to bustling **Manger Square,** where most of the Christian sights are clustered. **Rachel's Tomb,** on the northern outskirts of Bethlehem, is a 30-minute walk (or NIS2 *service*) from there. Manger St. forks into Star St.; **Paul VI Road** branches off this, and a right turn leads into Manger Sq. Alternatively, take a *service* from Rachel's Tomb to **Bab az-Zaqaq,** the transportation hub for the region, at Hebron Rd. and Paul VI Rd. The walk from Bab az-Zaqaq to Manger Sq. takes about 15 minutes. Star St. and **Najajreh Street** are home to the town's shopping district and open-air market.

Buses: Buses make the 8km trip from Suleiman St. Station in East Jerusalem (30min., daily every 15-30min. until 5pm, NIS2) to **Bab az-Zaqaq.** Buses stop running after dark.

Taxis: Taxis are the only local transportation; to find them, head downhill facing away from the Al-Andalus Hotel in Manger Sq. and bear left on Bait Sahur Rd. Taxis gather in the parking lot. To get back to Jerusalem, take a taxi to Bab az-Zaqaq or Rachel's Tomb (NIS1-2) and flag down a Jerusalem-bound *service*. A private taxi from the checkpoint to Jerusalem is NIS20-25; set a price before you leave. **Nativity Street** (tel. 274 19 23) is next door to the pharmacy near Manger Sq. Open Sa-Th 8am-7pm.

Tourist Office: PNA Ministry of Tourism, in the yellow hut in Manger Sq., has everything you need to know (including special Christmas and Easter info). Another office under Al-Andalus Hotel in Manger Sq. (tel. 647 70 50). Open M-Sa 8am-2:30pm.

Tours: Alternative Tourism Group, (tel. 277 21 51; fax 277 22 11; www.patg.com), in Bait Sahour, runs inexpensive tours of Palestinian cities and refugee camps throughout the West Bank. 3hr. refugee camp tour NIS35, full day Nablus-Ramallah NIS90.

Currency Exchange: Mercantile Discount Bank (tel. 274 39 88), in Manger Sq. Open M-Th 8:30am-12:30pm, F 8:30am-noon.

Emergency: Police: (tel. 274 49 07 or 274 49 03), on Al-'Ain St., downhill from Qanah St. **Tourist Police:** (tel. 647 70 50), in Manger Sq.

Pharmacy: Ar-Razi (tel. 274 16 47), on Nativity St. near Manger Sq. Open M-Sa 8am-8pm.

Post Office: (tel. 274 27 92), in Manger Sq. Open Sa-Th 8am-2:30pm. Send and receive mail via Israel and buy telecards and stamps good only within Palestinian territory.

⚡ ACCOMMODATIONS

There's no problem finding a place to stay during the off season, but at Christmas there's no room in the inn unless you reserve a year in advance. One attractive addition to Bethlehem's options is a **bed and breakfast** program, intended to give individuals a taste of Palestinian family life at a reasonable cost.

Tourist Bedouin Village (tel. 277 38 75; fax 277 38 76), in Bait Sahour's Shepherd's Valley, has tent accommodations with modern bath facilities and breakfast (NIS60). Occasional storytelling and Bedouin dinners. Open Apr.-Oct.

Franciscan Convent Pension (Franciscaines de Marie) (tel. 274 24 41), on Milk Grotto St. (look for the "White Sisters" plaque), offers flower- and Bible-bedecked rooms run by friendly nuns who will make you feel like you're in Catholic school again with the painful 9am check-out and 9pm curfew (in winter 8:30pm). Dorms NIS70; singles NIS120. Breakfast included. Dinner NIS45. Reservations recommended.

Alternative Tourism Group (ATG) (tel. 277 21 51; fax 277 22 11; www.patg.com). This B&B program overseen by ATG has 27 double rooms in private homes, all with clean private baths and some with telephones. NIS95 per person with breakfast. Lunch or dinner NIS25. Contact George Rishmawi at ATG in Beit Sahour.

Casa Nova (tel. 274 39 81/2; fax 274 35 40), off Manger Sq., has modern rooms and hot water. B&B NIS95; additional meals NIS25. 5% service charge. Check-out a cruel 8am. Flexible midnight curfew. Faxed reservations recommended.

Azzaitune Guest House (tel./fax 274 20 16; mobile 052 360 769), off Paul VI Rd. in Beit Jala'a. From Bab az-Zaqaq, take Paul VI Rd. away from Manger Sq. The closest thing Bethlehem has to a youth hostel. Dorms NIS55; singles NIS95; doubles NIS140.

Bethlehem Hotel, Manger St. (tel. 277 27 02; fax 277 07 06). Halfway between Rachel's Tomb and Manger Sq.; main entrance to the hotel not from the main street but from the adjacent small downhill sidestreet. Brand-new development project built especially for heavy 2000 tourism. Large dining rooms and grand lobby. Nice but antiseptic rooms. Singles NIS260/US$60; doubles NIS320/US$75; triples NIS390/US$90. Breakfast included, other meals NIS45. Check-out noon.

🖸 FOOD

Cheap falafel and shawarma stands in Manger Sq. and on Manger St. provide *fuul* for church-hopping excursions. **Granada** (tel. 274 72 33), in Manger Sq. along the line of souvenir shops, sells sandwiches (NIS7-15) and hot and cold drinks (open daily 8am-evening). Bethlehem's one-and-only nightspot, **Balloons,** on Hebron Rd. near Rachel's Tomb, dishes up renowned pizza. They only serve soft drinks, but don't let that burst your balloon—the alcohol pours at **Memories,** the pub upstairs (open W-M until late). **St. George** (tel. 274 37 80), in Manger Sq. next door to the post office, gets most of the tourist traffic from the Basilica with its impressive bar and extensive menu (salads NIS12, omelettes NIS17, meat plates NIS35; open daily 8am-midnight). One of Bethlehem's nicer options is the young and beautiful **Sababa** (tel. 274 40 06), on Manger St. opposite Alexander Hotel (hummus breakfast plate NIS10, grilled meats NIS45; open daily 9am-4pm). **Al-Bustan Restaurant** (tel. 274 77 66), in the Oriental Palace Hotel, satisfies with its three-course meal (soup or salad, entree, and dessert NIS70; open daily 10am-11pm).

🖸 SIGHTS

There are two ways to "do" Bethlehem. Traditionally, tourists arrive from Israel, hop from one Christian holy place to another in several hours, and are back in Jerusalem before dinner. A more interesting option is to spend an evening in Bethlehem and take a peek into the window of Palestinian life. Because no reliable public transportation is available, the best way to see the sights is to hire a guide with a vehicle for an afternoon. Guides gather in Manger Sq.; be sure to choose someone wearing a P.A.-issued ID tag, which indicates licensing. Tours should cost no more than US$8-10 per hour, including transportation. To explore the villages and other West Bank cities from Bethlehem, contact ATG (see **Tours,** p. 384).

MANGER SQUARE

🖾BASILICA OF THE NATIVITY. Manger Sq. is dominated by the Basilica of the Nativity, a massive basilica honoring the spot generally considered to be Jesus's birthplace and the oldest continuously used church in the world. Erected in 326 CE by Constantine under the supervision of his mother **Helena,** it was spared the Persian invasion (when virtually every other Christian shrine in the Holy Land was demolished) because of its mosaic of the three (Persian) wise men. The church lapsed into disrepair after the Crusader kingdom fell, but its importance as a holy shrine never waned: during the ensuing centuries, struggle for its control repeatedly led to bloodshed. In the 1840s, the church was restored to its former dignity, but squabbles between the various sects continue. Established in 1751 and finalized 100 years later, an elaborate system of worship schedules has worked through competing claims, but the confusion resulting from the Greek Orthodox Church's rejection of summer daylight savings time demonstrates the teetering balance of this arrangement.

DOOR OF HUMILITY. Though it has an impressive history, the Basilica of the Nativity is not particularly attractive, and bursts with pilgrims and tourists. The main entrance and windows were blocked up as a safety precaution during medieval times. To enter, assume a kneeling position and step through the narrow Door of Humility—a remnant of Christian attempts to prevent Muslims from entering on horseback. Marvel at the fragments of mosaic floor—all that remains of Constantine's church—beneath the huge wooden trap doors in the center of the marble Crusader floor. England's King Edward IV offered the oak ceiling as a gift; the Russian royal family bequeathed the handsome icons adorning the altar in 1764.

GROTTO OF THE NATIVITY. The sanctuary beneath the church is the Grotto of the Nativity. Crosses are etched into the columns on both sides of the cramped doorway—religious graffiti from centuries of pilgrims. The focus of the hubbub is a silver star bearing the Latin inscription: *Hic De Virgine Maria Jesus Christus Natus Est* ("Here, of the Virgin Mary, Jesus Christ was born"). The 14 points represent the 14 stations of the Via Dolorosa (see p. 273)—thus the end of Jesus' life is poetically married to its beginning. The star, added by Catholics in 1717, was removed by Greeks in 1847 and restored by the Turkish government in 1853. Quarrels over the star are said to have contributed to the outbreak of the Crimean War. (*In Manger Sq. Basilica complex open daily in summer 5:30am-7pm; in winter 5am-5pm. Free, donations encouraged. Tour guides often roam the square and nave offering tours; a reasonable fee is NIS15 for a 1hr. tour with a licensed guide. Modest dress required.*)

ST. CATHERINE'S CHURCH. Built by the Franciscans in 1881, this simple and airy church is a welcome contrast to the grim interior of the adjacent basilica. Superbly detailed wood carvings of the 14 stations of the cross line the walls. The first of the downstairs crypt rooms, the **Chapel of St. Joseph,** commemorates the carpenter's vision of an angel who advised him to flee with his family to Egypt. The burial cave of children slaughtered by King Herod (Matthew 2:6) lies below the altar and through the grille in the **Chapel of the Innocents.** Beyond the altar, a narrow hallway leads to the Grotto of the Nativity, although it is blocked by a thick wood door pierced by a peephole. During times of greater hostility between Christian sects, this glimpse was as close as Catholics could get to the Greek Orthodox shrine. To the right of the altar, a series of rooms contains celebrity sepulchres including the **Tomb of St. Jerome,** as well as those of St. Paula and her daughter Eustochia. These lead to the spartan cell where St. Jerome produced the **Vulgate,** the 4th-century translation of the Hebrew Bible into Latin. The Franciscan Fathers conduct a solemn procession to the basilica and underground chapels every day. To join in the 20 minutes of Gregorian cantillation and Latin prayer, arrive at St. Catherine's by noon. Saint Catherine's also broadcasts a **midnight mass** to a worldwide audience every Christmas Eve. (*Adjoins the Basilica. Use the separate entrance to the left of the Basilica entrance, or pass through the doorways left of the altar there. Open daily 6:30am-8pm.*)

NEAR MANGER SQUARE

MILK GROTTO CHURCH. The cellar of this church is thought to be the cave in which the Holy Family hid; Mary took refuge here and breast-fed baby Jesus when fleeing from Herod into Egypt. According to legend, some of Mary's milk fell while she was nursing the infant Jesus, whitewashing the rocks. The cave and church take their names from the original milky-white color of the rocks, which have now either been blackened by candle smoke or painted blue. Today, women with fertility problems eat some of the white dust as a charm. Don't miss the photo exhibit of suckling babies born to those whose prayers were rewarded. (*10min. walk from Basilica of the Nativity down Milk Grotto St. Facing the stores in Manger Sq., turn left down the alleyway to the Franciscan flag. Tel. 674 24 25. Open daily 8-11:45am and 2-6pm. Ring bell if locked.*)

O LITTLE TOWN OF BETHLE(MAY)HEM

Christmas in Bethlehem explodes with pilgrims and tourists, none of whom could say "how still we see thee lie." Come Dec. 25, the town becomes a huge festival. Falafel stands play *Jingle Bells* and *White Christmas*, red-robed Santa Clauses smile in the streets, and strings of colored lights adorn storefronts and church facades. Getting a ticket to midnight Mass isn't easy, but the service is broadcast on TVs throughout Manger Sq.

MUSEUMS. The two adjacent stores that comprise the **Palestinian Heritage Center** display and sell traditional crafts. The small but interesting exhibit features a "traditional Palestinian sitting room" complete with handwoven carpets and teapots. The stores sell inexpensive needlework and other crafts, sold at minimal profit. The new and still developing **Bethlehem Museum** showcases Palestinian crafts, traditional costumes, and a 19th-century Palestinian home. (*Heritage Museum: off Manger St. near the Bethlehem Hotel. Tel. 274 26 42. Open M-Sa 9am-7pm. Bethlehem Museum: down Star St., toward the basilica. Tel. 274 25 89. Open M-Sa 8am-2pm. Admission NIS3.*)

NEAR BETHLEHEM

TOMB OF RACHEL. *Kever Raḥel* is a sacred site for Jews, a spot where synagogues have been built and destroyed throughout history. On one side are fervently praying Ḥasidic men, on the other weeping Yemeni women. The beautiful and illustrious Rachel died in Bethlehem while giving birth to Benjamin (Genesis 35:19-20), and has been a timeless symbol of maternal devotion and suffering since. The tomb is revered as a place to pray for a child or a safe delivery. There are separate entries for women and men. Women should dress modestly; men must don a paper *kippah*, available at the entrance. The P.A. insists that the tomb is the property of the Islamic *Waqf*, though the Israeli government have recently constructed a watchtower and fortress-like casing around it, and plan to build a special access road linking the tomb to Jerusalem, bypassing Bethlehem. (*On the northern edge of town on the road to Jerusalem, at the intersection of Manger St. and Hebron Rd. A 30min. walk from the Basilica of the Nativity. All buses between Jerusalem and Bethlehem or Hebron pass the tomb. Tel. 678 75 07. Open Su-Th 5am-7pm, F 5am-2pm and 5-7pm.*)

BAIT SAHOUR. Bait Sahour, on the eastern edge of Bethlehem, is believed to be the setting for the biblical Book of Ruth, in which a wealthy local farmer falls in love with a poor young widow, a new convert to Judaism. Home to some 15,000 inhabitants, the town contains vast, open stretches of grazing land, including the **Fields of Ruth.** The name of the village means "House of the Shepherds" in Hebrew, and Christian tradition holds that this is **Shepherd's Field,** where those tending their flocks were greeted by the angel who pronounced the birth of Jesus (Luke 2:9-11). A sign points left toward an alternate Shepherd's Field, promoted as the real thing by the Fransiscans. The site includes a tiny chapel, monastery, and excavated Byzantine church. (*Buses from the parking lot below Manger Sq. run to Bait Sahour (NIS1); from the drop-off, it's a 20min. walk to the site. You can also walk the 1½km from Bethlehem. A taxi costs NIS15. Open daily 8-11:30am and 2-5pm.*)

HERODION. Herodion is one of the world's finest examples of well-preserved early Roman architecture. The flat-topped Mt. Herodion arrests the eye with its startling silhouette, 11km east of Bethlehem. Much of the road between Herodion and Bethlehem crosses over the "Valley of Fire," where fathers sacrificed their first-born sons by fire in biblical times. It was also the site of the New Testament suicide of Judas, betrayer of Jesus. Built as a summer palace by King Herod, the mammoth structure boasts a unique circular design—round towers, circular swimming pools, and bathouses surround round buildings. Herod's body is believed to be buried here, and although it has not yet been found, excavators have unearthed bones dating back to 2000 BCE (some of the oldest ever discovered) inside Kroutoon Cave.

Bypass the excruciating outdoor steps ascending Mt. Heredion and take the naturally air-conditioned 200 steps *inside* the mountain, carved into the cisterns, leading directly into the palace's central courtyard. At the top, the western defense tower is directly above the Kroutoon Cave. The red roofs below are those of the Jewish settlements of Teqoa, Noqedim and Ma'ale Amos, where the prophet Amos is buried. Take the outside steps to get back downstairs. The bridge was recently built directly over what used to be the palace's main gate. (*A round-trip private taxi from Bethlehem should cost NIS30, including waiting time. At press time, no buses served Herodion. Although located in the West Bank, Herodion is an Israeli National Park and continues to be managed by the Society for the Protection of Nature in Israel. Tel. 037 762 251. Open daily in summer 8am-5pm; in winter 8am-4pm. Admission NIS18, with ISIC NIS15.*)

JERICHO أريــحا יריחו

The first city to fly the Palestinian flag and the headquarters of the Palestinian Authority, Jericho vibrates with ground-breaking activity. Streets strewn with banners, flags, and portraits of Yassir Arafat convey Palestinian pride and optimism. Settled 10,000 years ago, Jericho is believed to be the world's oldest city; at 250m below sea level, it is also the world's lowest. Its location in the sweltering heart of the Judean Desert makes it scorching year-round; winter vacationers have flocked here for tans as far back as the 8th century, when King Hisham built a magnificent winter palace. Aside from several beautiful mosaic floors, the ruins themselves aren't that spectacular—after all, the walls are famous for having tumbled down.

After Joshua destroyed the city with a blast of his trumpet (Joshua 2:6), Jericho remained in shambles for centuries. The oasis town made a partial comeback under the Romans, Crusaders, and Mamlukes, but never grew to anything more than a palm grove village until 1967, when thousands of Palestinian refugees fled here from Israel. After it gained autonomy, the refugee camps were proudly replaced by apartment buildings and the standard of living drastically improved. In keeping with King Hisham's vision, today's Jericho is the site of several million-dollar investment projects, including a luxury resort popular with wealthy Palestinians, a cable-car/hotel complex at the foot of the Mount of Temptation, and the sin city known as the Oasis Casino Hotel.

⚠ ORIENTATION AND PRACTICAL INFORMATION

Jericho is on the road to Amman, 40km east of Jerusalem, at the junction of the highway to Galilee (for information on crossing to **Jordan**, see p. 379). The quickest and most reliable way to get to Jericho is by **service taxi.** Direct transportation from Jerusalem is infrequent; take a *service* from the parking lot outside the Suleiman St. bus station in East Jerusalem to **Al-Izariyyeh** (Bethany) or **Abu Dees** (both NIS2) and switch to a Jericho-bound *service* (NIS6), which will stop in the **central square** or at the **Oasis Casino.** The best way to get back to Jerusalem is actually to go in the opposite direction: because Jerusalem-bound *service* usually leave Jericho only when full, hail a *service* back to Jericho on the main road and catch another NIS6 *service* from the city center back to Jerusalem.

There is no public transportation within the city, but there are a multitude of **yellow taxis** (NIS30-40 per hour). Become your own taxi driver at **Orabi Rent-a-Car** (tel. 232 32 30), on Jerusalem Rd. Rates start at a reasonable NIS140/US$30 per day, but the blue license plates (indicating Palestinian ownership) might be problematic if touring in Israel. **Zaki Sale and Rent Bicycle** (tel. 232 24 76), in the central square, rents 21-speed mountain bikes with locks (NIS3 per hr.; open daily 7am-1pm).

The P.A.-run **Tourist Information Offices** (tel. 232 29 35 or 232 12 29) are opposite the old city parking lot and in the municipality building in the town center (open Sa-Th 8am-2:30pm). Satisfy your currency exchange cravings at **Cairo Amman Bank** (tel. 232 36 27), in the main square (open Sa-W 8-11:30am and 4-6pm, Th 8:30-11:30am). The **police** (tel. 232 21 00, 232 25 21, or 232 26 44) are on the northern side of the central square, next to the bank, while the **tourist police** (tel. 232 19 09) are across from Elisha's Spring (open daily 8am-6pm). **Arabi Pharmacy** (tel. 232 23 25), on 'Ain as-Sultan St. by Hisham's Palace Hotel, has the latest bedtime in town (open Sa-Th 8am-midnight). If it turns out to be more serious, go to **Jericho Government Hospital** (tel. 232 24 06), on Jerusalem St. Head down Amman St. from the police station to get to the **post office** (tel. 232 25 74; fax 232 36 09; open Sa-Th 8am-2:30pm). The blue public **telephones** in the West Bank take non-Bezek telecards.

🏠 ACCOMMODATIONS AND FOOD

With a relatively easy commute to Jerusalem, there isn't much reason to sleep here (hotels are expensive anyway). **Jerusalem Hotel** (tel. 232 24 44; fax 232 31 09), 1km down Amman St., has airy dorms (no A/C) with shared baths as well as clean rooms with air conditioning, telephones, and a few balconies (Dorms NIS95/US$20 per person; singles NIS240/US$50; doubles NIS334/US$70; triples NIS382/US$80.

WEST BANK

Breakfast included.) **Jericho Resort Village** (tel. 232 12 55; fax 232 21 89), off Qasr Hisham St. is a full-fledged resort complex with swimming pools, six restaurants, and luxurious lounge areas—a magnet for wealthy Palestinian families. (Singles NIS382/US$80; doubles NIS477/US$100.) There's nothing cheaper than **New Jericho Pension** (tel. 232 22 15), on Jerusalem Rd. across from New Jerusalem mosque; ring the caretaker Ibrahim next door to be checked in (singles NIS40; doubles NIS80).

There *is* such a thing as a free lunch in the West Bank; friendly locals may well bring you home to chat and dine on chicken. The city's best "locals" restaurant, catering to native tastes and pockets, is **Abu Nabil** (tel. 232 21 60), the red awning in the main square. A full lunch or dinner includes grilled meat, salad, pita, and hummus (NIS25; open daily 6:30am-midnight). **7 Trees** (tel. 232 27 81), on 'Ain as-Sultan St., serves local specialties in a bright, spacious setting (*musakhana*, a huge Bedouin chicken dish for two with nuts, vegetables, and bread NIS35; open daily 9am-midnight). The 700-seat **Temptation Restaurant** (tel. 232 26 14), underneath the Mount, tempts with a daily all-you-can-eat buffet (NIS35; open daily 6am-9pm).

♫ ENTERTAINMENT

The beautiful public **Spanish Garden,** near the center of town, was built recently through the contributions of the government of Spain. Reminiscent of a medieval Andalusian *hadeeka*, with two large fountains and lush greenery, the garden livens up after 6pm, when Jericho families, small children, and teenagers show up to enjoy Arabic music, coffee, and *argeileh*. A small cafe serves inexpensive snacks next to an arcade (open daily in summer sunset-2am; in winter sunset-9pm). Few visitors to this city of temptation can resist the **Oasis Casino Hotel,** several kilometers before the city center. This state-of-the art casino, with the full array of slot machines, blackjack, craps, poker, roulette, and other tables, would hold its head high even in Las Vegas. All gambling is in U.S. dollars, which can be exchanged from any currency at the door. Palms restaurant upstairs serves light meals and snacks. (Min. bids at most tables US$10-25, though some are US$5. No t-shirts. Passports required for entrance. Open daily 24hr.)

👁 SIGHTS

Hire a taxi for several hours from the city center and beat the heat (NIS30-40 per hour; set a price in advance). Visit Hisham's Palace first, as a cluster of restaurants and a cooling spring near the ancient city provides a pleasant post-tour rest stop.

HISHAM'S PALACE. Known as *Qirbet al-Mafraq* in Arabic, the palace was designed in 724 CE for the Umayyad Caliph Hisham as a lavish winter retreat from Damascus, and the jaw-droppingly extensive ruins here do not disappoint. The window in the courtyard, the site's most renowned feature, is in the shape of the six-pointed Umayyad star. A beautifully preserved mosaic depicts a sinister tableau in which a lion devours a gazelle as its naive playmates frolic beneath the Tree of Life. (3km north from Jericho's main square; follow the signs along Qasr Hisham St. to the turnoff at a guard post. Coming from ancient Jericho, take Jiftlik Rd., past the synagogue and the 'Ain as-Sultan refugee camp. After 1½km, turn right on the road back to Jericho; the turn-off for Hisham's Palace is on the left. Tel. 232 25 22. Open daily 8am-5pm. Admission NIS10, students NIS7.)

ANCIENT JERICHO. Thought to be the oldest city in the world, ancient Jericho is now a heap of ruined walls. Called **Tel as-Sultan,** the mound contains layer upon layer of garbage from cities ancient and modern. The oldest fortifications, 12m down, are 7000 years old. Some of the finds date from the early Neolithic period, leading archaeologists to suspect that Jericho was inhabited as early as the 8th millennium BCE. A limited amount of excavation has exposed many levels of ancient walls, some of them 3.5m thick and 5.5m high. Imagination will have to substitute for visible splendor at this site, which is distinctly unimpressive except for its great panoramas. (Follow 'Ain as-Sultan St. to its end. The entrance is through a parking lot around the corner. From Hisham's Palace, 2km away, turn right onto the road that runs past the Palace, cross a narrow bridge, then take a left at the next junction. Info. tel. 232 19 09. Open daily in summer 8am-6pm; in winter 8am-4pm. Admission NIS10, students NIS7.)

MOSQUE OF NABI MUSSA. About 8km from Jericho on the road to Jerusalem, the huge Mosque of Nabi Mussa stands in a sea of sand on a hill a short distance from the road, topped with a complex of white domes. Built in 1269 CE, this spot is revered throughout the Muslim world as the grave of the prophet Moses, and many Muslims yearn to be buried by his side. Islamic tradition holds that Salah ad-Din had a dream about the location of the place where God carried the bones of Moses. The tomb is said to have special powers—run your hands over the velvet cloth of Moses' Tomb while making a wish and see for yourself. Across from the tomb, stairs lead upward into a minaret with incredible views of the surrounding Judean desert. Ask the souvenir vendors to unlock the gate if it is wired shut. *(Private cab or taxi (NIS40) from Jericho are the only options for getting to the mosque. Open daily 8am-sunset. Free, but donations welcome.)*

MOUNT OF TEMPTATION MONASTERY. An imposing Greek Orthodox monastery stands on the edge of a cliff among the mountains west of Jericho; the peak is believed to be the New Testament's **Mount of Temptation,** where the Devil tried to tempt Jesus. The complex of buildings stands before a grotto, said to be the spot where Jesus fasted for 40 days and 40 nights at the end of his ministry (Matthew 4:1-11). Greek monks now live in the monastery, built in 1895. The summit of the mountain, named **Quarantal** after the Latin word for "forty," is also a pedestal for the Maccabean **Castle of Dok,** beside which lie the remains of a 4th-century Christian chapel. *(Monastery open daily 8am-2pm and 4-6pm. Modest dress required.)*

JERICHO SYNAGOGUE. This 6th-century synagogue, one of the oldest in the world, features an expansive mosaic floor (discovered while setting foundations for a summer house) with a *menorah, shofar* (ram's horn), *lulav* (palm branch), and the inscription *Shalom al Yisrael* ("Peace Be Upon Israel"). As part of extensive preliminary peace agreements, the P.A. has promised to watch over this synagogue, which is now a functioning *yeshiva. (Next to Ancient Jericho. Tel. 232 14 00. Open daily in summer 8am-6pm; in winter 8am-4pm. Admission NIS10, students NIS7.)*

NEAR JERICHO: WADI QELT

The three freshwater springs of Wadi Qelt nourish wildlife and lush greenery as they meander the 28km between limestone cliffs and undulating ridges of bone-white chalk. The *wadi* offers a brilliant hike, but a string of murders (presumably political) have taken place here in the past several years. The advice at press time was a resounding "Why risk it?" Inquire at SPNI to determine the relative safety of hiking in the area (main Tel Aviv office tel. (03) 638 86 36). SPNI offers one-day tours focusing on both natural and artificial attractions in the *wadi* (NIS260/US$59). The pace may be slower, but hiking with a group is much safer. The most interesting and accessible section of the *wadi* extends from the spring of Ein Qelt, past the 6th-century St. George's Monastery, and down into Jericho, 10km east. The trek takes about four hours. The best place to start is at the turn-off from the Jerusalem-Jericho Hwy., about 9km west of Jericho, marked by the orange sign for St. George's. *Service* to Jericho and Allenby Bridge stop here on request. By car, it is possible to skip the hike and drive most of the way to St. George's Monastery.

St. George's Monastery dates from the 5th or 6th century CE. Byzantine mosaics decorate the floor of the church; look for the likeness of a two-headed eagle, the Byzantine symbol of power. The neighboring St. John's Church houses a spooky collection of the skulls and bones of monks slaughtered when the Persians swept through in 614 CE. The Greek Orthodox monks who maintain the monastery can refill canteens for a journey into Jericho. (Open M-Sa in summer 8am-1pm and 3-5pm; in winter 8am-1pm and 3-4pm. Modest dress required, modest donation desired.) On the way to back to Jericho from St. George's, the ruins of **Tel Abu Alayia** are on the right. The palaces here, used by the Hasmoneans and later by King Herod, boast decorated walls, nearby bath houses, and pools.

RAMALLAH رام الله

Ramallah (perched with its demure sister Al-Bireh 900m above sea level) is the cultural capital of the West Bank, with a highly educated and self-consciously fashionable population. Before 1967, it was famous for its cool, pleasant mountain air and known as the "Bride of Palestine," a summer haven for Arabs from Jordan, Lebanon, and the Gulf. With vacationers long gone by the time of the *intifada*, Ramallah and the energetic young intellectuals at nearby Birzeit University joined Nablus as leaders of West Bank resistance. Now under P.A. control, the city has become a transportation hub and cosmopolitan center for much of the West Bank. When Palestinian self-rule expands, Ramallah (which already houses several important P.A. offices) will replace Gaza City as the administrative hub of the P.A.

Although it is still a political litmus test and just as restless as the rest of the West Bank, Ramallah has recently restored much of its traditional character. Today, Ramallah is known for its religiously relaxed atmosphere (alcohol flows freely and movie theaters are well attended) and the fabulous cafes along its main streets. With a large Christian population and many citizens who spend time in the U.S., Ramallah is among the least conservative cities in the West Bank; women can go out in pants and a t-shirt. Ramallah is also the hub of Palestinian feminist activity: the city's women frequently attend university rather than marry early, and several female-run cafes are used to fund local feminist organizations.

🛈 ORIENTATION AND PRACTICAL INFORMATION

It is possible to get from Ramallah to most northern West Bank towns by direct *service*. To get to Ramallah from **Jerusalem**, take a *service* from outside Damascus Gate (20min., NIS2.50), or an Arab bus from the station on Nablus Rd. (40min., NIS1.50). Buses and *service* to Jerusalem leave from Jaffa Rd., just off **Manara Circle** (Al-Manara), the town's epicenter. The last bus leaves at 5pm, the last *service* around 7pm. **Currency exchanges** are on all major streets and at Manara Circle. The only bank that accepts foreign ATM cards is **British Bank,** near Al-Bardoni's Restaurant on Yaffa St. **Jordan National Bank,** a 10-minute walk down the road to Jerusalem, gives advances on MC. The **police station** is on An-Nahda St., on the left past the Al-Wehdeh Hotel from Manara Circle. The **post office,** off Main St., downhill from Rukab's Ice Cream, sells beautiful Palestinian stamps. Cyber access is readily available at Internet "cafes," many of which do not actually serve food. The cheapest access is at **Carma Cyber Club** (tel. 298 48 54), in the Luluat al-Manara building, 6th floor, near Manara Circle (NIS4 per hr.; open Sa-Th 8am-midnight). **Ramallah General Hospital** (tel. 995 65 61 or 995 65 62) is more accessible than Ramallah's **pharmacies,** which close at 8pm or earlier.

⌂ ACCOMMODATIONS AND FOOD

Accommodations are expensive compared with nearby Jerusalem. **Miami Pension** (tel. 296 68 08), near the intersection of Jaffa St. and Faisal St., is a small, lovely hotel with a sunny lobby, hall balconies, and rooms with private bath, TV, and phone (singles NIS140/US\$35; doubles NIS200/US\$45; triples NIS230/US\$50). **Al-Wehdeh Hotel** (tel./fax 298 04 12), on An-Nahda St. near Manara Circle, is the cheapest accommodation, but not the cleanest. TVs and telephones circulate between rooms, some with balconies, all with private baths (NIS120-160/US\$25-35 per person; breakfast included). The excellent rooms at **Al-Hajal Hotel** (tel./fax 298 67 59), off Jaffa Rd. opposite Ramallah Park, pamper with satellite TV, phone, and private bath (singles NIS180/US\$40; doubles NIS225/US\$50; triples NIS260/US\$60; breakfast included).

○♪ FOOD AND ENTERTAINMENT

Budget restaurants and hangouts look down on the city from the tops of the taller buildings around Manara Circle. The **As-Siraj Theatre** (tel. 995 70 37), near Clock Circle, **Ashtar Theatre** (tel. 82 72 18 or (050) 512 285), on Radio St., and **Popular Arts Cinema** (tel. 995 38 91), on Al-Bireh St., host performing arts and dance shows: call or ask around town for details. Afterwards, head over to **Rukab's Ice Cream** (tel. 295 64 67), on Main St. at the corner of the post office, for possibly the best, gooiest ice cream in the hemisphere (multi-flavor cone NIS5; open daily 8am-1am).

🖎 **Layali Sultan** (tel. 298 02 75), on the 7th floor, on Main St. Groovy youths fill the palm-treed interior to nosh on cheap desserts and light meals (NIS7-25). Live *oud* every Th and Sa after 9pm, live Arabic singer F nights. Open daily noon-1am.

Angelo's (tel 295 64 08), a left turn off Main St., about 3 blocks after Manara Circle. Angelo flings pizza into the air and onto the plates of hungry travelers (NIS19-50). The garlic bread (NIS8 per basket) is a local favorite. Open daily 11am-midnight.

Rumours, off Main St., near the post office. Stylish cafe with world-weary cuisine (Italian, Chinese, and Middle-Eastern cuisine NIS18-30) and extensive alcoholic menu (Sex on the Beach NIS15). Tables cleared Sa nights for Ramallah's only weekly dance party, featuring Europop and Arabic hits. Open Su-F 11:30am-midnight, Sa 11:30am-2am.

Al-Aseel, off Main St. A tent on the roof of a building near Manara Circle. Nightly live music make this place as hot as the West Bank in July. Cool off with desserts, coffee, and light food (NIS5-15), or blow it all off with an *argeileh* (NIS10). *Oud* music Su-W, live Arabic singing Th-Sa. Open daily noon-midnight.

BBQ Za'rour (tel. 298 18 68), 5th floor of Faraḥ Building on Main St. (enter from rear). BBQ and kebab NIS18-35. Unlimited *argeileh* NIS15. Open daily 9am-midnight.

Taboun (tel. 298 05 05), 6th floor of Cairo-Amman Bank Building on Al-Ahaliya College St. Traditional Levantine dishes made with natural ingredients. Delicious fresh-squeezed juices. Full meal with drink around NIS40. Run by women, whose funds support a local women's science initiative. Open daily noon-midnight.

Urjuwan, in the Cultural Center on Al-Nahda St. near Manara Circle. Operated by women to fund local feminist organizations. Daily specials cooked on the spot with fresh ingredients. Clean and inexpensive. Open daily for lunch.

👁 SIGHTS

The main attraction in Ramallah is the city itself; on Saturdays, Manara Circle is a crammed, cosmopolitan jungle; on quieter days, the interested traveler can glimpse the pride and tension of a key Palestinian city.

MUSEUMS AND GALLERIES. The **Palestinian Folklore Museum** seeks to "revive Palestinian folklore and preserve it from theft or loss," and exhibits traditional costumes, handicrafts, and two rooms of a Palestinian house with a minimum of the expected propaganda. The **M. Sayem Gallery** displays Palestinian artwork in a space underneath the Ministry of Culture offices. (*Folklore Museum in the neighboring town of Al-Bireh, a few blocks away. Tel. 995 41 23. Gallery on the 3rd street on the right off Radio Blvd.*)

BIRZEIT UNIVERSITY. Birzeit University, the largest and most important university in the West Bank, is 12km northwest of Ramallah. Birzeit's 2500 students have a history of vocal opposition to the Israeli occupation; the university was often shut down by the Israeli Army during the 1980s, and was closed altogether from the first years of the *intifada* until April 1992. Today, Birzeit remains a vital presence; the university takes pride in its history and its strong leadership position in the West Bank, and has even developed an Internet training program. Travelers can attend some of Birzeit's frequent cultural events, which have recently included an international troupe of flamenco dancers and a Mormon orchestra. The university website (www.birzeit.edu) has info on Ramallah's present and past, an online travel guide, a performance schedule for university-sponsored events, and links to many local establishments. (*Service from Manara Circle NIS3. Tel. 998 20 59.*)

AL-IZARIYYEH (BETHANY) العزرية

Between Jerusalem and Jericho, near its western sister city, Abu Dees. Take a service from Jerusalem's Damascus Gate (NIS2) or from Jericho's central square (NIS6); ask for Al-Izariyyeh (ih-zar-EE-yeh). Service stop at the gas station next to the road to Al-Quds University. The sites are east, along the main road. Women should dress modestly and travel in groups.

This relatively prosperous Palestinian village is sacred to Christians as the home of Lazarus (and his sisters Mary Magdalene and Martha) and the place where Jesus miraculously raised him from the dead. A five-minute downhill walk from the gas station leads to a parking area on the left (with an unassuming grey gate labeled "Church"). The 1954 **Franciscan Church** (tel. 674 92 91) marks the spot where Jesus supposedly slept. (Church and excavations open daily Mar.-Oct. 8-11:30am and 2-6pm; Nov.-Feb. 8-11:30am and 2-5pm. Small donations appreciated.) The church features impressive mosaics depicting Lazarus's resurrection. Excavations have unearthed shrines here dating back to the 4th century. Signs from the Franciscan Church point uphill to the first-century **Tomb of Lazarus.** When the Crusaders arrived, they built a church over Lazarus's tomb, a monastery over Mary and Martha's house, and a tower over Simon the Leper's abode (Simon was another resident of Bethany cured by Jesus). In the 16th century, Muslims erected a mosque over the shrine, and in the following century Christians dug another entrance to the tomb so they too could worship there. Descend the steps and stoop down to see the tomb that does not contain Lazarus's body. (Tomb open daily 8am-7pm. Someone will come across the street to point out the light switch and ask for a donation; NIS2 is appropriate.)

HEBRON חברון الخليل

Service run to Bethlehem and Jerusalem (NIS5) from Bab az-Zawiyyeh St., the main drag. No regular visiting hours at the **mosque.** Security has been very tight since the shootings several years ago by a Jewish extremist, Baruch Goldstein. All Jews are officially barred from entering the mosque portion of the building, and all entrants are required to present a passport (without a Jewish-sounding last name) and pass through several metal detectors.

> **! HEBRON HAZARD.** Visitors should keep in mind that even native Palestinians sometimes regard Hebron as unsafe. Take along an Arabic-speaking guide, easily hired through **Alternative Tourism Group** in Bethlehem (see p. 384).

Lagging slightly behind other Palestinian cities, Hebron is not yet the most hospitable of tourist attractions. While recent months have seen relative peace and quiet, this hiatus comes after a history of bloody conflict, including the shooting of Muslim worshipers by an Israeli extremist several years ago. The city's once-famed masonries and vineyards remain economically depressed even under Palestinian self-rule. Many of the outdoor market shops remain closed. The enclave of about 500 Israelis who continue to live here was promised security as part of the redeployment agreements, but there are strong feelings of resentment from the Palestinian population of 130,000.

While Hebron is known for its turbulent political climate, it is also home to an extremely prominent religious site, the burial place of Abraham and Sarah, Isaac and Rebecca, and Jacob and Leah, patriarchs and matriarchs of both Judaism and Islam. Jews refer to the burial site as the **Machpelah Cave,** while Muslims call it the **Al-Ibrahimi Mosque** in honor of Abraham, the father of Ishmael and the man credited with founding monotheism. Half synagogue and half mosque, the rather grand structure standing there today is thought to lie directly above the underground tombs. It was renovated by Jewish philanthropist Sir Moses Montefiore in the 19th century, but no one knows how long this site has been venerated. While the synagogue is quite modest-looking, the interior of the mosque is a spectacular example of Islamic decor. Peek inside the metal bars to see the shrines for each of the patriarchs and matriarchs. The shrines are built directly above the supposed site of each tomb, and contain calligraphic script, Arabian carpets, and golden utensils. Note the huge stepped lectern (from which the *imam* delivers the Friday sermon), carved from a single block of wood. The longest Herodian cut stone ever discovered also forms part of the mosque's walls (lift the carpet or ask someone to point it out).

GAZA غزة

The distance separating Israel from the Gaza Strip is covered in a one-minute car ride from one side of the border checkpoint to the other, but once in Gaza City, it becomes apparent that the two regions are worlds apart. A 46km long and 6-10km wide sliver along the Mediterranean coast, the Gaza Strip is one of the most densely populated areas of the world. Gaza's population has increased dramatically in recent years, swelling to more than one million people with an influx of over 570,000 Palestinian refugees since 1951.

Gaza's history stretches back to 3000 BCE, when it was inhabited by Arab Canaanites. It grew as a stopping point for traders traveling from Africa and the Sinai to the southwest and from parts of the Middle East and Asia to the east. The Prophet Muhammad's grandfather, As-Sa'id Hashem Bin 'Abdumonaf, is said to have been one such trader, who died when passing through Gaza City and is purportedly buried in one of the city's mosques. Gaza is better-known for its recent history of occupation and uprising under Israel. The region was administered by Egypt from 1948 until the 1967 Six-Day War, when refugees flooded into the area after the Israeli occupation. Of the 770,000 refugees living in Gaza today, over 420,000 continue to live in the overcrowded United Nations-sponsored camps (see **Refugee Camps, p. 396**). The 1987 **Intifada** (see **p. 245**) uprising began in Gaza, in the Jabalaya camp near Gaza City. The peace process intensified with the onset of the *intifada*, and the Oslo and Cairo agreements of 1994 placed Palestinian Authority in control of the Gaza Strip.

Gaza prides itself on its long history as an intercontinental crossroads and now looks to reinvigorate that tradition, as evidenced by widespread construction and by the growing numbers of international trade and investment signs that line Gaza City's streets. Renewed attempts are being made to rehabilitate refugee camps with the help of the U.N., the European Community, and other international resources. Tourist officials hope that the sea and beaches will entice crowds of visitors to vacation in the Gaza Strip. However, it is the disorderly everyday life of Gaza's present—the mosques, churches, and unearthed archaeological finds that blend haphazardly into side-streets and vending stalls—that makes for the most fascinating and affordable random wandering for travelers. Gaza throbs with the activity of its capital's outdoor markets, chokes in the dust and cramped quarters of the refugee camps, and embraces visitors with a hospitable eagerness.

> **SAFETY WARNING.** Since 1994, the Gaza Strip has been governed by an autonomous Palestinian National Authority (PNA). Traveling is usually **safe** for foreign tourists; register with their respective consulates in Tel Aviv, Israel (p. 292) before going. Keep abreast of current events to avoid going to Gaza in times of unrest or tension. Women must dress **modestly**—long sleeves and a long skirt—and men should avoid wearing shorts. Have your **passport** on hand at all times.

PHONE FACTS | **Country Code:** 972. **Police/Emergency:** Tel. 100.

ENTRY

At time of publication, **Erez** is the only border checkpoint open for crossing from Israel into Gaza. From **Jerusalem**, *service* taxis meet across from Damascus Gate and go directly to the checkpoint (1hr.; infrequent, departs when full; NIS30). Though it is not possible to enter Gaza by car, it is helpful to understand the system of colored **license plates** that differentiates vehicles (see **Getting Around: Cars, p. 380**, for an explanation of the various plates).

Crossing the checkpoint takes three steps. First, Israeli soldiers will inspect your passport and record the reason for and proposed length of your stay in Gaza. They will then give you a slip of paper for presentation when entering Gaza. Taxis cross the border for NIS10, but the walk is very short. After crossing into Gaza, your information will once again be entered into a ledger. On the return trip to Israel, luggage is passed through an X-ray machine. On the Gaza side of the checkpoint, taxis heading into Gaza City center abound. A *service* taxi should cost NIS5 each to the central Palestine Sq. or the main street, Omar al-Mukhtar. A *special* taxi can cost anywhere from NIS20-50.

GAZA CITY

Despite an initial assault on the senses by the bustle, noise, sights, and smells of the city, the crowds of locals shuffling through the central market and along the main street and coastal road soon settle visitors into the remarkably laid-back rhythm of urban life. Roaming around the centers of activity brings a glimpse of present-day life but also offers encounters with the city's centuries-old architectural and cultural treasures.

⚡ ORIENTATION AND PRACTICAL INFORMATION

Taxis from Erez checkpoint let off in the heart of the city, **Palestine Square** (*Maidan Filisteen*). The main street, **Omar al-Mukhtar Street,** runs from Palestine Sq. to the coast. The grassy commercial strip **Norwegian Gardens** divides the lanes of Omar al-Mukhtar St. Almost all hotels are in the **Remal** (beach) district of the city, lined up along the coastal **Ar-Rashid Road,** which forms a T-junction with Omar al-Mukhtar St. Taxis along Omar al-Mukhtar St. cost NIS1. Most streets are labeled in English and Arabic, but establishments are rarely numbered.

Airplanes: Gaza Airport (tel. 213 42 99 or 213 42 89) is near **Rafah. EgyptAir** (tel. 282 15 30), on the corner of Aj-Jala'a St. and Al-Wihda St., has flights to **Cairo** (NIS235/US$50 one-way, NIS510/US$107 round-trip). Cash only.

Buses: In Palestine Square, beyond the municipality building. **Gaza Bus Company** (tel. 282 26 16) sends A/C-less buses to **Rafah** (1½hr., NIS2.50).

Taxis: *Service* taxis (NIS1 for trips along Omar al-Mukhtar St.) depart when full to **Rafah** (45min., NIS5). **Emad** will pick up passengers (tel. 285 53 90 or 286 40 00).

Car Rental: Al-'Ali Rent-a-Car, 84 Omar al-Mukhtar St. (tel. 282 85 34 or 282 72 96), near the top of the Norwegian Gardens, on the right coming from the beach (NIS350/US$85 for 2 days). Open Sa-Th 8am-8pm.

Tourist Offices: Gaza City's **public relations and information office** (tel. 282 47 00), in Palestine Sq., near the Arab Bank (marked by an English sign). Free outdated English map of the city, with an updated map for 2000 in the works. Open Su-Th 8am-2:30pm.

Human Rights Organizations: UNRWA (tel. 677 74 88), on Jamal 'Abd an-Nasser St. To get to the office, take a taxi to the "U.N." Tours to **Jabalaya refugee camp** (see p. 396). Call to arrange in advance. Donations requested. Open Su-Th 7:30am-3pm.

Currency Exchange: Commission-free exchanges line Omar al-Mukhtar St. and Palestine Sq. (look for the "$" signs). Open Sa-Th 9am-9pm. **Western Union** (tel. 286 57 75) is next door to the Cairo Amman Bank at the top of the Norwegian Gardens on Omar al-Mukhtar St. Open Su-W 8:30am-12:30pm and 2-4pm, Th 8:30am-12:30pm.

Emergency: Police (tel. 100), on Al-Maidal St., off Omar al-Mukhtar St.

Hospitals: 'Ali Arab Hospital (tel. 820 325), right on the first street past the taxi stand in Palestine Sq. **Shifa Hospital** (tel. 865 520, 860 109, or 864 009), on Izz ad-Din Al-Qassam St., left of Omar al-Mukhtar St. before the Rashad Shawra Cultural Center.

Pharmacy: Masoud (tel. 861 879), at the corner of Charles de Gaulle St. and Omar al-Mukhtar St., near the beach. Open daily 7:30am-midnight.

Post Office: On Omar al-Mukhtar St. between the Norwegian Gardens and Palestine Sq., Open Su-Th 8am-2pm. Palestinian (not Israeli) stamps are issued here.

Telephones: Al-Baz (tel. 238 21 910), on Omar al-Mukhtar St. up from the Norwegian Gardens, on the left. International calls NIS4 per min. Open Sa-Th 9am-10pm.

Telephone Code: 07.

▌ ACCOMMODATIONS

Gaza City has the only accommodations in the Gaza Strip, along the coastal Ar-Rashid road in the Remal district, a short walk from the end of Omar al-Mukhtar St. Proprietors generally speak English and are eager to offer suggestions of sights and places to eat. **⬛Cliff Hotel** (tel. 286 13 53), on Ar-Rashid St., claims to be the first hotel in Gaza, though you couldn't tell from its spacious and clean rooms with modern amenities like full bath, air conditioning, beach-view balcony, TV, fridge, and phone. (Singles NIS190/US$40, students NIS145/US$30; doubles NIS255/US$54, students NIS190/US$40. Breakfast included.) **Al-Amal Hotel** (tel. 821 798), on Omar al-Mukhtar St. near the beach's end, has fans (but no A/C) and a popular *sheesha* parlor downstairs. (Singles NIS145/US$30 with shared shower, NIS190/US$40 with bathroom; doubles NIS145/US$30-NIS235/US$50; triples NIS285/US$60. Breakfast included. Cash only.) **Marna House**, Ahmed 'Abd el-'Aziz St. (tel. 282 26 24 or 282 33 22), a right off Palestine Sq. onto Izz ad-Din Al-Qassam St., then another right. Marna house is yourna house: the large rooms (all with bath and satellite TV, some with A/C) are in a quiet, residential neighborhood with a lovely courtyard and garden. (Singles NIS285/US$60; doubles NIS335/US$70. Breakfast included. Traveler's checks accepted.)

◖ FOOD

Gaza City's speciality is its **seafood,** served up in restaurants along the coastal road that offer the most after-dark activity in the city. For basics, try **An-Nowra Supermarket** (tel. 864 331) on Omar al-Mukhtar St., opposite Al-Amal (open Sa-Th 7am-3am).

Ad-Diwanieh Restaurant, (tel. 282 50 62), on Aj-Jala'a St. off Omar al-Mukhtar St., serves sandwiches (chicken NIS15; hot dogs NIS4; cheese NIS3) and traditional Palestinian fare (soup, salad, rice, and meat NIS25-50). Call ahead for Palestinian meals.

As-Samaq Restaurant, (tel. 286 43 85), Ar-Rashid St. You wont know whether to ogle the beautiful ocean view or the gaily-costumed waitstaff. Spicy seafood dishes NIS20-60. Large selection of salads (NIS3) and soups (NIS10). Open Sa-Th 10am-11pm.

Loveboat Restaurant (tel. 823 450). Come aboard via the Cliff Hotel courtyard on Ar-Rashid St. Set a course for new romance with full meat (NIS40) or fish (NIS50) dishes including salad and coffee/tea. Weighs anchor daily 7am-midnight.

Al-Moluki, at Mustafa Hafez and Omar al-Mukhtar St. Great for a cheap, in-and-out falafel or shawarma fix (in- and outdoor seating). Open Sa-Th 9am-midnight, F noon-midnight.

Pizza Inn (tel. 284 04 25), at the top of the Norwegian Gardens. Westerners rejoice: salad bar NIS12, hamburgers NIS9, spaghetti NIS14, or pizza (with all the fixings small NIS21, medium NIS28, large NIS42). Open daily 11am-midnight.

REFUGEE CAMPS There are eight Palestinian refugee camps scattered throughout Gaza. Most are clustered in the north, in the vicinity of Gaza City: **Jabalaya** is a 15-minute car ride and **Beach Camp** a mere five-minute walk from the city. There also are sizable camps in the Strip's other two major cities to the south, Khan Yunis and Rafah. From Gaza City, visitors can walk into Beach Camp, though the most meaningful way to understand a camp is to set up a tour to Jabalaya with Gaza City's United Nations Relief and Works Agency (UNRWA; see **Human Rights Organizations,** p. 395). UNRWA guides visitors through the camp to the educational, health, and community facilities it has helped establish to aid refugees.

Delice, 4 Izz ad-Din Al-Qassam St. (tel. 282 25 69), left off the the beach, delights with small meals (pita pizza NIS4, spinach-and-cheese croissant NIS3), warm drinks, and delectable sweets (½kg of cookies NIS17, eclairs NIS5). Open daily 8am-midnight.

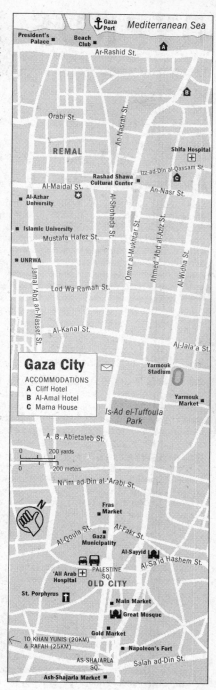 SIGHTS

GREEK ORTHODOX CHURCH OF ST. PORPHYRUS. Gaza's major historical church abuts the minaret of a small mosque to the right. The church was first built on the site in the beginning of the 5th century and was named after Saint Porphyrus of northern Greece, who was charged with spreading Christendom in Gaza. When he predicted the birth of the empress' child, St. Porphyrus won a mandate for the city's temples to be torn down and for a Christian church to be built. March 10, the day of the saint's death, is still celebrated by Gazan Christians. The church has a remarkable, sky-blue arched ceiling dotted with white stars. There also is an impressive collection of dark Orthodox icons along the walls of the church. *(Across Palestine Sq. on the 2nd street that curves down to the right beyond the bus station. Tel. 282 68 06. Open daily 8am-8pm.)*

NAPOLEON'S FORT. Before Napoleon spent three nights here in 1799 during his war against Egypt and Syria, the building had been occupied by Gaza governors of both the Mamluke and Ottoman eras. Today, this monument to *machismo* is home to a quaint garden and a girls' school. *(Streets branching off to the left from the main market and the gold market lead to al-Wihda St. and the fort. No regular hours, but a caretaker from the girls' school inside the gate may allow a quick peek.)*

AS-SA'ID HASHEM MOSQUE. The grandfather of the Prophet Muhammad, who died while traveling through Gaza City on business, is said to be buried under one of the four porticoes of this mosque's courtyard. *(10min. walk down Al-Wihda St. toward Palestine Sq. Take a right on the side street with a "White Goose" sign and bear left.)*

GAZA

CYPRUS Κυπρος

100 CYPRIOT CENTS (100¢)=1 CYPRIOT POUND (£1)

US$1=£0.55	£1=US$1.81
CDN$1=£0.37	£1=CDN$2.72
UK£1=£0.89	£1=UK£3.06
AUS$1=£0.36	£1=AUS$2.81
SAR1=£0.09	£1=SAR11.12
EUR1=£0.58	£1=EUR1.75
NIS1 (NEW ISRAELI SHEKEL)=£0.13	£1=NIS7.71

PHONE FACTS | **Country Code:** 357. **Police/Emergency:** Tel. 199.

The ancient playwright Euripides once wrote that Cyprus is "where the Loves who soothe mortal hearts dwell." The lovely port cities of Limassol and Paphos (easy ferry trips from Haifa) will surely soothe you with their sunny beaches, breezy ruins, and friendly locals, who have grown accustomed to the growing number of tourists that pass through their hometowns. For coverage of the sights and sounds of all of Cyprus, check out *Let's Go: Greece (including Cyprus) 2000*.

GETTING THERE. Ferries from **Haifa, Israel** (p. 310) leave frequently for Limassol and Paphos. Residents of Australia, Canada, New Zealand, the U.K., and the U.S. need only present a valid **passport** for entry into Cyprus (good for 90 days). Residents of South Africa will need a **visa** to enter (NIS40), available from the South African consulate in **Tel Aviv** (see p. 292).

LIMASSOL Λεμεσος

Equal parts fast-paced industrial hub and laid-back resort town, Limassol is a cordial introduction to Cyprus. A barrage of cultural festivities entertains visitors and natives year-round, while the city's elegant restaurants, designer stores, and architecture add an air sophistication lacking in most other Cypriot cities.

ORIENTATION AND PRACTICAL INFORMATION

Passenger boats arrive at the **new port,** 5km southwest of the town center. Bus #1 runs to the port from the station near Anexartisias Market, and bus #30 runs from the port to downtown (every 30min., Sa every hr.; 35¢). Buses wait near the customs building or outside the port gates. Taxis to town cost £2.50. The blocks neighboring the town hall house tourist services. A number of dining and entertainment venues are on **Agiou Andreou,** parallel to the waterfront two blocks inland.

Ferries: Poseidon Lines (tel. 745 666; fax 745 577) and **Salamis Tours** (tel. 355 555; fax 364 410) run to: **Haifa, Israel** (11hr., 2 per week, £50); **Rhodes, Greece** (18hr., 2 per week, £44); and **Piraeus, Greece** via **Rhodes, Greece** (45hr., 2 per week, £47).

Cruises: Salamis Tours (tel. 355 555; fax 364 410), **Louis Tourist Agency** (tel. 363 161; fax 363 174), and **Paradise Island Tours** (tel. 357 604; fax 370 298) stop at **Haifa, Israel,** and **Port Said, Egypt.**

Buses: KEMEK (tel. 747 532), 400m north of the castle at Irinis and Enosis, serves **Nicosia** (M-F 5 per day, Sa 3 per day; £1.50) and **Paphos** (10 per week, £1.50). **Kallenos** (tel. 654 850) by the old port, heads for **Larnaca** (M-Sa 3-4 per day, £1.70).

Service Taxis: Taxis run 6am-6:30pm to **Nicosia** (£3.45), **Larnaca** (£3), and **Paphos** (£2.50). Contact **Makris** (tel. 365 550) or **Kyriakos.** Free port pickup.

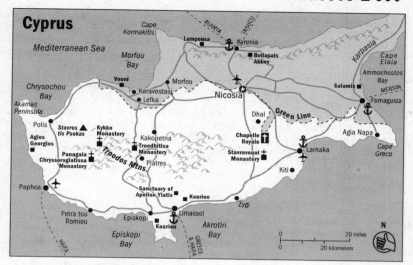

Cyprus

Mediterranean Sea

Cape Kormakitis

Morfou Bay

Chrysochou Bay

Akamas Peninsula

Lampousa
Kyrenia
Bellapais Abbey
Karpasia
Cape Elaia
Ammochostos Bay
MERSIN

Vouni
Morfou
Karavostasi
Lefka
Nicosia
Salamis
Famagusta

Polis
Stavros tis Psokas
Kykko Monastery
Kakopetria
Dhali
Green Line
Agia Napa

Aglos Georgios
Panagaia Chryssorogiatissa Monastery
Troodhitisa Monastery
Platres
Troodos Mtns.
Chapelle Royale
Stavrovouni Monastery
Larnaka
Cape Greco

Paphos
Sanctuary of Apollon Ylatis
Kourion
Kiti

Petra tou Romiou
Episkopi
Kourion
Limassol
Zygi

Episkopi Bay
Akrotiri Bay

0   20 miles
0   20 kilometers

N

Tourist Office: CTO, Spiro Araouzos 15 (tel. 362 756), on the waterfront a block east of the castle. Open M-Tu and Th-F 8:15am-2:30pm and 4-6:30pm, W 8:15am-2:30pm, Sa 8:15am-1:15pm. Office at the **port** (tel. 343 868) open immediately following arrivals.

Police: Tel. 330 411, on Gladstone and Leonidos next to the hospital.

Hospital: Government General Hospital, outside Limassol near the village Polemidia; take the #15 bus. There are many private doctors and clinics.

Post Office: Tel. 330 190, next to the central police station. Open May-Sept. M-Tu and Th-F 7:30am-1:30pm and 4-6pm, W 7:30am-1:30pm, Sa 9-11am.

Internet Access: Cybernet Café, Eleftherias 79 (tel. 745 093). £1.50 for 1st hr.; £1 per additional hr. Open 1pm-2am.

Telephone Office: CYTA on the corner of Markos Botsaris and Athinon. All telephones in Limassol use phonecards (available at the post office) except a few in the port.

Telephone Code: 05.

ACCOMMODATIONS

Quirky downtown guest houses are Limassol's budget best, but solo travelers (especially women) may prefer the upscale hotels on the waterfront. The ■**Guest House Ikaros,** Eleftherias 61 (tel. 354 348), may make you giddy with its tapestries, fish tanks, animal skins, and chandeliers, but you'll come to your senses once you settle down in the spacious rooms with shared bath. (Singles £5; doubles £10; 1st daily shower free, 2nd 50¢.) **Luxor Guest House,** Ag. Andreou 101 (tel. 362 265), has an understated decor that lends a simple elegance to this well-located guest house (singles £5; doubles £10; shared baths). **Continental Hotel,** Spiro Araouzos 137 (tel. 362 530), offers privacy but not much light. All guests get private baths, phones, and a free breakfast (singles £15; doubles £25; triples £35; A/C £2 extra).

FOOD AND ENTERTAINMENT

You'd be crazy to pass up a meal at ■**Cuckoo's Nest,** Agiou Andreou 228 (tel. 362 768). Cheap village wine (£2.25 per bottle) flows freely (*mezze* £4, entrees £1.25-3). **Mikri Maria,** Ankara 3 (tel. 357 676) serves exquisite food cooked over hot coals. Try the grilled *lountza* and *halloumi* or the refreshing *tzatziki*. Live guitar music entertains in winter (entrees £3-5.50; Cypriot brandy sour 65¢; open

M-Sa until 10:30pm). **Ta Kokkina,** Agiou Andreou 239 (tel. 340 015), has an exotic garden and bar to match its exotic African menu (ostrich steak and South African sausage entrees £5-11). **Richard and Berengaria,** Irinis 23 (tel. 363 863), opposite the castle, serves local specialties like *sheftalia* (£1.20) and *halloumi* sandwiches (80¢).

Cafes and bars are everywhere in cosmopolitan Limassol. Well dressed twenty-somethings congregate at **Graffiti,** Agiou Andreou 244, a tree-laden open-air bar with great live music. **Symio,** Agiou Andreou 248, is also a popular hangout replete with paintings and funky furniture designed by the artist owner. The mansion and patio at **Passatempo,** on the corner of Agiou Andreou and Souzou, is a great place to passatime sipping on cappuccino (forego the expensive *Gucci* and *Rolex* appetizers). There's no exkoozi to miss **Skoozi!,** Agiou Andreou 292, one block from the Guest House Luxor. Young Cypriots enjoy jazz, trance, opera music while noshing on delicious crepes (banana and *ganache* £2.60) and all kinds of coffee (65¢).

📷 SIGHTS

KOURION. The ruins at Kourion were colonized by wandering Achaïans in the 14th and 13th centuries BCE. The **Sanctuary of Apollo** (8th century BCE) and the **stadium** (2nd century CE) have been reconstructed to their former glory after an earthquake leveled them in the 17th century. The earliest structure on the site is a 2nd-century BCE **theater** used in Roman times for staging dramas, animal fights, and professional wrestling. Across the road from the main site are a group of ruins under excavation. In the northwest corner are the remains of the **House of Gladiators** and its mosaic gladiator pin-ups. The **House of Achilles,** facing the highway at the end of the excavation site, is fenced off, but you can get the key at the ticket office or climb in through the narrow path following the fence along the road. The nearby **Museum of Kourion** provides clear explanations of the artifacts. *(12km west of Limassol. Buses from Limassol Castle leave every hr. on the hr. (9am-1pm), returning at 11:50am, 2:50, 4:50pm (70¢). Site open June-Sept. 8am-7:15pm; Oct.-May 8am-5pm. Admission £1. Museum: open M and W-F 7:30am-2:30pm, Th 3-6pm. Admission £1.)*

LIMASSOL CASTLE. The Limassol castle, where Cyprus's King Richard married Queen Berengaria in 1191, was destroyed by earthquakes and Genoese assaults. The castle is best known as a prison: the Knights of St. John converted the chapel into a series of jail cells, and the West Hall was used as a prison under the British until 1940. Now the castle houses the **Cyprus Medieval Museum,** which has medieval armor and religious objects. *(Tel. 330 419. Open M-F 9am-5pm, Sa-Su 10am-1pm. £1.)*

SPECIAL EVENTS. At summer's end, Limassol's gardens (also home to Cyprus's largest **zoo**) are transformed into a tribute to Dionysus for the Limassol **wine festival,** where participants are given a bottle to fill with as much of the local vintage as they can handle. The general intoxication is compounded by music, dance, and theater (admission £1.50). At the end of June, actors from around the world trek to Limassol for **Shakespeare Nights** (tel. 363 015 for more information). **Carnival,** which takes place in February 50 days before Orthodox Easter, is celebrated with more vigor in Limassol than anywhere else in Cyprus. Details of these events are available at the CTO and in *This Month's Principal Events.*

🏖 BEACHES

The city's long stone beach might be a little too rocky for the discerning beach-goer, but a new breakwater has made the area more pleasant for swimming. **Dassoudi Beach,** 3km east of Limassol, is famous throughout Cyprus (take bus #6 from the Kanaris market every 15min., 50¢). The ebullient **Ladies' Mile Beach,** just west of the new port, is also popular (take bus #1).

PAPHOS Πάφος

More than just a beach town, Paphos was the favorite city of Aphrodite, the goddess of love, and a cosmopolitan hotspot in Roman times. After being leveled by an earthquake in the 7th century, it has re-emerged as the tourist capital of Cyprus.

⚑ ORIENTATION AND PRACTICAL INFORMATION

Paphos is divided into two sections: the upper section, **Ktima Paphos** (referred to as "Paphos") is centered around **Plaza Kennedy,** with its shops, budget hotels, and services. **Kato Paphos** is roughly 1km south, with luxury hotels, holiday villas, and the city's nightlife. Unless otherwise noted, everything below is in Ktima Paphos.

City Buses: Bus #11 runs between Ktima and Kato (every 15min., 50¢). Catch them in Ktima up the road from the post office; in Kato at any of the yellow benches on the road to town. Bus #10 goes to **Coral Bay** (20 per day, 50¢). Schedules at tourist office.

Service Taxis: To **Limassol** (every 30min. M-Sa 5:45am-6:30pm, Su 7am-5:30pm; £2.50). Contact **Makris** (tel. 232 538) or **Kyriakos** (tel. 232 538).

Moped Rental: There are several shops in Kato and Ktima Paphos. £2.50-6.50 per day.

Tourist Office: CTO, Gladstone 3 (tel. 253 341; fax 232 841). Open M-Tu and Th-F 8:15am-2:30pm and 3-5:15pm, W and Sa 8:15am-1:30pm.

Travel Agency: Iris Travel, Gladstone 10A (tel. 237 585), opposite CTO. Ferry tickets to **Rhodes, Crete,** and **Israel** (student discounts up to 20%). Airline tickets to **London** and **Greece** (student discounts up to 40%). Open M-F 8am-1pm and 4-7pm, Sa 8am-1pm.

Police: Tel. 806 060, on Grivas Digenes, in Pl. Kennedy. English spoken. Open 24hr.

Hospital: Paphos General (tel. 240 111), on Neophytos Nicolaides, offers free first aid. English spoken. **St. George's Private Hospital,** El. Venizelou 29 (tel. 247 000), on the way to the youth hostel; casualty and ambulance services. English spoken. Open 24hr.

Internet Access: Limanaki (tel. 239 616), by Kato Paphos fort. £2 per hr. Open 5pm-2am.

Post Office: Main branch on El. Venizelou. Open M-F 7:30am-1:30pm and (except W) 3-6pm, Sa 8:30-10:30am. **Kato Paphos** (tel. 240 226) branch on Ag. Antoniou.

Telephone Office: CYTA (tel. 230 228), on Grivas Digenes. Open 7:30am-7:30pm.

Telephone Code: 06.

▟ ACCOMMODATIONS

Finding affordable accommodations in Paphos is a chore. Solo travelers should stick to the youth hostel; groups might try renting a flat. Prices are higher in Kato Paphos. ◪**Kiniras Hotel,** Makarios 91 (tel. 241 604), is a friendly guest house with luxurious rooms, bath, air conditioning, TV, and phone (singles £20; doubles £30; breakfast included). The **Youth Hostel (HI),** El. Venizelou 45 (tel. 232 588), is a 15-minute walk from the *plateia* on Pallikaridi to Venizelou, on the right (£5 for the 1st night, £4 each additional night). **Violetta Flats,** Dionissiou 7 (tel. 234 109; fax 220 734), in Kato Paphos, has flats with kitchens and private baths, and is well situated for enjoying the nightlife (singles £12; doubles £15; A/C £2 extra). **Zenon Gardens Geroskipou Camping** (tel. 242 277), east of the tourist beach, 3km from the harbor, has a mini-market, restaurant, and kitchen. (Open Mar.-Oct.; £2 per site; £2 per 3 people; £1 per small tent.)

◖▮ FOOD AND ENTERTAINMENT

Putting on pounds in Kato Paphos will cost a lot of them, but Ktima Paphos is affordable and elegant. **Peggy's Miranda Cafe,** in Pl. Kennedy, is run by and for British expats with a continental breakfast (£2) and a book swap (open M-Sa 8am-4pm). **Hondros,** Ap. Pavlou 96 (tel. 234 256), in Kato Paphos, is one of Kato Paphos's oldest and least touristy restaurants. Eat lamb *kleftiko* off the spit (£4) while sitting beneath grapevines on a bamboo-covered terrace. (Entrees £3.50-6; open 11am-4pm and 7pm-midnight.) **Euro Surfcafe,** Gladstone 1 (tel. 239 239), has reasonably priced light meals (sandwiches £1-1.50, beer 80¢) and Internet access (£2 per hr.; open until 9pm). The elegant **Park Mansion Hotel** (tel. 245 645), one block from the tourist office, dishes up Cypriot fare with a French flair (entrees £4.50-8).

Virtually all of the area's nightlife centers around Agias Napas St., a couple blocks inland from the waterfront in Kato Paphos. **Summer Cinema,** on the waterfront past Geroskipou Beach, is a trendy open-air club just far enough from packaged tour hotels for the locals to call it their own. **Shotts,** Poseidon 91, is popular despite the £5 cover. **Boogies** is Paphos's favorite karaoke bar; after 2am, slurred but earnest Spice Girls renditions give way to a hot dance floor.

👁 SIGHTS

ANCIENT HOUSES. The mosaic floors of the House of Dionysus, the House of Theseus, and the House of Aion in Kato Paphos are the city's most dazzling ancient relics. Discovered accidentally in 1962 by a farmer plowing his fields, they were excavated by a Polish expedition that found mosaics covering 14 rooms of the expansive Roman **House of Dionysus.** Using the stones' natural varying hues, the floors depict vibrant scenes from mythology and daily life. Toward the water rests the **House of Theseus** (dating from the 2nd to 6th centuries CE), a luxurious building with marble statues, columns, and mosaic floors. *(Tel. 240 217. Admission £1.)*

CATACOMBS OF AGIA SOLOMONI. The musty catacombs—decorated with Byzantine frescoes and containing a chapel dedicated to St. Solomoni—were built on the site of an old synagogue. Part of the deepest chamber is filled with water, which you may not notice until you're drenched in it. A tree that is said to cure the illnesses of those who tie a cloth to it marks the entrance to the catacombs. St. Paul was whipped for preaching Christianity to the Greeks at the nearby **St. Paul's Pillar.** *(Opposite the Apollo Hotel on A. Pavlos. Open 24hr. Free.)*

OTHER SIGHTS. The remnants of an *agora* are north of the mosaics beside the 3000-person, 2nd-century **odeon,** a roofed limestone theater that is still in use today. Built in the 7th century on a hill overlooking the harbor, the **Byzantine Castle** *(Saranda Kolones)* was intended to protect inhabitants from Arab pirates. When an earthquake destroyed the castle in 1222, the Lusignans built the impressive **Paphos Fort** at the end of the pier. *(Odeon: open 7:30am-7pm. Admission 50¢. Byzantine Castle is on Sophia Vembo off A. Pavlou. Paphos Fort: open 10am-5:45pm. Admission 75¢.)*

🏖 BEACHES

The two most popular beaches are the touristy **Geroskipou** to the east and the bigger, sandier **Coral Bay** to the north. For Geroskipou, take bus #11 from Ktima Paphos (3 per hr., 50¢); to reach Coral Bay, take bus #15 from Geroskipou (every 20min., 50¢). **Cape Lara** is host to sandy beaches and is a nesting site for Green and Loggerhead Turtles. As both species have seen a steady decline in population, the Lara Sea Turtle Project was conceived in 1971 to protect the turtles by ensuring that nesting continues. Turtle nests can be viewed in the Project's hatchery enclosure. There's no public transportation to Cape Lara; your best bet is a jeep excursion or motorbike.

JORDAN الاردن

US$1=0.71 JORDANIAN DINAR (JD)
CDN$1=JD0.48
UK£1=JD1.13
AUS$1=JD0.45
SAR1=JD0.12
EUR1=JD0.75
E£1 (EGYPTIAN POUND) =JD0.21
NIS1 (NEW ISRAELI SHEKEL) =JD0.17
S£100 (SYRIAN POUNDS) =JD1.70

JD1=US$1.40
JD1=CDN$2.09
JD1=UK£0.88
JD1=AUS$2.23
JD1=SAR8.53
JD1=EUR1.34
JD1=E£4.79
JD1=NIS5.94
JD1=S£58.70

PHONE FACTS | **Country Code:** 962. **Police:** Tel. 191/192.

Take it from the late King Hussein, the longest-ruling head of state in the world: "Jordan is a beautiful country: wild, with limitless deserts where the Bedouin roam....The mountains of the north are clothed in green forests, and where the Jordan River flows it is fertile and warm in winter. Jordan has a strange, haunting beauty and a sense of timelessness. Dotted with the ruins of empires once great, it is the last resort of yesterday in the world of tomorrow."

In ancient times, the Hashemite Kingdom of Jordan was where John the Baptist baptized Jesus, desert trade routes flourished during the Roman Empire, and the mysterious Nabatean people carved an entire city into red rock at Petra—all in the course of a few decades. Modern Jordan *(Al-Urdun)* is now sandwiched between some of the roughest players in a rough neighborhood: Saudi Arabia, Israel, Syria, and Iraq. The memory of Black September, 1970 (a brutal suppression of Palestinian political activity by Jordanian authorities) has not disappeared, nor has the trauma of the Gulf War, in which Jordan supported Saddam Hussein. However, Jordan's former King Hussein (and his ever-gracious wife, U.S.-born and educated Queen Noor) did much to raise morale within its borders and raise support from without. A growing tourism industry has been the key to opening Jordan to the hearts (and pockets) of outsiders, but despite this growth, most of the country and its sites of interest are largely untouched by the sticky fingers of gross commercialism. Close your eyes as you wander through Jordan's many natural and human-made wonders—you could be in any century.

HIGHLIGHTS OF JORDAN

■ Hit spectacular **Azraq and the Desert Castles** (p. 433) en route to the lost Nabatean city of **Petra** (p. 442).
■ The only thing better than the desert beauty of **Wadi Rum** (p. 454) is the hospitality of its Bedouin community (no wonder Lawrence of Arabia stayed here for so long).
■ Be sure to visit the impressive Roman ruins at **Jerash** (p. 426), which is also home to the **Jerash Festival,** a summertime musical and cultural extravaganza.

ESSENTIALS

ENTRY

Visas can be obtained at Amman's **Queen Alia International Airport** and are valid for one month but renewable at any police station (US$44). Visas may also be obtained in person or by mail from any Jordanian embassy or consulate (takes up to five days). Requirements include a passport (valid for at least six months), a completed application form with one photo, and a self-addressed, stamped envelope. A **group visa** can be issued for tours of five or more.

EMBASSIES AND CONSULATES

Embassies and consulates within Jordan are all located in **Amman** (see **Practical Information**, p. 417). Jordanian embassies and consulates abroad include: **Australia,** 20 Roebuck St., Red Hill ACT 2603, Canberra (tel. (02) 6295 9951; fax 6239 7236); **Canada,** 100 Bronson Ave. #701, Ottawa, Ont. K1R 6G8 (tel. 613-238-8090; fax 232-3341); **U.K.,** 6 Upper Philimore Gardens, London W8 7HB (tel. (171) 937 3685; fax 937 8795); and **U.S.,** 3504 International Dr. NW, Washington, D.C. 20008 (tel. 202-966-2664; fax 966-3110) or 866 United Nations Plaza #554, New York, NY 10017 (tel. 212-355-9342; fax 826-0830).

✈ BORDER CROSSINGS

Getting a **visa** to enter Jordan is a breeze, as the government issues visas at all international border crossings (except King Hussein/Allenby Bridge). Note that there are three separate **departure taxes:** JD4 for departure by land (except for travel to the West Bank); JD6 by sea (from Aqaba); and JD10 by air (does not apply to transit travelers in Jordan under 72 hours).

TO EGYPT. A **ferry** shuttles between Aqaba and Nuweiba'. The slow ferry supposedly leaves at noon (3½hr. or more, JD6), and a faster, less crowded, and more punctual **speedboat** also leaves around noon (1hr., JD20 plus JD4 departure tax). Tickets can be purchased at any travel agency in Aqaba; be sure to show up a few hours before departure. You can get a free **Sinai-only visa** if you plan to stay in the Sinai; otherwise, you'll need an **Egyptian visa** (2-week or 1-month), which can be obtained in one day at the Egyptian Consulate in Aqaba for JD12 (see p. 451). Visas can also be obtained on board the ferry for an extra charge, or you can risk it and wait to obtain a tourist visa upon arrival in Nuweiba'.

TO IRAQ. There are two JETT buses from Amman to Baghdad (14hr., 8:30am and 2pm, JD12). Citizens of Western countries are unlikely to be granted Iraqi visas.

TO ISRAEL. There are two border crossing points between Israel and Jordan. There is no entrance fee into Israel and **free visas** are given at the border, though most Western citizens do not need visas (see **Israel: Entry,** p. 237). However, a **departure tax** is required if crossing in either direction. The simple crossing between **Aqaba** and **Eilat** should take less than an hour; take a taxi from Aqaba to the border (JD3-4), then walk the 1km no-man's land between the two countries (there's no transport). Once over the border, the Israeli authorities will call you a taxi into Eilat (NIS15-20). There is no bus service on either side of the border. Though it is much more of a hassle, travelers in northern Jordan can cross the **Sheikh Hussein Bridge** (*Jisr Sheikh Hussein*) to the town of Beit She'an in Galilee, either by bus or *service* taxi (JD3-4; border open Su-Th 6:30am-10pm, F-Sa 8am-8pm).

TO SAUDI ARABIA. The official crossing points between Jordan and Saudi Arabia are located on the coast of the Gulf of Aqaba at Ad-Durra and farther east at Al-Mudawwara. JETT and SAPTCO buses (JD31) run from Amman to: **Jeddah** (10am), **Dammam** (11am), and **Riyadh** (11:30am). The hardest part about traveling to Saudi Arabia from Jordan is getting a **visa:** tourists can only register for transit visas, which sometimes let you travel along the Trans-Arabia Pipeline but usually only let you spend a day in Riyadh.

TO SYRIA. The official road crossing into Syria runs through the town of **Dera.** Daily buses and *service* run from Amman to **Damascus** and **Aleppo.** Although *service* are faster (and more expensive) than the buses, they are usually detained longer at the border, meaning *service* travelers may end up spending more money for a trip that takes just as long as the cheaper bus route. The painfully slow **Hijazi** railway chugs between Amman's Abdali Bus Station and Damascus.

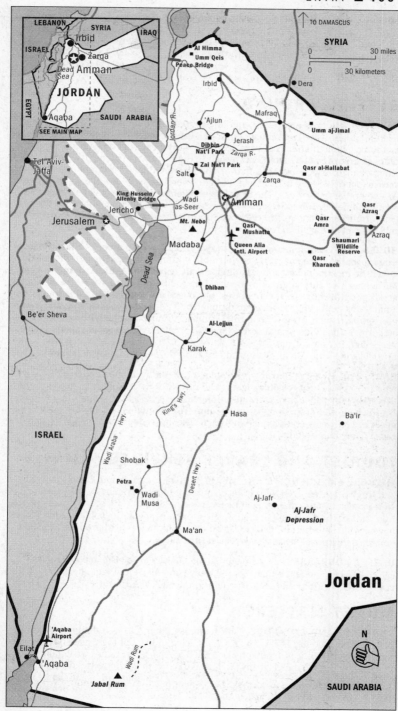

TO THE WEST BANK. The **King Hussein/Allenby Bridge** between Amman and the West Bank is a very popular (and crowded) option (border open Su-Th 8am-10:30pm, F-Sa 8am-1pm). Visas are not issued at this border, but most Western citizens do not need a visa to enter the West Bank. Take a JETT bus (45min., daily 6:30am, JD6) from either station in Amman or a minibus or *service* taxi (45min., JD1.5*)* from Abdali Bus Station.

GETTING AROUND

TAXIS. **Private taxis** are yellow and have "taxi" written on them. They are most useful (and crowded) in Amman. Insist that drivers use the meter; the starting fare is 150fils. Women should always sit in the back seat, whether or not there are other passengers. Men should always sit in the front when alone. It's rude to give exact change; drivers expect you to round up from the meter fare. Public taxis or **service** (ser-VEES) are usually white or gray Mercedes with a white sign written in Arabic on the roof (جرعل). The front doors display the fixed route and number (in Arabic numerals only). *Service* travel set routes in Amman and between the central terminals of larger cities. Schedules are unpredictable—*service* leave when full, but can be hailed en route.

BUSES. The government owns a monopoly on intercity bus service, so the **Jordan Express Tourist Transport (JETT)** is your only option. However sparse, these buses cover the most popular routes, including daily trips from Amman to Aqaba, Petra, Ma'an, the King Hussein/Allenby Bridge, Damascus, and Cairo via Aqaba. Bus fares are slightly lower than *service* rates, but buses are slower and their routes are sometimes confusing. The air-conditioned JETT luxury coaches cost about 20% more than regular buses; those from Amman to Aqaba come with hosts, professional wrestling videos, and screeching Egyptian movies. Booking ahead is often necessary. In Amman, most buses follow the pattern of *service*, with traffic to the north leaving from Abdali Station and buses to the south from Wahdat Station.

CARS. For groups of four to six, renting a car can be an affordable and efficient way to reach less accessible sights. The beautiful Kings' Highway route, barely served by other modes of transportation, can be seen by private car in a full day. Desert heat and police regulations require fire extinguishers in cars. **Four-wheel drives** are only needed to reach Wadi Rum. The law requires **seatbelts** (JD5 fine for those flying unfettered).

TOURIST AND TRAVEL SERVICES

MEDICAL EMERGENCIES AND HEALTH. Health care is quite good in Jordan, and the World Health Organization's figures show that even in the mid-1980s, safe water and adequate sanitary facilities were accessible to 100% of the urban population and 95% of the rural population. Most doctors speak English and pharmacies have a wide selection of medicines and other pharmaceutical products, including condoms. In case of **medical emergencies,** dial 193.

USEFUL ADDRESSES. In Amman, try the **Ministry of Tourism and Antiquities** (tel. (06) 642311) to collect a map, some glossy pamphlets, and fact sheets about the country. There's also a branch at Amman's Queen Alia Airport (tel. (06) 445 12 56).

MONEY MATTERS

CURRENCY AND EXCHANGE. The **Jordanian dinar (JD)** is a decimal currency, divided into 1000 **fils**. Prices are always labeled in fils, but the usual spoken practice is to call 10fils a *piaster* (pt, also called a *qirsh*). Prices are written in Arabic numerals, although the currency itself is marked with Western-friendly numbers.

Bank exchange hours are regularly 8:30am to 12:30pm, with some banks opening from 4 to 5:30pm as well. There are many ranches of the national **Housing Bank**

(*Bank al-Iskan*) outside Amman; there are also exchange offices located in many of the *souqs*. Queen Alia International Airport has exchange facilities for incoming passengers. A passport is required to change **traveler's checks. Credit cards** are only accepted in expensive hotels. **ATMs** work only for local bank cards.

TIPPING. A tip of 10% is expected in restaurants, unless "service included" appears on the menu; servers at fancier establishments expect a little something even if service is included. Taxi drivers do not expect tips, but will round off fares to their advantage. Members of large sightseeing groups tip the bus driver about 500fils. A small tip (500fils) to room cleaners and porters in hotels is appropriate.

BUSINESS HOURS. Most stores and offices are open from 8 or 9am until 1pm, then reopen around 3 or 4pm. In the larger cities, the stores may remain open all afternoon. In Amman, retail stores close around 8 or 9pm. Banks and government offices retain only a skeleton crew in the afternoon.

ACCOMMODATIONS

HOTELS. Regulated tourist hotels charge prices as high as Jordan's mid-summer temperatures. Bargaining is difficult, but hotel owners may be more flexible in the off-season winter months. Fall and spring are the busiest times, though sunny Aqaba sees the most activity during the winter and spring. Single women may feel uncomfortable at cheaper hotels and may not be admitted. Jordanian law bars unmarried couples from sharing a room; for foreign travelers, a "don't ask, don't tell" policy seems to be the norm. Most budget hotels do not abide by government prices; "official" prices are listed in Arabic and cheaper ones in English. Most hotels add a 10% service charge; ask whether it's included in the price. Hotel owners may ask to hold your passport for the length of your stay, but they will return it after a night if you need to change money. There are no hostels in Jordan.

CAMPING. Camping is an option at government-approved sites, though facilities are virtually nonexistent. Approved areas include the beach north of Aqaba, Dibbin National Park, and the Dana Wildlands Campsite. Camping is allowed next to most government **Rest Houses** (free or JD1-2 per person per night, plus 10% tax). You'll need a sleeping bag or blanket for cool summer nights; winter evenings can bring freezing temperatures. You can also spend the night in a **Bedouin camp** on the outskirts of most towns and scattered around the desert. Tea, Arabic coffee, and meals are always included in an invitation, though showers and toilets are rare. While the Bedouin won't accept money, a pack of cigarettes is always appreciated.

KEEPING IN TOUCH

MAIL. Most post offices have **Poste Restante. American Express** offices (Amman and Aqaba) also hold mail. **Airmail letters** to North America cost 400fils, aerogrammes or postcards 300fils (to Europe 300fils/150fils). Mail from Jordan to North America and Europe takes one to two weeks if you're lucky. International **Express Mail Service (EMS)** is available in major post offices and costs less than Western companies like DHL and FedEx.

TELEPHONE AND INTERNET ACCESS. Although the telephone system was recently revamped, international lines are often overloaded, especially around holidays. **Phonecards** have made a welcome appearance, and are probably the easiest way to make both local and international calls as **no collect calls** can be made except from a private phone. **Calling card** calls can only be placed from private phones. You can make **international calls** from telephone offices (JD6.6 per 3min. to the U.S.) or luxury hotels (fast but expensive). Use a private phone and reimburse the owner (to U.S., Europe, or Australia JD1.83-2.2 per min.; 30% less 10pm-8am). **International operator:** tel. 0132. **Information:** tel. 121.

In most major cities, almost every place—from the hostel to the supermarket—is wired to the Internet, often at a cheaper rate (JD1-1.5) than cybercafes.

JORDAN

WOMEN TRAVELERS

Jordan is a modernized country and women will generally feel quite comfortable, although harassment is not uncommon (just ignore it). Women should dress conservatively, as those dressed inappropriately will suffer higher prices from offended merchants and possibly even pinches. For more tips, see **Women Travelers,** p. 29.

DRESS AND ETIQUETTE

Jordan is socially conservative by Western standards, making modest dress a necessity for both sexes. Neither sex can wear shorts (except in hedonistic Aqaba), and women's skirts must be at least ankle-length. Shirts should cover the shoulders and upper arms. Sandals that expose feet are acceptable. Amman slackens its dress code at night and by the pool.

Jordanians have a very strong hospitality ethic. Bedouin invitations to coffee or tea should be strongly considered, as declining an invitation is often interpreted as a direct insult. If you choose to reject an offer, be calm and firm and repeat yourself until the point sinks in. Lone women should never accept an invitation from a single man. Most people who offer to help you, feed you, or take you somewhere are probably not con artists; they often represent the best of a culture that is serious about kindness to visitors.

LIFE AND TIMES

ANCIENT HISTORY

Sometime in the Middle Bronze Age (around the 18th century BCE), a mysterious martial people known as the **Hyksos** (a Greek bastardization of the Egyptian *hkaw haswt,* "rulers of foreign lands") descended on Egypt and Arabia from the north. Their new-fangled horse-drawn chariots and bronze weapons helped them easily conquer the area and permanently change military practices in the region. The identity of these strangers is still up for debate, but most archaeologists agree that they came from the region that is modern-day Jordan.

For all their innovative power, the Hyksos' rule was short-lived; the Egyptian pharaohs eventually took over and ruled Jordan (along with Palestine and Syria) as one empire called **Canaan.** During the **Iron Age** (c. 1200-332 BCE), small city-states that initially developed along trade routes rose into three major kingdoms in Jordan. These kingdoms bickered constantly, both with their Israelite neighbors across the Jordan river and among themselves, even when the **Persian Empire** took over and ruled the region as a minor governate. The arrival of Macedonian superstar **Alexander the Great** in 332 BCE ushered in an age of social and artistic development heavily influenced by Greek culture. The Greeks founded new cities (such as Umm Qeis) and renamed others (Jerash became Antioch and Amman became Philadelphia). Hellenistic influence lasted through the reign of Alexander's successor Ptolemy, invasion by the Seleucids, and conquest of the area by the Romans under Pompey in 63 BCE.

Before Alexander's conquest, however, a thriving new civilization had emerged when a nomadic tribe from Arabia known as the **Nabateans** settled in southern Jordan during the 6th century BCE. The Roman scholar Strabo wrote that their capital was at **Petra** (see p. 442), where they carved buildings, temples, and tombs out of solid sandstone rock. As desert dwellers, the Nabateans were also skilled water engineers who irrigated their land using an extensive system of dams, canals, and reservoirs. Petra became a center of trade routes between Assyria, China, India, Egypt, Syria, Greece, and Rome, and the dialect of Arabic spoken by its inhabitants (versus the Aramaic that most tribes in the area spoke) helped spread that language around the region. Sometime during the 4th century CE, the Nabateans left their capital at Petra without explanation. Everything from localized famine to alien invasion has been cited as the cause for their exodus.

The departure of the Nabateans inaugurated a period of Roman control that would last four centuries. In northern Jordan, the Greek cities of Philadelphia (Amman), Antioch (Jerash), Gadara (Umm Qeis), Pella, and Irbid joined with cities in Palestine and southern Syria to form the **Decapolis League,** a fabled confederation linked by bonds of economic and cultural interest. Jerash became the most splendid city in the flourishing League and one of the greatest cities in all of the Roman provinces, while Pella was a center for Christian refugees fleeing Roman persecution. The cities were noted for their impressive Byzantine mosaics, the most beautiful of which can be found at **Madaba** (see p. 437)—including the intricately detailed 6th-century **Map of the Holy Land.** At the same time the Map was being created, however, Jordan suffered severe depopulation: the **plague** of 542 CE wiped out much of the population, while many more were wiped out by the **Sassanian** invasion of 614 CE. The invading Sassanians paved the way for the invading **Ottomans,** who would rule the area until the outbreak of WWI in 1916.

MODERN HISTORY

Once the Ottoman Empire breathed its last at the end of WWI (in part due to Arab revolts led by **Lawrence of Arabia**), the weak but well-intentioned League of Nations gave Western European powers control over the Levant in order to prepare these territories for independence. Great Britain was given control over Iraq and Palestine (which included modern-day Israel, the West Bank, the Gaza Strip, and Jordan), and in 1921 established the area east of the Jordan River as the **Emirate of Transjordan. Abdullah** (a 40th-generation direct descendant of the Prophet Muhammad) was set up as *emir* (prince), and the British-controlled emirate spent most of the period until the end of WWII keeping the peace between local Arabs and immigrant Jews fleeing into Palestine from Europe. Shortly after the end of World War II, exhausted Great Britain handed the Palestine problem over to the newly-formed United Nations, which granted Jordan independence. After Israel became a state in May 1948, Jordan offered refugees full citizenship (the only Arab country to do so), much to the chagrin of most Arab leaders.

Unification efforts with the Palestinians were cut short in 1951, when Abdullah was assassinated by a Palestinian youth while praying at Al-Aqsa Mosque in Jerusalem. Abdullah's eldest son, Talal, ruled for six months before resigning, and Talal's son **Hussein** (who had also been shot but survived thanks to a well-placed medal) took over the throne just before his 18th birthday. King Hussein ruled for 48 years until his death on February 7, 1999—the longest serving executive head of state in the world (see **In The News,** p. 410). Hussein's moderate political stance (a result of his British education) and two (of four) gracious Western wives (including his widow, **Queen Noor,** a California-born Princeton graduate) have made him a darling of the West. Even domestically he was known as *Al-Malik al-Insan* ("The Humane King"), particularly for his reception of Palestinian and (more recently) Kuwaiti refugees. Hussein opened his powerful cabinet to Palestinians and Bedouin, who form the bedrock of the monarchy's support.

The aftermath of the 1967 war with Israel did not shine so favorably upon Hussein. Over 400,000 Palestinians fled to Jordan, throwing the Jordanian government and the Palestinian Liberation Organization (PLO) into a tense relationship: King Hussein wanted to hold secret peace negotiations with the Israelis, while the PLO hoped to use Jordan as a base for attacks on Israeli-held territory. In September 1970 (known as **Black September**), King Hussein made a bold move by declaring war on the PLO after it hijacked several commercial airliners. He imposed martial law, and clashes between Jordanian and PLO troops took over 3000 lives. After Arab League mediation and Egyptian president Nasser's personal intervention, an agreement was forged requiring the PLO to move its headquarters to Lebanon.

The **Gulf War** of 1990-1991 brought its own problems. A tide of pan-Arabism and resentment of Western power led many Jordanians to support Saddam Hussein. Jordan's refusal to join the U.S.-led anti-Iraq coalition devastated both the nation's economy and its international political clout after the war. Most foreign aid was suspended, and the annual per capita income fell from US$2000 (1990) to US$1400 (where it stands today). Unlike its Arab neighbors, Jordan has neither oil reserves nor abundant natural resources, and is dependent upon Arab and American financial aid to augment its income, which consists largely of the export of phosphates and vegetables grown in the Jordan Valley. The country's main source of income had been money sent home from Jordanian workers in the Gulf States, but after the war they were largely replaced by Egyptian workers (whose country was considered more acceptable by the anti-Iraq coalition).

Hussein improved international relations in August 1994, when he and Israeli Prime Minister Yitzhak Rabin signed the **Washington Declaration,** ending the state of war between the two countries and opening the border between Aqaba and Eilat. The monetary umbilical cord from the West was reconnected, and the U.S. and Great Britain relieved millions of dollars of Jordan's foreign debt. An increase in tourism, heartily encouraged by Hussein and his successor, has given the country a much-needed economic boost.

IN THE NEWS

On February 7, 1999, **King Hussein** died of cancer-related health complications. The King's brother, former **Crown Prince Hassan,** was to inherit the throne from Hussein; just days before his death, however, Hussein announced that his eldest son, 37-year-old **Abdullah,** would succeed him. Hussein criticized Hassan for jumping the gun when the king went abroad, running the country as though Hussein would never return. Though Hassan did dismiss the King's loyalists in the army and altered some of Jordan's domestic policies, many have speculated that King Hussein acted out of fear that if Hassan became king, it would be his sons and not Hussein's who would ascend to the throne in later years. Many have also questioned whether the young and relatively inexperienced Abdullah is capable of being king (though he is a 43rd generation descendant of the Prophet). However, Abdullah is in an ideal position to encourage the peace process in the Middle East: he is boarding one of the most politically troubled ships of state carrying no political baggage. The Palestinian heritage of his wife, **Queen Rania,** has also made the couple popular with the dueling sectors of Jordan's population.

RELIGION AND ETHNICITY

The vast majority of Jordanians are **Sunni Muslims,** though pockets of Shi'ite Muslims exist as well. Centuries of Byzantine rule and Crusader occupation have left their mark; Jordan has a sizeable community of **Christians** (roughly 4% of the population). Most Jordanians are ethnic Arabs (including many Palestinian expats and refugees), but about 2% of the population are Armenian, Circassian, or Druze.

LANGUAGE

The official language of Jordan is **Arabic,** but the spoken dialect differs from classical Arabic and the variations spoken in Egypt, the Gulf States, and North Africa. Due to decades of British colonial rule, **English** is Jordan's second language, taught at both public and private schools. Most signs are written in both Arabic and English, and Jordan Television's second channel broadcasts subtitled British and American programs as well as some French programs after 8:30pm.

THE ARTS

POPULAR AND FOLK CULTURE. Jordanians have a strong oral tradition of storytelling and ballad singing. Eavesdrop on a wedding for a taste of traditional folk music and for the women's salutatory shouts and ululations (*ha-WEEE-ha!*), known as **zaghroutah. Dabke** is a popular traditional line dance performed to the rhythmic beat of feet pounding on the floor. Skillful **weavers** use techniques developed over countless centuries to make traditional Jordanian rugs and tapestries out of wool and goat hair. Leather handicrafts, pottery, ceramics, and coral curios are also very common, but **wood-carving** is the Jordanian specialty.

VISUAL AND PERFORMING ARTS. Both the Jordanian government and private groups are taking measures to promote and foster the **visual arts,** and Jordan's architecture, painting, and sculpture have all developed substantially in this century. Jordanian art is often an expression of Arab and Muslim identity, but the county's mix of cultures also results in themes relating to traditional Bedouin life or a desire to return to the Palestinian homeland. Two decades ago, Queen Noor founded the annual **Jerash Festival.** The summer festival features diverse international offerings, from Romanian choirs to Indian dance troupes. Traditional Arab and Bedouin arts are displayed, and Arab music and theater features prominently among the events. For more information on the Jerash Festival, see p. 429.

LITERATURE. The Jordanian region itself has a long tradition of prose: the oldest example of a Semitic script, the 9th century BCE relic known as the **Mesha Stele,** was found in Karak. Jordanian literature does not exist as its own genre as Egyptian or Lebanese literature does; yet many Jordanian writers publish frequently. **Diana Abu-Jaber** recently achieved prominence for her first novel, *Arabian Jazz,* which was a finalist for the national PEN/Hemingway award. Many exiled Palestinian authors have written from Jordan, the most famous of whom is **Mahmous Darwish.** Of Western non-natives writing in and about Jordan, the most famous is the British rabblerouser T.E. Lawrence, also known as **Lawrence of Arabia.** His *Seven Pillars of Wisdom* contains vivid descriptions of the battles fought and the territory explored during the Arab Revolt of 1916. Even if you don't reach Lawrence's old haunts at Wadi Rum, don't miss David Lean's swooning and romanticized movie *Lawrence of Arabia.* Gertrude Bell, one of the first female Western travelers in the region, writes of her journeys through Jordan and Syria in *The Desert and the Sown* (for more info on Bell's life, see **An Englishwoman in Arabia,** p. 440). The last word in desert mystery is Agatha Christie's *Argument with Death,* which introduces readers to the mesmerizing power of Petra.

FOOD AND DRINK

Jordanian cuisine has evolved through centuries of Bedouin and Palestinian cooking. The national dish is **mensaf,** and its main ingredients appear in most other Jordanian dishes. *Mensaf* consists of rice on a large tray of flat bread, topped with pine nuts, an entire lamb or goat, and a tangy yogurt-based sauce known as *jamid.* It is eaten from a communal dish while standing: the right hand is used to ball the rice while the flat bread is used to pull off chunks of meat and dip them into the warm sauce. The Bedouin serve the head of the lamb on top, reserving the prize delicacies (tongue and eyes) for speechless guests.

A combination of hummus, cheese, honey, jam, bread, and sometimes *fuul* form a standard breakfast. Traditional dinners are served around 2 or 3pm; popular dishes include *musakhan,* chicken baked with olive oil, onions, and spices, served on bread; and *mahshi,* a tray of vine leaves, squash, or eggplant stuffed with mincemeat, rice, and onions. Supper is usually smaller and lighter. A staple at any time of the day is *za'tar,* a sauce of thyme mixed with sesame seeds and spices, eaten either by dipping the bread into olive oil and then into the mix, or pizza-style (*mana'eesh*).

JORDAN

SUGAR AND SPICE Jordan has long been a safe haven and cultural breeding ground for Syrian and Palestinian refugees. Nevertheless, immigrant kitchens compulsively guarded their native dessert recipes—that is, until the **Jabri** and **Habiba** pastry chains came onto the scene around 1950. Jabri introduced Damascene **ba'laweh,** while Habiba hooked the country on **kinafeh** from the Palestinian villages of Nablus. Half a century later, the Jordanian sweet tooth can only be satisfied by the honey-coated, nut-filled pockets of filo-dough joy that have become an inseparable part of the country's more established traditions.

Drink bottled water (300fils, more at restaurants and tourist haunts) or use iodine tablets. **Coffee** and **tea** are expressions of Jordanian hospitality, and tourists are likely to be offered refreshment many times a day. If a hot drink doesn't tickle your fancy, ask for *barid* (Arabic for "cold"). Jordanians drink tremendous amounts of tea *(shay)*, almost always made with mint *(na'na')*. Stereotypes hold that bumpkin *fellaheen* (country people) drink their tea syrupy sweet; restaurants will assume you do too unless you prove your gentility by asking for *sukkar aleel* (just a little sugar). A cup of the thick, black, bittersweet Arabic coffee *(ahwa)* is stronger than espresso. Drinking **alcohol** is prohibited by Islam, so imbibing in Jordan is subject to some restrictions and conventions. Anyone who looks older than 16 may buy at a liquor store (usually owned by Christians). Locally-brewed Amstel is the most popular alcoholic drink (600fils); imports are also available. 'Araq is a popular aniseed hard alcohol (similar to the Greek *ouzo* and Turkish *raki*) that is mixed with water until it turns cloudy and white.

AMMAN عمان

The automobiles ricocheting off Amman's street corners leave scattered pedestrians in their wake as horns catapult visitors onto sidewalks. The sidewalks in Amman are as packed with people as its streets are with cars, and the entire frenetic tableau is set to the beat of the popular Arabic music pouring out from storefronts. Five times a day, the noisy pinball game of urban Jordanian life is paused when the *muezzin* calls the people to prayer, its lone voice echoing from the minarets that dot the skyline. When the sun goes down and the lights come up, the jasmine-scented streets provide the perfect setting for lazy summertime strolls across the city's seven hills.

Though it was the Ammonite capital in Biblical times, modern-day Amman was a mere village in the decades preceding 1948, when its population of 6000 could have easily fit inside the city's Roman Theater. Following the Arab-Israeli wars of 1948 and 1967, however, many Palestinian refugees ended up here, and Amman began to expand exponentially. Descendants of these original Palestinians now make up about 70% of Jordan's population. Many feel that they don't have it any better than their fathers and grandfathers did in Palestine; some Palestinians are highly successful doctors, businesspeople, bankers, and politicians, but many still live in Amman's huge refugee camps. Egyptian and Southeast Asian workers also make up a large part of the city's population, and after the Gulf War in 1991, they were joined by immigrants from Iraq and Kuwait. Today, Amman's more than one million inhabitants make up roughly one-third of Jordan's total population.

Amman's central location has made it the country's principal transportation hub and the base for exploring Jordan's other sights. Its entertainment, government services, and reasonable hotel prices are typical of a cosmopolitan capital city, but Amman's charm resists such generic classifications. The people of downtown Amman are the city's most valuable treasure. The greetings you hear are quite sincere, and chances are a "welcome" will lead to a cup of tea, a conversation, and experiences you'll never forget. Seasoned globetrotters agree—travelers are welcome in Amman as in few places on earth.

✦ ORIENTATION

Take advantage of Amman's summits to get a perspective on this roller-coaster city. Rocky **Jabal al-Qala'a** ("Fortress Hill"), where the Archaeological Museum sits amid Roman and Umayyad ruins, provides a panoramic view of winding streets, tall buildings, mosques, and ruins, all of which serve as useful landmarks.

Amman's downtown district, **Al-Balad,** is neatly framed by the city's seven hills and is the best location from which to orient yourself. Al-Balad has three major landmarks: the **Al-Husseini Mosque (Masjid Malik Hussein),** the **Roman Theater** (known only by its English name to locals), and the **Central Post Office** *(maktab al-bareed).* With your back to the mosque, the city's focal point, you face **King Faisal**

Street, which leads northwest to the post office and numerous budget hotels. Turn right, and you look up **Hashemi St.**, which leads to the Roman Theater. To the left is the city's main **fruit and vegetable souq**. The **gold souq** is on the right-hand side of King Faisal St. as you walk up the street toward the post office. The **clocktower** and the recently-built piazza are just past the Roman Theater on Hashemi St.

Amman's eight **numbered traffic circles** follow a line leading westward out of town and through **Jabal Amman** on Zahran St. Beyond 3rd Circle (Amman's diplomatic center and home of most embassies), traffic circles have been replaced by busy intersections. Although the city is earnestly attempting to rename these intersections "squares," each is still fondly called a "circle," or *duwwar*. From 7th Circle, traffic heads south to Queen Alia International Airport and the Desert Highway (Aqaba is 335km south), to the Kings' Highway via Madaba (35km), Karak (125km), and Petra (260km), and via Na'ur to the Dead Sea and the border of Israel (90km). From 8th Circle, you can continue west to Wadi as-Seer or head north to Jerash (50km).

Following King Hussein St. northwest from the city center brings you to **Jabal al-Weibdeh,** a tree-lined middle-class neighborhood perched on a hill. The **JETT** and **Abdali Bus Stations,** two of the city's major transportation hubs, are in this neighborhood. The blue dome and octagonal minaret of the Jabal's enormous **King Abdullah Mosque (Masjid Malik 'Abdullah)** are visible from all surrounding heights. To the north of the city lies **Jabal Hussein,** a largely residential district dominated by the Housing Bank complex *(mujamma' bank al-iskan)*, next to the Forte Grand Hotel. This area is bordered to the northwest by the Ministry of Interior Circle *(duwwar ad-Dakhiliyyeh)* and the modern suburb of **Shmeisani,** complete with luxury hotels and American-style fast food restaurants. **Abdoun** and **Sweifiyeh,** Amman's two runners-up for Western-style decadence, lie west of Al-Balad. The fertile Jordan Valley lies beyond the city limits to the north and west; the city recedes into desert in the south and east. To the southeast of the city, in the direction of the airport, rises **Jabal al-Ashrafiyyeh.** Its ornate **Abu Darwish Mosque** can be seen above the **Wahdat Bus Station** and the Wahdat Palestinian Refugee Camp.

The government has installed some street signs in downtown Amman; most have English translations. Although most people know King Faisal and Hashemi St., other inquiries are likely to produce blank stares. Successful navigation of Amman means knowing its landmarks. In addition to remembering the Al-Husseini Mosque, Roman theater, and Wahdat and Abdali Bus Stations, try to find out which numbered circle your destination is near and you'll have an easier time finding your way. Don't hesitate to ask locals for assistance—they'll usually be glad to help you out.

GETTING THERE AND AWAY

Airplanes: Queen Alia International Airport (tel. 445 33 33 or 445 32 00), 35km south of Amman. **24-hr. buses** connect Abdali Bus Station and the airport (40min., every 30min., JD1). A private **taxi** to the airport costs JD10 (JD15 at night; 2 pieces of luggage free, additional pieces 200fils). No *service* run to the airport. **Housing Bank** and **Jordan Bank** (open 24hr.) and a **tourist office** (open 9am-2pm) are in the airport. There is a JD10 exit fee when leaving Jordan by air (JD4 if by land, JD6 if by sea).

Intercity Buses: Minibuses to the north central and northwestern parts of the country (including the Jordan Valley) leave from **Abdali Bus Station** on King Hussein St. at Jabal al-Weibdeh. To: **Jerash** (300fils); **'Ajlun** (400fils); **Irbid** (800fils); **Salt** (150fils); and **King Hussein/Allenby Bridge** (JD1.5). **Hashemi St. Station** (a.k.a. **Raghadban Interchange**), near the Roman Theater, launches traffic to the northeast, including Zarqa, Mafraq, and points east of Irbid. Traffic to and from the south is based at **Wahdat Station,** several kilometers from downtown Amman, between the Abu Darwish Mosque and the Wahdat Refugee Camp. Buses go to **Madaba, Karak, Ma'an, Wadi Musa, Petra,** and **Aqaba.** The **JETT bus station** (tel. 56 64 146, international 56 96 151/2) has 2 offices on King Hussein St., past Abdali Bus Station and opposite Army Headquarters. A/C buses to: **King Hussein/Allenby Bridge** (45min., 6:30am, JD6); **Petra** (3½hr.; 6:30am; JD5.5, round-trip JD11, round-trip tour including guide, horse, and lunch

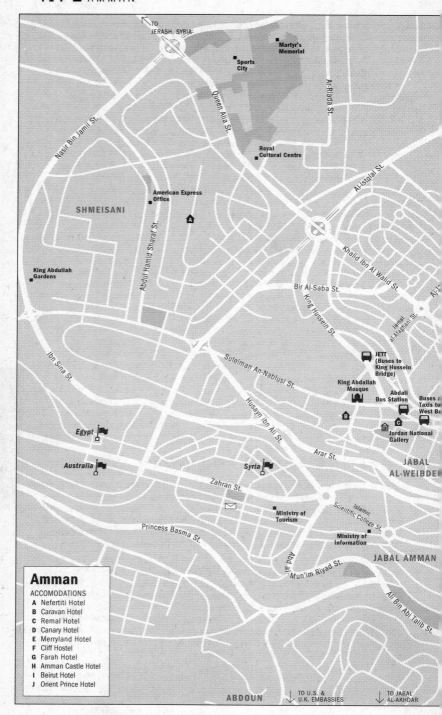

TO
JERASH, SYRIA

Martyr's
Memorial

Sports
City

Ar-Riada St.

Queen Alia St.

Royal
Cultural Centre

Al-Istiqlal St.

American Express
Office

SHMEISANI

Abdul Hamid Sharaf St.

Khalid Ibn Al Walid St.

King Abdullah
Gardens

Bir Al-Saba St.

King Hussein St.

Jamal al-Afaghani St.

Nasir Bin Jamil St.

Ibn Sina St.

Suleiman An-Nablusi St.

JETT
(Buses to
King Hussein
Bridge)

King Abdallah
Mosque

Abdali
Bus Station

Buses a
Taxis to
West Ba

Husayn Ibn Ali St.

Egypt

B

Jordan National
Gallery

Australia

Arar St.

JABAL
AL-WEIBDE

Syria

Zahran St.

Islamic
Scientific College St.

Ministry of
Tourism

Princess Basma St.

Ministry of
Information

JABAL AMMAN

Abd al-Mun'im Riyad St.

Ali Bin Abi Talib St.

Amman

ACCOMODATIONS
A Nefertiti Hotel
B Caravan Hotel
C Remal Hotel
D Canary Hotel
E Merryland Hotel
F Cliff Hostel
G Farah Hotel
H Amman Castle Hotel
I Beirut Hotel
J Orient Prince Hotel

ABDOUN

TO U.S. &
U.K. EMBASSIES

TO JABAL
AL-AKHDAR

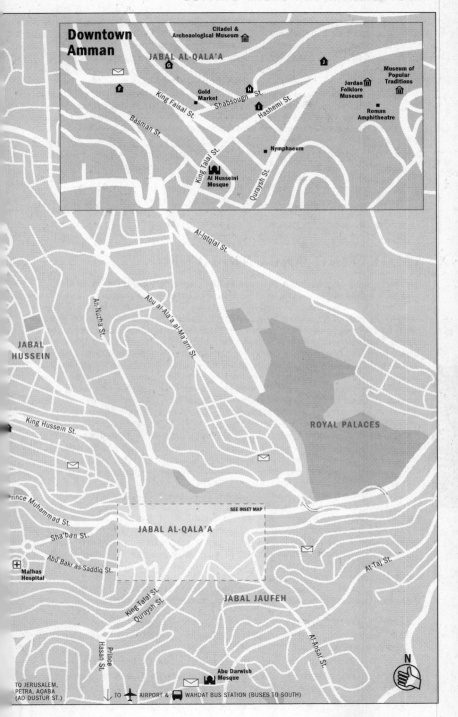

Downtown Amman

Citadel & Archeaological Museum

JABAL AL-QALA'A

Museum of Popular Traditions

Jordan Folklore Museum

Gold Market

King Faisal St.

Shabsough St.

Hashemi St.

Roman Amphitheatre

Basman St.

King Talal St.

Nymphaeum

Quraysh St.

Al Husseini Mosque

Al-Istqlal St.

Abu al-Ala'a al-Ma'arri St.

An-Nuzha St.

JABAL HUSSEIN

King Hussein St.

ROYAL PALACES

Prince Muhammad St.

Sha'ban St.

SEE INSET MAP

JABAL AL-QALA'A

Abu Bakr as-Saddiq St.

Malhas Hospital

At-Taj St.

King Talal St.

Quraysh St.

JABAL JAUFEH

Prince Hasan St.

Al-Ansar St.

Abu Darwish Mosque

N

TO JERUSALEM, PETRA, AQABA (AD DUSTUR ST.)

TO ✈ AIRPORT & 🚌 WAHDAT BUS STATION (BUSES TO SOUTH)

JD32.5); **Aqaba** (4hr., 11 per day, JD4); **Damascus** (4-5hr., 7am and 3pm, JD4.5, visa required); **Cairo** (20-24hr., Tu and Sa 6:30am, JD33); and **Beirut** (8hr., M and Th 9am, JD15). Office open daily 6am-8pm. Reserve 1 day in advance.

Intercity Service Taxis: Intercity *service* leave from the same stations as buses and go to the same regions, but tend to be 40-50% more expensive. From **Abdali Bus Station,** *service* to: **Jerash** (470fils), **'Ajlun** (750fils), **Irbid** (880fils), **Salt** (350fils), and **King Hussein/Allenby Bridge** (JD1.5). From **Wahdat Bus Station,** *service* to: **Madaba** (500fils), **Karak** down the King's Highway (JD1.5), **Ma'an** via the newer Desert Highway (JD3.5), **Petra** (JD4), and **Aqaba** (JD6). All prices, bus and *service* alike, are government-regulated, but government regulations are not always observed.

Car Rental: Local agencies have fewer restrictions. **Reliable Rent-a-Car** (tel. 592 96 76 or 079 52 13 58). JD25-35 per day gets you insurance, unlimited mileage, and 24-hr. breakdown service for a 1998 Nissan. The manager will send someone to pick you up at your hotel and bring you out to their office in Abdoun. If you prefer name recognition, try **Avis** (tel. 569 94 20; fax 562 10 12) or **Budget** (tel. 569 81 31; fax 567 33 12). For a real cheapie, check out **Firas** (tel. 560 20 82; fax 461 68 74), at 1st Circle, with unlimited mileage on economy cars (JD18 and up). **Valid driver's license** and **passport** required by all agencies. Reserve in advance in summer and the high season. Drivers under 21 may have more luck with local agencies than with corporate heavyweights.

⌷ GETTING AROUND TOWN

To reach locations within the city or to find the departure point for buses and *service*, ask a downtown shopkeeper. You can flag **buses** and **service** anywhere along their routes, but *service* are often full (they take five passengers) from the beginning to the end of their prescribed courses. Public transportation stops at 8 or 9pm, and a couple of hours earlier on Fridays; walking is a safe alternative. Metered **taxis** prowl the streets and honk their horns at potential passengers. After 11pm, taxi drivers expect about double the daytime fare; make sure you bargain before getting in. 500fils is about right for a trip from downtown to 3rd Circle or from 3rd to 6th Circle; 350fils is about right for the downtown-Abdali route. A taxi between the two bus/*service* stations should cost 800fils. The trip along Jabal Amman from 1st to 8th Circle should cost no more than JD1.1; check to make sure the meter is running (see **Getting Around,** p. 406). It is an Arab custom for men to ride in the front seat of taxis. Women should always ride in the back seat.

Buses traveling within Amman cost about 100fils; it's a little more if you're heading for the suburbs. Flag any bus traveling in your direction and ask the driver if it stops where you want to go, or find out at any bus station. Pay your fare after the ride has begun. Drivers and their assistants don't like making change, so carry 100fils in change with you. Most buses have the name of their destination written in Arabic on the front, sides, or both. Some have numbers, but since buses going on different routes may display the same number, what worked one time may not the next. Asking around is the best way to find a bus.

Although it may cost a few more fils, transportation by **service** or white taxi is much easier on the nerves than bus travel and offers frequent opportunities to meet Jordanians. *Service* routes are clear and comprehensive, with their numbers and the names of their routes listed on the doors in Arabic. All routes within the city originate downtown. Stopping a *service* en route is difficult—many drive at breakneck speed, so make yourself visible without stepping into the street, and then stick out your arm with the palm down. Some popular routes are:

#1 (١): On Jabal Amman, from Center City through 1st–3rd Circles (100fils).

#2 (٢): From Basman St. (behind Cliff Hotel) along Jabal Amman to Malik 'Abd Ribiya St. and between 2nd and 3rd Circles (90fils).

#3 (٣): From Basman St. along Jabal Amman to 3rd and 4th Circles (100fils).

#4 (٤): From Omar al-Khayyam St. (opposite the Cliff Hotel) to Al-Amaneh Circle and gardens, passing near all points of interest on Jabal al-Weibdeh (90fils).

#6 (٦): From Cinema al-Hussein St. (aka Malik Ghazi St.), along King Faisal and King Hussein St. to Ministry of Interior Circle, passing Abdali and JETT bus stations (100fils).

#6a (٦•): From Cinema al-Hussein St. to Shmeisani near the Ambassador Hotel (110fils).

#7 (٧): From Cinema al-Hussein St. past Abdali to Shmeisani near Arab Bank (70fils).

Service and minibuses to Wahdat Bus Station start at Kureisha St. (aka Sakfi Seil) near Petra Bank and pass near Abu Darwish Mosque on Jabal Ashrafiyyeh. *Service* directly to Wahdat Bus Station from Abdali cost 120fils. Another route starts at Shabsough St. near the gold *souq* downtown, passing Abdali Bus Station and Jabal Hussein to Ministry of Interior Circle (80fils). Some prices will be higher or lower than those listed, but drivers rarely cheat passengers, even tourists.

▓ PRACTICAL INFORMATION

TOURIST AND FINANCIAL SERVICES

Ministry of Tourism: (tel. 464 23 11/2; fax 464 84 65), P.O. Box 224. From 3rd Circle on Jabal Amman, take the first left on Fareed as-Sa'd St., then take the first left again to reach the imposing building on your left. Distributes free maps, hotel price lists, and lovely color brochures. Open Sa-Th 8am-2pm.

Embassies:

Australia (tel. 593 02 46, visa info 593 27 80), on Jabal Amman between 4th and 5th Circles, across from a large grassy knoll. Helpful with foreign visas. Open Su-Th 7:30am-3pm, visas M and W 9am-noon.

Canada (tel. 566 61 24; fax 568 92 27), in Shmeisani near the Petra Bank. Open Su-W 8am-4:30pm, Th 8am-1:30pm, visas 9-11am.

Egypt (tel. 560 51 75; fax 560 40 82), Jabal Amman between 4th and 5th Circles. Take a right off Zahran St. after the grassy space; it's 50m down on the right. Bring a photo and JD9 before noon; pick up your visa that afternoon. Open Sa-Th 9:30am-3pm, visas 9:30am-noon.

Israel (tel. 552 54 07; fax 552 19 71), 4th Circle on Jabal Amman. Far from any *service* route; take a yellow taxi. Visas JD13. Open Su-Th 9am-4pm.

Lebanon (tel./fax 592 91 11), Abdoun, behind U.K. Embassy. 1-month visa JD14; 3-month visa JD28. Open M-Th and Sa 8am-2pm, visas 8am-11am.

Syria (tel. 464 19 35 or 45), Jabal Amman up from 3rd Circle toward the reflecting building. Take a left at the intersection and head up the hill. Look for the Syrian flag (red, white, and black stripes with 2 green stars). In theory, a visa costs JD34, but virtually nobody gets one—you must have a Jordanian entry stamp and no evidence of visits to the West Bank or Israel. Open Su-Th 8:30am-2pm, visas 9-11am.

U.K. (tel. 592 31 00; fax 592 37 59), in Abdoun on Damascus St. Instead of turning right to the U.S. Embassy, continue on the road until you reach the Orthodox Club (the walled-in playground with the red jungle-gym protruding above the walls). Make a right, then 2 quick lefts. Open daily 8:30am-noon, visas all day.

U.S. (tel. 592 01 01, visa info 592 32 93; fax 592 41 02), in Abdoun. Heading north on Jabal Amman (Zahran St.), make a left at 5th Circle and continue to the 1st intersection. Make a left on Cairo St. and take the 3rd right. The fortress-like complex is 500m down that road. Open Su-Th 8am-4:30pm, visas 7-10am.

Currency Exchange: Banks are generally open Sa-W 8:30am-12:30pm and 4-5:30pm, Th 8:30am-2pm, and closed Friday. Many authorized **money changers** (found downtown between the Al-Husseini Mosque and the post office) are open daily, usually late into the evening. They offer roughly the same exchange rates as banks but will not ask for a bank's commission. Passport required. Most **ATMs,** including the one next to the Arab Bank on King Faisal St., can give **cash advances** on Visa and MC.

American Express: 58 'Abdul Hamid Sharaf St., P.O. Box 408 (tel. 560 70 14; fax 566 99 05; email traders@nets.com.jo), opposite Shmeisani's Ambassador Hotel. Holds mail. Obtains visas when cardholders purchase plane tickets. Open Sa-Th 8:30am-6pm.

LOCAL SERVICES

English Bookstores: Al-'Ulama Bookshop (tel. 463 61 92; fax 465 60 17), just uphill from the post office. History books, travel guides, dictionaries, and a couple of American news magazines. Fax and photocopier available. Open Su-Th 8am-7pm. **Istiqlal Library** has 3 locations in Amman: downtown opposite the post office (tel. 462 24 75); Shmeisani (downhill from the KFC; tel. 566 31 30); and Sweifiyeh (around corner from Turino Hotel; tel. 582 11 69). These book and stationery stores have a helpful English-speaking staff. Downtown branch open Su-Th 7:30am-5:30pm; other 2 open Su-Th 8am-1:30pm and 3-6:30pm. **Amman Bookshop** (tel. 464 40 13), at 3rd Circle. Walk down Prince Muhammad St.; the bookstore is on your left, across from the large Kodak sign. A huge store replete with trashy novels, esoteric art history books, CDs, and oodles of stationery. Visa, AmEx accepted. Open Su-Th 8:30am-2pm and 3:30-6:30pm.

Local Press: *Your Guide to Amman,* published monthly and available free at larger hotels, bookstores, and travel agencies, is full of helpful info. *The Jordan Times* (150fils), a daily newspaper with excellent coverage of the Middle East and Africa, lists useful telephone numbers, 24-hour pharmacies, and cultural events in Amman. *Jordan Today,* published monthly and available at larger hotels, has invaluable information on tourism, culture, and entertainment. The *International Herald Tribune* arrives after 3pm one day late at newsstands; *Time, Newsweek,* and *The Economist* are sporadically available. The weekly *Jerusalem Star* (350fils) lists cultural events and all the piddling details from the lives of the royals. The *New York Times* is sometimes available one day late at the gift shop in the Marriott and Inter-Continental Hotels.

Cultural Centers: American Cultural Center (tel. 585 91 01), Abdoun, inside the American Embassy Complex. Free American films every Su and Th and cable TV. Lectures by scholars and politicians visiting Jordan are open to the public. Library has American periodicals, comfy couches, a video library, and a good selection of books, mostly non-fiction. Center and library open Su-Th 8am-5pm. **British Council** (tel. 463 61 47 or 48; fax 465 64 13), on Rainbow St. Facing uphill at 1st Circle, go left. The British Council is past the Saudi Embassy on the right hand side. Sponsors films, lectures, and various other activities. Office open Su-Th 8am-3pm; A/C library open Su-Th 10am-6pm.

Laundromat: Laundromats are generously scattered throughout Amman. **Dry Clean** (tel. 464 19 55), 3rd Circle, Jabal Amman, 50m down the street from the Ministry of Tourism, charges 500fils for shirts and 750fils for pants. **Aj-Jami'a Laundry** (tel. 534 78 57), on your first right heading away from the city past the main gate of Jordan University, is a do-it-yourself joint (wash and dry JD2).

EMERGENCY AND COMMUNICATIONS

Emergency: Ambulance: Tel. 193 or 199. **Traffic Accidents:** Tel. 896 390.

Pharmacies: *Jordan Times* and *Your Guide to Amman* list all-night pharmacies and doctors, both rotating weekly. Pharmacies open Sa-Th 8:30am-7pm. The **Rawhi Pharmacy** (tel. 464 44 54), between 3rd and 4th Circles, has an English-speaking staff. For non-prescription medicine, try **Safeway** (tel. 568 53 11), on the edge of Nasir Bin Jamil St. near the northwestern edge of Shmeisani; another in 7th Circle (open daily 24hr.).

Hospitals: The *Jordan Times, Jordan Star,* and *Your Guide to Amman* list doctors and hospitals. The **Shmeisani Hospital** (tel. 560 74 31) is reputable; others include the **Jordan Hospital** (560 75 50) in 4th Circle, and the **Arab Heart Surgical Hospital** (tel. 592 11 99), an ultramodern research institute in 5th Circle.

Post Office: The main post office is at the base of Prince Muhammad St., just before it joins King Faisal St. downtown. Stamps and **Poste Restante.** Cables and **faxes** can be sent from this office. Open Sa-Th 8:30am-7pm, F 8am-noon. **EMS** (tel. 568 81 90) is on Lifta St., a dead end behind Qawar Arthroscopy Center. From downtown, go up King Hussein St. past the Abdali and JETT bus stations. Take a right on Bir as-Sab'a St. and look left. Open daily 8am-8pm; holidays 8am-2pm.

Internet Access: Amman is dotted with cybercafes offering connections at JD1-1.5 per hr.

Telephones: Overseas calls can be made from hotels or the post office (only place you can pay in cash for overseas calls). **Phonecards** can be used at payphones around Amman. **Alo** and **JBB** cards are available at most newsstands and some restaurants in denominations of JD1, JD5, and JD15 and work for both local and international calls. There is a plethora of private phone offices on Omar al-Khayyam St. To get there, exit to your left from the post office and take your first left up the street across from the Cliff Hotel.

Telephone Code: 06.

ACCOMMODATIONS

Most backpackers are **downtown,** which is overgrown with small, seedy hotels conveniently located near the main post office, the telephone office, a large market, and many affordable restaurants. Many clean and reputable (but more expensive) hotels are near the **Abdali Bus Station** in Jabal al-Weibdeh, an area close to the city center and convenient for transport out of Amman. Just beyond Jabal al-Weibdeh is the opulent **Shmeisani** district, with a few reasonably priced accommodations worth the hunt. Rooms have private baths unless otherwise noted.

DOWNTOWN/AL-HUSSEINI MOSQUE AREA

Farah Hotel (tel. 465 14 43 or 48; fax 465 14 37), on Cinema al-Hussein St. Follow red and yellow signs at the intersection of King Hussein and King Faisal St. through an alley and across a street to this 6-story behemoth. Each floor has 4 smallish rooms with local phone, TV, 2 bathrooms (free showers, no toilet paper), and a large fridge. Relax with a *sheesha* in the cafeteria or read a book on the straw-covered terrace. International phone office with high rates downstairs. Internet JD2 per hr. Rooftop mattresses JD2; shared rooms JD3.5 per person; singles JD7; doubles JD9; triples JD10.5; quads JD14.

Cliff Hostel (tel. 462 42 73), on Prince Muhammad St. With your back to the post office, cross to the left-most of the 2 streets in front of you (toward the blue "Citizen" sign); take a left and walk ½ block to an alley beneath a Coca-Cola-postered terrace. The Cliff competes with the Farah for the backpacker market. Clean, spacious, high-ceilinged rooms with fans. Called "The U.N. headquarters of the Middle East" by manager Abu Suleiman, Cliff also offers more honest information and directions than the Ministry of Tourism. Terrace mattress JD2; singles JD5; doubles JD6; triples JD9; quads JD10. Showers 500 fils. Reception sells bottled water and other conveniences. Lockout at midnight, but a knock will get you in until 1am. Reserve in advance.

Beirut Hotel (tel. 463 69 86 or 463 80 99; fax 465 09 16), Al-Hashemi St. Between Al-Husseini Mosque and the Roman Theater. Walking from the mosque, look for the blue sign with white English letters on the left side of the street after about 90m. Eager-to-please manager caters to Arab and Western clientele. Carpeted rooms small but clean. Private telephones and common bath. Singles JD5; doubles JD8; triples JD15.

Orient Prince Hotel (tel. 465 65 90; fax 465 65 90), on Al-Hashemi St., between the Roman Theater and McDonald's on the opposite side of the street. Entrance in an alley by the camera shop. Ask to stay on the theater side; the views make the large dreary rooms more appealing. Private phones. Singles JD8; doubles JD10; triples JD15.

Amman Castle Hotel (tel./fax 464 27 66), on Shabsuq St. between Al-Husseini Mosque and the Roman Theater, 90m down on the right hand side of the mosque "HOTEL" in red letters on yellow background. Proprietors speak minimal English, but small rooms are comfortable, clean, and have nice mosaic floors. Few foreigners. Shared bath. 3rd floor common kitchen. JD2 for empty bed in occupied room. Doubles JD8.

NEAR ABDALI STATION

Caravan Hotel, P.O. Box 9062 (tel. 566 11 95/7; tel./fax 566 11 96; email caravan@go.com.jo), Al-Ma'moun St. on Jabal al-Weibdeh. Only 100m northwest of Abdali Bus Station, across from King Abdullah Mosque. Entrance is a short walk down the street directly opposite the mosque, across from an Orthodox church. Spacious, spotless rooms have green carpeting and soft beds. For true luxury, ask for a balcony, relax on the vine-shaded terrace, or take a seat on the roof. Ihsan Twal will enrich your stay with Arabic food to fit your budget. Free local calls, Internet JD2 per ½hr. Singles JD18; doubles JD22; triples JD26. Visa, MC accepted. 15% *Let's Go* discount.

Canary Hotel (tel. 463 83 53; tel./fax 465 43 53; email canary_h@hotmail.com), Karmaly St. on Jabal al-Weibdeh near Terra Sancta College, P.O. Box 9062. Facing downhill from Abdali Station, walk 1½ blocks along the right side of King Hussein St. When the main road forks downhill to the left, continue straight on Al-Ba'oniyah St. Take your first right on Karamaly St. and try to survive the final 1½-block climb to this placid neighborhood. Khaleel Twal welcomes you to his vine-entwined, canary-filled courtyard. Family-style meals; breakfast included, lunch and dinner available. Comfy beds and satellite color TV. Singles JD16; doubles JD22; triples JD24; quads JD28; add 10% service charge. Reserve a few days in advance in summer. Visa, MC accepted.

Merryland Hotel (tel. 463 03 70 or 71; fax 463 03 72), on King Hussein St., P.O. Box 9122. Walk downhill with the traffic on King Hussein St. about 90m past Abdali Station; the Merryland will appear on the right. Perhaps the nicest 2-star hotel you'll ever see, the Merryland has spruced up the typical hotel restaurant with glass chandeliers, a small bar, and a prohibitively expensive Arabic disco downstairs. Huge rooms off black marble hallways feature springy mattresses, comfortable sofas, refrigerators, and a variety of art on the walls. Some have radios, and the priciest ones are equipped with A/C. 2-room suites with small kitchenettes also available. Worth the splurge. Singles JD12-17; doubles JD18-25; triples JD25-35. Summer rates JD5-7 higher. Visa, MC accepted.

Remal Hotel, 4 Sa'id Bin al-Harith St., P.O. Box 910477 (tel. 463 06 70; fax 465 57 51). Look downhill from the Abdali Bus Station for the police station on the right; the hotel is 100m up the small street next to the station. Small rooms are brightened by fresh paint and balconies; beds are large and comfy and come with fluffy feather pillows. Attached restaurant offers traditional Arab fare. Singles JD12; doubles JD18; triples JD24; add 10% service charge. Price includes breakfast for *Let's Go* users.

SHMEISANI

Nefertiti Hotel, 26 Aj-Jahed St. (tel. 560 38 65 or 560 35 53), 2 streets downhill from and directly in line with the Ambassador Hotel. Rooms come in differing shapes and sizes, but all are quite large. Some have gigantic glass-enclosed terraces, delightful places to enjoy this quiet neighborhood. Others have glass-enclosed bathrooms that afford spectacular toilet-seat views of Amman without compromising your privacy. Be sure to check out several rooms before you commit; they differ enough that one may suit your taste more. Singles JD11.5; doubles JD14.5; triples JD18. Cash only.

◪ FOOD

The better sit-down restaurants in Amman cluster near 3rd Circle, in Shmeisani, and along Mecca St.; these places usually add a 10% service charge to the bill. The **Umm 'Uthaina** district, by 6th Circle past Amra Hotel, offers a variety of appetizing, cheap foods. The jewels of the city's offerings are the street foods. If the listings are in Arabic, ask the vendor to translate. The **souq** is near the Al-Husseini Mosque (with your back to the mosque turn left and walk about four blocks); prices are steady and bargaining unnecessary (open Su-Th 8:30am-sundown). For some cool treats after these cheap eats, try **Crema Creme** or **Frosti** on Paris St.

Anyone who is anyone mingles at the **Caffe Moka** in Abdoun, which serves strawberry tarts (JD1.250) and cappuccino (JD1). Also try **Ma'atouk's** in 3rd Circle (coffee 300fils), or the absurdly named **Eco-Tourism Cafe** on King Faisal St., where a friendly mix of young and old Jordanians shoot the breeze over *ahwa* (Arabic coffee) and *nargeileh* (300fils). Jordanian society reserves such entertainments for men. Although Western women may enter such establishments, they may feel more comfortable (bring a male friend) at such places as **Reem al-Bawady,** Tla' al-'Ali, Al-Ubeel Circle, which offers *nargeileh* for smoking in traditional Bedouin camel-hair tents. **Babiche Cafe** and **Geneva** in Shmeisani and the new **Caffe Moka** in Abdoun serve coffee, drinks, and pastries to a *chi-chi* co-ed crowd.

Westerners and wealthy Ammanites swear by the **Safeway** stores on the edge of Shmeisani and at 7th Circle (any taxi driver will get you to one in no time), where you can also get dry cleaning, shoe repair, a hardware store, Internet access, and a branch of the American sandwich shop **Subway** (open 24hr.). American grease-to-go has also invaded Jordan: **McDonald's, Pizza Hut, Arby's,** and **Kentucky Fried Chicken** draws both locals and tourists—you can't miss the neon signs in Shmeisani (taxis know the route well). For a real taste of Americana, head to **Cheers Elite Cafe** in Sweifiyeh's Turino Hotel, where everyone knows your name and blues and Top 40 music serenade you as you chow down on affordable buffalo wings, pizzas, and burgers. **Hard Rock Café** has also recently opened in Abdoun.

Hashem Restaurant (tel. 463 64 40), on Prince Muhammad St., in the alley directly across from the Cliff Hotel. Arabic fast food at its best. The final word in hummus since the 50s, Hashem is a great place to see, hear, and taste Amman's frantic pace. Hummus and *fuul* served with an amazing pickled pepper concoction; bread freshly baked across the street; everything garnished with mint leaves and onions grown fresh in their garden. Tea, hummus, and an evening's conversation with locals totals well under 650fils. Take-out makes good packed lunches for daytrips. Open daily 24hr.

Abu Ahmad's New Orient Restaurant (tel. 464 18 79), 3rd Circle, Jabal Amman, behind the Amman Surgical Hospital. Splurge at this luxurious restaurant among vines, green checkered tablecloths, and a hyper-attentive staff. Award-winning *nouveau* Arabic cuisine. Grilled dishes JD2.25-4.5; appetizers 600fils-JD4.5. Open daily noon-4pm and 7pm-midnight. Traveler's checks, Visa, MC accepted.

Al-Quds Restaurant (Jerusalem Restaurant) (tel. 463 01 68), on King Hussein St. around the corner from the post office. From the Cliff Hotel, cross the street and go around the corner to your right. Look for a greenish awning. Although it looks like an American pancake house, Al-Quds serves authentic Arabic food in a wonderfully clean setting. Try their variation on *mensaf,* made with chicken instead of lamb (JD2), or sample their more standard fare such as kebab (JD1.9) or hummus (500fils). Top it all off with a selection from their mounds of tempting, artistically arranged sweets. Open daily in summer 7am-11pm; in winter 7am-10pm.

Salam Restaurant (tel. 462 26 26), on King Faisal St., half a block up from the Al-Husseini Mosque on the left-hand side of the street, next to the Bata shoe store. Very small English sign; look for spitted chickens in the window. Come for the colorful crowd, tasty food, and enticing aroma; stay for the pastries. JD3.3 buys bread, bird, and fries at the tables upstairs. *Sfiehah* and *mana'eesh* 200fils. The menu is in Arabic, but servers can describe the dishes in English. Open daily 8am-10:30pm.

Indian Restaurant (tel. 581 98 29), 8th Circle. A step inside the Indian Restaurant and you know you've come to someplace different. Scantily clad waitresses bring copious amounts of alcohol to adventure-seeking guests. No hummus or *mensaf* here: feast on vegetarian curry, basmati rice, and fresh-squeezed juice. The food is spicy and delicious. Entrees JD1.5-3. Open daily noon-4pm and 6:30pm-midnight. Visa, MC accepted.

Cairo Restaurant (tel. 462 45 27), on the left on a side street 2 blocks from the Al-Husseini Mosque. With your back to the mosque, head left past the clothes booths and look for the big red and white sign. Eat a lot for a little: roasted ½-chicken 1.250fils, kebab 1.4fils, *fasulya* (green beans cooked with lamb in tomato sauce) 300fils, breakfast *fuul* plates 300fils, and a ½-head of lamb (including eyes and tongue) JD1.3. Vegetarians beware: this place is an orgy of flesh. Open daily 5am-11pm.

Romero (tel. 464 42 27 or 28), 3rd Circle, Jabal Amman. Walking towards 2nd Circle from 3rd take the second right and, across from the Ambassador Hotel, *voilà*: Ristorante Romero. This romantic outdoor cafe with a sunny Mediterranean ambience serves the best Italian food in Amman. Glitzy indoor section has French and Italian artists' works on the walls. Pasta JD2.75-4; meat and seafood JD3.5-8. Open daily 1-3:30pm and 8-11:30pm. Reserve in advance. Visa, MC, and AmEx accepted.

Abu Khamis and Abu Saleh Restaurant (tel. 462 27 82), on King Faisal St., 1 alley over from the Cliff in the direction of the Al-Husseini Mosque. A deceptively small facade leads to a spacious, brightly-lit interior. There are English translations opposite the Arabic dishes listed on the menu, but prices are conveniently left untranslated. Half-chicken and kebab go for about JD1.250 each. Open daily 7am-10:30pm.

⬛ SIGHTS

SWEIFIYEH MOSAIC. Amman's finest Byzantine artifact was found during construction at the western edge of the city in 1970. The mosaic illustrates the passing of the seasons and once belonged to a 6th-century church. Ask the caretaker to hose down the floor for a better look at the bizarre creatures: leaf-bearded men, eagles with ears, and eel-men. The most worthwhile sight north of Madaba. (*Follow the signs from the first left west of 6th Circle. Open Sa-Th 9am-4pm, F 9am-1:30pm. Free.*)

ROMAN THEATER. The Roman Theater, on Jabal al-Qala'a downtown is the most renowned of Amman's historical sights. Built by Roman Emperor Antonius Pius (138–161 CE), the Roman Theater could once accommodate all 6000 of Amman's inhabitants. (*Open daily 8am-7pm. Admission free.*)

HERITAGE MUSEUMS. Two museums are built into the foundations of the theater on either side of the enclosed stage area. On the right, the **Folklore Museum** has exhibits on the diverse heritages of the Jordanian people—from Circassian military weaponry to Palestinian embroideries and Bedouin encampments. The **Museum of Popular Traditions** shows off attire and accessories from the country's past. The gallery to the right of the entrance displays 6th-century mosaics from Madaba and Jerash. Students can try begging for free admission, which has sometimes worked if there aren't many other visitors. Otherwise, the hefty JD1 fee keeps away all those who are not specifically interested in Jordanian culture and costumes. (*Folklore Museum: tel. 465 17 42. Open Su-Th 9am-5pm, F and official holidays 10am-4pm. JD1. Museum of Popular Traditions: tel. 465 17 60. Open daily 9am-5pm. JD1.*)

CITADEL HILL. From the Roman theater or any other downtown locale, you can climb the steep steps and streets to the flat top of Citadel Hill. A trip to the top of Citadel Hill is a good idea for your first day in Amman, as the view will give you the best perspective on the city's labyrinthine ups and downs. The trip is best taken with a companion (especially for women traveling alone); in the event that locals are a bit overzealous in their desire to make friends. The citadel is the site of ancient Amman, called Rabbath-Ammon or "The Great City of the Ammonites"—an ancient people who make several cameos in the Bible. Guides charging an outrageous JD5 can skillfully decipher the visually impoverished sight's historical wealth, more of which Spanish and American archaeological teams are uncovering all the time. Tours leads visitors from the three remaining columns of the Roman **Temple of Hercules** to the much later **Umayyad Palace**, which is still in good condition. Informative signs aid independent discovery of the area.

ARCHAEOLOGICAL MUSEUM. This museum on Citadel Hill contains a chronologically organized series of finds from ancient sites throughout Jordan. Fragments of the **Dead Sea Scrolls** and 200,000-year-old rhinoceros teeth share the limelight with Iron Age anthropomorphic sarcophagi, minimalist Nabatean portraits, and sublime Roman marble statuary. In front of the museum are the foundations of a 2nd-century Roman temple that housed a 10m statue of Hercules, to whom the temple was likely dedicated. Three of the statue's giant marble fingers hint at the shrine's former glory. (*Tel. 463 87 95. Open daily 9am-5pm; official holidays 10am-4pm. JD2.*)

ANCIENT ROMAN RUINS. The best-preserved and most intriguing of Amman's ruins lie behind the museum. Vaulted chambers tower 10m over a spacious courtyard where elaborate floral decorations can still be seen in the stonework. The 7th-century structure once supported a huge stone dome and was used as a mosque, audience hall, and residence. Below the Roman walls, directly to the north, an open pit leads into the underground passageway that connected the fortified city to a hidden water supply. With a flashlight and fancy footwork you can enter the cavernous rock-hewn cistern by this route (the more conventional approach is from the gate on the street below). Avoid the grassy area across from the Temple of Hercules: despite its location, it's not part of the ruins but a youthful 40-year-old cemetery. A path between the two leads to a hard-to-see shortcut down the steep steps and backyards of the hillside neighborhood. Like most places in Amman, the route is safe and offers local color, but *Let's Go* does not recommend it to women alone.

AL-HUSSEINI MOSQUE AND ENVIRONS. The Citadel was the heart of ancient Amman, but today the pulse emanates from downtown, in and around this noted mosque (aka *Masjid Malik Hussein*). The Ottoman-style structure was built in 1924 on the site of an ancient mosque built by Umar, the second caliph of Islam. The nearby **Nymphaeum** was a sacred fountain and bathing ground for the ancient city. At the center of the triangle formed by the citadel, the mosque, and the post office is Amman's **gold souq,** featuring row upon row of gold jewelry, and a few shops selling antique Bedouin silver jewelry. Although bargaining is a way of life in much of Amman, prices in the gold market are fixed (JD10 per gram), as jewelry is priced strictly by weight. *(Open Sa and M-Th 9am-9pm, Su 9am-1pm.)*

KING ABDULLAH AND ABU DARWISH MOSQUES. Barely out of a *muezzin*'s range from Al-Husseini Mosque is Abdali's own place of worship, the *Masjid Malik 'Abdullah.* Constructed over seven years in memory of the late king (the current Abdullah's great-grandfather), King Abdullah Mosque's blue mosaic dome can shelter 3000 Muslims kneeling in prayer. The black-and-white checkered dome of the nearby Abu Darwish Mosque *(Masjid Abu Darwish)* peeks over Jabal Ashrafiyyeh. In the 1940s, Circassians built this mosque, one of the most unusual religious structures in the Middle East, entirely from white rock and black basalt, brought from quarries in the northern part of the country. The two colors were also used for the mosque's decoration and ornamentation.

JORDAN NATIONAL GALLERY. This gallery displays a vast amount of contemporary artwork representing the cultural output of the entire Middle East and the Islamic world. Many of the works are surprisingly critical of daily life. Shift gears to this day and age to take a break from the ancient ruins. *(On Jabal al-Weibdeh at Muntazah Park. Tel. 463 01 28. Open W-M 9am-5pm. JD1.)*

⬚ ENTERTAINMENT

BARS

For less trendy elitism and more good old-fashioned drinking, try the limitless Guinness at the **Irish Pub** in the basement of the Dove Hotel, between 4th and 5th Circles, next door to the Egyptian Embassy. Beer JD3. Happy hour M 7-9pm. Open daily 6:30pm-2am. **The Cellar** lies in the cozy basement of **Al-Qasr Hotel** between the Ambassador and Nefertiti Hotels in Shmeisani. This mellow jazz bar features live music, mixed drinks, and potato skins—sure to please any hepcat expat. Another good watering hole is **Rover's Return** in Sweifiyeh, below the Comfort Inn Hotel. There are also a variety of grimy dives in Al-Balad; one is as good as another, and the **Kit Kat Bar,** behind the Cliff Hotel, is easy to find; just ask Sally Bowles.

CINEMA AND THEATER

There are four **cinemas** that show English-language films: the **Philadelphia** (tel. 463 41 49), 3rd Circle, 100m after the tower building; **Concord** (tel. 567 74 20), Abdali; **Plaza** (tel. 569 92 38), at the Forte Grande in Shmeisani; and the luxurious **Galery 1 and 2** in Abdoun. A few scattered theaters show B-grade action movies from India and the U.S., as well as 1970s soft porn. The word on the street says the censors have cut these to ribbons by the time they hit the screens, though: buyers beware. **Cinema al-Hussein,** downhill from the Farah Hotel is a good spot for such titillating fare. The **Nabil & Hisham's Theater,** Rainbow St. (tel. 462 51 55), 1st Circle, sometimes produces English-language plays.

CLUBS

Amman has its fair share of nightclubs. The scene picks up discernibly in the summer, when the sweltering days give way to cool evenings. Even the moniest men and the glammest girls bed down by 1 or 2am. Thursdays rage by all accounts, Sundays and Mondays also produce a fair-to-middling crowd, but the rest of the week is **dead**. Many of the hippest discos have members-only policies. One consistently popular hotspot is **Salute**, between 1st and 2nd Circles, under the Villa d'Angelo Italian restaurant. If you can squeeze yourself onto their breezy patio, consider yourself a member of the "in" crowd. Unaccompanied men not admitted (drinks JD2-5; no cover; Happy Hour Th 11:45pm-12:45am). Dress well and a silver tongue (or silver of another variety) will get you into **Yesterday's**, in 4th Circle. **JJ's**, in the basement of the Hyatt Hotel in 3rd Circle, is harder to get into; only the smoothest operators should attempt it—all other operators should just stand by. Ask anyone wearing Levis and carrying a cellular phone for the most up-to-date hipster info.

TRADITIONAL ENTERTAINMENT

Lone men and progressive couples interested in a more authentic (if slightly seedier) experience should explore the nightlife on Prince Muhammad St., about 300m downhill from the 3rd Circle. **Arizona** and her neighbor down the hill, **Kinz,** boast live Arabic music and belly dancers in a restaurant-style setting. No nudity, no cover. At JD5 for a beer, though, don't expect your excursion into Amman's slightly sketchier underbelly to be cheap. **Caesar's Palace Restaurant,** on Jabal al-Weibdeh, offers more traditional Jordanian music and dancing, including belly dancing on Thursday nights. For traditional Arab singing and music, brave the hefty cover at the **Roof Garden** (tel. 465 88 51), near Salute and Gengiskhan Restaurant. Waitresses in red body suits with shiny chest ornaments will bring large Amstels to you and your 18+ companions (drinks JD2-2.5; cover JD5-6, includes first drink).

NEAR AMMAN

WADI AS-SEER. Burgeoning Amman has begun spreading westward into the quiet valley of **Wadi as-Seer,** a region first settled by the fair-skinned Circassians. At Wadi as-Seer, the high desert plateau suddenly gives way to the Jordan Valley, where a little stream (*"wadi,"* hence the name) snakes through the countryside on its way to the Dead Sea. The narrow asphalt road that follows this valley out of town is ideal for daytripping motorists and tramping backpackers, even on scorching summer days. Groups of friendly children wander through the verdant pomegranate plants and olive trees that line the 12km road that runs southwest to the remains of Qasr al-Abd. *(The easiest path begins from the Al-Husseini Mosque in Amman. Walk left past the screeching taxis to a fork in the road (10min.). Head left at the fork; the lines of* **minibuses** *off to the right will drop you off at Wadi as-Seer (100fils). The Wadi as-Seer* **bus** *leaves from 5th or 6th Circle; hail the bus going north, away from downtown. From Wadi as-Seer, catch a minibus headed down the valley road (150fils). The whole trip takes 45min.-1½hr., depending on your driver's skill at avoiding stray chickens. Buses leave when full. Bring plenty of water and patience—you may have a bit of a wait for the return trip.)*

AL-BASSA SPRINGS. Soon after leaving Wadi as-Seer, you'll pass **Al-Bassa Springs,** the source of the valley's fertility and the site of a local swimming pool. Carved into the face of the cliff above the left bank of the *wadi* is **Ad-Deir,** the monastery. This extraordinary building merits the 20-minute climb, even if you don't find any of the Roman gold that villagers claim is buried under the floor. Each of the ossuary's thousands of triangular wall-niches once cradled a monk's skull.

QASR IRAQ AL-EMIR (CASTLE OF THE PRINCE'S ROCK). The story behind the creation of this impressive rock palace is almost as fascinating as the monolithic carvings on its walls. Local legend holds that a love-smitten slave named Tobiah built **Qasr al-Abd** (Castle of the Slave) to win the hand of his master's daughter.

Tobiah carved lions, panthers, and eagles into its walls while his master was away. Unfortunately, the master returned before Tobiah could finish, and the slave's efforts went unrewarded save the Aramaic inscription "Tobiah" carved near the entrance of one of the 11 hand-dug **caves**, 500m back up the valley road. Kill-joy historians, however, explain the inscription and the castle remains with references to Tobiah the Ammonite Servant (of God), a rich priest in Jerusalem. Ancient historian Josephus records yet another story about a wealthy Tobiah family and the exploits of the young son Hyrcanus, who built a strong fortress constructed entirely of white marble and enclosed by a wide, deep moat.

Regardless of who actually built the palace, two red stone lions remain intact, though there is no roof. The most impressive is the lioness (without a mane) on the northwest corner, but both lions have a unique twist: the male (with the flowing mane) is breast-feeding a baby with its female nipples, and the female lioness, prowling the corner alone, has male genitals. (Qasr Iraq al-Emir is the last stop at the end of the road from Amman through Wadi as-Seer. The guard or his son should let you in for free; a small donation of 100-200fils, however, is appreciated.)

NORTH OF AMMAN

SALT السلط

Salt (pronounced like SULTry) thrived as an administrative center during Ottoman rule, making it a likely choice for the capital of the new mandate of Transjordan when it was formed in 1921 (see **Modern History**, p. 409). The more centrally-located village of Amman won that honor, however, and Salt's main connection to governmental administration today is that the swanky preparatory school there can claim almost all of Jordan's high officials as its alumni.

Nevertheless, Salt's position as a regional Ottoman stronghold is still very evident: whole sections of archways from a church destroyed during the reign of the Ottomans snuggle up beside older local homes. The Ottoman barracks (built over a 13th-century fortress destroyed to prevent its capture by Crusaders) also remain intact, and Salt's large Christian community has peppered the hillsides with church towers. In the second half of the 19th century, Salt again became the center of regional society when industrious Saltis built Jordan's first hospital, its first modern church, and its first secondary school. Downhill from the bus station in Salt lies **Wadi Sh'eib**. Refreshing but unpalatable natural streams bubble out of the ground and break through the pavement of the main road. Unexplored caves, abandoned stone houses, and numerous dirt paths wrap around the *wadi* and the lush terraced farmlands and eucalyptus groves, making a minibus up Wadi Sh'eib the most dramatic approach to Salt.

🖪 PRACTICAL INFORMATION. From Amman, corner an Abdali bus driver to find the **minibus** going to Salt (30min., 175fils). Minibuses depart when full; be prepared to wait. Return minibuses run until early evening. The **post office** (tel. 554 96 85) is located uphill on the main road, a good 10min. walk from the circle at the bottom (open Sa-Th 7:30am-7pm, F 7:30am-1:30pm). Salt's **telephone code** is 05.

🗓 ACCOMMODATIONS AND FOOD. Although Salt has no hotels, Saltis are proud to uphold the Bedouin tradition of *khuttar*, whereby prominent (and not-so-prominent) local families take it upon themselves to host any visitors that cross their paths or knock on their doors. The tourist office, across the hall from the Archaeological Museum, is empty more often than not, but the **municipal building,** up the street from the Abu Jaber House (see **Sights,** below), is a good source of information.

Delicious food is easy to find. For the best kebab north of Amman, head to **Al-Amad's,** established in 1927 by Radi Al-Amad (whose portrait adorns the walls) and inherited by his son, who runs it today. Amad's is just downhill from the town center and the Abu Jaber house but it is hard to find—ask a local. JD1.250 will buy you kebab and the privilege of seeing his guest book, which has been signed by digni-taries who ate there as students in Salt; a detailed documentation of what they ate supplements their signatures. Open daily 8am-10pm. For good hummus, *fuul*, and the like, the **Canam Restaurant** (downhill from the Archaeological Museum) is a good, cheap bet. Hummus, *mezze*, and tea are all available at 300fils, and various enticing mincemeat dishes weigh in around JD1. Finish up with freshly-baked pastries at **Al-Habiba,** up the road from Canam and across from the Archaeological Museum (the *warbaht* is especially good).

◙ SIGHTS. Constructed in 1894, the famous but dilapidated **Abu Jaber house** serves as a reference point for just about everything in the city. It lies right below the plaza in the city center, and even if you can't get in to see the Italian fresco-cov-ered ceilings, a street-side perspective is enough to appreciate why this building is one of Jordan's finest architectural works (open Sa-Th 8am-11pm). To get to the free **Salt Archaeological and Folklore Museums,** go 300m uphill from the bus station, veering right; on the right you'll see a white building ringed with red stone and hung with a rather obscure blue sign. The Archeological Museum (tel. 355 65 51) consists of two rooms with lots of coins, pottery, and jewelry dating from the Chal-colithic period (4000 BCE) to the Islamic period (1516 CE). The Folklore Museum (tel. 355 36 53) is one flight up from the Archaeology Museum (both open Sa-Th 8am-6pm, F 9am-5:30pm). The highest point in Salt is the mosque on **Jabal Yushah,** which, according to Muslim legend, covers the site of the tomb of the prophet Hosea, or Yushah. The awe-inspiring view of the West Bank will make the trip up the hill worth your while: in the morning, you can see from the Dead Sea to Lake Tiberias. A round-trip taxi from downtown Salt costs JD2.

JERASH جرش

Although buried by sand and not volcanic lava, Jerash maintains much the same feel as the perfectly preserved Italian town of Pompeii. Stumbled upon by German traveler Ulrich Seetzen in 1806, Jerash is one of the most extensive provincial Roman cities still in existence. In ancient times it was dubbed Gerasa and was an important member of the Decapolis League, a loose association of trading cities allied with Rome (see **Ancient History,** p. 409). Because of Jerash's isolation in a remote valley, it survived long after the other nine cities were destroyed.

Jerash is typically Roman in design; indeed, the city's builders trampled over earlier settlements, so little evidence of pre-Roman days remains. Inscriptions calling the town **Antioch** reveal that the Seleucid king of that name had a prominent outpost here, but Jerash entered its golden age only after its conquest by the Roman general Pompey in 64 BCE. Over the following three centuries, Jerash experienced a period of prosperity rivaled only by the city's tourist boom of the 1990s. Granite was brought from as far away as Aswan and old temples were razed and rebuilt according to the latest architectural fads. In 106 CE, the Emperor Tra-jan annexed the surrounding Nabatean lands and built a highway from Damascus to Aqaba that passed through Jerash. Hadrian visited the town in 129; the Trium-phal Arch built for the occasion still stands. The town was converted to Christian-ity and had a bishop by the mid-4th century.

Following the destruction of the Syrian trading center at Palmyra (see p. 510) and the decline of the Nabatean kingdom, trade routes shifted from the desert to the sea. Frantic construction continued through the 6th century, but without their former wealth, the citizens of Jerash could only replace the older monuments with inferior structures that were plundered by invading Persians in 635. The great earthquake of 747 left few remnants for the Muslim Arabs, who controlled the city at that time. The Crusaders described Jerash as uninhabited, and it remained abandoned until its rediscovery in the 19th century. After the invasion of the Ottoman Turks, Circassians built the modern town in what was once the main residential area.

🛂 ORIENTATION AND PRACTICAL INFORMATION

Getting to Jerash is gleefully easy. **Minibuses** (280fils) and air-conditioned **buses** (350fils) leaving from Amman's Abdali Station make the one-hour journey routinely throughout the day. **Service** are a bit pricier, somewhat faster, and also leave from Abdali. Ask the driver to stop at the Hadrianic Arch; otherwise you'll be let off across the river, next to the Eastern baths. To reach the ruins, retrace your steps uphill and hang a left; the **Visitors Information Center** will appear on the right after a five-minute walk (tel. 645 12 72 open daily 8am-5pm). Jerash dazzles along the 1km walk from the South Gate down the Street of Columns to the North Gate. The tiny Chrysoras (Golden) River separates the ancient ruins on the western bank from the new town on the eastern bank. Groups can hire **guides** for JD5 (a JD1 tip is also expected). Booklets including maps and explanations of the sights invite leisurely exploration (JD1-6). The **post office** is behind the bus station (open daily 8am-7pm). The **tourist police** station stands across the street. Jerash's **telephone code** is 02.

Buses and **service taxis** leave town from the **Jerash bus station,** on the western edge of the new city in front of the mosque. Buses serve Abdali Station in **Amman** (1hr.; 280fils, with A/C 350fils), **'Ajlun** (250fils), and **Irbid** (320fils). *Service* generally cost 50% more than buses. Public transportation shuts down at around 7pm in summer and 6pm in winter. Hitchers to Amman, Dibbin, or 'Ajlun are known to walk south about 1km from the Visitors Center to the intersection with Hwy. 20. Turning right (west) leads to 'Ajlun and Dibbin National Park. Going straight will lead to Amman, and the main road continues through town, north to Irbid. Buses pass frequently toward Amman and are easy to flag. Stand back from the road as you signal the bus—drivers seem to consider time and speed infinitely more important than toes.

🛏🍴 ACCOMMODATIONS AND FOOD

Because Jerash is such an easy daytrip from Amman, there are no accommodations in the town. You might consider either **camping** at Dibbin National Park, about 8km away, or taking a room at the Dibbin Rest House (see p. 429). One might also "camp" in the backyard or basement of the **Jerash Rest House** (tel. 635 11 46), a stomping ground for tour bus groups. Ask the manager nicely—if he lets you stay, it might be for free. Rest House soft drinks are a rip-off at JD1, and bottled water goes for a throat-drying JD1; stock up before you arrive. At the **Al-Khayyam Restaurant** (tel. 635 10 18), just past the visitors center on the right, JD3 buys bread, salad, and grilled meat (open daily 8am-10pm). Escape the scorching sun on their open-air patio, complete with a fountain and ceiling fans. Street stands surrounding the bus station sell cheap falafel and *fuul* (100-200fils). Walking into town saves money and brings you into the lively streets of un-touristed Jerash.

👁 SIGHTS

Jerash's claim to fame is its ruins; nevertheless, over 90% of ancient Jerash still awaits excavation. *(Open daily in summer 7am-7pm; in winter 7am-5pm. Admission JD5. From April to October there is an hour-long sound and light show, with special JETT buses to get you there. Ask at the JETT office (tel. 566 41 46) in Amman.)*

TRIUMPHAL (HADRIANIC) ARCH AND ENVIRONS. This arch, 400m south of the ancient walls, was built to honor Emperor Hadrian's arrival in the winter of 129 CE. Examine the spare parts strewn about to get a feel for how big the structure once was. After your own majestic passage through the arch, you'll come upon the remaining stables and spectator seats of the **Hippodrome.** This arena hosted chariot races and other contests of skill for the amusement of up to 15,000 spectators. Continuing north, you'll see the Visitors Center and enter the site proper at the **South Gate,** followed by the **Forum** or Oval Plaza, the most photographed part of the city. The Ionic columns encircling the plaza have been reconstructed to 1st-century CE form. The central podium was once topped with a statue.

SOUTH THEATER. A footpath to the left of the Forum leads to this theater, where Greek doodles reveal that 4000 of Jerash's wealthiest citizens could reserve seats for their bloodthirsty viewing pleasure. The two-story backstage was once furnished with curtains and marble statues. At "the spot," a groove in the floor of the lower stage, your voice will carry and magnify to several times its regular volume. The circular niches below the first row of seats are ancient telephones—speak into any one and your voice will be audible at any other "receiver." The top row of theater seats offers the best view of the ruined Temple of Zeus, which lies between the theater and the South Gate.

THE CARDO. Otherwise known as **The Street of Columns,** the Cardo runs from the Forum to the **North Gate.** Its 260 pairs of columns are Corinthian replacements for earlier Ionic columns and were once capped by aqueducts carrying water throughout the ancient city. The holes in the floor drained rainwater into a sophisticated sewer system. Massive sidewalk coverings protected pedestrians from the sun, but only traces of these metropolitan parasols remain. The main avenue's first intersection is named the **South Tetrapylon** after its four huge slabs of stone, once accompanied by pillars and a large statue. Going west (left) at the cross street brings you to the remains of a 7th-century Umayyad building. Back on the Cardo, frescoes depicting lizards, cats, and turtles decorate the floor of the 4th-century **Cathedral** to the left, unsanctimoniously built from, and on top of, the remains of a 2nd-century temple to Dionysus. Next along the avenue of arches is the **Nymphaeum,** built in 191 CE. Intricate stone carvings and the incorporation of marble and gypsum indicates that this two-story fountain was assembled at the height of Jerash's fortune, and was later used in an annual reenactment of the Miracle at Cana, where Jesus changed water into wine (John 2:1-11). The gigantic bowl in front of the fountain was not the water dish of an oversized canine but a pool that caught water as it cascaded over the Nymphaeum's facade.

JERASH ANTIQUITIES MUSEUM. Well hidden to the right, this museum lies a short way down the pillared promenade. Tall display cases mounted along the walls show neatly arranged artifacts from the Neolithic to the Ottoman periods. Coins, jewelry, theater "tickets" made of stone, and a three-dimensional model of the ruins highlight the museum's small collection. Opposite the museum and across the Cardo is the city's **Agora,** a newly-restored meeting place with a central fountain. This small area served as the city's meat and fish market. *(Museum open Sa-Th 8am-5pm, F 10am-2:30pm. Free.)*

TEMPLE OF ARTEMIS. A short jaunt farther down the Cardo brings you to the impressive Artemis Temple Stairway. Two flights up, the ominous columned structure at the top of the hill to the left of the Cardo is the Temple of Artemis. The patron goddess of Jerash, daughter of Zeus, and sister of Apollo, Artemis held special significance throughout the Decapolis, once the territory of similar goddesses Ishtar and Anat. Her temple consisted of a Great Gate, a shrine-topped podium, and a courtyard surrounded by giant pillars. Retracing your steps, descend Artemis' staircase and continue on the Cardo until you reach the **West Baths,** including a 2nd-century cold bath *(frigidarium)*, warm bath *(tepidarium)*, hot bath *(caldarium)*, and changing rooms. The **East Baths,** across the *wadi* by the bus station, were built on an even larger, more majestic scale. Taking a left at the **North Tetrapylon** leads to the **North Theater.** Though the theater is undergoing restoration, crafty tourists can sneak in and catch a glimpse of the marble stage, vaguely resembling a squashed coat of arms when viewed from above.

CHURCH OF ST. COSMOS AND ST. DAMIUS. A good 200m to the left (facing the temple), behind Artemis's monument, lie a series of Byzantine churches built in the 6th century CE. Especially worth the walk is the Church of St. Cosmos and St. Damius, dedicated to a twin brother team of doctors who treated their patients for free. Though entrance to the church is barred by barbed wire, peering over the edge from above affords great views of its mosaic floor. Depicting the doctors surrounded by animals, it is one of the few pieces of art to survive Umayyad Caliph

JERASH FESTIVAL The immensely popular Jerash Festival was instituted in 1981 by the beautiful and ever-gracious Queen Noor and takes place every summer in the second half of July. The South Theater and Artemis Steps provide a dramatic setting for musical, theatrical, and dance groups who come from all over the world to perform in celebration of Jordanian and international culture, past and present. Performers have ranged from superstar Umm Kulthum to the Royal Jordanian Orchestra, and from Spanish flamenco dancers to the Royal Shakespeare Company. The festival has become very popular in recent years thanks to the presence of beloved Arab pop star Majdah Ar-Roumi (a Lebanese Celine Dion). Tickets for all three days cost JD10 (JD1 after 6pm) and are sold all over Amman (and usually sell out) in the weeks beforehand. The easiest place to get them is the JETT office in Abdali (tel. 566 41 46). Transport to and from Jerash is chaotic. Get a group together and share a private taxi. For details and lineups, check with the Jerash Festival Office, P.O. Box 910 582, Amman (tel. (06) 467 51 99 or 567 51 99), look on the web at www.jerashfestival.com.jo, or read *The Jordan Times*. Also see **Jerash Festival,** p. 411.

Yazid II's attempt to destroy all images and likenesses of God's creations in 720 CE. Walking into the adjoining Church of St. John may make you an amateur archaeologist as you reveal hidden mosaics with a gentle scuffing of the feet.

NEAR JERASH: DIBBIN NATIONAL PARK

The pines and oaks of this fertile woodland are a sight for sore eyes in the middle of the desert wasteland. Located in the hills 10km southwest of Jerash and 65km north of Amman, the **Dibbin National Park** (pronounced dib-EEn) encompasses some 20km of forest stretching south from the town of the same name. On the old road to Jerash near Dibbin village is the **Dibbin Rest House** (tel. (02) 633 97 10; fax 635 11 46), offering private "bungalows." Though run-down, they do come with refrigerators, TVs, and porches (singles JD15; doubles JD20; triples JD30; indoor "camping" JD2 per person). The access road leaves the Amman-Jerash Highway about 2km south of Jerash; look for the signs. You'll have to take a car or hire a taxi (round-trip JD5), as neither buses nor *service* access the park. Another option is the bus from Jerash to the nearby village of Dibbin; the hike from the village to the park is about 2km uphill. The park offers **campgrounds** free of charge and equally free of facilities.

'AJLUN عجلون

Overlooking the highest peak of the town of 'Ajlun is the ancient **Qal'at ar-Rabadh** ('Ajlun Castle), loosely translated from Arabic as "the castle that straddles a hill." Izz ad-Din Usama, a nephew of Salah ad-Din, built this huge castle in 1184 to contain the progress of the Crusaders. The original building was erected to outdo the Castle of Belvoir on Lake Tiberias, but with its four corner towers and seven floors, Qal'at ar-Rabadh more closely resembles Karak Castle, south of Amman (see **Karak,** p. 439). Filled with secret passages, dark corridors, and winding, crumbly staircases, the castle makes every explorer feel like Indiana Jones.

🛈 **ORIENTATION AND PRACTICAL INFORMATION.** 'Ajlun lies a hilly 24km west of Jerash, an easy bus ride from Amman or Irbid. The **bus** from Abdali Station in Amman (1½hr., 450fils) will drop you off a few streets down from the main circle. Follow the sound of honking cars and the smell of roasting shawarma uphill toward the towering minaret of the mosque and the center of town. From the circle, the castle is 4km up a gently sloping road. You can catch a **taxi** for 500fils-JD1 (be sure to negotiate a price before getting in) or try to find one of the infrequent **minibuses** (50fils). Especially on Fridays, public transportation can be slow—start walking uphill and flag the bus on the way. Generous passers-by may also give you a lift if you're looking tired. 'Ajlun's **Directorate of Tourism** (tel. 642 01 15), located about 200m downhill from the castle, gives out free maps and brochures and can arrange for a guided tour of the castle. Exchange money at the **Arab Bank,** next

JORDAN

door to the post office, or the **Housing Bank,** on the center circle (both open Sa-Th 8:30am-1:30 pm and 4-6pm). The **post office** is located on Amman St., to your right as you enter the town, a few hundred yards from the circle (open Sa-Th 8am-5pm).

▐▐▐ ACCOMMODATIONS AND FOOD. There are two hotels in 'Ajlun, both within short walking distance of the castle along the road to town. The **'Ajlun Hotel** (tel./fax 642 01 15), closer to the castle, offers clean, bright rooms with built-in closets, therapeutically hard mattresses, and awesome views (singles JD18; doubles JD22; breakfast included). As the place is often uninhabited, be sure to bargain.) At the **Ar-Rabadh Castle Hotel** (tel. 642 02 02), new rooms come with TV, phone, balcony with sunset view, and immaculate bathrooms. Unless you plan on staying longer than a week, the management is reluctant to stray from official rates (singles JD24; doubles JD32; breakfast included, but add a 10% service charge). The restaurants of both hotels offer a lunch with a view for a whopping JD4-5. The 'Ajlun Restaurant looks like a fully-enclosed ski chalet with an Islamic twist, while the Ar-Rabadh sports a multi-tiered outdoor cafe with a fountain and umbrellas. The view from both is affordable if you stick to the 300-400fils *mezze* plates. Those who prefer to fill their bellies rather than their eyes should stop in at the **Green Mountain Restaurant** (tel. 642 09 05), just off 'Ajlun's center circle. A half-chicken goes for JD1.250, kebab sandwich 300fils, and hummus or *fuul* 400fils; 700fils buys a complete meal including rice, meat, and a vegetable (open daily 6:30am-9:30pm; in winter 6:30am-8pm). The **Abu al-Izz Restaurant** (tel. 420 625) is in front of the Green Mountain. This sprawling outdoor cafe with leafy trellises offers the usual Middle Eastern food for higher prices than the Green Mountain, but with more ambience (half-chicken JD1.5, hummus 500fils). As always, street vendors provide economical and delicious alternatives.

◙ SIGHTS. '**Ajlun Castle** once controlled a long stretch of Jordan's northern valley and protected lines between Jordan and Syria. Crusaders spent decades trying to capture the castle and nearby village. After the Crusader threat dissipated, Salah ad-Din used the castle as a base to control nearby iron mines and transmit messages by beacon and pigeon; from Baghdad to Cairo, the relay could be made in 12 hours. During the Ottoman period, 50 soldiers were stationed in the castle at all times. After that, the castle was mostly uninhabited until 1812, when the Swiss explorer J.L. Burkhardt (better known for discovering Petra the same year) found 40 members of the Barakat family living there. Two major earthquakes in 1837 and 1927 did the damage that the Crusades never could. While the castle is in quite good condition today, parts of it are still under restoration by the Department of Antiquities. Guides are cheap (JD3), but it's more fun just to poke around with a flashlight. *(Open daily in summer 8am-6pm; in winter 8am-5pm. Admission JD1.)*

IRBID اربد

The streets that were once crowded with the residents of ancient Dion (a city in the Decapolis League) are now a fluorescent maze of merchants and Kung Fu theaters catering to the students of Yarmouk University, one of the biggest institutions of higher learning in Jordan. The bohemian charm that Yarmouk's strolling students lend to Irbid makes the city an enjoyable base from which to plan trips to Umm Qeis or Damascus. The university's free **Museum of Jordanian Heritage,** near the campus's North Gate, provides the nation's biggest and best narrative of Jordan's history from prehistoric times to the present.

▐ TRANSPORTATION

Many travelers hitch to Irbid via Jerash, but the quickest and safest way to the city from Amman is with the A/C **Hijazi Bus Co.** (1¼hr., 820fils). Taxis from the private bus station to downtown cost 500fils. **Minibuses** from Amman, Jerash, and 'Ajlun are cheaper but slower; they drop you off at New South Station, from which you can take a *service* downtown (70fils). **Taxis** to Yarmouk cost 500fils (JD1 after midnight). **Service** to Yarmouk (75fils) leave from Abu Bakr as-Siddiqa St. Take a right on Baghdad St., a left at the obelisk monument, and walk three blocks until you see the line of white *service*. For a *service* to North Station, take the first left after the Omayed Hotel toward the post office. Continue straight, across the street, until the road ends at a diagonal intersection. Turn right, walk for about five minutes, then go right again when you see the big purple sign on your left. *Service* line up here and will drop you off one street up from the station.

Buses to **Al-Himma** and **Umm Qeis** leave often from North Station. **Taxis** between the two bus stations cost 700fils. To leave Irbid, go to **New South Station** (ask for *Bas ila 'Amman*). From here a minibus runs regularly to 'Ajlun (250fils) and to Amman's Abdali Station (500fils). The last buses depart for Amman at about 8pm (in winter as early as 5pm). *Service* also leave New South Station for **Damascus, Syria** (3-4hr. depending on border crossings, JD5). Bring your visa and JD4 exit fee for the border crossing; it should be fairly painless as long as you have no evidence of a trip to Israel in your passport and you carefully follow your *service* taxi driver's instructions (for details, see **Border Crossings,** p. 404). You will cross first through Jordanian customs and, about a mile later, through Syrian customs. Irbid is also a convenient departure place for **Israel**. To get there, take *service* from Al-Aghwar Station to the Ash-Sheikh Hussein Bridge (bring passport and JD4 exit fee). *Service* run regularly from downtown to Yarmouk and to North Station.

☑ ORIENTATION AND PRACTICAL INFORMATION

Facing downhill from the **main circle** (next to the Al-Amin Hotel), the town **mosque** and **market** are down the street to the right. The **tourist office** (tel. 724 17 44) is nearby. The Bank of Jordan and Abu Bakr Hotel are up the street to the left. To get to the currency exchange centers, walk downhill 50m and take the first left after the Al-Amin Hotel onto Baghdad St. At your back lies another circle with an obelisk monument. Continue down Baghdad St. past the Omayed Hotel up to **ANZ Grindlay's Bank,** which exchanges cash and traveler's checks (open Sa-Th 8:30am-12:30pm). The **post office** (tel. 729 89 48) will be across the street (open Sa-Th 7:30am-6pm, F and holidays 7:30am-1:30pm). **Yarmouk University** is across town to the south, a *service* taxi ride away. The taxi should let you off just a bit before the North Gate. Backtrack to the circle and turn left and you'll be on the main drag of the Yarmouk region, packed with restaurants and **Internet providers** (500fils per hr. is a good rate). All six digit **telephone numbers** in Irbid are now seven digits (dial a 7 at the beginning of the original six digit number). Irbid's **telephone code** is 02.

▟ ACCOMMODATIONS

Al-Amin Al-Kabir Hotel (tel. 724 23 84), on Maidan Malek 'Abdullah St., one block from the city center and Ministry of Antiquities building, has bright and breezy rooms, spotless communal showers, and courteous management, but no electric fans. Interior rooms are lit by a glass-covered "atrium;" rooms overlooking the street have balconies but can be noisy. (Singles JD5; doubles JD8; hot shower 500fils; bargain in off-season.) The clean, homey **Hotel Al-Wehdeh Al-Arabiah** (tel. 724 20 82) sits at the top of Aj-Jaish St.; prepare to be plied with tea and coffee in the "Bedouin tent" on the right as you enter. Some of the rooms have balconies, and the friendly Egyptian management is ready to bargain (dorm beds JD2; singles JD4; doubles JD6; free showers). Around the corner from the Al-Amin on Wasfi et-Tal St., **Abu Bakr Hotel** (tel. 724 26 95) is in the same building as the Bank of Jordan. Windows make up entire walls and upstairs rooms afford great views of Irbid (for what it's worth). The stuffiness is combatted by ceiling fans (singles JD3; doubles JD5; triples JD6; free showers). At **Omayed Hotel** (tel./fax 724 59 55), above Irbid Supermarket on Baghdad St., all rooms have phones, fans, private baths (some with bidet), and curious three-window television nooks. The upstairs restaurant has tremendous views and serves tasty JD2 student specials. Receptionist Ahmad Mansour can tell you how to get anywhere you want to go (singles JD14; doubles JD18; add 10% tax).

⌕ FOOD

The streets around Yarmouk University are lined with wall-to-wall restaurants that are in turn crammed from wall to wall with everyone from students to local for-tune-tellers in search of a good meal and a chance to argue about politics. Pop-eye's Fried Chicken, Subway, and Pizza Hut are just a short jaunt away, but even if you've been unimpressed with falafel and shawarma so far, give the food stands on the main street a second chance. Fresh and hot, with no spice spared, the cheapest food in Irbid is some of Jordan's best (falafel 150fils, shawarma 250-300fils). The local market is held around the mosque.

The "Nest of Happiness" known as **Ish Al-Hama Restaurant** (tel. 769 23 11), across from the mosque, is the local favorite for sit-down dining, featuring plentiful por-tions at cheap prices. If you're really hungry, don't miss the generous JD1.8 mixed plate. (Hummus 350fils, cheese omelettes 500fils. Open 7am-1am.) **Hadramout Res-taurant** (tel. 724 42 48), directly off of the main university circle, offers reasonable local fare and drinks on a sprawling patio (entrees JD1-2.5; open daily in summer 7:30am-1am; in winter 7:30am-11pm). **Andalusia Restaurant** (tel. 724 15 86), on the 6th floor of the building above Grindlay's Bank, across from the post office, offers a four-star dining experience that's far nicer on the palate and far harder on the wallet than most Irbid fare. (Grilled lamb cutlets and filet of fish JD2.25, appetizing buffet JD5, plus 20% tax. Open daily 8am-midnight.) Grab a drink or a pipe at **Nine Classic Cafe** (tel. 726 72 27), on the third floor of the building across from the mosque, and see if you have the (cue) balls to beat Irbid's best billiard players (open 9am-2am).

UMM QEIS أم قيس

Umm Qeis was the Biblical **Gadara**, where Jesus turned a sinner's demons into a herd of pigs that stampeded down the hill to drown in the Sea of Galilee. This thriving town was one of the ten cities of the Decapolis League, founded by Pompey after his conquest of Syria and Palestine in 64 BCE. Its name comes from a Semitic word meaning "stronghold," reflecting the city's role as a fortified border town guarding the crucial land routes between southern Syria and northern Pales-tine. Once a resort for Romans vacationing at Al-Himma's therapeutic hot springs, Umm Qeis was renowned for its arts and its legendary orgiastic extravagances. However, earthquakes and plagues in the 7th and 8th centuries CE left Umm Qeis nothing more than a hamlet.

⚑ PRACTICAL INFORMATION. There is a **post/telephone office** (tel. 750 00 04) along the main road through modern Umm Qeis (open in summer 7:30am-7:30pm; in winter 7:30am-3pm). Knock if the door is locked. Get stamps, post cards, and loads of historical information from Abu Aloush at the reasonably priced **Sara Umm Qeis Gift Shop** (tel. (07) 956 202).

▟▛ ACCOMMODATIONS AND FOOD. The **Umm Qeis Hotel** (tel. 750 00 80) is about 100m uphill from the ruins, on the left. New rooms are freshly painted and sparsely furnished. The roof offers an enjoyable view (JD5 per person, with bath JD7; breakfast JD2.5, dinner JD3). The beautiful **Umm Qeis Rest House** (tel. 750 05 55), just past the museum to the right, is an offshoot of Amman's glitzy Romero restaurant and serves up refreshments at not-so-refreshing prices. For JD4-5, you can sit overlooking the Golan Heights and the Sea of Galilee and eat your fill of soup, salad, or pasta; ice cream drips for 750fils (open 9am-10pm). Middle Eastern food is available at a few cheap places along the main road.

▨ SIGHTS. Visitors to Umm Qeis will wander among a mix of Greco-Roman, Byzantine, and Ottoman architecture that reflects the various cultures who con-quered or just passed through this strategically located town. Today, the two-story white **Umm Qeis Museum** (the building flying the Jordanian flag) is the main point of interest in Umm Qeis. Check out **Tyche,** the patron goddess of Gadara; she lacks a few important appendages, but still holds onto her fruit-filled cornucopia, a symbol of fertility. The foundation of the **North Theater,** which once accommodated 5000, is hardly visible just outside the museum. The Ottomans took the actual stones of the structure to build the village on the hill; German archaeologists are now attempting to reconstruct parts of it. (Open daily in summer 9am-5pm; in winter 9am-4pm. Free.)

Journey back in time through the **Roman ruins** nearby. The Romans were nothing if not a practical people: they named the main road through their town the **Decumanus Maximus,** which not-so-roughly translates to "Main Road." To the left of this road overlooking the Golan Heights and the Sea of Galilee is the **Basilica Terrace,** whose black basalt Corinthian columns surround the octagonally arranged white limestone columns of what was once a Byzantine church. Farther along the Main Road, built into the perimeter of the Basilica Terrace, are 14 barrel-vaulted rooms that used to be street-front **shops.** The shops have been reconstructed to look as they did in Roman times. Just left past the shops are the weed-embraced ruins of the **East Baths** and **Nymphaeum.** At the end of the Decumanus sits a circular building of basalt rocks; adjacent to that is an **underground mausoleum,** the only completely intact structure from **Ancient Gadara.** The holes in the ceiling were used to drop food to the spirits of the interred, and now provide enough light to peek through the locked gate into the underground caverns. The main burial room, with six chambers on each of three walls, was expanded and re-used in the Byzantine era. The **Eastern Necropolis** is a cemetery just outside the city walls where the Greco-Roman and later the Arab residents of Umm Qeis were interred. On your left will be the entrance to the Roman **aqueduct,** which brought water from Ezra in Syria. Just before the aqueduct is the **Temple of Zeus,** which is being restored. The mass of Ottoman Buildings on the top of the hill covers what used to be an **acropolis,** the most important quarter of ancient Gadara.

EAST OF AMMAN

AZRAQ AND THE DESERT CASTLES الازرق و القصور الصحراوية

The springs at Azraq were once the only permanent bodies of water in more than 2500km^2 of sun-scorched, sand-and-scorpion desert. However, so much water is now pumped into Amman that the area has dried up significantly. As recently as three years ago, the palm trees were green, the animals abundant, and the sky was colored with hundreds of species of exotic birds. Now no evidence of the vast springs remains: what used to be green is a parched brown, and the only movement is that of trucks passing through. Water isn't the only thing to have disappeared from Azraq. The most remarkable records of human habitation are the scattered Umayyad castles (*qusur*; singular *qasr*), a group of structures that originally formed a chain from the north of Damascus to Khirbet al-Mafjar, near Jericho. Built in the 7th and 8th centuries CE by the Umayyads, the castles were mysteriously abandoned a century later. The imposing stonework of **Qasr Kharaneh** and strategic location of **Qasr Azraq** support speculation that the castles sheltered caravans along the trade route between Syria, Arabia, and the Far East. The baths near **Qasr al-Hallabat** and the magnificent frescoes at **Qasr Amra** provided respite from the vast, unforgiving desert. Still relatively tourist-free, these quietly majestic ruins will awe you with the strength of their standing arches and the warmth of their Bedouin gatekeepers.

◪ ORIENTATION AND PRACTICAL INFORMATION. A trip to the Azraq Oasis and the Desert Castles is fraught with uncertainty and difficult to arrange, but it's worth every annoyance. There are only three options for transportation to the castles. First, you can hire a **taxi** from Amman at the official rate of JD24 (try bargaining it down to JD20). This will provide half a day's wheels and someone who knows the route (full day over JD30). Second, if you're over 18 and have a few people with you, renting a **car** for the day is by far the most enjoyable way to do the desert loop. You can rent a car in Amman for JD25-35 or more for a day, with unlimited mileage and the option to return it in Aqaba or at the airport. Reliable Rent-a-Car (tel./fax 592 96 76) offers the best deals (see **Car Rentals,** p. 416). The third and easiest way to get to the desert castles, in terms of both your pocketbook and your peace of mind, is to arrange a daytrip through the **Cliff Hostel** (see p. 419) for JD10. This tour offers less mobility, but it typically skips the least spectacular castle, Qasr al-Hallabat. Also, it will likely bring you in contact with the charismatic Fouad, a five-year veteran of the castle route whose close relationships with the Bedouin make for a memorable journey. Arrange a few days in advance; at least four people must sign up before the trip will leave.

As always, **hitchhiking** is discouraged and, in a worst-case scenario, potentially suicidal. Hitchhikers should beware of the intense sun and the vast, desolate spaces involved in the desert loop. Travelers report that the ever-friendly Jordanians are quick to pick hitchers up, but vehicles can be few and far between in these parts. Those who decide to try their luck by thimb (or downward turned palm, as tradition has it here), should bring a head covering and much more water than they think they will need, and tell hostel where they have gone and when they expect to return. *Let's Go* does not recommend hitchhiking as a viable means of transport, though many travelers have and will continue to travel this way.

The following description details a three-part, **clockwise road trip** that allows a traveler to take in all the castles and Azraq: (1) north from Amman to Zarqa (30km); (2) east from Zarqa to Azraq (87km), passing the unimpressive Qasr al-Hallabat (30km from Zarqa); and (3) returning west along the southern highway from Azraq back to Amman, passing Qasr 'Amra (25km from Azraq), Qasr Kharaneh (40km from Azraq), and Qasr Mushatta (about 90km from Azraq and 40km from Amman). Going the other way (Amman-Azraq-Zarqa) is deadly for hitchhikers, since cars come as frequently as snowstorms in the desert. *Service* from Abdali Station in Amman can take you to Zarqa quickly and cheaply (300fils). Accepting rides from the army is **illegal,** and will take you only as far as some lonely desert depot anyway. The **telephone code** for the area is 06, the same as in Amman.

QASR AL-HALLABAT قصر الحلابات

Qasr al-Hallabat's ruined arches appear in the desert approximately 30km east of Zarqa. Angle off at the right, turn onto the paved road, and turn left up the track to the gate. The gatekeeper's tent is to the right of the main gate, far removed from the crumbling castle; you're free to roam around whatever is left (keep in mind that any gatekeeper who gives you information will expect a few hundred fils in return). Originally constructed by the bath-obsessed emperor Caracalla (198-217 CE) as a Roman fort, Qasr al-Hallabat was reused by the Byzantines as a monastery during the reign of Anastasius (491-518). The Umayyads rebuilt it as a residential palace in the 8th century and added a mosque just meters away from the main defense structure. Look for the Byzantine carvings on the remaining walls and on fallen slabs of stone. More rewarding sights are still to come; if your time is limited, you may want to skip Qasr al-Hallabat.

Back on the main highway, the sand and limestone desert to the south contrasts sharply with the gray volcanic desert to the north. Just off the road to the south is **Hammam As-Sarh,** the ruined bathhouse modeled after Amra (below). A 1000-year-old well, covered by a rusty metal grating, lurks to the left of the bathhouse. Though some daredevils have been known to climb onto the grating and peer into the abyss below, *Let's Go* does not recommend taking the risk (or the water).

AZRAQ الازرق

On the long and grinding road east of Zarqa, you'll hear nothing but the entreaties of your overheating engine until suddenly, after ages of drab desert, the formerly lush gardens of the **Azraq Oasis** appear. Once Jordan's only permanent body of fresh water, the oasis is quickly drying up today, but **Azraq Junction** is still a great place to relax and reassemble your bearings (both mental and mechanical). The junction is located where the highway to the northeast goes to Iraq and the southeastern road leads to the southern castles and Saudi Arabia.

About 13km north of Azraq Junction on the highway to Iraq stands **Qasr Azraq,** still in excellent condition thanks to extensive restoration. The black basalt fort, built by the Romans in 300 CE and later rebuilt by the Ayyubids in 1237, rose to three levels. Only parts of the second level survived a 1926 earthquake, including a ceiling that exposes a web of huge basalt beams. The Druze gatekeeper will haul open the remarkable three-ton stone portal of the castle and, if he's feeling friendly, will show you his photocopied **Lawrence of Arabia** photograph collection (Many of the photographs look suspiciously like the gatekeeper's grandfather). The most interesting attractions lie within a few meters of the entrance. Looking up from the main door, you'll see the *machicoulis* (holes) through which boiling oil and molten lead were conveniently poured on invaders. Carved into the pavement behind the main gate is a Roman board game: if time permits, ask the gatekeeper to show you how to play this fun game. In the center of the courtyard lies a small cube of a mosque, originally built as a Roman church. Just above the entrance is the room used by Lawrence of Arabia himself, who used the fort as his headquarters during the height of the Arab revolt against Ottoman rule in 1917.

Throughout the trip, keep an eye out for the desert wildlife making a comeback ever since Jordan started protecting its fragile habitat. In the **Shaumari Wildlife Preserve,** near Qasr Amra, the government is reintroducing armadillos, Himalayan dwarf hamsters, ostriches, Syrian wild asses, and Arabian oryxes (admission 500fils, students 300fils). Cheetah and desert wolves roam in regions to the northeast and southwest of Azraq.

There are many small markets and stands in town that provide cheap nourishment. You'll also find a **post office** (open Sa-Th 8am-3pm, F 7:30am-1pm) and a **Housing Bank** (open for exchange Sa-W 9am-1pm and 4-5pm, Th 9am-1pm). For a true oasis experience, stay at the **Sayad Hotel** (tel. 464 49 88), visible from the Azraq castle. Graced with an olive grove, a rose garden, and a beautiful mosaic pool (open only in summer), Sayad is also graced with high prices: singles JD24; doubles JD32; add 10% service charge. Located on the north side of Azraq, down a tree-lined road, is the government-run **Azraq Resthouse** (tel. 383 40 06; fax 383 52 15). Rooms include bath, A/C, color TV, minibar, and a view of the pool, which non-guests can use for JD2. Singles JD15; doubles JD20; triples JD25. The overpriced restaurant in the Resthouse serves usual fare (complete meal JD5).

QASR AMRA قصر عمرة

For a sneak preview of Qasr Amra, simply look at any *½-dinar* bill. Constructed under the auspices of Umayyad Caliph al-Walid ibn 'Abd al-Malik, the hunting lodge and bath complex of Qasr Amra impress visitors with the elegant simplicity of their designs. The interior is also the best preserved of the desert palaces: its vaulted stucco ceilings are splashed with lively frescoes, and mosaics cover two of the floors. As you walk in, look to the right at the **mural** depicting the enemies of Islam—among them the emperors of Byzantium, Persia, and China as well as Roderique, then King of Spain. The similarity in the faces to traditional depictions of Jesus suggests a Roman rather than a Muslim artist. An early portrayal of the zodiac covers the domed ceiling of the *caladarium* (hot room). Since they ignore the Muslim tradition forbidding the pictorial representation of human beings, the frescoes throughout the castle are all the more riveting. Especially surprising are the many portrayals of nude women, which somehow escaped the decree of Umayyad Caliph Yazid II (720-724 CE), a weekend visitor of the castle who ordered all human images and likenesses destroyed. (*Reach Qasr Amra on the road heading southwest of Azraq Junction, 28km from Qasr Azraq. The very hospitable gatekeeper expects a small* bakhsheesh; 250-500fils per person should do.)

QASR KHARANEH قصر الخرانة

Qasr Kharaneh is named for the small black stones that blanket the area. Some experts believe Kharaneh was a defensive fort; they point to the four corner towers and the square plan of a Roman fortress, as well as to the enigmatic arrow slits in the walls. Others believe these slits were part of an elaborate ventilation system and argue that Kharaneh served as a retreat for Umayyad leaders to discuss matters of state. Most historians, however, believe it was a *khan*, or inn—the first of the Islamic world. This is further evinced by the architectural style of the castle, which would later come to typify an Umayyad inn. A painted Arabic dedication in a 2nd-story room dates the building's construction to 710-711 CE. Greek inscriptions on the doorjambs imply that the Umayyads built upon an earlier structure. For a good view of the courtyard and the barren landscape stretching to Saudi Arabia and Iraq, climb the staircase on your left as you enter. You'll also see the neighboring military base and the maneuverings of Jordanian troops. When you've finished exploring, the gatekeeper will let you ride his camel for some *bakhsheesh* (500fils should do). As he leads you around the castle, listen carefully: he insists that the ghosts of horses, camels, and people roam the ruins.

QASR MUSHATTA قصر مشتة

This final castle is a hassle to get to and a downer after sights past. Those determined to find it can take any turn-off to Queen Alia International Airport. Hitchhikers often hire *service* from the village of **Muwaqaar** in the north to reach the castle. The castle is on the left as you approach the airport from the north, but the public access road turns off to the right and loops about 4km around the airport. If you're walking from the airport, don't take this marked turn-off; instead, continue to the left of the airport, past the Alia cargo terminal, until Mushatta appears on the left (a 30min. walk). Soldiers at checkpoints will ask to see your **passport,** may take it temporarily, and possibly turn you away.

The entrance to the 8th-century castle once beckoned travelers with wonderfully carved floral designs, but most of the carved stones were delivered to Kaiser Wilhelm II as a gift from Ottoman Sultan Abdulhamid II; only fragments remain. An entire piece of the wall now resides in the Berlin Museum. Although the size of the ruins attest to the ambition of the construction, the castle, for unknown reasons, was never completed; indeed, Mushatta was constructed with smaller, weaker bricks than other Catch a **taxi** or **bus** back to Amman via the airport.

SOUTH OF AMMAN

Three roads link Amman and Aqaba: the **Wadi Araba Highway** (aka Jordan Valley) the **Desert Highway,** and the **Kings' Highway.** Of these routes, the Kings' Highway (Wadi Mujib Rd.) is the best way to travel the length of Jordan. This ancient route journeys through spectacular canyons, passing Biblical sites, Crusader castles, and Byzantine churches and mosaics along the way. This road was supposedly traveled by the Israelites during their exodus from Egypt, and later became a popular spice route (for more on the ancient spice trade, see **Yemen: Ancient History,** p. 408). Amman to Petra is a whopping 282km along the Kings' Highway (262km along the Desert Highway), but the distances between sights along the way are more manageable: Amman to Madaba 33km, Madaba to Karak 98km, and Karak to Petra 150km. The only indoor accommodations are in Karak and Madaba (most camp in the *wadis* north of Karak or between Karak and Petra). The easiest route is to see Madaba before heading to Karak for the night. Leaving early in the morning from Karak, the trip to Petra can be done comfortably in a day, stopping in Shobak and at the Dana Nature Reserve along the way.

Service and **minibuses** run most of the way from Amman to Petra, but generally in the mornings only. **Hitchhiking** south of Amman is possible (hitchers stick their right arm out, palm down), but is risky and difficult along the deserted Kings' Highway. It is illegal to hitchhike on the Wadi Araba, which runs along the Israeli border. To get to the Desert Highway from downtown Amman, hitchhikers head south on Jerusalem St. (in Jabal Nadhif across Wadi 'Abdoun), which becomes Rt. 15 (the Desert Highway). To get to the Kings' Highway, hitchers take a *service* from Amman's Wahdat Station to Madaba, then try their luck on the road to Karak, which passes out of Madaba by the Apostles' Church. Small groups of hitchers stand by the mini-obelisk marking the intersection of the Kings' Highway and the Desert Highway, 18km south of Amman. People reach the intersection by taking a Madaba-bound *service* from Wahdat Station or by hitching south from 7th Circle.

DEAD SEA البحر الميت

More than 400m below sea level, the Dead Sea is the lowest point on earth. Now a serenely quiet shore, the Dead Sea region is thought by many to be the site of five biblical cities: Sodom, Gomorrah, Admah, Zeboin, and Zowr. Indeed, a dried pillar of salt nearby is believed to be the remains of Lot's wife, who, upon fleeing the damned city of Sodom, disobeyed God's command to not look back. Four times as salty as regular sea water, the peculiar buoyancy of this briny liquid forces even the densest swimmer into a back float, and the wealth of salts and minerals gives it renowned curative powers (recognized for over 2000 years). The awful tasting salt water makes a tiny paper cut feel like an amputation; don't get any in your eyes, or you'll have to beg to use one of the eye-flushing plastic water bottles that those in the know tote along to the beach. The Dead Sea is easier to reach by public transport and cheaper if visited from Israel (see **Israel: Dead Sea,** p. 350); its northeastern shore, about an hour from Amman or Deir Alla, hosts the only stretch of sand open to visitors on the Jordanian side. During the middle of the day, the sun reflects off the sea's still surface, creating the illusion that the entire body of water is about to spill into the Jordan Valley.

Buses connect to the Dead Sea from Amman's Muhajeren Station, located near the police station. Take a taxi there and indicate that your destination is the Dead Sea, as it is possible the driver will not understand the station name. Don a Panama hat, bring plenty of water, and don't forget your passport—several military roadblocks along the way may demand identification. Buses generally leave every 30 minutes but schedules can be precarious, so set aside plenty of time. Some buses go to **Shouna** (1hr., 400fils), where you can catch a second bus to the **Rest House** (30min., 200fils). Arrange group daytrips with the JETT and Alpha bus companies (JD10-20) or with many of Amman's hotels (Cliff Hotel charges JD10 per person). **Taxis** to the Dead Sea from Amman can be found for as little as JD8, but most will demand JD25; try bargaining.

The **Dead Sea Rest House** (tel. (05) 546 110) offers showers to relieve you of Lot's wife's encrusted fate. Unless you swim around the barrier to the north, which closes off the nicest section of beach, you'll have to pay JD2.5 to enter the resort enclave. The complex contains showers, the Rest House (bungalow with A/C, bathroom, TV, and telephone JD35), and an overpriced restaurant (entrees JD3-7, soft drinks 700fils, water 800fils). The rocky walk into the water can be tough—consider foot protection. Shelters are available to ward off the merciless sun. The last bus leaves at 6pm, but if you get stranded, the sunset over the West Bank will almost make it worthwhile (Rest House open daily 8am-11pm; swimming allowed until sundown). About 12km south of the Rest House, the natural spring of **Zara** nestles between the colorful Jordan Valley cliffs. Less than 30km south on the highway to Aqaba (Rte. 35) is **Zarqa Ma'in,** a cascading hot spring.

MADABA مادبا

Madaba is perched atop a plateau of orange groves overlooking the Jordan Valley. The scanty Roman columns hardly evoke visions of the flourishing trade center that Madaba once was, but archaeologists at work in the new downtown "Archaeological Park" are rapidly uncovering past glories; a Roman road, a burnt palace, and several churches have been discovered only meters away from the Church of St. George (home of the famous mosaic **Map of the Holy Land**). The elaborate mosaic masterpieces scattered throughout this "City of Mosaics" attest to Madaba's importance as a Byzantine ecclesiastical center; the town received its own bishop as early as the 5th century CE. Persians attacked Madaba in 614 CE, slaughtering the residents and damaging many Roman and Byzantine artifacts, and an 8th-century earthquake finished off the job. Madaba remained a ghost town for the next 1100 years, until Christian clans from Karak reinhabited the city in the late 1800s. Now a peaceful rural town that relies heavily upon tourism, Madaba is equipped with a plethora of souvenir shops and convenience stores, but has little to offer tourists besides a peaceful home base from which to daytrip to **Mt. Nebo** (p. 439) and **Jerash** (p. 426). Women report that this town is particularly high on the nuisance list—expect to be talked to and stared at from the moment you arrive. Look out for tourist traps but don't miss the carpet shops, if only to watch the mesmerizing process of loom weaving.

▨ PRACTICAL INFORMATION

Minibuses shuttle between Madaba and Amman's **Wahdat** (180fils), **Raghadan** (220fils), and **Abdali** Stations (260fils) until 7pm in summer, 5pm in winter (1hr.); *service* don't service this route. **Hitchhiking** probably doesn't get any easier than on this road (but *Let's Go* does not recommend hitchhiking). To reach the city center from Madaba's bus station, take a *service* (70fils) or hike uphill toward the Church of St. George (20min.). The **tourist office** (tel. 545 527) is around the corner from St. George (open Sa-Th 8am-2pm). **Bank of Jordan** (open Su-Th 8am-2pm and 4-6pm) and **Housing Bank** (open Su-Th 8:30am-5pm) are on King Abdullah St., around the corner from the tourist office. For the **police**, dial 192; in a general **emergency**, dial 191. In case of **medical emergency**, dial 193. The nearest public hospital is **Nadim Hospital** (tel. 541 700), 1km from Madaba. The new, private **Mahabba Hospital** stands near the entrance to the town. The central **post office** is next to the banks on King Abdullah St., around the corner from the tourist office (open Sa-Th 7:30am-7pm, F 7:30am-1:30pm). Madaba's **telephone code** is 05.

▨ ◘ ACCOMMODATIONS AND FOOD

Madaba's increasing popularity has led to the construction of several new hotels that have undermined the monopoly held by ◪**Lulu's Pension** (tel. 543 678), a gorgeous bed-and-breakfast. Lulu's features clean bathrooms and a quaint kitchen with tablecloths, doilies, and fake flowers. The remodeled rooms on the second floor are among the nicest in Jordan. The pre-bargaining price for a royal room with a king-sized bed is JD15 (students JD12), or sleep on the roof for JD6. Ring the bell if the door is locked. The **Madaba Hotel,** around the corner from the church, offers more affordable, spotless rooms, extremely hospitable management, and a mosaic-friendly location (JD9 per person; breakfast included). Slightly more expensive, but worth the extra money, is the **Black Iris Hotel** (tel. 541 959), located just off the main street near Al-Mouhafada Circle. With spacious rooms and a congenial family atmosphere, it's tough to turn down this gem when you see the size of their breakfast, served in the upstairs family-style dining room. Singles JD18; doubles JD25. Try to bargain for the five-person room downstairs (JD5 per person) or rooftop mattresses (JD1). **Camping** is also available (JD1).

Join Germans in short-shorts at the **Rest House** (tel. 544 069), next to the tourist office. The Rest House caters mainly to groups, but anyone who can shell out JD6 is welcome to fill up at the buffet lunch. A snack of hummus and Coke costs JD1.5 (open daily 8am-8pm; buffet lunch noon-4pm.) The **Ayola Coffee Shop,** on Yarmouk St., serves deli-style sandwiches (JD1) in a pleasant Bedouin restaurant full of Madaba's young hipsters (open daily 9am-11pm). For the best falafel in town (150fils), try **Shaheen's Restaurant,** off King Abdullah St. (open daily 10am-late).

◉ SIGHTS

MAP OF THE HOLY LAND. Built in 1896 atop the foundation of a Byzantine church, the prominent Greek Orthodox **Church of St. George** stands in the center of town, right off the square. Parts of the 6th-century CE **Map of the Holy Land** (originally composed of 2.3 million tiles) are housed within the church's yellow brick walls. The Map is the oldest preserved and most detailed ancient map of this region. At one time the map depicted the entire Middle East (as shown by the few remaining tiles of Turkey, Lebanon, and Egypt), but now only the Palestinian cities of Byzantium, Nablus, Hebron, and Jericho remain. The most well-known section of the map is the inset map of Jerusalem at its center, with representations of the buildings that existed in the 6th century (including the Church of the Holy Sepulchre). The church is also known by some devout local Christians and Muslims for supposedly hosting the Virgin Mary in 1978. A small shrine in the crypt contains an icon of Mary with a third arm and blue "healing hand" supernaturally imprinted on the icon during the Madonna's visit. *(Open M-Th and Sa 7am-6pm, F and Su 10:30am-6pm. Admission JD1.)*

MADABA MUSEUM. Madaba's museum, tucked in an alley down the hill from the Apostles' Church off Prince Abdullah St., is divided into three sections: the Old House of Madaba, the Folklore Museum, and the Archaeological Museum. The complexes feature an extensive collection of mosaics, including a depiction of the Garden of Eden, traditional Jordanian dresses, and pottery dating as far back as 4500 BCE. *(Open W-M 9am-5pm. Admission JD3, includes Archaeological Park and Apostles' Church.)*

ARCHAEOLOGICAL EXCAVATIONS. The **Archaeological Park,** around the corner from the Church of St. George, is a 1000-square-meter playground of ancient finds, featuring the **Church of the Virgin Mary** and **Hippolytus Hall.** In addition to a recently uncovered **Roman road,** the park is home to mosaics from the days of Herod the Great (1st century BCE) to the Umayyad period (8th century CE). Madaba's largest intact mosaic, from 758 CE, lies within the remains of the **Apostles' Church,** on the southern edge of town. *(Open in summer W-M 8am-7pm; in winter 8am-5pm. Admission JD3.)*

NEAR MADABA: MOUNT NEBO

*No buses go to Mt. Nebo. Take a **taxi** (round-trip JD4, 30min. wait at the site included). You can also take a **service** from Madaba to Feisaliyyeh (150fils), then walk or bargain with the driver once the other passengers get off. JD2.50 should get you the extra 3km up, a 30min. wait, and the trip back to Madaba. Without a prearranged ride, the only way off Mt. Nebo is to walk back to Feisaliyyeh. Buildings and Siyagha Peak are open in summer 7am-7pm; in winter 7am-5pm. Pay the guard 500fils to stay and see the sunset. Admission 500fils.*

The view of the sunset from Mt. Nebo is so spectacular that Moses' last request to God was for a view from its heights. Although the Bible says that "no man knows the place of his burial to this day" (Deuteronomy 34:6), Moses' grave is rumored to be in a secret cave somewhere along 'Ain Musa. On Nebo's **Siyagha Peak,** the Christians of Madaba built a three-nave **Memorial Church,** next to which looms an imposing serpentine cross. Archaeological work has revealed a complete mosaic floor in the church dating from 531 CE, as well as foundations of monasteries from the 3rd century CE. In the 7th century, the **Chapel of the Theotokos** (or Mary, Mother of God) was added, with lavish decorations adorning the walls.

Just beyond Feisaliyyeh, a marked turn-off leads to **Khirbet al-Mukheiyat,** once known as the ancient village of **Nebo,** on the southern base of the mountain. A one-hour hike (round-trip) will allow you to see the secular scenes of fishing, hunting, and wine-making that decorate another finely preserved Byzantine church floor. Despite repeated warnings by the Surgeon General, cigarettes are the preferred *bakhsheesh* for the Bedouin gatekeeper who lives on the hill at the end of the paved road (open until dusk, or whenever the gatekeeper leaves). The trip out here is worth it; the mosaic is astounding and the views are, well, enough to make it onto a dying prophet's wish list. If the opportunity arises, head out to the waterfall **'Ain Musa** (Spring of Moses) to cool off. To get there, don't go chasing waterfalls: take a right before the Mt. Nebo sign and follow the road down into the valley. Walk around the old pump buildings and follow the path down to the right.

KARAK الكرك

Once the ancient capital of Moab, Karak now humbles itself in the shadow of **Karak Castle,** the largest of the mountaintop Crusader castles that stretch from Turkey to the Sinai. Home to some of Jordan's most influential clans, the prosperous modern town of Karak extends away from the castle on its northern and eastern slopes and serves as an ideal resting place for travelers on the Kings' Highway.

⚄ ORIENTATION AND PRACTICAL INFORMATION. Travel to Karak from Amman's Wahdat Station by **minibus** (2hr., 750fils) or **service taxi** (JD1.2) along the Desert Highway. To reach **Petra** from Karak, take a minibus from the city center to Tafilah (30min., 500fils), and from Tafilah to Shobak (30min., 250fils, departures erratic, but often at 7am). At times, no buses run to **Shobak;** those who hitch say it's easy, though *Let's Go* does not recommend hitchhiking. **Minibuses** sometimes run from Shobak to Petra. A direct bus from Karak to Petra leaves at 9am, depending on the volume of tourist traffic. No *service* travel these routes, but a **private taxi** will take you directly from Karak to Petra for a hefty JD40. **Buses** also run from Karak to Petra through Ma'an (JD1). There are more connections to Petra through Ma'an, but they may take a little longer than if you try your luck going through Shobak. If you are traveling in the late afternoon, cars are very rare and lodgings along the way are limited to hospitable locals or camping at Shobak Castle. It can get cold and lonely at night on the desert mountains, so many find it better to stay the night in Karak and leave on the 9am bus.

The two main landmarks in town are the castle at the top of the hill and the town's center circle at the bottom, which has a statue of horse-and-rider in the middle. Karak's newly renovated **tourist office** is right next to the Castle Hotel (usually open Sa-Th 8am-2pm). The **Housing Bank** (tel. 351 142), four blocks downhill from the castle and to the right, will change traveler's checks and cash (open for exchange Sa-Th 8:30am-2pm). For **medical emergencies,** dial 193. Karak's **Italian Hospital** (tel. 351 145 or 045), is downhill from the road up to the castle, or in the direction of the dagger if you orient yourself using the manic horseman in the center circle. The **police station** is located down the street and on the right of the tourist office, next to the huge radio tower. Karak's **post and telephone office** (open Sa-Th 8am-2pm) is located across the street from the tourist office and the Tower Hotel. The **telephone code** for Karak is 03.

⚄⚄ ACCOMMODATIONS AND FOOD. The best domicile for your dinar is at the **Towers Castle Hotel** (tel. 352 489), to the right of the main circle. The Towers Castle offers spacious rooms and helpful management. (Singles JD6, with bath JD12; doubles JD12, with bath JD16.) **New Karak Hotel** (tel. 351 942), down the hill from the castle, has noisy, stuffy rooms, but you can't go wrong with the hot showers and low prices (singles JD3; triples JD7.5). The **Rum Cottage Hotel** (tel. 351 351; fax 354 293), around the corner from the Towers Castle, has newly carpeted singles for JD8 (doubles with private bath JD6; with private bath, TV, and small refrigerator JD10). All prices are negotiable, especially during the off season.

For a tasty sit-down meal at a price that'll make you stand up and cheer, try the **Rum Cottage Restaurant** (tel. 353 789), across the street from the police station and the radio tower. Oven-warmed frozen pizza starts at JD1.5, and a tasty grill or

AN ENGLISHWOMAN IN ARABIA Wrapped in a heavy sun hood, with her skirts and petticoats whipping up the dry sands, **Gertrude Bell** traveled throughout the Arabian desert advising sheiks, documenting archaeological sites, and hosting proper teas on her Wedgwood china. In the 1880s, Bell was one of the first women to study at Oxford University; she gained high honors but shocked professors with her brazenness. Her family sent her to Bucharest to be schooled in the ways of Victorian femininity, but Bell's insatiable wanderlust would have none of it. Soon Bell was traveling farther East and in 1909, with a bevy of male servants in caravan, she set out for "Mesopotamia." Dubbed an "honorary man" by the Arabs she met, Bell befriended graduate student T.E. Lawrence (later to be known as **Lawrence of Arabia**) and became the only woman to be drafted to Cairo's Arab Bureau as an intelligence agent when WWI broke out. She ignited controversy during the war with her support of Arabic self-determination and her indisputable femininity. Later, she helped carve out the nascent state of Iraq and served as one of King Faisal's closest aides. Nevertheless, Bell still took her own life in 1926. The next day, Baghdad's crowds filed past to pay respects to this "uncrowned queen of Iraq."

mensaf with salad and coffee or tea starts at JD3 (open daily 8am-10pm). **Fida Restaurant** (tel. 352 677), down the street from the Ram Hotel, serves an open buffet luncheon (JD5) popular with tourist groups (open 8am-10pm). The **Government Rest House** (tel. 351 148), near the castle entrance, offers a great view of the Jordan Valley's descent to the Dead Sea and huge JD6 meals (open until 10pm). Cheap falafel and fruit from the stalls lining the street to the left of the Ram Restaurant make great fixings for a picnic atop the ruins.

◙ SIGHTS. Built into and on top of the hill overlooking its sleepy hamlet, **Karak Castle** is full of secret passageways and hidden rooms; bring a flashlight for easier exploration and allow at least two hours. In 1142 CE, Baldwin I of Jerusalem built the castle midway between his capital and Shobak, on the site of an Iron Age citadel mentioned in the Mesha Stele of 850 BCE. The castle was renovated in 1188 under Salah ad-Din, and although the fortress's walls have mostly collapsed since then, its building blocks remain large enough to inspire starry-eyed wonder. Inside, vaulted stone ceilings span only a few meters, resulting in a network of long, narrow halls and barracks. You can still see the bolt holes for mammoth stone doors that have since turned to dust. To the west across the dry moat are battlements from which the charming Renauld de Chatillon cast prisoners 40m to their deaths (with wooden boxes fastened around their heads so that they would not lose consciousness too quickly). When Salah ad-Din took the castle after the 1187 Battle of Hittim, he personally saw to it that Chatillon's head was removed. Below, a 50m tunnel leads out of town through an arched gateway. Ask the museum guard to unlock the underground chamber opposite the museum entrance; the 150m long vaulted room used to be the main entrance to the castle. Steep, jagged walls atop an even steeper hill turn a tour of the windblown ruins into a challenge. To the right of the castle entrance is a stone staircase that descends to the **Archaeological Museum.** A copy of the Mesha Stele rests alongside original Nabatean, Roman, and Mamluke artifacts (open daily 8am-4pm; admission to castle and museum JD1).

NEAR KARAK

West of Karak, Highway 49/80 (some call it 50 for added confusion) drops over 20 meters from the Kings' Highway to the Dead Sea "port" of **Mazra'a** and the Al-Lisan ("Tongue") Peninsula. Five kilometers before reaching Mazra'a and the Wadi Araba Highway to Aqaba, Highway 49/80 passes **Bab adh-Dhira.** The cemeteries here contain 20,000 shaft tombs enshrining 500,000 bodies (an unfortunate 25-to-1 body-to-tomb ratio) and over three million pottery vessels. The length of the bones indicates that the average height in Bab adh-Dhira was a sturdy 2m (over 6½ ft.). Reaching this site may be more trouble than it's worth for all but the most morbidly curious.

Hitchers report that there is very little traffic between Mazra'a and Karak. For assistance, stop in at the **Mazra'a Police Post,** 5km north of the junction. Heading out of Mazra'a is the Wadi Araba Highway, where hitchhiking is always prohibited. In the towns surrounding Karak, tourist services are non-existent. If you're lost or need a ride or a place to stay, approach a friendly looking store owner or businessperson and ask for help (offer a tip of 500fils or JD1 in return). Solo women should refuse hospitality from single men.

The mosques at **Mu'tah** and at the nearby village of **Mazar** (bus 150fils) commemorate the Islamic generals who died in the first great battles between the forces of Islam and Byzantium in 632 CE. The green-domed mosque in Mazar houses a small **Islamic museum** on the first floor (usually open 9am-4pm).

SHOBAK شوبك

Amman-bound minibuses (500fils) reach Shobak from Wadi Musa (near Petra), departing from Wadi Musa gate in the early morning. Around the same time of day, minibuses make the trip from Karak to Tafilah (30min., 250fils). If you hire a taxi (no more than JD7 from Karak, no more than JD3 from Wadi Musa), make sure the driver waits while you explore.

King Baldwin's first castle at Shobak pales in comparison to his later creation at Karak. **Shobak Castle,** known to locals as "Mons Realis" or "Montréal," is 4km from the marked turn-off at the northern edge of Shobak town. The castle first fell to Salah ad-Din in 1189, just 74 years after it was built. In 1260, the Mamlukes gained possession of the castle, restored it, and inscribed records of their work on its main walls and towers. Most of the castle is gone today, but the view from the approaching road across the natural moat is inspiring: colossal white stones silhouetted against desert brush and a cobalt sky. Villagers who lived inside the castle walls depended upon the water from the rock-hewn well, 375 steps deep. They have long since abandoned the area, leaving a secluded spot for free camping.

DANA NATURE RESERVE

Buses between Tafilah and Shobak (JD1) will drop you off along the Kings' Highway, but they are rare and you'll have to hitch or hike the last few km to the reserve. As always, taxis are a more efficient option (around JD5 from Karak).

Located 50km south of Karak and just west of the Kings' Highway, the Dana Nature Reserve harbors an impressive array of ibex, mountain gazelles, jackals, and the occasional red fox. Founded in 1990, Dana is Jordan's newest national reserve, but the site has an incredibly long history. Archaeological evidence of Paleolithic, Edomite, Nabatean, and Roman settlements have all been found within the reserve's borders. There are several well-marked trails for day **hiking** and an expensive **campground** whose price seems to fluctuate depending upon how much the caretaker likes you. For more information on Dana or any other reserve, contact the Royal Society for the Conservation of Nature (tel. (06) 533 79 31).

PETRA البتـراء

Match me such marvel save in Eastern clime,
a rose-red city 'half as old as Time'!

—Dean Burgon, *Petra*

As one approaches the once-lost city of Petra, towering sculptures peek out from the walls of a natural 3m-wide fissure to reveal raw mountains that were fashioned by human hands into impossibly delicate structures. Petra ("stone" in ancient Greek) is perhaps the most astounding ancient city left to the modern world, and certainly a must-see for visitors to the Middle East.

For 700 years, Petra was lost to all but the few hundred members of a Bedouin tribe who guarded their treasure from outsiders. In the 19th century, Swiss explorer Johann Burkhardt heard Bedouin speaking of a "lost city," and he vowed to find it. Though initially unable to find a guide willing to disclose the city's location, he guessed that the city he sought was the Petra of legend, the biblical Sela, which should have been near Mt. Hor, the site of Aaron's tomb. Impersonating a Christian pilgrim, Burkhardt hired a guide, and on August 22, 1812, he became the first non-Bedouin in thousands of years to have walked between the cliffs of Petra's *siq* (the mile-long rift that was the only entrance to Petra). In the nearly two centuries since Burkhardt's discovery, Petra has become a feature tourist attraction, admired by visitors from all over the world (including the film crew of *Indiana Jones and the Last Crusade*). Petra now has its own camel corps to protect the blushing ruins from the many overzealous pilgrims who follow in Burkhardt's footsteps.

Humans first set foot in the area back in the 8th millennium BCE. By the 6th century BCE, the Nabateans (a nomadic Arab tribe) had quietly moved onto land controlled by the Edomites and had begun to profit from the trade between lower Arabia and the Fertile Crescent. Over the next three centuries, the Nabatean Kingdom flourished, secure in its easily defended capital. The Nabateans carved their monumental temples out of the mountains, looking to Egyptian, Greek, and Roman styles for inspiration. Unique to the Nabateans are the crow-step (upside-down staircase) patterns that grace the crowns of many of the memorials. The crow-steps so decidedly resemble inverted stairways that the people of Meda'in Salih (in Saudi Arabia) claimed that God threw Petra upside down and turned it to stone to punish its people's wickedness.

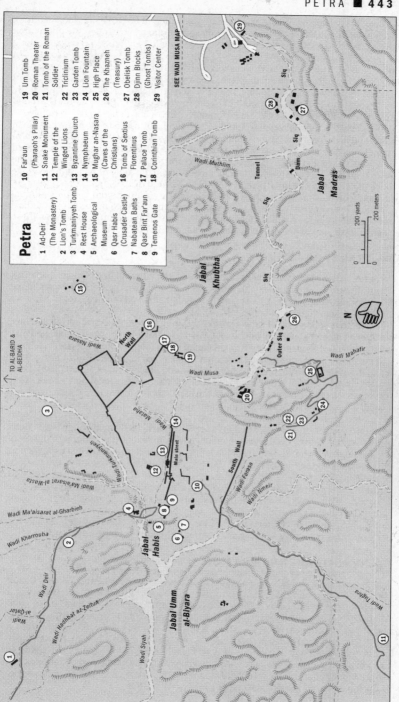

Petra

1 Ad-Deir
(The Monastery)
2 Lion's Tomb
3 Turkmaniyeh Tomb
4 Rest House
5 Archaeological
Museum
6 Qasr Habis
(Crusader Castle)
7 Nabatean Baths
8 Qasr Bint Far'aun
9 Temenos Gate
10 Far'aun
(Pharaoh's Pillar)
11 Snake Monument
12 Temple of the
Winged Lions
13 Byzantine Church
14 Nymphaeum
15 Mughar an-Nasara
(Caves of the
Christians)
16 Tomb of Sextius
Florentinus
17 Palace Tomb
18 Corinthian Tomb
19 Urn Tomb
20 Roman Theater
21 Tomb of the Roman
Soldier
22 Triclinium
23 Garden Tomb
24 Lion Fountain
25 High Place
26 The Khazneh
(Treasury)
27 Obelisk Tomb
28 Djinn Blocks
(Ghost Tombs)
29 Visitor Center

SEE WADI MUSA MAP

JORDAN

More historically verifiable evidence suggests that, in 63 BCE, the Nabatean King Aretes defeated Pompey's Roman Legions. The Romans controlled the entire area around Nabatea, however, prompting the later King Rabel III to strike a deal: as long as the Romans did not attack during his lifetime, they would be permitted to move in after he died. In 106 CE, the Romans claimed the Nabatean Kingdom and inhabited the city of rosy Nubian sandstone (see **Ancient History**, p. 408). In its heyday, Petra housed as many as 30,000 people, but after an earthquake in 363 CE, a shift in the trade routes to Palmyra (Tadmor) in Syria, the expansion of the sea trade around Arabia, and another earthquake in 747, much of Petra had deteriorated to rubble.

For decades, the Bedouin adapted to the influx of tourists by providing them with food and accommodations inside Petra, a practice outlawed in 1984-85 out of concern for the monuments. While many of Petra's Bedouin have been relocated to a housing project near Wadi Musa, a large portion still make their homes in the more remote caves and hills of the city (spanning 50km, most of which the average tourist never sees). Many Bedouin sell souvenirs and drinks amidst the ruins; others tend goats—don't be surprised to hear a *baaa* or a barnyard smell emanating from inside an ancient tomb. If you venture on paths that go beyond the standard one-day itinerary, you will notice stones piled into neat columns. As long as these cairn markers are in sight, you're near a trail, and Bedouin will pass by.

⌐ TRANSPORTATION

Petra lies in the rocky wilderness near the southern extreme of the Kings' Highway, about 282km from Amman (262km via the Desert Highway). **JETT buses** leave Amman daily (3hr., 6:30am, JD5; pricey but all-inclusive complete round-trip tour including lunch, guide, and horse JD32.5). Reservations should be made in person at JETT stations well ahead of time, especially during the busy fall and spring seasons; questions can be handled by phone (tel. 664 146). You'll be dropped off at the Petra Visitor's Center. More than one day is needed to do longer hikes, but the JETT tour will cover the most impressive (and most frequented) sights. **Service** to Petra from Wahdat Station in Amman takes about five hours, plus a wait in Ma'an (JD2). Drivers will drop you off at either the **Al-Anbat** or the **Musa Spring Hotel;** from Wadi Musa you can walk the 3km or take a **private taxi** (JD1) to Petra. From Aqaba, a two-hour **minibus** trip costs JD3. Start early in the morning to make any of these connections.

To reach Petra from the Kings' Highway, take the well-marked turn-off and head west into the colorful, steep-sided town of **Wadi Musa**. Halfway through Wadi Musa on the way to Petra, you'll pass the main traffic circle and travel through the main market area. A tortuous 1km from the traffic circle, the spur road leaves town and ends at the entrance to Petra. The cluster of buildings here includes the visitors center, the Government Rest House, a group of five-star hotels for the rich and boring, and the gatehouse to the valley that leads to the *siq* and Petra proper.

To leave Petra, catch a **minibus** or **service** to Aqaba (JD3), Amman (JD3), or Wadi Rum (JD3) at the center of Wadi Musa near the post office or at the Musa Spring Hotel. Buses leave at 6, 8am, and 3:30pm. A local **bus** to Ma'an often leaves in the early morning (one-way 500fils); ask at your hotel for exact information.

ⓜ PRACTICAL INFORMATION

The **tourist police** (tel. 215 64 41) munch on cigar ends at the **Petra Visitor's Center** (tel. 215 60 20; open daily 7am-6pm), where you can hire an official guide for a "low tour" of the city center (2½hr., JD8). More comprehensive guided tours go to Al-Madbah (JD8), Ad-Deir (JD9), and Jabal Harun (JD35). Arrange trips to more remote areas directly with the guide; a full day tour costs JD35. You can rent a horse for JD7 (you're also responsible for renting the guide's horse), but it's more interesting to remain on foot. It's easy to tag along behind a group with a guide or to form a group of your own. The various guidebooks available at the Visitor's Center are helpful, but there's no substitute for the expertise of an official guide, especially for the more remote sites of Al-Barid or Al-Madras.

On the other side of the Visitor's Center are the rest house and the swinging gate that mark the beginning of the trail down to the *siq*. There are almost as many banks and money exchanges in Wadi Musa as there were dead Nabateans in Petra. The two largest, **Arab Bank** (tel. 215 68 02) and **Housing Bank** (tel. 215 60 82), are both located next to the main traffic circle (open Sa-Th 8:30am-12:30pm). **Cairo Amman Bank,** in the Mövenpick Hotel, just outside the entrance to Petra, is open daily 8:30am-3pm. All banks extract exorbitant commissions. You can get a Visa **cash advance** from any bank. The **Wadi Musa Pharmacy** (tel. 215 64 44) is on the main traffic circle (open 24hr.). The **government health center** (tel. 215 60 25), a 15-minute walk uphill from the main traffic circle, is open 24 hours. The **Petra Polyclinic** (tel. 215 66 94) at the traffic circle, costs more but has modern equipment. Wadi Musa has a **post office** with Poste Restante (tel. 215 62 24) next to the Musa Spring Hotel (open Sa-Th 7:30am-7pm, F 7:30am-12:30pm). A second branch is behind the Visitor's Center, by the entrance to the *siq* (tel. 215 66 94; opendaily 8am-7pm). Plug in at **Petra Internet Cafe** (tel. 215 72 64) for an exorbitant JD4 per hour, just off the main circle in Wadi Musa across from Ar-Rashid Hotel. Petra's **telephone code** is 03.

▐ ACCOMMODATIONS

Since Jordan and Israel signed a peace treaty, visitors from all over the world have flooded the Jordanian hillside, and construction has boomed in Wadi Musa. Most of the development revolves around luxury resorts, but there are plenty of cheapies to go around. Prices become negotiable in the off season (May-July and Dec.-Feb.). **Camping** inside Petra is illegal, but lingering explorers (especially women) may receive invitations for overnight stays from Bedouin. Others pick off-the-beaten-path caves for the night. Camping is available in Wadi Musa at some of the hotels.

Al-Anbat 1 Hotel (tel. 215 62 65; fax 215 68 88). Follow the trough down from the spring. Has the best views around. Free and frequent buses to Petra. Witness the most beautiful sunset in Wadi Musa from mattresses in the "greenhouse" (JD2). Camping facilities (tents and showers) available for JD2. The basement of this 2-star hotel offers cavernous student rooms (JD4) and clean communal baths. Upstairs singles JD9; doubles JD15; triples JD18. Buffet dinner (JD4) and breakfast (JD2) available.

Petra Gate Hotel (tel. 215 6908), 40m up the hill from the main circle in Wadi Musa on the right, overlooking the valley. A homey atmosphere with smallish rooms and tasty home-cooked dinners. Cordial, helpful employees live up to the "funky and friendly staff" slogan. Free billiards, so you can bet all the money you're saving by staying here. Rooftop mattresses JD1. Dorm room JD3. Singles JD5, with bath JD8; doubles JD10.

Sunset Hotel (tel. 215 65 79; fax 215 69 50), about 200m uphill from the visitor's center. If your feet are sore and your bottom hurts from a Petra camel ride, this is the place for you—the first inexpensive and clean option outside the mega-hotel complex. Singles JD7, with shared bath JD15; doubles JD10/JD18. Breakfast JD2.

Musa Spring Hotel and Restaurant, Wadi Musa Gate (tel. 215 63 10; fax 215 69 10). The first hotel as you enter town from Amman, but a trek from Petra proper. Plenty of budget traveler companionship. Free shuttle to Petra at 7 and 8am, returning 6pm. Free use of kitchen. Rooftop mattresses with hot showers JD2; singles JD4; doubles JD8, with private bath JD1.5. Breakfast JD1.5, all-you-can-eat buffet lunch or dinner JD3.

Araba Hotel (tel. 215 61 07), 200m uphill from the main circle in Wadi Musa. Pastel-hued rooms with small, private baths and soft, colorful mattresses. Rooftop mattresses JD1; singles JD6; doubles JD10. Breakfast JD1.

Cleopatra Hotel (tel./fax 215 70 90), 50m uphill from the main traffic circle, on the left. Colorful rooms with relatively clean private baths. Friendly manager gives maps and info. Singles JD10; doubles JD14; triples JD18. Breakfast JD1.500.

Orient Hotel and Restaurant (tel./fax 215 70 20), left of the traffic circle facing downhill. Small, cozy rooms have sparkling baths. Two neighboring mosques and their competing *muezzins* make for an interesting aural experience. Make sure to get a room with a downhill view and balcony. Singles JD5; doubles JD10; triples JD12. Breakfast JD1.5.

FOOD

The farther you go from the ruins, the less you'll pay for falafel. Wadi Musa boasts the best bargains, especially in the streets to the right of its main circle as you approach from Petra. Many hotels have all-you-can-eat buffets at reasonable prices; others offer filling meals with pasta, rice, chicken, salad, and bread for JD2-3 (open daily 6-9pm). The **Star Supermarket** (on the left and uphill from the traffic circle) has the cheapest water (300fils) and the most reasonably-priced basics for bag lunches. **Papazzi** (tel. 215 70 87), uphill from the Visitor's Center, is an Italian chain restaurant with great pizza (medium JD5-7).

■ **Al-Wadi Restaurant** (tel. 215 71 63), located right in the city center on the main circle. Christmas-colored decoration and somewhat unsavory odors upstairs do not detract from the awesome food served here. Most appetizers under JD2.5, main meals JD1-3. Ask about student deals.

Rose City Restaurant (tel. 215 73 40), just uphill from the site. Attentive staff provides energy for the hike uphill with delicious grills (JD2.5-3) in a spacious dining room with eclectic decor. Hummus 600fils, soda 300fils. Open daily 6am-10pm.

Aj-Janoub Restaurant (tel. 215 75 65), on the 1st street on the right before reaching the main circle from Petra. Modest kebabs are the cheapest in town at only 500fils. Hummus 500fils, falafel 150fils, soda bottles 200fils. Open daily 5am-midnight.

Cleopatra Restaurant, to the left of the main circle facing downhill. Friendly Egyptian cooks will serve you rice, salad, bird, and bread for JD1.5. Falafel 200fils, shawarma 600fils, soda 500fils. Open daily 10am-10pm.

The Petra Pearl, across the street and 10m uphill from Cleopatra. Serves up a chicken buffet (JD3.5) and *ad hoc* lessons in Arabic. Open 6am-midnight.

Red Cave Restaurant (tel. 215 77 99), just up the street from Petra. Well-decorated, bamboo-covered restaurant with red brick covering has delicious food to match the elegant setting. Daily specials and *mensaf* (JD3) are good options. Appetizers around JD1.

SIGHTS

This is why you came to Petra. Many spectacular monuments are close enough to be viewed in a day, but a few require multi-day expeditions. Guides are expensive but recommended for 4 of the more remote hikes in Petra. It's best to bring water bottles from outside; Bedouin sell water throughout the park, but at JD1-1.5 per bottle, you'll need to empty the Treasury to stay hydrated. **Open** *in summer daily 6am-6pm; in winter 6am-5pm, but these hours are only loosely enforced. If you stay to see the sunset, you should have no problem getting out.* **Admission** *for 1 day JD20, 2 days JD25, 3 days JD30, under 12 50% off for 2 or 3 days.*

Although the Nabateans worshiped only two deities—Dushara (the god of strength) and Al-Uzza (or Atargatis, the goddess of water and fertility)—the number of temples and tombs in Petra seems infinite. Climbing will allow you to escape the tour groups crowding the inner valley.

OBELISK TOMB. As you head toward the canyon-like *siq*, large *djinn* monuments (ghost tombs) and caves will stare down at you from distant mountain faces. The Obelisk Tomb is built high into the cliff on the left. Closer to the entrance of the *siq*, rock-cut channels once cradled the ceramic pipes that brought 'Ain Musa's waters to the city and the surrounding country. A nearby dam burst in 1963, and the resulting flood killed 28 tourists in the *siq*. While designing the new dam, the Nabateans' ancient dam was uncovered and used as a model.

■ **KHAZNEH.** As you enter the *siq*, 200m walls on either side begin to block out the sunlight, casting enormous shadows on the niches that once held icons meant to hex unwelcome visitors (you should be safe if you've paid the admission fee). The *siq* winds around for 1½km, then slowly emits a faint pink glow at the first peek of the Khazneh (Treasury). At 90m wide and 130m tall, the Khazneh is the best preserved of Petra's monuments, though bullet holes are clearly visible on the upper urn. Believing the urn to be hollow and filled with ancient pharaonic treasures, Bedouin periodically fired at it, hoping to burst this petrified piñata. Actually, the Treasury is a royal tomb and quite solid. The Khazneh's rock face is like a geological mood ring: in the morning, the sun's rays give the monument a rich peach hue, in late afternoon it glistens rose, and by sunset it drips blood red.

ROMAN THEATER. Down the road to the right as you face the Khazneh, Wadi Musa opens up to the 7000-seat Roman Theater. The long row of Royal Tombs on the face of Jabal Khubtha stands to the right. The Romans built their theater under the red stone Nabatean necropolis, and the ancient carved caves still yawn above it. The theater has been restored to its 2nd-century appearance and audiences are returning after a 1500-year intermission. A marble Hercules (now in the museum) was discovered just a few years ago in the curtained chambers beneath the stage.

ROYAL TOMBS. Across the Wadi are the Royal Tombs. The **Urn Tomb,** with its unmistakable recessed facade, commands a soul-scorching view of the still-widening valley. The two-tiered vault beneath the pillared facade is known as the **prison,** or *sijin.* A Greek inscription on an inner wall describes how the tomb, originally dedicated to the Nabatean King Malichus II in the 1st century CE, was converted to a church 400 years later. Nearby sits the **Corinthian Tomb** (allegedly a replica of Nero's Golden Palace in Rome) and the **Palace Tomb** (or the Tomb in Two Stories), which juts out from the mountainside. Laborers completed the tomb by attaching pre-assembled stones to its upper left-hand corner. Around the corner to the right is the **Tomb of Sextus Florentinus,** who was so enamored of these hewn heights that he asked his son to bury him in this ultimate outpost of the Roman Empire.

MAIN STREET. Around the bend to the left, a few restored columns are all that remain of the paved Roman main street. Two thousand years ago, columns lined the full length of the street, shielding markets and residences. At the beginning of the street on the right, the **Nymphaeum** ruins outline the ancient public fountain near its base. On a rise to the right, before the triple-arched gate, recent excavations have uncovered the Temple of Al-Uzza (Atargatis), also called the **Temple of the Winged Lions.** In the spring you can watch the progress of U.S.-sponsored excavations that have already uncovered several workshops and some cracked crocks.

BYZANTINE CHURCH. A joint Jordanian-American team has also recently excavated an immense Byzantine church with a wealth of mosaics. The site lies several hundred meters to the right of the Roman street, near the Temple of the Winged Lions, from which some of the church's column bases and capitals were probably lifted. Each of the church's side aisles is paved with 70 square meters of remarkably preserved mosaic, depicting humans of various professions, representations of the four seasons, and indigenous, exotic, and even mythological animals. Recent studies attest that the church was the seat of an important Byzantine bishopric in the 5th and 6th centuries, an assertion that challenges the belief that Petra was in decline by 600 CE. The archaeologists on the site are constantly digging, scraping, and sniffing. They also protect their site quite jealously—entrance may require charm and luck.

SOUTHERN TEMPLE AND ENVIRONS. A team from Brown University is unearthing the Southern Temple. White hexagonal paving stones cover an extensive tunnel system that marks the importance of this holy site. Farther along, the triple-arched **Temenos Gate** was once the front gate of the **Qasr Bint Far'aun** (Palace of the Pharaoh's Daughter), a Nabatean temple built to honor the god Dushara. On your left, just before the gate, are the **Nabatean Baths.** On the trail leading off behind the temple to the left, a single standing column, **Amoud Far'aun** (Pharaoh's Pillar), gloats beside its two fallen comrades.

MUSEUMS. To the right of the Nabatean temple, a rock-hewn staircase leads to a small **archaeological museum** holding the spoils of the Winged Lions dig as well as carved stone figures from elsewhere in Petra. On the way to the monastery, the **Nabatean Museum** has good artifacts and air-conditioned restrooms with what is probably the ■**world's best toilet seat view.** *(Both museums open daily 9am-4pm; free.)*

▟ HIKES: AROUND PETRA

Many people go home raving about Petra's most accessible ten percent, content with what they can see in a single day at the site. However, the Bedouin say that in order to appreciate Petra, you must stay long enough to watch your nails grow long. The following seven treks fill two days, but you can easily spend a week wandering, especially if you venture beyond the ancient city limits. Four of these seven hikes require a guide (JD35): **Sabra**, the **Snake Monument, Jabal Numair,** and **Jabal Harun**. The requirement is not enforced, but it's unwise to hike the remote hills alone. If you feel lost, keep a sharp Turkimaniyyeh eye out for remnants of donkey visits which can, ironically enough, serve as a trail of crumbs.

WADI TURKIMANIYYEH وادى تـركما نية

The shortest and easiest of the hikes leads down the *wadi* to the left of and behind the Temple of the Winged Lions. Fifteen minutes of strolling down the road that runs through the rich green gardens of **Wadi Turkimaniyyeh** leads you to the only tomb at Petra with a Nabatean inscription. The lengthy invocation above the entrance beseeches the god Dushara to safeguard the tomb and to protect its contents from violation. Unfortunately, Dushara took a permanent sabbatical and the chamber has been stripped bare.

QASR HABIS قصر حا بس

A second, more interesting climb begins at the end of the road that descends from the Pharaoh's Pillar to the cliff face, a few hundred meters left of the museum. The trail dribbles up to the **Qasr Habis** (Crusader Castle). While the steps have been restored recently, they don't lead up to much. A path winds all the way around the mountain, however, revealing gorgeous canyons and (you guessed it) more tombs on the western side. The climb to the top and back takes less than an hour.

JABAL HARUN جبـل هارون

This climb begins just to the right of Jabal Habis, below the museum. A sign points to **Ad-Deir** (the Monastery) and leads northwest across Wadi Siyah, past the Forum Restaurant, and on to Wadi Deir and its fragrant oleander. As you squeeze through the narrowing canyon along an endless, twisting stairway, you will confront a human-shaped hole in the facade of the **Lion's Tomb**. A hidden tomb awaits daredevils who try to climb the cleft to the right; less intrepid wanderers can backtrack to the right and spot the tomb a few minutes later.

Back on the path, veer left to reach Petra's largest monument. Ad-Deir, 50m wide and 45m tall, is larger but less ornate than the Khazneh. With a single inner chamber that dates back to the 1st century CE, most scholars believe that Ad-Deir was originally either a Nabatean temple or an unfinished tomb dedicated to one of the later Nabatean kings. It picked up its orthodox appellation in the Byzantine period. On the left, a lone tree popping through a crack in the rock marks more ancient steps, which continue all the way up to the rim of the urn atop the monastery. Those with more courage than caution may actually step out onto the ancient urn. Straight across the *wadi* looms the highest peak in the area, **Jabal Harun** (Aaron's Mountain or Mt. Hor). On top of the mountain, a white church reportedly houses the **Tomb of Aaron**. The whole trip takes a few hours, a couple more if you detour into **Wadi Siyah** and visit its seasonal waterfall on the way back.

JABAL UMM AL-BIYARA جبـل أم البيارة

It takes a grueling three-hour hike to ascend **Jabal Umm al-Biyara** (Mother of Cisterns Mountain), which towers over the Crusader castle on Jabal Habis. Follow the trail from the left of the Nabatean temple past the Pharaoh's Pillar and down into the *wadi* to the right. A 50m scramble up the rock chute to the left of the blue sign leads to the beginning of a stone ramp, which leads to the top.

Exercise caution on the ramp, since the footing is fickle. It was here, at the site of Petra's original acropolis and the biblical city of Sela, that a Judean king supposedly hurled thousands of Edomites over the cliff's edge. The gigantic piles of shards, over 8000 years old, are the only remnants of the mountains' first inhabitants.

If instead of climbing Umm al-Biyara you continue south along Wadi Tughra (which runs by its base), you'll eventually reach the **Snake Monument,** one of the earliest Nabatean religious shrines. From here it's about two hours to Aaron's Tomb on Jabal Harun. The path meanders around Jabal Harun before ascending it from the south. When it disappears on the rocks, follow the donkey droppings. As you start to climb Jabal Harun you'll see a lone tent. Inside, a Bedouin, the official holder of the keys, will escort you the rest of the way and open the building for you to explore. The entire trek takes five or six hours.

THE HIGH PLACE الاماكن العليا

One of the most popular hikes is the circular route to the **High Place** on **Jabal al-Madbah,** a site of sacrifice with a full view of Petra—even the tourist police come here to watch the sunset. A staircase sliced into the rock leads to the left just as the Roman Theater comes into view. Follow the right prong when the trail levels and forks at the top of the stairs. On the left, **Obelisk Ridge** presents one obelisk to Dushara and another to Al-Uzza. On the peak to the right, the High Place supports a string of grisly sights: two altars, an ablution cistern, gutters for draining away sacrificial blood, and cliff-hewn bleachers for an unobstructed view of the animal sacrifices. Head downhill past the cerulean blue Pepsi stand, leaving the obelisks behind you, and backtrack under the rugged western face of the High Place. A hard-to-find staircase leads down to a sculptured **Lion Fountain.** The first grotto complex beyond it is the **Garden Tomb.** Below it is the **Tomb of the Roman Soldier** (named for the tough guy carved in the facade) and across from it a rock **triclinium** (feast hall), which has the only decorated interior in Petra. The trail then leads into Wadi Farasa and ends near the Pillar. The circle, followed in either direction, takes about one and a half hours.

AL-MADRAS AND AL-BARID المدرس و البارد

Beyond Petra, tourist groups and commercialism disappear. Bedouin here remain stoically unaffected by modernity, and varied wildlife roam free. The isolated antiquities can be reached only at length by donkey or foot. All roads lead back to the Kings' Highway.

A trail branching to your left just past the Obelisk Tomb and before the entrance to the *siq* leads to **Al-Madras,** an ancient Petran suburb with almost as many monuments as Petra itself. On the way, watch for the short-eared desert hare and a full spectrum of long, lanky lizards in dazzling purple, fuchsia, and irridescent blue. Come with water, a snack, and a guide. The round-trip takes four to eight hours to complete.

Past the Tomb of Sextus Florentinus and the **Mughar an-Nasara** (Caves of the Christians), a trail chisels into the rock that leads to the northern suburb of **Al-Barid.** A road passing the new hotel in Wadi Musa also approaches this archaeological site. Al-Barid is a curious miniature of Petra, complete with a short *siq*, several carved tombs, and caves. If you don't feel like hoofing it, a Wadi Musa **taxi** will take you there and wait at the entrance for an hour (JD7). Also off the new road past the hotel is **Al-Beidha.** Excitement runs high among the members of the excavating expedition here; they've uncovered traces of a pre-pottery Neolithic village, a sedentary society dating from the 8th millennium BCE. Conclusive evidence of this site's age would make Al-Beidha one of the oldest known farming communities in the world (along with Jericho). A Bedouin guide can lead you here via a painless trail (about 3hr. each way). Bring an extra JD2-3 or some of your own native trinkets (such as cigarettes) to trade.

AQABA العقبة

Set in a natural theater beneath a crescent of rugged hills, Aqaba is Jordan's sole link to the sea. Beneath the water, legions of brilliantly colored creatures flit through a surreal universe of coral. Aqaba's reefs are a world apart from the damaged reefs of Eilat, mainly due to a lesser tourism impact, but they aren't quite on par with the spectacular snorkeling spots that circle the southern Sinai. Above the water, Aqaba serves as an important trade and military center and has become the darling of an Arab elite in need of periodic respite from dry cityscapes. At the tip of the gulf of the same name, Aqaba's strategic setting has been apparent since biblical times, when King Solomon's copper-laden ships embarked from here. The Romans stationed their famous Tenth Legion at this point, and the Crusaders fortified the port and Pharaoh's Island, 7km off the coast (now in Egyptian territory). During the 1917 Arab Revolt, Faisal Ibn Hussein and T.E. Lawrence staged a desert raid on the Ottoman fortifications and captured the port. In 1965, King Hussein not-so-shrewdly traded the Saudis 6000km of southeastern desert (before he knew there was oil beneath the sand) for 13km of coastline, and started developing the city. After the reopening of the Suez Canal in 1957 and the increased traffic caused by the Iran-Iraq War, the harbor became packed with leviathan tankers bulging with cargo. During the 1991 Gulf War, Aqaba was Iraq's chief illicit outlet, but a blockade slowed traffic considerably. Aqaba has bounced back in recent years—trade has resumed, and the open border with Israel has exposed the city to tourism.

✵ ORIENTATION

Aqaba consists of one elongated beach extending from the royal villa on the Israeli border to the huge, fenced-in port facilities 4km southeast down the arching corniche. Luxury hotels and military complexes have gobbled up a good part of the beach near town. **Four countries** come together in the small northern tip of the Gulf of Aqaba: Egypt meets Israel near the conspicuous resort hotels at Taba, Israel's Eilat faces Jordan's Aqaba across the border, and Saudi Arabia looms to the southeast (for information on **border crossings,** see p. 404).

Shops line the streets of central Aqaba, branching around the post office and behind the **Hussein Ibn 'Ali Mosque.** South of the port and 10km from central Aqaba, the **ferry dock** handles the thousands of Egyptian workers and occasional foreign travelers who cross the Gulf of Aqaba to Nuweiba' in Egypt. About 1km past the ferry port, you'll come to the **Marine Research Center** building; past that lie Aqaba's finest coral reefs and a sandy beach that stretches south to the Saudi border.

⬓ TRANSPORTATION

Airplanes: Royal Jordanian (tel. 201 24 03) has 2 regular flights per day to and from Amman (1hr., JD30). Their office is a 10-min. walk northeast of town on Ash-Sharif al-Hussein Ibn 'Ali St., just past the rotary. Some hotels run buses from Aqaba International Airport to the center of the city. Taxis cost JD2 per person.

Buses and Service: The **minibus station** (tel. 201 63 78) is uphill past the post office; turn right onto King Talal St. and walk 2 blocks. Daily minibuses to **Petra** leave when they're full (2hr.; officially at 8:30, 10:30am, noon; JD3). Sometimes another bus departs in early afternoon. Another way to Petra is to take a minibus to **Ma'an** (1½hr., JD1) and catch a Petra bus from there (1½hr., JD1). There is normally only 1 minibus to **Wadi Rum** (1½hr., 7:30am, JD1.50), but during the busy season others also sometimes leave after noon. Check times in advance. **JETT buses** (tel. 201 52 22), just north of the Miramar Hotel, go to Amman (4hr.; 7, 9, 10:30am, 2, 3:30, 4:30pm; JD4).

Taxis: Talal (tel. 201 24 77) offers groups (max. 4 people) quick transport to **Petra** (3hr., JD30), **Wadi Rum** (1¼hr., JD20), and the Aqaba **ferry terminal** (10km, JD3).

Car Rental: Government-controlled prices are US$25-80 per day, plus 44-88¢ per km. Rental agencies include **Rum** (tel. 201 35 81), across from the post office, which is perhaps the cheapest; **Avis** (tel. 202 28 83), downhill from the Jordan National Bank; and **Hertz** (tel. 201 62 06), across from the Aquamarina II Hotel.

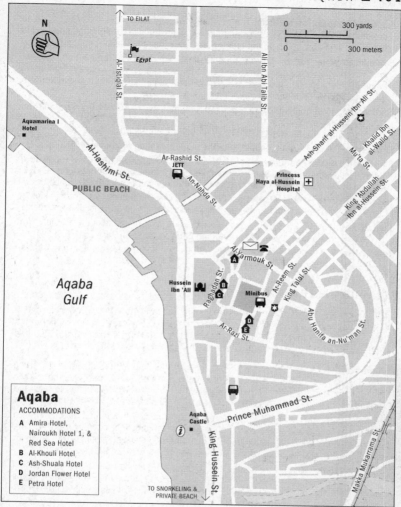

Aqaba

ACCOMMODATIONS

A Amira Hotel,
   Nairoukh Hotel 1, &
   Red Sea Hotel
B Al-Khouli Hotel
C Ash-Shuala Hotel
D Jordan Flower Hotel
E Petra Hotel

ⓘ PRACTICAL INFORMATION

Visitors Center: Tel. 201 33 63 or 37 31. A worthwhile stop on the grounds of the new Islamic Museum, about halfway to the port from the town center. A short walk or a 500fils taxi ride. Maps, brochures, and information on travel to nearby cities. Open Sa-Th 8am-1pm and 5-7pm.

Tourist Police: Tel. 201 35 13, at the Israeli border. **Tourist Office:** tel. 313 363.

Egyptian Consulate: Tel. 201 61 71, on Al-Istiqlal St.; turn right along the curve about 800m northwest of the Aquamarina II Hotel and look for the guard booth in front. Same-day service for **Egyptian visas.** Bring your passport, a photo, and JD12. Open Sa-Th 9am-2pm. Apply for visa 9am-noon, pick-up at 2pm.

Currency Exchange: Arab Bank (tel. 201 35 45), just north of the park in the main square, has an **ATM** that accepts Visa (open Su-Th 8:30am-3pm). **Jordan National Bank** (tel. 202 23 51), 10m downhill from the post office on the 1st right, allows withdrawal with MC. Hefty JD5 commission on traveler's checks. Open Su-Th 8:30am-3pm.

American Express: International Traders Travel Agency Office (tel. 201 37 57). Walk downhill from the post office, take your first left, and continue for 30m; the office is just before the Ali Baba. Will hold mail for anyone. Open daily 8:30am-1pm and 4-7pm.

English Bookstore: Yamani Bookshop (tel. 201 22 21), opposite the post office. Excellent selection of newspapers, magazines, and travel guides. Also sells film, snorkeling equipment, sunscreen, and odds and ends. Open daily 9am-1:30pm and 6-9:30pm. Visa, MC, Diner's Club accepted.

Laundromat: Most hotels provide expensive laundry service. **Al-Abbi Dry Cleaning** (tel. 201 57 22), 1 block down from the minibus and *service* station on King Talal St., is cheaper. Shirts 500fils, pants 700fils. Open Sa-Th 8am-9pm.

Emergency: Police: Tel. 192, across from the minibus station. **Ambulance:** Tel. 193.

Pharmacies: Aqaba Pharmacy (tel. 201 22 37), next to Jordan Flower Hotel (open Sa-Th 24hr., F midnight-8am and 8pm-midnight; Visa, MC). **Jerusalem Pharmacy** (tel. 201 47 47), on Tunisiyya St. next to the Az-Zeitouna Hotel (open Sa-Th 7:30am-midnight).

Hospital: Princess Haya al-Hussein (tel. 201 41 11), near Royal Jordanian Office. One of Jordan's best hospitals, with decompression chambers and staff who deal with diving accidents.

Post Office: (tel. 201 39 39). Turn left out of the bus station, and take the next left. Next to the large radio tower. **Poste Restante** and **EMS.** Open Sa-Th 7am-7pm, F 8am-1pm.

Telephones: Next to post office. Open daily 7:30am-10pm. Cheaper after 8pm and Fridays.

Telephone Code: 03.

ACCOMMODATIONS

While Aqaba has some of the highest prices in Jordan (after Petra), there are several good values. Many hotels add a 10% tax to prices. The only legal **camping** north of the port is in the lots beside some of the larger hotels; the Aqaba Hotel also has a small site, and the JD6 fee admits you to the private beach and showers.

Nairoukh Hotel 1 (tel. 201 92 84/5), behind Ata 'Ali and 'Ali Baba restaurants. There are 2 Nairoukhs; this one is between the Amira and Red Sea Hotels. The staff cleans incessantly, and the place sparkles. Spacious rooms with A/C, TV, fridge, towels, and phone. Singles JD14; doubles JD18; triples JD25. Breakfast JD1.5. Add 10% tax.

Red Sea Hotel (tel./fax 201 21 56). Next door to Nairoukh I. Somewhat dark and dingy, with basic rooms and bathrooms. Be sure to get a room with a "Western toilet." The manager 'Amer is a great resource, and can arrange snorkeling excursions with lunch for JD18. Singles with bath JD7; doubles JD10. Add JD4-5 for A/C, TV, fridge.

Ash-Shuala Hotel (tel. 201 51 53; fax 201 51 60), on Raghadan St., behind the Hussein Ibn 'Ali Mosque. A luxury hotel with low prices. Color TV and refrigerators; some rooms have bidets, balconies, free breakfast, and a charming view of Eilat. Singles JD16; doubles JD28. 10% tax added to prices.

Amira Hotel (tel. 201 88 40; fax 201 25 59), next to Nairoukh I. You're sure to A(d)mira the TV, towels, fridge, private baths, and A/C. Singles JD14; doubles JD18; triples JD25.

Al-Khouli Hotel (tel. 203 01 52), in the square behind Ash-Shuala Hotel. Small entrance, bigger rooms. A/C, fans, and phones. Singles JD14; doubles JD16. Be sure to bargain.

Jordan Flower Hotel (tel. 201 43 77; fax 201 43 78), in the commercial area across the park from the Arab Bank. Dreary entrance with comfortable rooms, some with balcony seaview. Ceiling fans and outside bathrooms. Singles JD5, with A/C and fridge JD7.5; doubles JD6/12; triples JD12/18.

FOOD

Fresh fish, the obvious staple of a seaside town, is surprisingly hard to find in Aqaba. The low plankton count in the clear northern waters of the Gulf of Aqaba forces hungry sea creatures to forage elsewhere. Jordanians are not permitted to fish the richer Saudi waters, and the Egyptian export tax is outlandish. A **market,** where you can fill up on fresh fruit, bread, and cheese, sprawls behind the Ash-Shuala Hotel, though your delicate nostrils may be overwhelmed on windless summer days (open daily 7am-11pm). Shops around the square sell everything from ice cream to **fried sloth.** Many restaurants cluster around the Aquamarina II Hotel, and lamb, beef, and falafel are everywhere around the Hussein Ibn 'Ali Mosque. **Gelato Uno,** near Tikka Chicken, serves frozen treats (open 10am-midnight).

Ash-Shami Restaurant (tel. 201 61 07), next to Ash-Shuala Hotel, across from the mosque. Probably the best food for your fils in the main district. Go with a group and get a mixed appetizer plate (JD3) and a mixed grill (JD2.5). Open 10:30am-1am.

'Ali Baba Restaurant (tel. 201 39 01), near the Nairoukh I Hotel, next door to Hani 'Ali Restaurant. 'Ali Baba's outside terrace is a great place to people-watch. Top-notch *baba ganoush* 500fils, hamburgers JD1.75, and a huge variety of steaks (JD7). Open daily 9am-11pm. Visa, MC, AmEx accepted.

Hani 'Ali Restaurant (tel. 201 52 00), next to Ali Baba Restaurant. Hani 'Ali is always crowded with customers noisily munch, munch, munching on its reasonably priced, world-class pastries. Open daily 7am-10pm.

Captain's Restaurant (tel. 201 69 05), on An-Nahda St., by the Aquamarina II Hotel. Look for the blue and white veranda. One of Aqaba's best, but it goes a bit overboard on the naval decor. Spaghetti with fresh cheese JD1.75, meat dishes JD2.5-5.5, and simple omelettes 500fils. Open daily 9am-11pm.

China Restaurant (tel. 201 44 15), on the 3rd floor of the building behind the post office. Gaudy red interior and varied menu of quality food (entrees JD2-4). Hits the spot for those with a hankering for Chinese. Open daily 11:30am-3pm and 6:30-11pm.

Tikka Chicken (tel. 201 36 33), An-Nahda St., west of the Aquamarina II Hotel on the right. Seven different chicken dishes with various side dishes JD1.75-2.5. Herbivores will enjoy the veggie salad (500fils) and hummus (500fils). Open daily noon-midnight.

SIGHTS

RUINS OF AILA. Aqaba should thank its lucky starfish for its aquatic splendors, because the sights above sea level are all washed up. The recently discovered ruins of **Aila** are the only exception; in a plain beachside lot across from the Miramar Hotel, archaeologists have uncovered the original 120m by 160m city. From the 7th to 10th centuries CE, Aila ("god" in Aramaic) was an early Islamic port, trading as far away as China. Visitors are free to wander amid signs explaining the paltry ruins. Items recovered in the excavations, including Greek and Arabic inscriptions and pottery shards, are displayed in the recently completed **Aqaba Museum,** in the same building as the Visitor's Center, between the castle and the southern waterfront. *(Open W-M in summer 8am-1pm and 4-6pm; in winter 3-5pm. Admission JD1.)*

PHARAOH'S ISLAND. An accord between Jordan and Egypt has recently opened up the Egyptian **Pharaoh's Island** (known in Arabic as **Jeziret Far'aun**), 7km off shore, to tourists from Jordan (see p. 166). The **Aquamarina Hotel** (tel. 201 62 50) runs full-day trips to the island for JD24 (reserve at least 2 days ahead). The Aquamarina also runs day-long snorkeling jaunts (JD10) and daytrips to **Wadi Rum** (JD38.5).

UNDERWATER ADVENTURES

BEACHES. A free and relatively clean **public beach** awaits near the Miramar Hotel. The majority of Aqaba's cleaner, emptier, and more scenic public beaches are quite far away. The **Aqaba Hotel** has a gorgeous white sand beach, but will gouge you JD2.2 for the privilege of burning your feet (shade and lounge chairs are reserved for guests). Southeast of downtown, a free **pebble beach** hides behind a "Restricted Area—No Camping" sign. It's mostly a male scene, and women may become the focus of unwanted attention. The beaches south of the port, off the road leading to Saudi Arabia, are more remote but have beautiful views and great snorkeling.

SNORKELING. **Yemeniyyeh Reef,** just south of the Marine Research Center beyond the port, ranks among the world's best for scoping fish. The **Royal Diving Center** (tel. 201 70 35; fax 201 70 97) in the Yemeniyyeh area can help you get into the water. They rent snorkeling gear (JD3) and conduct beach dives (JD10, for two JD17). Novices can enroll in a six-day dive course for JD300. Entrance to the center costs JD2, which includes use of the beach next door. A bus runs to and from all major hotels in Aqaba (to the diving center at 9am, back to Aqaba at 4-5pm) for JD1. Otherwise, it is a 15min. taxi ride south of the city. Most luxury hotels also rent out equipment and organize outings. Armed with a mask, snorkel, and pair of fins, aquatic adventurers can wander off on their own to some of the more isolated spots near the Saudi border, where the fish run on super-octane. For important information on snorkeling and scuba diving, see **Scub-etter Watch Out,** p. 159.

SCUBA DIVING. The **Seastar Watersports Center** (tel. 201 41 31 or 32; fax 201 41 33), in the Al-Cazar Hotel, conducts dives daily at 9am and 2pm (arrive 30min. early; 1 dive JD24, 2 JD38, discounts for multiple dives). JD7 rents snorkeling gear for a day (prices include transportation). Beginners can take a test dive for JD34; a full PADI scuba course costs JD280. The **Yamani Bookshop,** oddly enough, has a good selection of masks and fins (see **Practical Information,** p. 452). The **Aquamarina Club** (tel. 201 62 50), at the Aquamarina Hotel, offers a number of **water sports,** including waterskiing (JD4), wind surfing (JD5 per hour), or tubing (JD2).

NEAR PETRA AND AQABA: WADI RUM وادي رام

Taxis constantly run to Wadi Rum (1hr. from Aqaba, 2hr. from Petra; JD15-20). *Buses* and *service* along the Desert Highway can drop passengers off 25km north of Aqaba at the turnoff marked "Rum 30km." From here it is possible to hitch a ride to the Government Rest House at Wadi Rum. Hitching, always risky, is feasible in the summer due to the lack of traffic. Another option is to rent a car in Aqaba (see p. 450). Four-wheel drive vehicles are not necessary unless you plan to explore the desert on your own. The Aquamarina Hotel in Aqaba arranges daytrips to Wadi Rum (see p. 450). Buses leave Wadi Rum in the morning for **Petra** (2hr., 8:30am, JD3) and **Aqaba** (1½hr., JD1.5)—inquire about exact times. **Admission** JD1, includes a complimentary cup of tea or coffee; JD5 extra if you bring in your own car.

Two tectonic plates split to create the sublime desert valley of Rum. At the northern end of the *wadi* lies the village of Rum, home to hundreds of Bedouin, the Desert Police, and the Government Rest House. At the southern end of the valley stands the fort of the **Desert Camel Corps,** the descendants of the British-trained Arab Legion. The unabashed members of the Desert Patrol proudly pose for photographs in their green robes and red *kafiyas.* When not posing for visitors, they chase smugglers and renegade Bedouin or offer desert jaunts to beautiful star-gazing areas.

Just beyond the village of Rum, a vast wilderness of sand and rock begins. Massive, rust-colored cliffs tower over the desert floor, some shooting up to heights of 1700m. Although there is little escape from the sun during the day, the evening brings fantastic shadows, transforming the desert into a vast jigsaw puzzle of light and dark. The whopping slabs of granite and sandstone erupted from beneath the desert floor millions of years ago; it's easy to imagine that Wadi Rum has not changed a bit since then. In *Seven Pillars of Wisdom,* **T.E. Lawrence** (better known as Lawrence of Arabia) wrote that when he passed between these rusty crags, his

A ROCKIN' GOOD TIME A fabulous but little-known way to enjoy Wadi Rum is by **rock climbing.** Many Europeans (especially the French) arrive each year, suited up for sheer-face scaling in this spectacular region. Experienced climbers will take thrillseekers on trips, and their prices generally won't put you between a rock and a hard place. One recommended guide to seek out is Sabbah Atieeq. Inquire at the Rest House for the rock climbing book, containing descriptions of a number of different climbing routes and visitors' accounts of their adventures. If you want to climb but don't have equipment, you can rent some from a Bedouin guide. One day of climbing, including equipment rental and a guide, costs around JD35. Rock on!

"little caravan fell quiet, ashamed to flaunt itself in the presence of such stupendous hills." The hills and dunes are still as stupendous as they were in Lawrence's time, and provide a magnificent setting for a few days of desert exploration and camping.

With its other-worldly lavender mountains backdropped by an empty sky, Wadi Rum had earned the name **Valley of the Moon.** For JD5, a Bedouin will lead you by camel to a crack in the rocks, the origin of the springs that support all of the *wadi*'s life. Dark stains point out the conduits carved by the ancient Nabateans to conserve the precious water. You may also be shown **Lawrence's Well,** where T.E. used to doze beside a small spring bursting forth from the rocks. A large concrete cistern now holds the spring's water. The Bedouin can point out the many mammoth boulders inscribed with millennia-old graffiti. Other sights include the **Rock Bridge,** a massive rock with an arch through the middle, and the elusive **moving sand dune,** an enormous red mountain of sand.

The village is the base for desert explorations. While a camel ride certainly gets you and your backside into the spirit of things, jeeps cover more ground. A sign in the Rest House lists possible destinations. Camel rides start at JD7 for a two-hour trip to the Well, and go up to JD30 for an overnight trip. Trips can be arranged through the **tourist police** (tel. 218 215) at the Rest House. The **tourist office** is also helpful (tel. 332 115). For jeep trips, try to gather a group of up to six at the Rest House to share the cost. A full-day jeep itinerary, with climbs through narrow *siqs* and hikes up sand dunes, goes for JD40. A good option is to take a four- to five-hour jeep or truck trip that visits a number of the sights. Plan to visit at dusk, when the *wadi* explodes with color. The only place to stay in the village is the **Government Rest House** (tel. 201 88 67). Guests can sleep on the roof (JD2) or in one of the tents (JD3). Breakfast costs JD3, other meals JD6. A half dozen supermarkets provide pricey provisions. A large tent beside the Rest House is often the site of traditional Bedouin music and singing in the evenings. You can arrange an **overnight** in the desert for the official Rest House price of JD30-40—save JD10-15 by arranging a trip directly with a Bedouin. A night in the desert is truly unforgettable.

JORDAN

LEBANON لبنان

US$1=L£1519.50 LEBANESE POUNDS
CDN$1=L£971.52
UK£1=L£2489.32
AUS$1=L£859.96
SAR1=L£237.80
EUR1=L£1661.73
JD1 (JORDANIAN DINAR) =L£2146.19
S£100 (SYRIAN POUNDS) =L£3630

L£1000=US$0.66
L£1000=CDN$1.03
L£1000=UK£0.40
L£1000=AUS$1.16
L£1000=SAR3.05
L£1000=EUR0.60
L£1000=JD0.47
L£1000=S£27.54

PHONE FACTS   Country Code: 961. Police: Tel. 112.

Lebanon has long enjoyed its privileged position at the crossroads of three continents, proving its resilience over millennia of razings by foreign invaders and natural disasters. Before the recent 15-year civil war, Lebanon was the multi-faceted "jewel of the Middle East," with clean *souqs*, ritzy hotels, hot fashions, and dirt-cheap prices. The self-proclaimed sophistication of the Lebanese is a blend of Mediterranean and Arab elements with a healthy dose of panache from the French, whose 1918-1943 occupation of the area left a lasting impression on the cuisine, language, and culture. In the political sphere, four major religious groups—Sunni and Shi'ite Muslims, Druze, and Christians of different denominations—vie for power and influence. In times of peace, this diversity adds flavor to the famed sights and natural splendor of the country; tension can make it explosive.

The country has emerged from the civil war with its spirit (if not its structures) intact, and it now welcomes back a growing number of tourists. Beirut in particular is rising from the ashes of its internal strife more alive than ever. Large areas of the capital are being rebuilt and rejuvenated. Ba'albeck's international festival, world famous in the 1960s, is once again a hot ticket. Ancient cities, pristine mountains, hot springs, and other historical and natural monuments make Lebanon a worthwhile destination; the ambitious and worldly spirit of its people make it unique.

HIGHLIGHTS OF LEBANON

■ Shop, Rock, 'n Roll: sample the international flavor of **Beirut** (p. 463), best known for its cheap-cheap, *chi-chi* shopping and party-til-dawn discotheques and nightclubs.
■ The stellar Roman ruins and world-famous cultural festival at **Ba'albeck** (p. 482) will make you long for the days of pagan abandon.
■ The amazing Umayyad ruins at **A'anjar** (p. 484) are some of the best in the Middle East

ESSENTIALS

ENTRY

Travelers need a visa to enter Lebanon, and many will need to arrange for one well in advance. Citizens of **Canada, Ireland,** the **U.K.,** and the **U.S.** can obtain a visa upon arrival at Beirut International Airport or at any official surface-entry border post. Single entry visas cost US$35 and are valid for three months; multiple entry visas cost US$70. Travelers with an **Israeli stamp** in their passports will be denied entry. If you need to obtain a visa in advance, print out an application online at www.embofleb.org/visas.htm#Tourist Visa. You can also send a letter of request to the nearest embassy or consulate, specifying length of stay and the reason for your trip. Applications must include one passport-sized photo, a contact address

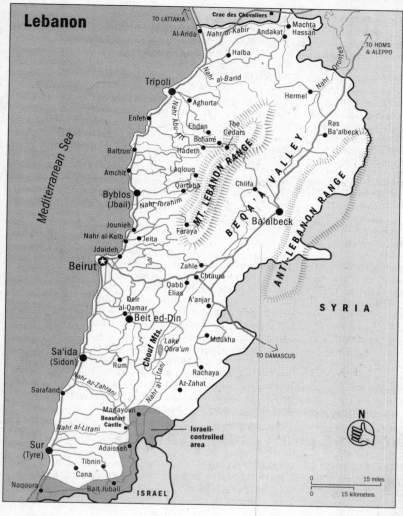

Lebanon

TO LATTAKIA
Crac des Chevaliers
Al-Arida
Nahr al-Kabir
Andakat
Machta Hassan

TO HOMS & ALEPPO

Halba
Orontes

Nahr al-Barid
Tripoli
Aghorta
Hermel

Enfeh
Nahr Abu-'Ali
Ehden
The Cedars
Ras Ba'albeck

Baltrun
Bcharré
Hádeth

Amchit
Laqlouq

Byblos (Jbail)
Qartaba
Chlifa

Nahr Ibrahim

Jounieh
Faraya
Ba'albeck

Nahr al-Kalb
Jeita

Jdaideh
Beirut
Zahle

Qabb Elias
Chtaura

Deir al-Qamar
A'anjar

Beit ed-Din

Mediterranean Sea

MT. LEBANON RANGE

BEQA-A VALLEY

ANTI-LEBANON RANGE

Sa'ida (Sidon)
Rum
Lake Qara'un
Mdukha

Chouf Mts.

TO DAMASCUS

Sarafand
Nahr az-Zahrani
Nahr al-Litani
Rachaya
Az-Zahat

Marjayoun
Beaufort Castle
Nahr al-Litani

Sur (Tyre)
Adaisseh
Israeli-controlled area

Tibnin

Naqoura
Cana
Bait Jubail
ISRAEL

SYRIA

N

0   15 miles
0   15 kilometers

LEBANON

in Lebanon (any Beirut hotel is fine), a money order for the type of visa you are requesting, your passport, and a self-addressed stamped envelope.

EMBASSIES AND CONSULATES

Embassies and consulates for other countries in Lebanon are all located in **Beirut** (see **Practical Information,** p. 467). Lebanese embassies and consulates abroad include: **Australia,** 27 Endeavour St., Red Hill ACT 2603, Canberra (tel. (02) 6295 7378; fax 6239 7024) or Level 5-70 William St., Sydney NSW 2000; **Canada,** 640 Lyons St. Ottawa, Ontario, K1S 3Z5 (tel. 613-236-5825 or 5855; fax 232-1609) or 40 Ct. St. Catherine, Montreal, Quebec H2V 2A2 (tel. (514) 276-2638; fax 276-0090); **U.K.,** 21 Kensington Palace Gardens, London W84QN (tel. (020) 7229 7265/7266; fax 7243 1699); and **U.S.,** 2560 28th St. NW, Washington, D.C. 20008 (tel. 202-939-6300; fax 939-6324) or 9 E. 76th St., New York, NY 10021 (tel. 212-744-7905; fax 794 1510).

⚑ BORDER CROSSINGS

TO SYRIA. Crossing into Syria may take a long time due to hyper-security at the border. Daily buses run from Tripoli or Beirut to Damascus, and from Beirut north to Aleppo and Lattakia. Though costly, it's possible to hire a *service* to Damascus. Citizens of Australia, Canada, the U.K., the U.S., and most European countries must obtain a Syrian visa before embarking on the border crossing; visas should be procured from one's home country in advance, as there is no Syrian representation in Lebanon and it is difficult to get a visa at the Syrian embassy in Amman. In a pinch, go to the Immigration Office in Marseh Sq. in Damascus and request an **exit visa** that entitles you to another visa at the Syrian border. This unusual request will require much bureaucratic dilly-dallying and is to be avoided if possible.

TO ISRAEL. Though Lebanon borders Israel, direct travel between the two countries is impossible at this time. Most travelers go to Syria, then into Jordan, where the Israeli border is open (see **Border Crossings: To Israel**, p. 404).

GETTING AROUND

Taxis and **service** are indistinguishable. Most *service* cast aside their plebeian airs and become ultra-expensive private taxis the minute they see a newly arrived foreigner. Be firm when approaching a taxi and have a landmark or region of the city in mind. When the taxi slows down, shout the name of your destination through the window. If the taxi driver already has passengers, he will either invite you inside or quickly drive off. If the cab is empty, say *"service"* and the taxi should stop. *Service* stop around 11pm or midnight. Most **buses** are privately owned and efficient. Some are luxury Pullmans, while others are older school bus-style vehicles with vinyl seats, no air conditioning, and tacky interiors. The only way to find out schedules is to ask locals. While it is possible to rent a **car** in Beirut, it is not advisable. There are few universally understood or respected traffic signals in Lebanon, and most drivers are graduates of the bat-out-of-hell school of driving. While **hitchhiking** is common in some rural areas, it is dangerous and not recommended by *Let's Go* due to the tense political situation in the mountains of southern Lebanon. Most places are accessible by *service* or bus anyway.

TOURIST AND TRAVEL SERVICES

MEDICAL EMERGENCIES AND HEALTH. In a medical emergency, dial 140 for an **ambulance** or 865 561 for the **Red Cross**. In Beirut, head to the **American University Hospital** in Hamra (see p. 468). **Pharmacies** generally have someone on hand who can prescribe medication for those who know what they need.

USEFUL ADDRESSES. For tourist information, contact one of the **Lebanon Tourist Offices** abroad: in **Egypt,** 1 Talaat Harb St., Maidan At-Tahrir, Cairo (tel./fax 202 393 75 29); in **France,** Office du Tourisme Libanais, 124, Rue du Faubourg St. Honoré, 75008 Paris (tel. (33) 1 4359 1036; fax 1 4359 1199 or 1 4359 1213); and in the **U.K.,** Lebanon Tourist and Information Office, 90 Piccadilly St., London W1V 9HB (tel. (44) 20 7409 2031; fax 7493 4929; email abdallah@lebanon.demon.co.uk).

MONEY MATTERS

CURRENCY AND EXCHANGE. The basic unit of currency is the **Lebanese pound** (L£), sometimes known locally as the **lira**. Bills are in denominations of L£500, 1000, 10,000, 50,000, and 100,000, while coins of L£250 and 500 are now in circulation. U.S. dollars are widely accepted, especially at restaurants and hotels, although all transactions are officially supposed to be made in Lebanese pounds.

BUSINESS HOURS. Government offices are open M-Sa 8:30am-2pm and F 8-11am. Banks are open M-Sa 8:30am-12:30pm. Businesses are usually open M-Sa 9am-6pm. Muslim shops may close on Fridays. The Lebanese week ends on Sunday.

TIPPING AND BAKHSHEESH. *Bakhsheesh* (see p. 12) may be necessary in out of the way places, but is not as widespread as in Egypt, Jordan, and Syria. Since prices are higher and travelers tend to be wealthier than those in other countries, spoiled guards and officials may expect more palm-greasing than their counterparts in other countries. Liberal tipping at restaurants is expected; *service* drivers do not expect tips, but taxi drivers should get a little something extra (especially for long rides or ones that include many military checkpoints).

ACCOMMODATIONS

Accommodations are neither plentiful nor cheap. Wartime inflation caused prices to skyrocket, and lodging prices are particularly astronomical. Accommodations fall under three unofficial categories: uninhabitable but very cheap, "middle range" establishments that start at around US$20 per night, and luxury resort havens patronized mostly by vacationing Arabs from the Gulf States. **Campsites** are not well publicized; ask at the tourist office to reserve a spot.

KEEPING IN TOUCH

MAIL. Poste Restante is not the reliable service it was before the war. Mail sent to the main post office in Beirut has been known to disappear. There are many **DHL** offices (but no Federal Express), and as of press time, mail took longer to get to the U.S. than to Europe and Australia due to the dearth of trans-Atlantic flights in or out of Beirut. Packages take up to four days for international express delivery.

TELEPHONE, FAX, AND INTERNET ACCESS. International calls can be placed from public telephone offices—there is one in every Beirut district, though not in every Lebanese city. **Phonecards** are also becoming increasingly common. **AT&T operators** can be accessed from any phone: dial 426 801 in Beirut, and add 01 outside Beirut (charged as a call to Beirut). Telex and **fax** services are available, mostly in Beirut. **Internet access** is easy to find in all the urban centers. In major cities like Beirut and Tripoli, Internet access might be easier to find than a phone with a reliable long-distance connection. Rural villages lag behind in this respect, but everything in Lebanon is only a daytrip from Beirut.

WOMEN TRAVELERS

Women traveling alone should not have much trouble: gender relations in Lebanon are arguably the most comfortable in the Middle East, thanks mostly to the influence of the French. Women should be aware that Lebanese men may give them unwanted attention: this may be nothing more than leers and catcalls, but many women report unsavory offers ranging from a night on the town to proposals of marriage. There is little violent crime. For more tips, see **Women Travelers**, p. 29.

DRESS AND ETIQUETTE

Lebanon's Westernization is reflected in its liberal attitudes toward dress and demeanor. In the big cities and along the coast, tank tops and shorts are perfectly acceptable for men and women. Both sexes should dress modestly when touring the country's rural areas and when visiting monasteries and other religious sites.

LIFE AND TIMES

ANCIENT HISTORY

The earliest settlers of Lebanon were the **Phoenicians** from the Arabian Peninsula (3500 BCE), who spread their 22-letter alphabet wherever they went and established Beirut, Ba'albeck, and the important port cities of Byblos, Sidon, and Tyre. The people of **Tyre** were particularly resourceful, building one of the first business empires in history nearly 3000 years ago. The sailing-savvy Phoenicians from Tyre also founded the city of **Carthage** in the 9th century BCE and left it under the rule of **Queen Dido**, who eventually went mad with love and hurled herself atop a sword. The remaining Tyrian settlers cut their own swathe through the heart of the Mediterranean, colonizing parts of Cyprus, Rhodes, and the Aegean Islands before sailing around Africa and discovering the Straits of Gibraltar.

Egyptian domination of the Phoenician cities began in 1500 BCE and was long-lived but fairly ineffective, like any modern-day Egyptian bureaucracy. Life under the invading **Assyrians** was downright brutal. The relative prosperity of the age of city-states only returned once Phoenicia became part of the **Persian Empire** under King Cyprus in 538 BCE. **Alexander the Great** overthrew the Persians in 332 BCE, marking the beginning of the Greco-Macedonian cultural domination of the Middle East during the following centuries. Phoenicia was thoroughly Greek when the Romans (themselves a belligerent carbon copy of the Greeks) made Phoenicia a part of the province of Syria under **Pompey** in 64 BCE. Phoenicia was a rather safe and uneventful place throughout the Roman and Byzantine era, and its geographical inaccessibility made it a refuge for minorities fleeing persecution during those religiously volatile times. In the 7th century CE, the Christian sect that later became the **Maronite Church** settled in the northern districts of the Lebanese mountains to avoid conversion to Islam by the Arabs that controlled the area until the arrival of the Christian Crusaders in the 11th century. The Shi'ite Muslim sect also sought refuge there during the 9th century, and the Druze followed suit two centuries later. This situation would have serious repercussions in modern times.

MODERN HISTORY

Muslim Druze and Christian Maronites co-existed peacefully under **Ottoman** rule, but once the Turks' power began to decline, the two sects started fighting ruthlessly until the end of WWI, when the League of Nations authorized the **French** government to pick through the ruins of faction-ravaged Lebanon and institute reforms in everything from politics to health care. Educational reforms formalized the study of the Arabic language, which fed into the rising tide of Pan-Arabism washing over much of the Middle East in the postwar era.

In 1926, Lebanon became a republic in name only: the French did not grant independence until November 22, 1943. The infant government that came to power was militantly nationalistic and tried to cut itself off from France immediately and completely; riots erupted when the French refused to comply and strong-armed their way back into the Lebanese government. The country reeked so much of anti-French sentiment, however, that the French finally departed after WWII. The U.S. has been the most important Western influence on Lebanese society since—an interesting cultural clash evidenced by modern-day Beirut's many McDonald's-lined *rues* and *boulevards*.

Postwar Western leanings concentrated governmental power in the hands of Lebanon's Christian population, to the exclusion of the Muslim citizenry. When Yassir Arafat moved the headquarters of the **Palestinian Liberation Organization (PLO)** to Beirut from Amman, Jordan in 1970, however, the stormy political climate in Lebanon turned torrential. The PLO added their numbers to the growing Muslim population, making Christians the minority. Fearing PLO guerilla activity, the Christian government (with the help of the Lebanese National Army) retaliated as a "defense" measure—an act of outright aggression in the eyes of many Lebanese Muslims. Many soldiers defected and joined anti-Christian opposition factions, leaving the National Army weakened by 1980.

In the 1970s, Israel began attacking the southern half of the country, where PLO forces were stationed. Much of the predominantly Shi'ite Muslim population in the area migrated to Beirut to escape these attacks, cinching the western half of the capital with an impoverished **"Belt of Misery"** that barely contained the overflowing gut of Maronite wealth in the eastern half of Beirut. On June 6, 1982, Israel initiated **Operation Peace for Galilee**, a cheerful-sounding plan that actually involved surrounding and shelling Beirut at an immense civilian cost. This attack led to a public outcry against the ruthless Israeli military tactics, which in turn led to the formation of the fundamentalist Muslim group **Hezbollah** ("Party of God"), determined to act with more immediacy and extremity than the PLO had.

The Lebanese civil war came to the global forefront in 1982 (although it had officially begun in 1975), after Islamic fundamentalists started taking hostages. The target for kidnappings were Westerners who lived and worked in Beirut, particularly those who lived in the expat **Hamra** district. In July, **David Dodge** (president of the American University of Beirut) became the first foreign hostage, and such tactics persisted until the last hostage was released in June 1992; by then, 50 foreigners had been taken, some kept chained and blindfolded for five years. The U.S. government instituted a ban on American citizens' travel to Lebanon that lasted until 1997; the U.S. government still does not consider travel in Lebanon to be safe. Europeans visited the country for several years before the U.S. ban was lifted.

Part of the rebuilding of the country has required restructuring the government. Until 1990, an unwritten agreement called the **National Pact** required that the President be a Maronite Christian, the Prime Minister a Sunni Muslim, the speaker of Parliament a Shi'ite Muslim, and the Chief of the Armed Forces a Druze. This arrangement had contributed to the civil war: because of high Muslim birth rates and Christian emigration, Muslims began to outnumber Christians and became discontent with Christian minority rule. Under the reforms of the **peace accord** that ended the civil war in 1990, many of the powers of the Christian president were shifted to a half-Christian, half-Muslim cabinet, and the Muslim Prime Minister was required to countersign presidential decrees.

Parliamentary elections were held in 1992, with Hezbollah winning the largest number of seats. Current Lebanese President **Emile Lahoud** was elected in October 1998 with the hope that his work reforming the Lebanese National Army in the aftermath of the civil war would meet with similar success in the political world. Lahoud assumed the Presidency over a country in a politically uncertain but eager position. Political apathy is discouraged by law; voting is mandatory for all males 21 years and over. Women, on the other hand, can petition for the right to vote when they reach age 21 if they have an elementary-school education.

Because Lebanon has virtually no natural resources, the economy is dependent on banking, commerce, and tourism. Before the war, the country was the "gateway to the Mediterranean"—backpackers and royalty frolicked side by side. It was also the banking capital of the Middle East, holding half the wealth of the Arab world in secret bank accounts. Wartime inflation forced the economy to adopt a more stable currency than the Lebanese pound; the invisible hand chose the U.S. dollar.

IN THE NEWS

June 3, 1999 saw the withdrawal of the Israel-backed **South Lebanon Army (SLA)** from Jezzine, a town outside of the "security zone" formed by Israel as a buffer against attacks from Hezbollah. This withdrawal marks the end of 14 years of SLA occupation and is the first step in Israeli Prime Minister Barak's pledge to pull Israeli troops out of Lebanon within a year. According to General Lahad, the leader of the SLA, troops are being pulled out because they cannot "handle any more deaths;" however, Israeli officials say the removal is a test of the Lebanese government's willingness to prevent Hezbollah from using evacuated areas for attacks on Israel. The Lebanese government seemed to have failed the test: as the SLA moved out, Hezbollah guerrillas resumed missile attacks (resulting in the death of two SLA soldiers), and Israeli and Hezbollah forces are now embroiled in a tit-for-tat bombing struggle. The 200-odd SLA men who stayed behind in Jezzine have surrendered and may face trial for collaborating with Israeli forces. Nevertheless, Lebanese president Emile Lahoud received a warm welcome when he made a surprise visit to the town, so things may be looking up.

RELIGION AND ETHNICITY

Lebanon's religious composition differs greatly from that of the rest of the Arab world. The country has more **Shi'ite** than Sunni Muslims (who are the Islamic majority most everywhere else in the world) and also has a sizeable **Druze** population of about 300,000. **Maronite Christians** are rare in most of the world, but in Lebanon (the birthplace of their sect) they are the most prevalent Christian denomination. The beginnings of Maronite Christianity are unclear; the sect is named after St. Maron, a 5th-century hermit from Syria, and St. John Maron, a monk who later preached St. Maron's theology. For the most part, religious groups have remained geographically separate. Before the start of the war, Shi'ite Muslim communities dominated southern Lebanon (including Sur) and the northeast region along the Syrian border. The Maronite Christian population held the majority in central Lebanon, including Eastern Beirut, and the northwestern coastline approaching Tripoli. Tripoli, northern Lebanon, and western Beirut were populated primarily by Sunni Muslims.

LANGUAGE

The official language of Lebanon is **Arabic,** but it is unique among its neighbors in the degree of **French** that is spoken. Many people speak **English** as well (English is the most widely spoken language in most of Beirut). Street signs throughout Lebanon are written in Arabic and French. Radio programming airs in French, English, and Arabic. French is taught in predominantly Christian areas, while English is more common as a second language among Muslims; there is also a minority of Armenian speakers. There is no local English daily newspaper, but newsstands carry an assortment of British and American dailies and weekly magazines. A local English-language weekly, *Monday Morning,* reviews local news and social events. The local French newspaper is *L'Orient le Jour.*

THE ARTS

LITERATURE. Largely because of its liberal political history, Lebanon has one of the richest and most diverse literary traditions in the Arab world. In the 19th century, Beirut led a broad Arab cultural renaissance. Mystic, metaphysical poet, novelist, and artist **Khalil Gibran** is most famous for his work *The Prophet;* a museum in his hometown, Bcharré (p. 481), is devoted to his life and works. **Amin Ma'alouf** has published four historical novels in French that have established his presence as a Lebanese writer. He made history when his novel *The Rock of Tanios,* about a 19th-century Lebanese village, won the distinguished French *Prix de Goncourt* in 1993. **Amin Rihani** is another well-known 20th-century poet whose work is classified as *Adab Al-Mahjar,* or "Literature of the Migration." Influenced by American poet Walt Whitman, Rihani introduced free verse into Arabic poetry. These writers and many modern Lebanese authors often wrote from abroad. What makes their work "Lebanese" is its enduring fascination with and love of Beirut, its interest in the problems of war and strife, and its form. Lebanese **poetry** has developed a distinctive form, the *zajal,* where verses are sung rather than recited. World literature has also contemplated the civil war. Kamal Salibi's *A House of Many Mansions—The History of Lebanon Reconsidered* recounts events of the war.

Robert Fisk's *Pity the Nation: Lebanon at War* gives a first-hand account of the conflict and its major players. Italian journalist Oriana Fallaci's *Insh'allah* also tackles the topic of the civil war through a personal account of her time in the capital city, and the book has been translated into numerous languages.

VISUAL AND PERFORMING ARTS. Lebanon's cities and villages come alive with annual festivals that feature traditional folk dancing and music. The largest of these is in Ba'albeck (see Ba'albeck, p. 482). **Belly dancing** is a popular form of entertainment at nightclubs and even at private parties. A type of provincial dance is the **dakle,** in which dancers wearing traditional mountain garb enact themes from village life. The national dance is the **dabke,** a line dance performed to the rhythmic beat of feet pounding on the floor.

Modern **theater** in Lebanon took off in the 1950s and 60s, and was featured in many of the annual festivals around the country. The luxurious Hotel al-Bustan in Beit Meri, a suburb of Beirut, hosts Lebanon's main dramatic and musical festival, the **International Festival of the Performing Arts,** for five weeks in February and March. The war has colored theatrical themes: most contemporary theater ponders the effects of conflict. **Cinema** has undergone a similar evolution; the Lebanese film industry now revolves around documentaries somehow incorporating the civil war. Popular movie theaters play mainly American and European films.

FOOD AND DRINK

Lebanese food is known all over the Middle East for its variety, flavor, and quality. Vegetarian dishes are common. **Tabbouleh** is the national dish, made with parsley, *burghul* (cracked wheat), onions, tomatoes, lemon juice, and spices. **Fattoush** is a salad of lettuce, tomato, and cucumber with small pieces of toasted pita mixed in to soak up the dressing. Lebanese *mezze* (appetizers) include any combination of green peppers, cucumbers, radishes, scallions, olives, pickles, hummus, *baba ghanoush*, eggplant, and fuzzy raw almonds. *Mujeddra* is a lentil stew cooked with sauteed onions and spices. *Kibbeh naye* is raw beef and spices, whipped into a dip and eaten with pita. There are different varieties of **pita** as well: *marqooq* is a paper-thin bread cooked on a metal dome in a wood fire, common both in the mountains and at stands in Beirut; *ka'ak* is a sesame bread, molded either into little round balls or breadsticks. These are customarily dipped into coffee.

Lebanese meals often finish with cornucopias of fresh fruit, but sweets are also popular. The best are made with secret recipes closely guarded by those who possess them (mostly Sunni Muslims). Tripoli is especially famous for sweets like *halawat aj-jibn:* unsalted cheese kept in a warm place for a few days and then rolled out with semolina into long sheets with sugar, syrup, and *'ashta* (sweet cream). Lebanon is most famous for its **'araq,** an aniseed liquor similar to Greek *ouzo,* produced in small villages by families that have passed on techniques for years. The non-alcoholic specialty is *jellab,* a raisin syrup served with pine nuts.

BEIRUT بيروت

In the 60s, Beirut was the gateway to the Mediterranean, the meeting point of East and West. Europeans could sample the flavors of the Orient while lounging in familiar comfort, and wealthy Arabs could sneak away to a hedonistic haven of social pleasures condemned by their conservative nations. A tightly knit group of international jet-setters, journalists, and socialites unwound at seaside cafes, casinos, and resorts. During its golden years, Beirut was home to people of many religions and ethnicities, and seemed like a paradise shared by all. The reality, however, was that a growing underclass of disaffected refugees was barely surviving on the edges of the city; exiled Palestinians and Shi'ites were silently witnessing the extravagant lifestyle of the expats and *chi-chi* crowds.

Beirut

ACCOMMODATIONS
A Pension Home Valery
B YWCA
C Mayflower Hotel
D Embassy Hotel
E University Hotel
F West House Residence
G Mushrek Hotel

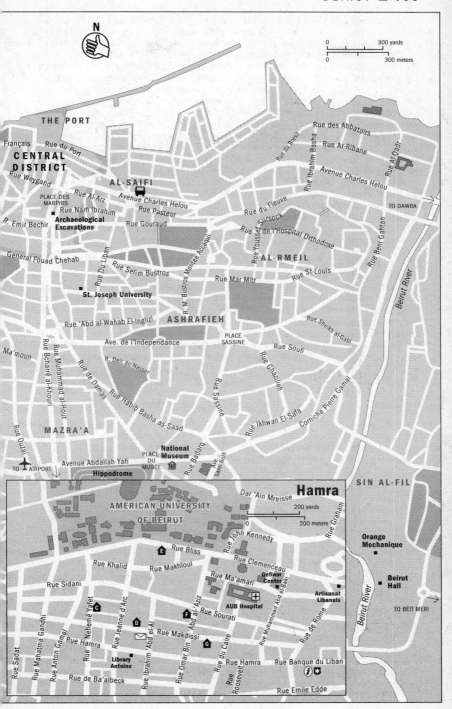

The civil war blew away the illusion of the city as a content, multicultural melting pot, but an overriding sense of nationalism has survived the class and ethnic conflict. Beirut has been dubbed "The City That Would Not Die" by the Ministry of Tourism, and the epithet is well-earned. Some parts of the city were ravaged more than others, but 15 years of constant conflict took its physical and psychological toll on every district. Astounding evidence confirms that Beirut has actually been destroyed seven times—by a tidal wave, fire, several earthquakes, and war—since first gaining fame as the site of a Roman law school in the 3rd century BCE. In spite of present efforts to improve and standardize the city's dishevelled, inconsistent appearance, Beirut remains a town of much visual contrast. At opposite ends of the spectrum lie glittering high-rises and the abject remains of shellshocked neighborhoods, battered into an eerie silence by years of sniper attacks. Rather than fading into obscurity, though, Beirut continues to blossom. Buildings are springing up at a staggering pace, and the city is looking to restake its claim as the Arab world's most cosmopolitan city. For those who can afford the Western-style prices, Beirut is as hedonistic and forward-thinking as any European metropolis. The city's dedication to the capitalist credo is in full effect in its many Internet cafes, jazz clubs, and opulent shopping districts, and its future in the global marketplace seems assured. Arab tourists are returning in force, and even Europeans (and to a lesser extent, Americans) are exploring this erstwhile Paris of the East.

✛ ORIENTATION

Situated on a promontory jutting into the Mediterranean, Beirut is bounded to the north and west by the sea and in all other directions by a mass of closely packed commercial and residential areas. The tourist office and the vast majority of budget accommodations, restaurants, shops are congregated in the **Hamra** district, a roughly rectangular area marked by **Rue Bliss** to the north, **Rue de Rome** to the east, **Rue Emile Edde** to the south, and **Rue Sadat** to the west. This area has also become home to many administrative buildings that used to be downtown until they were destroyed in the war. Just to the north of Rue Bliss is the beautiful **American University of Beirut (AUB)**. The quieter streets of **'Ain Mreisse** are home to even cheaper hotels. To get there, follow **Rue John Kennedy** away from the AUB and turn left on **Rue Graham** towards the sea. The area in front of the Hard Rock Cafe marks the start of the **Corniche**, a nice place to see Beirutis at play.

Avenue de Paris runs parallel to the sea. Following this west for several kilometers brings you to the wealthy district of **Raouche** (RA-oo-sheh), home to many of Beirut's finest restaurants and the famed **Pigeon Rocks**. Heading south, the street becomes **Avenue du General de Gaulle** and passes the fishing harbor before again becoming **Boulevard Sa'ed Salam**, which heads inland. Passing first **Cola Bridge**, then the horse-racing **Hippodrome**, this road arrives finally at the **National Museum**. Just seaward lies the elegant district of **Ashrafieh**, centered around **Place Sassine**. Further north is **Downtown**, once the heart of the city but now one big construction site. Continuing east on Ave. Charles Helou, you come first to the **Charles Helou Bus Terminal** (shar la-LOO) and, several kilometers later, to the transport hub of **Dawra**.

▤ TRANSPORTATION

There are three main transport hubs for **buses** and **service**: Cola Bridge, Charles Helou Bus Terminal, and Dawra. Buses and *service* to all points south of Beirut and the Beqa'a Valley (including Ba'albeck) congregate at **Cola Bridge** in southern Beirut, accessible by any intracity bus heading to the National Museum. Points north of Beirut, as well as buses to Damascus and Amman, depart from the brand-new **Charles Helou Bus Terminal** near the port in western Beirut. Shorter journeys to the north (e.g. Jounieh and Byblos) and intercity *service* taxis all leave from **Dawra** in western Beirut, across the river. Both Dawra and Charles Helou are easily accessible by the intracity buses that terminate at Dawra. For more general information about transportation, see **Getting Around**, p. 458.

GETTING THERE AND AWAY

AIRPLANES. Beirut International Airport (tel. 629 065 or 066), 5km south of downtown, has regular flights to Damascus, Amman, and London. **Taxis** to the airport should cost no more than L£10,000.

BUSES AND SERVICE. Buses depart when full, so schedules are unpredictable. **Lebanese Commuting Company** buses service **Sur** and **Sa'ida** for L£500 from Cola. Buses leave from **Charles Helou** to: **Tripoli** (2hr.; A/C Pullman bus L£2000, less comfy coaches L£1000); **Amman** (8hr., US$20); and **Damascus** (3½hr., L£10,000). Buses depart from **Dawra** to **Byblos** (1½hr., L£500) via **Jounieh** (45min.). Buses stop running at 8 or 9pm. Like buses, **service** depart when full. **Cola Bridge** to: **Sur** (3½hr., L£5000) via **Sa'ida** (2hr., L£1000); **Ba'albeck** (3hr., L£7000); and **Beit ed-Din** (1½hr., L£5000).

CAR RENTAL. There are many car rental companies in Beirut, but by driving you risk life and limb. **Europcar** (tel. 480 480 or 502 200) has an office in the Sa'arti building on Hayek Ave. in Sin al-Fil, and another in 'Ain Mreisse (tel. 602 223). **Budget Rent-a-Car** (tel. 741 740/1) is in the Minkara building on Rue Clemenceau.

GETTING AROUND TOWN

The best way to get around Beirut is on foot. Almost all listings are centrally located in Hamra, and even the walk from 'Ain Mreisse to the Pigeon Rocks takes no more than a pleasant 30 minutes.

BUSES. Intracity buses all cost L£500 and are surprisingly easy to use. Over 20 different lines criss-cross the city, and are ideal for going to well-traveled destinations such as Cola Bridge, the National Museum, Dawra, or the Pigeon Rocks (Raouche). Rather than trying to memorize the route schedule that the Ministry of Tourism hands out, you should treat them like *service* taxis. Stand on the proper side of busy streets and shout your destination as the bus slows down. Intracity buses finish their runs around 7 or 8pm; after that you're left with *service* or private taxis.

SERVICE TAXIS. *Service* within Beirut should cost L£1-2000, and you should rarely pay more than L£5000 for a private taxi except for trips late at night or all the way across town. *Service* stop running around 11pm or midnight, and all "taxis" (as opposed to private cars) have red licence plates. Private taxis can be called 24 hours. **Radio Taxi** (tel. 804 026 or 352 250) and **Lebanon Taxi** (tel. 340 717/8 or 353 152/3) are among the cheapest and most reliable.

■ PRACTICAL INFORMATION

Tourist Office: Ministry of Tourism (tel. 343 073), at the intersection of Rue de Rome and Central Bank St. in Hamra, to the left of Pizza Hut. The best of its kind in the Middle East. Fluent English speakers distribute sleek, up-to-date maps and brochures for every region of the country. Open M-F 8am-4pm, Sa 8am-1pm.

Tours: Nakhal Tour Company (tel. (01) 389 389 or (03) 234 747; fax 389 282) offers 6-day tours of Lebanon leaving from Beirut for US$35-55 per day (lunch included), 1-day tours to Ba'albeck, 'Anjar, and other sights, and week-long tours to Syria, Jordan, Cyprus, Egypt, Turkey, and Greece. The **Ministry of Tourism** also arranges tours.

Embassies: Australia (tel. 789 010 or 789 030; fax 789 025), on Rue Bliss in Ras Beirut. **Canada,** 434 Jabal Dib Highway (tel. 521 163 or 415; fax 521 167). **Egypt** (tel. 867 917, 862 932, or 802 734; fax 863 751), on Rue Thomas Edison in Ramlet Baida. **Jordan** (tel. 922 500/1; fax 922 502), on Elias Helou St. in Ba'abda. **U.K.** (tel. 403 640 or 405 070), in Chancellerie. Another branch in Raouche (tel. 805 898 or 812 849; fax 866 437). **U.S.** (tel. 402 200 or 403 300; fax 407 112), in Awkar. Take a *service* headed anywhere north of Beirut (e.g. Byblos, Tripoli) and ask to be dropped off at Dbayye. From Dbayye, the only way to the embassy is by taxi (L£5000).

Currency Exchange: Foreign currency can be exchanged at any bank or currency exchange shop. U.S. dollars are universally accepted at shops, on buses, and in hotels. **ATMs** give cash advances on Visa or MC; many are plugged into the Cirrus network. **Fransabank** (tel. 340 180/8) is located across from the tourist office in Hamra. Open M-F 8:15am-2:30pm, Sa 8:15am-noon.

American Express: (tel. 602 225/6), in the Gefinor Center on Rue Clemenceau in western Hamra. Will not hold mail. Open M-F 9am-4pm, Sa 8:30am-1:30pm.

English Bookstores: Naufal Booksellers (tel. 354 898), on Rue Sourati, across from the Idriss Market. One of the best English-language magazine and travel guide selections in the Middle East. *Time, Newsweek, Financial Times,* and a wide selection of English novels and Penguin classics. Open M-F 9:30am-6pm, Sa 9:30am-2pm. **Librairie Antoine,** (tel. 341 470/1), on Rue Hamra near Rue Jeanne d'Arc. Mostly French, with a smaller selection of English books and dailies. Open M-F 8:30am-6pm, Sa 8:30am-1:30pm.

Laundromat: Five Star Cleaners (tel. 742 856), on Rue Nehme Yafet just off Rue Sidani. Laundry and dry cleaning services. Shirts (L£3000), trousers (L£4000), and socks (L£1000) all cleaned to perfection. Open M-F 8am-6pm, Sa 8am-4pm.

Emergency: Ambulance: Tel. 140. **Police:** Tel. 112. **Fire:** Tel. 175.

Tourist Police: Tel. 343 286, in the same building as the Tourist Office. Some English spoken. Start here with minor complaints or if you're the victim of petty crimes; more serious issues should be directed to the city police (*al-amn al-'amm*). Open 24hr.

Pharmacy: Pharmacie Rishani (tel. 342 831), on Rue Sourati opposite Naufal Booksellers in Hamra. Staff speaks English, French, and Arabic. Open daily 8am-8pm. **Mazen Pharmacy** (tel. 313 362), in Mazra'a, is open 24hr.

Hospital: American University of Beirut Hospital (tel. 340 460 or 350 000), in Hamra, at the intersection of Rue Ma'amari and Rue Claire. The best in Beirut.

Post Office: On Rue Makdissi, nearly opposite Embassy Hotel, on the 2nd floor of a nondescript, hard-to-find building with few signs. With the Embassy Hotel on your left, turn right into the doorway next to the sign that reads "Amin A. Faris, MD, Neurology." **Poste Restante** is unreliable. Open M-Th 8:15am-2pm, F 8:15-11am, Sa 8:15am-1pm.

Internet Access: You can have your web and eat it too at **Web Cafe,** on Makhoul St. next to Flying Pizza in Hamra. L£8000 for 1st hr., L£6000 each additional hr. Open daily noon-midnight. **PC Club** (tel. 745 339), on Rue Mahatma Gandhi; walk along Rue Bliss keeping the AUB to your right, and take a left at Popeye's Chicken. Play network games or write email (L£5000 per hr.), or rack it up on the pool table (L£1000). Open 24hr.

Telephones: The **telephone office** (tel. 348 903) in Hamra is in a small, glassy room in the same building as the Ministry of Tourism. To the U.S. or U.K. 7am-10pm L£2100 per min., 10pm-8am L£1800; to Australia L£2400/2100; to New Zealand or South Africa L£3600/3300; to Europe L£2100/1800. 3min. minimum. Open daily 8am-11pm.

Telephone Code: 01.

▟ ACCOMMODATIONS

Finding decent budget lodging can be difficult, as most of it was destroyed in the war. There are a few "hostels" that are barely habitable and a full host of luxury resorts, but little in the middle range. The cheapest options are in 'Ain Mreisse, a short walk from Hamra.

▧ **Mayflower Hotel** (tel. 340 680 or 347 080), on Rue Nehme Yafet, 2 blocks off Rue Hamra. A splurge, but like a Pilgrim in search of a new world, the Mayflower is the first to reach the realm of excellence. Normally, singles are US$65, plus a 16% tax, *plus* a 5% service fee, but if you request the budget room, the price is slashed to US$35 plus the 5% service fee. You still get the TV, A/C, private bath, maid service, and the cleanest rooms in town.

▧ **Pension Home Valery** (tel. 362 169 for 2nd floor; 364 906 for 3rd floor), in 'Ain Mreisse. With the Hard Rock Cafe on your left, walk 100m down the street and take a right; enter just after the Wash Me Carwash. Beirut's rock bottom; offers clean but boxy rooms with fans, sofas, and tile floors. The 2 floors have different management (3rd floor is friendlier). 2- to 4-bed dorms US$5. Hot showers free on 2nd floor, L£2000 on 3rd.

University Hotel (tel. 365 391), just off the Rue Bliss in Hamra across from the AUB. Its private bathrooms and excellent location in the heart of budget Beirut help compensate for the fanless rooms (although some rooms come with A/C). US$20 per person. Student rates are for monthly stays only: US$150 per month.

Mushrek Hotel (tel. 345 773/2), Rue Makdissi, 2 blocks down from the post office in Hamra. Green checkered floor, huge wardrobes, refrigerators, fans, and large balconies. Communal bathrooms with peeling paint fall somewhere between not great and bearable. Singles L£25,000; doubles L£35,000; triples L£40,000; suites with kitchenette, private bath, and A/C L£50,000.

Y.W.C.A. (tel. 367 750/1) in 'Ain Mreisse, around the corner from the Valery. This international center is usually populated by students and is **open only to women.** Comfortable rooms with bath and fridge. Dorm beds US$15; singles US$25; doubles US$30. Night owls beware: curfew Su-F 9pm, Sa 1am.

West House Residence (tel. 350 450), near the corner of Rue Sourati and Rue 'Abd el-'Aziz. Oh my brothers, these ultra-funky 70s apartments out of *A Clockwork Orange* are the cheapest "furnished apartments" in town. Viddy the fully-equipped suites with mini-fridge, A/C, private bath, TV, and kitchenette. Streetside rooms are noisy, but worth it for the pretty polly you'll save. Private room for 1 or 2 US$32, US$200 per week, US$650 per month. Visa, MC, AmEx with min. US$300. 5% tax added.

Embassy Hotel (tel. 340 814; fax 340 815), Rue Makdissi, across from the post office. Pleasant lobby and dark rooms with A/C, TV, mini-fridge, private bath, and springy mattresses. Plant-filled indoor and outdoor restaurant and Beirut's only hotel garden present a bucolic escape from the urban jungle outside. Singles L£50,000; doubles L£70,000; triples L£82,000; add a 14% service charge. Breakfast US$3.

FOOD

European pub grub, Western fast food, glitzy and exotic foreign cuisine, cafe fare, and Lebanese favorites are all part of Beirut's food scene. "Snacks" are sandwich shops with little ambience but good value. The Hamra district, especially around AUB, is packed with small, affordable eateries. Raouche is home to many of Lebanon's most renowned restaurants, some with sunset views of the Pigeon Rocks.

Flying Pizza (tel. 351 904 or 353 975), on Rue Makhloul at Rue Jeanne d'Arc, next door to Web Cafe. You'll feel like you're in a sushi bar when you're handed a checklist rather than a menu. Create your own Italian-Lebanese pizza with artichokes, beef pepperoni, or ham, all featuring a secret spicy tomato sauce on thick or thin crust. Small pizza L£5500, toppings L£1250 each. Open daily 11am-midnight. Delivery free in Hamra.

Web Cafe (tel. 348 881 or 880), on Rue Makhloul in Hamra, adjacent to Flying Pizza. For caffeine and **Internet** addicts. A slick, polished joint where slick, polished AUB students hang out to rack up their trend points. Gourmet sandwiches (L£6000-9500), espresso drinks (L£2000-3000), and beer (L£3500-4500). Open daily noon-midnight.

China (tel. (01) 739 314 or (03) 756 655), on Rue Sourati in Hamra. Near East meets Far East, hot meets sour, and spring meets roll in A/C splendor. Chicken with cashew nuts (L£10,500) and fried banana over ice cream (L£2750) sing a sweet duet. Student discount (15%) does not apply to takeout. Open daily noon-midnight.

Hamadeh Snack (tel. 342 670), at the corner of Rue de Rome and Central Bank St. in Hamra, across the street from the Ministry of Tourism. Popular morning stop for commuting Beirutis. Delicious *mana'eesh* with *za'tar*, lamb, and cheese L£1000-2500. Nothing beats a *beetza* with olives (L£3500). Open daily 6am-5pm.

Al-Amadouli (tel. 340 552), on the corner of Rue Makdisi and Rue Nehme Yafet, diagonal from the White Tower Hotel. Downstairs is a take-away bar, upstairs is a sit-down restaurant whose interior design is a fight to the death between swaths of gold and pastel, fake greenery, over-sized chandeliers, and Christmas decorations. Tasty dishes (L£6000-8000) and live lute player (performances W-Su evenings; cover L£1000). Beer L£2000. Open daily noon-midnight.

LEBANON

Hard Rock Cafe, at the Bayview Hotel in 'Ain Mreisse (tel. 373 023, 373 024, or 371 247; fax 369 079). It's a Hard-Rock life for those who blow all their lira on the typically overpriced burgers (L£12,000-16,000) and beers (L£4500-8000) served at this paraphernalia-cluttered hall. Open noon-midnight.

👁 SIGHTS

For a city with a 5000-year heritage, Beirut is a bit slim on sights of archaeological importance. Since the war ended in 1991, the reconstruction effort and urban digging initiatives have peeled back otherwise inaccessible layers of destroyed cityscape. Although archaeological teams have uncovered ancient ruins, most are not currently available for public viewing. Some in the process of being catalogued and taken apart to be deposited in city parks.

NATIONAL MUSEUM. This museum was ready to open its doors in 1938, but tension leading to WWII delayed the opening until 1942. When civil war broke out in 1975, the museum again closed its doors (see **Ars Longa, Bellum Breve,** p. 471). Extensive restoration and renovation was completed within the last few years, and today visitors can again walk through the halls of the most glorious museum in the Middle East. Especially impressive are the intricately carved Roman sarcophagi, the mosaics from Ba'albeck, and the set of 27 eerily lit, anthropomorphic coffins in the basement. *(Ave. Abdullah Yafi near the race track. Open W-Su 10am-5pm. Admission L£5000; students and under 18 L£1000.)*

PIGEON ROCKS. Ministry of Tourism pamphlets proclaiming these rocks Beirut's major natural landmark neglect to describe the neon signs and fast food-riddled landscape that make the whole scene more discouraging than uplifting. The mere geological uniqueness of the rocks merits a brief visit, and it's worth scrambling down to the rocks for the stunning cliff views. Formed by an earthquake eons ago, the two rocks are huge formations just off the coast; one has a hole in the center through which small boats pass. Today home to daredevil divers, the shores near Pigeon Rocks have yielded the oldest evidence of human existence in Beirut. The flints and tools that were found here are now displayed in the American University of Beirut (AUB) Archaeological Museum. *(Off the coast of Raouche.)*

SURSOCK MUSEUM. Donated in 1912 by the Lebanese philanthropist Nicholas Ibrahim Sursock, the museum is housed in a mansion whose *fin de siècle* Lebanese-Italian architectural style is a spectacle in and of itself. The temporary exhibits revolve around Lebanese themes and culminate in an annual Salon D'Automne, which showcases the best in modern Lebanese art. *(Rue Sursock in Ashrafieh. Open daily 8am-2pm and 4-8pm during exhibits only. Free.)*

AUB ARCHAEOLOGICAL MUSEUM. This museum is small but full of local history, excellent glazed work, and sublime ivory carvings. The campus is also a nice place for a picnic or a stroll: runners or walkers can use their track, carved into the hillside and offering great views over the valley. *(On the AUB campus on Rue Bliss, in the Hamra district. Museum open M-F in summer 9am-2:30pm; in winter 9am-4pm. Free.)*

RUINS, ANCIENT AND MODERN. Behind Central Bank St. near the Port are the remains of a large **Roman bath.** Originally discovered in 1968, it underwent a thorough excavation and cleaning over the past two years. For a living testament to the ravages of contemporary warfare and the modern ruins it has created, the best place to go is not downtown. Though this area was the epicenter of the fighting, it has been completely razed and is now the site of a massive **reconstruction project** supervised by the Solidere Company (which offers tours of the rebuilding sites upon request; tel. 646 129). Instead, walk up from downtown on Rue de Damas toward the National Museum: nearly every building in the area is pocked with bullet holes, and many are barely standing. Unfortunately, poor Beirutis are forced to eke out a living in what remains of their homes here.

LEBANON

ARS LONGA, BELLUM BREVE When the officials at Beirut's National Museum realized that civil war was about to break out, they moved quickly to save the thousands of pieces of precious artwork in their care. The Roman sarcophagi and statuary (arguably the most impressive works) could not be moved due to their massive weight, so they were entombed in nearly three feet of concrete. Many of the smaller pieces were sent to Germany or stored in National Bank vaults. Space and time were limited, however, and much of the pottery could only be unceremoniously dumped in cardboard boxes and stored in the basement to wait out the hostilities. Unfortunately, the intense humidity in the flooded basement caused the cardboard boxes to disintegrate, damaging many of the ceramics and other pottery pieces. The war itself caused inevitable damage: snipers poked holes through priceless mosaics, the museum's majestic columns were so badly bullet-pocked that they were left barely standing, and giant exhibit halls brimmed with debris. Nevertheless, a remarkable percentage of the art was preserved. Since the war ended, the museum's facade has received a facelift, the bank vaults have been emptied, the oil and grime staining the pottery has been removed, and most gloriously, the cement cases have been opened. Today's National Museum is as much a monument to the resilience and ingenuity of the modern Lebanese people as it is to their fascinating and varied history.

♫ ENTERTAINMENT

Beirutis who can afford it support a thriving dance and party scene. During the war, clubs in the northern suburbs of Jounieh and Kaslik helped people forget about life for a while. When the darkest years of conflict ended, discos and bars filled with optimistic youth re-energized by the end of sniper threats and car bombings. Ras Beirut now throbs with a new beat after years of boarded-up silence, rivaling the club meccas of the suburbs. An added incentive to shake it on down to downtown Beirut is that after-hours public transportation to and from suburbia is limited to expensive private taxis. All places listed below are accessible from Beirut by bus or *service* before midnight and should cost no more than L£8000 for return taxi fare to Beirut.

CLUB-HOPPING

Orange Mechanique, Sin al-Fil, 300m up from Beirut Hall along the river. The most popular and notorious discotheque in Beirut, and one of the very few that tends to attract gay patrons. Follow the eclectic crowds and professional dancers for a melange of New York techno, acid jazz, and rave. Drinks US$7. Crowds come at 10pm and dance at midnight. No cover. Open Th-Sa and holidays.

B018, have Scotty beam you up to the Beirut Forum. This spawn of Orange Mechanique is a jazzy hip-hop joint equipped with Star Trek control deck seats and a retractable roof with a great view of the starry Beirut nights. Open daily 7pm-dawn, but the superstars don't really come out until after 10pm. Beer L£10,000; mixed drinks L£15,000.

Monkey Rose (tel. 362 666). Monkey see, Monkey Rose: word-of-mouth has made this place extremely popular with a younger crowd (mostly hip teens barely clearing the 18+ age restriction) that grooves the night away to rave, trance, and acid jazz. Drinks L£8000-12,000. No cover. Open 8pm-dawn.

Oliver's, in Ma'ameltein, on the main seaside drag. The first disco to open in the area has seen better days, leading some to say "thank you sir, but may I have another (disco)?" Nevertheless, this mirrored *boite* is often crowded to capacity. Usually no cover for foreigners, who bounce around to commercial hip-hop and dance music. Drinks L£8000-14,000, beer L£5000. Open 9:30pm-4am.

Crazy, on the main road in Kaslik. Loud music attracts "alternative," cell-phoned Beirutis. Strictly rave, with cage dancers galore—ow! Mixed drinks L£10,000. Cover US$15.

BAR-HOPPING

Henry J. Bean's, "but his friends call him Hank," on Rue Madame Curie. From Rue Hamra, head towards the AUB campus; bear right and keep going until you see it on the right. The bar and its English-speaking staff hold Happy Hour daily (4-8pm), when you can satisfy your Hankering for beers at half-price (normally L£5000-6500). The place keeps hopping t-hanks to everyone's favorite heavily-hopped brew, Guinness. Open noon-1am.

L'Escroc (Cheap Shots), on Rue Al-Inglisi Ashrafieh. With your back to Circuite Empire in Place Sassine, walk 100m down the large street leaving the Chase on your right. Although this local favorite's name means "crook" in French, you won't be swindled (cheap shots only L£2500). If you'd rather inhale smoke than alcohol, have an *argeileh.* Open noon-1am.

Pacifico, off Rue Monot in Ashrafieh. "The goddess made me a cup of tea with a spot of rum, but she herself drank only the rum." Heine's words on the menu may inspire you to imitate the goddess with the L£6500-10,500 shooters. Alternately, you can worship her with cigars (L£9500-33,500), fancy meals (L£14,500-24,500), Almaza beer (L£4000), and even Corona (L£6000). Happy Hour M-Sa 6:30-8pm.

Janneh, Bait Meri. A.pain to reach—take a *service* from Dawra to Mkalles, then another to Bait Meri; do it early, or else private taxis are the only way home. This tropical food and drink complex nearly lives up to its name ("heaven" in Arabic). Waterfall, pond, and crossbridge flow through 2 restaurants serving Chinese and Western entrees (L£14,000-30,000). Drinks L£4000-10,000. Open 9am-5am.

Blue Note, on Rue Makhoul, Hamra. An excessively ambient jazz joint, serving pasta lunches (US$15-20) and pricey dinners (US$20-25). A budget-friendlier option is to fill up on the *mezze.* Live music Friday and Saturday nights. Local beer L£3900, imported L£5200. Tack on 20% tax. Cover L£6000. Open M-Th noon-1am, F-Sa noon-2am.

■ S-HOPPING (AND OTHER SPORTS)

Beirut is known for its cheap, high-quality luxury goods (and we don't mean the slicksters at the discos): gold-leaf calligraphy and filigree, silver jewelry, traditional crafts, perfume, and intricate embroidery are all dirt cheap. Beautiful and affordable Lebanese crafts can be found at the **Artisanat Libanais,** on Rue Clemenceau opposite the old French embassy, and at the branch next to the St. Georges Hotel downtown. *Les Artisans,* as cooperative craft unions are called, are nonprofit—all revenue goes to the artists themselves. There are jewelry shops on every corner in Beirut, but it is a good idea to ask a trustworthy local for directions to an honest shop. Bargaining for gold and silver is usually acceptable, but prices are fixed at the Artisanat. Beirut's traditional *souqs* were once world renowned, but were destroyed during the war and have not been restored.

Virile sporting urges may be quenched at the **Beirut Racetrack,** where purebred Arabian horses run every Sunday (Saturday in summer). Beirut's posh **Golf Club** (tel. 822 470) is open to foreigners, who can use the nine-hole course, swimming pool, and squash and tennis courts for a fee (varies with activity; around L£20,000). The Club survived some difficult times: in 1982 the Israeli army bulldozed the gold club pavilion, and in 1989 alone 360 shells landed on the course. The **Mediterranean** is quite polluted around Beirut, but locals don't seem to mind. There are also several **swimming pools** open to visitors. The cleanest and best is at the St. George Hotel downtown (L£20,000 per day for use of pool and facilities).

NEAR BEIRUT

JOUNIEH جونية

Take a service to Dawra (L£500) and hop another service (L£500): some go directly to Jounieh, but those headed for Byblos or Tripoli can also drop you off at Jounieh.

High-stakes risktakers gamble and bikini-clad women gambol at the casinos, clubs, and luxurious beach resorts of Jounieh, Lebanon's capital of hedonism. Wealthy

Beirutis and well-heeled visitors jaunt 21km north of Beirut to frolic at the three coastal towns—Kaslik, Jounieh, and Ma'ameltein—that compose the area collectively referred to as Jounieh. Though it undoubtedly possesses as ancient a history as neighboring Beirut and Byblos, Jounieh now betrays no hint of antiquity to taint its many disco floors (see **Club-Hopping**, p. 471) and Western-style steakhouses, pizza factories, and falafel stands. Food in Jounieh is fairly expensive, but there are several budget options. Look for cheap Arab eats on the main street parallel to the sea. **Sailor's Snack** (tel. (09) 635 700) serves up munchies like *shish tawouq* and kebab sandwiches (L₤2500; open 24hr.).

◪ **SWIMMING.** Jounieh's primary attraction during hot summer days is its swimming. The beach resorts along the city's coast typically charge L₤10,000-15,000 for use of their pool facilities, but a cheaper, more fun option is to swim in the **ocean**, thankfully devoid of the floating debris that characterizes much of the Lebanese and Syrian coast. Free surf, sand, and sun are everywhere—just walk toward that big, blue wet thing on the left.

HARISSA MOUNTAIN. Check out the stunning views from the heights of Harissa Mountain. The preferred mode of ascension is via **téléphérique,** a nine-minute gondola skyride that provides spectacular views of the heavily developed coastline. When it gets too steep for the cable cars, a funicular takes over the ascent to the pinnacle *(Tel. 914 324. Entrance left of Hospital St. Louis, just off the main seaside drag. Téléphérique runs Tu-Su 10am-midnight. Admission L₤7500, ages 4-10 L₤3500.)*

CASINO DU LIBAN. The world-famous Casino du Liban towers over Ma'ameltein to the north. In its heyday, the casino dueled with Monte Carlo for Mediterranean gaming supremacy and was filled with celebrities, international jet-setters, and suave British spies sipping martinis. War shut down the funhouse, but it has recently reopened to tourists from all over the world. The opulent excess of the three gaming rooms, five restaurants, two auditoriums, and eight bars will shake you, but not stir you. The doorman may sneer at dirty backpackers, and those in sandals will be turned away. *(21+ admitted. Open daily 8pm-4am.)*

CHURCHES. At the top of Harissa Mountain is the ultramodern **Church of the Virgin of Lebanon.** The interior may sport tacky electric candles and a statue of questionable aesthetic value, but the exterior spiral staircase leads to unmatched vistas. Gamblers can also pray for big bucks at the modernist **Maronite Cathedral,** a magnificent glimmering glass building. *(Both churches open to the public daily from 10am to 9pm. Services M-Sa 6:30, 7:30am, 4, 5, 6pm; Su and holidays every hr. 6am-7pm.)*

JEITA GROTTO مغارة جيتا

*Getting to Jeita (20km north of Beirut) without shelling out a lot of cash for a private taxi is a struggle. Try hopping a **bus** at Dawra for Jounieh or Byblos (L₤500) and asking to be let off at "Mafra' Jeita." Or, walk uphill for 5min. into the modern town. From there hail a **service taxi** to "Mafra' maghaarat Jeita;" the driver should let you out at the turn-off to the caverns (L₤1000). The grotto is a 2km downhill walk. The parking attendant specializes in hooking carless visitors up with rides, but some must brave the uphill climb on the return journey. Open Tu-Su 9am-5pm; closed Jan. 5-Feb. 5. Admission L₤16,500, under 13 L₤9250, under 4 free.*

The Jeita Grotto formed where the Nahr el-Kalb (Dog River) hollowed out the insides of a wooded mountain off the coastal highway near Beirut, forming one of the largest and most intricately carved caverns in the world. The caverns house the river's source and a soaring cathedral of latticed stalactites and stalagmites. The Jeita Grotto has been known to humans since the Paleolithic age, but credit for the most recent and well-publicized discovery goes to an American, Reverend William Thomson, a missionary who ventured 50m into the cave. Once he reached the underground river, he fired his gun, and the gunshot echoes revealed the subterranean immensity. In his honor, the still water in the cavern's lower gallery is named Thomson's Pool.

The Lebanese Minister of Tourism Nicolas Fattouche (no relation to the salad) was responsible for reopening the grotto after the war. He hired the German company Mapas to overhaul the attraction and make it kitschy enough to satisfy generations weaned on Disney. Mapas did not disappoint. After paying the outrageously high (but worthwhile) admission fee, visitors are whizzed to the entrance of the **upper cave** in one of four "Austrian" cable cars. Discovered years after Thomson's gunshot, the upper cave is now entered through a 100m tunnel drilled into the mountain. The upper caverns are more spectacular than the lower caverns and contain remarkable mineral formations, many of them resembling the statues found in Lebanon's museums. Next to the tunnel is a snack bar and theater showing a 23-minute film detailing the caves' history. A little replica of a steamboat tugs you the 100m to the entrance of the **lower cave**, but only in the summer; the trip to the lower cave can only be made over water, and in the winter the water level is too high to be navigable.

FAQRA AND FARAYA

Venture just east of Beirut into the Mt. Lebanon area, and the fact that the country's nickname is "Little Switzerland" begins to make sense. It is difficult to believe that the beaches of the coast are so close to the ski resorts of the alpine interior. Faqra and Faraya rank highest among the nation's resorts; at 1600m above sea level, the reason for their superiority is eminent.

⚑ PRACTICAL INFORMATION. Faqra (45km from Beirut) and Faraya (50km from Beirut) are difficult to reach. Neither service nor white minivans trek up to this area, and private taxis cost a prohibitive US$20-30 each way, making a daytrip unworthy of the cost unless you have a private car.

⚑ ACCOMMODATIONS. Hotel prices in "Little Ritzerland" are as steep, fast, and as out of control as you'll be on the slopes. One reasonable option in Faqra is the **Faqra Club** (tel. (09) 300 501/2/3/4 or (09) 300 600), where comfortable, spotless quarters are rented as single rooms (doubles US$150, weekends US$225; triples US$188/275). There are bigger "junior" and "executive" suites suitable for large groups (junior suites US$235, weekends US$325; executive suites US$255/365). All rooms feature private bath and satellite TV; junior suites include a sitting area, and executive suites have a kitchenette as well. All prices are negotiable during the week and the off-season (mid-Apr. to late-May, and again from early-Oct. to mid-Dec.).

The hotels in Faraya are a little more accommodating to the wallet. Very near the main traffic circle, **Old Bridge Hotel and Restaurant** is marked by an Arabic sign only (*al-(H)otel aj-Jisr al-'Adeem*). Rooms are large, well-maintained, two-bed suites with kitchenettes (singles US$25; doubles US$40; triples US$45). The in-house restaurant features *mezze* (L$2000-2500) and grills (L$15,000-25,000). With the Old Bridge Hotel on the left, walk down the main street to reach the **Coin Vert Hotel and Restaurant** (tel. (09) 720 812), a relatively inexpensive place with clean rooms and private baths (some with balconies) (singles US$30; doubles US$40; triples US$50). Ask for summer or student discounts, sometimes as much as 15% off.

For leafy outdoor seating and an equally wholesome meal in Faqra, head to **An-Nahr al-Hawi Restaurant** (Arabic sign only; tel. (09) 720 260), just past the main traffic circle. *Mezze* runs about L$3500 per dish, and entrees range between L$4000 and L$7000. Elegant sit-down meals and spectacular views are served up in Faraya at **Al-Qanatir Restaurant** (tel. (03) 710 818 or (09) 300 818), about 2km before the Faqra Club on the main road from Beirut. *Mezze* can be yours for about US$12 per person with *'araq*, whiskey, or wine included (open daily noon-midnight).

◉ ⚐ SIGHTS AND ENTERTAINMENT. Over 3000 years of continuous settlement in this region have left their mark in the form of a few interesting ruins: the **Grand Temple** in Faqra is believed to have been built by the Romans in the first century CE (open W-M 8:30am-dusk; admission for foreigners L$2000, Lebanese nationals L$1000). But let's face it: the real reason to visit these villages is for the **skiing**. Faqra has four slopes, ranging from beginner to advanced levels, while Faraya boasts 13 slopes (including some "professional level"). Ski season runs from December to April (slopes open daily 8am-4pm). Lift tickets cost around US$10, and full equipment rental typically costs the same. Call Solipro (tel. (01) 257 220) with general inquiries about skiing in Faqra; Mr. Christien Rizk (tel. (09) 341 034/5 or (03) 771 211/2) will answer all your questions about skiing in Faraya.

NORTH OF BEIRUT

BYBLOS (JBAIL) جبيل

Byblos is still duking it out with Jericho, Damascus, and Aleppo for the title of old-est city in the world. Ancient myths relate how after the beautiful youth Adonis was killed by a boar in nearby Afqa Grotto, he would emerge from Hades every summer to frolic in Byblos with Aphrodite. Better substantiated is the 7000-year-old city's historical origin as a small fishing village in the Neolithic age. Even the ancients considered Byblos an ancient city; it first grew to prominence at the beginning of the 3rd millennium BCE by providing Egyptian pharaohs with much-needed timber from the famed cedars of Lebanon. One of the most important Phoenician city-states, Byblos became a great supplier of papyrus, a legacy that survives in the etymology of words like Bible and bibliography. Roman, Muslim, Crusader, and Turkish rulers all punched in their timecards before the city finally evolved into modern-day Jbail. A favored playground for the international crowd before the war, Byblos has emerged from the conflict relatively unscathed and ready to welcome visitors back to its ancient ruins, a splendid foil to the city's hyper-chic port district and the trendy cell-phone toters that frequent it.

🛈 ORIENTATION AND PRACTICAL INFORMATION

Byblos's layout is straightforward and simple to master. The main drag of the mod-ern town is **Rue Jbail.** Buses from Dawra (L£500) will let you off along this street near the modern Diab Brothers building. **Service taxis** to Amchit bunch up on Rue Jbail opposite the Mobil station (L£1000). Getting to Beirut is easy up until about 9pm—walk up towards the highway past Diab Brothers and you'll soon see a battal-ion of **buses** waiting to take you back to Dawra (L£500). If you bear right and don't get on the highway, you'll soon reach the entrance to the sandy **Tam Tam Beach.** Across the street from the police station on Rue Jbail, **Byblos Bank** exchanges trav-eler's checks (open M-F 8am-5:30pm, Sa 8am-1pm). Rue Jbail soon makes a nearly 90-degree turn to the right at the KFC. Taking a left just before this curve leads to the *souqs* of the **Old City,** the wax museum, the entrance to the archaeological site, and the small **Ministry of Tourism** (tel. 540 325; supposedly open in summer M-Sa 9am-4:30pm, Su 10am-1pm; in winter 10am-2pm). The street directly across from the KFC leads over to the **Byblos Harbor.** Farther along the on way to Amchit, look to

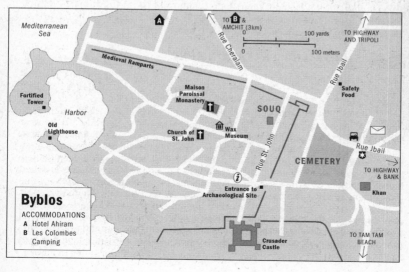

Byblos

ACCOMMODATIONS
A Hotel Ahiram
B Les Colombes
  Camping

Mediterranean Sea

TO B &
AMCHIT (3km)

100 yards

TO HIGHWAY
AND TRIPOLI

Medieval Ramparts

Rue Cheralam

Rue Jbail

Maison
Paroissal
Monastery

Safety
Food

Fortified
Tower

Harbor

SOUQ

Old
Lighthouse

Church of
St. John

Wax
Museum

Rue St. John

CEMETERY

Rue Jbail

Entrance to
Archaeological Site

TO HIGHWAY
& BANK

Khan

Crusader
Castle

TO TAM TAM
BEACH

LEBANON

the right for the **Central Telephone Office,** where you can call the U.S., U.K., and any-where in Europe for L£2100 per minute (Australia L£2400, South Africa L£3600; 3min. minimum; open daily 8am-midnight). A right just past Diab Brothers leads to the nondescript **post office** (tel. 540 003; open M-Th and Sa 8am-2pm, F 8-11am). A little farther along Rue Jbail on the left is the **police station** (tel. 541 142 or 945 853). For an **ambulance,** call the **Red Cross** (tel. 125). Byblos's **telephone code** is 09.

■ ACCOMMODATIONS AND FOOD

Finding a place to stay in Byblos itself is nearly impossible without shelling over an arm and a leg. Fortunately, one of the best budget options in all of Lebanon is just a short *service* ride (L£1000) or a 3km northward walk away. ◨**Les Colombes Camping** (tel. 540 322) in Amchit, is at a beautifully lush cliffside site. A path leads down the cliff to the sea, which is ideal for swimming. Rent a tent (US$1) and a campsite (US$3 per person, on weekends US$5). If this is too rustic for your liking, you can stay in a "tangalow," a combination tent and bungalow shaped like the former but featuring the bathroom of the latter (singles US$15; doubles US$20). Some say having one's own tent is nicer, as tangalows often have noisy neighbors and feature more than the occasional cockroach. Chalets (US$30 each), equipped with a dining room and kitchenette, are available for longer term guests. The complex is so pleasant that many nature-loving travelers use it as the base for their visit to Lebanon. The **Hotel Ahiram** (tel. 540 440 or 541 540; fax 944 726) is the cheaper of the two downtown options. To get to this large hotel and its two restaurants, take the last right before the sea on the harbor road. Modern rooms with air conditioning, TV, refrigerators and private bath feature windswept balconies with sea views (singles US$48; doubles US$68; triples US$78; Visa, MC, AmEx accepted). Breakfast included; bargain if staying longer than two nights.

The **food** options in Byblos run the gamut from imported grease-to-go (KFC, Pizza Hut) to the ultra chic snack machines lining the port. For an upscale meal, rig up the HMS Digestive Tract and weigh ankur at the **Seven Seas Restaurant** on St. John's St., next to the wax museum. The stone-vaulted restaurant offers a lunch of salad, fish and chips, or *shish* for L£8500. Cap off a meal with a bottle of local wine from their extensive list (Visa accepted). Once the most glamorous restaurant in the Middle East, the **Byblos Fishing Club** and its eccentric owner Pépé "the Pirate" Abed prompted a French critic to remark, "visiter le Liban sans connaitre Pépé...c'est passer sa lune de miel avec un eunuque!" ("to visit Lebanon without knowing Pépé...that is like spending your honeymoon with a eunuch!"). Pictures of Pépé with Marlon Brando, Charles de Gaulle, and David Rockefeller confirm: it's chic. The prix-fixe menu with meat (US$17) or fish (US$25) may be too pricey, but the Fishing Club remains *the* place for a sunset drink.

■ SIGHTS AND ENTERTAINMENT

Remnants spanning nearly all of Byblos's 7000 odd years of continuous inhabitation can be found at this archaeological site. Enter the site via the largest and best preserved of the ruins, the **Crusader Castle.** Built by the Franks in the 12th century out of stones pillaged from earlier buildings, the towers of the castle afford panoramic views that serve as a useful orientation to the rest of the ruins. To the west are columns from an ancient **Roman Colonnade** in front of a small **Roman Theater,** reconstructed to only half of its original size. Walking toward the boarded-up modern building, be careful not to fall into the **King's Well,** a remarkably deep depression that remained in use until Hellenistic times. Nearby rest the crushed limestone floors of Byblos's earliest settlements. Some dating from the Neolithic (5th millennium BCE) and others from the Chalcolithic (4th millennium BCE) Era, these settlements are among the earliest human remains in the world. (*Site open daily 8am-sunset. Admission L£6000.*) Walking to the east away from the sea, you'll soon come to the **Obelisk Temple,** comprising a forecourt and a slightly raised sanctuary. Originally built on the site of the 5000-year-old Temple of Resheph, the obelisks were moved to the new site to ease excavation. Only one of the 26 sandstone obelisks carries an inscription: a hieroglyphic dedication to an Egyptian god. Those who want a closer look at the inscriptions will be disappointed, however, as the Lebanese government erected a fence around them last year to prevent vandalism. While broiling at the top of Crusader Castle, you may gaze longingly at the gleaming waters of **Tam Tam Beach.** An easy 20-minute walk from town, the soft sands of this free shoreline convulse with Bob Marley-listening, beer-swilling, sunscreen-neglecting youth, savoring the salvos that they flick at the ironsides of old S.S. Morality in the process. Avoid crowds by going on weekdays.

TRIPOLI طرابلس

Tripoli (*Trablos* in Arabic) is the "capital of the North," a city perhaps different in character from any other region in Lebanon. While the general flavor of Tripoli is that of Mashriq (Eastern) Arab culture—with mosques, *souqs*, and *hammams*—the subtle taste of the Mediterranean definitely tinges the Al-Mina district.

Tripoli's rich history began when the Phoenicians established a small port in the Al-Mina area in 9th century BCE. Before the turn of the millennium, it was taken over by the Persians, the Macedonians, and then the Romans—but a 551 CE earthquake and tidal wave ultimately claimed Tripoli as its own. The Mamlukes resettled the area a century later and lifted the city into a golden age during the 11th century, when Tripoli flourished as an intellectual center complete with an extensive library. After staving off one Crusading leader by bribery and persuasion in the 1090s, its leaders succumbed to the fierce Raymond Saint-Gilles in 1099. The occupation lasted for 180 years, but in 1289 the Mamlukes had their revenge: years of scheming and minor skirmishes paid off when they were finally able to send the Crusaders packing, and they set to work fortifying the peninsula from further attacks. Mamluke Sultan Qalaoun even razed the old Crusader city to the ground and built a new one (now known as Al-Madina) at the foot of the hill near the castle. The city's second great Mamluke age lasted until 1516, and the *khans, hammams*, mosques, and *madrasas* that dot the city today remain from that period. When the Ottomans came to power, Sultan Suleiman I, who ruled from 1520 to 1566, kept the city unchanged and even restored many of its treasures.

Today's Tripoli is a crossroads both of moods and of cultural outlooks matching its geographically criss-crossed flavor. The Tripolitanians shuffling along the seaside corniche are dressed in fashions ranging from miniskirts to *hijabs* (traditional women's head scarves). While cars zip past each other in a chaotic race, the lazy Mediterranean sun lingers on the Lebanese horizon, sending the message for Tripoli's fishermen to call it a day and begin their cafe-side lounging.

✳ ORIENTATION

The major north-south road of Tripoli is **Rue Fouad Chehab.** Approaching from Beirut on this road, you will first hit **Al-Karami** roundabout with its distinctive "Allah" sign in the middle. The next major intersection sends **Rue Remayzat** off to the left and Rue 'Abd al-Hamid Karami, popularly known as **Rue Tall,** off to the right. On the left of Rue Tall is the landmark **At-Tal clocktower,** and across the street is the dusty **Jamal 'Abd an-Nasser Square.** This area forms the heart of modern Tripoli and is filled with *service* drivers boisterously plying their trade. Taking the first right after An-Nasser Sq. leads to **Koura Square,** and a left here takes you to **An-Nejmeh Square.** From here you can see the towering citadel, and almost all of the sights are a short walk away. To find your way to the sights, however, it's best to either ask a local or go to the Ministry of Tourism Office (on Al-Karami roundabout) to pick up their excellent map, as the streets around here defy any attempt at city planning. **Al-Mina** is 2km from the city center towards the sea. *Service* taxis (L₤500), which leave directly across the street from the clocktower, will get you to the main seaside drag, **Rue Ibn Sina,** also known as the **corniche.**

🛈 PRACTICAL INFORMATION

Buses: From the **Ahdam Bus Station,** just west of An-Nasser Sq. (open daily 5am-7pm). To **Beirut** (every 15min.; L£2000, students L£1500). The **Karnak office** is on Rue Fouad Chehab around the right-hand corner from Ahdam. To: **Damascus** (4½hr.; Sa, Tu, Th 4:30am; US$3); **Homs** (2½hr., daily every hr. 8:30am-midnight, US$4); **Hama** (3hr., US$4); **Aleppo** (5hr., US$5); and **Lattakia** (3½hr., 3:30pm, US$3) via **Tartus** (2hr., US$3).

Service: Depart from the south side of the square. To **Beirut** (L£4000) and nearly every other destination in Syria and Lebanon. *Service* to **Bcharré** (L£3500) and the mountains leave from Koura Sq., near the Ahram Hotel. No regular *service* go to Ba'albeck.

Tourist Office: (tel. 433 590), in Karami Sq. near the "Allah" sign. Provides an enormous historical map and pamphlets on all major tourist regions in Lebanon. The trilingual staff is an excellent resource for honest information about hotels all over Lebanon. Open M-Sa 8am-6pm, Su 8am-1pm.

Laundromat: Express Laundry (tel. 625 825), around the corner from the mall housing Compugames (see below) and opposite Krameh Palace. Shirts L£2500, pants L£4000. Open in summer M-Th and Sa 7:30am-6pm, F 7:30am-3pm; in winter M-Th and Sa 7:30am-4:30pm, F 7:30am-3pm.

Emergency: Police: Tel. 17. **Red Cross:** Tel. 140. **Ambulance:** Tel. 430 017.

Pharmacy: Ayoub Pharmacy (tel. 624 295), in An-Nasser Sq., directly across from the clocktower. Trilingual staff. Open M-F 8am-5pm, Sa 8am-1:30pm.

Post Office: (tel. 432 101), on Fouad Chehab St., 100m south of the "Allah" roundabout. Open Sa and M-Th 8am-1:30pm, F 8-11am. **DHL office** (tel. 433 205), off Fouad Chehab St. in Helou Plaza, about 500m north of Big Bite. Documents and parcels up to ½kg US$50 (students US$25) for any destination worldwide. Each additional ½kg US$20; $US25 flat fee per parcel. Open M-F 8am-5pm, Sa 8am-3pm.

Internat Access: Easily accessible in Tripoli. **Compugames,** in the mall on Riyad as-Salah St. With the Big Bite on your right, walk away from the clocktower until you reach the 1st traffic roundabout. Take a right and pass the Hallab Brothers Patisserie. The modern mall housing Compugames will follow on the left. L£5000 per hr. Open daily 9am-2am. **EasyNet** (see below) charges L£6000 per hr.

Telephones: EasyNet (tel. 447 041 or (03) 495 548), off Al-Koura Sq., facing the Az-Zahree Building. The Marhaba brothers speak English and place international calls to the U.S., U.K., Australia, and Canada (L£1000 per min.). Much better than the Central Telephone Office. Open daily 9am-midnight.

Telephone Code: 06.

⌂ ACCOMMODATIONS

Tripoli's accommodations are generally much cheaper and less crowded than those in Beirut. Many tourists make Tripoli a long daytrip from Beirut, but a few nights' stay allows more leisurely exploration of the northern half of the country. Most budget hotels in Tripoli accept both Lebanese pounds and U.S. dollars, but credit cards tend not to be accepted. **Pension Haddad** (tel. 624 392), lies down an alley to the right off Tall St., just past An-Nasser Sq. The clean rooms are overflowing with crosses, icons, and embroidered tapestries that would make your grandmother proud. The rock-hard beds would straighten her gnarly spine (singles US$5; doubles US$10; triples US$15). **Palace Hotel** (tel. 432 257), on Tall St., stands just past An-Nasser Sq. and the friendly watch salesmen of Haddad Alley. The palatial reception area with a lovely Orientalist ceiling seems to have earned the hotel its name, making the rooms and their spotty floors seem anticlimactic. Beautiful stained-glass windows adorn the hotel throughout. (Singles L£15,000, with bath US$15; doubles L£30,000, with bath US$30; triples L£45,000, with bath $US45. Laundry service.) **Al-Koura Hotel** (tel. (03) 326 803) lies down an alley named Rue Izz ad-Din, the second right-hand turn past the outdoor cafe on An-Nasser Sq. Spotless rooms have tasteful cedar rafter ceilings and original Ottoman-era brickwork, and come with private bath, breakfast, and air conditioning. (Singles US$20; doubles US$30; triples US$45; less well-maintained 3-bed dorms US$5. Laundry service.)

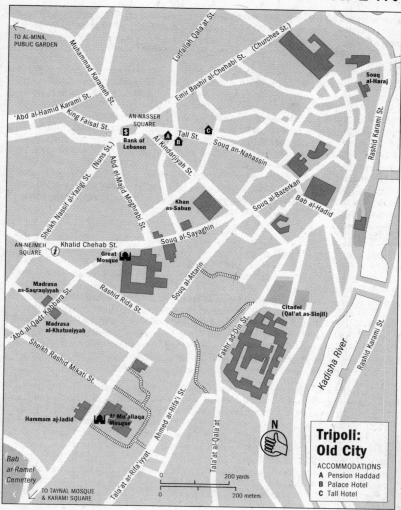

Tripoli:
Old City

ACCOMMODATIONS
A Pension Haddad
B Palace Hotel
C Tall Hotel

LEBANON

FOOD

Find fast **food** with a Middle Eastern twist at **Big Bite** (tel. 430 156 or 440 965), a bistro on the corner of Tall St. and Fouad Chehab St. Falafel and french fry—together at last! Garnish your burger (L£3000) with a side of hummus (L£2000) or go for straight almost-Americana with a respectable vegetarian pizza (L£4500; open daily 4am-10pm). For a pleasant and affordable sit-down meal, try the **Continental Rest** (tel. 445 475), on Tall St. under the green awning, across the street from the building with the "ABC" sign. Here, kebab and hummus can be yours for under L£6500 (open daily 8am-10:30pm). For those with a fishy craving, head no further than the **Captain Fish Restaurant** (tel. 613 031), off Ibn Sina St. in Al-Mina, with its air-conditioned interior and pick-a-fish meals. Half a kilo of fish is enough for two (L£45,000; open daily noon-midnight). Tripoli is famous for sweets containing a special kind of cream called *'ashta* (see **Food and Drink**, p. 463). Some of the best sweets in town are at **Hallab Brothers** (tel. 444 433 or 445); one branch is on the right side of Tall St. Try their syrupy baklava (L£3750 per ¼kg) or Tripoli's specialty, *halawat aj-jibn* (L£3000; open daily 5:00am-10pm). **Al-Mawiyye**, near Hammam aj-Jadeed, serves up similar sweetness in an old city atmosphere.

♫ ENTERTAINMENT

After a long day dodging traffic in Al-Madina, Tripoli's nighthawks usually converge around two activities: walking and smoking (which are sometimes combined). The **corniche walk** in Al-Mina is a splendid place to sit on the sea-side rocks and watch the sun set. Many restaurants and cafes dot the corniche, but unfortunately, Ilan Sina Ave. runs between these and the water. A more scenic option is a ride on one of the many **boats** that tour the nearby islands during the day (tours L£3000-5000). Boats usually run between 9am and 6pm, and dock at sundown to serve as cafes during the evenings. Try **Al-Badi Cafe** for a more landlocked smoking and coffee experience. With the sea on your left, head to the end of the corniche walk; the cafe will face you. This is the only place on the corniche directly on the water. The fare is a bit pricey (*argeileh* and Turkish coffee L£6000), but the atmosphere is worth it (open daily 9am-1am).

👁 SIGHTS

TAYNAL MOSQUE. Tripoli is divided into two sections: **Al-Mina**, the old but destroyed area around the port, and **Al-Madina**, the new section built by Sultan Qalaoun in 1289 CE. To start your sightseeing tour, take the second left off the "Allah" roundabout as you approach it from downtown Tripoli; you'll soon approach the green-domed **Taynal Mosque**. The most beautiful mosque in Tripoli, it was built in 1336 by Saif ad-Din Taynal on the site of a ruined Carmelite church. This location was outside the limits of the Mamluke city and was originally a Roman Temple to Zeus, then a Byzantine church, and finally the Carmelite structure. Visitors are sometimes allowed to climb the minaret, but entry depends on the presence of the guard. *(Free. Women must wear a full-length cloak and are requested not to enter during prayers, normally between 11:30am and 1pm. No shoes.)*

BAB AL-HADEED. After leaving the mosque, turn right and then left into the neighborhood of Bab al-Hadeed. **Ahwa Moussa**, one of the oldest coffee houses in the city, calls this area home. **Hammam aj-Jadeed** is the largest bathhouse in Tripoli, built in 1740 but non-functional since the 1970s. It's still worthwhile to take a look at the faded grandeur of the interior. *(Free. The keymaster hangs out in a local shop, and will ask for a L£2000 "donation.")* Through the arch in the same direction is a **souq** replete with overflowing stalls and the smell of rotting organic matter underfoot. Don't slip on the fish heads, beef entrails, or chicken claws that litter the cobblestones. A street running perpendicular to the *souq* leads to two *madrasas* (Qur'anic schools): the **Madrasa al-Khatuniyyah**, built in 1373, and the **Madrasa as-Saqraqiyyah**, built in 1359. The inscriptions above the door of Khatuniyyah list the details of the *waqf*, or endowment left by the founder for the students and the poor. On the other wall is the image of a cup, a symbol that recalls the Mamlukes' days as slaves. Saqraqiyyah was founded by a soldier, and its dome stands over a former Mamluke tomb.

GREAT MOSQUE. Continuing on to the right is the Great Mosque, built from 1294 to 1315 on the remains of a ruined 12th-century Crusader cathedral. Remains of Western architecture from the old church have been incorporated into the mosque structure; most notably, a Lombard-style bell tower was transformed into the minaret. Near the mosque are two *madrasas* from the same period, the Madrasa ash-Shamsiyat and Madrasa al-Mashad. *(Free. Modest dress required. Women must cover themselves with a full-length cloak available at the entrance and are requested not to enter during the prayer hour. No shoes.)*

SCRUBBING DOWN (HAMMAMS AND SOAP FACTORIES). Beyond the Great Mosque, the road forks on the left to reach the **Khan as-Sabun**, the soap factory.

Though this Ottoman building was used as recently as 1970, it looks like it needs a good wash. The first left down a long alley after the soap factory leads to the **Hammam al-'Abd** (Bath of the Slave), Tripoli's only functional *hammam*. *(Tel. 446 583. Men only. Open daily 7am-midnight. All-inclusive admission L£15,000.)* Retracing your steps to the soap factory, a right and then a left leads back to the main north-south *souq*. At the end of the main street is the brass *souq*. A right turn after that takes you to the large **Hammam Izz ad-Din,** the oldest Turkish bath in the city (completed in 1298 CE). Vendors can give directions to another soap factory (still in use), which produces colorfully swirly soap bars.

CITADEL (QAL'AT SINJIL). A visit to the Citadel takes you to the heart of Al-Madina. The Citadel, towering over the *souqs, hammams,* mosques, and *madrasas,* is known as **Qal'at Sinjil** (Citadel of St. Gilles), after Raymond Saint-Gilles, the Crusading tough guy who took the city from the Mamlukes in 1099 CE. An octagonal Fatimid construction was converted to a church by the Crusaders. Some visibly layered Mamluke and Ottoman additions are also visible. A stroll to the top of the building yields an impressive view of Tripoli. *(Open daily in summer 8am-7pm; in winter 8am-5pm. Admission L£5000, students L£2500.)*

NEAR TRIPOLI

BCHARRÉ بشرى

Though a bus (L£2500) sometimes runs in the morning from near the Ministry of Tourism in Tripoli, Bcharré is most reliably reached by service from Koura Sq., across from the Ahram Hotel (L£5-6000). Service traffic back to Tripoli becomes thin later in the day, so it makes sense to start your trip early. Gibran Museum open July-Sept. daily 9am-5pm; Oct.-June Tu-Su 9am-5pm. Admission L£3000, students L£2000.

Bcharré's height almost reaches the statuesque proportions its most famous citizen achieved in life: trilingual writer, artist and mystic philosopher **Khalil Gibran** hailed from this tiny alpine hamlet. At 1400m above sea level, the quiet mountain air is a refreshing break from the noise and pollution of Lebanon's bigger cities. Moreover, the **Kadisha Valley,** which this red-roofed, predominantly Christian village overlooks, is among the most scenic spots in the country.

The **Gibran Museum** in itself is worth the trip to Bcharré. It houses the author's personal library and many of his drawings, manuscripts, and letters. The useful guidebook costs US$5, but copies can be borrowed from the museum. The guide contains pertinent aphorisms reflecting the sentiments that inspired Gibran's works. It also assigns titles to the artist's often enigmatic paintings. Gibran was a romantic, fascinated by the interplay of humans with each other and with God. Born here in 1883, he immigrated to Boston, Massachusetts, at a young age. In 1898 he returned to Lebanon to spend the summer with his father and then attend the Sagesse College in Beirut, where he studied Arabic and French. After traveling through Paris (where he met artist Auguste Rodin in 1908), Gibran returned to Boston. There, he wrote his English masterpiece, *The Prophet.* By the time he died in 1931, he had published 17 works in Arabic and English. His body was returned to the Bcharré hermitage for burial; as the last room of the museum, it provides a haunting epilogue to Gibran's life and work.

Since the town's two budget hotels closed down, the only reasonably priced accommodation is the **Palace Hotel** (tel. 671 4005; fax 671 460), 100m past the imposing St. Saba Church on the left. It offers fluffy carpeting, private baths, and a cavernous downstairs restaurant with a well-apportioned bar to complement its superb mountain views (singles US$25-30; doubles US$35-50; triples US$45-60; bargain in the off-season). **Shallal Rest** (tel. (03) 448 625), next to the waterfall up the road from the museum, serves filling, cheap sandwiches (L£1500-3000) and beer (L£2000) in a pleasant outdoor setting, made all the better by the tributary that flows through it to the waterfall (open daily 9am-9pm).

LEBANON

THE CEDARS

Getting to the Cedars is difficult. Arrange for a Bcharré-bound service to continue on to the Cedars (L£3-4000), or your only option will be the private taxis from Bcharré, which charge an outlandish US$10 for the return journey. A donation is requested.

The **Cedars of Lebanon** (*Arz ar-Rab*, "Cedars of God"), perched in the mountains about 5km from Bcharré, are more than a grove of gigantic, rare trees. The cedars are a symbol of ancient Phoenician trading history, a revered image of the modern Lebanese nation, and backdrop of some of the most beautiful ski slopes on the Mediterranean Coast. Most of the woods (all but 12 trees) were decimated for timber trade with Egypt (where the resin was used for mummification), Phoenician ship-building, and Roman temple and tomb construction. The few remaining patches have been protected since 1876. Near the end of the roped path through the grove, a dead tree has been skinned and varnished to create a curious monument.

The grove is especially elegant when cloaked with snow. The tourist office in Beirut (see **Beirut: Practical Information,** p. 467) has detailed information on winter skiing and snowboarding in the area. Accommodations in the area are generally expensive ski resorts waiting for the high season, usually between December and March. The **Alpine Hotel** (tel. 671 057) offers very clean mountainview rooms with spotless baths and satellite TV (singles with breakfast US$25, with half board US$35, full board US$45). The hotel can also set you up with a lift ticket (US$25 per day) and suit you up with skis (rentals US$10 per day).

EAST OF BEIRUT

BA'ALBECK بعلبك

Ba'albeck, 86km from Beirut, is the site of Lebanon's greatest Roman treasure—a majestic **temple complex** towering over the fertile Beqa'a plain. The temple alone is reason enough to visit the country. To the founding Phoenicians, the city was the center of worship for their leading deity, Ba'al. When Alexander and his band of merry Macedonians conquered the city in the 4th century BCE, however, they saw fit to make a few alterations. The city was redubbed Heliopolis (City of the Sun), and the names of the leading Phoenician gods were changed to honor three Roman deities: Jupiter (the Roman version of Ba'al), Venus (a Roman correlate to Ba'al's consort Astarte), and Mercury (the messenger of the gods, with no known Phoenician equivalent). When Christianity became the official religion of the Roman Empire in 325 CE, Emperor Constantine closed the Ba'albeck temples. Not to be outdone by polytheism's remains, Emperor Theodosius tore down Jupiter's altars in the **Great Court** of the complex and used the stones to build a **basilica.** The remains of the three apses of this basilica, originally oriented to the west, can still be seen in the upper part of the stairway in the Temple of Jupiter. After the Arab conquest in 636 CE, the temples were transformed into a **fortress** (*qala'a*) and the original Phoenician city's name restored. Over the next millennium-and-a-half, the same litany of conquerors that appears in every place in the Middle East (Umayyads-'Abbasids-Toulounids-Fatimids-Ayyubids-Mamlukes-Ottomans) had their way with Ba'albeck. The ruins were not restored until the late 19th century by Germany's Kaiser Wilhelm II and, after World War II, by the French. Today, Ba'albeck has achieved infamy in the West as home to the headquarters of **Hezbollah** (see **Modern History,** p. 461), and until six years ago was a no-go for tourists. Though Ba'albeck beckons to Western tourists today, visitors should respect local customs, avoid revealing clothing, and keep abreast of potential conflict in the area.

☷ ORIENTATION AND PRACTICAL INFORMATION

The approach to Ba'albeck from Beirut is via **Rue 'Abd el-Halim Hajar,** one of two main streets and home to two of Ba'albeck's three hotels. The other main drag is **Ras al-'Ain Boulevard,** intersecting Rue Hajar just past Ash-Shams Hotel. A left at the intersection leads to the temples; a right takes you along the river, past a park in Ba'albeck's most attractive area. On the other side of the park are the **Hezbollah Headquarters.** Following the boulevard east for about 5km takes you to its namesake, **Ras al-'Ain,** a pleasant spring. Off Rue Hajar on Sheikh 'Abdullah Hill, about 1km before town, the **quarry** is home to the world's largest stone.

The most common way to get to Ba'albeck is by **service** from Cola Bridge in Beirut (L£6000). You may have to change cars in Shtawra, the Beqa'a Valley's transport hub, but you should only pay once. **Buses** also run from Beirut's Cola Bridge (L£3000). Leaving Ba'albeck, *service* can be hired to Shtawra (L£2000), and from there to most destinations, including Homs and Sa'ida (30min., US$5).

The **post office** is several kilometers out of town along Ras al-'Ain Blvd. (open M-F 8-11am, Sa 8am-2pm). The **Central Telephone Office** is off to the left of Ras al-'Ain Blvd., about 150m from the main intersection. If you can't find it, ask locals for directions to the "Markaz Telephone Centrale." The small office is open 24 hours (U.S., Europe, Australia L£2000 per min.). **Fransabank** (tel. 371 870), along Ras al-'Ain Blvd., does not exchange travelers checks; do that at one of the **exchange booths** along Rue Hajar. Employees of **Pharmacy Ghassan** (tel. 370 320), on Rue Hajar across the street and up from Ash-Shams Hotel, speak a little English and a lot of French (open M-Sa 8am-10pm). **Police** (tel. 112) or the 24-hour **tourist police** (tel. 371 177) may be contacted in emergencies. Ba'albeck's **telephone code** is 08.

ACCOMMODATIONS AND FOOD

There are three hotels in Ba'albeck. Rock-hard beds come with a spectacular temple view at **Pension Shuman** (tel. 370 160), right in front of the temples on Ras al-'Ain Blvd. (US$6 per person). Softer, lunar-surfaced beds accompany slightly obstructed views at **Ash-Shams Hotel** (tel. 373 284), on Rue Hajar just before the intersection (US$6 per person). Both are squeaky clean and have sweet-smelling communal bathrooms. For a step back into the heyday of Victorian tourism, powder your nose at the **Palmyra Hotel** (tel. 370 230). Built in 1874, its guestbook includes Kaiser Wilhelm II, Kemal Atatürk (who is he, you ask? see p. 541) and Charles de Gaulle. The vine-lined cafe casually serves dinner on temple fragments, and the hotel's beautiful rooms preserve a bygone era of European decadence (singles L£57,000; doubles L£79,500; triples L£94,500).

Cheap Arab sandwich shops line Rue Hajar. The best of the lot is **Sindibad** (tel. 370 271), where the friendly owner will wrap up tasty vegetables or meat for immediate consumption (L£1500-2500). Several quality outdoor restaurants serving copious portions of traditional Lebanese *mezze* line Ras al-'Ain Blvd. Peruse the bill carefully, as some restaurants specialize in ripping off tourists.

SIGHTS AND ENTERTAINMENT

TEMPLE COMPLEX. The **Temple of Jupiter** (the tallest in the world) is easily recognizable by its six remaining Corinthian columns, each towering 22m high. How the massive stones were placed with such astonishing precision still remains a mystery. The columns hint at the immensity of the original standing structure, which was completed around 60 BCE. Jupiter's **Propylaea** and **Hexagonal Court,** the first structures you pass after paying the entrance fee, were added in the 3rd century CE. The circular **Temple of Venus,** outside the present-day tourist site to the left, dates from this time as well. The misnamed **Temple of Bacchus** is the most well-preserved building in the complex; its size and the intricate detail of its adornments make it one of the greatest Roman temples in the world. The temple was actually dedicated to Venus/Astarte, but exquisite reliefs of grapes and poppies on the main door indicate that this newer place of worship (completed in the 2nd century CE) was consecrated to a small cult of Bacchus, which drank wine and smoked opium during rituals. *(Open daily 8:30am to 30min. before sunset. Admission L£10,000, free with a letter from the Beirut Ministry of Tourism saying you're a student.)*

LEBANON

BA'ALBECK FESTIVAL. The temple complex, and more specifically, the **Great Court,** is the site of the world-famous **Ba'albeck Festival.** The festival began in 1955 and continued until 1974, drawing performers like Ella Fitzgerald, Rudolf Nureyev, and Margot Fonteyn. Over the last couple of years, the festival has been revived and has proven wildly successful. Get tickets in advance for next year's July through August bash—almost the whole country attends. *(During the festival, buses are available there and back from Beirut for around US$6, and service run to Ba'albeck from both the Cola and Barbir bridges in Beirut (L£10,000). For more info, call (01) 373 150 or email baalbeck@inco.com.lb. Festival tickets L£30,000-150,000.)*

ZAHLE

Zahle is accessible by service from Cola Bridge in Beirut (L£2000). Another option is to take a minivan headed for either Ba'albeck or Shtawra and ask to be dropped off at Zahle. If your ride won't go directly to Zahle, get off at Shtawra, 6km away, and take a service to Zahle (L£1000). If it's too late at night for service transport, you will have to rely on private taxis, which may charge L£5000-10,000.

A day in Zahle, an enchanting red-roofed city renowned for the quality of its wine and the quantity of poetry its wine-imbibing poets have produced, will cause even the most leaden sensibilities to fly off into grandiloquent verse. Founded about three centuries ago, Zahle's first 150 years were a bit less uplifting than a Mediterranean love poem. The town was destroyed three times, each time by fire. Ever unflappable, Zahle rose like a phoenix: by 1885, a newly constructed railroad made the town a vital internal port used by Beirut, Damascus, Mosul, and even Baghdad. Today, dozens of restaurants, most with outdoor seating, line the northern bank of the **Bardouni** river. It's even easier to find excellent, economical accommodations here than it is to get drunk on the well-priced *'araq.* Situated on Rue Brazil, directly across from the Khowry Hospital, the **Hotel Akl** (tel. (08) 820 701) is set in a beautiful old house with high ceilings. The rooms are spotless, the management friendly and trilingual, and the communal areas sunlit and inviting (L£25,000 per person, with private bath L£30,000; tea or coffee L£1500). Next door, the **Hotel Traboulsi** (tel. (08) 812 661), also inside a charming old house, is run by the friendly Umm George (George's mom). Though not quite as well maintained as the Hotel Akl, rooms are kept quite tidy and feature big beds and lovely patio sitting areas (L£20,000 per person, private bath included). Fine restaurants abound in Zahle; **Restaurant Le Coin** (tel. (03) 320 144), at the end of Rue Brazil, is a good one. Walk toward the restaurant area with the Hospital on your right. *Mezze* can be yours for L£11,000 (Burak L£7500 per dozen, local wine L£30,000 per bottle, *'araq* L£3000 per glass).

A'ANJAR

Service from Shtawra run to Mafra A'anjar (L£1000), where signs direct you down the 500m road to the site. To get to Shtawra, catch service from Beirut's Cola Bridge (L£2000) or from Ba'albeck (L£1000). You can also ask to be dropped off at Shtwarma on minivans from Beirut bound for Zahle or Ba'albeck (1-1½hr.). Open daily 7am-7pm. Admission L£6000.

This amazing locale dating from the Umayyad dynasty (705-715 CE) is the largest and best preserved Umayyad site in all of Lebanon, and perhaps in the entire Middle East. Built by Caliph Walid Ibn 'Abd al-Malik as a prosperous trade hub, A'anjar covers a staggering 114,000 square meters constructed in almost a perfect square. Roman influences are everywhere: like most Roman towns, A'anjar is oriented around the north-south **Cardo Maximus** and the east-west **Decumanus Maximus,** both lined with the remains of a columned arcade. The first building after the entrance on the left side is the **public bath,** complete with a vestiary (where bathers undressed and relaxed) and three separate rooms for cold (*frigidarium*), warm (*tepidarium*), and hot (*caldarium*) baths. The **Little Palace,** about 20m down the Cardo Maximus, is the best place to examine the intricate details that once adorned each building in the site. The **Tetrapylon,** at the intersection of the Cardo Maximus and the Decumanus Maximus, shows a Greek influence with Greek lettering on the bases and acanthus leaves on the Corinthian columns. On the same side of the Cardo Maximus is a mosque and the monumental **Great Palace.**

SOUTH OF BEIRUT

BEIT ED-DIN بيت الدين

17km down the coastal highway, 26km inland, and 850m below Beirut. Accessible by service (1hr., L£4000) from Cola Bridge in Beirut. The Beirut tourist office has a floor plan and site map worth picking up. Palace and museums open Tu-Su 9am-6pm. Admission L£6000.

The Beit ed-Din ("House of Faith") Palace is a breathtaking example of early 19th-century Lebanese and Italian Baroque architecture. It was built over a 30-year period by the dashing Emir Bechir ash-Shehab II, ruler of Mount Lebanon for over half a century, and bears triumphant testimony to his long reign. The ground floor houses a less-than-inspiring **museum** dedicated to the life of Druze leader Kamal Jumblatt, a member of Parliament and cabinet minister. Flanking the outer courtyard (Dar al-Baraniyya), where courtiers used to mingle, **Al-Madafa** is a two-story structure once used for receiving guests and now home to two museums. The ground level exhibits collections of photographs by well-known Lebanese and European shutterbugs. Upstairs, the long corridors of the **Rashid Karami Archaeological and Ethnographic Museum** display an impressive model of the palace complex, Bronze and Iron Age pottery, and Roman glass. The **Emir Amine Palace** perches just up the hill to the right of Beit ed-Din. The facade of the **central courtyard** (Dar al-Wusta) is among the palace's most beautiful features. Downstairs, a museum located in the former stables displays fantastic Byzantine mosaics, mostly from the ancient city of Porphyrion. Emir Bechir built three palaces, one each for his sons—Qassim, Khalil, and Amine. Qassim's is now in ruins and Khalil's is used as Beit ed-Din's seat of local government, but Amine's estate has proved to be Bechir's greatest investment. It is now a fully restored luxury hotel with 24 rooms, each with a private terrace and hanging garden. It's not quite budget (doubles US$167), but looking is free. Grab a beer but not much else at the pricey **Al-Hatemia Restaurant** (tel. 500 526), near the town's main square (shawarma L£7500-8000, beer L£3000-4000; open daily 7:30am-4am). The **Beit ed-Din Festival** is held annually in July and August in the palace's **outdoor courtyard**. It draws thousands of visitors and features international performers. Ask at the tourist office for details.

SA'IDA (SIDON) صيدا

Sa'ida, known as Sidon to the Phoenicians, is located 48km south of Beirut and was one of the three great Phoenician city-states (the other two were Byblos and Tyre). Although many of Sa'ida's ancient artifacts were plundered and sold by treasure hunters in the 19th century (some have even turned up on the black market recently), several sights merit a daytrip to Lebanon's third largest city. Sa'ida has a rich history, with evidence of habitation dating from 4000 BCE. The port flourished in the Phoenician era (12th-10th centuries BCE), and the city peaked during the occupation of the Persian Empire (550-330 BCE). Although glass manufacture was Sidon's biggest industry, it became most famous for its purple dye, made from the small shell of the Murex snail (see **Princes' Dye and Nymph's Charming**, below). Like other Phoenician city-states, Sidon suffered under a succession of conquerors, including Alexander the Great, the Romans, the Crusaders, and Salah ad-Din. Skirmishes continued until 1291 CE, when the city was finally conquered by the Mamlukes. It fell into obscurity during the French Mandate, but revived as an urban center over the past century. Modern Sa'ida is not as fun-filled as its ancient incarnation no doubt was: streets are clogged with garbage, the architecture is of the Mediterranean semi-modern cement school, and decent budget room and board do not exist. However, the Phoenician and Crusader ruins, as well as a lively *souq*, make Sa'ida a worthwhile daytrip from Beirut.

🔃 ORIENTATION AND PRACTICAL INFORMATION

Though Sa'ida is large, almost all sights (and the only hotel) fall within a concentrated area. Buses and *service* arrive and depart from **Sahet an-Nejmeh,** a bustling roundabout filled with patisseries on **Rue Riad as-Solh,** the main north-south street. Buses from Beirut follow this road past the beach and fun fair. The street continues past Sahet en-Nejmeh to the Castle of St. Louis, but changes its name to **Rue Fakhr ad-Din.** A right turn off Riad as-Solh leads to the parallel **Rue Shakrieh,** home to the only hotel in town. Follow Rue Shakrieh north towards the sea to reach the entrance to the Sea Castle.

Buses from Beirut's Cola Bridge should cost LS500, while **service** cost around LS2500. Both buses (LS500) and *service* (LS3000) depart regularly from Sahet an-Nejmeh for **Sur.** It's also possible to catch a *service* to **Shtawra** (US$5) in the Beqa'a Valley. Just south of Sahet an-Nejmeh, on the left of Rue Riad as-Solh and next to Grand Stores, is **Kotob Exchange** (tel. 720 322), one of the few places that will exchange traveler's checks (US$2 charge per check; open M-Sa 8:30am-2pm, F 8:30am-noon). As always, in an emergency, call the **police** (tel. 112) or an **ambulance** (tel. 125). Just across the street from the Kotob Exchange is **Pharmacy Atef Bissat,** an extensive drugstore with the longest hours in town (tel. 721 821; open daily 8am-10:30pm). **Hamond Hospital** (tel. 723 111) is the best in town. The **post office** is about 200m north of Sahet an-Nejmeh (towards Beirut) on the left of Rue Riad as-Solh (open M-Th 8am-2pm, F 8am-1pm). Sa'ida's **telephone code** is 07.

🍴🛏 ACCOMMODATIONS AND FOOD

The only hotel in Sa'ida proper is the **Hotel d'Orient** (tel. 720 364) on Rue Shakrieh, 200m up from the Sea Castle; (Arabic sign only, *Nazel ash-Sharq*). Grimy floors, back-poking mattress springs, and a smelly communal bathroom are LS20,000 per person. Comfortable upstairs rooms with TVs and fans are cleaner (singles/doubles LS25,000; triples LS30,000). The four-star **Mounes Hotel** (tel./fax (03) 666 657), halfway between Sa'ida and Sur in Sarafand, is a beautiful splurge with a pool, a dock for ocean swimming, an outdoor restaurant, A/C, private baths and refrigerators. Hop a bus or *service* bound for Sur and ask to be let off at the Mounes (singles US$40; doubles US$60; triples US$70; use of pool for non-guests LS5000).

The **Government Rest House** (tel. 722 469) provides outdoor patio seating amid palm trees and excellent views of the Sea Castle. Factor in the 20% tax when choosing *a la carte* among salads (LS3000-7500) and meat or fish entrees (LS5500-17,000), or get the spectacular tourist menu (LS18,000, tax included), reserved for groups of six or more (open daily 11am-midnight; Visa, MC accepted). **Al-'Arabi** is the first restaurant you pass when coming from Beirut, about 2km out of central Sa'ida on Rue Riad as-Solh. Out in Sarafand, try the **'Aroosat Kheyzaran** (no English sign; tel. (03) 249 231), 350m up the main road towards Sa'ida. This restaurant specializes in weddings, but you'll betrothe yourself to its free pool and deck. Fish and *mezze* for two *(quelle romantique!)* LS20,000, wine or beer LS15,000 (open noon-midnight). **Pastries** are a Sa'ida specialty, and easy to find.

🏛 SIGHTS

The **Old City** developed at the end of the Crusader period and contains *souqs, khans,* and other medieval remnants. The most interesting site in Sa'ida proper is the **Sea Castle,** a Crusader fortress built on a small island, connected to the shore by a stone walkway. Fishermen mend their nets on the foul-smelling and polluted beach by the entrance. Impressive *souqs* lie between the Sea Castle and the **Castle of St. Louis,** a ruined 13th-century structure erected on top of a Fatimid fortress during a crusade led by French King Louis IX. The **Great Mosque** is south of the *souq* on the way to the Castle of St. Louis. **Murex Hill** (see **Princes' Dye and Nymph's Charming,** p. 488) is just south of the Castle of St. Louis. (Open daily 8am-6pm. Admission LS2000, children under 10 LS1000.) The most important site is the **Temple**

of Echmoun, about 2½km out of town along the fast flowing Nahr al-Awali. Built in the 7th century BCE to commemorate Sidon's favorite god, Echmoun, this is the most complete Phoenician site remaining today. This god of healing and medicine, represented by a snake coiled around a staff, lives on in the medical symbol known as a caduceus, a symbol also adopted by the Romans for the wing-footed god Mercury. The large, pyramid-like temple is the oldest part of the complex, while the colonnade, surrounded on both sides by mosaics, was a later Roman addition. The **Throne of Astarte,** carved out of granite and flanked by two sphinxes, is one of the temple's most impressive features. (Follow the Rue Riad as-Solh north, with the beach on your left. After the fairgrounds, take a right and then bear left following the bank of the river. The temple is on the left. A taxi (ask for Bustan ash-Sheikh) will cost about L£4000 (open daily 8am-6pm; free).

SUR (TYRE) صور

The modern city of Sur sits alongside and atop the remains of the ancient Phoenician city-state of Tyre, 79km south of Beirut. When Herodotus (the so-called "Father of History") visited Tyre's Temple of Hercules in the 5th century BCE, the city had already existed for over 3000 years. The original settlement consisted of two islets, joined by King Hiram with a landfill in the 10th century BCE. During the next two centuries, the city passed through a golden age under the Phoenicians; its most famous citizen was the doomed queen Dido, the founder of Carthage. Indeed, Tyre was so important at the time that it lent its name to the ever-important Mediterranean, which was then known as the Tyrean Sea. During the 6th century BCE, the Babylonian Nebuchadnezzar laid siege to the city as headstrong Tyreans resisted for 13 years. The 4th century BCE brought Alexander the Great, cutting his bloody swathe to Persia. For seven months the Tyreans held the city, frustrating the great Macedonian so much that he destroyed half the city and massacred or sold into slavery the city's 30,000 residents after breaking through. Next were the Romans in 64 BCE; the Umayyads in 634 CE; the Crusaders in 1124; the Mamlukes in 1291; and the Ottomans in the 16th century.

Visit modern-day Sur for the amazing Roman ruins, including history's biggest hippodrome. Though the city stands just over 10km north of the Israeli-occupied security zone, travel there is safe except during particularly politically tense times. Check the news and ask locals about the present situation in Sur before going.

▶ ORIENTATION AND PRACTICAL INFORMATION

Modern Sur rests on a promontory that was once an island but has long since been silted over. The two harbors are named according to what they face, with the **Sidonian harbor** to the north and the **Egyptian harbor** to the south. The **taxi stand** and **bus station** are in the center of town, a few meters from the Sidonian port. Walk south, toward the Egyptian harbor, and take the first left to reach **Rue Abu Dib,** the main shopping thoroughfare of Sur. The first right off this street leads to the impressive ruins known as **Area One** (locals refer to it as **Assar Ja'fariyya**). A 25-minute walk farther along Rue Abu Dib leads to Sur's highlight, the **Roman Ruins,** known as **Assar Romaniyya.** The **Rest House** lies 150m towards the sea from the entrance to the ruins.

White **vans** (L£500) and air-conditioned Pullman **buses** (L£1500) connect Sur to Sa'ida. To get to Sur from Beirut by bus, change at Sa'ida (full trip L£1000). Direct **service** from Beirut's Cola Bridge run around L£5000. The **post office** (tel. 740 018) is 200m east of the taxi stand across from the UN building on Bawaba St. (open M-Th 8am-2pm, F-Su 8-11am). The same building also serves as the **telephone office** (open daily 24hr.; to Europe or U.S. 7am-10pm L£2100 per min., 10pm-7am L£1800; to Australia L£2400/2100; 3min. minimum). About 200m down the street, with the post office on the right, awaits the **Ezzedine Pharmacy** and its helpful, English-speaking staff (open M-Sa 7:30am-6pm, Su 7:30am-2pm). In an emergency, call the **police** (tel. 740 009) or an **ambulance** (tel. 140). Sur's **telephone code** is 07.

LEBANON

PRINCES' DYE AND NYMPH'S CHARMING

Since antiquity, the royal wardrobes of the world have been made from fabrics of the deepest purple hue. The color's regal associations originated off the coast of Sa'ida, where two species of **mollusk**, *Murex* and *Buccinum*, live in great numbers. Legend has it that the intense purple ink within their shells was discovered when the lovesick god **Melkart** was wooing the nymph **Tyrus**. One day Melkart's dog playfully bit into a shell and his muzzle came away purple. Tyrus then demanded that Melkart make her a purple garment from the shell in exchange for the consummation of his passion. Melkart quickly pulled some strings, establishing a powerful precedent for the dye's importance in trade, romantic and otherwise. The Phoenicians' mercantile production of purple dye was considerably more complex and messy, and probably less rewarding. Narrow-necked baskets baited with frog or mussel meat were placed in the sea; when a quantity of mollusks were gathered, they were brought to the factories. The yellowish sacs, which turn purple when exposed to light, were removed and boiled in lead pots. The Phoenicians did not like to clean up after themselves, and the snail shell refuse now forms the 50m high Murex Hill.

■ ACCOMMODATIONS AND FOOD

The cheaper of the only two accommodations in Sur is the **Elissa Hotel** (tel. (03) 287 855), named for Tyre's most famous resident and the founder of Carthage, Queen Dido (a.k.a. Elissa). With the Rest House on the left, walk 200m toward the Assar Ja'fariyya in the distance; the hotel is on the right. The Elissa offers two types of rooms: the luxurious, newly renovated kind, complete with private bath, TV, and air-conditioning (singles US$50; doubles US$65), or the less luxurious but adequate older type with no TV (singles US$35; doubles US$45). A large downstairs restaurant and nearby stretch of beach round off the amenities.

Cheap eateries cluster around the taxi stand. For a somewhat authentic taste of Italy, try **Pizzeria Italia** (tel. 742 562), on Rue Abu Dib across from Restaurant Abu Dib. Small (L£1500, toppings L£500) and large (L£6000, toppings L£3000) pizzas are the only things on the menu (open daily 9am-11pm).

■ SIGHTS

ROMAN RUINS. In **Assar Romaniyya**, it's possible to trace, as historian Edward Gibbon said, "the utmost lines of vice and virtue, the most exalted perfection and the meanest degeneracy"—in short, the lavish immensity of ancient Rome. The ruins begin with a monumental **archway** and **cardo** and include the remains of large civic buildings, an **aqueduct**, **baths**, and a **theater.** The **necropolis** holds hundreds of marble sarcophagi, some of which are also displayed at the National Museum in Beirut. Tyre's larger-than-life **hippodrome** (once buried under six meters of sand), is one of the largest and best preserved in the world, once capable of holding over 20,000 spectators. *(Open daily 7am-7pm. Admission L£5000, students L£2500.)*

AREA ONE. The small ruins at **Assar Ja'fariyya**, also called **Area One**, are filled with swirled colonnades, intricate mosaic floors, and remarkably well-preserved living quarters. What appear to be islands are actually the remains of Phoenician breakwaters. *(Open daily 8am-8pm. Admission L£5000, students L£2500.)*

LEBANON

SYRIA سوريا

US$1=41.85 SYRIAN POUNDS (S£)
CDN$1=S£28.11
UK£1=S£66.47
AUS$1=S£26.36
SAR1=S£6.88
EUR1=S£43.87
JD1 (JORDANIAN DINAR)=S£59.03
L£1 (LEBANESE POUND)=S£0.03
TL100,000 (TURKISH LIRA)=S£9.36

S£100=US$2.39
S£100=CDN$3.56
S£100=UK£1.50
S£100=AUS$3.79
S£100=SAR14.53
S£100=EUR2.28
S£100=JD1.69
S£1=L£35.88
S£=TL10,682

PHONE FACTS   **Country Code:** 963. **Police:** Tel. 112.

Syria's unique position at the meeting point of Asia, Africa, and Europe has made it a jewel of civilization. Encapsulated by the Caspian Sea, the Indian Ocean, the Black Sea, and the Nile River, the land records the presence of at least seven great empires. The silk route ran through Syria, a strong thread linking China with the Mediterranean and making Doura Europos (Salhieh) an ancient center of trade. It was here that copper was made pliable and bronze was invented. The kingdom of Ugarit (Ras Shamra) on the Mediterranean coast developed the first alphabet in history, and a royal palace at Ebla (Tel Merdikh) contains one of the largest documentary archives of the ancient world.

After a recent history of closed regimes and enmity with Israel, Syria is now open to travelers. From the sparsely populated Syrian Desert in the east to the west's balmy seashore, the country's natural beauty remains unmolested by masses of tourists. Backpackers are only beginning to pass through with increasing frequency, and organized tour groups are becoming more common. Get there before they do and discover magnificent Roman ruins, medieval castles, and prices that haven't changed since the dawn of time. Syria is one of the last frontiers of budget adventure in the Eastern Mediterranean.

HIGHLIGHTS OF SYRIA

■ Splendid stronghold of a city of rebels, the ruins of **Palmyra** (p. 510) defy the tug of time with the same flourish with which its queen once resisted the Romans.
■ This ain't just a castle—it's a castle on Crac. See **Crac des Chevaliers** (p. 516), the Crusader fortress that even Salah ad-Din couldn't conquer.

ESSENTIALS

ENTRY

Visa applications are available from any Syrian embassy. Send two completed applications (not photocopied), your passport (without evidence of a trip to Israel), two signed photos, a self-addressed envelope stamped for US$2, and payment (by money order only) to an embassy (3-month double-entry visas US$61). The embassy will return the passport with your tourist visa in it. If you visit **Israel** before a trip to Syria, insist that Israeli customs place **no stamp** in your passport, or more practically, have them stamp a piece of paper inserted in your passport that can be removed. Be warned that Syrian border officials may still refuse entry if they see that you have no Jordanian entry stamp or have an Egyptian exit stamp from Taba. All visitors staying in Syria for more than two weeks (even those with six-month visas) must apply for a **visa extension** on the 13th day of their stay. If possible, it makes sense to do this in one of the smaller cities where the bureaucracy is less entrenched and there are fewer people with similar requests.

EMBASSIES AND CONSULATES

Embassies and consulates within Syria are all located in **Damascus** (see **Practical Information,** p. 502). Syrian embassies abroad include: **U.K.,** 8 Belgrave Sq., London, SW1 X8PH (tel. (020) 7245 9012; fax 7235 4621) and **U.S.,** 2215 Wyoming Ave. NW, Washington, D.C. 20008 (tel. 202-232-6313; fax 797-1899).

✖ BORDER CROSSINGS

TO LEBANON. Crossing into Lebanon may take a long time due to the hyper-security at the border, but the path is well-trodden and simple. Daily buses run from Damascus to Tripoli or Beirut, and from Aleppo and Lattakia to Beirut. Though costly, it's possible to hire a *service* to drive across the border from Damascus. Citizens of Australia, Canada, Ireland, the U.K., the U.S., and most European countries can obtain a Lebanese visa at the border; Syrian visas, however, are not available if crossing from the other direction. If you want to visit Lebanon and then return to Syria, be sure to get a **multiple-entry Syrian visa,** since there is no Syrian representation in Lebanon and it is difficult to get a visa of any kind at the Syrian embassy in Amman. If you have a single-entry visa but wish to visit Lebanon and then return to Syria, go to the Immigration Office in Marseh Sq. in Damascus and request an **exit visa** that entitles you to be issued another visa at the Syrian border. This unusual request will require much bureaucratic dilly-dallying; avoid if possible.

TO JORDAN. The official road crossing into Jordan runs through the town of Dera. Daily buses run from Damascus or Aleppo to Amman. *Service* from Damascus are faster, but also more expensive. Jordanian visas are not available at the border; be sure to obtain one from an embassy or consulate before setting out. For true penny pinchers, the painfully slow Hejaz railway chugs (and chugs, and chugs) between Damascus and Amman.

TO TURKEY. Of the four official land crossings between Syria and Turkey, the Bab al-Hawa post on the Aleppo-Antakya road is the most popular, and often gets so congested that it takes a few hours to cross. Buses run from Damascus, Aleppo, and Lattakia to a number of Turkish destinations, most commonly Istanbul and the travel hubs of Antakya and Iskenderun near the border. Buy a Turkish visa at the border for US$20.

TO ISRAEL AND IRAQ. Syria's borders with Israel and Iraq are closed; neither situation is likely to change soon. The most common route between Syria and Israel is via Jordan and the West Bank. In the past few years, a few trade delegations have been permitted to travel by road between Baghdad and Damascus, but it remains to be seen whether a loosening of border restrictions will follow.

GETTING AROUND

TAXIS AND BUSES. Yellow private taxis, also known as **service** (ser-VEES), are user-friendly and relatively cheap. To hail one, hold out your hand with the palm down. Taxis have meters, but drivers rarely use them; negotiate a price before getting in. If a driver refuses to bargain, just point to the meter to get a fair rate. Beware and be firm—many drivers specialize in cheating newly arrived travelers.

Karnak, the government-run bus company, has extensive routes and low fares. Buses occasionally depart on schedule, and reservations are required. **Pullman** buses are a step below Karnak. Over 50 **private bus companies** now operate in Syria; they have ship-shape coaches and competitive prices. Reservations are a good idea for these buses too. Karnak, Pullman, and private buses usually leave from different stops—make sure you're at the right one. All tickets must be bought at the stations, as drivers do not handle money.

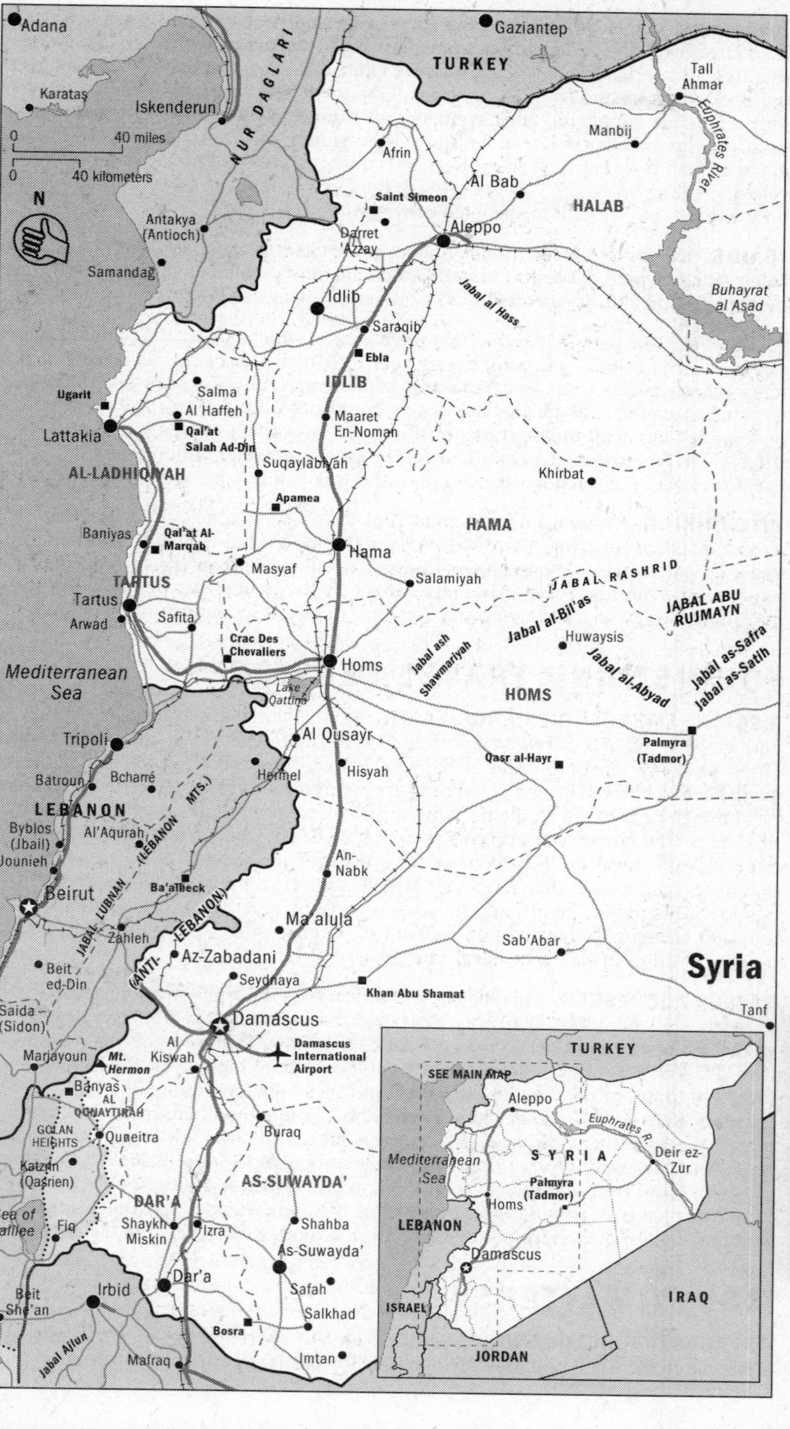
Syria
Adana
Gaziantep
TURKEY
Karataş
Iskenderun
NUR DAGLARI
0 40 miles
0 40 kilometers
N
Antakya (Antioch)
Samandağ
Tall Ahmar
Euphrates River
Manbij
Afrin
Al Bab
Saint Simeon
HALAB
Darret 'Azzay
Aleppo
Jabal al Hass
Buhayrat al Asad
Idlib
Saraqib
Ebla
IDLIB
Ugarit
Salma
Al Haffeh
Lattakia
Qal'at Salah Ad-Din
Maaret En-Noman
AL-LADHIQIYAH
Suqaylabiyah
Khirbat
Apamea
HAMA
Baniyas
Qal'at Al-Marqab
Hama
Masyaf
JABAL RASHRID
Salamiyah
TARTUS
Tartus
Arwad
Safita
JABAL ABU RUJMAYN
Jabal al-Bil'as
Huwaysis
Crac Des Chevaliers
Homs
Jabal ash Shawmariyah
Jabal al-Abyad
Jabal as-Safra
Jabal as-Satih
Mediterranean Sea
Lake Qattina
HOMS
Tripoli
Al Qusayr
Palmyra (Tadmor)
Qasr al-Hayr
Hisyah
Batroun
Bcharré
Hermel
LEBANON
Byblos (Jbail)
Al'Aqurah
(LEBANON MTS.)
Jounieh
An-Nabk
Ba'albeck
Beirut
JABAL LUBNAN
(ANTI-LEBANON)
Ma'alula
Zahleh
Sab'Abar
Az-Zabadani
Beit ed-Din
Seydnaya
Khan Abu Shamat
Saida (Sidon)
Damascus
Tanf
Al Kiswah
Damascus International Airport
Marjayoun
Mt. Hermon
Banyas
AL QUNAYTIRAH
GOLAN HEIGHTS
Quneitra
Buraq
Katzrin (Qasrien)
AS-SUWAYDA'
DAR'A
Sea of Galilee
Fiq
Shaykh Miskin
Izra
Shahba
As-Suwayda'
Dar'a
Safah
Beit She'an
Irbid
Salkhad
Bosra
Jabal Ajlun
Mafraq
Imtan
TURKEY
SEE MAIN MAP
Aleppo
Euphrates R.
Deir ez-Zur
Mediterranean Sea
SYRIA
Palmyra (Tadmor)
Homs
LEBANON
Damascus
ISRAEL
IRAQ
JORDAN

SYRIA

Microbuses (MEEK-ro-bus) are an easy, cheap, and relatively hassle-free way to travel between cities. They differ from clattery old **minibuses,** which are becoming less frequent on the roads. Microbuses are white minivans that drive on set routes within Damascus and to outlying areas. Like most *service,* they usually depart only when full. Untangling their confusing schedules may be difficult at first (destinations are often written in Arabic on the side of the vehicle), but they are cheaper than taxis for long rides. Fees in Damascus are set, but vary everywhere else depending on where you get off; ask the person next to you (not the driver) how much to pay or wait to see what other people are paying.

TRAINS. Strictly speaking, trains connect some cities in Syria. Frankly speaking, roller skates would serve you better. Trains are slow, crowded, and dirty, and in most places they drop you off about 30km out of town. Use the buses.

CARS. Very few people in Syria own private cars, which is why the public transportation is so good. If you want to risk your life driving one, cars can be rented at a few places in Damascus (see **Damascus: Car Rental,** p. 499). Cars are generally not worth the expense, as all the sights you could possibly want to see are easily accessible via cheap public transportation. For negotiable prices, some *service* drivers will be your private chauffeur for the day—a cheaper option than renting a car if you want the freedom to visit out-of-the-way places.

HITCHHIKING. There is no need to hitchhike in Syria. If you stand by the side of a road, an ultra-cheap microbus will eventually stop. It is not unusual, however, for truck drivers to pick up passengers in order to subsidize their trips (they usually expect S£1-2 per kilometer). Hitchers caught by the police may be hauled in for questioning or given a stern warning. *Let's Go* does not recommend hitchhiking.

TOURIST AND TRAVEL SERVICES

MEDICAL EMERGENCIES AND HEALTH. Syria is a clean and healthy country, and water in cities is normally chlorinated and safe to drink. Outside of the main cities, however, most tap water is likely to be unsterilized. Bottled water is readily available and advised in small towns. There are numerous pharmacies in Syria and no shortage of Western medicine. Quality and prices are regulated by the Ministry of Health. The government runs several hospitals and clinics, and there are also many private practices. With a doctor for every 2500 inhabitants, Syria has a better doctor-to-patient ratio than any other Middle Eastern country. However, its facilities are not state-of-the-art, and in cases of serious emergency, travelers should consider traveling to Lebanon or Jordan (or, ideally, Israel), or returning to their home countries. In case of **medical emergency,** dial 110.

USEFUL ADDRESSES. The **Ministry of Tourism** runs an office in Damascus (Rue Victoria, tel. (11) 223 7940; fax 224 2636; email min-tourism@syriatel.net; www.syriatourism.org) as well as a **Tourist Information Center** (29 May Street, tel. (11) 232 3953). Tourist police are strict, so locals don't hassle travelers much; in the event that they do, contact the **police** directly by dialing 112.

Syria's WWW Sites (leb.net/~hajeri/syria.html) is a comprehensive bibliography of web pages about Syrian politics, culture, and tourism. Find hard facts about visas, customs, and international embassies at the **World Travel Guide's** Syria site (www.wtgonline.com/data/syr/syr460.asp). In **Syria, A Photographic Journey** (www.manhal.com/), professional photos of Palmyra, Aleppo, and Damascus are accompanied by quotes from famous English authors who traveled in the region.

MONEY MATTERS

CURRENCY AND EXCHANGE. The basic unit of currency is the **Syrian pound,** abbreviated S£. Each pound is divided into 100 **piasters,** or *qirsh,* abbreviated pt.

You may bring as much foreign currency into the country as you like, but may not leave with more than you brought in. Amounts up to US$5000 do not need to be declared. The Commercial Bank of Syria has exchange desks at its many branches, as well as in major hotels. U.S. dollars are the preferred currency for exchange.

Credit cards cannot be used to obtain cash advances, though major cards like Visa, MasterCard, and American Express are increasingly accepted at large hotels and stores for purchases. If you are in a bind, some shopkeepers in the Damascus *souq* will disguise a cash advance as a purchase, although the exchange rate will be lower than the official bank rate. **Black market** exchange is most common in *souqs* or near Al-Marjeh Sq. in Damascus, where a thriving trade flourishes beneath the thumb of secret service agents on the lookout for offenders. Some hotels will unofficially change money for you at the black market rate, usually up to S$8 per US$1 more than the bank rate. (You should get no less than S$50 per US$1 using cash or traveler's checks.) Transactions using U.S. dollars are illegal (except to pay hotel bills): in 1986, a law was passed making illegal exchange or possession of hard currency punishable by up to three years in prison.

BUSINESS HOURS. The work week begins on Saturday and ends on Thursday. Friday is the official day off. Stores are generally open 8:30am-2pm, then again from 4-8pm in winter (4-9pm in summer). Some stores stay open all day in winter. Government offices are open 9am-2pm. Museums always close on Tuesdays, and are generally open 9am-5pm in winter, 9am-6pm in summer. Restaurant hours are variable. Most establishments serve food from 11am until the last few patrons leave (often after midnight).

TIPPING AND BAKHSHEESH. It used to be the case that nothing would get done in Syria without a bit of **palm-greasing.** Now, increased contact with the world market is changing the general attitude towards *bakhsheesh*. While bribes are no longer necessary to accomplish the smallest task (and are inappropriate when dealing with high government officials and police officers), tipping makes everything run a little smoother. Taxi drivers, waiters, and movie theater employees should be given at least a 10% tip. If you stay multiple nights at a hotel that cleans its rooms daily, a small thank you (S$20-40 per day) to the person responsible is appropriate.

ACCOMMODATIONS

There are no hostels in Syria, and the two hotel options span opposite ends of price and quality: expensive international chain resorts or basic hole-in-the-wall, bed-and-a-roof crash sites. The higher the quality of a room, the more likely it is that you'll have to pay in U.S. dollars; all two-star or higher hotels carry this requirement. In most places, there is an even split between hotels that charge Syrian pounds and those that demand U.S. dollars, but in heavily touristed towns like Palmyra, prepare to part with the dead Presidents. Different employees from the same establishment often quote contradictory rates; bargaining can save some money. Damascus and Aleppo hotels are less likely to respond to haggling, but if they look empty, give it a shot. Even posted rates can sometimes be brought down, if only by a few pounds. Unmarried couples may have a difficult time getting a room together; this is less of a problem in more expensive hotels.

KEEPING IN TOUCH

MAIL. Mail from Syria is inexpensive but slow (letters to the U.S. can take up to three weeks to arrive). Overseas letters cost about S$18, postcards S$11. Take packages to a post office for inspection before wrapping them up. **Poste Restante** service is available in Damascus's main post office; bring your passport and enough money to cover customs charges on parcels (letters carry no charge). The **American Express** office in Damascus (see **Practical Information,** p. 502) also holds mail.

TELEPHONE AND INTERNET ACCESS. Trials and tribulations abound. Damascus has a 24-hour telephone office where you can place international calls, but you'll need your passport, lots of money, and patience (at least an hour's worth). Some other cities have offices as well. Most hotels have direct-dial international capabilities, but rates from Syria are exorbitant (US$12 per 3min. to the U.S.), and hotels charge at least double the phone office rates. It's much cheaper to have your party call you back or to call collect. The access code for **MCI's World Phone** program is 0800, **AT&T's USADirect** 0801, and **Sprint** 0888. You can now use phonecards to make local calls; they are available at most post offices. Syria's **international phone code** is 963. Inside Syria, you need to dial 0 before the city code.

The Internet is not yet a viable means of communication in Syria. Cyber access is in its most rudimentary stage, and there are no Internet cafes open to the public. There are Internet terminals in the National Library in Damascus, but you must be supervised by an official, and the process is difficult and expensive. If you're dying to check your email, head over to Lebanon.

WOMEN TRAVELERS

Common sense is the best companion for women traveling in Syria. Men may make comments, but remember that ignorance is bliss; the best way to deal with harassers is simply to ignore them. If they prove persistent, raise your voice and threaten to call the police. If things get out of hand, alert the tourist police (tel. 112). Many female travelers have found that simply wearing a wedding band wards off many unwanted advances. For more tips, see **Women Travelers,** p. 29.

DRESS AND ETIQUETTE

Conservative dress is the norm for both sexes. Shorts, tank tops, and short skirts will invite stares, comments, and possibly sexual advances. Pants and skirts should fall to at least mid-calf and shirts should cover the shoulders and upper arms. It is considered impolite to point directly at someone or to point the sole of your shoe at someone (as when sitting down and placing an ankle on one knee). When a Syrian tips his or her head up and makes a clucking noise, this means "no"—Westerners have been known to mistake it for a sign of acknowledgment or a "get in the back seat" gesture by a taxi driver.

LIFE AND TIMES

ANCIENT HISTORY

"Each person has two homelands: his own and Syria." The words of Andrea Parrot, former director of the Louvre, may not be that far from the truth. The oldest alphabet in the world (and the precursor to most ancient and modern alphabets) was discovered at **Ugarit,** a site near Lattakia; **Ebla,** one of the oldest civilizations in the world (founded in the 3rd millenium BCE), was unearthed near present-day Aleppo; and the city of Damascus is the world's oldest continually inhabited city.

Greater Syria—a land area incorporating present-day Lebanon, Israel, Jordan, and Syria—has been the locus of countless land squabbles since ancient times and continues to be fought over today. The list of conquerors and rulers of the region reads like a who's-who of ancient history. After the rise and fall of Ebla around 2500 BCE, the Assyrian king **Shamshi-A'adad I** established his capital at Shubat Enlil (known today as Tel Leilan, in northeast Syria) around 1800 BCE. The **Hittites** moved in 200 years later and ruled until their rivals, the Egyptians, wrenched control of the area out their hands two centuries later. The **Arameans** migrated into Syria around 1200 BCE and established several minor kingdoms, the most important being Aram, near present-day Damascus. An endless array of ancient conquerors had their way with Syria in the years that followed: the Assyrians returned, quickly succeeded by the Babylonians, the Persians, and the Seleucids (who gave Syria its name). **Alexander the Great** added Syria to his empire during his massive land campaign in 333 BCE, establishing the city of **Antioch** as its capital. Next up were the Romans under Pompey, who made the entire region one of its many provinces in 64 BCE. It remained a province for several centuries.

The Arabs conquered Syria in 636 CE and established Damascus as the capital of the powerful **Umayyid** caliphate. The Abbasid caliphs were less drawn by Damascus' many charms, and moved the capital to Baghdad when they took over in 750 CE. Muslim rule ended in the 11th century when the Crusaders arrived and made Syria part of the Christian Kingdom of Jerusalem. Syria was freed from Christian control along with the rest of the Arab world when the great liberator **Salah ad-Din** overthrew the Kingdom of Jerusalem at the end of the 12th century. The Mamlukes moved in from Egypt around 1300 and ruled until the coming of the Ottomans.

MODERN HISTORY

Most of the coastal region of modern-day Syria officially became part of the **Ottoman Empire** in 1516. Syria's economy thrived over the following four centuries; the market towns of **Damascus** and **Aleppo** were particularly successful due to their locations along the trade routes between the desert, Persia, and Europe. During WWI, the German-backed Turks and the Suez-based British faced off in Syria. **Emir Faisal** and his Arab nationalist army backed the British, who promised pan-Arab independence. After emerging victorious, however, the British betrayed Faisal by carving up the Levant and placing Syria under the control of the French. In response, Faisal and British colonel T.E. Lawrence (better known as **Lawrence of Arabia**) conquered Damascus in October 1918. A bit peeved, the French strong-armed their way back into control (with the help of a 1920 mandate from the League of Nations) and battled nationalist rebels in and around Damascus until falling to Germany in 1940. British and Free French forces liberated the territory in July 1941, and **Syrian independence** came about when the last troops withdrew in April 1946.

The first few decades of independence were anything but peaceful. In March 1949, the country came under the first of a series of military dictatorships. **Pan-Arabism** became a major political force in Syria (and the rest of the Middle East) during the 1950s, heralded mainly by the rise of the **Ba'ath Party** (or Arab Socialist Resurrection Party). The Ba'ath Party has been and still is the strongest political force in Syria since rising to power in the 1963 **March Revolution.** The party was dealt a major blow by the **Six-Day War** against Israel in June 1967, which cost Syria the **Golan Heights.** The nation suffered further casualties, both in terms of lives and morale, when Syrian-backed Palestinian guerillas were defeated by Jordanian forces in the **Black September** hostilities of 1970 (see **Jordan: Modern History,** p. 409). After frantic finger-pointing among government officials, **Hafez al-Assad,** the Ba'ath's fair-haired boy and commander of the Syrian Air Force, seized control of the country and was sworn in as president on March 14, 1971.

Assad has since run the supposedly "democratic" nation of Syria as a tight-fisted dictatorship, though two events in the early years of his rule challenged his supremacy. In 1973, Assad and Egypt's Anwar Sadat launched a surprise attack on Israel known as the **Yom Kippur War** (see **Egypt: Modern History,** p. 48). After early Arab gains, the Israelis surged forward and came within 35km of Damascus, forcing Assad to cease fire and sign an armistice. In February 1982, the militant **Muslim Brotherhood** launched a rebellion from the town of Hama; most estimate that Assad's forces retaliated by killing between 5000 and 25,000 people. Assad's political skills proved more successful in the mid-1980s. When Israel invaded Lebanon in 1982, Assad responded by backing the main Lebanese Muslim militias, Amal and Hezbollah. Over the next few years, Israel and Syria clashed; by 1985, Israel withdrew from Lebanon, but Syria did not. Though formally an independent nation, Lebanon continues to take its major political cues from Damascus.

SYRIA

The money gained from **oil sales** in the 1970s allowed Assad to pursue a program of capital formation, but industries were haphazardly chosen and poorly run, leaving Syria with nothing but inefficient factories. The Syrian economy today suffers from the two-headed monster of rapid **population growth** and massive **inflation** (which reached 300% in late 1991, but has since dropped to a less stratospheric 22%). Unemployment stalled at 35% in the 70s and 80s, and the colossal bureaucracy (20% of workers are government-employed) is matched only by its colossal inefficiency. Western economic aid has been scarce due to Syria's connections with terrorist groups, support of Iran, and skirmishes with Western favorite Jordan. However, in exchange for support of the U.S.-led coalition against Iraq in the 1991 **Gulf War,** Syria received financial concessions and a free hand in Lebanon. Lately, Assad has actively sought Western aid to revitalize Syria's plodding economy: the loosening of travel restrictions for Syrian Jews and talks with Israel (see **In The News,** below) have curried favor with Western governments and investors.

In 1999, Assad was elected to his fifth term with 99% of the vote. Though Assad's policies have stabilized and even improved Syrian politics—he diluted the Ba'ath's centralized power by mandating the election of local councils (of which at least 51% must be workers or peasants)—his political longevity can also be attributed to the aggressive suppression of his enemies. The omnipresent internal security forces, known as the **Mukhabarat,** quell all anti-Assad sentiment. The government also has an abysmal human rights record, and has repeatedly been accused of harboring (some say training) terrorists. Today, all political parties are associated with the **National Progressive Front (NPF),** a coalition dominated by the Ba'ath Party and run by Assad himself. The **People's Council** is a 250-member legislative body, but since it is controlled by the NPF, Ba'ath policies pass with a minimum of opposition.

IN THE NEWS

The world turned its eyes to the **Golan Heights** in the summer of 1999 when President Assad and Israeli prime minister Ehud Barak seemed closer than ever to forming an agreement about the territory, under Israeli control since 1967. Syria has long claimed that the land was seized unfairly, and Assad has stated that he will settle for nothing less than full Israeli withdrawal. After his election in May 1999, Barak announced that he wanted to restart peace talks with Damascus, and many predicted that the handover of the Golan Heights was imminent. By August 1999, Assad and Barak had not yet begun talks, but U.S. Secretary of State Madeleine Albright visited the two countries to encourage a settlement in the near future.

RELIGION AND ETHNICITY

Islam is the dominant religion of Syria, the faith of 88% of the country's 17 million people. Of these, about 74% are Sunni and 14% are Shi'ite. The Shi'ite branch is split into several sects, such as the Isma'ilis (2%), and the Alawites (12%). The latter group counts President Assad among its adherents. About 10% of Syrians belong to the Catholic or Eastern Orthodox churches; 2% are Druze.

The statistics on Syria's ethnic composition vary, with different sources setting the number of Arabs between 82% and 90%. The rest of the population is Kurdish, Turkish, Armenian, and Circassian. Part of the Kurdish minority would like to create an independent state, which would also include the Kurds in Turkey, Iran, and Iraq. Their grievances have not yet been accompanied by constructive action; pamphlets distributed in 1992 brought about the arrest of 200 Kurdish activists. For more on the struggle for Kurdish independence, see **Turkey: Religion and Ethnicity,** p. 542.

LANGUAGE

Although only 82-90% of Syrians claim Arab ancestry, all speak **Arabic,** the official state language. **French** has long been a second language, but English is becoming more prevalent. Minority groups, such as the Kurds in the east and the Armenian population centered in Aleppo, continue to use their own languages. In some villages, you may encounter Turkish or possibly even Aramaic, the language spoken during Jesus' time. For some handy Arabic phrases, consult the **Glossary,** p. 702.

THE ARTS

Although the alphabet was first discovered in Syria, only recently has the world has discovered anything noteworthy in Syrian letters. One of the greatest poets in contemporary Syrian literature is the iconoclast **Adonis** (Ali Ahmad Sa'id). Adonis's experiments in modernism have earned him international fame; some claim he transformed Islamic culture as radically as Dante influenced Christianity. Adonis was the central figure of the **New Poets,** a group of Arabs who used poetry to challenge language, religion, and authority in the 1960s and 70s. The first of Adonis's seven poetry collections, *Aghani Mihyar al-Dimashqi* (*Songs of Mihyar the Damascene,* 1961) is the most readily available in English translation.

Possibly the most popular Syrian poet is **Nizar al-Qabbani.** Born in Damascus, Qabbani had a special passion for Beirut: he believed this "Lady of the Universe" was so beautiful that Arabs tried to destroy her out of envy. Such lover's passion characterized Qabbani's early work, mainly poems that scandalized traditional Arab society. His poems were so popular that they were set to music by famous singers including Umm Kulthum (see **Umm Kulthum,** p. 53). After serving as a Syrian ambassador, Qabbani abandoned the practice of politics and began writing about it. His strong nationalism led him to pen poems and essays ridiculing Arab dictators for their military failures, social backwardness, and human rights abuses. When Jordan and the Palestinians signed peace accords with Israel, Qabbani provoked fierce debate with the poem "When will they announce the death of the Arabs?" Newspapers and magazines printing his writings were banned in several countries. Other poems treat the oppression of women as a metaphor for Arab political problems.

FOOD AND DRINK

Syrian meals feature the typical Levantine staples: hummus, falafel, shawarma, shish kebab, and *shish tawouq,* among others. A particularly common dish is **farooj,** roasted chicken served with chilis and onions. Syrian desserts are delicious: **ba'laweh** is pistachio- or almond-filled filo dough; **burma** is shredded, fried dough with pistachios; and **basbouseh** is wheat pastry with syrup. Don't leave without trying the desert banana **bybil;** its short growing season (culminating in a harvest around Oct. 1) makes it one of the most prized fruits in the world. Other fruits are available in abundance; the **aseer** (fruit juice) available at stands is one of the best ways to rehydrate. Arabic coffee is a potent and bittersweet brew known as **ahwa.** Be careful when adding milk, though—Syrian milk is not always pasteurized. **Mandarin** is the Syrian-brewed soft drink. Liquor ranges from locally brewed beers such as Sharq and Barada (as well as Amstel smuggled from Lebanon) to **'araq,** an anise-flavored liqueur mixed with water and consumed from shot glasses. Ask for **booza** and you'll get ice cream, not alcohol.

MARY ATE A LITTLE LAMB
Anyone with knowledge of Middle Eastern cuisine will likely claim that the Syrian kitchen is one of the region's best. Such a claim should not be put forth sheepishly; it is supported by the large numbers of high-quality patisseries and Arab eateries that dot the streets of most major cities. The uninitiated should note, however, that some dishes are acquired tastes. The notorious "sheep's eggs"—actually sheep testicles—are the most famous example. Sheep also get special treatment in a Damascene favorite, *ma'adim,* which consists of sheep's hooves drenched in a hummus-like dressing and served over bread. Moving up the sheep's anatomy we arrive at mukh, sheep's brains: these are normally mixed with lettuce and lemon to produce "Brain Salad." If such a mix proves to be a gastrointestinal disaster, consider washing it down with a soothing cup of *zghourat,* a tea made from "useful plants in the ground" that tastes curiously close to its rough English translation.

DAMASCUS دمشق

Pre-Islamic Arabs looked upon the site of present-day Damascus and named it *Balad ash-Sham*, a phrase denoting green hills, plentiful soil, and an otherwise blessed *Jannat ad-Dounia* ("Heaven on Earth"). In the intervening centuries, other colors—Roman red, the French tricolor, the *service* taxi yellow—have refracted through the prism of history to render a city as colorful as the rainbow.

Though Aleppans will try to convince you otherwise, the Damascus area has been continuously inhabited longer than any other place in the world. Early historical references to the city include 3000 BCE Ebla tablets, as well as 15th-century BCE pharaonic inscriptions and records of city as the capital of the Aramaic kingdom. Centuries later, Roman invaders left their mark, most notably in the form of the Temple of Jupiter, built by Apolodor the Damascene. During the Byzantine era, Christians converted the temple into a church and built other monuments that still stand today. In 636 CE, Khaled Ibn al-Walid, otherwise known as the "Sword of God," conquered Damascus in the name of Islam. The city served as the capital of the Umayyad Empire for close to a century, at a time of enormous growth for the Islamic community. Damascus began to suffer when the Abbassids replaced the Umayyads and moved their capital to Baghdad. In the ensuing centuries, Damascus fell under the thumb of various Muslim dynasties and empires, including the Ottoman Turks, whose influence remains quite visible in existing Damascene architecture. During WWI, German and Turkish armies used Damascus as a base. After Syria came under French control, resistance raged hardest in Damascus; in 1925, the French crushed a popular revolt in the unruly city. Syria won its independence in 1946, and Damascus found itself the capital of a modern nation-state.

Today, the pulse, physical appearance, and odors of the city reflect contemporary realities rather than historical splendor. Damascus is a city of many faces: large fountains, parks, and wide avenues grace the newer part of town, while the winding cobblestone streets of the Old City house Damascus' Christian population and a plethora of small craft shops and bakeries. Downtown, pedestrians and cars constantly thrust and parry in an everyday street-level duel. Meanwhile, fruit stand owners and pastry makers pull chairs up to the curbs and look on, passing the day at a safe distance from the frenetic pace of bustling Damascus.

✦ ORIENTATION

With the help of a few landmarks, Damascus is easy to navigate on foot. The impressive **Hijaz Railway Station** is located at the intersection of **An-Nasr Street** and **Sa'ad aj-Jabri Street,** with an old railway car on display in front of its stone steps. Facing away from the station, Sa'ad aj-Jabri St. stretches directly in front of you. Walking down this street, the **post office** and **exchange bank** are on your left. Across the well-traveled footbridge crossing **Al-Quwatli Street**, Sa'ad aj-Jabri St. becomes **Port Said Street**. Continuing on Port Said St. brings you to **Yousef al-'Azmeh Square**. Radiating to the right of this landmark is **29 Mai Avenue** (called **29 Ayyar Avenue** in Arabic) and the **Tourist Information Center**. To the left is **Maysaloun St.** and the 5-star **Cham Palace Hotel** (pronounced *Sham*). Continuing past the Cham Palace brings you to **Abu-Roumaneh Street** (officially named **Aj-Jala'a Avenue**), a nicer residential area and home to several embassies and cultural centers.

Another important area, especially for those seeking cheap eats and hotels, pistachio desserts, or money changing, is **Al-Marjeh Square** (also named, but never called, Ash-Shuhada or Martyr's Square), two blocks off An-Nasr St. in line with the post office. Al-Marjeh Sq. has developed something of an ill reputation, as Russian prostitutes frequent many of the cheaper hotels here. In the center of the square, the **Barada River** surfaces from its underground lair in the form of a big fountain. Just up from Al-Marjeh Sq., across Quwatli St., and to the right of 'Azmeh Sq. is the **Bahsa** district, home to some of the nicest budget hotels in the Middle East. Continue right on An-Nasr St. from the Hijaz Station to enter the **Souq al-**

Hamidiyyeh and the **Old City.** A walk through the covered *souq* brings you to the **Umayyad Mosque** (at the very end of the *souq*).

A left turn from the Hijaz Station onto **Al-Baroudi Street** eventually leads to the **Foire Internationale de Damas,** site of the annual international exposition, where the Barada River flows and numerous fountains shoot high into the air. The **Taqiyyeh as-Suleimaniyyeh Mosque** and the **Military Museum** are on the right as you walk away from the station. The **National Museum** borders the river. The huge local **bus** and **service station** can be found under the **President Hafez al-Assad Bridge** on Quwatli St.

▣ TRANSPORTATION

Airplanes: Damascus International Airport lies southeast of Damascus. Buses to the airport leave from the Victoria Bridge on Al-Quwatli St. (S£10 for each piece of luggage, free if no luggage). A taxi to the airport costs S£300-500. There are regular flights to European and Arab capitals, and domestic 1-way flights daily to **Aleppo** (S£600), **Lattakia** (S£500), and **Deir ez-Zur** (S£600). Air travelers to **Beirut** must pay in U.S. dollars (US$60, 21-day round-trip ticket US$100). It is not uncommon for flights to be arbitrarily cancelled up to 24 hours before departure time. There is a S£100 **exit fee** if you leave Syria by air. The **SyrianAir** office (tel. 222 07 00) is on Sa'ad aj-Jabri St., across from the post office. Open daily 8:30am-7pm.

Buses: For **intercity transportation** north of Damascus, there are 30 private bus companies with competitive rates operating out of **Karajat Harasta,** on the eastern edge of the city. Arrive at any time and chances are a bus will be leaving for your destination within 30min. Among the most reliable operators are **Qadmoos** (tel. 512 22 60) and the **Damas Tour Co.** (tel. 511 90 67). Buses depart daily to: **Aleppo** (4½hr., noon, S£150); **Lattakia** (4hr., every hr., S£150); and **Hama** (3hr., noon, S£85). The government-run **Karnak Bus Co.** (tel. 231 14 93 or 231 61 36) is a 15min. walk west of Al-Marjeh Sq. Run-down buses service: **Bosra** (30min.; 11am, 2:30, 5, 7:30pm; S£50); **Amman** (4-6hr.; 7, 9am, 3, 4pm; US$6); and **Beirut** (3-3½hr.; 7:30, 8:30, 9:30am, noon, 1, 2:30, 3:30, 4:30pm; S£175). Similarly decrepit Karnak buses depart from Karajat Harasta to: **Aleppo** (4-4½hr., 7:30am and 4:30pm, S£130); **Homs** (2hr., every hr. 7:30am-6:30pm, S£60); **Lattakia** (4-4½hr., 8:30am and 2:30pm, S£125); **Tartus** (5hr., 2pm, S£100); and **Palmyra** (3hr.; 8:30, 9, 11am, 12:30, 2:30, 4:30, 6:30pm; S£100).

Service: Minibuses and **service** are fairly cheap and have the dubious advantage of leaving when full. *Service* travel to: **Aleppo** (3hr., S£300); **Amman** (4hr., S£400); **Beirut** (3hr., S£4-500); **Sidon** (4hr., S£500); and **Tripoli** (5hr., S£500). Domestic *service* leave from 'Abasseen Stadium; international *service* leave from Barumkeh.

Car Rental: Rental cars are remarkably expensive. There are a few places around the post office, but not much English is spoken. For helpful driving information in English, try **Hertz** (tel. 221 66 15; fax 222 61 81), at the Cham Palace Hotel. Rent with unlimited mileage for a day (US$60 per day) or on a weekly basis (US$55 per day).

Taxis: Private or **service taxis** (yellow cars) have meters and drivers are required by law to use them. If the meter isn't turned on (starting fare S£3), either demand that the driver use it or negotiate a fair price before getting in. Longer trips, like the one from Hijaz Station to Karajat Harasta, shouldn't cost more than S£80. If you think that the driver is cheating you, point to the side of the road and indicate that you are getting out; if this doesn't attract his attention, try opening the door. Although drivers are likely to get mad, they will usually concede a fairer price if you remain firm. Most drivers, however, will give you an honest rate and appreciate a small tip of S£5-10.

Microbuses: These white minivans (also called **service**) have predetermined routes and pick up passengers along the way. If one is going your way, flag it down and jump in. *Service* run to Mezzeh from the beginning of Ath-Thaura St. and to Muhajereen and Abu Roumaneh from under the President's Bridge (Jisr ar-Rais). A *service* also connects Baramkeh Station with Karaj Halab. As rides only cost S£3-10, even a short ride is usually worth it. Rap on the window when you want out.

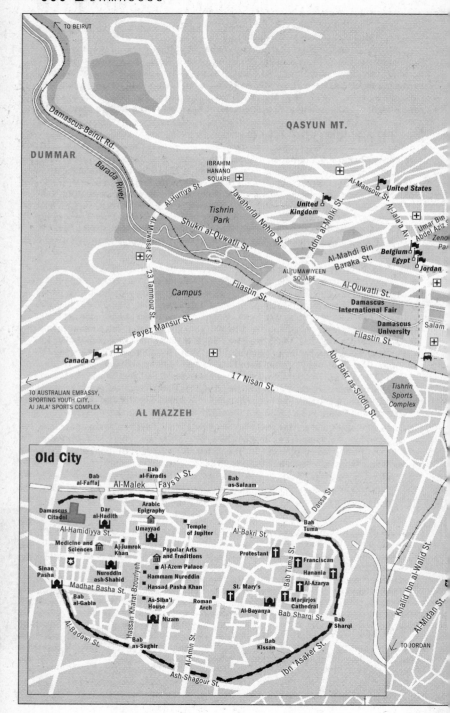

TO BEIRUT

QASYUN MT.

DUMMAR

Damascus-Beirut Rd

Barada River

IBRAHIM HANANO SQUARE

Al-Hurriya St.

Jawaherlal Nehro St.

Tishrin Park

Shukri al-Quwatli St.

Al-Muwasat St.

23 Tammouz St.

Campus

Filastin St.

Fayez Mansur St.

Canada

17 Nisan St.

Al-Mansour St.

Al-Jala'a Av.

United States

United Kingdom

Adna al-Malki St.

Al-Mahdi Bin Baraka St.

AL 'UMAWIYEEN SQUARE

Umar Bin Abdel Aziz

Zenoi Par

Belgium

Egypt

Jordan

Al-Quwatli St.

Damascus International Fair

Damascus University

Salam

Abu Bakr as-Siddiq St.

Filastin St.

Tishrin Sports Complex

TO AUSTRALIAN EMBASSY, SPORTING YOUTH CITY, AJ JALA' SPORTS COMPLEX

AL MAZZEH

Old City

Bab al-Faffaj

Bab al-Faradis

Al-Malek   Faysal St.

Bab as-Salaam

Dassa St.

Damascus Citadel

Dar al-Hadith

Arabic Epigraphy

Al-Hamidiyya St.

Umayyad

Temple of Jupiter

Al-Bakri St.

Bab Tuma

Medicine and Sciences

Aj-Jumrok Khan

Popular Arts and Traditions

Protestant

Franciscan

Sinan Pasha

Nureddin ash-Shahid

Al-Azem Palace

Hammam Nureddin

Hassad Pasha Khan

Bab Tuma St.

Hanania

Al-Azarya

Madhat Basha St.

Hassan Kharat Bzouriyeh

St. Mary's

Marjirjos Cathedral

Bab al-Gabia

As-Siba'i House

Roman Arch

Al-Bayanya

Bab Sharqi St.

Bab Sharqi

Nizam

Al-Badawi St.

Bab as-Saghir

Al-Amin St.

Bab Kissan

Ibn 'Asaker St.

Khalid Ibn al-Walid St.

Al-Midan St.

Ash-Shagour St.

TO JORDAN

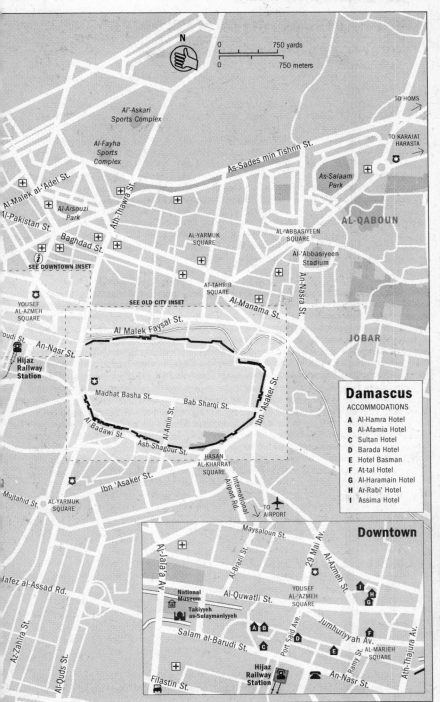

7 PRACTICAL INFORMATION

TOURIST AND FINANCIAL SERVICES

Tourist Office: 29 Mai Ave. (tel. 222 23 88). From Yousef al-'Azmeh Sq., walk to the right of the white modern building; the poster-coated office will be on your left. Maps and info in English. Open Sa-Th 8am-2pm and 4-7pm, F 9am-11pm.

Tours: Nawafir Travel and Tours (tel. 231 93 27; fax 231 94 57), in the basement of Al-Assima Hotel in Bahsa. Much more helpful than the disorganized official office, Nawafir serves as the *de facto* tourism info office for both Damascus and greater Syria. Ask 'Adnan Habbab and Martin about "Marhaba Service," which arranges transportation from the airport and a 1-night stay at a 2-star hotel for newly arrived travelers (US$45). Open daily Apr.-Sept. 9:30am-2pm and 5-9pm; Oct.-Mar. 9:30am-2pm and 4-8pm.

Embassies: Australia, 128 Al-Farabi St. (tel. 613 23 23; fax 613 24 78). Open Su-W 7:45am-4pm. **Canada,** Block 12, Al-Mezzeh (tel. 611 66 92; fax 611 40 00). Open Su-W 8:30-11:30am and 2-4pm, Th 8:30-11:30am. **Egypt** (tel. 333 35 61), on Aj-Jala'a Ave. in Abu Roumaneh. Open daily 9am-3pm. **Jordan** (tel. 333 46 42), in Abu Roumaneh. Open Sa-Th 9-11am. **Turkey,** 48 Ziad Ben Abi Sufyan St. (tel. 333 14 11; fax 333 92 43). Open Su-Th 8:30-11am. **U.K.,** Malki Kurd Ali St. (tel. 371 25 61/2; fax 373 16 00). Open M-Th 8:30-10:30am. **U.S.,** 2 Al-Mansour St. (tel. 333 23 15, emergencies 333 13 42; fax 224 79 38), in Abu Roumaneh. Take Aj-Jala'a Ave. (Abu Roumaneh) away from Al-Quwatli to Rawdat Abilalan Sq. The stars and stripes are flying to the left. Consular section open Su-Th 8-11am. Observes all U.S. and most Syrian holidays.

Visa Extension Office: Head down Sa'ad aj-Jabri St. towards the Hijaz Train Station. Turn left at the end of the Barada Hotel; the office will be on the left side. A near-flawless display of Syrian bureaucratic inefficiency. Travelers staying in Syria for longer than 2 weeks must register with the police and apply for a visa extension. You will be sent to various places, including a photocopy store (if they forget to use carbon paper) and possibly to a very special room downstairs where a uniformed man with your passport in his hand asks you for a tip. It is not required. Open 8am until sometime in early afternoon, usually just before you show up. Go in the morning.

Currency Exchange: Always a chore. Even though it's illegal, many shop owners and travel agents in Damascus will discretely offer to change foreign currency at higher rates than the banks. If you don't want to risk getting dragged to a Syrian detention center, take traveler's checks to the **American Express Office** (see below). Head to the bank only if that doesn't work. Banking hours are Sa-Th 8am-2pm; many are open 4-8pm as well. The **Commercial Bank of Syria,** at Yousef al-'Azmeh Sq., has a foreign cash exchange window. Open Sa-Th 9am-1:30pm. The branch in front of the Hijaz Station exchanges cash and traveler's checks. To change traveler's checks, bring your passport, your purchase record, and S£25 per check. Open Sa-Th 10am-6pm, F 10:30am-3pm.

American Express: (tel. 221 78 13; fax 221 79 38), to the right of the Sudan Airways office on Al-Mutannabi St. Heading away from Hijaz Station toward Yousef al-'Azmeh Sq., take a left on Fardous St.; Al-Mutannabi is the first left. Holds mail for AmEx clients, exchanges traveler's checks, and serves tea. One lump or two? Open Sa-Th 9am-1:30pm and 5-8pm.

LOCAL SERVICES

English Bookstores: The **Librarie Universelle** (tel. 223 23 00, ask to be transferred), in the Cham Palace Hotel near Yousef al-'Azmeh Sq., has 2 big shelves full of paperbacks. Yesterday's *International Herald Tribune* and last week's *Time* and *Newsweek* also available. Open daily 9am-9pm. The **Sheraton** and **Meridien Hotels** have smaller selections.

Cultural Centers: American Cultural Center, 87 Rue Ata Ayoubi (tel. 333 18 78). Frequent film screenings and concerts. Open Su-Th 8am-4:30pm. **British Council** (tel. 333 84 36), at Rawdah Sq. on the left side of Aj-Jala'a Ave. in Abu Roumaneh. A/C reading room. Open Sa-Th 9am-9pm.

Laundromat: Al-Akrami laundry service, next to Al-Haramain Hotel in Al-Bahsa, off Al-Marjeh Sq. Pants S£25, shirts S£20, socks S£5, underwear S£10. Open Sa-Th 7am-8pm.

EMERGENCY AND COMMUNICATIONS

Pharmacies: Hours are generally Sa-Th 9am-1:30pm and 5-9:30pm. Try **Kassar** (tel. 222 73 47), across from the post office on Sa'ad aj-Jabri St. Pharmacies rotate late hours; if you can't read the posted Arabic lists, inquire at a larger hotel. The all-night **Central Pharmacy,** on Saba' Abhar Sq., closes for lunch 1-5pm.

Emergency: Police: Tel. 112. **Ambulance:** Tel. 110. U.S. citizens can call the embassy (tel. 333 32 32). For medical problems call the **Red Crescent** (tel. 442 16 00) or **Al-Assad aj-Jami'i Hospital** (tel. 212 65 00).

Tourist Police: Tel. 222 00 00. Take Al-Quwatli St. past the National Museum; the Office of Tourist Police will be directly under Hafez al-Assad Bridge, on the left side of the street. English-speaking and open 24hr.

Post Office: Tel. 221 90 00, on Sa'ad aj-Jabri St., down the street directly in front of the Hijaz Railway Station on the left. Open Sa-Th 8am-7pm and F 9am-noon. **Poste Restante** charges only parcels. Rates depend on Syrian customs. The **EMS** (tel. 223 69 00) office is directly behind the post office, in a little building in the parking lot. Delivery to North America or Europe normally takes 3 days. Open Sa-Th 8am-6pm.

Telephone Office: On An-Nasr Ave., 1 block to the right of the Hijaz Station towards the Old City. Open daily 8am-10pm. For international calls, bring your passport, lots of cash, and a good supply of patience—placing calls can take up to an hour. A far easier way to place both domestic and international calls is to buy an **Easycomm phonecard** from the post office. Cards come in various denominations and can be used at any of the many Easycomm phone booths that dot the city.

Telephone Code: 11.

ACCOMMODATIONS

In two-star or better hotels, prices for foreigners are listed in U.S. dollars, though other Western currencies are often accepted. The Syrian government, eager to grab greenbacks, charges "wealthy" tourists two to three times what Syrians and those with residence permits pay in Syrian pounds. Most hotels accept traveler's checks and will give change in dollars, but it's a good idea to have small bills on hand to simplify exchange and avoid horrible hotel exchange rates. The best two-star hotels are located near Hijaz Station and the post office, but Al-Marjeh Sq. has cheaper, equally comfortable options. Many "hotels" in this area moonlight as brothels and may turn you away if you're not paying extra for a bedmate, but don't let the sleazy places keep you from finding jewels—inexpensive hotels with high ceilings, clean bathrooms, and bug-free beds. Many one-star hotels are both cheaper and cleaner than the "superior" two-star joints. Never forget to bargain, especially in the off-season or if a place looks empty.

AL-MARJEH SQUARE

Al-Haramain Hotel (tel. 231 94 89 or 231 42 99), on Bahsa St. With your back to the 'Umar al-Khayyam Hotel in Al-Marjeh Sq., walk down the small, one-way street to the left. Cross the big street (Al-Quwatli or Al-Bahsa St.) and go right, looking for the signs; the hotel is down an alley on the left. Clean and bright, this old Damascene house with an open courtyard and a fish-filled fountain is perhaps the best place to stay in Damascus. Schmooze with the super-friendly staff to get the inside scoop on "Dimashq." Singles S£235; doubles S£360-95; triples S£495. Hot showers included in fees (S£35 for non-guests). Breakfast S£65. Reserve 1-2 days in advance. Visa, MC accepted.

Ar-Rabi' Hotel (tel. 231 83 74; fax 231 18 75), next door to Al-Haramain and similar in style (though not as well maintained). A backpacker haven with a larger courtyard than Al-Haramain. International phone service, airport transport, aid with hotel reservations. 3-bed dorms S£175; singles S£250; doubles S£375; triples with bath S£525. Breakfast S£75. Staff recommends reservations up to 10 days in advance during summer.

Assima Hotel (tel. 231 85 67), in Bahsa. It's beside a big parking lot on the second right as you walk up Midan Yousef al-'Azmeh St. towards 'Azmeh Sq. Appliances don't always work, but 2-star rooms make up for what they lack in character with a nice rooftop cafeteria and a great *Let's Go* discount (about US$8 off). Manager Adnan Habbab, who also runs Nawafir Travel and Tours, can answer any and all questions about Syria. Singles US$17; doubles US$23; triples US$30-35.

Hotel Basman (tel. 221 80 03; fax 224 66 89), 1 block uphill from Al-Marjeh Sq. on the right corner of Rami St. Spacious and pleasant rooms with mini-fridge, TV, fans, and bath. Staff speaks little English. Singles US$17; doubles US$23; triples US$28.

At-Tal Hotel (tel. 231 55 82/3), next to Imad on Ash-Shuhada'a St., with an unmistakable yellow and green sign. Clean, A/C rooms are popular with Iranians. Windows afford great views of Al-Marjeh Sq. A 3-star hotel with great rooms but higher prices. Extras include TV/VCR (US$1), fridge (US$1), extra bed (US$8), and breakfast (US$3). Laundry service available. Singles US$24; doubles US$31; triples US$36.

NEAR HIJAZ STATION

Barada Hotel (tel. 221 25 46), directly across from Post Office on Sa'ad aj-Jabri. High-ceilinged, spacious rooms have hardish mattresses. Bathrooms have clean but stained floors. The price is right: singles US$14; doubles US$20; triples US$25; quads US$30. Private bath US$3. Hallway shower US$2.

Al-Afamia Hotel (tel. 222 91 52 or 89 63; fax 221 46 83), off Joumhouriyyah St. directly behind the post office; take the first left after the massive building. Enormous beds, TV, and private bathrooms, plus amiable management. Spotless rooms on the top floor are brand new and the best deal for those seeking European standards: singles US$25; doubles US$28; triples US$33. Lower floors are remarkably less immaculate, but cheaper as well: singles US$22; doubles US$25. Reserve at least 4 days in advance.

Sultan Hotel (tel. 222 57 68 or 221 69 10; fax 224 03 72), on Al-Barudi St. With your back to the station, turn left, and the Sultan is a block down across the street. Rooms are far more colorful than average with red and green carpets and stained glass windows. Small, multi-language library in the lobby. Singles with bath US$24; doubles US$25; triples US$30. Rooms with A/C US$1 extra. Breakfast US$6. No credit cards.

Al-Hamra Hotel (tel. 221 07 17 or 223 73 49), on Furat St. around the corner from Al-Afamia. Spacious, carpeted hallways lead to rooms that are well-furnished, but could use an extra scrubbing and more light. *Let's Go* discount prices: singles US$17; doubles US$23; triples US$28.

◨ FOOD

Hummus, falafel, and shawarma star as Damascene staples—there are as many food stands around Al-Marjeh Sq. as there are portraits of the big man. Fresh fruit stands serve juices that are meals unto themselves. Prices are fairly low (hummus S£30, falafel S£15, shawarma S£25, large juice S£40-50). The best pastry shops are around Al-Marjeh Sq.—don't miss the sinfully honey-glazed pistachio treats.

Maysaloun Street, just off Yousef al-'Azmeh Sq. past the Cham Palace Hotel, is home to numerous sit-down restaurants and ice cream parlors. In the evenings, the street fills with cologne-scented sweets-lovers, strolling with a sundae or large juice in hand. **Damer Patisserie**, on Maysaloun St., is the best ice cream parlor in Damascus (open Sa-Th 9am-12:30am). If you've had enough hummus, good pizzerias line Abu Roumaneh St., one block down from Damer. The **Christian Quarter** in the Old City (Bab Touma Sq.) has good atmosphere, great falafel, and a genuine fast-food pizza joint. Christians also flout their freedom from alcohol restrictions.

Nadi al-'Ummal (tel. 231 87 69). Turn right off 29 Mai St. near 'Azmeh St. at Cinema as-Sufara, then follow the lamp-lined path to the end of the street. You won't find many proletarians at this "Workers' Club," but you will find excellent appetizers (S£50-70) and grills (S£85-100) while relaxing in the *argeileh*-scented breezes of an old Damascene courtyard. Barada beer S£60. *Argeileh* S£80. Open Sa-Th 5pm-midnight.

(ALMOST) FINGER-LICKIN' GOOD Slower than its neighbors Lebanon and Jordan to import grease-to-go Western fast food chains, Syria may seem to be catching up based on the plethora of KFC advertisements that have recently sprung up. Contrary to the signs and to popular belief, though, there is no Kentucky Fried Chicken in Damascus. The Colonel and his artery-clogging fare opened for just one day before the government shut him down for being too Western. The unlucky but enterprising owner soon hit upon an ingenious solution: he made a few alterations on his sign and quickly re-opened shop as the Kuwaiti Food Company. Plans to garb the Colonel in traditional Arab headgear have been put on hold.

Abu al-Ezz (tel. 221 81 74 or 224 60 05). Facing away from the front of the Umayyad Mosque, walk through the arch of the Temple of Jupiter and take your first right; it's on the left. One of the best places in Damascus to soak up Syrian atmosphere and food. Enticing but pricey menu includes sheep eggs (S£300) and the usual Middle Eastern fare (boiled lamb in yogurt S£160). Lunch S£150-200, dinner around S£400. Reservations required for dinner. Live music and whirling dervishes in the Bedouin tent after 9:30pm. Open daily 8am-1am. No credit cards.

Ash-Shamiat (tel. 222 72 70), off Abu Roumaneh in An-Nijma Sq. This local favorite caters to an eclectic crowd of expats and Damascene intellectuals. Uncover the restaurant's kitsch conspiracy: beaded lamps, hanging baskets, and embroidered tablecloths are everywhere. Appetizers S£15-55, meat entrees S£60-100. Open daily 7am-3am.

Abu Kamal (tel. 222 42 65), Yousef al-'Azmeh Sq., in the Ministry of Labor building on the corner of Fardous St. Serves devastating Syrian fare at prices that are not. The dirt of Damascus' streets is nowhere to be found on the white, polished floors. Bow-tied waiters bring succulent entrees (S£110-200) while you gaze through large windows onto Yousef al-'Azmeh Sq. Delicious Aleppo-style kebab S£110. Appetizers S£35-50. Open daily 7am-2am. Visa, MC accepted.

'Ali Baba (tel. 222 54 34), Yousef al-'Azmeh Sq., in the basement of the Ministry of Labor building on the corner of Fardous St. You are received with open arms on the 1st floor and escorted to the basement, a womb of Arab decoration and decorum. Appetizers S£40-90, entrees S£100-200. Spirited performances by whirling dervishes (and dervishettes) Th and Sa 8:30-11pm. Open daily 9am-midnight. Visa, MC, AmEx accepted.

Umayyad Palace Restaurant (tel. 222 08 26), in the Old City. Walk to the right of the Umayyad mosque, turn right, and follow the many signs. The dark alley leading here may deter single women. Eat like a caliph in the spectacular (albeit expensive) downstairs restaurant. Everything you'd never dare to order is here to sample. Lunch buffet S£350, dinner S£700. Musicians or dervishes perform nightly 8pm-midnight. Open daily 12:30-4:30pm and 8pm-midnight.

Pizza Roma (tel. 331 64 34), off Maysaloun St., on the right just past the Cham Palace. A modern and authentic pizza joint with a rare (but rather feeble) salad bar (e.g., no lettuce). Create your own pizza with thick or crispy crust and a variety of swine-less toppings. Pizza margherita S£50. Open daily 8am-1am.

🎵 ENTERTAINMENT

As the evenings cool, Damascene-sters take to the streets. Outdoor cafes pepper the area behind the Umayyad Mosque. By the end of the evening, the place grows into a big street party as people pull up chairs to drink or smoke *argeileh*. One of the best of the Old City cafes is **An-Nawfara** (tel. 543 68 13), featuring Arabic storytelling nightly at around 9pm (*argeileh* S£50, Turkish coffee S£25; open daily 8am-midnight). To reach the cafe, head down Souq al-Hamidiyyeh toward the Umayyad Mosque. Turn right at the mosque and proceed around the mosque wall. Take the first right; the cafe is on the immediate right. **Maysaloun Street,** past the Cham Palace Hotel, hops until 1am, when the ice cream stores and juice stands close.

WHY YOU GOTTA (FORE)PLAY ME LIKE THAT?

No self-respecting Damascus movie theater lacks eye-catching advertisements. Go to any of these movie houses and you will likely encounter posters depicting couples in titillating positions, captured *in flagrante delicto,* adding a bit of erotic flair to the already frenzied Damascene streets. A striking example of this involves two healthy maidens clad in black bikinis, captured by the camera as they jump off a boat into the sea and expose just the requisite amount of flesh to set those raging hormones aflame. Anyone hoping that the promises made outside the theater will come to fruition inside, however, will be disappointed: Syrian censorship laws require that sexually explicit material be deleted from films. The laws say nothing about advertisements, however, and Damascene movie house managers accordingly exploit the loophole.

Most of the late-night and early-morning activity in Damascus takes place in the bars of the larger hotels and in the Christian quarter around Bab Touma, where the Muslim alcohol restrictions are thrown by the wayside. While the nicer bars in Bab Touma and the hotels are an exception, women will not be received warmly at most locals bars. It's prudent to enlist trustworthy male companionship. The closest approximation to a mellow Western bar is **Mar Mar** (tel. 541 00 41), in Bab Touma near Hammam Bakree, across from the Al-Issar Restaurant. Young, wealthy jetsetters drink beer (S£100) or eat steak (S£275) while listening to the fresh tunes of local constellations (open Th-Su until 2am; you may need reservations on Th and Sa nights). **Le Piano** (tel. 543 03 75), is on the last left off of Hanamia St. before Bab Sharqi in the Old City. It serves beer (S£120) and plays karaoke amid musically themed decor. There's no cover charge, but reservations are necessary and singles are admitted to the bar only (not to tables). For more classy Middle Eastern decor, head down the street to **Casa Blanca.** With a beautiful roofed courtyard and an open-air fountained terrace, Casa Blanca is a great place to go for a lap-of-luxury drink (beer S£100-150, wine S£450-900). Several embassies rotate hosting parties on Thursday nights; call the American or British embassies for details. The high-quality **Cham Palace Theater** has regular showings of American films at 12:30, 3:30, 6:30, and 9:30 (S£100). There are numerous **swimming pools** in Damascus (many at larger hotels) where you can take a dip for S£200. For a steamier time, you might consider 1 of the several *hammams* (Turkish baths) that gurgle around the *souq.* The **Hammam Nour ed-Din** (tel. 222 95 13), close to 'Azem palace. is the most luxurious establishment. Full massage, bath, soap, and sauna cost S£240. The baths here are for men only (opem daily 9am-midnight). Women who want to experience similar pleasures can go to **Hammam al-Ward** (tel. 231 43 07), near the black and white Al-Ward Mosque in Bahsa, two streets behind the Al-Haramein Hotel (open 9am-11pm; Tu-W for women, Th-M for men; the works S£200).

◉ SIGHTS

Today, the Old City harbors many of the most intriguing Damascene attractions, from bustling *souqs* to grand Ottoman architecture to some of the world's oldest Muslim and Christian places of worship. The sprawling rough that is modern Damascus also contains the occasional gem.

OLD CITY

CITADEL. The Citadel was built by the Seljuks in 1078 CE and once housed elaborate baths, mosques, and schools. During the crusader invasions, it functioned as a headquarters for Egyptian and Syrian sultans, including Salah ad-Din. The Ayyubid Sultan Malek al-'Adel demolished and rebuilt the Citadel in 1202 CE because he felt it was no longer suitable for contemporary warfare. The new fortress has 300 arrow slits and was once surrounded by a deep moat that has now been filled in to serve as the *souq* floor. Although the physically impressive Citadel is not officially a historical sight, its interior wonders may be accessed through an adequately *bakhsheesh*-greased palm. *(Next to the entrance of Souq al-Hamidiyyeh.)*

SOUQ AL-HAMIDIYYEH. The tin-covered Souq al-Hamidiyyeh teems with stall-owners peddling anything from Arabic-inscribed cutlery to tea and spices to snazzy clothing. It begins next to the Citadel and stretches to the Temple of Jupiter and the Umayyad Mosque. Children and store owners often bring visitors through the jumble of overcrowded stalls to have tea in their shops. Damascus's jet-setting young elites, newly-arrived Sudanese, and residents of the Old City are among the many groups seen in the city's most diverse locale.

UMAYYAD MOSQUE. In 705 CE, the Caliph Walid Ibn 'Abd al-Malek supervised the building of the Umayyad Mosque, one of the oldest and grandest mosques in the world. Originally the site of an ancient temple dedicated to Hadad (an Aramaean god revered around 1000 BCE), it was later the temple of Jupiter the Damascene. In the 4th century, a Byzantine church dedicated to St. John the Baptist was erected on this site. The church was destroyed to make room for the grand mosque; the only relic that survived was the head of St. John (known by Muslims as the prophet Yahya), now resting in its own shrine in the mosque's prayer hall. The shrine is a site of veneration for both Christians and Muslims. The mosque's three minarets were built in different styles and have been touched up by various empires since their original construction. Intricate mosaics decorate the walls of the mosque, and on the central dome are the names of some of the most significant figures in early Muslim history. *(Open daily 9:30am-9pm, closed for prayer F 12:30-2pm. S£10 includes entrance to Salah ad-Din's Tomb; S£50 may occasionally be charged in summer. Use the visitors' entrance left of the main entrance. Robes available.)*

SALAH AD-DIN'S TOMB. To the left of the Umayyad Mosque on the way to the visitors' entrance is Salah ad-Din's Tomb, built in 1193 CE and restored by Kaiser Wilhelm II of Germany in the late 19th century. The famed fighter's body lies under a red dome in a peaceful garden mausoleum. Inside the building, both a wooden and a marble tomb occupy the place of honor. The marble was a gift from the Kaiser; Salah ad-Din chose to stay in the wooden one. Just before the Umayyad Mosque at the end of Souq Al-Hamidiyyeh stand the remains of the 3rd-century CE **Temple of Jupiter,** now a source of shade for magazine and Qur'an sellers. The few remaining pillars harmonize with the frenetic symphony of the *souq*. *(Open in summer daily 9am-5pm; in winter 10am-5pm. Free with paid admission to the Umayyad Mosque.)*

'AZEM PALACE. On the side of the Umayyad Mosque (to the right when approaching from Souq al-Hamidiyyeh) is this 1749 palace, once the official home of As'ad Basha al-Azem, the Ottoman governor of Damascus. Through the modest door, a courtyard leads into the palace's specialized rooms: the bride's chamber, mother-in-law's chamber, instrument room (with a phonograph imported from New York), king's room, room of the pilgrimage (featuring impressive tiny Qur'ans), arms room, bath, and reception room. Inside, a **Museum of Popular Traditions** has the usual stonefaced mannequins in anatomically impossible poses, with French-only labels. While the museum is only occasionally interesting (especially the dazzling, multi-chambered *hammam*), the courtyard and Ottoman architectural embellishments are downright stunning. *(Palace and museum open in summer daily 9am-5pm; in winter 9am-3:30pm. Admission S£300, students S£15.)*

CHRISTIAN QUARTER. Behind the Umayyad Mosque, the narrow streets of the Old City begin their winding journey to the Christian Quarter, centered around Bab Touma Sq., at the end of Midhat Basha St. There you'll find the **Chapel of Ananias,** dedicated to the Christian disciple who restored sight to St. Paul. *(Open daily 9am-1pm and 4-7pm. Free.)* Directly across the street stands **St. Paul's Chapel,** the Armenian Orthodox church from which that same saint was lowered out of a window to escape arrest by his Jewish enemies. You may have to knock at the gate for entrance; the friendly multilingual staff will be happy to let you in and give you a religious history lesson. *(Open daily 8am-1:30pm. Free.)*

DOWNTOWN DAMASCUS

TAQIYYEH AS-SULEIMANIYYEH MOSQUE. While this mosque, on Salam al-Barudi St., is open only to Muslims, its exterior is a compelling expression of Ottoman architecture. Built in 1554 by the famed architect Sinan, its two lofty minarets frame a huge dome reflected in a courtyard fountain. The faithful pray at outdoor patios crowned with archways. The surrounding *madrasa* was converted into the **Artisanat,** an Ottoman market offering silver jewelry, oil paintings, and mother-of-pearl inlaid backgammon boards. *(Most shops open daily 9am-9pm. Visa, MC accepted.)*

MUSEUMS. The **Military Museum** stands at attention next door to the mosque and the market. The museum displays both ancient and modern weapons and photos that pay homage to those who have perished for their country. *(Open W-M 8am-1:30pm. Admission S£200, students S£5.)* One street over from the military museum, the **National Museum** has a shady green courtyard and an excellent collection of writings in Ugarit, the first alphabet, dating from the 14th century BCE; Aramaic, the language that Jesus spoke; and of course, Arabic. The museum's permanent collection contains Syrian sculpture, a Qur'an collection, Palmyran textiles from the first three centuries CE, and an entire reconstructed underground tomb from Palmyra. Beyond the door at the end of the last hall stand the frescoed walls of a synagogue excavated from the 3rd-century CE town of Doura Europos. Ask the guard to let you in if necessary. *(Open W-M 9am-6pm. Admission S£300, students S£15.)*

NEAR DAMASCUS

BOSRA بصرى

*Luxury **buses** from Damascus leave for Bosra from Karajat Barumkeh (2hr., every 2hr. 8am-8pm, S£50). Ask upon arrival what time buses return (the last bus usually departs at 8:30pm). **Microbuses** from Karaj Dar'a on the southern edge of Damascus go to Dar'a (2hr., S£45). However, it's still another 30min. and S£15 to Bosra. The **luxury bus** is a better option for travel to Bosra, since it's both quicker and cheaper. The Citadel is open daily 8am-7pm. Admission S£300, students S£15.*

Nineteen centuries ago, Bosra (20km from the Jordanian border) was the northern capital of the Nabatean kingdom (best known for building and abandoning the castles at Petra, Jordan). The Romans annexed the city in 106 CE, renamed it *Neatrajana Bustra*, and made it the capital of the Province of Arabia. Muslim control began in 634 CE, and the 6000-seat theater (with standing room for 3000 more) was converted into a citadel over the next 6 centuries: fortifications were added, a second outer wall was constructed, and more rooms were built to accommodate increasing numbers of horses and soldiers. The **Roman Theater-Arab Citadel** complex is still the most impressive structure in Bosra, making it second only to Palmyra in terms of Roman remains in Syria: the Roman Theater is one of the best preserved in the world, with secret stairways and an undamaged stage. Bosra is an easy and worthwhile daytrip: an afternoon can easily cover the sights. It is possible to spend a memorable night in the Citadel for S$200.

Bosra is not lacking in historically significant Muslim sights, either. The 7th-(some say 8th-) century **Mosque of 'Umar** is purportedly the third oldest mosque in all of the Islamic world, and still maintains some of its original form. Bosra also boasts the **Mabrak Mosque,** to which (legend has it) a camel brought the first copy of the Qur'an in Syria. Be sure not to miss the baths just across from the mosque—for a little extra money, the guard will open a back gate to the actual bathing and washing area. The 3rd-century **basilica,** is where Muhammad allegedly met the Nestorian monk Bahira (who first predicted The Prophet's future greatness). South of the gateway is a huge reservoir dug by the Romans. A branch of Wadi Zeid, supposedly fed by a conduit system, flowed down from the hills and emptied itself into the reservoir. Locals call it **Birkat al-Hajj,** the Pool of Pilgrimage.

MA'ALULA معلولا

*Ma'alula is an easy daytrip from Damascus, with frequent **minibuses** from Karaj Ma'alula on the east side of town (1hr., S£20). To get to the karaj, take a service to Abasseeyen Sq.; it's down An-Nasra St., on the left. Alternatively, take a **taxi** for approximately S£30.*

The tiny town of Ma'alula (56km northeast of Damascus) is tucked quietly into the Al-Qalamoun Mountains. Ancient churches and old mosques drowse among blue houses, precipitously clinging to steep slopes beneath staggering cliffs. Ma'alula is worlds away from the rapid developments of nearby Damascus—townspeople still speak **Aramaic**, the language in which Jesus preached and the Lord's Prayer was authored. Aramaic remained the vernacular of Syria until replaced by Arabic after the Islamic conquests of the 7th century. The language only survived among the few Christians who lived in isolated villages in the mountains.

The **Monastery of St. Taqla** was carved into the face of a nearby barren cliff in the 4th century to hold the remains of the young saint in a large cave. The daughter of a Seleucid prince, Taqla was a disciple of St. John and a convert to Christianity before such behavior became popular. She ran away from home when a servant revealed that her father had plans to kill her. While being pursued on the night she was to be burned, she was led by an angel toward safety: a mountain opened up for her and then quickly closed, crushing her father's soldiers.

Following the road around to the left of the town and the cliffs is the mountain-top chapel of **Mar Sarkis**, named after St. Sarkis, a Syrian horseman during the reign of King Maximus (3rd century CE). Continuing along the road past the Safir Hotel, at the bridge down the road to the left is the entrance to the mountain path leading to St. Taqla's Monastery. A right turn leads to cliffs and spectacular views.

SAYIDNAYA صيدنايا

*To get to Sayidnaya, take a bus from Karaj Ma'alula in Damascus (40min., S£15; see **Ma'alula** above for directions). Though infrequent minibuses connect Sayidnaya and Ma'alula, you'll likely have to backtrack to Damascus to do it all in one day.*

Sayidnaya (Arabic for "Our Lady") rests halfway between Damascus and Ma'alula, a 29km trip from either city. The hilltop **Chapel of the Virgin** in the center of town was built in 547 CE to honor the spot where the Virgin Mary appeared before a wealthy hunter. Within a maze of stone stairways, a shrine to the Virgin contains an **icon** (said to have been painted by St. Luke), to which miracles throughout the ages have been attributed. To the right of the church is the entrance to a small, underground **sanctuary** where Mary supposedly stood. It may be necessary to get the security guard to ask one of the nuns to open the mirrored doors protecting the icon and sanctuary. The inscription outside the entrance echoes the commandment Moses was given before the Burning Bush (Exodus 3:5): "Take off your shoes, for the ground you are treading upon is sacred." In the time of the Crusaders, Sayidnaya was second only to Jerusalem as a place of pilgrimage, and was called (redundantly) Notre Dame de Sayidnaya. Pilgrims and respectful passers-through may be allowed to spend one night in the clean, spacious rooms of the convent for free.

QUNEITRA قنيطرة

*Visitors must obtain permission from the Syrian Tourist Police in Damascus before going to Quneitra. Get the free permit in only 10min. at the office behind Palace Adnan al-Malki, up the stairs of the white monument, across the street to your left (look for men with rifles out front). Bring your **passport** (which will often be checked on the way to Quneitra as well). Permit office open Su-Th 8am-2pm; permit is good only for the next day. **Buses** leave Baramkeh Station for Khan Arnabeh (1½hr., S£20), then from Khan Arnabeh to Quneitra (15min., S£5). Buses leave every 10min. or when they fill up. More direct and expensive buses go from Damascus straight to Quneitra. You will pick up your mandatory guide/security officer between Khan Arnabeh and Quneitra. Do not take pictures of police officers or anything vaguely official-looking: you risk having your whole roll of film confiscated.*

The war-ravaged town of Quneitra (a diminished form of *qantara*, "bridge") owes its misfortune to its strategic location beside the Golan Heights at an intersection of roads leading to four countries. Quneitra was destroyed during the Syrian-Israeli conflict in 1967 (see **Modern History,** p. 495) and has recently been opened by the Syrian government as a "museum." The incident on the Golan was a major factor in the political destabilization that allowed the still-governing Ba'ath Party to seize control in November 1970. Quneitra is a fair distance from Damascus, but a visit to the town is worthwhile: although unimpressive as a memorial to those who perished during the bombings, the town does offer a firsthand look at the aftermath of military conflicts that have long plagued the Middle East. Visitors are given a guided tour of the modern ruins, including a walk through the crumbled main street, now overgrown with weeds. The partially-destroyed mosque, church, and hospital have been stripped bare and are riddled with bullet holes. Binoculars are provided at the eerily out-of-place Quneitra Restaurant (a spacious new dining facility) to gaze out over the U.N. Military Security Zone at Israel, just 500m away.

SUWEIDA

Service from Damascus to Suweida (130km southeast) leave from Karaj Dara'a (1½hr., S£140). Buses from Damascus to Suweida leave from Karaj Suweida (1½hr., S£30). Domas Tours also offers regular service to Suweida from Karaj Barumkeh (1½hr., S£50). To get to Suweida from Bosra, take a service from the town to Karaj Dara'a in Damascus (½hr., S£10).

In the 3rd century, the Romans considered Suweida (known at that time as Dionysis) one of the most important towns in the Province of Arabia by the Romans. Late in the Nabatean period, the area was called Suwada ("little black town") because it was constructed with black volcanic rock. In recent decades, however, this provincial town has been bulldozed to make way for the many new houses built to accommodate the growing population (currently a bloated 250,000). Suweida has little to offer travelers as a daytrip from Damascus except the well-arranged and informative **Suweida Museum,** 1km up the hill from the bus station. Many of Suweida's ruins have been preserved at this museum, built and organized in 1991 with the aid of the French. It contains artifacts dating from the Stone Age to the Roman Empire, including many well preserved basalt statues. The highlights are the mosaics from Shaba in the main room, especially the beautiful "Artemis surprised while bathing" from the mid-3rd century CE (open in summer 9am-6pm; in winter 9am-4pm; admission S£300, students S£15).

CENTRAL SYRIA

PALMYRA تدمــر

The desert oasis of Palmyra ("City of Palms," also known locally as Tadmor, "City of Dates") first offered travelers shade in the 1st century BCE, when it was a stopover for caravans passing from the Persian Gulf to the Mediterranean. Palmyrenes began to prosper from tax revenues collected from tired, thirsty traders and grew even wealthier after their city became a Roman colony in 129 CE. Most of the city's surviving ruins date from this period of prosperity, when Palmyra was the keystone of the thriving trade between the Roman Empire, the Middle East, and India.

During the middle of the 2nd century CE, reduced trade and increased distaste for Persian rule inspired Palmyran resident **Odenathus** to overthrow the city's senate and declare himself king. Odenathus and his son were assassinated in 267 CE after defeating the encroaching Persians, but his multilingual and strikingly beautiful second wife **Zenobia** took control of the city on behalf of her young son. Said to possess "manly understanding" by 18th-century historian Edward Gibbon, this Greek-Arab woman not only achieved full independence from Rome but also attacked the Roman territories and took possession of lower Egypt and much of Asia Minor. The minting of coins emblazoned with her image was the last straw: an infuriated Roman emperor Aurelian successfully attacked Palmyra (the capital of Zenobia's province) and carted Zenobia off to Rome.

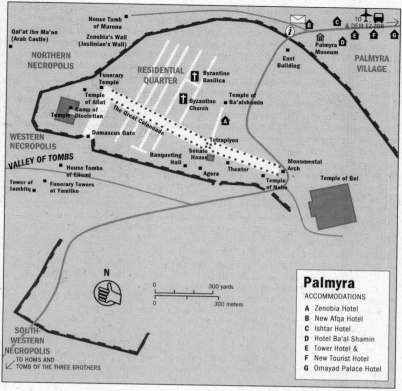

Map labels:
House Tomb of Marona
Qal'at Ibn Ma'an (Arab Castle)
Zenobia's Wall (Justinian's Wall)
NORTHERN NECROPOLIS
RESIDENTIAL QUARTER
Funerary Temple
Byzantine Basilica
East Building
Palmyra Museum
PALMYRA VILLAGE
Temple of Allat
Byzantine Church
Temple of Ba'alshamin
Camp of Diocletian
Temple
The Great Colonnade
Damascus Gate
WESTERN NECROPOLIS
Tetraplyon
VALLEY OF TOMBS
House Tombs of Eilami
Banqueting Hall
Senate House
Agora
Theater
Monumental Arch
Tower of Jambliq
Funerary Towers at Yamilko
Temple of Nabo
Temple of Bel
SOUTH-WESTERN NECROPOLIS
TO HOMS AND TOMB OF THE THREE BROTHERS
N
0   300 yards
0   300 meters

Palmyra
ACCOMMODATIONS
A Zenobia Hotel
B New Afqa Hotel
C Ishtar Hotel
D Hotel Ba'al Shamin
E Tower Hotel &
F New Tourist Hotel
G Omayad Palace Hotel

In succeeding years, Palmyra served as a Roman border fortress and was conquered by Muslims in the 7th century. Local emir Fakhr ad-Din built the castle overlooking the site in the early 1600s, but the ruined city itself was only sporadically inhabited. The modern town was first centered in the courtyard of the Temple of Bel, but between 1929 and 1932 was relocated northeast of the ruins. Today, Palmyra still maintains much of the grandeur of its days as an ancient Roman province: its majestic, column-lined avenues stand proudly in a lush oasis surrounded by miles of uninhabited desert. The ruins of Palmyra, though weathered by centuries of war and sandstorms, rank among the most spectacular in the Middle East. As a result of its well-deserved fame, Palmyra has fallen prey to the clutches of tourism, and new hotels are constructed each year. Nevertheless, sunsets over the ancient temples and castle still awe with their imperial silence.

🛈 ORIENTATION AND PRACTICAL INFORMATION

The **Karnak Station** (tel. 910 288) is near the circle by the post office. Karnak runs buses to: **Damascus** (3hr.; 10:15am, 12:30, 1:45, 5pm; S£100); **Homs** (2hr.; 7am, 2:30pm; S£65); and **Deir ez-Zur** (2hr.; 11:30am, 1, 1:30, 3:15, 5:30, 7, 9pm; S£75). **Service** and rattling **public buses** serve **Homs** (2hr., S£50) from the *service* station, a 5-minute walk down the main street past the post office. *Service* to **Damascus** leave just across the street, starting at 6am (S£75). **Qadmoos** and **Damas Tours** are among the most luxurious of the numerous private buses that travel to Damascus, Homs, and several smaller towns. Schedules are volatile; ask at hotels for updated info.

The **tourist office** (tel. 910 574) is on the highway between the ruins and the new city (open Sa-W 8am-2pm and 5-8pm, F morning only). They give out one informative brochure and a few backgammon hints; get more helpful books and guides at the entrance to the Museum of the Temple of Bel. A newer, considerably fancier office is scheduled to open in 1999 opposite the post office. **Currency exchange** is best done before coming to Palmyra, though some hotels change money (the Cham Palace does it most legally, but at the worst rates). The **pharmacy** (tel. 910 455) is just down from the Spring Restaurant on the right of the main street (open Sa-Th 9am-1pm, F 9am-noon). For **medical emergencies,** call the **hospital** (tel. 910 551). An English-speaking representative of the **tourist police** can be reached at the Temple of Bel (tel. 910 517), while the **police station** (tel. 910 158) is on the main street off the highway as you reach the first hotels in the new town. The **post office** is near the circle on the highway (open daily 8am-2pm). **Telephones** can be found outside the post office, inside the Temple of Bel, and outside the museum; purchase a phonecard in the post office. Palmyra's **telephone code** is 31.

■ ACCOMMODATIONS

The town of Palmyra has been steadily encroaching upon the ruins of Palmyra for years. Hotels are being renovated and prices are continually on the rise; however, a number of friendly and inexpensive options remain. Most hotels and restaurants are on the main street starting at the highway. The hotels that charge in dollars are more comfortable, but about six times as expensive. ◪**Ishtar Hotel** (tel. 913 073; fax 913 260), on the left at the beginning of the main street, is one of the first hotels you'll see when entering the city. Warren Beatty never had it this good: the four "backpacker" rooms are impeccably clean and very quiet, though they have minuscule windows and no private bathrooms. Service is excellent and quarters are cleaner than those in any other budget hotel around (singles S£300; downstairs doubles and triples S£200 per person; upstairs double with bath and breakfast US$20; Visa, MC, AmEx accepted). **Omayad Palace Hotel** (tel. 910 755), 250m down the main street to the right of the fountain, lets you rest like an Umayyad caliph in the beautiful, pastel-hued lobby and spacious, shaded courtyard of this former Palmyrene house (singles S£200; doubles S£300; triples S£450; breakfast S£50). The misnamed **New Tourist Hotel** (tel. 910 333), on the right side of the main street, is actually the oldest in Palmyra, with decent rooms (some with private bath) and more free tea than you can drink. The effusive guestbook confirms that this is a backpackers' haven (summer rooftop mattresses S£100; 3-bed dorms S£125, with bath S£150; singles S£200; doubles S£325). Rooms may be smallish at the **New Afqa Hotel** (tel. 910 386), near the post office and the new tourist office (before the Karnak station), but all have big fans, private bath, and the thickest mattresses in Palmyra (singles S£200; doubles S£400; breakfast S£50). **Hotel Ba'al Shamin** (tel. 910 537), one block south of the main street and a block down from the museum, boasts spacious rooms and the cheapest inhabitable singles in Palmyra. Rooms include private bath (singles S£150; doubles S£300; triples S£600). You can also **camp** under one of the backyard olive trees at the luxury **Hotel Zenobia,** yards away from the ruins, for S£200. Peak season is March to May; bargaining may work in the off-season, when simply walking away can cut a quoted price in half.

■ FOOD

Palmyra's main street abounds with restaurants catering to tourists' every desire. Each has a special feature, but value and quality don't differ much from place to place. Meals are universally mediocre, but vary in price depending on tourist traffic. Some of the hostels serve local beer (S£75) until 11pm. Up the street, the local diners are just as ready and eager to feed you, but don't let them rip you off. Be sure to sample the traditional dish **mensaf** (see **Jordan: Food and Drink,** p. 411). A refreshing oasis of a restaurant, **Palmyra Tourist Restaurant** (tel. 910 346) dazzles with fountains, canopies, an in-house boutique, and reasonably priced meals. *Mezze* with chicken, mineral water, and salad costs S£200. Beer, wine, and *'araq* are also served (open daily 7:30am-midnight). **Spring Restaurant** (tel. 910 307), on the right of the main street, offers tasty *mensaf* (S£175-200) or meat entrees (S£125) in the relaxing and super-comfortable upstairs Bedouin tent. A breakfast of omelettes and cheese goes for S£50 (open daily from 7am until the shawarma runs out). **Palmyra Traditional Restaurant** (tel. 912 155), on the left of the main street, gets more business from a positive guidebook review than from the quality of their food (they've converted the recommendation into a multilingual, larger-than-life sign). *Mensaf* is big but overpriced (S£250; open 8am-midnight). Next to the tourist office on the highway near the ruins, **Oasis Restaurant** (tel. 911 439) offers a large group buffet at the ruins with music and dancing in tents (open 7pm-midnight).

👁 SIGHTS

Palmyra takes a full day to explore. A popular and intelligent way to see the ruins in the intense heat of summer is to follow the sun: wake up at dawn, catch the spectacular sunrise, and begin exploring before the sun is directly overhead.

TEMPLE OF BEL. This mammoth building, enclosed in a high, largely recon-structed wall, is a good place to begin exploring Palmyra. The gatehouse has books on Syria and Palmyra, and the guides here (who may charge up to S£1000 per day, though bargaining can cut prices in half) are useful for a more in-depth appreciation of the ruins. The existing Temple of Bel was constructed in 32 CE over an older Hellenistic site. Bel is a Babylonian pronunciation of the Semitic word *Ba'al* ("master"), the name for the supreme deity who was also identified with the Greek god Zeus (Jupiter in Rome). The **sacrificial altar** in the middle of the temple was used for animal sacrifices: blood ran into the drain in the floor and was emptied into a sophisticated plumbing system (only a large stone pipe, sitting beside the drainage hole, remains). The impressive **cella** ("shrine")—the free-standing building in the center of the temple—was built from 17 to 32 CE. There are also small shrines to the right and the left, reflecting the multitude of deities that constituted the godhead of the mighty Bel. Just outside the entrance are several intricate carvings of grapes and pineapples (hinting at Palmyra's once-rich agricultural past), which can also be found on the bottom of the stone slab. *(Gatehouse open daily in summer 8am-1pm and 4-6pm; in winter 8am-4pm. Admission S£300, students S£15.)*

MONUMENTAL ARCH. The Great Colonnade once led from the Temple of Bel to the monumental arch and the rest of the city. Constructed in 200 CE, the oft-photo-graphed Monumental Arch is richly decorated with rows of pears, acorns, and palm trunks, as well as acanthus, oak, and grape leaves. On the left, just past the Arch, stands the **Temple of Nabo,** raised 2m off the ground. Dedicated to the Babylo-nian god of writing (later identified with Apollo), this 1st-century CE construction (along with **Zenobia's Baths** to the right) is largely in ruins. Up the colonnade and to the left is a newly renovated **theater.** More than half of it was reconstructed in the past two decades. The stage, the paved semi-circular orchestra where the chorus performed, and the foundations of the actors' dressing rooms remain visible.

AGORA AND ENVIRONS. Further down the street to the left are the not-so-dis-tinct remains of the **Agora** (public market) and the **Senate House.** Social position determined one's placement in the Agora: Palmyran and Roman officials sat in the northern portico, senators in the eastern portico, soldiers in the western portico, and merchants and caravan leaders in the southern portico. Next door to the Agora is the **Banqueting Hall,** where religious fraternities congregated to party down on deity-inspired holidays. The prominent Tetrapylon consists of four groups of poorly rebuilt columns. The pedestals in the center of each group of col-umns once supported statues, including ones of the great Zenobia and her husband, Odenathus. Nearby, vendors sell soda and beer. To the right of the Tetrapylon, near the Zenobia Hotel, is the **Temple of Ba'alshamin,** dedicated to Zeus Baalshamin, whose name means "Master of the Heavens," was the god of storms and fertilizing rains. The locked vestibule of the temple has six columns with platforms as bases for statues. Further to the right, the ruins partially covered by the Zenobia Hotel used to be a colonnaded courtyard surrounded by rooms and a chapel. This complex's role within the temple remains unknown.

QAL'AT IBN MA'AN. The imposing Qal'at Ibn Ma'an, or Arab Castle, is attributed to Fakhr ad-Din the Ma'anite, who once ruled the area between Mt. Lebanon and the Syrian desert. This fortress, built in the 12th or 13th century to protect Palmyra from eventual Crusader attacks, is *the* place to be at sunset, though busloads of photo-snapping tourists can mar the experience in the high season. You can climb the 150m slope for free (30-45min.) or bargain for a ride from town (aim for S£200 with a 2hr. wait). *(Open daily until just after sunset. Admission S£150, students S£15.)*

FUNERARY TOWERS. To the left of Qal'at Ibn Ma'an are funerary towers, known as "eternal houses" in Palmyra. Each of the most important families had its own mausoleum, though there are also individual sepulchers. From the main city, the tombs are a 30-minute walk. As always, there's a catch—the keymaster won't move a muscle until you've arranged transportation. If you haven't rented a car, this means getting a taxi (S£200 after bargaining), many of which prowl outside the museum around tour time. You can hire a guide to the tombs (prices start around S£300); once at the towers, however, most guides will let you latch on to their group for a small fee. *(Tombs are unlocked by a keymaster Apr.-Sept. W-M 8:30, 10, 11:30am, and 4:30pm; Tu 8:30, 9, 10, 11, 11:30am, and 4:30pm; Oct.-Mar. last opening at 2pm. Trips leave from the Palmyra Museum, where tickets can be purchased. Admission S£300, students S£15.)*

VALLEY OF THE TOMBS. The **Tomb of Elahbel,** which belonged to a rich Palmyran family, has stairs to its roof for a good view of the Valley of the Tombs. The impressive underground **Tomb of the Three Brothers** is southwest of the city. The center panel of the colorful wall frescoes in this tomb shows the manly Achilles hiding in feminine dress among the daughters of Lycomedes upon hearing the Delphic oracle foretell his death, which would come only after the cross-dressing hero suited up for war and was shot in his now-famous left heel.

MUSEUMS. The **Palmyra Museum,** at the entrance to the new town, is larger and more interesting than most Syrian museums. Statues from family tombs, coins with godly depictions, and a tacky model of an ancient Palmyran cave and its seminaked inhabitants highlight the collection. The **Ethnographic Museum** won't have Madame Tussaud melting with envy: the mildly interesting displays attempt to catalogue different aspects of Bedouin life with wax statues. *(Palmyra Museum: open daily Apr.-Oct. 8am-1pm and 4-6pm; Nov.-Mar. W-M 8am-1pm and 2-4pm. Admission S£300, students S£15. Ethnographic Museum: open daily 8am-2:30pm. Admission S£150, students S£20.)*

HOMS حمص

Any Syrian will tell you that oil is the most refined thing in Homs. All over the Levant, "Homsies" are the notorious butt of jokes ridiculing their supposed stupidity. Now an industrial wasteland strewn with bent telephone poles, hanging electrical wires, and rank streets, Homs has seen better days. In ancient Roman times (when it was known as Emesa), Homs was an important metropolis along the trade route that went through the small town of Palmyra. Most buildings of historical interest have been destroyed by wars and earthquakes, however, and the city is now little more than Palmyra's destitute, unemployed, older brother. As much as travelers try to avoid the smoke-belching city, Homs often serves as a default transportation hub: roads from Hama, Palmyra, Damascus, and Tartus converge here, and Crac des Chevaliers is only a short bus ride away. Be it ever so humble, there's no place like Homs.

❷ ORIENTATION AND PRACTICAL INFORMATION

The **bus station** sits at the intersection of **Al-Corniche** and **Hama Streets**. A right turn out of the station brings you to the intersection with Hama St., where you'll find food vendors and small, cheap restaurants. Hama St. intersects **Quwatli Street**, past the Khalid Ibn al-Walid Mosque, at a bus stop and fountain. A right onto Quwatli brings you to a clocktower and most of Homs's accommodations. The public **bus station** is past the small clocktower circle on Hama St., near Khalid Ibn al-Walid Mosque. **Minibuses** go to **Crac des Chevaliers** (1hr., every hour 8am-5pm, S£25). **Microbuses** make frequent runs to: **Damascus** (2hr., S£65); **Aleppo** (2½hr., S£85); **Tartus** (1hr., S£30-40); and **Hama** (45min., S£17). The Karnak station next door sends buses daily to: **Damascus** (2hr., 10 per day 6:30am-7pm, S£75); **Hama** (45min., 10 per day 5am-6:30pm, S£25); and **Tartus** (1hr., 3:30pm, S£40).

Don't expect much more than a smile from the **tourist booth** (tel. 473 898) on Quwatli St., in the middle of a small park past the hotels. Get visas and renewals at the **passport office** on the right side of Ibn Khaldoun St., at the Quwatli St. intersection. Take the right directly after the Turkish Airlines Office. You'll need four passport-sized photos, available from the photo office to the left of the passport office (open for visa extensions Sa-Th 9am-1pm). An **exchange booth** set up by the Commercial Bank of Syria changes money at the usual rates. With your back to the entrance of Hotel Nasser aj-Jadid, walk 50m up the street; it's on the left (open Sa-Th 8:30am-noon). The **police** (tel. 112) are headquartered in the government building on Hashem al-Atasi St., a sharp left turn from the clocktower on Quwatli St. Across from the mosque on Hama St., **Umaliyya Pharmacy** (tel. 466 249) stays open 24 hours. The government **hospital** (tel. 110 for an **ambulance**) is on al-Corniche St. at the intersection with As-Salamiyeh St. To get to the **post office** on Riad St., head away from the clocktower circle and the Army Club, which will be on the right side. The post office will immediately follow on the left-hand side. **Poste Restante** is also available. The tourist office at the large clocktower circle also serves as the **telephone office** (open daily 8am-2pm and 7-10pm). Homs's **telephone code** is 31.

❚❖ ACCOMMODATIONS AND FOOD

Hotel options in Homs border on awful, especially if you're traveling alone. Most rooms are in large, old buildings in various states of disrepair on Quwatli St. Unless you arrive late at night and/or simply cannot leave Homs for the night, you're better off finding a home away from Homs. The best of slim pickings is **Hotel Nasser aj-Jadid** (tel. 227 423), on Quwatli St. about 50m past the park. The friendly, English-speaking manager will show you to relatively clean rooms sporting super-cool fans and dirty bathrooms. (Singles S£200; doubles S£300; triples S£450; quads S£475; cold showers S£25; hot showers S£50.) **Ghazi Hotel** (tel. 222 160) sits on Quwatli St., one block from the Nasser aj-Jadid toward the park (English sign says HOTEL). The pretty tile floors and the curtains' leafy print are not enough to temper the overall gloominess and rock-hard mattresses. (Stuffy singles S£175; doubles S£275; triples S£375; hot showers S£35.) **Basman Grand Hotel** (tel. 225 009 or 700), on Abu Ala'a St., off Quwatli St. before the park, has clean checkered floors and relatively tidy private baths (singles US$17; doubles US$22; triples US$27).

Falafel, shawarma, and pastry shops line Hama St. between the bus station and Quwatli St.; most stay open until midnight. Roving merchants hawk fresh-roasted corn on the cob, fruits, vegetables, and nuts. Myriad juice and snack shops squeeze onto the street parallel to Quwatli, behind Hotel Nasser aj-Jadid. Most are open late and offer affordable sandwiches (S£15) and cocktails (S£25-50). Army officers from the Homs military headquarters have adopted the diners between the park and the hotels as their stomping ground. For a sit-down meal and a glass of beer (S£36-50), try the red-ceilinged, yellow-walled **Toledo Restaurant,** behind the tourist office and park. Appetizers begin at S£20, entrees at S£100. The nearby **Nile Restaurant's** special is *fatteh*, a huge bowl of hummus with pita, lemon juice, and olive oil (S£170)— real Homstyle cooking. The **Rawda Cafe,** across Quwatli St. from the Toledo and the

Nile, provides welcome relief from the thronging industrial decay. Sip tea (S$30-40) and watch Homsies play backgammon around a shaded, tree-lined fountain.

👁 SIGHTS

KHALID IBN AL-WALID MOSQUE. This silver-domed mosque should be your first (and perhaps your last) sightseeing trip in Homs. It is dedicated to the Arab commander known as "the Sword of God," who brought Islam to Syria in 636 CE; his alms-laden tomb lies inside. Built at the time of King adh-Dhaher Babyars and rebuilt in 1910 at the end of the Ottoman period, the mosque mixes Byzantine, Ottoman, and Arab styles. Ask the attendant in the office for a guided tour. *(On Hama St. between city center and bus station. Free. Non-Muslims are welcome and robes are provided.)*

GREAT AN-NOURI MOSQUE AND ENVIRONS. Built in 1162 by Ayyubid commander Nour ad-Din Zanki (Nuraddin), this mosque is famous for its square minaret and wooden pulpit. The nearby **souqs** date back to the Ayyubid, Mamluke, and Ottoman periods. In the old city, the fifth major right off Al-Hamidiyyeh St. brings you to the **Umm az-Zunnar Church,** built in 59 CE. Fearing persecution by their pagan rulers, Homs's earliest Christians worshiped here secretly. The church was expanded during the Christian era and now holds the so-called **Belt of the Virgin Mary,** found under the altar in 1953.

NEAR HOMS: QAL'AT AL-HISN (CRAC DES CHEVALIERS) قلعة الحصن

Buses and *service* leave the Homs station for Qal'at al-Hisn daily (1hr., every hr. 7am-5pm, S£25). Officially, the last bus returns to Homs around 5pm. In low season, shark-like service drivers may claim to be private taxis after 3pm and charge an outrageous S£300 for the return trip. It's only a 10min. walk down the hill (through the village) to catch a local service at the restaurant. Start the trip in the early morning to give yourself time to explore and to stay out of the heat. *Open* in summer W-M 9am-6pm; in winter W-M 9am-4pm, Tu 9am-3am. *Admission* S£300, students S£15. Guided tours available for S£200, S£500 for groups.

Get high on **Crac!** This must-see mountaintop Crusader castle, also known as *Qal'at al-Hisn*, ranks among the best sights in Syria; those who proclaim it the Greatest Castle in the World are not far off the mark. Crac des Chevaliers is really a castle within a castle, separated by a moat, with a larger moat surrounding the entire structure. A governor of Homs built the original structure in 1031 CE, leaving a Kurdish garrison in the castle to defend against enemy attacks on the Tripoli-Homs-Hama road. In 1110, Crusaders nearly destroyed the fortress while capturing it. They built a new castle on the ruins of the old and used it to control the "Homs Gap," a narrow pass linking the coast to the Orontes Valley. As the only break in over 250km of mountain, possession of this pass guaranteed control over inland Syria. The Crusaders held the medieval fortress for 161 years; Salah ad-Din supposedly withdrew his troops upon viewing the imposing castle. The stronghold finally fell to the Mamluke army under the command of Sultan Baybars in 1271, after a month of intense fighting. The Crusaders were allowed to leave the country peacefully. Perched on a hill 750m above sea level and spreading over 30,000 sq. meters, on a clear day the castle's high towers afford panoramic views of the Mediterranean, the Port of Tripoli, and Homs Lake.

Upon entering through the main door, continue up the ramp past the **guard rooms** and **stables.** Straight ahead, through the door of the first tower, are the moat and the outer wall. To get to the **main courtyard,** take a sharp right. In front of the courtyard, the **seven-arched facade** (with its two doors and five windows) is the castle's most aesthetically impressive feature. Behind it is the **main assembly room,** where Crusader kings were received by the knights of the castle under a vaulted Gothic roof. The long room against the castle's back wall contains a huge **oven,** 5m in diameter. To the right is a **cathedral** that was converted into a mosque in 1271. The intriguing nooks in the rest of the castle lend themselves to impromptu exploration; a map might cramp your style, but a **flashlight** makes a great companion. Be sure to trek up to the southern towers for an inspiring view of the Syrian countryside with Lebanon in the distance. Those accustomed to warmer climes should bring a sweater.

At the **Roundtable Restaurant and Hotel** (tel. 740 280), 150m to the left and up the hill from the castle entrance, passable beds and baths await for S£500, meals for S£200. **Camping** (S£125 a head, including shower) is also available. The **Restaurant Des Chevaliers** (tel. 740 411), in front of the main entrance, has slightly higher prices and similar food (hummus S£25, meals S£150, beers S£100, coffee/tea S£25). If you get hungry or thirsty exploring the castle, visit the **Restaurant Princess Tower** (tel. 740 007), located Rapunzel-style on the top level of the castle toward the northern end (*mezze* S£150; open 7am-8pm).

HAMA حماة

Although the city of Hama was once an important trade center, the only remaining monuments of its former glory that remain are the **norias** (Aramaic for "water wheels") scattered throughout the city. Their low-pitched groaning is produced by wood rubbing wood; the same sound has echoed through Hama since the norias' construction in the Middle Ages. The graceful turning of these irrigation devices, matched by the smooth flow of the Orontes River nearby, has long set the pace for this town. Hama's serenity makes it difficult to remember that the city was ground zero for the Syrian government's bloody quelling of the Muslim Brotherhood uprising of 1982. Nevertheless, its numerous shoreside parks and the excellent quality of its budget accommodations make Hama an ideal place to spend a relaxing couple of days. The best way to see Hama's sights is to make like a *noria* and roll along the banks of the river.

🛈 ORIENTATION AND PRACTICAL INFORMATION

Navigating the small city of Hama is easy and almost entirely possible on foot. The intersection of **Quwatli St.** and **Sadiq Ave.** marks the city center. Most budget hotels and restaurants are on Quwatli St., facing the bank and the post office across the intersection. Continuing in this direction leads to **Murabet St.** and the city's second major intersection. Walking toward the grinding sound will bring you to the river. **Al-Ahliah** bus station (tel. 522 551) has service to all major Syrian cities. Walking toward the post office, go past the Basman Grand Hotel, and take a left after the large, white government building—the station is on your left around the corner. Frequent service to: **Damascus** (3hr., S£90); **Aleppo** (2hr., S£65); **Homs** (40min., S£20); **Lattakia** (3hr., S£100) via **Tartus** (2hr., S£65); and **Raqqa** (4hr., S£145). The **Karnak** bus station (tel. 229 985), on the corniche in the middle of town (doubling as the Afamia Restaurant and pastry shop), has frequent service to **Damascus** (S£75), **Aleppo** (S£60), and **Homs** (S£25). **Ar-Rayyan Bus Company** is a high-quality third option (tel. 225 581 or 227 977) running to **Homs** (S£20), **Aleppo** (S£65), and **Damascus** (S£90). The **minibus station** is a left turn away from the river at the intersection of Murabet and Quwatli. Conquer the hill by foot (20min.) or take a city bus (S£2). Minibuses depart when full to: **Damascus** (3hr., S£35); **Aleppo** (2hr., S£25); **Homs** (45min., S£11); and **Suqelbia** (1hr., S£20). Impractical and hugely expensive **service taxis** (of the gas-guzzling, boat-sized sort) leave from the station across the street to **Damascus** (S£200), **Aleppo** (S£150), and **Homs** (S£40).

The **tourist office** (tel. 511 033) is on Sadiq Ave., across the river from the central intersection (open daily 8am-2pm). As likely holds true for all of Syria, you're better off finding a knowledgeable hotel manager to introduce you to the city. In Hama, the best person to contact is Anas, manager of the **Cairo Hotel**. He can provide you with anything from the price of a bus ticket to Raqqa to the visa requirements for almost any nationality. Take a right at the intersection of Murabet and Quwatli; the remarkably efficient **passport office** will be on your left. Bring four passport-sized photos and S£50 to renew visas (open Sa-Th 9am-1pm). The **Commercial Bank of Syria**, next to the post office, exchanges cash and traveler's checks (open daily 9am-2pm and 5-8pm). The **black market** is alive and kicking as well. In an emergency, call the **police** (tel. 112), an **ambulance** (tel. 110), or go to **Medical Center Hospital** (tel. 515 801/2/3), just uphill from the Al-Ahliah bus station. **Ummalia Pharmacy,** 8 March St.

(tel. 225 097), is open 24 hours. Contact your hotel manager first about getting ahold of medicine; they usually know where to procure necessary items at the best prices. The **post office,** on Quwatli St., just past the Sadiq Ave. intersection, has minimal services (open daily 8am-2pm). A phonecard from the post office is less expensive than placing calls at your hotel. Hama's **telephone code** is 33.

ACCOMMODATIONS AND FOOD

Hama's hotels are far preferable to those in almost any other Syrian city. Amenities abound, floors sparkle, and managers practically tap dance to keep visitors happy. Prices vary drastically between high season (summer) and low season (winter), and depending on how well business has been going. It never hurts to ask for a discount. **Cairo Hotel** (tel. 222 280; fax 237 206), on Quwatli St. near the intersection with Jamal Abd an-Nasr St., might as well be upgraded to a two-star hotel, but manager Anas wants to keep it cheap. Some travelers have dubbed this kind, helpful manager a Syrian National Treasure. Spotless rooms have fridges, beautiful bathrooms, and color TVs. (Roof mattresses S£100; dorm beds S£150; singles S£250-300; doubles S£400; triples S£525-600; prices S£50-150 higher June-Aug. Breakfast S£75. A/C S£100 extra. Visa, MC, AmEx accepted). Cairo's rival and next-door neighbor, the **Riad Hotel** (tel. 235 512 or 235 540; fax 517 776), is a worthy match: clean rooms have fridges and speakers connected to a central sound system. Bonus: the hotel sells beer out of the lobby cooler. (Rooftop mattresses and facilities S£75-100; singles S£280; doubles S£405; triples S£505. Full bath or shower S£35; breakfast S£75; Visa, MC, AmEx accepted.) Luxurious and welcoming, **Noria Hotel** (tel. 512 414; fax 511 715), across the street, is under the same impeccable management as the Cairo, but much more upscale than its budget-conscious cousin. One of the only two-star hotels to justify its prices, all rooms come with air conditioning, continental breakfast, and a bevy of four-star services. Magnificent suites (for 2-5 people) have a kitchen, living room, and views of the *norias* (US$40-60). Fax summer reservations a month in advance (Singles US$18; doubles US$28; triples US$33. Visa, MC, AmEx accepted.)

Most of Hama's restaurants are of the standard chicken, meat, and falafel variety. A full meal shouldn't cost more than S£100. The diners scattered along Quwatli St. have plumper chickens and larger portions; more expensive restaurants line the waterfront. **Sultan Restaurant** (tel. 235 104), behind the Hama Museum, provides a memorable riverside meal in an Ottoman insane asylum. If the grinding noise from the neighboring *noria* doesn't drive you mad, Hama's fit-inducing specialty, *batirsh*, surely will: layered eggplant, mincemeat, and tahini eaten with bread (S£55). **Dream House,** off Medina Sq. near the Grand Mosque, offers spring rolls (S£45), excellent pizzas (S£90-110), and genuine banana splits. Barada beer (S£75) and a variety of liquors and imported wines (S£90-750) help ensure happy dreams (open daily 10am-1pm). A 15-minute walk from the center of town (with the river on your left) leads to **Four Norias** (tel. 221 013), an upscale riverfront restaurant with views of its namesakes. A complete Middle Eastern meal costs S£200-250; *'araq* and Sharq beer (S£36) are also available (open daily 9am-2am).

SIGHTS

OLD CITY AND OTTOMAN BATH. When facing the Orontes from the center of town, walk left along the bank and enter the cobblestone-paved **Old City.** The narrow, winding streets were built to provide protection from the sun at all hours. A small sign above an old door on the left that reads "Automan Public Bath" marks the **Hammam Othmania,** a Turkish bath from the Ottoman era. A bath with soap and a massage is only S£100. *(Open for men 7am-noon and 7-11pm, women noon-5pm.)*

HAMA MUSEUM. The **Hama Museum,** in the Old Azem Palace, was built as a residence for As'ad Pasha al-Azem, governor of Hama from 1700 to 1742. After he was promoted to a Damascus post, he built an even grander structure of the same name. The palace's men's section (the *Salamlek*) and women's section (the *Haramlek*) conveniently join at the baths. The museum also houses the remarkable **Maryameen Mosaic,** which captures the lovely ladies of the house jamming on 18th-century lutes and other funk machines. *(Open W-M 9am-4pm. Admission S£300, students S£15.)*

AN-NOURI MOSQUE AND CITADEL. After passing the Aj-Jabariyya water wheel (home to daredevil child divers in the late afternoon), the road opens up at the **An-Nouri Mosque.** Built in 1162 by Ayyubid commander Nour ad-Din Zanki (Nuraddin), the mosque thrusts a square minaret into the Syrian sky, mirroring its cousin in Homs. A left turn at the mosque brings you to the **Citadel,** the center of the old city and a popular spot for evening strolls. Supposedly, relics from the 6th millennium BCE were unearthed beneath this hill. Today, the only digging is done by kids playing in the huge park planted on top. *(You may be asked to pay a S£10 entrance fee.)*

GRAND MOSQUE. Hama once hid its **Grand Mosque** behind the Citadel. The mosque contains the tombs of two Ayyubid kings, Muhammad II (d. 1284 CE) and Al-Muzaffar III (d. 1298 CE). The 1982 uprising struck this Umayyad structure, along with the tombs of Hama's 13th-century emirs, from the official literature. Greek writing from a previous edifice marks some of the fallen stones. *(Free. All faiths welcome.)*

NEAR HAMA: APAMEA افاميا

To reach Apamea, take a microbus from Hama to Suqelbia (S£20), then a service to Qasr al-Madiq (S£10). The Colonnade is 2km farther up. Leave early in the day, when transportation is more frequent. Open W-M in summer 8am-2:30pm; in winter 8am-2:30pm. Admission S£150, students S£10; combination ruins and museum S£350, students S£25.

Apamea lies on a hill overlooking the lush Ghab Valley and the Orontes River (Nahr al-Aussi), 55km north of Hama. The Macedonians knew the city as Barnakeh, but a smitten King Sahicos renamed the military stronghold after his beloved wife Afamia in 310 BCE. After Apamea fell in 64 BCE, the victorious Romans supplied the city with an impressive rock-hewn water canal and ornamented the stone **colonnades** (the longest of which is 1850m)—still the city's most impressive features. They also built an **amphitheater** and a **public bath** (about 500m downhill and to the left of the colonnade), which have weathered the years much less gracefully. While in Apamea, your will likely encounter several moped-riding sharks selling "antiques" supposedly found in nearby graves. Beware—these "antiques" are more likely to have been manufactured in nearby shops just hours before your arrival.

The **Cathedral,** to the left when facing the modern cafeteria, harbors a selection of well-preserved mosaic floors. While even the best of these floors have suffered centuries of erosion from weather and warfare, the cathedral still houses a cross and a set of jewels given to the King of Persia in 540 CE in hopes of staving off an invasion. The Persians nonetheless invaded and razed the city 33 years later, enslaving almost 300,000 Apameans. Muslim Arabs entered the city on peaceful terms under the leadership of Abu Obeida Bin Jarrah. The city was likely abandoned as a result of a series of earthquakes that struck between 1137 and 1170. One of the more impressive structures is the circular **Al-Madiq Castle,** about 2km from the colonnade, near the modern town of Apamea. The Ottoman Stan Pasha built a great *khan* (courtyard inn or caravanserai) inside the castle that contained an inn, a stable, and a market. Now a museum, the echoing domes of the *khan* are well worth checking out.

MEDITERRANEAN COAST

LATTAKIA اللاذقية

Lattakia is a decidedly practical city. Far from being the Mediterranean resort the Ministry of Tourism would have you think, Lattakia's tall buildings and crowded streets have a congested, big-city feel. As Syria's largest seaport and the country's major import-export center, Lattakia donates its entire coastline to industry and lends itself poorly to Mediterranean daydreaming. Plenty of cheap eats and budget accommodations, however, make Lattakia a good base for exploring the ruins at

Ugarit and the castle of Salah ad-Din. Constructed in the 2nd century BCE by the Seleucids, St. Peter and Mark Antony once relaxed upon Lattakia's shores, but the only remaining witnesses to its glorious past are a few columns, a Roman arch from 200 CE, and some Ugarit artifacts, all housed today at the overpriced museum inside the Ottoman Khan ad-Dukhan.

ORIENTATION AND PRACTICAL INFORMATION

The main thoroughfare is **14 Ramadan Street,** running northeast from the harbor and ending at the **tourist office** (tel. 416 926; open daily 9am-8pm). At the intersection with **Ibrahim Hanano Street, Hanano Place** is home to an **Assad statue,** the **police station** (tel. 112), and many budget hotels. Farther inland, running north-south from the beginning of 14 Ramadan St., is **8 Azar Street,** which turns into **Baghdad Avenue** at the **Al-Quds Street** intersection. Heading east on Al-Quds St. (which soon morphs into **Al-Ghafiqi Street**) leads to the large **Al-Yaman Place** roundabout. The **Commercial Bank of Syria** faces the sea on 8 Azar St. before the traffic circle (open daily 8am-2pm and 5-8pm; traveler's checks not exchanged in evening). **Sani Daker Pharmacy** (tel. 476 979), on 8 Azar St. and before the Karnak office, has excellent, multilingual service (open Sa-W 9am-1:30pm and 5-8:30pm). In a medical emergency, call the **Assad Hospital** (tel. 487 782), on 8 Azar St. To get to the **post office,** face away from the train station and take the second right off the circle; it's 50m down on the left (open daily 8am-6pm). **Mail service** is across the street (open Sa-Th 8am-8pm, F 9am-2pm; Visa, MC). From Baghdad Ave., a right on Haria St. leads to the surprisingly efficient **telephone office** (open daily 8am-8pm). Lattakia's **telephone code** is 41.

The **Karnak bus station** (tel. 472 096), at the corner of Baghdad Ave. and Haria St. (turn left off Baghdad Ave. after it intersects Al-Quds St.), sends buses daily to: **Damascus** (4hr., 6am and 2:30pm, S£125) via **Homs** (2hr., S£65); **Aleppo** (3½hr., 3pm, S£65); and **Beirut** (4-5hr., 6am, S£175). The **Pullman Bus Station,** at Al-Yaman Placeroundabout, the first right facing away from the train station, serves **Baniyas** (45min., S£15), which is not accessible by microbus. The **Ash-Shati' Transport Co.,** 14 Ramadan St. (tel. 467 149), has daily buses to cities in Turkey such as: **Antakya** (2½hr., S£400); **Adana** (4hr., S£700); **Mersin** (3hr., S£800); **Iskenderun** (3hr., S£800); **Istanbul** (16hr., S£2000); and **Ankara** (12hr., S£1600). Bring your passport and US$20 to get a **Turkish visa** at the border. Within the city, travel by **taxi** (refuse to pay more than S£25) or *service* (white minivans). To get to the **microbus station,** with regular departures to neighboring areas, walk down Ramadan St. toward the tourist office, break left on Al-Maghreb al-Arabi St. at the big traffic circle, take the first right, and walk 500m.

ACCOMMODATIONS AND FOOD

Hotel Lattakia (tel. 479 527) offers a remarkably good deal. Walk a direct line from Assad's much admired backside until you reach a sprawling outdoor coffeeshop. Look for the flashing yellow sign in the alley to the right. The friendly management provides clean rooms with comfy, high beds, fans, a balcony, and a welcoming cup of tea (rooftop mattress S£75; singles S£100, with bath £150; doubles S£200/250; triples S£300/375). **Dounia Hotel** (tel. 421 296) is also a great value, though its less-than-central location, lack of private baths, and occasionally stained floors make it a runner-up. Face away from the Assad statue and outdoor cafe, and take the second right after the gas station; the small hotel is on the left. An exceedingly comfortable bed with a pair of exceedingly comfortable slippers awaits (singles S£100; doubles S£200; triples £300; quads £400).

Eating meals in Lattakia works the usual way—walk around enough and the raw meat and overcooked chicken in the windows start to look appetizing. Budget foodstops line the area around the Assad statue, while more upscale restaurants sit pretty on and around **America Street.** An excellent choice is the **Italian Corner Restaurant and Bar** (tel. 477 207). Follow Ramadan St. toward the sea and take a right when it dead-ends. The staff serves up several noble attempts at Western meat dishes (filet mignon, chicken piccadilly S£140-165), a wide array of pizzas (S£80-140), and an excitingly extensive cocktail menu (S£90-115; beer S£75; open daily 1pm-12:30am). **Sindbad Restaurant**, in a tiny man-made cave, has good food and chairs that resemble Elvis's hair. Take a right after the Italian Corner and follow America St. for two blocks. A left at the Al-Atlal hotel leads to Sindbad's doorstep. They serve up pizza (S£110) and a few Arab dishes garnished with fries (S£130), as well as beer (S£50) and alcoholic drinks (S£130), but close at 10:30pm.

NEAR LATTAKIA

UGARIT (RAS SHAMRA) راس شمرة

Take the last left before the Assad statue and head to the first intersection on the right. Hop on a service (S£15) heading to Ras Shamra and ask to be dropped off at the ruins. To get back, hail a service on the main road; they come more frequently earlier in the day. Ruins open daily in summer 9am-6pm; in winter 9am-5pm. Admission S£300, students S£15.

The historic Kingdom of Ugarit once stood upon the site of this tiny town, 16km north of Lattakia. Ugarit's greatest gift to our time is its 28-letter **alphabet,** preserved in a stone tablet from the 14th century BCE that now sits in the National Museum in Damascus (see p. 508). The oldest phonetic alphabet in the world, Ugaritic is the probable ancestor of both the Phoenician and Hebrew alphabets (though not the languages), as well as those of Latin and Greek. In 1928, an unsuspecting peasant farmer discovered this site when he unearthed a few slabs of stone marking a spot originally settled in the 7th millennium BCE. Since the Kingdom of Ugarit built its structures of stone, it left an architectural legacy better preserved than almost all other Bronze Age cities, which typically consisted of mud-brick houses. Nevertheless, snail-covered weeds are winning the war against the ruins. Professional guides can help decipher the fascinating remains and explain the elaborate system of waterworks. English- and French-speaking guides hang out at the entrance and will show you around for S£250 or your best offer, depending on demand. As you enter, the **royal palace** (where the alphabet was found) is to the right; the **residential quarters** and **acropolis** are farther down.

QAL'AT SALAH AD-DIN قلعة صلاح الدين

From Lattakia, take a microbus from the main microbus station to Al-Haffeh (45min., S£10). For easy thrills, hire the services of one of the Honda motorcycles across the street (round-trip and 1hr. wait S£100). Taxis will ask for S£100 each way—they know how few cars drive along the 7km road to the castle (hitchers should think twice). Castle open W-M in summer 9am-6pm; in winter 9am-4pm. Admission S£300, students S£15.

This fortress, 35km east of Lattakia, is named for the exalted warrior who took the "impregnable" castle from the Crusaders in 1188. Perched on a plateau flanked by two deep gorges, the site's most impressive feature is the 156km long, 18m wide, and 28m deep trench that laborers cut by hand to completely isolate the fortress from the adjacent land—perhaps the pinnacle of the Crusaders' architectural achievements. The lone column of rock that stands in the gorge once supported a drawbridge. Inside the walls, you'll find the arched entry to a stable on your right and a **dungeon** in the drawbridge tower. Holes in the dungeon walls mark where prisoners' chains were drilled into the stone. Up the path and inside the next tower, a hollow column conceals a secret staircase that soldiers on the roof descended to attack the enemy from behind. Across from the entrance sits a huge **cistern** that collected rain water for 4000 soldiers' tea. To the left are remains of Byzantine and Crusader **churches,** and directly in front is the **mosque.** Views from the tops of many of the buildings take in the surrounding valley's sweep towards the Mediterranean. Though no warriors remain to guard it, the castle's highest point remains virtually impregnable due to the thick tangle of prickly briars.

TARTUS طرطوس

Syria's second major seaport is Tartus, the charming older sister to buck-toothed Lattakia 90km to the north. The Phoenicians called this Mediterranean town Antardus, reflecting its secondary importance to the more secure island of Arwad ("Anti-Arwadus" means "the town opposite Arwad"). The Crusaders called it Tortosa and not only fortified the town's seaport but built its **Cathedral Church of Our Lady of Tortosa,** which many consider the premier piece of Crusader religious architecture standing outside Jerusalem. Salah ad-Din made short work of the fortifications in 1188, while the Templar garrison cowered in the dungeon. Nonetheless, Tartus served as the last Crusader stronghold on the mainland, remaining secure until August of 1291, when the Crusaders retreated to Arwad for a decade of ineffectual revolt. Tartus offers the Mediterranean seascape that Lattakia lacks, and the patchwork architecture of its medieval city underscores its diverse past. Modern-day Tartusians still inhabit the narrow lanes and arched buildings of the old town.

◪ **ORIENTATION AND PRACTICAL INFORMATION.** Three main streets and the corniche bind the downtown area of Tartus into a rectangle. **First Street** and **Ibn al-Walid Street** run from the sea to **Ath-Thawra Avenue.** Most of Tartus's reasonably priced hotels and restaurants line First St., running east from the corniche at the **Arwad dock.** At the **clocktower circle,** a left on Ath-Thawra Ave. leads to the **police station.** A block farther and to the right of Ath-Thawra Ave. is the **telephone office,** where a call abroad runs S£90-115 per minute (open daily 8am-midnight). Backtracking to the clocktower circle and hanging a left on Ibn al-Walid St., a 150m uphill walk across another traffic circle leads to the new **post office** (open Sa-Th 7:30am-7pm). Walking downhill towards the sea on Ibn al-Walid St. takes you past the **Commercial Bank of Syria** on the left, which changes traveler's checks for those too morally upright to use the black market (open daily 8:30am-noon). The **tourist information office** (tel. 223 448) is on the right (open Sa-Th 8am-2pm). Ibn al-Walid St. finally deposits you back on the corniche in front of the **Old City.** Across from the Daniel Hotel is the friendly and efficient **Al-Iman Pharmacy** (open Sa-W 8:30am-1:30pm and 5-8pm, Th 8:30am-1:30pm). Tartus's **telephone code** is 43.

The **Kadmous Transportation Co.** (tel. 316 730 or 312 829), at the intersection of Ibn-al-Walid St. and Ath-Thawra Ave., sends buses to: **Hama** (1½hr.; 6am, 4:30, 9pm; S£65) via **Homs** (1hr., S£40); **Lattakia** (1hr., every 15min., S£30); **Baniyas** (30min., every 30min., S£12); **Aleppo** (3½hr.; 6, 11:30am, 4:30, 9pm; S£115); and **Damascus** (3½hr., every 2hr. 2:30am-9:30pm, S£110). The **microbus station,** a 15-minute walk from the town center, services nearby destinations. Take either of the two main streets away from the sea, pass Ath-Thawra Ave., and turn right on Tichrin Ave. To get to **Lebanon,** either hop on a bus bound for Homs and transfer to another bus there, or hire a *service* taxi from the clocktower or on a sidestreet about 50m before the microbus station (Tripoli S£200, Beirut S£300). Remember to have a Lebanese visa and a multiple-entry Syrian visa (or exit visa) for re-entry into the country.

▟▛ **ACCOMMODATIONS AND FOOD.** Tartus houses enough budget hotel and restaurant options to make any brief stay a pleasant one. ▨**Daniel Hotel** (tel. 220 581; fax 316 555), one of Syria's premier budget hotels, sits a block and a half up from the beach on First St. Large, spic-and-span rooms have fans and private baths; some even come with balconies. The hotel also rents mountain bikes and runs trips to beaches along the Syrian coast. (Singles S£350; doubles S£600; triples S£800. Breakfast S£75.) Up the street on the right of the next intersection is the **Republic Hotel** (tel. 222 580). Clean rooms come with a sink and occasional technicolor art. (Singles and doubles S£200; triples S£300. Hot showers £35.) A step down in quality and price, the **Hotel Seyaha (Tourism)** (tel. 221 763), farther up First St. on the left, offers very livable rooms for the lowest prices in town, but no private bathrooms (singles S£200; doubles S£250; triples S£350; hot showers S£25).

On the right of First St. as you approach the sea, **An-Nabil Restaurant** (tel. 220 959) offers choose-your-own seafood, with quality red fish (S£100), white fish (S£225), and shrimp (S£300). Meat dishes (S£100-150) and beer (S£50) round off the menu (open daily 6am-12:30am). At the **Venicia Restaurant,** near the corner of the corniche and First St., the fresh fish is a catch at S£1600 per kilo. The sign on the street lies—there is no pizza. Tables for two on the balcony overlook the sea. For more luxurious dining, explore **The Cave,** 300m from the dock, on the waterfront by the Old City. Chef Ahmed spent 18 years as a cook on a Greek ship and brews his own *'araq* (S£15). The calamari goes down easy for S£350 (open daily 9am-11pm).

🕿 **SIGHTS.** Almost entirely unrenovated, the sturdy walls of the medieval **Old City** enclose a hive of activity and chronologically jumbled architecture. The fortified, 12th-century **cathedral** claims to be the location of the world's oldest altar dedicated to the Virgin Mary. Now a **museum,** it houses an eclectic collection of artifacts from all over coastal Syria. *(Open W-M 9am-2pm. Admission S£300, students S£15.)*

NEAR TARTUS

ARWAD ارواد

Ferries run every 15min. or so from Arwad port in Tartus (round-trip S£20; pay on the island before returning). The last boat leaves at 8:30pm. There are no formal lodgings available on the island, so don't get stranded. Open W-M 9am-6pm. Admission S£300, students S£15.

Arwad, Syria's sole island, floats just 3km from the coast of Tartus. In ancient times, Arwad served as a sanctuary for those seeking protection from foreign invaders. As such, it was the last Crusader stronghold to return to Muslim hands. More recently, the French used it as a prison for Syrian nationalists. The Phoenician kingdom of Aradus was centered on the island, and though its renowned defensive walls no longer stand, two grand medieval forts remain; one of them now calls itself a museum. Wandering Arwad's narrow lanes and enjoying a seaside cup of tea are equally popular activities. Alternatively, take a 30-minute empathy walk around the island—the environmental police would have a heart attack over the litter scattered liberally over Arwad's backside. Some derive great amusement from the gaudy shell souvenirs sold in large numbers around the port.

CASTLE LE BLANC

To get to Castle le Blanc, take a microbus from Tartus to Safita (40min., S£10). From Safita center you can hop on a service, which will take you to the base of a cobblestone side road (ask for Al-Burj). On foot from Safita center, walk up the steepest street and look for the cobblestone side road on the right leading up to the tower. Site theoretically open daily 9am-7pm. Admission is free, but a tip (around S£10) may be expected on the way out.

Of the once majestic Castle le Blanc, only one remaining tower stands guard over the tiled roofed houses and olive trees of the small mountain town of Safita. A beautiful chapel graces the tower's entrance level; it has never been deconsecrated and continues to serve as a place of worship today. Upstairs are the spacious living quarters, which represent one of the finest examples of Romanesque architecture in Syria. Another flight of stairs leads to the roof, which offers panoramic views of Lebanon and, on a clear day, Crac des Chevaliers (see p. 516).

NORTHERN SYRIA

ALEPPO حلب

Aleppo (*Halab* in Arabic), the "second capital of Syria," 350km north of Damascus, has flourished since the 3rd millennium BCE. Biblical Abraham is said to have milked his grey cow on the acropolis here—hence the name *Halab ash-Shahba,* or "he milked the grey." Situated at the crossroads of several vital trade routes, ancient Aleppo controlled the "Great Syrian Passage" connecting Mesopotamia and Persia with the Mediterranean Sea. Though occupied by the Romans, Persians, and Byzantines (whose Christian influence is still felt), Aleppo reached its cultural peak in the days of the Arab **Hamadanis;** Sayf ad-Dawla, who established the Hamadani state in 944 CE, hosted great poets Al-Mutanabbi and Abu al-Firas, filled the city with splendid mosques, schools, and tombs, and built the city's towering **Citadel,** which dominates Aleppo to this day. The city's *khans* were built later to accommodate the many traders passing through; several still stand. Construction continued during Ottoman rule, when the Middle East's biggest and best covered *souqs* were built in the ancient city.

Aleppo continues to be a meeting point of different cultures. Along with the city's Arabo-Muslim population, today's Aleppans include Armenians, Russians, and Greek Orthodox Christians. The cafes and outdoor restaurants that crowd its wide, tree-lined streets make contemporary Aleppo a sophisticated metropolis, with some of the best shopping available along the Eastern Mediterranean and a freewheeling sense of fun not felt in the bigger, older capital to the south. Some tourists may be turned off by Aleppo's pollution and hunkering socialist architecture, but more and more flock here not just as a stop en route to other sights, but as an end in itself.

✴ ORIENTATION

Mastering Aleppo's square layout is simple. You'll find almost all budget accommodations and some restaurants in the area bounded by **Al-Ma'ari** and **Quwatli Streets** (running east-west), and **Baron** and **Bab al-Faraj Streets** (running north-south). Late-night walks in this area can be unpleasant, especially when the Kung Fu and porn movies let out. The National Museum, tourist office, private bus services, travel agents, and a few expensive restaurants all lie on Al-Ma'ari St. A sharp right onto **Al-Walid Street,** which soon turns into **Sa'adullah aj-Jabri Street,** brings you to the **Christian Quarter,** where the wealthy strut their stuff around the restaurants and cafes. Walking is enjoyable in the cool evenings, especially in the enormous **Public Garden** opposite the Christian Quarter. South of Bab al-Faraj St. runs the congested **Al-Mutanabbi Street,** which eventually leads to the **Citadel.** Any right turn will land you in the bustling **souqs.** The easiest way to get perspective on Syria's second-largest city is to hike up the Citadel's bridge and climb the western wall.

🛈 PRACTICAL INFORMATION

Airplanes: Aleppo International Airport (tel. 233 67 00 or 233 54 05), 30km east of the city center. Buses leave for the airport from the bus stop across from the tourist office, but *service* taxis are more flexible (don't pay more than S£200).

Buses: To ride a local bus, purchase a card valid for 4 rides (S£10). Intercity **microbuses** depart from the Pullman Station to: **Homs** (S£75); **Hama** (S£60); **Damascus** (S£125); **Tartus** (S£150); and **Lattakia** (S£100). Many **private bus companies** have offices on Ibrahim Hanano St. (a few minutes walk to the right when facing the Amir Palace), and across the street from the Baron Hotel. The **Pan Bus Company** (tel. 222 42 76) has daily service to **Antakya, TUR** (3hr., 3 per day, 5:30am-2pm, S£250), and from there to many destinations in Turkey, including **Iskenderun** (4hr., S£300) and **Istanbul** (22hr., S£1100). US$20 buys a visa at the border. The **Karnak** station (tel. 221 02 48) faces the Baron; buses to: **Lattakia** (4hr., 7am, S£65); **Homs** (2½hr., 7 per day 5am-midnight, S£75) via **Hama** (2hr., S£60); **Damascus** (4½hr., 5am and 3:30pm, S£130); **Amman** (10pm, S£450); and **Beirut** (midnight, 1, 7, 10am, 1pm; S£75).

Taxis: Service stop next to the **Pullman Station,** behind the Amir Palace Hotel (S£2-5). Drivers of **private taxis** dislike the meter; few journeys should cost more than S£25.

Tourist Office: (tel. 222 12 00), on Al-Ma'ari St. at the intersection with Baron St., across from the National Museum. Get their map with bus and transportation information. Open Sa-Th 9am-2pm.

Aleppo

ACCOMMODATIONS

A Baron Hotel
B Ambassador Hotel
C Tourist Hotel
D Aj-Jawaher Hotel
E Hotel Najem Akhdar

Tourist Police: (tel. 222 12 00). The same number and building as the tourist office; ask to be transferred. Complaints about hideous over-charging on the part of taxi drivers, stores, hotels, and the like should be directed to tel. 119.

Currency Exchange: Changing anything but cash here is a hassle. The **Commercial Bank of Syria,** on Baron St. just past the Ugarit theater, accepts traveler's checks for a small commission; bring your passport and waiting shoes. Other branches on Al-Mutanabbi St. only change cash. All branches open daily 8am-noon. An **exchange booth** at the intersection of Quwatli and Bab al-Faraj St., changes cash only. Open Th-Sa 8am-8pm, F 9am-7pm. Some areas of the *souq* specialize in black market exchange at good rates.

English Bookstore: Kussa Library, on Homsi St. Go down Baron St., away from the tourist office and past the Kung Fu theaters. Take a right after Ma'had al-Mahaba School (a bombed-out looking building on the right); it's on the immediate left. Carries 3- to 4-day-old copies of *International Herald Tribune, Wall Street Journal,* and English versions of the Lebanese *Daily Star* and Egyptian *Al-Ahram.* Open daily 8am-2pm and 5-9pm.

Emergencies: Police and Medical: Tel. 112. **Hospital:** Tel. 110.

Pharmacies: The **Ummal An-Najl Pharmacy** (tel. 225 14 78), next to the entrance of Baghdad Station (open 24hr.). Most pharmacies in Aleppo open 9:30am-2pm and 5-9:30pm. They rotate late-night duties.

Medical Assistance: Dr. Faher (tel. 221 52 52) offers medical assistance in English.

Post Office: (tel. 144), on Aj-Jala'a St., just before the park, under a giant radio tower. Open daily 8am-8pm. **EMS** open Sa-Th 8am-2pm. Bring your passport. **DHL** (tel. 224 09 88); after Bab al-Faraj St., take the first right off Quwatli St. It's in a small alley to the left. Open Sa-Th 9am-2pm and 4-8pm.

Telephones: In the post office. Bring your calling card and pay at the desk after your call. Open daily 8am-10pm. S£120 per min. to the U.S., U.K., Canada, or Australia. Check hotel phone services and consider buying a Syrian phonecard.

Telephone Code: 21.

ACCOMMODATIONS

Hotels in Aleppo range from the seat of sleaze to the lap of luxury. Higher-priced options cluster on Baron St. in the center of town; more affordable places are scattered among the spare car parts and hole-in-the-wall eateries near the Bab al-Faraj clocktower. Those searching for very cheapest should be warned that some are frequented by Russian prostitutes. Look carefully before letting go of your cash.

Tourist Hotel (tel. 221 65 83), off Yarmouk St. across from the museum. Walking away from Bab al-Faraj clocktower on Al-Ma'ari St., take a right just before the Syria Hotel. It's 75m down on the left past an intersection. Spotless rooms (all with comfy beds and some with huge, beautiful balconies) are inspected by Madame Olga, the distinguished owner. Plant life galore adorns the communal areas. Singles S£350, with bath £400; doubles with bath S£700; triples with bath S£1050.

Aj-Jawaher Hotel (tel./fax 223 95 54), Bab al-Faraj. With your back to the clocktower, walk towards the Cultural Center (keeping it on your left), and take the first left. New, freshly painted rooms are very clean and have spotless bathrooms or pleasant balconies. Prices include bath. Singles S£350; doubles S£700; triples S£950. Breakfast S£75. Laundry service available.

Hotel Najem Akhdar (tel. 223 91 57). When facing the library from the clocktower, take a left and then a right around the mosque; the hotel is on your right. Rooms with pink bedspreads have comfortable beds, while rooms with balconies have lumpy beds and "showers" reminiscent of meatlockers. The hotel's friendly management and the rooftop restaurant with excellent Aleppan views make up for its gloomy ambience and the occasional roach sighting. Rooftop mattresses S£150; dorm beds S£200; singles S£300; doubles S£400, with bath S£500; triples S£600, with bath S£750. Breakfast S£75.

Baron Hotel (tel./fax 221 81 64), on Baron St. When Aleppo was the end of the line on the Orient Express, the Baron was a stopover for illustrious guests like T.E. Lawrence, Agatha Christie, and Kemal Ataturk. While still a majestic charmer, the most grandiose thing about it these days are its prices. The bar is the best place in Syria to drink (over-priced) local and German beer with other blasé expats and tourists. Singles US$30; doubles US$40; stunning suites US$80. Breakfast US$3-4. Reserve in advance.

Ambassador Hotel (tel. 221 02 31), on Baron St., next to the Baron Hotel. Rooms are cheerfully decorated with blue curtains, bedspreads, tablecloths, and Impressionist-style paintings, but the stained bathroom floors may give you a case of the blues. All rooms have wardrobes, some have balconies. Singles S£900/US$22; doubles S£1200/US$29; triples S£1500/US$36. Payment in U.S. dollars or European currencies is preferred. Breakfast S£100.

FOOD

For great inexpensive restaurants and cafes, go around the corner from the exchange booth on Quwatli St. onto Bab al-Faraj St. Take a right at the **fruit shake stands** and you'll see six or seven places on your right. Baron Street is lined with rooftop restaurants with bird's-eye views of the crowds. The Christian Quarter, near the park off Sa'adullah aj-Jabri St., is home to almost-Americana.

Beit Wakil (tel. 221 71 69 or 224 70 83), in the Christian Quarter. Head down Khayali St. towards Al-Hatab Sq. and take a right onto a small alley (Sirsi St.); the sweetest splurge in Syria is on the left. Munch on traditional Aleppan fare as an adept belly-dancer cuts a rug. Ottoman architecture and design provide an authentic backdrop, and the congenial manager offers to cater to "all budgets." Huge entrees S£300-500.

Abu Nouwas (tel. 221 03 88). From Bab al-Faraj clocktower, go up Al-Ma'ari St. and take the 1st right; it's 2 blocks uphill on the left. This clean, A/C diner has tasteful decor and an attentive staff. There are no menus: the manager gives tours of the kitchen to see what tempts your palate. Outstanding lentil soup (S£50); tasty kebab with warm pita, veggies, soup, salad, and drink (S£200). Breakfast S£75. Open daily 7am-midnight.

Al-Kindi (tel. 223 11 54 or 221 08 89). Walking uphill on Bab al-Faraj St. from the clock-tower, take the 2nd left; Al-Kindi is on the right. Synchronize your mastication with the whacking of a distant meat mallet in this cheap, down-to-earth local favorite. Extensive English (but not-so-vegetarian-friendly) menu featuring well-prepared kebab (S£80), shish tawouq (S£70), and even lamb eggs (S£70). Open daily 7am-2am.

Ali Baba Restaurant (tel. 221 50 24). From the clocktower, head up Bab al-Faraj St. and take the first left at the fruit shake stands. This rooftop restaurant's specialty is the kebab halabi (S£100). Copious amounts of Sharq beer (S£50) and 'araq (S£25) are sipped by the mostly male dinner guests. Open daily 8am-3am.

Patisserie Mousattat (tel. 212 747), the 3rd left up from the clocktower, just off of Bab Al-Faraj St., next to the exchange booth. A classic ba'lawa (baklava) bakery. Can't stomach shawarma before noon? Bring your morning munchies here and ask for ma'moniyya: a yummy cream-of-wheat-like starch drenched in warm syrup, doused with cinnamon, and eaten with pita bread (S£25). Open daily 5am-midnight.

👁️ 🎵 SIGHTS AND ENTERTAINMENT

CITADEL. Begin your sightseeing tour with an outstanding view of Aleppo from the soaring Citadel. Built in the 10th century CE by Sayf ad-Dawla, the Citadel stands 50m above the city on a hill (known as a tel), heightened by the remains of prior civilizations. In times of war, Aleppans equipped themselves with plentiful provisions and took refuge in this fortress. Its enormous entrance gate is fortified with three sets of steel doors, and the 12th-century **moat** (20m deep by 30m wide) is lined with smooth stones to make climbing difficult (some of the tiles are still in place today). The watery defense is now full of refuse, but not for the first time. Historical accounts describe in gruesome hyperbole how in 1400, Timor's Central Asian forces couldn't penetrate the Citadel until the moat brimmed with fallen soldiers' bodies.

Inside and to the immediate left of the main path lies a **bath** that was once used as a metal-working studio. Beyond that is the **small mosque** (with a well in the middle of its courtyard), the **great mosque** (only slightly bigger, but with a fountain rather than a well), and a cafeteria that serves overpriced food and drink (soda S£35) with an air of self-importance. Connected to the cafeteria are the **barracks**, now a museum displaying objects found during the Citadel's excavation. Below the barracks is a modern **amphitheater** that stages occasional performances. To the right of the main path are **storage rooms** for food and water to be consumed during sieges, followed by stairs that lead to the **Royal Palace.** One of the most interesting sections of the Citadel, this area has its own baths and a courtyard paved with black and white marble. From the palace, a passage leads to the opulent, graffiti-covered **Throne Room,** which sits directly above the main entrance. *(Open W-M in summer 9am-6pm; in winter 9am-4pm. Admission S£300, students S£15; museum S£150, students S£15.)*

HAMMAM YALBOAGHA AN-NASIRI. Outside the Citadel, the **Hammam Yalboagha An-Nasiri** awaits to steam, wash, and massage the sweat and grime off dirty, sore bodies. This beautifully restored 14th-century bath is heavily marketed by the Ministry of Tourism. *(Take a left with your back to the Citadel entrance. Open for women Su, Tu-W, and F 10am-1:30pm in summer; Sa, M, and Th 9am-1:30pm in winter. Open for men Su, Tu-W, and F 5pm-2am in summer; daily 5pm-1:30am in winter. Soaping, massage, and cup of coffee or tea S£415, S£200 if you bring your own soap and bathe unassisted.)*

MAIN SOUQ. Between the Hammam/Citadel area and the hotel district is the **best souq in the eastern Mediterranean.** All 9km of ancient, winding covered passageways burst with leather goods, wool, backgammon boards, carpets, tablecloths, Qur'ans, argeilehs, brass goods, and gold and silver jewelry. Several **khans** (caravanserais or courtyard inns) in the *souq* housed international traders during the Mamluke and Ottoman periods. On Friday evenings, the dark and deserted *souq* invites leisurely exploration on foot. Walking around the *souq* should be safe even during the less busy hours; women travelers are advised not to walk alone in the evenings. *(Open Sa-Th early morning until 7 or 8pm.)*

AJ-JAMI' AL-KABIR. Appropriately situated just behind the gold market, **Aj-Jami' al-Kabir,** the Great Mosque of the Umayyads (also called **Zacharias's Mosque,** after the Father of John the Baptist), is a real gem. Built on top of a Byzantine cathedral in the 8th century, its square minaret with five levels of arches is a remarkable piece of architecture. To the left of the main entrance is an empty 600-year-old **insane asylum** in good condition. Wander through to see where the insane, the not-so-insane, and the very rich were kept locked up by their families. The clean smell emanates from two **soap factories** around the corner; the excellent quality of Aleppo's soap (made out of olive or even laurel oil) is known throughout the Middle East. Both factories have been in the same spotless families for generations.

NATIONAL MUSEUM. Aleppo's National Museum is second only to Damascus's in its exhibit quality. Several 100,000-year-old Ugarit flint axes, a third-millennium BCE basalt altar from Ebla, and a stone lion from an 18th-century BCE temple will leave you reeling with the knowledge of your own temporal existence. The third floor includes a modern art wing; ask a guard to open it for you. *(Across from the tourist office on Baron St. Open in summer Sa-M and W-Th 9am-6pm, F 9am-12:30pm and 2-6pm; in winter Sa-M and W-Th 9am-4pm, F 9-11:30am and 2-6pm. Admission S£300; students S£15.)*

CHRISTIAN QUARTER. Fabulous 17th- and 18th-century homes line the narrow streets of the Christian Quarter. Within a few blocks, churches from four different denominations attract worshipers. Walk down Quwatli St. past Bab al-Faraj St. and take a left at the fascist-style stone gate. Down a narrow alley to the right is a 19th-century **Maronite Cathedral,** and to the right is a gorgeous **Greek Catholic Church.** At the store with underwear in the window, take a right to the **Greek Orthodox Church** and the **Armenian Church of the Forty Martyrs.** These magnificent buildings feature third-century artwork, engraved marble altars, and antique chandeliers.

NEAR ALEPPO

BASILICA OF SAINT SIMEON قلعةسمان

To reach St. Simeon from Aleppo, take a microbus to Darret 'Azzay (1hr., S£10). From this small town, negotiate with locals for the 8km ride to the cathedral. Service minivans will ask for S£100 one-way, but locals in brightly-colored Suzuki 3-wheelers might do a round trip for S£150-200. Open daily 9am-6pm, in winter 9am-4pm. Admission S£300, students S£15.

Born in a small mountain village in 386 CE, **Saint Simeon of Stylites** acquired the first and last parts of his name by spending almost 40 years preaching from atop a stylite (from the Greek *sylos*, meaning "pillar"). Simeon chained himself to a railing atop a pillar after receiving divine instruction in a dream, and received only two rations of supplies per week for the rest of his life. Peasants began to ask the local legend for advice, and the game of "Simon Says" was born. Before long, people came from all around to hear Simeon preach. With such a rapidly growing fan club, Simeon had to find higher and higher pillars to sanctify; he eventually ended up 15m in the air. While he would gladly answer male pilgrims' spiritual questions, Simple Simeon refused to talk to women.

Simeon's death in 459 CE did not stop pilgrims from visiting his pillar, and the emperor Zenon had a **cathedral** built around his home, considered a masterpiece of pre-Islamic architecture. A large dome covered the octagonal courtyard where the pillar stood, surrounded by four basilicas that formed a giant cross. One basilica was a chapel; the other three housed pilgrims. The rear wall of the chapel was decorated with delicate acanthus leaves and Byzantine crosses, widespread at the time. An earthquake destroyed the structure less than 50 years after its completion, causing pilgrims to question the site's holiness and deterring pious investors from rebuilding the cathedral. The 5th-century remains are still impressive, but years of chipping away at the pillar by souvenir seekers has reduced it to a large boulder. In the 10th century, the site was converted to a Byzantine fort with 27 towers along an enclosing wall. The fortifications are easily distinguishable from the cathedral ruins and afford excellent panoramic views of the rocky terrain leading up to Turkey.

If your taxi driver refuses to lower his price, insist on a side trip to **Qatura** to better justify the expense. This Roman tomb, resting place of the warrior Taitus Flavius Julianus, is carved into rock about 1km off the road to St. Simeon. Above the entrance to the main tomb, an eagle with spread wings—identical to one in Palmyra's Temple of Bel (see p. 513)—symbolizes the soul.

EBLA أبلا

From the Aleppo station, take a microbus headed to Ma'aret En-No'man (S£25) and ask to get off at the road to Ebla. It's a 30min. walk to the site, and there is no food or water available, but able will you be, ere you see Ebla. Back on the highway, it's easy to catch a bus back to Aleppo; they come frequently from both Ma'aret En-No'man and Hama. Open daily 6am-6pm. Admission S£200, students S£15, if the guy is there to collect it.

This *tel*, 60km south of Aleppo, was discovered in 1964, and excavations are still in progress. Ebla is thought to have been the oldest city in Syria, dating back to the 3rd millennium BCE. Over 17,000 **cuneiform tablets** have been recovered in an ancient **palace library,** revealing much about Syria's early history. Apparently, Ebla was the center of an important north Syrian empire during the 3rd millennium BCE, but as fate would have it, the city was to prove itself a rather irritating obstacle to the expansion of empires. Both Sargon of Akkad (in about 2300 BCE) and the Hittites (around 1600 BCE) razed Ebla almost in its entirety. Today, signs insist that you remain on the edges of the site; this shouldn't come as too much of a disappointment unless you have a strong interest in archaeology.

EASTERN SYRIA

DEIR EZ-ZUR

Tourists may consider Deir ez-Zur remote, but throughout the city's history, location has been its greatest asset. The city first flourished because of its strategic position next to the Euphrates River, at the crossroads of the two major communication routes. During the 1980s, oil was discovered beneath the city's sands, leading to the massive growth spurt that made contemporary Deir ez-Zur one of the largest towns in eastern Syria. However, Deir ez-Zur is first and foremost a city of the Euphrates. Even the Turkish dams harnessing the river's hydraulic force have not stripped it of its splendor. Enjoy its troubled waters from a safe distance on the **suspension bridge** built by the French. Aside from one rather good museum and magnificent views of the river, dry and distant Deir ez-Zur offers travelers little more than a hub for visiting the nearby ruins at Rasafeh, Halabiyyeh, and Zalabiyyeh, and a glimpse into the life of the nomadic desert people of easternmost Syria.

⚡ ORIENTATION AND PRACTICAL INFORMATION. Deir ez-Zur is easy to navigate; the major hotels, restaurants, and shopping areas are centered around the main intersection of **8 Azar** and **Al-Iman Streets.** Use the statue of President Assad on a horse as a handy landmark—nearly everything is a five-minute walk away. Very few signs are written in English or French; rely on maps and landmarks. The **bus/micro station** is about 1km out of town on 8 Azar St. Hourly **microbuses** go to **Raqqa** (2hr., S£60), **Mari** (2hr., S£50), and other southern areas. Old **buses** leave less frequently for **Damascus** via **Palmyra** (S£110), **Aleppo** (S£70), and **Homs** (S£75). The **luxury bus station** is about 2km out of town past the bus/micro station. **Karnak Bus Co.** (tel. 221 885) runs to: **Damascus** (6hr.; 8, 10, 11am, noon, 3, 10pm; S£160) and **Palmyra** (2hr., same times as Damascus, S£75). **Qadmoos** (tel. 212 920) runs buses to: **Palmyra** (2hr., S£85); **Damascus** (6hr.; 1, 7, 9, 11am, 2:15, 3, 5, 11, 11:15, 11:30pm, midnight; S£175); **Homs** (4hr.; 2, 11, 11:45pm, 1:15am; S£150); **Raqqa** (2hr.; 5, 10:30am, 5pm; S£75); and **Aleppo** (6hr.; 1, 6:30, 9am, 2:30, 8pm; S£135). **Furat Tours** (tel. 223 934) sends buses to: **Damascus** (6hr.; 9:30, 11pm, 1am; S£175); **Palmyra** (4hr., 12:45pm, S£135); and **Raqqa** (2hr.; 9:30am, 1pm; S£75).

The **tourist office** (tel. 226 150) is east of the square, one block south of Khalid Ibn Al-Walid St. English skills are tenuous, and resources like maps are rarely available (open Sa-Th 9am-2pm). Exchange cash at the **Commercial Bank of Syria**, a 10-minute walk along Al-Iman Ali St. (open Sa-Th 8am-4pm). The **police** (tel. 112) are around the corner from the museum on 6 Ayyar St., across from the river. Call 110 for an **ambulance**. **Ash-Shifa'a Pharmacy** (tel. 221 241) is next to Aj-Jamia'a Hotel, east of the main square. There are two **post offices:** the new one is near the bus/micro station on 8 Azar St.; the old one is a five-minute walk west of the square on Al-Iman Ali St. (both open 8am-2pm and 6:30-8pm). The only **public phones** are around the corner from the old post office; get **phonecards** inside. Deir ez-Zur's **telephone code** is 51.

▗◪ ACCOMMODATIONS AND FOOD. Lodgings in Deir ez-Zur are limited to dingy-looking buildings in disrepair. Don't count on hot showers, and be prepared for some not-so-clean beds. **Hotel Damas** (tel. 221 481), across the street from the Euphrates on 8 Azar St., is the best of slim pickings. Rooms overlooking the main street are breezy but loud at night (singles S£200; doubles S£325; triples S£425). **Hotel Aj-Jamia'a Al-'Arabia** (tel. 221 371) jams on Grande St., about two blocks away from the central square. A cool sitting room with a TV and balconies make this hotel somewhat cheery, but rumors of bedbugs abound (singles S£200; doubles S£325; triples S£425). **Hotel Al-'Arabi al-Kabir** (tel. 222 070), east of the square on Khalid Ibn Walid St., is brighter and cleaner than other options in town, but the unpleasant setting is a drawback (singles S£150; doubles S£300; triples S£350).

Don't expect fine dining—most culinary options come from the small falafel, shawarma, and pastry shops and the fresh produce **souq** around 8 Azar Sq. If the stand-up routine grows tiresome, there are a few sit-down places around the square and on the river. **Lucost** is a beautiful restaurant along the main branch of the Euphrates. Grab a decent meal (S£200) or just sit with a beer (S£100) and enjoy the view (open past midnight). **Sahara Restaurant,** a short walk west of the square, provides cheap, fresh, filling meals for S£65-75. **As-Sa'id Restaurant,** at the central square, offers sit-down or takeout skewered chicken or kebab (S£150-170).

◎ SIGHTS. Deir ez-Zur's **National Museum,** considered one of the best in Syria, was opened in response to growing archaeological discoveries in the area. It was established on this site in 1996 as a joint venture between the Syrian Antiquities Department and the Frei Universität of Berlin, Germany. The museum presents the region's history starting with the Biblical era, moving through Arab-Islamic culture, and ending in the present day. Especially interesting are the lifesized models and artifacts. The museum also pays particular attention to the region's sensitive environmental situation (open W-M 9am-6pm; admission S£300, students S£15).

RAQQA

Looking around contemporary Raqqa, one would hardly guess that this bustling market town possesses a glorious past. Located on the left bank of the Euphrates between Aleppo and Deir ez-Zur, Raqqa was founded in the 4th century BCE by Alexander the Great and rebuilt by many empires throughout the ages, though few ruins remain to attest to its former splendor. In 662 CE, 'Abbasid Caliph Mansur built a new city atop of Raqqa's ruins, with a semicircular plan inspired by Baghdad. The southern, straight side of this horseshoe-shaped city was determined by the course of the Euphrates. Raqqa reached its apex in the beginning of the 9th century under the notorious 'Abbasid Caliph Harun ar-Rashid, but virtually ceased to exist after Mongol invasions in 1260. It was not until the end of WWII that the city was revitalized as a Euphrates basin commercial site, once again built over its own ruins.

ZENOBIA, WARRIOR PRINCESS Previously called **Zenobia** (after the Palymrene queen under whose auspices it was built), the 3rd-century CE town of **Halabiyyeh** once guarded trade routes along the Euphrates and the desert. The Romans took Halabiyyeh after destroying Palmyra; in the following years, the town was a stronghold against the threatening Sassanian Persians. Its citadel was once heralded as the greatest Byzantine fortification outside Constantinople itself. The city was destroyed and eventually abandoned after sieges in 540 and 610. Nevertheless, Halabiyyeh's outer walls and upper fortifications remain relatively intact, and it is still possible to make out the foundations of some churches and baths. What isn't difficult at all to discern is the incredible view of the Euphrates. The twin fortress town of **Zalabiyyeh**, 3km downstream on the opposite bank, once defended the approaches to Halabiyyeh. With the exception of the main gateway, the site is almost completetly destroyed. Getting to these towns is an arduous process. From Deir ez-Zur, take a **microbus** to **Tibne** (S£15, every hr., 30min.). From this turnoff, you'll have to hitch or suffer the two-hour walk to Halabiyyeh. Getting to Zalabiyyeh is much harder and probably not worth it. From Halabiyyeh, cross the bridge just beyond town, walk for three hours along the main road, pass through the tunnel under the railway (just after the station), and proceed up the hill.

◪ ORIENTATION AND PRACTICAL INFORMATION. Orientation around Raqqa is easy from the **clocktower** in the central square and the requisite **Assad statue** down the hill to the south. The **microbus station** is about 200m south of the clocktower past the Assad statue. Microbuses leave regularly to **Al-Mansura** (30min., S£15) and **Aleppo** (3hr., S£75). The main **bus station** is across the street. The cheapest of the luxury bus lines is **Karnak** (tel. 224 097), with buses to **Damascus** (7hr., noon, S£160) and **Homs** (5hr., noon, S£100). The nicer **Qadmoos** (tel. 221 628) runs to **Damascus** (7hr.; 8:30am, 2:30pm, midnight; S£190), **Aleppo** (2hr.; 12:45, 7:15pm; S£85), and **Homs** (5hr.; 8:30am, 2:30pm, midnight; S£120). **Al-'Aliah,** another luxury bus line, services **Aleppo** (2hr.; 7, 8, 9, 11am, 1, 3:30, 6:30, 9pm; S£85). Don't expect much help from the **tourist office** (tel. 244 445; open Sa-Th 8:30am-2pm). In contrast, the **hospital** (tel. 222 340), just west of the clocktower on Ash-Shahid Bassel al-Assad St., is clean, economical, and friendly. The **post office** (tel. 235 899), just south of the clocktower on the east side of the street, is the only place to make **international phone calls.** You must buy an S£1000 **phonecard,** available outside. Very little English and an unhealthy suspicion of foreigners means that it's hard to get any information; even placing simple calls can strain the patience. Raqqa's **telephone code** is 22.

◪◪ ACCOMMODATIONS AND FOOD. Hotel Tourism (tel. 220 725), on the main street just east of the clocktower, is the best bet in town, with a pleasant sitting room and perks like showers, fridges, and TVs. Ask the manager to turn on the hot water or you'll be in for a frigid shower (doubles S£450; triples S£600). The nondescript rooms at **'Ammar Hotel** (tel. 222 612), on a side street one block north of the clocktower, are a little cheaper, with sinks but no showers in the rooms (singles S£200; doubles S£400; students S£150). **Hotel Karnak** (tel. 232 266) is a five-minute hike west of the Assad statue along the winding Ash-Shahid Bassel al-Assad St. The receptionist is helpful even to non-guests, and big rooms come with clean baths, air conditioning, and fridges. Ask for a top-floor room with a balcony and tremendous views (singles US$17; doubles US$23; triples US$27; traveler's checks accepted).

Many falafel and shawarma stands cluster around the main square, and delightful pastry shops beckon the hungry north of the clocktower. Finding a sit-down is often as rewarding as it is difficult. **Ar-Rashid Restaurant** (tel. 241 919) is about a block west of the clocktower through a small park. Enjoy a splendid Syrian meal (S£250) and beer (S£100) in the comfort of their air-conditioned dining room with views onto the garden. The **Hotel Karnak Restaurant** also offers cheap eats (S£200) that can be enjoyed on the patio overlooking the main street and lawn.

◉ SIGHTS. Most of Raqqa's former splendor has been lost over time, but there are a few exceptions. To the east and northeast of the clocktower, parts of the 'Abbasid wall still remain. Raqqa's 12th-century **city gate** is a 10-minute walk east of the clocktower. To the northwest lie the remains of the old **Grand Mosque**, built during the reign of the 'Abbasid caliph Al-Mansur in the 8th century CE. Only parts of the enclosure wall and the arcade of the sanctuary wall still stand. Syrian and French archaeologists have uncovered parts of the 'Abbasid palace, known as the **Palace of the Maidens,** to the north of the mosque. A small **museum** a few blocks to the east of the clocktower provides a two-tiered analysis of the region: the first floor details the archaeology from the province of Raqqa, and the second floor contains items from the city of Raqqa proper (open F-W 8am-4pm; admission S£150, students S£35). A newmuseum is scheduled to open on the banks of the Euphrates in late 2000.

NEAR RAQQA: RASAFEH

Service depart from Raqqa to Al-Mansura (30min., S£15), where local taxi drivers circle like sharks in search of tourists. A **taxi** ride to Rasafeh and back costs S£200. Hitchhiking is a popular option, though Let's Go does not recommend it. Hitchers first walk the short distance to Al-Mansura's main road to look for a lift. It may take about an hour and possibly require a few different rides, so bring water, small bills to offer your driver(s), and plenty of patience.

The towering walls of Rasafeh (30km south of Raqqa and the Euphrates), one of the most extraordinary desert cities in the Middle East, appear suddenly out of the vast, flat desert expanses. Around 303 CE, **Sergius,** a Christian officer in the Roman army, was brutally tortured for his refusal to worship the Roman god Jupiter. His horrible death sent shockwaves though Syria's Christian community, and Sergius became the patron saint of the immense, walled city of Rasafeh, where his shrine became a major pilgrimage site. The city was even renamed Sergiopolis in the 5th century. Sergiopolis fell to Persian Muslims in the 7th century, and eventually the Umayyads depopulated and deserted the area. Layers of archeological history chronicle the rise and fall of generations and the story of battles over religious beliefs. The relative difficulty of accessing Rasafeh means that few tourists crowd the town.

Enter Rasafeh through the Byzantine **North Gate,** often called one of the loveliest city entrances in Syria. Three Corinthian columns support the richly decorated triple entrance and serve as a graceful frame for the city beyond. Climb the ramparts for a better view of the whole fortress. The bulk of the site has not been excavated, so the interior looks somewhat like a lunar landscape, with high ground where walls once stood and depressions where roofs hung. In front of the gate is a run-of-the-mill Roman **basilica,** and about 100m farther lies the **khan** (market). To the west, the arched openings of the enormous **cisterns** lead to vast underground caverns, supplied by aqueducts connected to a huge open reservoir. These caverns were capable of holding enough water to supply the entire city for two to three years. To the east stands the early 6th-century **Basilica of St. Sergius,** the best preserved building in Rasafeh and one of the most lavishly decorated cathedrals in the region.

TURKEY (TÜRKİYE)

US$1=447,000 TURKISH LIRA (TL)	100,000TL=US$0.22
CDN$1=300,369TL	100,000TL=CDN$0.33
UK£1=720,384TL	100,000TL=UK£0.14
AUS$1=285,933TL	100,000TL=AUS$0.35
SAR1=73,930TL	100,000TL=SAR1.35
EUR1=475,049TL	100,000TL=EUR0.21
S£100 (SYRIAN POUNDS)=10,695TL	100,000TL=S£9.35

PHONE FACTS **Country Code:** 90. **Emergency:** Tel. 112.

At only 77 years old, Turkey is a young nation that has inherited the combined riches of the ancient Greeks and Romans, the Byzantines, and the Ottomans. Asia Minor has seen more than 10,000 years of cultural traffic, and each passing civilization has left a layer of debris for travelers to discover and explore. And the travelers *are* coming, tempted by tourist posters offering sun-soaked beaches and scantily-clad belly dancers. Along with the Sultanahmet district of Istanbul, the Mediterranean and Aegean coasts have an established tourist industry that makes enjoying Turkey easy. Still, the rest of Anatolia awaits exploration: pristine alpine meadows, cliffside monasteries, medieval churches, and countless cups of çay (tea) offered by people who take great pride in their tradition of hospitality.

For centuries now, the word Turkey has conjured up disconnected images of Ottoman sultans and their debauched harems, ferocious and proud fighters, and Islamic fundamentalists. While Bodrum nightclubs may resemble harem fantasies on most nights, Turkey's reality is not quite as fantastical. Young professionals tote cell phones and the country becomes increasingly wired to the Internet, but the devastating earthquake of August 1999 reminded the world that Turkey's infrastructure is still developing. Aware of itself as merely another itinerant civilization inhabiting a land that has seen more than 10,000 years of cultural traffic, Turkey refuses to commit to self-definition. A lengthy laundry list of civilizations has left inestimable physical and cultural imprints on a country whose infinite complexity is both its virtue and its burden. For the traveler, Turkey offers a fabulously rich artistic, cultural, and physical reservoir to explore. For full coverage of the sights and sounds of Turkey, check out *Let's Go: Turkey 2000*.

HIGHLIGHTS OF TURKEY

■ In **Istanbul** (p. 544), bargain your way out of the **Grand Bazaar,** relive the intrigue of the **Topkapı Palace Harem,** then take a breather at the **Hagia Sophia** before heading out to one of the city's nomadic discos.
■ The **Aegean coast** (p. 563) of Turkey is home to countless ancient ruins, including two of the seven wonders of the ancient world (at **Ephesus,** p. 568, and **Bodrum,** p. 572).
■ The shimmering beaches and Bohemian flavor of **Sinop** (p. 599) make it one of the undiscovered treasures of the Black Sea coast (p. 596).

ESSENTIALS

ENTRY

Citizens of Canada, New Zealand, and South Africa do not need **visas** to enter Turkey. Canadians and New Zealanders can stay in Turkey for three months; South Africans are permitted to stay for one month. Citizens of Australia, Ireland, the U.K., and the U.S. need visas to enter Turkey. Though visas can be obtained from any Turkish embassy or consulate, it is most convenient to get one upon arrival in

Turkey. Three-month, multiple entry sticker visas are available for cash at all official points of entry (AUS$30 for Australians, UK£10 for British and Irish citizens, US$45 for Americans). Visitors on a tourist visa need a **work permit** to hold a job in Turkey. Exchange students must obtain a **student visa.**

EMBASSIES AND CONSULATES

Embassies and consulates within Turkey are in **Ankara** (p. 586) and **Istanbul** (p. 550); there are British and American consulates in smaller cities. Turkish embassies and consulates abroad include: **Australia,** 60 Muggaway, Red Hill, Canberra ACT 2603 (tel. (02) 6295 0227/8; fax 6239 6592; email turkembs@ozemail.com.au); **Canada,** 197 Wurtemburg St., Ottawa, ON K1N 8L9 (tel. (613) 789-4044 or 789-3440; fax 789-3442); **New Zealand,** 15-17 Murphy St., Level 8, Wellington (tel. (4) 472 1290 or 472 1292; fax 472 1277; email turkem@xtra.co.nz); **South Africa,** 1067 Church St., Hatfield, Pretoria 0181 (tel. (12) 342 6053/4; fax 342 6052; email pretbe@global.co.za) and 6 Sandown Valley Crescent 2nd Floor, Sandown-Sandton, Johannesburg 2001 (tel. (11) 884 9060/1/2; fax 884 9064); **Syria,** 48 Ziad Ben Abi Sufyan St., Damascus (tel. (11) 333 14 11; fax 333 92 43); **U.K.,** 43 Belgrave Sq., London SWIX 8PA (tel. (020) 7393 0202 or 7393 9552; fax 7393 0066; email turkish.embassy@virgin.net); and **U.S.,** 1714 Massachusetts Ave. NW, Washington, D.C. 20036 (tel. 202-659-8200 or 659-0032; fax 659-0744; email turkish@erols.com).

⚑ BORDER CROSSINGS

TO SYRIA. Daily buses connect Antakya (p. 584) to **Aleppo** (3-4hr.) and **Damascus.** The border crossing is hassle-free, but you must get a visa beforehand in Ankara (p. 586), Istanbul (p. 550), or another Syrian embassy or consulate (see p. 490). Ideally, obtain the visa in your home country; it is not always easy, or even possible, to get one from an embassy or consulate in Turkey.

TO GREECE AND EUROPE. Buses leave from Istanbul's **Esenler Otobüs Terminal** and trains from Istanbul's **Sirkeci Gar** station (see p. 545) to various cities in Europe, including Athens, Sofia, Vienna, Munich, Bucharest, and Moscow. **Ferries** also leave from many cities on the Aegean coast to the Greek islands, which are in turn connected by boat to Athens. Citizens of the U.S., Canada, Australia, New Zealand, and E.U. countries do not need a visa to enter Greece. South Africans must obtain a visa beforehand from any Greek embassy or consulate.

TO NORTHERN CYPRUS. The best place to catch ferries from mainland Turkey is Taşucu, which sends fast seabuses (2½hr.) and slower ferries (5hr.) daily to **Girne,** in northern Cyprus. Less frequent ferries also travel to Girne from Alanya and Anamur, and three night ferries per week embark from Mersin to Mağusa. Turkish air carriers are the only ones that fly into northern Cyprus; flights run between Lefkoşa's Ercan airport and most major airports in Turkey.

GETTING AROUND

BY AIR. Turkish Airlines (THY) flies to over 30 cities in Turkey. **Istanbul** and **Ankara** are the hubs for domestic flights. Domestic flights are about US$90 one-way (some discounts for ages 12-24). It is often cheaper to purchase tickets for domestic flights while in Turkey. In some cities, an airport shuttle bus leaves from the downtown ticket office 30 to 90 minutes before flights (for an extra charge). There are reduced fares for passengers who book an international flight with THY.

BY BUS. Modern, cheap **buses** run frequently between all sizeable cities. In large cities, the *otogar* (bus station, accessible by free shuttles called *servis*) is often a distance from the city center, but many bus companies have branch offices downtown. Buy tickets in advance (10% ISIC discount on some lines). Fares may increase during summer and religious holidays. In rural areas, it is customary to

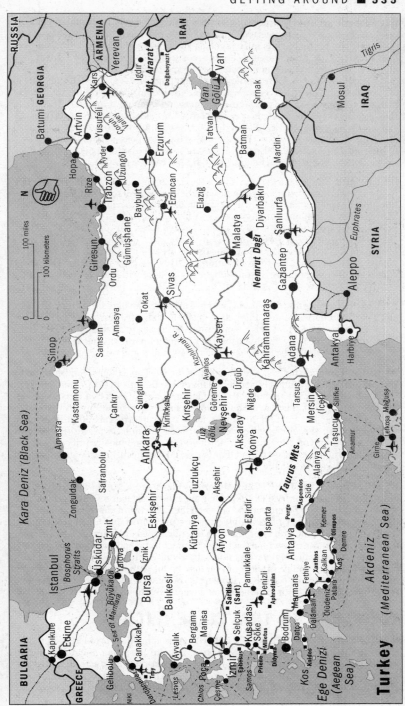

TURKEY

flag buses down from the roadside without reserving a seat in advance. Because road safety is a serious concern in Turkey, *Let's Go* strongly recommends that you only travel on reputable bus lines (such as **Varan, Ulusoy,** and **Kamıl Koç**), particularly for long trips. Although these are the most expensive tickets, the extra money allows companies to take additional safety precautions.

Fez Travel, 15 Akbıyık Cad., Sultanahmet, Istanbul (tel. (212) 516 90 24; fax 518 50 85; email feztravel@feztravel.com; www.feztravel.com), Turkey's flexible "backpacker bus" service, makes a loop encompassing Istanbul, Çanakkale, Gallipoli, the Aegean and Mediterranean coasts, Konya, Cappadocia, Ankara, and Bursa. A season pass (June-Oct. US$190, under 26 US$173) allows you to get on and off along the route at your whim. There are also cheaper passes for smaller portions of the route. Buses have an English-speaking staff full of info on accommodations and activities. Fez also sells tickets through **STA Travel** (see p. 25).

BY DOLMUŞ. Extensive *dolmuş* (shared taxi, usually vans or minibuses) service follows fixed routes within larger cities and between small towns, departing when full (*dolmuş* means "stuffed"). These are almost as cheap as municipal buses and allow you to get on and off anywhere you like. *Dolmuş* post their final destinations in their front windows, but if you're headed to an intermediate destination, ask locals *"Bu dolmuş [destination] gidiyor mu?"* ("Does this *dolmuş* go to [destination]?"). To ask your neighbor or the driver how much it costs to go to your destination, ask *"X kadar ne kadar?"* ("How much is it to X?"). The driver may remember your stated destination and stop there without any reminder; otherwise, say *"inecek var"* ("getting off").

BY TRAIN. Despite low fares, trains within Turkey are no bargain, as they are slow and follow circuitous routes. First class gets you a slightly more padded seat, but most Turks travel second class. Since couchettes are available, overnight train trips are preferable to overnight buses. Lock your compartment and keep valuables on your person. Make reservations at least a few hours in advance at the station.

BY BOAT. Ferries do not serve most cities on the west coast, but a **Turkish Maritime Lines** (TML) cruise ship sails between Istanbul and İzmir (21hr., 1 per week). A weekly boat connects Istanbul with destinations on the Black Sea coast. Istanbul has frequent service to Bandırma and Yalova. Larger ports have ship offices; otherwise, get on the boat and find the purser. Most Turkish ferries are comfortable and well equipped; the cheapest class sometimes includes a reclining chair or couchette where you can sleep. Avoid the often astronomically priced cafeteria cuisine by bringing your own food. Fares rise sharply in July and August. Student discounts are often available.

BY MOPED AND MOTORCYCLE. Motorized bikes are a good way to tour the coastal areas and countryside: they don't use much gas, can be put on trains and ferries, and are a good compromise between the high cost of car travel and the limited range of bicycles. Unfortunately, they are uncomfortable for long distances, dangerous in the rain, and unpredictable on rough roads and gravel. Always wear a helmet, and never ride with a backpack. Expect to pay about US$20-35 per day; remember to bargain. **Motorcycles** normally require a license. Ask if the quoted price includes tax and insurance, or you may be hit with an additional fee. Avoid handing your passport over as a deposit; if you have an accident or mechanical failure, you may not get it back until you cover all repairs.

TOURIST AND TRAVEL SERVICES

MEDICAL EMERGENCIES AND HEALTH. Serious medical problems should be taken to the *klinik* or **hospital** *(hastane)*. Private hospitals, located in urban areas, provide much better care than state-run institutions *(devlet hastanesi)*, and are not much more expensive for foreigners. Most doctors speak some English, and cash payments are expected. **Pharmacies** *(eczane)* in each town stay open all night on a rotating basis; signs in their windows and local newspapers tell which is on duty *(nöbetçi)*. For **medical emergencies,** dial 112 or call your consulate; they can provide a list of English-speaking doctors. If your problems are not urgent, go to the nearest tourist office before trying the police.

USEFUL ADDRESSES. Turkish cities and popular tourist towns have tourist offices with maps and lists of accommodations in the area. Turkish tourist office abroad include: **U.K.,** First Floor, 170-173 Piccadilly, London W1V 9DD (tel. (0171) 629 777, brochure request line (0891) 887 755; fax (0171) 491 0773; email tto@turkishtourism.demon.co.uk) and **U.S.,** 821 U.N. Plaza, 4th floor, New York, NY 10017 (212-687-2194; fax 599-7568; email tourny@idt.net; www.turkey.org/turkey). Surf on over to **Türkiye on the Web** (www.columbia.edu/İsss31/Turkiye) or **All About Turkey** (web.syr.edu/~obalsoy/Turkiye).

MONEY MATTERS

CURRENCY AND EXCHANGE. The **Turkish lira (TL)** is the main unit of currency in Turkey. Western currency, particularly U.S. dollars and German marks, will sometimes be accepted. Credit cards are generally accepted by larger businesses. *Let's Go* quotes prices effective in summer 1999, when Turkey experienced a drop in tourism and prices. Combined with fluctuating exchange rates and Turkey's high inflation, prices could increase by 10-30% by 2000. Prices are quoted in U.S. dollars to minimize unexpected increases.

Since Turkey has a high inflation rate, it's best to convert small amounts of money on a regular basis despite the commission charges. Using an ATM or a credit card will often get you the best possible rates. **ATM machines** are widespread in Turkey; larger banks usually accept Cirrus and PLUS, and major credit cards—particularly MasterCard and Visa—can also be used for cash advances.

BUSINESS HOURS. Most stores and offices are open Monday to Friday 8:30am-12:30pm and 1:30-5:30pm. Unlike the rest of the Islamic world, the official weekend is on Saturday and Sunday. Government offices and many other establishments close for the afternoon during the summer months, particularly on the Aegean and Mediterranean coasts.

TIPPING AND TAXES. Tips are usually not expected, but leaving a bit of small change (around US$1 regardless of the total price) at your table after a meal or with a taxi driver or hotel porter is appreciated. Only luxury restaurants require a 15-20% service charge *(servis dahil),* usually included in the bill; an additional small tip is customary. Turkey has a 10-20% **value-added tax,** known as the *katma değer vergisi* or **KDV,** which is included in the prices of most goods and services (including meals, lodging, and car rentals). Before you pay, check if the KDV is included in the price to avoid paying it twice. It can be theoretically reclaimed at most points of departure, but this requires much persistence.

ACCOMMODATIONS

HOSTELS. Hostels are generally dorm-style accommodations, often in large single-sex rooms with bunk beds, though most also offer private rooms for families and couples. Some have kitchens, bike or moped rentals, storage areas, and laundry facilities, and generally do not have daytime "lock-out" hours or a curfew. A bed in a hostel will average around US$5-8. There are very few accredited International Youth Hostels in Turkey, and if you ask for a hostel *(yurt),* you will most likely be directed to university dormitories. With its head office in Istanbul, the national **Youth Hostel Association-Turkey** (tel. (212) 513 61 50/52; fax 512 76 28; email info@hostelsturkey.org; www.hostelsturkey.org) has only 17 members, located mainly in Istanbul, Cappadocia, and the Aegean and Mediterranean coasts.

HOTELS AND PENSIONS. Clean, cheap accommodations are available nearly everywhere in Turkey in hotels *(otel)* and pensions *(pansiyon)*. Basic **hotel** rooms generally cost US$6-8 for a single and US$12-16 for a double. Some have dorm-style rooms; others allow travelers to sleep on their roofs for reduced rates. It is wise to make reservations at accommodations along the Aegean and Mediterranean coasts during the peak season. Cozy **pensions** are by far the most common form of lodging. Often they are private homes with extra rooms, and hosts will sometimes give personalized tours or offer home-cooked meals; unfortunately, many pensions do not provide phones, TVs, or private bathrooms. Pensions that call themselves **aile** (family-style) try to maintain a wholesome atmosphere, and are the preferred choice for women traveling alone in remote parts of Turkey, particularly Eastern Anatolia and the Black Sea coast. In the more touristed areas along the Aegean and Mediterranean coasts, Turks are accustomed to **unmarried couples** staying together, but such relations are often culturally unacceptable in rural and conservative regions, including the Black Sea coast and southeastern Turkey. It is generally a good idea to wear rings to help gain admittance.

DORMS. Many **universities** open their residence halls to travelers when school is not in session—some do so even during term-time. These dorms are often close to student areas in larger cities such as Ankara and Istanbul. Getting a room may take a couple of phone calls and require advanced planning, but rates tend to be low.

KEEPING IN TOUCH

MAIL. **Aerogrammes** are available at post offices: mark it *uçak ile* ("airmail") and tell the vendor the mail's destination: *Avustralya, Kanada, Büyük Bretanya* (Great Britain), *Yeni Zelanda* (New Zealand), *Güney Afrika* (South Africa), or *Amerika*. Airmail from cities in Turkey takes on average one to two weeks to reach its destination. If regular airmail is too slow, there are a few faster, more expensive options such as *Acele Posta Servisi* (APS). **Poste Restante** is available at the **PTT** (post, telegraph, and telephone office) in most towns.

TELEPHONE AND INTERNET ACCESS. A **calling card** is your best and cheapest bet. You can usually make direct international calls from public phones at the **PTT** (post and telephone office). A **prepaid card (telekart)** or a token-like **jeton** (both available at the PTT) must be deposited to activate the phone. To call home with a calling card, dial the appropriate access numbers for Turkey: **AT&T,** tel. 00 800 12277; **Sprint,** tel. 00 800 14477; **MCI WorldPhone Direct,** tel. 00 800 11177; **CanadaDirect,** tel. 00 800 16677; **BTDirect,** tel. 00 800 44 1177; **Australia Direct,** tel. 00 800 61 1177; or **Telkom South AfricaDirect,** tel. 00 800 27 1177. To make a **collect call,** dial 115 for an international Türk Telekom operator. An English-speaking operator can be reached by dialing the appropriate service provider listed above; they will usually place a collect call even if you don't have their phonecards.

Internet access is available in most regions for about US$1.50-3 per hour. Access is widespread in the touristed areas of Istanbul, Cappadocia, and the Aegean and Mediterranean coasts, but thins out along the Black Sea and in Eastern Turkey.

WOMEN TRAVELERS

Foreign women, especially those traveling alone, attract significant attention in Turkey. Because Western movies and TV often depict women as seductive sex symbols, female travelers are frequently perceived as likely sexual partners; however, although verbal harassment is common, physical harassment is rare. If harassed, women can attract attention by making a scene and using the expression *ayıp!* ("shame!") or *haydi git* ("go away"). If a situation becomes threatening, holler *imdat* (eem-DAHT, "help") or *polis* (PO-lees, "police"). More touristed parts of Turkey—Istanbul, Northwestern Turkey, the Aegean and Mediterranean coasts, Cappadocia, and Ankara—may be more comfortable for women. Only confident, experienced female travelers should venture into Central and Eastern Anatolia and along the Black Sea coast. For more tips, see **Women Travelers,** p. 29.

DRESS AND ETIQUETTE

Shorts scream "I am a tourist." Women will find a head scarf or bandana handy (even essential) in more conservative areas. Skin-baring clothes are more widely accepted in Istanbul and the resort towns of the Aegean and Mediterranean coasts, but not anywhere else. Long skirts and lightweight pants are most acceptable (and practical), but T-shirts are fine (though it would be wise to cover your arms in the more religious parts of the country). While topless bathing is common in some parts of the Aegean and Mediterranean coasts, it is not as acceptable in other regions of the country. Nude sunbathing is officially illegal.

Turks value hospitality and will frequently go out of their way to offer travelers a meal or cup of *çay.* If you are invited as a guest, it is customary to bring a small gift such as flowers or chocolates and to remove your shoes before entering. When making conversation, do not speak with disrespect or skepticism about Atatürk, the founder of modern Turkey, and avoid other sensitive subjects such as the Kurdish issue, the PKK, Northern Cyprus, Armenia, and Turkey's human rights record.

LIFE AND TIMES

ANCIENT HISTORY

Humanity has been mixing Asian and Western influences in what is now Central Turkey (known as "Anatolia" or "Asia Minor") since the 8th millennium BCE, making it one of the world's oldest continuously inhabited areas. By the start of the 2nd millennium BCE, the iron-forging **Hittites** had migrated from the Caucasus into central Anatolia to establish a millennium-long feudal empire headquartered at Hattuşaş (modern **Boğazkale,** p. 589). Despite Hittite dominance in central Anatolia (and beyond—the Hittites even managed to acquire Syria), other groups established themselves in the area of present-day Turkey, the most notable among them being the Phrygians (sometimes called the Trojans). **Troy** sprung up at the mouth of the Dardanelles, and archaeological excavations suggest that the Trojans unsheathed their swords for the Trojan War around 1250 BCE. After the collapse of the Hittites came the Persians, who used Turkey as a base for forays into Greece. Next in line was **Alexander the Great,** who invaded the region and took it from the Persians in less than a year. The Mediterranean coast's importance in the Roman province of Asia Minor paved the way for the creation of the East Roman Empire, centered in the city of **Constantinople** (now Istanbul). Constantinople, founded by Emperor Constantine in 324 CE over the Greek city of Byzantium, became the center of Greek Orthodox culture and the capital of a renewed empire stretching from the Balkans through Greece to the Levant and Egypt.

By the 9th century, the ancestors of the Turks had begun to migrate from central Asia and resettle everywhere from Iran to India. In the 11th century, **Selçuk Turks** from inner Mongolia established states in Persia (today's Iran) and Anatolia. Great Selçuk Sultans from this latter state—namely Tughril-Beg and Alp Arslan—led raids into the Byzantine realm they bordered, and the Selçuks in Anatolia became increasingly independent of the Great Selçuk Sultanate, centered in Persia. The Turks gained a foothold in Anatolia in 1075, when **Suleyman** (the son of Alp Arslan) captured Nicaea from the Byzantines, renamed it İznik, and set it up as the capital of the newly reorganized **Sultanate of Rum,** which declared its independence from the Great Selçuks in Persia a decade later. By its heyday in the 13th century, the Sultanate of Rum had developed into one of the most important Islamic states of its time, with thriving trade, agriculture, and arts.

When Selçuk rule broke down in the 14th century, separate Turkish principalities picked up the pieces. A general named **Osman** claimed the northwest corner of

Anatolia and united several fiefdoms against the Byzantines, laying the religious and cultural foundations for one of the largest and most enduring empires in the history of civilization: the *Osmanlı*, or **Ottoman**, Empire. From the mid-14th to the mid-15th century, Ottoman rulers slowly gnawed away at the Byzantine Empire. In 1453, after a 54-day siege, Constantinople fell to **Mehmet the Conqueror**, who went directly to the great Byzantine basilica Hagia Sofia and prayed to Allah (thus converting it into a mosque). The city came to be called **Istanbul** and became the capital of his new and vigorous empire, which grabbed up Greece, Cyprus, and the Balkans as far as Belgrade. **Selim I** (1512-1520) added Syria, Palestine, Egypt, and the Arabian Peninsula to the Empire, making the Ottoman Sultan the guardian of the three holy places of Islam—Mecca, Medina, and Jerusalem—in one fell swoop.

Such a vast and heterogeneous empire could be nothing but politically decentralized; the hinterland regions developed almost entirely independently—a fact that would lead to the Ottomans' eventual downfall. Non-Muslims were left to practice their religions freely, but in accordance with Islamic law they had to pay the **cizye**, a special head tax. Many of the empire's minorities, including Greeks and Jews, were peacefully incorporated into Ottoman society, and many fared better under Muslim authority than they had under the Crusaders and Spanish Monarchs.

When **Süleyman** became Sultan (1520-66), the Ottoman Empire grew still further. He doubled the size of the empire, securing borders that stretched from the Balkans and Greece north to the Black Sea (and even knocked on the gates of Vienna), west to Iraq, and south into the Arabian Peninsula and Africa. Süleyman's military conquests and lavish lifestyle earned him the sobriquet of "Magnificent" among Europeans. Süleyman's administrative, artistic, literary, and architectural legacies were equally dramatic. His commitment to legislation earned him the title of **Kanuni** (the Lawgiver), and his patronage of Mimar Sinan, the great Ottoman architect, resulted in some of the greatest of Ottoman monuments. Süleyman the Magnificent appointed his son Selim the not-so-magnificent (a.k.a. **Selim the Sot**), who transferred all his political power to the Grand Vizier and presided over an era of palace infighting (before he drowned in his tub in a drunken stupor in 1574). This period is sometimes referred to as the **"rule of the women,"** as mothers of potential sultans vied for power and had rivals' sons knocked off.

MODERN HISTORY

The Ottomans had lost all of their territories north of the Black Sea by 1812, and the government was growing weaker militarily as it went deeper into debt. A series of administrative reforms collectively known as the **Tanzimat** ("Reorganization") were instituted, beginning in 1839 with the Noble Edict of the Rose Chamber that declared all Ottoman citizens equal regardless of ethnicity, race, or religion. Despite major reforms, European and Russian diplomats feared that time was up for the **"sick man of Europe"** (as the empire was known), and feared even more what would happen to the European balance of power as a result. European powers intervened in the 1821 Greek War of Independence and fought the bloody **Crimean War** (1853-56). The 19th century saw one rebellion after another in the Ottoman domains (including uprisings among the Albanians, Serbs, Bulgarians, and Armenians). In response to an impending sense of doom, a group of bourgeois intellectuals that included the poet Namık Kemal (see **Literature**, p. 543) formed a group known as the **Young Turks.** Among other things, they sought to draft a Western-style constitution providing for an elected parliament—a wish that was fulfilled in 1876 upon the ascension of **Sultan Abdülhamid II** (1876-1909), who suddenly suspended the constitution and all democratic reforms two years later. In 1908, the **Young Turk Revolution** ended Abdülhamid's strangle-hold on power and restored the 1876 constitution. The new leaders, known as the **Committee for Union of Progress (CUP),** embarked on a reform program designed to increase centralization and promote industrialization. CUP leaders continued with reforms, but these were far overshadowed by such bloodbaths as the Albanian uprisings and the **Balkan Wars** (1912-13). Bloody disaster was all the Ottoman Empire saw in WWI, when they sided with Germany and were completely humiliated save at the **Battle of Gallipoli** (1916), when the Turks defended the Dardanelles against the Allies. Festering internal strife erupted in 1915's Armenian disaster, when some 600,000 to 800,000 Armenians were killed. The Unionists were not gone or forgotten, and under Ottoman general **Mustafa Kemal** they plunged head-long into the **Turkish War of Independence** (1920-22) against the Allies, who were looking to partition Anatolia amongst themselves. An armistice was signed on October 11, 1922. The new Grand National Assembly (under new President Kemal) abolished the sultanate on November 1, 1922 and set up the Turkish Republic by 1923.

As part of his obsessive campaign to Westernize Turkey (and forge a distinctly Turkish identity), Kemal required that all Turks adopt surnames, taking the surname **Atatürk,** or "father of the Turks," for himself (many place names also changed, such as Angora, which became Ankara). Atatürk oversaw the adoption of a Western-style constitution, abolished (Islam-sanctioned) polygamy, prohibited the use of the fez (traditional Islamic headgear), instituted secular law codes, adopted the Gregorian calendar, and closed religious schools and courts. By 1928, Islam was no longer the official state religion. As Alexander the Great had purged the country of Persians before, Atatürk purged Turkish of all Arabic and Persian influences, replacing the Arabic alphabet with a Latin version, and declaring that the *adhan* (call to prayer) be recited in Turkish instead of classical Arabic.

Shortly before WWII, the increasingly auto(tür)kratic Atatürk died and was replaced by his associate **İsmet İnönü.** The government remained neutral until the Turkey joined the Allies at the very end of the war. During the Cold War, Turkey's position within firing range of the Soviet Union and its control over the Bosphorus made it strategically vital to both Soviet and U.S. interests. Even today, Turkey remains one of the largest recipients of U.S. economic and military aid. Politics became increasingly polarized during the turbulent 1970s, reaching a fever pitch when **Abdullah Öcalan** formed the **Workers' Party of Kurdistan (PKK)** for Kurdish sovereignty. Turkey's foreign relations were no calmer than its domestic affairs. Fearing that Cyprus would be annexed by Greece, Turkey invaded the island in 1974; economic and arms embargoes soon followed, and Turkey responded by closing foreign military installations. The "Turkish Republic of Northern Cyprus" is still unrecognized by the U.N.

In September 1980, General **Kenan Evren** led a bloodless coup against the government and instituted brutally-enforced martial law throughout the country until 1983. Elections that year brought the **Motherland Party** (ANAP) of **Turgut Özal** to power. Özal's government encouraged such positive principles as free-market and foreign trade, but the worldwide recession of the following years sent Turkey into massive inflation, deficit, and unemployment. Based in Syria and Iraq and filled with ranks of disaffected young people, the PKK waged guerilla warfare against the government, catching many civilians in the crossfire. The government in turn banned the use of the Kurdish language and outlawed expressions of sympathy for the Kurds.

While discussion of the Kurdish issue has been forcibly silenced, the secularist tenets of the Turkish state have been the subject of increasing debate. In May 1993, the True Path Party elected **Tansu Çiller** the first female prime minister. Controversy arose around Turkey's secular **dress code,** which attempted to curb religious attire such as head scarves in academies and universities. Religious female students have protested and circumvented this rule by holding street demonstrations and wearing showy blond wigs over their head scarves (since the code dictates that the women's hair must be showing).

In early 1995, Turkey was accepted into the European Customs Union (after being rejected in 1989) on the condition that the Turkish Parliament make hundreds of new laws and changes to the constitution by that October. The European Union again denied Turkey candidacy for membership in December 1997. The E.U.'s simultaneous selection of Cyprus as a potential candidate greatly incensed Turkey, who threatened in late March 1998 to begin a new war with Cyprus.

IN THE NEWS

Recent news has been dominated by the devastating **earthquake** that struck north-western Turkey on August 17, 1999. At the time of publication, over 14,000 people were confirmed dead (mostly due to collapsing, poorly constructed apartments), with hundreds of thousands still missing. In the aftermath of the quake (which seismologists had predicted), the government came under increasing criticism for its failure to prepare the country. Luckily, relief poured into Turkey from all over the globe, including contributions from long-time rival Greece. Turkey's economy was seriously impacted by the quake, and many wondered how Turkey would cope with the tens of thousands left homeless as cold weather approached.

March 1999 saw the capture of **Abdullah Öcalan,** the leader and founder of the PKK and the man whom most Turks blame for the undeclared civil war against the Kurds (see p. 541). His capture triggered public demonstrations of joy in many of Turkey's cities, and Kurdish demonstrations of outrage throughout Europe and in Turkey. In June 1999, a three-judge panel convicted Öcalan and sentenced him to death (although, at time of publication, his sentence was under appeal). The Turkish public mostly greeted the conviction with relief, but many have questioned how the execution of Öcalan will solve the Kurdish problem. Indeed, the week after Öcalan's conviction saw a rise in terrorist incidents, including bombings in Istanbul. In August 1999, the PKK declared a **ceasefire** to negotiate with the Turkish government. Turkish leaders were initially dismissive of the PKK announcement, and it remains to be seen whether the conflict will deteriorate or improve.

RELIGION AND ETHNICITY

Although Atatürk set modern Turkey on a secular course, Islam has played a key role in the country's political and cultural evolution (see **Modern History,** p. 540). About 99% of Turks are Muslim. **Jews** represent a population of about 26,000 in Turkey today, concentrated mainly in Istanbul with large communities in İzmir and Ankara. **Orthodox Christians** of Greek, Armenian, and Syrian backgrounds compose the other religious minority. The **Alevi** are Shi'ites who follow simple moral norms rather than the *Sharia* (Islamic law) and the traditional pillars of Islam. "Alevi" refers to the numerous heterodox communities that make up 15-25% of the population. Roughly 12 to 15 million **Kurds** make up a quarter of Turkey's population, making them the largest ethnic group in the world without its own nation. Kurdish nationalist movements have existed since before the fall of the Ottoman Empire, but the most famous and extremist of these, the **Workers' Party of Kurdistan** (or **PKK**) was founded by Abdullah Öcalan in 1978 (see **Modern History,** p. 541, and **In The News,** p. 542). Until the early 20th century, ethnic **Armenians** comprised approximately 10% of the Anatolian population, but after the deportation and slaughter of about 600,000 to 800,000 Armenians in 1915, almost none are left in Eastern Anatolia today. In the past few decades, Armenians and their supporters have demanded that Turkey officially recognize the genocide and provide some form of apology or compensation. The **Laz, Hemşin,** and **Circassian** people are Caucasian minorities that live in Eastern Turkey and the northern Caucasus region.

LANGUAGE

In his effort to forge a secular Turkish identity, Atatürk ordered that the Turkish language be written in the Roman alphabet rather than Arabic script, purging Turkish of many Arabic and Persian borrowings. English is widely spoken wherever tourism is big (mostly in the major coastal resorts). In the rest of Anatolia, only university students know English. French and German are also widely spoken in cities. For pronunciation tips and handy phrases, see the **Phrasebook,** p. 706.

THE ARTS

LITERATURE. Although modern Turkish literature has adopted the Western literary forms of the novel and the essay, it often looks back to pre-Ottoman writings. The **Sufi poetry** of Celaleddin-i-Rumi and Yunuş Emre survived the Ottoman centuries relatively unscathed, as did *The Book of Dede Korkut*, a collection of 12 legends that recounts the travels and trials of the noble Oğuz Turks, the ancestors of modern Turks. Of the folk literature rediscovered in the 19th century, the tales of **Nasrettin Hoca**—a friendly, anti-authoritarian, religious man—are particularly popular, plastered on *ayran* cups and well known by children.

Satire has historically been an important element in Turkish literature. Poet **Namık Kemal** is particularly famous for his satire of the Ottoman Empire during its final years. A fervent republican and free-speech advocate, **Aziz Nesin,** is the provocative Alevi writer around whom the 1993 Sivas incident occurred. **Yaşar Kemal,** author of *Memed, My Hawk*, has been nominated several times for the Nobel Prize for Literature. He has been charged with anti-Turkish activities by the government for his *corpus* of work that consistently criticizes Turkish society and government. The magical realism of **Orhan Pamuk** has made him the best-selling author in Turkish history, and one of the few Turkish writers whose works have experienced international acclaim, particularly for his three major novels, *The White Castle*, *The New Life*, and *The Black Book*.

VISUAL ARTS. Long before Atatürk's revolution, Ottoman painting had gradually begun to adopt Western forms. In 1883, the **Academy of Fine Arts** was founded by the Ottoman artist, museum curator, and archaeologist, **Osman Hamdi Bey.** Staffed by Europeans, the Academy flourished under Hamdi's direction in a turn-of-the-century Istanbul society fascinated with French mannerisms. In 1914, the Ottoman government opened an Academy of Fine Arts for Women headed by the painter **Mihri Müşfil Hanım,** whose work blended the world of veiled ladies in Istanbul with the Parisian flair for Levantine fashions. The two eventually merged, and the Academy (as the combined institution is known) has had an unparalleled influence on the artistic movements of modern Turkey: the **Çallı group** of the 20s, the **'D' Group** of the 30s, and the **New Group** of the 40s, 50s, and 60s.

FOOD AND DRINK

Contemporary Turkish cuisine reflects its Ottoman heritage. Popular dishes such as **kebap** (kebab) and **pilav** (rice) are flavored by the cuisine of the nomadic Central Asian tribes that swept through Asia Minor. Fans of Greek, Armenian, and Levantine food will surely recognize their favorite dishes on Turkish menus. Lunch and dinner often begin with **meze,** which can be anything from simple *beyaz peynir* (feta cheese) to more complicated olive oil and vegetable dishes. Almost every meal involves meat (usually meaning lamb), and many restaurants specialize in **köfte** (small, spiced meatballs) or **mantı** (tiny meat-filled ravioli). The world of *kebap* is a wild one, and the varieties are limitless—from the burrito-style *döner kebap* to *iskender kebap*, served over pita cubes, immersed in spicy tomato sauce, and topped with garlicky yogurt. Save room for dessert: highlights include **baklava** (a flaky, sweet nut pastry with pistachio), *kadayif* (shredded pastry dough filled with nuts and drenched in syrup), *tavukgöğsu* (a creamy sweet of pulverized chicken fibers), and *helva* (sesame paste).

Despite the international fame of Turkish coffee, Turkey's national drink is without a doubt the strong, black tea known as **çay,** served in small, hourglass-shaped glasses. *Elma çayı* (apple tea), which tastes like warmed cider, is a good alternative to conventional Turkish tea's strong brew. A demitasse-full of pure caffeine, **kahve (Turkish coffee)** can be ordered *sade* (black), *orta* (medium sweet), or *şekerli* (very sweet). When you finish your *kahve*, read your fortune in the goop remaining in the bottom of your cup.

Alcohol is widely available but frowned upon in the more conservative parts of the country. Restaurants that post *içkisiz* have no alcohol, while those with *içkili* posted do have it. **Bira** (beer) is ever-popular: *Efes Pilsen* and *Tüborg* are the leading brands. The best domestic white wines are *Çankaya*, *Villa Doluca*, and *Kavaklıdere*, made in Cappadocia. The best red wines are *Yakut* and *Kavaklıdere*. Ice-cold **rakı**, a clear anise-seed liquor with the taste of licorice, is Turkey's national alcohol. Customarily mixed in equal parts with water, *rakı* is similar to Greek *ouzo* or Levantine *'araq*, but even stronger. Istanbul's local specialty is *balyoz* ("sledge hammer" or "wrecking ball"). Demolition is the appropriate concept here: *balyoz* is *rakı*, whiskey, vodka, and gin mixed with orange juice.

ISTANBUL (İSTANBUL)

Straddling two continents and almost three millennia of history, Istanbul exists on an incomprehensible scale. The city unfolds against a densely historic landscape of Ottoman mosques, Byzantine mosaics, and Roman masonry. In its current incarnation, Istanbul is the most crowded and cosmopolitan city in the Turkish Republic. This urban supernova explodes out into the surrounding countryside behind an ever-expanding front of new construction sites, but no crane or cement truck could possibly hope to keep up with the pace of Istanbulian life.

Legend has it that in the 7th century BCE, **Byzas**, a Greek speculator looking for prime real estate, consulted the infallible Oracle at Delphi, who told him to settle "opposite the Land of the Blind." Byzas and his crew settled here in 667 BCE, and the city was first named **Byzantium** in his honor. Roman infighting at the beginning of the 4th century CE determined the city's fate for the next millennium. The victorious Constantine declared Byzantium **"New Rome"** and renamed it **Constantinople,** the capital of what came to be the Byzantine Empire. Justi7nian, the most famous Byzantine emperor, doubled the city's glory with the Aya Sofia and other architectural monuments, only to have many of them destroyed centuries later by marauding Crusaders. Why did Constantinople get the works? That's nobody's business but the Ottoman Turks, whose rise was paralleled by the decline of the Byzantine Empire. Constantinople fell to the Ottomans on May 29, 1453, and the new sultan, **Mehmet II,** transformed the city into the exalted administrative, cultural, and commercial center of his empire. Under Ottoman rule, the city, which came to be called Istanbul (a Turkish corruption of the Greek phrase *"steen poli,"* or "to the city"), remained one of the world's major cosmopolitan centers and an architectural treasure trove, best known for its collection of Imperial mosques.

Ankara is now the governmental capital of the Republic of Turkey, but Istanbul remains its cultural heart. Between 1960 and today, the city's population has increased tenfold to over 13 million inhabitants. Even as Istanbul's centuries-long expansion has engulfed entire towns, each neighborhood of the city retains a distinct character: the poverty of Istanbul's *gecekondus* coexists with an ambitious commercialism as audacious and ostentatious as any to be found in New York or London. The challenge is to see beyond the Ottoman palaces, carpet salesmen, and backpacker bars, and venture out into neighborhood produce markets, back-alley tea shops, and remaining Byzantine fortifications.

■ ORIENTATION

Waterways divide Istanbul into three sections. The **Bosphorus Strait** (Boğaz) separates Asia from Europe. Turks call the western (European) side **Avrupa,** and the eastern (Asian) side **Asya.** The **Golden Horn,** a sizeable river originating just outside the city, splits Avrupa into northern and southern parts. Directions in Istanbul are usually further specified by city precinct or district. **Sultanahmet, Taksim** (both on the European side), and **Kadıköy** (on the Asian side) are the most relevant for sightseers. Most of the famous mosques, historical sites, and tourism facilities are south of the Golden Horn, towards the eastern end of the peninsula in Sultanahmet. The other half of "Europe" is focused on **Taksim Square,** the commercial and social center of the northern European bank. Two major arteries radiate from the square: **İstiklâl Caddesi,** the main downtown shopping street; and **Cumhuriyet Caddesi,** which is lined with airline offices and hotels. The Asian side of Istanbul is primarily residential.

⊏ TRANSPORTATION

Airplanes: Istanbul's airport, **Atatürk Havaalanı,** is 30km from the city. The domestic and international terminals are connected by a **bus** (every 20min. 6am-10pm). To get to **Sultanahmet,** take a Havaş shuttle bus from either terminal to Aksaray (every 30 min., $6). At Aksaray, walk 1 block south to Millet Cad. and take an Eminönü-bound **tram** to the Sultanahmet stop. You can also take a **taxi** ($4) to the Yeşilköy train station and take the commuter rail *(tren)* to the end of the line in Sirkeci. A direct taxi to Sultanahmet costs $17-20. To get to **Taksim,** take the Havaş shuttle bus to the end of the line (every 30 min., $6). To get to the airport, have a private service such as **Karasu** (tel. 638 66 01) pick you up from your hostel ($5.50), or take the Havaş airport shuttle from the McDonald's in Taksim (45 min., every 30min., $6).

Public Transportation: AKBİL is an electronic ticket system that lets you save 15-50% on fares for municipal ferries, buses, trams, seabuses, and the subway (but not *dolmuş*). Initial deposit of $5, add money in 1,000,000TL increments from any of the white IETT public bus booths that have the sign "AKBİL *satılır.*"

Trains: It's quicker and cheaper to take the bus to and from Istanbul. **Haydarpaşa Garı** (tel. (216) 336 04 75), on the Asian side, sends trains to Anatolia. Take the ferry from Karaköy pier #7 (every 20min., $0.50), halfway between Galata Bridge and the Karaköy tourist office, where rail tickets for Anatolia can be bought in advance at the **TCDD** office upstairs. To **Ankara** (6½-9hr., 5 per day, $7-12) and **Kars** (11-14½hr.; M, W, F, 9am and 11pm; $10). **Sirkeci Garı** (tel. (212) 527 00 50), in Eminönü sends trains to Europe via: **Athens** (24hr., 1 per day, $60); **Bucharest** (27hr., 1 per day, $30); and **Budapest** (40hr., 1 per day, $90).

Intercity Buses: Esenler Otobüs Terminal (tel. 658 00 36). Take the tram to Yusufpaşa ($0.50), walk to the Aksaray Metro, and take it to the *otogar* (15min., $0.50). Most companies have courtesy buses, called *servis,* that run to the *otogar* from Eminönü, Taksim, and other points in the city (free with bus ticket purchase). From Istanbul, buses travel to every city in Turkey. Destinations on **Ulusoy** (tel. 658 30 00; fax 658 30 10) include: **İzmir** (6hr.; every hr.; $20, students $17); **Bodrum** (8hr.; 2 per day; $23, students $20); and **Athens** (21hr.; M-Sa 1 per day; $60, students $51). **Varan** (tel. 658 02 74 or 658 02 77) runs to **Ankara** (6hr.; 7 per day; $22, students $20) and **Bodrum** (13hr.; 3 per day; $28, students $25.50). **Kamil Koç** (tel. 658 20 00) runs to: **Ankara** (6hr.; every hr.; $13, students $12). **Pamukkale** (tel./fax 658 22 22) runs to: **Pamukkale** (10hr.; 6 per day; $14, students $13). Unlicensed **international** companies have been known to offer discounts on trips to Western European destinations and then abandon their passengers in Eastern Europe.

Ferries: Turkish Maritime Lines (tel. 249 92 22), near pier #7 at Karaköy, to the left of the **Haydarpaşa** ferry terminal (blue awning marked "Denizcilik İşletmeleri"), ferries travelers to **İzmir** (combo ticket $10-25) via **Bandırma.** Buy the schedule *(feribot tarifesi)* for $0.60 at any pier, or call **Seabus Information** (tel. (216) 362 04 44).

Local Buses: Run 5am-midnight, less frequently after 10:30pm, arriving every 10min. to most stops. Hubs are Eminönü, Aksaray (Yusuf Paşa tram stop), Beyazit, Taksim, Beşiktaş, and Üsküdar. Signs on the front indicate destination, and signs on the right-hand side list major stops. **Dolmuş** are more comfortable but less frequent than buses. Most *dolmuş* gather on the side streets north of Taksim Sq.

Trams: The **tramvay** runs from Eminönü to Zeytinburnu (50¢ per ride). A ramshackle **commuter rail** (known locally as *tren*) runs between Sirkeci Gar and the far western suburbs. A 2-stop **metro** runs from the Karaköy side of Galata Bridge to Tünel, where an old-fashioned trolley car continues along İstiklâl Cad. to Taksim.

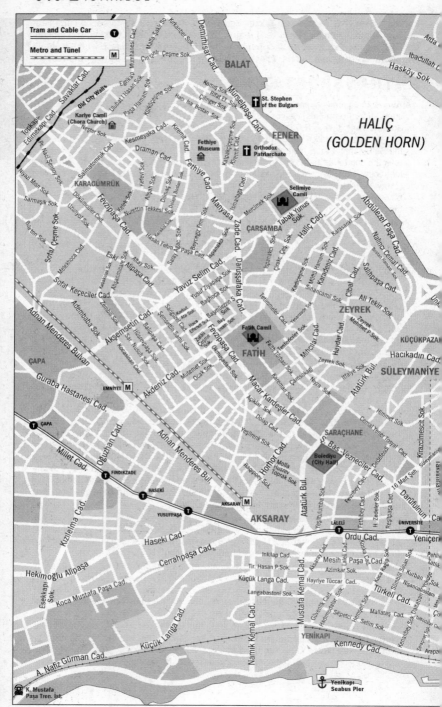

Tram and Cable Car Ⓣ
Metro and Tünel Ⓜ

Old City Walls

BALAT

St. Stephen of the Bulgars

FENER

HALIÇ (GOLDEN HORN)

Kariye Camii (Chora Church)

Fethiye Museum

Orthodox Patriarchate

Selimiye Camii

KARAGÜMRÜK

ÇARŞAMBA

Tabak Yunus Sok.

ZEYREK

KÜÇÜKPAZAR

ÇAPA

Yavuz Selim Cad.

Fatih Camii

FATİH

Hacıkadın Cad.

SÜLEYMANIYE

Guraba Hastanesi Cad.

EMNİYET Ⓜ

Adnan Menderes Bulvarı

SARAÇHANE

ÇAPA Ⓣ

Millet Cad.

Adnan Menderes Bul.

Belediye (City Hall)

FINDIKZADE Ⓣ

HASEKİ

AKSARAY Ⓜ

LÂLELİ

ÜNİVERSİTE Ⓣ

YUSUFPAŞA Ⓣ

AKSARAY

Ordu Cad.

Yeniçeri

Haseki Cad.

İnkılap Cad.

Mesih Paşa Cad.

Türkeli Cad.

Hekimoğlu Alipaşa

Cerrahpaşa Cad.

Küçük Langa Cad.

Koca Mustafa Paşa Cad.

Namık Kemal Cad.

Mustafa Kemal Cad.

Küçük Langa Cad.

YENİKAPI

A. Nafiz Gürman Cad.

Kennedy Cad.

K. Mustafa Paşa Tren. İst.

Yenikapı Seabus Pier

Istanbul

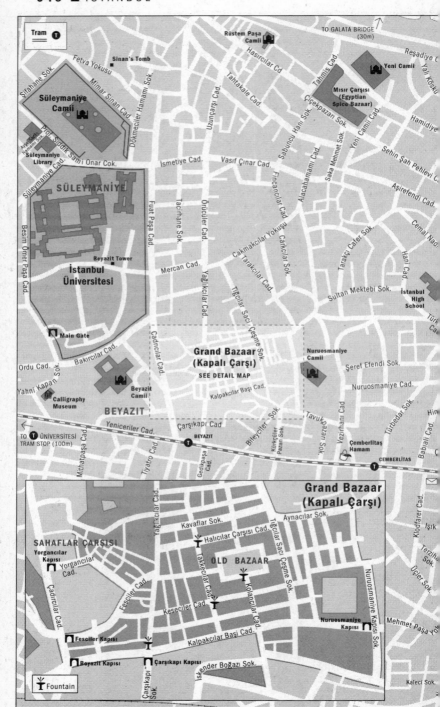

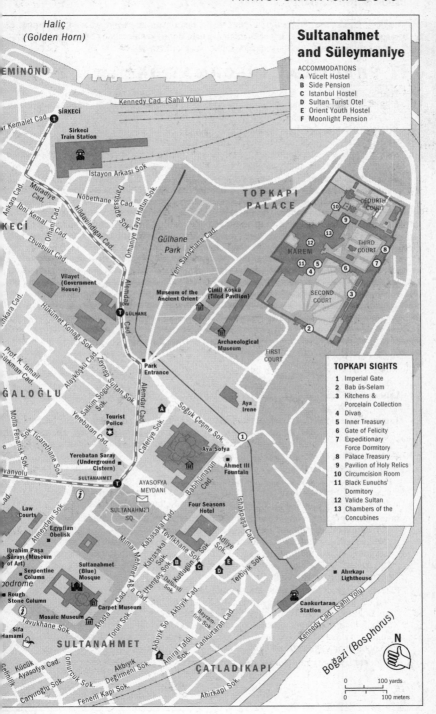

Sultanahmet and Süleymaniye

ACCOMMODATIONS
A Yücelt Hostel
B Side Pension
C Istanbul Hostel
D Sultan Turist Otel
E Orient Youth Hostel
F Moonlight Pension

TOPKAPI SIGHTS

1 Imperial Gate
2 Bab üs-Selam
3 Kitchens & Porcelain Collection
4 Divan
5 Inner Treasury
6 Gate of Felicity
7 Expeditionary Force Dormitory
8 Palace Treasury
9 Pavilion of Holy Relics
10 Circumcision Room
11 Black Eunuchs' Dormitory
12 Valide Sultan
13 Chambers of the Concubines

Haliç (Golden Horn)

EMİNÖNÜ

Kennedy Cad. (Sahil Yolu)

SİRKECİ

Sirkeci Train Station

İstayon Arkası Sok.

TOPKAPI PALACE

Gülhane Park

Museum of the Ancient Orient

Çinli Köşkü (Tiled Pavilion)

FOURTH COURT

HAREM

THIRD COURT

SECOND COURT

FIRST COURT

Archaeological Museum

Aya İrene

Vilayet (Government House)

GÜLHANE

Park Entrance

Tourist Police

Yerebatan Saray (Underground Cistern)

SULTANAHMET

Aya Sofya

Ahmet III Fountain

AYASOFYA MEYDANI

SULTANAHMET SQ.

Four Seasons Hotel

Law Courts

Egyptian Obelisk

İbrahim Paşa Sarayı (Museum of Art)

Serpentine Column

Rough Stone Column

Mosaic Museum

Sifa Hamamı

Sultanahmet (Blue) Mosque

Carpet Museum

SULTANAHMET

Ahırkapı Lighthouse

Cankurtaran Station

ÇATLADIKAPI

Boğazı (Bosphorus)

N

0   100 yards
0   100 meters

Taxis: Little. Yellow. Fiats. Better? Not really; taxi drivers are even more reckless and speed-crazed than other Istanbul drivers. 1 light on the meter means day rate; 2 mean night rate. Rides within the city shouldn't cost more than $5.

⑦ PRACTICAL INFORMATION

Tourist Office: 3 Divan Yolu (tel./fax 518 87 54), at the north end of the Hippodrome in Sultanahmet. Open daily 9am-5pm. Branches in the Takism's Hilton Hotel Arcade on Cumhuriyet Cad., Sirkeci train station, Atatürk Airport, and Karaköy Maritime Station.

Budget Travel: Indigo Tourism and Travel Agency, 24 Akbıyık Cad. (tel. 517 72 66; fax 518 53 33), in the heart of the hotel cluster in Sultanahmet. GO25 cards $5. Also sells bus, plane, and ferry tickets, arranges airport shuttle service, and holds mail. Open daily 8:30am-7:30pm in summer; M-Sa 9:30am-6pm in winter.

Consulates: Australia, 58 Tepecik Yolu, Etiler (tel. 257 70 52). Open M-F 10am-noon. **Canada,** 107/3 Büyükdere Cad., Gayrettepe (tel. 272 51 74; fax 272 34 27). **New Zealand,** 100-102 Maya Akar Center, Büyükdere Cad., Esentepe (tel. 211 11 14; fax 211 04 73). **South Africa,** 106 Büyükdere Cad., Esentepe (tel. 275 47 93; fax 288 76 42). Open M-F 9am-noon. **U.K.,** 34 Meşrutiyet Cad., Beyoğlu/Tepebaşı (tel. 293 75 40; fax 245 49 89). Open M-F 8:30am-noon. **U.S.,** 104-108 Meşrutiyet Cad., Tepebaşı (tel. 251 36 02; fax 251 32 18). Open M-F 8:30-11am.

Currency Exchange: *Bureaux de change* around the city open M-F 8:30am-noon and 1:30-5pm. Most don't charge commission. **ATMs** generally accept all international cards. Most banks exchange **traveler's checks.** Exchanges in Sultanahmet have poor rates and a 2% commission, but are open late and on the weekends.

American Express: Türk Express, 4½ Cumhuriyet Cad., 3rd floor (tel. 235 95 00), uphill from Taksim Sq. Open M-F 9am-6pm. Branch in Hilton Hotel, Cumhuriyet Cad. (tel. 241 02 48). Open daily 8:30am-8pm. Neither give cash advances or accept wired money.

English Bookstores: In Sultanahmet, *köşk* (kiosks) at the Blue Mosque, on Aya Sofia Meydanı, and on Divan Yolu, sell international papers. **Galeri Kayseri,** 58 Divan Yolu, caters to thinking tourists with books on Turkish, Islamic, and Byzantine history, as well as a host of guidebooks in multiple languages.

Laundromat: Star Laundry, 18 Akbıyık Cad. (tel. 638 23 02), below Star Pension in Sultanahmet. Wash and dry $1 per kg; 2kg min. Open daily 8am-10pm.

Tourist Police: In Sultanahmet, at the beginning of Yerebatan Cad. (24hr. hotline tel. 527 45 03 or 528 53 69; fax 512 76 76). They speak better English than any other local police, and their mere presence causes hawkers and postcard-selling kids to scatter. In an **emergency,** dial 155 from any phone.

Hospitals: American Hospital, Admiral Bristol Hastanesi, 20 Güzelbahçe Sok., Nişantaşı (tel. 231 40 50). Applauded by Istanbul natives and tourists, with many English-speaking doctors. **German Hospital,** 119 Sıraselviler Cad., Taksim (tel. 251 71 00), also has a multilingual staff and is conveniently located for Sultanahmet hostelers.

Internet Access: In low-rent corners and ambitious hostels all over Sultanahmet and Taksim. **Sinem Internet Cafe,** 16 Dr. Emin Paşa Sok. (tel. 513 62 29), in an alley off Divan Yolu by the Metro stop. Waits are rare at this pleasant Sultanahmet cafe with tapestries, cushions, and full drink service. $1.80 per hr. Open 9am-10pm. **Cafein Internet Cafe,** 21A Bekar Sok. (tel. 252 18 66), near the upper end of İstiklâl Cad. Cheap at $1.20 per hr. Open 10am-11:30pm.

PTT: All PTTs accept packages. **Main branch** in Sirkeci, 25 Büyük Postane Sok. Stamp and currency exchange services open 8:30am-7pm. 24hr. phones. The branch off Taksim Sq. at the mouth of Cumhuriyet Cad. is convenient for mailing packages or making calls. 24hr. international phone office. No collect calls allowed. Open M-F 8am-8pm, Sa 8am-6pm. Phonecards available 30, 60, or 100 *kontür* (credits); 1 credit lasts 2-10 seconds during international calls.

Telephone Code: 212 for the European side, 216 for the Asian side.

ACCOMMODATIONS

Budget accommodations are concentrated in **Sultanahmet** (a.k.a. Türist Şeğntral), bounded by Aya Sofia, the Blue Mosque, and the walls of the Topkapı Palace, The side streets around **Sirkeci** railway station and **Aksaray** have dozens of dirt-cheap and pretty dirty hotels. Hotels in **Lâleli** are the center of prostitution in Istanbul and should be avoided. Rates sometimes rise by 20% in July and August. All accommodations below are in Sultanahmet.

Istanbul Hostel, 35 Kutlugün Sok. (tel. 516 93 80; fax 516 93 84), down the hill from the Four Seasons Hotel. If you had to choose a hostel floor to eat off of, this would be a good choice. Happy hour 6:30-9:30pm (beer $2). Dorms $5; singles $11.

Sultan Hostel, 3 Terbıyık Sok. (tel. 516 92 60; fax 517 16 26), at Fez Travel Office entrance. Great views of the Sea of Marmara from the rooftop restaurant and bar. Happy hour 5-8pm. Dorms $5; singles $9. Laundry services. Visa, MC accepted.

Yücelt Hostel/Interyouth Hostel, 6/1 Caferiye Cad. (tel. 513 61 50; fax 512 76 28; email info@backpackersturkey.com; www.yucelthostel.com). Free beer until 9pm! Amenities out the wazoo and 3 free meals a day (including all-you-can-drink beer, wine, and tea). Dorms $7; singles $16; doubles $10. Did we mention free beer?

Moonlight Pension, 87 Akbıyık Cad. (tel. 517 54 29; fax 516 24 80). Away from the madness of the backpacker scene. Rooftop views. Kitchen. Also moonlights as a laundromat and Internet-service provider. Dorms $5; doubles $16; triples $21.

Orient Youth Hostel, 13 Akbıyık Cad. (tel. 517 94 93; fax 518 38 94; email orienthostel@superonline.com; www.hostels.com/orienthostel), near Topkapı Palace. It's happy hour daily until 10pm. At night, the festivities move into the bar for Turkey's biggest Australian invasion since Gallipoli (see **Entertainment,** p. 553). Dorms $5; doubles $12.50; quads $5.25 per person. Breakfast included.

Side Pension/Hotel Side, 20 Utangaç Sok. (tel 517 65 90; fax 517 65 90), near the entrance of the Four Seasons Hotel. This charming hotel/pension occupies the 2 buildings by the corner of Tevfikhane Sok. and Utangaç Sok. Pension singles $20; doubles $25; triples $35. Add $10 for bath. Hotel singles $40; doubles $50; triples $60. $5 less in winter. Visa, MC accepted.

FOOD

Istanbul's restaurants, like its clubs and bars, often stick by the golden rule that if it's well advertised or easy to find, it's not worth doing. Sultanahmet's heavily advertised "Turkish" restaurants aren't difficult to find, but much better meals can be found on İstiklâl Cad. and around Taksim. Small Bosphorus suburbs such as **Arnavutköy** and **Sarıyer** (on the European side) and **Çengelköy** (on the Asian side) are the best places for fresh fish. **Vişne suyu** (sour cherry juice) is sold by vendors in Ottoman costume wearing big steel teapots on their backs (20-30¢). The best open-air market is the daily one in **Beşiktaş**, near Barbaros Cad.

Dârüzziyâfe (tel. 511 84 14/5; fax 526 18 91), behind the Sultanahmet Camii on the Hippodrome. The specialty, *Süleymaniye çorbası* (meat and veggie soup, $2), is a must, as is the *çilek keşkül* (strawberry pudding, $1.50). No alcohol—they serve rosehip nectar instead. Open noon-11pm.

Cennet, 90 Divan Yolu Cad. (tel. 513 14 16), on the right side of the road as you walk from Sultanahmet toward Aksaray. Watch women make *gözleme* (Anatolian pancakes), particularly divine with cheese ($1). Live Turkish music and dancing nightly. Open daily 10am-midnight. $1 service charge added per person.

Haci Baba, 49 İstiklâl Cad. (tel. 244 18 86 or 245 43 77), has perfected a wide range of Turkish standards in its 78 years. Large, stylish dining room and a terrace overlooking the courtyard of Aya Triada. Entrees about $7. Open 10am-10pm.

Doy-Doy, 13 Şifa Hamamı Sok. (tel. 517 15 88). The best-best and cheapest-cheapest of Sultanahmet's cheap eats, the 3-story Doy-Doy keeps locals and backpackers coming back for more-more. Tasty *kebap* and salads ($3.50 and under). Open 8:30am-late.

Can Restaurant, 10 Divan Yolu Cad. (tel. 527 70 30), across the street from the tourist information office. Yet another cheap spot on Divan Yolu. Can you believe how delicious the green beans in tomato sauce are? Open 8am-9pm.

Pudding Shop, 6 Divan Yolu Cad. (tel. 522 29 70; fax 512 44 58). A major pitstop on the Hippie Trail to the Far and Middle East during the 70s. The setting for the drug deal scene in *Midnight Express* is now clean but tasty.

🎭 ENTERTAINMENT

HAMAMS (TURKISH BATHS)

While most Istanbul baths have either separate women's sections or women's hours, not all have designated female attendants. For details of the *hamam* experience, see **Just the Facts, Hamam,** below.

JUST THE FACTS, HAMAM Because of the Islamic emphasis on cleanliness, the **hamam** (Turkish bath) has been a part of Turkish daily life since medieval times. They also function as social centers, especially for women, who were often not allowed to leave the house. Men and women use separate bath houses or the same place on different days. A sign on the door may indicate the schedule for women *(kadınlar)* and men *(erkekler)*. Enter the bath house, deposit your clothes and lock your valuables in a cubicle *(camekan),* don the provided towel *(peştemal),* and proceed to the warm main room *(hararet)* with its large, heated stone *(göbek taşı).* Bring your own shampoo, soap, and towel, or pay to use theirs. Bathe yourself at the basins *(kurnas)* lining the walls, pouring the water over yourself with the provided bowl. Basins should only be shared by friends, and soapsuds should be kept clear of the basin water. Take care not to douse your neighbors, as they may have just finished a ritual cleansing. You usually pay extra to be washed and receive a **massage.** Typically, masseuse and client are of the same gender (you can request opposite-sex pairings if you so desire). The massage can be harder than Westerners are accustomed to; *"lütfen daha yumuşak"* (gentler please) is a useful phrase to know. After the massage comes a scrub-down with a **kese** (abrasive mitt), which strips excess skin cells and then some. Following the massage and *kese,* you will be sponged gently and shampooed. After reaching optimum cleanliness, you can return to your cubicle, order a drink, and relax before returning to the dusty streets outside. Men should never drop their *peştemal.* Turkish women frequently strip naked in the bath, but it's a good idea to wear underwear under your *peştemal* until you can gauge the sensibilities of a given *hamam.*

🛁 **Çemberlitaş Hamamı,** 8 Verzirhan Cad. (tel. 522 79 74), just a soap-slide away from the Çemberlitaş tram stop. One of the cleanest and most beautiful *hamams* in Istanbul, built by Sinan in 1584. Both the men's and women's sections have marble interiors under large domes. Vigorous "towel service" after the bath requires a tip of $1.50-3. Bath $14, with massage $18; students $8/12.

🛁 **Çinli Hamamı,** in Fatih, near the butcher shops at the end of Itfaiye Cad. Built for the pirate Barbarossa, this excellent authentic bath still has a few of its original İznik and Kütahya tiles. Both sections open 9am-8pm. Bath $4; massage $4

Cağaloğlu Hamamı (tel. 522 24 24), on Yerebatan Cad., 2km up from Yerebatan Cistern in Sultanahmet. Scenes from *Indiana Jones* were shot at this famous *hamam.* Stone and water tend toward a chilly lukewarm. Men's section open daily 7am-10pm; women's section 8am-8pm. $8 for self-service; $30 for massage and scrubdown.

NIGHTLIFE

Turkish nightlife generally falls into one of three categories. The first includes male-only çay houses, backgammon parlors, and dancing shows. Women are not prohibited but are unwelcome and should avoid these places. The second category includes **café-bars, rock bars,** and **backpacker bars.** Café-bars are smaller and more relaxed than the sometimes cavernous rock bars. Backpacker bars, the best places to meet fellow travelers, are concentrated in the Sultanahmet area. **Clubs** and **discos** comprise the third nightlife category. The hippest Istanbul clubs often move from unlisted locations in Taksim in the winter to unlisted open-air summer locations throughout the city. Even taxi drivers can't keep up with the scene.

Nightlife is centered around **Taksim** and **İstiklâl Cad.** In **Sultanahmet,** all pubs are within 100m of another and have standardized beer prices ($1-1.25). The Beşiktaş end of **Ortaköy** is a maze of upscale hangouts; along the coastal road toward Arnavutköy are a string of open-air clubs. Cover charges are high ($18-45), and bouncers highly selective, but wander along between Ortaköy and **Bebek** and try your luck.

Jazz Spot, at the end of Büyük Parmakkapı Sok in **Taksim.** Live bands lay the funk on thick as a mixed group of music lovers look on. Live music hits the spot nightly at 11pm. Beer $3. June-Aug. no cover; Sept.-May F-Sa cover $10. Open 11am-4am.

Mordi Cafe Bar, 47 Akbıyık Cad., down the street from the Orient Hostel in **Sultanahmet.** Leagues above the other backpacker bars in cleanliness and ambience, this spot was formerly a private residence. Happy hour until 10pm.

Peyote, İmam Adnan Sok. (tel. 293 32 62), next to Leman Kültür, in **Taksim.** This humble spot is one of the area's cheapest venues for live music. Live music Tu-Sa at 11:30pm will blow your mind. F-Sa cover $7.50; 1 drink included. Open M-Sa 6pm-4am.

Madrid Bar, İpek Sok., off Küçük Parmakkapı Sok., which is off İstiklâl Cad. in **Taksim.** Small, mellow spot is popular with Turkish students and young foreigners. Play spot-the-*madrileno* as you sip the cheapest brew in Taksim ($1). Open 2pm-2am.

Orient Bar, 13 Akbıyık Sok. (tel. 517 94 93), in the Orient Youth Hostel in **Sultanahmet.** Revelry abounds in this boisterous basement bar. *Nargile* (water pipe) nights (Th, Su at 9pm) attract international types, while evening belly dancing shows (M, W, F at 10pm) are inauthentic but entertaining. Open 8pm-2am; happy hour until 10pm.

👁 SIGHTS

Istanbul's incomparable array of world-famous churches, mosques, palaces, and museums can keep an ardent tourist busy for weeks. Most budget travelers spend a lot of time in **Sultanahmet,** the area around the **Aya Sofia,** south of and up the hill from Sirkeci. Merchants crowd the district between the **Grand Bazaar,** east of the university, and the less touristy **Egyptian Bazaar,** just southeast of Eminönü.

SULTANAHMET AND ENVIRONS

AYA SOFİA (HAGIA SOPHIA)

Open Tu-Su 9:30am-4:30pm. Gallery open Tu-Su 9:30-11:30am and 1-4pm. Admission $4.80, students free.

Aya Sofia was built by Justinian in 537 CE, and at that time its area (7570m^2) and height (55.6m) made it the grandest building in the world. Upon entering the church, which was even larger than King Solomon's temple in Jerusalem (see p. 269), Emperor Justinian exclaimed, "Solomon, I have outdone you!" Twenty years later, an earthquake brought the dome crashing to the ground, and in 1453 the entire building fell to the Ottomans and was converted into a mosque (as it remained until 1932, when Atatürk declared it a museum).

Aya Sofia's austere interior amplifies its awesome size. The nave is overshadowed by the massive, gold-leaf mosaic dome lined with hundreds of circular windows that make it seem as though the dome is floating on a bed of luminescent pearls. The **mihrab,** the calligraphy-adorned portal pointing towards Mecca, stands in the **apse,** the space that housed the altar during the mosque's Orthodox incarnation. The marble square on the floor marks the spot where Byzantine emperors were once crowned. On either side of it stand what must be two of the biggest candles in the history of wax. The **minbar,** the platform used to address the crowd at prayer time, is the stairway right of the *mihrab*. The **gallery** contains Byzantine mosaics uncovered from beneath a thick layer of Ottoman plaster as well as the famed **sweating pillar,** sheathed in bronze. The pillar has a hole where you can insert your finger to collect the odd drop of water, believed to possess healing powers.

BLUE MOSQUE (SULTANAHMET CAMİİ)

Sultanahmet is a functioning mosque that is closed at prayer times. Dress modestly. Open Tu-Su. Donation requested. Tomb open Tu-Su 9:30am-4:30pm. Admission $1, students free.

The mosque between the Hippodrome and Aya Sofia is the ⚑**Blue Mosque** (Sultanahmet Camii), so named for the beautiful blue İznik tiles that decorate the interior. Completed in 1617, it was Sultan Ahmet's "size doesn't matter" response to Justinian's larger Aya Sofia. The mosque has several "modern" constructions: the internal framework of iron bars across its domes allows the entire structure to bend in earthquakes (it's withstood 20 so far), and an underground pool moderates the mosque's interior temperature (heating in winter and cooling in summer). Numerology is the name of the game at the Blue Mosque: Sultan Ahmet was the 16th sultan of the Ottoman state and the sixth since the Turkish conquest of Constantinople; consequently, the mosque has 16 balconies and six **minarets.** These minarets are the primary source of the mosque's fame. Only the mosque at Mecca had six minarets at the time of the Blue Mosque's construction, and the thought of equalling that sacred edifice was considered heretical. Sultan Ahmet got around this difficulty by financing the construction of a seventh minaret at Mecca. The mosque copies the "floating light" motif of the Aya Sofia; the interior was originally lit with candles, the chandelier structure intended to create the illusion that tiny starlights floated freely in the air. A small stone from the **Ka'aba** at Mecca is almost invisible from the tourists' area. The small, square, single-domed structure in front of the Blue Mosque is **Sultanahmet'in Türbesi,** or Sultan Ahmet's Tomb, which contains the sultan's remains and those of his wife and sons; it also has İznik tiles. The reliquary in the back contains strands of the prophet Muhammad's beard.

HIPPODROME (AT MEYDANI)

Though all of the major Sultanahmet sites provide insight into pre-Ottoman and Ottoman history, few conjure images of the glory of Byzantine Constantinople like the **Hippodrome** *(At Meydanı),* behind the Blue Mosque. Built by the Roman Emperor Septimus Severus in 200 CE, it served as a place for chariot races and public executions. The politically opposed **Hippodrome Factions** arose out of the Hippodrome's seating plan, which was determined by social standing. The "blues" were wealthy citizens seated in the front rows and the "greens" urban plebians in cheap seats. In 532 CE, a tax protest turned into the full-out Nika Revolt. The city was ravaged in the ensuing melee, and Justinian's post-revolt reconstruction efforts culminated in the building of the Aya Sofia. The tall, northernmost column with hieroglyphics is the **Dikili Taş,** an Egyptian obelisk erected by the Pharaoh Thutmosis III in 1500 BCE and brought to Constantinople in the 4th century by Emperor Theodosius I. Farther south, the subterranean bronze stump is all that remains of the **Serpentine Column,** originally placed at the Oracle of Delphi. The southernmost column is the **Column of Constantine,** whose original gold-plated bronze tiling was looted by Crusaders during the sack of Constantinople.

MUSEUMS

MUSEUM OF TURKISH AND ISLAMIC ART. This superb museum (also known as İbrahim Paşa Sarayı) features a large Islamic art collection organized by period. The museum's main wing consists of a long hall with carpet and silver displays, off of which are rooms containing works from specific periods. The Selçuk displays and the Ottoman calligraphy with *tuğras* (seals) of sultans are particularly impressive. (*Open Tu-Su 9:30am-4:30pm. Admission $2, students $1.20.*)

YEREBATAN SARAYI (UNDERGROUND CISTERN). This underground "palace" is actually a vast underground cavern whose shallow water eerily reflects the images of its 336 supporting columns, all illuminated by colored ambient lighting. The echoing sounds of continuously dripping water and the muted strains of classical tunes will accompany your stroll across the elevated wooden walkways. Underground walkways originally linked the cistern to Topkapı Palace, but were blocked to curb rampant trafficking in stolen goods and abducted women. (*Stand with your back to Aya Sofia; the entrance is 175m from the cami in the stone kiosk on the left side of Yerebatan Cad. Open daily 9:30am-5:30pm. Admission $3, students $2.50.*)

TOPKAPI PALACE AND ENVIRONS

TOPKAPI PALACE (TOPKAPI SARAYI)

Main entrance is on Babıhümayun Cad., the cobblestone street off Aya Sofia Sq. Open W-M 9am-4:30pm. Admission $4, students free. Harem open Su-M and W-Sa. Mandatory tours leave every 30min. 9:30am-3:30pm. Harem $2.50, students $1.50.

Towering from the high ground at the tip of the old city and hidden behind walls up to 12m high, Topkapı Palace (Topkapı Sarayı) was the nerve center of the Ottoman Empire. Topkapı offers unparalleled insights into the wealth, excess, cruelty, and artistic vitality that characterized the Ottoman Empire at its peak. Built by Mehmet the Conqueror between 1458 and 1465, the palace became an imperial residence during the reign of Süleyman the Magnificent. The palace is divided into a series of courts, all surrounded by the palace walls.

FIRST AND SECOND COURTYARD. The **first courtyard**, through the **Imperial Gate,** was the popular center of the Palace. The general public was permitted entrance to watch executions, trade, and view the nexus of the Empire's glory. At the end of the first courtyard, the capped conical towers of the **Bab üs-Selam** (Gate of Greeting) mark the entrance to the **second court.** To the right beyond the colonnade, the **Imperial kitchens,** with their distinctive conical and vaulted chimneys, house three collections of porcelain and silver. The last set of doors on the left of the narrow alley open into the palace's deservedly world-famous Chinese and Japanese **porcelain collections.** Across the courtyard, where ostriches and eunuchs once roamed, lies the divine **Divan** (also known as Kubbealtı), with its window grilles, awnings, walls, and ceilings slathered in gold leaf. The **Council Chamber,** the room closest to the Harem, retains its original classical Ottoman *faience* decor. The plush Rococo-style room abutting the Council Chamber was where the Grand Vizier would receive foreign dignitaries. Next door and to the right is the **Inner Treasury,** where various instruments of cutting, bludgeoning, and hacking are kept.

THIRD COURTYARD. The **third court,** officially known as **Enderun** (inside), is accessible through the **Gate of Felicity.** In the **Expeditionary Force Dormitory** is a costume collection that traces the evolution of imperial costumes. Moving along down the colonnade brings you to the awesome **Palace Treasury.** One of the highlights is the legendary ✦**Topkapı dagger** (essentially three giant emeralds with a knife sprouting out of them), a gift Sultan Mahmut I intended to present to Shah Nadir of Iran in return for the solid-gold throne displayed elsewhere in the treasury. Wrestle your way to the front of the line leading up to all 86 karats of the Pigot Diamond, better known as the **Spoonmaker's Diamond** because it was traded to a spoonmaker in exchange for three spoons. A nearby glass compartment reportedly contains some of John the Baptist's bones. This display is excellent preparation for the **Pavilion of Holy Relics,** just on the other side of the courtyard and leagues ahead in beauty and elegance. Even the most İzniked-out traveler will be amazed by the calligraphied tiles of this holy site. The pavilion holds the booty taken from Egypt by Selim the Grim as well as relics from Mecca, including the **staff of Moses,** hairs from **Muham-**

mad's beard, and some of the Prophet's personal effects (including his bow and mantle, a hand-written letter, and two swords).

FOURTH COURTYARD. Three passages lead into the **fourth courtyard.** If Topkapı was the nerve center of the Ottoman Empire, then the fourth courtyard certainly qualifies as its pleasure center, as it was amongst these pavilions, gardens, and fountains that they really got their mojo working in the Ottoman age. Uninterrupted vistas of the Sea of Marmara and the Bosphorus extend from the broad marble terrace at the west end. At one end of the portico is the **Circumcision Room,** an octagonal chamber that hangs over the edge of the pavilion, built by Ibrahim the Mad.

HAREM. The Harem's 400-plus rooms housed the sultan, his immediate family, and an entourage of servants, eunuchs and general assistants. The mandatory tour begins at the **Black Eunuchs' Dormitory,** which is just what its name says it is (although there seems to be something missing...). Next up is the women's section of the harem, the center of which are the lavish chambers of the **Valide Sultan,** the sultan's mother and the most powerful woman in the Harem. Surrounding the room of the queen mum are the chambers of the **concubines,** the women who put the slut back in sultanate. If a particular woman attracted the sultan's affections or if the sultan spent a night with her, she would be promoted to coveted "odalisque" status (immortalized in Ingres' nudes), which meant she had to stay in Istanbul (concubines were allowed to leave after nine years) but got nicer quarters in exchange for her undying ministrations. Another stop on the harem tour is the **bedroom** of Mehmet I, the site of many of the sultan's greatest erections (the Blue Mosque aside); it was the randy Mehmet who was responsible for bringing the harem closer to the sultan's palace (it used to be in the distant Divan Yolu area).

ARCHAEOLOGICAL MUSEUM COMPLEX

150m downhill from the Topkapı Palace's first courtyard. When the palace is closed, enter the museums through Gülhane Park, where a separate road next to the park ticket booths leads to the museum complex. A single ticket gets you into all 3 museums, although one or another is often closed. Museum complex open Tu-Su 9:30am-4:30pm. Admission $3, students free.

TILED PAVILION AND ANCIENT ORIENT MUSEUM. The **Tiled Pavilion** (*Çinli Köşk*) exposes more than you ever wanted to know about the omnipresent İznik tiles. The once fully-tiled pavilion was built in 1472 by Mehmet to view the athletic competitions below, but fires and earthquakes have destroyed much of the original *faience.* The displays cover the full spectrum of Ottoman tilemaking, including some rare early İznik tiles. The smaller cement building adjacent to the Tiled Pavilion is the **Ancient Orient Museum,** which houses treasures so rare that the curator seems reluctant to let anyone see them. If you catch this place when it's open, don't miss the excellent collection of 2nd millennium BCE stone artifacts from the ancient Middle East (including Anatolia, Mesopotamia, and Egypt). The pride of this museum is the **Treaty of Kadesh,** the world's oldest-known written treaty, drafted after a battle between Ramses II of Egypt and the Hittite King Muvatellish (a copy graces the entrance to the United Nations).

ARCHAEOLOGY MUSEUM. The 19th-century Archaeology Museum has one of the world's great collections of Classical and Hellenistic art. The first portion of the building is a walking tour through the evolution of Classical sculpture. The highlight is the misnamed **Alexander Sarcophagus,** modeled on a Greek temple and covered with intricate carvings but actually holding the remains of the Sidonese king Abdalonymous. Other exhibits include "Istanbul Through the Ages" and "Ancient Turkey."

GRAND BAZAAR

From Sultanahmet, follow the Askaray tram tracks until a mosque appears on the right; enter its side gate and keep walking (virtual visit: www.grand-bazaar.com). Open M-Sa 9am-7pm.

Consisting of over 4000 shops, several banks, mosques, police stations, and restaurants, the enormous **Grand Bazaar** (*Kapalı Çarşısı,* "covered bazaar") could be a city in itself. Now the largest covered bazaar in the world, the Grand Bazaar began in 1461 as a modest affair during the reign of Mehmet the Conqueror. Today, the enormous Kapalı Çarşısı forms the entrance to the massive mercantile sprawl that starts at Çemberlitaş and covers the hill down to Eminönü, ending at the **Egyptian Spice Bazaar** *(Mısır Çarşısı)* and the Golden Horn waterfront. This colorful, chaotic, labyrinthine world combines all the best and worst of shopping in Turkey. Though the bazaar is loosely organized according to specific themes, much of it is a jumble of shops selling hookah pipes *(nargeileh)*, bright baubles, copper filigree shovels, Byzantine-style icons on red velvet, Turkish daggers, rugs, embroidered pillows, amber jewelry, silver flintlock guns with mother-of-pearl handles, musical instruments, chess sets, hand puppets, ornaments, and the ubiquitous evil-eye bedecked keychains. Through banter and barter, haggle and hassle, a day spent at the Kapalı Çarşısı is bound to tempt and tantalize on a scale unmatched by even the most frenetic of *souqs* elsewhere in the Middle East. You'll surely get lost, so enjoy the ride.

SÜLEYMANİYE COMPLEX

Down Divan Yolu in Beyazit. Walk along the tracks or actually take the tram to the ÜNIVERSITE stop, walk across the square, and take Besim Ömer Paşa Cad. past Istanbul University to Süleymaniye Cad. Mosque open Tu-Su 9:30am-4:30pm, except during prayer times. Tomb open Tu-Su 9:30am-4:30pm. Donation expected.

To the north of Istanbul University stands the massive, elegant **Süleymaniye Camii**, one of Ottoman architect Sinan's great masterpieces. The Süleymaniye Camii is part of a larger *külliye* (complex), which includes **tombs,** an **imaret** (soup kitchen), and several **madreses** (Islamic schools). Prof. Sıddık Sami Onar Sok. is the major street running between the university and the mosque. Passing through the graveyard brings you to the similarly decorated **royal tombs** of Süleyman I and his wife, Haseki Hürrem. Süleyman's tomb is a superb example of the Ottoman integration of İznik tiles, stained glass, and painted patterns. Walk along the Süleymaniye Camii's southwest side to the large arch just below the dome and enter the mosque's central courtyard through the smaller tourist entrance to the left of the main door. After removing your shoes and covering your head, proceed inside the vast and perfectly proportioned mosque—the height of the dome, 53m, is exactly twice the measurement of each side of the square base. The **stained-glass windows** are the sobering work of the master Sarhoş İbrahim (İbrahim the Drunkard). The İznik tile İnzanity all started here: the area around the *mihrab* showcases Sinan's first experiment in blue tiles.

NORTHWESTERN TURKEY

The cradle of the Ottoman Empire, Northwestern Turkey envelops the Sea of Marmara with a diverse collection of cities and towns—fantastic quick escapes from Istanbul's urban sprawl. The terracotta hue of the soil and the silvery olive groves recall fertile Tuscany; after all, this is the region that nourished the young Ottoman Empire, and it has two Ottoman capitals, **Bursa** (p. 559) and **Edirne** (p. 557) to show for it. The region's artistic achievements, including Edirne's masterful architecture and Bursa's silk, are world-famous. The **Gallipoli Battlefields** (p. 562) remain a major pilgrimage site for those commemorating the bloody WWI battle for the Dardanelles.

EDİRNE

Edirne has worn many masks throughout its almost 2000 years of historical prominence: founded as the Roman outpost Hadrianopolis by the humble Emperor Hadrian, Edirne has been an Ottoman capital (and is still home to the greatest Ottoman mosque in all of Turkey, Selimiye Camii) as well as a modern Greek military possession. In the 19th century, Edirne was still the seventh-largest city in Europe, but now the city has a quiet frontier town feel unlike any other spot in Turkey. Some report that the population in Edirne enjoys alcohol more than most places in Turkey (not coincidentally, the finest brand of *rakı* is produced nearby).

🗗 ORIENTATION AND PRACTICAL INFORMATION. At the heart of Edirne is the triangular **Hürriyet Meydanı**, bounded on three sides by **Hükümet Caddesi, Talat**

Paşa Caddesi, and Üç Şerefeli Camii. *Dolmuş* from the bus station stop here. Talat Paşa Cad. is the city's main east-west thoroughfare, starting behind the **Eski Camii** and running through town to the Tunca River. The city's main shops are on **Saraçlar Caddesi**, reached by taking Talat Paşa Cad. away from the Selimiye Camii mosque. The tourist office and cheap accommodations are around **Maarif Caddesi**.

Buses depart from the **otogar**, 2km from the city center, to: **Ankara** (8hr., 2 per night, $15); **Antalya** (15hr., 2 per day, $18.75); **Bursa** (Apr.-Dec. 2 per day, Nov.-Mar. 1 per day; $12.50); **Çanakkale** (5hr., 5 per day, $11.50); **Istanbul** (3hr., every 30min., $6.50); and **İzmir** (11hr., 2 per day, $12.50). **Dolmuş** leave from the dusty gravel lot behind the Rüstem Paşa Kervansaray Hotel (25-45¢).

The **tourist office**, 17 Talat Paşa Cad. (tel. 213 92 08), 300m down the road from the center of town, hands out free maps (open M-F 8:30am-5:30pm). **Türkiye İş Bankası**, on Saraçlar Cad., exchanges **traveler's checks** and has an **ATM** (open M-F 9am-12:30pm and 1:30-5:30pm). Take *dolmuş* #1 to the Mega Park stop (10min., 25¢) to reach the **police** (tel. 213 92 40). For pharmaceutical fancies, go to **Şifa Eczanesi** (tel.

NATAŞAS The world's oldest profession is legal in Turkey, and trafficking in **prostitutes** from the former Soviet Union (hence their Turkish name, *Nataşas*, from the common Russian name Natasha) has increased dramatically since 1989. Turkish brothels are supposed to be officially licensed and regulated by health and social service authorities. Aspiring prostitutes must attain a certificate and agree to regular AIDS and venereal disease check-ups, and a 1990 law set the penalty for abducting or raping a prostitute to be equal to that for crimes against any other woman (rather than two-thirds of the penalty, as it had been previously). According to officials, there are 56 brothels in Turkey and 2376 prostitutes, but a more realistic estimate would be close to 100,000 *Nataşas*. Many of these women are the victims of what has grown into a billion-dollar trafficking business. **Pimps** lure desperate former-Soviet-bloc women to Turkey under the pretense of employment offers, marriage, or modeling. These women are frequently abused, threatened, drugged, and raped by pimps who hold their passports and demand that they work to repay the "debt" they have accrued for being taken abroad. As illegal immigrants, they are often left with no political recourse, and their life expectancy averages a grim 35 years.

---

225 46 36), on Talat Paşa Cad. (open M-F 8:30am-7:30pm). There are two **hospitals** in town: the private **Özel Trakya Hastanesi** (tel. 213 92 00) and the public **Edirne Devlet Hastanesi** (tel. 225 46 03). The **PTT** is at 17 Saraçlar Cad. (post open 8:30am-5pm; phones open 8:30am-10pm). **Telephone code:** 284.

⌂⌂ ACCOMMODATIONS AND FOOD. Cheapies cluster around Maarif Cad. Call ahead when visiting Edirne in July, when the town is home to the Kırkpınar Grease Wrestling Festival (see **Sights**, below). ■ **Hotel Kervansaray** (tel. 225 21 95; fax 225 04 62), also known as Rüstempaşa, runs the length of Hürriyet Meydanı on Eski Camii Altı. Exquisite gardens, a cloistered courtyard, and stone hallways complement modern facilities (bath, TV, phone) and a billiards/Internet parlor (singles $30; doubles $60; triples $90; breakfast included). **Hotel Aksaray** (tel. 225 39 01), at the intersection of Maarif Cad. and Ali Paşa Ortakapı Cad., has small rooms, most without bath (singles $6.25; doubles $10, with bath $15; triples $11.25/$18.75).

Saray Restaurant (tel. 212 13 92), behind the PTT (look for a red awning), serves daily lunch specials at 50¢-$1 per serving (open for lunch only). **Yudum Tava Ciğer Salonu** (tel. 212 43 52), on the road stretching down from the Bedesten, serves Edirne's beefy specialty, *Tava Ciğer* ($1). The **teahouses** of Edirne are world-famous; the standout is **Antik Park Cafe**, 22 Tahmis Cad. (tel. 212 22 53).

⌂ SIGHTS. Every July, competitors from all over Turkey travel to Edirne, don giant leather breeches, slather themselves in oil, and hit the mats. The champions of the ▨Kırkpınar Grease Wrestling Festival are assured lasting fame and a portrait in the wrestling room of the Islamic Art Museum (see below). Despite the infamy of the festival, Edirne is *really* famed for its magnificent mosque architecture.

▨Selimiye Camii is considered the finest mosque in all of Turkey, surpassing Aya Sofia (Hagia Sophia) in size, structural stability, and aesthetic unity. Construction of the famous Ottoman architect Sinan's self-proclaimed masterpiece did not actually begin until 1567, the year after Sinan died. The four minarets are echoed in the eight massive interior columns supporting the large outer dome. The interior fills with light from 999 windows, illuminating the colorful lace patterns and calligraphic inscriptions on the 32m interior dome (as well as the *minbar* and *mihrab*). The former *madrasa* of the mosque houses the Turkish and Islamic Art Museum, which has a multitude of Islamic artwork and a special room recounting the history of the Kırkpınar Wrestling Festival. Approach the mosque from the west, as Sinan intended: pass the Kavaflar Arasta (cobbler's market) and head up the staircase, marked "Camii Giriş." (Museum open Tu-Su 8am-noon and 1:30-5:30pm. Admission 75¢, students free.) Edirne's two other mosques (both on Hürriyet Meydanı) trace the architectural transition from the Selçuk style of Konya and Bursa to the distinctly Ottoman style of Selimiye Camii. Look, but don't enter: most of these mosque interiors are being closed for renovations. The nine-domed Eski Camii ("Old Mosque") and its marble *mihrab* are an excellent example of pre-conquest Ottoman architecture. The limestone Üç Şerefeli Camii ("Three Balconies Mosque") replaced Eski Camii as the Friday afternoon hangout for Muslims upon its completion in 1447. Named for the three balconies gracing its minarets, the mosque is better known for its 23m dome, the largest Ottoman dome of its time.

BURSA

Surrounded by fertile plains and blessed with vast gardens and parks, the city has earned the moniker "Green Bursa"—a name with double significance, as Bursa is one of Turkey's holiest cities (green is the color of Islam). While the city's 14th-century mosques and tombs still receive visitors, Bursa's rapid economic growth has spawned a wealthy resort area, including one of Turkey's most popular skiing spots. Silk trade remains a major industry here, as attested by the silkworm cocoon harvests held every June and September. The town also claims a number of culinary triumphs: the *İskender kebap* and *İnegöl Köfte* (a type of meatball) were both invented in Bursa's kitchens. Anticipating the gastric distress such tasty victuals would conjure, Sultan Süleyman's Grand Vizier had several mineral baths (said to cure everything from heart trouble to athlete's foot) constructed here.

🛈 ORIENTATION AND PRACTICAL INFORMATION

Bursa's sights are along a 3km stretch of Atatürk Caddesi, and most of the hotels and restaurants are within a block of Atatürk Cad. in an area called Heykel. Bursa's terminal, 20km outside the city center, is reached by local bus #90/A (every 30min. 6:20am-midnight, 60¢). Buses go to: Ankara (5½hr., every hr., $10.25); Istanbul (3½hr., $9); and İzmir (5hr., every hr., $9.50). Four-passenger dolmuş (40-60¢ per person) leave from Atatürk Cad., behind the *Adliye*, and from the Atatürk statue in Heykel. The tourist office (tel. 220 18 48), is on Atatürk Cad. near the Atatürk statue, down the stairs and to the left (open daily May-Sept. 8:30am-6pm; Oct.-Apr. 8am-5pm). Something strange in the neighborhood? Call the police (tel. 221 35 12). Hospitals come in private (Vatan Hastanesi; tel. 220 10 40; on İnönü Cad.) and public (Devlet Hastanesi; tel. 220 00 20) varieties. Get yourself connected at Elite Internet Cafe, 37 Yeşil Cad. (tel. 327 03 34), before the overpass leading to Emir Sultan Camii ($1.20 per hr.; open daily 10am-1am). The PTT is opposite Ulu Camii (open daily 8am-11pm; airmail and currency exchange until 5:30pm). Telephone code: 224.

ACCOMMODATIONS AND FOOD

Bursa's budget hotels are off Atatürk Cad., south of the PTT. **Saray Oteli,** İnönü Cad., 1 Matbaa Çık (tel. 221 28 20), boasts spacious, well-lit rooms with communal toilets (singles $8; doubles $19; triples $23.80). Clean, quiet **Otel Güneş,** 75 İnebey Cad. (tel. 222 14 04) also has shared baths (singles $8.30; doubles $12; triples $18; quads $21.40). The birthplace of *İskender kebap* has many restaurants claiming to be its mother. ■ **Kebapçı İskender** (tel. 221 46 15) is the tastiest of the claimants, with two locations (7 Ünlü Cad. and on Atatürk Bul. by the cultural center) serving the same *İskender kebap* ($4.30) since 1867 (open daily 11am-9pm). ■ **Lalezar,** 14/C Ünlü Cad. (tel. 221 84 24), has tasty vegetarian appetizers ($1.40) and desserts ($1; open M-Sa 7:30am-9:30pm). **Çiçek Izgara,** 15 Belediye Cad. (tel. 221 65 26), in the square behind the town hall on Atatürk Cad., serves delicious *köfte* and *kasarlı köfte* (meatballs and cheese) for $3 (open daily 11am-4pm and 6-7:30pm).

ENTERTAINMENT

Entertainment in Bursa means winding down at a mineral bath, not getting liquored up. The bars and clubs of **Arap Şükrü** district, next to the park near Altıparmak Cad., are as close to nightlife as Bursa gets.

MINERAL BATHS. Bursa's fabled mineral baths are in the Çekirge ("Grasshopper") area west of the city. The three-bath complex **Yeni Kaplıca** ("New Baths") was constructed by Süleyman the Magnificent's Grand Vizier atop the remains of an even older bath built by Justinian (men only; bath $3-5.25, massage $3.50, *kese* $2; open 5am-11pm). The **Kaynarca** is a women's bath ($3, massage $3.50, *kese* $2; open 7am-10:30pm). Soak in a tub of smooth, pasty mud at **Karamustafa** ($4; open for men 7am-5pm, for women 8am-4pm). One of the finest Turkish baths in a country of Turkish baths, ■ **Eski Kaplıca** ("Old Bath") features a hot pool, a *hotter* pool, and a great massage room (open daily 7am-11pm; admission for men $7, women $5.35). *(Take bus #40 from Heykel or any dolmuş with a "Çekirge" sign (60¢). Get off on Çekirge Cad. by the Atatürk Museum. For Eski Kaplıca, walk west and bear right at the fork onto Yeni Kaplıca Cad. Signs point down the stairs toward the baths.)*

MARKETS. The **Koza and Emir Hans** have been the centers of the city's silk *(ipek)* trade for the past 500 years. Restored by the Aga Khan, the **Koza Han** draws silk cocoon dealers every July and September. During the rest of the year, the *han* is home to a slew of silk shops, which sell the fine local fabric by the bolt, tie, and scarf. The **Emir Han** concerns itself strictly with the sale of the finished product. Both *hans* open into the 14th-century **bedesten** (covered market), architecturally similar to Istanbul's Grand Bazaar. *(On Atatürk Cad. behind the Ulu Camii.)*

SIGHTS

ULU CAMI. The unique layout and domed splendor of the immense Ulu Cami, in the heart of town on Atatürk Cad., was a compromise between Sultan Beyazıt I and Allah. Beyazıt promised he would build 20 mosques in exchange for victory, but when he squashed his enemy, he built one mosque with 20 domes. The interior columns and walls are bedecked with Selçuk calligraphic excerpts from the Qur'an. The *mihrab* contains an astronomical guide with pictures of the planets.

YEŞIL TÜRBE AND YEŞIL CAMII. The gorgeous **Yeşil Türbe** (Green Tomb) stands atop a hill, its blue-green, tile-sheathed octagonal form rising out of the surrounding foliage (right off Atatürk Cad., along Yeşil Cad.). Inside, everything is covered with beautiful İznik tiles, even the sarcophagus of Ottoman hero Sultan Mehmet I (who is best known as the patron of the Harem of the Topkapı Palace in Istanbul, see p. 555). Across the street stands the 15th-century **Yeşil Camii** mosque, whose Selçuk influence is apparent in its brick-and-stone construction and its almost onion-shaped minarets. The mosque's real beauty lies within, where intricately stenciled İznik tiles adorn the walls. The balcony that hangs low above the entrance is where the sultan could enter and pray unobserved, while keeping his eyes peeled for potential assassins. The large, central dome is one of the first used in Ottoman architecture. *(Tomb open daily 8:30am-noon and 1-5:30pm.)*

MURADIYE. *Şehade* (royal sons) are buried in the tombs surrounding the Muradiye Camii, a testament to the early Ottoman practice of fratricide. In order to ensure a smooth succession, the eldest son would execute his younger or weaker brothers. The complex includes 12 tombs, but at the time of publication, only four were open to the public. Cem Sultan's tomb, covered in fine İznik tiles, is particularly spectacular. Adjacent to the tomb is the Muradiye or **Murat II Camii,** built in the same style as the Yeşil Camii. Hexagonal tile patterns adorn the walls, and at the back stands a beautiful *mihrab* with subtly shaded inscriptions. *(Catch one of the frequent "Muradiye" dolmuş or buses from the Atatürk Cad./Heykel area. Open daily 8:30am-noon and 1-5:30pm. Admission 60¢.)*

ÇANAKKALE

Modern Çanakkale presides over the mythic and eternally strategic Dardanelles, straits that have seen poets and soldiers come and go for centuries. With its inexpensive accommodations and frequent bus connections, Çanakkale is an easy base from which to explore Gallipoli and Troy. It is not, however, an overwhelmingly pleasant place, suffering from the noise, pollution, and frenzy expected in a city of its size (around 60,000). Nevertheless, Çanakkale is particularly hospitable to the thousands of Australians and New Zealanders who make the pilgrimage to Gallipoli around ANZAC Day (Apr. 25th), when every hotel in town is sure to be overbooked.

⊠ ORIENTATION AND PRACTICAL INFORMATION. Most everything relating to the mechanics of budget travel is within the one-block area around the ferry dock and the clocktower. From the *otogar*, turn left along **Atatürk Caddesi,** make a quick right onto **Demircioğlu Caddesi,** and follow the signs marked FERIBOT. **Buses** run to: **Ankara** (11hr., 5 per day 9am-10:30pm, $12.50); **Bursa** (4½hr., 13 per day until 12:30am, $6.25); **Edirne** (5hr., 5am and 1pm, $7.50); **Istanbul** (5hr.; every hr. until 7pm, every 2hr. afterwards; $10); **İzmir** (5hr.; every hr. until 7pm, every 2hr. afterwards; $7.50); **Konya** (11hr., 2 and 2:30pm, $12.50); and **Selçuk** (6hr., 1:15am, $8.75). *Dolmuş* (50¢-$1) leave from near the small bridge over the Sarı Çay inlet.

The English-speaking staff at the **tourist office,** 67 İskele Meydanı (tel./fax 217 11 87), distributes free maps and helps find rooms (open daily 8:30am-7:30pm). Several **banks** with Cirrus/PLUS **ATMs** stand in a sequestered part of the city. Walk up Demircioğlu Cad. and take the fourth right from Anzac House; follow this street to a four-way intersection (banks open M-F 9am-12:30pm and 1:30-5:30pm). The **police** (tel. 212 14 66) are off İnönü Cad., next to the PTT. Local hospitals include **Devlet Hastanesi** (public; tel. 217 10 98), off İnönü Cad. across from the PTT, and **Özel Hastanesi** (private; tel. 217 74 61), 1km from the tourist office. A pharmacy, **Pelini Eczanesi** (tel. 217 12 60), is on Demircioğlou Cad. just down from Anzac House. The **PTT** is on İnönü Cad. (open 8:30am-5pm). **Telephone code:** 286.

⌐ ACCOMMODATIONS. Budget accommodations cluster around the clocktower, with good restaurants and bars only a few steps away. Many feature a nightly screening of *Gallipoli*, starring Mel "the Aussie Tosser" Gibson, and can arrange Gallipoli and Troy tours. **Anzac House,** 61 Cumhuriyet Meydanı (tel. 217 01 56; fax 217 29 06), across from the taxi stand, is a popular spot for Aussies and Kiwis, with refurbished rooms and clean communal baths with hot showers. Perks include laundry service, Internet access ($4 per hr.), and a barbecue every evening. (Dorms $4; singles $8.15; doubles $10; triples $12; quads $15. Breakfast $1.50.) Another backpacker hangout, **Yellow Rose Pension,** 5 Yeni Sok. (tel./fax 217 33 43), is around the corner, 50m from the clocktower, with a garden, moderately clean single-sex dorms, laundry facilities, Internet access ($4 per hr.), and international phone and fax services. ($5 per person, with bath $6; breakfast $1.50.)

📷📀 **FOOD AND ENTERTAINMENT.** Çanakkale's restaurants serve the catch of the day along the waterfront, and its bars and clubs are close by on the streets behind. Nightlife can get going when enough people come to town, but off-season visitors often choose to stay in and make it a *Gallipoli* night. **The Yeni Entellektüel** ("New Intellectual;" tel. 217 56 03) suffers not from the pretentiousness expected from a name more appropriate for a Marxist magazine. Fish is brain food, and they serve lots of it, as well as distinctive dishes like *ahtapot* (octopus) and calamari (meals $7-8; open until 2am). Excellent *İskender kebap* ($2.50) and *lahmacun* (45¢), combined with local popularity, have forced the expansion of **Doyum Pide ve Kebap Salonu** (tel. 217 46 87), on the right side of Demircioğlu Cad., up from Anzac House. The best of the bars is the explosive **TNT Bar/Garden** (tel. 217 07 71), on Saat Kulesi Meydanı, which draws in hostelers to play pool ($4 per hr.) in a big wooden house. The garden serves drinks and quality standard fare (meals $4-6), and an acoustic guitarist croons nightly at 10pm (open daily until late).

NEAR ÇANAKKALE

Several agencies provide group tours of Troy and the Gallipoli Battlefields, which generally include round-trip transportation, breakfast or lunch, an English-speaking guide, and admission. **Gallipoli tours** leave daily, regardless of weather or group size; **Troy tours** only depart if there are enough people. While Gallipoli is best seen with a guided tour, Troy can easily by reached by *dolmuş*, and a self-tour allows more freedom and romantic imagination (you'll need plenty of it). Çanakkale-based **Ana-Tur**, Cumhuriyet Meydanı, Özay 30 İşhanı Kat. 2, (tel. 271 54 82 or 217 07 71), leaves from in front of Anzac House in Çanakkale around 10am. Anzac House sells tickets for $14; Yellow Rose Pension sells tickets for the same tour (under a different name) for $17. The cheaper **Down Under Travel Agency**, İsmetpaşa Mah., 14 Atatürk Cad. (tel. 814 24 31), operates out of nearby Eceabat.

BATTLEFIELDS OF GALLIPOLI (GELIBOLU)

If you want to visit on your own, take a ferry from Çanakkale to **Eceabat** *(every hr. 6am-midnight, in winter every 2hr.; 60¢). From Eceabat, take a dolmuş to the* **Kabatep Müzesi.** *Tel. 814 12 97. Open daily 8:30am-noon and 1-5:30pm. Admission $0.75.*

The strategic position of the Gallipoli Peninsula on the Dardanelles made it the site of one of the most catastrophic Allied offensives in WWI. According to a plan proposed by Britain's young First Lord of the Admiralty, **Winston Churchill**, the Allies could conquer Constantinople, drive Turkey out of the war, and open communications with Russia attacking at this spot. Eighty thousand Turks and more than 200,000 soldiers of the British Empire—including a disproportionate sacrifice by the Australian-New Zealand Army Corps (ANZAC)—lost their lives in the hideous, entrenched stalemate in December 1915. This battle launched its hero, **Atatürk**, on a rapid rise toward his status as Turkey's founding father. Each year, thousands of Aussies and Kiwis make pilgrimages to Gallipoli's war cemeteries, and April 25, the date of the Allied landing, is an important day of remembrance Down Under. The battle sights and accompanying memorials are spread out, so your best bet is to take an organized tour.

TRUVA (TROY)

32km south of Çanakkale. In summer, Troy-bound **dolmuş** *leave from the Çanakkale lot M-Sa every 30min. until dark (75¢). On Su, evenings, and in winter, take the Ezine* **minibus** *from the otogar or Atatürk Cad. to the intersection with the Troy road (20km; 50¢). From there, it's a relatively flat 5km walk. Site and Excavation House open daily in summer 8:30am-7:30pm; in winter, spring, and fall 8am-5pm. Admission to both $2.50, students $1.25.*

For the casual visitor with no romantic attachment to Homer ("The Face That Launched a Thousand Quips"), Troy's jumbled, partially excavated ruins may well prove a disappointment. People raised on stories of the Trojan War should not expect imposing ruins—the city Homer wrote about came tumbling down 3000 years ago. When Heinrich Schliemann rediscovered Troy in the 1880s, it had been a ghost town for at least 13 centuries. The site is confusing and not immediately striking to the imagination, a situation hardly improved by the hokey wooden horse and academic dryness of the displays in the excavation house. The site's presentation focuses more on what people ate or how they made pottery than on the quasi-historical legacy of Homer, who was quite a storyteller but not exactly a stickler for details. Troy offers extensive ruins of unmatched significance; nine distinct strata contain the remains of different cities that stood here, dubbed Troy I (from 3200 BCE) through Troy IX. The city of Homer's *Iliad* is now believed to be Troy VI, not Troy II, the city Schliemann excavated. An illustrated explanation of each stratum is available in the Excavation House (on your right after passing the horse). Look out for house foundations, city walls, a temple, and a theater.

AEGEAN COAST

Fabulous classical ruins and a sinuous coastline concealing sublime beaches have helped transform Turkey's once-tranquil Aegean coast into an increasingly popular destination. Framed by 5000-year-old mythology and history, the region's intensely rich culture is an eyeful for photographers, archaeologists, nature-lovers, and hedonistic nomads alike. Hellenistic ruins—especially extensive at Pergamon, Ephesus, Aphrodisias, and Pamukkale—stand as weathered testaments to the coast's glorious heritage.

İZMİR

İzmir, formerly ancient **Smyrna** (reputed to be the birthplace of Homer), has risen from the rubble of the 1922 Turkish War of Independence to become Turkey's third-largest city. Due to İzmir's sheer size, many travelers find themselves here for a bus transfer or even an overnight stay en route to the Aegean coast's more impressive sights. The city is only worth a more extended visit between June and August, when it hosts the **International İzmir Festival,** attracting world-renowned musical, dance, and theater performers.

🖪 **ORIENTATION AND PRACTICAL INFORMATION.** İzmir's principal boulevards radiate from roundabouts, called *meydan*. **Cumhuriyet Meydanı,** on the waterfront, is the city's financial center. Many budget hotels and inexpensive restaurants, along with several bus company offices and the **Basmane train station,** are located around **9 Eylül Meydanı,** the center of the Basmane district. To get to the city center and to Basmane from the **Yeni Garaj,** İzmir's new intercity bus station, take bus #601 to its end on **Sehit Fethibey Bulvarı** in museum-laden **Konak** or bus #605 to Basmane. Alternatively, walk the short distance from Konak to Basmane.

Airport Adnan Menderes, 20km south of İzmir, connects Turkey to major European cities and other cities in Turkey. Take the Havaş bus from the tourist office (45min., every hr., $2.50). **Turkish Airlines,** 1/F Gazi Osman Paşa (airport office tel. 274 24 24 or 274 28 00; ticket office tel. 484 12 20; reservations tel. 425 82 80), just up from the tourist office, runs flights to **Istanbul** and **Ankara** (both $75, students $63; open daily 8am-5:30pm). Intercity bus destinations include: **Ankara** (8hr., every 30min., $12.50); **Antalya** (8hr., every hr., $12.50); **Bodrum** (4hr., every 30min., $7); **Bursa** (5hr., every 30min., $7.50); **Istanbul** (9hr., every 30min., $15); **Kuşadası** (1½hr., every 30min., $3); and **Marmaris** (5hr., every hr., $8.75). To get to **Selçuk,** take a Bodrum or Kuşadası bus and ask to be let off (1hr., $2.50). A number of **banks** have offices along the waterfront. **Telephone code:** 232.

🖪 **ACCOMMODATIONS AND FOOD.** Head for 9 Eylül Meydanı and don't look back. 🖪**Hotel Oba,** 1369 Sok. No. 27 (tel. 441 96 05/6; fax 483 81 98), four blocks west of 9 Eylül Meydanı (away from the train station), has a rare combination of cheap, clean lodgings and great amenities, including a lobby bar. Each room has a private bath, TV, and air conditioning. (Singles $12; doubles $16. Breakfast included.) **Güzel İzmir Hotel,** 1368 Sok. No. 8 (tel. 483 50 69), offers clean rooms at budget prices, all with private showers. There's luggage storage, a TV room, and a public phone in the lobby. (Singles $7.50; doubles $15; triples $21.) A display case at the front of **Basmane Kebap Salonu,** 157/A Fevzipaşa Bul. (tel. 425 50 19), on the dead-end leading to the train station, holds the meats from which you create a fantasy *şiş* mix ($2.80-3.50). Ask for the specialty, *içli köfte* (meatballs with deep-fried batter, 50¢ each; open daily 11am-midnight). **Güzel İzmir Lokantaları,** 1368 Sok. No. 8/B (tel. 445 05 31), at the Basmane end of the 1369 Sok., is the best *lokanta* in the vicinity, offering an excellent selection of eight traditional dishes in a clean setting (*mousaka* and other meat dishes $1.50, vegetable dishes $1).

PERGAMON (BERGAMA)

Pergamon gazes across the river at the modern town of Bergama. It can easily be visited as a daytrip from Çanakkale, İzmir, Bursa, or Kuşadası. Buses run directly to Bergama from: İzmir (1½hr., 2 per hr., $2.75); Ankara (9hr., 10:30pm, $13.75); and Istanbul (9hr., 11pm, $15). Acropolis and Asclepion open daily in summer 8:30am-7pm; in winter 8:30am-5:30pm. Admission to each $2.50, students $1.25.

A dazzling center of cultural activity in antiquity, Pergamon was once the capital of the Roman province of Asia and had one of the two largest libraries in the ancient

---

BLACK, WHITE, AND READ WITH ENVY In ancient times, only the **Great Library of Alexandria** (see p. 130) surpassed Pergamon's, which contained over 200,000 volumes in repositories all over the city. So great was Alexandria's jealousy of the Pergamenes' literary hoard that they made what they thought was a brilliant strategic move: they limited the flow of Egyptian papyrus to Pergamon. The Pergamenes countered by writing all subsequent volumes on parchment pages made from goat hide, an exponentially more durable, manageable medium. The scheming Alexandrians were foiled only temporarily. After the Alexandrian library burned down, **Marc Antony** and his boys plundered Pergamon's shelves and presented the pilfered publications, as a token of his love, to Cleopatra to replace the charred editions. In 640 CE, the ill-fated collection was put to the torch by the **Caliph Omar:** if the books agreed with the Qu'ran, Omar argued, they were superfluous, and if they disagreed with the Qu'ran, they were heretical and fit for combustion.

---

world. The ruins of this great Hellenistic and Roman city dominate the top of the hill, while buildings from later eras, when the city's stature and importance declined, cling lower down at the hill's feet. Pergamon traces its roots back to the Aeolian Greeks, who built a settlement here in the 9th century BCE. The city was beautified by Philataeros, a successor of Alexander the Great, but all his work was undone by an earthquake in the 2nd century CE and subsequent kicks to the proverbial stomach from various ancient conquerors.

From the river (near the Pension Athena), cross the bridge and head up the hill through the old town. Follow the paved road until you come upon a gate, and take the path to the right of the gate (which eventually turns into a stone-paved road) up to the temples and marble ruins of the **Acropolis** looming over the city. On your way up, take in the breathtaking view of the Hellenistic **theater** that once seated 10,000. Farther up, try to land three coins on top of the column inside the **wishing well** for good luck. Follow the yellow signs from Atatürk Meydanı on the west side of town to reach the famed **Asclepion,** an ancient healing center where the foremost doctor of the ancient world, Galen (born in Pergamon), once worked. A marble colonnade, theater, and healing rooms remain visible today. Near the river and the old part of Bergama stand the remnants of **Kızıl Avlu,** a pagan temple that

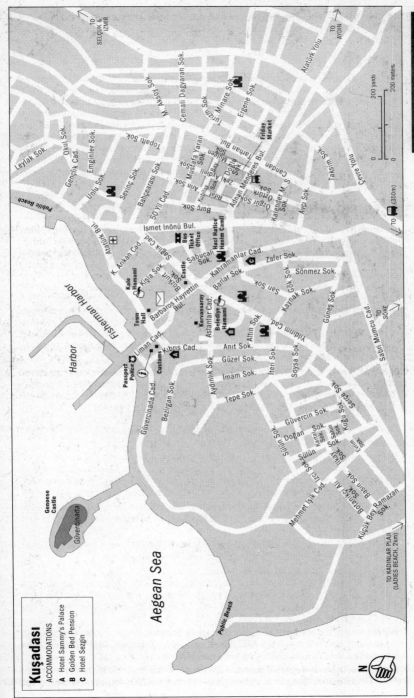

TURKEY

Kuşadası
ACCOMMODATIONS
A Hotel Sammy's Palace
B Golden Bed Pension
C Hotel Sezgin

Aegean Sea

Genoese Castle
Güvercinada

Fisherman Harbor
Harbor

Public Beach

Public Beach

TO KADINLAR PLAJI
(LADIES BEACH, 2km)

N

became one of the Seven Churches of the Apocalypse mentioned in the Book of Revelations—"this is where Satan has his altar" (Rev. 2:3).

KUŞADASI

Named for the pigeons that make their home in the town's 14th-century Genoese castle, Kuşadası ("Bird Island") transformed a few decades ago from a quiet town to a grand resort, thanks to its picturesque setting on sea-sloping hills and excellent sandy beaches, as well as its proximity to the magnificent archaeological wonders at Ephesus and Selçuk. Kuşadası's broad tourist apparatus accommodates every group: backpackers arrive by ferry from the Greek island of Samos and by bus from the north, while wealthy Americans and Europeans flood the carpet shops whenever their luxury cruise liners dock in the small harbor. Excellent budget hotels and towering luxury palaces are surrounded by myriad high-end jewelry and carpet shops, and reputedly over 100 pubs dot the city.

☒ ORIENTATION AND PRACTICAL INFORMATION

The duty-free shop, tourist office, and customs office are all in the port area. **Dolmuş** depart from a separate *dolmuş* stop on **Adnan Menderes Bulvarı**, about 1½km southeast of the intersection of **Atatürk Bulvarı** and **İnönü Bulvarı**, two of the main streets. **Kıbrıs Caddesi** runs uphill and inland from the tourist office, passing an ancient **kervansaray** and a covered bazaar. On the other side of the *kervansaray*, the broad, pedestrian-only **Barbaros Hayrettin Paşa Bulvarı** is home to the PTT, travel agencies, and several banks.

Airplanes: Airport Adnan Menderes, 20km south of İzmir, connects Turkey to most major European cities. Take the Havaş bus from the tourist office (45min., every hr., $2.50). **Turkish Airlines** sales office, 1/F Gazi Osman Paşa (tel. 484 12 20, reservations 425 82 80; fax 483 62 81), just up from the tourist office. Open daily 8am-5:30pm. To **Istanbul** and **Ankara** both $75, students $63.

Buses: The *garaj* is on Kahramanlar Sok., 2km south of the town center. Most hotels will either provide or pay for transportation from the *garaj*. To: **Ankara** (9hr., 4 per day 8:30am-7:30pm, $15); **Antalya** (7hr., 12:30 and 11pm, $12); **Bodrum** (2½hr., 4 per day 8:30am-7:30pm, $6); **Fethiye** (5½hr., 9:30am, $12); **Istanbul** (9hr., 6 per day 9:30-11:15pm, $18); **İzmir** (1½hr., every hr. 6am-9pm, $3); **Konya** (8hr., 11:15am and 7pm, $12); **Marmaris** (4hr., 9:30am, $9.50); and **Pamukkale** (3½hr.; 8:45am, returns 5pm; $7). Call ahead for bus tickets on weekends.

Dolmuş: Intercity *dolmuş* depart from a stop on Adnan Menderes Bul., about 1½km southeast of the intersection of Atatürk Bul. and İnönü Bul. To: **Selçuk** (20 min., every 15min. 6:30am-11:30pm, $1) via **Ephesus** (ask to be let off). City *dolmuş* run between the *dolmuş* stop on Adnan Menderes Bul. and the lot adjacent to the *garaj*.

Ferries: Ekol Travel (see **Travel Agencies,** below) beats the official rate. Port taxes ($10) are included in the ticket price. To: **Samos, Greece** (in summer daily 8:30am and 4:30pm; in winter 2 per week).

Tourist Office: 13 Liman Cad. (tel. 614 11 03; fax 614 62 95), at the corner of Liman Cad. and Güvercin Ada Sok. Open M-F 8am-noon and 1:30-5:30pm.

Travel Agencies: Ekol Travel with **WorldSpan,** Kıbrıs Cad., 9/1 Buyral Sok. (tel. 614 92 55 or 614 55 91; fax 614 26 44). Cheap flights, ferry tickets, temporary baggage storage, help finding accommodations, message board, car rentals, and emergency aid finding English-speaking doctors. Flash *Let's Go* for a 15% discount on ferry tickets. Open daily May-Nov. 8:30am-10pm; Dec.-Apr. 8:30am-5:30pm.

Banks: Several dot the waterfront area. **Türkiye İş Bankası,** on the corner of Atatürk Bul. and Liman Cad., offers a 24hr. **ATM** (Cirrus, Visa, MC). **Koç Bank,** by the police station on Atatürk Bul., has an **ATM** linked to Visa and MC.

English Bookstores: Kuydaş Kitabevi, 8/B İnönü Bul. (tel. 614 18 28; fax 614 26 83), sells newspapers, magazines, guidebooks, and novels. Open daily 9am-midnight. **Art**

Kitabevi, 57 Sağlık Cad. (tel. 614 64 54), near the intersection of Sağlık Cad. and Barbaros Cad., has cheaper used books and postcards. Open until 12:30am.

Hamam: Kaleıçı Hamamı (tel. 614 12 92), behind the PTT. Bath and massage $20; drink included. Half-price for guests of Hotel Sammy's Palace.

Police: (tel. 614 53 50), on Hükümet Cad. Finds translators in emergencies. **Tourist Police:** 6 Atatürk Bul. (tel. 614 10 22), past the *kervansaray.*

Hospital: Kuşadası Devlet Hastanesı, 30 Atatürk Bul. (tel. 614 10 26 or 614 16 14; fax 612 24 38), on the waterfront, at the northern edge of town. Little English spoken.

PTT: (tel. 614 10 22 or 614 15 79), next to the *kervansaray,* up Barbaros Hayrettin Paşa Bul. from the sea. Open daily 7am-11pm. **Phones** available 24hr. **Currency exchange** open 8am-midnight.

Telephone Code: 256.

ACCOMMODATIONS

Most of the budget accommodations are along Kıbrıs and Aslanlar Cad.

Hotel Sammy's Palace, 14 Kıbrıs Cad. (tel. 612 25 88 or (532) 274 21 29; fax 612 99 91; email sammy@superonline.com). There's no better option in Kuşadası. Run by the amiable and increasingly famous Salman "Sammy" Kurt. Spotless, well-decorated rooms all with balcony and bath. Laundry $2 per kg. Half price at *hamam* Kaleıçı Hamamı (see above). Internet access $4 per hr. Free transportation to and from Ephesus. Roof $3; dorms $5; singles $8; doubles $12. Sammy will pay for your cab fare from the *garaj.* Beware of Sammy impostors at the *garaj* and ferry docks.

The Golden Bed Pansiyon (tel./fax 614 87 08), off Aslanlar Cad. Though marked by signs, this *pansiyon* is somewhat hard to find. Owner Hasan "Mr. Happy" Değirmenci always seems to be smiling. Rooms have private bath; some have balconies too. Free transportation to and from the *garaj* and Ephesus. Laundry $3 per kg. *Hamam* half price. Rooms $6 per person. Breakfast included.

Hotel Sezgin, 15 Kahramlar Cad., Zafer Sok. (tel. 614 42 25; fax 614 64 89; email sezgin@ispro.net.tr). A comfortable atmosphere minutes away from the town center. Clean rooms with bath, 24hr. hot water, central heating, and satellite TV. Laundry $2.50 per kg. Internet access $3 per hr. Lounge and bar area. Singles $8; doubles $18; triples $28. Breakfast $2; BBQ dinner $3.

FOOD

Çınaraltı Restaurant (tel. 614 33 32 or 614 62 81). Take the *dolmuş* heading to Selçuk and ask to be let off at Çınaraltı. Serves exceptional Turkish fare ranging from *pancar salatası* (beet-root salad, $1) to various fish and meat dishes, including their specialty, *Çoban Kavurma* (a mixture of grilled meats, $3.20).

Avlu Restaurant (tel. 614 79 95), the 1st left off Barbaros Hayrettin Paşa Bul. A favorite among locals, this *lokanta* serves inexpensive, fresh meals. Large selection of vegetarian entrees ($1). Meat dishes $1.50-2.

Sammy's Kebap House and Cafe, 1 Hitit Sun Pasaji, Kıbrıs Cad., Buyraı Sok. (tel. 612 60 42), near the waterfront. Choose from various *kebaps* ($1.50) and sandwiches. Vegetarians can snack on one of their many omelette options ($2-3). Open 8am-1am.

Seyhan Restaurant, 63 Sağlık Cad. (tel. 614 79 85). Sunny restaurant with a friendly staff and a menu in 4 languages. Huge, *grand, groß, büyük* selection. Ask for the *sebzeli güveç,* a vegetable stew not listed on the menu. Open noon-midnight.

ENTERTAINMENT

The nighttime music and madness of the appropriately named **Barlar Sokak** ("bars street") gushes out for blocks, drizzling onto side streets like **Tuna Sokak,** where roofless bars with live European and Turkish bands are the norm. The killer combination of dozens of discos and no weekday cover charge makes club hopping easier than standing still. **Heaven** (tel. 613 24 56), on Tuna Sok., is one of the larger and more popular clubs. Decorated in a mock-Roman style with vines and a columned entrance, Heaven offers live Turkish pop in its inner courtyard weekend nights (Sa cover $7, 1 drink included). Those of a more secular ilk can pass on Heaven and pop on over to **Ecstasy** (tel. 612 81 90), a disco with sleek decor and plenty of polished steel that plays house and soul with occasional live music (free).

👁 SIGHTS

Kuşadası's best known sights are its shopping areas and its clean (but crowded) beaches. Contrary to the claims of the carpet and jewelry store owners, the **Grand Bazaar** and **Barbaros Hayrettin Paşa Bul.** are expensive places to shop, but browsing's always free. Kuşadası also hosts the **Kuşadası Music Festival,** an annual contest during which Turkish pop bands vie for bubble-gum glory. For tourists, this means free concerts in the last week of June.

BEACHES AND ISLANDS. Kuşadası's beaches are clean and sandy, but everyone this side of the Aegean knows it. Head to the Mediterranean coast for more secluded sunbathing. **Kadınlar Plajı** (Ladies Beach), 3km from the city, is easily accessible by a 40¢ *dolmuş* ride (beach chairs $2, with umbrella $4). **Balcı Pension** (tel. 614 14 10; fax 614 17 30) offers **scuba** courses ($40). A trip to Kuşadası would be incomplete without a visit to **Güvercinada** (Pigeon Island), the jutting peninsula that Kuşadası's namesake birds call home. Roam around the 14th-century Genoese castle, which the Ottomans turned into a military outpost, and enjoy a glass of *çay* at the tea houses along the old lookout point.

DILEK NATIONAL PARK. Dilek National Park, 26km from Kuşadası, contains four beaches and over 30 animal species. While overnight camping is not permitted, Dilek offers daytime canyon hiking (6km from entrance gate), sandy beaches (**İçmeler Beach,** 1km from the gate), and sand-and-pebble shores (**Aydınlık Beach,** 5km from the gate; **Karvakı Beach,** 7km from the gate). Don't leave without seeing **Zeus Mağarası** (Zeus's Cave), a small cavern opposite the sea, 100m outside the park entrance. Once rumored as the site of hidden treasure, the cave is filled with water bubbling up from the ground. *(Open daily in peak season 8am-8pm; extended hours July-Aug.; off-season 8am-5pm. Canyon open Oct.-June. Admission $1.20 per person, $1.60 per motorcycle, $5 per car.)*

NEAR KUŞADASI

EFES (EPHESUS) ΕΦΕΣΟΣ

*The easiest way to visit Ephesus either from **Kuşadası** or **Selçuk** is to take advantage of the free shuttle service offered by hotels. You can also take a Selçuk-bound **dolmuş** from the Kuşadası otogar and tell the driver to stop at Ephesus (20min., $1). From the Selçuk otogar, take any dolmuş toward Kuşadası (5min., frequent in summer, $0.50). **Taxis** run from Selçuk to the site ($5). The site is also an easy **walk** from Selçuk. Tel. (232) 892 64 02. Open 8am-6pm. Admission $5, students free.*

The ancient traveler Pausanias deemed Ephesus "the most beautiful work ever created by humankind." Ephesus's glorious prosperity has not gone the way of other notable ancient cities: to this day, it boasts a concentration of classical art and architecture surpassed only by Rome and Athens. The ruins rank first among Turkey's ancient sites in terms of sheer size and state of preservation.

On the left, just before the site's main entrance, is the **Vedius Gymnasium**, built in 150 CE; beyond the vegetation are the horseshoe-shaped remains of the city's **stadium.** After the main entrance gate, the tree-shaded road leads straight ahead to the colonnaded **Arcadiane**, Ephesus' main drag. Uphill along the **Street of Curetes** or **Marble Road,** you'll see the imposing ruins of the **Temple of Hadrian** on the left. A little farther up the hill on the left are the ruins of the exquisite **Fountain of Trajan.** The building on the left as you walk up the ramp is the **Prytaneion**, dedicated to the worship of **Vesta,** which contained an eternal flame that was tended by **Vestal Virgins.** The road that runs by the top entrance (as opposed to the main one) leads to the **House of the Virgin Mary** (8km, 1-1½hr. walking), where, according to pious belief, she lived after leaving Jerusalem.

SELÇUK

> *Buses* run between Selçuk's otogar, at the intersection of Sabahattındede Cad. and the road just east of Atatürk Cad., and: **İzmir** *(every 30min., $2.50);* **Bodrum** *(3hr., every 30min., $6);* **Fethiye** *(5½hr., every 2hr., $11.25);* **Marmaris** *(4hr., every hr., $7.50);* **Istanbul** *(every hr., $17.50);* and **Ankara** *(9hr., 1 per day, $15).* **Minibuses** run between Selçuk and **Kuşadası** *(30min., every 30min., $1).* Ruins open 8:30am-5:30pm. Free. Museum open daily 8:30am-noon and 1-5:30pm. Admission $2.50, students free.

Although it lingers in the shadow of nearby Ephesus, Selçuk offers several notable archaeological sites of its own. The colossal **Basilica of Saint John** lies off Atatürk Cad. on the supposed site of St. John's grave, about 400m from the intersection with Sabahattındede Cad. The entrance to the Byzantine church is inaccurately called the Gate of Persecution, referring to a frieze believed to depict a Christian being thrown to a lion, though it actually shows Achilles slaying a lion. A few hundred meters down Sabahattındede Cad. in the opposite direction are the sad remains of the **Temple of Artemis,** one of the **seven wonders of the ancient world,** but now more of a washout. Once one of the largest temples in existence, it now consists of a lone reconstructed column twisting upwards from a bog that approximates the area of the temple's foundation. The stunning 14th-century **İsa Bey Camii** lies at the foot of the hill on which the Basilica of St. Johns and the Ayasoluk castle stand. Back in town, directly across from the tourist office, **Efes Müzesi** (Ephesus Museum) houses a world-class collection of recent finds from Ephesus.

PAMUKKALE (HIERAPOLIS)

Whether as modern Pamukkale ("Cotton Castle") or ancient Hierapolis ("Holy City"), this village has been drawing the weary and the curious to its thermal springs for more than 23 centuries. The Turkish name refers to the extraordinary surface of the shimmering, snow-white limestone, shaped over millennia by calcium-rich springs. Legend has it that the formations are actually solidified cotton (the area's principal crop) that giants left out to dry. Most of the terraces are currently under restoration; plans are in the works to open new calcium pools as early as the summer of 2000. In any case, the site remains impressive, even if it is not open for bathing. Overshadowed by natural wonders, Pamukkale's well-preserved Roman ruins and museum have gone unadvertised by travel agencies.

☑ ORIENTATION AND PRACTICAL INFORMATION

Pamukkale is roughly divided into two areas: **Pamukkale Köyü,** or village, is home to hotels and restaurants; the **Pamukkale site** contains the pools and the ruins of Hierapolis. The road to the tourist complex begins from the central square, curves around to the left (past bus company offices), and heads uphill to the site, tracing the course of an ancient road. It's also possible to ascend to the top of the deposits by climbing up the calcium mountain face starting from the main square.

Buses stop in the center of Pamukkale Köyü. Most direct buses come from **Selçuk** or **Kuşadası** (4½hr., 5-6 per day, $6), but the usual route is through **Denizli,** 22km to the south. **Dolmuş** run between Denizli and Pamukkale's main square (25min., every 30min. until 10pm, $1); Pamukkale pensions can arrange free pick-up from the Denizli *otogar.* Direct buses from Pamukkale rarely exist, despite claims to the contrary. At the top of the hill within the site gates are: the **PTT** (tel. 272 21 21; open daily 8:30am-7pm); **tourist office** (tel. 272 20 77; fax 272 28 82; open in summer daily 8:30am-7pm; in winter M-F 8:30am-5pm); and **tourist police** (tel. 272 29 09; open 24hr.). **Pharmacies** are down in the village. **Telephone code:** 258.

ACCOMMODATIONS AND FOOD

Both of these hotels have swimming pools filled with Pamukkale thermal water and offer free pickup from the Denizli bus station. **Koray Hotel,** 27 Fevzi Çakmak Cad. (tel. 272 23 00; fax 272 20 95), features bathtub-blessed rooms that face a beautiful inner courtyard. The rooftop bar/restaurant features the best breakfast ($2) and dinner ($5) buffets in town (singles $10; doubles $16; cheaper in winter). **Venüs Hotel** (tel. 272 21 52), on Namık Kemal Cad., screams newness with its well-appointed rooms worthy of a goddess, all with balconies and spotless private bathrooms (singles $8; doubles $13; triples $15; breakfast $2, dinner $5).

Most of the pensions serve better dinners than those available in town. The large buffet at the **Koray Hotel** is the best option. The outdoor dining at **Gürsoy Aile Restaurant** (tel. 272 22 67), on Atatürk Cad. in the center of Pamukkale Köyü, is tasteful in more ways than one. The special is *görsoy börek,* but salads ($1-2) and pasta dishes ($2) will satisfy vegetarians (open 8am-midnight). **Han Restaurant** (tel. 272 27 92), next to Gürsoy Aile, specializes in *kebap* dishes. Try the *saç kebap* ($3.60), appetizers ($1.70), or salads ($2; open 24hr.). Although Pamukkale's nightlife doesn't rage like the coast's, there are still some drinking and dancing dives. Try **Tiffany's,** 4 Şirin Sok. (tel. 272 22 57; open 6:30pm-2am), but not for breakfast.

SIGHTS

BATHS. A favorite getaway for vacationing Romans almost two millennia ago, the warm baths at Pamukkale still bubble away. Elegant, shallow pools at the top of the hill gradually deepen farther down the slope, while the center of the formation is graced with intricately shaped terraces. All pools are now off-limits to public bathing due to overuse, but small walkways leading down the slope still allow barefoot visitors to touch the thermal waters. Don't leave Pamukkale without a savory dip in the **Sacred Spring** at the Pamukkale Motel, the only place where you can still swim in the warm, fizzy waters. On the pool's floor rest remains of Roman columns, toppled by the earthquake that created the spring. *(Ancient site open 24hr. Admission $3, students free. Sacred Spring open daily 8am-8pm. Admission $4 for 2hr.)*

RUINS OF HIERAPOLIS. Carved into the side of the mountain, the enormous **Grand Theater** is one of the best-preserved in Turkey; many carved stage decorations and much of the 25,000-person seating area remain intact. In front of the theater are the lesser preserved remains of the 3rd-century **Temple of Apollo** and the **nymphaeum,** a fountain temple dedicated to those frisky nymphs. Ancient priests performed rituals at the nearby **Plutonium** (a.k.a. *Cin Deliği* or "Devil's Hole"), a pit emitting toxic carbonic acid gas. After demonstrating the hole's potency by killing off a couple birds, the priests would duck inside while holding their breath, then reemerge having supposedly made a trip to the underworld. Down the road to Karahayıt are the north **city gate,** the ruins of a 5th-century Christian **basilica** dedicated to St. Philip (martyred here 1000 years ago), and a **necropolis,** holding some 1200 tombs and sarcophagi. These plots were prime real estate; it was believed that proximity to the hot springs and vapor-emitting cracks would ease one's trip to the underworld. *(Located behind the Pamukkale Motel.)*

NEAR PAMUKKALE: GEYRE (APHRODISIAS)

Perfect for a daytrip from Pamukkale. Buses leave daily at 10am and return at 5pm (2hr., round-trip $6.50. Site open daily in summer 8:30am-7:30pm; in winter 8:30am-5pm. Museum open daily in summer 8:30am-6pm; in winter 8:30am-5pm. Admission to site and museum $2.40, students free.

The ruins of Aphrodisias are still very much under excavation, but some archaeologists predict that they will eclipse Ephesus in grandeur after another 50 to 60 years. Ancient Greeks came here to pay respects to the goddess of love, **Aphrodite,** and ask for her blessing. Aphrodisias was well-known as a center for astronomy, medicine, and mathematics, but above all as a showcase for sculpture chiseled

TURKEY

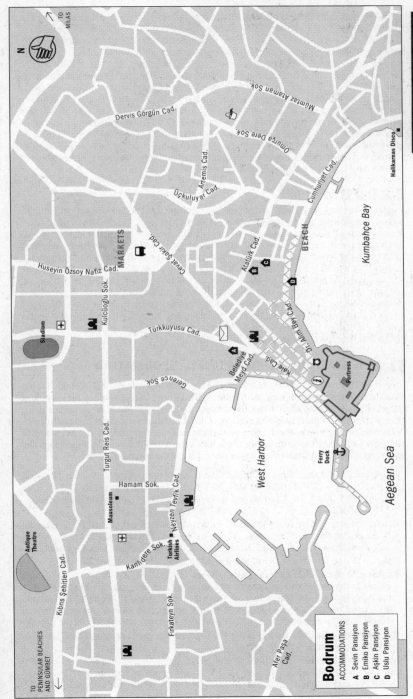

N

TO
MILAS

Dervis Görgün Cad.

Mumtaz Ataman Sok.

Omurca Dere Sok.

Artemis Cad.

Üçkuluyar Cad.

Cevat Şakir Cad.

MARKETS

Huseyin Özsoy Nafız Cad.

Kulcüoğlu Sok.

Türkkuyusu Cad.

Gerence Sok.

Belediye
Meyd Cad.

Stadium

Atatürk Cad.

Cumhuriyet Cad.

Halikarnas Disco

Kumbahçe Bay

BEACH

Dr. Alım Bey Cad.

Kale Cad.

Fortress

West Harbor

Ferry
Dock

Aegean Sea

Turgut Reis Cad.

Hamam Sok.

Mausoleum

Neyzen Tevfik Cad.

Turkish
Airlines

Kamı çere Sok.

Kıbrıs Şehitlen Cad.

Antique
Theatre

TO PENINSULAR BEACHES
AND GÜMBET

Fırkateyn Sok.

Afer Paşa
Cad.

Bodrum
ACCOMMODATIONS
A Sevin Pansiyon
B Emiko Pansiyon
C Aşkın Pansiyon
D Uslu Pansiyon

from the famed white and bluish-gray marble quarried in the nearby foothills. The highlights of a visit to Aphrodisias are the three magnificent structures located at the back of the site. The soaring Ionic columns of the **Temple of Aphrodite** mark the original home of a famous statue of the goddess. Sculpted nearly 2000 years ago, the statue was similar in appearance to the many-breasted Artemis of Ephesus. So far, only copies of the original have been unearthed. The grand **tetrapylon,** the gateway into the ancient city, has elegant spiral-fluted Corinthian columns and floral reliefs on its pediment. Its name, which means "four gateways" in Greek, refers to the four rows of four columns that comprise the structure. The ancient 30,000 seat **stadium** is one of the most intact ever excavated. Even the marble blocks that once marked the starting line for foot races remain in the central arena. The new **museum,** located near the site entrance, displays an impressive collection of Roman-era sculpture. Among the highlights are the large statues of Aphrodite, her priests, and a satyr carrying the child Dionysus.

BODRUM

Before it became the "Bedroom of the Mediterranean," the ancient city of Halicarnassus was known for Herodotus, the "father of history," and the 4th-century BCE Mausoleum of Haicarnassus. The latter's tomb was so magnificent that it was declared one of the Seven Wonders of the Ancient World, and the king's memory lives on in the word "mausoleum." A saying goes that we all have a bit (or more) of Bodrum in us. While Bodrum's night scene is the most notorious in Turkey, the surrounding Acadian Peninsula is famous for its silica beaches, lush forests, secluded swimming coves, and ancient ruins. As multitudes of Turkish jetsetters, international yachtsmen, backpackers, and package tourists attest, it's easy to get sucked into Bodrum's daily rhythm of sun, shopping, sight-seeing, and water sports—but all of these relatively innocent activities are a mere prelude to the bacchanalian delights that begin once night falls.

■ ORIENTATION AND PRACTICAL INFORMATION

Streets in Bodrum are poorly marked. The city's most prominent and easily recognizable landmark is the central **Castle of St. Peter** *(kale)*, from which several streets radiate. From the castle, **Cumhuriyet Caddesi,** the main commercial drag, runs along the beach, twisting slightly inland to allow room for a small beach before returning to the sea. Ferries and yacht cruises depart from the breakwater and **Kale Caddesi,** which runs from the left of the castle and ends at a mosque. The ever-popular **Atatürk Caddesi** stems to the right off **Cevat Şakir Caddesi.**

Airplanes: The **Bodrum Airport** is about 30min. out of town. Buses to the airport depart from the *otogar* ($4). **Turkish Airlines,** 208 Neyzen Tevfik Cad. (tel. 313 31 72). Open daily 8am-5:30pm. To: **Istanbul** and **Ankara** (both 1hr.; 4 per day 6:10am-9:15am; $70, students with ID $61). International flights go through Istanbul.

Buses: The *otogar* is on Cevat Şakir Cad. To: **Antalya** (8hr.; 4 per day; $12-13); **Istanbul** (12hr., 6 per day, $19-26); **İzmir** (4hr., 2am-6pm, $7); **Kuşadası** (2½hr., 2am-6pm, $6); **Pamukkale** (5hr.; 8:30, 10:30am, 3:30pm; $7); and **Selçuk** (3hr., 2am-6pm, $6).

Dolmuş: Depart from the *otogar* to **Marmaris** (3hr., every hr. 7am-8pm, $6).

Ferries and Hydrofoils: Bodrum Express Lines (tel. 316 40 67; fax 313 00 77) has offices in the *otogar* and near the castle. All ferries and hydrofoils run from the end of the jetty May-Sept. To: **Marmaris** (2hr.; Th and Su 8am, return 5:30pm; $24, round-trip $29, open return $39) and Greek islands such as **Kos** and **Rhodes.** Arrive at the jetty 30min. early for passport check. Call for schedule; it changes depending on the season.

Car and Moped Rentals: Botur Agency (tel. 313 90 52), on Cevat Şakir Cad. Cars $36-96 per day, mopeds $14-72 per day.

Tourist Office: 48 Barış Meydanı (tel. 316 10 91; fax 316 76 94), at the foot of the cas-tle. Pension information and room listings. Free brochures with maps. Open Apr.-Oct. daily 9am-8pm; Nov.-Mar. M-F 8am-noon and 1-5pm.

Travel Agencies: Botur, 24/A Cevat Şakir Cad. (tel 316 90 52; fax 316 82 08). Bus trips to: **Pamukkale** and **Ephesus** (2 days, 1 night in a 4-star hotel included; W and Sa 7:30am; $45); and a **village tour** (daily 11am, $8). Office open 9am-10:30pm.

Consulate: U.K. (tel. 316 70 51), Tepecik. Open M-Sa 8:30am-5:30pm.

Currency Exchange: Türkiye İş Bankası (tel. 316 10 12), on Cevat Şakır Cad., halfway between the *otogar* and the castle. Open M-F 9am-12:30pm and 1:30-5:30pm. Most of the exchange booths by the harbor on Kale Cad. and Cumhuriyet Cad. do not charge commission. **ATMs** located throughout the shopping areas and at the PTT.

Bookstores: A 24hr. **book fair** is on Cumhuriyet Cad. Open from late June-Aug.

Laundromat: Many on Türkkuyusu Cad., Cevat Şakir Cad., and Atatürk Cad. $4 per load. Most open daily 8am-10pm.

Hamam: (tel. 316 11 59). Walk inland on Cevat Şakir Cad., turn right onto Atatürk Cad., and turn left at the sign for the *hamam*. Open for men Su-Tu and Th-F 8:30am-6pm, W and Sa 8:30am-noon; for women W and Sa noon-6pm. Admission $6.

Police: 50 Barış Meydanı (tel. 316 10 04), at the foot of the castle, next to the tourist office. Open 24hr. **Emergency Police:** Tel. 316 12 15.

Hospital: Bodrum Devlet Hastanesi (tel. 313 14 20/21-27), Kıbrıs Şehitleri Cad. uphill from the amphitheater. Public. Open 24hr. **Private Bodrum Hospital** (tel. 313 65 66). Walk inland on Cevat Şakir Cad., take a left onto Artemis Sok., turn left onto Kulcuoğlu Sok., take the 3rd right, and then make the 1st right. English spoken. Open 24hr.

Pharmacies: Especially prevalent on Cumhuriyet Cad., Cevat Şakir Cad., and Atatürk Cad. All open daily 8:30am-8pm. All post the nighttime on-duty pharmacy, or call 118 to find out which one is open 24hr. that day.

Internet Access: Palmiye Internet Cafe (tel. 313 91 84; fax 313 91 81; email palmiye1@efes.net.tr), on Neyzen Tevfik Cad. From the mosque in front of the castle, walk along Neyzen Tevfik Cad. for 300m; the cafe is on the right. $3 per hr. Open M-Sa 10am-midnight, Su noon-midnight.

PTT: (tel. 316 12 12), Cevat Şakir Cad., 4 blocks from the *otogar* (heading towards the castle). Poste Restante, international phone, fax service. Open daily 8:30am-midnight.

Telephone Code: 252.

ACCOMMODATIONS

Finding a bedroom in the "Bedroom of the Mediterranean" is easy (pensions are plentiful) but requires advance planning. Single travelers should call ahead in the summer. Cheap pensions cluster behind the bank right of the castle as you face inland. There are also some finds off Türkkuyusu Sok. and on Atatürk Cad.

Emiko Pansiyon, Atatürk Cad., 11 Uslu Sok. (tel./fax 316 55 60). From the *otogar*, follow Cevat Şakir Cad. toward the castle and turn left onto Atatürk Cad. After 50m, turn right down the alley plastered with signs. Turn right on the street after Taşlık Sok. Peaceful *pansiyon* with tidy rooms, some with hardwood floors and bath. Guest kitchen. Break-fast $2, laundry $3. $8-10 per person.

Uslu Pension, 35 Cumhuriyet Cad. (tel. 313 68 46). Bar Street pension with bright rooms, lush plants in the hallways, great views of the sea, and communal bathrooms. Ask for a room in the back if you want quiet. $7 per person.

Aşkin Pansiyon (tel. 313 31 67). From the *otogar*, follow Cevat Şakir Cad. toward the castle, turn left onto Atatürk Cad., right down a passageway about 20m past the sign for Emiko, then left down a corridor with the *pansiyon's* yellow sign. Has a terrace with a splendid view of the sea and rooms with bath. $8 per person; off-season $4.

TURKEY

Sevin Pansiyon (tel. 316 76 82), on the left side of Türkkuyusu Cad. when heading inland. Modern rooms with comfortable mattresses and unique carved doors. Most rooms with bath. Laundry $3. $8 per person; off-season $4.

🍴 FOOD

Cheap eats in Bodrum consist of the usual *kebap* stands and the small cafeteria-style joints on Cevat Şakir Cad. Steaming corn on the cob (50¢) is sold from small carts along the main streets, and wherever you turn, the doughy beginnings of fresh pizzas ($4-6) are being tossed in the air.

Tarçın (tel. 313 87 50). Turn onto Atatürk Cad. from Cevat Şakir Cad. and make a left into the 2nd alleyway. Serves sumptuous homemade dishes ($2-9) that change according to the owner's creative whims and the day's market selection. Open M-F 8am-6pm.

06 Lokanta, 115 Cumhuriyet Cad. (tel. 316 83 83), near the 24hr. book fair. A popular meeting spot in the hub of the Cumhuriyet Cad.'s action. Savory Turkish cuisine in an elegant atmosphere. Many vegetarian options, like the excellent vegetable soup ($2), and a variety of fresh hot dishes ($4-5). Open 24hr.

Golden Gate (tel. 313 11 32). From Cevat Şakir Cad., turn left onto Atatürk Cad; it's 300m on the left. Friendly and relaxed atmosphere where devoted regulars sip the cheapest beers in Bodrum (50¢). Entrees come with soup, bread, starters, salad, potatoes, vegetable, rice, and fresh fruit ($4-8). Did we mention they've got the cheapest beers in Bodrum? Open daily 9am-3am.

Shirley Valentine (tel. 313 07 10), on Atatürk Cad. Eclectic decor of funky proportions: Turkish carpets on colorful walls, plastic aliens in iron candelabras, and twinkling white lights. After dinner, smoke a *nargile* in a corner filled with soft rugs and pillows. Starters $1.50-3; veggie omelette $4; Shirley Valentine Special Chicken Dinner $7. Open 24hr.

🎵 ENTERTAINMENT

Bodrum, a.k.a. the "Bedroom," is a wild flesh-pot whose excesses seem to bring out everyone's extremes. Loud, exciting discos and calm, sophisticated bars are merely the foreplay to what happens later. All of the following hotspots are on Cumhuriyet Cad. For a taste of wild Turkey, hop over the western ridge of Bodrum to Gümbet, where more discos and bars glitter in the night (30min. walk or 10min. *dolmuş* ride; *dolmuş* leave the *otogar* every 10min., 40¢).

Halikarnas Disco, Z. Müren Cad. at the end of Cumhuriyet Cad., 1½km from the center of town. This famed open-air disco sparkles with flashy opulence and impeccable service. The dress-to-be-scene clientele makes serious moves under the gaze of spectators who pay to sit in the VIP seats. Hourly shows, great music, and a celebrity-style entrance tunnel make this club *the* Bodrum experience. $16 cover charge. Beer $3; cocktails $6.

Hadi Gari (tel. 313 80 97). Set right next to the luminous castle, the oldest disco in Bodrum fuses classy elegance and funkiness. Stylish customers dance in a pagan-like trance on the large outdoor dance floor. Others recline on plush rose and silver cushions in the softly lit interior. Beer $2.40; *rakı* $3.60; cocktails $4-8. Restaurant by "day" (6pm-midnight), dance club by night (midnight-4am).

Greenhouse (tel. 313 09 11). A much-favored alternative dance bar where customers write their names on the walls in fluorescent paint and hang their T-shirts on the ceiling. Excellent international and Turkish DJs. Everyone seems to end up here at some point. Beer $1.80; *rakı* $3; cocktails $5. Open daily midnight-5am.

Karşı (tel. (532) 256 44 17). Sexy bartenders and an attractive clientele make for a sultry evening of come-hither glances. Bar dispenses underground, jazz, blues, and mixed pop plus beer ($2.40), *rakı* ($3), and cocktails ($4-8). Open daily 10am-5am.

👁 SIGHTS

RUINS OF HALICARNASSUS. Despite what everyone says about the nightlife, the ruins of ancient Halicarnassus are Bodrum's most noteworthy attraction. Unfortu-

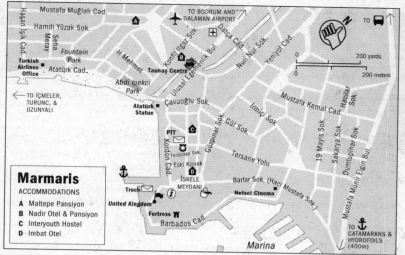

Marmaris

ACCOMMODATIONS

A Maltepe Pansiyon
B Nadir Otel & Pansiyon
C Interyouth Hostel
D Imbat Otel

nately, most of the remains were either destroyed, buried beneath the modern town of Bodrum, or shipped to London's British Museum. The old **city walls** and the large but uninspiring remains of the **theater** are still partly visible. The **Mausoleum,** one of the **seven wonders of the ancient world,** once rose to a height of 50m, but Crusaders demolished the structure to fortify the Castle of St. Peter (see below). Covered with a pyramidal roof, the mausoleum was crowned by a statue of Mausolus driving a chariot drawn by four horses. Today the mausoleum site houses a small porch with reconstructions of the mausoleum's friezes and an open-air museum with columnar fragments. *(To reach the theater, head towards Gümbet on Kıbrıs Şehitler Cad. To reach the mausoleum, turn onto Kirkateyn Sok. from Neyzen Tevfik Cad. Theater and "mausoleum" open Tu-Su 8am-noon and 1-5:30pm; until 5pm in the off-season. Admission $1.60, students $1.)*

CASTLE OF ST. PETER. Crusaders from the Knights of St. John decimated the nearby Mausoleum of Halicarnassus to construct Bodrum's formidable castle over the ruins of an ancient acropolis during the 15th and 16th centuries. Decorated with 249 coats-of-arms, the castle towers have been dubbed the English, French, German, and Italian Towers after the nations responsible for their construction. Despite their extensive fortifications, the Crusaders' towers were no match for Süleyman the Magnificent's forces, who overpowered the knights in 1523. Under Ottoman rule, the castle's importance waned, and in 1895 it was converted into a prison. The fortress now houses a museum with maritime and cultural exhibits. *(The most central landmark in Bodrum, the castle is right on the harbor. Tel. 316 25 16. Open Tu-Su 8am-noon and 1-5pm. Admission $3.80, students free.)*

MEDITERRANEAN COAST

Alternately chic, garish, and remote, the Mediterranean coast stretches along lush national parks, sunsoaked beaches, and pine forests. Natural beauty and ancient ruins have made the western Mediterranean one of Turkey's most touristed regions. Though increasingly overrun with pushy touts, Armani sportswear, and mega-hotels, the western coast also caters to the backpacker circuit. By day, travelers take tranquil boat trips, hike among waterfalls, and explore submerged ruins; by night, they exchange stories over Efes, dance under the stars, and fall asleep in seaside *pansiyons* and treehouses.

MARMARİS

Marmaris contains all the beach-town necessities: eclectic tourist shops, seaside restaurants, expensive yachts, a boisterous beach front, and decadent after-hours festivities. Rumor has it that Marmaris derived its name from Süleyman the Magnificent's order to "hang the architect" *(mimarı as)* of the local fortress. Exactly what was so distasteful about this understated castle is hard to say, as throngs of appreciative international tourists swarm to the landmark each summer. Some claim that the best part of Marmaris is getting away from it: boats set off from Marmaris for spectacular nearby coves and the Greek island of Rhodes.

⚡ ORIENTATION AND PRACTICAL INFORMATION

From the bus station, outside of town on Mustafa Münir Elgin Bul., take a *dolmuş* (40¢) or taxi ($3) to the town center on **Ulusal Egemenlik Bulvarı**, where the **Tansaş Shopping Center**, bus offices, and the *dolmuş* hub can be found. Located at the intersection of Ulusal Egemenlik Bul. and the sea, the **Atatürk Statue** is a good reference point. Facing the water at the monument, turn left down **Kordon Caddesi** to reach the tourist office and harbor. **Barlar Sokak** (Bar St.) and the **castle** are also to the left. **Atatürk Caddesi** and **Uzunyalı Caddesi** run from the right of the statue. Atatürk Cad. leads to the popular waterfront walkway and public beach before veering right and becoming **Kemal Seyfettin Elgin Bulvarı**.

Buses: The *otogar* (tel. 412 30 37) is down Ulusal Egemenlik Bul. and to the right on Mustafa Münir Elgin Bul. Buses run to: **Ankara** (11hr., 4 per day 9am-11pm, $22); **Antalya** (7hr., 10am and 11pm, $10); **Bodrum** (4hr.; in summer 8:30am-8pm, in winter 8:30am-2pm; $6); **Göreme** (14hr., 10:30am, $16); **Istanbul** (12½hr., 9am-1am, $20-23); **İzmir** (4½hr., 5:15am-2am, $9); and **Kuşadası** (5hr., $9). To get to **Fethiye**, take an intercity *dolmuş* from Tansaş Shopping Center (4hr., 7:30am-10pm, $6).

Travel to Rhodes: **Yeşil Marmaris** (tel. 412 64 86 or 412 64 88), on the harbor, runs **catamarans** (1hr.; May-Oct. daily, Nov.-Apr. Tu and F; 9:15am, return 4pm; round-trip $15-25, open return $30), **hydrofoils** (1hr.; May-Oct. daily 9:45am and 4:30pm, return 3pm; $15-25), and **ferries** (departs when full; 1½hr.; $20, round-trip $25). There's more to pay: $10 port tax, then $10 to get out of Greece, $10 more to get back into Turkey, plus the cost of another $45 Turkish visa if required for your nationality.

Local Dolmuş: *Dolmuş* leave from Tansaş Shopping Center and head down Ulusal Egemenlik Bul. to **Beldibi,** or down Atatürk Cad. to **Armutalan.**

Tourist Office: (tel. 412 72 77 or 412 10 35), 250m along Kordon Cad. English-speaking and very helpful. Open in summer daily 9am-6pm; in winter M-F 8am-5:30pm.

Budget Travel: Interyouth Hostel, Tepe Mah., 42 Sok No. 45 (tel. 412 36 87; fax 412 78 25), can help find cheap airline, bus, and boat tickets. Jeep and moped rentals. Extraordinary Backpacker's Cruise on the hostel's beautiful yachts ($200 for 5 days).

Consulates: U.K. (tel. 412 64 86/7; fax 412 50 77), in Yeşil Marmaris office building on the harbor, around corner from tourist office. Open M-F 7:30am-noon and 2:30-5pm.

Police: (tel. 412 14 94), on 49 Sok., 3 blocks from the tourist office.

Hospital: Esen Sağlık Medical Center (office tel. 413 13 16; mobile 0532 321 39 11; home 413 37 71; fax 413 13 16), on Kemal Seyfettin Elgin Bul. English-speaking doctors and nurses. 24hr. emergency and non-emergency treatment.

PTT: (tel. 412 12 12), on Fevzipaşa Cad., off Kordon Cad. **Currency exchange** 9am-10pm; **phone service** 8am-midnight; **direct money transfer** 8:30am-12:30pm and 1:30-5:30pm. **Postal truck** outside the tourist office. Open daily 8am-11pm.

Telephone Code: 252.

■ ACCOMMODATIONS

🏠 **Interyouth Hostel**, Tepe Mah., 42 Sok. No. 45 (tel. 412 36 87; fax 412 78 23), deep within the bazaar; follow the signs. Not to be confused with the imposter Interyouth Hostel at Kemeraltı Mah., 14 İyilikataş Mevkii, which doesn't offer what this place does—book exchange, Internet access ($4 per hr.), international phones, laundry ($6), and sunset cruises every other night in the summer ($10). Breakfast in the terrace bar and nightly spaghetti dinners (7:30pm, free for hotel guests). Dorms $5; private room $13; $1 discount for ISIC, HI, and IYTC holders.

İmbat Otel, 5 Eski Çarşı Sok. (tel. 412 14 13 or 413 63 20). Facing the tourist office, walk down the side street to the left, take the first left, and continue straight into the bazaar. Cheerful establishment run by "Rakı Man," who loves to indulge his guests in his namesake. Laundry $6. Breakfast $1.80. Free tea, coffee, and soda for guests. Dorms in summer $8 per person, in winter $6.

Maltepe Pansiyon, 64 Sok. No. 7 (tel. 412 16 29 or 412 84 56). Walk 400m down Ulusal Egemenlik Bul. from the Atatürk statue, turn left on G. Mustafa Muğlalı Cad., and left again 25m from Eet Cafe. Free use of washing machine and kitchen help you sleep easy in airy rooms, 15 with bath. Roof with outside beds or bungalows $4. Singles $12; doubles $16; triples $18; quads $24. Breakfast included.

Nadir Otel and Pansiyon, Kemeraltı Mah., 56 Sok. (tel. 412 11 67 or 412 18 06), next to the rocky outcrop behind the Tansaş Shopping Center. Comfy lounge with TV and Turkish carpets. Laundry 60¢ per item. Polished doubles with bath $17 per room, off-season $14. *Pansiyon* $6-7 per person. Breakfast included.

⚪ FOOD

Kervansaray Restaurant (tel. 412 64 84). Head straight on Ulusal Egemenlik Bul., turn left on Datça Yolu, and make another left on Yunus Nadi Cad. Or catch an Armutalan-bound *dolmuş*, which goes past the restaurant. Large meal ($12) comes with bottom-less booze and a side order of Turkish music and wrestling culminating in a performance by the most famous male bellydancer in Turkey. Open daily Apr.-Oct.

İdil Mantı Evi, 138 Barlar Sok., close to the harbor, serving *mantı* (meat-filled ravioli in yogurt, $4) and many varieties of *gözleme* ($2). Open daily noon-5am.

Eet Cafe Mozart, Org. Muğlalı Cad. #1-2-4 (tel. 413 87 64). Head down Ulusal Egemenlik Bul. and turn left on the street after the Tansaş Shopping Center. The chef at this Dutch *patisserie*-restaurant wants you to eet what you like: he prepares authentic European meals (fish and chips in newspaper $8.50) and is open to creating new dishes. Turkish breakfast $2, English breakfast $3. Open 8:30am-12:30am.

Internet Cafe (tel. 413 72 37), Yat Limanı, near the harbor. The breezy patio is perfect for munching on Turkish dishes and vegetarian options ($2-5). Moist homemade cakes and cookies $1.50. Open daily 9am-2am.

🎵 ENTERTAINMENT

It's hard to tell which is hotter in Marmaris: the burning sun or the blazing night-life. Showtime is 11pm for Barlar Sok., Uzunyalı, and Barbados Cad. (the harbor), when bars and clubs kick into high gear. To reach **Barlar Sok.** (Bar St.), take the left road next to the tourist office and veer left into the bazaar at the next corner. **Uzunyalı** is on the opposite side of Marmaris, right on the waterfront. **Barbados Cad.** is the pavement along the harbor. At bars with both indoor and outdoor seating, drinks are usually cheaper outside.

Greenhouse (tel. 412 50 71), on Bar St., has A/C, cutting-edge music, and a comfortable setting that has earned it most-favored-bar-and-dance-club status for years running. Beer $2, *rakı* $3.50, cocktails $5-10. Open 9pm-5am.

Backstreet (tel. 412 40 48), on Bar St. An open-air oasis (faux palm trees included) where *Everybody* goes to *Quit Playin' Games* and begin shaking it to international pop. *I'll Never Break Your Heart* or your bank with beer for $2.40, *rakı* at $3.50, cocktails $4-8. Open May-Sept. 9am to *As Long As You Love Me* (about 4am).

Escape Bar (tel. 412 74 17), on Bar St., is just what its name says: an escape from the flashy nightclubs. Features a pool table and cheap beer ($1.50). Open 8pm-2:30am.

Cheers (tel. 412 67 22), Uzunyalı. Everyone may not know your name, but this disco "theme park" featuring *Grease* and *Saturday Night Fever* is still oodles of fun with a mega sound system blasting 60s and 70s music. The festivities reach a hilarious climax during the screening of *Grease,* when excited patrons impersonate Travolta atop a real '67 Chevy in the middle of the bar. Beer $1.80, *rakı* $3.60, cocktails $4-6 (try the special "fishbowls" and you'll be swimming home, $20). Open Apr.-Oct. 8am-4am.

Davy Jones (tel. 412 06 07), Bar St. Don't ask us why everyone's favorite Monkee has a bar in Turkey named after him. Say "hey, sailor" to worn-out anchors, boat medals, and a colorful ocean mural. Alternative rock and blues play in the background.

🌊 SAND AND SURF

BEACHES. Only 1500m away, **Günlücek National Park** offers a small, quiet beach and picnic tables set against a lush forest with fragrant frankincense trees. Follow the harbor road past the marina and across the wooden footbridge, or catch a *dolmuş* from in front of the Tansaş Shopping Center (40¢). While the crowded beach in Marmaris proper is properly lively, quieter and prettier beaches in the area are accessible only by boat. Pleasant **İçmeler beach** is an easily reached exception. (*Dolmuş from the front of Tansaş Shopping Center or anywhere along Atatürk Cad go to İçmeler (10min., every 5min. 8am-1am, 50¢), or take the water dolmuş to İçmeler from the waterfront next to the tourist office (20min., in summer daily 7am-7pm, $4).*)

BOAT TRIPS. Water *dolmuş* going to **Turunç Beach** depart from the waterfront behind the Atatürk statue (45min., in summer every hr. 7am-7pm, $1). Full-day boat tours stop at **Paradise Island Beach,** the **Akvaryum** (aquarium), some phosphorous caves, and the popular **Turunç Beach.** Most continue to the **Gölenye Springs,** whose waters reputedly cure intestinal ills; the less crowded **Kumlu Buk Beach,** near the remains of a fortress; and the tiny village of **Keçi,** in the heavily-wooded Nimara Peninsula ($10-15 per person; lunch included). Legend has it that Marc Antony imported the Red Sea's white sand to the beaches of **Kleopatra's Island** (a.k.a. Sedir Adası) to impress Cleopatra. Fossilized are the real cause of the sand's whiteness, but a girl can dream, can't she? (*Take a boat to Kleopatra's Island through an organized tour; 45min., in summer 17 per day from 10:30am, return 7pm. Book one through a travel agency.*)

FETHİYE

Fethiye rests peacefully on a harbor surrounded by pine forests and mountains. Most visitors take daytrips to Ölüdeniz and the Butterfly Valley by day and enjoy Fethiye's winding streets and low-key nightlife come sundown.

🚩 ORIENTATION AND PRACTICAL INFORMATION. The *otogar* is 2km from the center of town, on the way to Ölüdeniz. If there are no *servis* shuttles to the town center, leave the terminal, cross the street, and wait for a *dolmuş* heading to Fethiye (10min., 40¢). The *dolmuş* runs on the main street, **Atatürk Caddesi,** past a mosque, the PTT, and an Atatürk bust. The ritzy **Çalış Beach** is to the right along **Sedir Sokak,** which becomes **Akdeniz Caddesi.** The *otogar* is on **Ölüdeniz Caddesi.** Buses running along the coastal road can drop passengers off anywhere en route to: **Ankara** (9hr.; 10, 10:30, 11pm; $19); **Antalya** (4hr., 2:30pm and 2:30am, $7); and **Kaş** (2hr., 4am-5:30pm, $3.60). **Dolmuş** run from the intersection of Hastane and Atatürk Cad. to **Çalış Beach** (5min., every 5min. 7am-1am, 40¢) and **Ölüdeniz** (20-25min., every 10min. 7am-9pm, $1). **Dolmuş boats** to **Çalış Beach** leave from the waterfront (every 20min. 9:30am-8pm, every 30min. 10pm-midnight; $1). The **Tourist Office,** 1/A İskele Meydanı (tel./fax 614 15 27), is down Atatürk Cad. past the PTT (open daily in summer 8:30am-7pm; in winter M-F 8am-5pm). **Travel Agencies** like **Fetur** (tel. 614 20 34 or 614 24 43), past the tourist office on Fevzi Çakmak Cad., arrange flights and daily boat tours (open daily 9am-5:30pm). The **police** (tel. 614 10 40) are around the corner from tourist office, near the ancient theater. A larger branch (tel. 614 13 09) is located on Atatürk Cad., across from the PTT. The **PTT** is on Atatürk Cad. (open 8am-midnight). **Telephone code:** 252.

▐▖▐▖ ACCOMMODATIONS AND FOOD. Cheap *pansiyons* cluster around Hastane Cad. and Fevzi Çakmak Cad. █**Ferah Pansiyon,** 2 Karagözler Ordu Cad. No. 21 (tel./fax 614 28 16; call for free pickup from the *otogar*), is one of the best hostels in Turkey, with spacious rooms (most with bath) and a free pool (dorms $3.60; rooms $10-12). **Sinderella Motel and Pansiyon** (tel. 266 46 11), on Çarşı Cad., can be reached by walking right down Atatürk Cad., taking a right opposite the hospital onto a small street, then making a left onto Çarşı Cad. It's a hip pension with stepsister-free, cheerful rooms and a lively outdoor eating area with a pool table ($8 per person, including breakfast). █**Meğri Lokantası,** Cumhuriyet Mah. 13/A Çarşı Cad. (tel. 614 40 74; fax 612 04 46), off Atatürk Cad. by the harbor, features an enormous selection of sumptuous Turkish fare (*meze* $1.40, *şiş* $3.60; open 24hr.). **Yörükoğlu** (tel. 612 20 64), on Çarşı Cad., serves huge "Turkish burritos" ($2; open 8am-1am). **Sedir Restaurant,** 3 Tütün Sok. (tel. 614 10 95), left off Çarşı Cad., has pizzas ($4-6) and grills ($4.80; open 7am-midnight).

▐▌ ENTERTAINMENT. Car Cemetery Bar, 33 Hamam Sok. (tel. 614 11 81), is just what you think it is: have a cold beer ($1.80) or *rakı* ($2) amid deceased car parts (open 10am-4am). Everybody dance now at tourist favorite **The Music Factory** (tel. 617 51 72), on Hamam Sok., a pumping metallic cage with two levels of flashing dance floors (open daily 5pm-5am). Sail the high seas by boarding the **Mare Nostrum** (tel. 0535 725 15 86; ask at the Ferah Pansiyon for information). The boat's friendly owners limit the cruise size to 12 guests and change the itinerary depending on the guests' interests ($95 for 3 days and 2 nights, $120 for 4 days and 3 nights; guests can stay on the boat for free the night before and after the cruise).

NEAR FETHİYE: ÖLÜDENİZ AND THE BUTTERFLY VALLEY

Dolmuş boats to Butterfly Valley leave from Ölüdeniz (45min.; 11am, 2, 6pm; return 8am, 1, 5pm; $2 each way). *Blue Lagoon* is a 20min. walk or $4.80 taxi ride from the dolmuş station. Park and lagoon open 6:30am-9pm. Admission $1.20, students 60¢. *Butterfly Valley* admission $1, students 50¢.

The town of Ölüdeniz's main attraction is the **Blue Lagoon,** an idyllic peninsula cradled in wooded hills and lapped by shining clear water. Enter from Tabiat Park, on the right of the road from Fethiye, where potable water, bathrooms, and showers are available. The next best thing to swimming in the Blue Lagoon is seeing it from above by tandem **paragliding,** available through **Sky Sports Paragliding** (tel. 617 05 11). Passengers are driven to the top of Baba Dağı and given take-off and landing instructions (2hr., $115; book in advance). The tiny turquoise bay known as █**Butterfly Valley** near Ölüdeniz is home to waterfalls and several species of butterfly, including the nocturnal orange and black Jersey Tiger. From the entrance to the valley, follow the blue dots up the rocky path to the two **waterfalls.** Spending the night means camping on the beach ($1.60 per tent), renting a mattress in the treehouse ($3 per person), or bedding down in **The Greek Home** ($3 per person). All accommodations have toilets and showers. Food is readily available at the local eatery ($4 per plate). It isn't hard to find **The Rock Cafe,** built into the sides of the cliffs (juices and stronger drinks $1).

KAŞ

Sandwiched between the depths of the sea and the stunning heights of the mountains, cosmopolitan Kaş is pretty shallow as far as nightlife goes but refreshingly hassle-free. Kaş is a great base for exploring the sunken city of Kevova and the beautiful beaches of the Blue Caves nearby.

TURKEY

⚑ ORIENTATION AND PRACTICAL INFORMATION. Most of the activity centers around the small harbor along the main street, **Cumhuriyet Caddesi.** At its west end near the mosque, Cumhuriyet Cad. intersects **Hastane Caddesi** before becoming **Atatürk Caddesi.** At its east end near the Atatürk statue, Cumhuriyet Cad. intersects **Çukurbağlı Caddesi** (also known as Şübe Sok.), which leads to the PTT. From the Atatürk statue, **Hükümet Caddesi** passes above the harbor to the two beaches. The street going uphill behind the tourist office—the one with most of the souvenir shops—is **Uzun Çarşı Caddesi.** Buses run from the *otogar*, uphill on Atatürk Cad., to **Antalya** via **Olimpos** (3hr., every 30min. 8am-10pm, $5.40) and **Fethiye** (2hr., 6 per day 9:30am-10pm, $3.60). The **tourist office,** 5 Cumhuriyet Meydanı (tel. 836 12 38), is to the left of the Atatürk statue (open daily in summer 8am-noon and 1-7pm; in winter M-F 8am-5pm). Nearly all **travel agencies** have tours to **Kevova. Bougainville Travel,** 10 Çukurbağlı Cad. (tel. 836 37 37; fax 836 16 05), offers diving courses, **kayaking** trips to Kekova ($35), and **Internet access** ($4 per hr.; open daily 8:30am-10pm). **Simena Tours,** 1 Elmalı Cad. (tel. 836 14 16), near the *otogar*, books popular daytrips to **Kevova.** For emergencies, try the **police** (tel. 836 10 24), across the entrance to Küçük Çalık Plaj (Little Pebble Beach). The **hospital** (tel. 836 11 85) is on Hastane Cad., 500m past the mosque by the tourist office. The **PTT** (tel. 836 14 50 or 836 14 78), on Çukurbağlı Cad., does **currency exchange** until 5pm (open daily 8:30am-midnight). **Telephone code:** 242.

🍴 ACCOMMODATIONS AND FOOD. There are many *pansiyons* on the side streets to the right of Atatürk Bul. **Hotel Nisa** (tel. 836 35 81), on Hastane Cad., has international phone service, TV and stereo, and a communal kitchen stocked with beer ($1.60; doubles $12). **Motel Korsan Karakedi,** 17 Yenicami Sok. (tel. 836 18 87; fax 836 30 86), is east along Hastane Cad. towards the theater, right on Yenicami Cad., and left after the mosque. The motel features sea-view rooms with bath, fan, and balcony ($12 per room). **Oba Pansiyon** (tel. 836 25 41), down a small side street near the *otogar*, has clean rooms with attractive balconies (singles $9; doubles $15; breakfast $1.60). **▧Smiley's Restaurant,** 11 Uzun Çarşı Gürsoy Sok. (tel. 836 28 12), has a great breakfast and Turkish specialties (*pide* $2.80), but it's the energetic İsmail and his wife that will make you smile: travelers who eat breakfast and dinner in the restaurant can crash for free on mats in their living room (and don't forget the 10% *Let's Go* discount on meals!). **▧Chez Evy,** 2 Terzi Sok. (tel. 836 12 53), up the street from the Red Point Bar, is the place to savor French food *de rigueur* in Ottoman splendor (broiled lamb $9, salad *niçoise* $3.60; open M-Sa 8am-2am).

🏖 BEACHES. Kaş's two main beaches rock—both are tucked in rocky coves surrounded by rocky cliffs—and have names to prove it. The entrance to **Küçük Çalık Plajı** (Little Pebble Beach) is at the top of the hill on Hükümet Cad., while the less crowded **Büyük Çalık Plajı** (Big Pebble Beach) is 15 minutes down the road to the left of the tourist office. Most travelers who paş through Kaş take a dip in the **Blue Caves,** 15km from Kaş and home to the Mediterranean's only **seal colony.**

NEAR KAŞ

KEVOVA

*If you don't go to Kevova through a tour, split a taxi from Kaş (tel. 836 19 33) to Üçağız ($30). Once there, ask **Smart Tourism** (tel. 874 20 40; fax 874 20 39), on the main dirt path in Üçağız, for help finding boats ($10-12 per hr.) to Kekova and the Blue Caves (open 8am-midnight). Glass-bottom boat trips cost $12-25 and may include lunch.*

The Lycian city of Kekova lies submerged beneath the clear Mediterranean waters as a result of an earthquake that struck in 25 CE. During the Hellenistic and Arab eras, the city served as a lookout post and refuge from marauding pirates. From craggy Kevova Island, it is possible to see through calm water to the underwater walls and staircases (calm seas afford views sharp enough to discern details on amphoras). Above sea level on Kevova Island, a motley assortment of doors and walls still bear evidence of long-gone floors and ceilings. The highlight of the trip is the partially submerged Lycian sarcophagus near the village of Kale.

OLİMPOS

Ask to be let off a Kaş- or Demre-bound bus from Antalya or an Antalya-bound bus from Kaş. You'll be dropped off at a rest station on the main road, where dolmuş leaves for the tree-houses (15min., every hr. 9:30am-6:30pm, $1.15).

Enchanting Olimpos is a true backpacker's town, one of the few budget spots along the Turkish Riviera. Olimpos brings travelers closer to the heavens by giving them the chance to make a nighttime ascent of the Chimaera, where a naturally occurring flame has burned since ancient times, and sleep in **treehouses**, rickety but charming *pansiyons* that perch in the trees along the dirt road to the beach and ruins. All prices for treehouses include breakfast and dinner. The best of the seeing-is-believing treehouses is ▉**Şaban Pansiyon** (tel. 892 12 65), a relaxed and welcoming family-run pension with tasty diner fare and 24hr. service to Antalya airport ($7 per person; private doubles $20; camping $6; airport service $42). **Orange Pansiyon** (tel. 892 12 42 or 892 13 17), perched in a grove of the eponymous trees, is the sturdiest treehouse pension in Olimpos ($6.65 per person; styrofoam-insulated bungalows with toilets $9.30; pension rooms $12). Staying at **Kadir's Yörük Treehouses** (tel. 892 12 50; fax 892 11 10), the first pension at the bottom of the road, is like going to a kid's summer camp, complete with volleyball and table tennis (dorm beds $6; doubles $14; bungalows $10 per person). Kadir's hits puberty after dark, though, when it becomes the focus of nightlife (beer $1.15, cocktails $2.35).

▉**CHIMAERA.** Olimpos's proximity to this perpetual natural flame in the mountainside (once so bright that ships navigated by it) inspired the residents of the city to worship Hephaestos, god of fire and the forge. Today's Olimpians are less reverent: most bring marshmallows to toast. The ancients believed the flame to be the breath of the Chimaera, a mythical beast that was part lion, part goat, part serpent, and all evil. Geologists have not produced a better explanation, but they suspect natural methane gas plays some role—implying that Hephaestos was the ancient god of fire, forge, and flatulence. *(Best seen at night. Ask pension owners about bus tours; 2½hr., 9:30pm, $2.80. Ironically, you need to bring a flashlight for the 20min. uphill trek to the flame.)*

RUINS. Ancient ruins choked with vines become more frequent farther from the cluster of pensions and towards the sea. You'll know you've arrived at the "jungle ruins" when the menagerie of fellow backpackers hanging from the trees is replaced with crabs, frogs, multi-colored birds, lizards, and butterflies darting among the sun-dappled trees and vine-covered ruins. A sign marked TEMPLE points through an imposing archway to the **mausoleum**, which holds two hefty sarcophagi—one inscribed with Greek characters, the other with the scratchings of tourists hoping to achieve similar immortality. Past the mausoleum is the exquisite 5th-century **mosaic house,** whose floors were entirely covered with intricate geometric tilework until an earthquake diverted the course of a stream that flooded the building. On the other side of the road and across the stream is the decrepit **theater,** uninspiring save the opportunity it offers to swim out under crumbling archways shrouded in vines, shrubs, and flowering bougainvillea. Continue along the main path to the surf, where the best preserved group of ruins looms over the water on a rocky cliff to the right. *(Unlimited-day admission to the ruins and beach $2.80, students $1.85. Hold on to your ticket stub.)*

ANTALYA

Capital of the so-called Turquoise Riviera and linked by air with Munich, Moscow, and Amsterdam, Antalya has spawned modern white buildings along its shoreline cliffs. Contemporary Antalya encircles Kaleiçi ("inside the fortress"), the crescent-shaped old city that brims with cobblestone streets, Ottoman houses, pensions, restaurants, boutiques, and carpet dealers. At Kaleiçi's heart, pricey eateries and cutting-edge nightclubs line the ancient walled harbor that once sheltered Roman galleys. Tourism has made Antalya *très* chic and *très* Western (from its Burger King head to its Benetton toes)—so much so that it even has its own cinema celebration, the Antalya Altın Portakal ("Golden Orange") Film Festival, held every fall.

ORIENTATION

In 1997, Antalya gave birth to a gargantuan shopping-mall-like **otogar**—replete with fountains, several **ATMs,** and sprawling, labyrinthine bathrooms with seat toilets—4km out of town at **Anadolu Kavşağı,** the intersection of Namık Kemal Cad. and Dumlupınar Bul. Frequent *dolmuş* (35¢) run to the city center, near **Kaleiçi,** the old city. **Işıklar,** at the intersection of **Kazım Özalp Caddesi** and **Cumhuriyet Caddesi,** is marked by a brick-red fluted minaret and a stone clocktower. Hostels and restaurants, as well as historically important ruins and buildings, are in this area.

Airplanes: Antalya International Airport (domestic info tel. 330 30 30; international info 330 36 00), 15km from town. **THY** (tel. 243 43 81/2), has an office on Cumhuriyet Cad. next to the tourist office. Open M-F 8:30am-8pm, Sa-Su 8:30am-5:30pm. Buses run between THY and the airport in summer (10 per day 4:45am-2:30am, $3). Flights to **Istanbul** ($61, students $47; round-trip $79/61) and many foreign cities.

Buses: To: **Ankara** (8hr., 7am-midnight, $9.50); **Fethiye** (5hr., every hr. 8am-11pm); **Cappadocia** (10hr., 8:30 and 10pm, $14); **Istanbul** (12hr., 6:30am-11pm, $14); **İzmir** (8hr., 9am-midnight, $9.50); and **Kaş** (3hr., every 30min. 8am-10pm, $4).

Ferries: Fener Turizm (tel. 242 16 53; fax 242 08 59) plans to start seabus service to **Girne** in Northern Cyprus (4½hr.; F 9am; $70, students $55) and to **Rhodes** in Greece (4hr.; Tu, Th 6am; $75, students $50). To get to their office, walk down Atatürk Cad. until it becomes Işıklar Cad. and turn right after the stadium. The office is on the right, on the 2nd floor of a building 200m down the road.

Dolmuş: Antalya has two *dolmuş* hubs. **Doğu Garaj** sends *dolmuş* to **Lale** and **Lara Beaches.** To get here from Atatürk Cad., turn right on Ali Çetinkaya Cad, walk 1 block, and turn right at the Start Hotel. The **Meydan Garajı,** at the intersection of Mevlâna Cad., Aspendos Bul., and Ali Çetinkaya Cad., 1½km from the city center, has *dolmuş* to **Perge** and **Aspendos.** *Dolmuş* to the **Museum** and **Konyaaltı Beach** run from Konyaaltı Bul. or Işıklar. Most *dolmuş* trips cost around 30¢.

Trams: A new tram system runs from the Antalya Museum along Cumhuriyet Cad., then down Atatürk Cad. to the stadium (every 20 min., 25¢).

Tourist Office: (tel. 241 17 47), on Cumhuriyet Cad., to the left of the red fluted minaret, past the military complex. Helpful, English-speaking staff distributes free maps. Open in summer M-F 8am-5pm, Sa-Su 9am-5pm; in winter M-F 8am-5pm, Sa-Su 10am-5pm.

Consulates: U.K., Dolaplıdere Cad. Pırıltı Sitesi, 1st Fl. (tel. 247 70 00; fax 824 67 03). **Turkish Republic of Northern Cyprus (TRNC),** Kışla Mah. 35th Sok. Dörteldemir Apt. 11 P.K. 633 (tel. 248 98 47).

Tourist Police: (tel./fax 243 10 61). Face the water and turn left on a little street left of the Atatürk bust at the harbor.

Hospital: The closest hospital to Kaleiçi is **Akdeniz Sağlık Vakfı Hastanesi,** 17 Ali Çetinkaya Cad. (tel. 247 90 01/2; fax 247 90 03), on the left side of Cumhuriyet Cad., 400m past the intersection with Atatürk Cad.

PTT: To get to the **main branch** (tel. 243 45 79), head west on Cumhuriyet Cad. and take the 1st major right onto Anafartalar Cad. Open daily 8:30am-5:30pm for stamps and **currency exchange.** Telephones and **Internet.**

Telephone Code: 242.

ACCOMMODATIONS AND FOOD

The best place to stay is in the pensions of **Kaleiçi,** which all include private showers and breakfast. ■**Sabah Pansiyon,** Kaleiçi Kılıçarslan Mah., 60 Hesapçı Sok. (tel. 247

53 45; fax 247 53 47), is a popular backpackers' hangout serving delicious vegetarian and meat dinners ($3) and cheap beer (60¢). (Singles $6; doubles $13, with A/C $18; bike/scooter rental $20 per day, car rental $24 per day.) All the furniture may be blue at **Mavi Pansiyon,** 13 Tabakhane Geçidi Kılıçarslan Mah. (tel. 247 63 73), but you won't say you blew all your money on a room (singles $12; doubles $16; 10% discounts for stays longer than 7 days). **Anı Pansiyon,** 26 Tabakhane Sok., Hesapçı Sok. (tel. 247 00 56) is understated and luxurious (singles $12; doubles $19).

    Cumba Restaurant and Cafe Bar, Atatürk Cad. 3 Kocatepe Sok. (tel. 248 67 67), dishes up green beans ($1.20), *cacık* (cucumber yogurt, $1), and an excellent mixed grill ($3.50) on beautifully tiled tables in an outdoor garden area (open 8am-midnight). The poolside **Hotel Alp Paşa Restaurant,** 500m from Hadrian's gate along Hesapçı Sok., in the courtyard of an Ottoman mansion-*cum*-hotel, serves fancy dinners without the fancy-dinner prices. Your nation's flag will be placed at the table in true U.N. fashion (Turkish and international dishes $3.50-7, all-you-can-eat buffet $7.70). Savor the cheap snacks (cheeseburgers $1.20) and beautiful harbor view of **Tophane Çay Bahçesi,** on the top of the ramparts.

🎵 ENTERTAINMENT

Whether you're looking for an elegant dance club or a more rowdy bar, there's no shortage of nightlife in Antalya. **Oscar,** Zafer Sok., in the Old City, shows Hollywood blockbusters and other foreign films ($3.50, students $2.35). ⬛**Club Ally,** above the harbor, is easily identified by the green laser it shoots out across the water at night. The be-all and end-all of nightlife for Antalya's young and wealthy, eight independently owned bars encircle a central bar in this spacious outdoor establishment. (Beer and *rakı* $4.65, cocktails $8.15. Cover F-Sa $11.65, Su-Th $8.15. Open 8pm-4am.) **Club 29** (tel. 241 62 60 or 247 59 37), along the harbor after Denizcinin, throbs with mega-bass Euro, Turkish, and American pop. (Beer $3.50; *rakı* $4.65. M-Th cover $8.15, F-Sa cover $10.50. Open 11pm-4am.) If y'all just want some cheap beer, yelken head on over to the **Yelken Cafe Bar,** which serves $1.15 brewskies.

👁 SIGHTS

⬛**ANTALYA MUSEUM.** This museum is one of Turkey's best and a winner of the 1988 European Museum of the Year Award. The exhibits chronicle the history of Turkey from prehistoric times to the founding of the Turkish Republic. One of the museum's highlights is the **Salon of the Gods,** with large 2nd-century BCE statues of Nemesis, Zeus, Aphrodite, Tyche, Athena, Artemis, Hermes, and Dionysus, and their Egyptian sidekicks Serapis, Isis, and Horus. The **Salon of Small Objects and Underwater Remains,** to the right, houses several gorgeous silver and ivory Phrygian statuettes; the gem of the collection is a magnificently painted Grecian urn, mysteriously labeled "Tibet Crater." The adjoining **Icon Hall** is home to a small collection of Orthodox Christian icons, among them a portrait and bones of St. Nicholas. The **Hall of Money and Jewelry** contains a few of the world's first coins, minted between 640 and 630 BCE by the Lydians from white gold or electrium (an alloy of gold and silver). *(2 Konyaalı Cad., about 2½km from town along Cumhuriyet Bul., which changes its name to Konyaaltı Bul. Dolmuş labeled "Konyaaltı/Liman" head along this street, stopping at the large "D" signs (30¢). Ask to be let off when you see the yellow museum signs. The train also runs to the museum for 25¢. Tel. 241 45 28. Open in summer Tu-Su 9am-6pm; in winter 8am-5pm. Admission $3.50, students $2.35.)*

OTHER SIGHTS. Near the entrance to Kaleiçi, at the intersection of Cumhuriyet Cad., stands the symbol of Antalya, the unique red-tinted **Yivli Minare** (fluted minaret). Dating from the 13th century, this minaret was constructed by the Selçuk Sultan Alaeddin Keykubad. Down Atatürk Cad., on the right, stands the three-arched **Hadrian's Gate,** built in 130 CE to commemorate the visit of the emperor Hadrian. Through this gate to the old city, about halfway down Hesapçı Sok., is the **Kesik Minare** (Broken Minaret). The ruined mosque traces Antalya's history: it was once a Roman temple, then a three-nave basilica, and finally a Selçuk mosque. At the far end of Hesapçı Sok. is the **Hıdırlık Tower,** which resembles a Roman-era mausoleum but is believed to have been built as a lighthouse in the 2nd century.

BEACHES

Antalya's two beaches, **Lara** and **Konyaaltı,** are both accessible by *dolmuş* (from the Doğu Garaj to Lara, from Konyaaltı Bul. to Konyaaltı; 30¢). Konyaaltı is free, while Lara charges 50¢ for admission and $3.50 for an umbrella and two chairs. On the way to Lara, you might want to stop at the **Lower Düden Waterfall,** a cascade that tumbles 20m into the sea. The spectacular **Upper Düden Falls,** about 10km from Antalya, are included in most half-day tours of Termessos. Antalya has two water parks: **Aqua Park,** before Lower Düden in the direction of Lara Beach (admission $12), and **Aqua Land,** beyond Konyaaltı Beach (admission $9.30, after 2pm $7).

ANTAKYA (HATAY)

In Antakya, site of the ancient city of Antioch, the throngs of tourists thin out and the Mediterranean resort atmosphere subsides considerably to give way to sprawling markets, manicured tea gardens, and the world-famous Hatay Museum. It was in Antioch that "the disciples were called Christians for the first time," and nearby St. Peter's Grotto is where Peter is said to have "christened" the religion in 40 CE (and re-christened the city Theopolis, "City of God") in an attempt to curb the city's excesses. The original sin was committed by Seleucus I Nicator, one of Alexander the Great's chief generals, who founded Antioch as the capital of his Asian empire in 300 BCE. Antioch fell from grace when it became a vice-ridden, decadent stop along the silk road and a comparable sin city under the Romans. Thanks to St. Peter's work, the city cleaned up its act and became a thriving theological and cultural capital. A second earthquake in the 6th century was the cause of its present state of disrepair, although crumbling ruins around this city of 150,000 hint at its former glory.

ORIENTATION AND PRACTICAL INFORMATION

The **Asi River** divides Antakya into two parts. At the center of town in the western half of the city, a theater, the PTT, a government office, and the museum snuggle up to the Atatürk statue rotunda. The eastern half has the budget hotels, restaurants, markets, *otogar*, and old neighborhoods. To reach the center of town, turn left at the exit of the *otogar*, make another left onto **İstiklâl Caddesi,** and continue 700m to the river. Cross the second bridge into the square with the Atatürk statue, without which everyone would be lost.

The *otogar* runs buses to: **Ankara** (10hr., 6 per day 10am-10pm, $13.50); **Aleppo, Syria** (3-4hr., 4 per day 9am-6pm, $8); and **Damascus, Syria** (9hr., 9:30am and noon, $15). *Dolmuş* leave opposite the station to **İskenderun** (30min., every 15min., $1.25), a popular border crossing town. For more information on crossing the border into Syria, see p. 534. The **tourist office,** 47 Atatürk Cad. (tel. 216 06 10), is an inconvenient 15-minute walk down Atatürk Cad. (open M-F 8am-noon and 1:30-5:30pm). **Türkiye İş Bankası** has branches on İstiklâl Cad. and on Hürriyet Cad. down from the Saray Hotel, both with **currency exchange** and 24-hour **ATMs.** The *otogar* and the exchange office on İstiklâl Cad. change Syrian pounds at better rates. **Devlet Hastanesi** (tel. 214 54 30), 4km from town, is the best **hospital** in Antakya (take a taxi for $3-4). The **PTT,** in the center of town, has 24-hour phone service (mail service daily 8:30am-6pm). **Telephone code:** 326.

ACCOMMODATIONS AND FOOD

Most accommodations are not well suited to the budget traveler. **Hotel Saray,** 3 Hürriyet Cad. (tel./fax 214 90 01), across the river from the square, offers a pleasant breakfast salon and new rooms with bath (singles $11; doubles $15; breakfast included). **Hotel Orontes,** 58 İstiklâl Cad. (tel. 214 59 31; fax 214 59 33), has rooms with A/C and TV (singles $31; doubles $44; triples $55; breakfast included). Culinary enthusiasts will swoon over Antakya's specialty, *içli köfte* (a.k.a. *oruk*), a spicy bulgur wheat and red pepper shell stuffed with seasoned lamb and pine nuts. If you're visiting Turkey after traveling through the Levant, you may miss your old friend *hummus*. Fear not! Antakya is humm(us)ing with stores peddling the stuff, such as local fave ⊠**Anadolu Restaurant,** 50/C Hürriyet Cad. (tel. 215 15 41), down the street from the Saray Hotel (full meal $5-6; open 10am-midnight). ⊠**Han Restaurant** (tel. 214 17 16), on Hürriyet Cad., is a great place to hang out and sip drinks or *cacık* (garlicky yogurt with cucumbers). Full meals run $5-6 (open 10am-midnight). **'46 Edem Dondurma** (tel. 214 53 36), on Atatürk Cad., 100m from the center of town, scoops up your favorite fruit flavors and three varieties of *dövme* ("pounded," thick ice cream; $1; open 8pm-1am). Those who are sick of Turkish fare and looking for Turkish fair should head to the year-round **carnival,** 500m south of the square on İnönü Cad., the road that hugs the east side of the river.

👁 SIGHTS

HATAY MUSEUM. The famous Hatay Museum is all that is left of ancient Antioch's magnificence, displaying possibly the world's best collection of **Roman mosaics.** The museum is divided into six numbered rooms. In **Salon I,** fated lovers Atalanta and Meleager hunt down a well-rendered boar in a panel from the 2nd-century mosaic *The Four Seasons.* The *Theater Scene* in Salon II is not as well-preserved, but **Salon III** makes up for it with its small, priapic hunchback *(The Happy Hunchback)* that bears the Greek superscript *kai su* ("and you?"). Salon III also contains the *Evil Eye,* with a scantily clad man running in horror from an enormous levitating eye radiating farm implements. **Salon IV** has a giant 5th-century floor mosaic. Mosey away from the mosaics to the coin collection in the back salon or the sarcophagi in the garden. *(Open Tu-Su 8:30am-noon and 1:30-5pm. Admission $2.50, students $1.50.)*

ST. PETER'S CHURCH (SEN PİYER KİLİSESİ). Founded by the apostle Peter and carved into a cave so that services could be conducted in secret, this is the cave where the congregation coined the word "Christianity" to describe their new religion. A delegate of the French Commissary in Syria donated the nearby statuette of St. Peter. The hillside above the church, riddled with the remains of carved tunnels, natural caves, and bits of Antioch's city walls, has been a holy place since pagan times. A path zigzags 200m to a high relief of an obscure veiled figure, alternately described as a wind-blown Mary and the Syrian goddess of Hierapolis, flanked by Charon, boatman of Hades. *(Turn left from the otogar and make an immediate right onto İstiklâl Cad. After 1 block, turn right at the twin gas stations and continue 1.2km to a sign on the right. The church is 250m uphill. Take bus #6 or a taxi from town ($2.20). Church open Tu-Su 8am-noon and 1:30-4:30pm. Admission $1.25. Mass Su 3-4:30pm. Women traveling alone have been assaulted when climbing up past the Grotto.)*

CENTRAL ANATOLIA

While the Aegean and Mediterranean coasts suffer from rampant tourism, the high, dry mountain ranges of beautiful Central Anatolia hosts some of the country's most authentic, hospitable towns.

ANKARA

The capital of the Turkish Republic and once the domain of King Midas, Ankara hides its ancient roots of gold beneath modern cinder block. In 1923, Atatürk built this planned city overnight from a few goat pastures and swampland that were dredged to make way for the garish Gençlik Park. Today, Ankara is an administrative metropolis and the nation's premier college town. The Museum of Anatolian

Civilizations may well be Turkey's best museum, and one can begin to understand Atatürk's pivotal place in the national consciousness after visiting his mausoleum. Ankara is also a convenient base for securing visas to the rest of the Middle East.

⚡ ORIENTATION AND PRACTICAL INFORMATION

The city's main street, **Atatürk Bulvarı**, runs north-south. At its north end is the **Ulus** precinct, centered around an Atatürk statue. The traditional village of **Hisar** (Citadel) is east of Ulus and crowned by the 9th-century **Ankara Fortress** (*Ankara kale*). Ulus and Hisar comprise **Eskişehir** (Old City). Farther south along Atatürk Bul. is **Kızılay**, the center of **Yenişehir** (New City). West of Kızılay is **Maltepe**, a district full of grim nightclubs and cheap student dorms. **Kavaklıdere, Çankaya,** and **Gaziosmanpaşa**, south of Kızılay, have lush residential areas, embassies, and nightclubs. Bus #413 runs the length of Atatürk Bul., from the Atakule tower to the equestrian statue in Ulus. The **Ankaray suburban railway line** is the subway system in Ankara, running east-west from its center in Kızılay.

Airplanes: *Havaş* buses (every 30min. 4am-10:30pm, $5) to **Esenboğa Airport** (tel. 398 00 00) depart Hipodrom Cad. (next to train station). **Turkish Airlines** (THY), 154 Atatürk Bul., Kavaklıdere (info and reservations tel. 419 28 00) has flights to: **Antalya** (1hr., 3 per day, $60); **Istanbul** (1hr., 25 per day, $73); **İzmir** (1¼hr., 6 per day, $74); and **Trabzon** (1¼hr., 3 per day, $60). Open M-F 8:30am-8pm, Sa-Su 8:30am-5:30pm.

Buses: The **otogar** is the westernmost stop on the Ankaray subway line (take any train to Kızılay). To get to Ulus, take a *dolmuş* (60¢), city bus (50¢), or taxi ($6.25), or ride the metro 2 stops north to Cumhuriyet Cad. Buses to **Boğazkale** via **Sungurlu** (3hr., 20 per day 6am-1am, $5). **Varan**, 34/1 İzmir Cad., Kızılay (tel. 418 27 06 or 224 00 43) is safer and more comfortable for all major cities.

Dolmuş: At Haci Bayram Camii and at Denizciler-Adnan Saygun Cad. intersection.

Subway: The east-west Ankaray line (stations marked by a white "A" on green) connects the bus station to Dikimevi, with stops in Tandoğan, Maltepe, Kızılay, and the Colleges (Kolej). The north-south Metro line (white "M" on red background) also stops in Kızılay, running north from there to Sıhhiye, Ulus, and the northwestern suburbs. Runs 6:15am-midnight. 5-ride passes $2.50, students $1.50.

Tourist Offices: 121 Gazi Mustafa Kemal Bul. (tel. 231 55 72), at Maltepe Ankaray stop. English-speaking staff can interpret for **tourist police** (tel. 303 63 53). Open daily 9am-5pm. Ankara also has a 24hr. **airport tourist office** (tel. 398 03 48).

Embassies: Australia, 83 Nenehatun Cad., Gaziosmanpaşa (tel. 446 11 80; fax 446 11 88). Open M-Th 8am-4:35pm, F 8am-3:25pm. **Canada,** 75 Nenehatun Cad., Gaziosmanpaşa (tel. 436 12 75; fax 446 44 37). Citizen services M-Th 9am-5:30pm, F 9am-1pm. **Greece,** 9-11 Ziaürrahman Cad., Gaziosmanpaşa (tel. 436 88 60; fax 446 31 91). Visa applications M-F 9:30am-noon. **New Zealand,** 13/4 İran Cad., Kavaklıdere (tel. 467 90 56; fax 467 90 13). Open M-Th 8:30am-12:30pm and 1:30-5:30pm, F 8:30am-1pm. **South Africa,** 27 Filistin Sok., Gaziosmanpaşa (tel. 446 40 56; fax 446 64 34). Open M-F 8am-12:30pm and 1-4:30pm. **Syria,** 40 Sedat Simavi Sok., Çankaya (tel. 440 96 57). Visa applications M-F 8:30-9:30am. **U.K.,** 46A Şehit Ersan Cad., Çankaya (tel. 468 62 30; fax 468 32 14). Open M-F 9am-1pm and 2:30-5:30pm. **U.S.,** 110 Atatürk Bul., Kavaklıdere (tel. 468 61 10; fax 467 00 19). Citizen services M-Th 8:30-11:30am and 2:30-5:30pm, F 8:30-11:30am.

American Express: Koçbank or **Türkiye İş Bankası** will cash AmEx and usually MC **traveler's checks.** Akbank does not charge commission. AmEx cardholders can send and receive moneygrams at the Koçbank by the equestrian statue in Ulus Meydanı.

Hospital: Sevgi Hastanesi, 28 Tunus Cad., Kavaklıdere (tel. 419 44 44 or 419 44 60), and **Bayındır Tıp Merkezi,** Kızılırmak Mah. #3-3A, 28th Sok., Söğütözü (tel. 287 90 00), are among Ankara's best private hospitals.

TURKEY

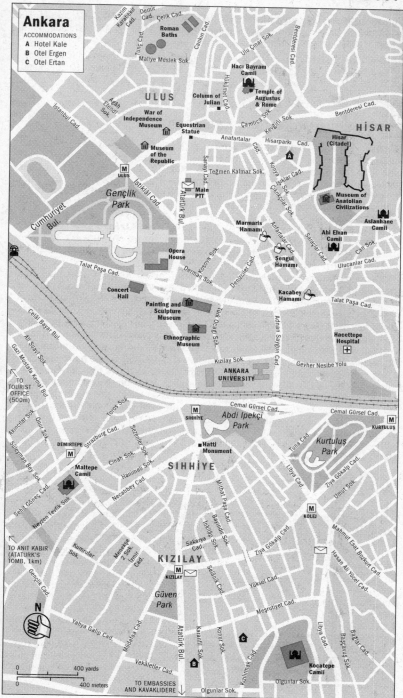

Ankara

ACCOMMODATIONS
A Hotel Kale
B Otel Ergen
C Otel Ertan

Internet Access: **Internet Center Cafe,** 107 Atatürk Bul. (tel. 419 27 54; fax 425 79 27), on the 3rd floor of the Engürü İş Hanı. Before noon $1.90 per hr., after noon $2.50 per hr. Open daily 9am-11pm.

PTT: In **Ulus,** on Atatürk Bul., just south of the equestrian statue. Open 24hr. In **Kızılay,** on Atatürk Bul. just off Kızılay Sq. Open M-Sa 8am-8pm, Su 8:30am-12:30pm and 1:30-5:30pm. In the **train station,** on Talat Paşa Cad. Open daily 7am-11pm.

Telephone code: 312.

ACCOMMODATIONS AND FOOD

The lively, student-oriented **Kızılay** is more expensive but more pleasant than the dustier, noisier **Ulus** (which is nearer the sights). To get to ■**Hotel Kale,** Anafartalar Cad., 13 Alataş Sok., Ulus (tel. 311 33 93 or 310 35 21), follow Anafartalar Cad. toward the Citadel, bear right before it becomes Hisarparkı Cad., and take the third left onto Şan Sok; it's at the intersection of Şan Sok. and Alataş Sok. All of the sunny rooms have baths; most have TVs (singles $14; doubles $24; triples $34). **Otel Ertan,** 70 Selânik Cad. (tel. 418 40 84 or 425 15 06), has the cheapest rooms in Kızılay (singles $13.75; doubles $20). **Hotel Ergen,** 48 Karanfil Sok., Kızılay (tel. 417 59 06/7; fax 425 78 19), the first right off Meşrutiyet Cad., is an elegant two-star hotel with private showers, baths, and TVs (singles $27.50; doubles $37.50).

The main culinary hotspots are Gençlik Park (cheap), Kızılay (mid-range), and Hisar and Kavaklıdere (embassy worker-filled upscale). **Hoşdere Cad.,** southeast of Atakule Tower, lays claim to many good restaurants. The supermarket **Gima** has branches on Atatürk Bul. in Kızılay and on Anafartalar Cad. in Ulus. ■**Göksu Restaurant,** 22/A Bayındır Sok. (tel. 431 22 19), one of the classier places in Kızılay (despite the poorly-executed "Hittite reliefs" on the walls) offers cheap and tasty Turkish and European food (filet mignon $4.50; open daily 11am-midnight). ■**Daily News Cafe,** 1 Arjantin Cad., Kavaklıdere (tel. 468 46 13), lets patrons peruse a free copy of the English-language *Turkish Daily News* or just pore over the newspaper decor (fusilli with porcini mushrooms $6; open daily 9am-midnight). **Cafe M,** 42 Selânik Cad., Kızılay (tel. 419 36 65), is so chic it doesn't even need a full name; its desserts—*muzlu süt* (banana milk) or tiramisu ($1 each)—will surely leave you full (open daily 7am-10:30pm). There's nothing rotten at the Danish **Kristiansen,** 24 Arjantin Cad., Kavaklıdere (tel. 466 13 46). Escape cafe fare with salads ($7), *smørrebrød* (sandwiches, $7-8), and, of course, danishes ($2; open daily 8am-11pm).

ENTERTAINMENT

Like so many other aspects of the city, Ankara's low-key, sit-a-spell nightlife is centered around Kızılay. Pub life thrives on **İnkilâp Sok.** and **Bayındır Sok.,** east of Kızılay Sq. Bar prices are fairly uniform: a pint of Efes, the local favorite, goes for $1.10-1.50; mixed drinks range from $3-4. **Gölge Bar,** 1-2-3 S.S.K. İşhane (tel. 434 09 78), is Ankara's #1 rock bar, playing nightly host to distortion-heavy cover bands and crowds who dig the cheap beer ($1.25). There's a cover charge only after 9pm on Friday and Saturday ($2.50, includes a beer; open daily 1pm-4am). **Nil Bar,** 19/C Bayındır Sok. (tel. 431 07 73), and **Alesta Bar** (tel. 431 12 04) open onto the street next door to each other, both with pleasant outdoor tables and deafening cover bands playing a mix of Turkish and American rock (beer $1.35; open daily 9am-1am). **Zx Bar Disco,** 14/A Bayındır Sok. (tel. 431 35 35), packs a three-floor Turkish pop punch: disco downstairs, live music upstairs, and a bar in the middle of it all (open daily noon-midnight). **The North Shield,** 111 Güvenlik Cad., Kavaklıdere (tel. 466 12 66; fax 468 86 91), one of the most popular bars in the area, is a Scottish pub with argyle carpeting and studded leather barstools (local beers $3.75, whiskies $6.25 and way up; open daily noon-1am).

◉ SIGHTS

◙MUSEUM OF ANATOLIAN CIVILIZATIONS. This museum, at the foot of the Citadel, recently won Europe's Museum of the Year Award and *Let's Go's* "Where All the Artifacts From Surrounding Sights Are" Award. This restored 15th-century Ottoman building houses a collection of astoundingly old artifacts tracing the history of Anatolia from the 6th millennium BCE onward). Some of the greatest hits include: artifacts from Çatalhöyük, which vies with Jericho (see p. 388) for the title of Oldest City in the World; perfectly preserved Hittite bull vessels; and a life-sized reproduction of King Midas's tomb. *(Adjacent to the Citadel. Open Tu-Su 8:30am-5:15pm. Admission $3, students $2.)*

ATATÜRK'S MAUSOLEUM (ANIT KABİR). Upon Atatürk's death, Turkey held an international contest to select a plan for his mausoleum; the winner, Emin Onat, designed the Hittite-influenced Anıt Kabir. Now covering 750,000m² near Tandoğan Sq., the building took nine years to complete, simple in execution but monumental in scope (like Atatürk himself). Six unhappy statues at the mausoleum's entrance represent Turkey's grief for their father's death, and 24 paired lions (symbols of power) line the broad stone promenade leading to the mausoleum. Across the courtyard is the tomb of **İsmet İnönü,** first prime minister of the Republic. The mausoleum complex has such Atatürkana as his 1936 Lincoln sedan, his rowing machine, his tie clips, and even photographs taken after his death showing cloud formations shaped like his profile. *(Ankaray: Tandoğan. Follow the signs to the entrance, guarded by 2 soldiers. Open M 1:30-5pm, Tu-Su 9am-5pm. Free.)*

MOSQUES. Completed in 1987, ◙**Kocatepe Mosque** is a 20th-century take on 16th-century piety, complete with electric chandeliers, digital clocks blipping away prayer times, and an underground shopping strip. Inside is a model of the mosque at Medina (the second holiest Muslim site in the world), a gift from Saudi Arabia's King Fahd. Amidst the nearby Roman ruins is one of Ankara's most important mosques, the **Haci Bayram Camii,** built alongside the tomb of dervish saint Haci Bayram Veli. The mosque first did time as the Roman Temple of Augustus. *(Kocatepe: east of Kızılay on Mithat Paşa Cad. Haci Bayram: east of Ulus' equestrian statue on Anafartalar Cad.; take a left at Gima supermarket.)*

NEAR ANKARA: SUNGURLU AND BOĞAZKALE

Nowhere is the former glory of the 4000-year-old Hittite civilization more evident than at its ruined capital, Hattuşaş, on the outskirts of present-day Boğazkale (just over 200km east of Ankara and 30km off the Samsun highway). Beginning in 1600 BCE, the great Hittite kings occupied Hattuşaş for four centuries, competing with the Egyptians for control of the fertile lands and trade routes of Mesopotamia. The 8km loop passing through the site makes for a beautiful hike through a wild landscape of cliffs and valleys. Two kilometers northeast of the site is Yazılıkaya, an open air temple with bas-reliefs of 100 of the 1000 or so Hittite gods. On the main road, Boğazkale's museum maintains a collection of the site's artifacts.

🛈 ORIENTATION AND PRACTICAL INFORMATION

Sungurlu is nothing more than a jumping off point for Boğazkale. **Lise Caddesi** runs from the main highway to the center of town, passing the large, green **Gençlik Park** before intersecting **Cengiztopel Caddesi,** marked by the Hotel Fatih. Buses to Sungurlu stop on the main highway or at the *otogar*, which sits just off the highway across from a Petrol Ofisi gas station. **Buses** leave the *otogar* for: **Ankara** (3hr., 13 per day 7:15am-9pm, $3.75); **Bodrum** (10hr., 6:30pm, $15); **Fethiye** (10hr., 7pm, $16.25); and **Istanbul** (9hr., 8:30pm, $12.50). **Türkiye İş Bankası,** within sight of the Hotel Fatih, cashes traveler's checks and has an **ATM.** The local hospital is **Devlet Hastanesi** (tel. 311 80 07). **Telephone code:** 364.

TURKEY

🔦📷 ACCOMMODATIONS AND FOOD

If you're stuck in Sungurlu, crash at the **Hotel Fatih,** 23 Cengiztopel Cad. (tel. 311 34 88; singles $10; doubles $16.25). Hit the **Hitit Motel** (tel. 311 84 09), 1km farther along the highway away from Ankara, for a pool and rooms with TV and private bath (breakfast $4, dinner $9). To get to the elegant **Birand Restaurant** (tel. 311 99 16), inside Özel İdare İşhanı, follow Lise Cad. past the intersection with Cengiztopel Cad. and take the next right onto Çorum Cad. The comprehensive menu includes *dolma* (90¢), cold *mezes* (90¢), and grills ($1.50-2; open daily 5:30am-12:30am). Crunchy *leblebi* (roasted chickpeas), a regional specialty, are available at dozens of shops throughout town.

🏛 BOĞAZKALE

To get to Boğazkale, take *a dolmuş* next to Gençlik Park (25min., every 30min. 7am-5:30pm, 75¢), or catch a private taxi ($15-20 round-trip). Both of these impressive Hittite ruins are open daily in summer 8am-7pm; in winter 8am-5:30pm. Admission to both is $1.75, students $1.

HATTUŞAŞ. Hattuşaş is where many of the Hittite artifacts housed at the Museum of Anatolian Civilizations in Ankara (see p. 589) were unearthed. Walking the loop around Hattuşaş in a counter-clockwise direction, you'll first pass the **Büyük Mabet,** a temple dedicated to the storm god Teshub and the sun goddess Hepatu in which everything is in groups of three (the Hittite holy number). The green Egyptian stones inside the entrance were the altar for animal sacrifices. Farther in are attendants' quarters and the temple's **warehouses,** where thousands of cuneiform tablets were found in 1907. Downhill from the temple were the offices of Assyrian merchants, where the "Rosetta Stone" of Hittite was found: a text translated into Akkadian and Hittite hieroglyphs allowed scholars to translate the elusive Hittite language. (The real Rosetta Stone, which helped historians translate hieroglyphs, was found in Rashid, Egypt; see p. 132.) On the right of the forked road is the *Aslanlıkapı,* or **Lion's Gate,** outfitted with special grooves for the hubs of entering chariot wheels to pass through unscratched. A photographic computer reproduction posted nearby shows what the gate might have looked like in the 13th century BCE. Follow the restored city walls running atop the embankment to the *Sfenksli Kapı,* or **Sphinx Gate,** once guarded by four sphinxes (only one remains). The plum tree to the left of the gate marks the point where the cuneiform- and hieroglyphic-inscribed Boğazkale tablets at Ankara's Museum of Anatolian Civilizations were found. Eastward and downhill along the wall are two hieroglyphic chambers, 50m apart on the right side of the road. **Chamber 2** was commissioned around 1200 BCE by King Shuppiluliuma II, the last king of Hattuşaş, and has a relief of this king holding a symbol with an inscription mentioning a "divine earth road," the symbolic entrance to the underworld. Last on the tour is the **Büyük Kale,** a ruined complex of archives, offices, and royal apartments linked by courtyards and containing over 8000 cuneiform tablets (including a treaty between Hattuziliz II and the pharaoh Ramses II).

YAZILIKAYA. The nearby holy shrine of Yazılıkaya was originally a series of narrow ravines in the rock (Yazılıkaya means "inscribed rock" in Turkish) with reliefs of gods and goddesses on parade. Goddesses appear in profile, wearing long, trailing robes; gods face forward, and their rank can be inferred by the number of horns on their hats. Archaeologists believe that **Chamber A** was used to celebrate the Hittite New Year every spring. The chamber definitely proves that the Hittites had never heard of the Beach Boys ("Two girls for every boy..."): reliefs of 42 male gods face half as many goddesses. On the far wall, the sculpture culminates in the marriage of the Hittite's most powerful deities, **Teshub,** the storm god, and **Hepatu,** the sun goddess. Facing the procession of deities is the famous 2.6m high relief representing **King Tudhaliya IV** (c. 1250-1220 BCE), who stands astride two mountains and under a winged sun disk. **Chamber B,** accessible via a passage to the right

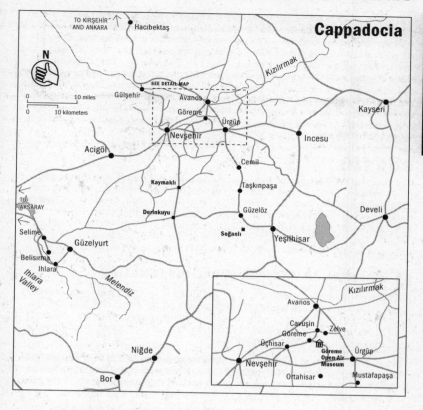

TURKEY

of the entrance, was the site of animal sacrifice and contains a relief of 12 sword-carrying gods that are believed to represent the months of the year.

CAPPADOCIA

No other place on earth looks quite like Cappadocia. The unique landscape began to take shape 10 million years ago, when volcanic lava and ash hardened into a layer of soft rock called *tufa*. Rain, wind, and flooding from the Kızılırmak River shaped the *tufa* into a striking landscape of cone-shaped monoliths called *peribaca* ("fairy chimneys"), which are grouped in cave-riddled valleys and along gorge ridges. Throughout Cappadocia's other-worldly moonscapes, stairs, windows, and sentry holes have been carved into the already eerily-eroded rock.

⬛ GETTING AROUND

Nevşehir is the region's transportation hub; even when tickets appear to be direct to Göreme or Ürgüp, what you're really getting is a *servis* shuttle to Nevşehir, then a regular bus onward from there. During the high season, a *dolmuş* follows the Ürgüp-Göreme-Çavuşin-Zelve-Avanos circuit (June-Sept. leaves Ürgüp every 2hr. 10am-6pm; returns from Avanos every 2hr. 9am-5pm). In winter, most connections within Cappadocia must be made via Nevşehir, from where buses depart every 30min. for all major Cappadocian towns. Transportation within this region should cost less than $1. Most visits to southern Cappadocia must be made though Aksaray. Buses from Nevşehir to Ankara stop in Aksaray (every hr., $2.50 to Aksaray).

Many backpackers choose to travel around Cappadocia by moped or motorcycle. Rental agencies in Göreme and Ürgüp rent **mopeds** ($6 per hr., $20 per day), **motorcycles** ($46 per day), and **bicycles** ($2 per hr., $12 per day). **Car rentals** start at about $30 per day, though prices skyrocket for automatic transmission. **Europcar** (tel. 341 34 88 or 341 43 15) in Ürgüp rents automatics with air conditioning for $88 per day. **Guided tours** of Cappadocia's major sites are available from agencies in Göreme (see p. 592) and Ürgüp (see p. 595). These agencies typically provide daylong tours of the region including transportation, lunch, and admission to all the sights ($25, students $23).

GÖREME

The village of Göreme may be small, but it is indisputably a bigshot in the Cappadocian tourist industry. Located in the heart of Cappadocia, Göreme has no fewer than 120 pensions, mostly cave dwellings carved into the soft *tufa*. Similarly grotesque numbers of tour groups operate here, yet a small-town charm prevails: Göreme still looks and feels like a rural Turkish village, with donkey-drawn carts and hundreds of fairy chimneys. Göreme's central location makes it the best base for exploring Cappadocia, and the surreal Open-Air Museum is just a short walk away.

■ ORIENTATION AND PRACTICAL INFORMATION

Navigating Göreme is not difficult. Most everything is along the **main road,** the only street in town paved with asphalt. The **otogar,** just off the main road, is at the eastern end of the town center. Nearby, a road up to the Open-Air Museum breaks off from the main road, heading south up a hill. Restaurants are mostly near the main road, and *pansiyon*s are everywhere.

Buses: From the *otogar,* buses travel via **Nevşehir** to: **Ankara** (4hr., 14 per day, $7.50); **Bursa** (10hr., 3 per day, $14); **Istanbul** (11hr., 8 per day 6:30-8:30pm, $15); **Pamukkale** (10hr., 6 per day, $14); **İzmir** (11hr., 3 per day, $15); **Olimpos** (12hr., 7 per day, $19); **Marmaris** (14hr., 5 per day, $20); and **Bodrum** (14hr., 6 per day, $19).

Tourist Office: This hotel-run cooperative in the *otogar* only gives info on lodgings.

Travel Agencies: The most reputable are **Zemi Tours** (tel. 271 25 76; fax 271 25 77), on the left side of the road leading from the *otogar* to the Open-Air Museum, and **Neşe Tours** (tel. 271 25 25 or 271 26 43; fax 271 25 24; www.prizma.net.tr/~nesecafe), next to the Internet Cafe. Popular full-day tours hit all the highlights (departs 9:30am, returns at sunset; $25, students $23; lunch and all admission fees included). **Kapadokya Balloons** (tel. 271 24 42; fax 271 25 86; www.kapadokyaballoons.com) offers 90-min. **balloon tours,** a.k.a. "aerial nature walks," held Apr.-Oct. daily at dawn, weather permitting; $210-230; book at least the day before.

Banks: Two are next to the Open-Air Museum. Open daily 9am-5:30pm.

Laundromat: Tel. 271 25 79, behind the *otogar,* across from the Göreme Belediye Handicrafts Market. Wash and dry $5, with ironing $5.50. Open daily 9am-8pm.

Medical Assistance: Göreme Sağlık Ocağı Hospital (tel. 271 21 26), near the PTT, is more of a clinic, but it will do in a pinch.

Pharmacy: On the main road near the hospital. Open daily 8am-8pm.

PTT: On the main road just after the turn-off for the Open-Air Museum. The best exchange rate in town. Open daily 8:30am-12:30pm and 1:30-5:30pm.

Telephone Code: 384.

ACCOMMODATIONS

The government of Göreme has set the prices for the town's hostels according to the following scale: dorms $5; singles $6, with shower $8. The prices may soon rise to $5, $7, and $10, respectively. Though this eliminates haggling and undercutting, establishments designated as starred hotels can charge higher rates. The tourist office in the *otogar* advertises dozens of pensions; most will pick you up if you call.

Köse Pansiyon (tel. 271 22 94; fax 271 25 77), just behind the PTT. Makeshift Ottoman divans, vine-covered ceilings, a swimming pool, a bookshelf replete with guidebooks to Turkey and Cappadocia, and helpful Scottish-Turkish owners leave nothing left to be desired. Breakfast $1.25; vegetarian and 4-course dinners $4. Dorms (bring your own sleeping bag, if possible) and private rooms, some with bath.

Kookaburra Pansiyon (tel. 271 25 49), up on the hill behind the bus terminal. The name's meant to attract backpackers from Down Under, but the attractive rooms, some with private showers and stunning views, could have done the trick on their own.

Paradise Pension (tel./fax 271 22 48). The name fits, if "paradise" means an excellent pension located on the road to the Open-Air Museum. Two fairy chimney rooms, each with 5 beds and shared bath, as well as 9 smaller rooms. Turkish breakfast $1.60. Special meals offered most nights. Laundry $6.

Kelebek Motel-Pension (tel. 271 25 31; fax 271 27 63), a 5min. hike up from the *otogar*. Göreme's most elevated *pansiyon*, with elevated prices to boot. Beautiful hardwood-floored dorm rooms, as well as singles and doubles, some with showers. English-language videos shown in the cave bar. Breakfast $1.50-2, dinner $4-5. Laundry $5. Doubles $10-12; Ottoman doubles $25; other cave rooms $14-18. Visa, MC accepted.

FOOD AND ENTERTAINMENT

Cafe Doci@ (tel. 271 29 03; www.indigotourizm.com.tr/cafedoci@), to the left as you exit the *otogar* on the road toward Nevşehir. Run by young entrepreneurs and pun lovers Arman and Haluk, whose flawless English has an Australian twang. Mammoth burgers $4. Good beer ($2) and good times make this the place to be on a night out on the town. Big-screen TV offers American movies, *Mr. Bean*, *Friends*, and *South Park*, and 2 computer terminals provide access to the 'net for $4 per hr. $2 after 8pm. Open late.

Flintstones Bar (tel. 657 32 81), at the turn-off for the Open-Air Museum. In the town of Bed-*rakı*, fans of Britpop will have a yabba-dabba-doo time. American movies and BBC news during the day. No food, but a well-stocked bar. Beer $1.50. Open until dawn.

Pacha Bar (tel. 271 23 40). In the middle of Göreme's central promenade, Pacha is the busiest bar in town. Enjoy drinks (beer $1.50) either at the bar or on cushioned benches. Open until no one's left.

Escape Bar (tel. 543 27 14), below a giant fairy chimney flying the Turkish flag. This converted donkey barn is Göreme's only dance club; writhe along with the featured nightly belly dancers. Beer $2. Happy hour 10pm. Open until morning.

SIGHTS

GÖREME OPEN-AIR MUSEUM. Containing seven Byzantine churches, a convent, and a kitchen/refectory, the Open-Air Museum offers the most impressive concentration of frescoed churches in Cappadocia. In the 4th century, St. Basil founded one of the first Christian monasteries here, setting down religious tenets that influenced the teachings of St. Benedict and, subsequently, the entire Western monastic tradition. The most spectacular frescoes adorn the recently renovated **Karanlık Kilise** ("Dark Church"). **Çarıklı Kilise** ("Sandal Chruch") was so named because of the footprint on the ground, reportedly a mold of Jesus' sole. **Yılanlı Kilise,** marked by a hermaphroditic-looking figure, is also known as St. Onuphrius Church. According to one legend, the Egyptian girl Onophirios was so beautiful that she could not drive away all the men seeking to ravish her. She prayed for assistance and was granted a long white beard and mustache, which solved all her problems. If only it were still that easy. (*1km out of Göreme on the Ürgüp road. Walk 100m from the Göreme bus station and take a right at the 1st major intersection. Open June 15-Oct. 15 8am-6:30pm; Oct. 16-June 14 8am-5:30pm. Admission $4, students $2. Additional charge for Karanlık Kilise $7.80, students $4.*)

◤ HIKING: NEAR GÖREME

When good Christians die, they go to heaven; when good hikers die, they go to Cappadocia. Mountain ranges with spectacular views and eerie rock formations are all within throwing distance of Göreme. Follow the road leading to the Open-Air Museum 1km past the museum itself, take a left on the dirt road by Kaya Camping, turn left again at the next paved road, and walk 3km to reach **Sunset Point** ($0.60, students $0.40). From there, you can descend into the **Rose Valley,** where bizarre, multi-colored rock formations make for one of the area's better hikes. After getting lost a few times, you'll eventually end up in Çavuşin; take the Avanos-Nevşehir **bus** or the Avanos-Zelve-Göreme-Ürgüp minibus back to Göreme (every 30min. until 6pm, weekends every hr.), or take a **taxi** instead ($4). Follow the canal west of the bus terminal to reach **Pigeon Valley,** whose namesakes have unfortunately been hunted almost to extinction. This hike is also somewhat confusing, but ultimately you'll end up in Uçhisar. Located to the north of Göreme is **Love Valley,** affectionately known as "Penis Valley" because of the phallic rock formations that would give even Dirk Diggler a complex. If you're short on time, consider a **guided tour** of the nearby terrain. Tour companies all peddle similar trips, typically departing at 9:30am and returning around sunset ($25, students $23).

NEAR GÖREME: KAYMAKLI AND DERİNKUYU

By dolmuş, Kaymaklı and Derinkuyu are about 30min. and 45min. from Göreme, respectively. From Göreme, dolmuş run to Nevşehir (every 30min. 6:30am-7pm, 40¢), then go to Kaymaklı (50¢) and Derinkuyu (75¢). Both sites are open daily 8am-7pm; off-season 8am-5:30pm. Kaymaklı admission $2.50, students $2. Derinkuyu admission $2.50, students $1.50.

In 1962, a farmer stumbled upon the underground city of Derinkuyu after searching his farm for a lost chicken. Though Cappadocia contains almost 200 such **underground cities,** Kaymaklı and Derinkuyu are the largest. The earliest written mention of Hellenic communities in Derinkuyu and Kaymaklı appears in Xenophon's *Anabasis,* which dates them to at least the 4th century BCE. All carved from *tufa,* the underground complexes were designed with mind-boggling ingenuity: low, narrow passages blocked off by massive boulders hindered would-be invaders, and sudden drops hidden behind corners threw intruders to their deaths. It was forbidden for anyone to leave while the cities were occupied, lest their departure give away the hideouts. Strangely, no toilets or other evidence of a permanent settlement have been conclusively found in either Derinkuyu or Kaymaklı.

Derinkuyu, 85m deep with a 120m well, is slightly more impressive. With eight levels open to the public, Derinkuyu has sizable rooms and halls, good lighting, and is relatively easy to access. **Kaymaklı,** smaller than Derinkuyu at 35m below ground, boasts a more complex structure. The modern village has been built around the underground city, so residents can enter storage areas through tunnels in their courtyards. One of Cappadocia's famous "blocked" tunnels is rumored to span 9km from Kaymaklı back to Derinkuyu. In both sites, red arrows lead down, blue arrows up. Both cities have uncharted tunnels, so be careful—these cities were designed to kill potential trespassers, and that means you.

ÜRGÜP

Göreme and Ürgüp vie for control of the Cappadocian tourist industry. Göreme's central location, proximity to hikes, and staggering excess of *pansiyons* and tour groups make it the more popular choice, but Ürgüp offers the double whammy of a less touristed atmosphere and a better organized information network. The town emerges from a collage of bizarre rock formations and early Christian dwellings interspersed among sunny vineyards and old Greek mansions, and its *otogar* and rental agencies offer access to most Cappadocian points of interest.

◪ ORIENTATION AND PRACTICAL INFORMATION. The main square, marked by a bath house and an Atatürk statue, is 20m down **Güllüce Caddesi** from the *otogar*. This road forks uphill into two smaller roads, both full of pensions and hotels. **Buses** head to: **Ankara** (5hr., 13 per day, $7.50); **Pamukkale** (10hr., 1 per day, $14); **Istanbul** (12hr., 5 per day, $15); **İzmir** (12hr., 1 per day, $15); **Kuşadası** (13hr., 1 per day, $17.50); **Selçuk** (13hr., 1 per day, $17.50); **Bodrum** (14hr., 1 per day, $19); **Fethiye** (15hr., 1 per day, $19); and **Marmaris** (15hr., 1 per day, $19). Aydın "the English speaker" Altan of **Nevtur** (tel. 341 43 02) can answer bus-related questions.

Run by İhsan "Mr. Jolly" Tarhan, the **tourist office** (tel. 341 40 59) is inside the garden on Kayseri Cad. (open daily Apr.-Oct. 8am-7pm; Nov.-Mar. 8am-5pm). **Erko Tours** (tel. 341 32 52 or 341 51 61; fax 341 37 85), in the *otogar*, organizes tours of Cappadocia. Several **rental agencies** are located near the *otogar* (bikes $5-10 per day, mopeds $15-20, cars from $30). **Tarihi Şehir Hamamı**, in the main square, is co-ed, so bring a friend; a complete bath with massage/scrub and sauna goes for $5 (open daily 7am-11pm). Several **pharmacies** cluster near the *otogar*. For medical assistance, call the **hospital** (tel. 341 40 31) or the **Cappadocia Health Center**, 28 Dumlupınar Cad. (tel. 341 54 27/8; fax 341 34 92). Surf the web at **Asia Teras** (tel. 341 38 39), about 20m to the left when exiting the tourist office ($2.50 per hr.; open 9am-midnight). To reach the **PTT**, head right from the tourist office and take the first right uphill (open daily in summer 8am-7pm; in winter 8am-5pm; **currency exchange** closed noon-1:30pm). **Telephone code:** 384.

⌂⌂⌂ ACCOMMODATIONS AND FOOD. The town's only backpacker hostel, **◪ Bahçe Hostel** (tel. 341 33 14; fax 341 48 78), is directly opposite the *hamam*. The Australian-Turkish management goes out of its way to provide information, organize tours, and ensure its clients the best deal on any purchase or rental. The cave bar and disco are a good environment for making alliances with fellow travelers. (Dorm beds $5; rooms $5, with bath $6; breakfast $1.25.) Sleep in splendor at **Hotel Asia Minor** (tel. 341 46 45; fax 341 27 21), behind the Atatürk statue, in a beautiful 150-year-old Greek mansion with a lovely garden and frescoes. Rooms have wood-panelled floors and Ottoman divans. ($30 per person; breakfast included.) **Hotel Akuzun** (tel. 341 38 69; fax. 341 37 85), across from Hotel Asia Minor, offers clean, modern rooms with showers; some even have balconies and bathtubs. Drinks are served on a rooftop terrace, breakfast outside in a rose garden. (Singles $27; doubles $52; triples $65; half price in off-season.)

Han Çirağan (tel. 341 41 69), between the *hamam* and the Harem Disco, has appropriated a 300-year-old *kervansaray* whose rooms are still used by merchants in horse-drawn carriages (*menemen* $2, *güveç* $2.50, mixed grill $3, *tandir kebap* $4.50). The tourist-oriented **Şömine Cafe**, in the center of the town square, specializes in the sketchily named *testi kebap*. It's actually a mix of lamb, tomatoes, onions, and garlic roasted in a clay pot; after six hours, the pot is broken to reveal a meal for two ($8; other entrees $2-4). **Cappadocia Restaurant** (tel. 341 40 29), a few blocks from the center of town on Kongre Salonu Yanı Cad., dishes up a mean *dolma* ($1.50), as well as plenty of vegetarian dishes.

♫ ENTERTAINMENT. Cappadocia is one of Turkey's major viticultural regions, and Ürgüp is its cork. Uphill to the right behind the Atatürk statue, the renowned **◪Turasan Winery**, supplier of 60% of Cappadocia's wines, offers free tours and tastings in its rock-carved cellar. Buy the cheap "wino specials" (most bottles $2.50-4) or splurge on the more robust '89 vintage ($7.50) and the notable '97 Kalecik Karası ($15; open 8am-8pm; tours available until 5pm). Several wine shops around the main square also offer free tastings. In the fall, the Ürgüp **wine festival** brings eager, full-bodied competitors from France, Italy, Argentina, and the U.S.

If you find yourself still energized after a day of trooping through Ürgüp's narrow cobblestone streets, get ready to dance. **Harem Disco,** at the foot of the road to the winery, blasts Turkish and European techno in a candlelit cave with a fireplace and disco ball (open daily until 4am). **Armağan Disco,** across the street from the Kapadokya Market (under the "Born To Be Free" sign), occasionally interrupts the 70s tunes and Turkish pop with a belly dancing act. Upstairs, several (relatively) quiet stone-cut rooms with divans and carpets sometimes host live traditional music (beer and *rakı* $2.50; open until 5am).

BLACK SEA COAST

Along the shores of the Black Sea, the heat of Anatolia gives way to sea breezes and tall fir forests. Where forests thin out, fields of tobacco and cherries alternate with sloping pastures spotted with grazing cattle. Traveling between towns often requires hours of transit in a crowded *dolmuş* careening treacherously around narrow mountain roads. The relative brevity and regular afternoon rainshowers of the summer season on the Black Sea coast may have left the area untouched by international tourism, but its allures are no secret to Turks. The beaches of Amasra and Sinop teem with vacationing Turkish college students. First settled by Phoenician and Greek colonists, the ancient trading posts of Sinop, Trabzon, and Amissos (now Samsun) were once pivotal links on the Byzantine Silk Road. Until recently, NATO naval bases dotted the coast, staring down Soviet fleets on the horizon. Of late, commerce with Georgia and other former Soviet republics has brought prosperity, but has also led to a marked increase in prostitution in urban areas like Trabzon.

SAFRANBOLU

The entire old Ottoman town of Safranbolu has been preserved, with development relegated to the new city 3km away. The restoration effort began in 1975, and today many of the refurbished houses have been converted to hotels or *gezi evleri*

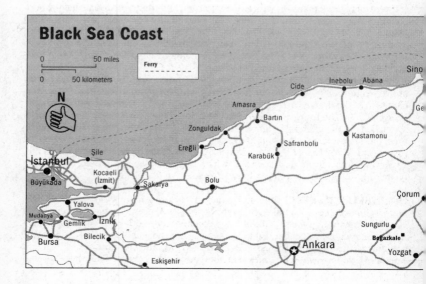

(open houses). Safranbolu remains one of the best places in Turkey to laze like a 19th-century *paşa* and soak in Ottoman domestic and culinary traditions.

⌖ ORIENTATION AND PRACTICAL INFORMATION. Safranbolu has two distinct sections: the beautiful old town, called **Çarşı**, and the dusty, uninteresting new one, called **Yeni Safranbolu** or **Kıranköy**. The main square, **Mehmet Kurtulanı Meydanı**, is Çarşı's center of transportation. If you stand in the square and look toward the old baths, you will see three streets. On the extreme left, **Kastamonu Caddesi** leads to the Çarşı Pansiyon. The next street, **Akın Sokak** runs to the Cinci Han, an old *kervansaray*. To the right, **Yukarı Çarşı Sokak** leads to the Arasna and the tourist office. Behind you, **Hilmi Bayramgil Caddesi** runs to the new town.

While direct **buses** do travel to Safranbolu, you may have to take a *dolmuş* from **Karabük**, a less-than-lovely steel manufacturing town 10km away (15min., frequent 7am-7pm, 40¢). Avoid Karabük entirely by getting off on the road to Safranbolu and waiting for the Karabük-Safranbolu *dolmuş* there. Buses and *dolmuş* will most likely stop in the new town. To get to Çarşı from there, catch any *dolmuş* running along the broad boulevard (5min., frequent 7:10am-11pm, 25¢). To return to Karabük, which has more bus options, take a *dolmuş* from Çarşı. Buses from new Safranbolu go to: **Amasra** via **Bartın** (2¾hr., 8am, $3.50); **Ankara** (3hr., 5 per day 5am-5:45pm, $6); **Antakya** (14hr., 3:30pm, $19); **Bursa** (8hr., 8pm, $14.30); **Istanbul** (6hr.; 8, 11am, 11:30pm; $12); **İzmir** (12hr., 8pm, $19); and **Trabzon** (12hr., 5:30pm, $19). **Taxis** between the old and new town cost about $3.60.

The **tourist office**, 5 Arasta Sok. (tel./fax 712 38 63), offers maps (open 8:30am-6pm). **T.C. Ziraat Bankası**, behind Cinci Han, has an **ATM** (open M-F 8:30am-noon and 1:30pm-6pm; currency and traveler's check exchange until 4:30pm). The **hospital** (tel. 712 11 87) is in the new town, near Kaya Erdem Cad., behind the Kız Sağlık Meslek Lisesi. The **PTT** is on Hamamönü Sok., near the Çarşı Pansiyon (open M-Sa 8:30am-12:30pm and 1:30-5:30pm). **Telephone code:** 370.

⌖⌖⌖ ACCOMMODATIONS, FOOD, AND ENTERTAINMENT. Since Safranbolu is popular year-round, try to make reservations a few days in advance. From the square, signs lead to **Çarşı Pansiyon**, 1 Bozkurt Sok. (tel. 725 10 79). The best deal in town, Çarşı gives the choice of standard rooms with shared

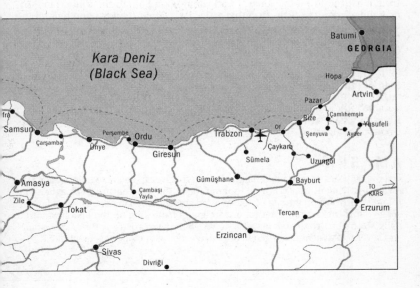

bath, or rooms with private bath and floor mattresses. (Singles $12; doubles $24; triples $28.50. Breakfast included.) If you aren't looking for luxuries, **Otel Gülen**, 2 Utku Sok., Ulu Camii Karşısı (tel. 725 10 82), is the cheapest place around, with one shared bath for all. Walk from the roundabout in new Safranbolu towards Çarşı and take the second right onto Cumhuriyet Cad.; the hotel is about 150m ahead. (Singles $2.40; doubles $4.75; triples $5.35; quads $7.10.) **Havuzlu Konak**, 18 Beybağı Sok. (tel. 725 28 83; fax 712 38 24), is an opulent restored Ottoman villa with lace bedspreads, couches, and brass tables. Stop in for *çay* even if you can't afford to stay—it's worth a look (singles $35-40; doubles $50-60; triples $70-80).

Kadıoğlu Şehzade Sofrası, 8 Arasta Sok. (tel. 712 50 91; fax 712 56 57), on the main square, serves the regional specialty *kuyu kebap* ($3.80), made by hanging a whole lamb in an underground pit and roasting it for hours. Ottoman couches, low tables, and a bubbling fountain create a slick, though touristy, atmosphere (most entrees $2.50-3; open 8am-midnight). Join locals for inexpensive, ambience-free meals at **Merkez Lokantası**, 1 Yukarı Çarşı (tel. 725 14 78). *Köfte* can't be beat at $1.80; chickpeas are a cheap $1 (open Su-F 7:30am-3am, Sa 7:30am-8pm).

Most nightspots are clustered together in a nest of buildings behind the Cinci Han. **Beyaz Ev Pub**, 18-20 Pazar Yeri (tel. 712 52 53), has a friendly environment, great live music, and $1.60 draft beer (live guitar and *saz* music W, F, Sa; open daily 11am-2am). **Turkuaz Cafe Bar**, 22 Pazar Yeri (tel. 712 85 55), has cheaper brews (beer $1.50) and live music on the first floor (W and F-Sa 8:30pm-2am; open noon-2am). Next door, **Hangar Disco** (tel. 712 67 27) won't conjure up visions of John Travolta, but you can work on your moves (beer $2.40; open 1pm-2am; cover $2.40 from 1pm-6pm, $3.80 from 7pm-3am; first drink included).

🔲 **SIGHTS.** The highlight of Safranbolu is unquestionably its Ottoman architecture. The traditional wooden mansions are characterized by an overhanging second floor and highly ornate ceiling decorations. The complex and contradictory floor plans were designed to maximize comfort and to keep men and women separated. To see the architecture up close, take a peek inside the fancier hotels or visit the *gezi evleri*, restored houses that accept visitors for a small fee. The best place to start is **Kaymakamlar Evi (Governor's Residence)**, the local museum. From the square, walk along Akın Sok. to the Cinci Han; Kaymakamlar is on the little street past the T.C. Ziraat Bankası and behind the Cinci Han. (Open in summer 9am-10pm; in winter 9am-5pm. Admission 60¢.) Other *gezi evleri* include the **Karaüzümler Evi**, on Mescit Sok. past the Otel Teras (admission 60¢; open 9am-2:30pm), and the **Mümtazlar Evi** (tel. 712 63 59), on Hükümet Sok., past the Tahsin Bey Konağ (admission 60¢; open 8:30am-midnight). Walk up the narrow broken street past Kaymakamlar Evi to reach **Hıdırlık Tepesi,** a lookout point with fantastic views of Safranbolu in all its antiqued glory. Hıdırlık Tepesi houses the **tomb of Hasan Paşa,** an Ottoman notable exiled to Safranbolu in 1843. On Manifaturacılar Sok. past the Cinci Han, the **İzzet Paşa Camii,** built in 1796, verges on Baroque excess with its decorative squiggles.

AMASRA

Over 3000 years of trade and fishing have left Amasra the same quiet beach getaway that Queen Amastris was looking for in the 4th century BCE, when she founded the town on the site of Sesamos, an ancient Miletian port. The midday sun sees young Turks and a handful of foreigners frolicking on the beaches until a daily afternoon drizzle dampens the town's half-paved roads. A Byzantine citadel and several 19th-century Ottoman houses coexist with modern cement block.

🛈 ORIENTATION AND PRACTICAL INFORMATION. Amasra sits on a peninsula that juts out into the Black Sea, forming two harbors. The western harbor is known as **Küçük Liman,** the eastern one as **Büyük Liman.** Küçük Liman Cad. runs along the western harbor by the hotels before winding left into the fortress. There is a small square on the western harbor, surrounded by the PTT and a number of hotels and restaurants. There are some direct buses to and from Amasra, but you will probably have to go through **Bartın,** about 15km to the south and accessible by frequent *dolmuş.* Buses run directly to: **Ankara** (4½hr., 4 per day 8am-10:30pm, $8.30); **Istanbul** (7hr., 4 per day 8am-10:30pm, $11); and **Karabük** (3 hr., 6:30pm, $4). A string of *dolmuş* connect Amasra to **Sinop** via Karabük and Kastamonu (8hr., $10). In the square, the **Türkiye İş Bankası** has an **ATM** and exchanges cash and **traveler's checks** (open M-F 9am-12:30pm and 1:30-6:30pm). The **PTT,** on the square by the western harbor, also has a currency exchange (open daily 8am-11pm). For information in English, visit the **Aydın Eczanesi** (tel. 315 23 23), a pharmacy next door to the PTT. Friendly chemist Aydın Söğüt can help with currency exchange and, of course, offers medical assistance. **Telephone code:** 378.

🛏🍴 ACCOMMODATIONS AND FOOD. Since Amasra swells with Turkish tourists in the summer, small household *pansiyon*s pick up the hotels' slack. The **Nur Turistik Pansiyon,** Küçük Liman Mah. Çamlık Sok. (tel. 315 10 15), along the waterfront road, offers cheap, high-quality rooms, some with waterfront balconies (singles $7; doubles $14.50; triples $21.50). Along the road toward the town center, **Otel Belvü Palas,** 20 Küçük Liman Cad. (tel. 315 12 37), has rooms with balconies and clean common bathrooms (no singles; doubles $12; triples $18; quads $24).

The restaurants along Amasra's western harbor dish out the port's predictable specialty, fish. The large and luxurious ▨ **Canlıbalık Restaurant,** 8 Küçük Liman Cad. (tel. 315 26 06), recognized as the town's best, provides an open-air setting with harbor views (full meal $5-8; open noon-midnight). In the park on the western harbor, the **Yakamoz Aile Çay Bahçesi,** Çamlık Sok. (tel. 315 11 77), is a great place to grab a morning coffee (70¢) or watch the sunset over a beer ($1). A small village **market** in the square offers local fruits, vegetables, and other treats.

📷 SIGHTS. Amasra is a sleepy resort draped in Byzantine ramparts. Although the town was fortified as far back as the 3rd century BCE, the **citadel** that stands today dates from the 9th century CE. Walk uphill from the bridge to the **Fatih Camii,** a ruined 9th-century Byzantine church that was converted into a mosque when Sultan Mehmet II conquered Amasra in 1460. The town's **museum** has items from the Hellenic through Ottoman eras, including a collection of Ottoman pistols (open Tu-Su 8:30am-5:30pm; admission $1.20, students 60¢). The local **woodworking market** on Çekiciler Cad. features local crafts and fine traditional musical instruments (open in summer 9am-9pm). *Dolmuş* from Amasra run east to pristine beaches in **Bozköy** and **Çakraz.**

SİNOP

Sinop takes its name from Sinope, a mythical nymph who spurned the advances of the thunderbolt-hurling god Zeus. Hoping to lure her into his Olympian sack, he offered to grant her a single wish; slyly, she asked for eternal virginity. Bound to his promise, Zeus isolated her on the tiny mountainous peninsula where modern Sinop now slumbers, a town yet to be deflowered by tourists. Uncrowded but slightly littered beaches and a festive nightlife provide escape from the industrial sprawl and seediness of Samsun and Trabzon to the east. College students in town for a beach holiday and old-timers nostalgic for friends from the recently closed NATO base warmly welcome the few foreign travelers who straggle into town.

🛈 ORIENTATION AND PRACTICAL INFORMATION. The Sinop peninsula juts northeast into the Black Sea. The town's main street, **Sakarya Caddesi,** runs from the city center southwest past the **otogar** towards the mainland. In the center of town at a large roundabout, Sakarya Cad. intersects **Atatürk Caddesi,** which runs south towards the harbor and a large square, **Uğur Mumcu Meydanı.** **Buses** from the *otogar* run to: **Ankara** (9hr., 9:30am and 9pm, $15); **Antalya** (21hr., 2pm, $23.75); **Bursa** (12hr., 2:30pm, $19); **İstanbul** (12hr., 3-5 per day 9am-8:30pm, $20); **İzmir** (18hr., 2:30pm, $23.75); **Kastamonu** (3hr., 3-5 per day 9am-8:30pm, $8.75); **Samsun** (3hr., 8pm, $6.50); and **Trabzon** (9hr., 8pm, $13). Connect at Kastamonu for **Amasra** and **Safronbolu;** connect at Samsun for **Amasya.** **Atatürk Hastanesi Hospital** (tel. 261 45 10) is open 24 hours, and there are plenty of pharmacies on Sakarya Cad. **Sinop Bilgisayar,** Yeni Mah., 3/A Nolu Konak Çıkmazı (tel. 260 47 44), just outside the square, offers **Internet access** ($1.25 per hr., one drink included; open 9am-3am). The **PTT** is in Uğur Mumcu Meydanı (open 8:30am-11pm, full services until 5pm). **Telephone code:** 368.

█ █ █ ACCOMMODATIONS, FOOD, AND ENTERTAINMENT. A popular spot for young Turks on vacation, Sinop has plenty of reasonably priced rooms, mostly next to the fortifications along the quiet waterfront. **Otel Denizci,** 13 Kurtuluş Cad. (tel. 261 09 04), has rooms with new baths, does laundry for free, and hosts a family of pigeons through a door between the second and third floors (singles $5; doubles $10, with bath $15; triples $15/22.50). **Uğur Aile Pansiyon,** 4 İskele Cad. (tel. 261 59 47), along the waterfront, is a budget-friendly place with large rooms, common baths, kitchen, and free laundry. The **restaurant** offers good fish and an entertaining █ **monkey** named Çapkın ("Playboy"). (Singles $4.75; doubles $9.50; triples $14.30; quads $19.) Yuvam Belediye Plajı and Karakum Plajı have beachside **campsites** ($4.75 per tent or caravan; open mid-Apr. to Oct.).

If the monkey at Uğur Aile Pansiyon isn't in your plans, try the fresh crabs at **Balık Restaurant** next door (meals $2-9; open in summer 9am-4am; in winter 9am-midnight), or follow the waterfront past the tourist office to the ultra-cheap restaurants serving *mantı* and *gözleme.* After a day at the beach, Sinop vacationers play backgammon at the waterfront cafes on Kıbrıs Cad. **Burç Cafe** (tel. 260 05 94), atop the citadel's tower, is a great place to drink a beer and enjoy the view (live *saz* performances nightly at 9pm; open Apr.-Oct. 8am-midnight). Stay out 'til almost dawn at █ **Teleskop Disco,** where DJs spin Turkish and foreign dance music (beer $1.20; open 6pm-4am), or at █ **Diogenes Bar,** 5 İskele Cad. (tel. 261 57 21), across from Uğur Restaurant, the official watering hole of the American archaeological team digging around Sinop (beer $1.40; open in summer 8pm-4am).

▣ SIGHTS. Sinop's **fortifications** date from 770 BCE, when the port was settled by Miletian colonists. What stands today is a mish-mash of Pontic and Ottoman renovations. Most notable for a large Hellenistic sculpture of a deer strangely unconcerned about being devoured by lions, Sinop's **museum,** at the eastern end of Sakarya Cad., also houses a sizable collection of Greek, Roman, and Ottoman coins, early Bronze Age pottery, and various amphorae. In the back of the museum lie the remains of the **Temple of Serapis,** dating to the 4th century BCE. Serapis is closely associated with Asclepius, god of medicine, healing, and dreaming. (Open M-F 8am-noon and 1:30-5:30pm, Sa-Su 9am-noon and 1:30pm-5:30pm. Admission $1.25, students 75¢.) Sinop's two oldest Islamic monuments are the 13th-century Selçuk **Alaaddin Camii** and **Pervane Medresesi,** next to each other on the north side of Sakarya Cad. Abandoned and deteriorating rapidly, **Balatlar Kilisesi,** a 7th-century Byzantine church near the intersection of Radar Yolu and Kemalettin Sami Paşa Cad., 1km northeast of the museum, retains some beautiful frescoes.

◪ BEACHES. Beach-goers have a number of options in Sinop. The best bet is beautiful, uncrowded **Akliman Halk Plajı,** 12km from town on the western coast. *Dolmuş* leave from Uğur Mumcu Meydanı (20min.; every 30min. M-F 7:30am-6pm, Sa-Su 8am-10pm; 60¢). Nearby **Yuvam Belediye Plajı** and over-developed **Karakum Plajı** are crowded with sun-seeking college students (a 30min. walk or brief *dolmuş* ride (20¢) northeast from Uğur Mumcu Meydanı along Kıbrıs Cad.).

AMASYA

A fortuitous meeting of human and natural architecture, Amasya suggests a Turkish Venice, framed by towering cliffs, a quiet river, carved rock tombs, ornate Selçuk *hamams* and mosques, and stately Ottoman houses. The birthplace of the geographer Strabo, Amasya was the capital of Pontus, a kingdom of Greek-speaking Persians that arose after the death of Alexander the Great. Under the Ottomans, who arrived in 1391, Amasya became an important theological and cultural center with 18 *medreses* (Islamic theological schools) by the 18th century.

ORIENTATION AND PRACTICAL INFORMATION

Amasya is divided by the **Yeşilırmak (Green River),** which runs roughly east-west. The **north bank,** home to Ottoman houses and the Pontic cliff tombs, is the older part of town. The tourist office and most restaurants and hotels lie on the **south bank,** either on **Mehmet Paşa Caddesi,** the road running immediately along the river, or the more substantial **Atatürk Caddesi,** one block south. The city center *(şehir merkezi),* between these two roads, is a large plaza with an Atatürk monument. Arriving buses stop either at the city center or at the **otogar,** 3km northeast of town. To get to the center, take any of the city buses (20¢, students 15¢) or *dolmuş* (25¢, students 20¢) that stop across the street from the *otogar.* A taxi costs $2.50. Alternatively, turn left at the exit of the *otogar* and follow the road to the city center. Buses run from the *otogar* to: **Ankara** (4½hr., 7 per day 7am-12:30am, $6.25); **Antalya** (12hr., 3pm, $15); **Bursa** (11hr., 8:30pm, $15); **Istanbul** (10hr., 5 per day 11:15am-11:15pm, $15); **İzmir** (14hr., 5pm, $15); **Marmaris** (15hr., 4pm, $22.50); and **Trabzon** (8hr.; 11am, 5, 10pm; $10). The **tourist office** (tel. 218 74 28) is in a kiosk on the river's south bank (open in summer M-F 10am-noon and 2-6pm, Sa-Su 1-6pm; closed in winter). Many **banks** with **ATMs** line the south bank of the river. **Yapi ve Kredi,** across the street from the PTT, cashes traveler's checks (open M-F 9am-12:30pm and 1:30-6pm). The local hospital is **Devlet Hastanesi** (tel. 218 40 00). The **PTT** is on Mehmet Paşa Cad., 100m west of the main square (open daily 8:30am-5pm). **Telephone code:** 353.

ACCOMMODATIONS AND FOOD

Though the Ottoman houses along the river are more expensive than most lodgings in Turkey, their beautiful views and traditional decor make them worth the extra expense. The 180-year-old **İlk Pension,** 1 Hitit Sok. (tel. 218 16 89), down a small side street off Mehmet Paşa Cad. across the street from the tourist office, offers large rooms of an authentic ilk with private baths (singles $17-32; doubles $25-45; triples $30-64; quads $32-70; breakfast $3; 10% student discount). **Zümrüt Otel,** 28 Hazeranlar Sok. (tel. 218 26 75), on the way to the Emin Efendi Pension, offers 14 cheap rooms with TVs, fridges, and terrace views of the tombs ($10 per person, breakfast included). Amasya's several *kebap* and *pide* restaurants are filled all day with locals escaping the sun, sipping tea, and taking in the scenery. If you're in more of a do-it-yourself mood, stock up at **Yimpaş,** a supermarket just across from the tourist office (open daily 8am-10pm). **Ocakbaşı Restaurant,** 5 Ziya Paşa Cad. (tel. 218 56 92), on the river, serves Turkish dishes in an outdoor plaza *(lahmacun* 75¢; *pide* $2; open daily 6am-10:30pm).

SIGHTS

PONTIC RUINS. Carved out of the cliffs north of the city are the **Kralkaya mezarları,** the tombs of the Pontic kings. Though the graffiti-covered tombs are less impressive up close than from below, a climb up offers beautiful panoramic views of the valley and city. Dating to the 3rd century BCE, an ancient **fortress** *(kale)* looms high above Amasya. It was renovated first by the Ottomans and again in the

1980s. The extensive ruins and spectacular views of the entire gorge are worth the long, steep hike. *(To get to the Kralkaya mezarları, cross the bridge by the PTT and follow the yellow signs up the hill. Open daily 8am-6pm. Admission $1, students 50¢. To get to the fortress, follow signs marked "Kale" from Zubeyde Hanım Cad., on the north bank. The walk takes about 30min.; if you're in a hurry, catch a cab for $4 each way.)*

MUSEUMS. The **Ottoman House Museum (Hazeranlar Konağ)** on the north side of the river is one of Amasya's best preserved Ottoman houses, along with the İlk and Emin Efendi *Pansiyons*. The **Archaeological Museum** has an impressive collection of artifacts spanning the history of the region, including the grisly mummified remains of Mongol rulers and their children, on display in the old Selçuk *türbe. (On Atatürk Cad. Open Tu-Su 8:30am-5pm. Admission $1, students 50¢.)*

SELÇUK AND OTTOMAN SIGHTS. Follow the river a short way west from the PTT to the **Sultan Beyazit II Camii.** Amasya's largest Islamic monument, the mosque was completed in 1486 by Sultan Beyazit II's eldest son and heir apparent Ahmet, who lost the throne in 1513 to his younger brother. From here, continue west on Atatürk Cad., past the Archaeological Museum, to the Selçuk **Gökmedrese Camii** (Blue Seminary Mosque). The blue tiles that gave the mosque its name (*"gök"* means "sky") are now mostly gone, and the spectacular carved door is in the museum. Right across the street is the Ottoman **Yörgüç Paşa Camii,** with striking sections of red stone and pristine frescoes. East along the river, past the tourist office, is the early Ottoman **Mehmet Paşa Camii,** a sprawling complex that now houses a girls' Qur'an school. ▧ **Yildiz Hatun Medresesİ,** 20m east of the tourist office, was an insane asylum built in 1308 by the Mongol Sultan Olcaytuas. The intricately carved doorway and other features of the building look remarkably Selçuk and remarkably crazy.

TRABZON

Since the collapse of the Soviet Union and the re-opening of Turkey's northeastern borders, Trabzon has resumed its role as the button on the Black Sea's underbelly—a sieve for trade into Georgia, Armenia, Azerbaijan, and Iran. The cell phones, thick traffic, concrete edifices, visible prostitutes that emerged after the region's most recent boom are merely another incarnation of a city that for three millennia has sheltered smugglers, pimps, and dethroned emperors. Battered by marauding Crusaders, the Comnenus dynasty took refuge here until 1461, when they ran out of spare daughters to marry off to appease the usurping Ottomans. Despite its seedy central square, Russian bazaar, and frenzied pace, Trabzon is a good stop to organize trekking tours in the Kaçkar Mountains to the south.

▨ **ORIENTATION AND PRACTICAL INFORMATION.** All of the city's hotels, restaurants, and services are concentrated around **Atatürk Alanı,** the main square, just uphill and west from the city's central port. **Kahramanmaraş (Maraş) Caddesi** runs west out of Atatürk Alanı, leading past banks, the PTT, and a few historical sites before ending just below the ancient **Aya Sofia. Gazipaşa Caddesi** is the short main road between Atatürk Alanı's western edge and the coastal highway, **Sahil Yolu,** which leads to the intercity **otogar,** 3km east.

Airplanes: *Dolmuş* leave from Atatürk Alanı and the coastal highway. **THY** (tel. 321 16 80), at the corner of Atatürk Alanı, runs to **Ankara** (40min.; 5:45, 10am, 7:30pm; $59, students $45) and **Istanbul** (1½hr.; 5:40, 9:40am, 7:20pm; $72, students $55).

Buses: 3km east of the main square. **Ulusoy** (tel. 325 22 01) and **Metro** (tel. 325 72 86) run to: **Ankara** (12hr.; 7:30am and 6pm; $18, students $16); **Bursa** (15hr., 12:30pm, $17); **Istanbul** (17hr.; 7 per day 1-7:30pm; $23, students $19). Sinop, Amasya, Amasra, Safranbolu, and all points west can be reached via **Samsun.**

Ferries: Turkish Maritime Lines, inside the gate at the base of İskele Cad., runs between Trabzon, Samsun, and Istanbul (June 15-Sept. 15). Open M-F 8am-5pm.

Tourist Office: At the eastern end of Meydan Camii Sok. Brand-new and well-equipped government tourist office, with moderate English spoken.

Travel Agencies: Usta Tour, 4 İskele Cad. (tel. 326 18 70/71), opposite the northeast corner of Atatürk Alanı, organizes tours of **Trabzon** (10am-4:30pm, $20 per person) and **Sumela** (10am-4:30pm, $15 per person) including transport, lunch, and a certified guide. Open daily June 15-Sept. 15 8:15am-7pm. **Afacan Tour,** 40 İskele Cad. (tel. 321 58 04 or 321 58 06), 100m down from Usta, has cheaper and more flexible tours of Trabzon and Sumela ($4). Open daily 9am-7pm.

Banks: Most of Trabzon's larger banks are lined up on Maraş Cad., just west of Atatürk Alanı. Cash is easy to exchange, but **traveler's checks** may require some persistence.

Police: Tel. 326 30 77.

Hospital: Nümune Hospital (tel. 230 23 01), at the intersection of Maraş Cad. and Faik Dranaz Cad. ("*Hastane*" or "*Nümune*" *dolmuş*).

Internet Access: Internet Cafe, inside the Corner Hamburger and Pizza joint on the east edge of Atatürk Alanı. $2 per hr. Open daily 7am-11pm.

PTT: West down Maraş Cad. Open 24hr.

Telephone Code: 462.

ACCOMMODATIONS AND FOOD.

It's difficult to find a sinless and silent hotel in Trabzon. The cheaper hotels cluster around **İskele Cad.,** northeast of the square. The hotels below are currently off the prostitution circuit, but this could change: accepting *Nataşas* (see p. 558) means extra cash and a packed house for hotel owners. **Otel Anıl,** 12 Güzelhisar Cad. (tel. 326 72 82/3), 50m off İskele Cad., is a bland but welcoming oasis of peace and cleanliness (with carpets and hot water) in the red-light district (singles $12; doubles $19; triples $26; call ahead in summer). **Hotel Benli** (tel. 321 10 22), next to the tourist office, is a 1940s hotel that has fallen in to disrepair—an anomaly in this reconstructed city. Squat toilets and no showers make the price right (singles $5; doubles $7-10; triples $15). Look for **Gözde Aile Oteli,** 7 Salih Yazıcı Sok. (tel. 321 95 79), on the upper section of İskele Cad. *Aile* means family, so it should be *Nataşa*-free (singles $6, students $4; doubles $12/10).

Trabzon's cuisine is a melange of standard Turkish fare, fresh Black Sea fish, and corn, potatoes, and peas from the fertile highlands south of the city. The dense foot traffic around Atatürk Alanı supports a dazzling array of restaurants, including *Chez McDonald's*. Grocery stores are at the northeast corner of Atatürk Alanı. **Kıbrıs Restaurant,** on the east side of the square, has a sedate, uncrowded dining room where you can get beer and *köfte* with all the fixings for $5 (open roughly 10am-11pm). **Nil Restaurant,** 1 Maraş Cad. (tel. 321 17 18), on the corner of Maraş Cad. and Atatürk Alanı, serves the local specialties *akçaabat köfte* (flat meatballs with rice, tomatoes, and grilled pepper; $2) and *sütlaç* (similar to rice pudding, $1).

VIVALAS TRABZONSPOR! (AND OTHER ENTERTAINMENT).

Trabzon is a **football** town, and **Trabzonspor,** the adored local team, plays regularly from late August to late May (with half-length matches in Jan. and Feb.). The stadium is about 5km east of downtown, on the seaside Spor Cad. (sheltered seats $4, open seats $1). One of the cooler places in town is **Blue Sea Bar,** 51A Sahil Yolu (tel. 322 27 33), across the highway from the shore (beer $1.50; open daily 11am-1am). **Vivalas Disco,** a popular student hangout, is on Gazipaşa Cad. near the sea. If you're more likely to cry "Vivalas Massage" than "Vivalas Disco," head 2km out to **Sekiz Direkli Hamam** (tel. 322 10 12), Pazarkapı Mah. Follow the signs along Maraş Cad. until it turns downhill, or take a $2 taxi (scrub and massage $4; open daily to both sexes 6am-11pm, women only Th 8am-5pm).

HALLUCINOGENIC HONEY In the 5th century BCE, King Cyrus of Persia recruited a ragtag troop of jack-booted Greek thugs to pillage various villages in Asia Minor. Among the 10,000 Greeks was Xenophon, who recorded their misadventures in the *Anabasis*. According to Xenophon, after making a hasty retreat while laden with booty, the soldiers wandered into fields upon fields of beehives brimming with honey. The tired horde began to sample the combs, with disastrous results: some of the soldiers who sampled the nectar ended up unconscious or plagued with violent diarrhea and vomiting. Those who consumed the nectar in moderation reported fantastical visions (who knows what the bees were seeing). The morning after, the entire legion woke up with a wicked hangover and some rich but embarrassing flashbacks. After enduring a few days of rehab and de-tox from the deleterious effects of too many psychedelics, the iron-hearted Hellenes marched west to Trabzon. Travelers in the area along the Black Sea coast have reported similarly mind-altering effects, and scientists have concluded that the bees are procuring their heady honey from the flower *Azalea Pontica*, which grows everywhere in the area.

◎ SIGHTS. Aya Sofia and its peaceful garden have done time as a temple of Apollo, a basilica, an Orthodox church under Comnenian Emperor Manual I (who commissioned the construction of the present edifice), and a mosque. A 1960s restoration project uncovered some of Turkey's best frescoes, many about the life of Jesus. Carvings of sailboats on the eastern wall were made by Genoans and Venetians pining for their distant homelands. To get there, *dolmuş* it from Atatürk Alanı, or stop a *dolmuş* driver on the coastal highway (museum open daily 8:30am-5pm; closed M in winter; free). The 7th-century **St. Anne's Church**, in an alley of Maraş Cad., is the oldest extant Christian structure in town, but is currently closed for restoration. **Gülbaharhatun Camii** (the Mosque of the Spring Rose), on Uzun Cad. past Atapark, holds the remains of Ottoman Sultan Selim I's mother. Up the road on Amasya Sok., Selim I's wife gave birth to Süleyman the Magnificent. Farther down Maraş Cad., within the walls of the old city, is **Fatih Camii,** once the cathedral of the *Panagia Chrysokephelos*, the Golden-Headed Virgin. In 1461, Sultan Mehmet covered the Virgin in plaster, but a portion of the original is intact on the east side.

NEAR TRABZON: SUMELA MONASTERY

Accessible by dolmuş from Trabzon's Russian Bazaar (1hr., 8am-11am), or with private tours from Trabzon (p. 602). Tours include a 30min. hike through the adjoining park (park admission $1.50, students $1) and a fresh trout lunch ($5) at Sumela Restaurant. A private hiking trail also goes up to Sumela.

Nowhere else in northwestern Anatolia is the region's Byzantine legacy so breathtakingly combined with the jagged, forested landscape than at Sumela Monastery, which is built into a cliffside cave to provide natural protection from the elements. Approximately 45km southwest of Trabzon, high in the mountains, Sumela was founded in 385 CE by two Athenian monks who were allegedly visited by the Holy Virgin. The monastery's inner chapel is a spectacular display of three layers of secular, Old Testament, and New Testament frescoes (all of which are partially exposed) covering the chapel's interior and exterior, which is shielded from harsh weather by the overhanging cave. The cave couldn't save the monastery from a recent fire, though. Turkish authorities are currently restoring it, but to see Sumela in all its pre-conflagration flagrante, check out the postcards (2 for $1) in the gift shop of the adjacent park.

YUSUFELİ

Yusufeli is cradled in the gorgeous, undeveloped **Çoruh Nehri** (Çoruh Valley). The Çoruh River narrows as the valley walls steepen into dry, crumbling spires and cliffs. Yet at the confluence of the Çoruh and its Barhal tributary is a corridor of lush greenery that defies the barren slopes above. If arriving from the south, you'll drop down from rolling grasslands and the huge Tatum Reservoir into a canyon system utterly unlike Anatolia's hilly steppe. Yusufeli, Turkey's **white-water rafting** capital, was home to a 1993 rafting championship. Tekkale (6km up the valley) also makes a relaxing base for walks, hikes, and treks in the upper Çoruh Valley or the Kaçkars. Even a day or two is enough to see a few of the valley's Georgian churches.

⋈ ORIENTATION AND PRACTICAL INFORMATION. The tourist center of Yusufeli is the rectangular area enclosed by four streets named after Turkish politicians: **Enver Paşa, Fevzi Çakmak, Mustafa Kemal,** and **İnönü Caddesi.** Most hotels occupy the upstream end of İnönü Cad., the central street that passes the **otogar** lot, pharmacies, and some decent alcohol-free restaurants.

Artvin Express, in the *otogar* lot, runs to: **Ankara** (18hr., noon, $19); **Bursa** (22hr., 9am, $24); **Istanbul** (20hr., 10am, $24); and **Trabzon** (6hr., 9am, $7). *Dolmuş* head from the *otogar* up the Çoruh River Valley (midday-evening), and less frequently to the Barhal Valley (departs in late afternoon and evening, returns the next morning). The Belgian and Turkish staff at the **Kaçkar Outdoor Sports Center,** on the right side of İnönü Cad., 50m up from the *otogar*, can arrange hikes, treks, tours of Georgian church sites, and the safest (and only legal) **rafting trips** in the area (office open 9:30-10:30am, in the evenings visit them at Çemil Pension in Tekkale). The local **hospital** (tel. 811 20 15) and **police** station are small and not much help. The **PTT** is on İnönü Cad., at the downstream end of town. **Telephone code:** 466.

⋈⋈ ACCOMMODATIONS AND FOOD. Yusufeli's better hotels are all close to each other on İnönü Cad. There's not much variety, but all the places listed are clean and quiet. **Hotel Çiçek Palas** (tel. 811 21 02) and **Hacıoğlu Oteli** (tel. 811 35 66), both just off İnönü Cad. in the courtyard next to Kaçkar Outdoor Sports Center, offer basic, peaceful rooms (singles $3.50; doubles $7). While the more homey Hacıoğlu has hot showers, Çiçek Palas has a common stove. **Barhal Hotel** (tel. 811 31 51), about 20m upstream on İnönü Cad., offers sterile rooms with river views from a courtyard (singles $6; doubles $8; triples $10). The owner, Sıralı Aydur, heads the local rafting club. To reach **Greenpeace Camping,** cross the bridge by the Hotel Barhal, turn right, take another right at the T-intersection, then turn left. The grounds offer secluded campsites, cold showers, and light meals ($1-2 per night; open mid-June to mid-Sept.). One of the more popular meeting places is **Çınar Lokantası** (tel. 811 23 65), which overlooks the river beneath the Barhal Hotel. Its menu includes grilled meat, fresh trout, *rakı*, and vegetarian *meze* (full meal with beer $3.50; open daily 9am-midnight). The **Mavi Köşk Restorant** (tel. 811 23 29), off İnönü Cad. downhill from Barhal Hotel, has good food and a well-stocked bar (full meal about $3.50; open daily 8am-1am).

⋈ OUTDOOR ADVENTURES. Many hopeful trekkers are drawn to Yusufeli for its dry weather and rafting. Though self-guided trekking takes a little more effort (and research), there is an excellent guide service at **Kaçkar Outdoor Sports Center,** housed underneath the Çiçek Palas Hotel. The two head guides, Stefan and Kim, speak fluent English and German. With their local guides, they can set up two- to three-day treks in the famed Kaçkar Mountains along the six-finger ridge (an all-inclusive $130). Another two- to three-day trip uses the delightful Karahan Pension as a base for day-treks into the open plateaus and crater lakes.

HIKING: THE ÇORUH VALLEY

As the Çoruh River winds its way through a stunning, arid valley towards Yusufeli, it leaves a line of small farms, lush trees, and sleepy hamlets in its wake. The village of **Tekkale,** about 6km up the paved road from Yusufeli, makes an excellent base for hikes up tributary streams to the area's numerous abandoned **Georgian churches** and *yayla* (high-altitude meadow villages). Longer hikes lead up past the spring snow line to the peaks and freezing lakes of the southeastern Kaçkars. **Cemil's Pension** (tel. (466) 811 29 08) is the place to stay in Tekkale, thanks to its cushioned open-air lounge and porch, full meals (about $3), modest rooms, and some of the cheapest beer in Turkey (50¢). Infrequent *dolmuş* run to Tekkale only in the afternoon ($1.50); many travelers hitchhike. Taxis runs about $5.

From Tekkale, a rough side road climbs up towards **Barhal** (also accessible by a separate road from Yusufeli). This slightly more remote village is popularly known as a base camp for treks. *Dolmuş* head to Barhal at sporadic times in the late afternoon and early evening. At the south of town, the **Barhal Pension** (tel. (466) 826 20 31) has new wooden rooms occupying the second floor of a house ($10 per person; dinner and breakfast included). At the town center, the road splits right 4km to the **Karahan Pension,** 50m uphill from the Barhal Kilise (ask locals for directions). Run by Mehmet Karahan, the Karahan offers great lodging for the Kaçkars-bound, including an airy deck where meals are served ($12 per night; breakfast and dinner included). From the center of Barhal, the road splits left to various *yayla*, and right to **Barhal Kilise,** 4km away, a well preserved 10th-century Georgian church that now serves as the town's mosque. From Tekkale, follow the road to Yusufeli for 7km to **Dörtkilise** ("Four Churches"), now home to only one of the original four. The remaining Georgian church is a hauntingly beautiful place to spend the evening, and the grounds outside make a prime campsite.

EASTERN ANATOLIA

Welcome to Eastern Turkey, where sheep outnumber people, where you can search in vain for an English speaker for days on end, and where police identification checks are more common than Efes Pilsen. Almost no Turks raised in the western part of the country have been to Eastern Anatolia, having been taught that the region is war-torn, remote, and impoverished. The Armenian slaughter of 1915 occurred largely within Turkey's eastern border territory, and intermittent fighting persists between the PKK and the Turkish army. This negative image of Turkey's frontier land has permeated its global reputation, leaving the area untouched by all but the most intrepid of travelers. However, the region offers some of Turkey's most astonishing beauty, both natural and man-made.

TRAVEL WARNING. Travel in Eastern Turkey should be approached with caution. Travelers should be updated on all consular advisories and warnings, and should be careful to follow all relevant rules and laws. Cooperation with police and military personnel is imperative. The unpredictable nature of travel in Eastern Anatolia requires that travel schedules be flexible. *Let's Go* does not recommend that **women** travel alone to Eastern Turkey. Even with a head scarf and long, concealing clothes, females may be mistaken for *Nataşas* (prostitutes) at night. To avoid unwanted advances, dress very conservatively, memorize some key phrases, and stay in the more expensive hotels.

ŞANLIURFA

Though known as Şanlıurfa (Glorious Urfa), to the Turkish state, Muslims refer to the city as Peygamberler Şehri, the City of Prophets. Urfa is said to be the birthplace of the prophet Abraham and dwelling place of the prophet Job, making it a popular pilgrimage destination. It's also the best base from which to visit the spectacular 2000-year-old funerary ruins at **Nemrut Dağı** (see p. 608).

Eastern Anatolia

⚑ PRACTICAL INFORMATION. Urfa's **otogar**, 1½km from the town center, is a bustling transport hub that serves all points on the compass. Walk east from the *otogar* down an unmarked, busy road that passes through a huge cemetery, then enters a business district where it meets the main boulevard, **Atatürk Caddesi.** Some buses have free, sporadic shuttle service to the *otogar*, or you can take a taxi for $4-5. Buses run to: **Ankara** (12hr., 8 per day, $17); **Doğubayazıt** (16hr., 4 per day, $22); **Istanbul** (17hr., 9 per day, $20); İzmir (17hr., 2 per day, $20); **Kars** (20hr., 1 per day, $24); **Trabzon** (15hr., 4 per day, $22); and **Van** (12hr., 4 per night, $13). *Dolmuş* and minibus leave from the same parking lot. The **tourist office** (tel. (414) 215 24 67) is across from the park full of mosques and pools at the extreme southern end of town on the marble complex (open M-F 8am-noon and 1:30-5:30pm). **Telephone code:** 414.

⌂◨ ACCOMMODATIONS AND FOOD. Because Urfa's heat persists through the night, consider splurging on rooms with air conditioning. Clean and quiet **Hotel İpek Palas,** 4 Şanmed Hastanesi Arkası (tel. 215 15 46), behind the Şan-Med Hospital on Atatürk Cad. at the town center, has air conditioning, private hot showers, TVs, and phones (singles $12; doubles $18; triples $24). Cheaper rooms with fans are also available. **Otel Doğu,** 131 Sarayönü (Atatürk) Cad. (tel. 215 12 28), across from the Şan-Med Hospital, is a good choice if you don't want air conditioning; remember to buy bottled water for the night (singles $6; double $8; triples $10).

Urfa is renowned for its culinary wonders, but its kitchens have a down side: many foods (especially meats) become infested with bacteria in the sweltering heat, and visitors often leave the city with stomach issues. **Urfa Sofrası,** on the north part of Atatürk Cad. across from the stadium, serves the best *kaburga* (lamb chops with rice) in town (meals $5-8). One of the few welcoming places for vegetarians, **Güney Lokantası,** 17 Köprübaşı (tel. 313 22 37), across from Hotel İpek Palas, offers three dishes with absolutely no meat (full meal $2-3; open 6am-midnight).

☎ SIGHTS. Though Urfa contains some ancient ruins, the real marvels are at Nemrut Dağı to the north. Religious pilgrims, however, flock to Urfa's Old Testament holy sites. Behind the first mosque on Göl Cad. lies the large **Mevlid Halil Camii,** which houses the believed **birth cave** of the prophet Abraham. Women are able to forge all the way back into the sacred cave, while men may only look through a barred fence, praying in the proper direction (dress respectably). The entrance to the city's **citadel** is marked by Corinthian columns constructed in 242 BCE, from which, according to legend, Nemrut shot firebrands at Abraham (open daily 8am-6pm; admission $2, students $1). **Eyyüp Peygamber,** 3km south of the bazaar, contains the cave where the prophet Job lived for seven years while his body was being consumed by worms. Take an "Eyyübe" *dolmuş* (20¢) from Atatürk Cad., across from the tourist office (cave open daylight hours; admission $1).

NEAR ŞANLIURFA: NEMRUT DAĞI

*Accessible from Şanlıurfa, Malatya, Kahta, and Adiyaman. **Harran and Nemrut Tours** (tel. 215 25 75; fax 215 11 56), based in Şanlıurfa, offers transportation and tours. Site **open** during daylight hours. **Admission** $3.50, students $2. Allow at least 2hr. to explore the site; not including the walk up. The monument is at the base of a cone-shaped pile of rocks, at the bottom of which are 3 terraces on the north, west, and east. Rough winds can cause chills and dehydration: bring layers and more than enough water.*

Colossal stone heads top the highest peak in the region (2150m), marking the burial spot of Commagene **King Antiochus I.** Antiochus broke away from the Seleucids in the wake of Alexander the Great's death, leading his own kingdom to its zenith. Crowds tend to be fairly dense here during the high season, but you can still find quiet places of solitude. During his life, Antiochus delineated specific plans for the construction and dedication of this egomaniacal monument in true Ramsesian style. Originally, nine figures of the king surrounded by gods, each several meters tall, sat enthroned on both east and west terraces, flanked by animals. This juxtaposition of man and god was arranged to demonstrate the king's relation to these synchronistic deities. Earthquakes toppled the heads of these statues, which now rest scattered on the ground. With some careful observation, visitors can match fallen heads with the torsos that remain. The figures mirror each other from north to south: Lion, Eagle, Apollo, Tyche (Fortuna), Zeus, Antiochus, Hercules, Eagle, and Lion.

A HEAD OF HIS TIME Locked for centuries inside the peak of Mount Nemrut, a burial site described as the eighth wonder of the ancient world may soon reveal its splendors. The secret of **Antiochus' tumulus,** or burial mound, first discovered at Nemrut's summit in 1881, may soon be open to archaeologists (who have been banned from the tomb for years by Turkish bureaucrats). The site holds relics dating back to the Commagene kingdom, which attained its hegemonic and fiscal zenith under Antiochus, best remembered for installing a pantheon of syncretic gods like "Apollo-Mithras" and "Zeus-Oromazdes." He commissioned 10m high statues of these gods in their honor; they are depicted bestowing the divine mandate upon a 10m high statue of himself. The Herculean labor of constructing this shrine from six-ton stone blocks (not to mention the 50m tall peak of crushed rock hiding the tomb itself) has lead archaeologists to surmise that the tomb may rival that of Tutankhamun (which was found in Luxor, Egypt, p. 196) in its wealth and majesty. (Tutankhamun's wealth and majesty are now on display at the Egyptian Museum in Cairo, p. 96.) The carvings have begun to deteriorate dramatically, due largely to the wear and tear of visitors running amok over the barricade-free site. So exercise caution and remember the wisdom of the park ranger: if everyone took a six-ton head, there'd be no six-ton heads left.

VAN

For 3000 years, Van and the surrounding area has been Eastern Turkey's most vibrant cultural center. The natural beauty is a backdrop for the area's unique blend of Urartian, Armenian, and Kurdish influences, which have given rise to such fantastic attractions as Akdamar Church, Çavuştepe Fortress, and the Van and Hoşap Castles. In the past century, however, the Van area has been the stage on which Turkey's most dramatic conflicts have unfolded. The first organized Kurdish rebellion occurred here during the 1880s, and WWI brought on the forced exile and slaughter of 600,000 to 800,000 Armenians. Today, the focus of conflict in Van is militant Kurdish separatism. Southeastern Anatolia is largely under martial law, and violence in the countryside is fairly common. Visitors should check all possible sources of information before planning a trip to Van.

🛈 ORIENTATION AND PRACTICAL INFORMATION. Most travelers arrive via the airport or the bus station, 2½km from the town center. Frequent *dolmuş* marked "İskele-Otogar" make the trip from the station to town (20¢). An airline bus usually meets flights for transport to the city; taxi service costs $6-7. **Cumhuriyet Caddesi** runs the length of downtown. At the far north end, *dolmuş* arrive and depart from **Beş Yol.** The airline ticket, bus ticket, and tourist offices mark the far south end of Cumhuriyet Cad. at the intersection with **K. Karabekir Caddesi.** Because some roads close in the early afternoon, all **buses** leave between 7am and 2pm. Most companies have free transport to the bus station 30 minutes before departure. Buses run to: **Ankara** (18hr., 8 per day, $18); **Antakya** (18hr., 1 per day, $20); **Istanbul** (25hr., 5 per day, $26); **İzmir** (25 hr., 3 per day, $27); **Şanlıurfa** (10hr., 2 per day, $12); and **Trabzon** (12hr., 1 per day, $18). *Dolmuş* leave for **Doğubeyazıt** 200m west of Beş Yol (4 per morning, $4).

The **tourist office** (tel. 216 20 18 or 216 36 75), across from the Asur Otel in a yellow building marked "Turizm Müdürlüğü," offers brochures and a photocopied map, but the staff speaks little English (open M-F 8am-noon and 1:30-5:30pm). If you have more complicated needs, someone from the **Asur Otel** (tel. 216 87 92, ask for Ercan Bozbay) can translate. They've become the unofficial primary source of tourist information, and can arrange tours or simply show you around. **Türkiye İş Bankası** and **Vakıf Bank,** on Cumhuriyet Cad. near the PTT, exchange traveler's checks (both open 8am-noon and 1:30-5:30pm). **ATM** machines dot the main avenue. The **Devlet Hastanesi** (state hospital) is 300m south of Beş Yol on İskele Cad. The large **PTT** (tel. 214 34 90), on Cumhuriyet Cad. near Sokak 6, has Poste Restante service and a row of 15 Türk Telekom phones (mail service open 6am-11pm; phone service 24hr.). **Telephone code:** 432.

🛏🍴 ACCOMMODATIONS AND FOOD. Van's early 1990s tourist boom created many hotels, most of which now stand empty and charge refreshingly low rates. The cheap hotels are bunched together in the market district on a street parallel to and two blocks west of Cumhuriyet Cad. Mid- and upper-range accommodations line the main drag. ◾ **Hotel Ipek,** Cumhuriyet Cad., Sok. 1, #3 (tel. 216 30 33), is in the heart of the western market district near the baby chicken vendors. Ipek is a good bargain, with basic rooms and clean sheets. Some rooms have showers. (Singles $2.50; doubles $5; triples $7.50; with shower add $3.) Like Ipek, ◾ **Hotel Büyük Asur,** Cumhuriyet Cad. Turizm Sok. #5 (tel. 216 87 92), is a travel hub, but it's a major step up in quality. Singles have large beds, and all rooms are equipped with 24-hour hot water showers. The lobby boasts a breezy deck and a traditional *kilim*-pillow lounge, while the roof terrace affords nice views of Van, especially around sunset. (Singles $12; doubles $16; triples $17.) **Camping** along the lake shore is possible; check all available resources for the latest news in safety.

Most of the affordable restaurants lie on the south end of Cumhuriyet Cad. Kurdish cuisine has disappeared from menus, leaving behind largely standard Turkish fare. You may be invited into the **traditional wedding houses,** where Kurdish dancing and dining continue until about midnight. **Altın Şiş** ("Golden Skewer;" tel. 216 22

65), two doors down from İş Bankası on Cumhuriyet Cad., has tasty *Adana kebap* in their upstairs family salon. If you're shy about ordering in Turkish, choose from the picture menu on the wall (full meal $3-5; open 5am-11pm). **Altın Sofra** (tel. 216 47 73) is on Cumhuriyet Cad., 3km east of K. Karabekir Cad. The first floor houses a grocery store, the second and third a *lokanta*, the fourth a pizza and hamburger joint, and the fifth a pastry cafe (all open 7am-11pm).

🏛 🎭 **SIGHTS AND ENTERTAINMENT.** After the Russians destroyed the city of Tuşba, the Turks and local Kurds rebuilt the new city of Van 5km to the south. Consequently, Van's center offers little of historical importance aside from its extensive museum. From Cumhuriyet Cad., walk 200m east on K. Karabekir Cad., then 200m north at the yellow sign to reach **Van Museum,** which exhibits a collection of Urartian artifacts on the ground floor and large stone carvings of lions in the inner courtyard. Upstairs, in addition to a *kilim* collection, there is a gallery called the "Genocide section" that presents a misleading portrayal of the slaughter of Turks by Armenians. This biased exhibit omits discussion of the Armenian genocide, and neglects to mention that many of the "Turkish" victims were actually Kurds (open 8am-noon and 1:30-5:30pm; admission $1.50, students $1).

Van is a prime place to purchase **kilims** (woven tapestry mats); carpet and *kilim* sellers here distribute to western Turkish dealers, and often offer the same quality for up to 70% less. The waters of **Lake Van** are a mesmerizing reflecting pool, shining bright blue on sunny days and fiery red at sunset. The high alkaline content of the waters renders the liquid a smooth silk, and the mineral concentration makes the lake useful for cleaning clothing (no soap necessary).

NEAR VAN

ÇAVUŞTEPE AND ENVIRONS

Çavuştepe must be visited in the morning, as the road closes at 3pm. Dolmuş ($4) heading for Hoşap Castle via Çavuştepe depart 200m west of the Istanbul Airlines office on Cumhuriyet Cad. (daily 7am-1pm). Cavuştepe open 8am-6pm. Admission $1.50. Hoşap open 8am-5pm. Admission $1.50, students $1.

The Urartian peoples dominated the entire Van region from the 9th through the 6th centuries BCE, with an architecturally sophisticated kingdom featuring towering fortresses, extensive tunnels, highways, canals, and piers. The Urartians built shrines and temples around the holy Van "Sea," believed to purify their weapons and fulfill their desires. Three of their major fortresses still stand a short distance from Van. Closest to town lies the fortress constructed by King Sarduri I (840-830 BCE), known today as the Rock of Van, or **Van Kale.** Called Tuşba by the Urartians, it was the center of their vast kingdom, which extended from the Mediterranean to Iran. Of the three fortresses, this is the only one that visitors can explore extensively. **Toprakkale,** 4km southeast of Van, was built in 735 BCE to defend Urartu from invaders. Access to Toprakkale is prohibited, as it lies in a military zone. **Mehir Kapısı's rock niche,** a Urartian site between the bluff and the castle, may be open to visitors. In 764 BCE, Sarduri II (764-735 BCE) built a sprawling, three-sectioned castle 25km south of Van. Once more than 850m long and 80m high, the remains of **Çavuştepe** are today not as impressive as those of the other Urartian sights. Archaeologists are currently excavating the little-known fortress of **Ayanis,** 33km northeast of Van.

Built in 1643, **Hoşap Castle** is one of Turkey's greatest Kurdish castles. After the erection of his magnificent complex, which included a bridge over the Hoşap river, Kurdish feudal lord San Süleyman chopped off the hands of the architect to prevent him from building another of equal beauty. The walls are made of a mixture of dirt and pigeon eggs, and the entrance gate has two reliefs of lions with chains around their necks, denoting the gladiator matches between animals and men that occurred within the castle walls. The upper level contains royal rooms, the harem, and a *hamam*, all with a view of the valley and the village below.

AKDAMAR CHURCH

50km west of Van on Akdamar Island, 5km off the coast. Dolmuş headed for Gevaş will go the additional 9km to the dock if you clear it with the driver before boarding. Dolmuş depart from Van, 400m north of Cumhuriyet Cad. on K. Karabekir Cad. (every hr. 6am-5pm., $1.50.). Ferries run 6am-sundown (Sa-Su every 30min., M-F when full; $1.50, students $1). If you come on a weekday, you might wait for hours for a boat to fill. Commission an entire boat for $25.

Armenians flourished in the Van region for more than two millennia. The remaining Armenian churches are fascinating, especially in light of the fact that the majority have been destroyed or converted into mosques. One such marvel is the the **Church of the Holy Cross** at Akdamar Island (Akdamar Church). A major architectural and artistic feat, the sandstone church stands on a plateau at the center of the island, along with a monastery that remained active until 1900. The surviving reliefs on the outside of the church tell the story of human evolution, Armenian history, and Christian religious history. Those familiar with the Bible will quickly recognize many of the engraved stories: Adam and Eve, Samson and Delilah, David and Goliath, Mary holding a baby Jesus. The jewels originally placed in every figurine's eye sockets have long since been stolen.

DOĞUBEYAZIT

Doğubeyazıt is pure frontier land. The city is a bit rough around the edges, but nevertheless a fascinating product of the dichotomies and tensions it harbors, from the constant shadow cast by the PKK to the towering reminder presented by Mount Ararat (Ağrı Dağ), believed by many to be the spot where Noah's Ark landed. As you might expect, tanks and soldiers seem to be everywhere, and checkpoints are common. If you follow the rules, Doğubeyazıt is safe and interesting, with access to the stunning Işak Paşa Palace.

🚹 ORIENTATION AND PRACTICAL INFORMATION. Visitors arrive either at the *otogar* in the east end of town or the *dolmuş* stop at the other end of **Belediye Caddesi. Bus** service is limited and indirect, but runs to a few western locales such as **Ankara** (2 per day, $18) and **Istanbul** (2 per day, $25). **Dolmuş** leave hourly for **Van** ($4). At the far west end of Belediye Cad., near the *dolmuş* stop and above the *çay* house, stands the **THY office,** 5 Meyramane Cad. (tel. 312 67 72), which triples as the official **tourist information center** and **tourist agency** (open daily 7am-8pm). Cheap hotels inhabit the east end of Belediye Cad., and the PTT and **banks** are near the middle. Exchange cash at **İş Bankası** (open 8am-12:30pm and 1:30-5:30pm). Internationally linked **ATMs** are prevalent throughout town. The **PTT** has 24-hour phones that do not accept Türk Telekom cards (open daily from 8:30am to 5pm). **Telephone code:** 472.

🚹🛏 ACCOMMODATIONS AND FOOD. The tourist boom of the early 1990s left a plethora of hotels in Doğubeyazıt, now largely empty. A cluster of enjoyable, cheap accommodations lies on the far east end of Belediye Cad. The best of the bunch is **Hotel Saruhan,** a small, family-run establishment with two- and three-person dorm rooms and shared baths and showers. Rooms are carpeted and always have fresh sheets. ($3 per person; $2 in off-season.) Next door is the **Hotel Erzurum,** 22 Belediye Cad. (tel. 312 50 80). Rooms are basic, and hot water starts at 9pm. ($3.75 per person.) Most restaurants in town serve *lokanta*-style food, often a bit drab. Find better victuals at fresh markets or the hotel restaurants. The **Dorya Restaurant** (tel. 311 53 09) is across the street from the PTT. Near Hotel Erzurum, try the **Domak Restaurant** (tel. 312 56 44).

🔲 SIGHTS. Most visitors come to Doğubeyazıt to see the **Işak Paşa Palace,** built in 1685 by a local Kurdish chief. The intricacy and beauty of the structure are most apparent in the ornate entryway, covered in relief work and *muqarnas* (stalagtite ornamentation). The large entrance with lion reliefs leads to the **harem.** The **master's chamber** lies deep in the southwest corner, through the kitchen. If you see a hole in the ground that looks like a squatting toilet, you're right—the toilet seat affords a view of the ruler's kingdom out the window. If the stairs are unlocked when you visit, walk down to see the **sarcophagus.** Climb the stairs near the mosque entrance for a great view of the valley beyond. Up the hill and beyond the mosque is an even older mosque and Urartian fortress. *(Take the road east from the Hotel Saruhan past an army checkpoint and up 6km up to the palace, a 1-1½hr. walk or a $6 taxi. Open daily 6am-5:30pm. Admission $2, students $1.)*

🏛 **MT. ARARAT AND ENVIRONS.** "...and in the seventh month, on the seventeenth day of the month, the ark came to rest upon the mountains of Ararat" (Genesis 8:4). The Doğubeyazıt area includes the supposed spot where the biblical **Noah** first shouted, "Land ho!", but the once-popular expeditions to Mt. Ararat (5137m) are presently prohibited. Satisfy yourself with the views instead. Other highlights of the area include a **meteor crater,** two **hot springs,** and **horseback riding.** *(The English-speaking students at the THY office run a tour agency by the dolmuş stop and can explain how to get to these locales. Tel. 312 67 72. Open daily 8am-8pm.)*

KARS

The hardscrabble poverty of Kars, an industrial crossroads that weathers long brutal winters and blistering summers, contrasts sharply with the haunting beauty of the rugged, fertile, steppe that surrounds the town in all directions. Kars was occupied by Russia from 1877 through 1920, and the town's rigid, organized layout bears an unmistakable Russian imprint. Because of nagging worries about Kurdish Workers Party (PKK) separatists, the military presence is particularly strong here; the army frequently stops buses to check travel documents and may even frisk men. Kars itself has a few interesting historical relics, but the major draw is the fabulous Armenian ruins at Ani, 48km to the west.

🛈 **PRACTICAL INFORMATION.** The new **otogar** is 7km east of town and the **airport** 6km east. **THY,** 80 Atatürk Cad. (tel. (474) 212 38 38), flies to **Istanbul** (daily 11am, $68) via **Ankara** ($50). Buses go to: **Ankara** (8 per day, $16); **Istanbul** (5 per day, $20); and **İzmir** (2 per day, $20). **Eski Otogar,** the old bus station two blocks east of the town center, has become the *dolmuş* lot for regional destinations. A minibus or two leave daily for **Trabzon** ($12) and **Yusufeli** ($6). Doğubeyazıt can not be reached directly. Get a permit to visit Ani at the **tourist office** (tel. (474) 223 23 00), in a gray building on the corner of Karadağ Cad. and Atatürk Cad. in the downtown business district. Many **banks** downtown exchange cash and have 24-hour **ATMs. Telephone code:** 474.

🍴🛏 **FOOD AND ACCOMMODATIONS.** Skip town as soon as you've seen Ani—most of Kars's hotels are noisy, plagued by swarms of black flies, and experience periodic water and electricity outages. The best value is **Hotel Temel,** 4/A Kazımpaşa Cad. (tel. (474) 222 12 76), a quick walk from the *dolmuş* stop; go west on Halit Paşa Cad. and turn left one street before Kazımpaşa Cad. All rooms are clean and carpeted, with phones, private baths, and good beds ($8 per person). Centrally located **Hotel Kervansaray,** 204 Faık Bey Cad. (tel. (474) 223 19 90), is another budget option, with clean sheets and shared bath ($4 per person, showers $1). As with hotels, the food in Kars is cheap and tolerable, but not spectacular. Kars is known for its *Kaşar,* a yellow cheese (*kaşar* also means "kosher" in Turkish). The upbeat **Salon Sema Piknik,** 9 Faık Bey Cad. (tel. (474) 223 21 18), one block east of the Hotel Kervansaray, satisfies vegetarians with its *Kaşarli pide,* a cheese-*pide*-pizza with vegetables and egg (full meal $3; open daily 8am-10pm). Crowds gather at **Cafe Kristal,** 181 Atatürk Cad. (tel. (474) 223 22 67), for the tasty *döner kebap* (full meal $3.50; open 8am-10pm).

NEAR KARS: ANİ

*All visitors to Ani must obtain an approved **permit** from the Kars tourist office before setting out (see **Practical Information** above). No public transportation runs between Kars and Ani. Without a private car, either hire a **taxi** ($50) or take a **dolmuş** ($6-7), organized through the tourist office. Dolmuş drivers usually take passengers through the permit process and to the Ani museum, where tickets are sold. **Admission** $2, students $1. Çelil Ersözoğlu (tel. (474) 223 63 23) is the main tour guide and usually the dolmuş driver. Otherwise, Ani Tour (tel. (474) 223 99 90), in the old bus station, offers a similar package deal, though service varies with demand. Cameras and camping at Ani are illegal.*

Situated 45km east of Kars on the present-day Armenian border, the ancient Armenian capital of Ani is a tremendous site. A strategic point on a lucrative trade route, Ani prospered and grew to a population that (at over 100,000) rivaled Constantinople. Ani sits on a triangular plateau wedged between the Alaçay and Arpaçay Rivers, accessible through the **Aslan Kapısı (Lion's Gate)**, the only remaining entrance of the original seven gates. After dealing with the preliminary security, most tourists are set free to roam in Ani. Heading left from the entrance will enable you to make a wide circle, touching all the ruins.

The ruins of the **Church of the Holy Redeemer,** built in 1034, is the first step along the southeast path. Head downhill to find one of the three **Churches of St. Gregory (Tigorn Honents).** On the east wall, realistic frescoes depict the life and times of St. Gregory the Illuminator, who brought Christianity to Armenia. Soon after King Titridates tortured St. Gregory, he realized his sins and converted himself and soon his state to Christianity. Down in the valley stand the remains of the **Covenant of the Virgins,** from which you can see over the border into Armenia. Head up the plateau to the largest building in Ani, the **Cathedral of Virgin Mary,** designed by Titridates in 939 CE, who also collaborated in the restoration of Istanbul's Aya Sofia. A passage to the left of the altar leads up to a private room; bring a flashlight for safe exploration. Farther southwest lies the **Menüçehir Camii,** built in 1072 and said to be the first mosque in Anatolia. Its climbable minaret bears the uniquely non-Selçuk inscription of Allah's name. From the rotunda-style **Church of St. Gregory (Abighamrets),** northwest of the citadel, the view of the Alaçay River shows carved caves in the canyon gorge, where Armenian and Georgian frescoes are said to be painted. In the center of the plateau is the **Church of the Holy Apostles,** once converted into a *kervansaray,* but now mostly a lot of rubble. Note the variety of Islamic geometric designs and *muqarna*s (stalactite ornamentations). To the northwest is the third **Church of St. Gregory,** built by the Armenian king Gegik I, and the **Selçuk Palace.**

GULF STATES

Look beyond the stereotyped images of oil barons and the Persian Gulf War. The Gulf States have a lot more to offer: stunning beaches, legendary religious sites; and some of the best markets in the world. While journeying into the oil-rich Gulf is more expensive than travel in the rest of the Middle East, the juxtaposition of glistening skyscrapers and a traditional Muslim lifestyle is nowhere more startling. From the ultra-modern shopping haven of Dubai to the 17th-century castles and forts lining Oman's northern coast, old and new each hold a privileged place in Gulf society. The **United Arab Emirates (UAE)** and **Oman** welcome tourists into their borders and heartily encourage foreigners to sample new sights, sounds, and tastes. Far removed from the Gulf War conflicts of 1991, these countries are safe, politically stable, and hospitable to Westerners—though residents of smaller towns may be surprised to see a foreign face. The UAE and Oman reveal a different side of Arab life, one in which economic prosperity coexists with strict religious beliefs, where tradition has been molded by a surprisingly multicultural blend of East African, Indian, and Persian influences.

HIGHLIGHTS OF THE GULF STATES

■ Just a short jaunt from Dubai, **Sharjah** (p. 630) preserves the rich history and culture that the UAE's glitzier cities have forgotten in its traditional *souqs*, museums, and forts.
■ Oman's vacation capital, breezy **Salalah** (p. 667) is the center of a coastline full of spectacular beaches, ancient archaeological excavations, awesome hikes, and the tomb of the prophet Job, a pilgrimage site for multiple faiths.
■ Hands-down one of the most gorgeous spots in the world, the isolated, undeveloped **Musandem Peninsula** (p. 664) dazzles with its rugged coastline and serene fjords.

ESSENTIALS

ENTRY

Except for citizens of other Gulf nations, most foreign visitors need a **visa** to enter the UAE and Oman. Visas can be obtained from the UAE or Omani embassy or consulate in your home country, or they can be arranged through a sponsor in the Gulf, usually a hotel or tour company. Phone or fax a hotel in Dubai, Abu Dhabi, or Muscat at least 10 days before you plan to arrive. The hotel will need a copy of your passport, your flight information, a visa-processing fee, and the guarantee that you will stay in that hotel for a set length of time. The visa will be waiting in the airport upon your arrival; have the hotel fax a copy to you beforehand, as many airlines need confirmation of a visa before letting passengers board the plane. If you plan to enter either country by land, you must obtain the visa directly from an embassy or consulate. Allow a week to 10 days for processing. Travelers whose passports show evidence of travel to Israel will be denied a visa to either country.

UAE VISAS

There are two types of **UAE visas**: a 30- or 60-day **visit visa**, which costs 110dhs and can be extended, and a 14-day **transit visa**, which is faster to process but costs 120dhs and cannot be renewed. Citizens of most Western countries need a visa to enter the UAE. All travelers in transit who do not leave Dubai or Abu Dhabi airport do not need a visa. **U.K. citizens** automatically receive a 60-day visa upon arrival in the UAE, which can be renewed for another two months. **Visa renewals** for any nationality can be made at the Department of Immigration and Naturalization, near the Dubai World Trade Center roundabout. The visit visa can be extended twice, each time for an additional 30 days (500dhs). If you overstay your visa visit, there is a 10-day grace period; after that, there is a 100dhs fine for each day overstayed.

Embassies and consulates within the UAE are located in **Dubai** (see **Practical Information,** p. 626) and **Abu Dhabi** (see **Practical Information,** p. 635). UAE embassies and consulates abroad include: **Australia,** 36 Gulgoa Circuit, O'Malley ACT 2606 (tel. (2) 6286 8802; fax 6286 8804); **Oman,** Diplomatic Area, Al-Khuwair, P.O. Box 551 code 111 or P.O. Box 335 code 113, Muscat (tel. 600 302; fax 602 584); **South Africa,** 980 Park St., Arcadia 0083 or P.O. Box 57090, Arcadia 0007, Pretoria (tel. 342 77 36/9; fax 342 7738); **U.K.,** 30 Princes Gate, London SW7 IPT (tel. (020) 7581 1281; fax 7581 9616); and **U.S.,** 3000 K St. NW, Suite 600, Washington, D.C. 20007 (tel. 202-955-7999; fax 337-7029) or 747 Third Ave., 36th floor, New York, NY 10017 (tel. 212-371-0480; fax 371-4923).

OMANI VISAS

Tourist (US$36) and **business** (US$60) visas are valid for two years, allow multiple entries, and permit stays of up to six months. Embassies and consulates within Oman are located in **Muscat** (see **Practical Information,** p. 649). Omani embassies abroad include: **U.K.,** 167 Queens Gate, London, SW7 5HE (tel. (171) 225 00 01) and **U.S.,** 2535 Belmont Road, N.W., Washington, D.C. 20006 (tel. 202-387-1980).

⚒ BORDER CROSSINGS

BETWEEN THE UAE AND OMAN. Crossing the border between the UAE and Oman is incredibly easy; the biggest hassle may be getting the visas. The only official crossing point is via the border towns of Al-'Ain (UAE) and Buraimi (Oman); buses traveling between Dubai and Muscat pass through this checkpoint. If you would like to drive across this border, you must obtain a **road permit** in advance. It is also possible to cross into Oman's Musandem Peninsula through the UAE town of Sham, north of Ras al-Khaimah, but no public transportation travels this route. The roads at Dibba and Hatta are open, but if tourists cross the border this way, they are considered to be in transit and can incur fines for staying in the country longer than 48 hours. For more information, see **The Old In-Out,** p. 639.

UAE TO SAUDI ARABIA. Saudi Public Transport Company (SAPTCO) runs buses between Abu Dhabi and Dubai and Damman, Saudi Arabia three times per week (6-9hr.) However, obtaining a visa to enter Saudi Arabia is nearly impossible. Tourist visas are not offered. To get a visitor or business visa, you need a formal invitation from a Saudi company or individual sponsor. Muslims can apply for *hajj* or *umrah* visas in their home countries, but even these are difficult to obtain. The easiest option is to get a **transit visa,** which must be obtained from a Saudi embassy in advance, and allows up to seven days in the country.

UAE TO IRAN. There are no ferries strictly for passengers, but the state-run Valfajre-8 Shipping Company sells passenger tickets for its cargo boats. Ferries travel about once per week between Sharjah and Bandar-é Abbas, Iran. Westerners (with the exception of Israelis, who are barred entry) have been having more success in obtaining Iranian visas in recent years; however, results are always unpredictable. Contact an Iranian embassy for details.

OMAN TO YEMEN. There are conflicting reports about whether the road crossing the Yemeni-Omani border is open. There is no public transportation between the two countries, but travelers with their own cars may be able to drive across the border via the coastal highway through Salalah. Ask about the status of the highway in Salalah. A **visa** is required to enter Yemen (see p. 676).

GETTING AROUND

TAXIS AND BUSES. There are two types of taxis: **service** and **private** (or "engaged") taxis. *Service*, also called **share taxis**, carry a set number of passengers and usually travel on fixed routes, basically serving as a substitute for local buses. Since most cities in both the UAE and Oman are fairly spread out, it is impossible to avoid using taxis unless you rent a car. Taxis are also a fast, though expensive, way to travel between cities, and often the only way to travel between emirates. Always negotiate a price with the driver *before* getting in, as most taxis are unmetered and drivers are infamous for charging exorbitant amounts to unsuspecting foreigners. Even if a taxi has a meter, it is best to agree on a fare beforehand. Women should always sit in the back seat.

In the UAE, buses are not the omnipresent mode of transport that they are in many other countries. The only cities with **local bus service** are Abu Dhabi, Al-'Ain, and Dubai. Buses aren't much good for traveling between cities either; the one exception is the **Dubai Transport Corporation** (see p. 626), which runs buses from Dubai to the other emirates. In Oman, it's a whole different story: the state-operated **Oman National Transport Company (ONTC)** operates extensive local and intercity bus routes. The **local bus** system in Muscat is quite extensive, and rides only cost a few hundred baisa—by far the cheapest way to get around. The main **intercity bus** terminal is in Ruwi (Muscat) and complete timetables for all domestic routes are posted there. Reservations are only accepted for the express service to Salalah; book these tickets a day or two in advance. The only **international bus** service travels between Muscat and Dubai.

CARS. Renting a car isn't cheap, but it is relatively easy and usually worthwhile, given the spread-out nature of cities in the UAE and Oman. The road network in the UAE has doubled in the past decade, so renting a car allows much more freedom to explore the countryside, particularly since there are so few bus routes in the country. Rates start around US$36 per day for a small car, and there may be a limit on the number of kilometers you can drive before being charged. If outdoor sightseeing is your thing, get a **4-wheel drive** vehicle. Many of Oman's most spectacular sights are off the tarmac road. Most car rental agencies are located in Dubai, Abu Dhabi, and Muscat, and some of the airport branches are open 24 hours. Foreign driver's licenses are often accepted, but it is best to get an **International Driving Permit** (see p. 28) if you plan to rent a car in either country. Driving is on the right side of the road, right turns at red lights are prohibited, and the speed limit is 60kph in town, 100kph on highways. **Seatbelts** are mandatory—the UAE has the highest death rate from accidents in the world. Non-compliance in Oman results in a OR 10 fine. If you plan to cross the UAE-Oman border by car, you must get a **road permit.**

AIR. The main international airports in the UAE are in **Abu Dhabi** (tel. (02) 757 500), **Dubai** (tel. (04) 245 555), and **Sharjah** (tel. (06) 581 111). There are also smaller international airports at **Ras al-Khaimah** (tel. (07) 448 111), **Fujairah** (tel. (09) 226 222), and **Al-'Ain** (tel. (03) 855 555). The most traffic runs in and out of Dubai International Airport, a common hub for flights between Asia and Europe or North America, with 80 airlines operating to over 120 destinations worldwide. Most European capitals have direct flights to both Dubai and Abu Dhabi. There is also frequent service to other cities in the Middle East, as well as to India and southeast Asia. There is **no departure tax** upon leaving the UAE. **No internal flights** run between emirates; the country is so small that internal air travel is unnecessary.

Seeb International Airport, just outside of Muscat, handles all of Oman's international traffic. Over 60 international airlines operate out of Seeb, with frequent flights to Europe, North America, and southeast Asia. There is an OR 3 **departure tax** when leaving the country. **Oman Air** (tel. 707 222) has a monopoly on Oman's internal flights, offering air service between **Muscat** and **Salalah, Sur, Khasab** (on the Musandem Peninsula), and **Masirah Island** (see p. 646). As Oman is a small country, it takes no longer than 1½ hours to reach any domestic destination by air.

TOURIST AND TRAVEL SERVICES

MEDICAL EMERGENCIES AND HEALTH. Medical facilities in the UAE and Oman are quite modern, but not up to Western standards. Hospitals in major cities are far better than those in rural areas; if you think you may need serious medical attention, head to the nearest metropolis. Many luxury hotels have an English-speaking doctor on-call who can usually treat, or at least give referrals, to non-guests. There are a plethora of **pharmacies** in the UAE and Oman; in larger towns, at least one stays open 24 hours.

USEFUL ADDRESSES. There are no tourist offices in the UAE or Oman. Hotels and travel agencies can give brochures and advice, and many bookstores carry maps. In the UAE, the **Ministry of Information and Culture** offers insight on prominent sights; contact them at: P.O. Box 17, Abu Dhabi (tel. (02) 453 000 or 922; fax 452 504). In Dubai, try contacting the **Dubai Commerce and Tourism Promotion Board**, P.O. Box 594, Dubai (tel. (04) 511 600), near the ABN Bank Building, by the Bar Juman Shopping Mall. The **National Tourism Office of Oman** has information on visas and tourism in general. Contact them at: Directorate General of Tourism, P.O. Box 550, Muscat 113 (tel. 799 500 or 791 921; fax 794 213 or 239). Also try the **Omani Ministry of Information**, P.O. Box 600, Muscat 113 (tel. 600 591; fax 698 430) or the **Oman Chamber of Commerce and Industry**, P.O. Box 1400, Ruwi 112 (tel. 707 674; fax 708 497).

USEFUL WEB PAGES. The government's official **United Arab Emirates Home Page** (www.emirates.org/) provides a comprehensive introduction to the country, including a photo gallery, details about on the country's traditions, and information on travel to different regions. Another official **United Arab Emirates page** (www.uae.org.ae/) guides through a photo-intensive tour of the culture, outdoor activities, and architectural history of the region. Helpful web sites for Oman include **Oman Visitor** (www.geocities.com/RainForest/8883/omanvis.html), **OmaniaNet** (www.omania.net/), the home page of the German-based **Oman Studies Center** (www.oman.org/), and **Oman Infoworld** (Home.InfoRamp.Net/~emous/oman/).

MONEY MATTERS

CURRENCY AND EXCHANGE. The unit of currency in the UAE is the **dirham** (abbreviated as dhs or Dhs.), which is divided into 100 **fils.** In some places, you might see the currency referred to as AED (Arab Emirate Dirham). The monetary unit in Oman is the **Omani rial** (also spelled riyal, and abbreviated OR or RO), which is divided into 1000 **baisa** (or baiza). In 1995, the government issued new, redesigned notes for all denominations; look twice to make sure you're paying with the right bill. The exchange rates for all major currencies are published daily in the newspapers, or dial 1106 (in Oman) for exchange information in English.

While cash is the general method of payment in both countries, major **credit cards** (Visa, MC, AmEx, Diners Club) are widely accepted, especially in hotels and larger shops. Smaller shops may charge an extra five percent processing fee for credit card transactions. Banks can exchange most foreign currencies and traveler's checks, and can also **transfer money** and give **cash advances** on major credit cards. **Exchange centers** or money changers, often located near major *souqs*, offer better rates than the banks. Don't count on using **ATM** machines in the UAE; though most banks have them, few are linked to international networks. Omani ATMs, however, are prevalent throughout the country and are well-connected to international networks like Visa, MC, Cirrus, and PLUS. It's not necessary to bring **traveler's checks,** but if you do, be sure to bring American Express or Thomas Cook—it's nearly impossible to cash anything else.

TIPPING. Tipping is not compulsory, but it is the polite thing to do. Many restaurants add a service charge to the bill (which goes to the house, not to the waiter); otherwise, a 10% tip is standard. Some accommodations, particularly higher-end hotels, add a 14-17% tax and service charge. Be sure to ask if the nightly rate includes taxes before checking into a hotel. Taxi drivers are not tipped. Anyone who performs a service for you, such as carrying your bags, will appreciate a small tip.

BUSINESS HOURS. The working day generally begins early in the morning, around 7:30 or 8am, and includes a lunch and siesta break in the middle of the day. The official work week is from Saturday to Wednesday, and the traditional "weekend" is on Thursday and Friday, but increasingly many business close on Friday and Saturday instead. **Government offices** are open Saturday through Wednesday around 7:30am-1:30pm. **Banks** generally open their doors from Saturday to Wednesday 8am-noon and Thursday 8-11am. Business hours for **embassies** vary greatly; generally, they open only in the mornings, and are always closed on Fridays. **Private sector** offices and stores keep longer hours, but close for a lunch break in the middle of the day. Typical hours are Saturday through Thursday 8 or 9am until 1pm, then 4 or 4:30pm until 7 or 8pm. However, many stores now stay open on Fridays, and some big shopping malls don't close until as late as midnight.

ACCOMMODATIONS

Accommodations in the Gulf don't come cheap, and will generally absorb most of a budget traveler's allowance. If you've got the cash to splurge, you won't be disappointed, but budget lodgings are few and far between. Expect to pay at least US$30 per person each night, more in smaller towns or popular resort towns. If you plan to arrange a visa through a hotel, be aware that only the higher-end places offer this service, and they will expect you to stay in their abode for at least a few nights. There are a few Hostelling International **hostels** in Dubai, Abu Dhabi, and Sharjah, but none in Oman. For groups, another money-saving option is to rent a **furnished flat,** available for daily or weekly rental at a reduced rate in some cities; many have full kitchens and include maid service, making these flats a better value than hotel rooms. There are no **camping** options in the cities, but many people set up their tents in the surrounding desert.

KEEPING IN TOUCH

MAIL. The only **Poste Restante** facilities in the UAE are in the Dubai Central Post Office. For the most part, Poste Restante is a foreign concept to residents of the Gulf States, and it is unlikely that mail sent this way will be retrieved. Oman does not have Poste Restante. Instead, send mail to an **American Express Office** or directly to a hotel. American Express holds mail for cardholders, and has offices in Dubai (p. 627), Abu Dhabi (p. 635), Muscat (p. 649), and Salalah (p. 669).

Mail takes a week to 10 days to reach North America, Europe, or Australia. Airmail letters cost 3-6dhs/100-350 baiza (depending on weight), postcards 2dhs/150 baiza. Stamps can be purchased at post offices and many shops. In the UAE, drop outgoing mail into the **red mailboxes,** located at post offices and near many shopping centers. Hotels will often handle outgoing mail as well. In addition to the government-run postal service, international courier companies such as **DHL** and **Federal Express** operate out of Muscat.

TELEPHONE, FAX, AND INTERNET ACCESS. All telecommunications are provided by government monopolies, **Emirates Telecommunications Corporation (Etisalat)** in the UAE and the **General Telephone Office (GTO)** in Oman. Pay phones are a dime a dozen in cities, but most require **phonecards,** available from supermarkets and most local shops. Direct international calls and international collect calls can be made from all phones. Most hotels allow guests to make international calls, then pay for them at the reception desk. If you're using an **international calling card,** the access numbers in the UAE are: **AT&T** (tel. 800 121), **Sprint** (tel. 800 131), and **MCI** (tel. 800 111). International calling cards cannot be used in Oman, so phonecards are an economical alternative to expensive hotel calls. **Faxes** can be sent from telephone offices, as well as many shops and hotels. Within Oman, there are **no area codes,** though the first two or three digits of a telephone number reveal which region is being called.

The Internet is still in its infancy in the Gulf. The government controls Internet services, and bans access to web pages that violate the country's moral and cultural values. Cyber access is hard to come by, but Dubai, Abu Dhabi, Sharjah, and Muscat each have an Internet hall or cafe.

WOMEN TRAVELERS

In contrast to the widely-held conception of an Islamic fundamentalist society, women can drive and walk around unescorted in the UAE and Oman. Women will not have any problem checking into hotels alone, but they may feel uncomfortable in some of the cheaper urban lodgings. Stares and catcalls should simply be ignored, and lone women should not open the door of their hotel room if anyone knocks at night. All restaurants have a separate Family Room so females can eat unveiled and not be stared at; Western women should always eat in the Family Room as well. Women should not wear bikinis on the beach. The UAE and Oman pose fewer problems to female travelers than other Gulf countries, but the best way for women to avoid trouble is to dress conservatively (no tight clothing) and cover up as much as possible, particularly legs and arms. For more tips, see **Women Travelers,** p. 29.

DRESS AND ETIQUETTE

Though Oman and particularly the UAE are considered the most liberal of the Gulf States, their customs may still seem strict to Western visitors. Most locals wear the traditional long robes (the white *dishdasha* for men and the black *abaya* for women) and head-dress. Though there are no legal dress codes, be respectful and dress conservatively during the day, particularly in smaller towns. It is not necessary for foreigners to wear traditional Muslim clothing, but both men and women should cover their legs and upper arms at all times. Shorts, tank tops, and even t-shirts are inappropriate. Stay away from tight clothing that reveals the contours of the body. In hot weather, men should wear cotton pants and a loose, long-sleeved shirt; women should dress in long pants or an ankle-length skirt. In urban nightclubs, the clothing is tighter and more revealing, but upper arms and legs still remain covered.

Never take a photograph of anyone, particularly a woman, without asking permission first. During the month of Ramadan, it is inappropriate to eat, smoke, or drink in public. If visiting the home of a UAE citizen, it is customary to remove your shoes before stepping on the carpet and to avoid showing the soles of your feet.

LIFE AND TIMES

RELIGION AND ETHNICITY

Only 15-20% of the UAE's total population of 1.8 million are citizens. The remainder are mostly foreign workers and their families, with South Asians (mainly Indians and Pakistanis) constituting as much as half the population.

GULF STATES

Arabs from other countries (mainly Palestinians, Egyptians, Jordanians, Yemenis, and Omanis) account for more than 10%, as do Iranians. Western Europeans and Southeast Asians, including many Filipinos, have recently immigrated in increasing numbers and now comprise about 8% of the population. Islam is the official religion of the UAE, and 96% of the population is Muslim. Most are Sunni, but a 16% Shi'ite minority live mainly in Dubai and Sharjah. A majority of the expatriate workers are Muslim, though Hindus comprise a portion of the foreign population.

Islam is also the dominant religion in Oman. However, Oman is the only country to have a majority of **Ibidi** Muslims, one of the few remaining Khariji sects, the smallest of the three orientations of Islam. One of the earliest Muslim fundamentalist movements, the Kharijis broke with the majority of Muslims in 658, and are known for their strict rules on morals and contact with strangers. While Kharijis account for only 1% of Muslims worldwide, they comprise 75% of Oman's total population. About 10% of Omanis are Sunni Muslims. Hindus make up 14% of the population, and other religions count for about 1%. The population of the Sultanate is predominantly Arab, but sizable Indian and Pakistani populations live in the northern coastal areas. For the past 200 years, there has been an Indian merchant community in Muscat, and today around 300,000 expatriate workers from the Indian subcontinent comprise about 50% of the Omani work force. There are also minorities of Persian and **Baluchi** ancestries.

LANGUAGE

The official language of both the UAE and Oman is **Arabic,** though **English** is widely used in large cities and business circles. Many street and shop signs, as well as restaurant menus in the cities, are written in both Arabic and English. It is not uncommon to hear expatriate workers from the Indian subcontinent conversing in **Urdu, Hindi,** and **Farsi.** Though Arabic is used for education, official purposes, and the media, there are also a number of regional dialects. Thousands of UAE residents speak Farsi, **Pashto, and Somali.** The ethnic Baluch population, centered in Mutrah (Muscat), speak **Baluchi,** derived from an ancient Indo-Iranian language. Many locals in Salalah and other southern coastal towns in Oman speak a Dhofari dialect, and some residents of the isolated Musandem Peninsula speak **Kumzari,** a creole mixture of Hindi, Farsi, and Portuguese.

FOOD AND DRINK

Food in the Gulf is similar to cuisine in many other Middle Eastern countries. Typical Levantine food—such as hummus and tabbouleh—comprise the staples of meals. Typical ingredients in a dish include beef, mutton, lamb, chicken, seafood, rice, pistachios, dates, yogurt, and spices. Pork is absolutely taboo, as in all Muslim countries; you won't even find it on the menus of Western restaurants. Thanks to the large expat population from the Indian subcontinent, Indian dishes such as *biryani* and curries are ubiquitous in UAE and Omani restaurants.

Oman's historical role as an important center of the spice trade is still quite visible in its cuisine. Traditional Omani cooking centers around cardamom, cinnamon, cumin, ginger, pepper, tumeric, and saffron, but these spices are only used as subtle flavoring, so food is rarely hot. A mixture of these spices, ground and added to meats and poultry, is called **bizaar.** The main meal, eaten in the afternoon, is almost always accompanied by rice, potatoes, or bread. **Harees,** a dish made with boiled wheat, is flavored with chicken, tomato, and *bizaar*, and garnished with fried onion slices. A hearty meal with Pakistani roots, **qabouli** is made with meat, potatoes, and rice, and seasoned with *bizaar*, garlic, onions, and raisins.

The local coffee is known as **ahwa** (also spelled qahwa), an aromatic blend of ground beans and cardamom. It is acceptable to add a bit of sugar when developing a taste for *ahwa* (though locals always drink it black), but it is never taken with cream or milk. The cups hold no more than an ounce or two, and are often served alongside fruit or dates. **Halwa** is an Omani sweet made from flour, brown sugar, rose water, saffron, and cardamom—quite different from the Lebanese dessert of the same name. Fresh juices made from mango, banana, pineapple, and other tropical fruits are cheap and widely available from street stands. Yogurt, often served with nuts, is another popular drink; the local milk is a heavy, salty buttermilk called **laban.** In both countries, **alcohol** is restricted to establishments associated with hotels, usually adjoining restaurants and bars.

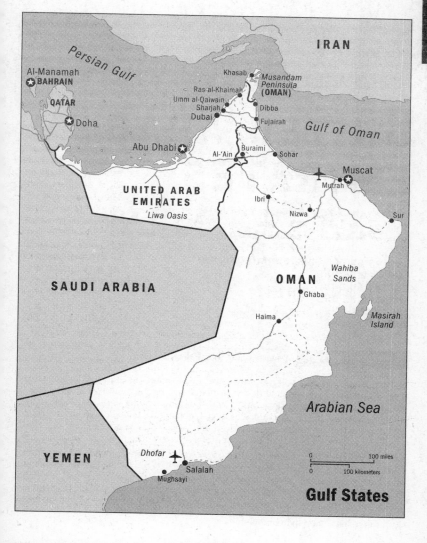

Gulf States

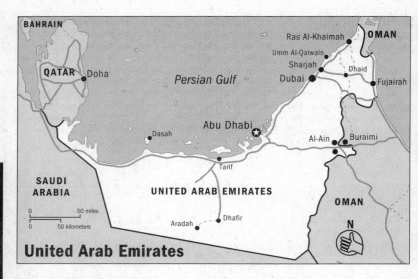

United Arab Emirates

UNITED ARAB EMIRATES

الامارات العربية المتحدة

US$1=3.67 DHS (UAE DIRHAMS)	**1 DH=US$0.27**
CDN$1=2.46 DHS	**1 DH=CDN$0.41**
UK£1=5.90 DHS	**1 DH=UK£0.17**
AUS$1=2.36 DHS	**1 DH=AUS$0.42**
SAR1=0.61 DHS	**1 DH=SAR1.65**
EUR1=3.92 DHS	**1 DH=EURO.26**
OR 1=9.54 DHS	**1 DH=OR 0.10**

PHONE FACTS | Country Code: 971. **Police:** Tel. 999.

In the past two decades, oil revenues have transformed the United Arab Emirates from a group of impoverished desert principalities into a wealthy, modern "Muslim Texas" with glittering skyscrapers and shopping rivaling Paris and Milan. Abu Dhabi and Dubai, the richest emirates, boast metropoles that seem to have sprung from the ground overnight. These cities barely existed 50 years ago, and the conservative, religious lifestyle of many Emiratis attests to the newness of the UAE's glitzy Western imports. Devout Muslims pray in traditional mosques, while blocks away jet-setters stream into the Hard Rock Cafe and international bigwigs bargain for gold in Dubai's famous *souqs*. Other emirates have less severe split personalities: Sharjah is known as the country's cultural capital for its preservation of historical and religious heritage, and less-developed northern emirates like Fujairah and Ras al-Khaimah reveal the natural beauty that must have existed before the skyscrapers and neon lights moved in.

HISTORY

While there are practically no historical documents from the UAE prior to the Islamic period, experts are certain that the area has been inhabited since the 4th millennium BCE. Tombs dating from 3000-2500 BCE, excavated at **Jabal Hafit** near Al-'Ain, reveal oasis-centered settlements with a farming economy—strong evidence that the climate back then was much more temperate than it is today. From 2500-2000 BCE, the **Umm an-Nar** fishing culture extended its control well into the interior of the Arabian Peninsula and down the Gulf coast into Oman.

By the time of the Greek and Roman empires, the main trade routes between the Mediterranean, Ethiopia, southwest Arabia, and India passed through the Gulf, exposing the coastal areas to multiple international influences. During the 7th century CE, the region's seafaring tribes were converted to Islam. In fact, **Dibba,** on the northern coast of Fujairah, was the site of the battle in 635 that marked the completion of the Islamic conquest of the Arabian Peninsula. During the Middle Ages, most of modern-day UAE was part of the **Kingdom of Hormuz.** With satellite ports at Qalhat (in eastern Oman) and **Julfar** (in the emirate of Ras al-Khaimah), Hormuz completely controlled the mouth of the Gulf and, therefore, most trade. After the Portuguese took Muscat in 1507, they went on to capture Hormuz and build a fort in Julfar. They remained there until 1633, when land attacks by hostile tribes and sea attacks from the British and Dutch forced them to abandon their holdings in the Gulf. During the next century, control of the lower Gulf passed through the hands of Oman's Al-Ya'ribi Imams, into those of the Persian Empire.

The land that is now the UAE has traditionally had a tightly-structured society divided into tribes, sub-tribes, and clans. The rise of British naval power in the Gulf coincided with the ascent of one of these tribes, the **Qawasim.** During the mid-18th century, the Qawasim built up ports at Sharjah and Ras al-Khaimah, where they rapidly raised an impressive fleet. Their newfound maritime strength brought the Qawasim into conflict with the Imams of Muscat, as their dominance of the high seas threatened Omani control of trade with India and East Africa. Meanwhile, Gulf access became increasingly vital to the British East India Company. When Napoleon Bonaparte's occupation of Egypt in 1798 blocked the Red Sea route, one British response was to enter into treaty relations with the Imam of Muscat, a move that inevitably placed them in opposition to the Qawasim. The Qawasim considered English ships fair targets for raids, a move that earned their land the nickname **Pirate Coast.** The British almost certainly exaggerated the Qawasim's involvement in piracy, but their series of attacks against the Pirate Coast climaxed in 1820, with the destruction of the Qasimi fleets and the first **Maritime Truce.** The truce was renewed several times until 1853, when the local sheikhs signed the permanent **Treaty of Peace in Perpetuity,** under which they accepted British military protection in exchange for abandoning piracy. The Pirate Coast was redubbed the **Trucial Coast,** a name that stuck until 1971.

After 1869, rivalry among the international powers began to threaten Britain's position in the Gulf. When the Ottomans occupied Al-Hasa and Qatar in 1871, they also claimed eight Trucial Coast settlements, and in 1887 a resurgent Persia took over some Qasimi territory as well. By the early 1890s, both France and Germany were also striving to establish themselves in the region. In an attempt to hold onto its sphere of influence, Britain secured **Exclusive Agreements** from the sheikhs of the Trucial Coast in 1892, written assurances that the local rulers would not ally, communicate with, or give residence to any other government. These Exclusive Agreements were the basis of Britain's relations with the Trucial States into the 20th century; from 1873 to 1947, the Trucial Coast was administered by the British India Company, and after 1947 by the London Foreign Office. However, the British never assumed full sovereignty; each Trucial State maintained full internal control.

The decline of the British Empire following World War II, particularly the granting of independence to India in 1947, accelerated changes in the Gulf. In the 1950s, the British sought to weld the distinct regimes of the Trucial States into a single administrative bloc. With British help, the **Trucial Oman Scouts** (a unified defense force) was set up in 1951. The following year, a **Trucial States Council** was formed to unite the various rulers (who had not all met together since 1905) in discussions on common problems and interests. When the British vacated the Persian Gulf in 1971, six of the Trucial States federated and became known as the United Arab Emirates. Ras al-Khaimah joined the federation in 1972, while Bahrain and Qatar opted for separate independence.

Today, the country consists of seven emirates—Abu Dhabi (the largest and officially the nation's capital), Dubai, Sharjah, Ajman, Fujairah, Umm al-Qaiwain, and Ras al-Khaimah. The loose federation allows joint policies in foreign relations, defense, and development, with each member state keeping a separate internal government headed by its own ruler, or *sheikh*. The UAE has one of the highest per capita incomes in the world (US$24,000 in 1997) and a sizable annual trade surplus, primarily due to its oil and gas output. At present levels of production, crude oil reserves should last for over 100 years. In recent years, the UAE government has encouraged increased privatization and industrial development.

IN THE NEWS

Territorial disputes between the UAE and Iran over a group of Gulf islands, **Abu Musa** and the **Greater and Lesser Tunbs,** have heightened in the past year. The importance of the islands rests in the strategic value of their location in the Strait of Hormuz, the entrance to the Persian Gulf. The islands have been in Iran's possession since 1971. The government in Abu Dhabi has long objected to the legitimacy of Tehran's pact with Sharjah, as it was signed before the UAE came into being. In early 1999, Iran built a town hall on Abu Musa and began conducting military exercises in nearby waters, reigniting antagonisms. The other members of the Gulf Cooperation Council (GCC) expressed their support of the UAE, and in July 1999 formed a committee to facilitate talks between the two countries. By the end of the summer, the conflict had not yet been resolved.

DUBAI دبي

Dubai is truly a shopper's oasis. Known as the "City of Merchants" since trade caravans from Mesopotamia began stopping here around 3000 BCE, the city's streets today seem lined with more shopping malls than mosques. Bargain for spices, textiles, and gold in the alleyways of Dubai's traditional *souqs*, window-shop for high-end European *couture* in the air-conditioned shopping malls, or pick up last-minute souvenirs at the world's largest duty free airport shopping complex. Dubai even has a month-long Shopping Festival beginning in mid-March. The array of imported goods available in Dubai is a reflection of the diversity of Dubai's natives. As the second-largest emirate, Dubai is a cosmopolitan blend of Arabs, Persians, Bengalis, Filipinos, Indians, and Brits. Aside from shopping, Dubai does have a few noteworthy gems to dazzle the budget traveler, who will undoubtedly spend a few days in this hub for Asia-bound international flights.

✴ ORIENTATION

Dubai is actually two towns separated by the **Dubai Creek** (Khor Dubai): **Deira** to the north and **Bur Dubai** to the south. The heart of the city is in Deira, but both towns are connected by the **Al-Maktoum Bridge** and the ever-chugging *abras*, wooden motorboats that serve as water taxis. **Beniyas Road** runs parallel to the creekfront on the Deira side. The next main street parallel to Beniyas is **Al-Maktoum Road,** which hits **An-Nasr Square** (also called Beniyas Sq.), Dubai's equivalent of London's Picadilly Circus or New York's Times Square. On the Bur Dubai side, **Al-Faheidi Street** runs alongside Bur Dubai's Old Souq about one block past the *abra* docks. Al-Faheidi St. turns into As-Seef Rd. at the **Al-Mussalla Rd. Roundabout,** just south of the Dubai National Museum. **Khalid Ibn al-Walid Road** runs parallel to As-Seef until the two roads connect at the **Strand Cinema Roundabout. Trade Center Road** connects Khalid Ibn al-Walid Rd. to Adh-Dhiyafah Rd., which leads south to Jumeira.

Dubai

ACCOMMODATIONS

A Shiraz Hotel
B Ma'arib Hotel
C Emirates Hotel &
   Imperial Palace Hotel

N

400 yards
400 meters
0
0

TO CLOCK TOWER ROUNDABOUT (1km)

Al-Mateena St.

Salah ad-Din St.

Al-Rigga St.

FISH ROUNDABOUT

Umar ibn al-Kattab St.

Kuwait

Deira Taxi Station

UNION SQ.

Sheraton Hotel

An-Nakhal St.

Al-Maktoum Hospital Rd.

Al-Maktoum Rd.

France

Benijas Rd.

Naif Rd.

St. 5

UMM HURER ROUNDABOUT

TO UMM HURER ROUNDABOUT (700m)

NAIF ROUNDABOUT

Deira St.

AN-NASR (BENIYAS) SQ.

St. 3

Rd. 14

UK

Al-Musalla St.

NAIF SOUQ

Al-Burj St.

St. 1

Dubai Creek (Khor Dubai)

Al-Khaleej Rd.

28th St.

38th St.

Naif South St.

As-Sabkha Rd.

DEIRA

COVERED SOUQ

As-Soor St.

Al-Baniyan St.

As-Souq al-Kabeer St.

As-Seef St.

TO HYATT REGENCY & GALERIA MALL (800m)

GOLD SOUQ

Sikkat al-Khail St.

Souq Deira St.

Old Baladiya St.

Abra (Ferry)

Ruler's Office

TO WORLD TRADE CENTRE (AUSTRALIAN, ITALIAN, TURKISH, & US CONSULATES, 3.5km)

Thega Centre Rd.

AL-FAHEIDI ROUNDABOUT

Deira Bus Station

Al-Ras St.

Al-Fahidi St.

DEIRA SOUQ

Abra (Ferry)

ETISALAT

Dubai Museum (Al-Fahaidi Fort)

Al-Mussalla Rd.

Al-Armadiya St.

DUBAI OLD SOUQ

Ali Ibn Abi Talib St.

Al-Faheidi Rd.

Egypt

SAFEDIYA ROUNDABOUT

TO GULF OF ADEN

Ash-Shindagha Tunnel

AL-GHABIBA ROUNDABOUT

ETISALAT

An-Nahda St.

BUR DUBAI

Al-Hisn St.

TO JORDANIAN & PAKISTANI CONSULATES (1km)

Port Rashid

Dubai Bus & Taxi Station

Al-Rifa'a St.

Al-Ghubaiba St.

Al-Falah Rd.

Al-Khaleej Rd.

Khalid Ibn al-Waleed St.

JUMEIRA (4km)

🖅 TRANSPORTATION

Airplanes: Dubai International Airport is on Airport Rd. (flight info tel. 206 66 66). Bus #4 runs between the Gold Souq bus station in Deira and the airport (25min., every 30min. 6am-11pm); routes #11, 15, and 44 also go to the airport, but take longer and depart less frequently. Jetsetters can fly to over 120 international destinations from Dubai. **Dubai National Airline Travel Agency (DNATA)** (tel. 222 151), at the old Flame Roundabout, near the Clocktower Roundabout, houses most major airline offices.

Buses: Dubai Municipality (tel. 861 616) runs over 20 **local routes** throughout the main commercial and residential areas of the city (6am-11pm, no afternoon service on F; 1-3.5dhs; pay the driver when you board). There are main bus stations both in **Deira,** off Al-Khor St. near the back of the Gold Souq, and in **Bur Dubai,** on Al-Ghubaiba Rd. Get a map of the bus routes at either station. **Dubai Transport Company** (tel. 273 840) offers **intercity minibuses** to Sharjah, Ajman, Umm al-Qaiwain, Ras al-Khaimah, Fujairah, Al-'Ain, and Abu Dhabi. Unfortunately, they only have outward service; no buses run *into* Dubai. **Oman National Transport Co.** (tel. 00 (968) 226 241 or 590 601) runs daily international buses to **Muscat** (5-6hr.; 7:30am, 5:30pm).

Ferries: Dubai's equivalent of a ferry across the Khor Dubai is the **abra,** a wooden motor-boat with two long benches that seat about 30 people. For 0.5dhs, you can go between Bur Dubai's Old Souq and the Deira creekfront at the intersection of Beniyas Rd. and As-Sabkha Rd. *Abras* run every 5min. from 5am until around midnight. You can also hire one at a negotiable price for an *abra* "cruise" up or down the creek.

Taxis: Dubai has both metered taxis and private taxis. The **metered taxis** are camel-colored and have the green-black-red Dubai Municipality Transport seal on them. The **private taxis** all have "TAXI" signs on top. Negotiate a price with the driver before entering a private taxi. When first arriving in town, it's best to use the metered taxis to become familiar with typical fares between destinations.

Car Rental: Foreign drivers need an International Driving Permit in Dubai. **Budget Rent-a-Car** (tel. 823 020; fax 823 574), on Al-Maktoum Rd. between the airport and central Deira, charges about 137dhs per day, but cost varies with the type of car. MC, Visa, AmEx accepted. Open 8am-1pm and 4-7pm. **United Car Rentals** (tel. 666 286; fax 692 001), behind the DNATA building off Ar-Rigga Rd., charges 120dhs per day plus 25dhs for collision insurance. Open 8am-8pm.

🏛 PRACTICAL INFORMATION

TOURIST AND FINANCIAL SERVICES

Tours: Dubai Travel and Tourist Services (DTTS) (tel. 515 153; fax 527 692), on the ground floor of the Europecar Building on Ar-Rola Rd., offers city tours, overnight desert safaris, and sandboarding or camel riding trips. Willing to negotiate on group and student discounts. Open Sa-Th 8am-1pm and 4-7pm. **Relax Tourism** (tel. 451 881; fax 451 886), on the ground floor of the Dune Center on Adh-Dhiyafah Rd., offers city tours and desert and mountain safaris. Open Sa-Th 9am-1pm and 3-7pm.

Budget Travel: Arabian Air Travel Agencies (tel. 04 284 046; fax 04 281 735; email arbtours@emirates.net.ae), on Al-Maktoum Rd. in An-Nasr Sq. International and local flights. Open 8:30am-1pm and 3-7pm.

Embassies and Consulates: Australia (tel. 313 444; fax 314 812), in the Dubai World Trade Center in Bur Dubai, next to the Trade Center Roundabout. Open Su-Th 8am-noon. **Canada** (tel. 521 717; fax 517 722), on Al-Hisn St. in the Juma' al-Majid building next to Citibank. Open Sa-W 8-11am. **Iran** (tel. 521 150; fax 512 069), off Khalid Ibn al-Walid Rd. near the Egyptian and Yemeni Consulates. Open Su-Th 7:30am-2:30pm. **Oman** (tel. 513 111; fax 514 214), off Khalid Ibn al-Walid Rd. next to the Egyptian Consulate. Can issue Omani visas in 2-3 working days. Open Sa-W 7:30am-1:30pm. **U.K.** (tel. 521 070; fax 525 750), on As-Seef Rd. opposite the Twin Towers. Open Sa-W 7:30am-2:30pm. **U.S.** (tel. 313 115; fax 314 043), in the Dubai World Trade Center in Bur Dubai. Open Sa-W 7:30am-5pm. **Yemen** (tel. 520 213; fax 522 901), off Khalid Ibn al-Walid Rd., next to the Iranian and Egyptian consulates. Open Su-W 8am-1pm.

Currency Exchange: Foreign currency can be exchanged at any bank or currency exchange shop, but exchange bureaus generally offer better rates than banks. Bank hours are generally Sa-Th 8am-1pm, money exchange centers Sa-Th 8:30am-1pm and 4:30-8:30pm. **Thomas Cook Ar-Rostamani** has several branches on both the Deira and Bur Dubai sides of the creek. They can cash traveler's checks and give cash advances on Visa and MC. Their ATMs are connected to the Visa, MC, Cirrus, and PLUS networks. In Bur Dubai, there are branches on the corner of Al-Faheidi Rd. and 34th St. (tel. 530 500) and on Sheikh Zayed Rd. near the Holiday Inn Crown Plaza Hotel (tel. 327 444). In Deira, there is one on Al-Maktoum Rd. in An-Nasr Sq. (tel. 223 564).

Bank: Citibank NA (tel. 800 40 00; fax 524 942), next to the Bur Juman shopping center on Trade Center Rd. The Deira branch is on Al-Maktoum Rd.

American Express: Kanoo Travel (tel. 521 100), on Za'abeel Rd. next to the GPO. Client letter service available; send mail c/o AmEx, Client Mail, P.O. Box 290, Dubai, UAE. Open Sa-Th 8:30am-7pm, F 9am-1pm.

LOCAL SERVICES

English Bookstores: Magrudy's Bookshop (tel. 444 192; fax 497 819; email books@emirates.net.ae; www.magrudy.com), on Jumeirah Beach Rd. in Magrudy Shopping Mall. Open Sa-Tu 8:30am-1:30pm and 4-8pm, W 8:30am-9pm, Th 8:30am-8pm, F 4:30-8:30pm. Great selection of novels, travel guides, and language books at reasonable prices. If Magrudy's doesn't have a book, they'll order it for you.

EMERGENCY AND COMMUNICATIONS

Emergency and Police: Tel. 999. **Ambulance:** Tel. 998. **Fire:** Tel. 997.

24-Hour Pharmacy: One pharmacy in each emirate stays open all night, but the duties rotate daily. Call 232 323 or look in *Gulf News*.

Hospital/Medical Services: American Hospital Dubai (tel. 367 777, emergency room 309 66 46), in Bur Dubai on Oud Metha Rd. near Lamcy Plaza and An-Nasr Leisureland. Most doctors are Americans, Canadians, or Brits, and all speak English. Emergency services are free for both residents and visitors in all Dubai hospitals.

Post Office: Dubai Central Post Office (tel. 371 500), on Za'abeel Rd. in Karama on the Bur Dubai side of the creek. **Poste Restante** available (open Sa-Th 8am-1pm and 4-7pm). There are additional post office branches in the World Trade Center and at the corner of As-Sabkha Rd. and Beniyas Rd. in Deira. Open Sa-Th 8am-midnight.

Telegrams and Fax: Telegram and fax services are available at the **Etisalat** Building (tel. 228 111), on Beniyas Rd. in Deira. It's the tall skyscraper with a giant golf ball on it.

Internet Access: Internet Cafe (tel. 453 441; email postmaster@intercaf.co.ae), in the Dune Center on Adh-Dhiyafah St. in Satwa. Minimum charge 15dhs per hr. Open Sa-Th 9:30am-3am, F 1:30pm-3am.

Telephones: Local calls within Dubai are free. Most public phones use phonecards, available at grocery stores, malls, and post offices. The **AT&T access code** within the UAE is 800 121. **Operator:** Tel. 100. **Directory assistance:** Tel. 180.

Telephone Code: 04.

▟ ACCOMMODATIONS

Emirates Hotel (tel. 222 01 91; fax 222 044), off As-Sabkha Rd. From the airport, take a bus to the As-Sabkha Bus Station and make a right onto As-Sabkha Rd. After 2 blocks, turn right at the bright neon sign for the Imperial Palace Hotel; it's at the intersection of 1st and 6th St. Provides crystal-clean rooms with A/C and private bath. As it's in a busy and noisy part of town, however, women may get harassed by men on the street right up until they reach the hotel door. Singles 90dhs; doubles 140dhs. No credit cards or personal checks accepted, but they can arrange visas into the UAE for 260dhs and a 3-night minimum stay. Contact them about 2 weeks in advance.

UAE

Imperial Palace Hotel (tel. 211 344; fax 222 37 70), next door to the Emirates Hotel. Although the Imperial is slightly cheaper than the Emirates, it's not quite as clean. Singles 80dhs; doubles 120dhs; triples 150dhs. They can process your visa for US$72 and the guarantee that you stay there for the duration of your visit to the UAE.

Shiraz Hotel (tel. 254 800; fax 254 867), at the entrance to Deira's New Gold Souq, opposite the bus stand on Al-Khor Rd. Take the bus from the airport to the Gold Souq; a bright neon sign with an arrow points you towards the hotel. The Shiraz is more expensive, but in a radiant part of town. Clean, A/C rooms with private baths. Singles 150dhs; doubles 180dhs; triples 200dhs. The Shiraz will process visas for 500dhs; they need about 2 weeks.

Ma'arib Hotel (tel. 266 050; fax 266 603), near the entrance to Deira's Gold Souq on Sikkat Al-Khail Rd. and Souq Deira St. Some of the cheapest rooms around, but in a male-dominated atmosphere. Singles 100dhs; doubles 250dhs. Visas cost 300dhs and take about 2 weeks.

⬢ FOOD

Lined with falafel and shawarma stands, Chinese restaurants, Lebanese cafes, Indian diners, and American fast food joints, Dubai is a city for all tastes. Find the cheapest grub in the **cafeterias** gracing nearly every street corner in Deira. The *biryanis* and curries in the ubiquitous Indian eateries are also a good deal. Fast food joints like McDonald's, Kentucky Fried Chicken, and Pizza Hut can satisfy your craving for familiarity, but not much else.

Gerard's French Patisserie and Confiserie (tel. 443 327), in Magrudy's Shopping Mall on Jumeirah Beach Rd. in Jumeirah. With the elegant ambiance of a Parisian cafe, Gerard's is a charming spot for a light lunch or snack. They mostly serve baked goods like croissants and pastries, but also have some ready-made sandwiches and salads.

Sharda Vegetarian Restaurant (tel. 267 263), in the Gold Souq, by the entrance closest to the bus stop, opposite Ary Jewelers and behind Indian Jewelers. There are dozens of Indian restaurants in Dubai, but the service here is top-notch and food is cheap, fast, and *spicy*. An animal lover's paradise, it offers vegetarian entrees like *dosas* and *puris* for less than 3dhs, as well as a variety of filling Indian sweets. Another location off of As-Sabakha Rd. behind Jaloos Hotel. Lunch 10am-2:30pm, dinner 7-11:45pm.

Station One Restaurant (tel. 398 55 81), on Adh-Dhiyafah Rd. across the street from the Dune Center. A small diner serving Lebanese dishes at reasonable prices, Station One is at its best with meat dishes. Vegetarians have plenty of options, however, including hummus, falafel, and exquisite salads.

The Bananas (tel. 536 262), on Al-Faheidi St. across from the National Bank of Dubai. Dubai's version of your favorite local pizza joint. Deep-dish pan pizzas with all the toppings imaginable, including bananas (no joke) and honey. Service is fast and friendly and after you've had your fill, you get to pick your own discount out of a box.

Hard Rock Cafe (tel. 399 28 88), at Dubai Park. Add another t-shirt to your collection, this time in Arabic! You know what to expect from this bastion of musical and capitalist imperialism. Live entertainment nightly, Club 4FM Night on F. Open daily noon-2am.

🎭 ENTERTAINMENT

Dubai is one of the few cities in the Gulf with kickin' nightlife. If clubbing and bar hopping aren't your thing, try relaxing with a hubble-bubble pipe at one of Dubai's **sheesha cafes.** The **Dhiyafah Coffee Shop** (tel. 398 73 73), on Dhiyafah Rd. directly across from the Dune Center, is a great place to relax. Amsterdam it's not, but there are backgammon boards and a variety of pipes (3-15dhs). The public beach at **Jumeira Beach Park** (tel. 443 245) shares the same waterfront as the locally famous Hilton Beach Club. The grassy expanse invites soccer games and picnics—pack a lunch, use the barbecue pits, or frequent the fast food stands (open Th-F 8am-

11:30pm, Sa-W 8am-11pm; Sa and Su women and children only; admission 5dhs).
Most of the bars and clubs are in the major **resort hotels** like the Hilton, Sheraton,
Metropolitan, and Hyatt Regency. Scenes change faster than a speeding camel, so
pick up a copy of *What's On* (on sale at bookshops and most hotels) to make sure
you're not left out by the "in" crowd. No matter which bar or club you choose, you'll
definitely be *outré* if you're underage: the **drinking age** is 21 and strictly enforced.

The Boston Bar (tel. 455 888), in the lobby of the Jumeira Rotana Hotel next to the Dune
Center. A restaurant and bar (decorated exactly like the infamous TV watering hole,
Cheers) that makes 30-something Yankee expats feel at home again. Beer runs the
gamut from Budweiser (9dhs) to Amstel (16dhs). Th nights tend to get crowded; popular bands play on Su. Happy Hour noon-8pm. Open daily noon-2am.

Humphrey's Tavern (tel. 314 000), in the lobby of the Hilton. Popular with a younger
crowd despite its wall of tribute to Humphrey Bogart. Large screen TV, dartboard, and
standard bar food served in a flash. Order the "traditional British ploughman's fayre" at
your own risk. Open Sa-Th noon-4pm and 6pm-2am.

Rattlesnake (tel. 343 00 00), at the Metropolitan Hotel. An expat crowd dances the
night away, usually to live Canadian rock bands. Designed like the set of an old Western, complete with a county jail for rabble-rousers. Drinks range between 25-30dhs.
Beer 20dhs per pint. Open for lunch noon-3pm, featuring nachos, buffalo wings, and
other American fare. Dinner 7pm-3am. No cover, pardner.

■ SIGHTS

Most of Dubai has been torn down and rebuilt within the past half-century, so only
a handful of places reflect the days before McDonald's and the Armani Exchange
moved to town. Although many companies offer city tours, intrepid budget adventurers armed with an adequate supply of water can blaze their own trails with **Dubai
Town Walk,** a city map with suggested walking routes on both sides of the creek
(.5dhs; limited availability—try the Dubai International Arts Center or Profiles in
Markaz aj-Jumeirah and Jumeirah Plaza). An **abra ride** across the creek to Bur
Dubai is the best way to view the emirate's trading ports and *dhows*. *Abras* embark
from the Deira creekfront at the intersection of Beniyas and As-Sabkha Rd.; just follow the crowds of workers, who use these water taxis as a cheap form of transportation (0.5dhs, every 5min. 5am-midnight). Passengers hit land at Bur Dubai's Old
Souq. For 30-50dhs, you can hire a boat and driver for a private half-hour river tour.

SOUQS. Deira's *souqs* are prime territory for exploration. Dubai is one of the
cheapest places in the world to buy gold, *sobi* sure to get a glimpse of the glittering
element responsible for most of Dubai's wealth at the **Gold Souq** (between Al-Khor
St. and Sikkat Al-Khail St). Prices fluctuate with the gold market, but don't let the
displays dazzle you into accepting a vendor's original price; haggling usually meets
with success. Many of the intricately-designed pieces were crafted by local artisans,
and supposedly, all pieces in the *souq* can boast at least 18 carats. Deira's Gold
Souq is world famous; about 25% of the world's annual gold production is traded
here. Nearby, between Ar-Ras St. and Beniyas Rd., the **Spice Souq** (also called **Deira
Old Souq**) has bustled since 1850. Just tell them what you want, what you really
really want: cardamom, saffron, paprika, cinnamon, nutmeg, frankincense, and
henna go by the ounce or the ton. At the **Dubai Old Souq**, near the *abra* dock on the
Bur Dubai side, Persian carpets, Indian tapestries, and embroidered textiles fill the
shop windows. *(Spice Souq open Sa-Th 9am-1pm and 4-8:30pm, F 4:30-8:30pm.)*

DUBAI NATIONAL MUSEUM. The **Dubai National Museum,** four blocks from the
Dubai Old Souq on Al-Faheidi Rd., is one of the few places that provides historical
insight on local life in days past. The museum is built inside Old Al-Faheidi Fort,
with a huge *dhow* sitting to the left of the building. Built for sea defense in the
early 19th century, today the fort is the oldest structure in a city where buildings
rise and fall faster than oil prices. The best part of the museum lies *under* the fort,

COOL VIBRATIONS Before the luxury of air conditioning arrived in Dubai, even the slightest breeze was a reprieve from the sweltering heat. The ancient ancestors of Dubai's contemporary air conditioning worshippers relied on **windtowers** to capture the briefest breeze and transform them into comfortable gusts through their homes. Windtowers are tall, chimney-like structures with four triangular vents inside. Many homes had multiple windtowers: the elaborately decorated one was above the main bedroom while another was used for the first floor, as Muslim law forbids opening windows on the ground floor. These towers can still be seen today in the **Bastakia Quarter** of Bur Dubai, near the Dubai National Museum—one of the few places left where you can still admire the emirate's old architecture and truly understand what non-electrical air conditioning meant in Dubai's earlier days.

though. Walk to the far left corner of the courtyard and continue down into a time warp: there is a life-sized replica of an old *souq* complete with a "live" blacksmith, jeweler, and tailor; continue down the alleyways to see Muslim children reciting verses from the Qur'an at Islamic School. On the outskirts of the town lies a Bedouin tent site at nightfall. The museum has a bizarre simulacrum reminiscent of Hollywood's Paramount Studios: life-sized replicas of camels, an oasis, and a campfire let you experience the desert without actually going there. *(Tel. 531 18 62. Open Sa-Th 8:30am-7:30pm, F 1:30-7:30pm. Admission 3dhs.)*

SHARJAH الشارجة

People go to Dubai to shop, but they visit Sharjah to explore Arabia's rich history and tradition. In 1998, UNESCO named this third-largest emirate the cultural capital of the Arab world for its commitment to preserving its traditional heritage. Only a 20-minute drive from super-Westernized Dubai, Sharjah brims with museums and some of the UAE's greatest architectural masterpieces. From the mosque-like design of the *souqs* to the gargantuan **plastic Qur'an** residing in Cultural Sq., Sharjah's aesthetic reflects its Islamic heritage. Cultural capital may seem like Sharjah's only asset today, but until recently the emirate's wealth and political stature outshone that of Dubai and Abu Dhabi. Throughout the 19th century, it reigned as one of the most important ports on the Gulf and the dominant city of the Trucial Coast. Though its fortunes waned when sea trade diverted to Dubai in the 1940s, things have been looking up for Sharjah's economy recently: in 1992, major new natural gas discoveries boosted the emirate's income, and the UAE's tourism industry now centers around the namesake city. The city's upbeat motto, "Smile You Are in Sharjah," makes a bit more sense in light of the wealth pouring in, but tourists will hardly be smiling at the price hikes that are sure to ensue.

✴ ORIENTATION

The main thoroughfare in central Sharjah is **Al-Arouba Road,** which runs through the city and across **Khalid Lagoon** (Khor Khalid) via the Sharjah Bridge. Coming from Dubai, you'll probably enter Sharjah on **King Faisal Road,** which runs perpendicular to Al-Arouba; Souq al-Markazi will be on your left and King Faisal Mosque on your right. Most of the museums, as well as the Old Souq and Al-Majarrah Souq, are on **Corniche Road,** which runs along the waterfront. The **Central Souq** (Souq al-Markazi) also lies on the waterfront, just southeast of Al-Arouba. **Az-Zahra Road,** parallel to Al-Arouba, has most of the cheap restaurants. **Al-Wahda Road** leads to Cultural Sq., home of the fabled plastic Qur'an. Take **Airport Road** from Cultural Sq. to get to the airport, the Natural History Museum, and Sharjah Library.

🛈 PRACTICAL INFORMATION

Sharjah International Airport (tel. 581 111, flight inquiry 581 000) is on the southeastern outskirts of town on Airport Rd., 15km from the city center. There are no buses to or from the airport, only fixed-rate airport taxis (tel. 06 508 1134) that transport passengers between the airport and central Sharjah (40dhs) or Dubai (60-70dhs). There's a **taxi stand** near the veggie *souq*, but *service* can be hailed on most major roads. Drivers make several stops throughout town until the vehicle fills up. *Service* to **Dubai** (where taxis to **Abu Dhabi** and **Al-'Ain** are available) are white cars with a black seal (5dhs). Catch them outside the Central Souq on the side facing King Faisal Mosque and Al-Ittihad Sq. To hire the taxi privately (or "engage" it), the cost is 20dhs per hour. Since there are **no buses** in Sharjah, this is a good option for groups. If your Arabic is rusty, try to find a driver with whom you can communicate. **Dubai Transport Co.** (tel. (04) 273 840) runs **minibuses** between Sharjah and **Dubai.** If you decide to rent a car, call on **Metro Rent-A-Car** (tel. 367 157, cell (050) 634 01 18; fax 368 066), near the Municipality Roundabout opposite the Plaza Hotel. Cars start at 90dhs per day, including insurance. Most foreign driver's licenses are accepted (open 8:30am-1pm and 4:30-9pm).

There are dozens of supermarkets in Sharjah, particularly facing the southwest entrance of the Al-Majarrah Souq. Additional supermarkets, such as **Argawani Stores** (tel. 510 603 or 358 957; fax 525 053), line Corniche Rd. between the Sharjah Arts Center and Al-Majarrah Souq. Open daily 8am-11pm. The **Department of Culture and Information,** P.O. Box 5119 (tel. 541 116; fax 362 126), on Al-Burj Rd. by the Old Souq, fulfills the basic tourist office duties. **Thomas Cook Ar-Rostamani** (tel. 363 656), on Al-Arouba St. near Ar-Rolla Sq., exchanges traveler's checks and gives cash advances on Visa and MC. Yearning for a good book? **Sharjah Library** (tel. 585 566; fax 585 611), on the Sharjah-Dhaid Hwy. next to the American University of Sharjah, has photocopy services, two **Internet** halls, and a full public library (open 8am-2pm and 4-9pm). **Dalia Laundry** (tel. 371 274), near the Municipality Roundabout, next to the Plaza Hotel and Metro Rent-A-Car charges 1.5dhs for shirts, 3dhs for pants (open 8:30am-2pm and 4:30-10pm). In an emergency, call the **police** or an **ambulance** at 999. If it's a medical problem you have, go to the **American Hospital in Dubai** (see p. 627). It's only 20 minutes away, and its facilities are the best around. One pharmacy in each emirate stays open all night, but the duties rotate daily (tel. 232 323 or look in *Gulf News*). **Rasha Pharmacy** (tel. 549 889), on Tariq Ibn Ziyad Rd. near Al-Gouwain Market, stays open nightly until midnight. The **Central Post Office** is on As-Soor Rd. at Government House Sq. (a.k.a. Municipality Roundabout). **Telegram** and **fax** services are available at **Etisalat,** the tall skyscraper on As-Soor Rd. with an enormous golf ball resting on top, near the Al-Kuwait Roundabout. Sharjah's **telephone code** is 06.

ACCOMMODATIONS AND FOOD

The best of Sharjah's budget accommodations is █**City Hotel** (tel. 355 600; fax 350 888), off Az-Zahra Rd. near the Municipality Roundabout. Sparkling rooms have private baths and air conditioning; indulge yourself with the room service. They can't arrange visas yet, but the manager says they will soon (singles 105dhs; doubles 126dhs; triples 140dhs; credit cards and traveler's checks accepted). **Ar-Rolla International Hotel** (tel. 512 000; fax 512 111; email rolahotl@emirates.net.ae; www.ebmanage.com/rolahotl) is off Al-Arouba Rd. and Bank St., facing Ar-Rolla Sq. This ritzy, well-scrubbed hotel in the heart of downtown is worth the extra dirhams. It's one of the few hotels in town (excluding the five-star resorts) that can arrange tourist **visas** (400dhs, must reside here for entire stay in Sharjah). Credit cards and traveler's checks are accepted (singles 150dhs; doubles 200dhs; triples 250dhs). The slightly cramped **Sharjah Plaza Hotel** (tel. 377 555; fax 373 311), behind City Hotel on Al-Qasimiya Rd. at the Municipality Roundabout, isn't exactly a steal, but amenities like TV, refrigerator, air conditioning, and private bath offer creature comforts. Singles are only 100dhs, but doubles and triples are a whopping 150dhs and 180dhs. The **Youth Hostel (HI)** (tel. 225 070), one of the few in the Gulf, is at Traffic Sq. in Sharqan, near the Sharjah Sports Club. All meals are available, and there is also a common kitchen and shared bathrooms (singles 30dhs; doubles 60dh).

Furnished flats are a more spacious and comfortable alternative to the overpriced hotel rooms. **Jawhrat Al-Ghuwair Furnished Apartments** (tel. 351 212; fax 355 656; email alareen@emirates.net.ae), next to Al-Ghuwair Market near the Clocktower Roundabout, has simply decorated one-bedroom apartments with a living room, bathroom, kitchen, and full amenities like air conditioning, TV, telephone, washing machine, and microwave—perfect for couples or even groups of three or four (provided that some don't mind crashing on the living room sofas). Sliding scale prices start at 180dhs per night and fall as low as 110dhs with longer stays; flats are also cheaper without housekeeping or with metered rates for water and electricity.

There's no shortage of coffee shops and cafeterias dishing out *biryani* and mutton burgers. Most of the cheap eateries lie on Az-Zahra Rd.; Al-Arouba Rd. has several fast food joints. **Deena Leena Restaurant** (tel. 357 161), on Az-Zahra Rd. near the Clocktower Roundabout, serves hot 'n' spicy *dosas* and *biryanis*. A full lunch or dinner includes soda, bread, *masala*, and Indian sweets (7-8dhs; open daily 5am-1am). Escape the sweltering heat and rehydrate in **Al-Hawaj Cafeteria** (tel. 360 330), an air-conditioned oasis with fresh fruit juices (3-5dhs) and *faloodas* (scrumptious ice cream sundaes, 5dhs). More substantial fare includes shawarma, falafel, and the meat-eater's choice of chicken or mutton burgers (open daily 8:30am-4pm).

◉ SIGHTS

If you're looking for a club or bar scene, forget it: the Sheikh of Sharjah banned alcohol and closed all of the emirate's discos back in 1985. Instead, smiley Sharjah takes its museums seriously. Most of the museums and architectural landmarks are within walking distance from the center of town, on Corniche Rd. between Al-Beirj Rd. and Bank St.

SHARJAH ARTS PLAZA AREA. Though only a few years old, the Sharjah Arts Plaza was built in the traditional style of the emirate's oldest buildings. A series of courtyards and alleyways divide the white, one-story stone buildings, which house art schools and studios. The imposing **Sharjah Art Museum** lies just outside the Arts Plaza Area, on the side farthest from the waterfront. Built in 1997 to house the Sheikh's personal collection, the museum also permanently displays 18th-century orientalist oil paintings and watercolors, as well as photographs of Islamic architecture from all over the Arab world. A rare series of prints depict an invasion by the British army and the local resistance against the attacks. *(Tel. 352 239; fax 511 222. Open Sa-Su and Tu-Th 9am-1pm and 5-8pm, F 5-8pm. Free.)*

HISN ASH-SHARJAH FORT. Built in 1820, the **Hisn Ash-Sharjah Fort** was formerly the home of Sharjah's ruling family, the Al-Qasimi clan, as well as the site of their court and prison. The fort was partially demolished in 1969, but by the efforts of Sharjah's current ruler, Sheikh Dr. Sultan Ibn Muhammad al-Qasimi, it was fully restored and renovated into a museum. If you haven't yet seen any of the ancient forts, it's worth exploring for an hour or so. Exhibitions range from the prison's old shackles to weaponry and jewelry, and an introductory video (in English and Arabic) provides a comprehensive overview of Sharjah's past. *(Tel. 375 500; fax 368 288. Open Sa-Su and Tu-Th 9am-1pm and 4pm-8pm, F 4:30-8:30pm, W evenings women and children only.)*

SHARJAH HERITAGE MUSEUM AND ISLAMIC MUSEUM. Housed in a renovated 200-year-old building, the **Islamic Museum**, contains rare manuscripts and exhibits relating the cultural lifestyle of Muslims over a period of 1400 years. The collection includes scientific instruments, pottery, coins, and the first map of the ancient world, drawn by Sharif al-Idrisi about 1200 years ago. At the ripe age of 155, the **Heritage Museum,** also known as **Bait An-Naboodah,** is one of the oldest houses still standing in Sharjah. Built around a traditional open courtyard and topped with windtowers, its 16 rooms are still furnished as they were over a century ago. *(Both museums located near Literature Sq. in Al-Gharb; from the Arts Plaza and Al-Hisn Fort, make a right away from Boorj Ave. and Bank St. Islamic Museum: Tel. 353 334; fax 353 746. Open Sa-Su and Tu-Th 9am-1pm and 5-8pm, F 4:30-8:30pm, holidays 9am-1pm and 4:30-8:30pm. Heri-*

tage Museum: Tel. 512 999; fax 368 288. Open Sa-Su and Tu-Th 9am-1pm and 4-8pm, F 4:30pm-8:30pm, W evenings women and children only. Free.)

SHARJAH ARCHAEOLOGICAL MUSEUM. If you choose to go to only one museum in Sharjah, **Sharjah Archaeological Museum** (tel. 366 466; fax 376 334), on Al-Hizam Al-Akhdar Rd. in Cultural Sq., should be it. This high-tech gem holds excavations dating back to the Stone Age. A series of films narrates the displays of artifacts and explains the science of archaeology. Most importantly, though, the museum is only ½-block away from the famously kitschy **plastic Qur'an** in Cultural Sq., Sharjah's answer to the plastic lawn flamingo. *(Open Sa and M-Th 9am-1pm and 5-8pm, F 4-8pm, W evenings women and children only.)*

SHARJAH SCIENCE MUSEUM. The supermodern science fair that is the **Science Museum** is supposedly designed for children, but very few 8-year-olds are likely to understand the exhibits about such esoteric topics as aerodynamics, cryogenics, and electrostatic generators. Nevertheless, the hands-on exhibits are fun even if you don't know quite what they're explaining. *(Tel. 514 777; fax 514 733. On Al-Hizam Al-Akhdar Rd. near Cultural Sq. Open in summer Sa and M-Th 9am-1pm and 5-8pm, F 5-8pm; in winter Sa and M-Th 9am-1pm and 4-8pm, F 4-8pm; W evenings women and children only.)*

NATURAL HISTORY MUSEUM. If natural history isn't your passion, save some cash and skip the **Natural History Museum**—it's in the middle of the desert, a distant 28km from the city center, and only accessible by cab. As far as natural history museums go, though, this one's a winner. The life-size dioramas depict life in the desert and under the sea, and there are also a variety of stuffed and live animal and plant exhibits. It would be an understatement to call the museum's **mechanical camel** a highlight. *(Tel. 311 411; fax 311 000. Hire a cab for a couple of hours and keep the driver waiting—otherwise you'll be stranded in the desert (round-trip 50-60dhs). Open Sa-W 9am-7pm, Th noon-7pm, F 2-8pm. Admission 5dhs adults, under 12 2dhs, under 6 free.)*

 SHOPPING

The majestic buildings of Sharjah's *souqs* are priceless sights, but within their walls await some of Arabia's greatest treasures from the past and present.

CENTRAL MARKET (SOUQ AL-MARKAZI). The Central Market, also known as Souq Al-Markazi, is the best place to buy hand-woven **carpets** in Sharjah, if not the UAE. The ornate, colorful building may look familiar: it's depicted on the 5dh bill. The market's long, split-level atria are filled with shops selling antiques, jewelry, and clothing in addition to those famed carpets. The second level of the *souq* farthest from King Faisal Rd. has the most carpet stores. Two shops with excellent selections and helpful salespeople are **Persian Carpets Kingdom** (tel. 573 50 98 or 574 16 08) and **Talriz Carpets** (tel. 723 672). Persian Carpets Kingdom has rugs from as near as Iran and as far as Russia, as well as an impressive selection of Afghani wool rugs (probably the cheapest to buy at around 500dhs). Their Persian carpets range in price depending on the material (silk is the most expensive), and can soar in price as high as a whopping 25,000dhs! Cotton and wool rugs can be purchased for around 2000dhs. Most of these stores can arrange cargo shipping back to your homeland. No matter how reasonable a price may sound, it's best to spend a couple of hours perusing the selections and comparing prices. Bargain fiercely and never settle for the first or even second price given. *(On King Faisal Rd. at the intersection with Al-Arouba Rd. near the Sharjah Bridge. Open daily 8:30am-1:30pm and 4:30-10pm.)*

SOUQ AL-ARSAH. Sharjah's Old Souq, the Souq Al-Arsah, takes shoppers back to the 19th century, when Sharjah was the center of the pearl trade in the Arabian Gulf. A few pearl traders still buy and sell in this magnificent building, made from coral, lime, and plaster and topped with palm fronds. Other shops deal in antiques, souvenirs, jewelry, and herbs. Many have intricately carved Zanzibar-style wooden doors. Forget the shopping—Souq Al-Arsah is a sight in itself. *(Located off Corniche Rd. toward* *the side of the Arts Complex farthest inland. It's confusing to find as it lies within a maze of court-yard and alleyways, so your best bet is to ask for directions. Open 9am-1pm and 5pm-9pm.)*

AL-MAJARRAH SOUQ. Located on the Corniche by Al-Khalij Sq. This *souq* is basically a modern shopping mall selling shoes and clothing, but its architecture is worth a glance: stained glass windows line its long gallery, and the top floor (under the mosque-like dome) is painted like the dark blue desert sky with the zodiac stars sparkling in gold paint. *(Open 8:30am-1:30pm and 4:30-10:30pm.)*

ABU DHABI أبوظبي

The energetic capital of the United Arab Emirates sprawls across a narrow island in the Arabian Gulf, a modern metropolis with a Manhattanesque skyline and designer outlets rivaling Beverly Hills and Paris. Legend has it that the city got its name from a group of 18th-century hunters chasing a gazelle. When the high-flying prey leapt from the mainland to the island, the hunters named the place Abu Dhabi, meaning "father (or possessor) of the gazelle." That's about all the history Abu Dhabi has to offer, as the island was barely developed (save a few fishing communities) before enormous oil reserves were discovered in the late 1960s. This unfinished city houses only a handful of buildings older than 30 years and seems to forever linger "under construction." Although Abu Dhabi offers little in the way of historical sights and other typical tourist attractions, it abounds with blooming gardens and sandy beaches. Prices are set for the wealthy oil baron or business executive, so unless you're doing a safari in the nearby Empty Quarter desert, there's really not much reason for a budget traveler to stay long.

ORIENTATION

The main city center lies on the northern end of the island, clustered between **Corniche Road,** which runs from the Hilton to the Sheraton Hotels, and the road alternately known as **Zayed the 1st** and **Zayed the 2nd Street.** The majority of hotels, shopping centers and restaurants are located between these roads, particularly on **Sheikh Hamdan Ibn Mohammed Street** (Sheikh Hamdan St.) and **Khalifa Ibn Zayed Street.** Many of the attractions geared towards tourists congregate on the pier known as the **Breakwater,** which splits from Corniche Rd. near the Hilton.

TRANSPORTATION

Airplanes: Abu Dhabi International Airport (tel. 757 500, flight inquiries 757 611 or 706 30 00), on the mainland, 35km from the city. Served by all major international carriers. No departure tax. **Oman Air** (tel. 311 144; fax 314 543) flies to **Muscat** (1hr.; daily 1:45, 10:45pm; OR 67). Ticket office open Sa-Th 8am-1pm and 4:30-7pm. The easiest way to get from the airport to the city is with the "specially registered" **Al-Ghazal Taxi** (tel. 706 27 28), which has a desk in the airport (65dhs to city center). Normal taxis should charge around 40dhs.

Intercity Transportation: The main **bus station** is on Hazza Ibn Zayed Rd. **Abu Dhabi Transport** (tel. 431 500) only sends buses to other cities within the emirate, such as **Al-'Ain** (2½hr., every hr. until 9pm, 10dhs). **Share taxis** and **minivans** to **Dubai** also leave from the bus station (30dhs).

Local Buses: Intracity buses are not very useful because they lack numbers and don't follow schedules or set routes. Most people either drive their own cars or take taxis. Bus rides should cost 1-5dhs within the city.

Taxis: Over 12,300 white-and-gold taxis swarm around Abu Dhabi. Fares are metered, starting at 2dhs and adding up to 5-10dhs for travel within the city.

Car Rental: Budget Rent-A-Car (tel. 334 200; fax 331 498), on An-Nasr St. at Khalid Ibn al-Walid St. (next to Al-Masood Travel and Services), has rates starting at 150dhs per day with unlimited mileage. Open Sa-Th 8am-7pm, F 9am-noon. **Avis Rent-A-Car** (tel. 323 760 or 345 651; fax 330 734 or 312 033), on Khalid Ibn al-Walid St. at the intersection with An-Nasr and Sheikh Hamdan St.

🛈 PRACTICAL INFORMATION

Tours: Sunshine Tours (tel. 449 914; fax 446 856; email sstours@emirates.net.ae), on Old Airport Rd. opposite Abu Dhabi Exhibition Center. Offers a variety of tours, safaris, and scuba trips with a multilingual staff. **Net Tours** (tel. 794 656; fax 721 188) leads half-day city tours (75dhs) and full-day excursion to other emirates (145-350dhs).

Embassies: Most embassies, unless otherwise noted, are in the diplomatic area on Airport Rd., about 10km south of the city center. **Australia** has a consulate in Dubai only (see p. 626). **Bahrain** (tel. 312 200; fax 311 202). Open Sa-W 8am-2pm. **Canada** (tel. 263 655; fax 263 424). Open Sa-W 8:30am-4pm. **Egypt** (tel. 445 566 or 445 656; fax 449 878). Open Sa-W 9am-noon. **Iran** (tel. 447 618; fax 448 714). Open Sa-W 9-11am. **Oman** (tel. 463 333; fax 464 633). Open Sa-W 8am-2pm. **South Africa** (tel. 726 200). **U.K.** (tel. 326 600; fax 341 744 or 345 968), on Khalid Ibn al-Walid St., between Corniche Rd. and An-Nasr St. Open Sa-W 8-11am. **U.S.** (tel. 436 691; fax 435 441), on As-Suoan St., between Al-Karamah St. and An-Nahyan St. Open Sa-W 1-3pm. **Yemen** (tel. 448 457; fax 447 978), on King Khalid Ibn 'Abdul 'Aziz St., between Al-Manhal St. and As-Suoan St. Open Sa-W 8am-2pm.

Currency Exchange: UAE Exchange Company (tel. 322 166), on Sheikh Hamdan St. in the *souq* area, near the intersection with 10th St. Cashes AmEx, Visa, MC traveler's checks, gives Visa and MC cash advances, and receives Western Union moneygrams. Open Sa-Th 8am-1:30pm and 4-9:30pm, F 9-11:30am and 4-9:30pm. Additional money changers line Sheikh Hamdan St. in the *souq* area, as well as the pedestrian underpass that runs under Sheikh Hamdan St. between HSBC Bank and the *souq*.

ATMs: HSBC Bank (also called British Bank of the Middle East), on Sheikh Hamdan St. opposite the *souq*, has Visa, MC, Cirrus, and PLUS connections. **National Bank of Abu Dhabi**, on Sheikh Hamdan St. near the Crowne Plaza Hotel, has Cirrus and PLUS links.

American Express: (tel. 213 045), on An-Nasr St. at Khalid Al-Walid St. Cash advances on AmEx cards. No traveler's check exchange. Client mail held for 1 month; address mail to: AmEx-Middle East, c/o Al-Masood Travel and Services, P.O. Box 806, Abu Dhabi, UAE. Open Su-Th 8:30am-1pm and 3-6:30pm.

English Bookstore: Book Corner (tel. 315 323), in Liwa Center (1st mezzanine) on Sheikh Hamdan St. Sells English language books and magazines. Open Sa-W 10am-2pm and 4:30-10:30pm, Th-F 10am-2pm and 4:30-11pm.

Markets: There are dozens of supermarkets on the small unnamed roads running parallel to Sheikh Hamdan St., particularly behind the Crowne Plaza Hotel.

Laundromats: No self-service laundromats, but there are plenty of small establishments offering laundry services for around 1dh per item. Look in the shopping strips behind the Crowne Plaza Hotel on Sheikh Hamdan St.

Emergency: Tel. 999. **Ambulance:** Tel. 998.

Pharmacy: 24hr. duty rotates daily among pharmacies. Call the info line (tel. 777 929) or check the newspaper. Most pharmacies are normally open Sa-Th 8:30am-1:30pm and 4:30-10:30pm, F 4:30-10:30pm.

Hospital: The government-run **Mafraq Hospital** (tel. 512 31 00) has 520 beds.

Post Office: GPO (tel. 302 52 11), on Old Airport Rd. Open Sa-W 8am-11pm and 4-8pm, Th-F 8am-noon. Another branch opposite Majestic Hotel on Khalifa Ibn Zayed St.

Fax: Services available at **Etisalat** (tel. 208 40 00), at Airport Rd. and Zayed the 2nd St.

Internet Access: The Cultural Foundation (tel. 619 53 75), on Zayed the 1st St. at Khalid Ibn al-Walid St. 10dhs per hr. Open Su-Th 8am-2pm and 5-9pm, F-Sa 9am-noon and 5-8pm. **Cyber Café** (tel. 319 000 or 312 323), 1st floor of Sahara Residences on Zayed the 2nd St. 20dhs per hr. Open daily 7am-12:30am.

Telephone Code: 02.

▚ ACCOMMODATIONS

Abu Dhabi's hotels cater to the business class traveler, not the budget explorer. Many hotels can set you up with a **UAE visa** from your home country, but unless you specifically need to fly into Abu Dhabi, it makes more sense to arrange your visa through a hotel in Dubai, as it has easier accessibility to the Northern Emirates, Sharjah, the Musandem Peninsula, and Oman.

Majestic Hotel (tel. 710 000; fax 741 221), on Khalifa Ibn Zayed St. near the intersection with Umm an-Naqr St. More than just a name: a marble-and-chandelier entryway leads to large rooms with kitchenettes and tiny bathrooms with tubs. Hotel complex includes 2 restaurants, a 24hr. coffee shop, and a massage parlor. Singles in summer 200dhs, in winter 250dhs; doubles 200/250dhs. Visas (400dhs) take 5 business days to process and require a 3-night stay. AmEx, MC, Visa accepted.

Federal Hotel (tel. 789 000; fax 794 728), on Khalifa Ibn Zayed St. near intersection with Umm an-Naqr St. A business class hotel with a tiny elevator. Rooms have attached kitchenette and bath. Singles 200dhs; doubles 225dhs. Stays over 3 nights warrant a small discount: singles 150dhs; doubles 175dhs. Arranges visas (400dhs, 3-night min. stay) for professionals only; students are out of luck. If the hotel processes your visa, you're not eligible for the discounted room rate.

Zakher Hotel (tel. 329 300 or 327 900; fax 326 306), at the intersection of Sheikh Hamdan St. and Khalifa Ibn Zayed St. Retro 70s decor complements the retro 70s smell of some rooms. Average-sized rooms lack kitchenettes (standard in Abu Dhabi). Rooms in the extension are larger and nicer. Singles 170dhs; doubles 230dhs; extension rooms 20dhs more. 15% service charge. Visas require 4 days to process, 400dhs, and a 3-night min. stay. Complementary airport-to-hotel transportation. Amex, Visa, MC, and traveler's checks accepted.

Mina Hotel (tel. 781 000; fax 791 000), at the intersection of As-Salaam St. and Al-Mina St., opposite Citibank near the Sheraton Hotel. Clean, comfy rooms with kitchenettes and bathtubs. Singles 180dhs; doubles 200dhs. Three-night stay reduces rates by 20dhs. No visa processing. AmEx, Visa, MC accepted.

◖ FOOD

The extensive culinary choices in this sprawling capital city reflect the multicultural nature of the UAE's population. The tourist traps (where guests dine on overpriced food in a Bedouin camp setting or aboard a restored *dhow*) congregate on the Breakwater. Most other eateries are in the hotels and shopping malls, though a handful of independent eateries hide on side streets behind the big complexes.

▨ Al-Maghrab al-'Arabi Restaurant (tel. 269 555), ground floor of Yusef Center on Sheikh Hamdan St. Elegant Moroccan restaurant with great food and reasonable prices. Cross your fingers and hope for a seat: there are only 5 tables amidst embroidered draperies, colored ceramic tiles, intricately carved ceilings, and stained glass light fixtures. Entrees 15-20dhs, including couscous with meat and grilled *hamour*. Open noon-midnight.

Amna al-'Arab Restaurant (tel. 272 705), on Khalifa Ibn Zayed St. opposite Mashriq Bank. Cheap and tasty Indian, Chinese, and Arab dishes battle it out for ethnic supremacy on the menu, while the decor clashes too: the Family Room is decked out in red, white, and blue, while the main dining room has green, orange, and white walls. Most entrees 12-18dhs. Open 11am-1am.

Cafe Moka (tel. 329 090), on Sheikh Hamdan St., top floor of Liwa Center. A lively, popular hangout with blaring TVs and music for blaring locals and expats. Sandwiches (20dhs), pasta (19-22dhs), pizza (18-24dhs), and pastries galore (3-5dhs). Specialty MoCola Shake is no mo' than an ice cream float (12dhs). Open daily 7:30am-11:30pm.

Le Boulanger (tel. 316 112 or 318 115), top floor of BHS Building on Sheikh Hamdan St., next to Crowne Plaza Hotel. A wannabe Parisian café where waitresses prance around in bright red berets and a baguette is always within eyeshot. All-you-can-eat Friday brunch (10am-3pm) attracts droves of locals and expats. Wolf down obscene quantities of pancakes, omelettes, grilled *hamour*, shrimp, pastries, salad, and soup for 30dhs. Teatime buffet 4-6pm. Open daily 7am-midnight.

As-Safina Restaurant (tel. 662 085), on the Breakwater opposite the Hilton. Set inside the renovated personal *dhow* of the Sheikh Zayed Ibn Sultan an-Nahyan. Good seafood and a great panoramic ocean view come for a hefty price: full meals 40-50dhs. Open noon-3:30pm and 7-11pm.

♫ ENTERTAINMENT

The major hotels—namely the Sheraton, Crowne Plaza, and Hilton—offer liquor-licensed, spirit-serving, alcohol-abundant bars with a range of kitschy themes. Check out the magazine *What's On*, available at bookshops, for a preview of the various theme nights. **Hemingway's Entertainment Complex** (tel. 681 19 00), the large building behind the Hilton, offers more opportunities for sin than spring break at Papa Hemingway's homestead in Key West, Florida. Boogie the night away at **Tequiliana's Discotheque** (open Su-Tu and F 10pm-2:30am, W-Th 10pm-3:30am; cover W-Th 50dhs); scat like a cat at the **Jazz Bar** (open Sa-Th 7pm-1am); or chow down on Latin American munchies at the **Bistro** (don't worry, there's a bar there too; open F-Tu noon-11:30pm, W-Th noon-12:30am). After 7pm, only bacchanalians over 21 can enter the complex. No local dress allowed; this place caters entirely to rich Western tourists and expats.

Near the Hilton, the corniche breaks away from rest of the island to form the **Breakwater,** a pleasure peninsula festooned with brightly lit restaurants, *sheesha* cafes, and miniature fun fairs. It's also the departure point for romantic **dhow cruises** around the harbor, which unveil superb views of the Abu Dhabi skyline. **Blue Dolphin Tours** (tel. 669 392) offers a reasonable priced one-hour *dhow* cruise for 10dhs per person. *Dhows* leave every hour from 5 to 11pm from a small dock behind the As-Sofon Dhow Restaurant on the Breakwater.

◉ SIGHTS

Since most of the cityscape has been built, torn down, and rebuilt within the last 30 years, Abu Dhabi offers surprisingly few tourist attractions for the capital city of a wealthy Gulf State.

AL-HISN PALACE AND CULTURAL FOUNDATION. The only historical site of interest is Al-Hisn Palace, also known as the White Fort or White Palace. The original fortress foundation was constructed in 1793 to protect the island's invaluable well, making it the only building in Abu Dhabi not constructed in the last 50 years. When the *sheikhs* of the emirate moved their capital from the Liwa Oasis to Abu Dhabi island, they commissioned a new facade and some showy towers, then declared the fort the royal residence. A new Presidential Palace was built on the western corner of the island in 1972, and the old one is currently undergoing extensive renovations, so access is limited. One of the few highlights is the brightly colored ceramic tile archway decorating the entrance. The palace is housed within the Cultural Foundation Complex on Sheikh Hamdan St.; the main entrance is on An-Nasr St. to the left of the mosque. The Cultural Foundation features an exhibition room, library, movie theater, and performance halls, and a free monthly guide gives the lowdown on what's happening in Abu Dhabi.

PARKS. Abu Dhabi calms the nerves with dozens of beautiful gardens and promenades. The **Public Garden** on Zayed Ibn Sultan St. is more tranquil than the garden of Eden. Fountains, manicured flowerbeds, and shady trees abound. Although all the city's parks are generally safe for unaccompanied females, women can breathe even easier at the **Ladies' Park** on Zayed the 1st St. The corniche is also a popular walking and picnicking spot for locals seeking out that elusive cool breeze. There are two corniches in Abu Dhabi; the **Main Corniche** runs along Corniche Rd. from the Hilton Hotel to the Sheraton, and the **New Corniche** extends down the eastern side of the island on Eastern Ring Rd. The government recently shelled out 200 million dirhams to give a stretch of the Main Corniche a "facelift;" the boardwalk is now dominated by the gigantic Volcano Fountain. *(Public Garden: open Sa-Th 4-11pm, F 9am-11pm. Follow the purple signs located throughout the city. Admission 1dh. Ladies' Park: open Sa-Th 3:30-10:30pm. F 10am-11:30pm. Women and children under 10 only.)*

BEACHES

Abu Dhabi Island offers a number of good beaches. **Ar-Raha Beach,** on the Abu Dhabi-Dubai Hwy. past Umm an-Nar Roundabout, has been rated one of the best public beaches in the area. It's partitioned into two sides—one for women only, the other for both sexes. (Open 10am-7pm; free.) More public sands stretch alongside the road opposite the Hilton leading to the Breakwater. The private beaches connected to hotels charge exorbitant sums for access; one of the more sanely priced is **Ad-Dana Ladies' Beach,** on Corniche Rd. past the Hilton, near the Khalidiya Palace Hotel. In addition to a well-manicured spot of secluded shoreline, facilities include a swimming pool and cafeteria. (Open W-F 10am-dusk, Sa-Tu 11am-dusk. Women only. Admission 5dhs.)

AL-'AIN العين AND BURAIMI البريمي

The barren desert landscape slowly blossoms into a small green oasis as one drives into Al-'Ain from Dubai or Abu Dhabi. The lush green tops of the palms lining the streets form a shady canopy for the small city of Al-'Ain ("the spring" in Arabic), which is otherwise completely surrounded by sandy desert. The gardens and oasis in Al-'Ain are a testament to the number of wells lying beneath this Garden City, as it is commonly dubbed. The miraculous water that fills these wells lies at **'Ain Al-Fayda,** a spring at the foot of **Jabal Hafit,** the tallest mountain in the area.

Al-'Ain and Buraimi straddle the UAE/Oman border, and in comparison to Al-'Ain's plushness, the Omani town of Buraimi seems caught in a time warp. The extravagant wealth of the UAE and the relative poverty of Oman is evident as soon as one crosses the border between the two towns. Bare, barren Buraimi is much less developed than Al-'Ain, particularly in terms of irrigation. Buraimi basically consists of two roads—one lined with shops and coffee stands, the other with car repair shops. While Al-'Ain appears to be a gleaming Emerald City, Buraimi is a reminder that this is indeed the middle of the desert.

ORIENTATION

Al-'Ain's main roads, **Zayed Ibn Sultan Road** and **Khalifa Ibn Zayed Street,** connect at Buraimi St. by the flyover, forming a boomerang that runs through the length of the town from the Hilton to the Rotana Hotels. Al-'Ain's roundabouts are named after the Alice-in-Wonderland-like scenes that sit in their centers. The **Coffeepot Roundabout** is at the intersection of Zayed Ibn Sultan Rd. and 'Umar Ibn Al-Khatab Rd. The Al-'Ain Museum Oasis and the bus and taxi stands are situated in this area. This road eventually leads to a flyover bridge, under which Buraimi St. runs to the left. If you continue over the flyover instead of bearing left towards Buraimi, you'll hit the **Clocktower Roundabout,** where the GPO and Etisalat are located. Buraimi is much smaller than Al-'Ain. There's really only one **main road,** and you hit it as soon as you cross the border from Al-'Ain. Banks, hotels, markets, coffee shops, and everything else are on this street. The two budget hotels and two forts in Buraimi are on opposite sides of the main road. The **Police Roundabout** is in front of the two forts, and a right turn at the roundabout leads to the isolated camel market.

PRACTICAL INFORMATION

Buses: The **Al-'Ain bus station** is in front of the Al-'Ain Oasis, off Zayed Ibn Sultan Rd. between the Clocktower Roundabout and Al-'Ain Fort Museum. Buses only run within the city of Al-'Ain and to **Abu Dhabi.** There are no local buses in Buraimi, but buses to

THE OLD IN-OUT. While Buraimi is technically in Oman, for all intents and purposes both Al-'Ain and Buraimi are part of the UAE. Anyone can freely cross back and forth between the two towns, and travelers coming from the UAE do not need an Omani **visa** to enter Buraimi. The actual **border checkpoint** is 53km (1½hr. by bus) into Oman, on the road to Muscat. Taking the bus across this checkpoint is easy. Once you reach the customs post, an officer will collect the passports of everyone on the bus and return them within 15 to 20 minutes. Travelers in Oman must have a UAE visa in order to get as far as Buraimi. For information on getting a visa, see p. 614.

Muscat via **Sohar** leave 3 times daily (express 7am and 1pm, regular 3pm) from the parking lot across the street from the Adh-Dharah Hotel. The schedule changes frequently; check the times posted at the bus stop or call **Oman National Transport Co.** (tel. 652 255 or 590 601). **Visas** cannot be issued at the border; make sure you already have one before boarding a bus into Oman.

Taxis: Share taxis to **Dubai** (30dhs) and **Abu Dhabi** run more frequently than the buses. These minivans have little room for luggage, so drivers may ask you to buy 2 seats—one for yourself and one for your luggage. The **Al-'Ain taxi stand** is next to the bus stand. Make a right out of the bus parking lot, and go around the curve toward the Al-'Ain Fort Museum; the taxi stand is on the right. The **Buraimi taxi stand** is at the roundabout past Al-Buraimi Hotel. Taxis in both towns can also be hailed on the main roads. Al-'Ain taxis are metered (2dhs base fee). Omani taxis, if shared, are often cheaper, but you must bargain over the fare. Taxis can go between the 2 towns, but Al-'Ain taxis charge a minimum 10dhs to go to Buraimi, whereas Omani taxis charge 5dhs or less.

Car Rental: The 5-star hotels in Al-'Ain all offer car rental services, but you'll need an International Driving Permit. Try **Al-'Ain Hilton** (tel. 686 666; fax 686 888), **Hotel Intercontinental Al-'Ain** (tel. 686 686), or the **Rotana Hotel** (tel. 515 111).

Tours: Al-'Ain Camel Safaris (tel. 688 006; mobile 477 268; fax 688 005) offers half-day and overnight camelback desert safaris. Prices run between 100-450dhs per person. City tours of Al-'Ain and Buraimi also available (100dhs per person).

Travel Agencies: There are several travel agencies on As-Sinaiyyah (Al-'Ain St.) between the GPO and An-Nafaka Bridge, including **Abu Dhabi Travel Agency** (tel. 641 159), across the street from Etisalat. Open Sa-Th 9am-1pm and 4:30-7:30pm, F 9am-2pm.

Currency Exchange: Both Omani rials and UAE dirhams can be used in either town. **Abu Dhabi Commercial Bank,** on As-Sinaiyyah St. (Al-'Ain St.) between the GPO and An-Nafaka Bridge. Has 2 **ATMs** with Visa, MC, PLUS, and Cirrus connections. Open Sa-W 8am-1pm, Th 8am-noon. **Thomas Cook Ar-Rostamani** (tel. 665 558), in Al-'Ain on Zayed Ibn Sultan Rd., between the flyover and the Al-Murabba' Roundabout (with a giant fort at its center). Buys and sells traveler's checks, gives cash advances on Visa and MC, and sells Omani rials, which are needed for the bus fare across the border. Open Sa-Th 8:30am-1pm and 4:30-9pm, 1st and 2nd F of the month 5-9pm. There are also currency exchanges on Buraimi's Main Rd.

Market: Anwar Al-'Ain Grocery (tel. 661 319), across the street from the Al-'Ain GPO (open daily 7am-2:30pm and 5-11:30pm). Additional markets are on Zayed Ibn Sultan Rd. In Buraimi, there are several groceries in the Buraimi Souq, the huge fort at the 1st roundabout past the border. Open 7am-noon and 3-9pm.

Laundry: New Tahrir Laundry (tel. 661 319), in Al-'Ain directly behind the Anwar Al-'Ain grocery store. Shirts 3dhs. Open daily 8am-7:30pm.

Emergency: Tel. 999 in both Al-'Ain and Buraimi.

Pharmacy: 24hr. pharmacies rotate; check *Gulf News* in Al-'Ain and *Times of Oman* in Buraimi for contact information.

Medical Services: The 5-star **Intercontinental, Hilton,** and **Rotana** hotels all have doctors on call. Even if you are not a guest, go there first.

Post Office: Al-'Ain GPO (tel. 642 200), on As-Sinaiyyah (Al-'Ain St.) by the Clocktower Roundabout. **Fax** services available. There is a post office in Buraimi, but the Al-'Ain GPO is so much more efficient that even the residents of Buraimi head there. Open Sa-W 8am-1pm and 4-7pm, Th 8am-4pm, F 8-11am.

Telephone Codes: Al-'Ain: 03. There are no city codes in Oman. Be aware that calls between Al-'Ain and Buraimi are considered **international calls** and charged as such. If calling Al-'Ain from Buraimi, dial the country and city codes first (00-971-3); if calling Buraimi from Al-'Ain, dial just the country code first (00-968).

▌ ACCOMMODATIONS

Hamasa Hotel (tel. 651 200; fax 651 210), about 1mi. past the border on the Buraimi side. On the right as you enter Buraimi opposite the Toyota dealer just before the Police Roundabout. The best of the 3 budget hotels: conveniently located, spacious, and well-lit. With A/C, TV, private bath, and comfy furnishings, the Hamasa offers the most dazzle for your dirham. Singles 130dhs; doubles 150dhs; add 12% tax and service charges. Credit cards accepted.

'Ain Al-Fayda Rest Houses (tel. 838 333; fax 838 900), in an isolated area approximately 25km from the center of Al-'Ain. Expect the charge for the taxi to the hotel to increase the cost of your room by over 50% (1-way fare from Al-'Ain about 30dhs). Spacious rooms with elegant Victorian-style decor. Singles 100dhs; doubles 165dhs; 2-person suites 220-330dhs; 1-bedroom chalets 330dhs; 2-bedroom chalets 440dhs.

Adh-Dharah Hotel (tel. 650 492 or 652 995; fax 650 881), on the Buraimi side, 500m past the Border Roundabout on the right. Average-sized rooms with attached baths are clean, but haunted by the smell of cigarettes past. Though the Adh-Dharah is cheaper, the nearby Hamasa Hotel delivers a better deal. Singles 110dhs; doubles 150dhs.

▌ FOOD

Several cafeterias and coffee shops line Al-'Ain's **Zayed Ibn Sultan Road** (also called Hilton Rd.) between the Grand Mosque and the Clocktower Roundabout. Make a run for the Buraimi side of the border if it's *biryani* or mutton burgers you're craving—that's all the cafeterias on the main road offer. Fresh fruits and vegetables are sold in the **Buraimi Souq**, the monumental fort-like market at the Police Roundabout.

Quetta Cafeteria and Restaurant (tel. 641 050 or 656 242), about 2 blocks past the Grand Mosque on the right. This colossal cafeteria, with a family room for women and kids, sports the usual Indian fare of *biryanis,* curries, and kebabs (5-8dhs). They also sell Indian sweets for around 2dhs. Open Sa-Th 5am-1am, F 5am-noon and 1pm-1am.

Golden Gate Restaurant (tel. 662 467), on As-Sinaiyyah Rd. next to the Commercial Bank of Abu Dhabi, on the right-hand side coming from the GPO. Need a change from mutton burgers and Indian curry? Chinese and Filipino entrees run 15-20dhs, veggie entrees are a bit cheaper at 10-12dhs. Fried rice dishes 8-15dhs, plain steamed rice 4dhs. Open Sa-Th noon-3pm and 6:30-11:30pm, F 11am-3pm and 6:30-11:30pm.

The Happiness Land Cafeteria (tel. 658 839), on As-Sinaiyyah Rd., about ½ mi. past the Golden Gate Restaurant coming from the GPO. If happiness means video games and American fast food, this is Nirvana. Hot dogs, fries, and burgers run 3-5dhs. Fresh fruit juices quench the toughest thirsts for as little as 4dhs. Open daily 8am-1am.

The 'Ain Al-Fayda (tel. 838 333, ext. 508). If you choose to stay at the distant 'Ain Al-Fayda Rest Houses, cabs may be hard to come by but food won't. There are several restaurants and coffeeshops in the complex, but this is the most upscale: a sit-down, tip-the-waiter sort of place. Entrees include pasta, chicken, and fish (8-20dhs). Sandwiches 15dhs. Open 6:30am-4:00pm and 6:30-11:30pm.

🎵 ENTERTAINMENT

For daytime entertainment, chill out at the **Hiltonia Resort, Golf, and Aquatic Club** (tel. 686 666), on Khalid Ibn Sultan Rd. in Al-'Ain; facilities include two pools, a golf course, and a restaurant (open daily 8:30am-7:30pm; admission Sa-W 50dhs, under 14 30dhs; Th-F and holidays 75dhs, under 14 50dhs; Hilton guests free). If you seek tranquility, head to the **Public Gardens,** in the Clocktower area of Al-'Ain, across from the Rotana Hotel. Palm trees, water fountains, and fragrant flowers line the stone paths crisscrossing the park. The gardens are frequented by families with children, making it a safe place at any hour, even for solo travelers (open daily 4-11pm; admission 1dh). Nightlife centers around two hotels in Al-'Ain: the **Hotel Intercontinental Al-'Ain,** east of town off Khalid Ibn Sultan St., and the **Rotana Hotel.** If you're up for shakin' it with the sheikhs, here's a list of the happening spots.

The Metro (tel. 686 686, ext. 272), in the basement of the Hotel Intercontinental Al-'Ain, is the only disco between these 2 towns. The dance floor and cushioned lounge area in the back are intimate (read: tiny), but it does make it easy to meet the mostly European expats that call the Metro their rave away from home. The club is technically open only to "members" (a free privilege the club grants at its discretion), but Western tourists are usually allowed in. Draft beer 17dhs, cans of beer 16dhs, spirits 14dhs and up. Must be 20 to enter, 21 to drink. Cover W-Th 25dhs (includes a free drink); no cover F-Su and Tu. Open W-Th 10pm-3am, F-Su and Tu 10pm-2:30am.

Trader Vic's Restaurant and Boathouse Bar (tel. 515 111), at the Rotana Hotel in Al-'Ain. The liveliest bar in Al-'Ain comes complete with faux-tropical decor and a nightly Cuban band that lays down sultry Latin beats to make the sweaty nights even steamier. Draft beer 15dhs, 10dhs during happy hour (3-8pm). Mixed drinks 20-25dhs. 21+ admitted. No cover. Open daily 12:30pm-12:30am.

The Horse and Jockey Pub (tel. 686 686, ext. 320), in the Hotel Intercontinental Al-'Ain. An upper-crust English pub with a dark oak and hunter green interior that suits the older, wealthier European crowd. Live lounge acts sing the latest in Western pop on W and Th nights. Members only, but Western tourists are usually let in. Pints of draft beer 16dhs, Guinness 18dhs, cocktails from 13dhs. 21+ to drink. No cover. Open daily noon-midnight. Happy Hour (2dhs off every drink) noon-2pm and 6-8pm.

La Bamba Bar and Disco (tel. 686 686), next to Metro in basement of Hotel Intercontinental Al-'Ain. Male clientele come to ogle scantily clad Filipino singers. Unaccompanied women should skip this scene. *Para bailar la bamba* on the dance floor, *se necesita* couples only. Live entertainment on W and Th. 20 to enter, 21 to drink. Cover 20dhs, including free drink. Open Su-F 8pm-1:45am.

👁 SIGHTS

Though Al-'Ain and Buraimi are fairly spread out, their main attractions can be explored in a day or two. Consider hiring a car and driver from Al-'Ain Camel Safaris as taxis cost an arm and a leg.

AL-'AIN

AL-'AIN MUSEUM, EASTERN FORT, AND ENVIRONS. The **Al-'Ain Museum** (tel. 641 595), on Zayed Ibn Sultan Rd. near the Coffeepot Roundabout, is the only museum between the two towns. While it boasts a stellar exhibit of Bedouin jewelry, handicrafts, and old weaponry, there's not much else of interest. The displays of archaeological excavations and the history of Omani oil production are yawn-inducing. The crumbling **Eastern Fort,** in front of the museum, makes a nice snapshot with its courtyard cannon, but there's nothing to see inside. Just outside the museum's stone walls lies the **Al-'Ain Oasis,** where narrow cobblestone paths wind through a shady forest of palm trees. On the other side of the museum, a large, brown fort-like structure houses Al-'Ain's **Livestock Souq.** (*Eastern Fort open Sa-Th 8am-2:30pm and 4:30-6:30pm, F 9am-noon and 4:30-6:30pm. Admission 50fils. Livestock Souq open all day, but busiest in the early morning and early evening.*)

JABAL HAFIT AND 'AIN AL-FAYDA. About 30km from the center of Al-'Ain, **Jabal Hafit,** the tallest mountain in the area, affords spectacular views of the surrounding area from its summit. On Thursday and Friday evenings, the mountain is packed with picnicking locals eating out of their parked cars. It is not possible to ascend to the peak without a car, but the round-trip taxi fare (60dhs) is well worth the price, particularly if you go in the early evening and watch the sunset. This is one of the rare times when a tour company actually offers a good deal; the most economical way to scale Jabal Hafit is with the tour offered by **Al-'Ain Camel Safaris** (see p. 639). The pool of spring water at **'Ain Al-Fayda** is believed to have healing properties. Swimming is not allowed as the pool is somewhat sulfuric, but the surrounding park is an ideal spot for picnicking and relaxing.

BURAIMI

AL-KHANDAQ FORT. Buraimi's 200-year-old **Al-Khandaq Fort** is a more imposing structure than the crumbling Eastern Fort in Al-'Ain, with a 7.3m deep moat and four intricately decorated towers. The camel-colored walls enclose a large courtyard, which was impressively restored a few years ago. First built by the Al-Bushamis, a local Na'im tribe, the fort was occupied a few years later by the Wahhabis, a group of puritanical Islamists. Unlike most forts in Oman and the UAE, Al-Khandaq is not a museum, but it's an interesting place to stroll through and explore. *(Open Sa-Th 8am-1:30pm and 4:30-6:30pm. Free.)*

BURAIMI SOUQ AND AL-HILLA FORT. Just north of the Al-Khandaq Fort, the **Buraimi Souq** adopted the imposing architectural style of the fortress next door. The small vendors inside sell fresh fruit, vegetables, and fish. A few shops peddle Omani souvenirs and handicrafts, including *khanajir*, the daggers traditionally worn by Omani men. While the selection can't compare to that in Muscat's *souqs*, prices may be somewhat cheaper depending on your bargaining skills. The **Al-Hilla Fort,** directly behind the *souq*, is currently under restoration and closed to the public. *(Buraimi Souq open 7am-noon and 3-9pm.)*

CAMEL MARKET. Follow As-Sahar Rd. about 4km away from the Buraimi Souq to check out the **camel market.** The market is a series of pens, each home to two or three camels lazily lounging and patiently waiting for their new owner to arrive—it could be you! Like Al-'Ain's livestock souq, Buraimi's camel market is open all day, but is busiest in the early morning before temperatures soar.'

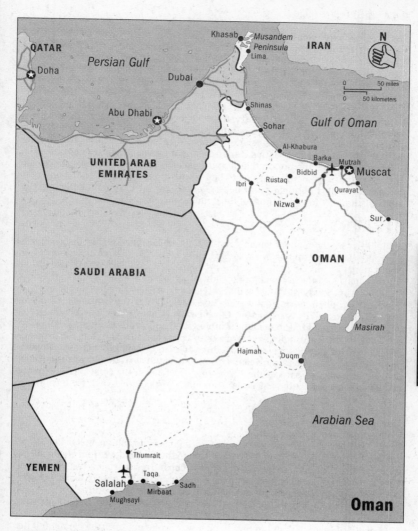

OMAN عمان

US$1=OMANI RIALS (OR) 0.39
CDN$1=OR 0.26
UK£1=OR 0.62
AUS$1=OR 0.25
SAR1=OR 0.06
EUR1=OR 0.40
1DH (UAE DIRHAM)=OR 0.10

OR 1=US$2.70
OR 1=CDN$3.83
OR 1=UK£1.60
OR 1=AUS$3.99
OR 1=SAR 15.72
OR 1=EUR 2.51
OR 1=DHS 9.54

PHONE FACTS **Country Code:** 968. **Emergency:** Tel. 999. There are no individual city codes in Oman.

643

Oman is the only country in the world whose name begins with the letter "O." Along with fellow Gulf state Qatar, it is one of only two countries that have a letter all to themselves. Aside from this alphabetical delight, Oman offers enchantments for nature lovers, history buffs, and sun worshippers alike. Isolated from the rest of the world until the 1970s, Oman has slowly become acquainted with modernity just as tourists have started to discover the bevy of natural wonders within its borders. The variety of landscapes on this horn of the Arabian peninsula is unmatched by any other Middle Eastern country, from the mountainous fjords of the northern Musandem Peninsula, to the temperate tropical beaches in the southern Dhofar region, to the central deserts where temperatures soar over 50°C (122°F). The medley of centuries old castles, fortresses, and mosques scattered across the country challenges the notion that if you've seen one fort, you've seen them all. Though at times the country seems to be rushing to meet progress head on, most Omanis are still traditionalists at heart, fiercely loyal to the monarchy and the small Islamic sect to which most of the population belongs.

HISTORY

While little is known about Oman's pre-Islamic past, archaeologists have discovered settlements dating back to the 3rd millennium BCE. Most people lived as desert nomads, but by 2000 BCE, the prosperous **Magan Empire** had spread out across Oman's northern coast, taking advantage of the copper found in the hills around Sohar. Southern Oman's Dhofar region flourished due to the presence of **frankincense,** one of the ancient world's most sought-after substances (see **Frankincense, My Dear,** p. 672). Around 630 CE, a missionary arrived in Oman bearing a letter from the Prophet Mohammed; brothers Abd and Jaifar al-Mustakabar, who ruled the land jointly, quickly embraced the Muslim faith. The first Ibadi Imam, **Julanda Ibn Mas'ud,** was elected in 751. From the 7th to the 15th centuries, Oman's maritime trade flourished and **Sohar** became one of the most important seaports in the Islamic world. As early as the 8th century, the fame of the great Omani seaman **Abu Ubaida Ibn Abdulla Ibn al-Qassim,** who made a 7000km voyage from Oman to Canton (Guangzhou) in China, was widely known.

In 1507, the Portuguese occupied Oman's northern coast, with Hormuz and later Muscat as their base of operations. The Portuguese realized, as the British later would, that control of the Gulf was vital for any European power with its eye on India. After nearly a century and a half of Portuguese occupation, **Sultan Ibn Saif al-Yarubi** reconquered Muscat in 1650 and expelled the Portuguese from Oman. Since then, no other foreign power has conquered Oman (apart from a brief period of Persian occupation). This 1650 victory is usually cited as the date of **Omani independence,** making Oman the oldest independent state in the Arab world.

The Ya'aruba Imams introduced a period of renaissance and wealth. Most of Oman's imposing castles and forts were built during their reign. However, after the 1718 death of Imam Sultan Ibn Saif II, civil war broke out over the election of his successor. Taking advantage of the country's weak state, Persian troops occupied Muscat but failed to take Sohar, which was defended by **Ahmad Ibn Sa'id.** In 1749, Sa'id was elected Imam, marking the start of Oman's present dynasty, the **Al-Busaid.** Within a few years, he managed to build the Omani navy into a formidable power, leading expeditions against pirates and the Persians. In 1786, with maritime trade becoming increasingly important to the nation, Sa'id's successor Hamad moved the capital from the interior to coastal Muscat. Around this time, he also adopted the title of Sultan, which implied temporal authority in a way that the religious title of Imam did not.

The Omani Empire reached its peak under the reign of **Sayyid Sa'id Ibn Sultan,** who exercised power from 1804-1856. While other Gulf states found themselves under the heel of imperialism, Oman was building up its own colonial empire. At its height, Oman's influence extended far down the east African coast, where it controlled the ports of **Mombasa** and **Zanzibar** (which served as Oman's second capital). Oman also controlled portions of Persia, Baluchistan, and the Indian subcontinent; in fact, it did not abandon its last outpost in Pakistan until 1947. During Sayyid Sa'id's reign, Oman also developed relations with a number of European countries and became the first Arab state to establish diplomatic relations with the U.S. After Sayyid Sa'id's death, however, the empire split: one of his sons became the Sultan of Zanzibar and the other the Sultan of Muscat and Oman.

By the early 20th century, the Sultan's power to control the interior of the country had decreased considerably. In February 1932, **Sultan Sa'id Ibn Taimur,** father of the present ruler, came to power. When he tried to exercise his nominal control in the interior in the early 1950s, the British (believing there might be oil inland) backed him up. The result was a territorial dispute over the **Buraimi Oasis** involving Oman, Saudi Arabia, and Abu Dhabi. Sultan Sa'id emerged the victor, and the Buraimi Oasis was placed firmly within Oman's borders.

Sultan Sa'id Ibn Taimur was, in the words of one British writer, "an arch-reactionary of great personal charm." He wanted no change of any sort in Oman and did all he could to isolate his country from the rest of the world. Omanis were not allowed to leave the country, and those who did were seldom allowed to return. He forbade travel between the interior and the coast and prohibited women from leaving their villages. Believing education was a threat to his power, he opposed it, and banned singing, dancing, and football as well. The Sultan's only contact with the outside world was through his British advisers and Muscat's merchant families, to whom he granted enormously lucrative import monopolies that provided most of the country's income. In exchange, the merchants stayed out of politics and imported nothing that sniffed of progress or the West, including radios, books, or even eyeglasses. Aside from this minority of rich merchants, most of Oman's population struggled in a subsistence economy and lived in extreme poverty. Deprivation led to disturbances in central and southern Oman, and in 1965, a nationalist rebel group called the **Dhofar Liberation Front (DLF)** attempted a revolt against the state. The tension further escalated after oil was discovered in Oman in 1967 and Sa'id refused to spend the new wealth on national infrastructure development.

Sa'id's son, **Qaboos,** who ironically received his education in Britain, was immediately placed under house arrest when he returned to Oman in 1964. In 1970, at the age of 30, Qaboos led a bloodless palace coup and sent his father into exile (Sa'id spent his exile in a London hotel, rumored to have subsisted on a diet of **fried Mars Bars**). Sultan Qaboos Ibn Sa'id quickly set to modernizing Oman's semi-feudal economy and repealing his father's oppressive social restrictions. Within a week, a national radio station was installed, and Oman's comparatively modest oil revenues were allocated to build much-needed roads, hospitals, and schools. Despite his ambitious modernization programs, the Sultan has demonstrated a strong desire to preserve Oman's traditional character. Modern construction has been largely confined to certain areas, both in Muscat and in provincial cities, and until the 1990s, the country was slow to open up to tourism.

To this day, Oman has no constitution or democratic representation. All power lies in the hands of Sultan Qaboos, who has full authority to act according to his own will. While he has lead his country forward in terms of infrastructure, he has only made a few democratic reforms. There is no legislation, nor any political parties. The judicial system is to a large extent based on the Islamic Sharia. The most notable door Qaboos has opened to citizen participation in the government was the establishment of the **Majlis ash-Shura** (State Consultative Council) in 1991. The 59 members of this council represent different regions of the country; in 1997, the Sultan appointed two female representatives, calling upon women to participate in Oman's social and political evolution. However, the Majlis ash-Shura and the Sultan's appointed cabinet of ministers play only a consultative role, and Qaboos has no obligation to follow their suggestions.

OMAN

IN THE NEWS

Oil prices reached 25-year lows at the end of 1998, causing unprecedented social and economic challenges for Oman as well as the other Gulf States. In December 1998, the **Gulf Cooperation Council** (GCC)—made up of Oman, Saudi Arabia, Kuwait, Qatar, the UAE, and Bahrain—gathered in a summit to discuss the destabilizing effects of the plummeting prices. Oman established trade with **Israel** in 1995, but froze all commercial relations when hardliner Benjamin Netanyahu came to power in 1996. After Ehud Barak was elected prime minister in May 1999, Sultan Qaboos quickly welcomed the new leader and sought to reestablish contact with the Israeli government after resumption of the peace process.

MUSCAT مسقط

Muscat is often referred to as the "Jewel of Arabia," and rightly so—the city is a glittering, multifaceted capital encompassing centuries of history and tradition. Muscat has long distinguished itself from the other cities along the Gulf: in the late 14th century CE it rose to prominence as a small but important trading post with lands as distant as Africa and the Far East. When the Portuguese invaded the Gulf years later, they were briefly headquartered in the city before the Omani army drove them out in 1650, thereby ending Portuguese occupation of the region. The currently ruling dynasty of Oman, the Al-Busaid, moved in two centuries later and remain there today. Modern Muscat's sparkling waters and honey-colored mountains serve as a backdrop for a vibrant meeting of the city's colorful past and cacophonous present. One of Oman's most authentic *souqs* is just blocks away from several modern-day shopping malls, and eccentrically decorated traffic roundabouts (such as the Incense Burner Roundabout) lead to aging forts and elegantly adorned mosques. The city limits are lined with relaxing parks and beaches, and the center is divided into the three regions of Ruwi, Mutrah, and Old Town Muscat (in addition to the major suburban areas of Al-Qurm, Al-Khuwair, and Medinat as-Sultan Qaboos). Each area has its own distinctive flavor, giving travelers many tasty samples of life along the Arabian Sea, old and new.

✳ ORIENTATION

Muscat stretches from the suburbs near Seeb to the beaches of Al-Bustan. The main highway is **As-Sultan Qaboos Street**, which links Seeb Airport to Ruwi, Mutrah, and Old Town Muscat. As-Sultan Qaboos St. becomes An-Nahdah St. at the Al-Qurm Roundabout. **Ruwi** is the commercial district of Muscat, where all the banks, many restaurants, and a couple of hotels are located. The main **Ruwi Roundabout** lies immediately after the exit off the highway. The roundabout is the start of **Aj-Jami' Street,** on which the Ruwi bus station and taxi stand are located. Aj-Jami' St. runs from the roundabout to the Sheraton Hotel, intersecting (in order): An-Noor St., Al-Fursan St., Bank Al-Markazi St., and Bait Al-Falaj St.

In **Mutrah, Al-Bahri Road** runs along the Mutrah **corniche** from the **As-Samakah Roundabout,** next to the Fish Market and bus stop, all the way to **Old Town Muscat.** The *souq*, hotels, small groceries, and coffee shops line this closest road to the Fish Market. **Old Town Muscat** is easily accessible from Mutrah via public transport. The main roads, **Bab al-Mutthaib Street** and **As-Saidiyah Street,** run from the fort-like entrance to Old Town Muscat and head out towards Sidab.

▣ TRANSPORTATION

Airplanes: Muscat is served by **Seeb International Airport** (flight info tel. 1101 or 519 223; airport info 519 809), about 35km (30-40min.) from the city center. Seeb is the only airport in Oman with international flights (though there are rumors that Salalah will

Muscat

ACCOMMODATIONS
A Al-Qurm Beach House
B Hotel Summer Sands
and Makha Hotel

Gulf of Oman

OMAN

Bab al-Mattaib

Al-Bustan
Palace Hotel

SEE INSET
BELOW LEFT

TO BANDAR JUSSA BEACH
(4km)

Qantab Rd.

As-Saidiyah St.

AL-BUSTAN

AL-BUSTAN
ROUNDABOUT

Al-Bustan
Palace Beach

Sidab Rd.

Hiramel Rd.

HIRAMEL

SIDAB

Incense
Burner
Monument

OLD TOWN
MUSCAT

Al-Bahri Rd.

Qalbuh
Bay Park

Mutrah
Watchtower

SEE MUTRAH
DETAIL MAP

Sultan's Armed Forces
Museum

Al-Fursan St.

SEE RUWI
DETAIL MAP,
P. 641

B

AL-WADI AL-KABIR

Bait al-Falaj St.

Al-Matha St.

MUTRAH

ARMY BASE

RUWI

Al-Matha St.

Darsait St.

Ras al-Hamra St.

Fuhud St.

AL-QURM

RUWI
ROUNDABOUT

Ruwi St.

Al-Mujama St.

AL-BURJ
ROUNDABOUT

Hillat St.

Sud Ruwi St.

Sud Ruwi St.

Bait al-Falaj St.

ROUNDABOUT

An-Nahdah
Hospital

An-Nahdah St.

An-Nahdah St.

Al-Amerat St.

Gulf of Oman

1 mile

1 kilometer

0

0

N

Police
Stadium

Maydan
al-Fath
Stadium

Al-Harthy
Center

Al-Walja St.

Maydan al-Fath St.

Fort
Jalali

Way 9332

200 yards

200 meters

0

0

Al-Khanus
Park

Al-Qurm Nature Reserve

Al-Qurm Amusement Park

SHEIKH AL-MALIK
ROUNDABOUT

Al-Qurm Heights Rd.

AL-QURM
ROUNDABOUT

Sabco
Center

AL-WUTAYYAH

Altam St.

A

Way 9331

Gulf of Oman

Al-Alaam Palace

Fort Mirani

Intercontinental
Hotel

Hyatt Regency
Hotel

Yemen

Syria

MEDINAT
AS-SULTAN
QABOOS

Way 3672

As-Sarooj St.

Medina as-Sultan

Sheikh al-Amin St.

Qaboos St.

Dawhat al-Adab St.

Qasr al-Alaam St.

Omani French Museum
(Bait Fransa)

As-Saidiyah St.

SHATI
AL-QURM

Bahrain

AL-KHUWAIR

Turkey

Bab al-
Kabir

Mutthaib St.

Old Town Muscat

Al-Bandar St.

St. 35

Minavans & Taxis

Bait
az-Zubair

TO SEEB
INTERNATIONAL
AIRPORT (15KM)

Natural
History
Museum

Jamat ad-Duwal St.

Al-Muzafat St.

Al-Khariya St.

United Arab
Emirates

Saudi Arabia

Qatar

France

Kuwait

Egypt

Jordan

Iran

USA

Jami' at ad-Duwal al-'Arabiyah

SEE
INSET
ABOVE

soon start handling international flights). The OR 5 **departure tax** for international flights is included in ticket prices. **Oman Air** (tel. 707 222), the only carrier for internal air travel, flies to: **Salalah** (1½hr.; 1 or 2 per day; OR 32, round-trip OR 60); **Sur** (1-way OR 14); **Masirah Island** (1½hr.; on Su, M, W, Sa; round-trip OR 34); **Khasab** (1½hr., 1 per day Sa-W, OR 20); **Abu Dhabi, UAE** (1hr.; daily noon, 9pm; OR 67); **Dubai, UAE** (1hr.; daily 8am, 2:30, 6, 9pm; OR 59); and **Doha, Qatar** (50min., daily 6pm).

Intercity Buses: Oman National Transport Co. (tel. 590 601 or 590 046; fax 590 152) runs intercity buses out of Muscat's 2 main terminals. **Ruwi Bus Station** (ticket office tel. 708 522) is on Aj-Jami' St., 2 blocks from the Ruwi Roundabout. Buses leave from Ruwi to: **Buraimi** via **Sohar** (express 7am, 1pm; regular 3pm); **Sur** (express 7:30am, 2:30pm; regular F 4:30pm); **Ibri** via **Nizwa** (express 8am, 2:30pm; regular 4pm); and **Salalah** (12-13hr.; Sept. 16-June 14 6am, 7pm; June 15-Sept. 15 6am, 6, 7pm; OR 8). **Mutrah Fish Market Bus Station** (ticket office tel. 714 422) is on Mutrah's corniche, to the left of the As-Samakah Roundabout. Buses depart from Mutrah (called Muscat on some timetables) to **Dubai, UAE** (5½hr.; 7:30am, 4:30pm; 1-way OR 9, round-trip OR 16). Some buses to **Salalah** also stop at the Mutrah Fish Market station.

Local Buses: Muscat's buses may be cheap (most trips cost no more than a few hundred baisa), but they are not the most popular mode of transport around the city. Because of the sweltering Gulf heat and the metal buses' lack of A/C, these ovens-on-wheels are like hell on earth. Local buses run 6:30am-11pm (every 20-30min.). **Route numbers** are as follows: **#01** (١) Al-Wadi Al-Kabir; **#02** (٢) Mutrah-Wadi Aday; **#04** (٤) Khoala Hospital; **#23** (٢٣) Airport/Al-Hayl/As-Seeb; **#25** (٢٥) Royal Hospital/Al-Udhaybal Heights; **28** (٢٨) Al-Khawd/University; and **#31/32** (٣١\٣٢) Medinat An-Nahdah.

Minivans: Minivans zoom up and down major roads in the city center and most parts of the Greater Muscat area. There are 2 **share taxi/minivan stands** in **Ruwi:** on the southern side of the Ruwi Roundabout and directly across the street from the Ruwi Bus Station on Aj-Jami' St. In **Mutrah,** minivans cruise up and down the corniche and rest in the parking lot by Mutrah Fish Market Bus Station. In **Old Town Muscat,** wait along As-Saidiyah St. or at any of the major roundabouts. All minivans are camel-colored and have orange Arabic signs on them. Minivans leaving from a stand leave only when full; hop on an moving vehicle for less of a wait. Minivans between the 3 central districts of Muscat cost 200 baisa or less; from Seeb Clocktower to any of the central districts 500 baisa; from suburbs such as Al-Khuwair and Al-Qurm to the central districts 250-300 baisa. **Minibuses** in this area can only be caught on the main highway through As-Sultan Qaboos St. Minibuses don't always have fixed routes; depending on his mood, the driver will either take you exactly to your destination or just as far as he's going.

Taxis: Share taxis wait in the same spots as the minivans, but are typically almost twice as expensive. Negotiate fares with the driver. Most of the share taxis will only deviate off the main routes to go to major destinations like the Al-Qurm Beach House, Jussa Beach, and the Al-Bustan Beach Club. **Engaged taxis** will rip off every rial in your possession; prices are neither fixed nor metered, so you are at the mercy of the driver when attempting to negotiate an affordable fare.

Car Rental: If you can afford it, renting a car in Muscat to caravan around Oman is strongly recommended. Some of Oman's most spectacular scenery is off the tarmac road, so if you plan to do a lot of outdoor sightseeing, hire a 4-wheel drive vehicle. Most cars are manual rather than automatic. Expect to pay OR 75-100 per week for a car, OR 180-260 for a 4-wheel drive vehicle. **Budget Rent-A-Car** has several locations in Muscat. The Seeb Airport branch (tel. 510 816/817) is open 24hr. Additional branches at the Mercure Al-Falaj Hotel (tel 702 311, ext. 890) and Ruwi Novotel (tel. 704 244, ext. 937). **Europcar** has a 24hr. location at the Seeb Airport (tel. 519 014) and an additional branch at the Muscat Holiday Inn (tel. 684 093). **Hertz** has a 24hr. location at Seeb Airport (tel. 521 187) and an additional office at National Travel and Tourism (tel. 566 208), on As-Sultan Qaboos St. in Hattayah, opposite An-Nahdah Hospital.

⑦ PRACTICAL INFORMATION

TOURIST AND FINANCIAL SERVICES

Tours: Arabian Sea Safaris (tel. 693 223; fax 693 224; email arabseas@gto.net.om) offers an array of diving, snorkeling, sailing, and desert camping safaris with multilingual guides to sites such as Sur, Ras al-Hadd, and the Wahiba Sands. **Al-Hashan Tours** (tel. 773 76 66 or 910 16 52), Al-Harthy Complex, 2nd floor, in Al-Qurm, offers fort tours and Wahiba Sands safaris. Open Sa-Th 8:30am-1pm and 4:30-7pm.

Embassies and Consulates: All foreign embassies in Muscat are in the Embassies District in Al-Khuwair, on Jami'at ad-Duwal al-'Arabiyah (League of Nations) St., unless otherwise stated. **Australia** has no diplomatic representation in Oman. **U.K.** (see below) handles emergencies for Australian citizens. The nearest Australian consulate is in Dubai, UAE (see p. 626). **Canada** has no diplomatic representation in Oman. The **U.K. Embassy** (see below) handles emergencies for Canadian citizens. **Iran** (tel. 696 944), between the Jordanian and Egyptian embassies. Open Sa-W 7:30am-3:30pm. **New Zealand** (tel 795 726), on Lane 3007, off Mutrah (High) St. in Mutrah Al-Kubra. Open Sa-W 7:30am-2:30pm. **Saudi Arabia** (tel. 601 744), between the embassies of the UAE and Qatar. Open Sa-W 8:30am-2pm. **UAE** (tel. 600 302), between the Egyptian and Saudi embassies. Open Sa-W 8am-1:30 pm. **U.K.** (tel. 693 077), the first embassy on Jami'at ad-Duwal al-'Arabiyah St., across the *wadi* from the U.S. Embassy. Handles consular services for Australians and Canadians. Open Sa-W 8:30am-12:30pm. **U.S.** (tel. 698 989), between the U.K. and the Jordanian embassies. Open Sa-W for American citizens 8am-12:30pm, for others 8-11am. **Yemen** (tel. 600 815), off Al-Kharijiyah St. in Shati' Al-Qurm; follow Way 2827 to Way 2840. Open Sa-W 9:30am-2:30pm.

Currency Exchange: Tel. 1106 or check the newspapers for daily exchange rates. Most banks cash American Express and Thomas Cook traveler's checks, but at considerably higher rates than the exchange centers. In general, banking hours are Sa-W 8am-noon, Th 8-11am. Most banks have **ATM** machines. **Oman and UAE Exchange Center** (tel. 750 830), in the shopping arcade across from the Ruwi Roundabout, on the side of As-Sultan Qaboos St. heading towards the airport. Cash advances on Visa, MC, and AmEx. Exchanges traveler's checks and cash. **ATMs** have Visa, MC, AmEx, PLUS, and Cirrus links. Open Sa-Th 8am-noon, and 4-8pm. Another branch inside the Mutrah Souq. **National Bank of Oman (NBO),** in the Mutrah Business District off Bait Al-Falaj St. Visa and MC links. There are a number of major banks in this area, just south of Al-Burj St. and the Star Cinema. **Oman International Bank (OIB),** on Aj-Jami' St. at the Ruwi Roundabout, behind the share taxi/minivan stand. Links to Visa and MC.

American Express: Represented by **Az-Zubair Tours** (tel. 708 08 17), on Way 3119, off Ruwi St. between the Ruwi Roundabout and the Al-Burj Roundabout. No exchange facilities, but they will hold mail for AmEx clients. Address letters to: AmEx–Client's Mail, P.O. Box 833, Ruwi, Oman. Open Sa-Th 8am-1pm and 4-6pm.

LOCAL SERVICES

English Bookstore: Al-'Oloum Bookshop has several locations: in the Hyatt Regency (tel. 602 888), the Sheraton Hotel (tel. 799 899), and the Al-Harthy Shopping Complex on An-Nahdah St. in Al-Qurm (tel. 566 196). **Family Bookshop** also has several locations: in the Muscat Intercontinental Hotel (tel. 600 500), on Souq Ruwi St. in Ruwi (tel. 786 463), and across from the Sabco Shopping Center in Al-Qurm (tel. 564 391).

Market: Sultan Shopping has a larger selection than most "foodstuff" shops. Two locations: off Al-Burj St. behind Star Cinema in Ruwi (tel. 797 276) and on Al-Qurm St. opposite the Qurm Amusement Park (tel. 563 207). Open daily 8am-1pm and 4-11pm.

Laundromat: Snow White Laundry (tel. 703 462), in the Star Cinema shopping complex in Ruwi. The hotels in Mutrah and Qurm also offer laundry services.

EMERGENCY AND COMMUNICATIONS

Emergency: Tel. 999

24-Hour Pharmacy: 24hr. duties rotate on daily. Check local papers for location and telephone number. Pharmacies are generally open Sa-Th 8am-1pm and 4-7pm, F 4-7pm.

Hospital: An-Nahdah Hospital (tel. 707 800), southwest of Ruwi Roundabout.

Post Office: There are post offices in every area of Muscat. Main branches are in: **Seeb** (tel. 519 922), near the Airport Roundabout (open Sa-W 7:30am-1:30pm and 3:30-5:30 pm); **Ruwi** (tel. 701 651), on Markaz Mutrah at-Tijari St., off Al-Burj St. next to Star Cinema (open Sa-W 8am-2pm and 3:30-5:30pm); **Mutrah** (tel. 711 633), at the Al-Mina Roundabout next to the Mina Qaboos Port Services building (open Sa-W 8am-2pm and 4-6pm); and **Old Town Muscat** (tel. 738 547), near the HSBC bank at Bait az-Zubair Museum on Al-Bareed St. (open 7:30am-1:30pm and 3:30-6pm).

Internet Access: Cyberworld (tel. 566 740), in Alasfoor Plaza in Al-Qurm, next to Sabco Commercial Center off An-Nahdah St. Open Sa-Th 9am-1pm and 4-8:30pm.

▓ ACCOMMODATIONS

Super-cheap hotels are hard to come by in most of Oman, and Muscat is no exception. Mid-range (read: semi-skanky) hotels are a dime a dozen. Mutrah's corniche, from the Fish Souq to the Old Souq entrance, is lined with several such establishments. Additional accommodations can be found in Ruwi's industrial area, but the ambience of auto repair shops and factories can't compete with the old world charm and atmosphere of Mutrah's corniche. If beach accessibility is a priority, Al-Qurm offers one reasonably priced (by Omani standards) establishment.

RUWI

Ruwi may not have the ambience of the Mutrah Corniche, but the accommodations there are cheaper and next to the main bus station and taxi stand, with easy access to restaurants and groceries.

▨ **Al-Wafa Hotel Flats** (786 522 or 786 540; fax 786 534), on Aj-Jami' St, ½-block past Qaboos Mosque, directly behind the Ruwi Bus Station on the left. For couples and larger groups, renting a 1- or 2-bedroom furnished flat is a cheaper, more spacious alternative to cramped, overpriced hotel rooms. All flats include a fully-equipped kitchen, living room, and 1 or 2 baths. 1-bedroom flat OR 20; 2-bedroom flat OR 25. Weekly rate OR 5 less per day. Cash only.

Hotel Summer Sands (tel. 771 382/3/4; fax 771 33 85). From Bait Al-Falaj St., turn on Al-Baladiyah St. between the Wadi al-Kabir Roundabout and the Sheraton, and follow signs for Makha Hotel and take the 3rd left; the hotel is on the right side. Despite what its name implies, this hotel is miles away from the nearest beach. Bright rooms (all with private bath) and fluffy beds are more than adequate. Singles OR 13; doubles OR 17; 4-person suite OR 26; add 15.5% tax and service charge. Visa and MC accepted.

Makha Hotel (tel. 771 44 71; fax 771 69 227). From Bait Al-Falaj St., turn on Al-Baladiyah St. between the Wadi al-Kabir Roundabout and the Sheraton. Following the signs. Motel-style lodgings with outdoor entrances on terrace. No frills here, just basic, uncarpeted rooms with shower, A/C, TV, and refrigerator. Singles OR 12; doubles OR 14. Visa, MC, AmEx accepted.

MUTRAH

▨ **Naseem Hotel** (tel. 712 418; fax 711 728), on the corniche, between As-Samakah Roundabout and the Mutrah Souq. The Naseem is hands down the corniche's best offering; in terms of comfort, no one else comes close. Enormous rooms with ceramic tile decor and bathtubs big enough to swim in. Singles OR 10.9; doubles OR 15.3; triples OR 17.45; tax included. Cash only.

Mina Hotel (tel. 711 828; fax 714 981), on the corniche directly across from the Fish Market and bus station. Rooms in the front have balconies overlooking the harbor and

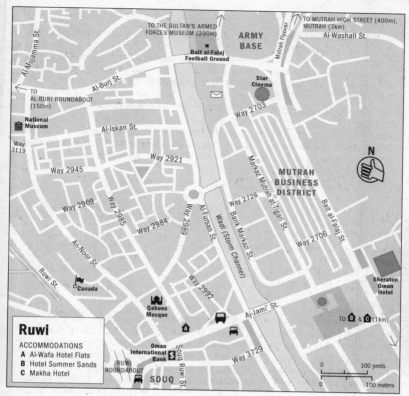

corniche. Basic amenities include fan, A/C, refrigerator, and attached bath. Singles OR 12.5; doubles OR 15.6; triples OR 18.8; tax included. Visa, MC, AmEx accepted.

Corniche Hotel (tel. 714 636 or 714 707; fax 714 770), on the corniche across from the Fish Market and bus station. A fake marble entryway leads upstairs to modest carpeted rooms with private baths. Room size and quality decrease as you move from the front of the hotel (facing the corniche) to the back. Singles OR 9.8, with sea view OR 10.9; doubles OR 15.3/16.4; tax included. AmEx, Diner's Club accepted.

AL-QURM

Qurm Beach House (tel. 564 070; fax 560 76 17). From Al-Qurm Roundabout, follow Al-Qurm St. past Al-Qurm Amusement Park. Continue around a curve until you see the beach, and turn right at the sign for Qurm International Hotel. Qurm Beach House is the first hotel on the left. Qurm Beach House offers simple but tight quarters that you may be forced to share with 6-legged guests. The main draw is its prime location—half a block from the beach. All rooms have private bath. Singles OR 14; doubles OR 20-25; add 17% tax and service charge. Visa, MC, AmEx, Diner's Club accepted.

☐ FOOD

Man O-man, will your taste buds ever thank you for visiting Muscat. The capital's lip-smacking smorgasboard of intercontinental eateries is a welcome change from the typical Omani standbys like shawarma and *biryani*.

RUWI

🦑 **Payalok Filipino Restaurant** (tel. 797 290), in the Oman International Bank shopping strip facing the flyover, near the Ruwi Roundabout. Nightclub dancers aren't the only spicy Filipino dishes in Muscat. Payolok serves authentic, freshly-prepared island entrees: sample "Filipino hot" chicken *adobo* or shrimp *fuyong*. A mainly Filipino clientele, friendly service, and a pleasant atmosphere (until they start up the karaoke). Open daily 9:30am-3pm and 5-11:30pm.

Omar Al-Khayyam Restaurant (tel. 703 035 or 707 082), in the Oman International Bank (OIB) shopping strip, to the right of the bank directly across from Fares Al-Farsi Trading. An extensive menu of Indian and Chinese entrees and a smattering of Continental cuisine, such as chicken à la king. Frequented mainly by locals working in Ruwi's Central Business District guaranteed to make a less-than-2-rial dent in your budget. Open daily 11am-3pm and 6pm-midnight.

Golden City Restaurant (tel. 790 949), to the left of 'Umar Al-Khayyam Restaurant in the OIB shopping strip. While the dining room is smaller than 'Umar Al-Khayyam's, the menu offers a broader selection of continental dishes. Prices are comparable to the other eateries in this area; a meal costs around 2 rials. Open Sa-Th 10am-3:30pm and 5:30pm-midnight, F 9am-midnight.

Chicken Tikka and **Kentucky Fried Chicken** (tel. 705 040). East meets greasy West in these joint dining areas on Aj-Jami' St. (across from Mosque al-Qaboos). Decide which culture has better mastered the art of poultry preparation. Both restaurants charge about OR 1.5 for a chicken meal.

MUTRAH

The majority of Mutrah's coffee shops and restaurants are seaside—they line the corniche from the *souq* entrance to the Mutrah Fish Market bus station. The entrance to the *souq* is at the traffic light between As-Samakah Roundabout and the Mutrah St. Roundabout. Despite the number of restaurants clustered in the area, however, there's not much variety. The hotels on the corniche have several good restaurants: **Ash-Shati'a Restaurant** (tel. 714 636), at the Corniche Hotel, serves both Indian and Arabic dishes, while **Al-Bahr Restaurant**, at the Mina Hotel (tel. 711 828), offers pricier Indian dishes.

🦑 **Taj Restaurant** (tel. 796 880), on the Ruwi end of Mutrah (High) St., a few blocks past the Mutrah Flyover. The Taj opened 21 years ago as the first Indian restaurant in Oman; today, it serves both Indian and Chinese entrees in lavish theme rooms decorated with Mughali murals and brightly-colored stained glass windows. The Taj's friendly service and hot, spicy food make dining here a memorable experience. A full meal costs just under OR 5. Open Sa-Th 12:30-3pm and 7pm-midnight, F 1-3pm and 7pm-midnight.

The Fast Food Restaurant (tel. 714 447), to the left of the *souq* entrance. Cheeseburgers, fries, sundaes, and shakes—just what you came all the way to Oman to eat. Open daily 8:30am-2pm and 5pm-2am.

AL-QURM AND AL-KHUWAIR

The suburbs (and expat havens) of Al-Qurm and Al-Khuwair offer some excellent alternatives to the already diverse restaurants in the central areas of Muscat. Make the trek out to Al-Khuwair (on the opposite side of the highway next to Medinat as-Sultan Qaboos) for traditional Omani dishes in an authentic ambience. Take a bus, microbus, or share taxi out to the Al-Khuwair Roundabout, and then hail a taxi.

🦑 **Al-Ofair Public Food Restaurant** (tel. 601 361 or 693 965), behind the Shell Station on the Al-Khuwair Hwy. A taste of traditional Oman, where guests sit on floor cushions and feast on native dishes like *thareed* (made with mutton and Omani bread). Custom dictates eating with your hands, but silverware is available upon request. Each group gets a private dining room, decorated with Persian rugs and artifacts. The food is rich,

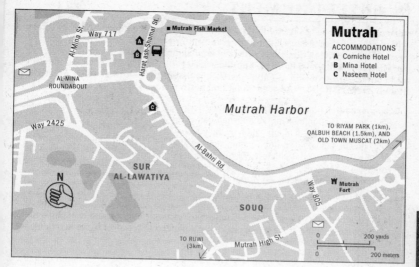

Mutrah

ACCOMMODATIONS
A Corniche Hotel
B Mina Hotel
C Naseem Hotel

O M A N

the portions large, and the prices gentle on the wallet: full meals OR 2. Dress conservatively. Open Sa-Th noon-4pm and 6pm-midnight, F 1-4pm and 6pm-midnight.

Prince's Restaurant (tel. 602 213), across the street from the Az-Zawahi Mosque, Al-Khuwair. If you aren't tired of Indian food, some of the best curries and *biryanis* around are cooked in Prince's kitchen. Eccentric decor ranges from Victorian Era portraits to paintings of Hindu gods. A full meal runs about OR 2. Open Sa-Th noon-3:20pm and 6:30pm-midnight, F 1-3:30pm and 6:30pm-midnight.

Le Bistro (tel. 565 356), facing Al-Khamis Plaza in Al-Qurm, next to Muscat Bakery. Take the Seeb bus from Muscat and get off at Sabco Commercial Center; Al-Khamis Plaza is opposite Al-Asfoor Plaza and Fanja House. Nibble on savory crepes, baguette sandwiches, and luscious chocolate and fruit mousse at this petit French cafe. OR 4 buys a full meal, soda, and dessert. Open Sa-Th 8am-11pm, F 4-11pm.

Bin Attique Restaurant for Traditional Omani Food (tel. 603 225), behind the Shell Station on the Al-Khuwair Hwy. The Al-Ofair's next-door neighbor and main competitor. Private dining rooms furnished with rugs and cushions, but Bin Attique serves Indian curries and *biryanis* as well. OR 2 for a full meal. Open daily 9am-1am.

OLD TOWN MUSCAT

Old Town Muscat does not have many culinary options aside from the following two restaurants. There are a couple of coffee shops on the main road that leads from Muscat to Sidab and Al-Bustan.

Golden Key Restaurant (tel. 738 595). Exit Old Town Market and head towards Sidab; it's on the 1st street to the right immediately after the sharply-curved underpass. Typical Levantine fare (falafel, hummus) as well as sandwiches. Dining room is spacious, cool, and clean—which is more than can be said of the other coffee shops in the area. Full meal including water or soda OR 1.5. Open daily 7:30am-1pm and 4:30pm-2am.

Al-Badiyah Restaurant (tel. 738 165), next door to the Golden Key. Offers mainly Indian cuisine. Prices are a bit higher—a full meal costs around OR 2. Open daily 7:30am-4pm and 6pm-12:30am.

🎵 ENTERTAINMENT

Muscat's nightlife is not particularly frisky, but there are a couple of bars and clubs where you can dance the night away. The trendiest (and liveliest) spots are at the **Hyatt Regency Hotel** in Shati Al-Qurm, the **Intercontinental Hotel** near the Hyatt, and the **Sheraton Oman Hotel** in Ruwi. **Star Cinema** (tel. 791 641), a UFO-shaped building at the intersection of Bait al-Falaj and Al-Borj St. in Ruwi, shows mainly American blockbusters as well as the occasional Indian film (tickets OR 1).

Copacabana (tel. 602 888), at the Hyatt Regency Hotel. Take a minibus heading towards Seeb to Sabco Commercial Center, then hail a cab (OR 3). The place to see and be seen in Muscat. Expect interrogation by the fashion police; don't provoke them by wearing shorts or sandals. The club's small, crowded dance floor is lit by floor-to-ceiling TVs, and the DJ pumps out the latest Western party tunes. Grab a table on the balcony and count the local-to-expat ratio. Relatively safe for unaccompanied women. 21+ admitted. Cover OR 3 per couple on W and Th. Open Sa-Th 9pm-1:30am.

Safari Bar (tel. 602 888), Hyatt Regency Hotel. Live Zairean music, a 4-wheel drive safari vehicle, and signs pointing the way to Mt. Kilimanjaro and the East African cities of Mombasa and Arusha give visitors a superficial and contrived glimpse of Oman's African influences. This 2-level bar and club is still popular with expats and a mainly male (90% men, 10% women) local crowd.

Al-Ghazal Pub (tel. 600 500), Intercontinental Hotel. This faux English-style pub caters mainly to an over–30, non-British, European crowd who have a jolly good time chatting up other expats over a pint or two. "Authentic" pub grub includes fish (scampi, to be exact) and chips (OR 5.9). Local bands showcased some evenings; themed nights like "quiz night" pack the house. Open daily noon-3pm and 6-11pm. 21+ admitted.

👁 SIGHTS

RUWI

THE SULTAN'S ARMED FORCES MUSEUM. Exhibits here depict Oman's brutal military history in vivid and gory detail. Photographs, weapons, military attire, and posted essays trace the violent narrative of Oman's major military battles, including the suppression of Marxist-Communist insurgents in the Southern Dhofar Region. Outside of the museum is a mini-amusement park for bloodthirsty military buffs, who can climb inside and explore preserved battleships and tanks. Imagine the carnage! (Tel. 796 880. Near the Mutrah flyover. From the Al-Burj Roundabout, follow Al-Burj St. and take the 1st left before the traffic light onto Al-Murarama St. Pass the Mercure Al-Falaj Hotel on your left and follow the winding road for 5min.; the museum is signposted on the right before the intersection with Bait Al-Falaj St. Open Su and W 8am-12:30pm. Admission OR 1.)

NATIONAL MUSEUM. A small but impressive exhibit of Oman's African influences (see **In and Out of Africa,** p. 663). Model *dhows*, latticed door designs, and carved furniture colorfully depict Oman's links with Zanzibar, the second capital of the Omani Empire in 1832. (Tel. 701 289. Near the Ruwi Roundabout and the Ruwi Bus Station. On An-Noor St., the road running from the corner of the Mosque al-Qaboos, close to the intersection with Al-Burj St. Open Sa-W 8am-2pm. Free.)

MUTRAH

SUR AL-LAWATIYA DISTRICT. A guarded gate and archway just after the Aj-Jami' Mosque mark the entrance to this UNESCO Human Heritage Site. Facing the entrance to the Mutrah Souq, head to the right. A labyrinth of alleyways winds through the traditional residential district of the **Lawatis,** members of a Shi'ite sect of Islam, who have lived here as merchants since the 16th century. The Lawatis are known for the delicate lattice work on the balconies of their homes; their white houses are also adorned with stained-glass Arabesque windows and Zanzibar-style carved doors. Some of the famed old balconies are still in good condition and can be appreciated from the adjacent corniche, as outsiders are not permitted within the city walls. Dress modestly and ask permission before snapping pictures.

MUTRAH WATCHTOWER. The Mutrah Watchtower is behind the Al-Inshirah Complex on the small peninsula opposite Riyam Park and the Incense Burner Monument. The watchtower gives spectacular views of the bay and corniche from the top of its 100 steps. To reach the entrance of the watchtower, walk to the right behind the Al-Inshirah Restaurant.

OTHER SIGHTS. Riyam Park, along the corniche, is more or less a children's amusement park, but the UFO-like **Incense Burner Monument** resting atop the highest cliff gives excellent views of the bay and is not as steep a climb as the watchtower. The monument was constructed in 1990 as part of the Omani National Day celebration. **Mutrah Fort,** on the corniche opposite Riyam Park, is closed to the public, but it's a scenic photo shot. *(Riyam Park open Sa-W 4-11pm, Th-F 9am-midnight.)*

AL-KHUWAIR AND MEDINAT AS-SULTAN QABOOS

NATURAL HISTORY MUSEUM. Oman's wildlife, including leopards and birds stuffed and displayed in their "natural" habitats, has never looked so vibrant. The skill of Oman's taxidermists and diorama-artists is more compelling than the nation's zoological legacy. Geological history section includes the exciting world of fossils—too bad you can't stuff a rock. A separate Hall of Whales is dominated by the skeleton of a randy 23-year old sperm whale (*physeter macrocephalus*, or *Lorentzus Xianus*); legend has it that he followed his mate up into the waters of Panama and back. *(Tel. 602 555 or 604 957, ext. 166. Take a microbus from the city center heading towards Seeb airport and get off at the Al-Khuwair Roundabout. Then hire a taxi to take you to the museum. Open Sa-W 8am-2pm, Th 9am-1pm, F and Su 4-7pm. Free.)*

OMANI MUSEUM. Perched atop a rocky cliff with a killer view, this two-story museum brims with insightful information about Oman's forts (a worthwhile first stop before embarking upon *Le Grand Tour des Forts* north of Muscat). The natural history and early history rooms offer the only detailed archaeological exhibits in Muscat. Traditional jewelry, clothing, and pottery displayed upstairs. *(Tel. 600 946. In Medinat as-Sultan Qaboos, bordering Al-Qurm, atop a hill called Information City. You'll need a cab to get there—minimum OR 6 round-trip from the Al-Khuwair Roundabout, OR 8-10 from the city center). Open Sa-W 8am-2pm, Th 9am-1pm. Free.)*

OLD TOWN MUSCAT

BAIT AZ-ZUBAIR. Far and away Muscat's finest heritage museum. Bait az-Zubair (House of Zubair) was once the home of Minister and State Council member Zubair Ibn 'Ali. When Zubair bought the Bait al-Bagh (House of Gardens, as it was then called) in 1914, it was one of the largest houses in Muscat and a frequent meeting place for scholars, poets, and statesmen. Today, the Zubair family's private collection of *khanajir* (traditional daggers; singular *khanjar*), jewelry, and traditional clothing is housed inside. Remarkably helpful guided tours are given for free. *(Tel. 736 688; email bazubair@gto.net.om. The museum is off of As-Saidiyah St. From Mutrah, follow Al-Bahri Rd. to Old Town Muscat, where the road curves and becomes As-Saidiyah St. The entrance to Bait az-Zubair is in a parking lot after the second sharp curve and the HSBC bank, the last right turn before the sign for the Omani French Museum appears. Open Sa 4-8pm; M and W 4-7pm; Su, Tu, and Th 9am-12:30pm. Admission OR 1.5.)*

OMANI FRENCH MUSEUM (BAIT FRANSA). This small museum commemorating France's relationship with Oman is located in the 19th-century Bait Fransa (House of France), the residence of the French consuls from 1896 until 1920. A vice-consul died here in 1908; the official record states that he was *assassiné par un coup de chaleur* ("assassinated by the heat"). Sultan Qaboos and France's President Mitterand opened the museum in 1992; its holdings range from traditional French and

Omani attire to photographs of diplomatic visits. *(Tel. 736 613. From Mutrah, follow the main road to Muscat, turn left on As-Saidiyah St., and go through the arched entryway of Bab al-Kabir onto Qasr al-Alam St. The museum is signposted on the right. Minibuses from Mutrah (200 baisa) only go as far as the Bab Al-Kabir archway. Open Sa-W 8:30am-1pm. Free.)*

FORT MIRANI AND FORT JALALI. Only dignitaries can enter these twin forts (built by the Portuguese in the 16th century), but the public can get their *phil* of the museums inside. Both forts flank the Al-Alam Palace overlooking the bay, and were once the scene of some vicious sea battles. Fort Jalali was used as a prison; its sole entrance is up a steep flight of stairs accessible only by sea. For the best views, make a right after exiting Bait Fransa and follow the main road to the bay.

SCENIC VIEWS. The most spectacular view in Muscat originates from the **Qantab Overlook.** Qantab Rd., the main route to Bandar Jussa Beach and the fishing community of Qantab, winds through breathtaking mountain scenery. A small car park overlook on the left side of the road offers a vista that would make Little Joe Cook gasp for air. Early birds can see the sun rise, but the view is awesome at any time of day. Follow signs for Qantab from the Al-Bustan Roundabout, or take a taxi from Ruwi (at least OR 6 round-trip). The hill and overlook on the main road to **Sidab,** a small fishing village, offer staggering views of the gleaming sea, rocky mountains, and Islamic architecture below. The best vistas are at the top of the hill closest to Muscat, before the road dips into Sidab's center. Follow As-Saidiyah St., the main road from Muscat; there are signs pointing the way to Sidab. **Hiramel,** another tiny fishing village just south of Sidab, offers a glimpse into traditional Muscati life and architecture. Follow the road from Sidab; the left turn for Hiramel is signposted on the main road. If you have a car, park on the tarmac road and wander by foot through the maze of narrow streets, as it is impossible to drive in this area.

🛍 SHOPPING

Muscat's shopping malls are clustered in Al-Qurm; the **Sabco Center** and the **Commercial Center** both have several crafts shops and tourist-geared *"souqs"* selling Omani handicrafts and weavings. However, the old *souq* on the Mutrah corniche is a more colorful (and authentic) place to buy the same goods.

Unlike many of the other Gulf State *souqs* (which are basically modern flea markets), the **Mutrah Souq** has managed to hold on to its heritage. The Souq is a maze of shops selling spices, *khanajir*, carved wooden boxes, jewelry, perfumes, modern clothing, and shoes. It is surrounded by traditional Islamic sights: white-washed buildings with delicate latticed balconies, a beautiful blue-domed mosque with intricate painting on the edges of its dome, and a *dhow*-filled harbor. Aside from the standard complement of spices and jewelry, the Mutrah Souq has some unusual goods available for purchase, such as carved, wooden jewelry boxes and concentrated perfume scents sold in delicate glass bottles. Prices range widely from shop to shop depending on quality; never settle for the first price offered, or even the second or third. Souvenir *khanajir* range in price from OR 5 to OR 60; the more expensive ones have been passed down through the ages, while the smaller, cheaper ones were probably made in Nizwa but still make attractive souvenirs. The entrance to the *souq* is at the first traffic light after the As-Samakah Roundabout heading towards Muscat (open 8am-1pm and 4-7:30pm).

◧ BEACHES AND PARKS

BANDAR JUSSA BEACH. Rocky cliffs and gleaming turquoise water surround this long stretch of bright sand, Muscat's most popular public beach, southeast of the city center. On weekends and holidays, locals pack the waterfront and fishermen suspend their daily work to shuttle tourists to secluded beaches along the coast. You can hire fishermen to go out to the beaches of **Jassah** and **Khayran,** where you can **snorkel** in the coral reefs (provided you have the equipment). Settle on a price before departing, and arrange for the fisherman to pick you up from the secluded shore of your choice at a specific time—otherwise you'll find yourself up the creek without a paddle. *(If driving, follow the signs from the Al-Bustan Roundabout in Qantab. Sea taxi fares are posted on a green sign board next to the snackshop by the beach entrance. Minibuses from any of Muscat's centers will go up to Bandar Jussa, though usually only on weekends when there's the most demand. During the week, you'll probably have to engage a taxi; expect to pay a minimum of OR 5 each way.)*

AL-QURM PARK AND NATURE RESERVE. In keeping with its commitment to protect the environment, the Omani government opened this 570,000 square meter nature reserve and adjacent black mangrove *(qurm)* forest in 1993. A local favorite on the weekends, thestretch of park—which includes rose gardens, fountains, and a lake—runs from Al-Qurm St. all the way to the sandy beach. At the far end of the park, the Nature Reserve has a sanctuary for many migratory birds. **Horseback rides** in winter from 4-11pm (short loop 500 baisa, full garden OR 3, 1hr. along beach OR 10). *(On Al-Qurm St. next to the Al-Qurm Amusement Park. From Muscat, take a bus heading towards Seeb and get off at the As-Sabco Commercial Ctr.; hail a cab from there for OR 1.5. **Sound and light shows** on M, Th, and F evenings. Open Sa-W 4-11pm, Th-F 9am-midnight.)*

AL-BUSTAN PALACE BEACH. In Al-Bustan, between Sidab and Qantab. This private hotel beach offers impressive but expensive pool, beach, tennis, and gym facilities. The long stretch of beach at the Al-Bustan is generally less crowded than the public sands in Al-Qurm and Bandar Jussa, and single women will arouse less unwanted attention. The Al-Bustan offers a full range of **water sports** (no, not that kind) for additional fees. Snorkeling trips, water skiing, and windsurfing can all be arranged at the beach. *(Tel. 799 666. Free for hotel guests, but a whopping OR 6 on weekdays and OR 10 on weekends for non-guests. Open 10am-sunset.)*

QALBUH BAY PARK. On the waterfront in Mutrah, less than 1km towards Muscat from the Riyam Roundabout. The town of Qalbuh is signposted on the main road; turn left into the parking area past white houses and a blue-domed mosque. A tranquil place to stroll in the early evening. Settle down on a bench or in the grassy picnic area and watch the sunset beyond Riyam Park's trippy Incense Burner Monument (see p. 655). *(Open Sa-Th 3-11pm, F and holidays 8am-midnight.)*

AL-KHARUS PARK. This long shell-strewn beach is dotted with palms, barbeque sites, and dried palm leaf umbrellas. At the far right end of the beach, fishermen dock their boats on the sandy cove. There are no food stands, so pack a picnic lunch. *(No minivans or buses go here; take a taxi from the Al-Qurm Roundabout near Sabco Commercial Ctr. for OR 2. Open 24hr. Free.)*

NEAR MUSCAT

What pyramids are to Egypt, forts are to Oman. The three forts in Muscat (see p. 656) are not open to the public, but several fortresses a few hours north are a veritable *Tour des Forts*. If you are traveling from Sohar to Muscat, these forts make convenient rest stops. With a car, you can see all the forts in one day; otherwise, take a **taxi**, as bus service to these towns is infrequent.

BARKA

***Microbuses** from Muscat go as far as the signposted junction on the Muscat-Sohar Hwy. (Ruwi to Seeb clocktower 500 baisa, Seeb clocktower to Barka junction 300 baisa). From the Barka junction, hop on a microbus heading to the Barka town center (100 baisa). The **fort** is along the main road leading to the town center. **Open** daily 7:30am-6pm. The **souq** and **beach** are across the lot from the fort. The **bullfighting arena** is 4km farther down the main road. Past the town center, there is a large clearing that extends for 1km, with a lone, white, fort-shaped building in the middle. The arena is 250m past this building before the roundabout. **Microbuses** from Barka will head down this way (150 baisa).*

Some say that Barka (48km from Muscat on the road to Sohar) is just another ordinary Omani town, but that's a load of bull. The village actually preserves one of the most unusual traditions in the region: **bullfighting.** On alternate Fridays, two Brahmin bulls (carefully matched in size, age, and weight) are pitted against each other. Unlike the sanguine standoffs in Spain, Omani bullfights end before either animal has shed a drop of blood; if you're thirsting for blood sports, you will be barking up the wrong tree. Indeed, the bulls even have ropes tied to them so they can be pulled apart should they become too violent. In a cultural variation of the universally known game of "Chicken," the first bull to run away is declared the loser. Fights last from around 4pm until sunset and are free and open to the public.

If you've come on the wrong Friday, Barka also offers a tremendous castle-fort, a busy *souq*, and serene beaches. The **Barka Fort,** one of the largest in Oman, puts the forts in Sohar and Mutrah to shame. The structure itself consists of several multi-level courtyards and towers linked by narrow winding stairways, with rooms almost entirely bare save a few pieces of old weaponry and Persian rugs. Catch good views of the coastline and town from the upper levels of the fort. The **souq** is on the beach, directly across from the fort. In the early morning, fishermen reel in the catch of the day, then sell their seafood alongside fresh produce vendors.

NAKHL

To get to the fort and hot springs, follow the directions from Muscat to Barka (see above). At the Barka junction, hop on a minibus heading for Nakhal (300 baisa). Under a tree at the base of the fort, share taxis and minibuses can transport you to the Ath-Thowara Hot Springs (150 baisa or less from Nakhal Fort to the Hot Springs).

By far Oman's most impressive of its kind, the **Nakhal Fort** resides approximately 25km from the Barka Roundabout atop a 200-foot mountain peak. It overlooks the lush rolling date plantations that make Nakhal one of the greenest spots in the Batinah Plain. The fort consists of six towers (each 30m tall), a mosque with an intricately carved entrance, and a dungeon (open daily 7:30am-5pm).

Dip into warm blue waters and relax in the shade of palm trees at **Ath-Thowarah Hot Springs,** a popular local picnic site. Children wade through the water trying to grab the tiny fish scurrying by while men and (fully clothed) women relax in separate areas of the springs. Tourists can also "swim" in the springs but must respect local customs: no tank tops, shorts, or bathing suits. Wear light cotton fabrics and jump in clothed as the locals do.

NORTHERN OMAN

NIZWA

The blazing glory of the 6th- and 7th-century capital of Oman has faded to the glimmer of a frenetically paced *souq* (the production site for most of the jewelry and *khanajir* sold in the Mutrah Souq in Muscat) and one of the country's most interesting forts. Although palm-enclosed Nizwa, bordered by an 8km long oasis of date plantations, is the largest city in the interior of Oman, it's only worth a one-night stopover to explore the town and nearby forts.

⚄ ORIENTATION AND PRACTICAL INFORMATION. The town of Nizwa consists of one long road that stretches from the first roundabout, past the posh Nizwa Hotel (approximately 20km from the town center), all the way to the **Bahla Roundabout,** half a block past the lively *souq* area and town center. Accommodations are scarce and pricey, but are all easily found on the main Muscat-Nizwa Hwy. **Buses, microbuses,** and **taxis** all park in the lot in front of the *souq*. There are three buses to and from Ruwi, Muscat, and Nizwa daily—two express and one regular (2½-3hr.). Purchase tickets on the bus (OR 2). If you're making this a daytrip from Muscat, take a microbus from the Seeb Clocktower Roundabout in Muscat. Unless you come in a taxi, it's not a good idea to stay overnight because there's little room for a backpack on the cramped minibuses (OR 1.8). **Bank Muscat** (tel. 410 988), half a block past the Falaj Daris Hotel, opposite the BP gas station before the second roundabout, cashes AmEx traveler's checks only, and has an **ATM** with Visa, MC, AmEx, Cirrus, and PLUS links. Continuing straight through the roundabout, Nizwa's larger **grocery stores** flank the road. Additional groceries are located in the *souq* area, but are smaller and offer less selection. The **post office** is inside the *souq*, at the corner farthest from the fort on the main road (open Sa-W 9am-2pm, Th 8-11am). Continue around the curve in front of the fort for additional restaurants and **Oman International Bank** (tel. 410 036), whose **ATM** has Visa and MC links. The last roundabout forks, with one branch leading to Bahla, the other to Muscat.

■■ **ACCOMMODATIONS AND FOOD.** Nizwa may be a self-proclaimed tourist haven, but the pickings here are slim and rather expensive. The newly-opened **Majan Guest House** (tel. 431 910; fax 431 911) is hard to miss, 500m from the first roundabout coming from Muscat. This gleaming white building features luxurious rooms with elaborate private entrances and a bright, endearing decor (singles OR 20; doubles OR 25). The **Falaj Daris Hotel** (tel. 410 500; fax 410 537) is more expensive and less stellar than those at the Majan Guest House. Despite the overpriced quarters, the rooms are quite comfortable, and there's even a swimming pool to provide much-needed relief from the Gulf heat (singles OR 21.8; doubles OR 29.5; credit cards accepted).

There are a couple of good restaurants in the *souq* area that serve traditional Omani dishes as well as Arabic and Indian cuisine. **Arab World Restaurant** (tel. 410 708) serves heaping portions of grilled chicken, kebabs, and shawarma with bread, hummus, and salad (OR 1.7; open daily 6:30am-midnight). There are two locations: one in the shopping strip that runs from the Bahla Roundabout to the Fort (next to Oman International Bank) and one at the end of the shopping strip between the Majan Guest House and the Falaj Daris Hotel. Inside the *souq* itself, the **Al-Agar Restaurant** (tel. 411 043), to the left of the entrance facing the watchtower and fort, serves flavorful Omani dishes in a colorful, authentic atmosphere (OR 2.5 for a full meal). Straw mats, Persian rugs, and cushions provide the only seating in the spacious dining room, and the old weapons and artifacts covering the walls give the impression that you've stumbled into a crafts shop rather than a restaurant. No matter where you are in Oman, **Pizza Hut** (tel. 412 096) can deliver a piping hot pan pizza to your door. If you'd like to dine under its glaring red roof, the popular fast food chain is between the Falaj Davis Hotel and Bank Muscat.

A DATED TRADITION Dates, often called the "brides of the desert," have long been a symbol of Bedouin hospitality. When camel-driven caravans used to cross the desert along ancient trade routes, they would often stop at Bedouin camps. The type of hospitality offered by the Bedouin indicated not only if they were pleased with the caravan's arrival, but also whether they would offer the caravan protection. If the merchants were offered **dates and coffee,** it was a sign that the Bedouin would assure the caravan's safety until it was out of sight of the camp. If the Bedouin offered a **meal** afterward, they would guarantee the caravan's safety for one day's journey. An offer to **stay overnight** meant that the Bedouin would ensure a safe journey for three days after departure. Bedouin tradition dictated that if the caravan were attacked during the indicated time period, the Bedouin hosts would be obligated to avenge the attack. Although caravans no longer traverse the desert, the tradition of offering dates, coffee, and even an overnight stay is still widely practiced. Wherever you go in Oman, you will more often than not be presented with dates and Arabic coffee *(ahwa)*. To refuse such hospitality is an insult to your Bedouin hosts, so accept the refreshments and consider yourself a guest of honor.

🔵 **SIGHTS.** Most items for sale in the Mutrah *souq* were made here in Nizwa, but the town's self-proclaimed status as a major tourist attraction has caused prices to skyrocket. Better bargains can be found in Muscat, but the **Nizwa Souq** is a sight in itself. The eclectic market sells everything from goats to silver *khanajir*, and the shops overflow with Omani handicrafts. The *souq* is busiest in the early morning and late evening (open Sa-Th 8am-1pm and 4:30-9pm). Nizwa's **fort** and **castle** are enclosed within the same high stone wall (called As-Salah) at the far end of the *souq*, but were constructed at different times. The castle, the oldest part of the complex, was built in 851 CE, when Nizwa was made the capital of Oman. It once contained a sheep farm, a ladies' jail, living quarters for the army, stables, wells, and even a secret conversation room. The fort, an imposing round tower 35m high and 45m in diameter, was added centuries later as a residence for the Imams and Walis (open daily in summer 8am-4:30pm; in winter 8am-5:30pm; free).

NEAR NIZWA: BAHLA AND JABRIN

*Take a **minibus** from Nizwa to the Jabrin bus stop, about 20min. down the Nizwa-Bahla-Jabrin road. The **Jabrin Fort** is approximately 3½km down the only road on your left from the Jabrin bus stop, 2min. from **Bahla**. Ask the driver if he'll go down to the fort, off the roundabout at the end of the road. If you're lucky, he will only charge 700-800 baisa for the completed journey from Nizwa. Otherwise, you can **walk** (if it's not too hot) or wait at the bus stop for a **taxi** to drive by. Alternately, you can catch a taxi to the Jabrin Fort from the bus stop in front of the Bahla Fort, but it will cost around OR 5 round-trip. Jabrin Fort **open** daily 8am-5pm.*

The large, crumbling structure on the left of the main road leading from Nizwa to the hilly green town of Bahla is the **Bahla Fort,** recently named a UNESCO World Heritage Site. The deteriorating, pre-Islamic era mudbrick walls don't appear too impressive at the moment, but the fort is currently undergoing major renovations that are scheduled to be completed in time for the arrival of the new millennium. Until the fort re-opens, stay in your minibus and look out the window on your left for a view of Bahla's ancient **city wall.** The wall begins near the bottom of the hill before the Bahla Fort and continues to the town center.

Once in Jabrin, spend some time exploring its own majestic fort. The **Jabrin Fort** was constructed in 1671 by the Imam Bal'arab Bin Sultan Al-Ya'ribi as a palace (the Imam is also buried in a tomb within the fort). The remains are majestic and well-preserved, and the rooms filled with furnishings and weaponry that give a good sense of what life was like in the home of 17th-century Arab nobility.

SOHAR

Although Sohar was once the largest and most important trading town in Oman, as well as the site of many battles between the Omanis and the Portuguese, there's not very much happening there today. Perhaps the stories of adventurous Sohar native **Sindbad the Sailor** (or *Sindibad*, in Arabic) were invented in hopes that a few misguided tourists would want to spend a night or two in his hometown; the only other real draw for tourists in Sohar is the fort. Although it is a coastal town, the beaches have dark sand, and garbage is strewn all along the shores.

🔳 ORIENTATION AND PRACTICAL INFORMATION

There are two central districts in Sohar. Both are by the **Sohar Roundabout,** marked by a massive globe. The bus stop, central market, GPO, and bank are all on **An-Nahda Street** in the Old Hospital Area. The other central district is near the **Old Fort** running parallel to the **corniche,** and is home to several coffee shops and supermarkets. The two hotels are located past the **Mosque-on-Stilts Roundabout,** near Sallan Roundabout, north of the center of town. There are four daily buses to **Muscat,** two express (4hr.) and two regular (6½hr.). **Express** buses leave from the gas station on the Dubai-Muscat Hwy., about 3km past the Globe Roundabout from either hotel. **Regular** buses leave from the bus stop in front of the Old Hospital. Both buses leave around 8am and 3pm, but the schedule changes frequently; check with **Oman**

National Transport Co. (tel. 590 046) for exact times. The only means of local transport in Sohar are **share taxis**. Trips between either of the central districts should cost about 100 baisa, but taxis are not metered, so settle on a price beforehand. **Women** should sit in the back seat if they are alone; otherwise, they may fall victim to unwelcome advances from the driver. **Bank Muscat** (tel. 841 784), on An-Nahda St. behind the GPO, has **ATMs** with Visa, MC, PLUS, and Cirrus connections. There are also several exchange bureaus around the Central Market. **Hakim Trading Stores** (tel. 851 144), directly across the street from the SPO, sells food, toiletries, and stationery (open daily 8:30am-1:30pm and 4:30-11pm). In an **emergency**, call 999. **Muscat Pharmacy** is on As-Souq St. next to Commercial Bank (open Sa-Th 8am-1pm and 4-10pm, F 9-11:30am and 5-8:30pm). One pharmacy in town stays open all night, but duties rotate; check the *Khalij Times* for the schedule. **Sohar Hospital** (tel. 840 166 or 840 544), is west of the city center. The **post office** (tel. 840 003; fax 840 052), on An-Nahda St., has **fax** and **telegram** services (open Sa-W 8am-2pm, Th 8-11am).

ACCOMMODATIONS

There are only two places to stay in Sohar, and neither is a bargain. Muscat's cheaper accommodations are only three hours away. If you do stay in Sohar, share taxis are the only means of transport to the hotels. A ride to either hotel from the share taxi stand or regular bus stop in front of the Old Hospital should cost around 300 baisa. Although fairly overpriced, **Al-Wadi Hotel** (tel. 840 058 or 841 995; fax 841 997), 9km from the center of Sohar on the Dubai-Muscat Hwy., is the cheaper of Sohar's two options. The hotel is shaped like a fort with rooms lining the circular courtyard, its entryway is decorated like a Persian sitting room, and rooms are *cabana* style with an average-sized bedroom and private bath. There's also a swimming pool, restaurant, and bar (singles OR 23.1; doubles OR 31.5; suite OR 52.5). The **Sohar Beach Hotel** (tel. 843 701; fax 843 776), is 5km north of town, off As-Souq Rd. Rooms here are bigger than at the Al-Wadi, and your bill will increase proportionally to size. The building is completely white on the exterior, brilliantly contrasting with the bright stained-glass windows. Although their pool is a landscaped masterpiece, the beachfront outside of the hotel is less than impressive (singles OR 29; doubles OR 35; add a whopping 17% hotel tax).

FOOD

There aren't too many culinary options in Sohar unless your budget is flexible enough to afford a *minimum* of OR 3 to dine at either of the hotels. Most of the cheap eateries are on An-Nahda St. by the Central Market and Old Hospital. The **Riyadh Restaurant** (tel. 841 719), next to the Central Market and across the street from the Old Hospital and the bus stop, serves *biryanis* and curries. A full meal, including soda, runs about 700 baisa. The **Naif Ash-Shisawi Trading Coffee Shop** (tel. 845 40) is farther up An-Nahda St. Facing the Central Market with the Old Hospital behind you, make a left and walk past the GPO; it awaits just past the fork in the road, on your left. Besides the obvious, the coffee shop also serves chicken and mutton burgers (300 baisa). Vegetarians should not be fooled by the "vegetable burger"—it's really just a mutton burger with lettuce and tomatoes (open 6am-midnight). There are similar coffee shops and restaurants along the corniche.

SIGHTS

Sohar's main attraction is the **Sohar Fort.** One of the largest forts in Oman, it dates back to the early 1300s and was once crucial in the defence of the Strait of Hormuz. Legend says that it took 1000 men to defend the fort, though it fell to the Portuguese in 1507 without a single cannon being fired. The **museum** (tel. 844 758) lies inside the crumbling walls of one of the fort's towers. Exhibits include a detailed photographic presentation of Sohar's history, archaeological excavations of ancient pottery and handicrafts, and some old weaponry. Check out the view of

OMAN

the Gulf and Sohar's architecture from the roof of the museum (open Sa-W 8am-2pm, Th-F 8am-noon and 4pm-6pm). Earlybirds can catch a glimpse of the **Fish Souq,** the wooden structure on the corniche, about 2km north of the Fort. Fishing is still one of Sohar's main industries (open 6-11am).

SUR صور

Sur once served as a port for trade with lands as distant as Africa and the Far East, and its architecture shows it: the old structures are dotted with intricately carved wooden doors and arabesque windows reminiscent of the whitewashed buildings of Zanzibar (see **In and Out of Africa,** p. 663). Today, Sur is a sleepy, seafaring town that offers tranquil beaches and a glimpse at the international influences that color Omani history. Its quiet residential districts and the lull of the wooden *dhows* bobbing up and down in the harbor make Sur a peaceful and relaxing refuge from noisy and overcrowded Muscat, about four hours away.

◪ ORIENTATION AND PRACTICAL INFORMATION. Few of Sur's streets have names. Arriving from Muscat, Sur's main road begins at the **Clocktower Roundabout.** Bearing left at the stop sign at the end of this road leads to the beach and the *dhow* building yards; bearing right puts you on **Souq Road,** which runs through the *souq* area in the central part of town. There are many **bus stops** (with posted bus schedules) all along this main road, usually next to the roundabouts. Two daily express buses and one regular bus shuttle over to **Muscat** (6hr., express 4hr.; OR 3.5); purchase tickets on board. **Minibuses** and **taxis** are also easily found along this road. The **National Bank of Oman** (tel. 440 246), down Souq Rd. away from Muscat, has an **ATM** with MC and Cirrus links and cashes AmEx traveler's checks only. Bear right at the curved side road that begins at the bank, and the Sur Hotel will appear on your left. **'Ali Khamis Supermarket** (tel. 440 851) vends its goods opposite the Sur Hotel (open daily 7:30am-1pm and 4:30-11pm). **Bank Muscat** (tel. 443 350), on the next corner on the right, has a better connected **ATM** (with Visa, MC, AmEx, Cirrus, and PLUS links) and also cashes AmEx traveler's checks. Make a left at Bank Muscat for a reliable travel agency, **Bahwan Travel** (tel. 444 712), on the first corner on the left (open 8am-1pm and 4:30-7:30pm). Several **laundries** are located in this area, as well as **Aj-Jawi Pharmacy** (tel. 441 188; open daily 8:30am-1pm and 4:30-11:30pm). Check a daily paper for the 24-hour pharmacy on duty. Follow the smell of fish back toward Bank Muscat and continue down the road to the **Fish Market** and **bus station.** Back on the main Sur-Muscat road, the **post office** is to the left of the roundabout between Sinesla Fort and the Bahwan Mosque, heading away from Muscat.

▟▙ ACCOMMODATIONS AND FOOD. Deciding on a place to crash in Sur won't be difficult considering the limited options: there are a whopping three hotels, and only two are reasonable choices for a traveler on a budget. (If you've got a backpack, expect to be sent away with an upturned nose at the snobbish Sur Mercure Hotel.) Of the two viable options, the better bet is the **Sur Beach Hotel** (tel 442 031; fax 442 228). Get off at the bus stop immediately before the Sinesla Fort-Pizza Hut Roundabout and take a taxi 3½km down the road (OR 1.5). Sur's self-proclaimed "oasis of comfort," this hotel lures travelers with bright, commodious rooms and balconies overlooking the sea. Such luxury does not come cheap: singles cost OR 28, doubles OR 35 (plus 17% tax). All major credit cards are accepted. The **Sur Hotel** (tel. 440 090; fax 443 798) is more centrally situated in the *souq* area, between the National Bank of Oman and Bank Muscat. It's within walking distance of the bus station by the market, and a taxi should cost OR 1. The management seems to have invested more money in decorating the impressive entryway with an elaborately carved Zanzibari doorway than it did in furnishing the rather small, dismal rooms. Quality and price vary, so look at a few rooms before settling down. According to several locals, the Sur Hotel isn't the safest place for women traveling alone (singles OR 12.6, with bath and toilet OR 13.8; doubles OR 17.25, with bath and toilet OR 28.75; cash only).

IN AND OUT OF AFRICA

Sur has been an important seafaring port since the 6th century CE, when local merchants began trading with cities along the East African coast. The boats they used to follow the Indian Ocean's monsoon winds were remarkably similar to those still constructed in Sur's *dhow* building yard (see p. 663). Trading routes stretched from Sur to the towns of Lamu, Mombasa, and Dar es-Salaam, now in Kenya and Tanzania. Some *dhows* even traveled as far south as the famed spice islands of **Zanzibar**, off the southern coast of modern-day Tanzania. The contact between these Arab traders and the Swahili people gave Omani life the distinctly African flavor one can still taste today. Arab traders influenced the language of **Kiswahili** so much that today it is a combination of Arab and African dialects, and is spoken both in East Africa and along the coast of Oman. East Africans also revolutionized fashion in Oman: men unwrapped their turbans and donned the small, boxy hats called **kamus** first worn in Zanzibar. The most distinct evidence of a cultural exchange between Africa and Oman is the magnificent architecture in both regions. The intricately carved **wooden doors** that dot the otherwise simple white architecture in Sur have their origin in East Africa, where such craftwork began on the islands of Lamu and Zanzibar. The architectural exchange went both ways: the arabesque windows so characteristic of much of the Arab world appear in East African buildings.

The *souq* area is crowded with *biryani* frying, shawarma grilling coffee shops. The **Turkish Sheep Restaurant** (signposted on the main Sur-Muscat road at the Muscat Pharmacy Roundabout) offers outdoor dining with a "scenic" view of the highway. The restaurant may be big, but the menu is not; nevertheless, the few dishes up for grabs are ample, delicious, and served in record time. Grilled chicken tikka comes with hummus, Arabic bread, and salad (OR 1.3). Fresh juice goes for 300 baisa. **Al-Mutailie Chinese Food Restaurant** (tel. 938 41 22), behind the Sur Hotel near Bahwan Travel and Aj-Jawi Pharmacy, serves up noodle and rice dishes for OR 1-1.4 and chicken entrees for OR 1-1.5. Seafood is a bit pricier: prawns and other aquatic delicacies cost as much as OR 3. American fast food chains are crammed into in every nook and cranny of Sur.

■ ♫ SIGHTS AND ENTERTAINMENT. Sur's main sights can all be enjoyed in a day. If you're not pooped come nightfall, head to the **Cheer's Bar,** on the second floor of the Sur Beach Hotel, for some low-energy diversion. The live Filipino entertainment is a telltale sign that this small bar is frequented mainly by older local men, joined by some hotel guests (21+ admitted; no cover; open daily 6pm-midnight).

BILAD AND SINESLA FORTS. The crumbling **Bilad Fort,** over 200 years old, is nestled in a small mud hut village enclosed by date palms. To reach it, hop on a **microbus** from the *souq* area or the main road (200 baisa), and ride approximately 6km away from the town center toward Muscat. Just past the Al-Maha Gas Station, on the right between the Sur Mercure Hotel and the Clocktower Roundabout, a green sign with a picture of the fort points down a narrow cobblestone path; the fort is at the end of this road. For a more majestic fort-going experience, take a minibus to the **Sinesla Fort** Roundabout. This fort is in less of a state of disarray than Bilad, but despite its fortuitous preservation, there's still not much to see inside. *(Bilad Fort open daily 7:30am-6pm. Sinesla Fort open daily 7:30am-6pm. Both forts are free.)*

AYEGA AND DHOW BUILDING YARD. Enclosed by a camel-colored wall, the **dhow building yard** houses these traditional wooden fishing boats in various stages of construction. The tiny fishing village of **Ayega,** which can be seen across the sound, is home to most of the men building the *dhows*, and offers some of Sur's best architecture in a peaceful excursion from the mainland. The ferry dock (just a stone stoop) is accessible through the parking lot directly before the yard. Two official government buildings with royal flags flank the entrance to this lot. Climb aboard the small wooden boat that ferries passengers across the water for free. Alternately, nice vistas of Ayega can be viewed under the shade provided by the verandas in the small park half a block before the *dhow* building yard. Continuing 2km farther down this road is another harbor where finished *dhows* bob in the water. The main **public beaches** where the locals hang-ten and play volleyball are along the coast between the turn-off from the main road near the town center and the park facing Ayega. Additional beaches line the area around the Sur Beach Hotel. All of these beaches are public, so local custom and modesty should be observed. *(Follow the main Sur-Muscat road to its end, make a left at the stop sign, and continue around the bend along the coast for 3km. Microbuses also head out this way (500 baisa). The dhow yard is on the left after the bend in the road, where there's a small park dotted with verandas.)*

NEAR SUR: RAS AL-HADD

These **beaches** comprise one of the largest nesting grounds in the Indian Ocean for the endangered sea turtle. Nesting season is in the fall (Sept.-Nov.), and access to the nesting grounds is closely monitored during this time: specific guidelines must be followed so as not to disturb the dwindling population of this almost extinct species. The best time to see the turtles is early dawn, when natural light allows for flashless photography. To get to Ras al-Hadd, you will need to make arrangements through a tour company in Muscat, as there are none in Sur. Taxis, minivans, and buses do not go out this way because of the condition of the road. If you have hired your own **four-wheel drive** vehicle, you can brave the road and drive to the beaches from Sur (approximately 3hr.). From Sur, follow the Muscat-Sur road to **Al-Kamil** (30min. away) by turning right off the main road and following the signs. In Al-Kamil, pass through the roundabout and follow signs for **Al-Askara.** Get on Route 23m, which will wind through the Wahiba Sands; 30 minutes along this road, a sign labeled "Ras al-Hadd" will point to the left down a dirt-gravel track leading to the turtle beaches. A **permit** is needed to enter the conservation site; get it from the Ministry of Regional Municipalities and Environment at the site before 9:30pm (OR 1). When you pick up your permit, be sure to get the leaflet with detailed guidelines about how to observe the turtles without disturbing them. **Camping** is allowed on the beach inland of the "No Entry" signs, but no fire, lights, or vehicles are allowed on the sands. Excessive noise, flash photography, and campfires will get you kicked off the beach and fined OR 125.

MUSANDEM PENINSULA

The breathtaking Musandem Peninsula is a land forgotten by oil derricks and skyscrapers. The isolated region is covered almost entirely by steep, rocky mountains that jut out into the turquoise waters of the Strait of Hormuz. The coastline of the Musandem curves in and out of dozens of peninsulas, creating the main fjords Khawr Habalayn, Khawr Najd, and Khawr ash-Shamm. Visiting the Musandem Peninsula will no doubt be one of your most memorable experiences in Oman. The serenity of floating in and out of fjords, almost completely surrounded by honey-colored mountains and glistening waters, or dozing on one of the dozens of secluded beaches, is truly unforgettable.

KHASAB

Khasab is the capital of the Musandem Peninsula region, but it's little more than a sleepy town that is an excellent base for exploring the seascape and the peninsula's handful of archaeological attractions. Camp on one of the nearby beaches or go exploring during the day to get a feel for what the Musandem is really all about.

☐TRANSPORTATION. Oman Air (tel. 830 543) operates flights five days a week (1-2hr., OR 20) from Muscat to **Khasab** (Sa, M, W 8:55am; Su, Tu 6:30am) and back from Khasab to **Muscat** (Su, M, W 10:20am; Su, Tu 8:50am). No special permits or visas are needed to visit the Musandem Peninsula. The town lacks a formal mode of public transport (no buses or taxis), and tour companies will probably claim that you are at their mercy. Ignore them. Elderly locals with **private vehicles** (either four-wheel drive or sedan) and *lots* of spare time serve as makeshift taxi drivers at reasonable rates. Call Mr. Mohammed Ahmed 'Ali as-Sam (tel. 937 38 71, pager 911 03 38), or talk to 'Abdullah, who works the evening shift at the Khasab Hotel. Sample fares from the Khasab Hotel: Khasab Airport (OR 2); Bukha (OR 5); Khawr Najd (OR 5); Tawi (OR 3); Bussa Beach (OR 1); Khasab Fort (OR 1); Kuzman Fort (OR 1); New Souq (500 baisa); and Khasab Port (OR 1).

⊠ ORIENTATION AND PRACTICAL INFORMATION. For such a small town, Khasab takes up a lot of space. Visitors will inevitably find themselves at either the airport or the Khasab Hotel, both south of town. Only one road leads into the "center" of town, which consists of the **New Souq** area and the **Souq Roundabout** (the second roundabout from the airport and hotel). Turning left at the Souq Roundabout and continuing past the Oman Air shopping strip leads to the **Old Souq** (1.5km) and the **corniche** (3km). Veer left at the corniche to get to Bukha via Khasab Port and Bussa Beach; turn right to reach the Khasab Fort.

The New Souq area spreads out to the east and west of the Souq Roundabout. **Oman Air** (tel. 830 543) is at the corner of the *souq*, to the left of the roundabout (open Sa-Th 8am-1pm and 5-7pm). On the right of the roundabout, **Bank Muscat** exchanges traveler's checks and has an **ATM** with Visa, MC, AmEx, Cirrus, and PLUS connections (open Sa-W 8am-noon, Th 8-11:30am). The **National Bank of Oman** and **Oman International Bank** keep the same hours and also have ATMs, but without AmEx links. Between the banks are **Muscat Pharmacy** (tel. 830 150; open Sa-Th 8am-1pm and 4-9pm), the fax-sending **post office** (open Sa-Th 8am-2:30pm), **Al-Hawashim Trading Laundry** (open Sa-Th 8am-noon and 4-10pm, F 8-11am and 4-10pm), and **Sayoub al-Mazyoud ash-Shehi Trading Grocery Store** (open Sa-Th 8am-1pm and 4-10pm, F 4-11pm). Continue past the banks and GPO to another roundabout; straight through this roundabout and to the right stands the **Khasab Hospital** (tel. 830 137). Dial 999 for **emergencies** of any kind.

⊠ ACCOMMODATIONS. The remote serenity of the Musandem Peninsula comes with a hefty price tag, due to the monopolistic practices of Khasab's sole tour company (which also happens to own the town's only hotel). The **Khasab Hotel** (tel. 660 267; fax 660 989) is the only place to stay. The rooms, all with private bath, are clean but somewhat drab and stale, reminiscent of an overused highway motel. Nonetheless, the management and staff will bend over backwards to please you, perhaps out of guilt for the small fortune they charge for rooms (singles OR 20.5; doubles OR 34). For groups occupying four rooms or guests staying more than two nights, there's a discount if you pay in cash (singles OR 17.5; doubles OR 29). Visa and MC are also accepted, but you won't get the reduced room rates. If planning a trip during the height of the tourist season or traveling as a large group, make reservations at least two months in advance. The hotel only has 15 rooms (though plans to expand are in the works).

It is possible to **camp** for free on the beaches outside Khasab. No permits are required, but you'll need an ample supply of water since the beaches don't offer any campsite amenities. **Bussa Beach,** closest to town, is about halfway between the Khasab Port and the coastal village of Quida. The kilometer-long strip of sand is far from secluded, considering its location right smack on the main road between Bukha and Khasab. However, it's a good site for a camper's final night on the Musandem because of its proximity to the airport. The turquoise waters of the Gulf of Oman gently lap the light sands of **Khawr Najd,** a small beach enclosed by a majestic fort that overlooks the fjords on the eastern side of the Musandem. Khawr Najd is wedged between two mountainous peninsulas, and its beauty is unsurpassed in the area, particularly at sunrise. No wonder the beach is such a popular weekend site for Omani and Emirati families, who dock their yachts along the shore. This spectacular camping spot is about a 30-minute drive south of Khasab. Private taxis charge OR 5 each way; make sure to prearrange a time for your driver to return and pick you up or you'll be marooned.

IRAN FOR THE BORDER Brace yourself: the speedboat owners carrying sheep into the Khasab Port are really **Iranian smugglers.** Early in the morning, drivers empty their livestock off at Khasab, where the goats and sheep are herded off to the UAE on the large pick-up trucks parked near the port. Meanwhile, the speedboat owners spend the day shopping for American brand cigarettes at Khasab's *souqs* and relaxing by the port as they wait for nightfall. After the sun has set, the Iranians load up their boats with the contraband cigarettes and make a mad dash for Iran, trying to evade the Iranian Coast Guard before daybreak. The cigarettes are then carried by land across Iran to Afghanistan and even Russia.

🛈 **FOOD.** Culinary choices in Khasab are limited to sandwiches and cheap Indian food. **Musandem Restaurant** (tel. 830 569) dishes out *biryanis* (800 baisa) and curries (200-600 baisa). Take a left at the Souq Roundabout; the restaurant is in the shopping strip that houses Oman Air (open 6am-11pm). Several doors down in the same shopping strip is **'Abdullah Bin Muhammad Bin 'Eid ash-Sheihi Coffeeshop** (tel. 830 426), one of the few restaurants in existence whose name is longer than its menu. This tiny cafe with golden foil walls serves only one thing—sandwiches (100 baisa). There are four sandwich options: egg, mutton, falafel, or mincemeat (open Sa-Th 7am-1pm and 4:30-11pm, F 7-11am and 4:30-10pm). The Khasab Hotel's small **hotel restaurant** (tel. 660 267) serves up tasty lemon-butter *hamour* fish, grilled or fried (OR 2.5). The *fattoush* salad is a treat for veggie-lovers (OR 1.5). The restaurant is connected to the hotel's bar and serves alcohol as well (open daily for breakfast 6:45-9am, lunch noon-2:20pm, dinner 7-10:15pm).

🕐 🍹 **SIGHTS AND ENTERTAINMENT.** Khasab's nightlife is a lot more than sleepy; it's verging on comatose. There are really only two options: a late stroll along the corniche to watch the sunset, or an early drink at the Khasab Hotel. The **hotel bar,** the only place in town that serves alcohol, is a popular hangout for local men. Women may feel uncomfortable alone at the bar, but can sit in either the hotel's restaurant or lounge and order drinks (tap beer OR 1.1-1.5, shots 700 baisa-OR 1.5; open Sa-Th noon-3pm and 7-11pm, F 2-4pm and 7-11pm).

While Khasab's nightlife scene is definitely not worth the trek up north, the majestic beauty of the surrounding seascape and the handful of archaeological attractions are. **Khasab Travel and Tours** (tel. 830 464; fax 830 364) holds an iron-tight monopoly on guided tours around the peninsula. Despite what they may tell you, it is possible to see most of the sights on your own (though it requires more effort), with more independence and more money left in your wallet at the end of the day.

KHASAB FORT AND PORT. Where the road from the town center hits the corniche, a right turn leads to the Khasab Fort, a left to the harbor and Khasab Port. The rather typical fort consists of five mismatched towers. Built in the 16th century by the Portuguese, the fort is strategically located on the cornice overlooking the Strait of Hormuz. The interior is more or less bare with the exception of a few old rifles and *khanajir* (daggers), but the friendly, elderly guard will give you a "grand" tour for free. Khasab Port, a small harbor with a handful of old *dhows* and dozens of speedboats, is really only worth seeing in the early morning or late evening for a glimpse of the Iranian sheep traders *cum* cigarette smugglers. *(Khasab Fort open Sa-W 7:30am-2:30pm. Private taxis OR 2 round-trip.)*

TAWI

Private taxis run to Tawi (OR 3 from Khasab Hotel). If driving, follow the main road to Bukha and turn left at the sign for Quida, 10km from Khasab Port. Follow the paved road to its end; it'll eventually turn into a gravel track. Go through the village until you reach a large beige house on a sharp right curve. Just before this house, the prehistoric carvings are at ground level on a large pile of rocks that look as if they've recently fallen from atop the mountain.

Although the stone houses of the coastal settlement of Tawi may be more visually striking, the town is best known for its smattering of **prehistoric rock carvings**, estimated to be more than 2000 years old. There are only five carvings and you'll need a keen eye to find them: three look like dinosaurs (though logic implies that they're more likely to be camels), the other two like humans. You can't see the carvings from a car; you'll have to get within a couple of meters of the rocks. Just before the rocks, there are small wooden shelters built into tiny caves and an ancient well that is still used by Tawi's present residents.

BUKHA

Bukha, 27km southwest of Khasab, is the closest the peninsula comes to having another town. As there are no hotels in Bukha, however, you'll have to make it a day trip from Khasab. **Bukha Fort,** a small square fort with three barrel-shaped watchtowers, overlooks the spectacular shoreline. The fort is not open to the public, but you can admire it, along with the town's towers and *dhows*, from the surrounding beach. There's another fort atop a hill slightly inland from Bukha, but it's little more than a lone watchtower surrounded by crumbling rocks.

The drive to Bukha is particularly scenic. Al-Harf, a small coastal village with spectacular views of the Strait of Hormuz, makes a quick photo-op on the way. On a clear day you can't quite see forever, but it is possible to see the Iranian coastline. The picturesque Aj-Jadi (2km before Bukha) woos travelers with a sandy white stretch of beach and two restored watchtowers. One of the towers is on the beach; another is farther inland atop a hill. Neither is open to the public. Private taxis to Bukha cost OR 10 round-trip and stop at Al-Harf or Aj-Jadi upon request.

KUMZAR AND THE FJORDS

The boat ride through the fjords to the small fishing village of Kumzar, located on the northern tip of the peninsula, is the best reason to visit the Musandem. Kumzar is a tiny settlement of stone-rock houses wedged between steep mountains, accessible only by sea. The inhabitants are known for speaking **Kumzari,** a language unknown to the rest of Oman (though Arabic is also used and understood here). This creole mixture of Hindi, Farsi, and Portuguese developed out of various fishing contacts in the past. The isolated village is a cool place to check out, but the main draw is the breathtaking boat ride there through the Strait of Hormuz, along the mountainous coastline and past the fjord **Khawr ash-Shamm.** Hire a fisherman to take you there and back (OR 35 per boat, not per person).

DHOFAR REGION

SALALAH صلالة

Salalah is the official capital of Oman's southern Dhofar region and the unofficial summer vacation capital of the entire country. Between the months of June and September, the region's climate is dramatically altered by monsoon rains sweeping in from the Indian Ocean, and everyone flocks here to cool off. While the rest of the country swelters in the summer heat, the Dhofar's plain desert and mountainous landscape transform into a tropical paradise of rolling green hills, flowering trees, and majestic waterfalls. The small city of Salalah offers decent accommodations and all the necessities, but is most important as a home base for exploring this magnificent countryside. East of Salalah are the ruins of ancient cities once known for their importance (and exportance) in the frankincense trade as well as their waterfalls and beaches. North of Salalah, the remains of An-Nabi Ayoub (the prophet Job) lie atop Jabal Ittin, an important pilgrimage site for many faiths. West of Salalah, the road leading to Yemen is replete with spectacular seascape views, a beach with blowholes, and serene mountain villages.

✹ ORIENTATION

Salalah's small city center is concentrated in the kilometer between the north-south **An-Nahdah** and **Al-Matar Streets,** with **Ar-Rabat Road** forming the northern boundary and **Ash-Shuruq Street** (the corniche) along the coast. The ocean is to the south. Al-Matar St., on the eastern end of the city center, has several hotels and small restaurants, and runs through the **Clocktower Roundabout** from the airport to the water. An-Nahdah St. runs south to the Sultan's Palace and the Al-Haffa Souq. The major east-west roads are **23rd July Street** and **As-Salaam Street.** Additional hotels and a cluster of grocery stores are located on these two roads.

⌐ TRANSPORTATION

Airplanes: Salalah Civil Airport (tel. 204 311), at the northern end of Al-Matar St., farthest from the waterfront. Coming from the city center, follow Al-Matar St. straight through the Clocktower Roundabout until it ends. **Oman Air** (tel. 204 263), in Haffa House at the Clocktower Roundabout, operates 2 flights per day M and W-Sa to Muscat, 1 flight Tu and Su (OR 32, round-trip OR 60). Additional daily flight added during the height of the monsoon season (mid-June to mid-Sept.).

Intercity Buses: Oman National Transport Co. (tel. 292 773; fax 291 003) sends out 2 buses per day, with an added bus during the monsoon season, from Salalah's Central Market to the Ruwi Bus Station in **Muscat** (12-13hr.; June 16-Sept. 16: 6am, 7pm; Sept. 17-June 15: 6am, 5pm, 6pm; OR 8), via **Nizwa** (11hr., OR 6) and **Seeb International Airport** (12-13hr., OR 8).

Local Transportation: Microbuses and **taxis** linger at the Central Market on 23rd July St., about 2 blocks past the An-Nahdah St. intersection heading towards Al-Matar St., and behind the HSBC Bank on As-Salaam St. Coming from the airport, take a left off Al-Matar St. onto As-Salaam St.; the bank is on the right a couple of blocks down the road. Fares within the city-center run around 300 baisa for a microbus, 500 baisa for a taxi.

Car Rental: If you plan to explore the outdoor sights, consider renting a 4-wheel drive vehicle. **Budget Rent-A-Car** (tel. 235 160 or 235 333), in the lobby of the Salalah Holiday Inn on Al-Khandaq St. Another location at Salalah Civil Airport (tel. 290 097). Other rental agencies include **Europcar** (tel. 297 948; fax 297 958), **Toyota Rent-A-Car** (tel. 290 908; fax 700 483), and **Thrifty Rent-A-Car** (tel. 294 901).

DRIVING TIPS. Renting a **car** is the best (though priciest) way to see the sights around Salalah. When driving at night, watch out for **stray camels** loose on the highway. They often seem to appear out of nowhere, and can cause serious damage to vehicles. Fill up your fuel tank every time you leave Salalah, as **gas stations** outside of town are few and far between.

ℤ PRACTICAL INFORMATION

Tours: Ettin Tours (tel. 235 333 or 949 15 77; fax 235 775), in the lobby of Salalah Holiday Inn. Leads city tours of Salalah and the surrounding countryside, including the lost city of Ubar, Khawr Rawri, and Job's Tomb. Also arranges overnight camping safaris, camel rides, and 4-wheel drive car hire. **Zubair Tours** (tel. 235 333), also in the lobby of Salalah Holiday Inn, offers group tours for US$80-95 per car (seats 1-4 people) or US$30-35 per person for groups over 10. The tours of the standard sights are pretty overpriced, considering that a taxi can be hired for OR 4-5 per hr. to visit the sights east and west of town, but the dolphin- and whale-watching trip is a unique opportunity to see the 22 species of marine mammals that make their home in the waters off Salalah.

Travel Agencies: The **Oman Air** office in Haffa House is the only place to buy domestic tickets in Salalah. **National Travel Agency** (tel. 290 699; fax 294 575), on As-Salaam St. opposite the Redan Hotel, sells international tickets to other Gulf countries (open Sa-Th 8am-1pm and 4-7pm, F 9-11am).

Currency Exchange: Bank Muscat, on An-Nahdah St. (½ block south of As-Salaam St.), has an ATM with MC, Visa, AmEx, Cirrus, and PLUS links, and cashes AmEx traveler's checks (open Sa-W 8am-noon, Th 8-11:30am). **Oman United Exchange Co.,** on An-Nahdah St. at the As-Salaam St. intersection, opposite Habib Bank, cashes traveler's checks and gives cash advances. **HSBC Bank** has **ATMs** linked to Visa, MC, Cirrus, and PLUS on Al-Matar St. in front of An-Nasr Hotel Center, and on As-Salaam St., 1½ blocks from An-Nahdah St. heading towards Al-Matar St.

American Express: Represented by **Zubair Tours** (tel. 235 333), in lobby of Salalah Holiday Inn. No cash advances or traveler's check exchange. Holds mail for clients only; address mail to: AmEx Client's Mail, c/o Zubair Travels and Service Bureau, Salalah Holiday Inn, P.O. Box 870, PC 211, Oman. Open Sa-Th 8am-1pm and 4-7pm, F 8-11am.

Laundromat: On As-Salaam St., opposite Redan Hotel. Additional laundries on Al-Matar St. near the Dhofar Hotel and An-Nasr Hotel Center. Shirts 100 baisa, pants 100 baisa.

Emergency: Tel. 999. **Police:** Tel. 290 099.

Pharmacy: Al-Mawasa Pharmacy (tel. 299 393), on 23rd July St. at the An-Nahdah St. intersection, underneath the Bridgestone sign. Open Sa-Th 8am-1pm and 4-10pm, F 4-10pm. Check local papers for the on-duty 24hr. pharmacy, as it changes daily.

Hospital: Sultan Qaboos Hospital (tel. 211 151), on As-Sultan Qaboos St. near the Al-Mustashfa ("Hospital") Roundabout, is the main hospital in the Dhofar province.

Post Office: On An-Nahdah St. next to the GTO (the building with the tall tower and phone). 24hr. **telegraph** service. Open Sa-W 7:30am-2:30pm.

International Operator: Tel. 195.

◤ ACCOMMODATIONS

The majority of Salalah's hotels are overpriced four- or five-star resorts whose prices rise as the mercury drops between late June and late August. If you plan to come during the height of the monsoon season, you're best off making reservations about two months in advance, as Gulf families flock to Salalah during this time. For couples and larger groups, hotel flats are the cheapest and most comfortable alternative to resorts. While these apartments are probably too pricey for solo travelers, Salalah also has a handful of mid-range hotels with decent rooms.

▨ **Paradise Oasis Hotel Flats** (tel. 296 955), on 23rd July St., 4 blocks east of An-Nahdah St. On the right corner next to small white mosque and blue citadel, with a large sign saying "Hotel Flats." Capacious, cozily-furnished 2-3 bedroom flats with fully-equipped kitchens, A/C, living rooms with large TVs, washing machines, and balconies. 2-bedroom (1 queen bed, 2 twin) OR 20; 3-bedroom (1 queen, 4 twin) OR 30.

▨ **Al-Hana'a Hotel** (tel. 298 305 or 298 306; fax 291 894), on 23rd July St. at Al-Matar St. Pristine white rooms gleam along with the splashes of blue on the ceramic tiles. Singles are a bit tighter than the spacious doubles and triples, but equally tidy. All rooms have private bath. Singles OR 11; doubles OR 17; triples OR 19. Breakfast included. Visa, MC, AmEx.

An-Nasr Hotel Center (tel. 949 41 87), on Al-Matar St. From the airport, go straight through Clocktower Roundabout; the hotel is in the first shopping plaza on the left, between the traffic light and As-Salaam St. A decent hotel with large rooms, attached baths, and a central location. Singles OR 17.55; doubles OR 21.1; quads OR 29.25.

Dhofar Hotel (tel. 290 484), on Al-Matar St. ½ block north of As-Salaam St.; the huge grey complex opposite the Bahar sign. Bright, carpeted rooms with flowery beds and attached baths fulfill the 2 C's: comfort and cleanliness. Singles OR 18; doubles OR 23.

Redan Hotel (tel. 292 266; fax 290 491), on As-Salaam St. 1 block west of Al-Matar St. A basic budget joint done up in midnight blue. Modest but adequate rooms with untidy attached baths and balconies overlooking As-Salaam St. Singles OR 12; doubles OR 15.

✂ FOOD

The majority of Salalah's restaurants have menus with three headings: Indian, Chinese, and Continental. Once you've exhausted the Asian and badly-imitated Western entrees, the only alternative to dining at the hotels (and shelling out a small fortune) are the handful of coffee shops that dish out typical Levantine foods like hummus and falafel. The restaurants on 23rd July St. and As-Salaam St. run the gamut of Salalah's dining options.

Ittin Tourist Recreation and Restaurant (tel. 949 22 23), on An-Nabi Ayoub Rd., the road to Job's Tomb that starts at the corner of the Hamdan Plaza Hotel. On the right after several km of gravel plains, before the road steepens and heads into the mountains. Most locals go here at night to relax and smoke *sheesha* against a backdrop of strutting peacocks. Smoke hubbly-bubbly or eat in traditionally decorated private rooms. This place is coolest at night in more ways than one: it's generally too hot to enjoy when the sun is up. Full meal OR 2.5.

Al-Fareed Tourist Restaurant (tel. 292 382), on 23rd July St., on the left heading from An-Nahdah St. to Al-Matar St. This A/C expat and tourist haven serves a bit of everything. Don't miss the Thursday and Friday night all-you-can-eat buffets with dishes like hummus, mixed grill, chicken, curry, and chow mein (OR 2.5). Open Sa-Th 11am-3:30pm and 6pm-midnight, F 1-3:30pm and 6pm-midnight.

Hassam Ibn Thabit Restaurant (tel. 291 010), on 23rd July St., between An-Nahdah St. and Al-Matar St., almost directly opposite Al-Fareed Tourist Restaurant. Locals flood the large, striped-carpet dining area and gaze at the wooden ceilings as they await the Indian, Chinese, or Continental dish of their choice. Portions are small but filling. Full meals run around OR 2. Open daily 6am-midnight.

Ahla Restaurant (tel. 294 040), on As-Salaam St. next to Redan Hotel, opposite the DHL Office. This small coffee shop, popular with locals, dishes out cheap Levantine food. Hummus 500 baisa, falafel 500 baisa, kebabs OR 1. Open daily 6am-3am.

🎵 ENTERTAINMENT

The only bar in town is at the **Salalah Holiday Inn** (tel. 211 025). A Filipino band plays the latest in 90s soft rock and the greatest in 80s pop during the early evening, but bellydancers take center stage after 11pm (open daily 8pm-1am). The only alternative to the bar scene at the Holiday Inn is smoking hubbly-bubbly under the stars. On An-Nabi Ayoub Rd., the street leading to Job's Tomb, there are several coffee shops with outdoor **sheesha cafes.** The Ittin Tourist Recreation and Restaurant (see **Food,** above) offers the best ambience with its traditional Persian decor and outdoor seating. The small shopping strip behind the Hamdan Plaza Hotel also houses three coffee shops and *sheesha* joints. Salalah's coastline has beautiful **beaches,** but sun-worshippers should head here after the monsoon has blown through. Unlike the rest of the country, the sun shines hardest in the Dhofar region from September through May. The best beach is behind the Al-Haffa Souq, east of the city center. The Holiday Inn shares the same sands a couple of kilometers down the coast, but they charge a pretty penny for access (OR 3 per day).

👁 SIGHTS

Salalah's most breathtaking sights all lie outside the city center in the surrounding countryside. Nevertheless, a half-day tour of Salalah's central district yields a handful of attractions with great historical importance. The Al-Haffa district along the water harbors some of the city's oldest landmarks, such as the **Al-Haffa Souq,** south of As-Sultan Qaboos St., and the beautiful **Al-Hisn Palace,** the Sultan's summer residence at the end of An-Nahdah St.

OMAN

SALALAH MUSEUM. Salalah's museum houses a small collection of jewelry, clothing, and handicrafts unique to the Dhofar region. The main attraction, however, is the work of a non-native—the black and white photographs shot by the British **Wilfred Thesiger**. Born in Ethiopia, Thesiger traveled through Oman with the Rashid Tribe from 1945-50 before the Sultan put a price on his Christian head. Fortunately for Thesiger, some of the Bedouin he had befriended in his desert sojourn were able to help him escape execution. *(On Markaz al-Muhafdhah St. From the An-Nahdah Roundabout near the GTO Building, head toward the city center and take the first right off An-Nahdah St. Follow this road past a small green-domed mosque on the right. The museum is in the large beige building on the right across from Nahal Tours. Free.)*

FOOTPRINTS OF PROPHET SALEH'S SACRED CAMEL. The camel of the Prophet Saleh is mentioned in the Qur'an as one of only 10 **animals allowed to enter heaven** (other heaven-bound creatures include Jonah's whale, Noah's dove, and the ram that Abraham sacrificed instead of Isaac). Fourteen of the camel's **footprints** are embedded in solid rock in the Al-Haffa district, enclosed in a sanctuary built by the Sultan. *(Coming from the Clocktower Roundabout, follow Al-Matar St. and take a left on 23rd July St. You will see a small mosque on your right; make the first right after this onto a gravel road near the Aj-Jazeera Paints store. Follow the gravel road through a small residential area until the road ends. The camel footprints are in the small beige building with a white Arabic sign to the left. Open daily 6am-10pm.)*

DHUFA (AL-BALAD ARCHAEOLOGICAL SITE). Closer to the Al-Haffa Souq lie the ruins of **Dhufa,** an ancient city that prospered between the 12th and 16th centuries BCE. Today the ruins are little more than stone rubble lying near a creek, officially called the **Al-Balad archaeological site.** Legend has it that a grand mosque, palace, houses, and tombs all stood here. There's not enough remaining to go out of your way to visit, but if you happen be en route to the beach or *souq* nearby, it's worth a stop. *(Follow Al-Matar St. to the closest road to the water (Al-Bahri St.). Turn left and follow Al-Bahri St. to its end at a roundabout. The ruins are on the left. The gate to the site is falling apart, and some people climb in through the many holes.)*

NEAR SALALAH

JOB'S TOMB (QABR AN-NABI AYOUB)

Minibuses do not go to the tomb, but it's possible to hire a taxi to take you there (OR 5 per hr.). Follow the road behind the Hamdan Plaza Hotel (An-Nabi Ayoub Rd.) up the mountain; the tomb is signposted along the way. The left turn from the main street is indicated by a sign; follow this steep road to the fork at the end. Bear left for the mosque and tomb, right for a small tourist restaurant.

The mountain of **Jabal Ittin** rises up north of Salalah. The cattle farm villages, steep forested gorges, and mountains covered with lush green trees along the uphill road contrast sharply with the seascape and frankincense groves lying west of Salalah. About 40km from Salalah on Jabal Ittin is the well-preserved tomb of An-Nabi Ayoub, speculatively identified as the prophet Job from the Old Testament. The prophet's putative remains are housed in a small white tomb with a green, satin-covered coffin. Incense burners filled with frankincense, a symbol of religious importance, have been placed at the foot of the coffin. Next to the tomb is a small green and white mosque open only to Muslims. The tomb is a pilgrimage site for many Muslims, Jews, and Christians. Visitors should respect Islamic decorum by removing shoes before entering and covering head, arms, and legs.

TAQAH

Microbuses run from Salalah to Taqah's main road (400 baisa). Follow the brown signs on Taqah St. to the castle. Walk 300m through the town and turn left on Al-Hisn St.; the castle is at the end of this road. Open Sa-W 7:30am-2:30pm.

The fishing village of **Taqah,** 36km from Salalah, houses old Dhofari architecture, a nondescript castle, and remnants of a once-thriving fishing industry. The old fishing boats scattered along Taqah's beach road are unique because they are sewn together with coconut fibers rather than held with nails. Farther from the shore, a simply designed square **castle** has beveled sides and two short watchtowers. Inside, the castle's rooms encircle a courtyard. The old castle fortifications border the graveyard of the **Sheikh al-Affif Mosque,** where Sultan Qaboos' mother, uncle, and grandfather are buried (his exiled father, Sultan Sa'id, is conspicuously missing). Make a left out of the castle and walk straight down the narrow paved road running alongside the mosque. The paved road turns into a gravel track before intersecting Taqah St., and the cemetery runs parallel to this gravel track. In the corner closest to the street lie the graves of the Sultan's relatives, decorated more elaborately than the others in white marble with black Arabic script. The grave with three markers is that of the Sultan's mother, who died in August 1992. Her brother is buried to the right, and the farthest marker is that of the Sultan's grandfather.

KHAWR RAWRI AND SUMHURAM

*The turn-off for Khawr Rawri is to the right of the main road and is signposted approximately 7km past Taqah. From this point you'll have to walk 2½km to the site. Follow the dirt road for 2km to the fork in the road. Bear right at the fork and continue to the archaeological site on the right. **Microbuses** from Salalah and Taqah go past the turn-off for Khawr Rawri en route to Mirbat (400-500 baisa from Salalah). **Taxis** from Salalah charge OR 5 per hr. Khawr Rawri is **open** Sa-W 8am-1:30pm. There are holes in the fence that some people crawl through to explore the site even when it's closed.*

About 7km beyond Taqah are the ancient ruins of the city of Sumhuram, which contain the remains of the famed Queen of Sheba's palace. This two-acre archaeological site overlooks the scenic Khawr Rawri, a sandy lagoon surrounded by cliffs and home to dozens of migratory birds, including pink flamingos, pelicans, and storks. Inscriptions in the ruined city reveal that its name was Sumhuram, but archaeologists believe that this is the same place referred to as **Moscha** in the 1st-century Greek mariners' guidebook to the Indian Ocean, *The Periplus of the Erythraean Sea.* The ancient city was built under the orders of King 'Azz II of Hadramawt (part of modern Yemen) in 100 BCE, and served as the collection site and port for the flourishing frankincense trade in Dhofar. Sumhurum has been excavated at least three times since 1952, and archaeological digs are still in progress. Finds include bronze coins, a Greek amphora, a stone bull's head, and

FRANKINCENSE, MY DEAR... I *do* give a damn. For

more than five millennia, frankincense was one of the most highly valued substances to the great cultures of the Middle East, Mediterranean, and even the Far East. This "pearl of the desert" was once worth as much as gold, and at the height of its popularity, the Dhofar region exported 3000 tons of frankincense resin annually. Although best known today as one of the gifts given to the baby Jesus by the three kings, frankincense once had many aromatic, medicinal, and spiritual uses. The ancient Egyptians used it when embalming their pharaohs, and when the tomb of King Tut was opened in 1922, the fragrance could still be detected from a sealed flask after 3300 years. Believing that frankincense had protective qualities, Arab doctors scented their clothing with the fragrance before visiting ailing patients to avoid contracting contagious diseases. Though this may seem like specious medicine, during the time of the Black Plague in Europe (1603-66), perfumers were immune presumably because they were constantly surrounded by this essential oil. This prized scent had spiritual purposes as well: many ancient cultures believed that the smoke from burning frankincense carried their prayers to their god(s) above. The Dhofar region's landscape is still covered in these stubbly trees with gnarled limbs. Today frankincense is sold widely throughout Oman as a popular perfume and is burned as an aromatherapy incense.

the temple of a moon goddess named Sin. A well in the temple area plunges over 30m deep, with walls more than 2.5m thick. The remains of what is believed to be the **Queen of Sheba's Palace** stand on a small hill overlooking Khawr Rawri. The Queen of Sheba used to travel to Dhofar for frankincense, which she often presented as a gift to King Solomon. Sheba had the palace built for her to reside in during her visits, and frankincense was stored inside before being shipped to Yemen.

TAWI ATAYR AND WADI DARBAT

Just before the turn-off for Khawr Rawri, there is a sign for Tawi Atayr pointing to the left. From the village, turn left down a gravel road signposted "Kalsis Adeen," which then forks to the right, to reach the sinkhole. If you have 4-wheel drive, take the left turn for Darbat immediately after the hairpin bends close to the base of the mountain.

Tawi Atayr is a mountain village surrounded by spectacular greenery, though the real trick is not to use your eyes, but your ears. Just outside of town, the cliffs plummet to form the largest **sinkhole** in the world, 150m in diameter and 211m in depth. Thousands of singing birds filling the sinkhole join together in a high-pitched symphony of tweets and chirps. Climb down to a metal platform overlooking an 80m drop to see water and fallen boulders at the bottom of the gorge.

At the beginning of the ascent to Tawi Atayr, a gravel track winds through tree-covered hills to Wadi Darbat. During the height of monsoon season, a magnificent 100m **waterfall** cascades to the bottom of the Darbat valley. Though the falls dry up when the monsoon ends, a pool of water always sits at the bottom of the *wadi*. About 2½km from the start of the road leading to Darbat, there are three small huts on the right. Climb up the hill behind these huts to a small arch at the crest of the mountain. Through the arch you can witness a stupendous view of the coastal plain and the Darbat valley, with its mountains, waterfalls, lakes, and lush vegetation. Continue down the road to reach **caves** filled with old stalactites and stalagmites. Some of these caverns have been used by local shepherds for shelter, and their animal paintings (colored with coal, iron, and ochre) are still preserved on the walls. At the end of the road, about 8½km down, the cavern on the left side is believed to be the largest natural cave in Oman.

MARBAT

Marbat, 66km east of Salalah, lies on the main coastal road, past the turn-offs for Tawi Atayr, Jabal Shamhan, and Khawr Rawri. Microbuses go from Salalah to Marbat for 600 baisa. Marbat's castle is signposted once you reach the town. Ibn 'Ali's mosque is within walking distance from the main road. Turn right on Ibn 'Ali Rd. and continue for 1km to its end.

Formerly the capital of the Dhofar region, Marbat was famed in the 9th century for the breeding and exporting of horses. In fact, its name is believed to have come from the Arabic *"Marbat al-Khail,"* which literally means "place where horses are tied." Now a fishing village on a small inlet, Marbat can still hold its head high thanks to its great beaches and architectural significance. One of the less significant buildings in town is the **castle**. Constructed similarly to the one in Taqah, the fortification has carved wooden windows and a tower overlooking the sea. Its cannons lie several meters away, pointing out to sea. A couple of kilometers before Marbat, a blue Arabic sign points to the **Tomb of Ibn 'Ali**. Ibn 'Ali died in 1135 CE, and a mosque and tomb were built in commemoration not long afterward. Only Muslims are allowed to enter; non-Muslims can admire the remarkable mosque from the parking lot. Instead of a single colored dome capping the building, there are two completely white onion-shaped domes—a common form of mosque architecture during medieval times in Dhofar and Yemen's Hadramawt region. Inside, the tomb is covered with a green sheet and is marked by a large, elaborate wooden headstone with a carved Arabic inscription. A Muslim graveyard surrounds the building.

AL-MUGHSAYL

Catch microbuses to Al-Mughsayl from Salalah's central market or the HSBC parking lot on As-Salaam St. (around OR 1).

OMAN

The small town of Al-Mughsayl, 40km west of Salalah, has one of Oman's most enchanting beaches, comprised of sculptured cliffs, turquoise lagoons, and bursting blowholes. The sands stretch over 4km, dotted with sun pavilions and herds of camels. In the steep cliffs at the far end of the beach lies **Al-Manrif Cave,** an imposing cavern of dark black limestone hanging over the sea. On the other side of the cave, the sandy cliff gives way to limestone deposits so porous that water spouts out of these **blowholes** after the waves crash into the cliff. Al-Mughsayl Beach is a popular weekend spot for local Omanis and a must-see for visiting tourists.

RAKHYUT

> *The drive through Rakhyut is difficult without a 4-wheel drive vehicle, particularly if there's been recent rainfall. It's possible to take a **minibus** from Salalah heading to **Sarfayt** (just before the Yemeni border), then disembark at the Rakhyut turn-off and hitchhike from there. Let's Go does not recommend hitchhiking. Hiring a 4-wheel drive in Salalah is a pricier option. There are **no gas stations** between Salalah and the border, so fill the tank before leaving.*

Continuing west past Al-Mughsayl, the road winds up and down eight hairpin bends in the mountains, and the landscape offers spectacular views of honey-colored mountain cliffs converging with the sparkling turquoise sea. After the bends, the road traverses frankincense groves and rolling green hills until reaching the Yemeni border some 140km away. Approximately 40km before the border, a left turn-off leads to the Jabali mountain village of **Rakhyut,** home of local fishermen and cattle herders, nestled atop a steep forested gorge. Jabali men dress in a manner distinctly different from other Omanis; rather than wearing a *dishdasha*, they don dark shirts with long cloth skirts. Jabali males all have beards and usually carry long wooden staffs. At the end of the turnoff to Rakhyut, there's a small **beach** with a **camping area;** ask permission before sleeping there.

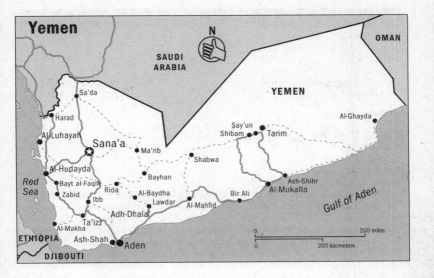

YEMEN اليمن

US$1=YR 141.5 (YEMENI RIALS)
CDN$1=YR 94.94
UK£1=YR 224.59
AUS$1=YR 89.49
SAR1=YR 23.22
EUR1=YR 147.92
OR 1 (OMANI RIAL)=YR 417.4

YR 100=US$0.70
YR 100=CDN$1.05
YR 100=UK£0.44
YR 100=AUS$1.11
YR 100=SAR4.30
YR 100=EUR0.67
YR 100=OR 0.24

PHONE FACTS | **Country Code:** 967. **Police:** Tel. 199.

Situated at a favorable position on the Arabian Peninsula, Yemen is a verdant, beach-lined interruption of vast seas of sand that was once the prosperous heart of the ancient frankincense trade. Historians have long celebrated its richly diverse history of wealth: the ancients referred to the country as *Arabia Felix*, or "Happy Arabia," and its most famous queen, the Bible's Queen of Sheba, has become a worldwide symbol for decadence and power. Modern Yemen is not nearly as prosperous, although many foreign development projects have been launched to modernize the economy in recent years. Agriculture remains the most important economic activity. Before a 1962 revolution, Yemenis saw little reason to improve the economy for fear of attracting foreign involvement.

For travelers, this means visiting an area mostly untouched by the outside world. Yemen's appeal is its history of indifference to the rest of the globe, as well as the legacy this insularity has left in its culture, architecture, and politics. The honey-colored, rain-thirsty mountains and valleys in the north and the tropical, *dhow*-lined beaches in the south frame a society living in millennium-old structures. In spite of the hassles of being in a place so radically different from the West, most travelers find a visit to Yemen the adventure of a lifetime.

675

ESSENTIALS

ENTRY

You'll need a **visa** to enter Yemen, and a lot of time and patience to get it: the government has been known to require a day-by-day itinerary, including the names of the hotels you'll be staying in. Anyone whose passport shows evidence of a trip to **Israel** will be denied a visa. Prices depend on the type of visa and your nationality: Americans pay US$30 for a single entry tourist visa, US$60 for a multiple entry visa. Other nationalities range from US$65-70. Visits must be completed within three months of the visa's issuance. Extensions, obtainable through the Immigration Office, are free for the first two weeks. Upon arrival, visitors receive a **permit** good for one month, during which they do not need to register with the police or get a departure permit. However, **departure taxes,** payable at the port of departure, apply to everyone.

EMBASSIES AND CONSULATES

Embassies and consulates for other countries in Yemen are all in **Sana'a** (see **Practical Information: Embassies,** p. 684). Yemeni embassies and consulates abroad include: **Canada,** 350 Spark St., # 1100, Ottawa, K1R 7S8, ON, (tel. 613-729-6627; fax 729-8915); **U.K.,** 57 Cromwell Rd., London, SW72ED, (tel. (0171) 584 6607; fax 589 3350); and **U.S.,** 2600 Virginia Ave., NW, Washington, D.C. 20037 (tel. 202-965-4760; fax 337-2017). Yemen does not have diplomatic representation in **Australia, Ireland, New Zealand,** and **South Africa;** apply through the nearest office.

⚒ BORDER CROSSINGS

TO OMAN. There are conflicting reports about whether the highway across the Yemen-Oman border (through the town of Habrut) is open; ask the authorities once in Yemen. There is no public transportation between the two countries. A visa and sponsor are required to enter Oman (see **Oman: Entry,** p. 676).

TO SAUDI ARABIA. Crossings are possible at the border towns of Haradh and Al-Buq, but getting an entry visa is incredibly difficult, requiring a friend in the government, an act of Allah, or both. To get a visitor or business visa, you need a formal invitation from a Saudi company or individual sponsor. Muslims can apply for *hajj* or *umrah* visas in their home countries, but even these are difficult to obtain. The easiest option is to get a **transit visa,** which must be obtained from a Saudi embassy in advance, and allows up to seven days in the country.

GETTING AROUND

AIR TRAVEL. Yemenia, the national carrier, operates domestic and international flights. The major international airport is at Sana'a, but there are entry ports at the airports in Aden, Al-Hudayda, Ar-Rayan, and Ta'izz as well. Most flights to and from Yemen stop in European or Middle Eastern hubs (such as Cairo, Amman, and Jeddah). Bumpy domestic flights are available but unreliable.

ROAD TRAVEL. Road travel in Yemen is extremely hazardous. Avoid buses and minivans that are overcrowded, and do not travel at night or in bad weather. There is often no railing between the road and the valley's (distant) bottom. A modern road system is in the works, and already exists between Sana'a, Al-Hudayda, and Ta'izz. Visitors will travel mostly by bus, taxi, and *service*. White **service taxis** are identifiable by their horizontal stripes and routes written in Arabic on the front door. Routes are fixed but schedules are not. *Service* travel between cities but not within them; they depart when full. **Private taxis** drive around major cities (Sana'a and Aden); negotiate a price before beginning your trip.

CAR RENTAL. Travel agencies handle car rentals. Rented cars usually come with drivers, as it is not advisable to tackle the roads on your own; make sure the driver is included in the price of the car. Insist that the driver not chew *qat* (a narcotic plant) while operating the vehicle, as it often requires a free hand (or two) to tear off the leaves. Do not believe drivers who claim they have never had an accident. Drivers consistently disobey traffic laws. Many roads are subject to tribal law, so drivers involved in accidents can end up in the custody of local tribes.

TOURIST AND TRAVEL SERVICES

Most luxury hotels have resident **doctors** or can get one in an emergency. **Pharmacies** are harder to miss than to find. The **Yemeni Ministry for Culture and Tourism** (housed with the General Tourism Authority) gives general travel advice (including itineraries) for travel in Yemen and issues the proper **permits** for doing so. Inquiries must be made in person at the office on 26 September St. in Sana'a (tel. (01) 252 317/9 or 200 001; fax 252 316 or 261 925). Brochures and maps are available by mail; write to: General Tourism Authority, Al-Hasabah, Beer Sha'if, P.O. Box 129, Sana'a, Yemen. For more info, go to www.nusacc.org/yemen/home.htm.

MONEY MATTERS

CURRENCY AND EXCHANGE. The Yemeni currency unit is the **rial (YR),** which starts in denominations of five rials. There are no coins in circulation. **Credit cards** will only be accepted at Western-style businesses and most travel agencies. Be forewarned that there are **no ATMs** anywhere in Yemen. Currency exchanges take cash only, and should all have the same daily rates, with slightly better rates on US$100 bills. Banks change traveler's checks at a fee of about US$8.

PRICES AND TIPPING. Bargain on everything but meal and room prices (which are lower in the summer). Pay what the locals are paying (listen for the numbers in Arabic or watch the bills being forked over). **Tipping** is not neccessary anywhere in Yemen except fancy Western establishments; everyone will ask for money, but only tip those who have given you a ride or a place to sleep for the night.

BUSINESS HOURS. Business hours vary from place to place and day to day, but count on businesses generally being open from 8am to noon and then reopening after a lengthy *qat* chew from 4 to 8pm. Most close Friday afternoons for prayer.

ACCOMMODATIONS

Budget accommodations are everywhere, but ask to see the rooms (and sheets) before deciding. There is no hotel tax. Take the opportunity if locals offer you the chance to sleep in their home for a night: it's an excellent opportunity to see the inside of an old Yemeni house. Women, especially those traveling alone, should absolutely refuse such an offer, as it likely has different connotations. Once inside the house, sleep with your bag comfortably attached to you, as being visibly suspicious of crime will offend your host. Always offer about YR 400-500 the next morning, and be pleasantly surprised if your offer is refused.

KEEPING IN TOUCH

MAIL. Mail to Yemen is faster than mail from Yemen. All towns have a post office, but it is best to send mail only from Sana'a and Aden, as service from rural areas is unreliable. **Poste Restante** is available in Sana'a, but is also unreliable. No postal code is necessary when sending mail or packages to Yemen. Insure your package by using a Western express mail service such as **DHL,** 37 Az-Zubairy St., Sana'a (tel. (01) 249 878; fax 268 858). When addressing international letters, have someone write the address (or at least "Sana'a" or "Aden") in Arabic. Aerogrammes from Sana'a to Europe, Australia, or North America cost under YR 140 (postcards YR 20) and take anywhere from seven to 25 days to arrive.

TELEPHONES AND INTERNET ACCESS. Telecom offices are everywhere and are surprisingly hassle-free. Almost all have local, long distance, and fax services (hotels usually have fax services as well). Long distance calls cost YR 200-400 with a **phonecard,** which may be purchased from post offices, Telecom offices, and news kiosks. Almost all offices offer AT&T, USADirect, or WorldConnect **collect calls:** dial (01) 0080 0101 (leave out the initial 01 in Sana'a); it will be charged as a local call from anywhere in Yemen. Check before you leave home about other international services. Some hotels and Telecom offices have **Internet access;** most towns have at least one cybercafe, with prices around YR 12-15 per hour.

WOMEN TRAVELERS

Female tourists should be aware of just how unusual their presence is in Yemen, not only because of the sexual segregation of Yemeni society but because of the rarity of foreign travelers in the country. Act modestly and adhere to Yemeni social restrictions. Do not expect to chew *qat* with the men and be prepared to be refused admission to certain establishments on given days. Westerners should also be forewarned that gender segregation and polygamy are markers of a Yemeni man's wealth and success; to criticize either practice is extremely offensive and can result in being forbidden from visiting parts of the country. For more tips, see **Women Travelers,** p. 29.

DRESS AND ETIQUETTE

Neither men nor women should wear shorts. Women should cover themselves from the neck to the ankles and wear long sleeves (no plunging necklines or visible bra straps). Wearing a face-covering veil is not necessary for foreign women, but it does minimize the amount of staring (see **Who's That Girl?,** below). Do not make extended eye contact with men, as it is considered provocative.

LIFE AND TIMES

ANCIENT HISTORY

Yemen's commercial successes and agricultural know-how made it one of the major movers and *sheikh*-ers of the ancient world. It had its heyday in the age of the **frankincense** trade (roughly 200 BCE to 300 CE), when the Romans appropriately referred to it as **Arabia Felix,** or "Happy Arabia." Yemen's known history actually extends back to 3000 BCE, when five principal kingdoms—Saba (the oldest

WHO'S THAT GIRL? *Shershefs* ("sheet" in Arabic) are the long, black traditional garments that most Westerners think of when they think of Middle Eastern women. A *shershef* consists of an *'abbaya* (the outer cloaklike garment) worn over a *sirwal* (the pants) with a two-piece veil covering the head and hanging down over the collar of the *'abbaya*. The outer portion is the facial veil, which snaps in place above the ears and consists of an opaque bottom layer with a narrow slit for the eyes and a sheer, slit-less outer layer that more conservative women pull down over the bottom layer to cover the eyes. The second piece of the head covering is the scarf that covers the top of the veil, pinning it in place and hiding the hair. The scarf is tied in a variety of knots, depending on the woman's personal style. Today, the *souq* in Sana'a sells such modern adaptations as zip-front *'abbayas* and nifty velcro facial veils. Many women also wear funky socks (some have even been seen wearing "Merry Christmas" stockings) as signs of individuality.

and most powerful), Hadramawt, Ausan, Qataban, and Ma'in—began trading and fighting with each other in Southern Arabia. In the 11th century BCE, camels began to be used to carry gold, frankincense, myrrh, and other precious goods from the Yemeni production center at Qana to Rome, Greece, and Egypt. The caravans returned with Mediterranean artwork and ideas, resulting in a diverse, sophisticated, and incredibly wealthy culture that would prosper for 14 centuries, and even invent the **astrolabe** (a device that measures the distance between stars) in the 15th century BCE. Jealous Greeks and Romans failed to capture the region, but succeeded in finding a new trade route to India (via Egypt) in the first century BCE. This signalled the downfall of the Sabaeans and the other Southern Arabian empires (save the Himyarites, who continued to prosper on the Red Sea coast of Yemen). With the arrival of the **caliphs** (headquartered at Damascus and Baghdad), Yemen became just a far-flung corner of a massive Islamic empire. Nevertheless, when Muhammad united the Arab world in 630 CE, Yemenis constituted almost half of Arabia's population.

MODERN HISTORY

After the country became part of the Ottoman Empire in 1517, its real power was still in the hands of the Zaydi **imams** who had come to power in the 9th century CE. The *imams*, who essentially forced Yemen into a millennium-long isolation from the rest of the world, ultimately did more harm than good to the country, though they did protect Yemen's national identity from various corrosive forces: the strict Islamic culture of Damascus and Baghdad, Turkish Ottoman society, and the dangers of colonialism in later centuries. The *imams* also founded the Islamic school at Zabid in the 9th century, which was older than Al-Azhar in Cairo (now the oldest continuously operating university in the world) and once the most important Islamic center in southern Arabia.

Britain seized Aden in 1839 and established control of the neighboring sheikhdoms before granting the country independence in 1925. Imam Yayha and his son Ahmad ruled Yemen for the next few decades, continuing a program of isolation and very little development. Only a week after Ahmad's death in 1962, **Colonel 'Abdullah as-Sallal** led a military coup and proclaimed the country the **Yemen Arab Republic** (YAR). The deposed *imam* fled to the northern mountains, and a civil war raged for eight years between the YAR and the *imam*'s Royalist forces (backed by Egypt and Saudi Arabia until 1965, when Nasser and Saudi King Faisal pulled support). The civil war continued through the ousting of the British from Aden (the only place where they had maintained a presence) in the late 1960s and the exile of President as-Sallal in 1967. The fighting finally ceased in 1970, when the last *imam* was exiled to England and the YAR was recognized by Saudi Arabia. However, with the closure of the Suez Canal in 1967, Yemen's economy was on the verge of ruin. The new **People's Republic of South Yemen** was formed on November 30, 1967 with support from Communist countries. It was the first, last, and only Arab Marxist state and one of the most radically Marxist programs in the world.

Relations were horrible at best between southern Yemen (renamed the People's Democratic Republic of Yemen or PDRY) and the Western- and Saudi-supported northern republic; there were two assasinations, two full-scale wars, and countless border skirmishes between 1970 and 1980 alone. Under President **'Ali 'Abdullah Saleh,** elected in 1978, the stability of the YAR steadily improved; by 1989, the two countries developed civil relations, mainly due to mutual economic concerns about oil deposits. On May 22, 1990, the two Yemens were formally united as the **Republic of Yemen** under President Saleh, a five-member council, and a combined house of representatives.

But the political upheaval wasn't over yet. Yemen's sympathies with the Iraqis in the **Persian Gulf War** of 1991 led to the suspension of Arab aid and the expulsion of some 800,000 Yemenis from Saudi Arabia. The economy was further strained by an influx of starving refugees from war-torn Somalia. The democratic elections that were held on April 27, 1993 were the first ever in the Arabian Peninsula, although some claim that they were actually corrupt. Yemen entered the international conscience in November 1993 when a U.S. diplomat was abducted by tribal kidnappers, then released several days later. Constant internal strife, coupled with this new-found notoriety, escalated into yet another civil war in May 1994. The region's first democratic experiment has been walking a wobbly tightrope between peace and discord ever since, though many express optimism about the future.

IN THE NEWS

In December of 1998, 16 Western tourists were **kidnapped** by warring Yemeni tribes; three Brits and an Australian were **killed,** leading the U.S. State Department and other countries to issue warnings against travel in the country. Tourism has waned after the incident, and many Yemenis are as confused and concerned about the incident as foreigners are. Hours after a Yemeni court sentenced the man responsible for the killings to death in July 1999, a bomb exploded in Sana'a, killing three. Tribal kidnappings have taken place before (and continue to take place), but had never been violent before this instance.

The future of tribe-government relations may be decided with the next round of elections. Yemen's first direct presidential elections are scheduled to be held in September 1999, one week before the end of the President Saleh's term of office. In the interim, Saleh has made headlines for his efforts to embrace Western-style democracy, renounce narcotic *qat* chewing, and strengthen ties with the rest of the Arab world to erode Yemen's long-standing tradition of insularity.

RELIGION AND ETHNICITY

Yemen is an Arab country in both language and culture, though tribal and religious distinctions abound. The people of the Tihama coastal plain, for example, are of mixed Arab and African descent. The **Zaydi** dynasty, one of the oldest and most important tribes in Yemen, counts the current president and former *imams* among its members. The Zaydis are Shi'ite Muslims who inhabit the northern mountain region; their religious and political beliefs have exerted a major influence on Northern Yemen since the 9th century. The northern and southern lowland regions are dominated by the **Shafi'i** community of Sunni Muslims, who differ widely in their cultural and economic structure and have often been at odds with the Zaydi. Yemen was home to a small minority of **Jews,** who dominated many aspects of the economy before mostly emigrating to Israel in 1949-50. The few **Christians** in Yemen practice at the country's only functioning church in Aden.

LANGUAGE

The official language of Yemen is Arabic. Some English is spoken in the south and by businessmen. Street signs are generally in Arabic only, though larger cities have signs in English as well, and many businesses have—badly spelled—English signs. All radio and most newspapers are in standard modern Arabic, except for the English-language weeklies *Yemen Times* and *Yemen Observer*.

THE ARTS

LITERATURE. There is very little modern Yemeni literature translated and circulated in the West, and Yemeni art is little-known despite a rich heritage. Yemen has a rich oral tradition dating back several millennia, and its written tradition (outside of Himyaritic and Sabaean rock inscriptions) is considered to have begun with the Middle Ages, when the two greatest figures were Nashwan Ibn Sa'id al-Himyari and Al-Hamdani. **Al-Hamdani** was a historian and geographer affectionately known as "the tongue of Yemen," who has been brought to world prominence in the upsurge of interest in "Oriental" (Near and Far Eastern) literature in the last century.

ARCHITECTURE. The 3000 years of Yemeni architecture is renowned among archaeologists and historians for its many diverse regional styles. The four- to six-story **tower houses** found in the highlands have separate rooms for men and women and a large room on the top floor called the *mafraj*, where the head of the household meets to talk and chew *qat* with his friends in the afternoons. The most spectacular example of Yemeni architecture is the city of **Shibam** (see p. 697), called the "Manhattan of the Desert" for its anachronistic collection of ancient skyscrapers. Yemeni architecture was also one of the first to use stone for construction, which became common practice around the time of a cultural boom Yemen experienced in tandem with the peak of Hellenism in Greece. Yemeni builders used their knowledge of stone quarrying and building to build some of the earliest irrigation devices.

FOOD AND DRINK

Yemeni breakfasts feature fresh fruit, *lahuh* (pancake-like sorghum bread), *fatoot* (strips of *lahuh* fried with bananas and honey), and scrambled "red eggs" made with onions and tomatoes. Lunch is the main meal, eaten without any utensils except a piece of bread. Dinner is light and consists of little more than fruit and bread (*qat* chewers are typically not hungry after an afternoon of indulging). **Salta**, the national dish, is a highly spiced and somewhat greasy stew of chicken or lamb with lentils, chickpeas, beans, and cilantro, served over rice. *Shurba* (Arabic for "soup") is made with lentils (*shurba bilsan*), fenugreek (*hulba*), or lamb *(shurba wasabi)*. Shawarma is the same as it is everywhere else, but Yemeni hummus is a watery goop that gives its Levantine cousins a bad name. **Bread** comes in several varieties, including *ruti*, *khubz tawwa*, and *lahuh*. *Bint as-Sahn* is a popular dessert of sweet bread topped with melted honey and clarified butter and sprinkled with charred sesame seeds or black pepper seeds. *Mumzipu*, a sweet confection made of baked apples, cinnamon, and a buttery crust (known in Ta'izz as *zubayda*), is similar to the pastry known as the Danish Puff, but sprinkled with the popular black pepper seeds.

Most Yemenis drink a very sweet tea flavored with mint and called **shai** (milk is optional). The strong, spicy coffee known as *ahwa* is rarely consumed, even though the country is the birthplace of coffee (the über-popular American chain Starbucks even named a brand of its brew Sanani Java, after Sana'a). A popular treat is the sweet and spicy **qishr,** made from the ground husks of coffee beans blended with ginger and cardamom. **Alcohol** is banned under strict Islamic law, but is available at Western establishments.

SANA'A صنعاء

Sana'a is one of the greatest cities on the Arabian Peninsula, though at present it is in a fairly lamentable condition. Legend has it that after the Biblical flood, Noah's son Shem founded Sana'a as a sparkling metropolis; as recently as 50 years ago, residents claimed the streets of this Yemeni capital were clean enough to eat off. With the sudden introduction of plastic and other disposables—and absolutely no sanitation or recycling systems to deal with them—the streets became flooded with trash in biblical quantities. Sana'a has been cleaning up its act in recent years, but Westerners may still recoil at the refuse.

The Sana'a that rises out of the rubbish is like no other city in the world. It has been a capital of the Sabaeans and Himyarites as well as the Islamic Yemenis, forcibly relinquishing that role during periodic occupations by Ethiopian, Persian, European, and Ottoman conquerors. Since Islam first swept into Yemen in the 7th century, Sana'a has been destroyed several times in revolts against caliphs from Baghdad. Internal power struggles have also left their wear and tear over the years, especially during the revolution and civil war. Yet Sana'a's resilience has shaped and reshaped it into something of an exhibit. A government tourist brochure proudly calls Sana'a's Old City "the world's largest open air museum," a claim not far from the mark. Ignoring the noise of automobiles and motorcycles, one could easily be centuries removed from the present day, walking along narrow streets and blind alleys while being watched over by the stained-glass eyes of the impressive tower houses.

✴ ORIENTATION

The teeming capital of Sana'a sprawls out across roughly 15km of terrain, but most places of interest are close to the center. There are two major landmarks in central Sana'a. The first is **Bab al-Yemen** ("Yemen Gate"), in the southern part of the Old City, the largest of five gates that once led into the Old City. It is the starting point for **Souq al-Milh** (Salt Souq), Sana'a's largest *souq*. **Az-Zubairy Street** also begins at Bab al-Yemen and continues westward to the suburb of **Hadda**, home to most of the expats and affluent Yemenis who live in Sana'a. Hadda is best reached by taking a minibus from Tahrir to the Hadda Hotel and then catching a private taxi from there. There are also a number of cheap hotels near Bab al-Yemen. The Old City's western gate, **Bab as-Sabah**, faces Tahrir from the east.

The other major landmark in Sana'a is **Maidan At-Tahrir** ("Tahrir Square," commonly referred to simply as **Tahrir**), in the middle of the western part of the Old City. Tahrir is the city's lively modern center and home to a wide range of restaurants and hotels. The north-south street bordering Tahrir to the north is **'Ali 'Abdul Moghni Street,** home to the five-star **Taj Sheba Hotel**—a minor landmark that's easy to spot. An overpass is in construction at the intersection of 'Ali 'Abdul Moghni St. and Az-Zubairy St. near the southwestern corner of the Old City, forcing vehicular traffic to take a complicated detour. The busy **Qa'al Yahud** (formerly the Jewish Quarter) is west of the Old City, but its many shops and restaurants have wiped out any vestiges of the area's historical and ethnic identity. For unexplained reasons, this area is also known as **Bir 'Azab**, or "the well of unmarried men." The suburb of **Hasaba**, almost halfway between the Old City and airport, is the departure point for intercity traffic heading north.

▣ TRANSPORTATION

Airplanes: Sana'a International Airport (tel. 250 858) is served by **Yemenia** (Yemen Airways), which has flights to: **Aden** (45min., 8 per day); **Al-Hudayda** (30min., 3 per day); **Cairo** (3hr., 5 per day); **Damascus** (5hr.); **London** (7½hr., 2 per week); **New York** via Europe; and **Ta'izz** (30min., 7 per day except Tu and Th). Pricier options include Lufthansa, Royal Jordanian, KLM and AirFrance. Aeroflot runs cheap flights via Moscow.

Sana'a

ACCOMMODATIONS
A Al-Mostaqbal Tourism Hotel
B Al-Muraisi Hotel
C Sultan Palace Hotel
D Taj Talha Hotel
E Hemyar Land Hotel

YEMEN

Upon arrival at the airport, take a **taxi** from the official stand and make certain the driver understands your intended destination before departing (YR 200 or less).

Buses: Government and private buses both leave from **Bab al-Yemen,** except those going to Ma'arib, which leave from **Hasaba.** Government buses run to: **Aden** (8hr., 2 per day, YR 700); **Al-Hudayda** (5hr., 4 per day, YR 500); **Ma'arib** (3hr., 8am, YR 360); and **Ta'izz** (4½hr., 4 per day, YR 500). Tickets for government buses should be purchased in advance from **General Land Transport Corporation** in Bab al-Yemen by the bus stop; arrive as early as 6am to get tickets for morning buses. **Yemen International Transport Co.** (tel. 275 088) runs buses to: **Al-Baida** (5hr., 6:30am, YR 1440); **Aden** (7½hr., 6:30am, YR 2200); **Al-Hudayda** (5½hr., 6:30am, YR 1600); **Ma'arib** (2½hr., 8am, YR 1300); and **Ta'izz** (5hr., 6:30am, YR 1800). Buy tickets for private buses in advance from **Yemen Felix Travel** (tel. 275 092/1), on Az-Zubairy St., 30m west of 'Ali 'Abdul Moghni St. (open Sa-Th 8:30am-1pm and 4:30-9pm).

Service Taxis: *Service* taxis to **Ta'izz** (5hr., YR 600), **Al-Hudayda** (5½hr., YR 600), and **Aden** (7½hr., YR 800) leave from the **Mammoth Taxi Station** on Ta'izz Rd., 200m south of Bab al-Yemen. Taxis to **'Amran** (1½hr., YR 300), **Hajja** (3½hr., YR 500), and **Sa'ada** (6hr., YR 650) depart from the **Hasaba Station.**

Local Transportation: Black-striped **minibuses** (YR 15-30) cruise the main streets of Sana'a in a complicated network of routes that either begin or end at Bab al-Yemen or Tahrir. Tahrir is the main minibus depot in Sana'a, sending buses out to Hadda, Bab al-Yemen, and Hasaba. Ask for your destination before getting in; just because a minibus is on a main street doesn't mean it will follow that road all the way to the end. **Private taxis** are plentiful as well, but far more expensive (YR 150 within Sana'a, YR 200 to Hasaba, YR 350 to Hadda). Every **motorcycle** in Sana'a is a taxi, but their disregard for traffic lights and one-way streets makes them unsafe (YR 50 between Tahrir and Bab Al-Yemen, YR 100 to the Sheraton or American embassy, YR 150-200 to Hadda).

Car Rental: The only place where it is possible to rent a car without an accompanied driver is **Hertz** (tel. 272 861), represented at Universal Travel's Al-Bawnya St. office, 10m east of the Egyptian embassy. Small, late-model Nissans go for US$50 per day. Limited mileage makes extended tours expensive.

🛈 PRACTICAL INFORMATION

TOURIST AND FINANCIAL SERVICES

Tourist Office: For maps and brochures, try the branch of the **General Corporation for Tourism** at the western end of Tahrir. To get permission to travel in Yemen, you must go to the **Main Office** (tel. 226 623) on Hasaba St., 50m south of the Sab'a Towers Hotel (next to the Osaimi Mosque). Getting here by minibus is impractical; ask a taxi driver to take you to *bolice seeyaha* for YR 150. The process takes about 30min. and is free. Open Su-Th 9am-noon.

Tours: Universal Tours (tel. 272 861; fax 272 834), the biggest travel agent in Yemen, has its main office on Al-Bawnya St., 10m east of the Egyptian embassy (see below); another branch is on Az-Zubairy St., 150m west of 'Ali 'Abdul Moghni St. Helpful, English-speaking staff. Open Su-Th 8am-12:30pm and 4-8pm. Visa, MC, AmEx. **Yemen Felix Travel and Tours** (tel. 275 091/2), on Az-Zubairy St., 40m west of 'Ali 'Abdul Moghni St., is another well-run, English-speaking travel agency, which books seats on the comfortable private buses and makes reservations for domestic and international flights. Open Su-Th 8:30am-1pm and 4:30-9pm. Visa, MC, AmEx.

Visa Extensions: Visas can be extended for 1 month at the **Jamal Jemi Police Station** (tel. 273 352), on 'Ali 'Abdul Moghni St. across from the National Museum. Extensions are free and take about 30min. Visas issued Sa-Th 8am-noon.

Embassies: Egypt (tel. 275 948/9; fax 275 196), Al-Bawnya St., 700m west of Tahrir. Little English spoken. Visas Su-Th 9-11am. **Jordan** (413 276/7; fax 414 516), Hadda Rd., across the street from Hadda Apartments. Visas Su-Th 8am-2pm. **Oman** (tel. 208

874/5; fax 204 586), Naukshout St. Take Zubairy St. 2km west from 'Ali 'Abdul Moghni St., turn left on Baghdad St., then right onto Naukshout St. after 500m. The embassy is on the left. Visas (US$36) Sa-Th 8am-1:30pm. **Saudi Arabia** (tel. 240 529/429; fax. 240 589), Al-Quds St., 500m east of Hadda Rd. Visas for Saudi are notoriously difficult to obtain. The best one can hope for is a transit visa, which will not be considered unless the passport already contains permission to enter a bordering country. Visas Su-Th 9-11am. **Syria** (tel. 414 891; fax 414 494), Hadda Rd., across from Hadda Post Office. Visas Su-Th 9-11am. **U.K.** (tel. 264 081; fax 263 059), on Hadda Rd. south of Djibouti St., by 70th Park. Also represents **Canada, Australia,** and **New Zealand.** Open Su-Th 8am-2pm. **U.S.** (tel. 238 842/9; fax 251 563), Ring Rd., near the Sheraton Hotel. Although they'll give you the standard "didn't we tell you not to come to Yemen?" speech, they register Americans and give up-to-date information on trouble spots. Consular services 11am-1pm; telephone inquiries Sa-W 2-4pm.

Currency Exchange: Sana'a moneychangers are easy to find anywhere in town but are most densely clustered around Tahrir and Bab al-Yemen. To have traveler's checks exchanged for U.S. dollars, try **Arab Bank** (tel. 276 585), on Az-Zubairy St., 1 block west of 'Ali 'Abdul Moghni St. (open Su-Th 9am-noon); or **National Yemen Bank** (tel. 272 071), also on Az-Zubairy St., 100m farther west (open Su-Th 9am-noon).

American Express: Represented by **Marib Travel and Tourism** (tel. 272 432/5; fax 274 199), on 'Ali 'Abdul Moghni St. They can book flights and will hold mail even for non-members, but do not exchange traveler's checks. Open Su-Th 8am-1pm and 4-7:30pm.

LOCAL SERVICES

English Publications: The Yemen Times and **The Yemen Observer** are small, weekly English-language newspapers that report on current events within Yemen. These publications are also good sources of information about cultural performances and English-language movies. Both are sold at newsstands for YR 30. *Time* and *Newsweek* can be found at the Taj Sheba and Sheraton Hotels for YR 400, and sometimes at the newsstand in front of the Bilqis Cinema, 50m south of Tahrir, for the cover price of YR 250.

Bookstore: Yemen Bookshop, on Al-Qasr St., west of 'Ali 'Abdul Moghni St., is the only option in Sana'a for books in English. Open 8am-noon and 4-8pm. The adventurously named **Book Shop,** 2 stores down, has the most extensive collection of Yemeni literature in Sana'a. Open 8am-noon and 4-8pm. **Aj-Jeel Aj-Jadeed Bookshop** (tel. 213 162; fax 213 163), in the middle of the western edge of Tahrir, is better stocked than most bookstores and has an English-speaking staff. Open Su-Th 8am-noon and 4-9pm.

EMERGENCY AND COMMUNICATIONS

Police: Gemal Gemi Police Station (tel. 273 352), on 'Ali 'Abdul Moghni St.

Pharmacy: Sana'a is full of pharmacies, but none of them are open 24hr. There are 3 in Tahrir on 'Ali 'Abdul Moghni St. All open daily 9am-1pm and 3-9pm.

Hospital: Azal Hospital (tel. 200 000), on 60 Meter Rd. on the eastern end of town, is the recommended private hospital. Both the American and British embassies have medical sections which, while not authorized to treat non-embassy personnel without specific permission from the Ambassador, can recommend qualified private doctors. **Ath-Thawra Hospital** (tel. 246 966), 500m east and 1 block south of Bab Al-Yemen, is the city's major public medical facility.

Post Office: The **Central Post Office** is in the middle of Tahrir Sq. Open daily 7am-8pm.

Telephones: Telecom Offices pop up every 50m or so on Sana'a's main streets.

Internet Access: The ▓**Taj Sheba Hotel** offers 1hr. on the web, a soda, and a hamburger in the relaxing surroundings of their restaurant for YR 1800. **Hadda Internet Cafe** (tel. 254 446), on Az-Zubairy St., 2km west of 'Ali 'Abdul Moghni St. and across from Tadramon Bank, charges a cheaper YR 12 per min. but takes a YR 100 service charge. Open 8am-1pm and 3-8pm.

Telephone Code: 01.

✂ ACCOMMODATIONS

Sana'a has the widest range of lodgings in Yemen. The cheapest hotels are close to Bab al-Yemen and Tahrir, while the Old City proper has a unique class of accommodations known as "Palace Hotels," housed in beautiful, centuries-old buildings. These tend to charge an exorbitant rate, payable in U.S. dollars.

▨ Sultan Palace Hotel (tel. 273 766; fax 289 581), on Golden St. in the Old City, near Bab as-Sabah. From Bab as-Sabah, follow the 1st street heading into the Old City for 50m, then turn right at the faded yellow sign with red lettering. This thick-walled old building is a favorite with backpackers. Staff and neighbors like to hone their English, French, and Dutch skills over afternoon *qat* sessions. Spotless rooms and hallway bathrooms, with large bathtubs and enough hot water to fill them. Lunch and dinner cooked to order (YR 300-400). Singles YR 1000; doubles YR 1300; triples YR 1600. Tours US$50, no matter where you go.

Al-Mostaqbal Tourism Hotel (tel. 284 668; fax 289 128), on Al-Qasr St. From Tahrir, walk 100m south on 'Ali 'Abdul Moghni St. and turn right onto Al-Qasr St. The hotel is 1 block down, marked by a blue and white sign. Simple, ultra-clean rooms have private bath and satellite TV. Singles YR 700; doubles YR 1500; triples YR 1800.

Taj Talha Hotel (tel. 287 130; fax 287 212), in the middle of the Old City; follow the signs from both Bab al-Yemen and the 2nd As-Sailah bridge. The location (and its friendly staff) are impossible to beat, but the prices aren't. Singles US$15; doubles US$20, with bath US$25. Breakfast included.

Al-Muraisi Hotel (tel. 272 824), directly behind the post office, on the 1st side street south of Tahrir. Mediocre Yemeni budget lodging epitomized. Singles YR 500; doubles YR 700; triples YR 1000.

Hemyar Land Hotel (tel. 244 257), across from Bab al-Yemen, with an entrance in back. A no-frills dive with decent rooms and bathrooms. The Kalishnikov-toting men playing dominoes and chewing *qat* around the common TV are about as close as you can get to Yemeni rednecks. Singles YR 300; doubles YR 500; triples YR 800.

⌨ FOOD

There is plenty of cheap food all over Sana'a: Az-Zubairy St. in particular is full of excellent eateries. In the Old City, food is served only in hotels and homes. Hotel meals are more expensive and less tasty than street food. Sana'a is one of the only places where it's possible to dine on non-Yemeni cuisine, so consider splurging on an "exotic" meal of pizza or pasta. Getting to Western-style restaurants can be difficult, since the clientele tend to be expats with cars or drivers; their haunts are scattered throughout Hadda. The two spots to sip tea are the **Garden Teahouse** in front of the Taj Sheba Hotel and the **Teahouse** just left of Bab al-Yemen as you leave the Old City. At YR 10 per cup (with milk YR 15), drinking tea is almost cheaper than doing nothing at all.

Koreana (tel. 413 491), in a residential part of Hadda, about 1km and many dark twists and turns from the Hadda Hotel. Take a taxi. Korean and Chinese entrees. All dishes are Spicy with a capital S. Enormous main courses YR 1100. A great respite from the heavily milked and sugared Yemeni tea. Open noon-3pm and 6-11:30pm.

Pizza Hut (tel. 263 752), on Az-Zubairy St., 200m west of 'Ali 'Abdul Moghni St. Deep dish, thin crust, extra cheese, chili peppers—hit the Hut for whatever your pizza-craving taste buds desire (unless they desire anchovies). For a truly authentic experience, head to the red-roofed branch in Hadda (tel. 240 794), on Djibouti St. on the north side of 70th Park. Both open 1-11:30pm.

Villa Di Angelo (tel. 412 581), on Hadda Rd., near Hadda Hotel, is the Old Faithful of the expat dining circuit, but dinner (mamma mia—no wine!) costs a hefty YR 2000-3000.

Ash-Shazarwan Restaurant. (tel. 279 692), on 'Ali 'Abdul Moghni St., 50m south of Tahrir, across from the Bilqis Cinema. Widely recognized as home of the best roasted chicken in Sana'a. The chicken roasts on spits in front of the restaurant all day; if you arrive too early it won't be ready, but if you come too late you'll feast on a dry bird. A half chicken costs YR 250. Open 11am-10:30pm.

🎵 ENTERTAINMENT

Sana'a does not swing, and the only place where alcohol can be swigged is at the obscenely overpriced **Sheraton Hotel** on the north edge of town (beer YR 800). The bar has a big screen TV tuned to ESPN, and there's an adjoining nightclub where a synthesized band soothes the hotel's savage beasts with the likes of John Denver and Barry Manilow (bar open daily until midnight; nightclub open M-F 8pm-1am). A taxi will go from Tahrir to the Sheraton for YR 150, but getting back costs YR 500. A better bet for socializing is the **American Club** in Hadda. The club is private, but members tend to be open with invitations; if you're thirsty, strike up a conversation with an expat. Another tactic is to visit the American Embassy to register, then innocently inquire where one might find a beer in town.

The **Bilqis Cinema** (tel. 251 749), on 'Ali 'Abdul Moghni St. 50m south of Tahrir, shows dubbed US and Hindi action flicks for YR 50 to an enthusiastic, noisy male crowd (women forbidden). For something tamer, head to Hadda, where several nights a week the **Shahara Hotel** (tel. 269 688) shows Anglo films six months behind their western release to both sexes (YR 50; showtimes in the *Yemen Observer*).

👁 SIGHTS

OLD CITY AND SOUQ AL-MILH. The main entrance to the Old City is **Bab al-Yemen,** the southern gate that separates the Old City from modern-day Az-Zubairy St. However, this giant portal manages to separate neither space nor time: the feverish activity of the Old City's **Souq al-Milh** spills over onto outside streets, and *souq* vendors and customers haggle over prices as they have done for centuries—though now they argue over the cost of lighters and ammunition belts in addition to those of more traditional goods. The *souq* is busiest once inside the Old City, where it separates into several specialty areas, including an aromatic spice *souq* (a welcome relief from the more pungent odors of the rest of Sana'a). West of Bab al-Yemen, the Old City is divided by **As-Sailah,** a *wadi* that is now a roadway prone to flooding. The largest and best preserved part of the Old City is east of As-Sailah.

TOWER HOUSES. The tower houses in old Sana'a are about five stories tall, though some rise to eight. Windows are set with stained glass in a cheerful array of colors, cut in unusual geometric patterns that evoke Matisse and Picasso more than the abstract natural forms of ancient Islamic architecture. The first two floors serve as a foundation for the house and are built of stone; upper floors are made of mud. A single family usually owns the house, and living arrangements are divided by both sex and generation. Some travelers are invited to see the inside of one these tower houses, a unique opportunity. For more information on tower houses, see **The Arts: Architecture,** p. 681.

QAT SOUQ. Not as big as Souq al-Milh but even busier, the Qat Souq is worth visiting even if you haven't acquired the habit. Livestock and produce change hands here along with the leafy drug, and people pack like sardines to get in on the action. Now that President Saleh is trying to cut down on *qat* use in a very visible way, the future of the Qat Souq is unclear. *(Morning and evening are the best times to check in to this open-air asylum, just east of the Old City.)*

GREAT MOSQUE AND ENVIRONS. The much-touted "Great Mosque" *(Aj-Jami' al-Kabir)* hides most of its beauty behind high walls, and poking around by non-Muslims is not encouraged. The mosque was built around 630 CE at Muhammad's behest, making it one of the oldest mosques still in existence. The inside is stun-

QAT LIVE WITH IT, QAT LIVE WITHOUT IT

Yemen's national drug is *qat*, the leafy branch of the tree bearing the same name. *Qat* is absolutely everywhere; in Sana'a and other cities, an entire *souq* is devoted to its sale. The effects of *qat* are similar to those of a mild amphetamine mixed with those of a mild relaxant, both raising the user's energy level and inspiring a calm, contemplative mood. There are no known permanent side effects to *qat*, although some users may experience nervousness or melancholy. First time users who chew too late into the evening may also have temporary insomnia. *Qat* is taken in a similar manner to chewing tobacco: the leaves are crushed with the teeth and then slid as a pasty mass into the cheek with the tongue. More leaves are added as the afternoon progresses, and the wad grows over a period of several hours. The leaves are spat out at the end of the session, but the bitter juice is swallowed as it mixes with saliva. Women chew the stuff behind veils or closed doors, but the male population forgoes this decorum: many men strut through the streets every afternoon with billiard ball-sized bulges in their cheeks.

ningly beautiful, and those who wish to sneak a peek can try on the western side of Souq al-Milh, some 70m inside of Bab al-Yemen. There are many more mosques in old Sana'a. Head due east from Souq al-Milh to admire the **Salah ad-Din Mosque** and the **Qubbat al-Bakiliya** beyond it.

MUSEUMS. Once you've had your fill of the open-air museum of the city, avail yourself of Sana'a's two indoor museums. The larger and more interesting of the two is the **National Museum,** which houses four floors of pre-Islamic and even pre-historical artifacts as well as a fine collection of Islamic and folk art. Its smaller and newer neighbor is the **Museum of Folklore and Popular Traditions,** which exhibits the artifact spillover from its elder neighbor in slightly less detail. *(Both museums are 10m from the northeast corner of Tahrir. The National Museum (tel. 271 696) is on 'Ali 'Abdul Moghni St. just outside of the square, and the Museum of Folklore and Popular Traditions (tel. 271 648) is just inside the square, around the corner. National Museum open Su-Th 9am-noon and 3-5pm. Admission YR 30. Museum of Folklore and Popular Traditions open Su-Th 9am-noon and 3-5pm. Admission YR 30.)*

NEAR SANA'A

WADI DHAHR

Taxis leave from Matbah, west of Hasaba in Sana'a (30min., YR 100). Dar al-Hajar Museum will be open daily 9am-12:30pm. Admission YR 30.

This lush valley, 12km northwest of Sana'a, makes for an easy half-day trip. Friday mornings are particularly eventful, as young couples are married here on Thursday nights and their future happiness is celebrated throughout the night and into Friday afternoon. Drums and rifles perform percussion for *jambiya* dances in which everyone participates. A less animated but widely photographed attraction is **Dar al-Hajar,** the rock palace built in 1786 as a leisure spot for Imam Mansur 'Ali Bin Mehdi 'Abbas. Built in the style of the Old City palaces but on a larger scale, Dar al-Hajar perches atop a giant rock flanked by guard towers. The palace is now a museum that had not yet opened to the public at press time. Among the ingenious devices employed in its construction are a deep well cut into the rock and refrigerators that use the rock and a system of air currents to keep their contents cool.

'AMRAN

A taxi from Hasaba in Sana'a brings you to the center of 'Amran (2hr., YR 300) and will pick you up from here for a trip back to Sana'a. The old town is 100m north of the taxi station.

The small, walled town of 'Amran, 50km northwest of Sana'a, lies in a stretch of farmland just south of where the mountains begin in earnest. 'Amran is a great place to stop for lunch and a look around on the way up into the misty peaks. Its small-town feel is evident in the muddy old lanes, where chickens and goats indolently pass the time. Homes are mostly unadorned, but have a welcoming air with their circular windows and rounded corners. People are more open to visitors than in other areas, though their English is no better than anywhere else in the country. One way to delve a little deeper into 'Amran's hospitable soul is by eating at one of the **Salta Restaurants** by the taxi station, where groups of men chow down from a communal plate. The quality and selection of all dishes are about the same; choose a crowded one and sit down with whichever fellows look most appealing. Women are not welcome here. It is very possible you won't be allowed to pay. If you are forced to spend the night, there is a comfortable and clean **Dormitory Hotel** 50m west of the taxi station (YR 100 per person).

IBB AND JIBLA

Although its Old City is extraordinary even by Yemeni standards, modern Ibb is little more than a busy transportation hub with easy access to the surrounding countryside—particularly the charming town of Jibla, 8km away. Jibla was the political and cultural capital of the As-Sulaydid empire (which once rivaled the Zaydi *imams*) under **Queen Arwa,** one of the only two women ever to rule in Yemen. She was one of the oldest rulers as well, holding power until the ripe old age of 92. Aside from Jibla, natural wonders are the big draw: lush mountains surround Ibb, and locals' rooftops afford spectacular views of the vast expanses of terraced fields where *qat* is grown in massive quantities. Crops flourish with the copious amounts of rain: showers occur almost daily in the summer months. Bring sturdy shoes and a small umbrella—Ibb is a great place to hike around and explore.

⚡ ORIENTATION AND PRACTICAL INFORMATION

Ibb is on the **Sana'a-Ta'izz highway,** accessible by bus or *service* from either city. *Service* will take you to the center of town, but intercity buses drop passengers at a roundabout 3km west of the city center. Catch a black-striped minivan from the roundabout to the BP gas station in town (YR 10). You can take a **minibus** west to Mafraq (YR 10) and walk from there to Jibla (about 30min.). Alternately, mini-buses run from the BP gas station to the **service taxi station** at the center of town (a few meters up the right-hand fork of Ta'izz Rd.). *Service* depart to **Jibla** from here (45min., YR 40), as well as to **Sana'a** (YR 600) and **Ta'izz** (YR 180). Minibuses cruise along the north-south **Ta'izz Road,** Ibb's main drag. The hill that begins in the center of town and rises eastward is the spectacular **Old City,** at most a 10-minute walk from any hotel on Ta'izz Rd. It is also possible to flag down a **bus** on the Sana'a-Ta'izz highway; some drivers will pick up hitchhikers. There are numerous **police stations** in Ibb, one of which is in the central market area (tel. 402 579). The **post office** is behind the soccer stadium (open daily 8am-2pm). Ta'izz Rd. is lined with **pharmacies, telecom offices** (call overseas from Ibb, as Jibla's rates are prohibitively high), and **currency exchanges.** The **telephone code** for Ibb and Jibla is 04.

■.□ ACCOMMODATIONS AND FOOD

Unless you arrive in Ibb at night, stay at Jibla's one hotel, at the base of town (YR 1000). The rooms are just as comfortable as in Ibb and infinitely quieter. Snort derisively and head for the door, and the price may fall to YR 500. In Ibb, the hotels around the taxi station are the cheapest, but you get what you pay for: the noise level borders on intolerable. **Hotel Nogum** (tel. 406 832 or 410 323), on Ta'izz Rd. 1500m south of the taxi station, is the best deal in Ibb: lots of amenities and an amenable staff (doubles YR 600; triples YR 900). **Ma'in Hotel** (tel. 640 321), a few meters up the left-hand fork of Ta'izz Rd., is clean and cheap, with an occasionally fulfilled promise of hot water (singles YR 200; doubles YR 400).

Ibb's culinary prospects are more cheerful than its lodgings. Ta'izz Rd. once again takes center stage: the upper part of the road is full of restaurants that tend to serve only one main dish. All restaurants are open daily 8am-10:30pm. **Aj-Jibli Restaurant,** south of the taxi station, has an excellent chicken dish with rice and bread (YR 250). Opposite Aj-Jibli and just south of the taxi station is the gold store-front of **Restaurant Al-Kebab,** which serves meatballs, bread, a dipping sauce, and a salad (YR 200). The **Youth's Buffet,** near the Old City, is manned by an ancient cook who sells a frying pan full of tasty scrambled eggs and vegetables with two baguette-style rolls (YR 70). To get here, take the right hand fork of Ta'izz Rd. uphill toward the Old City, then turn right at the mouth-watering beer glass cutout. Walk uphill to the next intersection and turn left.

■ SIGHTS

▨JIBLA. Jibla lives and breathes within the skeleton of its former glory. Queen Arwa is buried in a beautifully inscribed tomb in the **Mosque of Queen Arwa,** on the first street off the road into Jibla. The mosque and attached Qur'anic school (or *kattab,* both of which are still functional) are one of the most beautiful of such complexes in all of Yemen. In the terraced hills around town are further evidence of the greatness of Queen Arwa's age: an old **aqueduct** still brings water to Jibla from the two *wadis* that surround the town, passing by the ruins of the **Palace of Queen Arwa.**

IBB'S OLD CITY. The Old City is a settlement of four- and five-story houses devoid of decoration save their brightly-colored doors, which are constructed at the welding shop at the southern end of Ta'izz Rd. The city's improbably narrow streets exist in a time warp: turn a corner on a deserted street and you'll be transported to a modern-day market that's scarcely navigable for all its activity. The most welcome surprise is the **Aj-Jiyla Mosque** at its heart, a dilapidated but still impressive landmark built in 1773.

TA'IZZ

The museums in this pre-revolutionary seat of power are dedicated to remembering and preserving Imam Ahmad's past glories, but Ta'izz's inhabitants are much more interested in looking to the future and securing the city's position as one of Yemen's most modernized cities. Most buildings are brand-new. Many of the already chaotic streets have been dug up to make way for telecommunications cables, creating a crowded and dynamic atmosphere that can be exhilarating (and somewhat grating) compared to the rest of sleepy Yemen. More people sleep in the streets here than in any other Yemeni town, offsetting economic hopefulness while highlighting the need for modernization. Even Ta'izz's Old City is remarkable less for its physical aspect than for the feverish activity of its market. Take a breather by heading out to the surrounding mountainside or trekking through the small, quiet communities of the nearby Jabal Sabir.

❷ ORIENTATION AND PRACTICAL INFORMATION

Ta'izz's tangled streets are spread out across hilly countryside, making navigation difficult. The "city center" is **Bab Al-Kabir,** the main gate between the northern New City and the southern **Old City.** Bab al-Kabir is on **26 September Street,** the smaller of Ta'izz's two main east-west thoroughfares. **Tahrir Street** begins at Bab Al-Kabir and runs perpendicular to 26th September St. to connect it with the larger main thoroughfare **Gamal 'Abd an-Nasser Street** (Gamal St.), about 500m north. Two kilometers east of Tahrir, Gamal St. forks and becomes **Sana'a Street** on the left and **13th June Street** on the right. East of town are the zoo and Salah Palace, as well as the Sana'a and Aden Highways. The towns of Al-Hudayda and Al-Makha lie to the west. The looming peak of **Jabal Sabir** is always visible to the south.

Buses and *service* run daily to Ta'izz from Sana'a, Aden, and Al-Hudayda. **Service** taxis (4½hr., YR 400) to Sana'a and Aden wait for passengers just beyond the point where Gamal St. turns into Sana'a St. Wherever *service* are found, there will also be **motorcycle taxis** that generally charge less. Government buses leave farther down Sana'a St.; private buses leave from 13 June St. about 1500m past the end of Gamal St. **Yemen International Transport Co.** sends buses to **Sana'a** (5hr., 6:30am, YR 1800) and **Aden** (3hr., 10:30am, YR 1000).

Minibuses run along Gamal St. (YR 15-20), as do motorcycle taxis. YR 40-50 gets you across town on a **bike,** while a **car** can be rented for YR 70. For medical attention, go to **As-Sa'id Specialized Hospital** (tel. 213 246) on 26 September St., across from the National Museum. The **police station** (tel. 215 515) is near the eastern end of 26 September St. on the left-hand side, and the **post office** (tel. 215 515) is just before it. Internet access is available at **Al-Khatib Telecom** (tel. 221 208), on 26 September St., about 700m from Bab al-Kabir (YR 20 per min.; open Su-Th 8am-10pm). Ta'izz's **telephone code** is 04.

■□ ACCOMMODATIONS AND FOOD

Most hotels in Ta'izz are near the intersection of Gamal St. and Tahrir St. **Qasr Hemyar Tourist Hotel** has put up its name in glowing lights over the "commercial center" at the intersection to better advertise its clean, new rooms with private bathrooms (singles YR 1000; doubles YR 2000). One block east and 50m to the south, **Al-Walid Hotel** (tel. 227 165; fax 227 545) is equally new but pricier: singles with private bath are YR 1500, doubles YR 2000. The **◪Pepper Restaurant,** on Gamal St. about 1½km from Tahrir St., may be just what the doctor ordered. Head toward the Al-Hudayda taxis and look to the right for the English sign. The fish and rice dishes (YR 250) are quite good, and pizza is also served (open until 1am). Vegetarians (or anyone tired of meat-heavy Yemeni food) will appreciate the hearty bean-based *shurba* that's the only offering of a nameless **restaurant** near the intercity *service* depot (look for the blue doors under the pharmacy sign 20m east of the intersection on Gamal St.). On the southwest corner of Gamal St. and Tahrir St., **Modern Yemen Restaurant** dishes out *salta* and boiled beef for YR 300.

COFFEE TALK Yemen is often credited with being the first spot on the globe to cultivate coffee. Legend has it that farmers first reaped a jittery harvest there in 575 CE, although written evidence of the bean doesn't appear until the 10th century (when the physician **Avicenna of Bukhara** extolled the medicinal virtues of munching on the little brown *bunchum* bean). Regardless of where it was first gathered, coffee cultivation in Yemen has traditionally been centered in the eastern highland mountains. By the start of the 17th century, coffee was all the craze in Europe (appearing first in Amsterdam in 1616), and when Europeans arrived at the port town of **Al-Makha** (near present-day Ta'izz) in search of the coveted plant, they found a cosmopolitan city filled with lavish villas built by prosperous coffee merchants. Al-Makha had such a monopoly on coffee that it lent its name to the variety of bean known as **mocha.** The plant was soon smuggled out of Yemen to other locales, and mornings have never been the same. Although it once was a classy trade port on par with ancient Alexandria, run-down Al-Makha doesn't amount to a hill of beans today. Those still interested in seeing the namesake city can grab a taxi from the western end of Gamal St. in Ta'izz (YR 250).

👁 SIGHTS

JABAL SABIR. The mountain country surrounding Ta'izz is dry and sparsely vegetated, but it has a rugged beauty that can only really be appreciated from the vantage point atop Jabal Sabir. Most people acknowledge that the best *qat* in Yemen is grown on this hill, and the rival farmers here have been known to resort to open gunfights over who controls the *wadi* in times when water is scarce. Ask your hotel manager if Jabal Sabir is safe for travel before making your ascent. Those tiring of natural beauty can take in the unnaturally beautiful **Fortress of Cairo.** See with your eyes, not with your hands: the fort is used as a military base and is closed to visitors. *(Take a service (YR 60) from Bab al-Kabir.)*

OLD CITY. A sea of people wheel and deal in the Old City's **Central Market,** just inside of Bab al-Kabir. Silver is sold here (look for the white sign in English), but most of the activity revolves around the trading of food: brightly colored spices and dried peppers vie with giant piles of dried fish for olfactory domination. The twin minarets of the **Al-Ashrafiyya Mosque** preside over the section of the Old City in the foothills of Jabal Sabir. Since it's no longer used as a functioning house of worship (although the *madrasa*, or Qur'anic school, still churns out scholars), visitors stand a chance of getting inside if they ask one of the locals to let them in.

NATIONAL MUSEUM. The National Museum preserves the decadent household of the last *imam* as a monument to the corruption and astounding inequality of prerevolutionary Yemen. Don't expect mythical opulence from the small collection; some jewelry is on display, but the centerpieces are more along the lines of electric blankets and rusty film projectors. *(Tel. 215 599 or 215 302. On 26 September St., 1½km east of Bab al-Kabir. The service to Ghamelia passes by (YR 15). Motorcycle taxis go there for YR 30-40, private taxis a bit more. Open Su-Th 8am-12:30pm. Admission YR 50.)*

SALAH PALACE. Like the National Museum, the well-organized Salah Palace is a converted residence dedicated to preserving the treasures of the *imam* who once lived there. The exhibits display Yemen's world-renowned silver jewelry and manuscripts, documents, and photographs from the *imam's* reign. The walls are covered with recent photographs of Yemen's major towns. *(Service run from Bab al-Kabir to Ghamelia (YR 15), where another taxi can take you to Salah (YR 20; 30min. total). Open Su-Th 9am-12:30pm. Admission YR 150. No photography allowed.)*

ADEN

It's easy to forget the rest of Yemen once you're in Aden, Yemen's most famous city. The emerald sea is visible from almost anywhere along Aden's clean, peaceful streets, and the silhouetted islands in the distance evoke the tropics. Aden has a long history as a colonial enclave and as a pawn in Western power plays. It was the headquarters of the British presence, and the hand of colonialism has shaped everything from the grand old dame of the Crescent Hotel to the appropriately self-abasing monument Little Ben (the bratty younger sibling of the famous clocktower in London). The grandeur of Aden's colonial-era luxury hotels has long faded, but there's been a spate of recent building in the hopes that Aden will rise anew as an international hotspot. Until recently, the French consulate was housed in the former residence of the renegade poet Arthur Rimbaud, whose home also did time as a now-defunct museum. The effects of the secular, Marxist People's Democratic Republic of Yemen are also visible in the city's culture and architecture. Aden is the most socially westernized city in Yemen: far more women go unveiled here than in the north, and one can even get an alcoholic drink without undue trouble or expense. But while Pizza Hut, cold beer, and a swim may be a welcome change from the rest of Yemen, antiquity's dusty past still lies strewn around the city in its buildings, traditions, and people, and its inescapably Yemeni character remains.

✦ ORIENTATION

The city of Aden consists of three basically independent towns spread out over a peninsula enclosing one side of the **Bay of Aden.** The main town and city center of

Aden is **Crater** (so named because it sits in the center of an active volcano), on the peninsula's eastern side facing the open sea. The oldest part of Aden, Crater contains most of the city's historical attractions and its *souq* (as well as that most modern of Yemen's offerings, Pizza Hut). The minibus and taxi station is about 800m east of the *souq*. A road runs out of Crater to nearby **Sira Island,** with its picturesque fortress. The second town, **At-Tawahi,** occupies the western side of the peninsula. The nicest beaches are on the southern outskirts of At-Tawahi, in **Gold Mohur Bay** and **Elephant Bay.** Between Crater and At-Tawahi is the third town, **Ma'alla,** home to a few restaurants but little else. Just to the north of Aden are the suburbs of **Khormaksar** and **Sheikh 'Uthman,** with the **airport** between the two. Intercity buses and taxis arrive and leave from Sheikh 'Uthman.

🛈 PRACTICAL INFORMATION

Walking is the easiest way to get around within each of these small towns, even in the intense heat of midsummer, but you'll want to catch a minibus for travel between them, as well as between At-Tawahi and the beaches. **Minibuses** leave from the small gardens near the Crescent Hotel (YR 20). Private **taxis** charge at least YR 200 to get across town. **Renting a car** is not an efficient way to travel in Aden, but those looking to do so can turn to the **Avis Car Rental** (tel. 232 911) at the Aden Movenpick Hotel in Khormaksar (US$50 per day negotiable down to US$35 per day; non-negotiable YR 30 per km over 100km). At 6:30am, **Yemen International Transport Co.** gives its buses the royal send-off to: **Sana'a** (7½hr., YR 2200); **Al-Hudayda** (4hr., YR 2000); **Ta'izz** (3hr., YR 1000); and **Al-Mukalla** (10½hr., YR 3400).

Police are south of the market in Crater and have several offices around the main wharf in At-Tawahi. The Saudi-built **Friendship Hospital** (tel. 384 577) is on the waterfront in Crater, 500m west of Pizza Hut. Services for **money changing, international telephone calls,** and **pharmacies** are most abundant in Crater's central market, though few employees speak English. The **Central Post Office** is on Queen Arwa Rd. in eastern Crater, near the stadium. At-Tawahi also has a post office one block in from the waterfront, about 500m west of the main wharf. Right across the street, Internet access is available at **Qureish for Printing Services** (tel. 235 803) for YR 15 per minute (open Su-Th 8am-8pm). Aden's **telephone code** is 02.

🏠🍴 ACCOMMODATIONS AND FOOD

Cheap hotels are in relatively short supply in Aden. There are only three real budget hotels in the city. Find clean rooms and hallway baths at the **Red Sea Hotel** (tel. 252 402), three blocks west of the taxi station (quads YR 400 regardless of how many beds are occupied). The sparkling bathrooms of **Al-Wafa Hotel** (tel. 256 340) are 50m west of the taxi station, across the street from the Hurricane Cinema (doubles YR 1300; triples YR 1700). To get to the **Seera Tourist Hotel** (tel. 255 526), steera yourself 200m down the street that begins across from the now-defunct Military Museum, two blocks south of Queen Arwa Rd. (singles YR 2200; doubles YR 2250; triples YR 3190). Though much pricier, you'll moon over the **Crescent Hotel** (tel. 203 471; fax 204 597), by the public gardens in At-Tawahi, where beautiful rooms are decorated in a style reminiscent of Yemen's days as a royal empire (US$38 and up).

The cheapest eats can be found at the many food stands that dot the streets of the town. **Reem Tourist Restaurant,** on Gandi St. in Crater, one block north of the bus and taxi depot, is excellent and affordable. **Osan Broast Tourist Restaurant,** in the center of At-Tawahi opposite the public gardens, also offers low-price fare. **Ching Sing Chinese Restaurant,** on Ma'alla's main street, is an unquestionable local fave with questionably authentic Chinese decor. Admire the paper lamps, calligraphy, and rice paper screens as you chow down on chow mein (YR 600), served with painted chopsticks in "Ming" bowls. Prices are fairly high because Ching Sing is a frequent stop on the expat gravy train. A trip to Aden wouldn't be complete without a visit to the local **Pizza Hut,** indistinguishable from any other link in that worldwide chain (medium pizza YR 900). The familiar red-roofed temple to extra cheese is by the water in Crater, across from the National Museum.

♫ ENTERTAINMENT

Believe it or not, there are actually nightclubs in Aden, complete with live music, belly dancing, and liquor. **Ash-Shadrawn** (tel. 203 876), next to the Crater Pizza Hut, has a great view of the fortress on Sira Island and a large outdoor patio-*cum*-dance floor that serves food and drinks to the beat of the live Yemeni cover band. A belly dancer also makes periodic appearances throughout the evening, much to the delight of the mostly male patrons (appreciation for her talent is shown by scattering money over her head). Food prices are pretty standard (YR 300 for a half-chicken), but at YR 400, each beer costs more than a main course. Cover for this rather tame den of iniquity is YR 100 (open 5pm-4am). Even more surprising than the presence of spirits is the unheard-of-in-Yemen cross-dressing scene at the **Sailor's Club Restaurant and Hotel** (tel. 203 209; fax 203 559), in At-Tawahi. Sailor's is set up like Ash-Shadrawn, with an outdoor patio and dance floor (and several Russian belly dancers). The crowd is made up mostly of straight males, but some transvestites frequent the club, which is nothing short of extraordinary in this very traditional Islamic country. Beer goes for a reasonable YR 350, and food is expensive but delicious: YR 1000 buys lobster in a spicy tomato sauce (cover YR 100).

👁 SIGHTS

CISTERNS OF AT-TAWILA. The Cisterns of At-Tawila are along the slopes of Jabal Shemsan. This astounding ancient system of waterworks, once used to store rainwater and direct excess runoff into the sea, was not discovered until 1854. However, it is estimated that they were built in or before the first century CE. The drainage channels to the waterfront have now been filled in and are used as streets, which precipitated serious flooding in 1993, when heavy rains filled the cisterns beyond capacity. A popular **park** surrounds the lowest tanks, which have steps leading down into their empty beds. The majority of the cisterns are higher up on Jabal Shemsan and accessible only by a railing-less, winding pathway that leads into the heart of the mountain. Those who choose to take a half-day to explore the mountain (only an hour or so is needed for the park) should be warned that higher up the mountain, the path is much more challenging than it appears. The path leading up to the higher cisterns is on the left-hand side of the canyon into which the park disappears. Early morning and evening are the best times to visit. Always hike in a group, and inform someone in town about your plans before leaving. *(To reach the park from the taxi station, head straight down the street where An-Nasser Bookshop sits. Free.)*

MOSQUES. The most beautiful mosques are in Crater, the city's oldest neighborhood. If you walk along the road beginning at Pizza Hut, you'll first encounter the **Al-Khawja Mosque,** with its distinctive Indian-influenced architecture, immediately followed by the **Al-Aydarus Mosque,** 200m past the Al-Khawja. The older Al-Aydarus Mosque was built in the 14th century and has been razed and raised several times since then by various attackers and architects. The white, mosque-less **Aden Minaret** looms above neighboring houses some 50m east of the Crater post office.

SIRA ISLAND FORTRESS. Built by the Turks and used by the British during their tenure in Aden, this fortress was occupied until very recently by the military, who closed it to the public. Fortunately, the venerable low-tech installation is now open to anyone, revealing a panoramic view of Crater by day and cutting a striking figure against the night sky. *(To get to Sira Island, take the 300m long causeway (200m east of Pizza Hut) leading out of Crater. It's an easy walk, but taxis only cost YR 100.)*

OTHER SIGHTS. Churches are a rare sight in Yemen, but Aden is home to two of them. The **Catholic Church of St. France,** near the post office in At-Tawahi, serves as the lone functioning outpost of Christian worship in the entire country. The hilltop **Protestant Church** is visible from the intersection 50m west of the Crater post office. No longer used for religious purposes, it currently serves as an administrative office for the police. The **National Museum,** across the street from Pizza Hut, is housed in a grand old building that's more impressive than the small collection inside it. *(Museum open Su-Th 10:30am-1:30pm. Admission YR 30.)*

> ## SITTIN' ON THE DOCK OF THE BAY
> If you spend any time in Aden, you'll notice that the line of ships sitting out in the Gulf clearly aren't going anywhere. These are **Iraqi oil tankers,** trapped just off Aden's coast since 1991 by the United Nations embargo against their home country. It's impossible to tell from the shore view, but anyone who's been around boats can imagine how much these ship must have deteriorated over the course of seven unattended years. It's unlikely these tankers could return to active service even if the embargo were lifted today. A local group is petitioning the government for permission to go out and salvage whatever remains functional aboard, and either sell the rest for scrap or sink it.

◩ BEACHES

Among the beautiful beaches of At-Tawila, the public **Elephant Bay** is the biggest and the most littered. The next bay over is **Mohen Bay,** home to the **Mohen Gold Beach Club** (tel. 204 174; open 8am-11pm), where YR 100 buys access to a cleaner strip of sand and a restaurant/beach bar with radical food and drinks at radically jacked-up prices (grilled lobster tail YR 1000). Just on the other side of the hill behind the Mohen Gold is **Shipwreck Beach,** a preferable (and free) alternative to Elephant Bay. There can be a strong undertow in the late summer months and drownings have been known to happen, so ask about the swimming conditions before heading out and never swim alone. You can also hire fishermen to take you to those beaches not accessible from the road (boats YR 500-1000). Most beaches are accessible by taxi (YR 200-300) or minibus (YR 20) from At-Tawahi.

AL-MUKALLA

Al-Mukalla's appeal comes from its dramatic vistas, where houses seem to rise up from the sea itself. Because trade has traditionally fostered foreign contact, Al-Mukalla synthesizes Arab, African, and Indian elements in a kind of Yemeni melting pot that nearly matches the diversity of its northwestern counterpart, Tarim. Gentrification has recently put a pretty face on the city: a newly built sea wall and noisy promenade run across the length of the city. Bring a camera: not only is the city itself one of Yemen's most photogenic, but a vicious storm some years back dashed a pair of ships onto the coast to create a dramatic display.

◪ ORIENTATION AND PRACTICAL INFORMATION

Most places of interest are between the dry but still-bridged *wadi* and the old town at the eastern end of the city. A waterfront combination of *souq*, auction house, and junk yard is on the western side of the *wadi*. Most services are available in the older, nicer parts of town. For airline tickets, call the **Yemen Airline Office** (tel. 302 414). Private **buses** run by **Yemen International Transport Co.** leave from Ash-Sharq, 500m inland from the banks of the *wadi*, to **Aden** (10hr., 6:30am, YR 3400). **Taxis** and government buses depart almost directly across the *wadi* next to the Saba Hotel. Buses (6hr., 6:30am, YR 350) and *service* taxis (5hr., until early afternoon, YR 600) to **Say'un** leave from the Hai October suburb, 1km north of the sea to the west of the *wadi*. **Riyan Airport** is 25km north of Al-Mukalla off the Say'un road and can only be reached by private taxi. The **police station** is just east of the dry *wadi* on the west side of the street. Contact the **Ba-Sharahil Hospital** (tel. 302 012) in the event of a medical emergency. The **post office** (tel. 302 268) is across the street from the Mosque of 'Umar, just east of the promenade cafe. Internet connections can be accessed at **Computer Home** (tel. 352 063), in Hai October, 700m south of the taxi station, for an expensive YR 50 per minute.

◫◪ ACCOMMODATIONS AND FOOD

Al-Mukalla's hotels may be cheap, but solo travelers who arrive in the evening will likely have to pay for a double or triple. The **Saba Hotel** (tel. 304 755), on Al-Mukalla

Rd. on the eastern side of the dry *wadi*, boasts squeaky-clean rooms with chilly air conditioning and refrigerators (singles YR 1300; doubles YR 1500; triples YR 2000). The **Star Hotel** (tel. 303 925; fax 304 366) shines about 500m from the waterfront on the third street west of the *wadi*. A vertical white sign identifies the Star by its Arabic name, "An-Nujum" (triples YR 1500). If you're heading for Say'un and want an early start, **Ausan Hotel** (tel. 304 305; fax 304 306), on the main street just north of the taxi station, is the best deal in the area. All of their tidy rooms (except the singles) are air conditioned (singles YR 700; doubles YR 1500; triples YR 1700).

The waterfront harbors several restaurants, none of them spectacular. The meat patties, *samosas*, and sweet buns sold on the street are tastier and cheaper (YR 5-10). Tea, soda, and snacks are also available from the **promenade cafe.** In the Hai October suburb, across the street from the Say'un taxi station, the lively **Golden Dawn Restaurant** is known for savory food and wallet-friendly prices (entrees YR 200). The ground floor of the **Ausan Hotel** hosts a restaurant and teahouse whose specialty is a spicy chicken stew (YR 200).

👁 SIGHTS

🗺 HISN AL-GHUWAYZI. Along the Riyan road, about 1km north of the Say'un taxi station, the mini-fortress Hisn al-Ghuwayzi seems to defy the laws of engineering. This small mud building makes a wild sight, perched atop an outcropping of rock scarcely wider than its own base. The fortress itself is closed, but there are steps leading up the rock to the locked door. Hisn al-Ghuwayzi has the greatest visual impact from a distance, so travelers on their way north out of Al-Mukalla wouldn't miss much if they just convince a taxi driver to pull over for a quick photo stop.

PROMENADE AND OTHER SIGHTS. Crowds come out on the **promenade** to watch the waves break in the evenings, making the shore scene quite lively at dusk. Behind the first row of buildings, 100m east of the promenade cafe, is the stunning **Mosque of 'Umar.** The mosque itself is on a diagonal inside a large, elevated courtyard whose walls house street-level shops. The bright white building is graced with ornate pastel blue trimmings, their colors enhanced after dark by a creative lighting scheme. The other large mosque at the eastern end of this street is the **Ar-Rawda Mosque.** About 100m east of the *wadi* is the **Sultan's Palace,** which was a museum until 1994, when many of its exhibits were looted in the civil war. In western Al-Mukalla, on the other side of the *wadi*, sits a **junk souq:** ancient appliances are auctioned from the back of pickup trucks while goats and camels look on disinterestedly. The palm fronds and driftwood blown around everywhere by the wind make this collection even more eclectic.

WADI HADRAMAWT

The Wadi Hadramawt, a fertile valley extending across almost 200km, contains a variety of geologic and geographic terrains ranging from barren rocky plains to lush fields of terraced crops laid out in long, green stripes. Many traditional tribes still live in the region, which has been inhabited for thousands of years by nomadic herders and farmers. At the heart of the *wadi* are the three amazing towns of **Say'un, Shibam,** and **Tarim,** each renowned in its own right for visual beauty, architectural oddity, and stunning natural geography. These towns can and should be easily reached from the hub of Al-Mukalla.

SAY'UN

In stark contrast to dense and narrow Shibam, Say'un is full of open spaces, its large structures visible from almost anywhere in town. With a population of 30,000, Say'un is by far the largest town in Wadi Hadramawt, a fact belied by its many palm trees, spread-out settlements, and dusty roads. Say'un has been the administrative capital of Wadi Hadramawt for over 500 years, and is the ostensible destination of any public transport into the region.

⚡ ORIENTATION AND PRACTICAL INFORMATION. Even the biggest town in Wadi Hadramawt is small enough to conquer by foot. The **central souq** area, where Say'un's services and most of its hotels are located, spans only a few blocks. The *souq* would be hard to miss even without all the activity, as Say'un's main attraction, the **Sultan's Palace**, looms above it like the mammoth cliffs that shadow the city's southwestern edge. The **airport** is nearby to the north (10min., YR 100 by taxi). *Service* taxis don't operate in Wadi Hadramawt, but **buses** to Al-Mukalla, Shibam, and Tarim all leave from the public park just east of the town center in the morning. Blue buses serve **Shibam** (YR 60) and **Tarim** (YR 120) from 7am to about 10am, but there's only one bus to **Al-Mukalla** daily, leaving between 6 and 6:30am (YR 350). **Shared taxis** go to Shibam (YR 100), Tarim (YR 150), and Al-Mukalla (YR 600) until around 6pm. Most shops close around 6pm and on Fridays, but restaurants and tea houses stay open into the late evening. Call the **police station** (tel. 402 111) or the **Say'un Hospital** (tel. 403 260) for emergencies. **Postal services** leaving from here are unreliable: wait to get to Al-Mukalla to send mail. **Telecom offices** dot the central *souq*, and prices are commensurate with those all over Yemen.

⚏⚏ ACCOMMODATIONS AND FOOD. A range of hotels is easily accessible from the central *souq* area. The cheap, clean **At-Tawila Hotel** (tel. 405 264) hides in an alley across from the Sultan's Palace. Small, barren rooms and a lack of air conditioning are drawbacks (singles YR 500; doubles YR 800). In the streets behind At-Tawila is the **Rayboon Tourist Hotel** (tel. 405 393; fax 402 686), with comfortable rooms complete with air conditioning, satellite TV, telephones, and private bath (singles 800, with A/C YR 1000; doubles with A/C YR 1500; triples with A/C 2000). Take a swim (YR 50 per hr.) at the **Trade and Housing Tower Hotel** (tel. 403 575), but be prepared to lighten your wallet if you dive into their rooms (singles YR 1526; doubles YR 1770; triples YR 2005). Say'un doesn't offer much in the way of culinary options, so it's lucky that one of its few restaurants is among the best in Yemen. ▨**Bahamdoon,** in the middle of the central area, 300m east of the Palace on the north side of the street, serves baked fish, egg sandwiches, chicken, and meat dishes for less than YR 250. The decent **Park Cafe and Restaurant** and the **Ash-Sha'ab Restaurant** sit opposite each other, 100m eastward.

⬛ SIGHTS. The great white hype that is the **Sultan's Palace** is the thing to see in Say'un–you couldn't miss its hulking wedding-cake form if you tried. The maze of rooms within the palace are open for unrestricted exploration, but have long been stripped bare. Wide terraces give great views out on Say'un. It also houses a small **folklore and antiquities museum** with displays on Islamic medicine and coffee (open 8am-12:30pm; admission YR 30). The Tomb of Habshi is better known as the **Turquoise Tomb** because of its giant turquoise dome. This relative baby was built in 1910, but blends seamlessly with the older buildings that surround it.

SHIBAM

Shibam is one of the main reasons tourists come to Yemen, and with good reason. The 500 earthen houses of this spectacular city rise out of the desert like a strange rock formation, crowned in white for protection against the ruthless heat. Shibam is the only town in the world with a crew-cut. Buildings begin at elevations varying as much as 5m but all end at the same height. Within the earthen ramparts of Shibam is a disconcerting grid of streets that borrows from the principles of the traditional Muslim city, whose spatial dictates come straight from the Qur'an and the Hadith. The misalignment of the streets from one block to the next destroys the possibility of panoramic views of the city within its limits, despite its small size (less than 1km from one end to the other). Buildings are grouped tightly together on the hill for better protection against floods, earning the town its moniker, "The Manhattan of the Desert."

🛈 PRACTICAL INFORMATION. Shibam is 20km from Say'un; take a taxi from Say'un (YR 60) or hop off the Al-Mukalla bus early. There are no hotels, telephone offices, or currency exchanges in Shibam, but there's a **pharmacy** and **police station** just inside the gate and a few small **restaurants** on the main street. If you're in town at sunset, get out to the cliffs of Sahil Shibam to snap a classic photo of the light refracting throughout the city.

🛈 SIGHTS. Intricate *mashrabiyya* windows and wooden doors (some dating from the 12th century), adorn the facades of these five- to nine-story skyscrapers. This fascinating architectural ensemble dates from the 16th century, although several of Shibam's mosques, such as the **Aj-Juma'a Mosque** built by the notoriously extravagant Haroun ar-Rashid, are even older. The gleaming white **Mosque of Sheikh Ma'aruf** is a relative newcomer at only 500 years, cradled in a grove of date palms. Shibam's long history includes several instances of severe flood damage and retaliatory reconstruction (the last time the city was destroyed was in the 14th century CE), but a good deal of money has been spent to safeguard Shibam ever since it was declared a UNESCO World Heritage Site in the 1980s.

TARIM

Tarim is the theological center of a region with a dynamic and influential faith system. Muslim tradesmen and missionaries left the town to do business but returned home once they had amassed a substantial amount of money, which they spent on building palaces and mosques. Many of these buildings are clearly influenced by the pointed arches and stacked architectural styles of India and Southeast Asia. These sojourners brought back international traditions as well as money, as testified by the cosmopolitanism of Tarim's wealthier residents.

🛈 PRACTICAL INFORMATION. Without a private car, the only way to get to Tarim is by bus (mornings only, YR 60) or taxi (all day, YR 150) from Say'un to the main square. To get back to Say'un, walk 500m out of town on the main road to the station by a small park. There are a few hotels, restaurants, and a post office in Tarim, but no money exchanges, so bring enough cash to get back to Say'un.

🛈🛈 ACCOMMODATIONS AND FOOD. There are three hotels in Tarim. The dingy rooms and hallway toilets of **Brothers Pension** are in the central square (daytime naps YR 150; dorm beds YR 250; singles YR 350; doubles YR 500; triples YR 750). The clean and simple **Kenya Hotel** (tel. 415 720) is 300m down the street from the park (singles YR 900, with A/C YR 1200; doubles YR 1500; triples YR 1800). Farther down the same road and to the left at the fork is the singular **Gobba Palace Hotel** (tel. 415 221), offering large walled gardens, a swimming pool, and rooms in a wild, colorful building (singles YR 1232, with A/C 1680; doubles YR 1450/2060; pool and garden YR 100 for a few hours). There are a few small **restaurants** on the road out of town; choose one that's not empty.

🛈 SIGHTS. Tarim is known for its abundance of mosques. Citizens who left to make their fortunes traditionally built one upon their triumphant return home, and the town's "official" count is 365 (one for every day of the year). The most famous of the alleged 365, **Al-Muhdar Mosque** (300m from the square), has a 40m tall shining white minaret, built in 833 CE, that was until recently the tallest in South Arabia. Religious scholars and calligraphy buffs flock to Tarim to study the texts at **Al-Ahqaf Library,** in the park by the taxi station. The collection of 14,000 volumes make it Yemen's second largest library, but its fame rests on its beautiful hand-written manuscripts, 5000 in total. For some exercise-*cum*-views, follow the hill leading up from the central square into the cliffs a little left of center. The walk takes about 40 minutes and is a good vantage point for glamor shots of Tarim.

APPENDIX

CLIMATE

Temp in °C/Rain in cm	January		April		July		October	
Rain in cm	Temp	Rain	Temp	Rain	Temp	Rain	Temp	Rain
Limassol, CYP	15/5	7.6	24/10	1.8	37/21	.1	28/14	2.5
Alexandria, EGY	18/11	4.8	23/15	.3	29/23	0	28/20	0.5
Aswan, EGY	23/10	0	36/19	0	41/26	0	37/22	0
Cairo, EGY	18/8	0.5	28/14	.3	36/21	0	30/18	0
Eilat, ISR (Aqaba, JOR)	21/10	0	31/18	.5	39/26	0	33/21	0
Jerusalem, ISR	11/6	13.2	23/10	2.8	29/19	0	27/15	1.3
Tel Aviv, ISR	19/10	20.2	27/15	3.0	37/25	0	32/20	2.0
Amman, JOR	12/4	6.9	23/9	1.5	32/18	0	27/14	.5
Beirut, LEB	17/11	19	22/14	5.6	31/23	0	27/21	5.1
Muscat, OMA	25/19	2.8	32/26	1	36/31	0	34/27	0.3
Aleppo, SYR	10/1	8.9	24/9	2.8	36/21	0	27/12	2.5
Damascus, SYR	12/2	4.3	24/9	1.3	36/18	0	27/12	1.0
Deir ez-Zur, SYR	12/2	4.1	27/11	2.0	41/26	0	30/13	0.5
Ankara, TUR	4/-4	3.3	17/4	3.3	30/15	1.3	21/7	2.3
Istanbul, TUR	8/3	10.9	16/7	4.6	28/18	3.4	20/13	8.1
Dubai, UAE	23/12	2.3	30/18	0.5	38/28	0	33/22	0
Aden, YEM	28/22	0.2	31/24	0	36/27	0.3	30/22	0

HOLIDAYS AND FESTIVALS

Islamic holidays are timed to local sightings of the moon, so dates are not set until the last minute and differ from country to country. **Jewish** holidays last from sundown the night before to nightfall the next day. For longer holidays, businesses are closed for the first day (in the case of Passover, the last day) but remain open the rest of the time. The **holy day** (when many business are closed) is Friday *(Juma'a)* in the Muslim world and Saturday *(Shabbat)* in Israel. Businesses typically close on national holidays (listed below) as well. **Christian** holidays listed are those of the Eastern Orthodox or Maronite Church, and are celebrated among Christians in Syria, Lebanon, and Cyprus.

DATE	FESTIVAL	TYPE
Nov. 1, 1999	All Saints' Day	**Christian**
Nov. 6	Isra' and Miraj	**Islamic**
Nov. 18-19	National Days	**Omani**
Nov. 22	Independence Day	**Lebanese**
Nov. 30	Independence Day	**Yemeni**
Dec. 2	National Day	**UAE**
Dec. 4-11	Ḥanukkah, 1999	**Jewish**
Dec. 10	First Day of Ramadan (approximation)	**Islamic**
Dec. 25	Christmas	**Christian**
Jan. 4	Laylat al-Qadr	**Islamic**
Jan. 6	Epiphany	**Christian**

DATE	FESTIVAL	TYPE
Jan. 10	'Eid al-Fitr (end of Ramadan)	Islamic
Jan. 30	King 'Abdullah's Birthday	Jordanian
Feb. 9	Mar Maroun (Feast of St. Maron)	Christian (Lebanon)
Mar. 8	Revolution Day	Syrian
Mar. 18	'Eid al-Adha (Feast of the Sacrifice)	Islamic
Mar. 21	Purim	Jewish
Mar. 21	Women's Day (Mother's Day)	Syrian
Mar. 22	Arab League Day	Syrian
Apr. 7	Muharram (Islamic New Year)	Islamic
Apr. 17	Ashoura	Islamic
Apr. 17	Evacuation Day (Independence Day)	Syrian
Apr. 20-27	Pesaḥ (Passover)	Jewish
Apr. 21	Good Friday	Christian
Apr. 23	Easter	Christian
Apr. 23	National Independence and Children's Day	Turkish
May 1	Labour Day	Cypriot, Jordanian, Yemeni
May 2	Yom Ha-Shoah	Israeli
May 6	Martyr's Day	Lebanese, Syrian
May 10	Yom Ha-Atzma'ut (Israel Independence Day)	Israeli
May 19	Atatürk's Commemoration/Youth & Sports Day	Turkish
May 25	Independence Day	Jordanian
June 10	Shavuot	Jewish
June 10	Army Day and Anniversary of the Great Revolt	Jordanian
June 16	Eid al-Mawlid an-Nabi (Birth of the Prophet)	Islamic
June 18	Evacuation Day (Liberation Day)	Egyptian
June 19	Pentecost	Christian
July 23	Revolution Day	Egyptian
Aug. 15	Assumption of the Virgin Mary	Christian
Aug. 30	Victory Day	Turkish
Sept. 26	Revolution Day 1963	Yemeni
Sept. 30-Oct. 1	Rosh Ha-Shana (Jewish New Year)	Jewish
Oct. 6	National Day (Armed Forces Day)	Egyptian
Oct. 6	October War Day	Syrian
Oct. 9	Yom Kippur	Jewish
Oct. 14	Revolution Day 1962	Yemeni
Oct. 14-15	Sukkot	Jewish
Oct. 21	Simḥat Torah	Jewish
Oct. 24	Suez & National Liberation Day	Egyptian
Oct. 28	Isra' and Miraj	Islamic
Oct. 29	Republic Day	Turkish
Nov. 1	All Saints' Day	Christian
Nov. 16	National Day	Syrian
Nov. 18-19	National Days	Omani
Nov. 22	Independence Day	Lebanese
Nov. 30	First Day of Ramadan	Islamic
Nov. 30	Independence Day	Yemeni
Dec. 2	National Day	UAE
Dec. 22-29	Ḥanukkah	Jewish
Dec. 23	Victory Day	Egyptian
Dec. 25	Christmas	Christian
Dec. 31	'Eid al-Fitr (end of Ramadan)	Islamic

TIME ZONES

The Middle East spans three continents, so time zones vary. During standard time, **Egypt**, the **Levant** (Israel, The West Bank, Gaza, Jordan, Lebanon, Syria), **Cyprus,** and **Turkey** are two hours ahead of Greenwich Mean Time (GMT). **Yemen** is three hours ahead of GMT, and the **Gulf States** are two hours ahead of GMT. Things get complicated during daylight savings, when countries switch over at different intervals.

MEASUREMENTS

The metric system is used throughout the Middle East.

1 inch (in.) = 25.4 millimeters (mm)	1 millimeter (mm) = 0.039 in.
1 foot (ft.) = 0.30 m	1 meter (m) = 3.28 ft.
1 yard (yd.) = 0.914m	1 meter (m) = 1.09 yd.
1 mile = 1.61km	1 kilometer (km) = 0.62 mi.
1 ounce (oz.) = 28.35g	1 gram (g) = 0.035 oz.
1 pound (lb.) = 0.454kg	1 kilogram (kg) = 2.202 lb.
1 fluid ounce (fl. oz.) = 29.57ml	1 milliliter (ml) = 0.034 fl. oz.
1 gallon (gal.) = 3.785L	1 liter (L) = 0.264 gal.
1 acre (ac.) = 0.405ha	1 hectare (ha) = 2.47 ac.
1 square mile (sq. mi.) = $2.59km^2$	1 square kilometer (km^2) = 0.386 sq. mi.

TELEPHONE CODES

CYPRUS	357	LEBANON	961
Limassol, Paphos	05, 06	Ba'albeck	08
EGYPT	**20**	Bcharré	06
Alexandria	03	Beirut	01
Aswan	097	Saida (Sidon), Sur (Tyre)	07
Bahariyya	010	Tripoli	06
Cairo	02	**OMAN**	**968**
Dakhla	092	**SYRIA**	**963**
Hurghada	065	Aleppo	21
Kharga	092	Damascus	11
Luxor	095	Hama	33
Port Said	066	Homs	31
Sinai Peninsula (incl. Suez)	062	Lattakia	41
ISRAEL	**972**	Palmyra	34
Be'er Sheva	07	**TURKEY**	**90**
Eilat	07	Ankara	312
Golan	06	Antalya	242
Haifa	04	Bodrum	252
Jerusalem	02	Göreme	384
Tel Aviv	03	Istanbul (Asia/Europe)	216/212
Tzfat	06	İzmir	232
WEST BANK	**972**	Marmaris	252
All locations	02	Trabzon	462
GAZA	**972**	**UNITED ARAB EMIRATES**	**971**
Gaza City	07	Abu Dhabi	02
JORDAN	**962**	Al-'Ain	03
Amman	06	Dubai	04
Aqaba	03	Sharjah	06
Azraq (Desert)	06	**YEMEN**	**967**
Dead Sea	05	Aden	05
Irbid	02	Sana'a	01
Madaba	08	Ta'izz	04

APPENDIX

PHRASEBOOK

ARABIC (AL-'ARABI) العربى

Dialects of Arabic vary from country to country, but the most pronounced difference is between Egyptian and Levantine tongues. The *q* sound is dropped in Levantine Arabic; the Levantine *j* sound (as in fu**dge**) becomes a hard *g* (as in **G**ulf) in Egypt and parts of the Gulf. Arabic is read from right to left, but numerals are read from left to right. Arabic uses eight sounds not heard in English. *Kh* (خ) is like the German *ch*; *gh* (غ) is like the French *r*. There are two *h* sounds; one (ه) sounds like the English "h" and the other (ح, in Muhammad) is somewhere between *kh* and plain *h*. The letter *'ayn* (ع) comes from the throat. *R* is pronounced as a trill, just as it is in Spanish. Vowels and consonants can be either long or short (it means the difference between a *hammam*, bathroom, and a *hamam*, pigeon). The definite article is the prefix *al*, in Egypt pronounced more like *el*. When *al* comes before the sounds *t, th, j, d, dh, r, z, s, sh,* or *n,* the *l* is not pronounced, and the *l* elides to become the letter which follows it (e.g., *al-noor* becomes *an-noor*).

ARABIC NUMERALS										
0	1	2	3	4	5	6	7	8	9	10
٠	١	٢	٣	٤	٥	٦	٧	٨	٩	١٠
sifir	waahid	ithnayn	thalaatha	arba'a	khamsa	sitta	sab'a	tha-maniya	tis'a	'ashara

EMERGENCY

ENGLISH	ARABIC
Help!	Al-haoonee!
Stop!	Yuaf!
I'm ill.	Nifsee ghamma 'aleya
It hurts me here.	Biyugani heena
Water	Mayya
Hospital	Mustashfa
Doctor	Duktoor
tourist police	Bolees as-seeyaaha
I'm calling the police	Hagiblak al-bolees
Leave me alone!	Imshee!
Passport	Basbor/jawaz (Levant), Gawaz (Egypt)
Embassy	Safaarah

GREETINGS

ENGLISH	ARABIC
Hello (formal/informal); Response; Goodbye	Marhaba/As-Salaamu aleikum; Wa Aleikum as–salaam; Ma' as-salaama
Good morning (response)	Sabah al-kheir (Sabah an-noor/Sabah al-ishta)
Good evening (response)	Masaa' al-kheir (Masaa' an-noor)
How are you? (Levant/Egypt)	Keefak?/Izzayyak? (m), Keefik?/Izzayek? (f)
I'm fine (Levant/Egypt)	Mabsuut/Kuwayyis (m), Mabsuuta/Kuwayyisa (f)
Yes; Yes (formal); No; Maybe	Eeh (Levant)/Aiwa (Egypt); Na'am; La; Yimkin
Never mind, No big deal	Ma'laysh
Thank you	Shukran
Please	Min fadlak (m), Min fadlik (f)
I'm sorry	Ana aasif (male), Ana aasifa (female)
Excuse me (to get attention)	'An iznak (m), 'An iznik (f)
God willing; Praise God	Inshallah; Al-hamdu lillah

ENGLISH	ARABIC
I don't know.	Ma rafsh.
What is your name? (Levant/Egypt)	Shoo ismak/Ismakeh (m), Shoo ismik/Ismikeh (f)
My name is...	Ismi...
student (m/f)	Talib/Taliba
tourist	Saa-ih (male), Saa-iha (female), Suwwaah (pl)
I don't understand (m/f)	Mish fehhim/fahma
I don't speak Arabic (Levant/Egypt)	Ma bahki 'arabi/Mish batkallim 'arabi
Do you speak English?	Levant: Bitihkee inglizi? Egypt: Bititkallim inglizi? (m), Bititkallimee inglizi? (f)
Please speak slowly	Kalimnee biraaha min fadlak
What do you call ____ in Arabic?	Tibayeh ____ bil 'Arabi?

DIRECTIONS

ENGLISH	ARABIC
Can you tell me how to get to [Sesame Street]?	[Sesame Street] fein?, [Sesame Street] ayna?
Straight	Dughree or 'Alatool
Right/Left	Yameen/Shimal or Yisaar
North/South/East/West	Ash-shamal/Al-ganoub/Ash-shar/Al-gharb
I'm lost.	Aana tuht.
From where does the bus leave?	Al-mahatta feyn?
Station	Mahatta (Mahattat when followed by name).
Public Square	Maidan
I would like a ticket for... (m/f)	('Awiz/'Awza) tazkara rehyeh...
One way/Round-trip	Bass/Gai
What time does the ____ leave?	Biyitla imta ____
bus	Al-Baas (Levant), Al-Autubeese (Egypt)
train	Al-Atr
automobile	As-Sayyaara (Levant), Al-'Arabiyya (Egypt)
airport	Mataar

SERVICES

ENGLISH	ARABIC
Room	Ghurfa (Levant); Odha (Egypt)
I'd like a (single/double) room.	'Awiz (f: 'Awza) ghurfa (bisrir wehid/litnein).
How much is a room?	Al-ghurfa bikam?
Hotel	Funduq or (h)otel
Lunch/Dinner	Al-ghada/Al-'asha
Coffee (Levant/Egypt); Tea	Ahwa/qahwa; shay
Bathroom	Hammam, twaleet
Restaurant	Matam
Telephone	Tilifohn
I'd like to make a call to the U.S.	'Awiz/'Awza aguiz mukalmali Amrika
Pharmacy	'Agzakhena, saidaleeya
Post Office	Maktab al-bareed (Levant)/Bosta (Egypt)
Street	Shaare' (Levant); Sharia (Egypt)
Market	Souq
Museum	Mathaf
Mosque	Masjid/jaame' (Levant), Masgid/gaame' (Egypt)
Church	Kineesa

DATE AND TIME

ENGLISH	ARABIC
What time is it?	Addeish as-saa'a? (Levant) Es-saa'a kaam? (Egypt)
Hour, Time	Saa'a
Day/Week/Month/Year	Yoam/Usbuu'/Shahr/Sana
Yesterday/Today/Tomorrow	Imbaareh/Al-yoam/Bukra
What time do you open/close?	Bi'ifta/Bi'ifil as-saa'a kaam?
Sunday/Monday/Tuesday/Wednesday	Yoam al-ahad/Yoam al-itnein/Yoam at-tala'at or Yoam ath-thulth/Yoam al-arba
Thursday /Friday/Saturday	Yoam al-khamees/Yoam aj-juma'a/Yoam as-sabt

MONEY

ENGLISH	ARABIC
How much is this?	Addaysh? (Levant) Bikam? (Egypt)
Will you take half?	Taakhud nuss? (male) Taakhdee nuss? (female)
I want... (Levant; Egypt)	Ishtee or Biddee; 'Ayiz (m), 'Ayza (f)
Is there a student discount?	Fi takhfid lit talaba?
Cheap/Expensive	Rikhees/ghehlee
No way!	Mish mumkin! or Mamnoo'
Money	Masaari (Levant), Fuloos (Egypt)
Change	Fraata (Levant), Fakka (Egypt)

HEBREW (IVRIT) עברית

The Hebrew language contains 22 characters, written from right to left. Although Hebrew is read from right to left, **numerals** are read from left to right. Vowels are generally left unwritten, but may appear underneath regular characters as smaller markings. Modern spoken Hebrew contains a large number of Hebraicized versions of English words that may be understandable to perky-eared English-speaking listeners. The transliterations *ḥ* (ח) and *kh* (כ and ך) are both guttural, as in the German word *ach*. The Hebrew *r* is close to the French *r*, although an Arabic (or even English) *r* is also understood. The definite article is the prefix *ha*. Feminine adjectives add an "-ah" at the end; feminine verbs usually add an "-at" or an "-et."

HEBREW NUMERALS

0	1	2	3	4	5	6	7	8	9	10
efes	eḥad	shtayim	shalosh	arba	ḥamesh	shesh	sheva	shmoneh	teisha	eser

EMERGENCY

ENGLISH	HEBREW
Help!	Hatzeeloo!
Stop!	Tafseek! (m)/Tafseekee! (f)
Don't touch me	Al teegah bee
I'm ill	Anee ḥoleh (m)/Anee ḥolah (f)
I'm hurt	Anee patzoo'ah (m)/Anee ptzoo'ah (f)
Water	Mahyim
Hospital	Beit-ḥolim
Doctor	Rofeh
I need a doctor	Anee tzariḥ rofeh (m)/Ani tzriḥa rofeh
I'm calling the police	Anee kore (m) (f: koret) lamishtara
Leave me alone	Azov otee
Go away/Go to hell	Tistalek/Lekh l'azazel
Police/Fire fighters/Ambulance	Mishtara/Meḥabei esh/Ahmboolance

GREETINGS

ENGLISH	HEBREW
Hello/Goodbye	Shalom
Good morning/Good evening	Boker tov/Erev tov
Could you help me?	Atah yaḥol la'azor lee(m)/At yeḥola la'azor lee (f)?
How are you?	Ma nishma?
Excellent/Fine/Not good	Metzuyan/Be-seder/Lo tov
Yes/No/Maybe	Ken/Lo/Oolai
Thank you	Todah
Please/You're welcome	Bevakasha
Excuse me/I'm sorry	Sliḥa
I don't know	Anee lo yodeah (m)/Anee lo yoda'at (f)
What is your name?	Eikh korim lekhah? (m) Eikh korim lakh? (f)
My name is...	Shmee...
I'm a student	Anee student (m)/studentit (f)
How do you say...?	Eikh omrim...
I don't understand	Anee lo mevin (m)/Anee lo mevinah (f)
I don't speak Hebrew	Anee lo medaber (f: medaberet) ivrit
Do you speak English?	Ata medaber ivrit? (m)/At medaberet ivrit? (f)
Please repeat	Tagid (m) (f: tagidi) od pa'am, bevakasha
Please speak slowly	Tedaber (m)/(f: tedabri) le'at bevakasha

DIRECTIONS

ENGLISH	HEBREW
Where is... ?	Eyfoh... ?
Straight	Washar
Right/Left	Yameen/Smol
North/South/East/West	Tzafon/Darom/Mizraḥ/Ma'arav
I'm lost	Ne'ebadetee
Do you know where... is?	Ata yodeah (f: Aht yoda'at) eifoh nimtzah... ?
Do you stop at...?	Ata otzer be-...?
From where does the bus leave?	Mi'eifo ha-otoboos ozev?
Center of town	Merkaz ha'ir
Central bus station	Taḥana merkazit
Bus stop	Taḥanat otoboos
I would like a ticket for...	Ani rotzeh kartees le...
One-way/Round-trip	Keevoon eḥad/Haloh ve'ḥazor
Please stop	Atzor, bevakasha
What time does the ___ leave?	Matai ha___ ozev?
Bus	Otoboos
Taxi	Monit/Taxi
Automobile	Mekhonit
Train	Rakevet

SERVICES

ENGLISH	HEBREW
Do you know of a cheap hotel?	Ata makeer (m) (f: makeera) malon zol?
Do you have a single/double room?	Yesh laḥem ḥeder le'yaḥeed/kafool?
How much is the room?	Kama oleh haḥeder?
Hotel/Hostel	Malon/Aḥsania
Breakfast/Lunch/Dinner	Aruḥat boker/Aruḥat tzohora'im/Aruḥat erev
Do you have vegetarian food?	Yesh laḥem oḥel tzimḥonee?

ENGLISH	HEBREW
I am vegetarian	Ani tzimḥonee/tzimḥoneet
Coffee/Tea	Kafeh/Teh
Bathroom	Sherutim
Room	Ḥeder
Restaurant	Mees'ada
Telephone	Telephon
I'd like to make a call to the U.S.	Anee rotzeh (m) (f: rotzah) letalfen le'america
Passport	Darkon
Pharmacy	Beit Markaḥat
Post office	Do'ar
Street	Reḥov
Market	Shuk
Museum	Muzaion
Synagogue	Beit knesset
Church	Knessia
Mosque	Misgad
Beach	Ḥof
Grocery store	Makolet

DATE AND TIME

ENGLISH	HEBREW
What time is it?	Ma hasha'ah?
Hour, Time	Sha'ah
Day/Week/Month/Year	Yom/Shavuah/Ḥodesh/Shanah
Early/Late	Mookdam/Me'ooḥar
Today/Yesterday/Tomorrow	Ha-yom/Etmol/Ma±ar
Morning/Afternoon/Evening/Night	Boker/Tzohora'im/Erev/Lyla
What time do you open/close?	Matai atem potḥim/sogrim?
Open/Closed	Patoo'aḥ/Sagoor
Sunday /Monday/Tuesday/Wednesday	Yom rishon/Yom shaini/Yom shlishi/Yom revi'i
Thursday /Friday/Sabbath (Saturday)	Yom ḥamishi/Yom shishi/Shabbat

MONEY

ENGLISH	HEBREW
Do you have... ?	Yesh lekhaõ? (m) Yesh lakhõ? (f)
How much is this?	Kama zeh oleh?
I want...	Anee rotzehõ (m)/Anee rotzahõ (f)
I don't want... (male/female)	Lo rotzehõ (male) Lo rotzahõ (female)
Is there a student discount?	Yesh hanaḥa le'studentim?
Cheap/Expensive	Zol/Yakar
Do you accept credit cards/traveler's checks?	Atem mekablim kartisei ashrai/hamḥaot nos'im
Money	Kesef
Change (literally "leftovers")	Odef

TURKISH (TÜRKÇE)

Turkish is phonetic: each letter has only one sound that is always pronounced distinctly (save ğ, which lengthens the vowels adjacent to it). Special vowel and consonant pronunciations include: c (**j**acket); ç (**ch**eck); ı (i without a dot, cous**i**n); i (p**ea**ce); j (zh, plea**s**ure); ö (d**eu**x); ş (**sh**ort); u (b**oo**t); ü (**cue**). Special letter combinations include: ay (pronounced **eye**); ey (pl**ay**); oy (t**oy**); uy (ph**ooey**)

TURKISH NUMERALS

0	1	2	3	4	5	6	7	8	9	10
sıfır	bir	iki	üç	dört	beş	altı	yedi	sekiz	dokuz	on
si-fihr	beer	ee-KEE	ooch	durt	besh	altih	ye-DEE	SEH-kuz	doh-KOOZ	ohn

EMERGENCY

ENGLISH	TURKISH
Help!	İmdat! (Eem-daht!)
Stop!	Ayıp! (Ah-yup!)
I'm ill	Hastayℂm (has-TA-yuhm)
Water	Su (soo)
Hospital	Hastane (has-ta-NE)
I need a doctor	Doktor ihtiyacim (DohkTOR eeh-tee-YA-cum)
Go away!	Haydı git! (Hah-dee git!)
Police	Polis (polees)

GREETINGS

ENGLISH	TURKISH
Hello /Goodbye (morning)/Goodbye (evening)	Merhaba (Mehrhaba)/İyi günler (eee-YEE goon-lehr)/ İyi akşamlar (eee-YEE ak-SHAM-lar)
How are you?	Ne haber (nah-behr?)
Fine	İyiyim
Yes/No/Maybe	Evet (eh-veht)/Hayır (hyer)/Belki (behl-kee)
Thank you	Teşekkur ederim (tesh-ekur edeh-rim)
You're welcome	Bir şey değil. (beer shey dee-eel)
Please	Lütfen (loot-fahn)
Excuse me/I'm sorry	Pardon (pahr-don)/Özür dilerim (oz-oor deel-er-rim)
What is your name?	Adın ne? (ad-uhn ne?)
My name is...	İsmim (Ees-meem)
I'm a student	Oğrenciyim (OH-ren-jee-yeem)
I don't understand	Anlamadım (ahn-luh-mah-dim)
I don't speak Turkish.	Turkçe bilmiyorum. (Toork-che BEEL-mee-YOR-uhm)
Do you speak English?	İnglizce biliyor musun? (een-gul-EEZ-je beel-ee-YOR muh-SUN?)
Please speak slowly	Yavaş lütfen (yah-vash loot-fahn)
Are you a pimp?	Pesevenk misin? (pehs-seh-vehnk mih-sihn?)

DIRECTIONS

ENGLISH	TURKISH
Where is... ?	...nerede? (...nehr-eh-deh?)
How far is...?	...a ne kadar uzakta (a neh kahdahr oozakta?)
Straight	düz (dooz; to a taxi driver); doğru (doh-oo; said in all other instances)
Right/Left	Sağ (saa)/Sol (sohl)
North/South/East/West	Hangisi (han-gee-see)/Güneye (goo-ne-YE)/Do■uya (do-ghoo-YA)/Batℂya (ba-tuh-YA)
I'm lost	Yolumu kaybettim (yol-oo-moo kay-bet-teem)
I'm going to...	...ya gidiyorum (yah geed-EE-yohr-uhm)
Central bus station	otogar (oh-tow-gar)
Bus stop	otobüs dura■i (oto-boos doo-raa)
I would like a ticket.	Bir bilet alabilir miyim? (beer bee-let ala-bee-LEER mee-yeem?)

ENGLISH	TURKISH
One-way/Round-trip	Gidi@ (gee-deesh)/Gidi@-dönü@ biletin (gee-deesh doo-noosh bee-le-teen)
What time does the ___ leave?	Saat kaçta kalkiyor? (sah-at kach-tah kahlk-ee-yor?)
Bus	otobüs (oto-boos)
Taxi	Taksi
Automobile	Bir araba (beer ah-ra-bah)

SERVICES

ENGLISH	TURKISH
Is there an available room?	Boş odanız var mı? (bosh odaniz vahr mih?)
Single/double	Tek (tehk)/Çift (cheeft)
How much is the room?	Bir günlük fiyat ne kadar?
Hotel/Pension	Otel (oh-tell)/Pansiyon (pan-see-yown)
Breakfast/Lunch/Dinner	Kahvaltı (kah-val-tuh)/
Do you have vegetarian food?	Etsiz yemek var mı? (eht seez yemek vahr mi?)
I am vegetarian	Vejetariyanım (vej-e-tar-iyan-im)
Coffee/Tea	Kahve (Turkish coffee, kah-veh)/Çay (chai)
Bathroom	Tuvalet (too-wallet) or Banyo
Restaurant	Restoranda (ress-to-RAN-duh)
Telephone	Telefon
Can I make a call to the U.S.?	Amerika'ya nasıl telefon edebilirim (ame-REE-kaya nasul telefon ede-bee-lee-reem?)
Passport	Pasaport
Pharmacy	Eczane (ej-ZAH-ne)
Post office	Postane
Market	Bedesten (be-de-STEN)
Museum	Müzesi (moo-zeh-seh)
Mosque	Camii (jamee-ee)

DATE AND TIME

ENGLISH	TURKISH
What time is it?	Saat kaç? (Sa-at ka-ch?)
Hour	bir saat (beer sa-AT)
Day/Week/Month/Year	Bir gün (beer goon)/Bir hafta (beer hahfta)/Bir ay (beer ay)/Bu (boo)
Today/Yesterday/Tomorrow	Bugün (boo-goon)/dün (doon)/Yanin (yah-rin)
Are you open/closed?	Açık/kapalı (mısın (a-chik/kah-pah-li misin?)
Sunday /Monday/Tuesday/Wednesday	Pazar (pa-ZAR)/Pazartesi (pa-ZAR-te-see)/ Salı (saluh)/Çarşamba (char-sham-ba)
Thursday /Friday/Saturday	Perşembe (per-shem-be)/Cuma (joo-ma)/ Cumartesi (joo-mar-tee-see)

MONEY

ENGLISH	TURKISH
How much is this?	Fiyatı ne kadar? (fee-ya-tuh NE ka-dar?)
I want...	Biraz .... istiyorum
I don't want...	...istemedim (eestemedim)
Is there a student discount?	Öğrenci var mı? (Oo-ren-jee var muh?)
Do you accept credit cards?	Kredi kartı alıyor musunuz? (kredee kartuh aluh-YOR moo-soo-nooz?)
Money	Para (pahrah)

INDEX

A

Abdullah, King of Jordan 410
Abraham 37, 270, 523, 608
Abu Dhabi (UAE) 634
Abu Ghosh (ISR) 287
Abu Qir (EGY) 131
Abu Simbel (EGY) 220
Abydos (EGY) 203
accommodations 22
Ad-Darazi 39, 88
Aden (YEM) 692
aerogrammes 23
AIDS 18, 20
airplane travel
 charter flights 27
 courier flights 27
airports
 Abu Dhabi 634
 Abu Simbel 220
 Aleppo 524
 Alexandria 121
 Amman (Queen Alia Int'l) 403, 413
 Ankara 586
 Antalya 582
 Aswan 210
 Beirut 467
 Bodrum 572
 Cairo 42
 Dakhla Oasis 228
 Damascus 499
 Dubai 626
 Eilat 370
 Gaza City 395
 Hurghada 175
 Istanbul 545
 Jerusalem (Ben-Gurion Int'l) 251
 Kharga Oasis 232
 Khasab 664
 Kuşadası 566
 Luxor 186
 Marsa Matrouh 136

Muscat 646
Salalah 668
Sana'a 682
Tel Aviv (Ben-Gurion Int'l) 290
Trabzon 602
'Ajlun (JOR) 429
Akhenaton 97
Akhziv (ISR) 321
Akko (ISR) 317
Al-'Ain (UAE) 638
Al-Azhar University 50, 85
Al-Bab 40
Al-Barid (JOR) 449
alcohol 16
 'araq 412, 497
 rakı 544
 Stella 54
 strange brews 75
Aleppo (SYR) 523
Alexander the Great 48, 192, 408, 539
Alexandria (EGY) 119–128
'Ali, Muhammad 55, 84
aliens 201, 408
Al-Izariyyeh (WB) 392
Al-Madras (JOR) 449
Al-Makha (YEM) 691
Al-Mughsayl (OMAN) 673
Al-Mukalla (YEM) 695
alternatives to tourism 32–34
 reincarnation 204
Amasra (TUR) 598
Amasya (TUR) 601
American Express 9, 11
American Red Cross 17
AmEx offices
 Abu Dhabi 635
 Alexandria 124
 Amman 417
 Ankara 586
 Aqaba 452
 Aswan 211
 Beirut 468
 Cairo 67

Damascus 502
Dubai 627
Haifa 311
Istanbul 550
Jerusalem 259
Luxor 184
Muscat 649
Port Said 168
Salalah 669
Sana'a 685
Suez 172
Tel Aviv 292
Amman (JOR) 412–424
'Amran (YEM) 688
Amun, see gods
Andromeda's Rock 302
Ani (TUR) 613
Ankara (TUR) 585
ankh 39
Antakya (TUR) 584
Antalya (TUR) 581
Antioch 426, 584
Antony, Marc 48, 138, 564
Apamea (SYR) 519
Aphrodisias (TUR) 570
Aqaba (JOR) 450
Arabic language & phrasebook 702
Arad (ISR) 364
Arafat, Yassir 137, 244, 245
Aramaic 509
'araq 412, 497
argeileh, see *sheesha*
Armageddon (ISR) 328
Armenian genocide 541, 610
Artisanat Libanais 472
Arwad (SYR) 523
Arz ar-Rab (LEB) 482
Ashkelon (ISR) 303
'ashta 463, 479
Assad, Hafez al- 246, 495
Aswan (EGY) 209
Aswan High Dam 217

U

V

W